SEVENTH EDITION

strategic
management

text and cases

Gregory G. Dess
University of Texas
at Dallas

G. T. Lumpkin
Syracuse University

Alan B. Eisner
Pace University

Gerry McNamara
Michigan State
University

Strategic Management: Text and Cases 7th Global Edition
Gregory G. Dess, G. T. Lumpkin, Alan B. Eisner, Gerry McNamara
ISBN-13 9780077161088
ISBN-10 0077161084

Published by McGraw-Hill Education
Shoppenhangers Road
Maidenhead
Berkshire
SL6 2QL
Telephone: 44 (0) 1628 502 500
Fax: 44 (0) 1628 770 224
Website: www.mcgraw-hill.co.uk

British Library Cataloguing in Publication Data
A catalogue record for this book is available from the British Library

Library of Congress Cataloguing in Publication Data
The Library of Congress data for this book has been applied for from the Library of Congress

Commissioning Editor: Peter Hooper
Marketing Manager: Geeta Kumar
Production Editor: James Bishop

ISBN-13 9780077161088
ISBN-10 0077161084

To my family, Margie and Taylor; my parents, Bill and Mary Dess; and Walter Descovich

–Greg

To my lovely wife, Vicki, and my students and colleagues

–Tom

To my family, Helaine, Rachel, and Jacob

–Alan

To my wonderful wife, Gaelen; my children, Megan and AJ; and my parents, Gene and Jane

–Gerry

about the
authors

Gregory G. Dess

is the Andrew R. Cecil Endowed Chair in Management at the University of Texas at Dallas. His primary research interests are in strategic management, organization–environment relationships, and knowledge management. He has published numerous articles on these subjects in both academic and practitioner-oriented journals. He also serves on the editorial boards of a wide range of practitioner-oriented and academic journals. In August 2000, he was inducted into the *Academy of Management Journal*'s Hall of Fame as one of its charter members. Professor Dess has conducted executive programs in the United States, Europe, Africa, Hong Kong, and Australia. During 1994 he was a Fulbright Scholar in Oporto, Portugal. In 2009, he received an honorary doctorate from the University of Bern (Switzerland). He received his PhD in Business Administration from the University of Washington (Seattle) and a BIE degree from Georgia Tech.

G. T. (Tom) Lumpkin

is the Chris J. Witting Chair and Professor of Entrepreneurship at Syracuse University in New York. Prior to joining the faculty at Syracuse, Tom was the Kent Hance Regents Endowed Chair and Professor of Entrepreneurship at Texas Tech University. His research interests include entrepreneurial orientation, opportunity recognition, strategy-making processes, social entrepreneurship, and innovative forms of organizing work. He has published numerous research articles in journals such as *Strategic Management Journal, Academy of Management Journal, Academy of Management Review, Journal of Business Venturing,* and *Entrepreneurship: Theory and Practice.* He is a member of the editorial review boards of *Strategic Entrepreneurship Journal, Entrepreneurship Theory & Practice,* and the *Journal of Business Venturing.* He received his PhD in management from the University of Texas at Arlington and MBA from the University of Southern California.

Alan B. Eisner

is Professor of Management and Department Chair, Management and Management Science Department, at the Lubin School of Business, Pace University. He received his PhD in management from the Stern School of Business, New York University. His primary research interests are in strategic management, technology management, organizational learning, and managerial decision making. He has published research articles and cases in journals such as *Advances in Strategic Management, International Journal of Electronic Commerce, International Journal of Technology Management, American Business Review, Journal of Behavioral and Applied Management,* and *Journal of the International Academy for Case Studies.* He is the former Associate Editor of the Case Association's peer reviewed journal, *The CASE Journal.*

Gerry McNamara

is a Professor of Management at Michigan State University. He received his PhD from the Carlson School of Management at the University of Minnesota. His research focuses on strategic decision making, organizational risk taking, and mergers and acquisitions. His research has been published in numerous journals, including the *Academy of Management Journal, Strategic Management Journal, Organization Science, Organizational Behavior and Human Decision Processes, Journal of Management,* and *Journal of International Business Studies.* His research on mergers and acquisitions has been abstracted in the *New York Times, Bloomberg Businessweek, The Economist,* and *Financial Week.* He is currently an Associate Editor for the *Academy of Management Journal.*

Welcome to the Seventh Edition of *Strategic Management: Text and Cases!*

We are all very pleased with the positive market response to our previous edition. Below is some of the encouraging feedback we have received from our reviewers:

The text is thorough and all-inclusive. I don't need to refer to another book as a back-up. It addresses all aspects of strategic management from the initial inspiration of a vision to the nuts and bolts of putting the plan to work. It is well structured; it is clear how each chapter not only builds on the previous ones, but also how analysis, formulation, and implementation are interrelated.

Lois Shelton, California State University, Northridge

I use *Strategic Management* in a capstone course required of all business majors, and students appreciate the book because it synergizes all their business education into a meaningful and understandable whole. My students enjoy the book's readability and tight organization, as well as the contemporary examples, case studies, discussion questions and exercises.

William Sannwald, San Diego State University

It is very easy for students to read because it presents strategy concepts in a simple but comprehensive manner. It covers important developments in the strategic management field that are usually ignored by other textbooks (e.g., concepts like social networks and social capital, the balanced scorecard, and new forms of organizational structure).

Moses Acquaah, University of North Carolina at Greensboro

Content is current and easy for students to grasp; good graphs and charts to illustrate important points in the chapter. Book is well organized around the AFI framework.

Lise Anne D. Slatten, University of Louisiana at Lafayette

It is the best written textbook for the undergraduate course that I have come across. Application materials tie concepts to real-world practice.

Justin L. Davis, University of West Florida

The Dess text takes a practical/easy approach to explain very difficult subject matter. It integrates a number of real-life scenarios to aid the student in their comprehension of key concepts. The standout of the text is the Reflecting on Career Implications. These end-of-chapter questions aid the student in applying their learning to their workplace in a manner that promotes career success.

Amy Patrick, Wilmington University

The Dess book overcomes many of the limitations of the last book I used in many ways: (a) presents content in a very interesting and engrossing manner without compromising the depth and comprehensiveness, (b) inclusion of timely and interesting illustrative examples, (c) includes an excellent array of long, medium, and short cases that can be used to balance depth and variety, and (d) EOC exercises do an excellent job of complementing the chapter content.

Sucheta Nadkami, Drexel University

We are always striving to improve our work, and we are most appreciative of the extensive and constructive feedback that many strategy professionals have graciously given us. As always, we have worked hard to incorporate their ideas into the Seventh Edition—and we acknowledge them by name later in the Preface.

We believe we have made valuable improvements throughout our many revised editions of *Strategic Management.* At the same time, we strive to be consistent and "true" to our original overriding objective: a book that satisfies three R's: relevant, rigorous, and readable. That is, our tagline (paraphrasing the well-known Secret deodorant commercial) is: "Strong enough for the professor; made for the student." And we are pleased that we have received feedback (such as the comments on the previous page) that is consistent with what we are trying to accomplish.

To continue to earn the support of strategy instructors (and students!) we try to use an engaging writing style that minimizes unnecessary jargon and covers all of the traditional bases. We also integrate some central themes throughout the book—such as globalization, technology, ethics, environmental sustainability, and entrepreneurship—that are vital in understanding strategic management in today's global economy. We draw on short examples from business practice to bring concepts to life by providing 85 Strategy Spotlights (more detailed examples in sidebars).

Unlike other strategy texts, we provide three separate chapters that address timely topics about which business students should have a solid understanding. These are the role of intellectual assets in value creation (Chapter 4), entrepreneurial strategy and competitive dynamics (Chapter 8), and fostering entrepreneurship in established organizations (Chapter 12). We also provide an excellent set of cases to help students analyze, integrate, and apply strategic management concepts.

In developing *Strategic Management: Text and Cases,* we certainly didn't forget the instructors. As we all know, you have a most challenging (but rewarding) job. We did our best to help you. We provide a variety of supplementary materials that should help you in class preparation and delivery. For example, our chapter notes do not simply summarize the material in the text. Rather (and consistent with the concept of strategy!), we ask ourselves: "How can we add value?" Thus, for each chapter, we provide numerous questions to pose to help guide class discussion, at least 12 boxed examples to supplement chapter material, and three detailed "teaching tips" to further engage students. Also, the author team completed the chapter notes—along with the entire test bank—ourselves. That is, unlike many of our rivals, we didn't simply farm the work out to others. Instead, we felt that such efforts help to enhance quality and consistency—as well as demonstrate our personal commitment to provide a top-quality total package to strategy instructors. With the seventh edition, we also benefited from valued input by our strategy colleagues to further improve our work.

Let's now address some of the key substantive changes in the Seventh Edition. Then we will cover some of the major features that we have had in previous editions.

What's New? Highlights of the Seventh Edition

We have endeavored to add new material to the chapters that reflects both the feedback that we have received from our reviewers as well as the challenges that face today's managers. Thus, we all invested an extensive amount of time carefully reviewing a wide variety of books, academic and practitioner journals, and the business press.

We also worked hard to develop more concise and tightly written chapters. Based on feedback from some of the reviewers, we have tightened our writing style, tried to eliminate redundant examples, and focused more directly on what we feel is the most important content in each chapter for our audience. The overall result is that we were able to update our material, add valuable new content, and—at the same time—shorten the length of the chapters.

Here are some of the major changes and improvements in the Seventh Edition:

- **All of the 12 opening "Learning from Mistakes" vignettes that lead off each chapter at totally new.** Unique to this text, they are all examples of what can go wrong, and they serve as an excellent vehicle for clarifying and reinforcing strategy concepts. After all, what can be learned if one simply admires perfection!

- **Well over half of our "Strategy Spotlights" (sidebar examples) are brand new, and many of the others have been thoroughly updated.** Although we have reduced the number of Spotlights from the previous edition to conserve space, we still have a total of 85—by far the most in the strategy market. We focus on bringing the most important strategy concepts to life in a concise and highly readable manner. And we work hard to eliminate unnecessary detail that detracts from the main point we are trying to make. Also, consistent with our previous edition, many of the Spotlights focus on three "hot" issues that are critical in leading today's organizations: ethics, environmental sustainability, and crowdsourcing.

- **We have added a new feature—Issue for Debate—at the end of each chapter.** We have pretested these situations and find that students become very engaged (and often animated!) in discussing an issue that has viable alternative points of view. It is an exciting way to drive home key strategy concepts. For example, in Chapter 1, Seventh Generation is faced with a situation that confronts their values, and they must decide whether or not to provide their products to some of their largest customers. In Chapter 3, some interesting tradeoffs arose when The World Triathlon Corporation expanded their exclusive branding of Ironman to products that didn't reflect the "spirit" of the brand. And, in Chapter 6, Microsoft's new, more vertically integrated structure and competitive advantage in software poses an issue for some interesting alternative points of view.

- **Throughout the chapters, we provide many excerpts from interviews with top executives from Adam Bryant's _The Corner Office_.** Such viewpoints provide valuable perspectives from leading executives and help to drive home the value and purpose of key strategy concepts. For example, we include the perspectives of Tim Brown (CEO of IDEO) on employee empowerment, John Stumpf (CEO of Wells Fargo) on strategy implementation, and Gordon Bethune (former CEO of Continental Airlines) on the importance of incentive systems.

- **We have completely rewritten the "Reflecting on Career Implications . . ." feature that we introduced in the Sixth Edition of _Strategic Management_.** Based on reviewer feedback, we directed our attention to providing insights that are closely aligned with and directed to three distinct issues faced by our readers: prepare them for a job interview (e.g., industry analysis), help them with current employers or their career in general, or help them find potential employers and decide where to work. We feel this feature is significantly improved and should be of more value to students' professional development.

Key content changes for the chapters include:

- **Chapter 1 makes a strong business case for environmental sustainability and draws on Porter's concept of "shared value" that was initially introduced in the Sixth Edition.** Such issues advance the notion that firms should go far beyond a narrow focus on shareholder returns. Further, shared value promotes practices that enhance the competitiveness of the company while simultaneously advancing the social and economic conditions in which it operates.

- **Chapter 2 makes the distinction between "hard trends" and "soft trends" that was articulated by Dan Burrus in his recent book _Flash Foresight_.** This distinction is important in determing the importance of current trends and their evolution over time. Soft trends are something that might happen and a probability with which it might happen can be assigned. In contrast, hard trends are based on measurable facts, events, or objects—they are something that will happen. We provide the example of how the identification of hard trends (in technology) led the renowned Mayo Clinic to develop a CD to help customers to access useful medical information. This initiative provided the Mayo Clinic with significant financial and nonfinancial benefits!

- **Chapter 4 addresses two issues that are important to not only developing human capital in organizations but also for students entering—or enhancing their success in—an organization: mentorship versus sponsorship and the "trap" of ineffective networks.** Knowing the distinction between mentors and sponsors has valuable implications for one's career. Mentors may provide coaching and advice, and prepare one for the next position. Sponsors, on the other hand, are typically somebody in a senior position who can advocate and facilitate career moves. We also draw on research that suggests three types of "network traps" that professionals should work hard to avoid: the wrong structure, the wrong relationship, and the wrong behavior.

- **Chapter 6 discusses when actions taken to change the scope of businesses in which a corporation competes lead to positive outcomes for the firm.** We highlight the characteristics of both acquisitions and divestitures that lead to positive outcomes. With acquisitions, we focus on how the characteristics of the acquiring firm as well as the acquisition itself lead to positive reactions by the stock market to the announcement of the deal. With divestitures, we draw on the work by the Boston Consulting Group to highlight seven principles for effective divestitures.

- **Chapter 7 looks into the hidden costs of offshoring.** In recent years, many firms have moved parts of their operations to lower wage countries. In many cases, they have found that the expected cost savings were illusory. We discuss seven reasons why firms would not achieve the anticipated savings through offshoring and provide examples of firms that have benefited by bringing their operations back home.

- **Chapter 8 includes an examination of crowdfunding, a rapidly growing means to finance entrepreneurial ventures.** Crowdfunding involves drawing relatively small amounts of funding from a wide net of investors to provide potentially large pools of capital for entrepreneurial ventures. We discuss both the tremendous potential as well as the pitfalls of crowdfunding for entrepreneurs. Knowing that some of our students may want to be investors in these ventures, we also discuss issues that crowdfunding investors should consider when looking into these investment opportunities.

- **Chapter 9 addresses how firms can build effective boards of directors.** We identify how firms need to go beyond standard categories, such as insider versus outsider board members, to develop favorable board dynamics. We also discuss how the structure of boards has changed over the past 25 years.

- **Chapter 10 examines the costs and benefits of nurturing strong relationships to ensure cooperation and achieve high levels of performance.** Over the past 30 years, many scholars have argued that relational systems, where decisions regarding how to facilitate control and coordination are driven by relationships rather than bureaucratic systems and contracts, are superior to more traditional control systems. We examine this issue and discuss how relational systems have both advantages and disadvantages. We conclude with a brief discussion of when managers may want to rely more on relationship systems and when they may want to rely more on formal structure and reward systems.

- **Chapter 11 introduces the concept of "competency companions," an important idea for managers to consider in developing their leadership ability.** The idea is that leaders can benefit most by identifying and developing complementary strengths instead of continually working on already great qualities that they may possess. For example, a leader who has a strong competence in developing innovative ideas can extend that competency by developing strong communication skills.

- **Chapter 13 updates our Appendix: Sources of Company and Industry Information.** Here, we owe a big debt to Ruthie Brock and Carol Byrne, library professionals at the University of Texas at Arlington. These ladies have graciously provided us with comprehensive and updated information that is organized in a range of issues. These include competitive intelligence, annual report collections, company rankings, business websites, and strategic and competitive analysis. Such information is invaluable in analyzing companies and industries.

- **The cases section has been revised and expanded to further enhance our excellent case package.**

  - Approximately half of our cases are author-written (much more than the competition).
  - We have updated our users' favorite cases, creating fresh stories about familiar companies to minimize instructor preparation time and "maximize freshness" of the content.
  - We have added 8 exciting new cases specifically for this Global edition, including IKEA, Netflix, and Apple.
  - We have also extensively updated familiar cases, including eBay, Johnson & Johnson, Yahoo and many others.
  - A major focus on fresh and current cases on familiar firms.
  - Many videos on the Online Learning Center (OLC) or Connect to match the cases.

What Remains the Same: Key Features of Earlier Editions

Let's now briefly address some of the exciting features that remain from the earlier editions.

- **Traditional organizing framework with three other chapters on timely topics.** Crisply written chapters cover all of the strategy bases and address contemporary topics. First, the chapters are divided logically into the traditional sequence: strategy analysis, strategy formulation, and strategy implementation. Second, we include three chapters on such timely topics as intellectual capital/knowledge management, entrepreneurial strategy and competitive dynamics, and fostering corporate entrepreneurship and new ventures.

- **"Learning from Mistakes" chapter-opening cases.** To enhance student interest, we begin each chapter with a case that depicts an organization that has suffered a dramatic performance drop, or outright failure, by failing to adhere to sound strategic management concepts and principles. We believe that this feature serves to underpin the value of the concepts in the course and that it is a preferred teaching approach to merely providing examples of outstanding companies that always seem to get it right! After all, isn't it better (and more challenging) to diagnose problems than admire perfection? As Dartmouth's Sydney Finkelstein, author of *Why Smart Executives Fail,* notes: "We live in a world where success is revered, and failure is quickly pushed to the side. However, some of the greatest opportunities to learn—both for individuals and organizations—come from studying what goes wrong."* We'll see how, for example, Borders went from enjoying enormous success as an innovative firm—with revenues of nearly $4 billion in 2005—to bankruptcy six years later. We will also explore why Daimler's "ultra-urban" Smart car—despite its initial acclaim—has cost the firm $5.3 billion in cumulative losses over the years. And we'll explore why Cisco's eagerness to enter the digital video market via its acquisition of Pure Digital Technologies didn't pan out.

- **Consistent chapter format and features to reinforce learning.** We have included several features in each chapter to add value and create an enhanced learning experience. First, each chapter begins with an overview and a set of bullets pointing to key learning objectives. Second, as previously noted, the opening case describes a situation in which a company's performance eroded because of a lack of proper application of strategy concepts. Third, at the end of each chapter there are four different types of questions/exercises that should help students assess their understanding and application of material:

  1. Summary review questions.
  2. Experiential exercises.
  3. Application questions and exercises.
  4. Ethics questions

Given the centrality of online systems to business today, each chapter contains at least one exercise that allows students to explore the use of the Web in implementing a firm's strategy.

- **"Reflecting on Career Implications" for each chapter.** This feature—at the end of each chapter—will help instructors drive home the immediate relevance/value of strategy concepts. It focuses on how an understanding of key concepts helps business students early in their careers.

- **Key Terms.** Approximately a dozen key terms for each chapter are identified in the margins of the pages. This addition was made in response to reviewer feedback and improves students' understanding of core strategy concepts.

- **Clear articulation and illustration of key concepts.** Key strategy concepts are introduced in a clear and concise manner and are followed by timely and interesting examples from business practice. Such concepts include value-chain analysis, the resource-based view of the firm, Porter's five-forces model, competitive advantage, boundaryless organizational designs, digital strategies, corporate governance, ethics, and entrepreneurship.

- **Extensive use of sidebars.** We include 85 sidebars (or about seven per chapter) called "Strategy Spotlights." The Strategy Spotlights not only illustrate key points but also increase the readability and excitement of new strategy concepts.

- **Integrative themes.** The text provides a solid grounding in ethics, globalization, environmental sustainability, and technology. These topics are central themes throughout the book and form the basis for many of the Strategy Spotlights.

- **Implications of concepts for small businesses.** Many of the key concepts are applied to start-up firms and smaller businesses, which is particularly important since many students have professional plans to work in such firms.

- **Not just a textbook but an entire package.** *Strategic Management* features the best chapter teaching notes available today. Rather than merely summarizing the key points in each chapter, we focus on value-added material to enhance the teaching (and learning) experience. Each chapter includes dozens of questions to spur discussion,

---

*Personal communication, June 20, 2005.

teaching tips, in-class group exercises, and about a dozen detailed examples from business practice to provide further illustrations of key concepts.

- **Excellent Case Studies.** We have selected an excellent collection of current and classic cases for this edition, carefully including a wide variety of cases matched to key strategic concepts and organized to create maximum flexibility. We have a balance of short, concise, and longer, comprehensive cases while maintaining currency and name recognition of our cases with many new and updated classroom-tested cases. We also have updated many of the favorites from the Sixth Edition, such as Apple, eBay, Ford, Johnson & Johnson, and many others.

Student Support Materials

Online Learning Center (OLC)

The following resources are available to students via the publisher's OLC at www.mcgraw-hill. co.uk/textbooks/dess:

- Chapter quizzes students can take to gauge their understanding of material covered in each chapter.
- A selection of PowerPoint slides for each chapter.
- Links to strategy simulations the Business Strategy Game & GLO-BUS. Both provide a powerful and constructive way of connecting students to the subject matter of the course with a competition among classmates on campus and around the world.

Instructor Support Materials

Instructor's Manual (IM)

Prepared by the textbook authors, along with valued input from our strategy colleagues, the accompanying IM contains summary/objectives, lecture/discussion outlines, discussion questions, extra examples not included in the text, teaching tips, reflecting on career implications, experiential exercises, and more.

Revised by Christine Pence of the University of California–Riverside, the test bank contains more than 1,000 true/false, multiple-choice, and essay questions. It has now been tagged with learning objectives as well as Bloom's Taxonomy and AACSB criteria.

- **Assurance of Learning Ready.** Assurance of Learning is an important element of many accreditation standards. Dess 7e is designed specifically to support your Assurance of Learning initiatives. Each chapter in the book begins with a list of numbered learning objectives that appear throughout the chapter, as well as in the end-of-chapter questions and exercises. Every test bank question is also linked to one of these objectives, in addition to level of difficulty, topic area, Bloom's Taxonomy level, and AACSB skill area.
- **AACSB Statement.** The McGraw-Hill Companies is a proud corporate member of AACSB International. Understanding the importance and value of AACSB accreditation, Dess 7e has sought to recognize the curricula guidelines detailed in the AACSB standards for business accreditation by connecting selected questions in Dess 7e and the test bank to the general knowledge and skill guidelines found in the AACSB standards. The statements contained in Dess 7e are provided only as a guide for the users of this text. The AACSB leaves content coverage and assessment within the purview of individual schools, the mission of the school, and the faculty. While

Dess 7e and the teaching package make no claim of any specific AACSB qualification or evaluation, we have labeled selected questions within Dess 7e according to the six general knowledge and skills areas.

- **Computerized Test Bank Online.** A comprehensive bank of test questions is provided within a computerized test bank and is compatible with Blackboard and other course management systems.
- **Test Creation.**
  - Author/edit questions online using the 14 different question type templates.
  - Create printed tests or deliver online to get instant scoring and feedback.
  - Create questions pools to offer multiple versions online—great for practice.
  - Export your tests for use in *WebCT, Blackboard, PageOut,* and Apple's *iQuiz.*
  - Sharing tests with colleagues, adjuncts, TAs is easy.
- **Online Test Management.**
  - Set availability dates and time limits for your quiz or test.
  - Control how your test will be presented.
  - Assign points by question or question type with drop-down menu.
  - Provide immediate feedback to students or delay until all finish the test.
  - Create practice tests online to enable student mastery.
  - Your roster can be uploaded to enable student self-registration.
- **Online Scoring and Reporting.**
  - Automated scoring for most question types.
  - Allows manual scoring for essay and other open response questions.
  - Manual rescoring and feedback is also available.
  - Export easily to your grade book.
  - View basic statistical reports.

PowerPoint Presentation

Prepared by Pauline Assenza of Western Connecticut State University and consists of more than 400 slides incorporating an outline for the chapters tied to learning objectives. Also included are instructor notes, multiple-choice questions that can be used as Classroom Performance System (CPS) questions, and additional examples outside of the text to promote class discussion. Case Study PowerPoint slides are available to facilitate case study coverage.

McGraw-Hill Connect™ Management

Less Managing. More Teaching. Greater Learning. McGraw-Hill *Connect Management* is an online assignment and assessment solution that connects students with the tools and resources they'll need to achieve success.

- **McGraw-Hill *Connect Management* Features.** *Connect Management* offers a number of powerful tools and features to make managing assignments easier, so faculty can spend more time teaching. With *Connect Management,* students can engage with their coursework anytime and anywhere, making the learning process more accessible and efficient. *Connect Management* offers you the features described below.
  - There are chapter quizzes for the 12 chapters, consisting of 15–25 multiple-choice questions, testing students' overall comprehension of concepts presented in the chapter.

- There are 2 specially crafted interactives for each of the 12 chapters that drill students in the use and application of the concepts and tools of strategic analysis.
- *Connect* also includes special case exercises for approximately half of the 24 cases in this edition that require students to develop answers to a select number of the assignment questions.
- Some of these cases include financial analysis exercises related to the cases.
- The majority of the *Connect* exercises are automatically graded, thereby simplifying the task of evaluating each class member's performance and monitoring the learning outcomes.

- **Student Progress Tracking.** *Connect Management* keeps instructors informed about how each student, section, and class is performing, allowing for more productive use of lecture and office hours. The progress-tracking function enables you to
  - View scored work immediately and track individual or group performance with assignment and grade reports.
  - Access an instant view of student or class performance relative to learning objectives.
  - Collect data and generate reports required by many accreditation organizations, such as AACSB.

- **Smart Grading.** When it comes to studying, time is precious. *Connect Management* helps students learn more efficiently by providing feedback and practice material when they need it, where they need it. When it comes to teaching, your time also is precious. The grading function enables you to
  - Have assignments scored automatically, giving students immediate feedback on their work and side-by-side comparisons with correct answers.
  - Access and review each response, manually change grades, or leave comments for students to review.
  - Reinforce classroom concepts with practice tests and instant quizzes.

- **Simple Assignment Management.** With *Connect Management,* creating assignments is easier than ever, so you can spend more time teaching and less time managing. The assignment management function enables you to
  - Create and deliver assignments easily with selectable test bank items.
  - Streamline lesson planning, student progress reporting, and assignment grading to make classroom management more efficient than ever.
  - Go paperless with online submission and grading of student assignments.

- **Instructor Library.** The *Connect Management* Instructor Library is your repository for additional resources to improve student engagement in and out of class. You can select and use any asset that enhances your lecture. The *Connect Management* Instructor Library includes
  - Instructor Manual
  - Case Teaching Notes
  - PowerPoint® files
  - Test Bank

Videos

A set of videos related to both chapters and selected cases can be found on the Online Learning Center (OLC) or Connect to support your classroom or student lab, or for home viewing. These thought-provoking video clips are available upon adoption of this text.

Online Learning Center (OLC)

The instructor section of *www.mcgraw-hill.co.uk/textbooks/dess* also includes the Instructor's Manual, PowerPoint Presentations, Case Grid, and Case Study Teaching Notes as well as additional resources.

The Business Strategy Game and GLO-BUS Online Simulations

Both allow teams of students to manage companies in a head-to-head contest for global market leadership. These simulations give students the immediate opportunity to experiment with various strategy options and to gain proficiency in applying the concepts and tools they have been reading about in the chapters. To find out more or to register, please visit *www.mhhe.com/thompsonsims*.

e-book Options

e-books are an innovative way for students to save money and to "go-green," McGraw-Hill's e-books are typically 40% of bookstore price. Students have the choice between an online and a downloadable CourseSmart e-book.

Through *CourseSmart,* students have the flexibility to access an exact replica of their textbook from any computer that has internet service without plug-ins or special software via the version, or create a library of books on their harddrive via the downloadable version. Access to the CourseSmart e-books is one year.

Features: *CourseSmart* e-books allow students to highlight, take notes, organize notes, and share the notes with other *CourseSmart* users. Students can also search terms across all e-books in their purchased *CourseSmart* library. *CourseSmart* e-books can be printed (5 pages at a time).

More info and purchase: Please visit *www.coursesmart.co.uk* for more information and to purchase access to our e-books. *CourseSmart* allows students to try one chapter of the e-book, free of charge, before purchase.

Additional Resources

Create

Craft your teaching resources to match the way you teach! With McGraw-Hill *Create,* *www.mcgrawhillcreate.com,* you can easily rearrange chapters, combine material from other content sources, and quickly upload content you have written, like your course syllabus or teaching notes. Find the content you need in *Create* by searching through thousands of leading McGraw-Hill textbooks. Arrange your book to fit your teaching style. *Create* even allows you to personalize your book's appearance by selecting the cover and adding your name, school, and course information. Order a *Create* book and you'll receive a complimentary print review copy in three to five business days or a complimentary electronic review copy (eComp) via email in about one hour. Go to *www.mcgrawhillcreate.com* today and register. Experience how McGraw-Hill *Create* empowers you to teach *your* students *your* way.

McGraw-Hill Higher Education and Blackboard

McGraw-Hill Higher Education and Blackboard have teamed up. What does this mean for you?

1.   **Your life, simplified.** Now you and your students can access McGraw-Hill's *Connect* and *Create* right from within your Blackboard course—all with one single sign-on. Say goodbye to the days of logging in to multiple applications.

2. **Deep integration of content and tools.** Not only do you get single sign-on with *Connect* and *Create,* you also get deep integration of McGraw-Hill content and content engines right in Blackboard. Whether you're choosing a book for your course or building Connect assignments, all the tools you need are right where you want them—inside of Blackboard.

3. **Seamless gradebooks.** Are you tired of keeping multiple gradebooks and manually synchronizing grades into Blackboard? We thought so. When a student completes an integrated Connect assignment, the grade for that assignment automatically (and instantly) feeds your Blackboard grade center.

4. **A solution for everyone.** Whether your institution is already using Blackboard or you just want to try Blackboard on your own, we have a solution for you. McGraw-Hill and Blackboard can now offer you easy access to industry-leading technology and content, whether your campus hosts it or we do. Be sure to ask your local McGraw-Hill representative for details.

McGraw-Hill Customer Care Contact Information

At McGraw-Hill, we understand that getting the most from new technology can be challenging. That's why our services don't stop after you purchase our products. You can e-mail our product specialists 24 hours a day to get product training online. Or you can search our knowledge bank of Frequently Asked Questions on our support website. For customer support, call 800-331-5094, email *hmsupport@mcgraw-hill.com,* or visit *www.mhhe.com/support.* One of our technical support analysts will be able to assist you in a timely fashion.

Acknowledgments

Strategic Management represents far more than just the joint efforts of the four co-authors. Rather, it is the product of the collaborative input of many people. Some of these individuals are academic colleagues, others are the outstanding team of professionals at McGraw-Hill/Irwin, and still others are those who are closest to us—our families. It is time to express our sincere gratitude.

First, we'd like to acknowledge the dedicated instructors who have graciously provided their insights since the inception of the text. Their input has been very helpful in both pointing out errors in the manuscript and suggesting areas that needed further development as additional topics. We sincerely believe that the incorporation of their ideas has been critical to improving the final product.

Second, the authors would like to thank several faculty colleagues who were particularly helpful in the review, critique, and development of the book and supplementary materials. Greg's colleagues at the University of Texas at Dallas also have been helpful and supportive. These individuals include Mike Peng, Joe Picken, Kumar Nair, John Lin, Larry Chasteen, Seung-Hyun Lee, Tev Dalgic, and Jane Salk. His administrative assistant, Mary Vice, has been extremely helpful. Three doctoral students, Brian Pinkham, Steve Saverwald and Ciprian Stan, have provided many useful inputs and ideas, along with a research associate, Kimberly Flicker. He also appreciates the support of his dean and associate dean, Hasan Pirkul and Varghese Jacob, respectively. Tom would like to thank Gerry Hills, Abagail McWilliams, Rod Shrader, Mike Miller, James Gillespie, Ron Mitchell, Kim Boal, Keith Brigham, Jeremy Short, Tyge Payne, Bill Wan, Andy Yu, Abby Wang, Johan Wiklund, Mike Haynie, Alex McKelvie, Denis Gregoire, Alejandro Amezcua, Maria Minniti, Cathy Maritan, Ravi Dharwadkar, and Pam Brandes. Special thanks also to Jeff Stambaugh for his valuable contributions. Tom also extends a special thanks to Benyamin Lichtenstein for his support and encouragement. Both Greg and Tom wish to thank a special colleague, Abdul Rasheed at the University of

Texas at Arlington, who certainly has been a valued source of friendship and ideas for us for many years. He provided many valuable contributions to all editions. Alan thanks his colleagues at Pace University and the Case Association for their support in developing these fine case selections. Special thanks go to Jamal Shamsie at Michigan State University for his support in developing the case selections for this edition. Gerry thanks all of his colleagues at Michigan State University for their help and support over the years. He also thanks his mentor, Phil Bromiley, as well as the students and former students he has had the pleasure of working with, including Becky Luce, Cindy Devers, Federico Aime, Mike Mannor, Bernadine Dykes, Mathias Arrfelt, Kalin Kolev, Seungho Choi, Rob Davison, Dustin Sleesman, Danny Gamache, Adam Steinbach, and Daniel Chaffin.

Third, we would like to thank the team at McGraw-Hill for their outstanding support throughout the entire process. As we work on the book through the various editions, we always appreciate their hard work and recognize how so many people "add value" to our final package!

Fourth, we acknowledge the valuable contributions of many of our strategy colleagues for their excellent contributions to our supplementary and digital materials. Such content really adds a lot of value to our entire package! We are grateful to Pauline Assenza, Western Connecticut State University, for her superb work on case teaching notes as well as chapter and case PowerPoints. We thank Doug Sanford, Towson University, for his expertise in developing several pedagogical features, including the teaching notes for the "Learning from Mistakes . . ." and carefully reviewing our Instructor Manual's chapters. Justin Davis, University of West Florida, along with Noushi Rahman, Pace University, deserve our thanks for their hard work in developing excellent digital materials for Connect. And finally, we thank Christine Pence, University of California–Riverside, for her important contributions in revising our test bank and Todd Moss, Oregon State University, for his hard work in putting together an excellent set of videos online, along with the video grid that links videos to chapter material.

Finally, we would like to thank our families. For Greg this includes his parents, William and Mary Dess, who have always been there for him. His wife, Margie, and daughter, Taylor, have been a constant source of love and companionship. He would like to acknowledge his late uncle, Walter Descovich. Uncle Walt was truly a member of Tom Brokaw's *Greatest Generation*. He served in the U.S. Navy during World War II—where he learned electronics—and later became a superintendent at Consolidated Edison in New York City. He, his wife, Eleanor, and his family have been an inspiration to Greg over the years. Tom thanks his wife, Vicki, for her constant love and companionship. Tom also thanks Lee Hetherington and Thelma Lumpkin for their inspiration, as well as his mom, Katy, and his sister, Kitty, for a lifetime of support. Alan thanks his family—his wife, Helaine, and his children, Rachel and Jacob—for their love and support. He also thanks his parents, Gail Eisner and the late Marvin Eisner, for their support and encouragement. Gerry thanks his wife, Gaelen, for her love, support, and friendship and his children, Megan and AJ, for their love and the joy they bring to his life. He also thanks his parents, Gene and Jane, for their encouragement and support in all phases of his life.

Finally, we would like to thank all those who contributed cases and examples for this Global edition, these are:

Douglas Bryson
Cyrlene Claasen
Irena Descubes
Helena Gonzalez
Sarah Hudson
Tom McNamara
Asha Moore-Mangin

Their work will ensure that this textbook is both pedagogically sound and academically challenging, while at the same time being enjoyable to read.

guided
tour

Learning Objectives

Learning Objectives numbered LO5.1, LO5.2, LO5.3, etc. with corresponding icons in the margins to indicate where learning objectives are covered in the text.

Business-Level Strategy:

Creating and Sustaining Competitive Advantages

After reading this chapter, you should have a good understanding of the following learning objectives:

LO5.1 The central role of competitive advantage in the study of strategic management, and the three generic strategies: overall cost leadership, differentiation, and focus.

LO5.2 How the successful attainment of generic strategies can improve a firm's relative power vis-à-vis the five forces that determine an industry's average profitability.

LO5.3 The pitfalls managers must avoid in striving to attain generic strategies.

LO5.4 How firms can effectively combine the generic strategies of overall cost leadership and differentiation.

LO5.5 What factors determine the sustainability of a firm's competitive advantage.

LO5.6 How Internet-enabled business models are being used to improve strategic positioning.

LO5.7 The importance of considering the industry life cycle to determine a firm's business-level strategy and its relative emphasis on functional area strategies and value-creating activities.

LO5.8 The need for turnaround strategies that enable a firm to reposition its competitive position in an industry.

Learning from Mistal

Some of the most widely known brands and snack foods arena have been owned Corporation.[1] Since the 1930s, Hostess Br founded as Interstate Bakeries) produce popular baked goods, including Wonder B Ring Dings, Yodels, Zingers, and many o Even with its iconic brands and sales in c year, Hostess Brands found itself in a perilo went into bankruptcy in 2012. Unable to f solution to remain viable, in November closed down all of its bakeries and was for and sell off its brands to other bakeries. W of their brands and their longstanding ma was a surprise to many seeing the firm wrong?

The viability of a firm's business-level stra by both the internal operations of a firm an and preferences of the market. Firms that a the appropriate resources and cost structur needs of the environment. Hostess had long themselves in the baked goods business simple yet flavorful baked snack goods that in kids' lunchboxes for generations. Their str the environment was undone by a combinat

Learning from Mistakes

Microsoft hits another bump in the road

Microsoft, the perennial leader in PC operating systems and software, is increasingly coming under fire for its perceived lack of product innovation. It seems like a day doesn't go by without Microsoft delivering more disappointing news about some product's lacklustre performance. Does anyone remember the Zune personal media player or the Kin phone?

To be fair, with almost $60 billion in gross profits, and 90,000 employees in over 190 countries, Microsoft is no garage start-up. Its main campus in Seattle has over 120 buildings, its own transportation system, basketball courts and a shopping mall.

Despite the many trappings of success, Microsoft is still considered by many tech analysts to be a second rate company when it comes to innovation, as compared to Google, Apple, Facebook and Amazon. Critics maintain that for years, Microsoft chose to rest on its laurels, content to receive a steady, if impressive, revenue stream from its virtual global monopoly on PC operating systems. But as people switch in

Learning from Mistakes

Learning from Mistakes are examples of where things went wrong. Failures are not only interesting but also sometimes easier to learn from. And students realize strategy is not just about "right or wrong" answers, but requires critical thinking.

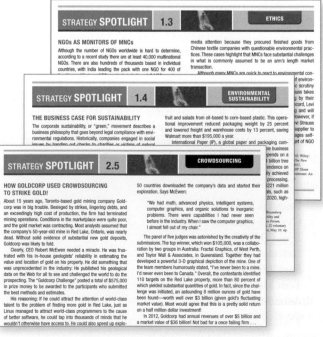

STRATEGY SPOTLIGHT 1.3 — ETHICS

NGOs AS MONITORS OF MNCs

Although the number of NGOs worldwide is hard to determine, according to a recent study there are at least 40,000 multinational NGOs. There are also hundreds of thousands based in individual countries, with India leading the pack with one NGO for 400 of

media attention because they procured finished goods from Chinese textile companies with questionable environmental practices. These cases highlight that MNCs face substantial challenges in what is commonly assumed to be an arm's length market transaction.

STRATEGY SPOTLIGHT 1.4 — ENVIRONMENTAL SUSTAINABILITY

THE BUSINESS CASE FOR SUSTAINABILITY

The corporate sustainability, or "green," movement describes a business philosophy that goes beyond legal compliance with environmental regulations. Historically, companies engaged in social

fruit and salads from oil-based to corn-based plastic. This operational improvement reduced packaging weight by 25 percent and lowered freight and warehouse costs by 13 percent, saving Walmart more than $195,000 a year.

International Paper (IP), a global paper and packaging com-

STRATEGY SPOTLIGHT 2.5 — CROWDSOURCING

HOW GOLDCORP USED CROWDSOURCING TO STRIKE GOLD!

About 15 years ago, Toronto-based gold mining company Goldcorp was in big trouble. Besieged by strikes, lingering debts, and an exceedingly high cost of production, the firm had terminated mining operations. Conditions in the marketplace were quite poor, and the gold market was contracting. Most analysts assumed that the company's 50-year-old mine in Red Lake, Ontario, was nearly dead. Without solid evidence of substantial new gold deposits, Goldcorp was likely to fold.

Clearly, CEO Robert McEwen needed a miracle. He was frustrated with his in-house geologists' reliability in estimating the value and location of gold on his property. He did something that was unprecedented in the industry: He published his geological data on the Web for all to see and challenged the world to do the prospecting. The "Goldcorp Challenge" posted a total of $575,000 in prize money to be awarded to the participants who submitted the best methods and estimates.

His reasoning: If he could attract the attention of world-class talent to the problem of finding more gold in Red Lake, just as Linux managed to attract world-class programmers to the cause of better software, he could tap into thousands of minds that he wouldn't otherwise have access to. He could also speed up explo-

50 countries downloaded the company's data and started their exploration. Says McEwen:

"We had math, advanced physics, intelligent systems, computer graphics, and organic solutions to inorganic problems. There were capabilities I had never seen before in the industry. When I saw the computer graphics, I almost fell out of my chair."

The panel of five judges was astonished by the creativity of the submissions. The top winner, which won $105,000, was a collaboration by two groups in Australia: Fractal Graphics, of West Perth, and Taylor Wall & Associates, in Queensland. Together they had developed a powerful 3-D graphical depiction of the mine. One of the team members humorously stated, "I've never been to a mine. I'd never even been to Canada." Overall, the contestants identified 110 targets on the Red Lake property, more than 80 percent of which yielded substantial quantities of gold. In fact, since the challenge was initiated, an astounding 8 million ounces of gold have been found—worth well over $3 billion (given gold's fluctuating market value). Most would agree that this is a pretty solid return on a half million dollar investment!

In 2012, Goldcorp had annual revenues of over $5 billion and a market value of $36 billion! Not bad for a once failing firm . . .

Strategy Spotlight

These boxes weave themes of ethics, globalization, and technology into every chapter of the text, providing students with a thorough grounding necessary for understanding strategic management. Select boxes incorporate crowdsourcing, environmental sustainability, and ethical themes.

Key Terms

Key Terms defined in the margins have been added to improve students' understanding of core strategy concepts.

> **competitive advantage**
> A firm's resources and capabilities that enable it to overcome the competitive forces in its industry(ies).

EXHIBIT 1.3 The Strategic Management Process

Exhibits

Both new and improved exhibits in every chapter provide visual presentations of the most complex concepts covered to support student comprehension.

Reflecting on Career Implications . . .

☒ **Creating the Environmentally Aware Organization:** Advancing your career requires constant scanning, monitoring, and intelligence gathering to find out not only future job opportunities but also to understand how employers' expectations are changing. Consider using websites such as LinkedIn to find job opportunities. Merely posting your resume on a site such as LinkedIn may not be enough. Instead, consider in what ways you can use such sites for scanning, monitoring, and intelligence gathering

☒ **SWOT Analysis:** As an analytical method, SWOT analysis is applicable for individuals as it is for firms. It is important for you to periodically evaluate your strengths and weaknesses as well as potential opportunities and threats to your career. Such analysis should be followed by efforts to address your weaknesses by improving your skills and capabilities.

☒ **General Environment:** The general environment consists of several segments, such as the demographic, sociocultural, political/legal, technological, economic, and global environments. It would be useful to evaluate how each of these segments can affect your career opportunities. Identify two or three specific trends (e.g., rapid technological change, aging of the population, increase in minimum wages) and their impact on your choice of careers. These also provide possibilities for you to add value for your organization.

☒ **Five-Forces Analysis:** Before you go for a job interview, consider the five forces affecting the industry within which the firm competes. This will help you to appear knowledgeable about the industry and increase your odds of landing the job. It also can help you to decide if you want to work for that organization. If the "forces" are unfavorable, the long-term profit potential of the industry may be unattractive, leading to fewer resources available and—all other things being equal—fewer career opportunities.

Reflecting on Career Implications

This new section before the summary of every chapter consists of examples on how understanding of key concepts helps business students early in their careers.

Go to library tab in Connect to access Case Financials.

Cases

Updated case lineup provides 10 new cases. The remainder have been revised to "maximize freshness" and minimize instructor preparation time.

support materials

Online Learning Center (OLC)

The website *www.mcgraw-hill.co.uk/textbooks/dess* follows the text chapter-by-chapter. OLC content is ancillary and supplementary germane to the textbook. As students read the book, they can go online to take self-grading quizzes, review material, or work through interactive exercises. It includes chapter quizzes, student PowerPoint slides, and links to strategy simulations The *Business Strategy Game* and GLO-BUS.

The instructor section also includes the Instructor's Manual, PowerPoint Presentations, Case Study Teaching Notes, Case Grid, and Video Guide as well as all student resources.

brief
contents

Preface vi

part 1 Strategic Analysis

1   Strategic Management: Creating Competitive
     Advantages 2

2   Analyzing the External Environment of the Firm 34

3   Assessing the Internal Environment of the Firm 70

4   Recognizing a Firm's Intellectual Assets: Moving
     beyond a Firm's Tangible Resources 104

part 2 Strategic Formulation

5   Business-Level Strategy: Creating and Sustaining
     Competitive Advantages 140

6   Corporate-Level Strategy: Creating Value through
     Diversification 178

7   International Strategy: Creating Value in Global
     Markets 210

8   Entrepreneurial Strategy and Competitive
     Dynamics 246

part 3 Strategic Implementation

9   Strategic Control and Corporate Governance 276

10   Creating Effective Organizational Designs 310

11   Strategic Leadership: Creating a Learning
     Organization and an Ethical Organization 344

12   Managing Innovation and Fostering Corporate
     Entrepreneurship 376

part 4 Case Analysis

13   Analyzing Strategic Management Cases 412

Cases C-1

Indexes I-1

contents

Preface vi

PART 1 Strategic Analysis

CHAPTER 1

Strategic Management: Creating Competitive Advantages 2

What Is Strategic Management?. 7
Defining Strategic Management 7
The Four Key Attributes of Strategic Management 8
The Strategic Management Process 9
Intended versus Realized Strategies 10
Strategy Analysis 11
Strategy Formulation. 13
Strategy Implementation. 13
The Role of Corporate Governance and Stakeholder Management 14
Alternative Perspectives of Stakeholder
    Management 15
Social Responsibility and Environmental
    Sustainability: Moving beyond the Immediate
    Stakeholders. 17
The Strategic Management Perspective: An Imperative throughout the Organization 20
Ensuring Coherence in Strategic Direction. . . . 22
Organizational Vision 23
Mission Statements. 25
Strategic Objectives 26
Summary. 29

CHAPTER 2

Analyzing the External Environment of the Firm: Creating Competitive Advantages 34

Creating the Environmentally Aware Organization 36
The Role of Scanning, Monitoring, Competitive
    Intelligence, and Forecasting. 36
SWOT Analysis. 41
The General Environment 42
The Demographic Segment. 42
The Sociocultural Segment 42
The Political/Legal Segment. 44
The Technological Segment 45
The Economic Segment 45
The Global Segment 46
Relationships among Elements of the General
    Environment 46
The Competitive Environment 48
Porter's Five-Forces Model of Industry
    Competition. 49
How the Internet and Digital Technologies
    Are Affecting the Five Competitive Forces. 55
Using Industry Analysis: A Few Caveats 59
Strategic Groups within Industries 61
Summary. 65

CHAPTER 3

Assessing the Internal Environment of the Firm. 70

Value-Chain Analysis 72
Primary Activities 74
Support Activities 76
Interrelationships among Value-Chain Activities
    within and across Organizations 79
The "Prosumer" Concept: Integrating Customers
    into the Value Chain. 80
Applying the Value Chain to Service
    Organizations. 81
Resource-Based View of the Firm. 82
Types of Firm Resources. 83

Firm Resources and Sustainable Competitive
    Advantages 85
The Generation and Distribution of a Firm's Profits:
    Extending the Resource-Based View of the Firm 90

**Evaluating Firm Performance: Two
Approaches 92**
Financial Ratio Analysis 92
Integrating Financial Analysis and Stakeholder
    Perspectives: The Balanced Scorecard 94
Summary 98

CHAPTER 4
**Recognizing a Firm's Intellectual Assets:
Moving beyond a Firm's Tangible
Resources 104**

**The Central Role of Knowledge in Today's
Economy 106**
**Human Capital: The Foundation of
Intellectual Capital. 109**
Attracting Human Capital 110
Developing Human Capital 112
Retaining Human Capital 116
Enhancing Human Capital: The Role of Diversity
    in the Workforce 117
The Vital Role of Social Capital 118
How Social Capital Helps Attract and Retain Talent 120
Social Networks: Implications for Knowledge
    Management and Career Success 120
The Potential Downside of Social Capital 125
**Using Technology to Leverage Human
Capital and Knowledge 126**
Using Networks to Share Information 126
Electronic Teams: Using Technology to Enhance
    Collaboration 127
Codifying Knowledge for Competitive Advantage 128
**Protecting the Intellectual Assets of the
Organization: Intellectual Property and
Dynamic Capabilities. 129**
Intellectual Property Rights 131
Dynamic Capabilities 131
Summary 133

PART 2 Strategic Formulation

CHAPTER 5
**Business-Level Strategy: Creating and
Sustaining Competitive Advantages 140**

**Types of Competitive Advantage
and Sustainability. 142**
Overall Cost Leadership 143
Differentiation 147
Focus 152
Combination Strategies: Integrating Overall
    Low Cost and Differentiation 154
**Can Competitive Strategies Be Sustained?
Integrating and Applying Strategic
Management Concepts. 157**
Atlas Door: A Case Example 158
Are Atlas Door's Competitive Advantages
    Sustainable? 159
**How the Internet and Digital
Technologies Affect the Competitive
Strategies 160**
Overall Cost Leadership 160
Differentiation 161
Focus 161
Are Combination Strategies the Key to E-Business
    Success? 162
**Industry Life-Cycle Stages: Strategic
Implications 162**
Strategies in the Introduction Stage 164
Strategies in the Growth Stage 165
Strategies in the Maturity Stage 165
Strategies in the Decline Stage 166
Turnaround Strategies 169
Summary 172

CHAPTER 6
**Corporate-Level Strategy: Creating
Value through Diversification. 178**

**Making Diversification Work:
An Overview 181**

Related Diversification: Economies of Scope and Revenue Enhancement 182

Leveraging Core Competencies 182

Sharing Activities 184

Enhancing Revenue and Differentiation. 185

Related Diversification: Market Power. 185

Pooled Negotiating Power 185

Vertical Integration 186

Unrelated Diversification: Financial Synergies and Parenting. 189

Corporate Parenting and Restructuring. 189

Portfolio Management 190

Caveat: Is Risk Reduction a Viable Goal of Diversification? 192

The Means to Achieve Diversification 193

Mergers and Acquisitions 193

Strategic Alliances and Joint Ventures 199

Internal Development 200

How Managerial Motives Can Erode Value Creation. 201

Growth for Growth's Sake 201

Egotism. 201

Antitakeover Tactics 202

Summary. 204

CHAPTER 7

International Strategy: Creating Value in Global Markets. 210

The Global Economy: A Brief Overview. 212

Factors Affecting a Nation's Competitiveness. 214

Factor Endowments. 214

Demand Conditions 214

Related and Supporting Industries 215

Firm Strategy, Structure, and Rivalry 215

Concluding Comment on Factors Affecting a Nation's Competitiveness .215

International Expansion: A Company's Motivations and Risks 217

Motivations for International Expansion 217

Potential Risks of International Expansion. 220

Global Dispersion of Value Chains: Outsourcing and Offshoring. 223

Achieving Competitive Advantage in Global Markets 225

Two Opposing Pressures: Reducing Costs and Adapting to Local Markets 225

International Strategy 228

Global Strategy. 228

Multidomestic Strategy. 230

Transnational Strategy 232

Global or Regional? A Second Look at Globalization. . . .233

Entry Modes of International Expansion. 234

Exporting. 235

Licensing and Franchising 236

Strategic Alliances and Joint Ventures 237

Wholly Owned Subsidiaries 238

Summary. 241

CHAPTER 8

Entrepreneurial Strategy and Competitive Dynamics 246

Recognizing Entrepreneurial Opportunities. 248

Entrepreneurial Opportunities. 248

Entrepreneurial Resources 251

Entrepreneurial Leadership. 255

Entrepreneurial Strategy. 256

Entry Strategies. 257

Generic Strategies 260

Combination Strategies. 262

Competitive Dynamics. 262

New Competitive Action. 263

Threat Analysis 264

Motivation and Capability to Respond 266

Types of Competitive Actions. .267

Likelihood of Competitive Reaction. 269

Choosing Not to React: Forbearance and Co-opetition. 270

Summary. 272

PART 3 Strategic Implementation

CHAPTER 9
Strategic Control and Corporate Governance 276

Ensuring Informational Control: Responding Effectively to Environmental Change 278
A Traditional Approach to Strategic Control 278
A Contemporary Approach to Strategic Control........279

Attaining Behavioral Control: Balancing Culture, Rewards, and Boundaries 281
Building a Strong and Effective Culture..............281
Motivating with Rewards and Incentives 283
Setting Boundaries and Constraints 284
Behavioral Control in Organizations: Situational Factors...........................286
Evolving from Boundaries to Rewards and Culture.....287

The Role of Corporate Governance 288
The Modern Corporation: The Separation of Owners (Shareholders) and Management.................290
Governance Mechanisms: Aligning the Interests of Owners and Managers...................291
CEO Duality: Is It Good or Bad? 297
External Governance Control Mechanisms 298
Corporate Governance: An International Perspective................................301
Summary............................. ..... .305

CHAPTER 10
Creating Effective Organizational Designs..... 310

Traditional Forms of Organizational Structure 312
Patterns of Growth of Large Corporations: Strategy-Structure Relationships.................312
Simple Structure 314
Functional Structure 314
Divisional Structure 316
Matrix Structure 319
International Operations: Implications for Organizational Structure 321

Global Start-Ups: A Recent Phenomenon.............322
How an Organization's Structure Can Influence Strategy Formulation.........................324

Boundaryless Organizational Designs 324
The Barrier-Free Organization 324
The Modular Organization 328
The Virtual Organization........................329
Boundaryless Organizations: Making Them Work......331

Creating Ambidextrous Organizational Designs 336
Ambidextrous Organizations: Key Design Attributes....336
Why Was the Ambidextrous Organization the Most Effective Structure? 337
Summary....................................338

CHAPTER 11
Strategic Leadership: Creating a Learning Organization and an Ethical Organization 344

Leadership: Three Interdependent Activities 346
Setting a Direction 347
Designing the Organization 348
Nurturing a Culture Committed to Excellence and Ethical Behavior 349

Getting Things Done: Overcoming Barriers and Using Power 350
Overcoming Barriers to Change 350
The Effective Use of Power 351

Emotional Intelligence: A Key Leadership Trait 354
Self-Awareness 354
Self-Regulation................................354
Motivation....................................355
Empathy 355
Social Skill 356
Emotional Intelligence: Some Potential Drawbacks and Cautionary Notes 357

Developing Competency Companions and Creating a Learning Organization 358
Inspiring and Motivating People with a Mission or Purpose 360

Empowering Employees at All Levels 360
Accumulating and Sharing Internal Knowledge. 361
Gathering and Integrating External Information. 362
Challenging the Status Quo and Enabling
    Creativity 363
Creating an Ethical Organization 364
Individual Ethics versus Organizational Ethics 365
Integrity-Based versus Compliance-Based
    Approaches to Organizational Ethics 366
Role Models 368
Corporate Credos and Codes of Conduct 368
Reward and Evaluation Systems. 369
Policies and Procedures 370
Summary. 372

CHAPTER 12

Managing Innovation and Fostering Corporate Entrepreneurship 376

Managing Innovation 378
Types of Innovation. 378
Challenges of Innovation 381
Cultivating Innovation Skills .382
Defining the Scope of Innovation 384
Managing the Pace of Innovation 385
Staffing to Capture Value from Innovation 386
Collaborating with Innovation Partners 386
Corporate Entrepreneurship. 387
Focused Approaches to Corporate
    Entrepreneurship 390
Dispersed Approaches to Corporate
    Entrepreneurship 391
Measuring the Success of Corporate
    Entrepreneurship Activities .393
Real Options Analysis: A Useful Tool 395
Applications of Real Options Analysis to Strategic
    Decisions 395

Potential Pitfalls of Real Options Analysis. 396
Entrepreneurial Orientation. 398
Autonomy 399
Innovativeness. 400
Proactiveness. 401
Competitive Aggressiveness 402
Risk Taking 403
Summary. 406

PART 4 Case Analysis

CHAPTER 13

Analyzing Strategic Management Cases 412

**Why Analyze Strategic Management
Cases? 413**
How to Conduct a Case Analysis 415
Become Familiar with the Material 418
Identify Problems 418
Conduct Strategic Analyses 419
Propose Alternative Solutions. 419
Make Recommendations. 421
**How to Get the Most from Case
Analysis 422**
**Useful Decision-Making Techniques
in Case Analysis 424**
Conflict Inducing Techniques. 427
**Following the Analysis-Decision-Action
Cycle in Case Analysis 432**
Summary. 436
Appendix 1 to Chapter 13: Financial Ratio
    Analysis. 437
Appendix 2 to Chapter 13: Sources of Company and
    Industry Information 447
Cases. C-1

cases

1 REINVENTING ACCOR
Hospitality, Corporate and International strategy
This case focuses on the Accor CEO's objective to become number three in the global hotel market and covers the progress to achieve this and the current strategy being followed C2

2 APPLE AND THE RETAIL INDUSTRY FOR SPECIALIST CONSUMER ELECTRONICS IN THE UNITED KINGDOM
Consumer Electronics
This case examines competitive conditions and Apple's competitive position within the consumer electronics retail industry in the United Kingdom C10

3 ROBIN HOOD
Hypothetical; Classic
Robin Hood and his Merrymen are in trouble, as wealthy travelers are avoiding Sherwood Forest. This classic case is an excellent introduction to strategic management using a nonbusiness solution C15

4 EBAY: EXPANDING INTO CHINA
Internet
eBay announced that its PayPal business would set up an international ecommerce hub in Chongqing, China, as the company tried to gain the local expertise it desperately needed to compete with China's top auction site, Taobao. However, little ground was gained and CEO John Donahoe would have to reconcile why one of the fastest-growing companies in history was moving so slowly C16

5 MICROFINANCE BANKS: GOING GLOBAL . . . AND GOING PUBLIC?
Banking
With the global success of the microfinance concept, the number of private microfinance institutions exploded and initial public offerings for these institutions was on the rise. This transfer of control to public buyers creates a fiduciary duty of the bank's management to maximize shareholder value. Will this be a good thing for these typically "do good" banks? C27

6 MCDONALD'S
Restaurant
McDonald's turnaround strategy was working, but the firm still faced a rapidly fragmenting market where changes in the tastes of consumers had made once-exotic foods like sushi and burritos everyday options C30

7 WHIRLPOOL AND THE BUILT-IN APPLIANCE INDUSTRY IN INDIA
New Product Management, Home Appliances
India's real estate boom led to the built-in appliances industry's biggest opportunity. Whirlpool was already an established player in the home appliances segment. Should Whirlpool tap this emerging market? If so, what might be its strategic objectives and positioning strategies for dealing with the competition and appealing to its prospective customers? C36

8 THE BEST-LAID INCENTIVE PLANS
Hypothetical; HBR Brief Case
Paragon Tool, a thriving machine tool company in an increasing tough industry, has been pouring money into growth initiatives. These efforts have shrunk the company's margins, but CEO Nikolas Anaptyxi believes they'll provide the foundation for a profitable future. Now Paragon is weighing the acquisition of MonitoRobotics, a company with proprietary technology for monitoring the functioning of robotics equipment C41

9 JOHNSON & JOHNSON
Pharmaceuticals, Personal Care Products, Medical Devices
Executives from health care conglomerate Johnson & Johnson had known about a critical design flaw with an artificial hip but decided to conceal this information from physicians and patients. Johnson & Johnson's DePuy Orthopaedics unit kept selling the hip replacement. Could more centralized control improve quality? C45

10 PROCTER & GAMBLE
Consumer Products

Procter & Gamble was the world's largest consumer products conglomerate, with billion-dollar brands such as Tide, Crest, Pampers, Gillette, Right Guard, and Duracell. However, sales were down as consumers were coping with the economic downturn by switching to P&G's lower-priced brands. C52

11 STUDIO 100: A SHOWCASE IN SHOW BUSINESS
Strategy Implementation, Innovation

This case study shows how Studio 100, a family entertainment initiative, gradually evolved into an international corporation with more than 1,000 employees, dozens of popular characters, and one of the largest independent catalogues of children's TV series in the world. C57

12 RHINO CAPTURE IN KRUGER NATIONAL PARK
Ethics, Funding

When government funding for South African National Parks was reallocated elsewhere, Head of Veterinarian Wildlife Services , Dr. Markus Hofmeyr, had find a new strategy to supplement their income. His solution was controversial. C67

13 HTC CORPORATION: A SMARTPHONE PIONEER FROM TAIWAN
Telecommunications

HTC evolved from a local subcontractor for PDAs to a global force in the smartphone industry by branding its own products. C79

14 INNOVATIVE TATA INC.—INDIA'S PRIDE!
Banking

With the global success of the microfinance concept, the number of private microfinance institutions exploded and initial public offerings for these institutions was on the rise. This transfer of control to public buyers creates a fiduciary duty of the bank's management to maximize shareholder value.
Will this be a good thing for these typically "do good" banks? C92

15 DATING AT IKEA CHINA: AN UNEXPECTED MANAGEMENT CHALLENGE
Emerging Markets, Culture

When IKEA opened its Shanghai Xuhui store in 2003, it adopted some strategies, such as opening the store in the city centre rather than in the suburbs, that were different from its norm. After all, the Chinese market was different and therefore required different strategies. However, little had it anticipated that 'being different' would entail a congregation of as many as 700 senior people at its restaurant for dating purposes! C101

16 GOOGLE VENTURES: DISRUPTING CORPORATE VENTURE CAPITAL?
Technology, Venture Capital

The case study discusses the concept of corporate venture capital (VC), Google's entry into the VC market through Google Venture (GV), its business strategy, and the challenges and potential for GV in the VC industry. C103

17 HEINEKEN
Beer

Heineken can lay claim to a brand that may be the closest thing to a global beer brand. But in the United States, Heineken has lost its leading position among imported beers to Corona, the Mexican beer that is often served with a garnish of lime. Would the move to acquire Asian Pacific Breweries and Tiger Beer brand help it in Asia? C109

18 YAHOO!
Internet

Marissa Mayer, Yahoo's new CEO, was determined to make the company a stronger force on smartphones and tablets. Would Mayer be able to lure back advertisers, reinvigorate a muddled brand, and improve morale at a company that has been marred by executive churn, constant cost-cutting, and mass layoffs? C114

19 NETFLIX: CAN IT RECOVER FROM ITS STRATEGY MISTAKES?
Entertainment

The home entertainment industry has been revolutionized over the last decade. This case examines some of the key strategic decisions Netflix has had to make to ensure its on-going success. C120

20 BUILDING THE NEW BOSCO-ZETA PHARMA (A)

Pharmaceuticals

After Bosco acquires Zeta AG, the company's chairman is unsure whether to merge the two firms using only internal resources or to enlist the help of an outside management consulting firm. This merger is the biggest in Bosco's history, and it is critical to mesh the companies' cultures and achieve ambitious cost savings C138

21 SILENCE IS NOT GOLDEN: GOLDEN AGRI-RESOURCES, GREENPEACE AND SUSTAINABLE PALM OIL

Corporate Responsibility, Crisis Management

The case covers the campaign by Greenpeace against the Indonesian company Golden Agri Resources (GAR), over allegations that GAR's palm oil production techniques were contributing to rapid deforestation and increasing CO_2 emissions. It also touches on the legitimacy and impacts of NGO campaigns. The case illustrates a number of important points such as a clash of management cultures; wise decision-making when facing a perfect storm of media swarming; and supply chains and reputational risks C149

22 GOING FLAT: PURSUIT OF A DEMOCRATIC ORGANIZATIONAL STRUCTURE

Organization Structure

An MBA graduate explored her options for full-time employment. She found the Ethical Business Company (EBC) and was instantly intrigued by their flat organizational structure. However, after three weeks at EBC, she wonders if a flat structure is right for all companies and all employees or if there are certain companies and people who fit better than others in the hierarchy more than others C153

23 PIXAR

Movies

Disney CEO Bob Iger worked hard to clinch the deal to acquire Pixar, whose track record has made it one of the world's most successful animation companies. Iger realized, however, that he must try to protect Pixar's creative culture while also trying to carry that culture over to some of Disney's animation efforts C157

24 APPLE INC.: STILL TAKING A BITE OUT OF THE COMPETITION?

Computers, Consumer Electronics

Apple was flying high on the success of the iPad mini and iPhone 5. However, CEO Tim Cook had big shoes to fill without founder Steve Jobs C161

Indexes   I-1

Company   I-1

Name   I-6

Subject   I-20

The Strategic Management Process

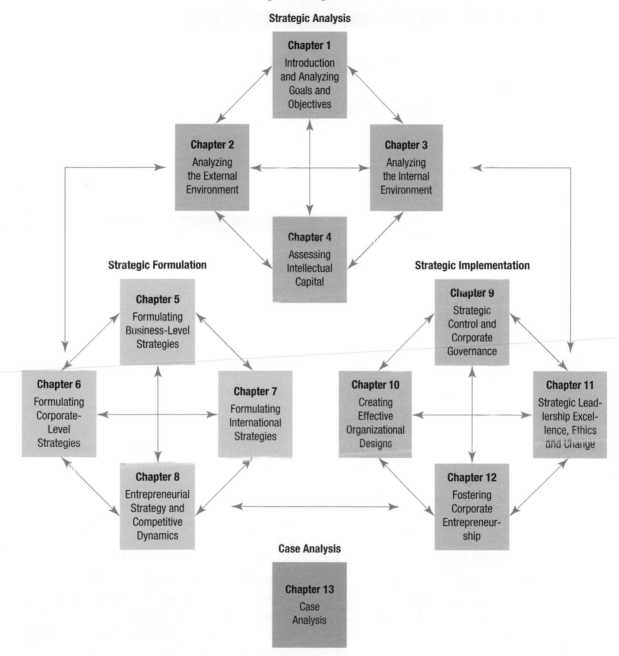

Strategic Analysis

Chapter 1
Introduction and Analyzing Goals and Objectives

Chapter 2
Analyzing the External Environment

Chapter 3
Analyzing the Internal Environment

Chapter 4
Assessing Intellectual Capital

Strategic Formulation

Chapter 5
Formulating Business-Level Strategies

Chapter 6
Formulating Corporate-Level Strategies

Chapter 7
Formulating International Strategies

Chapter 8
Entrepreneurial Strategy and Competitive Dynamics

Strategic Implementation

Chapter 9
Strategic Control and Corporate Governance

Chapter 10
Creating Effective Organizational Designs

Chapter 11
Strategic Leadership Excellence, Ethics and Change

Chapter 12
Fostering Corporate Entrepreneurship

Case Analysis

Chapter 13
Case Analysis

chapter 1

Strategic Management
Creating Competitive Advantages

After reading this chapter, you should have a good understanding of the following learning objectives:

LO1.1 The definition of strategic management and its four key attributes.

LO1.2 The strategic management process and its three interrelated and principal activities.

LO1.3 The vital role of corporate governance and stakeholder management, as well as how "symbiosis" can be achieved among an organization's stakeholders.

LO1.4 The importance of social responsibility, including environmental sustainability, and how it can enhance a corporation's innovation strategy.

LO1.5 The need for greater empowerment throughout the organization.

LO1.6 How an awareness of a hierarchy of strategic goals can help an organization achieve coherence in its strategic direction.

Learning from Mistakes

Microsoft hits another bump in the road

Microsoft, the perennial leader in PC operating systems and software, is increasingly coming under fire for its perceived lack of product innovation. It seems like a day doesn't go by without Microsoft delivering more disappointing news about some product's lacklustre performance. Does anyone remember the Zune personal media player or the Kin phone?

To be fair, with almost $60 billion in gross profits, and 90,000 employees in over 190 countries, Microsoft is no garage start-up. Its main campus in Seattle has over 120 buildings, its own transportation system, basketball courts and a shopping mall.

Despite the many trappings of success, Microsoft is still considered by many tech analysts to be a second rate company when it comes to innovation, as compared to Google, Apple, Facebook and Amazon. Critics maintain that for years Microsoft chose to rest on its laurels, content to receive a steady, if impressive, revenue stream from its virtual global monopoly on PC operating systems. But as people switch in

droves to smart phones and tablets (and competitors' operating systems) Microsoft is now seen as trying to play "catch up," and stumbling badly in the process.

The company recently took a $900 million write off due to poor sales of its Surface RT tablet—this compared to the estimated $25 billion that Apple made selling iPads over a comparable period. Microsoft's tablet device was supposed to be the showcase vehicle for the newest version of its flagship product—the Windows 8 operating system. Unfortunately, the latest Windows incarnation received a lukewarm reception and weak demand, which negatively impacted tablet sales. And while the Windows smart phone operating system (used primarily by Nokia) is more popular than the BlackBerry, it pales in comparison to Google's Android operating system, which commands an almost 80 percent market share.

Microsoft was also seen as tardy to the growing trend of "cloud computing" (although it *was* quicker than many rivals to capitalize on providing cloud services to large commercial customers). One bright spot for Microsoft would be the success of its Xbox entertainment centre, which accounts for about 14 percent of the company's revenue.

Still, there's a nagging perception that Microsoft is a runner up in the field of hi-tech, consistently presenting the wrong products for the markets that matter. In a swipe, Eric Schmidt (Chairman of Google) said that Microsoft is a well-run company but "they haven't been able to bring state-of-the-art products into the fields" that count. As proof, critics point out that once the Apple iPad was released, global PC sales started to stall. The iPad's position was then reinforced by the iPhone, a device that Microsoft's CEO Steve Ballmer mocked when released. Mr. Ballmer is probably laughing less now. He announced his "retirement" in August 2013 (some believe he was forced out as a result of Microsoft's perceived weakness and poor performance as compared to Apple and Google). In a final insult, on the day of Mr. Ballmer's announcement, Microsoft stock went up 7.3 percent.

In a nod to critics, the company unveiled a reorganization plan in July 2013, with the stated goal of becoming more of a "devices and services" company. Previously, Microsoft was comprised mainly of five divisions, with the "Windows" and "Server and Tools" divisions providing about 50% of revenue. The "Business" division provided about another 25 percent. This divisional arrangement was seen as a hindrance to innovation and communication, key characteristics needed to excel in the field of hi-tech. Microsoft now says that it is "rallying behind a single strategy as one company." It wants to avoid being a "collection of divisional strategies." Previously, complaints had been leveled about the prominence of the Windows division.

Microsoft's new strategy and organization intends to achieve a "holistic" approach by rearranging the company into four "engineering groups" that will operate along more functional lines. One division will house all of the operating systems regardless of the devices they will run. Actual devices will be located in another division. All technology related to searches (the Bing search engine for example) and productivity (the ubiquitous Office software suite) will be put together in a third group called "Application." A "Cloud" group will now be responsible for all of the company's data centers, databases and the service requirements of large commercial customers.

In one of its first major moves after the announced strategic reorganization, Microsoft revealed that it would be paying over $7 billion for Nokia's smartphone business. The acquisition will give Microsoft access to badly needed mobile skills and technology, and is a clear sign that the company plans to compete directly with Apple and Google for a bigger share of the ever growing smartphone market. But critics say Microsoft had no choice, since it was rumoured that Nokia was going to stop making Windows phones anyway.

What many people fail to realize about Microsoft is that, while possibly lacking "buzz," it still relies mainly on the steady loyalty of corporate IT managers for a large proportion of its revenue. These are a cautious bunch, not prone to chasing the latest fad when choosing a product. This cannot be readily said for the customers of Microsoft's competitors.

It's anyone's guess as to whether or not the new organization structure will just help clean up Microsoft's image problem, or genuinely help the company innovate and create. But shaking things up with regards to product development and strategy execution will certainly result in changes. One thing we can be sure of, with a market capitalization of $260 billion and over $70 billion in cash on hand, Microsoft won't be giving up the fight anytime soon.

By Tom McNamara and Erika Marsillac

Discussion Questions

1. What are some of the perceived problems and issues at Microsoft?
2. What steps has Microsoft taken to improve its strategic position?
3. What do you think the future holds for Microsoft?

The recent problems at Microsoft illustrate how even well-established firms can struggle in the marketplace if they do not anticipate and respond proactively to changes in the environment. Today's leaders face a large number of complex challenges in the global marketplace. In considering how much credit (or blame) they deserve, two perspectives of leadership come immediately to mind: the "romantic" and "external control" perspectives.[4] First, let's look at the **romantic view of leadership.** Here, the implicit assumption is that the leader is the key force in determining an organization's success—or lack thereof.[5] This view dominates the popular press in business magazines such as *Fortune, BusinessWeek,* and *Forbes,* wherein the CEO is either lauded for his or her firm's success or chided for the organization's demise.[6]

romantic view of leadership
situations in which the leader is the key force determining the organization's success—or lack thereof.

Consider, for example, the credit that has been bestowed on leaders such as Jack Welch, Andrew Grove, and Herb Kelleher for the tremendous accomplishments when they led their firms, General Electric, Intel, and Southwest Airlines, respectively.

Similarly, Apple's success in the last decade has been attributed almost entirely to the late Steve Jobs, its former CEO, who died on October 5, 2011.[7] Apple's string of hit products, such as iMac computers, iPods, iPhones, and iPads, are testament to his genius for developing innovative, user-friendly, and aesthetically pleasing products. In addition to being a perfectionist in product design, Jobs also was a master showman with a cult following. During his time as CEO between 1997 and 2011, Apple's market value soared by over $300 billion!

On the other hand, when things don't go well, much of the failure of an organization can also, rightfully, be attributed to the leader.[8] Micrsoft's leadership clearly failed to respond effectively to changes taking place in the technology industry. In contrast, Apple fully capitalized on emerging technology trends with a variety of products, including sophisticated smartphones.

The contrasting fortunes of Hewlett-Packard under two different CEOs also demonstrate the influence leadership has on firm performance.[9] When Carly Fiorina was fired as CEO of the firm, HP enjoyed an immediate increase in its stock price of 7 percent—hardly a strong endorsement of her leadership! Her successor, Mark Hurd, led the firm to five years of outstanding financial results. Interestingly, when he abruptly resigned on August 6, 2010, the firm's stock dropped 12 percent almost instantly! (To provide some perspective, this represents a decrease in HP's market value of about $12 billion.) And, since Hurd's departure, HP's market capitalization has dropped about 80 percent—as of early 2013!

However, this reflects only part of the picture. Consider another perspective, called the **external control view of leadership.** Here, rather than making the implicit assumption that the leader is the most important factor in determining organizational outcomes, the focus is on external factors that may positively (or negatively) affect a firm's success. We don't have to look far to support this perspective. Developments in the general environment, such as economic downturns, governmental legislation, or an outbreak of major internal conflict or war, can greatly restrict the choices that are available to a firm's executives. Borders, as well as several other book retailers, found the consumer shift away from brick and mortar bookstores to online book buying (e.g., Amazon) and digital books an overwhelming environmental force against which they had few defenses.

Major unanticipated developments can often have very negative consequences for businesses regardless of how well formulated their strategies are.

Let's look at a few recent examples:[10]

- Hurricane Katrina in 2007 had a disastrous effect on businesses located along the Gulf Coast.
- The financial meltdown of 2008 and the resultant deep recession during the following two years forced once proud corporations like General Motors and Citigroup to ask for government bailouts. Others, such as Merrill Lynch and Washington Mutual, had to be acquired by other firms.
- In the aftermath of BP's disastrous oil well explosion on April 20, 2010, the fishing and tourism industries in the region suffered significant downturns. BP itself was forced to pay a $20 billion fine to the U.S. government.
- On March 11, 2011, a 9.0 earthquake and tsunami devastated Japan and resulted in the loss of more than 20,000 lives. During the next two trading days, the country's stock exchange (Nikkei) suffered its biggest loss in 40 years. The disaster hit nearly every industry hard—especially energy companies. For example, Tokyo Electric Power Co., which operates a nuclear power plant that was severly damaged, fell 24.7 percent, and Toshiba Corp., a maker of nuclear power plants, slid 19.5 percent.

external control view of leadership situations in which external forces—where the leader has limited influence—determine the organization's success.

ECONOMIC CRISIS IN EUROPE:
THE FALLOUT CONTINUES

The European economic crisis increasingly appears to be an unending drama in slow motion. While finance ministers and central bankers propose and reject or implement and fail with one solution after another, unemployment keeps rising, banks falter, and public anger boils over. Greece is on the verge of a political and economic meltdown, Portugal and Spain are in prolonged recession, and Italy's problems now seem worse than anticipated. Only a decade ago, the 27-nation European Union, and the 17-nation Eurozone within that, was considered an economic powerhouse. Today, the very future of the Union and the Euro seems mired in uncertainty.

What are some of the implications of the economic crisis so far? First, it has led to widespread political protests. As governments like Portugal and Spain have been forced to cut government spending as part of the austerity programs they are implementing, public resentment has boiled over into often violent street protests. A public long used to generous welfare payments by the government finds it difficult to adjust to an environment without the safety nets that they have taken for granted for at least two generations. Second, political resentment has, in turn, led to changes in governments. In 2012, Francois Hollande was elected as president of France on a platform that threatened 75 percent taxes on the wealthy (which caused many prominent French citizens to change their citizenship!). Italy brought in Mario Monti, a seasoned economist, to lead the country out of the quagmire in place of the colorful, but highly controversial Silvio Berlusconi.

A major cause as well as consequence of the financial crisis has been the weakening of European banks, especially in countries such as Spain. As the real estate boom in Spain ended in an inevitable bust, banks found themselves holding too much real estate as collateral that did not cover the value of the loans. The resulting crisis of confidence in banks has forced the European Central Bank to pump in vast resources to prop up the tottering banks.

The joint effects of less government spending, inability of banks to lend, and civil unrest in various countries has been devastating on the employment situation in Europe. Spain currently has an unemployment rate of 24 percent. At the beginning of 2012, the under-25 unemployment rate in Spain stood at a staggering 51.4 percent. This compares to an overall unemployment rate of 7.9 percent in the United States as of early 2013—a rate that most Americans consider unacceptable. This certainly helps us to place the situation in perspective! The high unemployment rate among the youth has led to a number of social problems, such as increased crime rates, drug use, and depression. Because many young people in Europe do not expect the situation to improve in the foreseeable future, there has been a sudden increase in outward migration. Thousands of Portuguese youngsters, for example, have been migrating to their country's former colonies, such as Angola and Mozambique in Africa and Brazil in South America. One in ten college graduates now leave the country. In 2010 alone, the number of Portuguese workers in Brazil jumped by 60,000. Skilled Portuguese workers are also increasingly immigrating to countries such as the United States, Canada, and Australia. There are 50,000 Germans in Silicon Valley and over 500 start-ups in the San Francisco Bay area with French founders.

One industry that is feeling immense pain from the economic crisis is tourism. France, Spain, and Italy—the three biggest tourist destinations in Europe—have experienced double-digit declines in tourist arrivals and hotel occupancy rates in recent years. The tourism industry in France employs 900,000 people and generates $96 billion in revenues. In Spain, the industry employs 1.4 million people and generates about $110 billion in revenues. The decline in tourist arrivals has had a devastating effect on employment in tourism-related businesses such as hotels, restaurants, and travel.

Sources: Ash, L. 2011. Portugal's jobless graduates flee to Africa and Brazil. *bbc.co.uk*, August 31: np; Les miserables. 2012. *economist.com*, July 28, np; Clouds over the Mediterranean. 2012. *economist.com*, July 28: np; and Govan, F. 2012. Spain's lost generation: Youth unemployment surges above 50 percent. *telegraph .co.uk*, January 27: np.

Firms as diverse as Toyota, Honda, and Sony were forced to halt production because extensive damage to roads and distribution systems made it nearly impossible to move products.

The continuing economic in Europe has been a source of considerable uncertainty for firms doing business in Europe and throughout the world. Strategy Spotlight 1.1 discusses some of the causes and consequences of the ongoing European crisis.

Before moving on, it is important to point out that successful executives are often able to navigate around the difficult circumstances that they face. At times it can be refreshing to see the optimistic position they take when they encounter seemingly insurmountable odds. Of course, that's not to say that one should be naïve or Pollyannaish. Consider, for example, how one CEO is handling trying times:[11]

Name a general economic woe, and chances are that Charles Needham, CEO of Metorex, is dealing with it.

- Market turmoil has knocked 80 percent off the shares of South Africa's Metorex, the mining company that he heads.
- The plunge in global commodities is slamming prices for the copper, cobalt, and other minerals Metorex unearths across Africa. The credit crisis makes it harder to raise money.
- And fighting has again broken out in the Democratic Republic of Congo, where Metorex has a mine and several projects in development.

Such problems might send many executives to the window ledge. Yet Needham appears unruffled as he sits down at a conference table in the company's modest offices in a Johannesburg suburb. The combat in northeast Congo, he notes, is far from Metorex's mine. Commodity prices are still high, in historical terms. And Needham is confident he can raise enough capital, drawing on relationships with South African banks. "These are the kinds of things you deal with, doing business in Africa," he says.

What Is Strategic Management?

Given the many challenges and opportunities in the global marketplace, today's managers must do more than set long-term strategies and hope for the best.[12] They must go beyond what some have called "incremental management," whereby they view their job as making a series of small, minor changes to improve the efficiency of their firm's operations.[13] Rather than seeing their role as merely custodians of the status quo, today's leaders must be proactive, anticipate change, and continually refine and, when necessary, make dramatic changes to their strategies. The strategic management of the organization must become both a process and a way of thinking throughout the organization.

Defining Strategic Management

Strategic management consists of the analyses, decisions, and actions an organization undertakes in order to create and sustain competitive advantages. This definition captures two main elements that go to the heart of the field of strategic management.

First, the strategic management of an organization entails three ongoing processes: *analyses, decisions,* and *actions.* Strategic management is concerned with the *analysis* of strategic goals (vision, mission, and strategic objectives) along with the analysis of the internal and external environment of the organization. Next, leaders must make strategic *decisions.* These *decisions,* broadly speaking, address two basic questions. What industries should we compete in? How should we compete in those industries? These questions also often involve an organization's domestic and international operations. And last are the *actions* that must be taken. Decisions are of little use, of course, unless they are acted on. Firms must take the necessary actions to implement their **strategies.** This requires leaders to allocate the necessary resources and to design the organization to bring the intended strategies to reality.

Second, the essence of strategic management is the study of why some firms outperform others.[14] Thus, managers need to determine how a firm is to compete so that it can obtain advantages that are sustainable over a lengthy period of time. That means focusing on two fundamental questions:

- *How should we compete in order to create **competitive advantages** in the marketplace?* Managers need to determine if the firm should position itself as the low-cost producer or develop products and services that are unique and will enable the firm to charge premium prices. Or should they do some combination of both?
- *How can we create competitive advantages in the marketplace that are unique, valuable, and difficult for rivals to copy or substitute?* That is, managers need to make such advantages sustainable, instead of temporary.

strategic management
the analyses, decisions, and actions an organization undertakes in order to create and sustain competitive advantages.

L01.1
The definition of strategic management and its four key attributes.

strategy
The ideas, decisions, and actions that enable a firm to succeed.

competitive advantage
A firm's resources and capabilities that enable it to overcome the competitive forces in its industry(ies).

Sustainable competitive advantage cannot be achieved through operational effectiveness alone.[15] The popular management innovations of the last two decades—total quality, just-in-time, benchmarking, business process reengineering, outsourcing—are all about operational effectiveness. **Operational effectiveness** means performing similar activities better than rivals. Each of these is important, but none lead to sustainable competitive advantage because everyone is doing them. Strategy is all about being different. Sustainable competitive advantage is possible only by performing different activities from rivals or performing similar activities in different ways. Companies such as Walmart, Southwest Airlines, and IKEA have developed unique, internally consistent, and difficult-to-imitate activity systems that have provided them with sustained competitive advantages. A company with a good strategy must make clear choices about what it wants to accomplish. Trying to do everything that your rivals do eventually leads to mutually destructive price competition, not long-term advantage.

operational effectiveness
performing similar activities better than rivals.

The Four Key Attributes of Strategic Management

Before discussing the strategic management process, let's briefly talk about four attributes of strategic management.[16] It should become clear how this course differs from other courses that you have had in functional areas, such as accounting, marketing, operations, and finance. Exhibit 1.1 provides a definition and the four attributes of strategic management.

First, strategic management is *directed toward overall organizational goals and objectives.* That is, effort must be directed at what is best for the total organization, not just a single functional area. Some authors have referred to this perspective as "organizational versus individual rationality."[17] That is, what might look "rational" or ideal for one functional area, such as operations, may not be in the best interest of the overall firm. For example, operations may decide to schedule long production runs of similar products to lower unit costs. However, the standardized output may be counter to what the marketing department needs to appeal to a demanding target market. Similarly, research and development may "overengineer" the product to develop a far superior offering, but the design may make the product so expensive that market demand is minimal.

Second, strategic management *includes multiple stakeholders in decision making.*[18] **Stakeholders** are those individuals, groups, and organizations who have a "stake" in the success of the organization, including owners (shareholders in a publicly held corporation), employees, customers, suppliers, the community at large, and so on. (We'll discuss this in more detail later in this chapter.) Managers will not be successful if they focus on a single stakeholder. For example, if the overwhelming emphasis is on generating profits for the owners, employees may become alienated, customer service may suffer, and the suppliers may resent demands for pricing concessions.

stakeholders
individuals, groups, and organizations who have a stake in the success of the organization, including owners (shareholders in a publicly held corporation), employees, customers, suppliers, and the community at large.

Third, strategic management *requires incorporating both short-term and long-term perspectives.*[19] Peter Senge, a leading strategic management author, has referred to this need as a "creative tension."[20] That is, managers must maintain both a vision for the future of the organization as well as a focus on its present operating needs. However, financial

EXHIBIT 1.1
Strategic Management Concepts

Definition: Strategic management consists of the analyses, decisions, and actions an organization undertakes in order to create and sustain competitive advantages.

Key Attributes of Strategic Management

- Directs the organization toward overall goals and objectives.
- Includes multiple stakeholders in decision making.
- Needs to incorporate short-term and long-term perspectives.
- Recognizes trade-offs between efficiency and effectiveness.

markets can exert significant pressures on executives to meet short-term performance targets. Studies have shown that corporate leaders often take a short-term approach to the detriment of creating long-term shareholder value. Consider the following:

> According to recent studies, only 59 percent of financial executives say they would pursue a positive net present value project if it meant missing the quarter's consensus earnings per-share estimate. Worse, 78 percent say they would sacrifice value—often a great deal of value—to smooth earnings. Similarly, managers are more likely to cut R&D to reverse an earning slide if a significant amount of the company's equity is owned by institutions with high portfolio turnover. Many companies have the same philosophy about long-term investments such as infrastructure and employee training.[21]

Fourth, strategic management *involves the recognition of trade-offs between effectiveness and efficiency.* Some authors have referred to this as the difference between "doing the right thing" (**effectiveness**) and "doing things right" (**efficiency**).[22] While managers must allocate and use resources wisely, they must still direct their efforts toward the attainment of overall organizational objectives. Managers who only focus on meeting short-term budgets and targets may fail to attain the broader goals. Consider the following amusing story told by Norman Augustine, former CEO of defense giant Martin Marietta (now Lockheed Martin):

> I am reminded of an article I once read in a British newspaper which described a problem with the local bus service between the towns of Bagnall and Greenfields. It seemed that, to the great annoyance of customers, drivers had been passing long queues of would be passengers with a smile and a wave of the hand. This practice was, however, clarified by a bus company official who explained, "It is impossible for the drivers to keep their timetables if they must stop for passengers."[23]

Clearly, the drivers who were trying to stay on schedule had ignored the overall mission. As Augustine noted, "Impeccable logic but something seems to be missing!"

Successful managers must make many trade-offs. It is central to the practice of strategic management. At times, managers must focus on the short term and efficiency; at other times the emphasis is on the long term and expanding a firm's product-market scope in order to anticipate opportunities in the competitive environment. For example, consider Kevin Sharer's perspective. He is CEO of Amgen, the giant $17 billion biotechnology firm:

> A CEO must always be switching between what I call different altitudes—tasks of different levels of abstraction and specificity. At the highest altitude you're asking the big questions: What are the company's mission and strategy? Do people understand and believe in these aims? Are decisions consistent with them? At the lowest altitude, you're looking at on-the-ground operations: Did we make that sale? What was the yield on that last lot in the factory? How many days of inventory do we have for a particular drug? And then there's everything in between: How many chemists do we need to hire this quarter? What should we pay for a small biotech company that has a promising new drug? Is our production capacity adequate to roll out a product in a new market?[24]

Some authors have developed the concept of **"ambidexterity"** which refers to a manager's challenge to both align resources to take advantage of existing product markets as well as proactively explore new opportunities.[25] Strategy Spotlight 1.2 discusses ambidextrous behaviors that are required for success in today's challenging marketplace.

The Strategic Management Process

We've identified three ongoing processes—analyses, decisions, and actions—that are central to strategic management. In practice, these three processes—often referred to as strategy analysis, strategy formulation, and strategy implementation—are highly interdependent and do not take place one after the other in a sequential fashion in most companies.

effectiveness
tailoring actions to the needs of an organization rather than wasting effort, or "doing the right thing."

efficiency
performing actions at a low cost relative to a benchmark, or "doing things right."

ambidexterity
the challenge managers face of both aligning resources to take advantage of existing product markets as well as proactively exploring new opportunities.

strategic management process
strategy analysis, strategy formulation, and strategy implementation

LO1.2
The strategic management process and its three interrelated and principal activities.

AMBIDEXTROUS BEHAVIORS: COMBINING ALIGNMENT AND ADAPTABILITY

A recent study involving 41 business units in 10 multinational companies identified four ambidextrous behaviors in individuals. Such behaviors are the essence of ambidexterity, and they illustrate how a dual capacity for alignment and adaptability can be woven into the fabric of an organization at the individual level.

They take time and are alert to opportunities beyond the confines of their own jobs. A large computer company's sales manager became aware of a need for a new software module that nobody currently offered. Instead of selling the customer something else, he worked up a business case for the new module. With management's approval, he began working full time on its development.

They are cooperative and seek out opportunities to combine their efforts with others. A marketing manager for Italy was responsible for supporting a newly acquired subsidiary. When frustrated about the limited amount of contact she had with her peers in other countries, she began discussions with them. This led to the creation of a European marketing forum which meets quarterly to discuss issues, share best practices, and collaborate on marketing plans.

They are brokers, always looking to build internal networks. When visiting the head office in St. Louis, a Canadian plant manager heard about plans for a $10 million investment for a new tape manufacturing plant. After inquiring further about the plans and returning to Canada, he contacted a regional manager in Manitoba, who he knew was looking for ways to build his business. With some generous support from the Manitoba government, the regional manager bid for, and ultimately won, the $10 million investment.

They are multitaskers who are comfortable wearing more than one hat. Although an operations manager for a major coffee and tea distributor was charged with running his plant as efficiently as possible, he took it upon himself to identify value-added services for his clients. By developing a dual role, he was able to manage operations and develop a promising electronic module that automatically reported impending problems inside a coffee vending machine. With corporate funding, he found a subcontractor to develop the software, and he then piloted the module in his own operations. It was so successful that it was eventually adopted by operations managers in several other countries.

A recent *Harvard Business Review* article provides some useful insights on how one can become a more ambidextrous leader. Consider the following questions:

- **Do you meet your numbers?**
- **Do you help others?**
- **What do you do for your peers?** Are you just their in-house competitor?
- **When you manage up, do you bring problems—or problems with possible solutions?**
- **Are you transparent?** Managers who get a reputation for spinning events gradually lose the trust of peers and superiors.
- **Are you developing a group of senior-managers who know you and are willing to back your original ideas with resources?**

Source: Birkinshaw, J. & Gibson, C. 2004. Building ambidexterity into an organization. *MIT Sloan Management Review,* 45(4): 47–55; and, Bower, J. L. 2007. Solve the succession crisis by growing inside-out leaders. *Harvard Business Review,* 85(11): 90–99.

Intended versus Realized Strategies

Henry Mintzberg, a management scholar at McGill University, argues that viewing the strategic management process as one in which analysis is followed by optimal decisions and their subsequent meticulous implementation neither describes the strategic management process accurately nor prescribes ideal practice.[26] He sees the business environment as far from predictable, thus limiting our ability for analysis. Further, decisions are seldom based on optimal rationality alone, given the political processes that occur in all organizations.[27]

Taking into consideration the limitations discussed above, Mintzberg proposed an alternative model. As depicted in Exhibit 1.2, decisions following from analysis, in this model, constitute the *intended* **strategy** of the firm. For a variety of reasons, the intended strategy rarely survives in its original form. Unforeseen environmental developments, unanticipated resource constraints, or changes in managerial preferences may result in at least some parts of the intended strategy remaining *unrealized*. On the other hand, good managers will want to take advantage of a new opportunity presented by the environment, even if it was not part of the original set of intentions. For example, consider how China's growing middle class has helped cargo carriers rebound from a recent recession.

intended strategy
strategy in which organizational decisions are determined only by analysis.

EXHIBIT 1.2 Realized Strategy and Intended Strategy: Usually Not the Same

Source: From Mintzberg, H. & Waters, J. A., "Of Strategies: Deliberate and Emergent," *Strategic Management Journal,* Vol. 6, 1985, pp. 257–272. Copyright © John Wiley & Sons Limited. Reproduced with permission.

China's soaring demand for luxury goods and perishable foods from overseas has led to a dramatic increase in demand for air shipments. For example, Cathay Pacific, the largest carrier in Hong Kong, is flying 100 tons of lobster and 150 tons of grouper to China and Hong Kong every month from Australia and Indonesia. It also increased shipments of sashimi-grade fish to the country from Tokyo by 60 percent.

United Parcel Service, the world's largest package-delivery firm, has added two cargo planes in Hong Kong and one in Shanghai. FedEx, the world's largest air cargo carrier, is planning to buy more air freighters for its longest routes to Asia.[28]

Thus, the final **realized strategy** of any firm is a combination of deliberate and emergent strategies.

Next, we will address each of the three key strategic management processes: strategy analysis, strategy formulation, and strategy implementation and provide a brief overview of the chapters.

Exhibit 1.3 depicts the strategic management process and indicates how it ties into the chapters in the book. Consistent with our discussion above, we use two-way arrows to convey the interactive nature of the processes.

Strategy Analysis

> "The first thing I have to do is to have people understand where I'm going to take the company. And it has to be crystal clear. And not only does it have to be crystal clear, but everybody in the organization has to understand it, they have to have line of sight to that goal, and they have to understand how what they're doing is going to help us move into the future."
>
> —Joseph Jimenez, CEO of Novartis[29]

Strategy analysis may be looked upon as the starting point of the strategic management process. It consists of the "advance work" that must be done in order to effectively formulate and implement strategies. Many strategies fail because managers may want to formulate and implement strategies without a careful analysis of the overarching goals of the organization and without a thorough analysis of its external and internal environment.

Analyzing Organizational Goals and Objectives (Chapter 1) A firm's vision, mission, and strategic objectives form a hierarchy of goals that range from broad statements of intent and bases for competitive advantage to specific, measurable strategic objectives.

Analyzing the External Environment of the Firm (Chapter 2) Managers must monitor and scan the environment as well as analyze competitors. Two frameworks are provided: (1) the general environment consists of several elements, such as demographic and

realized strategy strategy in which organizational decisions are determined by both analysis and unforeseen environmental developments, unanticipated resource constraints, and/or changes in managerial preferences.

strategy analysis study of firms' external and internal environments, and their fit with organizational vision and goals.

EXHIBIT 1.3 The Strategic Management Process

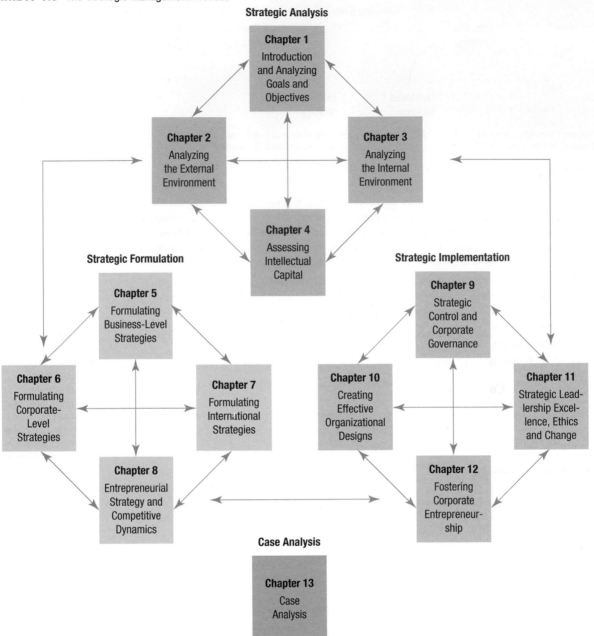

Strategic Analysis

Chapter 1
Introduction and Analyzing Goals and Objectives

Chapter 2
Analyzing the External Environment

Chapter 3
Analyzing the Internal Environment

Chapter 4
Assessing Intellectual Capital

Strategic Formulation

Chapter 5
Formulating Business-Level Strategies

Chapter 6
Formulating Corporate-Level Strategies

Chapter 7
Formulating International Strategies

Chapter 8
Entrepreneurial Strategy and Competitive Dynamics

Strategic Implementation

Chapter 9
Strategic Control and Corporate Governance

Chapter 10
Creating Effective Organizational Designs

Chapter 11
Strategic Leadership Excellence, Ethics and Change

Chapter 12
Fostering Corporate Entrepreneurship

Case Analysis

Chapter 13
Case Analysis

economic segments, and (2) the industry environment consists of competitors and other organizations that may threaten the success of a firm's products and services.

Assessing the Internal Environment of the Firm (Chapter 3) Analyzing the strengths and relationships among the activities that constitute a firm's value chain (e.g., operations, marketing and sales, and human resource management) can be a means of uncovering potential sources of competitive advantage for the firm.[30]

Assessing a Firm's Intellectual Assets (Chapter 4) The knowledge worker and a firm's other intellectual assets (e.g., patents) are important drivers of competitive advantages and wealth creation. We also assess how well the organization creates networks and relationships as well as how technology can enhance collaboration among employees and provide a means of accumulating and storing knowledge.[31]

Strategy Formulation

strategy formulation decisions made by firms regarding investments, commitments, and other aspects of operations that create and sustain competitive advantage.

"We measure, study, quantify, analyze every single piece of our business. . . . But then you've got to be able to take all that data and information and transform it into change in the organization and improvement in the organization and the formulation of the business strategy."

Richard Anderson, CEO of Delta Airlines[32]

Strategy formulation is developed at several levels. First, business-level strategy addresses the issue of how to compete in a given business to attain competitive advantage. Second, corporate-level strategy focuses on two issues: (a) what businesses to compete in and (b) how businesses can be managed to achieve synergy; that is, they create more value by working together than by operating as stand-alone businesses. Third, a firm must develop international strategies as it ventures beyond its national boundaries. Fourth, managers must formulate effective entrepreneurial initiatives.

Formulating Business-Level Strategy (Chapter 5)   The question of how firms compete and outperform their rivals and how they achieve and sustain competitive advantages goes to the heart of strategic management. Successful firms strive to develop bases for competitive advantage, which can be achieved through cost leadership and/or differentiation as well as by focusing on a narrow or industrywide market segment.[33]

Formulating Corporate-Level Strategy (Chapter 6)   Corporate-level strategy addresses a firm's portfolio (or group) of businesses. It asks (1) What business (or businesses) should we compete in? and (2) How can we manage this portfolio of businesses to create synergies among the businesses?

Formulating International Strategy (Chapter 7)   When firms enter foreign markets, they face both opportunities and pitfalls.[34] Managers must decide not only on the most appropriate entry strategy but also how they will go about attaining competitive advantages in international markets.[35]

Entrepreneurial Strategy and Competitive Dynamics (Chapter 8)   Entrepreneurial activity aimed at new value creation is a major engine for economic growth. For entrepreneurial initiatives to succeed viable opportunities must be recognized and effective strategies must be formulated.

Strategy Implementation

strategy implementation actions made by firms that carry out the formulated strategy, including strategic controls, organizational design, and leadership.

"We could leave our strategic plan on an airplane, and it wouldn't matter. It's all about execution."

John Stumpf, CEO of Wells Fargo[36]

Clearly, sound strategies are of no value if they are not properly implemented.[37] Strategy implementation involves ensuring proper strategic controls and organizational designs, which includes establishing effective means to coordinate and integrate activities within the firm as well as with its suppliers, customers, and alliance partners.[38] Leadership plays a central role to ensure that the organization is committed to excellence and ethical behavior. It also promotes learning and continuous improvement and acts entrepreneurially in creating new opportunities.

Strategic Control and Corporate Governance (Chapter 9)   Firms must exercise two types of strategic control. First, informational control requires that organizations continually monitor and scan the environment and respond to threats and opportunities. Second, behavioral control involves the proper balance of rewards and incentives as well as cultures and boundaries (or constraints). Further, successful firms (those that are incorporated) practice effective corporate governance.

Creating Effective Organizational Designs (Chapter 10)   Firms must have organizational structures and designs that are consistent with their strategy. In today's rapidly changing competitive environments, firms must ensure that their organizational boundaries—those internal to the firm and external—are more flexible and permeable.[39] Often, organizations develop strategic alliances to capitalize on the capabilities of other organizations.

Creating a Learning Organization and an Ethical Organization (Chapter 11)   Effective leaders set a direction, design the organization, and develop an organization that is committed to excellence and ethical behavior. In addition, given rapid and unpredictable change, leaders must create a "learning organization" so that the entire organization can benefit from individual and collective talents.

Fostering Corporate Entrepreneurship (Chapter 12)   Firms must continually improve and grow as well as find new ways to renew their organizations. Corporate entrepreneurship and innovation provide firms with new opportunities, and strategies should be formulated that enhance a firm's innovative capacity.

Chapter 13, "Analyzing Strategic Management Cases," provides guidelines and suggestions on how to evaluate cases in this course. Thus, the concepts and techniques discussed in these 12 chapters can be applied to real-world organizations.

Let's now address two concepts—corporate governance and stakeholder management—that are critical to the strategic management process.

LO1.3

The vital role of corporate governance and stakeholder management as well as how "symbiosis" can be achieved among an organization's stakeholders.

The Role of Corporate Governance and Stakeholder Management

Most business enterprises that employ more than a few dozen people are organized as corporations. As you recall from your finance classes, the overall purpose of a corporation is to maximize the long-term return to the owners (shareholders). Thus, we may ask: Who is really responsible for fulfilling this purpose? Robert Monks and Neil Minow provide a useful definition of **corporate governance** as "the relationship among various participants in determining the direction and performance of corporations. The primary participants are (1) the shareholders, (2) the management (led by the chief executive officer), and (3) the board of directors."[40] This relationship is illustrated in Exhibit 1.4.

The board of directors (BOD) are the elected representatives of the shareholders charged with ensuring that the interests and motives of management are aligned with those of the owners (i.e., shareholders). In many cases, the BOD is diligent in fulfilling its purpose. For example, Intel Corporation, the giant $54 billion maker of microprocessor chips, practices sound governance. Its BOD follows guidelines to ensure that its members are independent (i.e., not members of the executive management team and do not have close personal ties to top executives) so that they can provide proper oversight, it has explicit guidelines on the selection of director candidates (to avoid "cronyism"). It provides detailed procedures for formal evaluations of directors and the firm's top officers.[41] Such guidelines serve to ensure that management is acting in the best interests of shareholders.[42]

corporate governance
the relationship among various participants in determining the direction and performance of corporations. The primary participants are (1) the shareholders, (2) the management (led by the chief executive officer), and (3) the board of directors.

EXHIBIT 1.4 The Key Elements of Corporate Governance

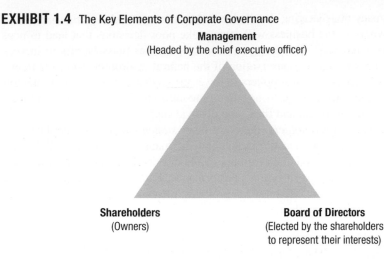

Management
(Headed by the chief executive officer)

Shareholders
(Owners)

Board of Directors
(Elected by the shareholders
to represent their interests)

Recently, there has been much criticism as well as cynicism by both citizens and the business press about the poor job that management and the BODs of large corporations are doing. We only have to look at the scandals at firms such as Arthur Andersen, Best Buy, Olympus, Enron, Tyco, and ImClone Systems.[43] Such malfeasance has led to an erosion of the public's trust in corporations. For example, a recent Gallup poll found that 90 percent of Americans felt that people leading corporations could not be trusted to look after the interests of their employees, and only 18 percent thought that corporations looked after their shareholders. Forty-three percent, in fact, believed that senior executives were in it only for themselves. In Britain, that figure, according to another poll, was an astonishing 95 percent.[44] Perhaps worst of all, in another study, 60 percent of directors (the very people who decide how much executives should earn) felt that executives were "dramatically overpaid"![45]

It is now clear that much of the bonus pay awarded to executives on Wall Street in the past few years was richly undeserved.[46] In the three years that led up to the collapse of seven big financial institutions in 2008, the chief executives of those firms collected a total of $80 million in performance bonuses and raked in $210 million in severance pay and earnings from stock sales. The trend continues. 2011 was a poor year for financial stocks: 35 of the 50 largest financial company stocks fell that year. The sector lost 17 percent compared to flat performance for the Standard & Poor's 500. However, even as the sector struggled, the average pay of finance company CEOs rose 20.4 percent. For example, JPMorgan CEO Jamie Dimon was the highest-paid banker—with $23.1 million in compensation, an 11 percent increase from the previous year. The firm's shareholders didn't do as well—the stock fell 20 percent.[47]

Clearly, there is a strong need for improved corporate governance, and we will address this topic in Chapter 9.[48] We focus on three important mechanisms to ensure effective corporate governance: an effective and engaged board of directors, shareholder activism, and proper managerial rewards and incentives.[49] In addition to these internal controls, a key role is played by various external control mechanisms.[50] These include the auditors, banks, analysts, an active financial press, and the threat of hostile takeovers.

Alternative Perspectives of Stakeholder Management

Generating long-term returns for the shareholders is the primary goal of a publicly held corporation.[51] As noted by former Chrysler vice chairman Robert Lutz, "We are here to serve the shareholder and create shareholder value. I insist that the only person who owns the company is the person who paid good money for it."[52]

stakeholder management
a firm's strategy for recognizing and responding to the interests of all its salient stakeholders.

Despite the primacy of generating shareholder value, managers who focus solely on the interests of the owners of the business will often make poor decisions that lead to negative, unanticipated outcomes.[53] For example, decisions such as mass layoffs to increase profits, ignoring issues related to conservation of the natural environment to save money, and exerting excessive pressure on suppliers to lower prices can harm the firm in the long run. Such actions would likely lead to negative outcomes such as alienated employees, increased governmental oversight and fines, and disloyal suppliers.

Clearly, in addition to *shareholders,* there are other *stakeholders* (e.g. suppliers, customers) who must be taken into account in the strategic management process.[54] A stakeholder can be defined as an individual or group, inside or outside the company, that has a stake in and can influence an organization's performance. Each stakeholder group makes various claims on the company.[55] Exhibit 1.5 provides a list of major stakeholder groups and the nature of their claims on the company.

Zero Sum or Symbiosis?   There are two opposing ways of looking at the role of stakeholder management.[56] The first one can be termed "zero sum." Here, the various stakeholders compete for the organization's resources: the gain of one individual or group is the loss of another individual or group. For example, employees want higher wages (which drive down profits), suppliers want higher prices for their inputs and slower, more flexible delivery times (which drive up costs), customers want fast deliveries and higher quality (which drive up costs), the community at large wants charitable contributions (which take money from company goals), and so on. This zero-sum thinking is rooted, in part, in the traditional conflict between workers and management, leading to the formation of unions and sometimes ending in adversarial union–management negotiations and long, bitter strikes.

Consider, for example, the many stakeholder challenges facing Walmart, the world's largest retailer.

> Walmart strives to ramp up growth while many stakeholders are watching nervously: employees and trade unions; shareholders, investors, and creditors; suppliers and joint venture partners; the governments of the U.S. and other nations where the retailer operates; and customers. In addition many non-governmental organizations (NGOs), particularly in countries where the retailer buys its products, are closely monitoring Walmart. Walmart's stakeholders have different interests, and not all of them share the firm's goals. Each group has the ability, in various degrees, to influence the firm's choices and results. Clearly, this wasn't the case when Sam Walton built his first store in Rogers, Arkansas, in 1962![57]

There will always be conflicting demands on organizations. However, organizations can achieve mutual benefit through stakeholder symbiosis, which recognizes that stakeholders are dependent upon each other for their success and well-being.[58] Consider Procter & Gamble's "laundry detergent compaction," a technique for compressing even more cleaning power into ever smaller concentrations.

EXHIBIT 1.5

An Organization's Key Stakeholders and the Nature of Their Claims

Stakeholder Group	Nature of Claim
Stockholders	Dividends, capital appreciation
Employees	Wages, benefits, safe working environment, job security
Suppliers	Payment on time, assurance of continued relationship
Creditors	Payment of interest, repayment of principal
Customers	Value, warranties
Government	Taxes, compliance with regulations
Communities	Good citizenship behavior such as charities, employment, not polluting the environment

NGOs AS MONITORS OF MNCs

Although the number of NGOs worldwide is hard to determine, according to a recent study there are at least 40,000 multinational NGOs. There are also hundreds of thousands based in individual countries, with India leading the pack with one NGO for 400 of its citizens. What are NGOs and what do they do? NGOs such as Greenpeace or World Wildlife Fund include a wide array of groups and organizations—from activist groups "reclaiming the streets" to development organizations delivering aid and providing essential public services. Other NGOs are research-driven policy organizations, looking to engage with decision makers. Still others see themselves as watchdogs, casting a critical eye over current events.

Some NGOs recently broadened their monitoring or watchdog role of multinational corporations (MNCs) to include not just the MNC itself but also the MNC's supply chain. As an example, Apple in 2011 received massive media scrutiny from Chinese environmental NGOs because the beloved U.S. technology giant ignored pollution violations of some of its Chinese suppliers. Following intense media pressure, Apple quickly arranged talks with the Chinese environmental NGOs and eventually increased environmental standards for its suppliers. However, the responsibility of MNCs does not stop with their immediate supplier base. International brands such as Nike and Adidas were targets of international media attention because they procured finished goods from Chinese textile companies with questionable environmental practices. These cases highlight that MNCs face substantial challenges in what is commonly assumed to be an arm's length market transaction.

Although many MNCs are quick to react to environmental concerns raised by NGOs, a more proactive management of environmental issues in their supply chain may prevent public scrutiny and other embarrassments. Apparel company Levi Strauss takes a proactive approach that encourages self-monitoring by their suppliers. For each false or misleading environmental record, Levi Strauss issues the supplier a "zero tolerance" warning and will terminate the relationship after three such warnings. However, if the supplier voluntarily reports environmental issues, Levi Strauss does not issue a warning, but instead works with the supplier to correct the problems. This proactive approach encourages self-monitoring and decreases the risk of becoming the target of NGO attention and media pressure.

Sources: Esty, D. C. & Winston, A. S. 2009. *Green to Gold*. Hoboken, NJ: Wiley: 69–70; Barboza, D. 2011. Apple cited as adding to pollution in China. *The New York Times*, September 1: np; Plambeck, E., Lee, H.L., and Yatsko, P. 2011. Improving environmental performance in your Chinese supply chain. *MIT Sloan Management Review*, 53(2): 43–51; and Shukla, A. 2010. First official estimate: An NGO for every 400 people in India. *www.indianexpress com*, July 7: np.

In the early 2000s, P&G perfected a technique that could compact two or three times as much cleaning powder into a liquid concentration. This remarkable breakthrough has led to a change not only in consumer shopping habits, but also a revolution in industry supply-chain economics. Here's how several key stakeholders are affected:

> *Consumers* love concentrated liquids because they are easier to carry, pour, and store. *Retailers,* meanwhile, prefer them because they take up less floor and shelf space, which leads to higher sales-per-square-foot—a big deal for Walmart, Target, and other big retailers. *Shipping and Wholesalers,* meanwhile, prefer reduced-sized products because smaller bottles translate into reduced fuel consumption and improved warehouse space utilization. And, finally, *environmentalists* favor such products because they use less packaging and produce less waste than conventional products.[59]

Strategy Spotlight 1.3 discusses the role of NGOs and their potential influence on companies' operations. While some organizations have been confronted for their controversial impact on the environment, others have made environmental concerns part of their business strategies and have been praised by watchdog groups for being proactive.

Social Responsibility and Environmental Sustainability: Moving beyond the Immediate Stakeholders

Organizations cannot ignore the interests and demands of stakeholders such as citizens and society in general that are beyond its immediate constituencies—customers, owners, suppliers, and employees. The realization that firms have multiple stakeholders and that evaluating their performance must go beyond analyzing their financial results has led to a new way of thinking about businesses and their relationship to society.

First, *social responsibility* recognizes that businesses must respond to society's expectations regarding their obligations to society. Second, *shared value,* views social responsibility not just as an added cost to businesses. Instead, it views businesses as creators of value that they then share with society in a mutually beneficial relationship. Finally, the *triple bottom line approach* evaluates a firm's performance. This perspective takes into account financial, social, and environmental performance.

Social Responsibility is the expectation that businesses or individuals will strive to improve the overall welfare of society.[60] From the perspective of a business, this means that managers must take active steps to make society better by virtue of the business being in existence.[61] What constitutes socially responsible behavior changes over time. In the 1970s affirmative action was a high priority, during the 1990s and up to the present time, the public has been concerned about environmental quality. Many firms have responded to this by engaging in recycling and reducing waste. And in the wake of terrorist attacks on New York City and the Pentagon, as well as the continuing threat from terrorists worldwide, a new kind of priority has arisen: the need to be vigilant concerning public safety.

Today, demands for greater corporate responsibility have accelerated.[62] These include corporate critics, social investors, activists, and, increasingly, customers who claim to assess corporate responsibility when making purchasing decisions. Such demands go well beyond product and service quality.[63] They include a focus on issues such as labor standards, environmental sustainability, financial and accounting reporting, procurement, and environmental practices.[64] At times, a firm's reputation can be tarnished by exceedingly poor judgment on the part of one of its managers. For example, BP CEO Tony Hayward's decision to withhold information from the public about the magnitude of the oil spill in the Gulf of Mexico further damaged the firm's reputation.

A key stakeholder group that appears to be particularly susceptible to corporate social responsibility (CSR) initiatives is customers.[65] Surveys indicate a strong positive relationship between CSR behaviors and consumers' reactions to a firm's products and services.[66] For example:

- Corporate Citizenship's poll conducted by Cone Communications found that "84 percent of Americans say they would be likely to switch brands to one associated with a good cause, if price and quality are similar."[67]
- Hill & Knowlton/Harris's Interactive poll reveals that "79 percent of Americans take corporate citizenship into account when deciding whether to buy a particular company's product and 37 percent consider corporate citizenship an important factor when making purchasing decisions."[68]

Such findings are consistent with a large body of research that confirms the positive influence of CSR on consumers' company evaluations and product purchase intentions across a broad range of product categories.

The Concept of "Shared Value" It is increasingly acknowledged that businesses acting as businesses, not as charitable donors, are the most powerful force for addressing the pressing issues that we face. This new conception of capitalism redefines the purpose of the corporation as creating shared value, not just profit per se. This will drive the next wave of innovation and productivity growth in the global economy.[69]

Shared value can be defined as policies and operating practices that enhance the competitiveness of a company while simultaneously advancing the economic and social conditions in which it operates. Michael Porter, one of strategic management's leading thinkers, argues that shared value creation focuses on identifying and expanding the connections between societal and economic progress.[70]

"I think the idea of shared value is fundamentally about the ability to both create economic value and . . . societal benefit simultaneously. It is really not about doing good and not about charity. Fundamentally, it is about business. Businesses create shared value when they can make a profit—create economic value—while simultaneously meeting important social needs or important social goals like improving environmental performance, reducing problems of health, improving nutrition, reducing disability, improving safety, and helping save for retirement. The basic idea of shared value is that there are many opportunities in meeting these societal needs to actually create economic value in the process. Shared value is where you do both."

The shared value perspective acknowledges that the congruence between societal progress and value chain productivity is far greater than traditionally believed. The synergy increases when firms consider societal issues from a shared value perspective and invent new ways of operating to address them. So far, however, relatively few firms have reaped the full productivity benefits.

Let's look at what Olam International is doing to reap "win-win" benefits by addressing societal challenges and, in so doing, enjoying higher productivity and profitability:

Olam International, a leading cashew producer, traditionally shipped its nuts from Africa to Asia for processing. By opening local processing plants and training workers in Tanzania, Mozambique, Nigeria, and the Ivory Coast, Olam cut its processing and shipping costs by as much as 25 percent and greatly reduced carbon emissions! Further, Olam built preferred relationships with local farmers. It has provided direct employment to 17,000 people— 95 percent of whom are women—and indirect employment to an equal number of people, in rural areas where jobs otherwise were not available.

The Triple Bottom Line: Incorporating Financial as Well as Environmental and Social Costs Many companies are now measuring what has been called a **"triple bottom line."** This involves assessing financial, social, and environmental performance. Shell, NEC, Procter & Gamble, and others have recognized that failing to account for the environmental and social costs of doing business poses risks to the company and its community.[71]

triple bottom line assessment of a firm's financial, social, and environmental performance.

The environmental revolution has been almost four decades in the making.[72] In the 1960s and 1970s, companies were in a state of denial regarding their firms' impact on the natural environment. However, a series of visible ecological problems created a groundswell for strict governmental regulation. In the U.S., Lake Erie was "dead," and in Japan, people died of mercury poisoning. More recently, Japan's horrific tsunami that took place on March 11, 2011, and Hurricane Sandy's devastation on the East Coast of the United States in late October 2012 have raised alarms. Clearly, the effects of global warming are being felt throughout the world.

Stuart Hart, writing in the *Harvard Business Review,* addresses the magnitude of problems and challenges associated with the natural environment:

The challenge is to develop a *sustainable global economy:* an economy that the planet is capable of supporting indefinitely. Although we may be approaching ecological recovery in the developed world, the planet as a whole remains on an unsustainable course. Increasingly, the scourges of the late twentieth century—depleted farmland, fisheries, and forests; choking urban pollution; poverty; infectious disease; and migration—are spilling over geopolitical borders. The simple fact is this: in meeting our needs, we are destroying the ability of future generations to meet theirs . . . corporations are the only organizations with the resources, the technology, the global reach, and, ultimately, the motivation to achieve sustainability.[73]

Environmental sustainability is now a value embraced by the most competitive and successful multinational companies.[74] The McKinsey Corporation's survey of more than 400 senior executives of companies around the world found that 92 percent agreed with former Sony President Akio Morita's contention that the environmental challenge will be one of the central issues in the 21st century.[75] Virtually all executives acknowledged their firm's responsibility to control pollution, and 83 percent agreed that corporations have an environmental responsibility for their products even after they are sold.

For many successful firms, environmental values are now becoming a central part of their cultures and management processes.[76] And, as noted earlier, environmental impacts are being audited and accounted for as the "third bottom line." According to a recent corporate report, "If we aren't good corporate citizens as reflected in a Triple Bottom Line that takes into account social and environmental responsibilities along with financial ones—eventually our stock price, our profits, and our entire business could suffer."[77] Also, a CEO survey on sustainability by Accenture debunks the notion that sustainability and profitability are mutually exclusive corporate goals. The study found that sustainability is being increasingly recognized as a source of cost efficiencies and revenue growth. In many companies, sustainability activities have led to increases in revenue and profits. As Jeff Immelt, the CEO of General Electric, puts it, "Green is green."[78]

Let's look at a few examples:[79]

- Adobe Systems recently earned $390,000 in energy rebates and reduced its annual operating costs by $1.2 million for a 121 percent return on an investment in heating, ventilation, and air-conditioning efficiency upgrades in San Jose, California.
- IBM saves at least $700 million a year in real estate costs alone by allowing approximately 25 percent of its 320,000 employees to telecommute.
- Sprint's eco-friendly packaging for mobile phones and accessories is expected to save the company $2.1 million annually and produce 647 fewer tons of waste each year.
- Boeing Corporation cut fuel use 3 percent on 737 airplanes by adding "winglets" to reduce air resistance, which were inspired by the biomechanics of bat and dragonfly wings.
- GM cut $12 million from disposal costs by sharing reusable packaging with its suppliers.

Let's look at how two well-known firms are increasing their operational effectiveness through their sustainable business practices. Strategy Spotlight 1.4 discusses Walmart's and International Paper's initiatives.

Many firms have profited by investing in socially responsible behavior, including those activities that enhance environmental sustainability. However, how do such "socially responsible" companies fare in terms of shareholder returns compared to benchmarks such as the Standard & Poor's 500 index? Let's look at some of the evidence.

SRI (socially responsible investing) is a broad-based approach to investing that now encompasses an estimated $3.07 trillion out of $25.2 trillion in the U.S. investment marketplace. SRI recognizes that corporate responsibility and societal concerns are considerations in investment decisions. With SRI, investors have the opportunity to put their money to work to build a more sustainable world while earning competitive returns both today and over time.

And, as the saying goes, nice guys don't have to finish last. The ING SRI Index Fund, which tracks the stocks of 50 companies, enjoyed a 47.4 percent return in a recent year. That easily beat the 2.65 percent gain of the Standard & Poor's 500 stock index. A review of the 145 socially responsible equity mutual and exchange-traded funds tracked by Morningstar also shows that 65 percent of them outperformed the S&P 500.[80]

LO1.5

The need for greater empowerment throughout the organization.

The Strategic Management Perspective: An Imperative throughout the Organization

Strategic management requires managers to take an integrative view of the organization and assess how all of the functional areas and activities fit together to help an organization achieve its goals and objectives. This cannot be accomplished if only the top managers in the organization take an integrative, strategic perspective of issues facing the firm

THE BUSINESS CASE FOR SUSTAINABILITY

The corporate sustainability, or "green," movement describes a business philosophy that goes beyond legal compliance with environmental regulations. Historically, companies engaged in social issues by handing out checks to charities or victims of natural disasters. While these forms of "green marketing" are here to stay, the new corporate sustainability movement wants not only to do good but also to save big bucks.

Companies across the world embrace the concept of sustainability as a powerful source of innovation and improving operational effectiveness. Companies that translate sustainable business practices into improved operational performance focus on the opportunity cost represented by waste instead of the short-term cost of implementing sustainable business practices. One industry in which sustainability creates competitive advantage is retailing. Take Walmart for example. Walmart is far ahead of its major competitors Target and Sears in terms of reducing waste and the weight of its packaging. In 2009, Walmart's Japanese Seiyu chain converted the packaging for its private-label fresh-cut fruit and salads from oil-based to corn-based plastic. This operational improvement reduced packaging weight by 25 percent and lowered freight and warehouse costs by 13 percent, saving Walmart more than $195,000 a year.

International Paper (IP), a global paper and packaging company, is another company that benefits from sustainable business practices. IP recognized that its future profitability depends on a steady supply of trees, and it has planted more than 4 billion tree seedlings since the 1950s. The company also cut dependence on fossil fuel by 21 percent from 2005 to 2010—partially achieved by burning limbs and other biomass debris from tree processing. These sustainability decisions paid off and saved IP $221 million annually. IP also formalized specific sustainability goals, such as reducing greenhouse gas emissions by 20 percent by 2020, highlighting the company's commitment to sustainability.

Sources: Stanford, D. 2011. Why sustainability is winning over CEOs. *Bloomberg BusinessWeek*, March 31: np; Gupta, N.J. & Benson, C. 2011. Sustainability and competitive advantage: An empirical study of value creation. *Competitive Forum*, 9(1): 121–136. International Paper. 2012. International Paper announces 12 voluntary sustainability goals to be achieved by 2020. *www.internationalpaper.com*, May 16: np.

and everyone else "fends for themselves" in their independent, isolated functional areas. Instead, people throughout the organization must strive toward overall goals.

The need for such a perspective is accelerating in today's increasingly complex, interconnected, ever-changing, global economy. As noted by Peter Senge of MIT, the days when Henry Ford, Alfred Sloan, and Tom Watson (top executives at Ford, General Motors, and IBM, respectively) "learned for the organization are gone."[81]

To develop and mobilize people and other assets, leaders are needed throughout the organization.[82] No longer can organizations be effective if the top "does the thinking" and the rest of the organization "does the work." Everyone must be involved in the strategic management process. There is a critical need for three types of leaders:

- *Local line leaders* who have significant profit-and-loss responsibility.
- *Executive leaders* who champion and guide ideas, create a learning infrastructure, and establish a domain for taking action.
- *Internal networkers* who, although they have little positional power and formal authority, generate their power through the conviction and clarity of their ideas.[83]

Top-level executives are key in setting the tone for the empowerment of employees. Consider Richard Branson, founder of the Virgin Group, whose core businesses include retail operations, hotels, communications, and an airline. He is well known for creating a culture and an informal structure where anybody in the organization can be involved in generating and acting upon new business ideas. In an interview, he stated,

> Speed is something that we are better at than most companies. We don't have formal board meetings, committees, etc. If someone has an idea, they can pick up the phone and talk to me. I can vote "done, let's do it." Or, better still, they can just go ahead and do it. They know that they are not going to get a mouthful from me if they make a mistake. Rules and regulations are not our forte. Analyzing things to death is not our kind of thing. We very rarely sit back and analyze what we do.[84]

STRATEGY AND THE VALUE OF INEXPERIENCE

Peter Gruber, chairman of Mandalay Entertainment, discovered that great ideas can come from the least expected sources. During the filming of the movie *Gorillas in the Mist,* his production company faced many problems. Rwanda—the site of the filming—was on the verge of revolution, the film needed to use 200 animals, and the screenplay required the gorillas to follow a script, that is, do what the script called for and "act." If that failed, the fallback position was to use dwarfs in gorilla suits on a soundstage—a strategy that usually failed.

Gruber explains how the "day was saved" by someone with very limited experience:

> We called an emergency meeting to solve these problems. In the middle of it, a young intern asked, "What if you let the gorillas write the story?" Everyone laughed and

wondered what she was doing in the meeting with experienced filmmakers. Hours later, someone casually asked her what she had meant. She said, "What if you send a really good cinematographer into the jungle with a ton of film to shoot the gorillas, then you could write a story around what the gorillas did on film." It was a brilliant idea. And we did exactly what she suggested: We sent Alan Root, an Academy Award–nominated cinematographer into the jungle for three weeks. He came back with phenomenal footage that practically wrote the story for us.

The upshot? The film cost $20 million to shoot—half the original budget. And it was nominated for five Academy Awards—including Sigourney Weaver for best actress—and it won two Golden Globe Awards.

Source: Gruber, P. 1998. My greatest lesson. *Fast Company,* 14: 88–90; and *imdb.com.*

To inculcate a strategic management perspective, managers must often make a major effort to effect transformational change. This involves extensive communication, incentives, training, and development. For example, under the direction of Nancy Snyder, a corporate vice president, Whirlpool, the world's largest producer of household appliances, brought about a significant shift in the firm's reputation as an innovator.[85] This five-year initiative included both financial investments in capital spending as well as a series of changes in management processes, including training innovation mentors, making innovation a significant portion of leadership development programs, enrolling all salaried employees in online courses in business innovation, and providing employees an innovation portal to access multiple innovation tools and data.

Many successful executives reward honesty and input, and show their interest in learning what others are thinking. Methods vary and include holding town-hall meetings, seeking the advice of people at all levels of the firm, and asking employees what they would do if they were in charge. As noted by Tim Brown, CEO of the premier design consulting firm IDEO: "The best can come from anywhere in an organization. So you'd better do a good job of spotting and promoting them when they come, and not let people's positions dictate how influential their ideas are."[86]

We'd like to close with our favorite example of how inexperience can be a virtue. It further reinforces the benefits of having broad involvement throughout the organization in the strategic management process (see Strategy Spotlight 1.5).

Ensuring Coherence in Strategic Direction

LO1.6

How an awareness of a hierarchy of strategic goals can help an organization achieve coherence in its strategic direction.

Employees and managers must strive toward common goals and objectives.[87] By specifying desired results, it becomes much easier to move forward. Otherwise, when no one knows what the firm is striving to accomplish, they have no idea of what to work toward. Alan Mulally, CEO at Ford Motor Company, stresses the importance of perspective in creating a sense of mission:

> I think the most important thing is coming to a shared view about what we're trying to accomplish—whether you're a nonprofit or a for-profit organization. What are we?

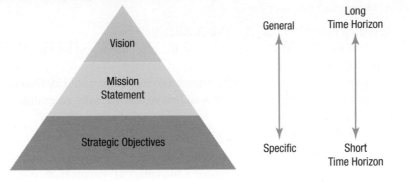

EXHIBIT 1.6 A Hierarchy of Goals

What is our real purpose? And then, how do you include everybody so you know where you are on that plan, so you can work on areas that need special attention. And then everybody gets a chance to participate and feel that accomplishment of participating and contributing.[88]

Organizations express priorities best through stated goals and objectives that form a **hierarchy of goals,** which includes its vision, mission, and strategic objectives.[89] What visions may lack in specificity, they make up for in their ability to evoke powerful and compelling mental images. On the other hand, strategic objectives tend to be more specific and provide a more direct means of determining if the organization is moving toward broader, overall goals.[90] Visions, as one would expect, also have longer time horizons than either mission statements or strategic objectives. Exhibit 1.6 depicts the hierarchy of goals and its relationship to two attributes: general versus specific and time horizon.

Organizational Vision

A **vision** is a goal that is "massively inspiring, overarching, and long term."[91] It represents a destination that is driven by and evokes passion. For example, Wendy Kopp, founder of Teach for America, notes that her vision for the organization, which strives to improve the quality of inner-city schools, draws many applicants:

> We're looking for people who are magnetized to this notion, this vision, that one day all children in our nation should have the opportunity to attain an excellent education. And that magnetizes certain people. And so it's more about them—it's their vision, it's not my vision. It's our collective vision.[92]

Leaders must develop and implement a vision. A vision may or may not succeed; it depends on whether or not everything else happens according to an organization's strategy. As Mark Hurd, Hewlett-Packard's former CEO humorously points out: "Without execution, vision is just another word for hallucination."[93]

In a survey of executives from 20 different countries, respondents were asked what they believed were a leader's key traits.[94] Ninety-eight percent responded that "a strong sense of vision" was the most important. Similarly, when asked about the critical knowledge skills, the leaders cited "strategy formulation to achieve a vision" as the most important skill. In other words, managers need to have not only a vision but also a plan to implement it. Regretfully, 90 percent reported a lack of confidence in their own skills and ability to conceive a vision. For example, T. J. Rogers, CEO of Cypress Semiconductor, an electronic chipmaker that faced some difficulties in 1992, lamented that his own shortsightedness caused the danger, "I did not have the 50,000-foot view, and got caught."[95]

hierarchy of goals
organizational goals ranging from, at the top, those that are less specific yet able to evoke powerful and compelling mental images, to, at the bottom, those that are more specific and measurable.

vision
organizational goal(s) that evoke(s) powerful and compelling mental images.

One of the most famous examples of a vision is Disneyland's: "To be the happiest place on earth." Other examples are:

- "Restoring patients to full life." (Medtronic)
- "We want to satisfy all of our customers' financial needs and help them succeed financially." (Wells Fargo)
- "Our vision is to be the world's best quick service restaurant." (McDonald's)
- "To organize the world's information and make it universally accessible and useful." (Google)
- "Connecting the world through games." (Zynga)

Although such visions cannot be accurately measured by a specific indicator of how well they are being achieved, they do provide a fundamental statement of an organization's values, aspirations, and goals. Such visions go well beyond narrow financial objectives, of course, and strive to capture both the minds and hearts of employees.

The vision statement may also contain a slogan, diagram, or picture—whatever grabs attention.[96] The aim is to capture the essence of the more formal parts of the vision in a few words that are easily remembered, yet that evoke the spirit of the entire vision statement. In its 20-year battle with Xerox, Canon's slogan, or battle cry, was "Beat Xerox." Motorola's slogan is "Total Customer Satisfaction." Outboard Marine Corporation's slogan is "To Take the World Boating."

Clearly, vision statements are not a cure-all. Sometimes they backfire and erode a company's credibility. Visions fail for many reasons, including the following:[97]

The Walk Doesn't Match the Talk   An idealistic vision can arouse employee enthusiasm. However, that same enthusiasm can be quickly dashed if employees find that senior management's behavior is not consistent with the vision. Often, vision is a sloganeering campaign of new buzzwords and empty platitudes like "devotion to the customer," "teamwork," or "total quality" that aren't consistently backed by management's action.

Irrelevance   Visions created in a vacuum—unrelated to environmental threats or opportunities or an organization's resources and capabilities—often ignore the needs of those who are expected to buy into them. Employees reject visions that are not anchored in reality.

Not the Holy Grail   Managers often search continually for the one elusive solution that will solve their firm's problems—that is, the next "holy grail" of management. They may have tried other management fads only to find that they fell short of their expectations. However, they remain convinced that one exists. A vision simply cannot be viewed as a magic cure for an organization's illness.

Too Much Focus Leads to Missed Opportunities   The downside of too much focus is that in directing people and resources toward a grandiose vision, losses can be devastating. Consider, Samsung's ambitious venture into automobile manufacturing:

> In 1992, Kun-Hee Lee, chairman of South Korea's Samsung Group, created a bold strategy to become one of the 10 largest car makers by 2010. Seduced by the clarity of the vision, Samsung bypassed staged entry through a joint venture or initial supply contract. Instead, Samsung borrowed heavily to build a state-of-the-art research and design facility and erect a greenfield factory, complete with cutting-edge robotics. Samsung Auto suffered operating losses and crushing interest charges from the beginning. And within a few years the business was divested for a fraction of the initial investment.[98]

An Ideal Future Irreconciled with the Present   Although visions are not designed to mirror reality, they must be anchored somehow in it. People have difficulty identifying with a vision that paints a rosy picture of the future but does not account for the often hostile environment in which the firm competes or that ignores some of the firm's weaknesses.

Mission Statements

A company's **mission statement** differs from its vision in that it encompasses both the purpose of the company as well as the basis of competition and competitive advantage.

Exhibit 1.7 contains the vision statement and mission statement of WellPoint Health Network, a giant $61 billion managed health care organization. Note that while the vision statement is broad based, the mission statement is more specific and focused on the means by which the firm will compete.

Effective mission statements incorporate the concept of stakeholder management, suggesting that organizations must respond to multiple constituencies. Customers, employees, suppliers, and owners are the primary stakeholders, but others may also play an important role. Mission statements also have the greatest impact when they reflect an organization's enduring, overarching strategic priorities and competitive positioning. Mission statements also can vary in length and specificity. The two mission statements below illustrate these issues.

> **mission statement**
> a set of organizational goals that include both the purpose of the organization, its scope of operations, and the basis of its competitive advantage.

- To produce superior financial returns for our shareholders as we serve our customers with the highest quality transportation, logistics, and e-commerce. (Federal Express)
- To be the very best in the business. Our game plan is status go . . . we are constantly looking ahead, building on our strengths, and reaching for new goals. In our quest of these goals, we look at the three stars of the Brinker logo and are reminded of the basic values that are the strength of this company . . . People, Quality and Profitability. Everything we do at Brinker must support these core values. We also look at the eight golden flames depicted in our logo, and are reminded of the fire that ignites our mission and makes up the heart and soul of this incredible company. These flames are: Customers, Food, Team, Concepts, Culture, Partners, Community, and Shareholders. As keeper of these flames, we will continue to build on our strengths and work together to be the best in the business. (Brinker International, whose restaurant chains include Chili's and On the Border)[99]

Few mission statements identify profit or any other financial indicator as the sole purpose of the firm. Indeed, many do not even mention profit or shareholder return.[100] Employees of organizations or departments are usually the mission's most important audience. For them, the mission should help to build a common understanding of purpose and commitment to nurture.

A good mission statement, by addressing each principal theme, must communicate why an organization is special and different. Two studies that linked corporate values and mission statements with financial performance found that the most successful firms

Vision
WellPoint *will redefine our industry:*
Through a new generation of consumer-friendly products that put individuals back in control of their future.

Mission
The WellPoint companies provide health *security* by offering a *choice* of quality branded health and related financial services *designed* to meet the *changing* expectations of individuals, families, and their sponsors throughout a *lifelong* relationship.

Source: WellPoint Health Network company records.

EXHIBIT 1.7
Comparing WellPoint Health Network's Vision and Mission

BACK TO (MANUFACTURING) BASICS FOR GENERAL ELECTRIC

By Tom McNamara and Erika Marsillac

General Electric (GE) is one of the largest, and one of the last, conglomerates on the planet. Originally descended in 1890 from a company started by the famous inventor Thomas Edison, it now sells a wide variety of products in 160 countries. Its broadly stated business goal is to focus on goods and services that are involved in "building, powering, moving and curing the world."

GE believes that the best way to provide value to its stakeholders is by working on things that matter, using the best people and the best technologies available to take on the toughest challenges. The challenges that GE wants to take on appear to be, more and more, in the manufacturing sector.

GE's renewed emphasis on manufacturing has caused it to make some prioritization changes. It has invested billions of dollars in new energy-related businesses, while at the same time it has sold off some peripheral activities, like a television network and commercial real estate holdings. The company, possibly concerned over the lingering aftershocks from the 2008 financial crisis and unwarranted risk, also announced that it is lowering its exposure to purely financial investments. For years, many analysts complained that GE was more of a bank than anything else. For example, in 2008 "GE Capital" had $600 billion in assets, which GE would now like to cut in half. These moves are expected to insulate the company from the vagaries of the market place, while at the same time promoting sustainable growth.

The investment research firm Morningstar believes that it makes good strategic sense for GE to get back to its historical industrial and manufacturing roots. "It's what they're really good at," says Morningstar, and "it's why they can continue to drive their competitive advantages."

So it appears that GE has come full circle. What started out as basically a famous inventor's laboratory and work shop is a company that once again is focusing on manufacturing. GE's industrial segments include its energy infrastructure, health care and aviation divisions. These units are responsible for almost two-thirds of GE's total revenue. With an estimated $70 Billion in cash holdings, and an average of 2000 patents filed every year, GE should have no problems making a go of it in the manufacturing sector, or, for that matter, any other business it desires.

Sources: John Waggoner, USA Today, May 30th, 2013 "Companies awash in cash, when will they spend it?"; ge.com; AP News, appearing in Bloomberg Business week News, September 27th 2012 "GE at 4-year high on industrial segment outlook"; Chris Kahn, The Associated Press, appearing in The Denver Post, July 7th 2012 "GE's net income drops 16 percent in second quarter".

mentioned values other than profits. The less successful firms focused almost entirely on profitability.[101] In essence, profit is the metaphorical equivalent of oxygen, food, and water that the body requires. They are not the point of life, but without them, there is no life.

Vision statements tend to be quite enduring and seldom change. However, a firm's mission can and should change when competitive conditions dramatically change or the firm is faced with new threats or opportunities.

Strategy Spotlight 1.6 explores General Electric's long and varied history from its beginning as a small manufacturing firm, its foray into activities such as television network and commercial real estate, and back to manufacturing. Its vision, however, has always remained the same: "building, powering, moving and curing the world."

strategic objectives
A set of organizational goals that are used to operationalize the mission statement and that are specific and cover a well-defined time frame.

Strategic Objectives

Strategic objectives are used to operationalize the mission statement.[102] That is, they help to provide guidance on how the organization can fulfill or move toward the "higher goals" in the goal hierarchy—the mission and vision. Thus, they are more specific and cover a more well-defined time frame. Setting objectives demands a yardstick to measure the fulfillment of the objectives.[103]

Exhibit 1.8 lists several firms' strategic objectives—both financial and nonfinancial. While most of them are directed toward generating greater profits and returns for the owners of the business, others are directed at customers or society at large.

| Strategic Objectives (Financial) | EXHIBIT 1.8 |

EXHIBIT 1.8
Strategic Objectives

Strategic Objectives (Financial)

- Increase sales growth 6 percent to 8 percent and accelerate core net earnings growth from 13 percent to 15 percent per share in each of the next 5 years. (Procter & Gamble)
- Generate Internet-related revenue of $1.5 billion. (AutoNation)
- Increase the contribution of Banking Group earnings from investments, brokerage, and insurance from 16 percent to 25 percent. (Wells Fargo)
- Cut corporate overhead costs by $30 million per year. (Fortune Brands)

Strategic Objectives (Nonfinancial)

- We want a majority of our customers, when surveyed, to say they consider Wells Fargo the best financial institution in the community. (Wells Fargo)
- Reduce volatile air emissions 15 percent by 2015 from 2010 base year, indexed to net sales. (3M)
- Our goal is to help save 100,000 more lives each year. (Varian Medical Systems)
- We want to be the top-ranked supplier to our customers. (PPG)

Sources: Company documents and annual reports.

For objectives to be meaningful, they need to satisfy several criteria. They must be:

- *Measurable.* There must be at least one indicator (or yardstick) that measures progress against fulfilling the objective.
- *Specific.* This provides a clear message as to what needs to be accomplished.
- *Appropriate.* It must be consistent with the organization's vision and mission.
- *Realistic.* It must be an achievable target given the organization's capabilities and opportunities in the environment. In essence, it must be challenging but doable.
- *Timely.* There must be a time frame for achieving the objective. As the economist John Maynard Keynes once said, "In the long run, we are all dead!"

When objectives satisfy the above criteria, there are many benefits. First, they help to channel all employees' efforts toward common goals. This helps the organization concentrate and conserve valuable resources and work collectively in a timely manner.

Second, challenging objectives can help to motivate and inspire employees to higher levels of commitment and effort. Much research has supported the notion that people work harder when they are striving toward specific goals instead of being asked simply to "do their best."

Third, as we noted earlier in the chapter, there is always the potential for different parts of an organization to pursue their own goals rather than overall company goals. Although well intentioned, these may work at cross-purposes to the organization as a whole. Meaningful objectives thus help to resolve conflicts when they arise.

Finally, proper objectives provide a yardstick for rewards and incentives. They will ensure a greater sense of equity or fairness when rewards are allocated.

A caveat: When formulating strategic objectives, managers need to remember that too many objectives can result in a lack of focus and diminished results:

> A few years ago CEO Tony Petrucciani and his team at Single Source Systems, a software firm in Fishers, Indiana, set 15 annual objectives, such as automating some of its software functions. However, the firm, which got distracted by having so many items on its objective list, missed its $8.1 million revenue benchmark by 11 percent. "Nobody focused on any one thing," he says. Going forward, Petrucciani decided to set just a few key priorities. This helped the company to meet its goal of $10 million in sales. Sometimes, less is more![104]

In addition to the above, organizations have lower-level objectives that are more specific than strategic objectives. These are often referred to as short-term objectives—essential components of a firm's "action plan" that are critical in implementing the firm's chosen strategy. We discuss these issues in detail in Chapter 9.

Seventh Generation's Decision Dilemma

A strike idled 67,300 workers of the United Food and Commercial Workers (UFCW) who worked at Albertsons, Ralphs, and Vons—all large grocery store chains. These stores sold natural home products made by Seventh Generation, a socially conscious company. Interestingly, the inspiration for its name came from the Great Law of the Haudenosaunee. (This Law of Peace of the Iroquois Confederacy in North America has its roots in the 14th century.) The Law states that "in our every deliberation we must consider the impact of our decisions on the next seven generations." Accordingly, the company's mission is: "To inspire a revolution that nurtures the health of the next seven generations," and its values are to "care wholeheartedly, collaborate deliberately, nurture nature, innovate disruptively, and be a trusted brand."

Clearly, Seventh Generation faced a dilemma: On the one hand, it believed that the strikers had a just cause. However, if it honored the strikers by not crossing the picket lines, the firm would lose the shelf space for their products in the stores they had worked so hard to secure. It would also erode its trust with the large grocery stores. On the other hand, if Seventh Generation ignored the strikers and proceeded to send its products to the stores, it would be compromising its values and thereby losing trust and credibility with several stakeholders—its customers, distributors, and employees.

Discussion Questions

1. How important should the Seventh Generation values be considered when deciding what to do?
2. How can Seventh Generation solve this dilemma?

Sources: Russo, M. V. 2010. *Companies on a Mission: Entrepreneurial Strategies for Growing Sustainably, Responsibly, and Profitably.* Stanford: Stanford University Press: 94–96; Seventh Generation. 2012. Seventh Generation's Mission—Corporate Social Responsibility. *www.seventhgeneration.com*: np; Foster, A. C. 2004. Major Work Stoppage in 2003. US Bureau of Labor and Statistics. Compensation and Working Conditions. *www.bls.gov*, November 23: np; and Fast Company. 2008. 45 Social entrepreneurs who are changing the world. Profits with purpose: Seventh Generation. *www.fastcompany*, np; and Ratical. nd. The six nations: Oldest living participatory democracy on earth. *www.ratical.org*, np.

Reflecting on Career Implications . . .

▣ **Attributes of Strategic Management:** The attributes of strategic management described in this chapter are applicable to your personal careers as well. What are your overall goals and objectives? Who are the stakeholders you have to consider in making your career decisions (family, community, etc.)? What tradeoffs do you see between your long-term and short-term goals?

▣ **Intended versus Emergent Strategies:** While you may have planned your career trajectory carefully, don't be too tied to it. Strive to take advantage of new opportunities as they arise. Many promising career opportunities may "emerge" that were not part of your intended career strategy or your specific job assignment. Take initiative by pursuing opportunities to get additional training (e.g., learn a software or a statistical package), volunteering for a short-term overseas assignment, etc. You may be in a better position to take advantage of such emergent opportunities if you take the effort to prepare for

them. For example, learning a foreign language may position you better for an overseas opportunity.

▣ **Ambidexterity:** In Strategy Spotlight 1.2, we discussed the four most important traits of ambidextrous individuals. These include looking for opportunities beyond the description of one's job, seeking out opportunities to collaborate with others, building internal networks, and multitasking. Evaluate yourself along each of these criteria. If you score low, think of ways in which you can improve your ambidexterity.

▣ **Strategic Coherence:** What is the mission of your organization? What are the strategic objectives of the department or unit you are working for? In what ways does your own role contribute to the mission and objectives? What can you do differently in order to help the organization attain its mission and strategic objectives?

▣ **Strategic Coherence:** Setting strategic objectives is important in your personal career as well. Identify and write

summary

We began this introductory chapter by defining strategic management and articulating some of its key attributes. Strategic management is defined as "consisting of the analyses, decisions, and actions an organization undertakes to create and sustain competitive advantages." The issue of how and why some firms outperform others in the marketplace is central to the study of strategic management. Strategic management has four key attributes: It is directed at overall organizational goals, includes multiple stakeholders, incorporates both short-term and long-term perspectives, and incorporates trade-offs between efficiency and effectiveness.

The second section discussed the strategic management process. Here, we paralleled the above definition of strategic management and focused on three core activities in the strategic management process—strategy analysis, strategy formulation, and strategy implementation. We noted how each of these activities is highly interrelated to and interdependent on the others. We also discussed how each of the 12 chapters in this text fits into the three core activities.

Next, we introduced two important concepts—corporate governance and stakeholder management—which must be taken into account throughout the strategic management process. Governance mechanisms can be broadly divided into two groups: internal and external. Internal governance mechanisms include shareholders (owners), management (led by the chief executive officer), and the board of directors. External control is exercised by auditors, banks, analysts, and an active business press as well as the threat of takeovers. We identified five key stakeholders in all organizations: owners, customers, suppliers, employees, and society at large. Successful firms go beyond an overriding focus on satisfying solely the interests of owners. Rather, they recognize the inherent conflicts that arise among the demands of the various stakeholders as well as the need to endeavor to attain "symbiosis"—that is, interdependence and mutual benefit—among the various stakeholder groups. Managers must also recognize the need to act in a socially responsible manner which, if done effectively, can enhance a firm's innovativeness. The "shared value" approach represents an innovative perspective on creating value for the firm and society at the same time. The managers also should recognize and incorporate issues related to environmental sustainability in their strategic actions.

In the fourth section, we discussed factors that have accelerated the rate of unpredictable change that managers face today. Such factors, and the combination of them, have increased the need for managers and employees throughout the organization to have a strategic management perspective and to become more empowered.

The final section addressed the need for consistency among a firm's vision, mission, and strategic objectives. Collectively, they form an organization's hierarchy of goals. Visions should evoke powerful and compelling mental images. However, they are not very specific. Strategic objectives, on the other hand, are much more specific and are vital to ensuring that the organization is striving toward fulfilling its vision and mission.

SUMMARY REVIEW QUESTIONS

1. How is "strategic management" defined in the text, and what are its four key attributes?

2. Briefly discuss the three key activities in the strategic management process. Why is it important for managers to recognize the interdependent nature of these activities?

3. Explain the concept of "stakeholder management." Why shouldn't managers be solely interested in stockholder management, that is, maximizing the returns for owners of the firm—its shareholders?

4. What is "corporate governance"? What are its three key elements and how can it be improved?

5. How can "symbiosis" (interdependence, mutual benefit) be achieved among a firm's stakeholders?

6. Why do firms need to have a greater strategic management perspective and empowerment in the strategic management process throughout the organization?

7. What is meant by a "hierarchy of goals"? What are the main components of it, and why must consistency be achieved among them?

key terms

romantic view of leadership 4
external control view of leadership 5
strategic management 7
strategy 7
competitive advantage 7
operational effectiveness 8
stakeholders 8
effectiveness 9
efficiency 9
ambidexterity 9
strategic management process 9
intended strategy 10
realized strategy 11
strategy analysis 11

strategy formulation 13 stakeholder management 15 hierarchy of goals 23 mission statement 25
strategy implementation 13 social responsibility 18 vision 23 strategic objectives 26
corporate governance 14 triple bottom line 19

experiential exercise

Using the Internet or library sources, select four organizations—two in the private sector and two in the public sector. Find their mission statements. Complete the following exhibit by identifying the stakeholders that are mentioned. Evaluate the differences between firms in the private sector and those in the public sector.

Organization Name			
Mission Statement			
Stakeholders (√ = mentioned)			
1. Customers			
2. Suppliers			
3. Managers/employees			
4. Community-at-large			
5. Owners			
6. Others?			
7. Others?			

application questions & exercises

1. Go to the Internet and look up one of these company sites: *www.walmart.com*, *www.ge.com*, or *www.fordmotor.com*. What are some of the key events that would represent the "romantic" perspective of leadership? What are some of the key events that depict the "external control" perspective of leadership?

2. Select a company that competes in an industry in which you are interested. What are some of the recent demands that stakeholders have placed on this company? Can you find examples of how the company is trying to develop "symbiosis" (interdependence and mutual benefit) among its stakeholders? (Use the Internet and library resources.)

3. Provide examples of companies that are actively trying to increase the amount of empowerment in the strategic management process throughout the organization. Do these companies seem to be having positive outcomes? Why? Why not?

4. Look up the vision statements and/or mission statements for a few companies. Do you feel that they are constructive and useful as a means of motivating employees and providing a strong strategic direction? Why? Why not? (*Note:* Annual reports, along with the Internet, may be good sources of information.)

ethics questions

1. A company focuses solely on short-term profits to provide the greatest return to the owners of the business (i.e., the shareholders in a publicly held firm). What ethical issues could this raise?

2. A firm has spent some time—with input from managers at all levels—in developing a vision statement and a mission statement. Over time, however, the behavior of some executives is contrary to these statements. Could this raise some ethical issues?

references

1. Gunther, M. 2010. Fallen angels. *Fortune,* November 1: 75–78.
2. Donahue, J. 2012. What do CEOs admire? *Fortune.* March 19: 143.
3. Austen, B. 2011. The end of Borders is not the end of books. *Bloomberg BusinessWeek,* November 14–20: 92–97;

Kary, T. & Sandler, L. 2011. Borders files bankruptcy, closing up to 275 stores. *www.businessweek.com,* February 16: np; Newman, R. 2011. 4 Lessons from the demise of Borders. *usnews.com,*; and Borders Group, Annual Report 2004. *media.corporate-ir.net.*

4. For a discussion of the "romantic" versus "external control" perspective, refer to Meindl, J. R. 1987. The romance of leadership and the evaluation of organizational performance. *Academy of Management Journal* 30: 92–109;

and Pfeffer, J. & Salancik, G. R. 1978. *The external control of organizations: A resource dependence perspective.* New York: Harper & Row.

5. A recent perspective on the "romantic view" of leadership is provided by Mintzberg, H. 2004. Leadership and management development: An afterword. *Academy of Management Executive,* 18(3): 140–142.

6. For a discussion of the best and worst managers for 2008, read: Anonymous. 2009. The best managers. *BusinessWeek,* January 19: 40–41; and, The worst managers. On page 42 in the same issue.

7. Burrows, P. 2009. Apple without its core*? BusinessWeek.* January 26/February 2: 31.

8. For a study on the effects of CEOs on firm performance, refer to: Kor, Y. Y. & Misangyi, V. F. 2008. *Strategic Management Journal,* 29(11):1357–1368.

9. Charan, R. & Colvin, G. 2010. Directors: A harsh new reality. *money.cnn.com.* October 6: np.

10. Dobson, C. 2010. Global airlines lost $1.7 billion due to Iceland ash cloud. *www.theepochtimes.com.* May 23: np, and Pylas, P. 2011. Nikkei slides 11 percent on radiation fears. *www.finance.yahoo.com.* March 14: np.

11. Ewing, J. 2008. South Africa emerges from the shadows. *BusinessWeek.* December 15: 52–56.

12. For an interesting perspective on the need for strategists to maintain a global mind-set, refer to Begley, T. M. & Boyd, D. P. 2003. The need for a global mind-set. *MIT Sloan Management Review* 44(2): 25–32.

13. Porter, M. E. 1996. What is strategy? *Harvard Business Review* 74(6): 61–78.

14. See, for example, Barney, J. B. & Arikan, A. M. 2001. The resource-based view: Origins and implications. In Hitt, M. A., Freeman, R. E., & Harrison, J. S. (Eds.), *Handbook of strategic management:* 124–189. Malden, MA: Blackwell.

15. Porter, M. E. 1996. What is strategy? *Harvard Business Review,* 74(6): 61–78; and Hammonds, K. H. 2001. Michael Porter's big ideas. *Fast Company,* March: 55–56.

16. This section draws upon Dess, G. G. & Miller, A. 1993. *Strategic management.* New York: McGraw-Hill.

17. See, for example, Hrebiniak, L. G. & Joyce, W. F. 1986. The strategic importance of managing myopia. *Sloan Management Review,* 28(1): 5–14.

18. For an insightful discussion on how to manage diverse stakeholder groups, refer to Rondinelli, D. A. & London, T. 2003. How corporations and environmental groups cooperate: Assessing cross-sector alliances and collaborations. *Academy of Management Executive,* 17(1): 61–76.

19. Some dangers of a short-term perspective are addressed in: Van Buren, M. E. & Safferstone, T. 2009. The quick wins paradox. *Harvard Business Review,* 67(1): 54–61.

20. Senge, P. 1996. Leading learning organizations: The bold, the powerful, and the invisible. In Hesselbein, F., Goldsmith, M., & Beckhard, R. (Eds.), *The leader of the future:* 41–58. San Francisco: Jossey-Bass.

21. Samuelson, J. 2006. A critical mass for the long term. *Harvard Business Review,* 84(2): 62, 64, and, Anonymous. 2007. Power play. *The Economist,* January 20: 10–12.

22. Loeb, M. 1994. Where leaders come from. *Fortune,* September 19: 241 (quoting Warren Bennis).

23. Address by Norman R. Augustine at the Crummer Business School, Rollins College, Winter Park, FL, October 20, 1989.

24. Hemp, P. 2004. An Interview with CEO Kevin Sharer. *Harvard Business Review,* 82(7/8): 66–74.

25. New perspectives on "management models" are addressed in: Birkinshaw, J. & Goddard, J. 2009. What is your management model? *MIT Sloan Management Review,* 50(2): 81–90.

26. Mintzberg, H. 1985. Of strategies: Deliberate and emergent. *Strategic Management Journal,* 6: 257–272.

27. Some interesting insights on decision-making processes are found in: Nutt, P. C. 2008. Investigating the success of decision making processes. *Journal of Management Studies,* 45(2): 425–455.

28. Leung, W. & Ling, C. S. 2010. Chinese consumers' appetites fatten air shippers. *International Herald Tribune,* July 30: 15.

29. Bryant, A. 2011. The corner office. *nytimes.com,* October 8: np.

30. A study investigating the sustainability of competitive advantage is: Newbert, S. L. 2008. Value, rareness, competitive advantages, and performance: A conceptual-level empirical investigation of the resource-based view of the firm. *Strategic Management Journal,* 29(7): 745–768.

31. Good insights on mentoring are addressed in: DeLong, T. J., Gabarro, J. J., & Lees, R. J. 2008. Why mentoring matters in a hypercompetitive world. *Harvard Business Review,* 66(1): 115–121.

32. Bryant, A. 2009. The corner office. *nytimes.com,* April 25: np.

33. A unique perspective on differentiation strategies is: Austin, R. D. 2008. High margins and the quest for aesthetic coherence. *Harvard Business Review,* 86(1): 18–19.

34. Some insights on partnering in the global area are discussed in: MacCormack, A. & Forbath, T. 2008. *Harvard Business Review,* 66(1): 24, 26.

35. For insights on how firms can be successful in entering new markets in emerging economies, refer to: Eyring, M. J., Johnson, M. W. & Nair, H. 2011. New business models in emerging markets. *Harvard Business Review,* 89(1/2): 88–95.

36. *Fortune.* 2012. December 3: 6.

37. An interesting discussion of the challenges of strategy implementation is: Neilson, G. L., Martin, K. L., & Powers, E. 2008. The secrets of strategy execution. *Harvard Business Review,* 86(6): 61–70.

38. Interesting perspectives on strategy execution involving the link between strategy and operations are addressed in: Kaplan, R. S. & Norton, D. P. 2008. Mastering the management system. *Harvard Business Review,* 66(1): 62–77.

39. An innovative perspective on organizational design is found in: Garvin, D. A. & Levesque, L. C. 2008. The multiunit enterprise. *Harvard Business Review,* 86(6): 106–117.

40. Monks, R. & Minow, N. 2001. *Corporate governance* (2nd ed.). Malden, MA: Blackwell.

41. Intel Corp. 2007. *Intel corporation board of directors guidelines on significant corporate governance issues. www.intel.com*

42. Jones, T. J., Felps, W., & Bigley, G. A. 2007. Ethical theory and stakeholder-related decisions: The role of stakeholder culture. *Academy of Management Review,* 32(1): 137–155.

43. For example, see The best (& worst) managers of the year, 2003.

BusinessWeek, January 13: 58–92; and Lavelle, M. 2003. Rogues of the year. *Time,* January 6: 33–45.

44. Handy, C. 2002. What's a business for? *Harvard Business Review,* 80(12): 49–55.

45. Anonymous, 2007. In the money. *Economist,* January 20: 3–6.

46. Hessel, E. & Woolley, S. 2008. Your money or your life. *Forbes,* October 27: 52.

47. Task, A. 2012. Finance CEO pay rose 20% in 2011, even as stocks stumbled. *www.finance.yahoo.com,* June 5: np.

48. Some interesting insights on the role of activist investors can be found in: Greenwood, R. & Schol, M. 2008. When (not) to listen to activist investors. *Harvard Business Review,* 66(1): 23–24.

49. For an interesting perspective on the changing role of boards of directors, refer to Lawler, E. & Finegold, D. 2005. Rethinking governance. *MIT Sloan Management Review,* 46(2): 67–70.

50. Benz, M. & Frey, B. S. 2007. Corporate governance: What can we learn from public governance? *Academy of Management Review,* 32(1): 92–104.

51. The salience of shareholder value is addressed in: Carrott, G. T. & Jackson, S. E. 2009. Shareholder value must top the CEO's agenda. *Harvard Business Review,* 67(1): 22–24.

52. Stakeholder symbiosis. 1998. *Fortune,* March 30: S2.

53. An excellent review of stakeholder management theory can be found in: Laplume, A. O., Sonpar, K., & Litz, R. A. 2008. Stakeholder theory: Reviewing a theory that moves us. *Journal of Management,* 34(6): 1152–1189.

54. For a definitive, recent discussion of the stakeholder concept, refer to Freeman, R. E. & McVae, J. 2001. A stakeholder approach to strategic management. In Hitt, M. A., Freeman, R. E., & Harrison, J. S. (Eds.). *Handbook of strategic management:* 189–207. Malden, MA: Blackwell.

55. Harrison, J. S., Bosse, D. A. & Phillips, R. A. 2010. Managing for stakeholders, stakeholder utility functions, and competitive advantage. *Strategic Management Journal,* 31(1): 58–74.

56. For an insightful discussion on the role of business in society, refer to Handy, op. cit.

57. Camillus, J. 2008. Strategy as a wicked problem. *Harvard Business Review,* 86(5): 100–101.

58. Stakeholder symbiosis. op. cit., p. S3.

59. Sidhu, I. 2010. *Doing both.* FT Press: Upper Saddle River, NJ: 7–8.

60. Thomas, J. G. 2000. Macroenvironmetal forces. In Helms, M. M. (Ed.), *Encyclopedia of management.* (4th ed.): 516–520. Farmington Hills, MI: Gale Group.

61. For a strong advocacy position on the need for corporate values and social responsibility, read Hollender, J. 2004. What matters most: Corporate values and social responsibility. *California Management Review,* 46(4): 111–119.

62. Waddock, S. & Bodwell, C. 2004. Managing responsibility: What can be learned from the quality movement. *California Management Review,* 47(1): 25–37.

63. For a discussion of the role of alliances and collaboration on corporate social responsibility initiatives, refer to Pearce, J. A. II. & Doh, J. P. 2005. The high impact of collaborative social initiatives. *MIT Sloan Management Review,* 46(3): 30–40.

64. Insights on ethical behavior and performance are addressed in: Trudel, R. & Cotte, J. 2009. *MIT Sloan Management Review,* 50(2): 61–68.

65. Bhattacharya, C. B. & Sen, S. 2004, Doing better at doing good: When, why, and how consumers respond to corporate social initiatives. *California Management Review,* 47(1): 9–24.

66. For some findings on the relationship between corporate social responsibility and firm performance, see: Margolis, J. D. & Elfenbein, H. A. 2008. *Harvard Business Review,* 86(1): 19–20.

67. Cone Corporate Citizenship Study, 2002, *www.coneinc.com.*

68. Refer to *www.bsr.org.*

69. This section draws on: Porter, M. E. & Kramer, M. R. 2011. Creating shared value. *Harvard Business Review,* 89 (1/2): 62–77.

70. Driver, M. 2012. An Interview with Michael Porter: Social entrepreneurship and the transformation of capitalism. *Academy of Management Learning & Education,* 11(3): 422.

71. An insightful discussion of the risks and opportunities associated with global warming, refer to: Lash, J. & Wellington, F. 2007. Competitive advantage on a warming planet. *Harvard Business Review,* 85(3): 94–102.

72. This section draws on Hart, S. L. 1997. Beyond greening: Strategies for a sustainable world. *Harvard Business Review,* 75(1): 66–76, and Berry, M. A. & Rondinelli, D. A. 1998. Proactive corporate environmental management: A new industrial revolution. *Academy of Management Executive,* 12(2): 38–50.

73. Hart, op. cit., p. 67.

74. For a creative perspective on environmental sustainability and competitive advantage as well as ethical implications, read Ehrenfeld, J. R. 2005. The roots of sustainability. *MIT Sloan Management Review,* 46(2): 23–25.

75. McKinsey & Company. 1991. *The corporate response to the environmental challenge.* Summary Report, Amsterdam: McKinsey & Company.

76. Delmas, M. A. & Montes-Sancho, M. J. 2010. Voluntary agreements to improve environmental quality: Symbolic and substantive cooperation. *Strategic Management Journal,* 31(6): 575–601.

77. Vogel, D. J. 2005. Is there a market for virtue? The business case for corporate social responsibility. *California Management Review,* 47(4): 19–36.

78. Esty, D.C. & Charnovitz, S. 2012. Green rules to drive innovation. *Harvard Business Review,* 90(3): 120–123.

79. Esty, D. C. & Simmons, P. J. 2011. *The green to gold business playbook.* New York: Wiley.

80. Kaahwarski, T. 2010. It pays to be good. *Bloomberg BusinessWeek,* February 1 to February 8: 69.

81. Senge, P. M. 1990. The leader's new work: Building learning organizations. *Sloan Management Review,* 32(1): 7–23.

82. For an interesting perspective on the role of middle managers in the strategic management process, refer to Huy, Q. H. 2001. In praise of middle managers. *Harvard Business Review,* 79(8): 72–81.

83. Senge, 1996, op. cit., pp. 41–58.

84. Kets de Vries, M. F. R. 1998. Charisma in action: The transformational abilities of Virgin's Richard Branson and ABB's Percy Barnevik. *Organizational Dynamics,* 26(3): 7–21.

85. Hamel, G. 2006. The why, what, and how of management innovation. *Harvard Business Review,* 84(2): 72–84.

86. Bryant, A. 2011. *The corner office.* New York: St. Martin's/Griffin, 6.

87. An interesting discussion on how to translate top management's goals into concrete actions is found in: Bungay, S. 2011. How to make the most of your company's strategy. *Harvard Business Review,* 89(1/2): 132–40.

88. Bryant, A. 2011. *The corner office.* New York: St. Martin's/Griffin, 171.

89. An insightful discussion about the role of vision, mission, and strategic objectives can be found in: Collis, D. J. & Rukstad, M. G. 2008. Can you say what your strategy is? *Harvard Business Review,* 66(4): 82–90.

90. Our discussion draws on a variety of sources. These include Lipton, M. 1996. Demystifying the development of an organizational vision. *Sloan Management Review,* 37(4): 83–92; Bart, C. K. 2000. Lasting inspiration. *CA Magazine,* May: 49–50; and Quigley, J. V. 1994. Vision: How leaders develop it, share it, and sustain it. *Business Horizons,* September–October: 37–40.

91. Lipton, op. cit.

92. Bryant, A. 2011. *The corner office.* New York: St. Martin's/Griffin, 34.

93. Hardy, Q. 2007. The uncarly. *Forbes,* March 12: 82–90.

94. Some interesting perspective on gender differences in organizational vision are discussed in: Ibarra, H. & Obodaru, O. 2009. Women and the vision thing. *Harvard Business Review,* 67(1): 62–70.

95. Quigley, op. cit.

96. Ibid.

97. Lipton, op. cit. Additional pitfalls are addressed in this article.

98. Sull, D. N. 2005. Strategy as active waiting. *Harvard Business Review,* 83(9): 120–130.

99. Company records.

100. Lipton, op. cit.

101. Sexton, D. A. & Van Aukun, P. M. 1985. A longitudinal study of small business strategic planning. *Journal of Small Business Management,* January: 8–15, cited in Lipton, op. cit.

102. For an insightful perspective on the use of strategic objectives, refer to Chatterjee, S. 2005. Core objectives: Clarity in designing strategy. *California Management Review,* 47(2): 33–49.

103. Ibid.

104. Harnish, V. 2011. Five ways to get your strategy right. *Fortune,* April 11: 42.

chapter 2

Analyzing the External Environment of the Firm

Creating Competitive Advantages

After reading this chapter, you should have a good understanding of the following learning objectives:

LO2.1	The importance of developing forecasts of the business environment.
LO2.2	Why environmental scanning, environmental monitoring, and collecting competitive intelligence are critical inputs to forecasting.
LO2.3	Why scenario planning is a useful technique for firms competing in industries characterized by unpredictability and change.
LO2.4	The impact of the general environment on a firm's strategies and performance.
LO2.5	How forces in the competitive environment can affect profitability, and how a firm can improve its competitive position by increasing its power vis-à-vis these forces.
LO2.6	How the Internet and digitally based capabilities are affecting the five competitive forces and industry profitability.
LO2.7	The concept of strategic groups and their strategy and performance implications.

Learning from Mistakes

Analyzing the external environment is a critical step in recognizing and understanding the opportunities and threats that organizations face. And here is where some companies fail to do a good job.

Consider the example of Salemi Industries and the launch of its product, Cell Zone, in 2005. Although it tried to carefully analyze its potential market, it misread the market's demand for the product and paid a steep price for its mistake.[1] Mobile phone usage was sharply increasing, and its founder observed that patrons in places such as restaurants would be annoyed by the chatter of a nearby guest having a private (but loud!) conversation. Salemi Industries interpreted this observation as an opportunity to create the Cell Zone: a "commercial sound resistant cell phone booth that provides a convenient and disturbance-free environment to place and receive phone calls . . . with a design feature to promote product or service on its curvilinear outer shell," according to the firm's website.

Salemi Industries' key error was that it failed to take into consideration an emerging technology—the increasing popularity of text messaging and other

nonvoice communication technology applications and how that would affect the sales of their product. For example, the Pew Internet & American Life Project estimated that the number of text messages that were sent each day would soar from 500,000 in 2001 to 4 billion in 2009. In addition to this technology shift, the target locations (restaurants) were not interested in or willing to give up productive square footage for patrons to hold private conversations. Not surprisingly, the firm has sold only 300 units (100 of them in college libraries), and Salemi Industries has lost over $650,000 to date.

Discussion Questions

1. What is the biggest stumbling block for Cell Zone?
2. Are there other market segments where Cell Zone might work?

Successful managers must recognize opportunities and threats in their firm's external environment. They must be aware of what's going on outside their company. If they focus exclusively on the efficiency of internal operations, the firm may degenerate into the world's most efficient producer of buggy whips, typewriters, or carbon paper. But if they miscalculate the market, opportunities will be lost—hardly an enviable position for their firm. As we saw from the Cell Zone example, misreading the market can lead to negative consequences.

In *Competing for the Future,* Gary Hamel and C. K. Prahalad suggest that "every manager carries around in his or her head a set of biases, assumptions, and presuppositions about the structure of the relevant 'industry,' about how one makes money in the industry, about who the competition is and isn't, about who the customers are and aren't, and so on."[2] Environmental analysis requires you to continually question such assumptions. Peter

Drucker labeled these interrelated sets of assumptions the "theory of the business."[3] The sudden reversal in Borders' fortunes (chapter 1) clearly illustrates that if a company does not keep pace with changes in the external environment, it becomes difficult to sustain competitive advantages and deliver strong financial results.

A firm's strategy may be good at one point in time, but it may go astray when management's frame of reference gets out of touch with the realities of the actual business situation. This results when management's assumptions, premises, or beliefs are incorrect or when internal inconsistencies among them render the overall "theory of the business" invalid. As Warren Buffett, investor extraordinaire, colorfully notes, "Beware of past performance 'proofs.' If history books were the key to riches, the Forbes 400 would consist of librarians."

In the business world, many once successful firms have fallen. Today we may wonder who will be the next Blockbuster, Borders, Circuit City, or *Encyclopaedia Britannica*.

Creating the Environmentally Aware Organization

LO2.1

The importance of developing forecasts of the business environment.

So how do managers become environmentally aware?[4] We will now address three important processes—scanning, monitoring, and gathering competitive intelligence—used to develop forecasts.[5] Exhibit 2.1 illustrates relationships among these important activities. We also discuss the importance of scenario planning in anticipating major future changes in the external environment and the role of SWOT analysis.[6]

The Role of Scanning, Monitoring, Competitive Intelligence, and Forecasting

LO2.2

Why environmental scanning, environmental monitoring, and collecting competitive intelligence are critical inputs to forecasting.

Environmental Scanning **Environmental scanning** involves surveillance of a firm's external environment to predict environmental changes and detect changes already under way.[7,8] This alerts the organization to critical trends and events before changes develop a discernible pattern and before competitors recognize them.[9] Otherwise, the firm may be forced into a reactive mode.[10]

Experts agree that spotting key trends requires a combination of knowing your business and your customer as well as keeping an eye on what's happening around you. Such a big-picture/small-picture view enables you to better identify the emerging trends that will affect your business.

Leading firms in an industry can also be a key indicator of emerging trends.[11] For example, with its wide range of household goods, Procter & Gamble is a barometer for consumer spending. Any sign that it can sell more of its premium products without cutting prices sharply indicates that shoppers may finally be becoming less price-sensitive with

environmental scanning

surveillance of a firm's external environment to predict environmental changes and detect changes already under way.

EXHIBIT 2.1 Inputs to Forecasting

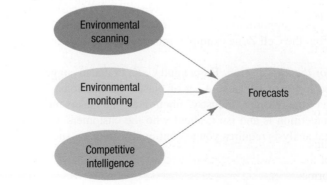

everyday purchases. In particular, investors will examine the performance of beauty products like Olay moisturizers and CoverGirl cosmetics for evidence that spending on small, discretionary pick-me-ups is improving.

Environmental Monitoring **Environmental monitoring** tracks the evolution of environmental trends, sequences of events, or streams of activities. They may be trends that the firm came across by accident or ones that were brought to its attention from outside the organization.[12] Monitoring enables firms to evaluate how dramatically environmental trends are changing the competitive landscape.

One of the authors of this text has conducted on-site interviews with executives from several industries to identify indicators that firms monitor as inputs to their strategy process. Examples of such indicators included:

- *A Motel 6 executive.* The number of rooms in the budget segment of the industry in the United States and the difference between the average daily room rate and the consumer price index (CPI).
- *A Pier 1 Imports executive.* Net disposable income (NDI), consumer confidence index, and housing starts.
- *A Johnson & Johnson medical products executive.* Percentage of gross domestic product (GDP) spent on health care, number of active hospital beds, and the size and power of purchasing agents (indicates the concentration of buyers).

Such indices are critical for managers in determining a firm's strategic direction and resource allocation.

In the last two sections on environmental scanning and monitoring, we discussed the importance of determining key trends and their evolution over time that can affect a firm's success. Projecting current trends into the future, however, is fraught with many risks. Dan Burrus, in his recent book *Flash Foresight,* has made an important distinction between **hard trends** and **soft trends** that we believe provides useful insights to managers who have to base their strategies on projections about the future.[13]

Dan Burrus provides a humorous example to illustrate a soft trend. When Elvis Presley died in 1977, there were about 100 professional Elvis impersonators. In the next five years, this number grew many fold. A straightforward projection of this trend would have shown that by the year 2000, one out of every three Americans would be an Elvis impersonator! Obviously, nobody made such a prediction, because the number of Elvis impersonators represents a soft trend. A soft trend is something that might happen, and the probability with which it might happen can be estimated. For example, continuing budget deficits is a soft trend. The choices government officials make about economic policy, taxation, and defense spending will have major implications for the size of the budget deficit. A number of important decisions that managers make are based on projections about future interest rates. These projections, however, are soft trends, because interest rates can be affected by a number of developments within and outside the country, such as decisions of the Federal Reserve, how the economic crisis in Europe unfolds, and China's decisions on buying U.S. treasury bonds.

A hard trend, on the other hand, is a projection based on measurable facts, events, or objects. It is something that *will* happen. The aging of the population is a hard trend. So is the increasing speed and decreasing cost of computers. Given the continuing depletion of fossil fuels and the increasing demand for automobiles in developing nations like China and India, a rise in oil prices is a hard trend, regardless of short-term fluctuations up or down.

In Strategy Spotlight 2.1, we discuss how Mayo Clinic benefited by acting on hard trends. Taking advantage of the increasing penetration of personal computers in American homes, Mayo Clinic transformed itself as a provider of health-related knowledge and expertise.

environmental monitoring
a firm's analysis of the external environment that tracks the evolution of environmental trends, sequences of events, or streams of activities.

hard trend
a projection based on measurable facts, events, or objects. It is something that will happen.

soft trend
something that might happen and for which the probability that it might happen can be estimated.

MAYO CLINIC'S TRANSFORMATION INTO A KNOWLEDGE ORGANIZATION: BENEFITING FROM HARD TRENDS

Very often when organizations project environmental trends into the future they see a bleak picture. Such "gloom and doom" scenarios, however, might actually be the result of a tendency to be selective about what we see or, even more often, our inability to see possible opportunities in what might seem like unrelated or peripheral developments.

Take the case of Mayo Clinic, the internationally known, Rochester, Minnesota, based not-for-profit hospital. Back in the 1980s, when they undertook an analysis of the future, what they saw was a depressing picture with an aging population, decreasing Medicare and Medicaid reimbursements, and ever-increasing losses in their emergency room operations. Thus, both the economic and demographic trends looked bleak. However, Dan Burrus, a consultant, discovered a number of significant hard trends occurring that many hospitals typically did not consider when making future plans. These technological trends included:

- Continuing declines in the prices of PCs
- Increasing speed and computing power of PCs
- Huge increases in the capacity to store, distribute, and search for information
- Increasing presence of PCs in virtually every home in the U.S and outside

Being a leading research hospital, the Mayo Clinic had developed over the years an enormous amount of knowledge about how to diagnose, manage, and cure a variety of diseases and health conditions. Although this knowledge was developed primarily to treat patients, Dan Burrus saw a huge opportunity for the Mayo Clinic to derive revenue from this knowledge by selling this information to a public that is hungry for reliable medical information written in an accessible fashion. The result was a CD that it sold to customers for $100. With this CD, the users could access information that would help them to determine, for example, whether their child's rash or fever was something they could treat with ibuprofen or something that needed an immediate trip to the emergency room. In the first year, 670,000 CDs were sold!

In addition to the extra revenue that the CD generated, Mayo's entry into the knowledge market had many unanticipated positive benefits. For example, the popularity of the CDs established the Mayo brand as a leader in healthcare, a name millions around the world would instantly recognize. Second, it helped Mayo transform itself from just another organization that delivers on-site healthcare to a one-of-a-kind organization that delivers health-related knowledge and expertise all around the world.

Today, when one visits MayoClinic.com, they see their slogan "Tools for healthier lives," which it claims draws on the expertise of more than 3,300 physicians, scientists, and researchers. The website lets one search for information on a wide variety of topics, including diseases and conditions, symptoms, drugs and supplements, and first aid. It also includes new and updated information on such topics as 2012 trends for cancer survivors, options for dealing with adversity, and how to spot and take action when experiencing job burnout.

Source: Burrus, D. 2011. *Flash foresight: How to see the invisible and do the impossible.* New York: HarperCollins; *www.mayoclinic.com*; and Ness, S.M. 2013. Reflections on 2012 trends from cancer survivors. *www.mayoclinic.com*.

---

competitive intelligence
a firm's activities of collecting and interpreting data on competitors, defining and understanding the industry, and identifying competitors' strengths and weaknesses.

Competitive Intelligence **Competitive intelligence** (CI) helps firms define and understand their industry and identify rivals' strengths and weaknesses.[14] This includes the intelligence gathering associated with collecting data on competitors and interpreting such data. Done properly, competitive intelligence helps a company avoid surprises by anticipating competitors' moves and decreasing response time.[15]

Examples of competitive analysis are evident in daily newspapers and periodicals such as *The Wall Street Journal, Bloomberg BusinessWeek,* and *Fortune.* For example, banks continually track home loan, auto loan, and certificate of deposit (CD) interest rates charged by rivals. Major airlines change hundreds of fares daily in response to competitors' tactics. Car manufacturers are keenly aware of announced cuts or increases in rivals' production volume, sales, and sales incentives (e.g., rebates and low interest rates on financing). This information is used in their marketing, pricing, and production strategies.

Keeping track of competitors has become easier today with the amount of information that is available on the internet. The following are examples of some websites that companies routinely use for competitive intelligence gathering.[16]

KEEPING TRACK OF THE COMPETITION THROUGH COMPETITIVE INTELLIGENCE SOFTWARE

By Sarah Hudson and Asha Moore-Mangin

Modern companies have a plethora of tools available for monitoring competitors' blogs, press releases, events, and any other content appearing online. Facebook, Twitter, and the use of RSS feeds through Google reader are some of the ways to receive a constantly updated stream of information on the competition. Competitive Intelligence (CI) consultancy agencies offer a bewildering variety of CI software solutions to deal with the problem of refining and tailoring the data to the needs of their corporate clients suffering from information overload.

The easy availability of data brings with it a morass of complex legal and ethical issues that can cost dearly if the company makes a mistake. Google recently backtracked on its decision to remove RSS support from Google Alerts after weighing the costs of dealing with compliance and privacy issues against the vast demand for information by its users.

On the other side of the fence, firms using CI in their daily business have their own problems to deal with, and many MNC's such as Coca-Cola and Dow Chemicals are now incorporating guidelines for competitive intelligence in their ethical codes. Unfortunately the pace of technological change is so fast that these guidelines can seem outdated, with the only reference to the use of technology in Coca Cola's Code of Business being "wiretapping" and "computer hacking" and none in Dow Chemical's Code, which refers only to "publicly available information."

Keeping track of the competition using CI software and the world wide web is a routine function of modern corporations. Keeping ethical codes up and running at the same pace as technological change seems to be a major challenge.

Sources: Garner, L. March 2013, "Another Reason Google Reader Died: Increased Concern About Privacy and Compliance," All Things D. allthingsd.com/20130324/another-reason-google-reader-died-increased-concern-about-privacy-and-compliance/; Kotenko, K. September 2013, "Google Reader Mourners, Rejoice! RSS Feeder is back Sort Of," Digital Trends. www.digitaltrends.com/social-media/google-reader-mourners-rejoice-rss-is-back-sort-of/; The Coca Cola Code of Business Conduct, August 2012 assets.coca-colacompany.com/45/59/f85d53a84ec597f74c754003450c/COBC_English.pdf; The Diamond Standard, Dow's Code of Business Conduct. www.dow.com/flipbook/Dow-Code-of-Conduct/#?page=16

- **Slideshare:** A Website for publicly sharing PowerPoint presentations. Marketing teams have embraced the platform and often post detail-rich presentations about their firms and products.
- **Quora:** A question-and-answer site popular among industry insiders who embrace the free flow of information about technical questions.
- **Ispionage:** A site that reveals the ad words that companies are buying, which can often shed light on new campaigns being launched.
- **YouTube:** Great for finding interviews with executives at trade shows.

At times, a firm's aggressive efforts to gather competitive intelligence may lead to unethical or illegal behaviors.[17] Strategy Spotlight 2.2 provides an example of how adhering to ethical codes whilst trying to keep up with technological change can be a major challenge.

A word of caution: Executives must be careful to avoid spending so much time and effort tracking the actions of traditional competitors that they ignore new competitors. Further, broad environmental changes and events may have a dramatic impact on a firm's viability. Peter Drucker, considered the father of modern management, wrote:

> Increasingly, a winning strategy will require information about events and conditions outside the institution: noncustomers, technologies other than those currently used by the company and its present competitors, markets not currently served, and so on.[18]

Consider the fall of the once-mighty *Encyclopaedia Britannica*.[19] Its demise was not caused by a traditional competitor in the encyclopedia industry. It was caused by new technology. CD-ROMs came out of nowhere and devastated the printed encyclopedia industry. An encyclopedia on CD-ROM, such as Microsoft *Encarta,* sells for only about $50. To make matters worse, many people receive *Encarta* free with their personal computers. The rise of Wikipedia has changed this industry even more. Thousands of contributors generate the content for free. Further, because it is Web-based, there is virtually no limit on how much information it can store.

environmental forecasting
the development of plausible projections about the direction, scope, speed, and intensity of environmental change.

Environmental Forecasting Environmental scanning, monitoring, and competitive intelligence are important inputs for analyzing the external environment. **Environmental forecasting** involves the development of plausible projections about the direction, scope, speed, and intensity of environmental change.[20] Its purpose is to predict change.[21] It asks: How long will it take a new technology to reach the marketplace? Will the present social concern about an issue result in new legislation? Are current lifestyle trends likely to continue?

Some forecasting issues are much more specific to a particular firm and the industry in which it competes. Consider how important it is for Motel 6 to predict future indicators, such as the number of rooms, in the budget segment of the industry. If its predictions are low, it will build too many units, creating a surplus of room capacity that would drive down room rates.

LO2.3

Why scenario planning is a useful technique for firms competing in industries characterized by unpredictability and change.

A danger of forecasting is that managers may view uncertainty as black and white and ignore important gray areas.[22] The problem is that underestimating uncertainty can lead to strategies that neither defend against threats nor take advantage of opportunities.

In 1977 one of the colossal underestimations in business history occurred when Kenneth H. Olsen, president of Digital Equipment Corp., announced, "There is no reason for individuals to have a computer in their home." The explosion in the personal computer market was not easy to detect in 1977, but it was clearly within the range of possibilities at the time. And, historically, there have been underestimates of the growth potential of new telecommunication services. The electric telegraph was derided by Ralph Waldo Emerson, and the telephone had its skeptics. More recently, an "infamous" McKinsey study in the early 1980s predicted fewer than 1 million cellular users in the United States by 2000. Actually, there were nearly 100 million.[23]

Obviously, poor predictions never go out of vogue. Consider some of the "gems" associated with the global financial crisis that began in 2008.[24]

- "Freddie Mac and Fannie Mae are fundamentally sound. . . . I think they are in good shape going forward."—Barney Frank (D-Mass.), House Financial Services Committee Chairman, July 14, 2008. (*Two months later, the government forced the mortgage giants into conservatorships.*)
- "I expect there will be some failures. . . . I don't anticipate any serious problems of that sort among the large internationally active banks."—Ben Bernanke, Federal Reserve Chairman, February 28, 2008. (*In September, Washington Mutual became the largest financial institution in U.S. history to fail. Citigroup needed an even bigger rescue in November.*)
- "In today's regulatory environment, it's virtually impossible to violate rules."— Bernard Madoff, money manager, October 20, 2007. (*On December 11, 2008, Madoff was arrested for allegedly running a Ponzi scheme that may have lost investors $50 billion. He was sentenced to 150 years in prison on July 29, 2009.*)

scenario analysis
an in-depth approach to environmental forecasting that involves experts' detailed assessments of societal trends, economics, politics, technology, or other dimensions of the external environment.

Scenario Analysis is a more in-depth approach to forecasting. It draws on a range of disciplines and interests, among them economics, psychology, sociology, and demographics. It usually begins with a discussion of participants' thoughts on ways in which societal trends, economics, politics, and technology may affect an issue.[25] For example, consider Lego. The popular Danish toy manufacturer has a strong position in the construction toys market. But what would happen if this broadly defined market should change dramatically? After all, Lego is competing not only with producers of similar products but also on a much broader canvas for a share of children's playtime. In this market, Lego has a host of competitors, many of them computer based; still others have not yet been invented. Lego may end up with an increasing share of a narrow, shrinking market (much like IBM in the declining days of the mainframe computer). To avoid such a fate, managers must consider

THE FUTURE OF ENERGY: SCENARIO PLANNING AT SHELL

By Tom McNamara and Erika Marsillac

Royal Dutch Shell (Shell) is a global energy powerhouse that is involved in both the upstream (exploration and extraction) and downstream (refinery and supply) elements of the petroleum business. Their operations take them to some of the most remote, and politically complicated, regions on the planet. A key component of their strategy making process is "scenario planning." Shell got started in scenario planning back in the 1970s and achieved fame by anticipating and successfully navigating both Middle East oil shocks in that decade.

Scenario planning is an organized and formal way for companies to think about how markets will behave in the future. In order to be effective, scenario planning relies on several disciplines; politics, economics, psychology, sociology, and demographics, to name just a few. Shell believes that by asking "what if?" questions it will be able to make more informed business decisions. The goal is not to develop a 100% accurate forecast of the future, but rather to envision a series of possible futures that managers might have to deal with. Sometimes these scenarios try to imagine what the world will look like decades into the future—no easy task. But with 40 years of experience of "looking into their crystal ball," Shell is confident that these exercises have value.

Shell is currently trying to give us a glimpse of what lies ahead in the next 50 years and, quite possibly, what the world might look like in the year 2100. As the world's population reaches 9 billion by the middle of this century, demand for energy could increase by 80%. Shell sees two possible futures. In one, there will be a continuation of the status quo, with present influential nations trying their best to maintain their influence and privileged access to resources. They call this a "rigid" system and believe that it will stifle economic growth and social mobility.

The other world they envision is one where power is diffused globally, with countries accommodating and compromising with one another. In this scenario there is dramatic growth in economic productivity offset by eroding social cohesion, and a degree of political uncertainty.

Shell believes that scenario planning deepens its partnerships with the companies it does business with, as well as its various stakeholders. Again, the goal is not to come up with a 100% accurate forecast of the future, but instead to challenge managers to ask more penetrating questions and to develop the competences that will allow them to better respond, and perhaps even anticipate, changes in the business environment.

Jeremy Bentham, a vice president at Shell, hopes that scenario planning will "provide quantified insights and a language for Shell's executives to apply when grappling with increasingly unfamiliar and challenging conditions." The results should be "a more reflective, responsive, and resilient business."

Sources: The Economist, August 29 2008 "Pierre Wack", The Economist, September 1 2008 "Scenario planning"; Shell website: shell.com.

a wider context than their narrow, traditional markets, by laying down guidelines for at least 10 years in the future to anticipate rapid change. Strategy Spotlight 2.3 provides an example of scenario planning at Royal Dutch Shell.

SWOT Analysis

To understand the business environment of a particular firm, you need to analyze both the general environment and the firm's industry and competitive environment. Generally, firms compete with other firms in the same industry. An industry is composed of a set of firms that produce similar products or services, sell to similar customers, and use similar methods of production. Gathering industry information and understanding competitive dynamics among the different companies in your industry is key to successful strategic management.

One of the most basic techniques for analyzing firm and industry conditions is **SWOT analysis.** SWOT stands for strengths, weaknesses, opportunities, and threats. It provides "raw material"—a basic listing of conditions both inside and surrounding your company.

The Strengths and Weaknesses refer to the internal conditions of the firm—where your firm excels (strengths) and where it may be lacking relative to competitors (weaknesses). Opportunities and Threats are environmental conditions external to the firm. These could be factors either in the general or competitive environment. In the general environment, one might experience developments that are beneficial for most companies such as improving economic conditions, that lower borrowing costs or trends that benefit some companies and harm others. An example is the heightened concern with fitness, which is a threat to some companies (e.g., tobacco) and an opportunity to others (e.g., health clubs).

> **SWOT analysis**
> a framework for analyzing a company's internal and external environment and that stands for strengths, weaknesses, opportunities, and threats.

Opportunities and threats are also present in the competitive environment among firms competing for the same customers.

The general idea of SWOT analysis is that a firm's strategy must:

- build on its strengths,
- remedy the weaknesses or work around them,
- take advantage of the opportunities presented by the environment, and,
- protect the firm from the threats.

Despite its apparent simplicity, the SWOT approach has been very popular. First, it forces managers to consider both internal and external factors simultaneously. Second, its emphasis on identifying opportunities and threats makes firms act proactively rather than reactively. Third, it raises awareness about the role of strategy in creating a match between the environmental conditions and the firm's internal strengths and weaknesses. Finally, its conceptual simplicity is achieved without sacrificing analytical rigor. (We will also address some of the limitations of SWOT analysis in Chapter 3.)

LO2.4

The impact of the general environment on a firm's strategies and performance.

The General Environment

The **general environment** is composed of factors that can have dramatic effects on firm strategy.[26] We divide the general environment into six segments: demographic, sociocultural, political/legal, technological, economic, and global. Exhibit 2.2 provides examples of key trends and events in each of the six segments of the general environment.

The Demographic Segment

Demographics are the most easily understood and quantifiable elements of the general environment. They are at the root of many changes in society. Demographics include elements such as the aging population,[27] rising or declining affluence, changes in ethnic composition, geographic distribution of the population, and disparities in income level.[28]

The impact of a demographic trend, like all segments of the general environment, varies across industries. Rising levels of affluence in many developed countries bode well for brokerage services as well as for upscale pets and supplies. However, this trend may adversely affect fast-food restaurants because people can afford to dine at higher-priced restaurants. Fast-food restaurants depend on minimum-wage employees to operate efficiently, but the competition for labor intensifies as more attractive employment opportunities become prevalent, thus threatening the employment base for restaurants. Let's look at the details of one of these trends.

The aging population in the United States and other developed countries has important implications. The U.S. Bureau of Statistics states that only 19.5 percent of American workers were 55 and older in 2010.[29] However, by 2020 that figure will increase to 25.2 percent, or about one in four, of all U.S. workers. At the same time, the United States is expected to experience a significant drop in younger workers aged 25 to 44 from 68 percent to 64 percent by 2018, making it increasingly important for employers to recruit and retain older workers.

The Sociocultural Segment

Sociocultural forces influence the values, beliefs, and lifestyles of a society. Examples include a higher percentage of women in the workforce, dual-income families, increases in the number of temporary workers, greater concern for healthy diets and physical fitness, greater interest in the environment, and postponement of having children. Such forces enhance sales of products and services in many industries but depress sales in others. The increased number of women in the workforce has increased the need for business clothing merchandise but decreased the demand for baking product staples (since people would

Demographic

- Aging population
- Rising affluence
- Changes in ethnic composition
- Geographic distribution of population
- Greater disparities in income levels

Sociocultural

- More women in the workforce
- Increase in temporary workers
- Greater concern for fitness
- Greater concern for environment
- Postponement of family formation

Political/Legal

- Tort reform
- Americans with Disabilities Act (ADA) of 1990
- Deregulation of utility and other industries
- Increases in federally mandated minimum wages
- Taxation at local, state, federal levels
- Legislation on corporate governance reforms in bookkeeping, stock options, etc. (Sarbanes-Oxley Act of 2002)
- Affordable Health Care Act (Obamacare)

Technological

- Genetic engineering
- Computer-aided design/computer-aided manufacturing systems (CAD/CAM)
- Research in synthetic and exotic materials
- Pollution/global warming
- Miniaturization of computing technologies
- Wireless communications
- Nanotechnology

Economic

- Interest rates
- Unemployment rates
- Consumer Price Index
- Trends in GDP
- Changes in stock market valuations

Global

- Increasing global trade
- Currency exchange rates
- Emergence of the Indian and Chinese economies
- Trade agreements among regional blocs (e.g., NAFTA, EU, ASEAN)
- Creation of WTO (leading to decreasing tariffs/free trade in services)
- Increased risks associated with terrorism

EXHIBIT 2.2

General Environment:
Key Trends and Events

OBESITY CREATES RETAILING OPPORTUNITIES

Adult obesity in the United States has increased from 12 percent in 1989 to 35 percent in 2010 and could rise to almost 50 percent by 2018. While these staggering numbers are frightening from a public health point of view, they create unexpected retailing opportunities. The big-and-tall market currently accounts for 8 percent of total menswear sales, yet more than a third of U.S. men are obese.

Retailers see opportunities to serve this growing market segment. Casual Male Retail Group, currently the market leader in the big-and-tall business, just started Destination XL, a new store concept that exclusively services obese men and offers wider aisles and greater selection of clothes. Competitors are following suit. Men's Wearhouse noticed a 40 percent revenue growth in oversized clothing and is currently testing big-and-tall stores.

While the market demand is promising, however, retailers also face challenges. Because the category is based on a physical attribute—and not a demographic, such as "middle-aged men"—big-and-tall stores long struggled with low public recognition. Rising obesity rates are slowly removing this social stigma and making the market segment attractive for mainstream retailers.

Retailers are reacting to this opportunity by offering a wide selection of clothing and added services. For instance, J.C. Penney recently launched "The Foundry Big & Tall Supply Co.," a specialty store that encompasses features of a microbrewery and a man cave, serving free beer and pretzels during happy hours.

Childhood obesity is also on the rise, with 41 percent of children now overweight or obese. Children at any age don't want to be set apart from their peers or recognized as different. JC Penney was one of the first retailers to offer larger clothing sizes for children on the rack, which saves children the embarrassment of digging through drawers of extended sizes. This strategy seems to be paying off: JC Penney reported that the children's plus-sized line has seen rapid sales growth. Overall, by offering new service and product concepts to the long-underserved but now socially accepted big-and-tall segment, retailers are benefiting financially from an unfortunate public health problem.

Sources: The last course. 2012. *The Economist,* December 14: 16; Townsend, M. 2011. Retailers see profits in big-and-tall menswear. *Bloomberg BusinessWeek.* June 27: 26–28; Park, M. 2012. Obese children outgrowing kids' clothing and furniture. *www.cnn.com,* February 15: np; and Keller, M. 2011. Retailers plump up childrens' clothing. *www.connectamarillo.com,* February 6: np

have less time to cook from scratch). This health and fitness trend has helped industries that manufacture exercise equipment and healthful foods but harmed industries that produce unhealthful foods.

Increased educational attainment by women in the workplace has led to more women in upper management positions.[30] Given such educational attainment, it is hardly surprising that companies owned by women have been one of the driving forces of the U.S. economy; these companies (now more than 9 million in number) account for 40 percent of all U.S. businesses and have generated more than $3.6 trillion in annual revenue. In addition, women have a tremendous impact on consumer spending decisions. Not surprisingly, many companies have focused their advertising and promotion efforts on female consumers. Consider, for example, Lowe's efforts to attract female shoppers:

> Lowe's has found that women prefer to do larger home-improvement projects with a man—be it a boyfriend, husband, or neighbor. As a result, in addition to its "recipe card classes" (that explain various projects that take only one weekend), Lowe's offers co-ed store clinics for projects like sink installation. "Women like to feel they're given the same attention as a male customer," states Lowe's spokesperson Julie Valeant-Yenichek, who points out that most seminar attendees, whether male or female, are inexperienced.[31]

Home Depot recently spent millions of dollars to add softer lighting and brighter signs in 300 stores. Why? It is an effort to match rival Lowe's appeal to women.

Another sociocultural trend that offers new business opportunities is the increasing level of obesity in the United States. We discuss this issue in Strategy Spotlight 2.4.

political/legal segment of the general environment how a society creates and exercises power, including rules, laws, and taxation policies.

The Political/Legal Segment

Political processes and legislation influence environmental regulations with which industries must comply.[32,33] Some important elements of the political/legal arena include tort reform, the Americans with Disabilities Act (ADA) of 1990, the repeal of the Glass-Steagall

Act in 1999 (banks may now offer brokerage services), deregulation of utilities and other industries, and increases in the federally mandated minimum wage.[34]

Government legislation can also have a significant impact on the governance of corporations. The U.S. Congress passed the Sarbanes-Oxley Act in 2002, which greatly increases the accountability of auditors, executives, and corporate lawyers. This act responded to the widespread perception that existing governance mechanisms failed to protect the interests of shareholders, employees, and creditors. Clearly, Sarbanes-Oxley has also created a tremendous demand for professional accounting services.

Legislation can also affect firms in the high-tech sector of the economy by expanding the number of temporary visas available for highly skilled foreign professionals.[35] For example, a bill passed by the U.S. Congress in October 2000 allowed 195,000 H-1B visas for each of the following three years—up from a cap of 115,000. However, beginning in 2006 and continuing through 2013, the annual cap on H-1B visas has shrunk to only 65,000—with an additional 20,000 visas available for foreigners with a Master's or higher degree from a U.S. institution. Many of the visas are for professionals from India with computer and software expertise. As one would expect, this is a political "hot potato" for industry executives as well as U.S. labor and workers' right groups. The key arguments against increases in H-1B visas are that H-1B workers drive down wages and take jobs from Americans.

Consider one of the proactive steps that Microsoft has taken to address this issue:

> Microsoft recently opened an office in Richmond, British Columbia, a suburb of Vancouver.[36] Here, it hopes to place hundreds of workers unable to obtain U.S. visas. Placing workers in the same time zone will help them to collaborate—given that the facility is located just 130 miles north of Microsoft's Redmond, Washington, campus. And it is just a 2 ½ hour drive on Interstate 5 if one needs face time.
>
> It certainly doesn't hurt that Canada does not place limits on visas for skilled workers. An unusually pointed press release by Microsoft stated: "The Vancouver area is a global gateway with a diverse population, is close to Microsoft's offices in Redmond, and allows the company to recruit and retain highly skilled people affected by immigration issues in the U.S."

The Technological Segment

Developments in technology lead to new products and services and improve how they are produced and delivered to the end user.[37] Innovations can create entirely new industries and alter the boundaries of existing industries.[38] Technological developments and trends include genetic engineering, Internet technology, computer-aided design/computer-aided manufacturing (CAD/CAM), research in artificial and exotic materials, and, on the downside, pollution and global warming.[39] Petroleum and primary metals industries spend significantly to reduce their pollution. Engineering and consulting firms that work with polluting industries derive financial benefits from solving such problems.

technological segment of the general environment innovation and state of knowledge in industrial arts, engineering, applied sciences, and pure science; and their interaction with society.

Nanotechnology is becoming a very promising area of research with many potentially useful applications.[40] Nanotechnology takes place at industry's tiniest stage: one billionth of a meter. Remarkably, this is the size of 10 hydrogen atoms in a row. Matter at such a tiny scale behaves very differently. Familiar materials—from gold to carbon soot—display startling and useful new properties. Some transmit light or electricity. Others become harder than diamonds or turn into potent chemical catalysts. What's more, researchers have found that a tiny dose of nanoparticles can transform the chemistry and nature of far bigger things.

The Economic Segment

The economy affects all industries, from suppliers of raw materials to manufacturers of finished goods and services, as well as all organizations in the service, wholesale, retail, government, and nonprofit sectors.[41] Key economic indicators include interest rates,

economic segment of the general environment characteristics of the economy, including national income and monetary conditions.

unemployment rates, the Consumer Price Index, the gross domestic product, and net disposable income.[42] Interest-rate increases have a negative impact on the residential home construction industry but a negligible (or neutral) effect on industries that produce consumer necessities such as prescription drugs or common grocery items.

Other economic indicators are associated with equity markets. Perhaps the most watched is the Dow Jones Industrial Average (DJIA), which is composed of 30 large industrial firms. When stock market indexes increase, consumers' discretionary income rises and there is often an increased demand for luxury items such as jewelry and automobiles. But when stock valuations decrease, demand for these items shrinks.

The Global Segment

global segment of the general environment
influences from foreign countries, including foreign market opportunities, foreign-based competition, and expanded capital markets.

More firms are expanding their operations and market reach beyond the borders of their "home" country. Globalization provides both opportunities to access larger potential markets and a broad base of production factors such as raw materials, labor, skilled managers, and technical professionals. However, such endeavors also carry many political, social, and economic risks.[43]

Examples of key elements include currency exchange rates, increasing global trade, the economic emergence of China, trade agreements among regional blocs (e.g., North American Free Trade Agreement, European Union), and the General Agreement on Tariffs and Trade (GATT) (lowering of tariffs).[44] Increases in trade across national boundaries also provide benefits to air cargo and shipping industries but have a minimal impact on service industries such as bookkeeping and routine medical services.

A key factor in the global economy is the rapid rise of the middle class in emerging countries. By 2015, for the first time, the number of consumers in Asia's middle class will equal those in Europe and North America combined. An important implication of this trend is the dramatic change in hiring practices of U.S. multinationals. Consider:

> Thirty-five U.S.-based multinational firms added jobs faster than other U.S. employers between 2009 and 2011, but nearly three-fourths of those jobs were overseas, according to a *Wall Street Journal* analysis. Those companies, which include Wal-Mart Stores Inc., International Paper Co., Honeywell International, Inc., and United Parcel Service, boosted their employment at home by 3.1 percent, or 113,000 jobs, at roughly the same rate of increase as the nation's other employers. However, they also added more than 333,000 jobs in their far-flung—and faster growing—foreign operations.[45]

Relationships among Elements of the General Environment

In our discussion of the general environment, we see many relationships among the various elements.[46] For example, a demographic trend in the United States, the aging of the population, has important implications for the economic segment (in terms of tax policies to provide benefits to increasing numbers of older citizens). Another example is the emergence of information technology as a means to increase the rate of productivity gains in the United States and other developed countries. Such use of IT results in lower inflation (an important element of the economic segment) and helps offset costs associated with higher labor rates.

The effects of a trend or event in the general environment vary across industries. Governmental legislation (political/legal) to permit the importation of prescription drugs from foreign countries is a very positive development for drugstores but a very negative event for U.S. drug manufacturers. Exhibit 2.3 provides other examples of how the impact of trends or events in the general environment can vary across industries.

Crowdsourcing: A Technology That Affects Multiple Segments of the General Environment Before moving on, let's consider the Internet. The Internet has been a leading and highly visible component of a broader technological phenomenon—the emergence

Segment/Trends and Events	Industry	Positive	Neutral	Negative
Demographic				
Aging population	Health care	√		
	Baby products			√
Rising affluence	Brokerage services	√		
	Fast foods			√
	Upscale pets and supplies	√		
Sociocultural				
More women in the workforce	Clothing	√		
	Baking products (staples)			√
Greater concern for health and fitness	Home exercise equipment	√		
	Meat products			√
Political/legal				
Tort reform	Legal services			√
	Auto manufacturing	√		
Americans with Disabilities Act (ADA)	Retail			√
	Manufacturers of elevators, escalators, and ramps	√		
Technological				
Genetic engineering	Pharmaceutical	√		
	Publishing		√	
Pollution/global warming	Engineering services	√		
	Petroleum			√
Economic				
Interest rate decreases	Residential construction	√		
	Most common grocery products		√	
Global				
Increasing global trade	Shipping	√		
	Personal service		√	
Emergence of China as an economic power	Soft drinks	√		
	Defense			√

EXHIBIT 2.3

The Impact of General Environmental Trends on Various Industries

of digital technology. These technologies are altering the way business is conducted and having an effect on nearly every business domain.

One application of digital technology is **crowdsourcing**, which will be a theme throughout the text. It has affected multiple elements of the general environment, such as technology, globalization, and economic. When and where did the term originate?[47] In January 2006, open sourcing was, for most businesspeople, little more than an online curiosity. At that time, Jeff Howe of *Wired* magazine started to write an article about the phenomenon. However, he soon discovered a far more important story to be told: Large—as well as small—companies in a wide variety of industries had begun farming out serious tasks to individuals and groups on the Internet. Together with his editor, Mark Robinson, they coined a new term to describe the phenomenon. In June 2006, the article appeared in which *crowdsourcing* was defined as the tapping of the "latent talent of the (online) crowd." It has become the term of choice for a process that is infiltrating many aspects of business life.

Clearly, crowdsourcing has claimed some well-known successes, particularly on the product development front. Consider:

- The Linux operating system, created as an open-source alternative to Windows and UNIX, can be downloaded for free and altered to suit any user's needs. And with all the firepower brought to bear by the online open-source community, bugs in the system get fixed in a matter of hours.
- One of Amazon's smartest moves was to invite their customers to write online reviews. The customers are neither paid nor controlled by the company, but the content that they create adds enormous value to other customers and, therefore, to Amazon.
- Roughly five million users per month swear by Wikipedia. The free online encyclopedia was created and updated by Internet volunteers to the tune of roughly two million articles and counting.

Throughout this book, we will introduce examples of crowdsourcing to show its relevance to key strategy concepts. For example, in Chapter 3, we discuss how Procter & Gamble used it to develop social connections through digital media that enable the firm to co-design and co-engineer new innovations with buyers. In Chapter 4, we discuss how SAP, the giant software company, uses crowdsourcing to tap knowledge well beyond its firm boundaries via the nearly 3 million participants in its Community Network. In Chapter 5, we explain how Unilever is using crowdsourcing to advance its sustainability initiatives. And, in Chapter 8, we discuss how firms use the power of the crowd to generate startup funding for new ventures.

Strategy Spotlight 2.5 explains how Goldcorp, a Toronto-based mining company, crowdsourced the expertise required to identify the best location to mine gold on the firm's property. Goldcorp invited geologists around the world to compete for $575,000 in prize money for analyzing its geological data. It was a remarkable success!

The Competitive Environment

Managers must consider the competitive environment (also sometimes referred to as the task or industry environment). The nature of competition in an industry, as well as the profitability of a firm, is often directly influenced by developments in the competitive environment.

The **competitive environment** consists of many factors that are particularly relevant to a firm's strategy. These include competitors (existing or potential), customers, and suppliers. Potential competitors may include a supplier considering forward integration, such as an automobile manufacturer acquiring a rental car company, or a firm in an entirely new industry introducing a similar product that uses a more efficient technology.

crowdsourcing
practice wherein the Internet is used to tap a broad range of individuals and groups to generate ideas and solve problems

industry
a group of firms that produce similar goods or services.

competitive environment
factors that pertain to an industry and affect a firm's strategies.

LO2.5

How forces in the competitive environment can affect profitability, and how a firm can improve its competitive position by increasing its power vis-à-vis these forces.

HOW GOLDCORP USED CROWDSOURCING TO STRIKE GOLD!

About 15 years ago, Toronto-based gold mining company Goldcorp was in big trouble. Besieged by strikes, lingering debts, and an exceedingly high cost of production, the firm had terminated mining operations. Conditions in the marketplace were quite poor, and the gold market was contracting. Most analysts assumed that the company's 50-year-old mine in Red Lake, Ontario, was nearly dead. Without solid evidence of substantial new gold deposits, Goldcorp was likely to fold.

Clearly, CEO Robert McEwen needed a miracle. He was frustrated with his in-house geologists' reliability in estimating the value and location of gold on his property. He did something that was unprecedented in the industry: He published his geological data on the Web for all to see and challenged the world to do the prospecting. The "Goldcorp Challenge" posted a total of $575,000 in prize money to be awarded to the participants who submitted the best methods and estimates.

His reasoning: If he could attract the attention of world-class talent to the problem of finding more gold in Red Lake, just as Linux managed to attract world-class programmers to the cause of better software, he could tap into thousands of minds that he wouldn't otherwise have access to. He could also speed up exploration and improve his odds of discovery.

Although his geologists were appalled at the idea of exposing their super-secret data to the world, the response was immediate. More than 1,400 scientists, engineers, and geologists from 50 countries downloaded the company's data and started their exploration. Says McEwen:

> "We had math, advanced physics, intelligent systems, computer graphics, and organic solutions to inorganic problems. There were capabilities I had never seen before in the industry. When I saw the computer graphics, I almost fell out of my chair."

The panel of five judges was astonished by the creativity of the submissions. The top winner, which won $105,000, was a collaboration by two groups in Australia: Fractal Graphics, of West Perth, and Taylor Wall & Associates, in Queensland. Together they had developed a powerful 3-D graphical depiction of the mine. One of the team members humorously stated, "I've never been to a mine. I'd never even been to Canada." Overall, the contestants identified 110 targets on the Red Lake property, more than 80 percent of which yielded substantial quantities of gold. In fact, since the challenge was initiated, an astounding 8 million ounces of gold have been found—worth well over $3 billion (given gold's fluctuating market value). Most would agree that this is a pretty solid return on a half million dollar investment!

In 2012, Goldcorp had annual revenues of over $5 billion and a market value of $36 billion! Not bad for a once failing firm . . .

Sources: de Castella, T. 2010. Should we trust the wisdom of crowds? *news.bbc.co.uk*, July 5: np; Libert, B. & Spector, J. 2008. *We are smarter than me*. Philadelphia: Wharton School Publishing; Tapscott, D. & Williams, A. D. 2007. Innovation in the age of mass collaboration. *www.businessweek.com*, February 1: np; and Tischler, L. 2002. He struck gold on the net (really). *fastcompany.com*, May 2: np.

Next, we will discuss key concepts and analytical techniques that managers should use to assess their competitive environments. First, we examine Michael Porter's five-forces model that illustrates how these forces can be used to explain an industry's profitability.[48] Second, we discuss how the five forces are being affected by the capabilities provided by Internet technologies. Third, we address some of the limitations, or "caveats," that managers should be familiar with when conducting industry analysis. Finally, we address the concept of strategic groups, because even within an industry it is often useful to group firms on the basis of similarities of their strategies. As we will see, competition tends to be more intense among firms *within* a strategic group than between strategic groups.

Porter's Five-Forces Model of Industry Competition

The "five-forces" model developed by Michael E. Porter has been the most commonly used analytical tool for examining the competitive environment. It describes the competitive environment in terms of five basic competitive forces.[49]

1. The threat of new entrants.
2. The bargaining power of buyers.
3. The bargaining power of suppliers.
4. The threat of substitute products and services.
5. The intensity of rivalry among competitors in an industry.

porter's five-forces model of industry competition
a tool for examining the industry-level competitive environment, especially the ability of firms in that industry to set prices and minimize costs.

Each of these forces affects a firm's ability to compete in a given market. Together, they determine the profit potential for a particular industry. The model is shown in Exhibit 2.4. A manager should be familiar with the five-forces model for several reasons. It helps you decide whether your firm should remain in or exit an industry. It provides the rationale for increasing or decreasing resource commitments. The model helps you assess how to improve your firm's competitive position with regard to each of the five forces.[50] For example, you can use insights provided by the five-forces model to create higher entry barriers that discourage new rivals from competing with you.[51] Or you may develop strong relationships with your distribution channels. You may decide to find suppliers who satisfy the price/performance criteria needed to make your product or service a top performer.

The Threat of New Entrants   The threat of new entrants refers to the possibility that the profits of established firms in the industry may be eroded by new competitors.[52] The extent of the threat depends on existing barriers to entry and the combined reactions from existing competitors.[53] If entry barriers are high and/or the newcomer can anticipate a sharp retaliation from established competitors, the threat of entry is low. These circumstances discourage new competitors. There are six major sources of entry barriers.

Economies of Scale   Economies of scale refers to spreading the costs of production over the number of units produced. The cost of a product per unit declines as the absolute volume per period increases. This deters entry by forcing the entrant to come in at a large scale and risk strong reaction from existing firms or come in at a small scale and accept a cost disadvantage. Both are undesirable options.

Product Differentiation   When existing competitors have strong brand identification and customer loyalty, differentiation creates a barrier to entry by forcing entrants to spend heavily to overcome existing customer loyalties.

threat of new entrants
the possibility that the profits of established firms in the industry may be eroded by new competitors.

economies of scale
decreases in cost per unit as absolute output per period increases.

product differentiation
the degree that a product has strong brand loyalty or customer loyalty.

EXHIBIT 2.4   Porter's Five-Forces Model of Industry Competition

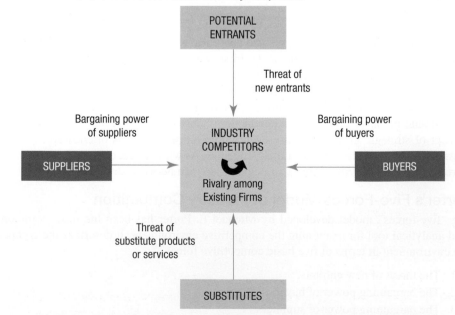

Capital Requirements   The need to invest large financial resources to compete creates a barrier to entry, especially if the capital is required for risky or unrecoverable up-front advertising or research and development (R&D).

Switching Costs   A barrier to entry is created by the existence of one-time costs that the buyer faces when switching from one supplier's product or service to another.

Access to Distribution Channels   The new entrant's need to secure distribution for its product can create a barrier to entry.

Cost Disadvantages Independent of Scale   Some existing competitors may have advantages that are independent of size or economies of scale. These derive from:

- Proprietary products
- Favorable access to raw materials
- Government subsidies
- Favorable government policies

In an environment where few, if any, of these entry barriers are present, the threat of new entry is high. For example, if a new firm can launch its business with a low capital investment and operate efficiently despite its small scale of operation, it is likely to be a threat. One company that failed because of low entry barriers in an industry is ProCD.[54] You probably never heard of this company. It didn't last very long. ProCD provides an example of a firm that failed because it entered an industry with very low entry barriers.

> The story begins in 1986 when Nynex (a former Baby Bell company) issued the first electronic phone book, a compact disk containing all listings for the New York City area. It charged $10,000 per copy and sold the CDs to the FBI, IRS, and other large commercial and government organizations. James Bryant, the Nynex executive in charge of the project, smelled a fantastic business opportunity. He quit Nynex and set up his own firm, ProCD, with the ambitious goal of producing an electronic directory covering the entire United States.
>
> The telephone companies, fearing an attack on their highly profitable Yellow Pages business, refused to license digital copies of their listings. Bryant was not deterred. He hired Chinese workers at $3.50 a day to type every listing from every U.S. telephone book into a database. The result contained more than 70 million phone numbers and was used to create a master disk that enabled ProCD to make hundreds of thousands of copies. Each CD sold for hundreds of dollars and cost less than a dollar each to produce.
>
> It was a profitable business indeed! However, success was fleeting. Competitors such as Digital Directory Assistance and American Business Information quickly launched competing products with the same information. Since customers couldn't tell one product from the next, the players were forced to compete on price alone. Prices for the CD soon plummeted to a few dollars each. A high-priced, high-margin product just months earlier, the CD phone book became little more than a cheap commodity.

The Bargaining Power of Buyers   Buyers threaten an industry by forcing down prices, bargaining for higher quality or more services, and playing competitors against each other. These actions erode industry profitability.[55] The power of each large buyer group depends on attributes of the market situation and the importance of purchases from that group compared with the industry's overall business. A buyer group is powerful when:

- ***It is concentrated or purchases large volumes relative to seller sales.*** If a large percentage of a supplier's sales are purchased by a single buyer, the importance of the buyer's business to the supplier increases. Large-volume buyers also are powerful in industries with high fixed costs (e.g., steel manufacturing).

- **The products it purchases from the industry are standard or undifferentiated.** Confident they can always find alternative suppliers, buyers play one company against the other, as in commodity grain products.
- **The buyer faces few switching costs.** Switching costs lock the buyer to particular sellers. Conversely, the buyer's power is enhanced if the seller faces high switching costs.
- **It earns low profits.** Low profits create incentives to lower purchasing costs. On the other hand, highly profitable buyers are generally less price sensitive.
- **The buyers pose a credible threat of backward integration.** If buyers are either partially integrated or pose a credible threat of backward integration, they are typically able to secure bargaining concessions.
- **The industry's product is unimportant to the quality of the buyer's products or services.** When the quality of the buyer's products is not affected by the industry's product, the buyer is more price sensitive.

At times, a firm or set of firms in an industry may increase its buyer power by using the services of a third party. FreeMarkets Online is one such third party.[56] Pittsburgh-based FreeMarkets has developed software enabling large industrial buyers to organize online auctions for qualified suppliers of semistandard parts such as fabricated components, packaging materials, metal stampings, and services. By aggregating buyers, FreeMarkets increases the buyers' bargaining power. The results are impressive. In its first 48 auctions, most participating companies saved over 15 percent; some saved as much as 50 percent.

Although a firm may be tempted to take advantage of its suppliers because of high buyer power, it must be aware of the potential long-term backlash from such actions. A recent example is the growing resentment that students have toward state universities in California because of a steep 32 percent increase in tuition. Let's see why they have so little bargaining power.

> Students protested by taking over a classroom building. As noted by *Forbes* writer Asher Hawkins: "It was a futile effort. Students who are already embarked on a four-year program are something of a captive audience, and California's state coffers are empty."[57] After all, students have high exit costs, primarily because of the difficulty in transferring credits to another university. Plus, there are fewer openings at other UC campuses due to budget cuts, and there is increasing demand for them from overseas students. All these factors erode student bargaining power.
>
> After the increase, the tuition and fees for in-state undergraduate students will come to about $10,000 for the academic year (this represents a compound annual increase of nearly 10 percent over the past decade). Although this may still seem like a reasonable price for a high-quality education, there could be more price increases ahead.

bargaining power of suppliers
the threat that suppliers may raise prices or reduce the quality of purchased goods and services.

The Bargaining Power of Suppliers   Suppliers can exert bargaining power by threatening to raise prices or reduce the quality of purchased goods and services. Powerful suppliers can squeeze the profitability of firms so far that they can't recover the costs of raw material inputs.[58] The factors that make suppliers powerful tend to mirror those that make buyers powerful. A supplier group will be powerful when:

- **The supplier group is dominated by a few companies and is more concentrated (few firms dominate the industry) than the industry it sells to.** Suppliers selling to fragmented industries influence prices, quality, and terms.
- **The supplier group is not obliged to contend with substitute products for sale to the industry.** The power of even large, powerful suppliers can be checked if they compete with substitutes.

- *The industry is not an important customer of the supplier group.* When suppliers sell to several industries and a particular industry does not represent a significant fraction of its sales, suppliers are more prone to exert power.
- *The supplier's product is an important input to the buyer's business.* When such inputs are important to the success of the buyer's manufacturing process or product quality, the bargaining power of suppliers is high.
- *The supplier group's products are differentiated or it has built up switching costs for the buyer.* Differentiation or switching costs facing the buyers cut off their options to play one supplier against another.
- *The supplier group poses a credible threat of forward integration.* This provides a check against the industry's ability to improve the terms by which it purchases.

The Threat of Substitute Products and Services   All firms within an industry compete with industries producing substitute products and services.[59] Substitutes limit the potential returns of an industry by placing a ceiling on the prices that firms in that industry can profitably charge. The more attractive the price/performance ratio of substitute products, the tighter the lid on an industry's profits.

Identifying substitute products involves searching for other products or services that can perform the same function as the industry's offerings. This may lead a manager into businesses seemingly far removed from the industry. For example, the airline industry might not consider video cameras much of a threat. But as digital technology has improved and wireless and other forms of telecommunication have become more efficient, teleconferencing has become a viable substitute for business travel. That is, the rate of improvement in the price–performance relationship of the substitute product (or service) is high.

> Teleconferencing can save both time and money, as IBM found out with its "Manager Jam" idea.[60] With 319,000 employees scattered around six continents, it is one of the world's largest businesses (including 32,000 managers) and can be a pretty confusing place. The shift to an increasingly mobile workplace means many managers supervise employees they rarely see face-to-face. To enhance coordination, Samuel Palmisano, IBM's new CEO, launched one of his first big initiatives: a two-year program exploring the role of the manager in the 21st century. "Manager Jam," as the project was nicknamed, was a 48-hour real-time Web event in which managers from 50 different countries swapped ideas and strategies for dealing with problems shared by all of them, regardless of geography. Some 8,100 managers logged on to the company's intranet to participate in the discussion forums.

Technological advancements have increased the mileage of gasoline-powered cars compared to that of hybrids. This has made hybrids less attractive from a price/performance ratio, as we discuss in Strategy Spotlight 2.6.

The Intensity of Rivalry among Competitors in an Industry   Firms use tactics like price competition, advertising battles, product introductions, and increased customer service or warranties. Rivalry occurs when competitors sense the pressure or act on an opportunity to improve their position.[61]

Some forms of competition, such as price competition, are typically highly destabilizing and are likely to erode the average level of profitability in an industry.[62] Rivals easily match price cuts, an action that lowers profits for all firms. On the other hand, advertising battles expand overall demand or enhance the level of product differentiation for the benefit of all firms in the industry. Rivalry, of course, differs across industries. In some instances it is characterized as warlike, bitter, or cutthroat, whereas in other industries

threat of substitute products and services the threat of limiting the potential returns of an industry by placing a ceiling on the prices that firms in that industry can profitably charge without losing too many customers to substitute products.

substitute products and services products and services outside the industry that serve the same customer needs as the industry's products and services.

intensity of rivalry among competitors in an industry the threat that customers will switch their business to competitors within the industry.

GAS VERSUS HYBRIDS: A BATTLE OF SUBSTITUTES

Hybrid cars such as the Toyota Prius have seen tremendous success since the first hybrids were introduced in the late 1990s. Yet the market share of hybrid cars in the U.S. fell from an all-time high of 2.8 percent in 2009 to 2.4 percent in 2010 and even further to 2.2 percent in 2011. These results are even more surprising given that the number of hybrid models on the market has increased each year from 17 in 2009 to 30 at the start of 2011. That's more choices, but fewer takers. While some may think that the hybrid car industry feels pressure from other novel car segments such as electric cars (e.g., Nissan Leaf), competition comes from an unusual suspect: plain old internal gas combustion cars!

The primary reason why environmental and cost-conscious consumers prefer gasoline-powered over hybrid cars is rather simple. Engines of gasoline-cars have increasingly challenged the key selling attribute of hybrid cars: fuel economy. While hybrid cars still slightly outcompete modern gasoline cars in terms of fuel

economy, consumers increasingly don't see the value of paying as much as $6,000 extra for a hybrid when they can get 40 mpg on the highway in a gasoline car such as the Hyundai Elantra or the Chevrolet Cruze.

Gasoline-powered cars may also outcompete hybrids on other selling attributes. For instance, buyers may prefer mature technologies such as gasoline-powered cars that don't come with the uncertainty of new technologies, such as doubts about the longevity of hybrid batteries. Moreover, new car generations like the Nissan Leaf and Chevrolet Volt allow consumers a sneak preview into the future. J.D. Power's most recent U.S. Green Automotive Study suggests that some customers would rather wait and invest their dollars in this new generation of electric cars. Customers holding out for electric cars that won't use any gasoline at all and the technological advancement of gasoline engines caused the unexpected comeback of the gasoline car.

Sources: Naughton, K. 2012. Hybrids' unlikely rival: Plain old cars. *Bloomberg BusinessWeek,* February 2: 23–24; Valdes-Dapena, P. 2011. Hybrid car sales: Lots of options, few takers. *money.cnn.com,* September 30: np; and Valdes-Dapena, P. 2011. Green cars are ready, car buyers aren't. *money.cnn.com,* April 27: np.

---

it is referred to as polite and gentlemanly. Intense rivalry is the result of several interacting factors, including the following:

- *Numerous or equally balanced competitors.* When there are many firms in an industry, the likelihood of mavericks is great. Some firms believe they can make moves without being noticed. Even when there are relatively few firms, and they are nearly equal in size and resources, instability results from fighting among companies having the resources for sustained and vigorous retaliation.
- *Slow industry growth.* Slow industry growth turns competition into a fight for market share, since firms seek to expand their sales.
- *High fixed or storage costs.* High fixed costs create strong pressures for all firms to increase capacity. Excess capacity often leads to escalating price cutting.
- *Lack of differentiation or switching costs.* Where the product or service is perceived as a commodity or near commodity, the buyer's choice is typically based on price and service, resulting in pressures for intense price and service competition. Lack of switching costs, described earlier, has the same effect.
- *Capacity augmented in large increments.* Where economies of scale require that capacity must be added in large increments, capacity additions can be very disruptive to the industry supply/demand balance.
- *High exit barriers.* Exit barriers are economic, strategic, and emotional factors that keep firms competing even though they may be earning low or negative returns on their investments. Some exit barriers are specialized assets, fixed costs of exit, strategic interrelationships (e.g., relationships between the business units and others within a company in terms of image, marketing, shared facilities, and so on), emotional barriers, and government and social pressures (e.g., governmental discouragement of exit out of concern for job loss).

Rivalry between firms is often based solely on price, but it can involve other factors. Take Pfizer's market position in the impotence treatment market. Pfizer was the first pharmaceutical firm to develop Viagra, a highly successful drug that treats impotence.

> In several countries, the United Kingdom among them, Pfizer faced a lawsuit by Eli Lilly & Co. and Icos Corp. challenging its patent protection. These two pharmaceutical firms recently entered into a joint venture to market Cialis, a drug to compete with Viagra. The U.K. courts agreed and lifted the patent.
>
> This opened the door for Eli Lilly and Icos to proceed with challenging Pfizer's market position. Because Cialis has fewer side effects than Viagra, the drug has the potential to rapidly decrease Pfizer's market share in the United Kingdom if physicians switch prescriptions from Viagra to Cialis. If future patent challenges are successful, Pfizer may see its sales of Viagra erode rapidly.[63] But Pfizer is hardly standing still. It recently doubled its advertising expenditures on Viagra.

Exhibit 2.5 summarizes our discussion of industry five-forces analysis. It points out how various factors, such as economies of scale and capital requirements, affect each "force."

internet
a global network of linked computers that use a common transmission format, exchange information and store data.

How the Internet and Digital Technologies Are Affecting the Five Competitive Forces

LO2.6
How the Internet and digitally based capabilities are affecting the five competitive forces and industry profitability.

The Internet is having a significant impact on nearly every industry. These technologies have fundamentally changed the ways businesses interact with each other and with consumers. In most cases, these changes have affected industry forces in ways that have created many new strategic challenges. In this section, we will evaluate Michael Porter's five-forces model in terms of the actual use of the Internet and the new technological capabilities that it makes possible.

The Threat of New Entrants In most industries, the threat of new entrants has increased because digital and Internet-based technologies lower barriers to entry. For example, businesses that reach customers primarily through the Internet may enjoy savings on other traditional expenses such as office rent, sales-force salaries, printing, and postage. This may encourage more entrants who, because of the lower start-up expenses, see an opportunity to capture market share by offering a product or performing a service more efficiently than existing competitors. Thus, a new cyber entrant can use the savings provided by the Internet to charge lower prices and compete on price despite the incumbent's scale advantages.

Alternatively, because digital technologies often make it possible for young firms to provide services that are equivalent or superior to an incumbent, a new entrant may be able to serve a market more effectively, with more personalized services and greater attention to product details. A new firm may be able to build a reputation in its niche and charge premium prices. By so doing, it can capture part of an incumbent's business and erode profitability.

Another potential benefit of Web-based business is access to distribution channels. Manufacturers or distributors that can reach potential outlets for their products more efficiently by means of the Internet may enter markets that were previously closed to them. Access is not guaranteed, however, because strong barriers to entry exist in certain industries.[64]

The Bargaining Power of Buyers The Internet and wireless technologies may increase buyer power by providing consumers with more information to make buying decisions and by lowering switching costs. But these technologies may also suppress the power of traditional buyer channels that have concentrated buying power in the hands of a few, giving buyers new ways to access sellers. To sort out these differences, let's first distinguish between two types of buyers: end users and buyer channel intermediaries.

EXHIBIT 2.5 Competitive Analysis Checklist

Threat of New Entrants Is High When:	High	Low
Economies of scale are		X
Product differentiation is		X
Capital requirements are		X
Switching costs are		X
Incumbent's control of distribution channels is		X
Incumbent's proprietary knowledge is		X
Incumbent's access to raw materials is		X
Incumbent's access to government subsidies is		X

Power of Buyers Is High When:	High	Low
Concentration of buyers relative to suppliers is	X	
Switching costs are		X
Product differentiation of suppliers is		X
Threat of backward integration by buyers is	X	
Extent of buyer's profits is		X
Importance of the supplier's input to quality of buyer's final product is		X

Power of Suppliers Is High When:	High	Low
Concentration relative to buyer industry is	X	
Availability of substitute products is		X
Importance of customer to the supplier is		X
Differentiation of the supplier's products and services is	X	
Switching costs of the buyer are	X	
Threat of forward integration by the supplier is	X	

Threat of Substitute Products Is High When:	High	Low
The differentiation of the substitute product is	X	
Rate of improvement in price–performance relationship of substitute product is	X	

Intensity of Competitive Rivalry Is High When:	High	Low
Number of competitors is	X	
Industry growth rate is		X
Fixed costs are	X	
Storage costs are	X	
Product differentiation is		X
Switching costs are		X
Exit barriers are	X	
Strategic stakes are	X	

End users are the final customers in a distribution channel. Internet sales activity that is labeled "B2C"—that is, business-to-consumer—is concerned with end users. The Internet is likely to increase the power of these buyers for several reasons. First, the Internet provides large amounts of consumer information. This gives end users the information they need to shop for quality merchandise and bargain for price concessions. Second, an end user's switching costs are also potentially much lower because of the Internet. Switching may involve only a few clicks of the mouse to find and view a competing product or service online.

BUYER POWER IN LEGAL SERVICES: THE ROLE OF THE INTERNET

The $240 billion U.S. legal services industry historically was a classic example of an industry that leaves buyers at a bargaining disadvantage. One of the key reasons for the strong bargaining position of law firms is high information asymmetry between lawyers and consumers, meaning that highly trained and experienced legal professionals know more about legal matters than the average consumer of legal services.

The Internet provides an excellent example of how unequal bargaining power can be reduced by decreasing information asymmetry. A new class of Internet legal services providers tries to accomplish just that and is challenging traditional law services

along the way. For instance, *LawPivot.com*, a recent startup backed by Google Ventures and co-founded by a former top Apple Inc. lawyer, allows consumers to interact with lawyers on a social networking site. This service allows customers to get a better picture of a lawyer's legal skills before opening their wallets. As a result, information asymmetry between lawyers and consumers is reduced and customers find themselves in a better bargaining position. Another example is *LegalZoom.com*, a service that helps consumers to create legal documents. Customers familiar with *LegalZoom.com* may use their knowledge of the time and effort required to create legal documents to challenge a lawyer's fees for custom crafted legal documents.

Sources: Jacobs, D. L. 2011. Google takes aim at lawyers. *Forbes,* August 8: np; and Alternative law firms: Bargain briefs. 2011. *The Economist,* August 13: 64.

In contrast, the bargaining power of distribution channel buyers may decrease because of the Internet. *Buyer channel intermediaries* are the wholesalers, distributors, and retailers who serve as intermediaries between manufacturers and end users. In some industries, they are dominated by powerful players that control who gains access to the latest goods or the best merchandise. The Internet and wireless communications, however, make it much easier and less expensive for businesses to reach customers directly. Thus, the Internet may increase the power of incumbent firms relative to that of traditional buyer channels. Strategy Spotlight 2.7 illustrates some of the changes brought on by the Internet that have affected the legal services industry.

The Bargaining Power of Suppliers   Use of the Internet and digital technologies to speed up and streamline the process of acquiring supplies is already benefiting many sectors of the economy. But the net effect of the Internet on supplier power will depend on the nature of competition in a given industry. As with buyer power, the extent to which the Internet is a benefit or a detriment also hinges on the supplier's position along the supply chain.

The role of suppliers involves providing products or services to other businesses. The term "B2B"—that is, business-to-business—often refers to businesses that supply or sell to other businesses. The effect of the Internet on the bargaining power of suppliers is a double-edged sword. On the one hand, suppliers may find it difficult to hold onto customers because buyers can do comparative shopping and price negotiations so much faster on the Internet.

On the other hand, several factors may also contribute to stronger supplier power. First, the growth of new Web-based business may create more downstream outlets for suppliers to sell to. Second, suppliers may be able to create Web-based purchasing arrangements that make purchasing easier and discourage their customers from switching. Online procurement systems directly link suppliers and customers, reducing transaction costs and paperwork.[65] Third, the use of proprietary software that links buyers to a supplier's website may create a rapid, low-cost ordering capability that discourages the buyer from seeking other sources of supply. *Amazon.com*, for example, created and patented One-Click purchasing technology that speeds up the ordering process for customers who enroll in the service.[66]

Finally, suppliers will have greater power to the extent that they can reach end users directly without intermediaries. Previously, suppliers often had to work through intermediaries who brought their products or services to market for a fee. But a process known as *disintermediation* is removing the organizations or business process layers responsible for intermediary steps in the value chain of many industries.[67] Just as the Internet is eliminating some business functions, it is creating an opening for new functions. These new activities are entering the value chain by a process known as *reintermediation*—the introduction of new types of intermediaries. Many of these new functions are affecting traditional supply chains. For example, delivery services are enjoying a boom because of the Internet. Many more consumers are choosing to have products delivered to their door rather than going out to pick them up.

The Threat of Substitutes   Along with traditional marketplaces, the Internet has created a new marketplace and a new channel. In general, therefore, the threat of substitutes is heightened because the Internet introduces new ways to accomplish the same tasks.

Consumers will generally choose to use a product or service until a substitute that meets the same need becomes available at a lower cost. The economies created by Internet technologies have led to the development of numerous substitutes for traditional ways of doing business.

Another example of substitution is in the realm of electronic storage. With expanded desktop computing, the need to store information electronically has increased dramatically. Until recently, the trend has been to create increasingly larger desktop storage capabilities and techniques for compressing information that create storage efficiencies. But a viable substitute has recently emerged: storing information digitally on the Internet. Companies such as Dropbox and Amazon Web Services are providing Web-based storage that firms can access simply by leasing space online. Since these storage places are virtual, they can be accessed anywhere the Web can be accessed. Travelers can access important documents and files without transporting them physically from place to place.

The Intensity of Competitive Rivalry   Because the Internet creates more tools and means for competing, rivalry among competitors is likely to be more intense. Only those competitors that can use digital technologies and the Web to give themselves a distinct image, create unique product offerings, or provide "faster, smarter, cheaper" services are likely to capture greater profitability with the new technology.

Rivalry is more intense when switching costs are low and product or service differentiation is minimized. Because the Internet makes it possible to shop around, it has "commoditized" products that might previously have been regarded as rare or unique. Since the Internet reduces the importance of location, products that previously had to be sought out in geographically distant outlets are now readily available online. This makes competitors in cyberspace seem more equally balanced, thus intensifying rivalry.

The problem is made worse for marketers by the presence of shopping robots ("bots") and infomediaries that search the Web for the best possible prices. Consumer websites like mySimon seek out all the Web locations that sell similar products and provide price comparisons.[68] Obviously, this focuses the consumer exclusively on price. Some shopping infomediaries, such as CNET, not only search for the lowest prices on many different products but also rank the customer service quality of different sites that sell similarly priced items.[69] Such infomediary services are good for consumers because they give them the chance to compare services as well as price. For businesses, however, they increase rivalry by consolidating the marketing message that consumers use to make a purchase decision into a few key pieces of information over which the selling company has little control.

Using Industry Analysis: A Few Caveats

For industry analysis to be valuable, a company must collect and evaluate a wide variety of information. As the trend toward globalization accelerates, information on foreign markets as well as on a wider variety of competitors, suppliers, customers, substitutes, and potential new entrants becomes more critical. Industry analysis helps a firm not only to evaluate the profit potential of an industry but also consider various ways to strengthen its position vis-à-vis the five forces. However, we'd like to address a few caveats.

First, *managers must not always avoid low profit industries (or low profit segments in profitable industries).*[70] Such industries can still yield high returns for some players who pursue sound strategies. As examples, consider Paychex, a payroll-processing company, and WellPoint Health Network, a huge health care insurer:[71]

> Paychex, with $2 billion in revenues, became successful by serving small businesses. Existing firms had ignored them because they assumed that such businesses could not afford the service. When Paychex's founder, Tom Golisano, failed to convince his bosses at Electronic Accounting Systems that they were missing a great opportunity, he launched the firm. It now serves nearly 600,000 clients in the United States and Germany. Paychex's after-tax-return on sales is a stunning 25 percent.

> In 1986, WellPoint Health Network (when it was known as Blue Cross of California) suffered a loss of $160 million. That year, Leonard Schaeffer became CEO and challenged the conventional wisdom that individuals and small firms were money losers. (This was certainly "heresy" at the time—the firm was losing $5 million a year insuring 65,000 individuals!) However, by the early 1990s, the health insurer was leading the industry in profitability. The firm has continued to grow and outperform its rivals even during economic downturns. By 2012, its revenues and profits were $61 billion and $2.5 billion, respectively.

Second, five-forces analysis implicitly *assumes a **zero-sum game**, determining how a firm can enhance its position relative to the forces.* Yet such an approach can often be short-sighted; that is, it can overlook the many potential benefits of developing constructive win–win relationships with suppliers and customers. Establishing long-term mutually beneficial relationships with suppliers improves a firm's ability to implement just-in-time (JIT) inventory systems, which let it manage inventories better and respond quickly to market demands. A recent study found that if a company exploits its powerful position against a supplier, that action may come back to haunt the company.[72] Consider, for example, General Motors' heavy-handed dealings with its suppliers:[73]

zero-sum game
a situation in which multiple players interact, and winners win only by taking from other players.

> GM has a reputation for particularly aggressive tactics. Although it is striving to crack down on the most egregious of these, it continues to rank dead last in the annual supplier satisfaction survey. "It's a brutal process," says David E. Cole, who is head of the Center for Automotive Research in Ann Arbor. "There are bodies lying by the side of the road."
>
> Suppliers point to one particularly nasty tactic: shopping their technology out the back door to see if rivals can make it cheaper. In one case, a GM purchasing manager showed a supplier's new brake design to Delphi Corporation. He was fired. However, in a recent survey, parts executives said they tend to bring hot new technology to other carmakers first. This is yet another reason GM finds it hard to compete in an intensely competitive industry.

Third, the five-forces analysis also has been criticized for *being essentially a static analysis.* External forces as well as strategies of individual firms are continually changing the structure of all industries. The search for a dynamic theory of strategy has led to greater use of game theory in industrial organization economics research and strategy research.

Based on game-theoretic considerations, Brandenburger and Nalebuff recently introduced the concept of the value net,[74] which in many ways is an extension of the five-forces

EXHIBIT 2.6 The Value Net

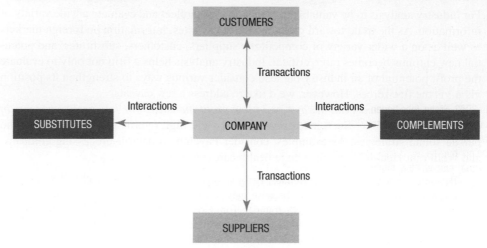

analysis. It is illustrated in Exhibit 2.6. The value net represents all the players in the game and analyzes how their interactions affect a firm's ability to generate and appropriate value. The vertical dimension of the net includes suppliers and customers. The firm has direct transactions with them. On the horizontal dimension are substitutes and complements, players with whom a firm interacts but may not necessarily transact. The concept of complementors is perhaps the single most important contribution of value net analysis and is explained in more detail below.

complements products or services that have an impact on the value of a firm's products or services.	**Complements** typically are products or services that have a potential impact on the value of a firm's own products or services. Those who produce complements are usually referred to as complementors.[75] Powerful hardware is of no value to a user unless there is software that runs on it. Similarly, new and better software is possible only if the hardware on which it can be run is available. This is equally true in the video game industry, where the sales of game consoles and video games complement each other. Nintendo's success in the early 1990s was a result of their ability to manage their relationship with their complementors. They built a security chip into the hardware and then licensed the right to develop games to outside firms. These firms paid a royalty to Nintendo for each copy of the game sold. The royalty revenue enabled Nintendo to sell game consoles at close to their cost, thereby increasing their market share, which, in turn, caused more games to be sold and more royalties to be generated.[76]

Despite efforts to create win–win scenarios, conflict among complementors is inevitable.[77] After all, it is naive to expect that even the closest of partners will do you the favor of abandoning their own interests. And even the most successful partnerships are seldom trouble free. Power is a factor that comes into play as we see in Strategy Spotlight 2.8 with the example of Apple's iPod—an enormously successful product.

We would like to close this section with some recent insights from Michael Porter, the originator of the five-forces analysis.[78] He addresses two critical issues in conducting a good industry analysis, which will yield an improved understanding of the root causes of profitability: (1) choosing the appropriate time frame and (2) a rigorous quantification of the five forces.

- *Good industry analysis looks rigorously at the structural underpinnings of profitability. A first step is to understand the time horizon.* One of the essential tasks in industry analysis is to distinguish short-term fluctuations from structural

APPLE'S IPOD: RELATIONSHIPS WITH ITS COMPLEMENTORS

In 2002, Steve Jobs began his campaign to cajole the major music companies into selling tracks to iPod users through the iTunes Music Store, an online retail site. Most industry executives, after being burned by illegal file-sharing services like Napster and Kazaa, just wanted digital music to disappear. However, Jobs's passionate vision persuaded them to climb on board. He promised to reduce the risks that they faced by offering safeguards against piracy, as well as a hip product (iPod and iPad Touch) that would drive sales.

However, Apple had a much stronger bargaining position when its contracts with the music companies came up for renewal in April 2005. By then, iTunes had captured 80 percent of the market for legal downloads. The music companies, which were receiving between 60 and 70 cents per download, wanted more. Their reasoning: If the iTunes Music Store would only charge $1.50 or $2.00 per track, they could double or triple their revenues and profits. Since Jobs knew that he could sell more iPods if the music was cheap, he was determined to keep the price of a download at 99 cents and to maintain Apple's margins. Given iTunes' dominant position, the music companies had little choice but to relent.

Apple's foray into music has been tremendously successful. Since the iPod's Introduction in 2001, Apple has sold over 300 million iPod units worldwide. In 2012, iPod sales reached $5.6 billion, and other music-related products came in at $8.5 billion. Despite tough competition, Apple still dominates the music player business.

Source: Reisinger, D. 2012. Why the iPod (yes, the iPod) still matters. *Fortune,* October 8: 79; Hesseldahl, A. 2008. Now that we all have iPods. *BusinessWeek,* December 15: 36; Apple Computer Inc. 10-K, 2010, 2012 Apple, Inc. Annual Report; and, Yoffie, D. B. & Kwak, M. 2006. With friends like these: The art of managing complementors. *Harvard Business Review,* 84(9): 88–98.

changes. A good guideline for the appropriate time horizon is the full business cycle for the particular industry. For most industries, a three- to five-year horizon is appropriate. However, for some industries with long lead times, such as mining, the appropriate horizon may be a decade or more. It is average profitability over this period, not profitability in any particular year, which should be the focus of analysis.

- *The point of industry analysis is not to declare the industry attractive or unattractive but to understand the underpinnings of competition and the root causes of profitability.* As much as possible, analysts should look at industry structure quantitatively, rather than be satisfied with lists of qualitative factors. Many elements of five forces can be quantified: the percentage of the buyer's total cost accounted for by the industry's product (to understand buyer price sensitivity); the percentage of industry sales required to fill a plant or operate a logistical network to efficient scale (to help assess barriers to entry); and the buyer's switching cost (determining the inducement an entrant or rival must offer customers).

Strategic Groups within Industries

In an industry analysis, two assumptions are unassailable: (1) No two firms are totally different, and (2) no two firms are exactly the same. The issue becomes one of identifying groups of firms that are more similar to each other than firms that are not, otherwise known as **strategic groups.**[79] This is important because rivalry tends to be greater among firms that are alike. Strategic groups are clusters of firms that share similar strategies. After all, is Kmart more concerned about Nordstrom or Walmart? Is Mercedes more concerned about Hyundai or BMW? The answers are straightforward.[80]

These examples are not meant to trivialize the strategic groups concept.[81] Classifying an industry into strategic groups involves judgment. If it is useful as an analytical tool, we must exercise caution in deciding what dimensions to use to map these firms.

strategic groups
clusters of firms that share similar strategies.

L02.7

The concept of strategic groups and their strategy and performance implications.

Dimensions include breadth of product and geographic scope, price/quality, degree of vertical integration, type of distribution (e.g., dealers, mass merchandisers, private label), and so on. Dimensions should also be selected to reflect the variety of strategic combinations in an industry. For example, if all firms in an industry have roughly the same level of product differentiation (or R&D intensity), this would not be a good dimension to select.

What value is the strategic groups concept as an analytical tool? *First, strategic groupings help a firm identify barriers to mobility that protect a group from attacks by other groups.*[82] Mobility barriers are factors that deter the movement of firms from one strategic position to another. For example, in the chainsaw industry, the major barriers protecting the high-quality/dealer-oriented group are technology, brand image, and an established network of servicing dealers.

The second value of strategic grouping is that it *helps a firm identify groups whose competitive position may be marginal or tenuous.* We may anticipate that these competitors may exit the industry or try to move into another group. In recent years in the retail department store industry, firms such as JCPenney and Sears have experienced extremely difficult times because they were stuck in the middle, neither an aggressive discount player like Walmart nor a prestigious upscale player like Neiman Marcus.

Third, strategic groupings *help chart the future directions of firms' strategies.* Arrows emanating from each strategic group can represent the direction in which the group (or a firm within the group) seems to be moving. If all strategic groups are moving in a similar direction, this could indicate a high degree of future volatility and intensity of competition. In the automobile industry, for example, the competition in the minivan and sport utility segments has intensified in recent years as many firms have entered those product segments.

Fourth, strategic groups are *helpful in thinking through the implications of each industry trend for the strategic group as a whole.* Is the trend decreasing the viability of a group? If so, in what direction should the strategic group move? Is the trend increasing or decreasing entry barriers? Will the trend decrease the ability of one group to separate itself from other groups? Such analysis can help in making predictions about industry evolution. A sharp increase in interest rates, for example, tends to have less impact on providers of higher-priced goods (e.g., Porsches) than on providers of lower-priced goods (e.g., Chevrolet Cobalt) whose customer base is much more price sensitive.

Exhibit 2.7 provides a strategic grouping of the worldwide automobile industry.[83] The firms in each group are representative; not all firms are included in the mapping. We have identified four strategic groups. In the top left-hand corner are high-end luxury automakers who focus on a very narrow product market. Most of the cars produced by the members of this group cost well over $100,000. Some cost many times that amount. The Ferrari F12 Berlinétta starts at $274,000, and the 2013 Lamborghini Gallardo will set you back $237,225 (in case you were wondering how to spend your employment signing bonus). Players in this market have a very exclusive clientele and face little rivalry from other strategic groups. At the other extreme, in the lower left-hand corner is a strategic group that has low-price/quality attributes and targets a narrow market. These players, Hyundai and Kia, limit competition from other strategic groups by pricing their products very low. The third group (near the middle) consists of firms high in product pricing/quality and average in their product-line breadth. The final group (at the far right) consists of firms with a broad range of products and multiple price points. These firms have entries that compete at both the lower end of the market (e.g., the Ford Focus) and the higher end (e.g., Chevrolet Corvette).

EXHIBIT 2.7 The World Automobile Industry: Strategic Groups

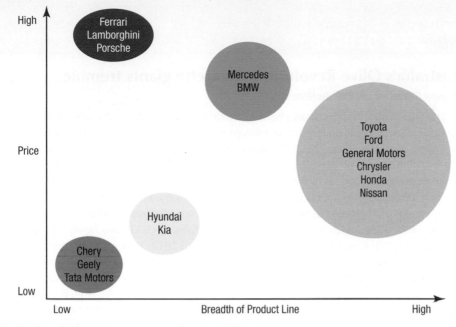

Note: Members of each strategic group are not exhaustive, only illustrative.

The auto market has been very dynamic and competition has intensified in recent years.[84] For example, some players are going more upscale with their product offerings. In 2009, Hyundai introduced its Genesis, starting at $33,000. This brings Hyundai into direct competition with entries from other strategic groups such as Toyota's Camry and Honda's Accord. And, in 2010, Hyundai introduced the Equus model. It was priced at about $60,000 to compete directly with the Lexus 460 on price. To further intensify competition, some key automakers are providing offerings in lower-priced segments. BMW, with their 1-series, is a well-known example. Such cars, priced in the low $30,000s, compete more directly with products from broad-line manufacturers like Ford, General Motors, and Toyota. This suggests that members of a strategic group can overcome mobility barriers and migrate to other groups that they find attractive if they are willing to commit time and resources.

Our discussion would not be complete, of course, without paying some attention to recent entries in the automobile industry that will likely lead to the formation of a new strategic group—placed at the bottom left corner of the grid in Exhibit 2.7. Three firms—China's Zhejiang Geely Holding Company, China's Chery Automobile Company, and India's Tata Motors—have introduced models that bring new meaning to the term "subcompact."[85] Let's take a look at these econoboxes.

> Chery's QQ model sells for between $4,000 and $7,000 in the Chinese market and sports horsepower in the range of 51 to 74. Geely's best-selling four-door sedan, the Free Cruiser, retails from $6,300 and $6,900. The firm is planning to go more upscale with the Geely KingKong ($7,500–$10,000), a four-door 1.5- to 1.8-liter sedan, and the Vision ($9,700–$15,300), a 1.8-liter four-door sedan. But, for price-points, India's Tata Motors has everyone beat. In January 2008, it unveiled the Nano with an astonishing retail price of only $2,500. It is a four-door, five-seat hatchback that gets 54 miles per gallon. But before you order one—keep in mind that it only comes with a 30 horsepower engine.

Australia's Olive Revolution: Cigarette giants tremble

By Irena Descubes and Tom McNamara

In 2011, the Australian government became the first country in the world to regulate the retail packaging and appearance of tobacco products by adopting the Tobacco Plain Packaging Act in December 2012. Tobacco companies are now required to print their names in a specific font on a unique-sized, plain, olive-green packaging emblazoned with public health warnings and images of smoking-related diseases. Why olive green? According to research, this is the color that is most unattractive to smokers. Furthermore, all company specific logos and branding used to differentiate one company from another are now banned.

The tobacco companies, led by British American Tobacco (BAT) and Japan Tobacco International (JTI) fought back in a legal dispute in April 2012. They said that they were selling a legal product and that for the Australian government to tell them how to package their goods infringed upon their intellectual property rights. BAT and JTI, later joined by Phillip Morris, Ltd. and Imperial Tobacco, lost in a decision made by the High Court of Australia, which sided in favor of the Australian government. Justice Kiefel wrote: "Many kinds of products have been subjected to regulation in order to prevent or reduce the likelihood of harm" and that labeling is required "to both protect and promote public health."

This landmark ruling was welcomed by the World Health Organization (WHO), which called upon the rest of the world to "follow Australia's tough stance on tobacco marketing." Should tobacco companies in other countries be worried?

Discussion Questions

1. What would be, in your opinion, the critical success factors needed to get such a legislative Act implemented in the United States of America?
2. What would be the major obstacles to its implementation?

Reflecting on Career Implications . . .

- **Creating the Environmentally Aware Organization:** Advancing your career requires constant scanning, monitoring, and intelligence gathering to find out not only future job opportunities but also to understand how employers' expectations are changing. Consider using websites such as LinkedIn to find opportunities. Merely posting your resume on a site such as LinkedIn may not be enough. Instead, consider in what ways you can use such sites for scanning, monitoring, and intelligence gathering.

- **SWOT Analysis:** As an analytical method, SWOT analysis is applicable for individuals as it is for firms. It is important for you to periodically evaluate your strengths and weaknesses as well as potential opportunities and threats to your career. Such analysis should be followed by efforts to address your weaknesses by improving your skills and capabilities.

- **General Environment:** The general environment consists of several segments, such as the demographic, sociocultural, political/legal, technological, economic, and global environments. It would be useful to evaluate how each of these segments can affect your career opportunities. Identify two or three specific trends (e.g., rapid technological change, aging of the population, increase in minimum wages) and their impact on your choice of careers. These also provide possibilities for you to add value for your organization.

- **Five-Forces Analysis:** Before you go for a job interview, consider the five forces affecting the industry within which the firm competes. This will help you to appear knowledgeable about the industry and increase your odds of landing the job. It also can help you to decide if you want to work for that organization. If the "forces" are unfavorable, the long-term profit potential of the industry may be unattractive, leading to fewer resources available and—all other things being equal—fewer career opportunities.

summary

Managers must analyze the external environment to minimize or eliminate threats and exploit opportunities. This involves a continuous process of environmental scanning and monitoring as well as obtaining competitive intelligence on present and potential rivals. These activities provide valuable inputs for developing forecasts. In addition, many firms use scenario planning to anticipate and respond to volatile and disruptive environmental changes.

We identified two types of environments: the general environment and the competitive environment. The six segments of the general environment are demographic, sociocultural, political/legal, technological, economic, and global. Trends and events occurring in these segments, such as the aging of the population, higher percentages of women in the workplace, governmental legislation, and increasing (or decreasing) interest rates, can have a dramatic effect on a firm. A given trend or event may have a positive impact on some industries and a negative, neutral, or no impact at all on others.

The competitive environment consists of industry-related factors and has a more direct impact than the general environment. Porter's five-forces model of industry analysis includes the threat of new entrants, buyer power, supplier power, threat of substitutes, and rivalry among competitors. The intensity of these factors determines, in large part, the average expected level of profitability in an industry. A sound awareness of such factors, both individually and in combination, is beneficial not only for deciding what industries to enter but also for assessing how a firm can improve its competitive position. We discuss how many of the changes brought about by the digital economy can be understood in the context of five-forces analysis. The limitations of five-forces analysis include its static nature and its inability to acknowledge the role of complementors. Although we addressed the general environment and competitive environment in separate sections, they are quite interdependent. A given environmental trend or event, such as changes in the ethnic composition of a population or a technological innovation, typically has a much greater impact on some industries than on others.

The concept of strategic groups is also important to the external environment of a firm. No two organizations are completely different nor are they exactly the same. The question is how to group firms in an industry on the basis of similarities in their resources and strategies. The strategic groups concept is valuable for determining mobility barriers across groups, identifying groups with marginal competitive positions, charting the future directions of firm strategies, and assessing the implications of industry trends for the strategic group as a whole.

SUMMARY REVIEW QUESTIONS

1. Why must managers be aware of a firm's external environment?
2. What is gathering and analyzing competitive intelligence and why is it important for firms to engage in it?
3. Discuss and describe the six elements of the external environment.
4. Select one of these elements and describe some changes relating to it in an industry that interests you.
5. Describe how the five forces can be used to determine the average expected profitability in an industry.
6. What are some of the limitations (or caveats) in using five-forces analysis?
7. Explain how the general environment and industry environment are highly related. How can such inter-relationships affect the profitability of a firm or industry?
8. Explain the concept of strategic groups. What are the performance implications?

key terms

environmental scanning 36
environmental monitoring 37
hard trend 37
soft trend 37
competitive intelligence 38
environmental forecasting 40
scenario analysis 40
SWOT analysis 41
general environment 42
demographic segment of the general environment 42
sociocultural segment of the general environment 42
political/legal segment of the general environment 44
technological segment of the general environment 45
economic segment of the general environment 45
global segment of the general environment 46
crowdsourcing 48
industry 48
competitive environment 48
Porter's five-forces model of industry competition 49
threat of new entrants 50
economies of scale 50
product differentiation 50
switching cost 51
bargaining power of buyers 51
bargaining power of suppliers 52
threat of substitute products and services 53
substitute products and services 53
intensity of rivalry among competitors in an industry 53
Internet 55
zero-sum game 59
complements 60
strategic groups 61

experiential exercise

Select one of the following industries: personal computers, airlines, or automobiles. For this industry, evaluate the strength of each of Porter's five forces as well as complementors.

Industry Force	High? Medium? Low?	Why?
1. Threat of new entrants		
2. Power of buyers		
3. Power of suppliers		
4. Power of substitutes		
5. Rivalry among competitors		
6. Complementors		

application questions & exercises

1. Imagine yourself as the CEO of a large firm in an industry in which you are interested. Please (1) identify major trends in the general environment, (2) analyze their impact on the firm, and (3) identify major sources of information to monitor these trends. (Use Internet and library resources.)

2. Analyze movements across the strategic groups in the U.S. retail industry. How do these movements within this industry change the nature of competition?

3. What are the major trends in the general environment that have impacted the U.S. pharmaceutical industry?

4. Go to the Internet and look up *www.kroger.com.* What are some of the five forces driving industry competition that are affecting the profitability of this firm?

ethics questions

1. What are some of the legal and ethical issues involved in collecting competitor intelligence in the following situations?

   a. Hotel A sends an employee posing as a potential client to Hotel B to find out who Hotel B's major corporate customers are.

   b. A firm hires an MBA student to collect information directly from a competitor while claiming the information is for a course project.

   c. A firm advertises a nonexistent position and interviews a rival's employees with the intention of obtaining competitor information.

2. What are some of the ethical implications that arise when a firm tries to exploit its power over a supplier?

references

1. Schneider, J. & Hall, J. 2011. Can You Hear Me Now? *Harvard Business Review,* 89 (4): 23; Hornigan, J. 2009. Wireless Internet use—Mobile access to data and information. *www.pewinternet .org,* July 22: np; and Salemi Industries. 2012. Home page. *www. salemiindustries.com,* Dec 20: np.

2. Hamel, G. & Prahalad, C. K. 1994. *Competing for the future.* Boston: Harvard Business School Press.

3. Drucker, P. F. 1994. Theory of the business. *Harvard Business Review,* 72: 95–104.

4. For an insightful discussion on managers' assessment of the external environment, refer to Sutcliffe, K. M. & Weber, K. 2003. The high cost of accurate knowledge. *Harvard Business Review,* 81(5): 74–86.

5. For insights on recognizing and acting on environmental opportunities, refer to: Alvarez, S. A. & Barney, J. B. 2008. Opportunities, organizations, and entrepreneurship: Theory and debate. *Strategic Entrepreneurship Journal,* 2(3): entire issue.

6. Charitou, C. D. & Markides, C. C. 2003. Responses to disruptive strategic innovation. *MIT Sloan Management Review,* 44(2): 55–64.

7. Our discussion of scanning, monitoring, competitive intelligence, and forecasting concepts draws on several sources. These include Fahey, L. & Narayanan, V. K. 1983. *Macroenvironmental analysis for strategic management.* St. Paul, MN: West; Lorange, P., Scott, F. S., & Ghoshal, S. 1986. *Strategic control.* St. Paul, MN: West; Ansoff, H. I. 1984. *Implementing strategic management.* Englewood Cliffs, NJ: Prentice Hall; and Schreyogg, G. & Stienmann, H. 1987. Strategic control: A new perspective. *Academy of Management Review,* 12: 91–103.

8. An insightful discussion on how leaders can develop "peripheral vision" in environmental scanning is found in: Day, G. S. & Schoemaker, P. J. H. 2008. Are you a "vigilant leader"? *MIT Sloan Management Review,* 49 (3): 43–51.

9. Elenkov, D. S. 1997. Strategic uncertainty and environmental scanning: The case for institutional influences on scanning behavior. *Strategic Management Journal,* 18: 287–302.

10. For an interesting perspective on environmental scanning in emerging economies see May, R. C., Stewart, W. H., & Sweo, R. 2000. Environmental scanning behavior in a transitional economy: Evidence from Russia. *Academy of Management Journal,* 43(3): 403–27.

11. Bryon, E. 2010. For insight into P&G, check Olay numbers. *Wall Street Journal.* October 27: C1.

12. Tang, J. 2010. How entrepreneurs discover opportunities in China: An institutional view. *Asia Pacific Journal of Management.* 27(3): 461–480.

13. Source: Burrus, D. 2011. *Flash Foresight: How to see the invisible and do the impossible.* New York: HarperCollins.

14. Walters, B. A. & Priem, R. L. 1999. Business strategy and CEO intelligence acquisition. *Competitive Intelligence Review,* 10(2): 15 22.

15. Prior, V. 1999. The language of competitive intelligence, Part 4. *Competitive Intelligence Review,* 10(1): 84–87

16. Hill, K. 2011. The spy who liked me. *Forbes,* November 21: 56–57.

17. Wolfenson, J. 1999. The world in 1999: A battle for corporate honesty. *The Economist* 38: 13–30.

18. Drucker, P. F. 1997. The future that has already happened. *Harvard Business Review,* 75(6): 22.

19. Evans, P. B. & Wurster, T. S. 1997. Strategy and the new economics of information. *Harvard Business Review,* 75(5): 71–82.

20. Fahey & Narayanan, op. cit., p. 41.

21. Insights on how to improve predictions can be found in: Cross, R., Thomas, R. J., & Light, D. A. 2009. The prediction lover's handbook. *MIT Sloan Management Review,* 50 (2): 32–34.

22. Courtney, H., Kirkland, J., & Viguerie, P. 1997. Strategy under uncertainty. *Harvard Business Review,* 75(6): 66–79.

23. Odlyzko, A. 2003. False hopes. *Red Herring,* March: 31.

24. Coy, P. 2009. Worst predictions about 2008. *BusinessWeek,* January 12: 15–16.

25. For an interesting perspective on how Accenture practices and has developed its approach to scenario planning, refer to Ferguson, G., Mathur, S., & Shah, B. 2005. Evolving from information to insight. *MIT Sloan Management Review,* 46(2): 51–58.

26. Dean, T. J., Brown, R. L., & Bamford, C. E. 1998. Differences in large and small firm responses to environmental context: Strategic implications from a comparative analysis of business formations. *Strategic Management Journal,* 19: 709–728.

27. Colvin, G. 1997. How to beat the boomer rush. *Fortune,* August 18: 59–63.

28. Porter, M. E. 2010. Discovering—and lowering—the real costs of health care. *Harvard Business Review,* 89 (1/2): 49–50.

29. Toossi, M. 2012. Labor force projections to 2020: A more slowly growing workforce. *Monthly Labor Review,* 135(1):43–64.

30. Challenger, J. 2000. Women's corporate rise has reduced relocations. *Lexington* (KY) *Herald-Leader,* October 29: D1.

31. Tsao, A. 2005. Retooling home improvement, *Businesssweek.com,* February, 14; and, Grow, B. 2004 Who wears the wallet in the family? *BusinessWeek,* August 16:10.

32. Watkins, M. D. 2003. Government games, *MIT Sloan Management Review* 44(2): 91–95.

33. A discussion of the political issues surrounding caloric content on meals is in: Orey, M. 2008. A food fight over calorie counts. *BusinessWeek,* February 11: 36.

34. For a discussion of the linkage between copyright law and innovation, read: Guterman, J. 2009. Does copyright law hinder innovation? *MIT Sloan Management Review,* 50(2): 14–15.

35. Davies, A. 2000. The welcome mat is out for nerds. *BusinessWeek,* May 21: 17; Broache, A. 2007. Annual H-1B visa cap met—already. *news.cnet.com,* April 3: np; and, Anonymous. Undated. Cap count for H-1B and H-2B workers for fiscal year 2009. *www.uscis.gov:* np.

36. Elliott, M. 2010. Opinion. *Fortune,* June 14: 56; and Greene, I. 2008. Case study: Microsoft's Canadian solution. *Bloomberg BusinessWeek,* January 28: 51.

37. Hout, T. M., Ghemawat, P. 2010. China vs. the world: Whose technology is it? *Harvard Business Review,* 88(12): 94–103.

38. Business ready for Internet revolution. 1999. *Financial Times,* May 21: 17.

39. A discussion of an alternate energy—marine energy—is the topic of: Boyle, M. 2008. Scottish power. *Fortune.* March 17: 28.

40. Baker, S. & Aston, A. 2005. The business of nanotech. *BusinessWeek,* February 14: 64–71.

41. For an insightful discussion of the causes of the global financial crisis, read: Johnson, S. 2009. The global financial crisis—What really precipitated it? *MIT Sloan Management Review.* 50(2): 16–18.

42. Tyson, L. D. 2011. A better stimulus for the U.S. economy. *Harvard Business Review,* 89(1/2): 53.

43. A interesting and balanced discussion on the merits of multinationals to the U.S. economy is found in: Mandel, M. 2008. Multinationals: Are they good for America? *BusinessWeek,* March 10: 41 64.

44. Insights on risk perception across countries are addressed in: Purda, L. D. 2008. Risk perception and the financial system. *Journal of International Business Studies,* 39(7): 1178–1196.

45. Thurm, S. 2012. U.S. firms add jobs, but mostly overseas. *wsj.com,* April 27: np.

46. Goll, I. & Rasheed, M. A. 1997. Rational decision-making and firm performance: The moderating role of environment. *Strategic Management Journal,* 18: 583–591.

47. Our discussion of crowdsourcing draws on the first two books that have addressed the concept: Libert, B. & Spector, J. 2008. *We are smarter than me.* Philadelphia: Wharton Books; and Howe, J. 2008. *Crowdsourcing.* New York: Crown Business. Eric von Hippel addressed similar issues in his 2005 book, *Democraticizing Innovation,* Cambridge, MA.: MIT Press.

48. This discussion draws heavily on Porter, M. E. 1980. *Competitive strategy:* Chapter 1. New York: Free Press.

49. Ibid.

50. Rivalry in the airline industry is discussed in: Foust, D. 2009. Which airlines will disappear in 2009? *BusinessWeek,* January 19: 46–47.

51. Fryer, B. 2001. Leading through rough times: An interview with Novell's Eric Schmidt. *Harvard Business Review,* 78(5): 117–123.

52. For a discussion on the importance of barriers to entry within industries, read Greenwald, B. & Kahn, J. 2005. *Competition demystified: A radically simplified approach to business strategy.* East Rutherford, NJ: Portfolio.

53. A discussion of how the medical industry has erected entry barriers that have resulted in lawsuits is found in: Whelan, D. 2008. Bad medicine. *BusinessWeek,* March 10: 86–98.

54. The ProCD example draws heavily upon Shapiro, C. & Varian, H. R. 2000. Versioning: The smart way to sell information. *Harvard Business Review,* 78(1): 106–114.

55. Wise, R. & Baumgarter, P. 1999. Go downstream: The new profit imperative in manufacturing. *Harvard Business Review,* 77(5): 133–141.

56. Salman, W. A. 2000. The new economy is stronger than you think. *Harvard Business Review,* 77(6): 99–106.

57. Staley, O. 2011. California universities feel the squeeze. *Bloomberg Businessweek,* January 24–January 30: 20–30.

58. Mudambi, R. & Helper, S. 1998. The "close but adversarial" model of supplier relations in the U.S. auto industry. *Strategic Management Journal,* 19: 775–792.

59. Trends in the solar industry are discussed in: Carey, J. 2009. Solar: The sun will come out tomorrow. *BusinessWeek,* January 12: 51.

60. Tischler, L. 2002. IBM: Manager jam. *Fast Company,* October: 48.

61. An interesting analysis of self-regulation in an industry (chemical) is in: Barnett, M. L. & King, A. A. 2008. Good fences make good neighbors: A longitudinal analysis of an industry self-regulatory institution. *Academy of Management Journal,* 51(6): 1053–1078.

62. For an interesting perspective on the intensity of competition in the supermarket industry, refer to Anonymous. 2005. Warfare in the aisles. *The Economist,* April 2: 6–8.

63. Marcial, G. 2000. Giving Viagra a run for its money. *BusinessWeek,* October 23: 173.

64. For an interesting perspective on changing features of firm boundaries, refer to Afuah, A. 2003. Redefining firm boundaries in the face of Internet: Are firms really shrinking? *Academy of Management Review,* 28(1): 34–53.

65. Time to rebuild. 2001. *Economist,* May 19: 55–56.

66. *www.amazon.com.*

67. For more on the role of the Internet as an electronic intermediary, refer to Carr, N. G. 2000. Hypermediation:

Commerce as clickstream. *Harvard Business Review,* 78(1): 46–48.

68. *www.mysimon.com*; and *www.pricescan.com.*

69. *www.cnet.com*; and *www.bizrate.com.*

70. For insights into strategies in a low-profit industry, refer to: Hopkins, M. S. 2008. The management lessons of a beleaguered industry. *MIT Sloan Management Review,* 50(1): 25–31.

71. Foust, D. 2007. The best performers. *BusinessWeek,* March 26: 58–95; Rosenblum, D., Tomlinson, D., & Scott, L. 2003. Bottom-feeding for blockbuster businesses. *Harvard Business Review,* 81(3): 52–59; Paychex 2006 Annual Report; and, WellPoint Health Network 2005 Annual Report.

72. Kumar, N. 1996. The power of trust in manufacturer-retailer relationship. *Harvard Business Review,* 74(6): 92–110.

73. Welch, D. 2006. Renault-Nissan: Say hello to Bo. *BusinessWeek,* July 31: 56–57.

74. Brandenburger, A. & Nalebuff, B. J. 1995. The right game: Use game theory to shape strategy. *Harvard Business Review,* 73(4): 57–71.

75. For a scholarly discussion of complementary assets and their relationship to competitive advantage, refer to Stieglitz, N. & Heine, K. 2007. Innovations and the role of complementarities in a strategic theory of the firm. *Strategic Management Journal,* 28(1): 1–15.

76. A useful framework for the analysis of industry evolution has been proposed by Professor Anita McGahan of Boston University. Her analysis is based on the identification of the core activities and the core assets of an industry and the threats they face. She suggests that an industry may follow one of four possible evolutionary trajectories— radical change, creative change, intermediating change, or progressive change—based on these two types of threats of obsolescence. Refer to: McGahan, A. M. 2004. How industries change.

Harvard Business Review, 82(10): 87–94.

77. Yoffie, D. B. & Kwak, M. 2006. With friends like these: The art of managing complementors. *Harvard Business Review,* 84(9): 88–98.

78. Porter, M. I. 2008. The five competitive forces that shape strategy. *Harvard Business Review,* 86 (1): 79–93.

79. Peteraf, M. & Shanley, M. 1997. Getting to know you: A theory of strategic group identity. *Strategic Management Journal,* 18 (Special Issue): 165–186.

80. An interesting scholarly perspective on strategic groups may be found in Dranove, D., Perteraf, M., & Shanley, M. 1998. Do strategic groups exist? An economic framework for analysis. *Strategic Management Journal,* 19(11): 1029–1044.

81. For an empirical study on strategic groups and predictors of performance, refer to Short, J. C., Ketchen, D. J., Jr., Palmer, T. B., & Hult, T. M. 2007. Firm, strategic group, and industry influences on performance. *Strategic Management Journal,* 28(2): 147–167.

82. This section draws on several sources, including Kerwin, K. R. & Haughton, K. 1997. Can Detroit make cars that baby boomers like? *BusinessWeek,* December 1: 134–148; and Taylor, A., III. 1994. The new golden age of autos. *Fortune,* April 4: 50–66.

83. Csere, C. 2001. Supercar supermarket. *Car and Driver,* January: 118–127.

84. For a discussion of the extent of overcapacity in the worldwide automobile industry, read: Roberts, D., Matlack, C., Busyh, J., & Rowley, I. 2009. A hundred factories too many. *BusinessWeek,* January 19: 42–43.

85. This discussion draws on: Wojdyla, B. 2008. The $2500 Tata Nano, unveiled in India. *jalopnik.com,* January 10: np; Roberts, D. 2008. China's Geely has global auto ambitions. *businessweek.com,* July 27: np; and, Fairclough, G. 2007. In China, Chery automobile drives an industry shift. *The Wall Street Journal,* December 4: A1, A17.

chapter 3

Assessing the Internal Environment of the Firm

After reading this chapter, you should have a good understanding of the following learning objectives:

LO3.1 The benefits and limitations of SWOT analysis in conducting an internal analysis of the firm.

LO3.2 The primary and support activities of a firm's value chain.

LO3.3 How value-chain analysis can help managers create value by investigating relationships among activities within the firm and between the firm and its customers and suppliers.

LO3.4 The resource-based view of the firm and the different types of tangible and intangible resources, as well as organizational capabilities.

LO3.5 The four criteria that a firm's resources must possess to maintain a sustainable advantage and how value created can be appropriated by employees and managers.

LO3.6 The usefulness of financial ratio analysis, its inherent limitations, and how to make meaningful comparisons of performance across firms.

LO3.7 The value of the "balanced scorecard" in recognizing how the interests of a variety of stakeholders can be interrelated.

Learning from Mistakes

Mercedes Benz and the failure of the Maybach: A question of too much luxury or not enough?

Mercedes Benz are an international leader in automobiles (they were actually the original inventors), famously known for combining "luxury with performance." Satisfying the customer is at the heart of everything they do, with their stated goal being to "inspire them with exciting premium automobiles" while setting the industry's standards. It was this focus on luxury and performance that led Mercedes to launch the Maybach in 2002.

The Maybach was expected to compete directly with such ultra-luxury cars as Bentley and Rolls-Royce. This is an extremely rarified niche market of high wealth consumers. Many people who buy cars in this bracket look at them as an investment, rather than just as a way to cruise around town in style. Proof of this is the supposed fact that three-quarters of all Rolls-Royces ever produced are still on the road.

With a clear commitment to quality and craftsmanship, each Maybach was hand built. Only the finest materials

were used and each car took from five to seven months to complete. Some models came with twin-turbo V12 engines capable of generating 630 horsepower, with an optional large, high-resolution cinema screen for passengers in the back. And just how much did all of this "old world tradition" cost? Models started at $343,250 for the Maybach 57 but the price could go as high as $1.3 million for the 62S Landaulet.

But there was one small problem. While customers recognized Mercedes as a world class leader in luxury, they unfortunately didn't see them in the same class as Bentley or Rolls-Royce (the brands that Maybach was expected to compete directly against) and were thus unwilling to buy the cars at those prices. Apparently, Mercedes had misjudged their own capabilities and over played their hand.

And the cost of all this? Car Magazine reported that Mercedes lost about $440,000 on each car built after having invested $1.32 billion in the project. It soon became clear that the Maybach was an unmitigated disaster, with rarely more than 150 to 300 being sold in any given year. In November 2011, Mercedes unceremoniously announced that they were closing the division. Production of the automobiles had stopped by the end of 2013.

After reevaluating the market Mercedes decided to replace the Maybach line with newer and more luxurious models of their existing Mercedes S-series. Whether or not these cars will ever be able to compete with Rolls-Royce and Bentley in the ultra-luxury market remains to be seen.

By Tom McNamara and Irena Descubes

Discussion Questions

1. Mercedes-Benz have an excellent reputation for quality, luxury and performance. Why do you think the Maybach was a failure?
2. What could Mercedes-Benz have done to better ensure the success of the Maybach?

In this chapter we will place heavy emphasis on the value-chain concept. That is, we focus on the key value-creating activities (e.g., operations, marketing and sales, and procurement) that a firm must effectively manage and integrate in order to attain competitive advantages in the marketplace. However, firms must not only pay close attention to their own value-creating activities but must also maintain close and effective relationships with key organizations outside the firm boundaries, such as suppliers, customers, and alliance partners.

The Maybach's sales have been well below expectations because Mercedes had misjudged its own capabilities and overplayed its hand. This was partly due to problems associated with several value chain activities. While a leader in high end luxury and performance, its skills and competences didn't translate well into the "ultra-luxury" market.

Before moving to value-chain analysis, let's briefly revisit the benefits and limitations of SWOT analysis. As discussed in Chapter 2, a SWOT analysis consists of a careful listing of a firm's strengths, weaknesses, opportunities, and threats. While we believe SWOT analysis is very helpful as a starting point, it should not form the primary basis for evaluating a firm's internal strengths and weaknesses or the opportunities and threats in the environment. Strategy Spotlight 3.1 elaborates on the limitations of the traditional SWOT approach.

We will now turn to value-chain analysis. As you will see, it provides greater insights into analyzing a firm's competitive position than SWOT analysis does by itself.

Value-Chain Analysis

value-chain analysis
a strategic analysis of an organization that uses value-creating activities.

Value-chain analysis views the organization as a sequential process of value-creating activities. The approach is useful for understanding the building blocks of competitive advantage and was described in Michael Porter's seminal book *Competitive Advantage.*[2] Value is the amount that buyers are willing to pay for what a firm provides them and is measured by total revenue, a reflection of the price a firm's product commands and the quantity it can sell. A firm is profitable when the value it receives exceeds the total costs involved in creating its product or service. Creating value for buyers that exceeds the costs of production (i.e., margin) is a key concept used in analyzing a firm's competitive position.

primary activities
sequential activities of the value chain that refer to the physical creation of the product or service, its sale and transfer to the buyer, and its service after sale, including inbound logistics, operations, outbound logistics, marketing and sales, and service.

Porter described two different categories of activities. First, five **primary activities**—inbound logistics, operations, outbound logistics, marketing and sales, and service—contribute to the physical creation of the product or service, its sale and transfer to the buyer, and its service after the sale. Second, **support activities**—procurement, technology development, human resource management, and general administration—either add value by themselves or add value through important relationships with both primary activities and other support activities. Exhibit 3.1 illustrates Porter's value chain.

support activities
activities of the value chain that either add value by themselves or add value through important relationships with both primary activities and other support activities; including procurement, technology development, human resource management, and general administration.

To get the most out of value-chain analysis, view the concept in its broadest context, without regard to the boundaries of your own organization. That is, place your organization within a more encompassing value chain that includes your firm's suppliers, customers, and alliance partners. Thus, in addition to thoroughly understanding how value is created within the organization, be aware of how value is created for other organizations in the overall supply chain or distribution channel.[3]

Next, we'll describe and provide examples of each of the primary and support activities. Then, we'll provide examples of how companies add value by means of relationships among activities within the organization as well as activities outside the organization, such as those activities associated with customers and suppliers.[4]

THE LIMITATIONS OF SWOT ANALYSIS

SWOT analysis is a tried-and-true tool of strategic analysis. SWOT (strengths, weaknesses, opportunities, threats) analysis is used regularly in business to initially evaluate the opportunities and threats in the business environment as well as the strengths and weaknesses of a firm's internal environment. Top managers rely on SWOT to stimulate self-reflection and group discussions about how to improve their firm and position it for success.

But SWOT has its limitations. It is just a starting point for discussion. By listing the firm's attributes, managers have the raw material needed to perform more in-depth strategic analysis. However, SWOT cannot show them how to achieve a competitive advantage. They must not make SWOT analysis an end in itself, temporarily raising awareness about important issues but failing to lead to the kind of action steps necessary to enact strategic change.

Consider the ProCD example from Chapter 2, page 51. A brief SWOT analysis might include the following:

Strengths	Opportunities
First-mover advantage	Demand for electronic phone books
Low labor cost	Sudden growth in use of digital technology

Weaknesses	Threats
Inexperienced new company	Easily duplicated product
No proprietary information	Market power of incumbent firms

The combination of low production costs and an early-mover advantage in an environment where demand for CD-based phone books was growing rapidly seems to indicate that ProCD founder James Bryant had a golden opportunity. But the SWOT analysis did not reveal how to turn those strengths into a competitive advantage, nor did it highlight how rapidly the environment would change, allowing imitators to come into the market and erode his first-mover advantage. Let's look at some of the limitations of SWOT analysis.

Strengths May Not Lead to an Advantage

A firm's strengths and capabilities, no matter how unique or impressive, may not enable it to achieve a competitive advantage in the marketplace. It is akin to recruiting a concert pianist to join a gang of thugs—even though such an ability is rare and valuable, it hardly helps the organization attain its goals and objectives! Similarly, the skills of a highly creative product designer would offer little competitive advantage to a firm that produces low-cost commodity products. Indeed, the additional expense of hiring such an individual could erode the firm's cost advantages. If a firm builds its strategy on a capability that cannot, by itself, create or sustain competitive advantage, it is essentially a wasted use of resources. ProCD had several key strengths, but it did not translate them into lasting advantages in the marketplace.

SWOT's Focus on the External Environment Is Too Narrow

Strategists who rely on traditional definitions of their industry and competitive environment often focus their sights too narrowly on current customers, technologies, and competitors. Hence they fail to notice important changes on the periphery of their environment that may trigger the need to redefine industry boundaries and identify a whole new set of competitive relationships. Reconsider the example from Chapter 2 of *Encyclopaedia Britannica,* whose competitive position was severely eroded by a "nontraditional" competitor—CD-based encyclopedias (e.g., Microsoft *Encarta*) that could be used on home computers.

SWOT Gives a One-Shot View of a Moving Target

A key weakness of SWOT is that it is primarily a static assessment. It focuses too much of a firm's attention on one moment in time. Essentially, this is like studying a single frame of a motion picture. You may be able to identify the principal actors and learn something about the setting, but it doesn't tell you much about the plot. Competition among organizations is played out over time. As circumstances, capabilities, and strategies change, static analysis techniques do not reveal the dynamics of the competitive environment. Clearly, ProCD was unaware that its competitiveness was being eroded so quickly.

SWOT Overemphasizes a Single Dimension of Strategy

Sometimes firms become preoccupied with a single strength or a key feature of the product or service they are offering and ignore other factors needed for competitive success. For example, Toyota, the giant automaker, paid a heavy price for its excessive emphasis on cost control. The resulting problems with quality and the negative publicity led to severe financial losses and an erosion of its reputation in many markets.

SWOT analysis has much to offer, but only as a starting point. By itself, it rarely helps a firm develop competitive advantages that it can sustain over time.

Sources: Shapiro, C. & Varian, H. R. 2000. Versioning: The Smart Way to Sell Information. *Harvard Business Review,* 78(1): 99–106; and Picken, J. C. & Dess, G. G. 1997. *Mission Critical.* Burr Ridge, IL: Irwin Professional Publishing.

EXHIBIT 3.1 The Value Chain: Primary and Support Activities

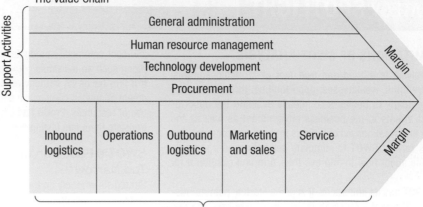

The Value Chain

Source: Reprinted with the permission of Free Press, a division of Simon & Schuster Inc., from *Competitive Advantage: Creating and Sustaining Superior Performance* by Michael E. Porter. Copyright © 1985, 1998 The Free Press. All rights reserved.

LO3.2

The primary and support activities of a firm's value chain.

inbound logistics
receiving, storing, and distributing inputs of a product.

EXHIBIT 3.2

The Value Chain: Some Factors to Consider in Assessing a Firm's Primary Activities

Primary Activities

Five generic categories of primary activities are involved in competing in any industry, as shown in Exhibit 3.2. Each category is divisible into a number of distinct activities that depend on the particular industry and the firm's strategy.[5]

Inbound Logistics   Inbound logistics is primarily associated with receiving, storing, and distributing inputs to the product. It includes material handling, warehousing, inventory control, vehicle scheduling, and returns to suppliers.

Inbound Logistics
- Location of distribution facilities to minimize shipping times.
- Warehouse layout and designs to increase efficiency of operations for incoming materials.

Operations
- Efficient plant operations to minimize costs.
- Efficient plant layout and workflow design.
- Incorporation of appropriate process technology.

Outbound Logistics
- Effective shipping processes to provide quick delivery and minimize damages.
- Shipping of goods in large lot sizes to minimize transportation costs.

Marketing and Sales
- Innovative approaches to promotion and advertising.
- Proper identification of customer segments and needs.

Service
- Quick response to customer needs and emergencies.
- Quality of service personnel and ongoing training.

Source: Adapted from Porter, M.E. 1985. *Competitive Advantage: Creating and Sustaining Superior Performance.* New York: Free Press.

Just-in-time (JIT) inventory systems, for example, were designed to achieve efficient inbound logistics. In essence, Toyota epitomizes JIT inventory systems, in which parts deliveries arrive at the assembly plants only hours before they are needed. JIT systems will play a vital role in fulfilling Toyota's commitment to fill a buyer's new car order in just five days.[6] This standard is in sharp contrast to most competitors that require approximately 30 days' notice to build vehicles. Toyota's standard is three times faster than even Honda Motors, considered to be the industry's most efficient in order follow-through. The five days represent the time from the company's receipt of an order to the time the car leaves the assembly plant. Actual delivery may take longer, depending on where a customer lives.

Operations Operations include all activities associated with transforming inputs into the final product form, such as machining, packaging, assembly, testing, printing, and facility operations.

> **operations**
> all activities associated with transforming inputs into the final product form.

Creating environmentally friendly manufacturing is one way to use operations to achieve competitive advantage. Shaw Industries (now part of Berkshire Hathaway), a world-class competitor in the floor-covering industry, is well known for its concern for the environment.[7] It has been successful in reducing the expenses associated with the disposal of dangerous chemicals and other waste products from its manufacturing operations. Its environmental endeavors have multiple payoffs. Shaw has received many awards for its recycling efforts—awards that enhance its reputation.

Outbound Logistics Outbound logistics is associated with collecting, storing, and distributing the product or service to buyers. These activities include finished goods, warehousing, material handling, delivery vehicle operation, order processing, and scheduling.

> **outbound logistics**
> collecting, storing, and distributing the product or service to buyers.

Campbell Soup uses an electronic network to facilitate its continuous-replenishment program with its most progressive retailers.[8] Each morning, retailers electronically inform Campbell of their product needs and of the level of inventories in their distribution centers. Campbell uses that information to forecast future demand and to determine which products require replenishment (based on the inventory limits previously established with each retailer). Trucks leave Campbell's shipping plant that afternoon and arrive at the retailers' distribution centers the same day. The program cuts the inventories of participating retailers from about a four- to a two-weeks' supply. Campbell Soup achieved this improvement because it slashed delivery time and because it knows the inventories of key retailers and can deploy supplies when they are most needed.

The Campbell Soup example also illustrates the win–win benefits of exemplary value-chain activities. Both the supplier (Campbell) and its buyers (retailers) come out ahead. Since the retailer makes more money on Campbell products delivered through continuous replenishment, it has an incentive to carry a broader line and give the company greater shelf space. After Campbell introduced the program, sales of its products grew twice as fast through participating retailers as through all other retailers. Not surprisingly, supermarket chains love such programs.

Marketing and Sales These activities are associated with purchases of products and services by end users and the inducements used to get them to make purchases.[9] They include advertising, promotion, sales force, quoting, channel selection, channel relations, and pricing.[10,11]

> **marketing and sales**
> activities associated with purchases of products and services by end users and the inducements used to get them to make purchases.

Consider product placement. This is a marketing strategy that many firms are increasingly adopting to reach customers who are not swayed by traditional advertising. A recent example is the starring role that BMW has in the film *Mission Impossible: Ghost Protocol*.[12]

In this latest in the series of *Mission Impossible* films, the i8 concept, a next-generation supercar from BMW, helps Tom Cruise and co-star Paul Patton race through Mumbai traffic. The car's appearance highlights the brand's return to Hollywood after a hiatus of more than a decade.

In addition to featuring the upcoming i8, BMW uses the film to promote its current X3 SUV, 6-series convertible, and 1-Series compact. In lieu of an upfront payment, the firm has promised to promote the film in its print and television ads, says Uwe Ellinghaus, head of brand management at BMW. As Ellinghaus claims, "*Mission Impossible* is a whole new dimension for BMW. It's what James Bond used to be."

At times, a firm's marketing initiatives may become overly aggressive and lead to actions that are both unethical and illegal.[13] For example:

- *Burdines.* This department store chain is under investigation for allegedly adding club memberships to its customers' credit cards without prior approval.
- *Fleet Mortgage.* This company has been accused of adding insurance fees for dental coverage and home insurance to its customers' mortgage loans without the customers' knowledge.
- *HCI Direct.* Eleven states have accused this direct-mail firm with charging for panty hose samples that customers did not order.
- *Juno Online Services.* The Federal Trade Commission brought charges against this Internet service provider for failing to provide customers with a telephone number to cancel service.

Strategy Spotlight 3.2 discusses how CrowdFlower, one of the world's leading crowd-sourcing service providers, has tapped into "collective intelligence" to help global brands such as Apple, eBay, Ford, and Microsoft.

service
actions associated with providing service to enhance or maintain the value of the product.

Service This primary activity includes all actions associated with providing service to enhance or maintain the value of the product, such as installation, repair, training, parts supply, and product adjustment.

Let's see how two retailers are providing exemplary customer service. At *Sephora.com*, a customer service representative taking a phone call from a repeat customer has instant access to what shade of lipstick she likes best. This will help the rep cross-sell by suggesting a matching shade of lip gloss. CEO Jim Wiggett expects such personalization to build loyalty and boost sales per customer. Nordstrom, the Seattle-based department store chain, goes even a step further. It offers a cyber-assist: A service rep can take control of a customer's Web browser and literally lead her to just the silk scarf that she is looking for. CEO Dan Nordstrom believes that such a capability will close enough additional purchases to pay for the $1 million investment in software.

Support Activities

Support activities in the value chain can be divided into four generic categories, as shown in Exhibit 3.3. Each category of the support activity is divisible into a number of distinct value activities that are specific to a particular industry. For example, technology development's discrete activities may include component design, feature design, field testing, process engineering, and technology selection. Similarly, procurement may include activities such as qualifying new suppliers, purchasing different groups of inputs, and monitoring supplier performance.

procurement
the function of purchasing inputs used in the firm's value chain, including raw materials, supplies, and other consumable items as well as assets such as machinery, laboratory equipment, office equipment, and buildings.

Procurement Procurement refers to the function of purchasing inputs used in the firm's value chain, not to the purchased inputs themselves.[14] Purchased inputs include raw materials, supplies, and other consumable items as well as assets such as machinery, laboratory equipment, office equipment, and buildings.[15,16]

THE POWER OF CROWDS: CROWDSOURCING COMES OF AGE

By Tom McNamara and Irena Descubes

Designing, producing, marketing and selling a new product that consumers will love is one of the most difficult activities a company can do. How do you develop a prototype? How do you figure out, strategically, what is the best course of action to take? How do you figure out what customers really want and what the public is expecting from your product or service? Well, one way is to just ask them. That's where "crowdsourcing" comes in.

Crowdsourcing, according to technology expert Raymon Ray, "is the act of tapping into a collective intelligence to complete a project or to come up with an idea." Instead of just using one person or one localized team to work on a project, you engage a variety of people, with multiple disciplines, from all over the country or all over the world. Some companies even use crowdsourcing as a contest, inviting people and organizations to provide them with ideas about some problem or issue, with the best submission winning a prize. The benefit is that you can get an almost exponentially greater number of possible solutions for a fixed cost.

A company that excels at this process is CrowdFlower, one of the world's leading crowdsourcing service providers. Their speciality is taking complicated projects and then breaking them down into "microtasks" (smaller discrete problems) which can be more readily distributed to experts to work on—similar to the way a person might work on a task in a production line. To help them, Crowd-Flower has at its disposal a global community of 5 million different contributors—people who are skilled mathematicians, statisticians, cartographers, musicians, psychologists, entrepreneurs, and information systems engineers. CrowdFlower completes thousands of tasks per week, specializing in problems related to search relevance, content moderation, business data verification/correction, and medical diagnoses.

Apple, AT&T, Autodesk, eBay, Ford, LinkedIn, Microsoft, Sears, Thompson Reuters, Toshiba, and Twitter would be just a few of the clients who have asked CrowdFlower for help with their problems. Recently, an important milestone was reached when CrowdFlower completed its one billionth task. The company's CEO said that "the volume of work we are seeing indicates crowd microtasking has gained widespread acceptance" and is proof that "CrowdFlower can accomplish large jobs rapidly and reliably."

Sources: PRNewswire-iReach, July 11 2013 "CrowdFlower Completes One-Billionth Crowd Judgment;" Ramon Ray, Business Insider, September 30 2011 "Crowdsourcing: What It Is & How to Use It;" CrowFlower website: crowdflower.com.

EXHIBIT 3.3 The Value Chain: Some Factors to Consider in Assessing a Firm's Support Activities

General Administration

- Effective planning systems to attain overall goals and objectives.
- Excellent relationships with diverse stakeholder groups.
- Effective information technology to integrate value-creating activities.

Human Resource Management

- Effective recruiting, development, and retention mechanisms for employees.
- Quality relations with trade unions.
- Reward and incentive programs to motivate all employees.

Technology Development

- Effective R&D activities for process and product initiatives.
- Positive collaborative relationships between R&D and other departments.
- Excellent professional qualifications of personnel.

Procurement

- Procurement of raw material inputs to optimize quality and speed and to minimize the associated costs.
- Development of collaborative win-win relationships with suppliers.
- Analysis and selection of alternative sources of inputs to minimize dependence on one supplier.

Source: Adapted from Porter, M.E. 1985. *Competitive Advantage: Creating and Sustaining Superior Performance.* New York: Free Press.

Microsoft has improved its procurement process (and the quality of its suppliers) by providing formal reviews of its suppliers. One of Microsoft's divisions has extended the review process used for employees to its outside suppliers.[17] The employee services group, which is responsible for everything from travel to 401(k) programs to the on-site library, outsources more than 60 percent of the services it provides. Unfortunately, the employee services group was not providing them with enough feedback. This was feedback that the suppliers wanted to get and that Microsoft wanted to give.

The evaluation system that Microsoft developed helped clarify its expectations to suppliers. An executive noted: "We had one supplier—this was before the new system—that would have scored a 1.2 out of 5. After we started giving this feedback, and the supplier understood our expectations, its performance improved dramatically. Within six months, it scored a 4. If you'd asked me before we began the feedback system, I would have said that was impossible."

Strategy Spotlight 3.3 addresses LG Electronics' exemplary procurement practices.

Technology Development   Every value activity embodies technology.[18] The array of technologies employed in most firms is very broad, ranging from technologies used to prepare documents and transport goods to those embodied in processes and equipment or the product itself.[19] Technology development related to the product and its features supports the entire value chain, while other technology development is associated with particular primary or support activities.

> **technology development**
> activities associated with the development of new knowledge that is applied to the firm's operations.

The Allied Signal and Honeywell merger brought together roughly 13,000 scientists and an $870 million R&D budget that should lead to some innovative products and services in two major areas: performance materials and control systems. Some of the possible innovations include:

- *Performance materials.* The development of uniquely shaped fibers with very high absorption capability. When employed in the company's Fram oil filters, they capture 50 percent more particles than ordinary filters. This means that cars can travel further with fewer oil changes.
- *Control systems.* Working with six leading oil companies, Honeywell developed software using "self-learning" algorithms that predict when something might go wrong in an oil refinery before it actually does. Examples include a faulty gas valve or hazardous spillage.[20]

Human Resource Management   Human resource management consists of activities involved in the recruiting, hiring, training, development, and compensation of all types of personnel.[21] It supports both individual primary and support activities (e.g., hiring of engineers and scientists) and the entire value chain (e.g., negotiations with labor unions).[22]

> **human resource management**
> activities involved in the recruiting, hiring, training, development and compensation of all types of personnel.

Like all great service companies, JetBlue Airways Corporation is obsessed with hiring superior employees.[23] But they found it difficult to attract college graduates to commit to careers as flight attendants. JetBlue developed a highly innovative recruitment program for flight attendants—a one-year contract that gives them a chance to travel, meet lots of people, and then decide what else they might like to do. They also introduced the idea of training a friend and employee together so that they could share a job. With such employee-friendly initiatives, JetBlue has been very successful in attracting talent.

Jeffrey Immelt, GE's chairman, addresses the importance of effective human resource management:[24]

> Human resources has to be more than a department. GE recognized early on—50 or 60 years ago—that in a multibusiness company, the common denominators are people and culture. From an employee's first day at GE, she discovers that she's in the people-development business as much as anything else. You'll find that most good companies have the same basic HR processes that we have, but they're discrete. HR at GE is not an agenda item; it is the agenda.

CREATIVE WHEN NO ONE'S LOOKING: PROCUREMENT AT LG ELECTRONICS

While LG Electronics spent $I.2 billon to market its many innovative electronic products in 2009, one of its truly pioneering actions has been the creation of a better supply chain. Although customers might not care about such investments, they would care about the price of one of the company's cell phones, the LG Cookie, which was 30 percent lower than its comparable direct competitors. This price reduction was due in part to cost reduction and innovation at the company's shipping bays. The Cookie has helped cement LG's status as the world's third-largest handset maker.

Previously, each of LG's divisions negotiated their own deals. Thus, even though they might purchase from the same supplier, different divisions could receive different prices. By centralizing purchases, LG has cut more than $2 billion from its annual $30 billion shopping bill. Thomas Linton, LG's first-ever procurement officer, has merged the various processes of the 115 factories and subsidiaries into a 50-page procurement manual and has worked more closely with suppliers, such as Taiwan's TSMC. In early 2009 the company forecast strong demand from China for

wafers, the silicon disks used to make chips. Linton quickly locked in suppliers, resulting in savings of $1 billion, according to the company. Other savings resulted from buying aluminum instead of higher-priced copper for the guts of electrical goods such as home appliances, thus saving $25 million in 2009. Moreover, Linton retained just enough control over LG's supply chain to find substantial cost savings other companies that outsourced their supply chain to top-tier suppliers were unable to find. For instance LG, together with its suppliers, benchmarked their power cords against the ones used in competing products and found surprising results: they were much longer! Shortening the cords and standardizing the color to all black resulted in $10 million annual cost savings.

As a result of implementing such lean procurement procedures, the company weathered the recent economic downturn better than many competitors. And, in 2010, it won the Institute for Supply Management's award for leadership and innovation in procurement.

Sources: Ihlwan, M. 2010. Creative when no one's looking: LG's re-engineering its supply chain so its innovative products will cost less. *Bloomberg BusinessWeek*, April 25: 37; Choi, T. & Linton, T. 2011. Don't let your supply chain control your business. *Harvard Business Review*, 89(12): 112–117.

General Administration   General administration consists of a number of activities, including general management, planning, finance, accounting, legal and government affairs, quality management, and information systems. Administration (unlike the other support activities) typically supports the entire value chain and not individual activities.[25]

Although general administration is sometimes viewed only as overhead, it can be a powerful source of competitive advantage. In a telephone operating company, for example, negotiating and maintaining ongoing relations with regulatory bodies can be among the most important activities for competitive advantage. Also, in some industries top management plays a vital role in dealing with important buyers.[26]

The strong and effective leadership of top executives can also make a significant contribution to an organization's success. As we discussed in Chapter 1, chief executive officers (CEOs) such as Herb Kelleher, Andrew Grove, and Jack Welch have been credited with playing critical roles in the success of Southwest Airlines, Intel, and General Electric.

Information systems can also play a key role in increasing the effectiveness of a wide variety of value chain activities and enhancing a firm's performance. Strategy Spotlight 3.4 discusses how CarMax has used its proprietary information system to enhance its competitive advantage.

Interrelationships among Value-Chain Activities within and across Organizations

We have defined each of the value-chain activities separately for clarity of presentation. Managers must not ignore, however, the importance of relationships among value-chain activities.[27] There are two levels: (1) **interrelationships** among activities within the firm and (2) relationships among activities within the firm and with other stakeholders (e.g., customers and suppliers) that are part of the firm's expanded value chain.[28]

> **LO3.3**
>
> How value-chain analysis can help managers create value by investigating relationships among activities within the firm and between the firm and its customers and suppliers.

> **general administration**
> general management, planning, finance, accounting, legal and government affairs, quality management, and information systems; activities that support the entire value chain and not individual activities.

COMPETITIVE ANALYTICS AT CARMAX

Organizations increasingly face the challenge to make sense of the enormous amount of data available for analysis. While not too long ago companies used data analytics almost exclusively for financial forecasting and supply chain management, businesses increasingly demand that their information systems generate competitive advantage. This development led to the emergence of a new breed of information systems, also known as competitive analytics systems.

Consider CarMax, the largest U.S. retailer of used cars, for an example of how competitive analytics looks in practice. With $9 billion in 2011 revenue, CarMax's success has many reasons, such as its compelling service offering, no haggle prices, and proven quality guaranteed by its 125-point inspection. Besides these more traditional sources of competitive advantage, CarMax also operates a proprietary information system that captures, analyzes, interprets, and disseminates information about all cars on the CarMax lot. CarMax's data analytics helps track "every purchase, number of test drives and credit applications per car and color preferences in every demographic and region," states

Katharine W. Kenny, CarMax vice president of investor relations. The ability to integrate various value chain activities in this proprietary system allows CarMax to realize a competitive advantage.

The key features of this system provide CarMax management with real-time business insights into different store operations, such as inventory management, pricing, and sales consultant productivity. This advanced information system allows CarMax to decrease uncertainties in traditionally hard to forecast areas such as inventory management, allowing management to improve operational efficiency, and anticipate future trends. Moreover, CarMax also invests heavily in store technology, with some CarMax stores using Apple iPads to assist customers, who are becoming more tech savvy. According to CEO Tom Folliard, all these IT initiatives are targeted to give customers "a better experience from the time they walk in the door to the time they leave, so they are more likely to buy a car and they're more likely to tell their friends about it."

Sources: Kiron, D. & Shockley, R. 2011. Creating business value with analytics. *MIT Sloan Management Review*, 51(1): 57–63; Felberbaum, M. 2012. CEO: CarMax focused on customer experience. *Bloomberg BusinessWeek*, June 25: np.

---

interrelationships
collaborative and strategic exchange relationships between value-chain activities either (a) within firms or (b) between firms. Strategic exchange relationships involve exchange of resources such as information, people, technology, or money that contribute to the success of the firm.

With regard to the first level, consider CarMax's proprietary information system. It provides management with real-time information about several aspects of store operations, including pricing, salesperson productivity, and inventory management.

With regard to the second level, Campbell Soup's use of electronic networks enabled it to improve the efficiency of outbound logistics.[29] However, it also helped Campbell manage the ordering of raw materials more effectively, improve its production scheduling, and help its customers better manage their inbound logistics operations.

The "Prosumer" Concept: Integrating Customers into the Value Chain

When addressing the value-chain concept, it is important to focus on the interrelationship between the organization and its most important stakeholder—its customers.[30] A key to success for some leading-edge firms is to team up with their customers to satisfy their particular need(s). As stated in a recent IBM Global CEO Study:

> In the future, we will be talking more and more about the "prosumer"—a customer/producer who is even more extensively integrated into the value chain. As a consequence, production processes will be customized more precisely and individually.[31]

Including customers in the actual production process can create greater satisfaction among them. It also has the potential to result in significant cost savings and to generate innovative ideas for the firm, which can be transferred to the customer in terms of lower prices and higher quality products and services.

In terms of how a firm views its customers, the move to create the prosumer stands in rather stark contrast to the conventional marketing approach in which the customer merely consumes the products produced by the company. Another area where this approach differs from conventional thinking concerns the notion of tying the customer into the company through, for example, loyalty programs and individualized relationship marketing.

How Procter & Gamble Embraced the Prosumer Concept In the early 2000s P&G's people were not clearly oriented toward any common purpose. The corporate mission "To meaningfully improve the everyday lives of the customers" had not been explicitly or inspirationally rolled out to the employees. To more clearly focus everyone's efforts, P&G expanded the mission to include the idea that "the consumer is the boss." This philosophy became one in which people who buy and use P&G products are valued not just for their money but also as *a rich source of information and direction.* "The consumer is the boss" became far more than a slogan in P&G. It became a clear, simple, and inclusive cultural priority for both employees and the external stakeholders such as suppliers.

The P&G efforts in the fragrance areas are one example. P&G transformed this small underperforming business area into a global leader and the world's largest fine fragrance company. They accomplished this by clearly and precisely defining the target consumer for each fragrance brand and by identifying subgroups of consumers for some brands. P&G still kept the partnerships with established fashion houses such as Dolce & Gabbana, Gucci, and Lacoste. However, the main point was to make the consumer the boss, focusing on innovations that were meaningful to consumers, including, for instance, fresh new scents, distinctive packaging, and proactive marketing. In addition, P&G streamlined the supply chain to reduce complexity and lower its cost structure.

The idea that "the consumer is the boss" goes even further. It also means that P&G tries to build social connections through digital media and other forms of interactions (thus incorporating the crowdsourcing concept that we introduced in Chapter 2). Baby diapers are one example. P&G used to use handmade diapers for its product tests. Today, however, this product is shown digitally and created in alternatives in an on-screen virtual world. Changes can be made immediately as new ideas emerge, and it can be redesigned on screen. Thus, P&G is creating a social system with the consumers (and potential consumers) that enable the firm to co-design and co-engineer new innovations with buyers. At P&G the philosophy of "the consumer is the boss" set a new standard.

Applying the Value Chain to Service Organizations

The concepts of inbound logistics, operations, and outbound logistics suggest managing the raw materials that might be manufactured into finished products and delivered to customers. However, these three steps do not apply only to manufacturing. They correspond to any transformation process in which inputs are converted through a work process into outputs that add value. For example, accounting is a sort of transformation process that converts daily records of individual transactions into monthly financial reports. In this example, the transaction records are the inputs, accounting is the operation that adds value, and financial statements are the outputs.

What are the "operations," or transformation processes, of service organizations? At times, the difference between manufacturing and service is in providing a customized solution rather than mass production as is common in manufacturing. For example, a travel agent adds value by creating an itinerary that includes transportation, accommodations, and activities that are customized to your budget and travel dates. A law firm renders services that are specific to a client's needs and circumstances. In both cases, the work process (operation) involves the application of specialized knowledge based on the specifics of a situation (inputs) and the outcome that the client desires (outputs).

The application of the value chain to service organizations suggests that the value-adding process may be configured differently depending on the type of business a firm is engaged in. As the preceding discussion on support activities suggests, activities such as procurement and legal services are critical for adding value. Indeed, the activities that may only provide support to one company may be critical to the primary value-adding activity of another firm.

Exhibit 3.4 provides two models of how the value chain might look in service industries. In the retail industry, there are no manufacturing operations. A firm such as Nordstrom

EXHIBIT 3.4 Some Examples of Value Chains in Service Industries

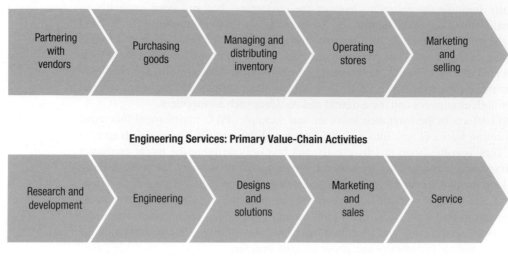

Retail: Primary Value-Chain Activities

Partnering with vendors → Purchasing goods → Managing and distributing inventory → Operating stores → Marketing and selling

Engineering Services: Primary Value-Chain Activities

Research and development → Engineering → Designs and solutions → Marketing and sales → Service

adds value by developing expertise in the procurement of finished goods and by displaying them in their stores in a way that enhances sales. Thus, the value chain makes procurement activities (i.e., partnering with vendors and purchasing goods) a primary rather than a support activity. Operations refer to the task of operating Nordstrom's stores.

For an engineering services firm, research and development provides inputs, the transformation process is the engineering itself, and innovative designs and practical solutions are the outputs. The Beca Group, for example, is a large consulting firm with over 2,500 employees, based in the Asia Pacific region. In its technology and innovation management practice, Beca strives to make the best use of the science, technology and knowledge resources available to create value for a wide range of industries and client sectors. This involves activities associated with research and development, engineering, and creating solutions as well as downstream activities such as marketing, sales, and service. How the primary and support activities of a given firm are configured and deployed will often depend on industry conditions and whether the company is service and/or manufacturing oriented.

Resource-Based View of the Firm

resource-based view of the firm
perspective that firms' competitive advantages are due to their endowment of strategic resources that are valuable, rare, costly to imitate, and costly to substitute.

L03.4

The resource-based view of the firm and the different types of tangible and intangible resources, as well as organizational capabilities.

The **resource-based view (RBV) of the firm** combines two perspectives: (1) the internal analysis of phenomena within a company and (2) an external analysis of the industry and its competitive environment.[32] It goes beyond the traditional SWOT (strengths, weaknesses, opportunities, threats) analysis by integrating internal and external perspectives. The ability of a firm's resources to confer competitive advantage(s) cannot be determined without taking into consideration the broader competitive context. A firm's resources must be evaluated in terms of how valuable, rare, and hard they are for competitors to duplicate. Otherwise, the firm attains only competitive parity.

As noted earlier (in Strategy Spotlight 3.1), a firm's strengths and capabilities—no matter how unique or impressive—do not necessarily lead to competitive advantages in the marketplace. The criteria for whether advantages are created and whether or not they can be sustained over time will be addressed later in this section. Thus, the RBV is a very useful framework for gaining insights as to why some competitors are more profitable than others. As we will see later in the book, the RBV is also helpful in developing strategies for individual businesses and diversified firms by revealing how core competencies embedded in a firm can help it exploit new product and market opportunities.

In the two sections that follow, we will discuss the three key types of resources that firms possess (summarized in Exhibit 3.5): tangible resources, intangible resources, and organizational capabilities. Then we will address the conditions under which such assets and capabilities can enable a firm to attain a sustainable competitive advantage.[33]

Types of Firm Resources

Firm resources are all assets, capabilities, organizational processes, information, knowledge, and so forth, controlled by a firm that enable it to develop and implement value-creating strategies.

Tangible Resources   These are assets that are relatively easy to identify. They include the physical and financial assets that an organization uses to create value for its

tangible resources
organizational assets that are relatively easy to identify, including physical assets, financial resources, organizational resources, and technological resources.

EXHIBIT 3.5

The Resource-Based View of the Firm: Resources and Capabilities

Tangible Resources	
Financial	• Firm's cash account and cash equivalents.
	• Firm's capacity to raise equity.
	• Firm's borrowing capacity.
Physical	• Modern plant and facilities.
	• Favorable manufacturing locations.
	• State-of-the-art machinery and equipment.
Technological	• Trade secrets.
	• Innovative production processes.
	• Patents, copyrights, trademarks.
Organizational	• Effective strategic planning processes.
	• Excellent evaluation and control systems.

Intangible Resources	
Human	• Experience and capabilities of employees.
	• Trust.
	• Managerial skills.
	• Firm-specific practices and procedures.
Innovation and creativity	• Technical and scientific skills.
	• Innovation capacities.
Reputation	• Brand name.
	• Reputation with customers for quality and reliability.
	• Reputation with suppliers for fairness, non–zero-sum relationships.

Organizational Capabilities

• Firm competencies or skills the firm employs to transfer inputs to outputs.
• Capacity to combine tangible and intangible resources, using organizational processes to attain desired end.

EXAMPLES:
• Outstanding customer service.
• Excellent product development capabilities.
• Innovativeness of products and services.
• Ability to hire, motivate, and retain human capital.

Source: Adapted from Barney, J. B. 1991. Firm Resources and Sustained Competitive Advantage. *Journal of Management:* 17: 101; Grant, R. M. 1991. *Contemporary Strategy Analysis:* 100–102. Cambridge England: Blackwell Business and Hitt, M. A., Ireland, R. D., & Hoskisson, R. E. 2001. *Strategic Management: Competitiveness and Globalization* (4th ed.). Cincinnati: South-Western College Publishing.

customers. Among them are financial resources (e.g., a firm's cash, accounts receivables, and its ability to borrow funds); physical resources (e.g., the company's plant, equipment, and machinery as well as its proximity to customers and suppliers); organizational resources (e.g., the company's strategic planning process and its employee development, evaluation, and reward systems); and technological resources (e.g., trade secrets, patents, and copyrights).

Many firms are finding that high-tech, computerized training has dual benefits: It develops more effective employees and reduces costs at the same time. Employees at FedEx take computer-based job competency tests every 6 to 12 months.[34] The 90-minute computer-based tests identify areas of individual weakness and provide input to a computer database of employee skills—information the firm uses in promotion decisions.

Intangible Resources Much more difficult for competitors (and, for that matter, a firm's own managers) to account for or imitate are **intangible resources,** which are typically embedded in unique routines and practices that have evolved and accumulated over time. These include human resources (e.g., experience and capability of employees, trust, effectiveness of work teams, managerial skills), innovation resources (e.g., technical and scientific expertise, ideas), and reputation resources (e.g., brand name, reputation with suppliers for fairness and with customers for reliability and product quality).[35] A firm's culture may also be a resource that provides competitive advantage.[36]

For example, you might not think that motorcycles, clothes, toys, and restaurants have much in common. Yet Harley-Davidson has entered all of these product and service markets by capitalizing on its strong brand image—a valuable intangible resource.[37] It has used that image to sell accessories, clothing, and toys, and it has licensed the Harley-Davidson Café in New York City to provide further exposure for its brand name and products.

Social networking sites have the potential to play havoc with a firm's reputation. Consider the unfortunate situation Comcast faced when one of its repairmen fell asleep on the job—and it went viral:

> Ben Finkelstein, a law student, had trouble with the cable modem in his home. A Comcast cable repairman arrived to fix the problem. However, when the technician had to call the home office for a key piece of information, he was put on hold for so long that he fell asleep on Finkelstein's couch. Outraged, Finkelstein made a video of the sleeping technician and posted it on YouTube. The clip became a hit—with more than a million viewings. And, for a long time, it undermined Comcast's efforts to improve its reputation for customer service.[38]

Organizational Capabilities **Organizational capabilities** are not specific tangible or intangible assets, but rather the competencies or skills that a firm employs to transform inputs into outputs.[39] In short, they refer to an organization's capacity to deploy tangible and intangible resources over time and generally in combination, and to leverage those capabilities to bring about a desired end.[40] Examples of organizational capabilities are outstanding customer service, excellent product development capabilities, superb innovation processes, and flexibility in manufacturing processes.[41]

In the case of Apple, the majority of components used in their products can be characterized as proven technology, such as touch screen and MP3 player functionality.[42] However, Apple combines and packages these in new and innovative ways while also seeking to integrate the value chain. This is the case with iTunes, for example, where suppliers of downloadable music are a vital component of the success Apple has enjoyed with their iPod series of MP3 players. Thus, Apple draws on proven technologies and their ability to offer innovative combinations of these.

intangible resources
organizational assets that are difficult to identify and account for and are typically embedded in unique routines and practices, including human resources, innovation resources, and reputation resources.

organizational capabilities
the competencies and skills that a firm employs to transform inputs into outputs.

Firm Resources and Sustainable Competitive Advantages

As we have mentioned, resources alone are not a basis for competitive advantages, nor are advantages sustainable over time.[43] In some cases, a resource or capability helps a firm to increase its revenues or to lower costs but the firm derives only a temporary advantage because competitors quickly imitate or substitute for it.[44]

For a resource to provide a firm with the potential for a sustainable competitive advantage, it must have four attributes.[45] First, the resource must be valuable in the sense that it exploits opportunities and/or neutralizes threats in the firm's environment. Second, it must be rare among the firm's current and potential competitors. Third, the resource must be difficult for competitors to imitate. Fourth, the resource must have no strategically equivalent substitutes. These criteria are summarized in Exhibit 3.6. We will now discuss each of these criteria. Then, we will examine how Dell's competitive advantage, which seemed secure as late as 2006, has eroded in recent years.

Is the Resource Valuable?   Organizational resources can be a source of competitive advantage only when they are valuable. Resources are valuable when they enable a firm to formulate and implement strategies that improve its efficiency or effectiveness. The SWOT framework suggests that firms improve their performance only when they exploit opportunities or neutralize (or minimize) threats.

The fact that firm attributes must be valuable in order to be considered resources (as well as potential sources of competitive advantage) reveals an important complementary relationship among environmental models (e.g., SWOT and five-forces analyses) and the resource-based model. Environmental models isolate those firm attributes that exploit opportunities and/or neutralize threats. Thus, they specify what firm attributes may be considered as resources. The resource-based model then suggests what additional characteristics these resources must possess if they are to develop a sustained competitive advantage.

Is the Resource Rare?   If competitors or potential competitors also possess the same valuable resource, it is not a source of a competitive advantage because all of these firms have the capability to exploit that resource in the same way. Common strategies based on such a resource would give no one firm an advantage. For a resource to provide competitive advantages, it must be uncommon, that is, rare relative to other competitors.

This argument can apply to bundles of valuable firm resources that are used to formulate and develop strategies. Some strategies require a mix of multiple types of resources— tangible assets, intangible assets, and organizational capabilities. If a particular bundle of firm resources is not rare, then relatively large numbers of firms will be able to conceive of and implement the strategies in question. Thus, such strategies will not be a source of competitive advantage, even if the resource in question is valuable.

Is the resource or capability . . .	Implications
Valuable?	• Neutralize threats and exploit opportunities
Rare?	• Not many firms possess
Difficult to imitate?	• Physically unique • Path dependency (how accumulated over time) • Causal ambiguity (difficult to disentangle what it is or how it could be re-created) • Social complexity (trust, interpersonal relationships, culture, reputation)
Difficult to substitute?	• No equivalent strategic resources or capabilities

EXHIBIT 3.6

Four Criteria for Assessing Sustainability of Resources and Capabilities

Can the Resource Be Imitated Easily?   Inimitability (difficulty in imitating) is a key to value creation because it constrains competition.[46] If a resource is inimitable, then any profits generated are more likely to be sustainable.[47] Having a resource that competitors can easily copy generates only temporary value.[48] This has important implications. Since managers often fail to apply this test, they tend to base long-term strategies on resources that are imitable. IBP (Iowa Beef Processors) became the first meatpacking company in the United States to modernize by building a set of assets (automated plants located in cattle-producing states) and capabilities (low-cost "disassembly" of carcasses) that earned returns on assets of 1.3 percent in the 1970s. By the late 1980s, however, ConAgra and Cargill had imitated these resources, and IBP's profitability fell by nearly 70 percent, to 0.4 percent.

Groupon is a more recent example of a firm that has suffered because rivals have been able to imitate its strategy rather easily:

> Groupon, which offers online coupons for bargains at local shops and restaurants, created a new market.[49] Although it was initially a boon to consumers, it offers no lasting "first mover" advantage. Its business model is not patentable and it is easy to replicate. Not surprisingly, there are many copycats. It seemed to represent a way to populate small businesses with an endless stream of enthusiastic customers. However, it has proven very hard to earn profits. For example, Groupon lost $256.7 million on $1.6 billion in revenues in 2011—and by late 2012, its stock was under $3 a share, a drop of about 80 percent from its value since its public trading debut. Privately-held LivingSocial, which is 31 percent owned by Amazon, had $558 million in losses on just $245 million in revenue. And even as Google and PayPal increased their coupon offers, there was a tremendous amount of churn in the industry in 2012. The number of daily deal sites in the United States rose by almost 8 percent (142 sites), according to Daily Deal Media, which tracks the industry. Meanwhile, globally, 560 daily deal sites closed over the same period!
>
> What are some of Groupon's main challenges? If they decrease their enormous marketing expenses, their growth could slow and their competitors would strengthen. But if they increase spending, they will have difficulty becoming a sustainably profitable company. And a key rival, LivingSocial, has been able to give discounts on Amazon products and gift cards because of Amazon's investment in it.

Clearly, an advantage based on inimitability won't last forever. Competitors will eventually discover a way to copy most valuable resources. However, managers can forestall them and sustain profits for a while by developing strategies around resources that have at least one of the following four characteristics.[50]

Physical Uniqueness   The first source of inimitability is physical uniqueness, which by definition is inherently difficult to copy. A beautiful resort location, mineral rights, or Pfizer's pharmaceutical patents simply cannot be imitated. Many managers believe that several of their resources may fall into this category, but on close inspection, few do.

path dependency
a characteristic of resources that is developed and/or accumulated through a unique series of events.

Path Dependency   A greater number of resources cannot be imitated because of what economists refer to as **path dependency.** This simply means that resources are unique and therefore scarce because of all that has happened along the path followed in their development and/or accumulation. Competitors cannot go out and buy these resources quickly and easily; they must be built up over time in ways that are difficult to accelerate.

The Gerber Products Co. brand name for baby food is an example of a resource that is potentially inimitable. Re-creating Gerber's brand loyalty would be a time-consuming process that competitors could not expedite, even with expensive marketing campaigns. Similarly, the loyalty and trust that Southwest Airlines employees feel toward their firm and its cofounder, Herb Kelleher, are resources that have been built up over a long period of time. Also, a crash R&D program generally cannot replicate a successful technology when research findings cumulate. Clearly, these path-dependent conditions build protection for the original resource. The benefits from experience and learning through trial and error cannot be duplicated overnight.

Causal Ambiguity   The third source of inimitability is termed **causal ambiguity.** This means that would-be competitors may be thwarted because it is impossible to disentangle the causes (or possible explanations) of either what the valuable resource is or how it can be re-created. What is the root of 3M's innovation process? You can study it and draw up a list of possible factors. But it is a complex, unfolding (or folding) process that is hard to understand and would be hard to imitate.

Often, causally ambiguous resources are organizational capabilities, involving a complex web of social interactions that may even depend on particular individuals. When Continental and United tried to mimic the successful low-cost strategy of Southwest Airlines, the planes, routes, and fast gate turnarounds were not the most difficult aspects for them to copy. Those were all rather easy to observe and, at least in principle, easy to duplicate. However, they could not replicate Southwest's culture of fun, family, frugality, and focus since no one can clearly specify exactly what that culture is or how it came to be.

Strategy Spotlight 3.5 describes Amazon's continued success as the world's largest online marketplace. Competitors recently tried to imitate Amazon's free shipping strategy, but with limited success. The reason is that Amazon has developed an array of interrelated elements of strategy which their rivals find too difficult to imitate.

Social Complexity   A firm's resources may be imperfectly inimitable because they reflect a high level of **social complexity.** Such phenomena are typically beyond the ability of firms to systematically manage or influence. When competitive advantages are based on social complexity, it is difficult for other firms to imitate them.

A wide variety of firm resources may be considered socially complex. Examples include interpersonal relations among the managers in a firm, its culture, and its reputation with its suppliers and customers. In many of these cases, it is easy to specify how these socially complex resources add value to a firm. Hence, there is little or no causal ambiguity surrounding the link between them and competitive advantage.

Consider how a Chinese beverage company succeeded by creating close partnerships with its distributors:[51]

> When Wahaha, the largest Chinese beverage producer, decided to take on Coca-Cola and PepsiCo, they began their attack in the rural areas of China. Why? They believed that they possessed a competitive advantage over the international giants because of the partnerships that they had built with the distributors across the more remote locations in China.
>
> Four years prior to the launch of a key product, "Wahaha Future Cola," the firm developed a policy for how to tie in "channel members" over the long term as a response to the increasing problem of accounts receivable and bad debt. This policy provided incentives for the channel members to pay an annual deposit in advance to cover any potential future bad debt and to operate according to Wahaha's payment policy.
>
> Sounds OK, but what did the distributors get in return? They received an interest rate from Wahaha that was superior to the bank rate. In addition, further discounts were offered for early payment, and annual bonuses were awarded to distributors that met the criterion for prompt payment.

Are Substitutes Readily Available?   The fourth requirement for a firm resource to be a source of sustainable competitive advantage is that there must be no strategically equivalent valuable resources that are themselves not rare or inimitable. Two valuable firm resources (or two bundles of resources) are strategically equivalent when each one can be exploited separately to implement the same strategies.

Substitutability may take at least two forms. First, though it may be impossible for a firm to imitate exactly another firm's resource, it may be able to substitute a similar resource that enables it to develop and implement the same strategy. Clearly, a firm seeking to imitate another firm's high-quality top management team would be unable to copy the team exactly. However, it might be able to develop its own unique management team.

---

causal ambiguity
a characteristic of a firm's resources that is costly to imitate because a competitor cannot determine what the resource is and/or how it can be re-created.

social complexity
a characteristic of a firm's resources that is costly to imitate because the social engineering required is beyond the capability of competitors, including interpersonal relations among managers, organizational culture, and reputation with suppliers and customers.

AMAZON PRIME: VERY DIFFICULT FOR RIVALS TO COPY

Amazon Prime, introduced in 2004, is a free-shipping service that guarantees delivery of products within two days for an annual fee of $79. According to *Bloomberg Businessweek,* it may be the most ingenious and effective customer loyalty program in all of e-commerce, if not retail in general. It converts casual shoppers into Amazon addicts who gorge on the gratification of having purchases reliably appear two days after they order. Analysts describe Prime as one of the main factors driving Amazon's stock price up nearly 300 percent from 2008 to 2010. Also, it is one of the main reasons why Amazon's sales grew 30 percent during the recession, while other retailers suffered.

Analysts estimate that Amazon Prime has more than 5 million members in the United States, a small slice of Amazon's 152 million active buyers worldwide. However, analysts claim that Prime members increase their purchases on the site by about 150 percent after they join and may be responsible for as much as 20 percent of Amazon's overall sales in the United States. Such shoppers are considered the "whales" of the $161 billion (in 2011) U.S. e-commerce market, one of the fastest-growing parts of U.S. retail. And, according to Hudson Square Research, Amazon, with a hefty 8 percent of the U.S. e-commerce market in 2010, is the single biggest online retailer in the United States.

Amazon Prime has proven to be extremely hard for rivals to copy. Why? It enables Amazon to exploit its wide selection, low prices, network of third-party merchants, and finely tuned distribution system. All that while also keying off that faintly irrational human need to maximize the benefits of a club that you have already paid to join. Yet Amazon's success also leads to increased pressure from both public and private entities. For a long time, Amazon was able to avoid collecting local sales taxes because Amazon did not have a local sales presence in many states. This practice distorts competition and strains already tight state coffers. Some states have used a combination of legislation and litigation to convince Amazon to collect sales taxes; Amazon began collecting Texas state sales tax in July 2012.

Moreover, rivals—both online and off—have realized the increasing threat posed by Prime and are rushing to respond. For example, in October 2010, a consortium of more than 20 retailers, including Barnes & Noble, Sports Authority, and Toys 'R' Us, banded together to offer their own copycat $79, two-day shipping program, ShopRunner, which applies to products across their websites. As noted by Fiona Dias, the executive who administers the program, "As Amazon added more merchandising categories to Prime, retailers started feeling the pain. They have finally come to understand that Amazon is an existential threat and that Prime is the fuel of the engine." Brick-and-mortar retailers are also trying to fight back by matching Amazon's prices, as they did during the 2012 holiday season, and by tightly integrating their on- and offline offerings.

Sources: Stone, B. 2010. What's in the box? Instant gratification. *Bloomberg Businessweek,* November 29–December 5: 39–40; Kaplan, M. 2011. Amazon Prime: 5 million members, 20 percent growth. *www.practicalcommerce.com,* September 16: np; Fowler, G. A. 2010. Retailers team up against Amazon. *www.wsj .com,* October 6: np; Halkias, M. 2012. Amazon to collect sales tax in Texas. *Dallas Morning News,* April 28: 4A.

Though these two teams would have different ages, functional backgrounds, experience, and so on, they could be strategically equivalent and thus substitutes for one another.

Second, very different firm resources can become strategic substitutes. For example, Internet booksellers such as *Amazon.com* compete as substitutes for brick-and-mortar booksellers such as B. Dalton. The result is that resources such as premier retail locations become less valuable. In a similar vein, several pharmaceutical firms have seen the value of patent protection erode in the face of new drugs that are based on different production processes and act in different ways, but can be used in similar treatment regimes. The coming years will likely see even more radical change in the pharmaceutical industry as the substitution of genetic therapies eliminates certain uses of chemotherapy.[52]

To recap this section, recall that resources and capabilities must be rare and valuable as well as difficult to imitate or substitute in order for a firm to attain competitive advantages that are sustainable over time.[53] Exhibit 3.7 illustrates the relationship among the four criteria of sustainability and shows the competitive implications.

In firms represented by the first row of Exhibit 3.7, managers are in a difficult situation. When their resources and capabilities do not meet any of the four criteria, it would be difficult to develop any type of competitive advantage, in the short or long term. The resources and capabilities they possess enable the firm neither to exploit environmental opportunities

Is a resource or capability . . .				
Valuable?	Rare?	Difficult to Imitate?	Without Substitutes?	Implications for Competitiveness?
No	No	No	No	Competitive disadvantage
Yes	No	No	No	Competitive parity
Yes	Yes	No	No	Temporary competitive advantage
Yes	Yes	Yes	Yes	Sustainable competitive advantage

EXHIBIT 3.7

Criteria for Sustainable Competitive Advantage and Strategic Implications

Source: Adapted from Barney, J. B. 1991. Firm Resources and Sustained Competitive Advantage. *Journal of Management,* 17: 99–120.

nor neutralize environmental threats. In the second and third rows, firms have resources and capabilities that are valuable as well as rare, respectively. However, in both cases the resources and capabilities are not difficult for competitors to imitate or substitute. Here, the firms could attain some level of competitive parity. They could perform on par with equally endowed rivals or attain a temporary competitive advantage. But their advantages would be easy for competitors to match. It is only in the fourth row, where all four criteria are satisfied, that competitive advantages can be sustained over time. Next, let's look at Dell and see how its competitive advantage, which seemed to be sustainable for a rather long period of time, has eroded.

Dell's Eroding (Sustainable?) Competitive Advantage In 1984, Michael Dell started Dell Inc. in a University of Texas dorm room with an investment of $1,000.[54] By 2006, Dell had attained annual revenues of $56 billion and a net income of $3.6 billion—making Michael Dell one of the richest people in the world. Dell achieved this meteoric growth by differentiating itself through the direct sales approach that it pioneered. Its user-configurable products met the diverse needs of its corporate and institutional customer base. Exhibit 3.8 summarizes how Dell achieved its remarkable success by integrating its tangible resources, intangible resources, and organizational capabilities.

Dell continued to maintain this competitive advantage by strengthening its value-chain activities and interrelationships that are critical to satisfying the largest market opportunities. It achieved this by (1) implementing e-commerce direct sales and sup port processes that accounted for the sophisticated buying habits of the largest markets and (2) matching its inventory management to its extensive supplier network. Dell also sustained these advantages by investing in intangible resources, such as proprietary assembly methods and packaging configurations, that helped to protect against the threat of imitation.

Dell recognized that the PC is a complex product with components sourced from several different technologies and manufacturers. Thus, in working backward from the customer's purchasing habits, Dell saw that the company could build valuable solutions by organizing its resources and capabilities around build-to-specification tastes, making both the sales and integration processes flexible, and passing on overhead expenses to its suppliers. Even as the PC industry became further commoditized, Dell was one of the few competitors that was able to retain solid margins. It accomplished this by adapting its manufacturing and assembly capabilities to match the PC market's trend toward user compatibility.

For many years, it looked as if Dell's competitive advantage over its rivals would be sustainable for a very long period of time. However, by early 2007, Dell began falling behind its rivals in market share. This led to a significant decline in its stock price—followed by a complete shake-up of the top management team.

EXHIBIT 3.8 Dell's Tangible Resources, Intangible Resources, and Organizational Capabilities

Inder Sidhu, the author of *Doing Both* (2010), provides a succinct summary of the central lesson in the Dell story:[55]

> Dell illustrates what can happen when a company emphasizes optimization to the exclusion of reinvention. Dell's obsession with operational excellence prevented it from delivering innovations that the market wanted, costing it a great deal of goodwill and prestige. When *Fortune* announced its annual list of "Most Admired Companies" in 2009, Dell, the leader from just four years prior, wasn't even mentioned in the top 50.

Not surprisingly, Dell's performance has sagged in recent years. Although its revenues slightly increased from $56 billion to $62 billion between 2006 and 2012, its net income was flat during the same period at about $3.5 billion and, more importantly, its market capitalization dropped about 75 percent from $64 billion to $16 billion.

The Generation and Distribution of a Firm's Profits: Extending the Resource-Based View of the Firm

The resource-based view of the firm is useful in determining when firms will create competitive advantages and enjoy high levels of profitability. However, it has not been developed to address how a firm's profits (often referred to as "rents" by economists) will be distributed to a firm's management and employees or other stakeholders such as customers, suppliers, or governments.[56] This is an important issue because firms may be successful in creating competitive advantages that can be sustainable for a period of time. However, much of the profits can be retained (or "appropriated") by its employees and managers or other stakeholders instead of flowing to the firm's owners (i.e., the stockholders).*

Consider Viewpoint DataLabs International, a Salt Lake City–based company that makes sophisticated three-dimensional models and textures for film production houses, video games, and car manufacturers. This example will help to show how employees are often able to obtain (or "appropriate") a high proportion of a firm's profits:

---

*Economists define rents as profits (or prices) in excess of what is required to provide a normal return.

Walter Noot, head of production, was having trouble keeping his highly skilled Generation X employees happy with their compensation. Each time one of them was lured away for more money, everyone would want a raise. "We were having to give out raises every six months—30 to 40 percent—then six months later they'd expect the same. It was a big struggle to keep people happy."[57]

Here, much of the profits are being generated by the highly skilled professionals working together. They are able to exercise their power by successfully demanding more financial compensation. In part, management has responded favorably because they are united in their demands, and their work involves a certain amount of social complexity and causal ambiguity—given the complex, coordinated efforts that their work entails.

Four factors help explain the extent to which employees and managers will be able to obtain a proportionately high level of the profits that they generate:[58]

- *Employee Bargaining Power.* If employees are vital to forming a firm's unique capability, they will earn disproportionately high wages. For example, marketing professionals may have access to valuable information that helps them to understand the intricacies of customer demands and expectations, or engineers may understand unique technical aspects of the products or services. Additionally, in some industries such as consulting, advertising, and tax preparation, clients tend to be very loyal to individual professionals employed by the firm, instead of to the firm itself. This enables them to "take the clients with them" if they leave. This enhances their bargaining power.

- *Employee Replacement Cost.* If employees' skills are idiosyncratic and rare (a source of resource-based advantages), they should have high bargaining power based on the high cost required by the firm to replace them. For example, Raymond Ozzie, the software designer who was critical in the development of Lotus Notes, was able to dictate the terms under which IBM acquired Lotus.

- *Employee Exit Costs.* This factor may tend to reduce an employee's bargaining power. An individual may face high personal costs when leaving the organization. Thus, that individual's threat of leaving may not be credible. In addition, an employee's expertise may be firm-specific and of limited value to other firms.

- *Manager Bargaining Power.* Managers' power is based on how well they create resource-based advantages. They are generally charged with creating value through the process of organizing, coordinating, and leveraging employees as well as other forms of capital such as plant, equipment, and financial capital (addressed further in Chapter 4). Such activities provide managers with sources of information that may not be readily available to others.

Chapter 9 addresses the conditions under which top-level managers (such as CEOs) of large corporations have been, at times, able to obtain levels of total compensation that would appear to be significantly disproportionate to their contributions to wealth generation as well as to top executives in peer organizations. Here, corporate governance becomes a critical control mechanism. For example, consider Henry Silverman, Cendant's CEO.[59] His total compensation for the period from 2000 to 2006 was an astonishing $481 million. The longtime head of Cendant, a travel and real estate services giant, once so infuriated investors with his outsized option grants that in the early part of the decade the firm ended up settling a shareholder lawsuit that protested the size of his pay package. The shareholders certainly didn't fare as well as Silverman—a $100 investment in Cendant shares in 2000 would have been worth only $51 in 2006!

Such diversion of profits from the owners of the business to top management is far less likely when the board members are truly independent outsiders (i.e., they do not have close ties to management). In general, given the external market for top talent, the level of compensation that executives receive is based on factors similar to the ones just discussed that determine the level of their bargaining power.[60]

In addition to employees and managers, other stakeholder groups can also appropriate a portion of the rents generated by a firm. If, for example, a critical input is controlled by a monopoly supplier or if a single buyer accounts for most of a firm's sales, their bargaining power can greatly erode the potential profits of a firm. Similarly, excessive taxation by governments can also reduce what is available to a firm's stockholders.

Evaluating Firm Performance: Two Approaches

This section addresses two approaches to use when evaluating a firm's performance. The first is financial ratio analysis, which, generally speaking, identifies how a firm is performing according to its balance sheet, income statement, and market valuation. As we will discuss, when performing a financial ratio analysis, you must take into account the firm's performance from a historical perspective (not just at one point in time) as well as how it compares with both industry norms and key competitors.[61]

The second perspective takes a broader stakeholder view. Firms must satisfy a broad range of stakeholders, including employees, customers, and owners, to ensure their long-term viability. Central to our discussion will be a well-known approach—the balanced scorecard—that has been popularized by Robert Kaplan and David Norton.[62]

financial ratio analysis
a technique for measuring the performance of a firm according to its balance sheet, income statement, and market valuation.

Financial Ratio Analysis

The beginning point in analyzing the financial position of a firm is to compute and analyze five different types of financial ratios:

- Short-term solvency or liquidity
- Long-term solvency measures
- Asset management (or turnover)
- Profitability
- Market value

Exhibit 3.9 summarizes each of these five ratios.

Appendix 1 to Chapter 13 (the Case Analysis chapter) provides detailed definitions for and discussions of each of these types of ratios as well as examples of how each is calculated. Refer to pages 437 to 446.

A meaningful ratio analysis must go beyond the calculation and interpretation of financial ratios.[63] It must include how ratios change over time as well as how they are interrelated. For example, a firm that takes on too much long-term debt to finance operations will see an immediate impact on its indicators of long-term financial leverage. The additional debt will negatively affect the firm's short-term liquidity ratio (i.e., current and quick ratios) since the firm must pay interest and principal on the additional debt each year until it is retired. Additionally, the interest expenses deducted from revenues reduce the firm's profitability.

A firm's financial position should not be analyzed in isolation. Important reference points are needed. We will address some issues that must be taken into account to make financial analysis more meaningful: historical comparisons, comparisons with industry norms, and comparisons with key competitors.

LO3.6

The usefulness of financial ratio analysis, its inherent limitations, and how to make meaningful comparisons of performance across firms.

Historical Comparisons   When you evaluate a firm's financial performance, it is very useful to compare its financial position over time. This provides a means of evaluating trends. For example, Apple Inc. reported revenues of $157 billion and net income of $42 billion in 2012. Virtually all firms would be very happy with such remarkable financial success. These figures represent a stunning annual growth in revenue and net income of 140 percent and 198 percent, respectively, for the 2010 to 2012 time period. Had Apple's revenues and net income in 2012 been $80 billion and $20 billion, respectively, it would still be a very large and highly profitable enterprise. However, such performance would have significantly damaged Apple's market valuation and reputation as well as the careers of many of its executives.

EXHIBIT 3.9 A Summary of Five Types of Financial Ratios

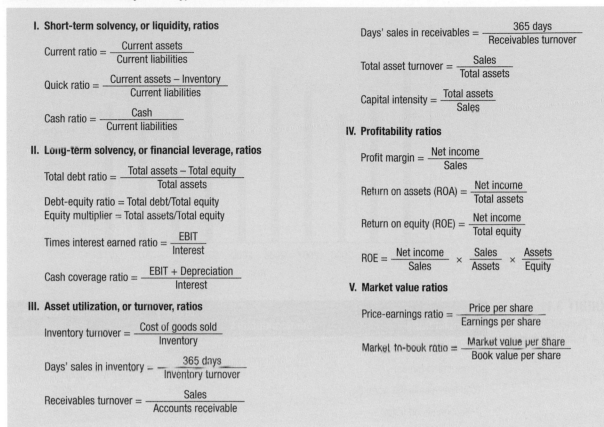

I. Short-term solvency, or liquidity, ratios

$$\text{Current ratio} = \frac{\text{Current assets}}{\text{Current liabilities}}$$

$$\text{Quick ratio} = \frac{\text{Current assets} - \text{Inventory}}{\text{Current liabilities}}$$

$$\text{Cash ratio} = \frac{\text{Cash}}{\text{Current liabilities}}$$

II. Long-term solvency, or financial leverage, ratios

$$\text{Total debt ratio} = \frac{\text{Total assets} - \text{Total equity}}{\text{Total assets}}$$

$$\text{Debt-equity ratio} = \text{Total debt/Total equity}$$

$$\text{Equity multiplier} = \text{Total assets/Total equity}$$

$$\text{Times interest earned ratio} = \frac{\text{EBIT}}{\text{Interest}}$$

$$\text{Cash coverage ratio} = \frac{\text{EBIT} + \text{Depreciation}}{\text{Interest}}$$

III. Asset utilization, or turnover, ratios

$$\text{Inventory turnover} = \frac{\text{Cost of goods sold}}{\text{Inventory}}$$

$$\text{Days' sales in inventory} = \frac{365 \text{ days}}{\text{Inventory turnover}}$$

$$\text{Receivables turnover} = \frac{\text{Sales}}{\text{Accounts receivable}}$$

$$\text{Days' sales in receivables} = \frac{365 \text{ days}}{\text{Receivables turnover}}$$

$$\text{Total asset turnover} = \frac{\text{Sales}}{\text{Total assets}}$$

$$\text{Capital intensity} = \frac{\text{Total assets}}{\text{Sales}}$$

IV. Profitability ratios

$$\text{Profit margin} = \frac{\text{Net income}}{\text{Sales}}$$

$$\text{Return on assets (ROA)} = \frac{\text{Net income}}{\text{Total assets}}$$

$$\text{Return on equity (ROE)} = \frac{\text{Net income}}{\text{Total equity}}$$

$$\text{ROE} = \frac{\text{Net income}}{\text{Sales}} \times \frac{\text{Sales}}{\text{Assets}} \times \frac{\text{Assets}}{\text{Equity}}$$

V. Market value ratios

$$\text{Price-earnings ratio} = \frac{\text{Price per share}}{\text{Earnings per share}}$$

$$\text{Market-to-book ratio} = \frac{\text{Market value per share}}{\text{Book value per share}}$$

Exhibit 3.10 illustrates a 10-year period of return on sales (ROS) for a hypothetical company. As indicated by the dotted trend lines, the rate of growth (or decline) differs substantially over time periods.

Comparison with Industry Norms   When you are evaluating a firm's financial performance, remember also to compare it with industry norms. A firm's current ratio or profitability may appear impressive at first glance. However, it may pale when compared with industry standards or norms.

Comparing your firm with all other firms in your industry assesses relative performance. Banks often use such comparisons when evaluating a firm's creditworthiness. Exhibit 3.11 includes a variety of financial ratios for three industries: semiconductors, grocery stores, and skilled-nursing facilities. Why is there such variation among the financial ratios for these three industries? There are several reasons. With regard to the collection period, grocery stores operate mostly on a cash basis, hence a very short collection period. Semiconductor manufacturers sell their output to other manufacturers (e.g., computer makers) on terms such as 2/15 net 45, which means they give a 2 percent discount on bills paid within 15 days and start charging interest after 45 days. Skilled-nursing facilities also have a longer collection period than grocery stores because they typically rely on payments from insurance companies.

The industry norms for return on sales also highlight differences among these industries. Grocers, with very slim margins, have a lower return on sales than either skilled-nursing facilities or semiconductor manufacturers. But how might we explain the differences between skilled-nursing facilities and semiconductor manufacturers? Health care facilities, in general, are limited in their pricing structures by Medicare/Medicaid regulations and

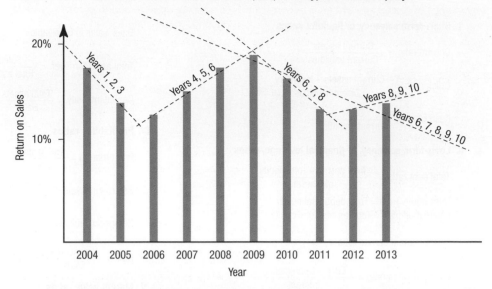

EXHIBIT 3.10 Historical Trends: Return on Sales (ROS) for a Hypothetical Company

EXHIBIT 3.11

How Financial Ratios Differ across Industries

Financial Ratio	Semiconductors	Grocery Stores	Skilled-Nursing Facilities
Quick ratio (times)	1.9	0.6	1.3
Current ratio (times)	3.6	1.7	1.7
Total liabilities to net worth (%)	35.1	72.7	82.5
Collection period (days)	48.6	3.3	36.5
Assets to sales (%)	131.7	22.1	58.3
Return on sales (%)	24	1.1	3.1

Source: Dun & Bradstreet. *Industry Norms and Key Business Ratios, 2010–2011.* One Year Edition, SIC #3600–3699 (Semiconductors); SIC #5400–5499 (Grocery Stores); SIC #8000–8099 (Skilled-Nursing Facilities). New York: Dun & Bradstreet Credit Services.

by insurance reimbursement limits, but semiconductor producers have pricing structures determined by the market. If their products have superior performance, semiconductor manufacturers can charge premium prices.

Comparison with Key Competitors   Recall from Chapter 2 that firms with similar strategies are members of a strategic group in an industry. Furthermore, competition is more intense among competitors within groups than across groups. Thus, you can gain valuable insights into a firm's financial and competitive position if you make comparisons between a firm and its most direct rivals. Consider a firm trying to diversify into the highly profitable pharmaceutical industry. Even if it was willing to invest several hundred million dollars, it would be virtually impossible to compete effectively against industry giants such as Pfizer and Merck. These two firms have 2012 revenues of $60 billion and $47 billion, respectively, and both had R&D budgets of $8 billion.[64]

Integrating Financial Analysis and Stakeholder Perspectives: The Balanced Scorecard

It is useful to see how a firm performs over time in terms of several ratios. However, such traditional approaches can be a double-edged sword.[65] Many important transactions—investments in research and development, employee training and development, and, advertising and promotion of key brands—may greatly expand a firm's market potential and create significant long-term shareholder value. But such critical investments are not reflected positively in short-term financial reports. Financial reports typically measure expenses, not the value created. Thus, managers may be penalized for spending money in the short term to improve their firm's long-term competitive viability!

Now consider the other side of the coin. A manager may destroy the firm's future value by dissatisfying customers, depleting the firm's stock of good products coming out of R&D, or damaging the morale of valued employees. Such budget cuts, however, may lead to very good short-term financials. The manager may look good in the short run and even receive credit for improving the firm's performance. In essence, such a manager has mastered "denominator management," whereby decreasing investments makes the return on investment (ROI) ratio larger, even though the actual return remains constant or shrinks.

The Balanced Scorecard: Description and Benefits   To provide a meaningful integration of the many issues that come into evaluating a firm's performance, Kaplan and Norton developed a **"balanced scorecard."**[66] This provides top managers with a fast but comprehensive view of the business. In a nutshell, it includes financial measures that reflect the results of actions already taken, but it complements these indicators with measures of customer satisfaction, internal processes, and the organization's innovation and improvement activities—operational measures that drive future financial performance.

The balanced scorecard enables managers to consider their business from four key perspectives: customer, internal, innovation and learning, and financial. These are briefly described in Exhibit 3.12.

Customer Perspective   Clearly, how a company is performing from its customers' perspective is a top priority for management. The balanced scorecard requires that managers translate their general mission statements on customer service into specific measures that reflect the factors that really matter to customers. For the balanced scorecard to work, managers must articulate goals for four key categories of customer concerns: time, quality, performance and service, and cost.

Internal Business Perspective   Customer-based measures are important. However, they must be translated into indicators of what the firm must do internally to meet customers' expectations. Excellent customer performance results from processes, decisions, and actions that occur throughout organizations in a coordinated fashion, and managers must focus on those critical internal operations that enable them to satisfy customer needs. The internal measures should reflect business processes that have the greatest impact on customer satisfaction. These include factors that affect cycle time, quality, employee skills, and productivity.

Innovation and Learning Perspective   Given the rapid rate of markets, technologies, and global competition, the criteria for success are constantly changing. To survive and prosper, managers must make frequent changes to existing products and services as well as introduce entirely new products with expanded capabilities. A firm's ability to do well from an innovation and learning perspective is more dependent on its intangible than tangible assets. Three categories of intangible assets are critically important: human capital (skills, talent, and knowledge), information capital (information systems, networks), and organization capital (culture, leadership).

- How do customers see us? (customer perspective)
- What must we excel at? (internal business perspective)
- Can we continue to improve and create value? (innovation and learning perspective)
- How do we look to shareholders? (financial perspective)

balanced scorecard
a method of evaluating a firm's performance using performance measures from the customers', internal, innovation and learning, and financial perspectives.

customer perspective
measures of firm performance that indicate how well firms are satisfying customers' expectations.

internal business perspective
measures of firm performance that indicate how well firms' internal processes, decisions and actions are contributing to customer satisfaction.

innovation and learning perspective
measures of firm performance that indicate how well firms are changing their product and service offerings to adapt to changes in the internal and external environments.

EXHIBIT 3.12
The Balanced Scorecard's Four Perspectives

Financial Perspective   Measures of financial performance indicate whether the company's strategy, implementation, and execution are indeed contributing to bottom-line improvement. Typical financial goals include profitability, growth, and shareholder value. Periodic financial statements remind managers that improved quality, response time, productivity, and innovative products benefit the firm only when they result in improved sales, increased market share, reduced operating expenses, or higher asset turnover.[67]

Consider how Sears, the huge retailer, found a strong causal relationship between employee attitudes, customer attitudes, and financial outcomes.[68] Through an ongoing study, Sears developed what it calls its total performance indicators, or TPI—a set of indicators for assessing their performance with customers, employees, and investors. Sears's quantitative model has shown that a 5.0 percent improvement in employee attitudes leads to a 1.3 percent improvement in customer satisfaction, which in turn drives a 0.5 percent improvement in revenue. Thus, if a single store improved its employee attitude by 5.0 percent, Sears could predict with confidence that if the revenue growth in the district as a whole were 5.0 percent, the revenue growth in this particular store would be 5.5 percent. Interestingly, Sears's managers consider such numbers as rigorous as any others that they work with every year. The company's accounting firm audits management as closely as it audits the financial statements.

A key implication is that managers do not need to look at their job as balancing stakeholder demands. They must avoid the following mind-set: "How many units in employee satisfaction do I have to give up to get some additional units of customer satisfaction or profits?" Instead, the balanced scorecard provides a win–win approach—increasing satisfaction among a wide variety of organizational stakeholders, including employees (at all levels), customers, and stockholders.

Limitations and Potential Downsides of the Balanced Scorecard   There is general agreement that there is nothing inherently wrong with the concept of the balanced scorecard.[69] The key limitation is that some executives may view it as a "quick fix" that can be easily installed. If managers do not recognize this from the beginning and fail to commit to it long term, the organization will be disappointed. Poor execution becomes the cause of such performance outcomes. And organizational scorecards must be aligned with individuals' scorecards to turn the balanced scorecards into a powerful tool for sustained performance.

In a recent study of 50 Canadian medium-size and large organizations, the number of users expressing skepticism about scorecard performance was much greater than the number claiming positive results. A large number of respondents agreed with the statement "Balanced scorecards don't really work." Some representative comments included: "It became just a number-crunching exercise by accountants after the first year," "It is just the latest management fad and is already dropping lower on management's list of priorities as all fads eventually do," and "If scorecards are supposed to be a measurement tool, why is it so hard to measure their results?" There is much work to do before scorecards can become a viable framework to measure sustained strategic performance.

Problems often occur in the balanced scorecard implementation efforts when there is an insufficient commitment to learning and the inclusion of employees' personal ambitions. Without a set of rules for employees that address continuous process improvement and the personal improvement of individual employees, there will be limited employee buy-in and insufficient cultural change. Thus, many improvements may be temporary and superficial. Often, scorecards that failed to attain alignment and improvements dissipated very quickly. And, in many cases, management's efforts to improve performance were seen as divisive and were viewed by employees as aimed at benefiting senior management compensation. This fostered a "what's in it for me?" attitude.

The World Triathalon's Initiatives to Extend Its Brand

World Triathlon Corporation (WTC) is a Florida-based company known for recognizing athletic excellence and performance. It provides events, products, and services under the Ironman and Ironman 70.3* branded names. Since its inception, *Ironman* has been identified with ambitious and courageous individuals who aren't afraid to push their limits. Tapping into athletes' desires to pursue their dream of becoming an Ironman was a successful business strategy for WTC. Given the extreme physical challenge, disciplined training, and camaraderie it offered its clients, WTC was able to grow its revenues and profits over the years.

In 2008, Providence Equity Partners, a private equity firm, acquired WTC for an undisclosed amount. The new owners started expanding the exclusive branding of Ironman to products and events that clearly didn't represent the "spirit" of the brand. For example, those who finished Ironman 70.3 races were allowed to be called "Ironmen," regardless of the shorter length and lesser degree of difficulty. Additionally, products such as cologne, mattresses, and strollers were branded with "Ironman." In October 2010, Ironman Access was launched as a membership program wherein individuals could get preferential registration access to Ironman events for a $1,000 annual fee. The response by the triathlete community was quick and decisive—and overwhelming negative. The athletes felt that WTC was losing its values in its pursuit of more profits. The company was trying to expand the brand, but it was alienating its base.

*Ironman 70.3 is the half triathlon; the number refers to the total distance in miles covered in the race—1.2 mile swim, 56 mile bike ride, and 13.1 mile run.

Discussion Questions

1. What actions should WTC take?
2. Is the World Triathlon Corporation acting too aggressively in trying to monetize the brand?
3. What are the long-term implications of their recent strategic actions?

Sources: Beartini, M. & Gourville, J.T. 2012. Pricing to create share value. *Harvard Business Review*, 90 (6): 96–104; and WTC. 2012. Corporate info. *www.ironman.com*, January 12: np.

Reflecting on Career Implications . . .

- **The Value Chain:** It is important that you develop an understanding of your firm's value chain. What activities are most critical for attaining competitive advantage? Think of ways in which you can add value in your firm's value chain. How might your firm's support activities (e.g., information technology, human resource practices) help you accomplish your assigned tasks more effectively? How will you bring your value-added contribution to the attention of your superiors?

- **The Value Chain:** Consider the most important linkages between the activities you perform in your organization with other activities both within your firm as well as between your firm and its suppliers, customers, and alliance partners. Understanding and strengthening these linkages can contribute greatly to your career advancement within your current organization.

- **Resource-Based View of the Firm:** Are your skills and talents rare, valuable, difficult to imitate, and have few substitutes? If so, you are in the better position to add value for your firm—and earn rewards and incentives. How can your skills and talents be enhanced to help satisfy these criteria to a greater extent? More training? Change positions within the firm? Consider career options at other organizations?

- **Balanced Scorecard:** Can you design a "balanced scorecard" for your life? What would be the perspectives that you will include in it? In what ways would such a "balanced scorecard" help you attain success in life?

summary

In the traditional approaches to assessing a firm's internal environment, the primary goal of managers would be to determine their firm's relative strengths and weaknesses. Such is the role of SWOT analysis, wherein managers analyze their firm's strengths and weaknesses as well as the opportunities and threats in the external environment. In this chapter, we discussed why this may be a good starting point but hardly the best approach to take in performing a sound analysis. There are many limitations to SWOT analysis, including its static perspective, its potential to overemphasize a single dimension of a firm's strategy, and the likelihood that a firm's strengths do not necessarily help the firm create value or competitive advantages.

We identified two frameworks that serve to complement SWOT analysis in assessing a firm's internal environment: value-chain analysis and the resource-based view of the firm. In conducting a value-chain analysis, first divide the firm into a series of value-creating activities. These include primary activities such as inbound logistics, operations, and service as well as support activities such as procurement and human resources management. Then analyze how each activity adds value as well as how *interrelationships* among value activities in the firm and among the firm and its customers and suppliers add value. Thus, instead of merely determining a firm's strengths and weaknesses per se, you analyze them in the overall context of the firm and its relationships with customers and suppliers—the value system.

The resource-based view of the firm considers the firm as a bundle of resources: tangible resources, intangible resources, and organizational capabilities. Competitive advantages that are sustainable over time generally arise from the creation of bundles of resources and capabilities. For advantages to be sustainable, four criteria must be satisfied: value, rarity, difficulty in imitation, and difficulty in substitution. Such an evaluation requires a sound knowledge of the competitive context in which the firm exists. The owners of a business may not capture all of the value created by the firm. The appropriation of value created by a firm between the owners and employees is determined by four factors: employee bargaining power, replacement cost, employee exit costs, and manager bargaining power.

An internal analysis of the firm would not be complete unless you evaluate its performance and make the appropriate comparisons. Determining a firm's performance requires an analysis of its financial situation as well as a review of how well it is satisfying a broad range of stakeholders, including customers, employees, and stockholders. We discussed the concept of the balanced scorecard, in which four perspectives must be addressed: customer, internal business, innovation and learning, and financial. Central to this concept is the idea that the interests of various stakeholders can be interrelated. We provide examples of how indicators of employee satisfaction lead to higher levels of customer satisfaction, which in turn lead to higher levels of financial performance. Thus, improving a firm's performance does not need to involve making trade-offs among different stakeholders. Assessing the firm's performance is also more useful if it is evaluated in terms of how it changes over time, compares with industry norms, and compares with key competitors.

SUMMARY REVIEW QUESTIONS

1. SWOT analysis is a technique to analyze the internal and external environment of a firm. What are its advantages and disadvantages?

2. Briefly describe the primary and support activities in a firm's value chain.

3. How can managers create value by establishing important relationships among the value-chain activities both within their firm and between the firm and its customers and suppliers?

4. Briefly explain the four criteria for sustainability of competitive advantages.

5. Under what conditions are employees and managers able to appropriate some of the value created by their firm?

6. What are the advantages and disadvantages of conducting a financial ratio analysis of a firm?

7. Summarize the concept of the balanced scorecard. What are its main advantages?

key terms

value-chain analysis 72
primary activities 72
support activities 72
inbound logistics 74
operations 75
outbound logistics 75
marketing and sales 75
service 76
procurement 76
technology
  development 78
human resource
  management 78
general administration 79

interrelationships 80
resource-based view
  of the firm 82
tangible resources 83
intangible resources 84
organizational
  capabilities 84
path dependency 86
causal ambiguity 87
social complexity 87
financial ratio
  analysis 92
balanced scorecard 95
customer perspective 95
internal perspective 95
innovation and learning
  perspective 95
financial perspective 96

experiential exercise

Caterpillar is a leading firm in the construction and mining equipment industry with extensive global operations. It has approximately 130,000 employees, and its revenues were $67 billion in 2012. In addition to its manufacturing and logistics operations, Caterpillar is well-known for its superb service and parts supply, and it provides retail financing for its equipment.

Below, we address several questions that focus on Caterpillar's value-chain activities and the interrelationships among them as well as whether or not the firm is able to attain sustainable competitive advantage(s).

1. Where in Caterpillar's value chain are they creating value for their customer?

Value-Chain Activity	Yes/No	How Does Caterpillar Create Value for the Customer?
Primary:		
Inbound logistics		
Operations		
Outbound logistics		
Marketing and sales		
Service		
Support:		
Procurement		
Technology development		
Human resource management		
General administration		

2. What are the important relationships among Caterpillar's value-chain activities? What are the important interdependencies? For each activity, identify the relationships and interdependencies.

	Inbound logistics	Operations	Outbound logistics	Marketing and sales	Service	Procurement	Technology development	Human resource management	General administration
Inbound logistics									
Operations									
Outbound logistics									
Marketing and sales									
Service									
Procurement									
Technology development									
Human resource management									
General administration									

3. What resources, activities, and relationships enable Caterpillar to achieve a sustainable competitive advantage?

Resource/Activity	Is It Valuable?	Is It Rare?	Are There Few Substitutes?	Is It Difficult to Make?
Inbound logistics				
Operations				
Outbound logistics				
Marketing and sales				
Service				
Procurement				
Technology development				
Human resource management				
General administration				

application questions & exercises

1. Using published reports, select two CEOs who have recently made public statements regarding a major change in their firm's strategy. Discuss how the successful implementation of such strategies requires changes in the firm's primary and support activities.

2. Select a firm that competes in an industry in which you are interested. Drawing upon published financial reports, complete a financial ratio analysis. Based on changes over time and a comparison with industry norms, evaluate the firm's strengths and weaknesses in terms of its financial position.

3. How might exemplary human resource practices enhance and strengthen a firm's value-chain activities?

4. Using the Internet, look up your university or college. What are some of its key value-creating activities that provide competitive advantages? Why?

ethics questions

1. What are some of the ethical issues that arise when a firm becomes overly zealous in advertising its products?

2. What are some of the ethical issues that may arise from a firm's procurement activities? Are you aware of any of these issues from your personal experience or businesses you are familiar with?

references

1. Reiter, C. 2012. BMW's Mini: Little but she is fierce!. *Bloomberg BusinessWeek,* February 6–12: 24–25. Cain, T. 2012. Smart fortwo sales figures. *www.GoodCarBadCar.net,* January: np. De Paula, M. 2012. How Smart's CEO plans to get its mojo back. *www.Forbes.com,* May 15: np. Levin, D. 2011. US sales of Smart cars hit wall. *www.money.cnn .com,* February 18: np. Smart USA. 2013. About us. *www.smartusa.com,* January: np.

2. Our discussion of the value chain will draw on Porter, M. E. 1985. *Competitive advantage:* chap. 2. New York: Free Press.

3. Dyer, J. H. 1996. Specialized supplier networks as a source of competitive advantage: Evidence from the auto industry. *Strategic Management Journal,* 17: 271–291.

4. For an insightful perspective on value-chain analysis, refer to Stabell, C. B. & Fjeldstad, O. D. 1998. Configuring value for competitive advantage: On chains, shops, and networks. *Strategic Management Journal,* 19: 413–437. The authors develop concepts of value chains, value shops, and value networks to extend the value-creation logic across a broad range of industries. Their work builds on the seminal contributions of Porter, 1985, op. cit., and others who have addressed how firms create value through key interrelationships among value-creating activities.

5. Ibid.

6. Maynard, M. 1999. Toyota promises custom order in 5 days. *USA Today,* August 6: B1.

7. Shaw Industries. 1999. Annual report: 14–15.

8. Fisher, M. L. 1997. What is the right supply chain for your product? *Harvard Business Review,* 75(2): 105–116.

9. Jackson. M. 2001. Bringing a dying brand back to life. *Harvard Business Review,* 79(5): 53–61.

10. Anderson, J. C. & Nmarus, J. A. 2003. Selectively pursuing more of your customer's business. *MIT Sloan Management Review,* 44(3): 42–50.

11. Insights on advertising are addressed in: Rayport, J. F. 2008. Where is advertising? Into 'stitials. *Harvard Business Review,* 66(5): 18–20.

12. Reiter, C. 2011. BMW gets its close-up, at Audi's expense. *Bloomberg BusinessWeek,* December 19–December 25: 24–25.

13. Haddad, C. & Grow, B. 2001. Wait a second—I didn't order that! *BusinessWeek,* July 16: 45.

14. For a scholarly discussion on the procurement of technology components, read Hoetker, G. 2005. How much you know versus how well I know you: Selecting a supplier for a technically innovative component. *Strategic Management Journal,* 26(1): 75–96.

15. For a discussion on criteria to use when screening suppliers for back-office functions, read Feeny, D., Lacity, M., & Willcocks, L. P. 2005. Taking the measure of outsourcing providers. *MIT Sloan Management Review,* 46(3): 41–48.

16. For a study investigating sourcing practices, refer to: Safizadeh, M. H., Field, J. M., & Ritzman, L. P. 2008. Sourcing practices and boundaries of the firm in the financial services industry. *Strategic Management Journal,* 29(1): 79–92.

17. Imperato, G. 1998. How to give good feedback. *Fast Company,* September: 144–156.

18. Bensaou, B. M. & Earl, M. 1998. The right mindset for managing information technology. *Harvard Business Review,* 96(5): 118–128.

19. A discussion of R&D in the pharmaceutical industry is in: Garnier, J-P. 2008. Rebuilding the R&D engine in big pharma. *Harvard Business Review,* 66(5): 68–76.

20. Donlon, J. P. 2000. Bonsignore's bid for the big time. *Chief Executive,* March: 28–37.

21. Ulrich, D. 1998. A new mandate for human resources. *Harvard Business Review,* 96(1): 124–134.

22. A study of human resource management in China is: Li, J., Lam, K., Sun, J. J. M., & Liu, S. X. Y. 2008. Strategic resource management, institutionalization, and employment modes: An empirical study in China. *Strategic Management Journal,* 29(3): 337–342.

23. Wood, J. 2003. Sharing jobs and working from home: The new face of the airline industry. AviationCareer. net, February 21.

24. Green, S., Hasan, F., Immelt, J. Marks, M., & Meiland, D. 2003. In search of global leaders. *Harvard Business Review,* 81(8): 38–45.

25. For insights on the role of information systems integration in fostering innovation refer to: Cash, J. I. Jr., Earl, M. J., & Morison, R. 2008. Teaming up to crack

innovation and enterprise integration. *Harvard Business Review,* 66(11): 90–100.

26. For a cautionary note on the use of IT, refer to McAfee, A. 2003. When too much IT knowledge is a dangerous thing. *MIT Sloan Management Review,* 44(2): 83–90.

27. For an interesting perspective on some of the potential downsides of close customer and supplier relationships, refer to Anderson, E. & Jap, S. D. 2005. The dark side of close relationships. *MIT Sloan Management Review,* 46(3): 75–82.

28. Day, G. S. 2003. Creating a superior customer-relating capability. *MIT Sloan Management Review,* 44(3): 77–82.

29. To gain insights on the role of electronic technologies in enhancing a firm's connections to outside suppliers and customers, refer to Lawrence, T. B., Morse, E. A., & Fowler, S. W. 2005. Managing your portfolio of connections. *MIT Sloan Management Review,* 46(2): 59–66.

30. This section draws on Andersen, M. M., Froholdt, M. & Poulfelt, F. 2010. *Return on strategy.* New York: Routledge: 96–100.

31. Quote from Hartmut Jenner, CEO, Alfred Karcher GmbH, IBM Global CEO Study, P. 27.

32. Collis, D. J. & Montgomery, C. A. 1995. Competing on resources: Strategy in the 1990's. *Harvard Business Review,* 73(4): 119–128; and Barney, J. 1991. Firm resources and sustained competitive advantage. *Journal of Management,* 17(1): 99–120.

33. For recent critiques of the resource-based view of the firm, refer to: Sirmon, D. G., Hitt, M. A., & Ireland, R. D. 2007. Managing firm resources in dynamic environments to create value: Looking inside the black box. *Academy of Management Review,* 32(1): 273–292; and Newbert, S. L. Empirical research on the resource-based view of the firm: An assessment and suggestions for future research. *Strategic Management Journal,* 28(2): 121–146.

34. Henkoff, R. 1993. Companies that train the best. *Fortune,* March 22: 83; and Dess & Picken, *Beyond productivity,* p. 98.

35. Gaines-Ross, L. 2010. Reputation warfare. *Harvard Business Review,* 88(12): 70–76.

36. Barney, J. B. 1986. Types of competition and the theory of strategy: Towards an integrative

framework. *Academy of Management Review,* 11(4): 791–800.

37. Harley-Davidson. 1993. Annual report.

38. Stetler, B. 2008. Griping online? Comcast hears and talks back. *nytimes.com,* July 25: np.

39. For a rigorous, academic treatment of the origin of capabilities, refer to Ethiraj, S. K., Kale, P., Krishnan, M. S., & Singh, J. V. 2005. Where do capabilities come from and how do they matter? A study of the software services industry. *Strategic Management Journal,* 26(1): 25–46.

40. For an academic discussion on methods associated with organizational capabilities, refer to Dutta, S., Narasimhan, O., & Rajiv, S. 2005. Conceptualizing and measuring capabilities: Methodology and empirical application. *Strategic Management Journal,* 26(3): 277–286.

41. Lorenzoni, G. & Lipparini, A. 1999. The leveraging of interfirm relationships as a distinctive organizational capability: A longitudinal study. *Strategic Management Journal,* 20: 317–338.

42. Andersen, M. M. op. cit. 209.

43. A study investigating the sustainability of competitive advantage is: Newbert, S. L. 2008. Value, rareness, competitive advantages, and performance: A conceptual-level empirical investigation of the resource-based view of the firm. *Strategic Management Journal,* 29(7): 745–768.

44. Arikan, A. M. & McGahan, A. M. 2010. The development of capabilities in new firms. *Strategic Management Journal,* 31(1): 1–18.

45. Barney, J. 1991. Firm resources and sustained competitive advantage. *Journal of Management,* 17(1): 99–120.

46. Barney, 1986, op. cit. Our discussion of inimitability and substitution draws upon this source.

47. A study that investigates the performance implications of imitation is: Ethiraj, S. K. & Zhu, D. H. 2008. Performance effects of imitative entry. *Strategic Management Journal,* 29(8): 797–818.

48. Sirmon, D. G., Hitt, M. A., Arregale, J.-L. & Campbell, J. T. 2010. The dynamic interplay of capability strengths and weaknesses: Investigating the bases of temporary competitive advantage. *Strategic*

Management Journal, 31(13): 1386–1409.

49. Scherzer, L. 2012. Groupon and deal sites see skepticism replacing promise. *finance.yahoo.com,* November 30: np; The dismal scoop on Goupon. 2011. *The Economist,* October 22: 81; Slater, D. 2012. Are daily deals done? *Fast Company;* and Danna, D. 2012. Groupon & daily deals competition. *beta.fool.com,* June 15: np.

50. Deephouse, D. L. 1999. To be different, or to be the same? It's a question (and theory) of strategic balance. *Strategic Management Journal,* 20: 147–166.

51. 2010. Wahaha . . . China's leading beverage producer. *www.chinabevnews.com,* April 11: np; and Anderson, M. M., Frohldt, M. & Pouflet, F. 2010. *Return to strategy.* New York: Routledge.

52. Yeoh, P. L. & Roth, K. 1999. An empirical analysis of sustained advantage in the U.S. pharmaceutical industry: Impact of firm resources and capabilities. *Strategic Management Journal,* 20: 637–653.

53. Robins, J. A. & Wiersema, M. F. 2000. Strategies for unstructured competitive environments: Using scarce resources to create new markets. In Bresser, R. F., et al., (Eds.), *Winning strategies in a deconstructing world:* 201–220. New York: John Wiley.

54. For an insightful case on how Dell was able to build its seemingly sustainable competitive advantage in the marketplace, refer to "Matching Dell" by Jan W. Rivkin and Michael E. Porter, Harvard Business School Case 9-799-158 (June 6, 1999).

55. Sidhu, I. op. cit., 61

56. Amit, R. & Schoemaker, J. H. 1993. Strategic assets and organizational rent. *Strategic Management Journal,* 14(1): 33–46; Collis, D. J. & Montgomery, C. A. 1995. Competing on resources: Strategy in the 1990's. *Harvard Business Review,* 73(4): 118–128; Coff, R. W. 1999. When competitive advantage doesn't lead to performance: The resource-based view and stakeholder bargaining power. *Organization Science,* 10(2): 119–133; and Blyler, M. & Coff, R. W. 2003. Dynamic capabilities, social capital, and rent appropriation: Ties that split pies. *Strategic Management Journal,* 24: 677–686.

57. Munk, N. 1998. The new organization man. *Fortune,* March 16: 62–74.

58. Coff, op. cit.

59. Adams, R. 2012. The decade's 10 best-paid CEOs. *Newsoxy.com,* June 7: np.

60. We have focused our discussion on how internal stakeholders (e.g., employees, managers, and top executives) may appropriate a firm's profits (or rents). For an interesting discussion of how a firm's innovations may be appropriated by external stakeholders (e.g., customers, suppliers) as well as competitors, refer to Grant, R. M. 2002. *Contemporary strategy analysis* (4th ed.): 335–340. Malden, MA: Blackwell.

61. Luehrman, T. A. 1997. What's it worth? A general manager's guide to valuation. *Harvard Business Review,* 45(3): 132–142.

62. See, for example, Kaplan, R. S. & Norton, D. P. 1992. The balanced scorecard: Measures that drive performance. *Harvard Business Review,* 69(1): 71–79.

63. Hitt, M. A., Ireland, R. D., & Stadter, G. 1982. Functional importance of company performance: Moderating effects of grand strategy and industry type. *Strategic Management Journal,* 3: 315–330.

64. *finance.yahoo.com.*

65. Kaplan & Norton, op. cit.

66. Ibid.

67. For a discussion of the relative value of growth versus increasing margins, read Mass, N. J. 2005. The relative value of growth. *Harvard Business Review,* 83(4): 102–112.

68. Rucci, A. J., Kirn, S. P., & Quinn, R. T. 1998. The employee-customer-profit chain at Sears. *Harvard Business Review,* 76(1): 82–97.

69. Our discussion draws upon: Angel, R. & Rampersad, H. 2005. Do scorecards add up? *camagazine.com.* May: np.; and Niven, P. 2002. *Balanced scorecard step by step: Maximizing performance and maintaining results.* New York: John Wiley & Sons.

chapter 4

Recognizing a Firm's Intellectual Assets

Moving beyond a Firm's Tangible Resources

After reading this chapter, you should have a good understanding of the following learning objectives:

LO4.1 Why the management of knowledge professionals and knowledge itself are so critical in today's organizations.

LO4.2 The importance of recognizing the interdependence of attracting, developing, and retaining human capital.

LO4.3 The key role of social capital in leveraging human capital within and across the firm.

LO4.4 The importance of social networks in knowledge management and in promoting career success.

LO4.5 The vital role of technology in leveraging knowledge and human capital.

LO4.6 Why "electronic" or "virtual" teams are critical in combining and leveraging knowledge in organizations and how they can be made more effective.

LO4.7 The challenge of protecting intellectual property and the importance of a firm's dynamic capabilities.

Learning from Mistakes

Yahoo buys Tumblr. Will corporate cultures collide or meld?

In May 2013, the CEO of Yahoo, Marissa Mayer acquired Tumblr for the pretty sum of $1.1 billion. Tumblr is a social micro blogging service with 300 million users, created by 26-year-old David Karp, a high school dropout, and it is very popular with young mobile users.

The question this raises is whether this acquisition will result in a culture clash or not. Unfortunately, Yahoo has a bad reputation for acquiring interesting young companies and then allowing them to die (Geocities, Flickr). However, Mayer addressed this issue straight away by writing on Yahoo's Tumblr "We promise not to screw it up." If Yahoo does not "screw it up" by neglecting or dismantling the company, Tumblr could be a wonderful platform for Yahoo's brand advertisers.

This deal is not about two tech companies merging together and using their strengths but about two very different ways of doing business being pitted against each other. One of the most pressing issues of this deal is what will become of each company's corporate culture. Yahoo

is a much older, more established, some say calcified corporate culture that has been short on innovation and creativity and user-focused designs and whose aim is to make money. Tumblr, on the other hand, is a young start up with a simple interface that allows all types of users to build a community however they want. Basically Tumblr is whatever its users want it to be and It is different for every user: that is why there are so many different communities on Tumblr and it has never made any money.

One of the major risks in strategic acquisitions is the loss of customers and the Tumblr community greeted the news of the merger with scorn. Some 300 million highly engaged young users are not easy to come by; 27 percent of the users are between 18 and 24 and 28 percent between 25 to 34 but young users are fickle when it comes to social networks and they hate aggressive advertising so Yahoo's heavy-handed techniques (banner ads, heavy branding) could alienate them.

Another major risk in strategic acquisitions is the inability to keep top talent in the acquired company because the corporate culture of the acquiring company is dramatically different. This has already occurred because just 11 days after its acquisition Tumblr lost its creative Director Jacob Bijani. In addition, Yahoo has a reputation of losing its best employees to rival firms. To prevent culture clash and key talent loss, it is important to consider corporate culture during due diligence and to ask important questions such as "Does the culture between the two companies match? Could two different cultures be sustained?" For the moment, Karp, who will get an estimated $220 million, will stay on in New York as CEO.

The web business is very different from other industries because there is a straight correlation between a company's ability to hire and keep key talent (this is one of the key challenges) and the quality of the product. Mayer is aware of this and in the year she has been at Yahoo the attrition rate has declined by nearly 60 percent and the number of former employees returning to Yahoo is increasing. In 2013, 12 percent of employees hired were former employees.

CEOs of tech businesses also have to create a good corporate culture. This does not mean that every company that has a great corporate culture is successful but research shows that tech firms with terrible corporate cultures are doomed. A necessary precondition of success is getting the culture right.

By Asha Moore-Mangin and Sarah Hudson

Discussion Questions

1. What are the main challenges facing Yahoo?
2. Do you think that the CEO of Yahoo will "screw it up"?

Managers are always looking for stellar professionals who can take their organizations to the next level. However, attracting talent is a necessary but *not* sufficient condition for success. In today's knowledge economy, it does not matter how big your stock of resources is—whether it be top talent, physical resources, or financial capital. Rather, the question becomes: How good is the organization at attracting top talent and leveraging that talent to produce a stream of products and services valued by the marketplace?

The opening case looks at how Yahoo, a company with a reputation for losing its best employees to rival firms, successfully managed its merger with Tumblr—an organization with a very different corporate culture. This was especially important for these two companies as in the web business, perhaps more so than in any other sector, the ability to hire and retain top talent is directly linked to the quality of the end product. For a technology company to succeed it has to manage its talent right.

In this chapter, we also address how human capital can be leveraged in an organization. We point out the important roles of social capital and technology.

The Central Role of Knowledge in Today's Economy

LO4.1

Why the management of knowledge professionals and knowledge itself are so critical in today's organizations.

Central to our discussion is an enormous change that has accelerated over the past few decades and its implications for the strategic management of organizations.[2] For most of the 20th century, managers focused on tangible resources such as land, equipment, and money as well as intangibles such as brands, image, and customer loyalty. Efforts were directed more toward the efficient allocation of labor and capital—the two traditional factors of production.

How times have changed. Today, more than 50 percent of the gross domestic product (GDP) in developed economies is knowledge-based; it is based on intellectual assets and intangible people skills.[3] In the U.S., intellectual and information processes create most of the value for firms in large service industries (e.g., software, medical care, communications, and education), which make up 77 percent of the U.S. GDP. In the manufacturing sector, intellectual activities like R&D, process design, product design, logistics, marketing, and technological innovation produce the preponderance of value added.[4] To drive home the point, Gary Hamel and the late C. K. Prahalad, two leading writers in strategic management state:

> The machine age was a physical world. It consisted of things. Companies made and distributed things (physical products). Management allocated things (capital budgets); management invested in things (plant and equipment).
>
> In the machine age, people were ancillary, and things were central. In the information age, things are ancillary, knowledge is central. A company's value derives not from things, but from knowledge, know-how, intellectual assets, competencies—all embedded in people.[5]

In the **knowledge economy,** wealth is increasingly created by effective management of knowledge workers instead of by the efficient control of physical and financial assets. The growing importance of knowledge, coupled with the move by labor markets to reward knowledge work, tells us that investing in a company is, in essence, buying a set of talents, capabilities, skills, and ideas—intellectual capital—not physical and financial resources.[6]

Let's provide a few examples. People don't buy Microsoft's stock because of its software factories; it doesn't own any. Rather, the value of Microsoft is bid up because it sets standards for personal-computing software, exploits the value of its name, and forges alliances with other companies. Similarly, Merck didn't become the "Most Admired" company, for seven consecutive years in *Fortune*'s annual survey, because it can manufacture pills, but because its scientists can discover medicines. P. Roy Vagelos, former CEO of Merck, the $47 billion pharmaceutical giant, during its long run atop the "Most Admired" survey, said, "A low-value product can be made by anyone anywhere. When you have knowledge no one else has access to—that's dynamite. We guard our research even more carefully than our financial assets."[7]

To apply some numbers to our arguments, let's ask, What's a company worth?[8] Start with the "big three" financial statements: income statement, balance sheet, and statement of cash flow. If these statements tell a story that investors find useful, then a company's market value* should roughly (but not precisely, because the market looks forward and the books look backward) be the same as the value that accountants ascribe to it—the book value of the firm. However, this is not the case. A study compared the market value with the book value of 3,500 U.S. companies over a period of two decades. In 1978 the two were similar: Book value was 95 percent of market value. However, market values and book values have diverged significantly. Within 20 years, the S&P industrials were—on average—trading at 2.2 times book value.[9] Robert A. Howell, an expert on the changing role of finance and accounting, muses, "The big three financial statements . . . are about as useful as an 80-year-old Los Angeles road map."

The gap between a firm's market value and book value is far greater for knowledge-intensive corporations than for firms with strategies based primarily on tangible assets.[10] Exhibit 4.1 shows the ratio of market-to-book value for some well-known companies. In firms where knowledge and the management of knowledge workers are relatively important contributors to developing products and services—and physical resources are less critical—the ratio of market-to-book value tends to be much higher.

As shown in Exhibit 4.1, firms such as Apple, Google, Microsoft, and Oracle have very high market value to book value ratios because of their high investment in knowledge resources and technological expertise. In contrast, firms in more traditional industry sectors such as Nucor and Southwest Airlines have relatively low market to book ratios. This reflects their greater investments in physical resources and lower investment in knowledge resources. A firm like Intel has a market to book value ratio that falls between the above two groups of firms. This is because their high level of investment in knowledge resources is matched by a correspondingly huge investment in plant and equipment. For example, Intel recently invested $3 billion to build a fabrication facility in Chandler, Arizona.[11]

Many writers have defined **intellectual capital** as the difference between a firm's market value and book value—that is, a measure of the value of a firm's intangible assets.[12] This broad definition includes assets such as reputation, employee loyalty and commitment,

knowledge economy an economy where wealth is created through the effective management of knowledge workers instead of by the efficient control of physical and financial assets.

intellectual capital the difference between the market value of the firm and the book value of the firm, including assets such as reputation, employee loyalty and commitment, customer relationships, company values, brand names, and the experience and skills of employees.

---

*The market value of a firm is equal to the value of a share of its common stock times the number of shares outstanding. The book value of a firm is primarily a measure of the value of its tangible assets. It can be calculated by the formula: total assets − total liabilities.

EXHIBIT 4.1

Ratio of Market Value to
Book Value for Selected
Companies

Company	Annual Sales ($ billions)	Market Value ($ billions)	Book Value ($ billions)	Ratio of Market to Book Value
Apple	157.0	510.0	117.2	4.4
Google	47.3	237.8	58.1	4.1
Oracle	37.1	162.4	44.1	3.7
Microsoft	73.7	229.4	66.4	3.5
Intel	53.8	106.1	45.9	2.3
Nucor	19.8	14.2	7.5	1.9
Southwest Airlines	17.0	7.9	6.9	1.1

Note: The data on market valuations are as of January 4, 2013. All other financial data are based on the most recently available balance sheets and income statements.

Source: *finance.yahoo.com.*

customer relationships, company values, brand names, and the experience and skills of employees.[13] Thus, simplifying, we have:

Intellectual capital = Market value of firm − Book value of the firm

How do companies create value in the knowledge-intensive economy? The general answer is to attract and leverage human capital effectively through mechanisms that create products and services of value over time.

human capital
the individual capabilities, knowledge, skills, and experience of a company's employees and managers.

First, **human capital** is the "*individual* capabilities, knowledge, skills, and experience of the company's employees and managers."[14] This knowledge is relevant to the task at hand, as well as the capacity to add to this reservoir of knowledge, skills, and experience through learning.[15]

social capital
the network of friendships and working relationships between talented people both inside and outside the organization.

Second, **social capital** is "the network of relationships that individuals have throughout the organization." Relationships are critical in sharing and leveraging knowledge and in acquiring resources.[16] Social capital can extend beyond the organizational boundaries to include relationships between the firm and its suppliers, customers, and alliance partners.[17]

explicit knowledge
knowledge that is codified, documented, easily reproduced, and widely distributed.

Third is the concept of "knowledge," which comes in two different forms. First, there is **explicit knowledge** that is codified, documented, easily reproduced, and widely distributed, such as engineering drawings, software code, and patents.[18] The other type of knowledge is **tacit knowledge.** That is in the minds of employees and is based on their experiences and backgrounds.[19] Tacit knowledge is shared only with the consent and participation of the individual.

tacit knowledge
knowledge that is in the minds of employees and is based on their experiences and backgrounds.

New knowledge is constantly created through the continual interaction of explicit and tacit knowledge. Consider, two software engineers working together on a computer code. The computer code is the explicit knowledge. By sharing ideas based on each individual's experience—that is, their tacit knowledge—they create new knowledge when they modify the code. Another important issue is the role of "socially complex processes," which include leadership, culture, and trust.[20] These processes play a central role in the creation of knowledge.[21] They represent the "glue" that holds the organization together and helps to create a working environment where individuals are more willing to share their ideas, work in teams, and, in the end, create products and services of value.[22]

Numerous books have been written on the subject of knowledge management and the central role that it has played in creating wealth in organizations and countries throughout the developed world.[23] Here, we focus on some of the key issues that organizations must address to compete through knowledge.

We will now turn our discussion to the central resource itself—human capital—and some guidelines on how it can be attracted/selected, developed, and retained.[24] Tom Stewart, former editor of the *Harvard Business Review,* noted that organizations must also undergo significant efforts to protect their human capital. A firm may "diversify the ownership of vital knowledge by emphasizing teamwork, guard against obsolescence by developing learning programs, and shackle key people with golden handcuffs."[25] In addition, people are less likely to leave an organization if there are effective structures to promote teamwork and information sharing, strong leadership that encourages innovation, and cultures that demand excellence and ethical behavior. Such issues are central to this chapter. Although we touch on these issues throughout this chapter, we provide more detail in later chapters. We discuss organizational controls (culture, rewards, and boundaries) in Chapter 9, organization structure and design in Chapter 10, and a variety of leadership and entrepreneurship topics in Chapters 11 and 12.

Human Capital: The Foundation of Intellectual Capital

L04.2

The importance of recognizing the interdependence of attracting, developing, and retaining human capital.

Organizations must recruit talented people—employees at all levels with the proper sets of skills and capabilities coupled with the right values and attitudes. Such skills and attitudes must be continually developed, strengthened, and reinforced, and each employee must be motivated and her efforts focused on the organization's goals and objectives.[26]

The rise to prominence of knowledge workers as a vital source of competitive advantage is changing the balance of power in today's organization.[27] Knowledge workers place professional development and personal enrichment (financial and otherwise) above company loyalty. Attracting, recruiting, and hiring the "best and the brightest," is a critical first step in the process of building intellectual capital. At a symposium for CEOs, Bill Gates said, "The thing that is holding Microsoft back . . . is simply how [hard] we find it to go out and recruit the kind of people we want to grow our research team."[28]

Hiring is only the first of three processes in which all successful organizations must engage to build and leverage their human capital. Firms must also *develop* employees to fulfill their full potential to maximize their joint contributions.[29] Finally, the first two processes are for naught if firms can't provide the working environment and intrinsic and extrinsic rewards to *retain* their best and brightest.[30]

These activities are highly interrelated. We would like to suggest the imagery of a three-legged stool (see Exhibit 4.2).[31] If one leg is weak or broken, the stool collapses.

To illustrate such interdependence, poor hiring impedes the effectiveness of development and retention processes. In a similar vein, ineffective retention efforts place additional

EXHIBIT 4.2 Human Capital: Three Interdependent Activities

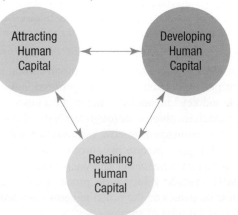

HOW GOOGLE ATTRACTS AND MAINTAINS TOP TALENT

By Sarah Hudson and Asha Moore-Mangin

Recruiting and keeping talented employees seems to hold no secrets for Google, who are routinely positioned at the top of "Best Employers" lists worldwide. How do they do it? Larry Page, Google CEO believes this is through creating a company culture where there is no fear and a flexible and innovative environment with a focus on ideas rather than "beating the competition," a more motivational approach.

Google practices what it preaches and has applied an innovative and flexible approach to its HR practices (termed "People Operations"). They use a data driven approach to their decision-making from recruitment to retirement and all the steps in between. They measure happiness, turnover, recruitment costs, and effectiveness; they research the factors of success for manager-team performance, communication, and pay structures. They have even studied how long the optimal lunch line should be at the cafeteria (3–4 minutes, enough to meet people without wasting time.)

This analytical approach lends legitimacy to decisions such as maintaining middle management in the organizational structure, extending and improving maternity leave, increasing salaries rather than offering bonuses, and having no more than four rounds of recruitment interviews.

The success of Google at attracting and keeping highly talented employees stems from basing their HR policies on facts rather than feelings and a guiding principle of ensuring the well-being of their employees.

Sources: Manjoo.F, January 2013 "The Happiness Machine; How Google became such a great place to work," www.slate.com/articles/technology/technology/2013/01/google_people_operations_the_secrets_of_the_world_s_most_scientific_human.single.html; Groth, A. April 2013, "Google's favourite psychologist explaines how the company retains top talent," www.businessinsider.com/adam-grant-on-google-2013-4#ixzz2aqntBfKu; Groth, A. February 2014, "Google's secret to attracting the best talent in the world," www.businessinsider.com/how-to-create-a-fearless-office-culture-2013-2#ixzz2aqnoTHiw

---

burdens on hiring and development. Consider the following anecdote, provided by Jeffrey Pfeffer of the Stanford University Business School:

> Not long ago, I went to a large, fancy San Francisco law firm—where they treat their associates like dog doo and where the turnover is very high. I asked the managing partner about the turnover rate. He said, "A few years ago, it was 25 percent, and now we're up to 30 percent." I asked him how the firm had responded to that trend. He said, "We increased our recruiting." So I asked him, "What kind of doctor would you be if your patient was bleeding faster and faster, and your only response was to increase the speed of the transfusion?"[32]

Clearly, stepped-up recruiting is a poor substitute for weak retention.[33] Although there are no simple, easy-to-apply answers, we can learn from what leading-edge firms are doing to attract, develop, and retain human capital in today's highly competitive marketplace.[34] Before moving on, Strategy Spotlight 4.1 examines how the Internet giant Google attracts and keeps highly talented employees with HR policies based firmly on facts.

Attracting Human Capital

> *In today's world, talent is so critical to the success of what you're doing—their core competencies and how well they fit into your office culture. The combination can be, well, extraordinary. But only if you bring in the right people.[35]*
>
> Mindy Grossman, CEO of HSN (Home Shopping Network)

The first step in the process of building superior human capital is input control: attracting and selecting the right person.[36] Human resource professionals often approach employee selection from a "lock and key" mentality—that is, fit a key (a job candidate) into a lock (the job). Such an approach involves a thorough analysis of the person and the job. Only then can the right decision be made as to how well the two will fit together. How can you fail, the theory goes, if you get a precise match of knowledge, ability, and skill profiles? Frequently, however, the precise matching approach places its emphasis on task-specific skills (e.g., motor skills, specific information processing capabilities, and communication skills) and puts less emphasis on the broad general knowledge and experience, social skills, values, beliefs, and attitudes of employees.[37]

Many have questioned the precise matching approach. They argue that firms can identify top performers by focusing on key employee mind-sets, attitudes, social skills, and general orientations. If they get these elements right, the task-specific skills can be learned quickly. (This does not imply, however, that task-specific skills are unimportant; rather, it suggests that the requisite skill sets must be viewed as a necessary but not sufficient condition.) This leads us to a popular phrase today that serves as the title of the next section.

"Hire for Attitude, Train for Skill"   Organizations are increasingly emphasizing general knowledge and experience, social skills, values, beliefs, and attitudes of employees.[38] Consider Southwest Airlines' hiring practices, which focus on employee values and attitudes. Given its strong team orientation, Southwest uses an "indirect" approach. For example, the interviewing team asks a group of employees to prepare a five-minute presentation about themselves. During the presentations, interviewers observe which candidates enthusiastically support their peers and which candidates focus on polishing their own presentations while the others are presenting.[39] The former are, of course, favored.

Alan Cooper, president of Cooper Software, Inc., in Palo Alto, California, goes further. He cleverly *uses technology* to hone in on the problem-solving ability of his applicants and their attitudes before an interview even takes place. He has devised a "Bozo Filter," an online test that can be applied to any industry. Before you spend time on whether job candidates will work out satisfactorily, find out how their minds work. Cooper advised, "Hiring was a black hole. I don't talk to bozos anymore, because 90 percent of them turn away when they see our test. It's a self-administering bozo filter."[40] How does it work?

> The online test asks questions designed to see how prospective employees approach problem-solving tasks. For example, one key question asks software engineer applicants to design a table-creation software program for Microsoft Word. Candidates provide pencil sketches and a description of the new user interface. Another question used for design communicators asks them to develop a marketing strategy for a new touch-tone phone—directed at consumers in the year 1850. Candidates e-mail their answers back to the company, and the answers are circulated around the firm to solicit feedback. Only candidates with the highest marks get interviews.

Sound Recruiting Approaches and Networking   Companies that take hiring seriously must also take recruiting seriously. The number of jobs that successful knowledge-intensive companies must fill is astonishing. Ironically, many companies still have no shortage of applicants. For example, Google ranked first on *Fortune*'s 2012 and 2013 "100 Best Companies to Work For," is planning to hire thousands of employees—even though its hiring rate has slowed.[41] The challenge becomes having the right job candidates, not the greatest number of them.

GE Medical Systems, which builds CT scanners and magnetic resonance imaging (MRI) systems, relies extensively on networking. They have found that current employees are the best source for new ones. Recently, Steven Patscot, head of staffing and leadership development, made a few simple changes to double the number of referrals. First, he simplified the process—no complex forms, no bureaucracy, and so on. Second, he increased incentives. Everyone referring a qualified candidate receives a gift certificate from Sears. For referrals who are hired, the "bounty" increases to $2,000. Although this may sound like a lot of money, it is "peanuts" compared to the $15,000 to $20,000 fees that GE typically pays to headhunters for each person hired.[42] Also, when someone refers a former colleague or friend for a job, his or her credibility is on the line. Thus, employees will be careful in recommending people for employment unless they are reasonably confident that these people are good candidates.

Attracting Millennials   This generation has also been termed "Generation Y" or "Echo Boom" and includes people that were born after 1982. Many call them impatient, demanding, or entitled. However, if employers don't provide incentives to attract and retain young workers, somebody else will. Thus, they will be at a competitive disadvantage.[43]

Why? Demographics are on their side—within a few years they will outnumber any other generation. The U.S. Bureau of Labor Statistics projects that by 2020 Millennials will make up 40 percent of the workforce. Baby boomers are retiring, and Millennials will be working for the next several decades. Additionally, they have many of the requisite skills to succeed in the future workplace—tech-savviness and the ability to innovate—and they are more racially diverse than any prior generation. Thus, they are better able to relate rapidly to different customs and cultures.

What are some of the "best practices" to attract Millennials and keep them engaged?

- **Don't fudge the sales pitch.** High-tech sales presentations and one-on-one attention may be attractive to undergrads. However, the pitch had better match the experience. Consider that today's ultra connected students can get the lowdown on a company by spending five minutes on a social networking site.

- **Let them have a life.** Typically, they are unenthusiastic about their parents' 70- or 80-hour workweeks. Millennials strive for more work-life balance, so liberal vacations become very important. They also want assurances that they can use it. At KPMG, 80 percent of employees used 40 hours of paid time off in the first six months of a recent year.

- **No time clocks, please.** Recent graduates don't mind long hours—if they can work them on their own schedule. Lockheed Martin allows employees to work nine-hour days with every other Friday off. And Chegg, the online textbook service, recently introduced an unlimited vacation policy—turnover rates among the younger workers dropped 50 percent. As noted by its CEO, Dan Rosensweig, "If you provide them with the right environment, they'll work forever."

- **Give them responsibility.** A chance to work on fulfilling projects and develop new ones on their own is important. Google urges entry-level employees to spend 20 percent of their time developing new ideas. PepsiCo allows promising young employees to manage small teams in six months.

- **Feedback and more feedback.** Career planning advice and frequent performance appraisals are keys to holding on to young hires. Several firms provide new hires with two mentors—a slightly older peer to help them get settled and a senior employee to give long-term guidance.

- **Giving back matters.** Today's altruistic young graduates expect to have opportunities for community service. Wells Fargo encourages its employees to teach financial literacy classes in the community. Accenture and Bain allow employees to consult for nonprofits.

A study from the Center for Work-Life Policy sums this issue up rather well: Instead of the traditional plums of prestigious title, powerful position, and concomitant compensation, Millennials value challenging and diverse job opportunities, stimulating colleagues, a well-designed communal workspace, and flexible work options. In fact, 89 percent of Millennials say that flexible work options are an important consideration in choosing an employer.

Developing Human Capital

It is not enough to hire top-level talent and expect that the skills and capabilities of those employees remain current throughout the duration of their employment. Rather, training and development must take place at all levels of the organization.[44] For example, Solectron assembles printed circuit boards and other components for its Silicon Valley clients.[45] Its employees receive an average of 95 hours of company-provided training each year. Chairman Winston Chen observed, "Technology changes so fast that we estimate 20 percent of an engineer's knowledge becomes obsolete each year. Training is an obligation we owe to our employees. If you want high growth and high quality, then training is a big part of the equation."

Leaders who are committed to developing the people who work for them in order to bring out their strengths and enhance their careers will have committed followers. According to James Rogers, CEO of Duke Energy: "One of the biggest things I find in organizations is that people tend to limit their perceptions of themselves and their capabilities, and one of my challenges is to open them up to the possibilities. I have this belief that anybody can do almost anything in the right context."[46]

In addition to training and developing human capital, firms must encourage widespread involvement, monitor and track employee development, and evaluate human capital.[47]

Encouraging Widespread Involvement   Developing human capital requires the active involvement of leaders at all levels. It won't be successful if it is viewed only as the responsibility of the human resources department. Each year at General Electric, 200 facilitators, 30 officers, 30 human resource executives, and many young managers actively participate in GE's orientation program at Crotonville, its training center outside New York City. Topics include global competition, winning on the global playing field, and personal examination of the new employee's core values vis-à-vis GE's values. As a senior manager once commented, "There is nothing like teaching Sunday school to force you to confront your own values."

Similarly, A. G. Lafley, Procter & Gamble's former CEO, claimed that he spent 40 percent of his time on personnel.[48] Andy Grove, who was previously Intel's CEO, required all senior people, including himself, to spend at least a week a year teaching high flyers. And Nitin Paranjpe, CEO of Hindustan Unilever, recruits people from campuses and regularly visits high-potential employees in their offices.

Mentoring and Sponsoring   Mentoring is most often a formal or informal relationship between two people—a senior mentor and a junior protégé.[49] Mentoring can potentially be a valuable influence in professional development in both the public and private sectors. The war for talent is creating challenges within organizations to both recruit new talent as well as retain talent.

Mentoring can provide many benefits—to the organization as well as the individual.[50] For the organization, it can help to recruit qualified managers, decrease turnover, fill senior-level positions with qualified professionals, enhance diversity initiatives with senior-level management, and facilitate organizational change efforts. Individuals can also benefit from effective mentoring programs. These benefits include helping newer employees transition into the organization, helping developmental relationships for people who lack access to informal mentoring relationships, and providing support and challenge to people on an organization's "fast track" to positions of higher responsibility.

Mentoring is traditionally viewed as a program to transfer knowledge and experience from more senior managers to up-and-comers. However, many organizations have reinvented it to fit today's highly competitive, knowledge-intensive industries. For example, consider Intel:

> Intel matches people not by job title and years of experience but by specific skills that are in demand. Lory Lanese, Intel's mentor champion at its huge New Mexico plant (with 5,500 employees) states, "This is definitely not a special program for special people." Instead, Intel's program uses an intranet and email to perform the matchmaking, creating relationships that stretch across state lines and national boundaries. Such an approach enables Intel to spread best practices quickly throughout the far-flung organization. Finally, Intel relies on written contracts and tight deadlines to make sure that its mentoring program gets results—and fast.[51]

Intel has also initiated a mentoring program involving a job titled technical assistants (TAs) who work with senior executives. This concept is sometimes referred to as "reverse mentoring" because senior executives benefit from the insights of professionals who have more updated technical skills—but rank lower in the organizational hierarchy. And, not surprisingly, the TAs stand to benefit quite a bit as well. Here are some insights offered by Andy Grove (formerly Intel's CEO):[52]

> In the 1980s I had a marketing manager named Dennis Carter. I probably learned more from him than anyone in my career. He is a genius. He taught me what brands are. I had no idea—I thought a brand was the name on the box. He showed me the connection of brands to strategies. Dennis went on to be Chief Marketing Officer. He was the person responsible for the Pentium name, "Intel Inside," he came up with all my good ideas.

Clearly, not everyone will have the opportunity to be a marketing manager at Intel and work directly with Andy Grove! So, when it comes to getting promoted, one might ask: How do sponsors differ from mentors?[53] Some have argued that in today's hot competition among professionals for advancement in an organization, having a mentor may provide many benefits—but sponsors are more likely to get one promoted. Why? A mentor may coach you, provide advice, and help prepare you for your next position. A sponsor, on the other hand, is someone in a senior position who's willing to advocate for and facilitate and enjoy more career moves, make introductions to the right people, translate and teach the secret language of success, and most important, "use up chips" for their protégé. Heather Forest-Cummings, a senior director of research at Catalyst claims: "A mentor will talk *with* you, but a sponsor will talk *about* you."

The idea of sponsorship has gained traction lately as more companies aim to move more women into corporate leadership. A recent study of 4,000 high-level employees found that 19 percent of men had a sponsor, but only 13 percent of women. However, women who had a sponsor were more likely to negotiate for raises, seek promotions and higher salaries, and self more career satisfaction—and get to the top. One of the co-authors of the study, Sylvia Ann Hewlett, president of the Center for Talent Innovation, boldly claims: "Sponsorship is the only way to get those top appointments."

Sponsorships, of course, involve a two-way street. Below, we provide some advice to those seeking sponsors and their responsibilities and obligations to their sponsors after the matchmaking process is completed.

- Your work must be of the highest quality. Executives need to be convinced that you are loyal, trustworthy, and dependable. After all, they are betting their own reputations on your career.
- Don't just put your head down and work hard. You need to be noticed and become a known quantity. Become active in your industry, volunteer for larger assignments, and attend conferences.
- Keep in mind that relationships evolve naturally. Don't simply ask someone to be your sponsor. And, be sure to hedge your bets. After all, your sponsor may leave the organization. So, be sure to nurture relationships with several people.
- Sponsors expect you to reciprocate with your loyal support. Sponsors also benefit from the "power of the posse" to enhance their own careers. After all, no one reaches the top of the organization on their own.

Monitoring Progress and Tracking Development   Whether a firm uses on-site formal training, off-site training (e.g., universities), or on-the-job training, tracking individual progress—and sharing this knowledge with both the employee and key managers—becomes essential. Like many leading-edge firms, GlaxoSmithKline (GSK) places strong emphasis on broader experiences over longer time periods. Dan Phelan, senior vice president and director of human resources, explained, "We ideally follow a two-plus-two-plus-two formula in developing people for top management positions." This reflects the belief that GSK's best people should gain experience in two business units, two functional units (such as finance and marketing), and in two countries.

Evaluating Human Capital   In today's competitive environment, collaboration and interdependence are vital to organizational success. Individuals must share their knowledge and work constructively to achieve collective, not just individual, goals. However, traditional systems evaluate performance from a single perspective (i.e., "top down") and generally don't address the "softer" dimensions of communications and social skills, values, beliefs, and attitudes.[54]

To address the limitations of the traditional approach, many organizations use **360-degree evaluation and feedback systems.**[55] Here, superiors, direct reports, colleagues, and even internal and external customers rate a person's performance.[56] Managers rate themselves to have a personal benchmark. The 360-degree feedback system complements teamwork, employee involvement, and organizational flattening. As organizations continue to push responsibility downward, traditional top-down appraisal systems become insufficient.[57] For example, a manager who previously managed the performance of 3 supervisors might now be responsible for 10 and is less likely to have the in-depth knowledge needed to appraise and develop them adequately. Exhibit 4.3 provides a portion of GE's 360-degree system.

Evaluation systems must also ensure that a manager's success does not come at the cost of compromising the organization's core values. Such behavior generally leads to only short-term wins for both the manager and the organization. The organization typically suffers long-term losses in terms of morale, turnover, productivity, and so on. Accordingly, Merck's former chairman, Ray Gilmartin, told his employees, "If someone is achieving results but not demonstrating the core values of the company, at the expense of our people, that manager does not have much of a career here."

> **360-degree evaluation and feedback systems** superiors, direct reports, colleagues, and even external and internal customers rate a person's performance.

Vision	• Has developed and communicated a clear, simple, customer-focused vision/direction for the organization.
	• Forward-thinking, stretches horizons, challenges imaginations.
	• Inspires and energizes others to commit to Vision. Captures minds. Leads by example.
	• As appropriate, updates Vision to reflect constant and accelerating change affecting the business.

Customer/Quality Focus

Integrity

Accountability/Commitment

Communication/Influence

Shared Ownership/Boundaryless

Team Builder/Empowerment

Knowledge/Expertise/Intellect

Initiative/Speed

Global Mind-Set

EXHIBIT 4.3

An Excerpt from General Electric's 360-Degree Leadership Assessment Chart

Note: This evaluation system consists of 10 "characteristics"—Vision, Customer/Quality Focus, Integrity, and so on. Each of these characteristics has four "performance criteria." For illustrative purposes, the four performance criteria of "Vision" are included.

Source: Adapted from Slater, R. 1994. *Get Better or Get Beaten:* 152–155. Burr Ridge, IL: Irwin Professional Publishing.

HCL'S EFFECTIVE 360-DEGREE EVALUATION SYSTEM

In order to foster innovation and encourage collaborative opportunities, leaders should be advised to set the tone by being good collaborators themselves. Collaborative leaders can inspire others in the organization to work with individuals outside of their formal line of work and depoliticize interactions. One method to encourage collaboration from the top is to increase transparency.

Take HCL, an Indian technology and IT enterprise operating in 31 countries, for example. CEO Vineet Nayar showed his commitment to collaboration by adopting a fundamentally different 360-degree evaluation for his top managers—he asked lower-level employees to weigh in on the evaluation of top executives. HCL in the past used a more traditional 360-degree evaluation in which each manager was assessed by a small number of people that made up this manager's work circle. As Nayar states, "Most of the respondents operated within the same area as the person they were evaluating. This reinforced the boundaries between the parts of the pyramid. But we were trying to change all that. We wanted

to encourage people to operate across these boundaries." To create a more collaborative environment, Mr. Nayar was the first to become more transparent, by posting his own 360-degree evaluation on the Web. Once the new transparency became a part of the organizational culture, more managers were included. Ultimately, HCL introduced a feature called "Happy Feet," allowing employees to evaluate managers who might affect or influence them.

Increased transparency also seems to be gaining acceptance in other companies and contexts. A third of U.S. executives, according to Aon Hewitt Associates, recognize the value potential of more transparency and share their 360 results with direct reports, up from 20 percent a few years ago. For instance, Dell Inc. is one U.S. company that actively encourages transparent 360-degree evaluations and considers it good management practice. As in the case of HCL, Dell CEO Michael Dell led by example and shared his 360 review with other members of the organization—emphasizing the need for CEOs to lead by example.

Sources: Ibarra, H. & Hansen, M.T. 2011. Are you a collaborative leader? *Harvard Business Review,* 89(7/8): 68–75; Lublin, J. S. 2011. Transparency pays off in 360-degree reviews. *Wall Street Journal. online.wsj.com*, December 8: np.

Strategy Spotlight 4.2 discusses HCL's unique approach to 360-degree evaluations.

Retaining Human Capital

It has been said that talented employees are like "frogs in a wheelbarrow."[58] They can jump out at any time! By analogy, the organization can either try to force employees to stay in the firm or try to keep them from jumping out by creating incentives.[59] In other words, today's leaders can either provide the work environment and incentives to keep productive employees and management from wanting to bail out, or they can use legal means such as employment contracts and noncompete clauses.[60] Firms must prevent the transfer of valuable and sensitive information outside the organization. Failure to do so would be the neglect of a leader's fiduciary responsibility to shareholders. However, greater efforts should be directed at the former (e.g., good work environment and incentives), but, as we all know, the latter (e.g., employment contracts and noncompete clauses) have their place.[61]

Identifying with an Organization's Mission and Values   People who identify with and are more committed to the core mission and values of the organization are less likely to stray or bolt to the competition. For example, take the perspective of the late Steve Jobs, Apple's widely admired former CEO:[62]

> When I hire somebody really senior, competence is the ante. They have to be really smart. But the real issue for me is: Are they going to fall in love with Apple? Because if they fall in love with Apple, everything else will take care of itself. They'll want to do what's best for Apple, not what's best for them, what's best for Steve, or anyone else.

"Tribal loyalty" is another key factor that links people to the organization.[63] A tribe is not the organization as a whole (unless it is very small). Rather, it is teams, communities of practice, and other groups within an organization or occupation.

Brian Hall, CEO of Values Technology in Santa Cruz, California, documented a shift in people's emotional expectations from work. From the 1950s on, a "task first" relationship—"tell me what the job is, and let's get on with it"—dominated employee attitudes. Emotions and personal life were checked at the door. In the past few years, a "relationship-first" set of values has challenged the task orientation. Hall believes that it will become dominant. Employees want to share attitudes and beliefs as well as workspace.

Challenging Work and a Stimulating Environment Arthur Schawlow, winner of the 1981 Nobel Prize in physics, was asked what made the difference between highly creative and less creative scientists. His reply: "The labor of love aspect is very important. The most successful scientists often are not the most talented.[64] But they are the ones impelled by curiosity. They've got to know what the answer is."[65] Such insights highlight the importance of intrinsic motivation: the motivation to work on something because it is exciting, satisfying, or personally challenging.[66]

One way firms keep highly mobile employees motivated and challenged is through opportunities that lower barriers to an employee's mobility within a company. For example, Shell Oil Company has created an "open sourcing" model for talent. Jobs are listed on its intranet, and, with a two-month notice, employees can go to work on anything that interests them.

Financial and Nonfinancial Rewards and Incentives Financial rewards are a vital organizational control mechanism (as we will discuss in Chapter 9). Money—whether in the form of salary, bonus, stock options, and so forth—can mean many different things to people. It might mean security, recognition, or a sense of freedom and independence.

Paying people more is seldom the most important factor in attracting and retaining human capital.[67] Most surveys show that money is not the most important reason why people take or leave jobs, and that money, in some surveys, is not even in the top 10. Consistent with these findings, Tandem Computers (part of Hewlett-Packard) typically doesn't tell people being recruited what their salaries would be. People who asked were told that their salaries were competitive. If they persisted along this line of questioning, they would not be offered a position. Why? Tandem realized a rather simple idea: People who come for money will leave for money.

Another nonfinancial reward is accommodating working families with children. Balancing demands of family and work is a problem at some point for virtually all employees.

Below we discuss how Google attracts and retains talent through financial and nonfinancial incentives. Its unique "Google culture," a huge attraction to potential employees, transforms a traditional workspace into a fun, feel-at-home, and flexible place to work.[68]

> Googlers do not merely work but have a great time doing it. The Mountain View, California, headquarters includes on-site medical and dental facilities, oil change and bike repair, foosball, pool tables, volleyball courts, and free breakfast, lunch, and dinner on a daily basis at 11 gourmet restaurants. Googlers have access to training programs and receive tuition reimbursement while they take a leave of absence to pursue higher education. Google states on its website, "Though Google has grown a lot since it opened in 1998, we still maintain a small company feel."

Enhancing Human Capital: The Role of Diversity in the Workforce

A combination of demographic trends and accelerating globalization of business has made the management of cultural differences a critical issue.[69] Workforces, which reflect demographic changes in the overall population, will be increasingly heterogeneous along dimensions such as gender, race, ethnicity, and nationality.[70] Demographic trends in the United States indicate a growth in Hispanic Americans from 6.9 million in 1960 to over

35 million in 2000, an expected increase to over 59 million by 2020 and 102 million by 2050. Similarly, the Asian-American population should grow to 20 million in 2020 from 12 million in 2000 and only 1.5 million in 1970. And the African-American population is expected to increase from 12.8 percent of the U.S. population in 2000 to 14.2 percent by 2025.[71]

Such demographic changes have implications not only for the labor pool but also for customer bases, which are also becoming more diverse.[72] This creates important organizational challenges and opportunities.

The effective management of diversity can enhance the social responsibility goals of an organization.[73] However, there are many other benefits as well. Six other areas where sound management of diverse workforces can improve an organization's effectiveness and competitive advantages are: (1) cost, (2) resource acquisition, (3) marketing, (4) creativity, (5) problem-solving, and (6) organizational flexibility.

- *Cost Argument.* As organizations become more diverse, firms effective in managing diversity will have a cost advantage over those that are not.
- *Resource Acquisition Argument.* Firms with excellent reputations as prospective employers for women and ethnic minorities will have an advantage in the competition for top talent. As labor pools shrink and change in composition, such advantages will become even more important.
- *Marketing Argument.* For multinational firms, the insight and cultural sensitivity that members with roots in other countries bring to marketing efforts will be very useful. A similar rationale applies to subpopulations within domestic operations.
- *Creativity Argument.* Less emphasis on conformity to norms of the past and a diversity of perspectives will improve the level of creativity.
- *Problem-Solving Argument.* Heterogeniety in decision-making and problem-solving groups typically produces better decisions because of a wider range of perspectives as well as more thorough analysis. Jim Schiro, former CEO of PriceWaterhouse Coopers, explains, "When you make a genuine commitment to diversity, you bring a greater diversity of ideas, approaches, and experiences and abilities that can be applied to client problems. After all, six people with different perspectives have a better shot at solving complex problems than sixty people who all think alike."[74]
- *Organizational Flexibility Argument.* With effective programs to enhance workplace diversity, systems become less determinant, less standardized, and therefore more fluid. Such fluidity should lead to greater flexibility to react to environmental changes. Reactions should be faster and less costly.

Strategy Spotlight 4.3 discusses Reckitt Benckiser's approach to diversity, which incorporates many different aspects of diversity

LO4.3

The key role of social capital in leveraging human capital within and across the firm.

The Vital Role of Social Capital

Successful firms are well aware that the attraction, development, and retention of talent *is a necessary but not sufficient condition* for creating competitive advantages.[75] In the knowledge economy, it is not the stock of human capital that is important, but the extent to which it is combined and leveraged.[76] In a sense, developing and retaining human capital becomes less important as key players (talented professionals, in particular) take the role of "free agents" and bring with them the requisite skill in many cases. Rather, the development of social capital (that is, the friendships and working relationships among talented individuals) gains importance, because it helps tie knowledge workers to a given firm.[77] Knowledge workers often exhibit greater loyalties to their colleagues and their profession

DIVERSITY AT WORK: RECKITT BENCKISER

At Reckitt Benckiser, the UK-based producer of home, health, and personal care products, workforce diversity is considered a competitive advantage and a key reason for net income growth of 17 percent annually, on average, from 1999 to 2010. In terms of traditional measures of diversity such as nationality, Reckitt Benckiser's senior team is not dominated by any nationality. Two executives are Dutch, one is German, two are British, one is South African, two are Italian, and one is from India. According to CEO Bart Becht, "It doesn't matter whether I have a Pakistani, a Chinese person, a Brit, or a Turk, man or woman, sitting in the same room, or whether I have people from sales or something else, so long as I have people with different experiences—because the chance for new ideas is much greater when you have people with different backgrounds. The chance for conflict is also higher—and conflict is good per se, as long as it's constructive and gets us to the best idea."

While nationality is an important measure of diversity, other less often discussed diversity measures become increasingly important for businesses. For instance, successful collaborations between divisions and people (whether measured in terms of patent citation, critical acclaim, or financial return) often involve a healthy mix of experienced employees and newcomers and also bring together people who have no working history with one another. The challenge for leaders is to make a concerted effort to promote this mix.

When given the choice, people will often choose to collaborate with others they know well or who have similar backgrounds, yet static groups breed insularity and may suffocate innovation. Take Nokia's former executive team as an example, which was 100 percent Finnish and had worked closely together for more than a decade. Many believe this homogeneity explains why Nokia failed to see the smartphone threat emerging from Silicon Valley. Moreover, diversity in corporate boardrooms has become increasingly important. Julie Causey, director at the Federal Reserve Bank of Minneapolis, highlights the importance of age diversity as "directors in their 30s and 40s can bring strong technical savvy, an appetite for innovation, and a fresh way of thinking."

Sources: Ibarra, H. & Hansen, M.T. 2011. Are you a collaborative leader? *Harvard Business Review*, 89(7/8): 68–75; Chase, S. 2012. Directors to watch 2012. *Directors & Boards*, 36(4): 53–58

than their employing organization, which may be "an amorphous, distant, and sometimes threatening entity."[78] Thus, a firm must find ways to create "ties" among its knowledge workers.

Let's look at a hypothetical example. Two pharmaceutical firms are fortunate enough to hire Nobel Prize–winning scientists.[79] In one case, the scientist is offered a very attractive salary, outstanding facilities and equipment, and told to "go to it!" In the second case, the scientist is offered approximately the same salary, facilities, and equipment plus one additional ingredient: working in a laboratory with 10 highly skilled and enthusiastic scientists. Part of the job is to collaborate with these peers and jointly develop promising drug compounds. There is little doubt as to which scenario will lead to a higher probability of retaining the scientist. The interaction, sharing, and collaboration will create a situation in which the scientist will develop firm-specific ties and be less likely to "bolt" for a higher salary offer. Such ties are critical because knowledge-based resources tend to be more tacit in nature, as we mentioned early in this chapter. Therefore, they are much more difficult to protect against loss (i.e., the individual quitting the organization) than other types of capital, such as equipment, machinery, and land.

Another way to view this situation is in terms of the resource-based view of the firm that we discussed in Chapter 3. That is, competitive advantages tend to be harder for competitors to copy if they are based on "unique bundles" of resources.[80] So, if employees are working effectively in teams and sharing their knowledge and learning from each other, not only will they be more likely to add value to the firm, but they also will be less likely to leave the organization, because of the loyalties and social ties that they develop over time.

How Social Capital Helps Attract and Retain Talent

The importance of social ties among talented professionals creates a significant challenge (and opportunity) for organizations. In *The Wall Street Journal,* Bernard Wysocki described the increase in a type of "Pied Piper Effect," in which teams or networks of people are leaving one company for another.[81] The trend is to recruit job candidates at the crux of social relationships in organizations, particularly if they are seen as having the potential to bring with them valuable colleagues.[82] This is a process that is referred to as "hiring via personal networks." Let's look at one instance of this practice.

> Gerald Eickhoff, founder of an electronic commerce company called Third Millennium Communications, tried for 15 years to hire Michael Reene. Why? Mr. Eickhoff says that he has "these Pied Piper skills." Mr. Reene was a star at Andersen Consulting in the 1980s and at IBM in the 1990s. He built his businesses and kept turning down overtures from Mr. Eickhoff.
>
> However, in early 2000, he joined Third Millennium as chief executive officer, with a salary of just $120,000 but with a 20 percent stake in the firm. Since then, he has brought in a raft of former IBM colleagues and Andersen subordinates. One protégé from his time at Andersen, Mary Goode, was brought on board as executive vice president. She promptly tapped her own network and brought along former colleagues.
>
> Wysocki considers the Pied Piper effect one of the underappreciated factors in the war for talent today. This is because one of the myths of the New Economy is rampant individualism, wherein individuals find jobs on the Internet career sites and go to work for complete strangers. Perhaps, instead of Me Inc., the truth is closer to We Inc.[83]

Another example of social relationships causing human capital mobility is the emigration of talent from an organization to form start-up ventures. Microsoft is perhaps the best-known example of this phenomenon.[84] Professionals frequently leave Microsoft en masse to form venture capital and technology start-ups, called "Baby Bills," built around teams of software developers. For example, Ignition Corporation, of Bellevue, Washington, was formed by Brad Silverberg, a former Microsoft senior vice president. Eight former Microsoft executives, among others, founded the company.

LO4.4

The importance of social networks in knowledge management and in promoting career success.

Social Networks: Implications for Knowledge Management and Career Success

Managers face many challenges driven by such factors as rapid changes in globalization and technology. Leading a successful company is more than a one-person job. As Tom Malone recently put it in *The Future of Work,* "As managers, we need to shift our thinking from command and control to coordinate and cultivate—the best way to gain power is sometimes to give it away."[85] The move away from top-down bureaucratic control to more open, decentralized network models makes it more difficult for managers to understand how work is actually getting done, who is interacting with whom both within and outside the organization, and the consequences of these interactions for the long-term health of the organization.[86]

Malcolm Gladwell, in his best-selling book *The Tipping Point,* used the term *connector* to describe people who have *used* many ties to different social worlds.[87] It's not the number of people that connectors know that makes them significant. Rather, it is their ability to link people, ideas, and resources that wouldn't normally bump into one another. In business, connectors are critical facilitators for collaboration and integration. David Kenny, president of Akamai Technologies, believes that being a connector is one of the most important ways in which he adds value:

> Kenny spends much of his time traveling around the world to meet with employees, partners, and customers. He states, "I spend time with media owners to hear what they think about digital platforms, Facebook, and new pricing models, and with Microsoft

leaders to get their views on cloud computing. I'm interested in hearing how our clients feel about macroeconomic issues, the G20, and how debt will affect future generations." These conversations lead to new strategic insights and relationships and help Akamai develop critical external partnerships.

Social network analysis depicts the pattern of interactions among individuals and helps to diagnose effective and ineffective patterns.[88] It helps identify groups or clusters of individuals that comprise the network, individuals who link the clusters, and other network members. It helps diagnose communication patterns and, consequently, communication effectiveness.[89] Such analysis of communication patterns is helpful because the configuration of group members' social ties within and outside the group affects the extent to which members connect to individuals who:

social network analysis
analysis of the pattern of social interactions among individuals.

- convey needed resources,
- have the opportunity to exchange information and support,
- have the motivation to treat each other in positive ways, and,
- have the time to develop trusting relationships that might improve the groups' effectiveness.

However, such relationships don't "just happen."[90] Developing social capital requires interdependence among group members. Social capital erodes when people in the network become independent. And increased interactions between members aid in the development and maintenance of mutual obligations in a social network.[91] Social networks such as Facebook may facilitate increased interactions between members in a social network via Internet-based communications.

Let's take a brief look at a simplified network analysis to get a grasp of the key ideas. In Exhibit 4.4, the links depict informal relationships among individuals, such as communication flows, personal support, and advice networks. There may be some individuals with literally no linkages, such as Fred. These individuals are typically labeled "isolates." However, most people do have some linkages with others.

To simplify, there are two primary types of mechanisms through which social capital will flow: *closure relationships* (depicted by Bill, Frank, George, and Susan) and *bridging relationships* (depicted by Mary). As we can see, in the former relationships one member is central to the communication flows in a group. In contrast, in the latter relationship, one person "bridges" or brings together groups that would have been otherwise unconnected.

Both closure and bridging relationships have important implications for the effective flow of information in organizations and for the management of knowledge. We will now briefly discuss each of these types of relationships. We will also address some of the implications that understanding social networks has for one's career success.

Closure   With **closure,** many members have relationships (or ties) with other members. As indicated in Exhibit 4.4, Bill's group would have a higher level of closure than Frank, Susan, or George's groups because more group members are connected to each other. Through closure, group members develop strong relationships with each other, high levels of trust, and greater solidarity. High levels of trust help to ensure that informal norms in the group are easily enforced and there is less "free riding." Social pressure will prevent people from withholding effort or shirking their responsibilities. In addition, people in the network are more willing to extend favors and "go the extra mile" on a colleague's behalf because they are confident that their efforts will be reciprocated by another member in their group. Another benefit of a network with closure is the high level of emotional support. This becomes particularly valuable when setbacks occur that may destroy morale or an unexpected tragedy happens that might cause the group to lose its focus. Social support helps the group to rebound from misfortune and get back on track.

closure
the degree to which all members of a social network have relationships (or ties) with other group members.

EXHIBIT 4.4   A Simplified Social Network

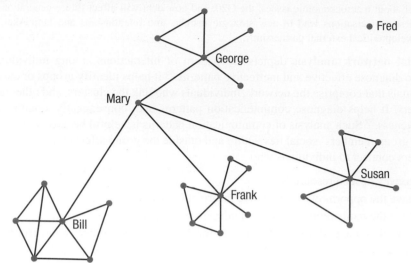

But high levels of closure often come with a price. Groups that become too closed can become insular. They cut themselves off from the rest of the organization and fail to share what they are learning from people outside their group. Research shows that while managers need to encourage closure up to a point, if there is too much closure, they need to encourage people to open up their groups and infuse new ideas through bridging relationships.[92]

bridging relationships
relationships in a social network that connect otherwise disconnected people.

Bridging Relationships   The closure perspective rests on an assumption that there is a high level of similarity among group members. However, members can be quite heterogeneous with regard to their positions in either the formal or informal structures of the group or the organization. Such heterogeneity exists because of, for example, vertical boundaries (different levels in the hierarchy) and horizontal boundaries (different functional areas).

Bridging relationships, in contrast to closure, stresses the importance of ties connecting people. Employees who bridge disconnected people tend to receive timely, diverse information because of their access to a wide range of heterogeneous information flows. Such bridging relationships span a number of different types of boundaries.

structural holes
social gaps between groups in a social network where there are few relationships bridging the groups.

The University of Chicago's Ron Burt originally coined the term **"structural holes"** to refer to the social gap between two groups. Structural holes are common in organizations. When they occur in business, managers typically refer to them as "silos" or "stovepipes." Sales and engineering are a classic example of two groups whose members traditionally interact with their peers rather than across groups.

A study that Burt conducted at Raytheon, a $25 billion U.S. electronics company and military contractor, provides further insight into the benefits of bridging.[93]

> Burt studied several hundred managers in Raytheon's supply chain group and asked them to write down ideas to improve the company's supply chain management. Then he asked two Raytheon executives to rate the ideas. The conclusion: *The best suggestions consistently came from managers who discussed ideas outside their regular work group.*
>
> Burt found that Raytheon managers were good at thinking of ideas but bad at developing them. Too often, Burt said, the managers discussed their ideas with colleagues already in their informal discussion network. Instead, he said, they should have had discussions outside their typical contacts, particularly with an informal boss, or someone with enough power to be an ally but not an actual supervisor.

Developing Social Capital: Overcoming Barriers to Collaboration   Social capital within a group or organization develops through repeated interactions among its members and the resulting collaboration.[94] However, collaboration does not "just happen." People don't collaborate for various reasons. Effective collaboration requires overcoming four barriers:

- The not-invented-here barrier (people aren't willing to provide help)
- The hoarding barrier (people aren't willing to provide help)
- The search barrier (people are unable to find what they are looking for)
- The transfer barrier (people are unable to work with the people they don't know well)

All four barriers need to be low before effective collaboration can take place. Each one is enough to prevent people from collaborating well. The key is to identify which barriers are present in an organization and then to devise appropriate ways to overcome them.

Different barriers require different solutions. Motivational barriers require leaders to pull levers that make people more willing to collaborate. Ability barriers mean that leaders need to pull levers that enable motivated people to collaborate throughout the organization.

To be effective, leaders can choose a mix of three levers. First, when motivation is the problem, they can use the **unification lever**, wherein they craft compelling common goals, articulate a strong value of cross-company teamwork, and encourage collaboration in order to send strong signals to lift people's sights beyond their narrow interests toward a common goal.

Second, with the **people lever**, the emphasis isn't on getting people to collaborate more. Rather, it's on getting the right people to collaborate on the right projects. This means cultivating what may be called **T-shaped management**: people who simultaneously focus on the performance of their unit (the vertical part of the T) and across boundaries (the horizontal part of the T). People become able to collaborate when needed but are disciplined enough to say no when it's not required.

Third, by using the **network lever**, leaders can build nimble interpersonal networks across the company so that employees are better able to collaborate. Interpersonal networks are more effective than formal hierarchies. However, there is a dark side to networks: When people spend more time networking than getting work done, collaboration can adversely affect results.

Implications for Career Success   Let's go back in time in order to illustrate the value of social networks in one's career success. Consider two of the most celebrated artists of all time: Vincent van Gogh and Pablo Picasso. Strategy Spotlight 4.4 points out why these two artists enjoyed sharply contrasting levels of success during their lifetimes.

Effective social networks provide many advantages for the firm.[95] They can play a key role in an individual's career advancement and success. One's social network potentially can provide three unique advantages: private information, access to diverse skill sets, and power.[96] Managers see these advantages at work every day but might not consider how their networks regulate them.

Private Information   We make judgments, using both public and private information. Today, public information is available from many sources, including the Internet. However, since it is so accessible, public information offers less competitive advantage than it used to.

In contrast, private information from personal contacts can offer something not found in publicly available sources, such as the release date of a new product or knowledge about what a particular interviewer looks for in candidates. Private information can give managers an edge, though it is more subjective than public information since it cannot be easily

---

unification lever
method for making people more willing to collaborate by crafting compelling common goals articulating a strong value of cross-company teamwork, and encouraging collaboration in order to send strong signals to lift people's sights beyond their narrow interests towards a common goal.

people lever
method for making people more willing to collaborate by getting the right people to work on the right projects.

T-shaped management
people's dual focus on the performance of their unit (the vertical part of the T) and across boundaries (the horizontal part of the T).

network lever
method for making people more willing to collaborate by building nimble interpersonal networks across the company.

PICASSO VERSUS VAN GOGH: WHO WAS MORE SUCCESSFUL AND WHY?

Vincent van Gogh and Pablo Picasso are two of the most iconoclastic—and famous—artists of modern times. Paintings by both of them have fetched over $100 million. And both of them were responsible for some of the most iconic images in the art world: Van Gogh's *Self-Portrait* (the one sans the earlobe) and *Starry Night* and Picasso's *The Old Guitarist* and *Guernica.* However, there is an important difference between van Gogh and Picasso. Van Gogh died penniless. Picasso's estate was estimated at $750 million when he died in 1973. What was the difference?

Van Gogh's primary connection to the art world was through his brother. Unfortunately, this connection didn't feed directly into the money that could have turned him into a living success. In contrast, Picasso's myriad connections provided him with access to commercial riches. As noted by Gregory Berns in his book

Iconoclast: A Neuroscientist Reveals How to Think Differently, "Picasso's wide ranging social network, which included artists, writers, and politicians, meant that he was never more than a few people away from anyone of importance in the world."

In effect, van Gogh was a loner, and the charismatic Picasso was an active member of multiple social circles. In social networking terms, van Gogh was a solitary "node" who had few connections. Picasso, on the other hand, was a "hub" who embedded himself in a vast network that stretched across various social lines. Where Picasso smoothly navigated multiple social circles, van Gogh had to struggle just to maintain connections with even those closest to him. Van Gogh inhabited an alien world, whereas Picasso was a social magnet. And because he knew so many people, the world was at Picasso's fingertips. From his perspective, the world was smaller.

Sources: Hayashi, A. M. 2008. Why Picasso Out Earned van Gogh. *MIT Sloan Management Review,* 50(1): 11–12; and Berns, G. 2008. *A Neuroscientist Reveals How to Think Differently.* Boston, MA: Harvard Business Press.

---

verified by independent sources, such as Dunn & Bradstreet. Consequently the value of your private information to others—and the value of others' private information to you—depends on how much trust exists in the network of relationships.

Access to Diverse Skill Sets   Linus Pauling, one of only two people to win a Nobel Prize in two different areas and considered one of the towering geniuses of the 20th century, attributed his creative success not to his immense brainpower or luck but to his diverse contacts. He said, "The best way to have a good idea is to have a lot of ideas."

While expertise has become more specialized during the past few decades, organizational, product, and marketing issues have become more interdisciplinary. This means that success is tied to the ability to transcend natural skill limitations through others. Highly diverse network relationships, therefore, can help you develop more complete, creative, and unbiased perspectives on issues. Trading information or skills with people whose experiences differ from your own, provides you with unique, exceptionally valuable resources. It is common for people in relationships to share their problems. If you know enough people, you will begin to see how the problems that another person is struggling with can be solved by the solutions being developed by others. If you can bring together problems and solutions, it will greatly benefit your career.

Power   Traditionally, a manager's power was embedded in a firm's hierarchy. But, when corporate organizations became flatter, more like pancakes than pyramids, that power was repositioned in the network's brokers (people who bridged multiple networks), who could adapt to changes in the organization, develop clients, and synthesize opposing points of view. Such brokers weren't necessarily at the top of the hierarchy or experts in their fields, but they linked specialists in the firm with trustworthy and informative relationships.[97]

Most personal networks are highly clustered; that is, an individual's friends are likely to be friends with one another as well. Most corporate networks are made up of several clusters that have few links between them. Brokers are especially powerful because they connect separate clusters, thus stimulating collaboration among otherwise independent specialists.

A Cautionary Note: Three Kinds of Network Traps   A recent study of over 300 companies explored how management teams can understand and capitalize on the formal and informal social networks of their employees.[98] Six common types of managers who get stuck in three types of network traps were identified. Such findings have important career implications:

- **The wrong structure.** The "formalist" relies too much on his firm's official hierarchy, missing out on the efficiencies and opportunities that come from informal connections. The "overloaded manager" has so much contact with colleagues and external ties that she becomes a bottleneck to progress and burns herself out.
- **The wrong relationships.** The "disconnected expert" sticks with people who keep him focused on safe, existing competencies, rather than those who push him to build new skills. The "biased leader" relies on advisers (same functional background, location, or values) who reinforce her biases, when she should instead seek outsiders to prompt more fully informed decisions.
- **The wrong behavior.** The "superficial networker" engages in surface-level interaction with as many people as possible; mistakenly believing that a bigger network is a better network. The "chameleon" changes his interests, values, and personality to match those of whatever subgroup is his audience, and winds up being disconnected from every group.

The Potential Downside of Social Capital

We'd like to close our discussion of social capital by addressing some of its limitations. First, some firms have been adversely affected by very high levels of social capital because it may breed **"groupthink"**—a tendency not to question shared beliefs.[99] Such thinking may occur in networks with high levels of closure where there is little input from people outside of the network. In effect, too many warm and fuzzy feelings among group members prevent people from rigorously challenging each other. People are discouraged from engaging in the "creative abrasion" that Dorothy Leonard of Harvard University describes as a key source of innovation.[100] Two firms that were well known for their collegiality, strong sense of employee membership, and humane treatment—Digital Equipment (now part of Hewlett Packard) and Polaroid—suffered greatly from market misjudgments and strategic errors. The aforementioned aspects of their culture contributed to their problems.

Second, if there are deep-rooted mindsets, there would be a tendency to develop dysfunctional human resource practices. That is, the organization (or group) would continue to hire, reward, and promote like-minded people who tend to further intensify organizational inertia and erode innovation. Such homogeneity would increase over time and decrease the effectiveness of decision-making processes.

Third, the socialization processes (orientation, training, etc.) can be expensive in terms of both financial resources and managerial commitment. Such investments can represent a significant opportunity cost that should be evaluated in terms of the intended benefits. If such expenses become excessive, profitability would be adversely affected.

Finally, individuals may use the contacts they develop to pursue their own interests and agendas that may be inconsistent with the organization's goals and objectives. Thus, they may distort or selectively use information to favor their preferred courses of action or withhold information in their own self-interest to enhance their power to the detriment of the common good. Drawing on our discussion of social networks, this is particularly true in an

groupthink
a tendency in an organization for individuals not to question shared beliefs.

organization that has too many bridging relationships but not enough closure relationships. In high closure groups, it is easier to watch each other to ensure that illegal or unethical acts don't occur. By contrast, bridging relationships make it easier for a person to play one group or individual off on another, with no one being the wiser.[101] We will discuss some behavioral control mechanisms in Chapter 9 (rewards, control, boundaries) that reduce such dysfunctional behaviors and actions.[102]

LO4.5

The vital role of technology in leveraging knowledge and human capital.

Using Technology to Leverage Human Capital and Knowledge

Sharing knowledge and information throughout the organization can be a means of conserving resources, developing products and services, and creating new opportunities. In this section we will discuss how technology can be used to leverage human capital and knowledge within organizations as well as with customers and suppliers beyond their boundaries.

Using Networks to Share Information

As we all know, email is an effective means of communicating a wide variety of information. It is quick, easy, and almost costless. Of course, it can become a problem when employees use it extensively for personal reasons. And we all know how fast jokes or rumors can spread within and across organizations!

Below is an example of how a CEO curbed what he felt was excessive time he spent on email.

> Brian Scudamore, CEO of 1-800-GOT-Junk, the $100 million clutter-removal service, found he was spending far too much time tackling his inbox.[103] He asked his assistant to take over and handle his emails. He says that getting rid of this "business killer" improved his productivity and made him a better manager. It also freed him to encourage and inspire his team. "It's given me time to walk around and talk to people," he says. Imagine that!

Email can also cause embarrassment, or worse, if one is not careful. Consider the plight of a potential CEO—as recalled by Marshall Goldsmith, a well-known executive coach:[104]

> I witnessed a series of e-mails between a potential CEO and a friend inside the company. The first e-mail to the friend provided an elaborate description of "why the current CEO is an idiot." The friend sent a reply. Several rounds of e-mails followed. Then the friend sent an e-mail containing a funny joke. The potential CEO decided that the current CEO would love this joke and forwarded it to him. You can guess what happened next. The CEO scrolled down the e-mail chain and found the "idiot" message. The heir apparent was gone in a week.

Email can, however, be a means for top executives to communicate information efficiently. For example, Martin Sorrell, chairman of WPP Group PLC, the huge $17 billion advertising and public relations firm, is a strong believer in the use of email.[105] He emails all of his employees once a month to discuss how the company is doing, address specific issues, and offer his perspectives on hot issues, such as new business models for the Internet. He believes that it keeps people abreast of what he is working on.

Technology can also enable much more sophisticated forms of communication in addition to knowledge sharing. Cisco, for example, launched Integrated Workforce Experience (IWE) in 2010.[106] It is a social business platform designed to facilitate internal and external collaboration and decentralize decision making. It functions much like a Facebook "wall": A real-time news feed provides updates on employees' status and activities as well as information about relevant communities, business projects, and customer and partner interactions. One manager likens it to Amazon. "It makes recommendations based on what you are doing, the role you are in, and the choices of other people like you. We are taking that to the enterprise level and basically allowing appropriate information to find you," he says.

Electronic Teams: Using Technology to Enhance Collaboration

LO4.6

Why "electronic" or "virtual" teams are critical in combining and leveraging knowledge in organizations and how they can be made more effective.

Technology enables professionals to work as part of electronic, or virtual, teams to enhance the speed and effectiveness with which products are developed. For example, Microsoft has concentrated much of its development on **electronic teams** (or e-teams) that are networked together.[107] This helps to accelerate design and testing of new software modules that use the Windows-based framework as their central architecture. Microsoft is able to foster specialized technical expertise while sharing knowledge rapidly throughout the firm. This helps the firm learn how its new technologies can be applied rapidly to new business ventures such as cable television, broadcasting, travel services, and financial services.

electronic teams
a team of individuals that completes tasks primarily through e-mail communication.

What are electronic teams (or e-teams)? There are two key differences between e-teams and more traditional teams:[108]

- E-team members either work in geographically separated work places or they may work in the same space but at different times. E-teams may have members working in different spaces and time zones, as is the case with many multinational teams.
- Most of the interactions among members of e-teams occur through electronic communication channels such as fax machines and groupware tools such as email, bulletin boards, chat, and videoconferencing.

E-teams have expanded exponentially in recent years.[109] Organizations face increasingly high levels of complex and dynamic change. E-teams are also effective in helping businesses cope with global challenges. Most e-teams perform very complex tasks and most knowledge-based teams are charged with developing new products, improving organizational processes, and satisfying challenging customer problems. For example, Hewlett Packard's e-teams solve clients' computing problems, and Sun Microsystems' (part of Oracle) e-teams generate new business models.

Advantages   There are multiple advantages of e-teams.[110] In addition to the rather obvious use of technology to facilitate communications, the potential benefits parallel the other two major sections in this chapter—human capital and social capital.

First, e-teams are less restricted by the geographic constraints that are placed on face-to-face teams. Thus, e-teams have the potential to acquire a broader range of "human capital" or the skills and capacities that are necessary to complete complex assignments. So, e-team leaders can draw upon a greater pool of talent to address a wider range of problems since they are not constrained by geographic space. Once formed, e-teams can be more flexible in responding to unanticipated work challenges and opportunities because team members can be rotated out of projects when demands and contingencies alter the team's objectives.

Second, e-teams can be very effective in generating "social capital"—the quality of relationships and networks that form. Such capital is a key lubricant in work transactions and operations. Given the broader boundaries associated with e-teams, members and leaders generally have access to a wider range of social contacts than would be typically available in more traditional face-to-face teams. Such contacts are often connected to a broader scope of clients, customers, constituents, and other key stakeholders.

Challenges   However, there are challenges associated with making e-teams effective. Successful action by both traditional teams and e-teams requires that:

- Members *identify* who among them can provide the most appropriate knowledge and resources, and,
- E-team leaders and key members know how to *combine* individual contributions in the most effective manner for a coordinated and appropriate response.

Group psychologists have termed such activities "identification and combination" activities and teams that fail to perform them face a "process loss."[111] Process losses prevent teams from reaching high levels of performance because of inefficient interaction dynamics among team members. Such poor dynamics require that some collective energy, time, and effort be devoted to dealing with team inefficiencies, thus diverting the team away from its objectives. For example, if a team member fails to communicate important information at critical phases of a project, other members may waste time and energy. This can lead to conflict and resentment as well as to decreased motivation to work hard to complete tasks.

The potential for process losses tends to be more prevalent in e-teams than in traditional teams because the geographical dispersion of members increases the complexity of establishing effective interaction and exchanges. Generally, teams suffer process loss because of low cohesion, low trust among members, a lack of appropriate norms or standard operating procedures, or a lack of shared understanding among team members about their tasks. With e-teams, members are more geographically or temporally dispersed, and the team becomes more susceptible to the risk factors that can create process loss. Such problems can be exacerbated when team members have less than ideal competencies and social skills. This can erode problem-solving capabilities as well as the effective functioning of the group as a social unit.

A variety of technologies, from email and Internet groups to Skype and Cisco's Umi TelePresence, have facilitated the formation and effective functioning of e-teams as well as a wide range of collaborations within companies. Such technologies greatly enhance the collaborative abilities of employees and managers within a company at a reasonable cost—despite the distances that separate them.

Codifying Knowledge for Competitive Advantage

There are two different kinds of knowledge. Tacit knowledge is embedded in personal experience and shared only with the consent and participation of the individual. Explicit (or codified) knowledge, on the other hand, is knowledge that can be documented, widely distributed, and easily replicated. One of the challenges of knowledge-intensive organizations is to capture and codify the knowledge and experience that, in effect, resides in the heads of its employees. Otherwise, they will have to constantly "reinvent the wheel," which is both expensive and inefficient. Also, the "new wheel" may not necessarily be superior to the "old wheel."[112]

Once a knowledge asset (e.g., a software code or a process) is developed and paid for, it can be reused many times at very low cost, assuming that it doesn't have to be substantially modified each time. Let's take the case of a consulting company, such as Accenture (formerly Andersen Consulting).[113]

> Since the knowledge of its consultants has been codified and stored in electronic repositories, it can be employed in many jobs by a huge number of consultants. Additionally, since the work has a high level of standardization (i.e., there are strong similarities across the numerous client engagements), there is a rather high ratio of consultants to partners. For example, the ratio of consultants to partners is roughly 30, which is quite high. As one might expect, there must be extensive training of the newly hired consultants for such an approach to work. The recruits are trained at Accenture's Center for Professional Education, a 150-acre campus in St. Charles, Illinois. Using the center's knowledge-management respository, the consultants work through many scenarios designed to improve business processes. In effect, the information technologies enable the consultants to be "implementers, not inventors."

Access Health, a call-in medical center, also uses technology to capture and share knowledge. When someone calls the center, a registered nurse uses the company's "clinical decision architecture" to assess the caller's symptoms, rule out possible conditions, and recommend a home remedy, doctor's visit, or trip to the emergency room. The company's

HOW SAP TAPS KNOWLEDGE WELL BEYOND ITS BOUNDARIES

Traditionally, organizations built and protected their knowledge stocks—proprietary resources that no one else could access. However, the more the business environment changes, the faster the value of what you know at any point in time diminishes. In today's world, success hinges on the ability to access a growing variety of knowledge flows in order to rapidly replenish the firm's knowledge stocks. For example, when an organization tries to improve cycle times in a manufacturing process, it finds far more value in problem solving shaped by the diverse experiences, perspectives, and learning of a tightly knit team (shared through knowledge flows) than in a training manual (knowledge stocks) alone.

Knowledge flows can help companies gain competitive advantage in an age of near-constant disruption. The software company SAP, for example, routinely taps the nearly 3 million participants in its Community Network, which extends well beyond the boundaries of the firm. By providing a virtual platform for customers,

developers, system integrators, and service vendors to create and exchange knowledge, SAP has significantly increased the productivity of all the participants in its ecosystem.

According to Mark Yolton, Senior Vice President of SAP Communications and Social Media, "It's a very robust community with a great deal of activity. We see about 1.2 million unique visitors every month. Hundreds of millions of pages are viewed every year. There are 4,000 discussion forum posts every single day, 365 days a year, and about 115 blogs every day, 365 days a year, from any of the nearly 3 million members."

The site is open to everyone, regardless of whether you are an SAP customer, partner, or newcomer who needs to work with SAP technology. The site offers technical articles, Web-based training, code samples, evaluation systems, discussion forums, and excellent blogs for community experts.

Source: Yolton, M. 2012. SAP: Using social media for building, selling and supporting. *sloanreview.mit.edu*, August 7: np; Hagel, J., III., Brown, J. S., & Davison, L. 2009. The Big Shift: Measuring the Forces of Change. *Harvard Business Review*, 87(4): 87; and Anonymous. undated. SAP Developer Network. *sap.sys-con.com*. np.

---

knowledge repository contains algorithms of the symptoms of more than 500 illnesses. According to CEO Joseph Tallman, "We are not inventing a new way to cure disease. We are taking available knowledge and inventing processes to put it to better use." The software algorithms were very expensive to develop, but the investment has been repaid many times over. The first 300 algorithms that Access Health developed have each been used an average of 8,000 times a year. Further, the company's paying customers—insurance companies and provider groups—save money because many callers would have made expensive trips to the emergency room or the doctor's office had they not been diagnosed over the phone.

The user community can be a major source of knowledge creation for a firm. Strategy Spotlight 4.5 highlights how SAP, in an example of effective crowdsourcing, has been able to leverage the expertise and involvement of its users to develop new knowledge and transmit it to their entire user community.

We close this section with a series of questions managers should consider in determining (1) how effective their organization is in attracting, developing, and retaining human capital and (2) how effective they are in leveraging human capital through social capital and technology. These questions, included in Exhibit 4.5, summarize some of the key issues addressed in this chapter.

Protecting the Intellectual Assets of the Organization: Intellectual Property and Dynamic Capabilities

> **LO4.7**
> The challenge of protecting intellectual property and the importance of a firm's dynamic capabilities.

In today's dynamic and turbulent world, unpredictability and fast change dominate the business environment. Firms can use technology, attract human capital, or tap into research and design networks to get access to pretty much the same information as their competitors. So what would give firms a sustainable competitive advantage?[114]

EXHIBIT 4.5 Issues to Consider in Creating Value through Human Capital, Social Capital, and Technology

Human Capital

Recruiting "Top-Notch" Human Capital

- Does the organization assess attitude and "general makeup" instead of focusing primarily on skills and background in selecting employees at all levels?
- How important are creativity and problem-solving ability? Are they properly considered in hiring decisions?
- Do people throughout the organization engage in effective networking activities to obtain a broad pool of worthy potential employees? Is the organization creative in such endeavors?

Enhancing Human Capital through Employee Development

- Does the development and training process inculcate an "organizationwide" perspective?
- Is there widespread involvement, including top executives, in the preparation and delivery of training and development programs?
- Is the development of human capital effectively tracked and monitored?
- Are there effective programs for succession at all levels of the organization, especially at the top-most levels?
- Does the firm effectively evaluate its human capital? Is a 360-degree evaluation used? Why? Why not?
- Are mechanisms in place to assure that a manager's success does not come at the cost of compromising the organization's core values?

Retaining the Best Employees

- Are there appropriate financial rewards to motivate employees at all levels?
- Do people throughout the organization strongly identify with the organization's mission?
- Are employees provided with a stimulating and challenging work environment that fosters professional growth?
- Are valued amenities provided (e.g., flex time, child-care facilities, telecommuting) that are appropriate given the organization's mission, strategy, and how work is accomplished?
- Is the organization continually devising strategies and mechanisms to retain top performers?

Social Capital

- Are there positive personal and professional relationships among employees?
- Is the organization benefiting (or being penalized) by hiring (or by voluntary turnover) en masse?
- Does an environment of caring and encouragement rather than competition enhance team performance?
- Do the social networks within the organization have the appropriate levels of closure and bridging relationships?
- Does the organization minimize the adverse effects of excessive social capital, such as excessive costs and "groupthink"?

Technology

- Has the organization used technologies such as email and networks to develop products and services?
- Does the organization effectively use technology to transfer best practices across the organization?
- Does the organization use technology to leverage human capital and knowledge both within the boundaries of the organization and among its suppliers and customers?
- Has the organization effectively used technology to codify knowledge for competitive advantage?
- Does the organization try to retain some of the knowledge of employees when they decide to leave the firm?

Source: Adapted from Dess, G. G., & Picken, J. C. 1999. *Beyond Productivity:* 63–64. New York: AMACON.

Protecting a firm's intellectual property requires a concerted effort on the part of the company. After all, employees become disgruntled and patents expire. The management of intellectual property (IP) involves, besides patents, contracts with confidentiality and noncompete clauses, copyrights, and the development of trademarks. Moreover, developing dynamic capabilities is the only avenue providing firms with the ability to reconfigure their knowledge and activities to achieve a sustainable competitive advantage.

Intellectual Property Rights

Intellectual property rights are more difficult to define and protect than property rights for physical assets (e.g., plant, equipment, and land). However, if intellectual property rights are not reliably protected by the state, there will be no incentive to develop new products and services. Property rights have been enshrined in constitutions and rules of law in many countries. In the information era, though, adjustments need to be made to accommodate the new realities of knowledge. Knowledge and information are fundamentally different assets from the physical ones that property rights have been designed to protect.

The protection of intellectual rights raises unique issues, compared to physical property rights. IP is characterized by significant development costs and very low marginal costs. Indeed, it may take a substantial investment to develop a software program, an idea, or a digital music tune. Once developed, though, their reproduction and distribution cost may be almost zero, especially if the Internet is used. Effective protection of intellectual property is necessary before any investor will finance such an undertaking. Appropriation of their returns is harder to police since possession and deployment are not as readily observable. Unlike physical assets, intellectual property can be stolen by simply broadcasting it. Recall Napster and MP3 as well as the debates about counterfeit software, music CDs, and DVDs coming from developing countries such as China. Part of the problem is that using an idea does not prevent others from simultaneously using it for their own benefit, which is typically impossible with physical assets. Moreover, new ideas are frequently built on old ideas and are not easily traceable.

Given these unique challenges in protecting IP, it comes as no surprise that legal battles over patents become commonplace in IP-heavy industries such as telecommunications. Take the recent patent battles Apple is fighting against smartphone makers running Android, Google's mobile operating system.[115]

> In 2012, Apple and HTC, a Taiwanese smartphone maker, agreed to dismiss a series of lawsuits filed against each other after Apple accused HTC of copying the iPhone. While this settlement may be a sign that Apple's new CEO, Timothy Cook is eager to end the distractions caused by IP-related litigation, other patent battles continue, including one between Apple and Samsung, the largest maker of Android phones. This legal battle involves much higher stakes, because Samsung shipped almost eight times as many Android smartphones as HTC in the third quarter of 2012. It remains to be seen how these IP-related legal battles eventually turn out, but Apple's new leadership seems to be more pragmatic about this issue. In Mr. Cook's words, "It is awkward. I hate litigation. I absolutely hate it," suggesting that he is not as enthusiastic a combatant in the patent wars as was his predecessor, Steve Jobs, who famously promised to "destroy Android, because it's a stolen product."

Countries are attempting to pass new legislation to cope with developments in new pharmaceutical compounds, stem cell research, and biotechnology. However, a firm that is faced with this challenge today cannot wait for the legislation to catch up. New technological developments, software solutions, electronic games, online services, and other products and services contribute to our economic prosperity and the creation of wealth for those entrepreneurs who have the idea first and risk bringing it to the market.

Dynamic Capabilities

Dynamic capabilities entail the capacity to build and protect a competitive advantage.[116] This rests on knowledge, assets, competencies, and complementary assets and technologies as well as the ability to sense and seize new opportunities, generate new knowledge, and reconfigure existing assets and capabilities.[117] According to David Teece, an economist at the University of California at Berkeley, dynamic capabilities are related to the

intellectual property rights
intangible property owned by a firm in the forms of patents, copyrights, trademarks, or trade secrets.

dynamic capabilities
a firm's capacity to build and protect a competitive advantage, which rests on knowledge, assets, competencies, complementary assets, and technologies. Dynamic capabilities include the ability to sense and seize new opportunities, generate new knowledge, and reconfigure existing assets and capabilities.

Are employees abandoning Apple?

By Asha Moore-Mangin and Sarah Hudson

Word is out in Silicon Valley that Apple employees are on the move. This comes as a bit of a surprise because Apple has a reputation for low staff turnover even though it offers lower pay and fewer perks then other companies. This reputation is changing as other technology companies such as Google, LinkedIn, Facebook, and Hewlett Packard are starting to receive more resume's from Apple employees. When questioned, job-seekers give two main reasons for looking elsewhere; the first is that start-ups pay more and secondly that the culture at Apple is changing due to the change of leadership.

CEO Tim Cook who took over from the visionary Steve Jobs in 2011 has found it hard to follow in Jobs' footsteps but in fairness who wouldn't have. Jobs was a visionary leader and creator of innovative products. He held bi-weekly meetings about the product-line and he made it possible for his employees to achieve the impossible. Cook is a business man who has given the company a more traditional direction and he believes in delegation, spreadsheets, and consensus. He does not attend product-line meetings and has not yet created anything revolutionary or innovative.

Another question being asked is whether Apple has run out of steam? Its stock has fallen, merchants are carrying iPhone inventories and its recent unveiling of a redesigned iOS 7 for the iPhones and iPads has failed to excite investors. For how much longer can Apple rest on its laurels?

Discussion Questions

1. Why are employees leaving Apple?
2. Are employees leaving because the stock price is falling or is the stock price falling because employees are leaving?

Sources: Nicholas Carson, Business Insider, April 15 2013, Apple Employees Are Sending Out CVs Like Never Before,; www.businessinsider.com/apple-executives-are-suddenly-more-willing-to-quit-the-company-to-work-at-startups-2013-4#ixzz2aLLW4UYI; Louis Bedigian, June 24 2013, Apple Employees Are Leaving for Google, LinkedIn, Facebook and Hewlett-Packard www.benzinga.com/analyst-ratings/analyst-color/13/06/3700262/apple-employees-are-leaving-for-google-linkedin-facebook#ixzz2aLLkncln; Chris O'Brien, June 24 2013, Apple stock drops to $400 amid reports of employee defections, www.latimes.com/business/technology/la-fi-tn-apple-stock-20130624,0,3190659.story; Rebecca Greenfield, August 22 2013, Apple CEO Tim Cook's Uninspiring Style Is Pushing Employees Away, www.theatlanticwire.com/technology/2013/08/apple-ceo-tim-cooks-uninspiring-style-pushing-employees-away/68608/

entrepreneurial side of the firm and are built within a firm through its environmental and technological "sensing" apparatus, its choices of organizational form, and its collective ability to strategize. Dynamic capabilities are about the ability of an organization to challenge the conventional wisdom within its industry and market, learn and innovate, adapt to the changing world, and continuously adopt new ways to serve the evolving needs of the market.[118]

Examples of dynamic capabilities include product development, strategic decision making, alliances, and acquisitions.[119] Some firms have clearly developed internal processes and routines that make them superior in such activities. For example, 3M and Apple are ahead of their competitors in product development. Cisco Systems has made numerous acquisitions over the years. They seem to have developed the capability to identify and evaluate potential acquisition candidates and seamlessly integrate them once the acquisition is completed. Other organizations can try to copy Cisco's practices. However, Cisco's combination of the resources of the acquired companies and their reconfiguration that Cisco has already achieved places them well ahead of their competitors. As markets become increasingly dynamic, traditional sources of long-term competitive advantage become less relevant. In such markets, all that a firm can strive for are a series of temporary advantages. Dynamic capabilities allow a firm to create this series of temporary advantages through new resource configurations.[120]

Reflecting on Career Implications . . .

- ▣ **Human Capital:** Identify specific steps taken by your organization to effectively attract, develop, and retain talent. If you cannot identify such steps by your organization, you may have fewer career opportunities to develop your human capital at your organization. Do you take advantage of your organization's human resource programs, such as tuition reimbursement, mentoring, and so forth?

- ▣ **Human Capital:** As workplaces become more diverse, it is important to reflect on whether your organization values diversity. What kinds of diversity seem to be encouraged (e.g., age-based or ethnicity-based)? In what ways are your colleagues different from and similar to you? If your firm has a homogeneous workforce, there may be limited perspectives on strategic and operational issues and a career at this organization may be less attractive to you.

- ▣ **Social Capital:** Does your organization have strong social capital? What is the basis of your conclusion that it has strong or weak social capital? What specific programs are in place to build and develop social capital? What is the impact of social capital on employee turnover in your organization? Alternatively, is social capital so strong that you see effects such as "groupthink"? From your perspective, how might you better leverage social capital toward pursuing other career opportunities?

- ▣ **Social Capital:** Are you actively working to build a strong social network at your work organization? To advance your career, strive to build a broad network that gives you access to diverse information.

- ▣ **Technology:** Does your organization provide and effectively use technology (e.g., groupware, knowledge management systems) to help you leverage your talents and expand your knowledge base? If your organization does a poor job in this regard, what can you do on your own to expand your knowledge base using technology available outside the organization?

summary

Firms throughout the industrial world are recognizing that the knowledge worker is the key to success in the marketplace. However, we also recognize that human capital, although vital, is still only a necessary, but not a sufficient, condition for creating value. We began the first section of the chapter by addressing the importance of human capital and how it can be attracted, developed, and retained. Then we discussed the role of social capital and technology in leveraging human capital for competitive success. We pointed out that intellectual capital—the difference between a firm's market value and its book value—has increased significantly over the past few decades. This is particularly true for firms in knowledge-intensive industries, especially where there are relatively few tangible assets, such as software development.

The second section of the chapter addressed the attraction, development, and retention of human capital. We viewed these three activities as a "three-legged stool"—that is, it is difficult for firms to be successful if they ignore or are unsuccessful in any one of these activities. Among the issues we discussed in *attracting* human capital were "hiring for attitude, training for skill" and the value of using social networks to attract human capital. In particular, it is important to attract employees who can collaborate with others, given the importance of collective efforts such as teams and task forces. With regard to *developing* human capital, we discussed the need to encourage widespread involvement throughout the organization, monitor progress and track the development of human capital, and evaluate human capital. Among the issues that are widely practiced in evaluating human capital is the 360-degree evaluation system. Employees are evaluated by their superiors, peers, direct reports, and even internal and external customers. We also addressed the value of maintaining a diverse workforce. Finally, some mechanisms for retaining human capital are employees' identification with the organization's mission and values, providing challenging work and a stimulating environment, the importance of financial and nonfinancial rewards and incentives, and providing flexibility and amenities. A key issue here is that a firm should not overemphasize financial rewards. After all, if individuals join an organization for money, they also are likely to leave for money. With money as the primary motivator, there is little chance that employees will develop firm specific ties to keep them with the organization.

The third section of the chapter discussed the importance of social capital in leveraging human capital. Social capital refers to the network of relationships that individuals have throughout the organization as well as with customers and suppliers. Such ties can be critical in obtaining both information and resources. With regard to recruiting, for example, we saw how some firms are able to hire en masse groups of individuals who are part of social networks. Social relationships can also be very important in the effective functioning of groups. Finally, we discussed some of the potential downsides of social capital. These include the expenses that firms may bear when promoting social and working relationships among individuals as well as the potential for "groupthink," wherein individuals are reluctant to express divergent (or opposing) views on an issue because of social pressures to conform. We also introduced the concept of social networks. The relative advantages of being central in a network versus bridging multiple networks was discussed. We addressed the key role that social networks can play in both improving knowledge management and promoting career success.

The fourth section addressed the role of technology in leveraging human capital. We discussed relatively simple means of using technology, such as email and networks where individuals can collaborate by way of personal computers. We provided suggestions and guidelines on how electronic teams can be effectively managed. We also addressed more sophisticated uses of technology, such as sophisticated management systems. Here knowledge can be codified and reused at very low cost, as we saw in the examples of firms in the consulting, health care, and high-technology industries.

In the last section we discussed the increasing importance of protecting a firm's intellectual property. Although traditional approaches such as patents, copyrights, and trademarks are important, the development of dynamic capabilities may be the best protection in the long run.

key terms

knowledge economy 107
intellectual capital 107
human capital 108
social capital 108
explicit knowledge 108
tacit knowledge 108
360-degree evaluation and
    feedback systems 115
social network analysis 121

closure 121
bridging
    relationships 122
structural holes 122
unification lever 123
people lever 123
T-shaped
    management 123
network lever 123
groupthink 125
electronic teams 127
intellectual property
    rights 131
dynamic capabilities 131

SUMMARY REVIEW QUESTIONS

1. Explain the role of knowledge in today's competitive environment.
2. Why is it important for managers to recognize the interdependence in the attraction, development, and retention of talented professionals?

3. What are some of the potential downsides for firms that engage in a "war for talent"?
4. Discuss the need for managers to use social capital in leveraging their human capital both within and across their firm.
5. Discuss the key role of technology in leveraging knowledge and human capital.

experiential exercise

Pfizer, a leading health care firm with $59 billion in revenues, is often rated as one of *Fortune*'s "Most Admired Firms." It is also considered an excellent place to work and has generated high return to shareholders. Clearly, they value their human capital. Using the Internet and/or library resources, identify some of the actions/strategies Pfizer has taken to attract, develop, and retain human capital. What are their implications?

application questions & exercises

1. Look up successful firms in a high-technology industry as well as two successful firms in more traditional industries such as automobile manufacturing and retailing. Compare their market values and book values. What are some implications of these differences?
2. Select a firm for which you believe its social capital—both within the firm and among its suppliers and customers—is vital to its competitive advantage. Support your arguments.
3. Choose a company with which you are familiar. What are some of the ways in which it uses technology to leverage its human capital?
4. Using the Internet, look up a company with which you are familiar. What are some of the policies and procedures that it uses to enhance the firm's human and social capital?

ethics questions

1. Recall an example of a firm that recently faced an ethical crisis. How do you feel the crisis and management's handling of it affected the firm's human capital and social capital?
2. Based on your experiences or what you have learned in your previous classes, are you familiar with any companies that used unethical practices to attract talented professionals? What do you feel were the short-term and long-term consequences of such practices?

Activity	Actions/Strategies	Implications
Attracting human capital		
Developing human capital		
Retaining human capital		

references

1. Touryalai, H. 2011. Meddling with Merrill: Merrill Lynch's profits are bolstering BofA. What is Merrill getting in return? *Forbes,* September 26: 45–47; Benoit, D. 2012. BofA-Merrill: Still a bottom-line success. *www.wsj .com,* September 28: np; Silver-Greenberg, J & Craig, S. 2012. Bank of America settles suit over Merrill for $2.43 billion. *www .nytimes.com,* September 28: np.

2. Parts of this chapter draw upon some of the ideas and examples from Dess, G. G. & Picken, J. C. 1999. *Beyond productivity.* New York: AMACOM.

3. An acknowledged trend: The world economic survey. 1996. *The Economist,* September 2(8): 25–28.

4. Quinn, J. B., Anderson, P., & Finkelstein, S. 1996. Leveraging intellect. *Academy of Management Executive,* 10(3): 7–27; and *https:// www.cia.gov/library/publications/ the=world=factbook/geos/us.html.*

5. Hamel, G. & Prahalad, C. K. 1996. Competing in the new economy: Managing out of bounds. *Strategic Management Journal,* 17: 238.

6. Stewart, T. A. 1997. *Intellectual capital: The new wealth of organizations.* New York: Doubleday/Currency.

7. Leif Edvisson and Michael S. Malone have a similar, more detailed definition of *intellectual capital:* "the combined knowledge, skill, innovativeness, and ability to meet the task at hand." They consider intellectual capital to equal human capital plus structural capital. *Structural capital* is defined as "the hardware, software, databases, organization structure, patents, trademarks, and everything else of organizational capability that supports those employees' productivity—in a word, everything left at the office when the employees go home." Edvisson, L. & Malone, M. S. 1997. *Intellectual capital: Realizing your company's true value by finding its hidden brainpower:* 10–14. New York: HarperBusiness.

8. Stewart, T. A. 2001. Accounting gets radical. *Fortune,* April 16: 184–194.

9. Adams, S. & Kichen, S. 2008. Ben Graham then and now. *Forbes,* November 10: 56.

10. An interesting discussion of Steve Jobs's impact on Apple's valuation is in: Lashinsky, A. 2009. Steve's leave—what does it really mean? *Fortune,* February 2: 96–102.

11. Anonyous. 2007. Intel opens first high volume 45 nm microprocessor manufacturing factory. *www.intel .com.* October 25: np.

12. Thomas Stewart has suggested this formula in his book *Intellectual capital.* He provides an insightful discussion on pages 224–225, including some of the limitations of this approach to measuring intellectual capital. We recognize, of course, that during the late 1990s and in early 2000, there were some excessive market valuations of high-technology and Internet firms. For an interesting discussion of the extraordinary market valuation of Yahoo!, an Internet company, refer to Perkins, A. B. 2001. The Internet bubble encapsulated: Yahoo! *Red Herring,* April 15: 17–18.

13. Roberts, P. W. & Dowling, G. R. 2002. Corporate reputation and sustained superior financial performance. *Strategic Management Journal,* 23(12): 1077–1095.

14. For a recent study on the relationships between human capital, learning, and sustainable competitive advantage, read Hatch, N. W. & Dyer, J. H. 2005. Human capital and learning as a source of sustainable competitive advantage. *Strategic Management Journal,* 25: 1155–1178.

15. One of the seminal contributions on knowledge management is Becker, G. S. 1993. *Human capital: A theoretical and empirical analysis with special reference to education* (3rd ed.). Chicago: University of Chicago Press.

16. For an excellent overview of the topic of social capital, read Baron, R. A. 2005. Social capital. In Hitt, M. A. & Ireland, R. D. (Eds.), *The Blackwell encyclopedia of management* (2nd ed.): 224–226. Malden, MA: Blackwell.

17. For an excellent discussion of social capital and its impact on organizational performance, refer to Nahapiet, J. & Ghoshal, S. 1998. Social capital, intellectual capital, and the organizational advantage. *Academy of Management Review,* 23: 242–266.

18. An interesting discussion of how knowledge management (patents) can enhance organizational performance can be found in Bogner, W. C. & Bansal, P. 2007. Knowledge management as the basis of sustained high performance. *Journal of Management Studies,* 44(1): 165–188.

19. Polanyi, M. 1967. *The tacit dimension.* Garden City, NY: Anchor Publishing.

20. Barney, J. B. 1991. Firm resources and sustained competitive advantage. *Journal of Management,* 17: 99–120.

21. For an interesting perspective of empirical research on how knowledge can adversely affect performance, read Haas, M. R. & Hansen, M. T. 2005. When using knowledge can hurt performance: The value of organizational capabilities in a management consulting company. Strategic *Management Journal,* 26(1): 1–24.

22. New insights on managing talent are provided in: Cappelli, P. 2008. Talent management for the twenty-first century. *Harvard Business Review,* 66(3): 74–81.

23. Some of the notable books on this topic include Edvisson & Malone, op. cit.; Stewart, op. cit.; and Nonaka, I. & Takeuchi, I. 1995. *The knowledge creating company.* New York: Oxford University Press.

24. Segalla, M. & Felton, N. 2010. Find the real power in your organization. *Harvard Business Review,* 88(5): 34–35.

25. Stewart, T. A. 2000. Taking risk to the marketplace. *Fortune,* March 6: 424.

26. Insights on the Generation X's perspective on the workplace are in: Erickson, T. J. 2008. Task, not time: Profile of a Gen Y job. *Harvard Business Review,* 86(2): 19.

27. Pfeffer, J. 2010. Building sustainable organizations: The human factor. *The Academy of Management Perspectives,* 24(1): 34–45.

28. Dutton, G. 1997. Are you technologically competent? *Management Review,* November: 54–58.

29. Some workplace implications for the aging workforce are addressed in: Strack, R., Baier, J., & Fahlander, A. 2008. Managing demographic risk. *Harvard Business Review,* 66(2): 119–128.

30. For a discussion of attracting, developing, and retaining top talent, refer to Goffee, R. & Jones, G. 2007. Leading clever people. *Harvard Business Review,* 85(3): 72–89.

31. Dess & Picken, op. cit.: 34.

32. Webber, A. M. 1998. Danger: Toxic company. *Fast Company,* November: 152–161.

33. Martin, J. & Schmidt, C. 2010. How to keep your top talent. *Harvard Business Review,* 88(5): 54–61.

34. Some interesting insights on why home-grown American talent is going abroad is found in: Saffo, P. 2009. A looming American diaspora. *Harvard Business Review,* 87(2): 27.

35. Grossman, M. 2012. The best advice I ever got. *Fortune,* May 12: 119.

36. Davenport, T. H., Harris, J. & Shapiro, J. 2010. Competing on talent analytics. *Harvard Business Review,* 88(10): 62–69.

37. Ployhart, R. E. & Moliterno, T. P. 2011. Emergence of the human capital resource: A multilevel model. *Academy of Management Review,* 36(1): 127–150.

38. For insights on management development and firm performance in several countries, refer to: Mabey, C. 2008. Management development and firm performance in Germany, Norway, Spain, and the UK. *Journal of International Business Studies,* 39(8): 1327–1342.

39. Martin, J. 1998. So, you want to work for the best. . . . *Fortune,* January 12: 77.

40. Cardin, R. 1997. Make your own Bozo Filter. *Fast Company,* October–November: 56.

41. Anonymous, 100 best companies to work for *money.cnn.com.* Undated: np.

42. Martin, op. cit.; Henkoff, R. 1993. Companies that train best. *Fortune,* March 22: 53–60.

43. This section draws on: Garg, V. 2012. Here's why companies should give Millennial workers everything they ask for. *buisnessinsider.com,* August 23: np; *worklifepolicy.com*; and Gerdes, L. 2006. The top 50 employers for new college grads. *BusinessWeek,* September 18: 64–81.

44. An interesting perspective on developing new talent rapidly when they join an organization can be found in Rollag, K., Parise, S., & Cross, R. 2005. Getting new hires up to speed quickly. *MIT Sloan Management Review,* 46(2): 35–41.

45. Stewart, T. A. 1998. Gray flannel suit? moi? *Fortune,* March 18: 80–82.

46. Bryant, A. 2011. *The corner office.* St. Martin's Griffin: New York: 227.

47. An interesting perspective on how Cisco Systems develops its talent can be found in Chatman, J., O'Reilly, C., & Chang, V. 2005. Cisco Systems: Developing a human capital strategy. *California Management Review,* 47(2): 137–166.

48. Anonymous. 2011. Schumpeter: The tussle for talent. *The Economist.* January 8: 68.

49. Training and development policy: Mentoring. nd. *opm.gov*: np.

50. Douglas, C. A. 1997. Formal mentoring programs in organizations. *centerforcreativeleadership.org*: np.

51. Warner, F. 2002. Inside Intel's mentoring movement. *fastcompany.com*, March 31: np.

52. Grove, A. 2011. Be a mentor. *Bloomberg BusinessWeek,* September 21: 80.

53. Our discussion of sponsorship draws on: Alsever, J. 2012. Want to move up? Get a sponsor. *Fortune,* May 21: 53–54; and Aguirre, D. 2010. When female networks aren't enough. *blogs.org/hbr/hewlett,* May 12: np.

54. For an innovative perspective on the appropriateness of alternate approaches to evaluation and rewards, refer to Seijts, G. H. & Lathan, G. P. 2005. Learning versus performance goals: When should each be used? *Academy of Management Executive,* 19(1): 124–132.

55. The discussion of the 360-degree feedback system draws on the article UPS. 1997. 360-degree feedback: Coming from all sides. *Vision* (a UPS Corporation internal company publication), March: 3; Slater, R. 1994. *Get better or get beaten: Thirty-one leadership secrets from Jack Welch.* Burr Ridge, IL: Irwin; Nexon, M. 1997. General Electric: The secrets of the finest company in the world. *L'Expansion,* July 23: 18–30; and Smith, D. 1996. Bold new directions for human resources. *Merck World* (internal company publication), October: 8.

56. Interesting insights on 360-degree evaluation systems are discussed in: Barwise, P. & Meehan, Sean. 2008. So you think you're a good listener. *Harvard Business Review,* 66(4): 22–23.

57. Insights into the use of 360-degree evaluation are in: Kaplan, R. E. & Kaiser, R. B. 2009. Stop overdoing your strengths. *Harvard Business Review,* 87(2): 100–103.

58. Kets de Vries, M. F. R. 1998. Charisma in action: The transformational abilities of Virgin's Richard Branson and ABB's Percy Barnevik. *Organizational Dynamics,* Winter: 20.

59. For an interesting discussion on how organizational culture has helped Zappos become number one in *Fortune's* 2009 survey of the best companies to work for, see: O'Brien, J. M. n 2009. Zappos knows how to kick it. *Fortune,* February 2: 54–58.

60. We have only to consider the most celebrated case of industrial espionage in recent years, wherein José Ignacio Lopez was indicted in a German court for stealing sensitive product planning documents from his former employer, General Motors, and sharing them with his executive colleagues at Volkswagen. The lawsuit was dismissed by the German courts, but Lopez and his colleagues were investigated by the U.S. Justice Department. Also consider the recent litigation involving noncompete employment contracts and confidentiality clauses of *International Paper v. Louisiana-Pacific, Campbell Soup v. H. J. Heinz Co.,* and *PepsiCo v. Quaker Oats's Gatorade.* In addition to retaining valuable human resources and often their valuable network of customers, firms must also protect proprietary information and knowledge. For interesting insights, refer to Carley, W. M. 1998. CEO gets hard lesson in how not to keep his lieutenants. *The Wall Street Journal,* February 11: A1, A10; and Lenzner, R. & Shook, C. 1998. Whose Rolodex is it, anyway? *Forbes,* February 23: 100–103.

61. For an insightful discussion of retention of knowledge workers in today's economy, read Davenport, T. H. 2005. *The care and feeding of the knowledge worker.* Boston, MA: Harvard Business School Press.

62. Fisher, A. 2008. America's most admired companies. *Fortune,* March 17: 74.

63. Stewart, T. A. 2001. *The wealth of knowledge.* New York: Currency.

64. For insights on fulfilling one's potential, refer to: Kaplan, R. S. 2008. Reaching your potential. *Harvard Business Review,* 66(7/8): 45–57.

65. Amabile, T. M. 1997. Motivating creativity in organizations: On doing what you love and loving what you do. *California Management Review,* Fall: 39–58.

66. For an insightful perspective on alternate types of employee–employer relationships, read Erickson, T. J. & Gratton, L. 2007. What it means to work here. *Harvard Business Review,* 85(3): 104–112.

67. Pfeffer, J. 2001. Fighting the war for talent is hazardous to your organization's health. *Organizational Dynamics,* 29(4): 248–259.

68. Best companies to work for 2011. 2011. *finance.yahoo.com,* January 20: np.

69. Cox, T. L. 1991. The multinational organization. *Academy of Management Executive,* 5(2): 34–47. Without doubt, a great deal has been written on the topic of creating and

maintaining an effective diverse workforce. Some excellent, recent books include: Harvey, C. P. & Allard, M. J. 2005. *Understanding and managing diversity: Readings, cases, and exercises.* (3rd ed.). Upper Saddle River, NJ: Pearson Prentice-Hall; Miller, F. A. & Katz, J. H. 2002. *The inclusion breakthrough: Unleashing the real power of diversity.* San Francisco: Berrett Koehler; and Williams, M. A. 2001. *The 10 lenses: Your guide to living and working in a multicultural world.* Sterling, VA: Capital Books.

70. For an interesting perspective on benefits and downsides of diversity in global consulting firms, refer to: Mors, M. L. 2010. Innovation in a global consulting firm: When the problem is too much diversity. *Strategic Management Journal,* 31(8): 841–872.

71. Day, J.C. undated. National population projections. *cps.ipums .org*: np.

72. Hewlett, S. A. & Rashid, R. 2010. The battle for female talent in emerging markets. *Harvard Business Review,* 88(5): 101–107.

73. This section, including the six potential benefits of a diverse workforce, draws on Cox, T. H. & Blake, S. 1991. Managing cultural diversity: Implications for organizational competitiveness. *Academy of Management Executive,* 5(3): 45–56.

74. *www.pwcglobal.com/us/eng/careers/ diversity/index.html.*

75. This discussion draws on Dess, G. G. & Lumpkin, G. T. 2001. Emerging issues in strategy process research. In Hitt, M. A., Freeman, R. E. & Harrison, J. S. (Eds.). *Handbook of strategic management:* 3–34. Malden, MA: Blackwell.

76. Wong, S.-S. & Boh, W. F. 2010. Leveraging the ties of others to build a reputation for trustworthiness among peers. *Academy of Management Journal,* 53(1): 129–148.

77. Adler, P. S. & Kwon, S. W. 2002. Social capital: Prospects for a new concept. *Academy of Management Review,* 27(1): 17–40.

78. Capelli, P. 2000. A market-driven approach to retaining talent. *Harvard Business Review,* 78(1): 103–113.

79. This hypothetical example draws on Peteraf, M. 1993. The cornerstones of competitive advantage. *Strategic Management Journal,* 14: 179–191.

80. Wernerfelt, B. 1984. A resource-based view of the firm. *Strategic Management Journal,* 5: 171–180.

81. Wysocki, B., Jr. 2000. Yet another hazard of the new economy: The Pied Piper Effect. *The Wall Street Journal,* March 20: A1–A16.

82. Ideas on how managers can more effectively use their social network are addressed in: McGrath, C. & Zell, D. 2009. Profiles of trust: Who to turn to, and for what. *MIT Sloan Management Review,* 50(2): 75–80.

83. Ibid.

84. Buckman, R. C. 2000. Tech defectors from Microsoft resettle together. *The Wall Street Journal,* October: B1–B6.

85. A study of the relationship between social networks and performance in China is found in: Li, J. J., Poppo, L., & Zhou, K. Z. 2008. Do managerial ties in China always produce value? Competition, uncertainty, and domestic vs. foreign firms. *Strategic Management Journal,* 29(4): 383–400.

86. Aime, F., Johnson, S., Ridge, J. W. & Hill, A. D. 2010. The routine may be stable but the advantage is not: Competitive implications of key employee mobility. *Strategic Management Journal,* 31(1): 75–87.

87. Ibarra, H. & Hansen, M. T. 2011. Are you a collaborative leader? *Harvard Business Review,* 89 (7/8): 68–74.

88. There has been a tremendous amount of theory building and empirical research in recent years in the area of social network analysis. Unquestionably, two of the major contributors to this domain have been Ronald Burt and J. S. Coleman. For excellent background discussions, refer to: Burt, R. S. 1992. *Structural holes: The social structure of competition.* Cambridge, MA: Harvard University Press; Coleman, J. S. 1990. *Foundations of social theory.* Cambridge, MA: Harvard University Press; and Coleman, J. S. 1988. Social capital in the creation of human capital. *American Journal of Sociology.* 94: S95–S120. For a more recent review and integration of current thought on social network theory, consider: Burt, R. S. 2005. *Brokerage & closure: An introduction to social capital.* Oxford Press: New York.

89. Our discussion draws on the concepts developed by Burt, 1992, op. cit.; Coleman, 1990, op. cit.; Coleman, 1988, op. cit.; and Oh, H., Chung, M. & Labianca, G. 2004. Group social capital and group effectiveness: The role of informal socializing ties. *Academy of Management Journal,* 47(6): 860–875. We would like to thank Joe Labianca (University of Kentucky)

for his helpful feedback and ideas in our discussion of social networks.

90. Arregle, J. L., Hitt, M. A., Sirmon, D. G., & Very, P. 2007. The development of organizational social capital: Attributes of family firms. *Journal of Management Studies,* 44(1): 73–95.

91. A novel perspective on social networks is in: Pentland, A. 2009. How social networks network best. *Harvard Business Review,* 87(2): 37.

92. Oh et al., op. cit.

93. Hoppe, op. cit.

94. This section draws on: Hansen, M. T. 2009. *Collaboration: How leaders avoid the traps, create unity, and reap big results.* Boston, MA: Harvard Business Press.

95. Perspectives on how to use and develop decision networks are discussed in: Cross, R., Thomas, R. J., & Light, D. A. 2009. How "who you know" affects what you decide. *MIT Sloan Management Review,* 50(2): 35–42.

96. Our discussion of the three advantages of social networks draws on Uzzi, B. & Dunlap. S. 2005. How to build your network. *Harvard Business Review,* 83(12): 53–60. For a recent, excellent review on the research exploring the relationship between social capital and managerial performance, read Moran, P. 2005. Structural vs. relational embeddedness: Social capital and managerial performance. *Strategic Management Journal,* 26(12): 1129–1151.

97. A perspective on personal influence is in: Christakis, N. A. 2009. The dynamics of personal influence. *Harvard Business Review,* 87(2): 31.

98. Cross, R. & Thomas, R. 2011. A smarter way to network. *Harvard Business Review,* 7/8 (89): 149–153.

99. Prusak, L. & Cohen, D. 2001. How to invest in social capital. *Harvard Business Review,* 79(6): 86–93.

100. Leonard, D. & Straus, S. 1997. Putting your company's whole brain to work. *Harvard Business Review,* 75(4): 110–122.

101. For an excellent discussion of public (i.e., the organization) versus private (i.e., the individual manager) benefits of social capital, refer to Leana, C. R. & Van Buren, H. J. 1999. Organizational social capital and employment practices. *Academy of Management Review,* 24(3): 538–555.

102. The authors would like to thank Joe Labianca, University of Kentucky, and John Lin, University of Texas at

Dallas, for their very helpful input in our discussion of social network theory and its practical implications.

103. Harnish, V. 2010. Stop doing these five business killers now. *Fortune,* December 6: 71.

104. Goldsmith, M. 2009. How not to lose the top job. *Harvard Business Review,* 87(1): 74.

105. Taylor, W. C. 1999. Whatever happened to globalization? *Fast Company,* December: 228–236.

106. Wilson, H. J., Guinan, P. J., Paris, S., & Weinberg, D. 2011. What's your social media strategy? *Harvard Business Review,* 7/8 (89): 23–25.

107. Lei, D., Slocum, J., & Pitts, R. A. 1999. Designing organizations for competitive advantage: The power of unlearning and learning. *Organizational Dynamics,* Winter: 24–38.

108. This section draws upon Zaccaro, S. J. & Bader, P. 2002. E-Leadership and the challenges of leading e-teams: Minimizing the bad and maximizing the good. *Organizational Dynamics,* 31(4): 377–387.

109. Kirkman, B. L., Rosen, B., Tesluk, P. E., & Gibson, C. B. 2004. The impact of team empowerment on virtual team performance: The moderating role of face-to-face interaction. *Academy of Management Journal,* 47(2): 175–192.

110. The discussion of the advantages and challenges associated with e-teams draws on Zacarro & Bader, op. cit.

111. For a recent study exploring the relationship between team empowerment, face-to-face interaction, and performance in virtual teams, read Kirkman, Rosen, Tesluk, & Gibson, op. cit.

112. For an innovative study on how firms share knowledge with competitors and the performance implications, read Spencer, J. W. 2003. Firms' knowledge sharing strategies in the global innovation system: Empirical evidence from the flat panel display industry. *Strategic Management Journal,* 24(3): 217–235.

113. The examples of Andersen Consulting and Access Health draw upon Hansen, M. T., Nohria, N., & Tierney, T. 1999. What's your strategy for managing knowledge? *Harvard Business Review,* 77(2): 106–118.

114. This discussion draws on Conley, J. G. 2005. *Intellectual capital management,* Kellogg School of Management and Schulich School of Business, York University, Toronto, KS 2003; Conley, J. G. & Szobocsan, J. 2001. Snow White shows the way. *Managing Intellectual Property,* June: 15–25; Greenspan, A. 2004. Intellectual property rights, The Federal Reserve Board, Remarks by the chairman, February 27; and Teece, D. J. 1998. Capturing value from knowledge assets, *California Management Review,* 40(3): 54–79. The authors would like to thank Professor Theo Peridis, York University, for his contribution to this section.

115. Wingfield, N. 2012. As Apple and HTC end lawsuits, smartphone patent battles continue. *New York Times. www.nytimes.com.* November 11: 57–63; and Tyrangiel, J. 2012. Tim Cook's freshman year: The Apple CEO speaks. *Bloomberg BusinessWeek,* December 6: 62–76.

116. E. Danneels. 2011. Trying to become a different type of company: Dynamic capability at Smith Corona. *Strategic Management Journal,* 32(1): 1–31.

117. A study of the relationship between dynamic capabilities and related diversification is: Doving, E. & Gooderham, P. N. 2008. *Strategic Management Journal,* 29(8): 841–858.

118. A perspective on strategy in turbulent markets is in: Sull, D. 2009. How to thrive in turbulent markets. *Harvard Business Review,* 87(2): 78–88.

119. Lee, G. K. 2008. Relevance of organizational capabilities and its dynamics: What to learn from entrants' product portfolios about the determinants of entry timing. *Strategic Management Journal,* 29(12): 1257–1280.

120. Eisenhardt, K. M. & Martin, J. E. 2000. Dynamic capabilities: What are they? *Strategic Management Journal,* 21: 1105–1121.

chapter 5

Business-Level Strategy:

Creating and Sustaining Competitive Advantages

After reading this chapter, you should have a good understanding of the following learning objectives:

LO5.1 The central role of competitive advantage in the study of strategic management, and the three generic strategies: overall cost leadership, differentiation, and focus.

LO5.2 How the successful attainment of generic strategies can improve a firm's relative power vis-à-vis the five forces that determine an industry's average profitability.

LO5.3 The pitfalls managers must avoid in striving to attain generic strategies.

LO5.4 How firms can effectively combine the generic strategies of overall cost leadership and differentiation.

LO5.5 What factors determine the sustainability of a firm's competitive advantage.

LO5.6 How Internet-enabled business models are being used to improve strategic positioning.

LO5.7 The importance of considering the industry life cycle to determine a firm's business-level strategy and its relative emphasis on functional area strategies and value-creating activities.

LO5.8 The need for turnaround strategies that enable a firm to reposition its competitive position in an industry.

Learning from Mistakes

How Showrooming almost destroyed Best Buy

In 2012, Best Buy, the world's largest electronics retailer was rocked by nearly nonstop turmoil. It saw three CEOs (who together were paid $26 million), a plunging stock price and several rounds of layoffs—both at the corporate level and at the stores. Best Buy also faced criticism that it had become a dinosaur in the digital age and that the alarming amount of "showrooming" occurring in its stores seriously eroded its market share.

Showrooming is where customers in the market for electronic items, for example, visit Best Buy to examine products and then use that information and advice to make informed online purchases at lower prices. Best Buy estimates that 40% of customers were visiting stores with no intention of buying anything. According to a Harris Interactive survey, 23% of respondents who said they had showroomed listed Best Buy as the bricks-and-mortar store they most frequently showroomed at. Best Buy knew that this was one of its biggest problems but was slow and inefficient in addressing the issue. It had also faced criticism for its poor customer service.

To address the latter issue, new CEO Hubert Joly decided to install Samsung-branded boutiques inside stores. The new stores-within-a-store model will go in 1,400 regular big-box

locations and the smaller mobile ones. Best Buy also invests more in online sales and uses promotions more efficiently in fighting competition such as Amazon which is not only a leader in the online sales business, but is also usually cheaper. In order to implement its new plans Best Buy updated its decade-old website which was part of its original woes. Currently programs such as "My Best Buy" are employed and recruitment of executives with experience in e-commerce is aggressively pursued. The retailer is also adding product reviews and buying guides to the site and enabling recommendations for other items the customer might want to buy.

It is believed that other Best Buy distributors like Google and Sony could follow Samsung's lead of partnering more with Best Buy. In fact the new Best Buy Canada plan includes a partnership with Microsoft to create Windows Stores at 500 Best Buy locations across the U.S. and more than 100 Best Buy and Future Shop locations in Canada. Samsung Electronics Canada will also be opening stores within Best Buy Canada and Future Shop stores. "They have great stores, in high traffic areas. It's a perfect, logical fit for bringing the Samsung experience to where consumers are shopping," said James Politeski, president of Samsung Canada.

David Strasser from Janney Capital Markets says "These vendors will also need to take up more space and invest more heavily in Best Buy as a distribution partner. This clearly is the death of showrooming at Best Buy."

Overall the news has been pretty good for Best Buy since Hubert Joly took over. Though the company is still laying people off, its stock has been one of the best performing on the Standard & Poor's 500 in the first half of 2013 and *Time* magazine recently proclaimed the company "back from the dead." In fact, 2013 was a renaissance year for Best Buy. After starting the year at a 10-year low, it rebounded 155 percent. Now we just have to wait and see whether Best Buy can keep this up.

By Cyrlene Claasen and Tom McNamara

Discussion Questions

1. Which factors contributed to Best Buy experiencing showrooming on such a high scale?
2. Does Best Buy have any real competitive advantage?

business-level strategy
a strategy designed for a firm or a division of a firm that competes within a single business.

The central role of competitive advantage in the study of strategic management, and the three generic strategies: overall cost leadership, differentiation, and focus.

generic strategies
basic types of business level strategies based on breadth of target market (industrywide versus narrow market segment) and type of competitive advantage (low cost versus uniqueness).

In order to create and sustain a competitive advantage, companies such as Best Buy need to analyze the needs and preferences of their customers and work to reinforce the value of their products for customers. They should not focus only on their internal operations. By not listening to their customers and responding to their evolving needs, Best Buy and many other firms have seen their performance drop and even their existence challenged.

Types of Competitive Advantage and Sustainability

Michael Porter presented three **generic strategies** that a firm can use to overcome the five forces and achieve competitive advantage.[2] Each of Porter's generic strategies has the potential to allow a firm to outperform rivals in their industry. The first, *overall cost leadership,* is based on creating a low-cost-position. Here, a firm must manage the relationships throughout the value chain and lower costs throughout the entire chain. Second, *differentiation* requires a firm to create products and/or services that are unique and valued. Here, the primary emphasis is on "nonprice" attributes for which customers will gladly pay a premium.[3] Third, a *focus* strategy directs attention (or "focus") toward narrow product lines, buyer segments, or targeted geographic markets and they must attain advantages either through differentiation or cost leadership.[4] Whereas the overall cost leadership and differentiation strategies strive to attain advantages industrywide, focusers have a narrow target market in mind. Exhibit 5.1 illustrates these three strategies on two dimensions: competitive advantage and strategic target.

Both casual observation and research support the notion that firms that identify with one or more of the forms of competitive advantage outperform those that do not.[5] There has been a rich history of strategic management research addressing this topic. One study analyzed 1,789 strategic business units and found that businesses combining multiple forms of competitive advantage (differentiation and overall cost leadership) outperformed businesses that used only a single form. The lowest performers were those that did not identify with any type of advantage. They were classified as "stuck in the middle." Results of this study are presented in Exhibit 5.2.[6]

For an example of the dangers of being "stuck in the middle," consider the traditional supermarket.[7] The major supermarket chains, such as Kroger, Ralphs, and Albertsons, used to be the main source of groceries for consumers. However, they find themselves in a situation today where affluent customers are going upmarket to get their organic and

EXHIBIT 5.1 Three Generic Strategies

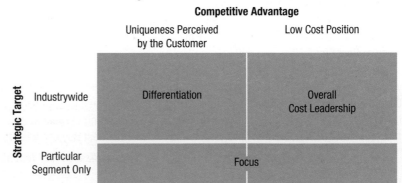

EXHIBIT 5.2 Competitive Advantage and Business Performance

	Competitive Advantage					
	Differentiation and Cost	Differentiation	Cost	Differentiation and Focus	Cost and Focus	Stuck in the Middle
Performance						
Return on investment (%)	35.5	32.9	30.2	17.0	23.7	17.8
Sales growth (%)	15.1	13.5	13.5	16.4	17.5	12.2
Gain in market share (%)	5.3	5.3	5.5	6.1	6.3	4.4
Sample size	123	160	100	141	86	105

gourmet foods at retailers like Whole Foods Market and budget-conscious consumers are drifting to discount chains such as Walmart, Aldi, and Dollar General.

Overall Cost Leadership

The first generic strategy is overall cost leadership. Overall cost leadership requires a tight set of interrelated tactics that include:

- Aggressive construction of efficient-scale facilities.
- Vigorous pursuit of cost reductions from experience.
- Tight cost and overhead control.
- Avoidance of marginal customer accounts.
- Cost minimization in all activities in the firm's value chain, such as R&D, service, sales force, and advertising.

Exhibit 5.3 draws on the value-chain concept (see Chapter 3) to provide examples of how a firm can attain an overall cost leadership strategy in its primary and support activities.

One factor often central to an overall cost leadership strategy is the **experience curve,** which refers to how business "learns" to lower costs as it gains experience with production processes. With experience, unit costs of production decline as output increases in most industries. The experience curve, developed by the Boston Consulting Group in 1968, is a way of looking at efficiency gains that come with experience. For a range of products, as cumulative experience doubles, costs and labor hours needed to produce a unit of product decline by 10 to 30 percent. There are a number of reasons why we find this effect. Among the most common factors are workers getting better at what they do, product designs being simplified as the product matures, and production processes being automated and streamlined. However, experience curve gains will only be the foundation for a cost advantage if the firm knows the source of the cost reduction and can keep these gains proprietary.

To generate above-average performance, a firm following an overall cost leadership position must attain **competitive parity** on the basis of differentiation relative to competitors.[8] In other words, a firm achieving parity is similar to its competitors, or "on par," with respect to differentiated products.[9] Competitive parity on the basis of differentiation permits a cost leader to translate cost advantages directly into higher profits than competitors. Thus, the cost leader earns above-average returns.[10]

overall cost leadership
a firm's generic strategy based on appeal to the industrywide market using a competitive advantage based on low cost.

experience curve
the decline in unit costs of production as cumulative output increases.

competitive parity
a firm's achievement of similarity, or being "on par," with competitors with respect to low cost, differentiation, or other strategic product characteristic.

EXHIBIT 5.3

Value-Chain Activities:
Examples of Overall
Cost Leadership

Support Activities

Firm Infrastructure

- Few management layers to reduce overhead costs.
- Standardized accounting practices to minimize personnel required.

Human Resource Management

- Minimize costs associated with employee turnover through effective policies.
- Effective orientation and training programs to maximize employee productivity.

Technology Development

- Effective use of automated technology to reduce scrappage rates.
- Expertise in process engineering to reduce manufacturing costs.

Procurement

- Effective policy guidelines to ensure low-cost raw materials (with acceptable quality levels).
- Shared purchasing operations with other business units.

Primary Activities

Inbound Logistics

- Effective layout of receiving dock operations.

Operations

- Effective use of quality control inspectors to minimize rework.

Outbound Logistics

- Effective utilization of delivery fleets

Marketing and Sales

- Purchase of media in large blocks.
- Sales force utilization is maximized by territory management.

Service

- Thorough service repair guidelines to minimize repeat maintenance calls.
- Use of single type of vehicle to minimize repair costs.

Source: Adapted from: Porter, M.E. 1985. *Competitive Advantage: Creating and Sustaining Superior Performance.* New York: Free Press.

The failure to attain parity on the basis of differentiation can be illustrated with an example from the automobile industry—the ill-fated Yugo. Below is an excerpt from a speech by J. W. Marriott, Jr., Chairman of the Marriott Corporation:[11]

> . . . money is a big thing. But it's not the only thing. In the 1980s, a new automobile reached North America from behind the Iron Curtain. It was called the Yugo, and its main attraction was price. About $3,000 each. But the only way they caught on was as the butt of jokes. Remember the guy who told his mechanic, "I want a gas cap for my Yugo." "OK," the mechanic replied, "that sounds like a fair trade."

Yugo was offering a lousy value proposition. The cars literally fell apart before your eyes. And the lesson was simple. Price is just one component of value. No matter how good the price, the most cost-sensitive consumer won't buy a bad product.

Gordon Bethune, the former CEO of Continental Airlines, summed up the need to provide good products or services when employing a low cost strategy this way: "You can make a pizza so cheap, nobody will buy it."[12]

Next, we discuss some examples of how firms enhance cost leadership position.

Aldi, a discount supermarket retailer, has grown from its German base to the rest of Europe, Australia, and the United States by replicating a simple business format. Aldi limits the number of products (SKUs in the grocery business) in each category to ensure product turn, to ease stocking shelves, and to increase its power over suppliers. It also sells mostly private label products to minimize cost. It has small, efficient, and simply designed stores. It offers limited services and expects customers to bring their own bags and bag their own groceries. As a result, Aldi can offer their products at prices 40 percent lower than competing supermarkets.[13]

Tesco, Britain's largest grocery retailer, has changed how they view waste in order to become more efficient. To cut their costs, they have begun shipping off food waste to bio-energy plants to convert the waste to electricity. This allows Tesco to both avoid landfill taxes of $98 per ton and also save on the cost of their electricity by providing the fuel for the power plant. Tesco is saving $3 million dollars a year alone in landfill taxes by simply sending their used cooking oil and chicken fat to be used to generate bioenergy rather than putting it in a landfill. Overall, Tesco estimates that energy saving efforts are shaving over $300 million a year from its energy bills.[14]

Harley Davidson has also worked to streamline its operations to significantly improve its cost position. In their York, Pennsylvania, plant, they have moved to a flexible production system that requires only five job classifications rather than the 62 they had before. Workers now have a wider variety of skills and can move where needed in the plant. They have also automated their production process, allowing them to reduce their production workforce from over 1,000 workers down to around 500. They have made similar changes in other plants. This has allowed them to keep production in the United States and cut production costs by at least $275 million. As a result, Harley's operating profit margin rose from 12.5 percent in 2009 to 16 percent in 2012.[15]

A business that strives for a low-cost advantage must attain an absolute cost advantage relative to its rivals.[16] This is typically accomplished by offering a no-frills product or service to a broad target market using standardization to derive the greatest benefits from economies of scale and experience. However, such a strategy may fail if a firm is unable to attain parity on important dimensions of differentiation such as quick responses to customer requests for services or design changes. Strategy Spotlight 5.1 discusses how Renault is leveraging a low cost strategy to draw in auto buyers in Europe.

Overall Cost Leadership: Improving Competitive Position vis-à-vis the Five Forces An overall low cost position enables a firm to achieve above-average returns despite strong competition. It protects a firm against rivalry from competitors, because lower costs allow a firm to earn returns even if its competitors eroded their profits through intense rivalry. A low-cost position also protects firms against powerful buyers. Buyers can exert power to drive down prices only to the level of the next most efficient producer. Also, a low-cost position provides more flexibility to cope with demands from powerful suppliers for input cost increases. The factors that lead to a low-cost position also provide substantial entry barriers position with respect to substitute products introduced by new and existing competitors.[17]

A few examples will illustrate these points. Harley Davidson's close attention to costs helps to protect them from buyer power and intense rivalry from competitors. Thus, they are able to drive down costs and enjoy relatively high power over their customers. By increasing productivity and lowering unit costs, Renault both lessens the degree of rivalry it faces and increases entry barriers for new entrants. Aldi's extreme focus on minimizing costs across its operations makes it less vulnerable to substitutes, such as discount retailers like Walmart and dollar stores.

> **LO5.2**
> How the successful attainment of generic strategies can improve a firm's relative power vis-à-vis the five forces that determine an industry's average profitability.

RENAULT FINDS LOW COST WORKS WELL IN THE NEW EUROPE

The European economic crisis has changed how Renault, a French car maker, designs and produces cars for European customers. Historically, European car buyers have been sophisticated, demanding well-designed, feature-laden cars from manufacturers. When the economic crisis hit Europe in 2007, automakers saw a dramatic shift in demand. Overall demand dropped, and the customers who did come in to buy became much more cost conscious.

In these difficult conditions, Renault has been able to carve out a profitable market for itself, selling low-cost, no-frills cars. Renault responded to this shift by creating an entry-level car group that was charged with designing and producing cars for these more cost conscious consumers. For example, they took an ultra-cheap car, the Logan, that was originally aimed for emerging markets and redesigned it to meet the new needs of the European market. The boxy sedan, which sells for around $10,000, is now one of Renault's best sellers. Its entry-level cars accounted for 30 percent of the cars sold by Renault in 2011 and generated operating profit margins over twice the profit margins of the higher priced cars Renault sold.

What is the recipe for success Renault has found to generate high profits on low-priced cars? It uses simple designs that incorporate components from older car designs at Renault and employs a no-discount retail policy. At the center of their design procedure is a "design-to-cost" philosophy. In this process, designers and engineers no longer strive for the cutting edge. Instead, they focus on choosing parts and materials for simplicity, ease of manufacturing, and availability. This often involves using components that were engineered for prior vehicle designs. When needing a new component, Renault begins by assessing how much customers would be willing to pay for certain features, such as air conditioning or power door locks, and then asks suppliers whether they can propose a way to offer this feature at a cost that matches what customers are willing to pay.

As they face imitation of this strategy by Volkswagen and Toyota, Renault is not sitting idle. As Carlos Ghosn, Renault's CEO, stated, "Our low-cost offering isn't low-cost enough. So we're working on a new platform that will be ultra low-cost."

Sources: Pearson, D. 2012. Renault takes low-cost lead. *wsj.com*, April 16: np.; and Ciferri, L. 2013. How Renault's low-cost Dacia has become a "cash cow." *Automotive News Europe*, January 3: np.

LO5.3

The pitfalls managers must avoid in striving to attain generic strategies.

Potential Pitfalls of Overall Cost Leadership Strategies Potential pitfalls of overall cost leadership strategy include:

- *Too much focus on one or a few value-chain activities.* Would you consider a person to be astute if he cancelled his newspaper subscription and quit eating out to save money, but then "maxed out" several credit cards, requiring him to pay hundreds of dollars a month in interest charges? Of course not. Similarly, firms need to pay attention to all activities in the value chain.[18] Too often managers make big cuts in operating expenses, but don't question year-to-year spending on capital projects. Or managers may decide to cut selling and marketing expenses but ignore manufacturing expenses. Managers should explore *all* value-chain activities, including relationships among them, as candidates for cost reductions.

- *Increase in the cost of the inputs on which the advantage is based.* Firms can be vulnerable to price increases in the factors of production. For example, consider manufacturing firms based in China which rely on low labor costs. Due to demographic factors, the supply of workers 16 to 24 years old has peaked and will drop by a third in the next 12 years, thanks to stringent family-planning policies that have sharply reduced China's population growth.[19] This is leading to upward pressure on labor costs in Chinese factories, undercutting the cost advantage of firms producing there.

- *The strategy is imitated too easily.* One of the common pitfalls of a cost-leadership strategy is that a firm's strategy may consist of value-creating activities that are easy to imitate.[20] Such has been the case with online brokers in recent years.[21] As of early 2013, there were over 200 online brokers listed on allstocks.com, hardly symbolic of an industry where imitation is extremely difficult. And according to Henry McVey, financial services analyst at Morgan Stanley, "We think you need five to ten" online brokers.

- *A lack of parity on differentiation.* As noted earlier, firms striving to attain cost leadership advantages must obtain a level of parity on differentiation.[22] Firms providing online degree programs may offer low prices. However, they may not be successful unless they can offer instruction that is perceived as comparable to traditional providers. For them, parity can be achieved on differentiation dimensions such as reputation and quality and through signaling mechanisms such as accreditation agencies.

- *Reduced flexibility.* Building up a low-cost advantage often requires significant investments in plant and equipment, distribution systems, and large, economically scaled operations. As a result, firms often find that these investments limit their flexibility, leading to great difficulty responding to changes in the environment. For example, Coors Brewing developed a highly efficient, large-scale brewery in Golden, Colorado. Coors was one of the most efficient brewers in the world, but their plant was designed to mass produce one or two types of beer. When the craft brewing craze started to grow, their plant was not well equipped to produce smaller batches of craft beer, and they found it difficult to meet this opportunity. Ultimately, they had to buy their way into this movement by acquiring small craft breweries.[23]

- *Obsolescence of the basis of cost advantage.* Ultimately, the foundation of a firm's cost advantage may become obsolete. In these circumstances, other firms develop new ways of cutting costs, leaving the old cost leaders at a significant disadvantage. The older cost leaders are often locked into their way of competing and are unable to respond to the newer, lower-cost means of competing. This is what happened to the U.S. auto industry in the 1970s. Ford, GM, and Chrysler had built up efficient mass manufacturing auto plants. However, when Toyota and other Japanese manufacturers moved into the North American car market using lean manufacturing, a new and more efficient means of production, the U.S. firms found themselves at a significant cost disadvantage. It took the U.S. firms over 30 years to redesign and retool their plants and restructure the responsibilities of line workers to get to where they were on cost parity with the Japanese firms.

Differentiation

As the name implies, a **differentiation strategy** consists of creating differences in the firm's product or service offering by creating something that is perceived *industrywide* as unique and valued by customers.[24] Differentiation can take many forms:

- Prestige or brand image (Adam's Mark hotels, BMW automobiles).[25]
- Technology (Martin guitars, Marantz stereo components, North Face camping equipment).
- Innovation (Medtronic medical equipment, Apple's iPhones and iPads).
- Features (Cannondale mountain bikes, Honda Goldwing motorcycles).
- Customer service (Nordstrom department stores, Sears lawn equipment retailing).
- Dealer network (Lexus automobiles, Caterpillar earthmoving equipment).

Exhibit 5.4 draws on the concept of the value chain as an example of how firms may differentiate themselves in primary and support activities.

Firms may differentiate themselves along several different dimensions at once.[26] For example, the Cheesecake Factory, an upscale casual restaurant, differentiates itself by

differentiation strategy
a firm's generic strategy based on creating differences in the firm's product or service offering by creating something that is perceived *industrywide* as unique and valued by customers.

EXHIBIT 5.4

Value-Chain Activities:
Examples of
Differentiation

Support Activities

Firm Infrastructure

- Superior MIS—To integrate value-creating activities to improve quality.
- Facilities that promote firm image.
- Widely respected CEO enhances firm reputation.

Human Resource Management

- Programs to attract talented engineers and scientists.
- Provide training and incentives to ensure a strong customer service orientation.

Technology Development

- Superior material handling and sorting technology.
- Excellent applications engineering support.

Procurement

- Purchase of high-quality components to enhance product image.
- Use of most prestigious outlets.

Primary Activities

Inbound Logistics

- Superior material handling operations to minimize damage.
- Quick transfer of inputs to manufacturing process.

Operations

- Flexibility and speed in responding to changes in manufacturing specifications.
- Low defect rates to improve quality.

Outbound Logistics

- Accurate and responsive order processing.
- Effective product replenishment to reduce customer inventory.

Marketing and Sales

- Creative and innovative advertising programs.
- Fostering of personal relationship with key customers.

Service

- Rapid response to customer service requests.
- Complete inventory of replacement parts and supplies.

Source: Adapted from Porter, M.E. 1985. *Competitive Advantage: Creating and Sustaining Superior Performance.* New York: Free Press.

offering high quality food, the widest and deepest menu in its class of restaurants, and premium locations.[27]

Firms achieve and sustain differentiation advantages and attain above-average performance when their price premiums exceed the extra costs incurred in being unique.[28] For example, the Cheesecake Factory must increase consumer prices to offset the higher cost of premium real estate and producing such a wide menu. Thus, a differentiator will always seek out ways of distinguishing itself from similar competitors to justify price premiums greater than the costs incurred by differentiating.[29] Clearly, a differentiator cannot ignore costs. After all, its premium prices would be eroded by a markedly inferior cost position. Therefore, it must attain a level of cost *parity* relative to competitors. Differentiators can do this by reducing costs in all areas that do not affect differentiation. Porsche, for example, invests heavily in engine design—an area in which its customers demand excellence—but it is less concerned and spends fewer resources in the design of the instrument panel or the arrangement of switches on the radio.[30]

Many companies successfully follow a differentiation strategy. For example, Zappos may sell shoes, but it sees the core element of its differentiation advantage as service. Zappos CEO Tony Hsieh puts it this way.[31]

> "We hope that 10 years from now people won't even realize that we started out selling shoes online, and that when you say 'Zappos,' they'll think, 'Oh, that's the place with the absolute best customer service.' And that doesn't even have to be limited to being an online experience. We've had customers email us and ask us if we would please start an airline, or run the IRS."

This emphasis on service has led to great success. Growing from an idea to a billion dollar company in only a dozen years, Zappos is seeing the benefits of providing exemplary service.

Lexus, a division of Toyota, provides an example of how a firm can strengthen its differentiation strategy by *achieving integration at multiple points along the value chain*.[32] Although the luxury car line was not introduced until the late 1980s, by the early 1990s the cars had already soared to the top of J. D. Power & Associates' customer satisfaction ratings.

> In the spirit of benchmarking, one of Lexus's competitors hired Custom Research Inc. (CRI), a marketing research firm, to find out why Lexus owners were so satisfied. CRI conducted a series of focus groups in which Lexus drivers eagerly offered anecdotes about the special care they experienced from their dealers. It became clear that, although Lexus was manufacturing cars with few mechanical defects, it was the extra care shown by the sales and service staff that resulted in satisfied customers. Such pampering is reflected in the feedback from one customer who claimed she never had a problem with her Lexus. However, upon further probing, she said, "Well, I suppose you could call the four times they had to replace the windshield a 'problem.' But frankly, they took care of it so well and always gave me a loaner car, so I never really considered it a problem until you mentioned it now." An insight gained in CRI's research is that perceptions of product quality (design, engineering, and manufacturing) can be strongly influenced by downstream activities in the value chain (marketing and sales, service).

Strategy Spotlight 5.2 discusses how Unilever, a global consumer products firm, uses crowdsourcing to differentiate itself through increased sustainability.

Differentiation: Improving Competitive Position vis-à-vis the Five Forces Differentiation provides protection against rivalry since brand loyalty lowers customer sensitivity to price and raises customer switching costs.[33] By increasing a firm's margins, differentiation also avoids the need for a low-cost position. Higher entry barriers result because of customer loyalty and the firm's ability to provide uniqueness in its products or services.[34] Differentiation also provides higher margins that enable a firm to deal with supplier power. And it reduces buyer power, because buyers lack comparable alternatives and are therefore less price sensitive.[35] Supplier power is also decreased because there is a certain amount of prestige associated with being the supplier to a producer of highly differentiated products and services. Last, differentiation enhances customer loyalty, thus reducing the threat from substitutes.[36]

Our examples illustrate these points. Lexus has enjoyed enhanced power over buyers because its top J. D. Power ranking makes buyers more willing to pay a premium price. This lessens rivalry, since buyers become less price-sensitive. The prestige associated with its brand name also lowers supplier power since margins are high. Suppliers would probably desire to be associated with prestige brands, thus lessening their incentives to drive up

CROWDSOURCING FOR DIFFERENTIATION IDEAS: UNILEVER'S EFFORTS TO PROPEL FORWARD ITS SUSTAINABILITY INITIATIVES

Unilever, a global manufacturer of consumer products such as Dove soap, Ben and Jerry's ice cream, Lipton ice tea, Axe deodorants, and many other widely used products, is aiming to lead the market in its ability to run a sustainable business enterprise. As part of this effort, they published their Sustainable Living Plan in November 2010. Included in this plan were their ambitious goals to reduce the environmental footprint of Unilever by 50 percent and source all of their agricultural inputs from sustainable growers by 2020.

Knowing that these goals will be challenging to achieve, Unilever turned to the power of the crowd to develop initiatives to meet these targets. In April 2012, they hosted a 24-hour global crowdsourcing event, called the Sustainable Living Lab, to generate creative ideas on how to improve their sustainability. Speaking of the challenges facing Unilever as they strive to lead the market in sustainability, Miguel Pestana, VP of Global External Affairs at Unilever, stated, "We can't solve these issues on our own. We need to engage with civil society, companies, government, and other key stakeholders." Unilever designed this as an invitation-only event where they would get input from sustainability leaders and experts. The response they received from invited participants was very positive, with over 2200 individuals, including over 100 Unilever managers, coming together to co-create ideas and solutions to advance Unilever's agenda of increasing the sustainability of their business and product line. They hosted discussion groups on four broad topics that encompassed activities across the entire value chain of Unilever. The topics discussed were sustainable sourcing, sustainable production and distribution, consumer behavior change, and recycling and waste.

The boards generated a large volume of discussion and also triggered a follow-up survey completed by over 400 participants. Unilever sees this event as a starting point, noting the need to remain committed to further developing the ideas generated in the event. Specifically, they plan to use the discussions as a basis on which to extend current and develop new partnerships with participating firms and organizations to help them achieve their sustainability goals. As one participant noted, "This was a great step to enable external specialists to collaborate with internal Unilever experts on key issues. This in itself was a significant step. The next step is to see how this could lead to collaboration that helps Unilever to drive more change to create a more sustainable sector."

Sources: Holme, C. 2012. How Unilever crowdsourced creativity to meet its sustainability goals. *Greenbiz.com*, June 7, np; and Peluso, M. 2012. Unilever to crowdsource sustainability. *MarketingWeek*, April 10, np.

---

prices. Finally, the loyalty and "peace of mind" associated with a service provider such as FedEx makes such firms less vulnerable to rivalry or substitute products and services.

Potential Pitfalls of Differentiation Strategies   Potential pitfalls of a differentiation strategy include:

- *Uniqueness that is not valuable.* A differentiation strategy must provide unique bundles of products and/or services that customers value highly. It's not enough just to be "different." An example is Gibson's Dobro bass guitar. Gibson came up with a unique idea: Design and build an acoustic bass guitar with sufficient sound volume so that amplification wasn't necessary. The problem with other acoustic bass guitars was that they did not project enough volume because of the low-frequency bass notes. By adding a resonator plate on the body of the traditional acoustic bass, Gibson increased the sound volume. Gibson believed this product would serve a particular niche market—bluegrass and folk artists who played in small group "jams" with other acoustic musicians. Unfortunately, Gibson soon discovered that its targeted market was content with their existing options: an upright bass amplified with a microphone or an acoustic electric guitar. Thus, Gibson developed a unique product, but it was not perceived as valuable by its potential customers.[37]

- *Too much differentiation.* Firms may strive for quality or service that is higher than customers desire.[38] Thus, they become vulnerable to competitors who provide an appropriate level of quality at a lower price. For example, consider the expensive

Mercedes-Benz S-Class, which ranged in price between $93,650 and $138,000 for the 2011 models.[39] *Consumer Reports* described it as "sumptuous," "quiet and luxurious," and a "delight to drive." The magazine also considered it to be the least reliable sedan available in the United States. According to David Champion, who runs their testing program, the problems are electronic. "The engineers have gone a little wild," he says. "They've put every bell and whistle that they think of, and sometimes they don't have the attention to detail to make these systems work." Some features include: a computer-driven suspension that reduces body roll as the vehicle whips around a corner; cruise control that automatically slows the car down if it gets too close to another car; and seats that are adjustable 14 ways and that are ventilated by a system that uses eight fans.

- *Too high a price premium.* This pitfall is quite similar to too much differentiation. Customers may desire the product, but they are repelled by the price premium. For example, Duracell (a division of Gillette) recently charged too much for batteries.[40] The firm tried to sell consumers on its superior quality products, but the mass market wasn't convinced. Why? The price differential was simply too high. At a CVS drugstore just one block from Gillette's headquarters, a four-pack of Energizer AA batteries was on sale at $2.99 compared with a Duracell four-pack at $4.59. Duracell's market share dropped 2 percent in a recent two-year period, and its profits declined over 30 percent. Clearly, the price/performance proposition Duracell offered customers was not accepted.

- *Differentiation that is easily imitated.* As we noted in Chapter 3, resources that are easily imitated cannot lead to sustainable advantages. Similarly, firms may strive for, and even attain, a differentiation strategy that is successful for a time. However, the advantages are eroded through imitation. Consider Cereality's innovative differentiation strategy of stores which offer a wide variety of cereals and toppings for around $4.00.[41] As one would expect, once their idea proved successful, competitors entered the market because much of the initial risk had already been taken. Rivals include an Iowa City restaurant named the Cereal Cabinet, the Cereal Bowl in Miami, and Bowls: A Cereal Joint in Gainesville, Florida. Says David Roth, one of Cereality's founders: "With any good business idea, you're faced with people who see you've cracked the code and who try to cash in on it."

- *Dilution of brand identification through product-line extensions.* Firms may erode their quality brand image by adding products or services with lower prices and less quality. Although this can increase short-term revenues, it may be detrimental in the long run. Consider Gucci.[42] In the 1980s Gucci wanted to capitalize on its prestigious brand name by launching an aggressive strategy of revenue growth. It added a set of lower-priced canvas goods to its product line. It also pushed goods heavily into department stores and duty-free channels and allowed its name to appear on a host of licensed items such as watches, eyeglasses, and perfumes. In the short term, this strategy worked. Sales soared. However, the strategy carried a high price. Gucci's indiscriminate approach to expanding its products and channels tarnished its sterling brand. Sales of its high-end goods (with higher profit margins) fell, causing profits to decline.

- *Perceptions of differentiation may vary between buyers and sellers.* The issue here is that "beauty is in the eye of the beholder." Companies must realize that although they may perceive their products and services as differentiated, their customers may view them as commodities. Indeed, in today's marketplace, many products and services have been reduced to commodities.[43] Thus, a firm could overprice its offerings and lose margins altogether if it has to lower prices to reflect market realities.

Overall Cost Leadership:

- Too much focus on one or a few value-chain activities.
- Increase in the cost of the inputs on which the advantage is based.
- The strategy is imitated too easily.
- A lack of parity on differentiation.
- Reduced flexibility.
- Obsolescence of the basis of cost advantage.

Differentiation:

- Uniqueness that is not valuable.
- Too much differentiation.
- The price premium is too high.
- Differentiation that is easily imitated.
- Dilution of brand identification through product-line extensions.
- Perceptions of differentiation may vary between buyers and sellers.

EXHIBIT 5.5

Potential Pitfalls of Overall Cost Leadership and Differentiation Strategies

focus strategy
a firm's generic strategy based on appeal to a narrow market segment within an industry.

Exhibit 5.5 summarizes the pitfalls of overall cost leadership and differentiation strategies. In addressing the pitfalls associated with these two generic strategies there is one common, underlying theme. Managers must be aware of the dangers associated with concentrating so much on one strategy that they fail to attain parity on the other.

Focus

A **focus strategy** is based on the choice of a narrow competitive scope within an industry. A firm following this strategy selects a segment or group of segments and tailors its strategy to serve them. The essence of focus is the exploitation of a particular market niche. As you might expect, narrow focus itself (like merely "being different" as a differentiator) is simply not sufficient for above-average performance.

The focus strategy, as indicated in Exhibit 5.1, has two variants. In a cost focus, a firm strives to create a cost advantage in its target segment. In a differentiation focus, a firm seeks to differentiate in its target market. Both variants of the focus strategy rely on providing better service than broad-based competitors who are trying to serve the focuser's target segment. Cost focus exploits differences in cost behavior in some segments, while differentiation focus exploits the special needs of buyers in other segments.

Let's look at examples of two firms that have successfully implemented focus strategies. LinkedIn has staked out a position as the business social media site of choice. Rather than compete with Facebook head on, LinkedIn created a strategy that focuses on individuals who wish to share their business experience and make connections with individuals with whom they share or could potentially share business ties. In doing so, they have created an extremely strong business model. LinkedIn monetizes their user information in three ways: subscription fees from some users, advertising fees, and recruiter fees. The first two are fairly standard for social media sites, but the advertising fees are higher for LinkedIn since the ads can be more effectively targeted as a result of LinkedIn's focus. The third income source is fairly unique for LinkedIn. Headhunters and human resource departments pay significant user fees, up to $8,200 a year, to have access to LinkedIn's recruiting search engine that can sift through LinkedIn profiles to identify individuals with desired skills and experiences. The power of this business model can be seen in the difference in user value for LinkedIn when compared to Facebook. For every hour that a user spends on the site, LinkedIn generates $1.30 in income. For Facebook, it is a paltry 6.2 cents.[44]

Marlin Steel Wire Products, a Baltimore-based manufacturing company, has also seen great benefit from developing a niche-differentiator strategy. Marlin, a manufacturer of commodity wire products, faced stiff and ever-increasing competition from rivals based in China and other emerging markets. These rivals had labor-based cost advantages that Marlin found hard to counter. Marlin responded by changing the game they played. Drew Greenblatt, Marlin's president, decided to go upmarket, automating his production and specializing in high-end products. For example, Marlin produces antimicrobial baskets for restaurant kitchens and exports its products globally. Marlin saw its sales grow from $800,000 in 1998 to $3 million in 2007.[45]

Strategy Spotlight 5.3 illustrates how BMW was able to build a strong niche position with its Mini line of cars.

MINI: STAKING OUT A SUCCESSFUL COMPACT CAR NICHE

BMW had a clear vision when it resurrected the vintage British automotive brand in 2001. It was simply to be the first premium brand in the compact car segment. Have they succeeded? Today, Mini sells nearly 300,000 cars a year and grew by over 20 percent from 2011 to 2012. It currently generates almost three times the sales of its most direct competing brand, Smart. BMW is also able to price the Mini at a premium relative to its key competitors, with a typical Mini selling for between $20,000 and $25,000. According to Jurgen Pieper, an analyst with Bankhaus Metzler, the Mini brand is quite profitable, earning about $250 million a year in a fairly difficult automotive market.

BMW was able to create this premium compact car niche using a business model with a set of mutually reinforcing attributes. First, they designed the car to offer a unique combination of modern features and capabilities with a classic design. The Mini nameplate was originally on a small British car in 1959. While the model launched by BMW in 2001 has little in common with the original, the basic style of the car reflects the look of the original and allowed it to clearly stand out from the modern SUVs and sedans that dominate today's car market. Thus, the look of the car was one of its key selling points. Second, they set the car apart from most other brands by using low-cost, event-focused advertisements to push the car. For example, rather than advertise on TV during sporting events, they placed a cardboard model of the car seated in football stadiums like a fan appearing to watch the game. BMW also benefited by having the car used as a central element in Hollywood movies, such as *Austin Powers in Goldmember* in 2002 and *The Italian Job* in 2003. Today, Mini continues their different advertising methods, spending over half their advertising budget on digital media, such as social networking, online videos, and ads targeted to mobile devices. Third, they have regularly extended Mini's product line while keeping a consistent look and styling. In addition to the basic model, they now have seven different models and could go up to 10 different models, but they all are easily recognizable as Minis.

The challenge that the leaders of Mini face is one that niche differentiators regularly face. They must regularly strive to freshen their product line and look for opportunities to grow their business without losing their focus on what makes Mini different.

Sources: Edmonson, G. & Eidam, M. 2004. BMW's Mini just keeps getting mightier. *businessweek.com*, April 4: np; Reiter, C. 2012. BMW's Mini: Little, but she is fierce! *Bloomberg Businessweek*, February 6: 24–25; and Foley, A. 2012. Online connections key to Mini's success, marketing chief says. *wardsauto.com*, October 24: np.

Focus: Improving Competitive Position vis-à-vis the Five Forces   Focus requires that a firm either have a low-cost position with its strategic target, high differentiation, or both. As we discussed with regard to cost and differentiation strategies, these positions provide defenses against each competitive force. Focus is also used to select niches that are least vulnerable to substitutes or where competitors are weakest.

Let's look at our examples to illustrate some of these points. First, by providing a platform for a targeted customer group, business people, to share key work information, LinkedIn insulated itself from rivalrous pressure from existing social networks, such as Facebook. It also felt little threat from new generalist social networks, such as Google+. Similarly, the new focus of Marlin Steel lessened the power of buyers since they provide specialized products. Also, they are insulated from competitors, who manufacture the commodity products Marlin used to produce.

Potential Pitfalls of Focus Strategies   Potential pitfalls of focus strategies include:

- ***Erosion of cost advantages within the narrow segment.*** The advantages of a cost focus strategy may be fleeting if the cost advantages are eroded over time. For example, Dell's pioneering direct-selling model in the personal computer industry has been eroded by rivals such as Hewlett-Packard as they gain experience with Dell's distribution method. Similarly, other firms have seen their profit margins drop as competitors enter their product segment.

- ***Even product and service offerings that are highly focused are subject to competition from new entrants and from imitation.*** Some firms adopting a focus strategy may enjoy temporary advantages because they select a small niche with few rivals. However, their advantages may be short-lived. A notable example is the multitude of dot-com firms that specialize in very narrow segments such as pet supplies, ethnic foods, and vintage automobile accessories. The entry barriers tend to be low, there is little buyer loyalty, and competition becomes intense. And since the marketing strategies and technologies employed by most rivals are largely nonproprietary, imitation is easy. Over time, revenues fall, profits margins are squeezed, and only the strongest players survive the shakeout.

- *Focusers can become too focused to satisfy buyer needs.* Some firms attempting to attain advantages through a focus strategy may have too narrow a product or service. Consider many retail firms. Hardware chains such as Ace and True Value are losing market share to rivals such as Lowe's and Home Depot that offer a full line of home and garden equipment and accessories. And given the enormous purchasing power of the national chains, it would be difficult for such specialty retailers to attain parity on costs.

LO5.4

How firms can effectively combine the generic strategies of overall cost leadership and differentiation.

Combination Strategies: Integrating Overall Low Cost and Differentiation

Perhaps the primary benefit to firms that integrate low-cost and differentiation strategies is the difficulty for rivals to duplicate or imitate.[46] This strategy enables a firm to provide two types of value to customers: differentiated attributes (e.g., high quality, brand identification, reputation) and lower prices (because of the firm's lower costs in value-creating activities). The goal is thus to provide unique value to customers in an efficient manner.[47] Some firms are able to attain both types of advantages simultaneously.[48] For example, superior quality can lead to lower costs because of less need for rework in manufacturing, fewer warranty claims, a reduced need for customer service personnel to resolve customer complaints, and so forth. Thus, the benefits of combining advantages can be additive, instead of merely involving trade-offs. Next, we consider three approaches to combining overall low cost and differentiation.

combination strategies
firms' integrations of various strategies to provide multiple types of value to customers.

Automated and Flexible Manufacturing Systems Given the advances in manufacturing technologies such as CAD/CAM (computer aided design and computer aided manufacturing) as well as information technologies, many firms have been able to manufacture unique products in relatively small quantities at lower costs—a concept known as **mass customization.**[49]

mass customization
a firm's ability to manufacture unique products in small quantities at low cost.

Let's consider Andersen Windows of Bayport, Minnesota—a $3 billion manufacturer of windows for the building industry.[50] Until about 20 years ago, Andersen was a mass producer, in small batches, of a variety of standard windows. However, to meet changing customer needs, Andersen kept adding to its product line. The result was catalogs of ever-increasing size and a bewildering set of choices for both homeowners and contractors. Over a 6-year period, the number of products tripled, price quotes took several hours, and the error rate increased. This not only damaged the company's reputation, but also added to its manufacturing expenses.

To bring about a major change, Andersen developed an interactive computer version of its paper catalogs that it sold to distributors and retailers. Salespersons can now customize each window to meet the customer's needs, check the design for structural soundness, and provide a price quote. The system is virtually error free, customers get exactly what they want, and the time to develop the design and furnish a quotation has been cut by 75 percent. Each showroom computer is connected to the factory, and customers are assigned a code number that permits them to track the order. The manufacturing system has been developed to use some common finished parts, but it also allows considerable variation in the final products. Despite its huge investment, Andersen has been able to lower costs, enhance quality and variety, and improve its response time to customers.

EXHIBIT 5.6
Effective Uses of
Flexible Production
Systems

- At Nikeid.com, customers can design an athletic or casual shoe to their specifications online, selecting almost every element of the shoe from the material of the sole to the color of the shoelace.
- Eleuria sells custom perfumes. Each product is created in response to a user profile constructed from responses to a survey about habits and preferences. Eleuria then provides a sample at modest cost to verify fit.
- Lands' End offers customized shirts and pants. Consumers specify style parameters, measurements, and fabrics through the firm's website. These settings are saved so that returning users can easily order a duplicate item.
- Cannondale permits consumers to specify the parameters that define a road bike frame, including custom colors and inscriptions. The user specifies the parameters on the firm's website and then arranges for delivery through a dealer.

Source: Randall, T., Terwiesch, C. & Ulrich, K. T. 2005. Principles for User Design of Custom Products. *California Management Review,* 47(4): 68–85.

Exhibit 5.6 provides other examples of how flexible production systems have enabled firms to successfully engage in mass customization for their customers:[51]

Exploiting the Profit Pool Concept for Competitive Advantage A profit pool is defined as the total profits in an industry at all points along the industry's value chain.[52] Although the concept is relatively straightforward, the structure of the profit pool can be complex.[53] The potential pool of profits will be deeper in some segments of the value chain than in others, and the depths will vary within an individual segment. Segment profitability may vary widely by customer group, product category, geographic market, or distribution channel. Additionally, the pattern of profit concentration in an industry is very often different from the pattern of revenue generation. Strategy Spotlight 5.4 outlines how technology giant Apple is expanding its profit pool through developing brand loyalty with its "Apple ecosystem."

profit pool
the total profits in an industry at all points along the industry's value chain.

Coordinating the "Extended" Value Chain by Way of Information Technology Many firms have achieved success by integrating activities throughout the "extended value chain" by using information technology to link their own value chain with the value chains of their customers and suppliers. As noted in Chapter 3, this approach enables a firm to add value not only through its own value-creating activities, but also for its customers and suppliers.

Such a strategy often necessitates redefining the industry's value chain. A number of years ago, Walmart took a close look at its industry's value chain and decided to reframe the competitive challenge.[54] Although its competitors were primarily focused on retailing— merchandising and promotion— Walmart determined that it was not so much in the retailing industry as in the transportation logistics and communications industries. Here, linkages in the extended value chain became central. That became Walmart's chosen battleground. By redefining the rules of competition that played to its strengths, Walmart has attained competitive advantages and dominates its industry.

Integrated Overall Low-Cost and Differentiation Strategies: Improving Competitive Position vis-à-vis the Five Forces Firms that successfully integrate both differentiation and cost advantages create an enviable position. For example, Walmart's integration of information systems, logistics, and transportation helps it to drive down costs and provide outstanding product selection. This dominant competitive position, serves to erect high entry barriers to potential competitors that have neither the financial nor physical resources to compete head-to-head. Walmart's size—with nearly $450 billion in sales in 2012— provides the chain with enormous bargaining power over suppliers. Its low pricing and wide selection reduce the power of buyers (its customers), because there are relatively few

HOW APPLE USES ITS 'ECOSYSTEM' TO GIVE MAC AN ADVANTAGE OVER WINDOWS

By Helena Gonzalez and Tom McNamara

With competition in the hi-tech world becoming fiercer, companies are finding it increasingly difficult to keep customers loyal to their products. As an answer to this problem, Apple developed what CEO Tim Cook calls the "Apple ecosystem." The term "ecosystem" refers to the seamless integration of Apple's hardware, operating systems, software, iCloud services, and stores.

After years of watching how Windows users were able to operate Apple's iOS platform on their PCs, Apple decided to offer these consumers a new reason to join the Apple world. Now users of the ecosystem can have all their devices synchronized automatically. For example, the moment a user checks out a restaurant on their Mac, the Calendar function will automatically add the restaurant's location, map, and directions. The ecosystem has given Apple a clear advantage over other providers. By integrating its systems, Mac has become the only device on which Windows, Linux, and OS X can run.

The Apple ecosystem is not driven by the hardware. Rather, it is driven by the integration of all of Apple's products, which puts it a step ahead of its competitors. It fulfills the five characteristics that a technology ecosystem should possess in order to give a firm a competitive advantage: It is holistic, seamless, interdependent, easy to use, and has lots of content.

It is holistic because it aims to include almost all of the electronic devices a person might need in the course of a day: Computer, phone, music, TV, etc.

It is seamless because all of the parts of the ecosystem work together easily and with little effort

It is interdependent because the proprietary format is compatible across all Apple devices and cannot be used on non-Apple devices.

It is easy to use. The average Apple user, however, does not need an instruction manual to get any of Apple's devices working.

Finally, Apple is the leader in the number of apps available and in the ability to access these apps from different devices.

Although Apple still needs to improve some areas of its ecosystem—social networking, office suite, TV, and cloud based software—its ecosystem certainly has important components that give it a competitive advantage in the high-tech world, allowing it to capture the attention of customers and retain their interests for longer periods of time.

Sources: "Apple delineates its ecosystem: The Mac's new advantage vs. Windows" by David The Apple Core, ZDNet, June 11 2013; "Apple's Ecosystem: Strength Or Liability?" Portfolio Management 101, November 14 2012.

---

competitors that can provide a comparable cost/value proposition. This reduces the possibility of intense head-to-head rivalry, such as protracted price wars. Finally, Walmart's overall value proposition makes potential substitute products (e.g., Internet competitors) a less viable threat.

Pitfalls of Integrated Overall Cost Leadership and Differentiation Strategies The pitfalls of integrated overall cost leadership and differentiation include:

- *Firms that fail to attain both strategies may end up with neither and become "stuck in the middle."* A key issue in strategic management is the creation of competitive advantages that enable a firm to enjoy above-average returns. Some firms may become "stuck in the middle" if they try to attain both cost and differentiation advantages. As mentioned earlier in this chapter, mainline supermarket chains find themselves stuck in the middle as their cost structure is higher than discount retailers offering groceries, and their products and services are not seen by consumers as being as valuable as those of high-end grocery chains, such as Whole Foods.

- *Underestimating the challenges and expenses associated with coordinating value-creating activities in the extended value chain.* Integrating activities across a firm's value chain with the value chain of suppliers and customers involves a significant investment in financial and human resources. Firms must consider the expenses linked to technology investment, managerial time and commitment, and the involvement and investment required by the firm's customers and suppliers. The firm must be confident that it can generate a sufficient scale of operations and revenues to justify all associated expenses.

- *Miscalculating sources of revenue and profit pools in the firm's industry.* Firms may fail to accurately assess sources of revenue and profits in their value chain. This can occur for several reasons. For example, a manager may be biased due to his or her functional area background, work experiences, and educational background. If the manager's background is in engineering, he or she might perceive that proportionately greater revenue and margins were being created in manufacturing, product, and process design than a person whose background is in a "downstream" value-chain activity such as marketing and sales. Or politics could make managers "fudge" the numbers to favor their area of operations. This would make them responsible for a greater proportion of the firm's profits, thus improving their bargaining position.

A related problem is directing an overwhelming amount of managerial time, attention, and resources to value-creating activities that produce the greatest margins—to the detriment of other important, albeit less profitable, activities. For example, a car manufacturer may focus too much on downstream activities, such as warranty fulfillment and financing operations, to the detriment of differentiation and cost of the cars themselves.

Can Competitive Strategies Be Sustained? Integrating and Applying Strategic Management Concepts

L05.5

What factors determine the sustainability of a firm's competitive advantage.

Thus far this chapter has addressed how firms can attain competitive advantages in the marketplace. We discussed the three generic strategies—overall cost leadership, differentiation, and focus—as well as combination strategies. Next we discussed the importance of linking value-chain activities (both those within the firm and those linkages between the firm's suppliers and customers) to attain such advantages. We also showed how successful competitive strategies enable firms to strengthen their position vis-à-vis the five forces of industry competition as well as how to avoid the pitfalls associated with the strategies.

Competitive advantages are, however, often short-lived. As we discussed in the beginning of Chapter 1, the composition of the firms that constitute the Fortune 500 list has experienced significant turnover in its membership over the years—reflecting the temporary nature of competitive advantages. Consider Dell's fall from grace. Here was a firm whose advantages in the marketplace seemed unassailable in the early 2000s. In fact, it was *Fortune*'s "Most Admired Firm" in 2005. However, cracks began to appear in 2007, and its competitive position has recently been severely eroded by both its traditional competitors and by an onslaught of firms selling tablets and other mobile devices. As a result, Dell's stock price declined by 56 percent over a five-year period ending at the start of 2013. In short, Dell focused so much on operational efficiency and perfecting its "direct model" that it failed to deliver innovations that an increasingly sophisticated market demanded.[55]

Clearly, "nothing is forever" when it comes to competitive advantages. Rapid changes in technology, globalization, and actions by rivals from within—as well as outside—the industry can quickly erode a firm's advantages. It is becoming increasingly important to recognize that the duration of competitive advantages is declining, especially in technology intensive industries.[56] Even in industries which are normally viewed as "low tech," the increasing use of technology has suddenly made competitive advantages less sustainable.[57] Amazon's success in book retailing at the cost of Barnes & Noble, the former industry leader, as well as Blockbuster's struggle against Netflix and, in turn, Netflix's difficulty in responding to Redbox in the video rental industry serve to illustrate how difficult it has become for industry leaders to sustain competitive advantages that they once thought would last forever.

In this section, we will discuss some factors that help determine whether a strategy is sustainable over a long period of time. We will draw on some strategic management concepts from the first five chapters. To illustrate our points, we will look at a company, Atlas Door, which created an innovative strategy in its industry and enjoyed superior performance for several years. Our discussion of Atlas Door draws on a *Harvard Business Review* article by George Stalk, Jr.[58] It was published some time ago (1988), which provides us the benefit of hindsight to make our points about the sustainability of competitive advantage. After all, the strategic management concepts we have been addressing in the text are quite timeless in their relevance to practice. A brief summary follows:

Atlas Door: A Case Example

Atlas Door, a U.S.-based company, has enjoyed remarkable success. It has grown at an average annual rate of 15 percent in an industry with an overall annual growth rate of less than 5 percent. Recently, its pre-tax earnings were 20 percent of sales—about five times the industry average. Atlas is debt free and by its 10th year, the company achieved the number one competitive position in its industry.

Atlas produces industrial doors—a product with almost infinite variety, involving limitless choices of width and height and material. Given the importance of product variety, inventory is almost useless in meeting customer orders. Instead, most doors can be manufactured only after the order has been placed.

How Did Atlas Door Create Its Competitive Advantages in the Marketplace? *First,* Atlas built just-in-time factories. Although simple in concept, they require extra tooling and machinery to reduce changeover times. Further, the manufacturing process must be organized by product and scheduled to start and complete with all of the parts available at the same time.

Second, Atlas reduced the time to receive and process an order. Traditionally, when customers, distributors, or salespeople called a door manufacturer with a request for price and delivery, they would have to wait more than one week for a response. In contrast, Atlas first streamlined and then automated its entire order-entry, engineering, pricing, and scheduling process. Atlas can price and schedule 95 percent of its incoming orders while the callers are still on the telephone. It can quickly engineer new special orders because it has preserved on computer the design and production data of all previous special orders—which drastically reduces the amount of reengineering necessary.

Third, Atlas tightly controlled logistics so that it always shipped only fully complete orders to construction sites. Orders require many components, and gathering all of them at the factory and making sure that they are with the correct order can be a time-consuming task. Of course, it is even more time-consuming to get the correct parts to the job site after the order has been shipped! Atlas developed a system to track the parts in production and the purchased parts for each order. This helped to ensure the arrival of all necessary parts at the shipping dock in time—a just-in-time logistics operation.

The Result? When Atlas began operations, distributors had little interest in its product. The established distributors already carried the door line of a much larger competitor and saw little to no reason to switch suppliers except, perhaps, for a major price concession. But as a startup, Atlas was too small to compete on price alone. Instead, it positioned itself as the door supplier of last resort—the company people came to if the established supplier could not deliver or missed a key date.

Of course, with an average industry order fulfillment time of almost four months, some calls inevitably came to Atlas. And when it did get the call, Atlas commanded a higher price because of its faster delivery. Atlas not only got a higher price, but its effective integration of value-creating activities saved time and lowered costs. Thus, it enjoyed the best of both worlds.

In 10 short years, the company replaced the leading door suppliers in 80 percent of the distributors in the United States. With its strategic advantage, the company could be selective—becoming the supplier for only the strongest distributors.

Are Atlas Door's Competitive Advantages Sustainable?

We will now take both the "pro" and "con" position as to whether or not Atlas Door's competitive advantages will be sustainable for a very long time. It is important, of course, to assume that Atlas Door's strategy is unique in the industry, and the central issue becomes whether or not rivals will be able to easily imitate their strategy or create a viable substitute strategy.

"Pro" Position: The Strategy Is Highly Sustainable Drawing on Chapter 2, it is quite evident that Atlas Door has attained a very favorable position vis-á-vis the five forces of industry competition. For example, it is able to exert power over its customers (distributors) because of its ability to deliver a quality product in a short period of time. Also, its dominance in the industry creates high entry barriers for new entrants. It is also quite evident that Atlas Door has been able to successfully integrate many value-chain activities within the firm—a fact that is integral to its just-in-time strategy. As noted in Chapter 3, such integration of activities provides a strong basis for sustainability, because rivals would have difficulty in imitating this strategy due to causal ambiguity and path dependency (i.e., it is difficult to build up in a short period of time the resources that Atlas Door has accumulated and developed as well as disentangle the causes of what the valuable resources are or how they can be re-created). Further, as noted in Chapter 4, Atlas Door benefits from the social capital that they have developed with a wide range of key stakeholders (Chapter 1) These would include customers, employees, and managers (a reasonable assumption, given how smoothly the internal operations flow and their long-term relationships with distributors). It would be very difficult for a rival to replace Atlas Door as the supplier of last resort—given the reputation that it has earned over time for "coming through in the clutch" on time-sensitive orders. Finally, we can conclude that Atlas Door has created competitive advantages in both overall low cost and differentiation (Chapter 5). Its strong linkages among value-chain activities—a requirement for its just-in-time operations—not only lowers costs but enables the company to respond quickly to customer orders. As noted in Exhibit 5.4, many of the value-chain activities associated with a differentiation strategy reflect the element of speed or quick response.

"Con" Position: The Strategy Can Be Easily Imitated or Substituted An argument could be made that much of Atlas Door's strategy relies on technologies that are rather well known and nonproprietary. Over time, a well-financed rival could imitate its strategy (via trial and error), achieve a tight integration among its value-creating activities, and implement a just-in-time manufacturing process. Because human capital is highly mobile (Chapter 4), a rival could hire away Atlas Door's talent, and these individuals could aid the rival in transferring Atlas Door's best practices. A new rival could also enter the industry with a large resource base, which might enable it to price its doors well under Atlas Door to build market share (but this would likely involve pricing below cost and would be a risky and nonsustainable strategy). Finally, a rival could potentially "leapfrog" the technologies and processes that Atlas Door has employed and achieve competitive superiority. With the benefit of hindsight, it could use the Internet to further speed up the linkages among its value-creating activities and the order entry processes with its customers and suppliers. (But even this could prove to be a temporary advantage, since rivals could relatively easily do the same thing.)

What Is the Verdict? Both positions have merit. Over time, it would be rather easy to see how a new rival could achieve parity with Atlas Door—or even create a superior competitive position with new technologies or innovative processes. However, two factors make it extremely difficult for a rival to challenge Atlas Door in the short term: (1) the success that Atlas Door has enjoyed with its just-in-time scheduling and production systems—which involve the successful integration of many value-creating activities—helps the firm not only lower costs but also respond quickly to customer needs, and (2) the strong, positive reputational effects that it has earned with multiple stakeholders—especially its customers.

Finally, it is important to also understand that it is Atlas Door's ability to appropriate most of the profits generated by its competitive advantages that make it a highly successful company. As we discussed in Chapter 3, profits generated by resources can be appropriated by a number of stakeholders such as suppliers, customers, employees, or rivals. The structure of the industrial door industry makes such value appropriation difficult: the suppliers provide generic parts, no one buyer is big enough to dictate prices, the tacit nature of the knowledge makes imitation difficult, and individual employees may be easily replaceable. Still, even with the advantages that Atlas Door enjoys, they need to avoid becoming complacent or suffer the same fate as the dominant firm they replaced.

LO5.6

How Internet-enabled business models are being used to improve strategic positioning.

digital technologies information that is in numerical form, which facilitates its storage, transmission, analysis and manipulation.

How the Internet and Digital Technologies Affect the Competitive Strategies

Internet and digital technologies have swept across the economy and now have an impact on how nearly every company conducts its business. These changes have created new cost efficiencies and avenues for differentiation. However, the presence of these technologies is so widespread that it is questionable how any one firm can use them effectively in ways that genuinely set them apart from rivals. Thus, to stay competitive, firms must update their strategies to reflect the new possibilities and constraints that these phenomena represent. In this section, we address both the opportunities and the pitfalls that Internet and digital technologies offer to companies using overall cost leadership, differentiation, and focus strategies. We also briefly consider two major impacts that the Internet is having on business: lowering transaction costs and enabling mass customization.

Overall Cost Leadership

The Internet and digital technologies create new opportunities for firms to achieve low-cost advantages by enabling them to manage costs and achieve greater efficiencies. Managing costs, and even changing the cost structures of certain industries, is a key feature of the digital economy. Most analysts agree that the Internet's ability to lower transaction costs has transformed business. Broadly speaking, *transaction costs* refer to all the various expenses associated with conducting business. It applies not just to buy/sell transactions but to the costs of interacting with every part of a firm's value chain, within and outside the firm. Think about it. Hiring new employees, meeting with customers, ordering supplies, addressing government regulations—all of these exchanges have some costs associated with them. Because business can be conducted differently on the Internet, new ways of saving money are changing the competitive landscape.

Other factors also help to lower transaction costs. The process of disintermediation (in Chapter 2) has a similar effect. Each time intermediaries are used in a transaction, additional costs are added. Removing intermediaries lowers transaction costs. The Internet reduces the costs to search for a product or service, whether it is a retail outlet (as in the case of consumers) or a trade show (as in the case of business-to-business shoppers). Not only is the need for travel eliminated but so is the need to maintain a physical address, whether it's a permanent retail location or a temporary presence at a trade show.

Potential Internet-Related Pitfalls for Low-Cost Leaders   One of the biggest threats to low-cost leaders is imitation. This problem is intensified for business done on the Internet. Most of the advantages associated with contacting customers directly, and even capabilities that are software driven (e.g., customized ordering systems or real-time access to the status of work in progress), can be duplicated quickly and without threat of infringement on proprietary information. Another pitfall relates to companies that become overly enamored with using the Internet for cost-cutting and thus jeopardize customer relations or neglect other cost centers.

Differentiation

For many companies, Internet and digital technologies have enhanced their ability to build brand, offer quality products and services, and achieve other differentiation advantages.[59] Among the most striking trends are new ways to interact with consumers. In particular, the Internet has created new ways of differentiating by enabling *mass customization,* which improves the response to customer wishes.

Mass customization has changed how companies go to market and has challenged some of the tried-and-true techniques of differentiation. Traditionally, companies reached customers using high-end catalogs, the showroom floor, personal sales calls and products using prestige packaging, celebrity endorsements, and charity sponsorships. All of these avenues are still available and may still be effective, depending on a firm's competitive environment. But many customers now judge the quality and uniqueness of a product or service by their ability to be involved in its planning and design, combined with speed of delivery and reliable results. Internet and digitally based capabilities are thus changing the way differentiators make exceptional products and achieve superior service. Such improvements are being made at a reasonable cost, allowing firms to achieve parity on the basis of overall cost leadership.

Potential Internet-Related Pitfalls for Differentiators Traditional differentiation strategies such as building strong brand identity and prestige pricing have been undermined by Internet-enabled capabilities such as the ability to compare product features side-by-side or bid online for competing services. The sustainability of Internet-based gains from differentiation will deteriorate if companies offer differentiating features that customers don't want or create a sense of uniqueness that customers don't value. The result can be a failed value proposition— the value companies thought they were offering, does not translate into sales.

Focus

A focus strategy targets a narrow market segment with customized products and/or services. With focus strategies, the Internet offers new avenues in which to compete because they can access markets less expensively (low cost) and provide more services and features (differentiation). Some claim that the Internet has opened up a new world of opportunities for niche players who seek to access small markets in a highly specialized fashion.[60] Niche businesses are among the most active users of digital technologies and e-business solutions, using the Internet and digital technologies to create more viable focus strategies.

Many aspects of the Internet economy favor focus strategies because niche players and small firms have been able to extend their reach and effectively compete with larger competitors. For example, niche firms can more easily employ Twitter and other social media to connect in personalized ways with their focused customer groups. With these social media tools, they can solicit input, respond quickly to customer feedback, and provide overall improvements in customer service. Thus, the Internet has provided many firms that pursue focus strategies with new tools for creating competitive advantages.

Potential Internet-Related Pitfalls for Focusers A key danger for focusers using the Internet relates to correctly assessing the size of the online marketplace. Focusers can misread the scope and interests of their target markets. This can cause them to focus on segments that are too narrow to be profitable or to lose their uniqueness in overly broad niches, making them vulnerable to imitators or new entrants.

What happens when an e-business focuser tries to overextend its niche? Efforts to appeal to a broader audience by carrying additional inventory, developing additional content, or offering additional services can cause it to lose the cost advantages associated with a limited product or service offering.

Are Combination Strategies the Key to E-Business Success?

Because of the changing dynamics presented by digital and Internet-based technologies, new strategic combinations that make the best use of the competitive strategies may hold the greatest promise.[61] Many experts agree that the net effect of the digital economy is *fewer* rather than more opportunities for sustainable advantages.[62] This means strategic thinking becomes more important.

More specifically, the Internet has provided all companies with greater tools for managing costs. So it may be that cost management and control will become more important management tools. In general, this may be good if it leads to an economy that makes more efficient use of its scarce resources. However, for individual companies, it may shave critical percentage points off profit margins and create a climate that makes it impossible to survive, much less achieve sustainable above-average profits.

Many differentiation advantages are also diminished by the Internet. The ability to comparison shop—to check product reviews and inspect different choices with a few clicks of the mouse—is depriving some companies, such as auto dealers, of the unique advantages that were the hallmark of their prior success. Differentiating is still an important strategy, of course. But how firms achieve it may change, and the best approach may be to combine differentiation with other competitive strategies.

Perhaps the greatest beneficiaries are the focusers who can use the Internet to capture a niche that previously may have been inaccessible. However, because the same factors that make it possible for a small niche player to be a contender may make that same niche attractive to a big company. That is, an incumbent firm that previously thought a niche market was not worth the effort may use Internet technologies to enter that segment for a lower cost than in the past. The larger firm can then bring its market power and resources to bear in a way that a smaller competitor cannot match.

A combination strategy challenges a company to carefully blend alternative strategic approaches and remain mindful of the impact of different decisions on the firm's value-creating processes and its extended value-chain activities. Strong leadership is needed to maintain a bird's-eye perspective on a company's overall approach and to coordinate the multiple dimensions of a combination strategy.

Strategy Spotlight 5.5 describes how fashion label Burberry is using digital technologies to combine potentially valuable first mover advantage with its luxury brand status.

industry life cycle
the stages of introduction, growth, maturity, and decline that typically occur over the life of an industry.

Industry Life-Cycle Stages: Strategic Implications

The **industry life cycle** refers to the stages of introduction, growth, maturity, and decline that occur over the life of an industry. In considering the industry life cycle, it is useful to think in terms of broad product lines such as personal computers, photocopiers, or long-distance telephone service. Yet the industry life cycle concept can be explored from several levels, from the life cycle of an entire industry to the life cycle of a single variation or model of a specific product or service.

Why are industry life cycles important?[63] The emphasis on various generic strategies, functional areas, value-creating activities, and overall objectives varies over the course of an industry life cycle. Managers must become even more aware of their firm's strengths and weaknesses in many areas to attain competitive advantages. For example, firms depend on their research and development (R&D) activities in the introductory stage. R&D is the source of new products and features that everyone hopes will appeal

STRATEGY **SPOTLIGHT** | 5.5

DIGITAL BURBERRY: DILEMMAS IN BRINGING LUXURY DIRECTLY TO THE CUSTOMER

By Glyn Atwal and Douglas Bryson

Fashionistas who were unable to attend the Burberry Spring/Summer 2013 show at London Fashion Week were not left disappointed. The live streaming of the show was able to captivate a global audience and items featured on the runway were available to order online—months in advance of their arrival in stores. With over 15 million fans on Facebook and 2 million followers on Twitter, Burberry has set out to leverage digital media to engage and interact with customers that would otherwise be difficult or more costly to reach. This strategy includes Burberry's e-commerce website that is helping to drive sales online; and of course this is beyond a simple 'transactional' relationship. Burberry Bespoke allows their clientele to customize their own Burberry trench coat, right down to a choice of buttons.

The latest in Burberry's quest to integrate the digital medium within a retail environment is showcased at its new flagship store on London's Regent Street. Technological initiatives include sales staff equipped with iPads and "clienteling" apps that give them a digital profile of customers' past choices and preferences.

Embedded RFID (radio frequency identification) tags are able to transform mirrors into screens that display video content of the "story" behind the product. The in store experience can be compared to an interactive Disneyland for adults.

With many iconic luxury brands still hesitant to embrace online luxury, Burberry is forging a potentially valuable first mover advantage over competitors. Expect copycats to attempt to claw into this space. However, luxury brands do need to be aware that the powerful blade of technology cuts two ways when developing the online component of their techno-marketing strategy. The growing popularity of online shopping portals, such as vente-privee. com, could erode the brand's exclusivity. An even more immediate threat is illustrated by the recent launch of Amazon's Luxury Beauty Store. It includes Burberry beauty products: this could simply be 'too democratic' for luxury brand elitists to bear. The ease of setting up a digital shop means that brand image is becoming dangerously virtual. Can Burberry's "clicks and bricks" approach offset the effects of egalitarian third-party online sales channels?

Sources: Dubois, D. (2013) 'Why luxury brands need social media,' South China Morning Post, 2 November, www.scmp.com/business/companies/article/1345609/why-luxury-brands-need-social-media; The Economist (2012) 'Burberry goes digital,' 22 September, www.economist.com/node/21563353

---

to customers. Firms develop products and services to stimulate consumer demand. Later, during the maturity phase, the functions of the product have been defined, more competitors have entered the market, and competition is intense. Managers then place greater emphasis on production efficiencies and process (as opposed to the product) engineering in order to lower manufacturing costs. This helps to protect the firm's market position and to extend the product life cycle because the firm's lower costs can be passed on to consumers in the form of lower prices, and price-sensitive customers will find the product more appealing.

Exhibit 5.7 illustrates the four stages of the industry life cycle and how factors such as generic strategies, market growth rate, intensity of competition, and overall objectives change over time. Managers must strive to emphasize the key functional areas during each of the four stages and to attain a level of parity in all functional areas and value-creating activities. For example, although controlling production costs may be a primary concern during the maturity stage, managers should not totally ignore other functions such as marketing and R&D. If they do, they can become so focused on lowering costs that they miss market trends or fail to incorporate important product or process designs. Thus, the firm may attain low-cost products that have limited market appeal.

It is important to point out a caveat. While the life cycle idea is analogous to a living organism (i.e., birth, growth, maturity, and death), the comparison has limitations.[64] Products and services go through many cycles of innovation and renewal. Typically, only fad products have a single life cycle. Maturity stages of an industry can be "transformed" or followed by a stage of rapid growth if consumer tastes change, technological innovations take place, or new developments occur. The cereal industry is a good example. When medical research indicated that oat consumption reduced a person's cholesterol, sales of Quaker Oats increased dramatically.[65]

EXHIBIT 5.7 Stages of the Industry Life Cycle

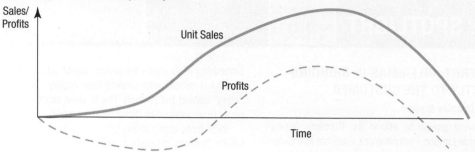

Stage / Factor	Introduction	Growth	Maturity	Decline
Generic strategies	Differentiation	Differentiation	Differentiation Overall cost leadership	Overall cost leadership Focus
Market growth rate	Low	Very large	Low to moderate	Negative
Number of segments	Very few	Some	Many	Few
Intensity of competition	Low	Increasing	Very intense	Changing
Emphasis on product design	Very high	High	Low to moderate	Low
Emphasis on process design	Low	Low to moderate	High	Low
Major functional area(s) of concern	Research and development	Sales and marketing	Production	General management and finance
Overall objective	Increase market awareness	Create consumer demand	Defend market share and extend product life cycles	Consolidate, maintain, harvest, or exit

introduction stage
the first stage of the industry life cycle, characterized by (1) new products that are not known to customers, (2) poorly defined market segments, (3) unspecified product features, (4) low sales growth, (5) rapid technological change, (6) operating losses, and (7) a need for financial support.

Strategies in the Introduction Stage

In the **introduction stage,** products are unfamiliar to consumers.[66] Market segments are not well defined, and product features are not clearly specified. The early development of an industry typically involves low sales growth, rapid technological change, operating losses, and the need for strong sources of cash to finance operations. Since there are few players and not much growth, competition tends to be limited.

Success requires an emphasis on research and development and marketing activities to enhance awareness. The challenge becomes one of (1) developing the product and finding a way to get users to try it, and (2) generating enough exposure so the product emerges as the "standard" by which all other rivals' products are evaluated.

There's an advantage to being the "first mover" in a market.[67] It led to Coca-Cola's success in becoming the first soft-drink company to build a recognizable global brand and enabled Caterpillar to get a lock on overseas sales channels and service capabilities.

However, there can also be a benefit to being a "late mover." Target carefully considered its decision to delay its Internet strategy. Compared to its competitors Walmart and Kmart, Target was definitely an industry laggard. But things certainly turned out well:[68]

> By waiting, Target gained a late-mover advantage. The store was able to use competitors' mistakes as its own learning curve. This saved money, and customers didn't seem to mind the wait: When Target finally opened its website, it quickly captured market share from both Kmart and Walmart Internet shoppers. Forrester Research Internet analyst Stephen Zrike commented, "There's no question, in our mind, that Target has a far better understanding of how consumers buy online."

Examples of products currently in the introductory stages of the industry life cycle include electric vehicles and 3D TVs.

Strategies in the Growth Stage

The **growth stage** is characterized by strong increases in sales. Such potential attracts other rivals. In the growth stage, the primary key to success is to build consumer preferences for specific brands. This requires strong brand recognition, differentiated products, and the financial resources to support a variety of value-chain activities such as marketing and sales, and research and development. Whereas marketing and sales initiatives were mainly directed at spurring *aggregate* demand—that is, demand for all such products in the introduction stage—efforts in the growth stage are directed toward stimulating *selective* demand, in which a firm's product offerings are chosen instead of a rival's.

Revenues increase at an accelerating rate because (1) new consumers are trying the product and (2) a growing proportion of satisfied consumers are making repeat purchases.[69] In general, as a product moves through its life cycle, the proportion of repeat buyers to new purchasers increases. Conversely, new products and services often fail if there are relatively few repeat purchases. For example, Alberto-Culver introduced Mr. Culver's Sparklers, which were solid air fresheners that looked like stained glass. Although the product quickly went from the introductory to the growth stage, sales collapsed. Why? Unfortunately, there were few repeat purchasers because buyers treated them as inexpensive window decorations, left them there, and felt little need to purchase new ones. Examples of products currently in the growth stage include cloud computing data storage services and high-definition television (HDTV).

Strategies in the Maturity Stage

In the **maturity stage** aggregate industry demand softens. As markets become saturated, there are few new adopters. It's no longer possible to "grow around" the competition, so direct competition becomes predominant.[70] With few attractive prospects, marginal competitors exit the market. At the same time, rivalry among existing rivals intensifies because of fierce price competition at the same time that expenses associated with attracting new buyers are rising. Advantages based on efficient manufacturing operations and process engineering become more important for keeping costs low as customers become more price sensitive. It also becomes more difficult for firms to differentiate their offerings, because users have a greater understanding of products and services.

An article in *Fortune* magazine that addressed the intensity of rivalry in mature markets was aptly titled "A Game of Inches." It stated, "Battling for market share in a slowing industry can be a mighty dirty business. Just ask laundry soap archrivals Unilever and Procter & Gamble."[71] These two firms have been locked in a battle for market share since 1965. Why is the competition so intense? There is not much territory to gain and industry

growth stage
the second stage of the product life cycle, characterized by (1) strong increases in sales; (2) growing competition; (3) developing brand recognition; and (4) a need for financing complementary value-chain activities such as marketing, sales, customer service, and research and development.

maturity stage
the third stage of the product life cycle, characterized by (1) slowing demand growth, (2) saturated markets, (3) direct competition, (4) price competition, and (5) strategic emphasis on efficient operations.

sales were flat. An analyst noted, "People aren't getting any dirtier." Thus, the only way to win is to take market share from the competition. To increase its share, Procter & Gamble (P&G) spends $100 million a year promoting its Tide brand on television, billboards, buses, magazines, and the Internet. But Unilever isn't standing still. Armed with an $80 million budget, it launched a soap tablet product named Wisk Dual Action Tablets. For example, it delivered samples of this product to 24 million U.S. homes in Sunday newspapers, followed by a series of TV ads. P&G launched a counteroffensive with Tide Rapid Action Tablets ads showed in side-by-side comparisons of the two products dropped into beakers of water. In the promotion, P&G claimed that its product is superior because it dissolves faster than Unilever's product.

Although this is only one example, many product classes and industries, including consumer products such as beer, automobiles, and athletic shoes, are in maturity.

Firms do not need to be "held hostage" to the life-cycle curve. By positioning or repositioning their products in unexpected ways, firms can change how customers mentally categorize them. Thus, firms are able to rescue products floundering in the maturity phase of their life cycles and return them to the growth phase.

Two positioning strategies that managers can use to affect consumers' mental shifts are **reverse positioning,** which strips away "sacred" product attributes while adding new ones, and **breakaway positioning,** which associates the product with a radically different category.[72] We discuss each of these positioning strategies below and then provide an example of each in Strategy Spotlight 5.6.

Reverse Positioning This assumes that although customers may desire more than the baseline product, they don't necessarily want an endless list of features. Such companies make the creative decision to step off the augmentation treadmill and shed product attributes that the rest of the industry considers sacred. Then, once a product is returned to its baseline state, the stripped-down product adds one or more carefully selected attributes that would usually be found only in a highly augmented product. Such an unconventional combination of attributes allows the product to assume a new competitive position within the category and move backward from maturity into a growth position on the life-cycle curve.

Breakaway Positioning As noted above, with reverse positioning, a product establishes a unique position in its category but retains a clear category membership. However, with breakaway positioning, a product escapes its category by deliberately associating with a different one. Thus, managers leverage the new category's conventions to change both how products are consumed and with whom they compete. Instead of merely seeing the breakaway product as simply an alternative to others in its category, consumers perceive it as altogether different.

When a breakaway product is successful in leaving its category and joining a new one, it is able to redefine its competition. Similar to reverse positioning, this strategy permits the product to shift backward on the life-cycle curve, moving from the rather dismal maturity phase to a thriving growth opportunity.

Strategy Spotlight 5.6 provides examples of reverse and breakaway positioning.

Strategies in the Decline Stage

Although all decisions in the phases of an industry life cycle are important, they become particularly difficult in the **decline stage.** Firms must face up to the fundamental strategic choices of either exiting or staying and attempting to consolidate their position in the industry.[73]

The decline stage occurs when industry sales and profits begin to fall. Typically, changes in the business environment are at the root of an industry or product group entering this stage.[74] Changes in consumer tastes or a technological innovation can push a product into

---

reverse positioning
a break in industry tendency to continuously augment products, characteristic of the product life cycle, by offering products with fewer product attributes and lower prices.

breakaway positioning
a break in industry tendency to incrementally improve products along specific dimensions, characteristic of the product life cycle, by offering products that are still in the industry but that are perceived by customers as being different.

decline stage
the fourth stage of the product life cycle, characterized by (1) falling sales and profits, (2) increasing price competition, and (3) industry consolidation.

REVERSE AND BREAKAWAY POSITIONING: HOW TO AVOID BEING HELD HOSTAGE TO THE LIFE-CYCLE CURVE

When firms adopt a reverse or breakaway positioning strategy, there is typically no pretense about what they are trying to accomplish. In essence, they subvert convention through unconventional promotions, prices, and attributes. That becomes a large part of their appeal—a cleverly positioned product offering. Next, we discuss Commerce Bank's reverse positioning and Swatch's breakaway positioning.

Commerce Bank

While most banks offer dozens of checking and savings accounts and compete by trying to offer the highest interest rates, Commerce Bank, a regional bank on the East Coast, took a totally different approach. It paid among the lowest rates in its market. Further, it offered a limited product line—just four checking accounts, for example. One would think that such a stingy approach would have scared off customers. However, Commerce Bank was very successful. Between 1999 and 2007, it expanded from 120 to 435 branches. Growing from a single branch in 1973, it was purchased by TD Bank in 2007 for $8.5 billion.

Why was it so successful? It stripped away all of what customers expected—lots of choices and peak interest rates and it *reverse positioned* itself as "the most convenient bank in America." It was open seven days a week, including evenings until 8 p.m. You could get a debit card while you waited. And when it rained, an escort with an umbrella walked you to your car. Further, the bank offered free coffee and newspapers for customers. Not too surprisingly, despite the inferior rates and few choices, customers regularly flocked to the bank, making it an attractive target for a larger bank to buy.

Swatch

Interestingly, the name "Swatch" is often misconstrued as a contraction of the words *Swiss watch.* However, Nicholas Hayek, chairman, affirms that the original contraction was *second watch*—the new watch was introduced as a new concept of watches as casual, fun, and relatively disposable accessories. And therein lies Swatch's *breakaway positioning.*

When Swatch was launched in 1983, Swiss watches were marketed as a form of jewelry. They were serious, expensive, enduring, and discreetly promoted. Once a customer purchased one, it lasted a lifetime. Swatch changed all of that by defining its watches as playful fashion accessories which were showily promoted. They inspired impulse buying—customers would often purchase half a dozen in different designs. Their price—$40 when the brand was introduced—expanded Swatch's reach beyond its default category (watches as high-end jewelry) and moved it into the fashion accessory category, where it has different customers and competitors. Swatch became the official timekeeper of the Summer Olympics in 1996, has continued to support the Olympics since, and has already signed on as a top sponsor of the 2016 Olympic Games in Rio.

Today, The Swatch Group is the largest watch company in the world. It has acquired many brands over the years, including Omega, Longines, Harry Winston, Calvin Klein, and Hamilton. Revenues have grown to $7.2 billion in 2011, and net income has increased to $1.4 billion. These figures represent increases of 44 percent and 85 percent, respectively, since 2009.

Sources: Moon, Y. 2005. Break free from the product life cycle. *Harvard Business Review,* 83(5): 87–94; *www.hoovers.com*; and *http://rio2016.com/en/sponsors/omega.*

---

decline. Compact disks forced cassette tapes into decline in the prerecorded music industry in the 1980s, and now digital devices have pushed CDs into decline.

Products in the decline stage often consume a large share of management time and financial resources relative to their potential worth. Sales and profits decline. Also, competitors may start drastically cutting their prices to raise cash and remain solvent. The situation is further aggravated by the liquidation of assets, including inventory, of some of the competitors that have failed. This further intensifies price competition.

In the decline stage, a firm's strategic options become dependent on the actions of rivals. If many competitors leave the market, sales and profit opportunities increase. On the other hand, prospects are limited if all competitors remain.[75] If some competitors merge, their increased market power may erode the opportunities for the remaining players. Managers must carefully monitor the actions and intentions of competitors before deciding on a course of action.

Four basic strategies are available in the decline phase: *maintaining, harvesting, exiting, or consolidating.*[76]

- *Maintaining* refers to keeping a product going without significantly reducing marketing support, technological development, or other investments, in the hope that competitors will eventually exit the market. Many offices, for example, still use typewriters for filling out forms and other purposes that cannot be completed on a PC. In some rural areas, rotary (or dial) telephones persist because of the older technology used in central switching offices. Thus, there may still be the potential for revenues and profits.

- **Harvesting** involves obtaining as much profit as possible and requires that costs be reduced quickly. Managers should consider the firm's value-creating activities and cut associated budgets. Value-chain activities to consider are primary (e.g., operations, sales and marketing) and support (e.g., procurement, technology development). The objective is to wring out as much profit as possible.

- *Exiting the market* involves dropping the product from a firm's portfolio. Since a residual core of consumers exist, eliminating it should be carefully considered. If the firm's exit involves product markets that affect important relationships with other product markets in the corporation's overall portfolio, an exit could have repercussions for the whole corporation. For example, it may involve the loss of valuable brand names or human capital with a broad variety of expertise in many value-creating activities such as marketing, technology, and operations.

- **Consolidation** involves one firm acquiring at a reasonable price the best of the surviving firms in an industry. This enables firms to enhance market power and acquire valuable assets. One example of a consolidation strategy took place in the defense industry in the early 1990s. As the cliché suggests, "peace broke out" at the end of the Cold War and overall U.S. defense spending levels plummeted.[77] Many companies that make up the defense industry saw more than 50 percent of their market disappear. Only one-quarter of the 120,000 companies that once supplied the Department of Defense still serve in that capacity; the others have shut down their defense business or dissolved altogether. But one key player, Lockheed Martin, became a dominant rival by pursuing an aggressive strategy of consolidation. During the 1990s, it purchased 17 independent entities, including General Dynamics' tactical aircraft and space systems divisions, GE Aerospace, Goodyear Aerospace, and Honeywell ElectroOptics. These combinations enabled Lockheed Martin to emerge as the top provider to three governmental customers: the Department of Defense, the Department of Energy, and NASA.

Examples of products currently in the decline stage of the industry life cycle include the video rental business (being replaced by video on demand), hard disk drives (being replaced by solid-state memory and cloud storage), and desktop computers (being replaced by notebook and tablet computers).

The introduction of new technologies and associated products does not always mean that old technologies quickly fade away. Research shows that in a number of cases, old technologies actually enjoy a very profitable "last gasp."[78] Examples include mainframe computers (versus minicomputers and PCs), coronary artery bypass graft surgery (versus angioplasty), and CISC (Complex Instruction Set Computing) architecture in computer processors versus RISC (Reduced Instruction Set Computing). In each case, the advent of new technology prompted predictions of the demise of the older technology, but each of these has proved to be resilient survivors. What accounts for their continued profitability and survival?

Retreating to more defensible ground is one strategy that firms specializing in technologies threatened with rapid obsolescence have followed. For example, while angioplasty may be appropriate for relatively healthier patients with blocked arteries, sicker, higher-risk patients seem to benefit more from coronary artery bypass graft surgery. This enabled the surgeons to concentrate on the more difficult cases and improve the technology itself. The advent of television unseated the radio as the major source of entertainment from American homes. However, the radio has survived and even thrived in venues where people are also engaged in other activities, such as driving.

Using the new to improve the old is a second approach. Carburetor manufacturers have improved the fuel efficiency of their product by incorporating electronic controls that were originally developed for electronic fuel injection systems. Similarly, CISC computer chip manufacturers have adopted many features from RISC chips.

Improving the price-performance trade-off is a third approach. IBM continues to make money selling mainframes long after their obituary was written. It retooled the technology using low-cost microprocessors and cut their prices drastically. Further, it invested and updated the software, enabling them to offer clients such as banks better performance and lower costs.

Clearly, "last gasps" may not necessarily translate into longer term gains, as the experience of the integrated steel mills suggests. When the first mini-mills appeared, integrated steel mills shifted to higher margin steel, but eventually mini-mills entered even the last strongholds of the integrated steel mills.

Turnaround Strategies

A **turnaround strategy** involves reversing performance decline and reinvigorating growth toward profitability.[79] A need for turnaround may occur at any stage in the life cycle but is more likely to occur during maturity or decline.

Most turnarounds require a firm to carefully analyze the external and internal environments.[80] The external analysis leads to identification of market segments or customer groups that may still find the product attractive.[81] Internal analysis results in actions aimed at reduced costs and higher efficiency. A firm needs to undertake a mix of both internally and externally oriented actions to effect a turnaround.[82] In effect, the cliché "you can't shrink yourself to greatness" applies.

A study of 260 mature businesses in need of a turnaround identified three strategies used by successful companies.[83]

- *Asset and cost surgery.* Very often, mature firms tend to have assets that do not produce any returns. These include real estate, buildings, etc. Outright sales or sale and leaseback free up considerable cash and improve returns. Investment in new plants and equipment can be deferred. Firms in turnaround situations try to aggressively cut administrative expenses and inventories and speed up collection of receivables. Costs also can be reduced by outsourcing production of various inputs for which market prices may be cheaper than in-house production costs.

- *Selective product and market pruning.* Most mature or declining firms have many product lines that are losing money or are only marginally profitable. One strategy is to discontinue such product lines and focus all resources on a few core profitable areas. For example, in the early 1980s, faced with possible bankruptcy, Chrysler Corporation sold off all its nonautomotive businesses as well as all its production facilities abroad. Focus on the North American market and identification of a profitable niche—namely, minivans—were keys to their eventual successful turnaround.

- *Piecemeal productivity improvements.* There are many ways in which a firm can eliminate costs and improve productivity. Although individually these are small gains, they cumulate over a period of time to substantial gains. Improving business processes by reengineering them, benchmarking specific activities against industry leaders, encouraging employee input to identify excess costs, increasing capacity utilization, and improving employee productivity lead to a significant overall gain.

Software maker Intuit is a case of a quick but well-implemented turnaround strategy. After stagnating and stumbling during the dot-com boom, Intuit, which is known for its QuickBook and TurboTax software, hired Stephen M. Bennett, a 22-year GE veteran, in 1999. He immediately discontinued Intuit's online finance, insurance, and bill-paying

turnaround strategy
a strategy that reverses a firm's decline in performance and returns it to growth and profitability.

LO5.8
The need for turnaround strategies that enable a firm to reposition its competitive position in an industry.

ALAN MULALLY: LEADING FORD'S EXTRAORDINARY TURNAROUND

Shortly after Alan Mulally took over as Ford's CEO in September 2006, he organized a weekly meeting with his senior managers and asked them how things were going. Fine, fine, fine were the responses from around the table. To this, an incredulous Mulally exclaimed: "We are forecasting a $17 billion loss and no one has any problems!" Clearly, there were cultural issues at play (such as denial and executive rivalry) but also very serious strategic and financial problems as well.

What a change a few years can make! Ford's profits for 2011 were $20 billion. This is quite a sharp contrast from its $14.7 billion loss in 2008—a time when high gasoline prices, bloated operations, and uncompetitive labor costs combined with the deep recession to create a perfect storm.

How did Mulally turn Ford around? It took many tough strategic decisions—involving not just company executives but Ford staff and the United Auto Workers (UAW). It involved downsizing, creating greater efficiency, improving quality, selling off the European luxury brands, and mortgaging assets to raise money. Ford's leaders and the United Auto Workers (UAW) also made transformational changes to lower the company's cost structure—a critical component to the company's long-term competitiveness.

Let's take a closer look at Mulally's strategic actions. We have to begin with the plan to undertake a dramatic refinancing of the business by raising bank loans secured against the company's assets. One of his first tasks was to finalize Ford's recovery plan and sell it to the banks. This financing enabled Ford to be the only major American automaker that avoided government-sponsored bankruptcy. And, as noted by Mulally, "The response that we received because we did not ask for the precious taxpayer's money has been tremendous." In fact, Jim Farley, head of marketing for Ford worldwide, estimates that Ford's standing on its own feet has been worth $1 billion in favorable publicity for the company and has attracted appreciative Americans into its dealers' showrooms.

Second, he decided that the firm would concentrate resources on the Ford brand and sell off the Premier Automotive Group (PAG) businesses—even if it meant taking a loss. Mulally had ridiculed the idea that top management could focus on Jaguar before breakfast, attend to Volvo or Land Rover before lunch, and then consider Ford and its Lincoln offshoot in North America in the afternoon. Accordingly, in 2007, Aston Martin was sold to private investors; Jaguar and Land Rover were sold to India's Tata Group in 2008; and a Chinese carmaker, Geely, bought Volvo in 2010. Further, the Mercury brand was phased out.

Third, Mulally realized that in addition to fewer brands, Ford needed a much narrower range of cars, albeit higher quality ones, carrying its familiar blue oval logo in all segments of the market. At one point Ford's designers had to deal with 97 different models—that was cut to 36 and may go lower.

Fourth, along with rationalizing the product range, Mulally insisted on raising the aspiration level with regard to quality. Although Ford used to talk about claiming parity with Toyota's Camry, Mulally shifted the emphasis to trying to make each car that Ford sells "best in class." A number of new cars being created under the One Ford policy are coming from Europe. Quality has improved dramatically according to some of the industry's outside arbiters, such as J. D. Power.

Fifth, to ensure that regional stars such as the Focus could become global successes, 8 of Ford's 10 platforms (the floor pan and its underpinnings) are now global platforms. More shared platforms enables Ford to build different models more quickly and economically to account for regional tastes in cars and variations in regulations. For example, the various Fiesta-based cars may look different, but they share about two-thirds of their parts. Such actions are particularly important as Ford focuses (no pun intended) its efforts toward smaller, more fuel-efficient automobiles which traditionally have smaller margins. As noted by Lewis Booth, Ford's finance director, "Customers' tastes are converging. Fuel efficiency matters everywhere."

Sixth, Mulally had to make many painful restructuring decisions in order to match production to the number of cars that Ford could sell. Since 2006, Ford cut half of its shop-floor workforce in North America and a third of its office jobs. By the end of 2011, a total of 17 factories had closed, and Ford's total employment fell from 128,000 to 75,000. In addition, the number of dealers has been cut by a fifth. Helped by union concessions, Ford has shed about $14 billion in annual operational costs and now can compete with Japan's "transplant" factories in America.

Regarding Ford's successful transformation, Mulally cliams: "We have earned the right now to make a complete family of best-in-class vehicles right here in the United States with U.S. workers and competing with the very best in the world. That's not only good for Ford and our customers and our stakeholders but that's good for the United States of America." Without doubt, such a statement a few years ago would have been dismissed as hyperbole.

Sources: Linn, A. 2010. For Ford's Mulally, big bets are paying off. *www.msnbc.com*. October 26: nd; Anonymous. 2010. Epiphany in Dearborn. *The Economist*. December 11: 83–85; Reagan, J. Ford Motor's extraordinary turnaround. December 10: np; and *www.finance.yahoo.com*.

operations that were losing money. Instead, he focused on software for small businesses that employ less than 250 people. He also instituted a performance-based reward system that greatly improved employee productivity. Within a few years, Intuit was once again making substantial profits and its stock was up 42 percent.[84]

Even when an industry is in overall decline, pockets of profitability remain. These are segments with customers who are relatively price insensitive. For example, the replacement demand for vacuum tubes affords its manufacturers an opportunity to earn above normal returns although the product itself is technologically obsolete. Surprisingly, within declining industries, there may still be segments that are either stable or growing. Although fountain pens ceased to be the writing instrument of choice a long time ago, the fountain pen industry has successfully reconceptualized the product as a high margin luxury item that signals accomplishment and success. In the final analysis, every business has the potential for rejuvenation. But it takes creativity, persistence, and most of all a clear strategy to translate that potential into reality.

Strategy Spotlight 5.7 discusses Ford's remarkable turnaround under the direction of CEO Alan Mulally.

ISSUE FOR DEBATE

Fast-Fashion Collaborations: Cheap but Chic

By Glyn Atwal and Douglas Bryson

It has never been easier for style conscious consumers to buy 'designer inspired' fashion. The High Street revolution started in 2004 when Karl Lagerfeld designed a collection for H&M under the unambiguous label "Karl Lagerfeld for H&M." A long line of collaborations has since seen H&M partner with high-end designers, including Jimmy Choo, Sonia Rykiel, Versace, and most recently Isabel Marant. Likewise, other mass retailers have launched similar collaborations, such as Jason Wu for Target, and Diane Von Furstenberg for Gap.

The media hype that follows the launch of these collections is often matched with consumer hysteria. Shoppers are not only willing to queue overnight, but there are even reports of scuffles and fights to secure a "must have" item of the designer collection. This is a global phenomenon and brings a new meaning to fast fashion. Media reports suggest that the Versace for H&M collection in Dubai and Beijing was sold out within 30 minutes.

The ongoing success of fast fashion collaborations has given mass retailers a compelling proposition to promote themselves as being at the forefront of fashion. It is no longer unusual to see an H&M advertisement alongside Gucci, Prada, or Louis Vuitton in *Vogue* or other fashion magazines. This trend may be good news for the bottom line for companies like H&M, but what's in it for the high-end designers?

High-end designers are able to broaden their brand awareness and appeal to new lifestyle segments. As a result, customers otherwise unable to afford to buy Versace or Jimmy Choo can garner a first experience of the designer brand. The gamble is that this will lead to future sales of affordable accessories or designer wear.

The downside of this strategy is that luxury fashion brands could lose the exclusivity that helped them to be perceived as luxurious to begin with. This might ultimately drive away the brand's core clientele who had been willing to pay a substantial premium for the brand's exclusivity.

Perhaps designer brand managers have in fact recognized that fast fashion collaborations reflect a new era of "democratized luxury." In a UK survey, 74% of luxury customers agreed that "luxury is for everyone" (Atwal et al., 2010). Will WalMart be the next stop for high-end fashion brands?

Questions for Discussion

1. Discuss the differences between a fashion and a luxury brand?
2. Discuss how a luxury brand can broaden its appeal without diluting its brand image?

Sources: Atwal, G., Bryson, D., and von Gersdorff, J. (2010) Deluxurification is in fashion, *Admap*, November, 44–45.

Reflecting on Career Implications . . .

- **Types of Competitive Advantage:** Are you aware of your organization's business-level strategy? What do you do to help your firm either increase differentiation or lower costs? Can you demonstrate to your superiors how you have contributed to the firm's chosen business-level strategy?

- **Types of Competitive Advantage:** What is your own competitive advantage? What opportunities does your current job provide to enhance your competitive advantage? Are you making the best use of your competitive advantage? If not, what organizations might provide you with better opportunities for doing so? Does your resume clearly reflect your competitive advantage? Or are you "stuck in the middle"?

- **Understanding *Your* Differentiation:** When looking for a new job or for advancement in your current firm, be conscious of being able to identify what differentiates you from other applicants. Consider the items in Exhibit 5.4 as you work to identify what distinguishes you from others.

- **Industry Life Cycle:** Before you go for a job interview, identify the life cycle stage of the industry within which your firm is located. You are more likely to have greater opportunities for career advancement in an industry in the growth stage than in the decline stage.

- **Industry Life Cycle:** If you sense that your career is maturing (or in the decline phase!), what actions can you take to restore career growth and momentum (e.g., training, mentoring, professional networking)? Should you actively consider professional opportunities in other industries?

summary

How and why firms outperform each other goes to the heart of strategic management. In this chapter, we identified three generic strategies and discussed how firms are able not only to attain advantages over competitors, but also to sustain such advantages over time. Why do some advantages become long-lasting while others are quickly imitated by competitors?

The three generic strategies—overall cost leadership, differentiation, and focus—form the core of this chapter. We began by providing a brief description of each generic strategy (or competitive advantage) and furnished examples of firms that have successfully implemented these strategies. Successful generic strategies invariably enhance a firm's position vis-à-vis the five forces of that industry—a point that we stressed and illustrated with examples. However, as we pointed out, there are pitfalls to each of the generic strategies. Thus, the sustainability of a firm's advantage is always challenged because of imitation or substitution by new or existing rivals. Such competitor moves erode a firm's advantage over time.

We also discussed the viability of combining (or integrating) overall cost leadership and generic differentiation strategies. If successful, such integration can enable a firm to enjoy superior performance and improve its competitive position. However, this is challenging, and managers must be aware of the potential downside risks associated with such an initiative.

We addressed the challenges inherent in determining the sustainability of competitive advantages. Drawing on an example from a manufacturing industry, we discussed both the "pro" and "con" positions as to why competitive advantages are sustainable over a long period of time.

The way companies formulate and deploy strategies is changing because of the impact of the Internet and digital technologies in many industries. Further, Internet technologies are enabling the mass customization capabilities of greater numbers of competitors. Focus strategies are likely to increase in importance because the Internet provides highly targeted and lower-cost access to narrow or specialized markets. These strategies are not without their pitfalls, however, and firms need to understand the dangers as well as the potential benefits of Internet-based approaches.

The concept of the industry life cycle is a critical contingency that managers must take into account in striving to create and sustain competitive advantages. We identified the four stages of the industry life cycle—introduction, growth, maturity, and decline—and suggested how these stages can play a role in decisions that managers must make at the business level. These include overall strategies as well as the relative emphasis on functional areas and value—creating activities.

When a firm's performance severely erodes, turnaround strategies are needed to reverse its situation and enhance its competitive position. We have discussed three approaches—asset cost surgery, selective product and market pruning, and piecemeal productivity improvements.

SUMMARY REVIEW QUESTIONS

1. Explain why the concept of competitive advantage is central to the study of strategic management.
2. Briefly describe the three generic strategies—overall cost leadership, differentiation, and focus.
3. Explain the relationship between the three generic strategies and the five forces that determine the average profitability within an industry.

4. What are some of the ways in which a firm can attain a successful turnaround strategy?
5. Describe some of the pitfalls associated with each of the three generic strategies.
6. Can firms combine the generic strategies of overall cost leadership and differentiation? Why or why not?
7. Explain why the industry life cycle concept is an important factor in determining a firm's business-level strategy.

key terms

mass customization 154
profit pool 155
digital technologies 160
industry life cycle 162
introduction stage 164
growth stage 165
maturity stage 165
reverse positioning 166
breakaway
 positioning 166
decline stage 166
harvesting strategy 168
consolidation strategy 168
turnaround strategy 169

business-level strategy 142
generic strategies 142
overall cost leadership 143
experience curve 143
competitive parity 143
differentiation
 strategy 147
focus strategy 152
combination
 strategies 154

application questions & exercises

1. Go to the Internet and look up *www.walmart.com*. How has this firm been able to combine overall cost leadership and differentiation strategies?
2. Choose a firm with which you are familiar in your local business community. Is the firm successful in following one (or more) generic strategies? Why or why not? What do you think are some of the challenges it faces in implementing these strategies in an effective manner?
3. Think of a firm that has attained a differentiation focus or cost focus strategy. Are their advantages sustainable? Why? Why not? (*Hint:* Consider its position vis-à-vis Porter's five forces.)
4. Think of a firm that successfully achieved a combination overall cost leadership and differentiation strategy. What can be learned from this example? Are these advantages sustainable? Why? Why not? (*Hint:* Consider its competitive position vis-à-vis Porter's five forces.)

ethics questions

1. Can you think of a company that suffered ethical consequences as a result of an overemphasis on a cost leadership strategy? What do you think were the financial and nonfinancial implications?
2. In the introductory stage of the product life cycle, what are some of the unethical practices that managers could engage in to enhance their firm's market position? What could be some of the long-term implications of such actions?

experiential exercise

What are some examples of primary and support activities that enable Nucor, a $19 billion steel manufacturer, to achieve a low-cost strategy? (Fill in the table below.)

Value-Chain Activity	Yes/No	How Does Nucor Create Value for the Customer?
Primary:		
Inbound logistics		
Operations		
Outbound logistics		
Marketing and sales		
Service		
Support:		
Procurement		
Technology development		
Human resource management		
General administration		

references

1. Kaplan, D. 2012. Hostess is bankrupt again. *Fortune,* August 13: 61–70; and Suddath, C. 2012. Hard choices: Gregory Rayburn on the dimming of Twinkies. *Bloomberg Businessweek,* November 26: 104.

2. For a recent perspective by Porter on competitive strategy, refer to Porter, M. E. 1996. What is strategy? *Harvard Business Review,* 74(6): 61–78.

3. For insights into how a start-up is using solar technology, see: Gimbel, B. 2009. Plastic power. *Fortune,* February 2: 34.

4. Useful insights on strategy in an economic downturn are in: Rhodes, D. & Stelter, D. 2009. Seize advantage in a downturn. *Harvard Business Review,* 87(2): 50–58.

5. Some useful ideas on maintaining competitive advantages can be found in Ma, H. & Karri, R. 2005. Leaders beware: Some sure ways to lose your competitive advantage. *Organizational Dynamics,* 343(1): 63–76.

6. Miller, A. & Dess, G. G. 1993. Assessing Porter's model in terms of its generalizability, accuracy, and simplicity. *Journal of Management Studies,* 30(4): 553–585.

7. Gasparro, A. & Martin, T. 2012. What's wrong with America's supermarkets? *WSJ.com,* July 12: np.

8. For insights on how discounting can erode a firm's performance, read: Stibel, J. M. & Delgrosso, P. 2008. Discounts can be dangerous. *Harvard Business Review,* 66(12): 31.

9. For a scholarly discussion and analysis of the concept of competitive parity, refer to Powell, T. C. 2003. Varieties of competitive parity. *Strategic Management Journal,* 24(1): 61–86.

10. Rao, A. R., Bergen, M. E., & Davis, S. 2000. How to fight a price war. *Harvard Business Review,* 78(2): 107–120.

11. Marriot, J. W. Jr. Our competitive strength: Human capital. A speech given to the Detroit Economic Club on October 2, 2000.

12. Burrus, D. 2011. *Flash foresight: How to see the invisible and do the impossible.* New York: Harper Collins.

13. Corstjens, M. & Lal, R. 2012. Retail doesn't cross borders. *Harvard Business Review,* April: 104–110.

14. Downing, L. 2012. Finally, a use for sandwich crusts. *Bloomberg Businessweek,* June 18: 18–19.

15. Hagerty, J. 2012. Hog maker Harley gets lean. *Wall Street Journal,* September 22: B1–B3.

16. Interesting insights on Walmart's effective cost leadership strategy are found in: Palmeri, C. 2008. Wal-Mart is up for this downturn. *BusinessWeek,* November 6: 34.

17. An interesting perspective on the dangers of price discounting is: Mohammad, R. 2011. Ditch the discounts. *Harvard Business Review,* 89 (1/2): 23–25.

18. Dholakia, U. M. 2011. Why employees can wreck promotional offers. *Harvard Business Review,* 89(1/2): 28.

19. Jacobs, A. 2010. Workers in China voting with their feet. *International Herald Tribune.* July 13: 1, 14.

20. For a perspective on the sustainability of competitive advantages, refer to Barney, J. 1995. Looking inside for competitive advantage. *Academy of Management Executive,* 9(4): 49–61.

21. Thornton, E., 2001, Why e-brokers are broker and broker. *BusinessWeek,* January 22: 94.

22. Mohammed, R. 2011. Ditch the discounts. *Harvard Business Review,* 89(1/2): 23–25.

23. Wilson, D. 2012. Big Beer dresses up in craft brewers' clothing. *Fortune.com,* November 15: np.

24. For an "ultimate" in differentiated services, consider time shares in exotic automobiles such as Lamborghinis and Bentleys. Refer to: Stead, D. 2008. My Lamborghini—today, anyway. *BusinessWeek,* January 18:17.

25. For an interesting perspective on the value of corporate brands and how they may be leveraged, refer to Aaker, D. A. 2004, *California Management Review,* 46(3): 6–18.

26. A unique perspective on differentiation strategies is: Austin, R. D. 2008. High margins and the quest for aesthetic coherence. *Harvard Business Review,* 86(1): 18–19.

27. Eng, D. 2011. Cheesecake Factory's winning formula. *Fortune,* May 2: 19–20.

28. For a discussion on quality in terms of a company's software and information systems, refer to Prahalad, C. K. & Krishnan, M. S. 1999. The new meaning of quality in the information age. *Harvard Business Review,* 77(5): 109–118.

29. The role of design in achieving differentiation is addressed in: Brown, T. 2008. Design thinking. *Harvard Business Review.* 86(6): 84–92.

30. Taylor, A., III. 2001. Can you believe Porsche is putting its badge on this car? *Fortune,* February 19: 168–172.

31. Mann, J. 2010. The best service in the world. *Networking Times,* January: np.

32. Markides, C. 1997. Strategic innovation. *Sloan Management Review,* 38(3): 9–23.

33. Bonnabeau, E., Bodick, N., & Armstrong, R. W. 2008. A more rational approach to new-product development. *Harvard Business Review.* 66(3): 96–102.

34. Insights on Google's innovation are in: Iyer, B. & Davenport, T. H. 2008. Reverse engineering Google's innovation machine. *Harvard Business Review.* 66(4): 58–68.

35. A discussion of how a firm used technology to create product differentiation is in: Mehta, S. N. 2009. Under Armor reboots. *Fortune.* February 2: 29–33 (5)

36. Bertini, M. & Wathieu, L. 2010. How to stop customers from fixating on price. *Harvard Business Review,* 88(5): 84–91.

37. The authors would like to thank Scott Droege, a faculty member at Western Kentucky University, for providing this example.

38. Dixon, M., Freeman, K. & Toman, N. 2010. Stop trying to delight your customers. *Harvard Business Review,* 88(7/8).

39. Flint, J. 2004. Stop the nerds. *Forbes,* July 5: 80; and, Fahey, E. 2004. Over-engineering 101. *Forbes,* December 13: 62.

40. Symonds, W. C. 2000. Can Gillette regain its voltage? *BusinessWeek,* October 16: 102–104.

41. Caplan, J. 2006. In a real crunch. *Inside Business,* July: A37–A38.

42. Gadiesh, O. & Gilbert, J. L. 1998. Profit pools: A fresh look at strategy. *Harvard Business Review,* 76(3): 139–158.

43. Colvin, G. 2000. Beware: You could soon be selling soybeans. *Fortune,* November 13: 80.

44. Anders, G. 2012. How LinkedIn has turned your resume into a cash machine. *Forbes.com,* July 16: np.

45. Burrus, D. 2011. *Flash Foresight: How to see the invisible and do the impossible.* New York: Harper Collins.

46. Hall, W. K. 1980. Survival strategies in a hostile environment, *Harvard Business Review,* 58: 75–87; on the paint and allied products industry, see Dess, G. G. & Davis, P. S. 1984. Porter's (1980) generic strategies as determinants of strategic group membership and organizational performance. *Academy of Management Journal,* 27: 467–488; for the Korean electronics industry, see Kim, L. & Lim, Y. 1988. Environment, generic strategies, and performance in a rapidly developing country: A taxonomic approach. *Academy of Management Journal,* 31: 802–827; Wright, P., Hotard, D., Kroll, M., Chan, P., & Tanner, J. 1990. Performance and multiple strategies in a firm: Evidence from the apparel industry. In Dean, B. V. & Cassidy, J. C. (Eds.). *Strategic management: Methods and studies:* 93–110. Amsterdam: Elsevier-North Holland; and Wright, P., Kroll, M., Tu, H., & Helms, M. 1991. Generic strategies and business performance: An empirical study of the screw machine products industry. *British Journal of Management,* 2: 1–9.

47. Gilmore, J. H. & Pine, B. J., II. 1997. The four faces of customization. *Harvard Business Review,* 75(1): 91–101.

48. Heracleous, L. & Wirtz, J. 2010. Singapore Airlines' balancing act. *Harvard Business Review,* 88(7/8): 145–149.

49. Gilmore & Pine, op. cit. For interesting insights on mass customization, refer to Cattani, K., Dahan, E., & Schmidt, G. 2005. Offshoring versus "spackling." *MIT Sloan Management Review,* 46(3): 6–7.

50. Goodstein, L. D. & Butz, H. E. 1998. Customer value: The linchpin of organizational change. *Organizational Dynamics,* Summer: 21–34.

51. Randall, T., Terwiesch, C., & Ulrich, K. T. 2005. Principles for user design of customized products. *California Management Review,* 47(4): 68–85.

52. Gadiesh & Gilbert, op. cit.: 139–158.

53. Insights on the profit pool concept are addressed in: Reinartz, W. & Ulaga, W. 2008. How to sell services more profitably. *Harvard Business Review,* 66(5): 90–96.

54. This example draws on Dess & Picken. 1997. op. cit.

55. A rigorous and thorough discussion of the threats faced by industries due to the commoditization of products and services and what strategic actions firm should consider is found in: D'Aveni, R. A. 2010. *Beating the commodity trap.* Boston: Harvard Business Press.

56. For an insightful, recent discussion on the difficulties and challenges associated with creating advantages that are sustainable for any reasonable period of time and suggested strategies, refer to: D'Aveni, R. A., Dagnino, G. B. & Smith, K. G. 2010. The age of temporary advantage. *Strategic Management Journal.* 31(13): 1371–1385. This is the lead article in a special issue of this journal that provides many ideas that are useful to both academics and practicing managers. For an additional examination of declining advantage in technologically intensive industries, see: Vaaler, P. M. & McNamara, G. 2010. Are technology-intensive industries more dynamically competitive? No and yes. *Organization Science.* 21: 271–289.

57. Rita McGrath provides some interesting ideas on possible strategies for firms facing highly uncertain competitive environments: McGrath, R. G. 2011. When your business model is in trouble. *Harvard Business Review,* 89(1/2): 96–98.

58. The Atlas Door example draws on: Stalk, G., Jr. 1988. Time—the next source of competitive advantage. *Harvard Business Review,* 66(4): 41–51.

59. Edelman, D. C. 2010. Branding in the digital age. *Harvard Business Review,* 88(12): 62–69.

60. Seybold, P. 2000. Niches bring riches. *Business 2.0,* June 13: 135.

61. Empirical support for the use of combination strategies in an e-business context can be found in Kim, E., Nam, D., & Stimpert, J. L. 2004. The applicability of Porter's generic strategies in the Digital Age: Assumptions, conjectures, and suggestions. *Journal of Management,* 30(5): 569–589.

62. Porter, M. E. 2001. Strategy and the Internet. *Harvard Business Review,* 79: 63–78.

63. For an interesting perspective on the influence of the product life cycle and rate of technological change on competitive strategy, refer to Lei, D. & Slocum, J. W. Jr. 2005. Strategic and organizational requirements for competitive advantage. *Academy of Management Executive,* 19(1): 31–45.

64. Dickson, P. R. 1994. *Marketing management:* 293. Fort Worth, TX: Dryden Press; Day, G. S. 1981. The product life cycle: Analysis and application. *Journal of Marketing Research,* 45: 60–67.

65. Bearden, W. O., Ingram, T. N., & LaForge, R. W. 1995. *Marketing principles and practices.* Burr Ridge, IL: Irwin.

66. MacMillan, I. C. 1985. Preemptive strategies. In Guth, W. D. (Ed.). *Handbook of business strategy:* 9-1–9-22. Boston: Warren, Gorham & Lamont; Pearce, J. A. & Robinson, R. B. 2000. *Strategic management* (7th ed.). New York: McGraw-Hill; Dickson, op. cit.: 295–296.

67. Bartlett, C. A. & Ghoshal, S. 2000. Going global: Lessons for late movers. *Harvard Business Review,* 78(2): 132–142.

68. Neuborne, E. 2000. E-tailers hit the relaunch key. *BusinessWeek,* October 17: 62.

69. Berkowitz, E. N., Kerin, R. A., & Hartley, S. W. 2000. *Marketing* (6th ed.). New York: McGraw-Hill.

70. MacMillan, op. cit.

71. Brooker, K. 2001. A game of inches. *Fortune,* February 5: 98–100.

72. Our discussion of reverse and breakaway positioning draws on Moon, Y. 2005. Break free from the product life cycle. *Harvard Business Review,* 83(5): 87–94. This article also discusses stealth positioning as a means of overcoming consumer resistance and advancing a product from the introduction to the growth phase.

73. MacMillan, op. cit.

74. Berkowitz et al., op. cit.

75. Bearden et al., op. cit.

76. The discussion of these four strategies draws on MacMillan, op. cit.; Berkowitz et al., op. cit.; and Bearden et al., op. cit.

77. Augustine, N. R. 1997. Reshaping an industry: Lockheed Martin's survival story. *Harvard Business Review,* 75(3): 83–94.

78. Snow, D. C. 2008. Beware of old technologies' last gasps. *Harvard Business Review,* January: 17–18. Lohr, S. 2008. Why old technologies are still kicking. *New York Times,* March 23: np; and McGrath, R. G. 2008. Innovation and the last gasps of dying technologies. *ritamcgrath. com,* March 18: np.

79. Coyne, K. P., Coyne, S. T. & Coyne, E. J. Sr. 2010. When you've got to cut costs—now. *Harvard Business Review,* 88(5): 74–83.

80. A study that draws on the resource-based view of the firm to investigate successful turnaround strategies is: Morrow, J. S., Sirmon, D. G., Hitt, M. A., & Holcomb, T. R. 2007. *Strategic Management Journal,* 28(3): 271–284.

81. For a study investigating the relationship between organizational restructuring and acquisition performance, refer to: Barkema, H. G. & Schijven, M. Toward unlocking the full potential of acquisitions: The role of organizational restructuring. *Academy of Management Journal,* 51(4): 696–722.

82. For some useful ideas on effective turnarounds and handling downsizings, refer to Marks, M. S. & De Meuse, K. P. 2005. Resizing the organization: Maximizing the gain while minimizing the pain of layoffs, divestitures and closings. *Organizational Dynamics,* 34(1): 19–36.

83. Hambrick, D. C. & Schecter, S. M. 1983. Turnaround strategies for mature industrial product business units. *Academy of Management Journal,* 26(2): 231–248.

84. Mullaney, T. J. 2002. The wizard of Intuit. *BusinessWeek,* October 28: 60–63.

chapter 6

Corporate-Level Strategy:

Creating Value through Diversification

After reading this chapter, you should have a good understanding of the following learning objectives:

LO6.1 The reasons for the failure of many diversification efforts.

LO6.2 How managers can create value through diversification initiatives.

LO6.3 How corporations can use related diversification to achieve synergistic benefits through economies of scope and market power.

LO6.4 How corporations can use unrelated diversification to attain synergistic benefits through corporate restructuring, parenting, and portfolio analysis.

LO6.5 The various means of engaging in diversification—mergers and acquisitions, joint ventures/strategic alliances, and internal development.

LO6.6 Managerial behaviors that can erode the creation of value.

Learning from Mistakes

The Flip video camera burst onto the scene in 2007 and took off, selling over two million of the simple, small, and easy-to-use cameras in two years. Sensing opportunity in the digital video market, Cisco Systems snapped up Pure Digital Technologies, the parent company of Flip, in 2009 for $590 million.[1] Just two years later, Cisco announced that it was pulling the plug on the Flip video camera and shutting down the Flip division. Why did Cisco, an experienced acquirer, fail with the Flip acquisition?

Cisco, a computer networking giant, has been extremely successful over the last several years, producing over $46 billion in sales and $8 billion in net income in 2012. As part of their business model, Cisco regularly undertakes acquisitions to extend its technology base and product portfolio. In the last decade, Cisco acquired over 80 firms as it extended its product portfolio.

Even with this experience with acquisitions, Cisco was unable to avoid failure with Flip for two reasons. First, Cisco's core business operations are in business networking equipment and software. Flip's business was selling video cameras to individual customers. This is a very different business, where Cisco's knowledge and other competencies were of little value. While Cisco has had some success extending into the consumer market, such as with their acquisition of Linksys, this success has come in the

home networking business, a market to which they can transfer some of their business networking competencies.

Second, in large, widely diversified firms, decision making can become slow and remote to market conditions. Cisco competes in a wide range of markets and had nearly 60 decision-making groups in its structure, with several layers separating John Chambers, the CEO of Cisco, from the individual markets. In such a large and diversified firm, the decision making in a small division with only $400 million in sales, 1 percent of the overall sales of Cisco, was not the top priority of corporate managers. Stephen Baker, an analyst with NPD Group, saw this and commented that "Cisco was never really committed to the product." As a result, Flip was slower and less responsive to market pressures than it was when it was an entrepreneurial firm.

These two factors left Flip unable to respond to the rapid changes occurring in the home market. Flip experienced a meteoric rise from 2007 to 2009, but this simply triggered an onslaught of competing cameras. Flip also faced an increasing threat from video-camera-enabled smartphones and tablets. There was also a shift in how customers used video devices during this period. Users increasingly wanted the ability to share videos in real time and also upload videos easily to YouTube, Flickr, and other social media sites. Cisco failed to see this shift and didn't add wireless transmission technology into the cameras. John Chambers, Cisco's CEO, admitted this failure. "With Flip, we missed the transition . . . it was about software that goes into the cloud—the way you're going to really deliver information in the future. We should have been developing our software for the cloud as opposed to the device. And we missed the window of opportunity."

In the end, Cisco didn't have the necessary vision to succeed in this market or the ability to respond quickly enough to the dynamic changes in customer desires.

Discussion Questions

1. Would Flip have had a better chance at success as a stand-alone firm than it did as part of Cisco? Why or why not?
2. Cisco didn't have the right market focus or competencies to win with Flip. What firms could have succeeded by acquiring Flip?

LO6.1

The reasons
for the failure
of many
diversification
efforts.

**corporate-level
strategy**
a strategy that focuses on
gaining long-term revenue,
profits, and market
value through managing
operations in multiple
businesses.

Cisco's experience with Flip is more the rule than the exception. Research shows that the vast majority of acquisitions result in value destruction rather than value creation. Many large multinational firms have also failed to effectively integrate their acquisitions, paid too high a premium for the target's common stock, or were unable to understand how the acquired firm's assets would fit with their own lines of business.[2] And, at times, top executives may not have acted in the best interests of shareholders. That is, the motive for the acquisition may have been to enhance the executives' power and prestige rather than to improve shareholder returns. At times, the only other people who may have benefited were the shareholders of the *acquired* firms—or the investment bankers who advise the acquiring firm, because they collect huge fees upfront regardless of what happens afterward![3]

There have been several studies that were conducted over a variety of time periods that show how disappointing acquisitions have typically turned out. For example:

- A study evaluated the stock market reaction of 600 acquisitions over the period between 1975 and 1991. The results indicated that the acquiring firms suffered an average 4 percent drop in market value (after adjusting for market movements) in the three months following the acquisitions announcement.[4]
- In a study by Solomon Smith Barney of U.S. companies acquired since 1997 in deals for $15 billion or more, the stocks of the acquiring firms have, on average, underperformed the S&P stock index by 14 percentage points and underperformed their peer group by 4 percentage points after the deals were announced.[5]
- A study investigated 270 mergers that took place between 2000 and 2003 in multiple countries and regions. It found that after a merger, sales growth decreased by 6 percent, earnings growth dropped 9.4 percent, and market valuations declined 2.5 percent (figures are adjusted for industry trends and refer to three years pre- or postmerger).[6]
- A study that investigated 86 completed takeover bids that took place between 1993 and 2008 noted a negative return of 2 percent per month in long-term performance for the 3-year postacquisition period.[7]

Exhibit 6.1 lists some well-known examples of failed acquisitions and mergers.

EXHIBIT 6.1 Some Well-Known M&A Blunders

Examples of Some Very Expensive Blunders

- Sprint and Nextel merged in 2005. On January 31, 2008, the firm announced a merger-related charge of $31 billion. Its stock had lost 76 percent of its value by late 2012 when it was announced that Sprint Nextel would be purchased by Softbank, a Japanese telecommunications and Internet firm. Softbank's stock price dropped 20 percent in the week after announcing it would acquire Sprint.
- AOL paid $114 billion to acquire Time Warner in 2001. Over the next two years, AOL Time Warner lost $150 billion in market valuation.
- Conseco paid $5.8 billion to buy Green Tree, a mobile home mortgage lender, in 1998 though the company's net worth was not even $1 billion. In the next two years, Conseco lost 90 percent of its market value!
- Daimler Benz paid $36 billion to acquire Chrysler in 1998. After years of losses, it sold 80.1 percent of the unit to Cerberus Capital Management for $7.4 billion in 2007. Cerberus didn't do any better, losing its ownership stake when Chrysler went into a government-managed bankruptcy in 2009.
- In 2012, Hewlett-Packard wrote off $9 billion of the $11 billion it paid for Autonomy, a software company that it purchased one year earlier. After they purchased it, HP realized that Autonomy's accounting statements were not accurate, resulting in a nearly 80 percent drop in the value of Autonomy once those accounting irregularities were corrected.
- Similarly, in 2012, Microsoft admitted to a major acquisition mistake when it wrote off essentially the entire $6.2 billion it paid for a digital advertising firm, aQuantive, that it purchased in 2007.

Sources: Ante, S.E. 2008. Sprint's wake-up call. *businessweek.com*., February 21: np; Gupta, P. 2008. Daimler may sell remaining Chrysler stake. *www.reuters .com*, September 24: np; Tully, S. 2006. The (second) worst deal ever. *Fortune*, October 16: 102–119.; and Wakabayashi, D., Troianovski, A. & Ante, S. 2012. Bravado behind Softbank's Sprint deal. October 16, *wsj.com*: np.

Many acquisitions ultimately result in divestiture—an admission that things didn't work out as planned. In fact, some years ago, a writer for *Fortune* magazine lamented, "Studies show that 33 percent to 50 percent of acquisitions are later divested, giving corporate marriages a divorce rate roughly comparable to that of men and women."[8]

Admittedly, we have been rather pessimistic so far.[9] Clearly, many diversification efforts have worked out very well—whether through mergers and acquisitions, strategic alliances and joint ventures, or internal development. We will discuss many success stories throughout this chapter. Next, we will discuss the primary rationales for diversification.

Making Diversification Work: An Overview

Clearly, not all diversification moves, including those involving mergers and acquisitions, erode performance. For example, acquisitions in the oil industry, such as British Petroleum's purchases of Amoco and Arco, are performing well as is the Exxon-Mobil merger. MetLife was able to dramatically expand its global footprint by acquiring Alico, a global player in the insurance business from AIG in 2010 when AIG was in financial distress. Since AIG was desperate to sell assets, MetLife was able to acquire this business at an attractive price. With this acquisition, MetLife expanded its global reach from 17 to 64 countries and increased its non-U.S. revenue from 15 to 40 percent.[10] Many leading high-tech firms such as Google, Apple, and Intel have dramatically enhanced their revenues, profits, and market values through a wide variety of diversification initiatives, including acquisitions, strategic alliances, and joint ventures, as well as internal development.

So the question becomes: Why do some diversification efforts pay off and others produce poor results? This chapter addresses two related issues: (1) What businesses should a corporation compete in? and (2) How should these businesses be managed to jointly create more value than if they were freestanding units?

Diversification initiatives—whether through mergers and acquisitions, strategic alliances and joint ventures, or internal development—must be justified by the creation of value for shareholders.[11] But this is not always the case.[12] Acquiring firms typically pay high premiums when they acquire a target firm. For example, in 2006 Freeport-McMoran paid a 30 percent premium to acquire Phelps Dodge in order to create the largest metals and mining concern in the U.S. In contrast, you and I, as private investors, can diversify our portfolio of stocks very cheaply. With an intensely competitive online brokerage industry, we can acquire hundreds (or thousands) of shares for a transaction fee of as little as $10.00 or less—a far cry from the 30 to 40 percent (or higher) premiums that corporations typically must pay to acquire companies.

Given the seemingly high inherent downside risks and uncertainties, one might ask: Why should companies even bother with diversification initiatives? The answer, in a word, is *synergy,* derived from the Greek word *synergos,* which means "working together." This can have two different, but not mutually exclusive, meanings.

First, a firm may diversify into *related* businesses. Here, the primary potential benefits to be derived come from *horizontal relationships;* that is, businesses sharing intangible resources (e.g., core competencies such as marketing) and tangible resources (e.g., production facilities, distribution channels).[13] Firms can also enhance their market power via pooled negotiating power and vertical integration. For example, Procter & Gamble enjoys many synergies from having businesses that share distribution resources.

Second, a corporation may diversify into *unrelated* businesses.[14] Here, the primary potential benefits are derived largely from *hierarchical relationships;* that is, value creation derived from the corporate office. Examples of the latter would include leveraging some of the support activities in the value chain that we discussed in Chapter 3, such as information systems or human resource practices. Cooper Industries has followed a successful strategy of unrelated diversification. There are few similarities in the products it

How managers can create value through diversification initiatives.

diversification
the process of firms expanding their operations by entering new businesses.

EXHIBIT 6.2

Creating Value through
Related and Unrelated
Diversification

Related Diversification: Economies of Scope

Leveraging core competencies
- 3M leverages its competencies in adhesives technologies to many industries, including automotive, construction, and telecommunications.

Sharing activities
- McKesson, a large distribution company, sells many product lines, such as pharmaceuticals and liquor, through its superwarehouses.

Related Diversification: Market Power

Pooled negotiating power
- ConAgra, a diversified food producer, increases its power over suppliers by centrally purchasing huge quantities of packaging materials for all of its food divisions.

Vertical integration
- Shaw Industries, a giant carpet manufacturer, increases its control over raw materials by producing much of its own polypropylene fiber, a key input to its manufacturing process.

Unrelated Diversification: Parenting, Restructuring, and Financial Synergies

Corporate restructuring and parenting
- The corporate office of Cooper Industries adds value to its acquired businesses by performing such activities as auditing their manufacturing operations, improving their accounting activities, and centralizing union negotiations.

Portfolio management
- Novartis, formerly Ciba-Geigy, uses portfolio management to improve many key activities, including resource allocation and reward and evaluation systems.

makes or the industries in which it competes. However, the corporate office adds value through such activities as superb human resource practices and budgeting systems.

Please note that such benefits derived from horizontal (related diversification) and hierarchical (unrelated diversification) relationships are not mutually exclusive. Many firms that diversify into related areas benefit from information technology expertise in the corporate office. Similarly, unrelated diversifiers often benefit from the "best practices" of sister businesses even though their products, markets, and technologies may differ dramatically.

Exhibit 6.2 provides an overview of how we will address the various means by which firms create value through both related and unrelated diversification and also include a summary of some examples that we will address in this chapter.[15]

Related Diversification: Economies of Scope and Revenue Enhancement

Related diversification enables a firm to benefit from horizontal relationships across different businesses in the diversified corporation by leveraging core competencies and sharing activities (e.g., production and distribution facilities). This enables a corporation to benefit from economies of scope. **Economies of scope** refers to cost savings from leveraging core competencies or sharing related activities among businesses in the corporation. A firm can also enjoy greater revenues if two businesses attain higher levels of sales growth combined than either company could attain independently.

Leveraging Core Competencies

The concept of core competencies can be illustrated by the imagery of the diversified corporation as a tree.[16] The trunk and major limbs represent core products; the smaller

related diversification

a firm entering a different business in which it can benefit from leveraging core competencies, sharing activities, or building market power.

economies of scope

cost savings from leveraging core competencies or sharing related activities among businesses in a corporation.

LO6.3

How corporations can use related diversification to achieve synergistic benefits through economies of scope and market power.

branches are business units; and the leaves, flowers, and fruit are end products. The core competencies are represented by the root system, which provides nourishment, sustenance, and stability. Managers often misread the strength of competitors by looking only at their end products, just as we can fail to appreciate the strength of a tree by looking only at its leaves. Core competencies may also be viewed as the "glue" that binds existing businesses together or as the engine that fuels new business growth.

Core competencies reflect the collective learning in organizations—how to coordinate diverse production skills, integrate multiple streams of technologies, and market diverse products and services.[17] Casio, a giant electronic products producer, synthesizes its abilities in miniaturization, microprocessor design, material science, and ultrathin precision castings to produce digital watches. These are the same skills it applies to design and produce its miniature card calculators, digital cameras, pocket electronic dictionaries, and other small electronics.

core competencies
a firm's strategic resources that reflect the collective learning in the organization.

For a core competence to create value and provide a viable basis for synergy among the businesses in a corporation, it must meet three criteria.[18]

- *The core competence must enhance competitive advantage(s) by creating superior customer value.* Every value-chain activity has the potential to provide a viable basis for building on a core competence.[19] At Gillette, for example, scientists developed the Fusion and Mach 3 after the introduction of the tremendously successful Sensor System because of a thorough understanding of several phenomena that underlie shaving. These include the physiology of facial hair and skin, the metallurgy of blade strength and sharpness, the dynamics of a cartridge moving across skin, and the physics of a razor blade severing hair. Such innovations are possible only with an understanding of such phenomena and the ability to combine such technologies into innovative products. Customers are willing to pay more for such technologically differentiated products.

- *Different businesses in the corporation must be similar in at least one important way related to the core competence.* It is not essential that the products or services themselves be similar. Rather, at least one element in the value chain must require similar skills in creating competitive advantage if the corporation is to capitalize on its core competence. At first glance you might think that computers and health care have little in common. However, Strategy Spotlight 6.1 discusses how IBM is leveraging its competencies in computing technology to provide health care services.

- *The core competencies must be difficult for competitors to imitate or find substitutes for.* As we discussed in Chapter 5, competitive advantages will not be sustainable if the competition can easily imitate or substitute them. Similarly, if the skills associated with a firm's core competencies are easily imitated or replicated, they are not a sound basis for sustainable advantages.

Consider Amazon's retailing operations. Amazon developed strong competencies in Internet retailing, website infrastructure, warehousing, and order fulfillment to dominate the online book industry. They used these competencies along with their brand name to expand into a range of online retail businesses. Competitors in these other market areas have had great difficulty imitating Amazon's competencies, and many have simply stopped trying. Instead, they have partnered with Amazon and contracted with Amazon to provide these services for them.[20]

Steve Jobs provided insight on the importance of a firm's core competence. The Apple CEO was considered one of the world's most respected business leaders:[21]

One of our biggest insights (years ago) was that we didn't want to get into any business where we didn't own or control the primary technology, because you'll get your head handed to you. We realized that for almost all future consumer electronics, the primary technology was going to be software. And we were pretty good at software. We could

IBM: THE NEW HEALTH CARE EXPERT

Watson, the supercomputer IBM used to win a competition against the best players on the quiz show *Jeopardy!* is now working toward becoming Dr. Watson. Over the decades, IBM has developed strong competencies in raw computing power. With Watson, a computer named after IBM founder Thomas J. Watson, IBM engineers and scientists set out to extend their competencies by building a computing system that can process natural language. Their goal was to build a system that could rival a human's ability to answer questions posed in natural language with speed, accuracy, and confidence. They took four years to develop the system and demonstrated its capabilities in beating two of the greatest champions of *Jeopardy!* in 2011.

Now, IBM is aiming to leverage their competencies in the health care arena. IBM is beginning this effort by allying with WellPoint, the nation's second largest health insurer, to provide medical advice using Watson. They have chosen to work initially on cancer treatment since the volume of research on cancer doubles every five years. As a result, it is very difficult for oncologists, the doctors treating cancer, to keep up with all of the medical advances. That is not a problem for Watson. IBM feeds massive amounts of data from hundreds of thousands of medical studies into Watson and updates the database as new research becomes available. Watson, which can analyze 66 million pages of data a second, has no

trouble keeping up. IBM then adds the individual patient's health history and current symptoms to the system. With its natural language capabilities, Watson can easily process and codify all of the information fed into it and within three seconds provide a personalized diagnosis and treatment plan. Watson can learn through the process. In its training phase, doctors assess Watson's answers and indicate whether they believe it is correct. This allows Watson to improve its decision making moving forward.

While oncology is the first medical specialty for Watson, IBM is looking to take the same approach to providing guidance for the treatment of diabetes, kidney disease, heart disease, and many other areas of medicine. In the future, IBM hopes to extend this system to remote medical treatment. Imagine a poor farmer in a village in Kenya who visits his doctor, complaining of chest discomfort. The doctor would simply talk into her phone to explain the symptoms and attach portable sensors to feed in EKG readings to the system. Watson would integrate this information with the patient's medical history and the latest research to provide cutting-edge medical advice on the treatment of the farmer.

With Watson, IBM aims to leverage their computing expertise to become medical experts.

Sources: Frier, S. 2012. IBM wants to put a Watson in your pocket. *Bloomberg Businessweek*, September 17: 41–42; Groenfeldt, T. 2012. IBM's Watson, Cedars-Sinai and Wellpoint take on cancer. *Forbes.com*, February 1: np; and *ibm.com*.

---

do the operating system software. We could write applications like iTunes on the Mac or even PC. And we could write the back-end software that runs on a cloud like iTunes. So we could write all these different kinds of software and tweed it all together and make it work seamlessly. And you ask yourself: What other companies can do that? It's a pretty short list.

Sharing Activities

As we saw above, leveraging core competencies involves transferring accumulated skills and expertise across business units in a corporation. Corporations also can achieve synergy by **sharing activities** across their business units. These include value-creating activities such as common manufacturing facilities, distribution channels, and sales forces. As we will see, sharing activities can potentially provide two primary payoffs: cost savings and revenue enhancements.

sharing activities
having activities of two or more businesses' value chains done by one of the businesses.

Deriving Cost Savings   Typically, this is the most common type of synergy and the easiest to estimate. Peter Shaw, head of mergers and acquisitions at the British chemical and pharmaceutical company ICI, refers to cost savings as "hard synergies" and contends that the level of certainty of their achievement is quite high. Cost savings come from many sources, including the elimination of jobs, facilities, and related expenses that are no longer needed when functions are consolidated, or from economies of scale in purchasing. Cost savings are generally highest when one company acquires another from the same industry in the same country. Shaw Industries, a division of Berkshire Hathaway, is the nation's largest carpet producer. Over the years, it has dominated the competition through a strategy of acquisition which has enabled Shaw, among other things, to consolidate its manufacturing operations in a few, highly efficient plants and to lower costs through higher capacity utilization.

Sharing activities inevitably involve costs that the benefits must outweigh such as the greater coordination required to manage a shared activity. Even more important is the need to compromise on the design or performance of an activity so that it can be shared. For example, a salesperson handling the products of two business units must operate in a way that is usually not what either unit would choose if it were independent. If the compromise erodes the unit's effectiveness, then sharing may reduce rather than enhance competitive advantage.

Enhancing Revenue and Differentiation

Often an acquiring firm and its target may achieve a higher level of sales growth together than either company could on its own. For example, Starbucks recently acquired a small bakery chain, La Boulange, and intends to sell La Boulange's products at Starbuck's cafes nationally. In leveraging Starbuck's national retail chain, La Boulange will be able to dramatically expand their market exposure and sales much beyond their current 19-store West Coast market.[22]

Firms also can enhance the effectiveness of their differentiation strategies by means of sharing activities among business units. A shared order-processing system, for example, may permit new features and services that a buyer will value. As another example, financial service providers strive to provide differentiated bundles of services to customers. By having a single point of contact where customers can manage their checking accounts, investment accounts, insurance policies, bill-payment services, mortgages, and many other services, they create value for their customers.

As a cautionary note, managers must keep in mind that sharing activities among businesses in a corporation can have a negative effect on a given business's differentiation. For example, when Ford owned Jaguar, they found that customers had lower perceived value of Jaguar automobiles when they found that the entry-level Jaguar shared its basic design with and was manufactured in the same production plant as the Ford Mondeo, a European midsize car. Perhaps, it is not too surprising that Jaguar was divested by Ford in 2008.

Related Diversification: Market Power

We now discuss how companies achieve related diversification through **market power.** We also address the two principal means by which firms achieve synergy through market power: *pooled negotiating power* and *vertical integration.* Managers do, however, have limits on their ability to use market power for diversification, because government regulations can sometimes restrict the ability of a business to gain very large shares of a particular market. For example, in 2011 AT&T attempted to acquire T-Mobile, a wireless service provider, but they were blocked by federal regulators who feared the combined firm would have too much market power in the telecommunications industry.

market power
firms' abilities to profit through restricting or controlling supply to a market or coordinating with other firms to reduce investment.

Pooled Negotiating Power

Similar businesses working together or the affiliation of a business with a strong parent can strengthen an organization's bargaining position relative to suppliers and customers and enhance its position vis-à-vis competitors. Compare, for example, the position of an independent food manufacturer with the same business within Nestlé. Being part of Nestlé provides the business with significant clout—greater bargaining power with suppliers and customers—since it is part of a firm that makes large purchases from

pooled negotiating power
the improvement in bargaining position relative to suppliers and customers.

suppliers and provides a wide variety of products. Access to the parent's deep pockets increases the business's strength, and the Nestlé unit enjoys greater protection from substitutes and new entrants. Not only would rivals perceive the unit as a more formidable opponent, but the unit's association with Nestlé would also provide greater visibility and improved image.

When acquiring related businesses, a firm's potential for pooled negotiating power vis-à-vis its customers and suppliers can be very enticing. However, managers must carefully evaluate how the combined businesses may affect relationships with actual and potential customers, suppliers, and competitors. For example, when PepsiCo diversified into the fast-food industry with its acquisitions of Kentucky Fried Chicken, Taco Bell, and Pizza Hut (now part of Yum! Brands), it clearly benefited from its position over these units that served as a captive market for its soft-drink products. However, many competitors, such as McDonald's, refused to consider PepsiCo as a supplier of its own soft-drink needs because of competition with Pepsi's divisions in the fast-food industry. Simply put, McDonald's did not want to subsidize the enemy! Thus, although acquiring related businesses can enhance a corporation's bargaining power, it must be aware of the potential for retaliation.

Vertical Integration

vertical integration
an expansion or extension of the firm by integrating preceding or successive production processes.

Vertical integration occurs when a firm becomes its own supplier or distributor. That is, it represents an expansion or extension of the firm by integrating preceding or successive production processes.[23] The firm incorporates more processes toward the original source of raw materials (backward integration) or toward the ultimate consumer (forward integration). For example, a car manufacturer might supply its own parts or make its own engines to secure sources of supply or control its own system of dealerships to ensure retail outlets for its products. Similarly, an oil refinery might secure land leases and develop its own drilling capacity to ensure a constant supply of crude oil. Or it could expand into retail operations by owning or licensing gasoline stations to guarantee customers for its petroleum products.

Vertical integration can be a viable strategy for many firms. Strategy Spotlight 6.2 discusses Shaw Industries, a carpet manufacturer that has attained a dominant position in the industry via a strategy of vertical integration. Shaw has successfully implemented strategies of both forward and backward integration. Exhibit 6.3 depicts the stages of Shaw's vertical integration.

Benefits and Risks of Vertical Integration   Vertical integration is a means for an organization to reduce its dependence on suppliers or its channels of distribution to end users. However, the benefits associated with vertical integration—backward or forward—must be carefully weighed against the risks.[24] The primary benefits and risks of vertical integration are listed in Exhibit 6.4.

Winnebago, the leader in the market for drivable recreational vehicles with a 20.4 percent market share, illustrates some of vertical integration's benefits.[25] The word *Winnebago* means "big RV" to most Americans. And the firm has a sterling reputation for great quality. The firm's huge northern Iowa factories do everything from extruding aluminum for body parts to molding plastics for water and holding tanks to dashboards. Such vertical integration at the factory may appear to be outdated and expensive, but it guarantees excellent quality. The Recreational Vehicle Dealer Association started giving a quality award in 1996, and Winnebago has won it every year.

In making vertical integration decisions, five issues should be considered.[26]

1. *Is the company satisfied with the quality of the value that its present suppliers and distributors are providing?* If the performance of organizations in the vertical chain—both suppliers and distributors—is satisfactory, it may not, in general,

VERTICAL INTEGRATION AT SHAW INDUSTRIES

Shaw Industries (now part of Berkshire Hathaway) is an example of a firm that has followed a very successful strategy of vertical integration. By relentlessly pursuing both backward and forward integration, Shaw has become the dominant manufacturer of carpeting products in the United States. According to CEO Robert Shaw, "We want to be involved with as much of the process of making and selling carpets as practical. That way, we're in charge of costs." For example, Shaw acquired Amoco's polypropylene fiber manufacturing facilities in Alabama and Georgia. These new plants provide carpet fibers for internal use and for sale to other manufacturers. With this backward integration, fully one-quarter of Shaw's carpet fiber needs are now met in-house. In early 1996 Shaw began to integrate forward, acquiring seven floor-covering retailers in a move that suggested a strategy to consolidate the fragmented industry and increase its influence over retail pricing. Exhibit 6.3 provides a simplified depiction of the stages of vertical integration for Shaw Industries.

Sources: White, J. 2003. Shaw to home in on more with Georgia Tufters deal. *HFN: The Weekly Newspaper for the Home Furnishing Network,* May 5: 32; Shaw Industries. 1993, 2000. Annual reports; and Server, A. 1994. How to escape a price war. *Fortune,* June 13: 88.

EXHIBIT 6.3 Simplified Stages of Vertical Integration: Shaw Industries

EXHIBIT 6.4

Benefits and Risks of Vertical Integration

Benefits

- A secure source of raw materials or distribution channels.
- Protection of and control over valuable assets.
- Proprietary access to new technologies developed by the unit.
- Simplified procurement and administrative procedures.

Risks

- Costs and expenses associated with increased overhead and capital expenditures.
- Loss of flexibility resulting from large investments.
- Problems associated with unbalanced capacities along the value chain. (For example, the in-house supplier has to be larger than your needs in order to benefit from economies of scale in that market.)
- Additional administrative costs associated with managing a more complex set of activities.

be appropriate for a company to perform these activities themselves. Nike and Reebok have outsourced the manufacture of their shoes for years, because they have found the independent suppliers capable of providing low-cost, acceptable quality shoes.

2. *Are there activities in the industry value chain presently being outsourced or performed independently by others that are a viable source of future profits?* Even if a firm is outsourcing value-chain activities to companies that are doing a credible job, it may be missing out on substantial profit opportunities. Consider Best Buy. When they realized that the profit potential of providing installation and service was substantial, they forward integrated into this area by acquiring Geek Squad.

3. *Is there a high level of stability in the demand for the organization's products?* High demand or sales volatility are not conducive to vertical integration. With the high level of fixed costs in plant and equipment as well as operating costs that accompany endeavors toward vertical integration, widely fluctuating sales demand can either strain resources (in times of high demand) or result in unused capacity (in times of low demand). The cycles of "boom and bust" in the automobile industry are a key reason why the manufacturers have increased the amount of outsourced inputs.

4. *Does the company have the necessary competencies to execute the vertical integration strategies?* As many companies would attest, successfully executing strategies of vertical integration can be very difficult. For example, Boise Cascade, a lumber firm, once forward integrated into the home-building industry but found that they didn't have the design and marketing competencies needed to compete in this market.

5. *Will the vertical integration initiative have potential negative impacts on the firm's stakeholders?* Managers must carefully consider the impact that vertical integration may have on existing and future customers, suppliers, and competitors. After Lockheed Martin, a dominant defense contractor, acquired Loral Corporation, an electronics supplier, for $9.1 billion, it had an unpleasant and unanticipated surprise. Loral, as a captive supplier of Lockheed, is now viewed as a rival by many of its previous customers. Thus, before Lockheed Martin can realize any net synergies from this acquisition, it must make up for the substantial business that it has lost.

Analyzing Vertical Integration: The Transaction Cost Perspective Another approach that has proved very useful in understanding vertical integration is the **transaction cost perspective**.[27] According to this perspective, every market transaction involves some *transaction costs*. First, a decision to purchase an input from an outside source leads to *search* costs (i.e., the cost to find where it is available, the level of quality, etc.). Second, there are costs associated with *negotiating*. Third, a *contract* needs to be written spelling out future possible contingencies. Fourth, parties in a contract have to *monitor* each other. Finally, if a party does not comply with the terms of the contract, there are *enforcement* costs. Transaction costs are thus the sum of search costs, negotiation costs, contracting costs, monitoring costs, and enforcement costs. These transaction costs can be avoided by internalizing the activity, in other words, by producing the input in-house.

A related problem with purchasing a specialized input from outside is the issue of *transaction-specific investments*. For example, when an automobile company needs an input specifically designed for a particular car model, the supplier may be unwilling to make the investments in plant and machinery necessary to produce that component for two reasons. First, the investment may take many years to recover but there is no guarantee the automobile company will continue to buy from them after the contract expires, typically in one year. Second, once the investment is made, the supplier has no bargaining power. That is, the buyer knows that the supplier has no option but to supply at ever-lower prices because the investments were so specific that they cannot be used to produce alternative products. In such circumstances, again, vertical integration may be the only option.

Vertical integration, however, gives rise to a different set of costs. These costs are referred to as *administrative costs*. Coordinating different stages of the value chain now internalized within the firm causes administrative costs to go up. Decisions about vertical integration are, therefore, based on a comparison of transaction costs and administrative costs. If transaction costs are lower than administrative costs, it is best to resort to market transactions and avoid vertical integration. For example, McDonald's may be the

transaction cost perspective
a perspective that the choice of a transaction's governance structure, such as vertical integration or market transaction, is influenced by transaction costs, including search, negotiating, contracting, monitoring, and enforcement costs, associated with each choice.

world's biggest buyer of beef, but they do not raise cattle. The market for beef has low transaction costs and requires no transaction-specific investments. On the other hand, if transaction costs are higher than administrative costs, vertical integration becomes an attractive strategy. Most automobile manufacturers produce their own engines because the market for engines involves high transaction costs and transaction-specific investments.

Unrelated Diversification: Financial Synergies and Parenting

LO6.4

How corporations can use unrelated diversification to attain synergistic benefits through corporate restructuring, parenting, and portfolio analysis.

With unrelated diversification, unlike related diversification, few benefits are derived from *horizontal relationships*—that is, the leveraging of core competencies or the sharing of activities across business units within a corporation. Instead, potential benefits can be gained from *vertical (or hierarchical) relationships*—the creation of synergies from the interaction of the corporate office with the individual business units. There are two main sources of such synergies. First, the corporate office can contribute to "parenting" and restructuring of (often acquired) businesses. Second, the corporate office can add value by viewing the entire corporation as a family or "portfolio" of businesses and allocating resources to optimize corporate goals of profitability, cash flow, and growth. Additionally, the corporate office enhances value by establishing appropriate human resource practices and financial controls for each of its business units.

Corporate Parenting and Restructuring

We have discussed how firms can add value through related diversification by exploring sources of synergy *across* business units. Now, we discuss how value can be created *within* business units as a result of the expertise and support provided by the corporate office.

Parenting The positive contributions of the corporate office are called the **"parenting advantage."**[28] Many firms have successfully diversified their holdings without strong evidence of the more traditional sources of synergy (i.e., horizontally across business units). Diversified public corporations such as Berkshire Hathaway and Virgin Group, and leveraged buyout firms such as KKR, and Clayton, Dublilier & Rice are a few examples.[29] These parent companies create value through management expertise. How? They improve plans and budgets and provide especially competent central functions such as legal, financial, human resource management, procurement, and the like. They also help subsidiaries make wise choices in their own acquisitions, divestitures, and new internal development decisions. Such contributions often help business units to substantially increase their revenues and profits. For example, KKR, a private equity firm, has a team of parenting experts, called KKR Capstone, that works with newly acquired firms for 12-24 months to enhance the acquired firm's value. They work to improve a range of operating activities, such as new product development processes, sales force activities, quality improvement, and supply chain management.

Restructuring Restructuring is another means by which the corporate office can add value to a business.[30] The central idea can be captured in the real estate phrase "buy low and sell high." Here, the corporate office tries to find either poorly performing firms with unrealized potential or firms in industries on the threshold of significant, positive change. The parent intervenes, often selling off parts of the business; changing the management; reducing payroll and unnecessary sources of expenses; changing strategies; and infusing the company with new technologies, processes, reward systems, and so forth. When the restructuring is complete, the firm can either "sell high" and capture the added value or keep the business and enjoy financial and competitive benefits.[31]

unrelated diversification
a firm entering a different business that has little horizontal interaction with other businesses of a firm.

parenting advantage
the positive contributions of the corporate office to a new business as a result of expertise and support provided and not as a result of substantial changes in assets, capital structure, or management.

restructuring
the intervention of the corporate office in a new business that substantially changes the assets, capital structure, and/or management, including selling off parts of the business, changing the management, reducing payroll and unnecessary sources of expenses, changing strategies, and infusing the new business with new technologies, processes, and reward systems.

Loews Corporation, a conglomerate with $16 billion in revenues competes in such industries as oil and gas, tobacco, watches, insurance, and hotels. It provides an exemplary example of how firms can successfully "buy low and sell high" as part of their corporate strategy.[32]

> Energy accounts for 33 percent of Loews' $30 billion in total assets. In the 1980s it bought six oil tankers for only $5 million each during a sharp slide in oil prices. The downside was limited. After all these huge hulks could easily have been sold as scrap steel. However, that didn't have to happen. Eight years after Loews purchased the tankers, they sold them for $50 million each.
>
> Loews was also extremely successful with its next energy play—drilling equipment. Although wildcatting for oil is very risky, selling services to wildcatters is not, especially if the assets are bought during a down cycle. Loews did just that. It purchased 10 offshore drilling rigs for $50 million in 1989 and formed Diamond Offshore Drilling. In 1995 Loews received $338 million after taking a 30 percent piece of this operation public!

For the restructuring strategy to work, the corporate management must have both the insight to detect undervalued companies (otherwise the cost of acquisition would be too high) or businesses competing in industries with a high potential for transformation.[33] Additionally, of course, they must have the requisite skills and resources to turn the businesses around, even if they may be in new and unfamiliar industries.

Restructuring can involve changes in assets, capital structure, or management.

- *Asset restructuring* involves the sale of unproductive assets, or even whole lines of businesses, that are peripheral. In some cases, it may even involve acquisitions that strengthen the core business.
- *Capital restructuring* involves changing the debt-equity mix, or the mix between different classes of debt or equity. Although the substitution of equity with debt is more common in buyout situations, occasionally the parent may provide additional equity capital.
- *Management restructuring* typically involves changes in the composition of the top management team, organizational structure, and reporting relationships. Tight financial control, rewards based strictly on meeting short- to medium-term performance goals, and reduction in the number of middle-level managers are common steps in management restructuring. In some cases, parental intervention may even result in changes in strategy as well as infusion of new technologies and processes.

Portfolio Management

During the 1970s and early 1980s, several leading consulting firms developed the concept of **portfolio management** to achieve a better understanding of the competitive position of an overall portfolio (or family) of businesses, to suggest strategic alternatives for each of the businesses, and to identify priorities for the allocation of resources. Several studies have reported widespread use of these techniques among American firms.[34]

Description and Potential Benefits The key purpose of portfolio models is to assist a firm in achieving a balanced portfolio of businesses.[35] This consists of businesses whose profitability, growth, and cash flow characteristics complement each other and adds up to a satisfactory overall corporate performance. Imbalance, for example, could be caused either by excessive cash generation with too few growth opportunities or by insufficient cash generation to fund the growth requirements in the portfolio.

The Boston Consulting Group's (BCG) growth/share matrix is among the best known of these approaches.[36] In the BCG approach, each of the firm's strategic business units

EXHIBIT 6.5 The Boston Consulting Group (BCG) Portfolio Matrix

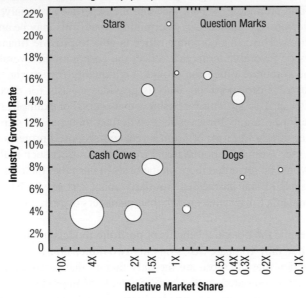

(SBUs) is plotted on a two-dimensional grid in which the axes are relative market share and industry growth rate. The grid is broken into four quadrants. Exhibit 6.5 depicts the BCG matrix. Following are a few clarifications:

1. Each circle represents one of the corporation's business units. The size of the circle represents the relative size of the business unit in terms of revenues.
2. Relative market share, measured by the ratio of the business unit's size to that of its largest competitor, is plotted along the horizontal axis.
3. Market share is central to the BCG matrix. This is because high relative market share leads to unit cost reduction due to experience and learning curve effects and, consequently, superior competitive position.

Each of the four quadrants of the grid has different implications for the SBUs that fall into the category:

- *Stars* are SBUs competing in high growth industries with relatively high market shares. These firms have long-term growth potential and should continue to receive substantial investment funding.
- *Question Marks* are SBUs competing in high-growth industries but having relatively weak market shares. Resources should be invested in them to enhance their competitive positions.
- *Cash Cows* are SBUs with high market shares in low-growth industries. These units have limited long-run potential but represent a source of current cash flows to fund investments in "stars" and "question marks."
- *Dogs* are SBUs with weak market shares in low-growth industries. Because they have weak positions and limited potential, most analysts recommend that they be divested.

In using portfolio strategy approaches, a corporation tries to create shareholder value in a number of ways.[37] First, portfolio analysis provides a snapshot of the businesses in a corporation's portfolio. Therefore, the corporation is in a better position to allocate resources among the business units according to prescribed criteria (e.g., use cash flows from the "cash cows" to fund promising "stars"). Second, the expertise and analytical resources in the corporate office provide guidance in determining what firms may be attractive (or unattractive) acquisitions. Third, the corporate office is able to provide financial resources to the business units on favorable terms that reflect the corporation's overall ability to raise funds. Fourth, the corporate office can provide high-quality review and coaching for the individual businesses. Fifth, portfolio analysis provides a basis for developing strategic goals and reward/evaluation systems for business managers. For example, managers of cash cows would have lower targets for revenue growth than managers of stars, but the former would have higher threshold levels of profit targets on proposed projects than the managers of star businesses. Compensation systems would also reflect such realities. Cash cows understandably would be rewarded more on the basis of cash that their businesses generate than would managers of star businesses. Similarly, managers of star businesses would be held to higher standards for revenue growth than managers of cash cow businesses.

Limitations   Despite the potential benefits of portfolio models, there are also some notable downsides. First, they compare SBUs on only two dimensions, making the implicit but erroneous assumption that (1) those are the only factors that really matter and (2) every unit can be accurately compared on that basis. Second, the approach views each SBU as a stand-alone entity, ignoring common core business practices and value-creating activities that may hold promise for synergies across business units. Third, unless care is exercised, the process becomes largely mechanical, substituting an oversimplified graphical model for the important contributions of the CEO's (and other corporate managers') experience and judgment. Fourth, the reliance on "strict rules" regarding resource allocation across SBUs can be detrimental to a firm's long-term viability. Finally, while colorful and easy to comprehend, the imagery of the BCG matrix can lead to some troublesome and overly simplistic prescriptions. For example, division managers are likely to want to jump ship as soon as their division is labeled a "dog."

To see what can go wrong, consider Cabot Corporation.

> Cabot Corporation supplies carbon black for the rubber, electronics, and plastics industries. Following the BCG matrix, Cabot moved away from its cash cow, carbon black, and diversified into stars such as ceramics and semiconductors in a seemingly overaggressive effort to create more revenue growth for the corporation. Predictably, Cabot's return on assets declined as the firm shifted away from its core competence to unrelated areas. The portfolio model failed by pointing the company in the wrong direction in an effort to spur growth—away from their core business. Recognizing its mistake, Cabot Corporation returned to its mainstay carbon black manufacturing and divested unrelated businesses. Today the company is a leader in its field with $3.3 billion in 2012 revenues.[38]

Caveat: Is Risk Reduction a Viable Goal of Diversification?

One of the purposes of diversification is to reduce the risk that is inherent in a firm's variability in revenues and profits over time. That is, if a firm enters new products or markets that are affected differently by seasonal or economic cycles, its performance over time will be more stable. For example, a firm manufacturing lawn mowers may diversify into snow blowers to even out its annual sales. Or a firm manufacturing a luxury line of household furniture may introduce a lower-priced line since affluent and lower-income customers are affected differently by economic cycles.

At first glance the above reasoning may make sense, but there are some problems with it. First, a firm's stockholders can diversify their portfolios at a much lower cost than a corporation, and they don't have to worry about integrating the acquisition into their portfolio. Second, economic cycles as well as their impact on a given industry (or firm) are difficult to predict with any degree of accuracy.

Notwithstanding the above, some firms have benefited from diversification by lowering the variability (or risk) in their performance over time. Consider GE, a firm that manufactures a wide range of products, including aircraft engines, power-generation equipment, locomotive trains, and large appliances. In addition to manufacturing these products, GE finances the purchase of them. GE's range of diversification has resulted in stable earnings over time and a low-risk profile. This allows them to borrow money at favorable rates, money that they, in turn, use to provide financing to buyers of their products.

Risk reduction in and of itself is rarely viable as a means to create shareholder value. It must be undertaken with a view of a firm's overall diversification strategy.

The Means to Achieve Diversification

LO6.5

The various means of engaging in diversification—mergers and acquisitions, joint ventures/strategic alliances, and internal development.

We have addressed the types of diversification (e.g., related and unrelated) that a firm may undertake to achieve synergies and create value for its shareholders. Now, we address the means by which a firm can go about achieving these desired benefits.

There are three basic means. First, through acquisitions or mergers, corporations can directly acquire a firm's assets and competencies. Although the terms *mergers* and *acquisitions* are used quite interchangeably, there are some key differences. With **acquisitions,** one firm buys another either through a stock purchase, cash, or the issuance of debt.[39] **Mergers,** on the other hand, entail a combination or consolidation of two firms to form a new legal entity. Mergers are relatively rare and entail a transaction among two firms on a relatively equal basis. Despite such differences, we consider both mergers and acquisitions to be quite similar in terms of their implications for a firm's corporate-level strategy.[40]

Second, corporations may agree to pool the resources of other companies with their resource base, commonly known as a joint venture or strategic alliance. Although these two forms of partnerships are similar in many ways, there is an important difference. Joint ventures involve the formation of a third-party legal entity where the two (or more) firms each contribute equity, whereas strategic alliances do not.

Third, corporations may diversify into new products, markets, and technologies through internal development. Called corporate entrepreneurship, it involves the leveraging and combining of a firm's own resources and competencies to create synergies and enhance shareholder value. We address this subject in greater length in Chapter 12.

acquisitions
the incorporation of one firm into another through purchase.

mergers
the combining of two or more firms into one new legal entity.

Mergers and Acquisitions

The most visible and often costly means to diversify is through acquisitions. Over the past several years, several large acquisitions were announced. These include:[41]

- InBev's acquisition of Anheuser-Busch for $52 billion.
- Pfizer's acquisition of Wyeth for $68 billion.
- Mittal Steel's acquisition of Arcelor for $33 billion.
- Boston Scientific's $27 billion acquisition of medical device maker Guidant.
- Microsoft's acquisition of Skype for $8.5 billion.
- Duke Energy's acquisition of Progress Energy for $25.5 billion.
- Softbank's acquisition of Sprint for $20 billion.

Exhibit 6.6 illustrates the dramatic volatility in worldwide M&A activity over the last several years. Several factors influence M&A activity. Julia Coronado, the chief economist at the investment bank BNP Paribas, highlights two of the key determinants, stating, "When mergers and acquisitions pick up, that's a good sign that businesses are feeling confident enough about the future that they're willing to become aggressive, look for deals, look for ways to grow and expand their operations. And it's also an indication that markets are willing to finance these transactions. So it's optimism from the markets and

EXHIBIT 6.6 Global Value of Mergers and Acquisitions

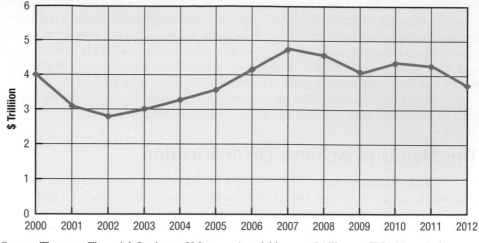

Source: Thomson Financial, Institute of Mergers, Acquisitions, and Alliances (IMAA) analysis.

from the businesses themselves."[42] Thus, the general economic conditions and level of optimism about the future influence managers' willingness to take on the risk of acquisitions. Additionally, the availability of financing can influence acquisition activity. During boom periods, financing is typically widely available. In contrast, during recessionary periods, potential acquirers typically find it difficult to borrow money to finance acquisitions.

Governmental policies such as regulatory actions and tax policies can also make the M&A environment more or less favorable. For example, increased antitrust enforcement will decrease the ability of firms to acquire their competitors or possibly firms in closely related markets. In contrast, increased regulatory pressures for good corporate governance may leave boards of directors more open to acquisition offers.

Finally, currency fluctuations can influence the rate of cross-border acquisitions, with firms in countries with stronger currencies being in a stronger position to acquire. For example, the Canadian dollar has increased in value from 80 U.S. cents to about $1 since 2009, making it relatively cheaper for Canadian firms to acquire U.S. firms.

Motives and Benefits Growth through mergers and acquisitions has played a critical role in the success of many corporations in a wide variety of high-technology and knowledge-intensive industries. Here, market and technology changes can occur very quickly and unpredictably.[43] Speed—speed to market, speed to positioning, and speed to becoming a viable company—is critical in such industries. For example, in 2010, Apple acquired Siri Inc. so that they could quickly fully integrate Siri's natural language voice recognition software into iOS, Apple's operating system.

Mergers and acquisitions also can be a means of *obtaining valuable resources that can help an organization expand its product offerings and services.* As noted earlier in the chapter, Cisco Systems, a computer networking firm, has undertaken over 80 acquisitions in the last decade. Cisco uses these acquisitions to quickly add new technology to their product offerings to meet changing customer needs. Then it uses its excellent sales force to market the new technology to its corporate customers. Cisco also provides strong incentives to the staff of acquired companies to stay on. To realize the greatest value from its acquisitions, Cisco also has learned to integrate acquired companies efficiently and effectively.[44]

Mergers and acquisitions also can *provide the opportunity for firms to attain the three bases of synergy—leveraging core competencies, sharing activities, and building market power.* Consider some of eBay's acquisitions. eBay has purchased a range of businesses in related product markets, such as GSI Commerce, a company that designs and runs online shopping sites for brick-and-mortar retailers, and StubHub, an online ticket broker. Additionally, they have purchased Korean online auction company Gmarket to expand their geographic scope. Finally, they have purchased firms providing related services, such as PayPal, the online payment system, and Zong, a mobile payment system provider.

These acquisitions offer the opportunity to leverage eBay's competencies.[45] For example, with the acquisition of GSI, eBay saw opportunities to leverage its core competencies in online systems as well as its reputation to strengthen GSI while also expanding eBay's ability to work with medium to large merchants and brands. eBay can also benefit from these acquisitions by sharing activities. In acquiring firms in related product markets and in new geographic markets, eBay has built a set of businesses that can share in the development of e-commerce and mobile commerce systems. Finally, by purchasing online and mobile payment firms, such as PayPal and Zong, eBay is able to integrate easy-to-use retail sites with flexible and secure payment systems. In doing so, they build market power relative to both retailers and customers as eBay stakes out ground as a full-service provider of online retailing systems.[46]

Merger and acquisition activity also can *lead to consolidation within an industry and can force other players to merge.*[47] The airline industry has seen a great deal of consolidation in the last several years. For example, Delta became the world's largest airline when it acquired Northwest in 2008, only to lose that position when United purchased Continental Airlines in 2010. In addition to these two acquisitions, there have been several others in the U.S. airline industry since 2000. In combining, these airlines are both seeking greater efficiencies by combining their networks and hoping that consolidation will dampen the rivalry in the industry.[48]

Corporations can also *enter new market segments by way of acquisitions.* As mentioned above, eBay, a firm that specialized in providing services to individuals and small businesses, moved into providing online retail systems for large merchants with its acquisition of GSI Commerce. Similarly, one of the reasons Fiat acquired Chrysler was to gain access to the U.S. auto market. Exhibit 6.7 summarizes the benefits of mergers and acquisitions.

Potential Limitations   As noted in the previous section, mergers and acquisitions provide a firm with many potential benefits. However, at the same time, there are many potential drawbacks or limitations to such corporate activity.[49]

First, *the takeover premium that is paid for an acquisition typically is very high.* Two times out of three, the stock price of the acquiring company falls once the deal is made public. Since the acquiring firm often pays a 30 percent or higher premium for the target company, the acquirer must create synergies and scale economies that result in sales and market gains exceeding the premium price. Firms paying higher premiums set the performance hurdle even higher. For example, Household International paid an 82 percent premium to buy Beneficial, and Conseco paid an 83 percent premium to acquire Green Tree Financial. Historically, paying a high premium over the stock price has been a poor strategy.

- Obtain valuable resources that can help an organization expand its product offerings.
- Provide the opportunity for firms to attain three bases of synergy: leveraging core competencies, sharing activities, and building market power.
- Lead to consolidation within an industry and force other players to merge.
- Enter new market segments.

EXHIBIT 6.7

Benefits of Mergers and Acquisitions

Second, *competing firms often can imitate any advantages realized or copy synergies that result from the M&A.*[50] Thus, a firm can often see its advantages quickly erode. Unless the advantages are sustainable and difficult to copy, investors will not be willing to pay a high premium for the stock. Similarly, the time value of money must be factored into the stock price. M&A costs are paid up front. Conversely, firms pay for R&D, ongoing marketing, and capacity expansion over time. This stretches out the payments needed to gain new competencies. The M&A argument is that a large initial investment is worthwhile because it creates long-term advantages. However, stock analysts want to see immediate results from such a large cash outlay. If the acquired firm does not produce results quickly, investors often divest the stock, driving the price down.

Third, *managers' credibility and ego can sometimes get in the way of sound business decisions.* If the M&A does not perform as planned, managers who pushed for the deal find their reputation tarnished. This can lead them to protect their credibility by funneling more money, or escalating their commitment, into an inevitably doomed operation. Further, when a merger fails and a firm tries to unload the acquisition, they often must sell at a huge discount. These problems further compound the costs and erode the stock price.

Fourth, *there can be many cultural issues that may doom the intended benefits from M&A endeavors.* Consider, the insights of Joanne Lawrence, who played an important role in the merger between SmithKline and the Beecham Group.[51]

> The key to a strategic merger is to create a new culture. This was a mammoth challenge during the SmithKline Beecham merger. We were working at so many different cultural levels, it was dizzying. We had two national cultures to blend—American and British—that compounded the challenge of selling the merger in two different markets with two different shareholder bases. There were also two different business cultures: One was very strong, scientific, and academic; the other was much more commercially oriented. And then we had to consider within both companies the individual businesses, each of which has its own little culture.

Exhibit 6.8 summarizes the limitations of mergers and acquisitions.

Strategy Spotlight 6.3 discusses the characteristics of acquisitions that lead investors to see greater value in the combinations.

Divestment: The Other Side of the "M&A Coin" When firms acquire other businesses, it typically generates quite a bit of "press" in business publications such as *The Wall Street Journal, Bloomberg Businessweek,* and *Fortune.* It makes for exciting news, and one thing is for sure—large acquiring firms automatically improve their standing in the Fortune 500 rankings (since it is based solely on total revenues). However, managers must also carefully consider the strategic implications of exiting businesses.

divestment
the exit of a business from a firm's portfolio.

Divestments, the exit of a business from a firm's portfolio, are quite common. One study found that large, prestigious U.S. companies divested more acquisitions than they had kept.[52] Well-known divestitures in business history include (1) Novell's purchase of WordPerfect for stock valued at $1.4 billion and later sold to Corel for $124 million, and (2) Quaker Oats' unloading of the Snapple Beverage Company to Triarc for only $300 million in 1997—three years after it had bought it for $1.8 billion!

EXHIBIT 6.8
Limitations of Mergers and Acquisitions

- Takeover premiums paid for acquisitions are typically very high.
- Competing firms often can imitate any advantages or copy synergies that result from the merger or acquisition.
- Managers' egos sometimes get in the way of sound business decisions.
- Cultural issues may doom the intended benefits from M&A endeavors.

THE WISDOM OF CROWDS: WHEN DO INVESTORS SEE VALUE IN ACQUISITIONS?

By some estimates, 70 to 90 percent of acquisitions destroy shareholder value. But investors do see value in some acquisitions. The question is, when does the wisdom of the investment crowd indicate there is value with acquisitions? Recent research suggests it rests in both the characteristics of the deal and the motivation of the acquiring firm.

The Characteristics of the Deal

Research has identified several deal characteristics that lead to positive investor reactions. Not surprisingly, investors see greater value in acquisitions when the acquiring and the acquired (target) firm are in the same or closely related industries. This is consistent with there being greater potential for synergies when the firms are in similar markets. Second, investors see greater value potential when acquiring managers are seen as responding quickly to new opportunities, such as those provided by the emergence of new technologies or market deregulation. Third, investors have a more positive reaction when the acquiring firm used cash to buy the target, as opposed to giving the target shareholders stock in the combined firm. Acquiring firms often use stock to finance acquisitions when they think their own stock is overvalued. Thus, the use of cash signals that the acquiring firm's managers have confidence in the value of the deal. Fourth, the less the acquiring firm relies on outside advisors, such as investment banks, the more investors see value in the deal. As with the use of cash, managers who rely primarily on their own knowledge and abilities to manage deals are seen as more confident. Finally, when the target firm tries to avoid the acquisition, investors see less value potential. Defense actions by targets are seen as signals that the target firm will not be open to easy integration with the acquiring firm. Thus, it may be difficult to leverage synergies.

The Motivation of the Acquirer

How much value investors see in the deal is also affected by the motivation of the acquirer. Interestingly, if the acquiring firm is highly profitable, investors see less value in the acquisition. The concern here is that strong performance likely leads managers to become overconfident and more likely to undertake "empire building" acquisitions as opposed to acquisitions that generate shareholder value. Second, if the acquiring firm is highly leveraged, having a high debt/equity ratio, investors see more value in the acquisition. Since the acquiring firm is at a higher risk of bankruptcy, managers of highly leveraged firms are likely to only undertake acquisitions if they are low risk and likely to generate synergistic benefits.

In total, the stock investors look to logical clues about the potential value of the deal and the motives of the acquiring firm managers to assess the value they see. Thus, there appears to be simple but logical wisdom in the crowd.

Sources: McNamara, G., Haleblian, J., & Dykes, B. 2008. Performance implications of participating in an acquisition wave: Early mover advantages, bandwagon effects, and the moderating influence of industry characteristics and acquirer tactics. *Academy of Management Journal*, 31: 113–130; and Schijven, M. & Hitt, M. 2012. The vicarious wisdom of the crowds: Toward a behavioral perspective on investor reactions to acquisition announcements. *Strategic Management Journal*, 33: 1247–1268.

Divesting a business can accomplish many different objectives.* As the examples on the previous page demonstrate, it can be used to help a firm reverse an earlier acquisition that didn't work out as planned. Often, this is simply to help "cut their losses." Other objectives include: (1) enabling managers to focus their efforts more directly on the firm's core businesses,[53] (2) providing the firm with more resources to spend on more attractive alternatives, and (3) raising cash to help fund existing businesses. For example, Pfizer embarked on a refocusing effort in 2011 where they decided to emphasize five therapeutic areas. As a result, Pfizer is divesting labs, facilities, and divisions that are outside these focal areas. Another example is Tyco International, the world's largest maker of security systems, which sold part of one of its businesses to raise cash for its share buyback—another reason for divestiture.

---

*Firms can divest their businesses in a number of ways. Sell-offs, spin-offs, equity carve-outs, asset sales/dissolution, and split-ups are some such modes of divestment. In a sell-off, the divesting firm privately negotiates with a third party to divest a unit/subsidiary for cash/stock. In a spin-off, a parent company distributes shares of the unit/subsidiary being divested pro-rata to its existing shareholders and a new company is formed. Equity carve-outs are similar to spin-offs except that shares in the unit/subsidiary being divested are offered to new shareholders. Dissolution involves sale of redundant assets, not necessarily as an entire unit/subsidiary as in sell-offs but a few bits at a time. A split-up, on the other hand, is an instance of divestiture where the parent company is split into two or more new companies and the parent ceases to exist. Shares in the parent company are exchanged for shares in new companies and the exact distribution varies case by case.

MEDTRONIC: FROM MEDICAL DEVICES TO SERVICES

By Cyrlene Claasen and Helena Gonzalez

In August 2013, Medtronic Inc. (MDT), the world's biggest maker of heart rhythm regulating devices announced its $200 million acquisition of Cardiocom which provides monitoring services to patients with chronic diseases. Through this move, Medtronic Inc. is expanding into the health-services industry, in emerging markets especially. The aim is to increase revenue growth in these regions to 20 percent from the current 15 percent.

Expansion in developing countries is a top priority for the device maker, which is coping with slow U.S. sales which range from pacemakers to insulin pumps as intensifying pressures to rein in healthcare spending take a toll on the once high-flying industry.

"Independent businesses do exist, but no one has the technical and clinical expertise that we have. Coupled with an elaborate infrastructure to manage patients, that's a pretty unique combination," CEO Omar Ishrak said.

The company is also working with administrators in Europe and the Middle East to improve hospital efficiency by developing new financing models and purchasing strategies.

Sources: Cortez, M. F. (2013). Medtronic Plans Expansion to Health Services, CEO Says, Bloomberg www.bloomberg.com. August 21: np.; Grayson, K. (2013) Medtronic CEO: We're not just devices anymore, Business Journals www.bizjournals.com. August 20: np.; Kelly, S. (2013). Medtronic aims to help countries build healthcare systems, Reuters n.reuters.com. August 21: np.

Divesting can enhance a firm's competitive position only to the extent that it reduces its tangible (e.g., maintenance, investments, etc.) or intangible (e.g., opportunity costs, managerial attention) costs without sacrificing a current competitive advantage or the seeds of future advantages.[54] To be effective, divesting requires a thorough understanding of a business unit's current ability and future potential to contribute to a firm's value creation. However, since such decisions involve a great deal of uncertainty, it is very difficult to make such evaluations. In addition, because of managerial self-interests and organizational inertia, firms often delay divestments of underperforming businesses.

The Boston Consulting Group has identified seven principles for successful divestiture.[55]

1. **Remove the emotion from the decision.** Managers need to consider objectively the prospects for each unit in the firm and how this unit fits with the firm's overall strategy. Issues related to personal relationships with the managers of the unit, the length of time the unit has been part of the company, and other emotional elements should not be considered in the decision.[56]

2. **Know the value of the business you are selling.** Divesting firms can generate greater interest in and higher bids for units they are divesting if they can clearly articulate the strategic value of the unit.

3. **Time the deal right.** This involves both internal timing, where the firm regularly evaluates all its units so that it can divest units when they are no longer highly valued in the firm but will still be of value to the outside market, as well as external timing, being ready to sell when the market conditions are right.

4. **Maintain a sizable pool of potential buyers.** Divesting firms should not focus on a single potential buyer. Instead, they should discuss possible deals with several hand-picked potential bidders.

5. **Tell a story about the deal.** For each potential bidder they talk with, the divesting firm should develop a narrative about how the unit they are interested in selling will create value for that buyer.

6. **Run divestitures systematically through a project office.** Firms should look at developing the ability to divest units as a distinct form of corporate competencies. While many firms have acquisition units, they often don't have divesting units even though there is significant potential value in divestitures.

CROWDSOURCING: HOW A STRATEGIC ALLIANCE WILL BENEFIT BOTH PARTIES

MRM Worldwide, a New York–based advertising firm, has entered into a strategic alliance with Aniboom, a "virtual" animation company. The alliance is designed to bring MRM's clients quicker and more cost-efficient animation services.

Aniboom, an Israeli company with offices in New York and San Francisco, was founded in 2006 by Uri Shinar, the former CEO of Israeli broadcaster Kesheet. It is a web-based platform that connects 8,000 animators in 70 countries around the world with clients in the TV, film, music, and video game sectors. Prospective clients submit Request for Proposals (RFPs) via the platform, and animators all over the world can respond. MRM global Chief Creative Officer Oren Frank believes that agencies are more likely to rely on this crowdsourcing approach in the future as clients seek more efficient ways of doing business.

MRM's plans are to have animators compete for work: "MRMs clients can launch a content creation competition in the Aniboom community for advertising solutions and have the community at large or a panel of judges select the top finalists and ultimate winner of the assignment. Or the competition could be private, with only the final results exhibited to the public."

Such competitions are part of a group of highly volatile trends that have become increasingly popular. They breed competition and bolster the idea that capitalism weeds out the weak links. It also becomes harder (or more unappealing) for established industries to bid on business that's sought through these methods, because costs can outweigh profits. However, there is one thing that it has done: The playing field has been leveled somewhat for new players. May the best _____ win!

Sources: Van Hoven, M. 2009. Strategic Alliances: MRM and Aniboom Team Up, Crowdsource. *www.mediabistro.com*. August 31: np; and McClellan, S. 2009. MRM, Aniboom Team Up. *www.adweek.com*. August 31: np.

---

7. **Communicate clearly and frequently.** Corporate managers need to clearly communicate to internal stakeholders, such as employees, and external stakeholders, such as customers and stockholders, what their goals are with divestment activity, how it will create value, and how the firm is moving forward strategically with these decisions.

Strategic Alliances and Joint Ventures

A **strategic alliance** is a cooperative relationship between two (or more) firms.[57] Alliances may be either informal or formal—that is, involving a written contract. **Joint ventures** represent a special case of alliances, wherein two (or more) firms contribute equity to form a new legal entity.

Strategic alliances and joint ventures are assuming an increasingly prominent role in the strategy of leading firms, both large and small.[58] Such cooperative relationships have many potential advantages.[59] Among these are entering new markets, reducing manufacturing (or other) costs in the value chain, and developing and diffusing new technologies.[60]

Entering New Markets Often a company that has a successful product or service wants to introduce it into a new market. However, it may not have the financial resources or the requisite marketing expertise because it does not understand customer needs, know how to promote the product, or have access to the proper distribution channels.[61]

Zara, a Spanish clothing company, operates stores in over 70 countries. Still, when entering markets very distant from its home markets, Zara often uses local alliance partners to help it negotiate the different cultural and regulatory environments. For example, when Zara expanded into India in 2010, it did it in cooperation with Tata, an Indian Conglomerate.[62]

Strategy Spotlight 6.5 discusses how a strategic alliance between two firms will help them crowdsource creative concepts.

Reducing Manufacturing (or Other) Costs in the Value Chain Strategic alliances (or joint ventures) often enable firms to pool capital, value-creating activities, or facilities in order to reduce costs. For example, SABMiller and Molson Coors, the number 2 and number 3 brewers in the United States, created a joint venture to combine their U.S. brewing

> **strategic alliance**
> a cooperative relationship between two or more firms.

> **joint ventures**
> new entities formed within a strategic alliance in which two or more firms, the parents, contribute equity to form the new legal entity.

operations in 2007. In combining brewery and distribution operations, they would benefit from economies of scale and better utilization of their facilities. The two firms projected $500 million in annual cost savings as a result of the integration of their operations.[63]

Developing and Diffusing New Technologies   Strategic alliances also may be used to build jointly on the technological expertise of two or more companies. This may enable then to develop products technologically beyond the capability of the companies acting independently.[64]

Verizon Wireless and ILS Technology announced an alliance in 2011 where Verizon would integrate technology developed by ILS to improve its machine-to-machine (M2M) data transmission systems. M2M systems allow firms to securely transmit data to and from various devices, including mobile devices and main office operations.[65]

Potential Downsides   Despite their promise, many alliances and joint ventures fail to meet expectations for a variety of reasons.[66] First, without the proper partner, a firm should never consider undertaking an alliance, even for the best of reasons.[67] Each partner should bring the desired complementary strengths to the partnership. Ideally, the strengths contributed by the partners are unique; thus synergies created can be more easily sustained and defended over the longer term. The goal must be to develop synergies between the contributions of the partners, resulting in a win–win situation. Moreover, the partners must be compatible and willing to trust each other.[68] Unfortunately, often little attention is given to nurturing the close working relationships and interpersonal connections that bring together the partnering organizations.[69]

Internal Development

| internal development
| entering a new business
| through investment
| in new facilities,
| often called corporate
| enterpreneurship and new
| venture development.

Firms can also diversify by means of corporate entrepreneurship and new venture development. **In today's economy, internal development is such an important means by which companies expand their businesses that we have devoted a whole chapter to it (see Chapter 12).** Sony and the Minnesota Mining & Manufacturing Co. (3M), for example, are known for their dedication to innovation, R&D, and cutting-edge technologies. For example, 3M has developed its entire corporate culture to support its ongoing policy of generating at least 25 percent of total sales from products created within the most recent four-year period. While 3M exceeded this goal for decades, a push for improved efficiency that began in the early 2000s resulted in a drop to generating only 21 percent of sales from newer products in 2005. By refocusing on innovation, 3M raised that value back up to 30 percent in 2011.

Biocon, the largest Indian biotechnology firm, shows the power of internal development. Kiran Mazumdar-Shaw, the firm's founder, took the knowledge she learned while studying malting and brewing in college to start a small firm that produced enzymes for the beer industry in her Bangalore garage in 1978. The firm first expanded into providing enzymes for other food and textile industries. From there, Biocon expanded on to producing generic drugs and is now the largest producer of insulin in Asia.[70]

Compared to mergers and acquisitions, firms that engage in internal development capture the value created by their own innovative activities without having to "share the wealth" with alliance partners or face the difficulties associated with combining activities across the value chains of several firms or merging corporate cultures.[71] Also, firms can often develop new products or services at a relatively lower cost and thus rely on their own resources rather than turning to external funding.[72]

There are also potential disadvantages. It may be time consuming; thus, firms may forfeit the benefits of speed that growth through mergers or acquisitions can provide. This may be especially important among high-tech or knowledge-based organizations in fast-paced environments where being an early mover is critical. Thus, firms that choose to diversify through internal development must develop capabilities that allow them to move quickly from initial opportunity recognition to market introduction.

How Managerial Motives Can Erode Value Creation

LO6.6
Managerial behaviors that can erode the creation of value.

Thus far in the chapter, we have implicitly assumed that CEOs and top executives are "rational beings"; that is, they act in the best interests of shareholders to maximize long-term shareholder value. In the real world, however, they may often act in their own self-interest. We now address some managerial motives that can serve to erode, rather than enhance, value creation. These include "growth for growth's sake," excessive egotism, and the creation of a wide variety of antitakeover tactics.

Growth for Growth's Sake

There are huge incentives for executives to increase the size of their firm. And these are not consistent with increasing shareholder wealth. Top managers, including the CEO, of larger firms typically enjoy more prestige, higher rankings for their firms on the Fortune 500 list (based on revenues, *not* profits), greater incomes, more job security, and so on. There is also the excitement and associated recognition of making a major acquisition. As noted by Harvard's Michael Porter, "There's a tremendous allure to mergers and acquisitions. It's the big play, the dramatic gesture. With one stroke of the pen you can add billions to size, get a front-page story, and create excitement in markets."[73]

In recent years many high-tech firms have suffered from the negative impact of their uncontrolled growth. Consider, for example, *Priceline.com's* ill-fated venture into an online service to offer groceries and gasoline.[74] A myriad of problems—perhaps most importantly, a lack of participation by manufacturers—caused the firm to lose more than $5 million a *week* prior to abandoning these ventures. Such initiatives are often little more than desperate moves by top managers to satisfy investor demands for accelerating revenues. Unfortunately, the increased revenues often fail to materialize into a corresponding hike in earnings.

At times, executives' overemphasis on growth can result in a plethora of ethical lapses, which can have disastrous outcomes for their companies. A good example (of bad practice) is Joseph Bernardino's leadership at Andersen Worldwide. Bernardino had a chance early on to take a hard line on ethics and quality in the wake of earlier scandals at clients such as Waste Management and Sunbeam. Instead, according to former executives, he put too much emphasis on revenue growth. Consequently, the firm's reputation quickly eroded when it audited and signed off on the highly flawed financial statements of such infamous firms as Enron, Global Crossing, and WorldCom. Bernardino ultimately resigned in disgrace in March 2002, and his firm was dissolved later that year.[75]

Egotism

A healthy ego helps make a leader confident, clearheaded, and able to cope with change. CEOs, by their very nature, are intensely competitive people in the office as well as on the tennis court or golf course. But sometimes when pride is at stake, individuals will go to great lengths to win.

Egos can get in the way of a "synergistic" corporate marriage. Few executives (or lower-level managers) are exempt from the potential downside of excessive egos. Consider, for example, the reflections of General Electric's former CEO Jack Welch, considered by many to be the world's most admired executive. He admitted to a regrettable decision: "My hubris got in the way in the Kidder Peabody deal. [He was referring to GE's buyout of the soon-to-be-troubled Wall Street firm.] I got wise advice from Walter Wriston and other directors who said, 'Jack, don't do this.' But I was bully enough and on a run to do it. And I got whacked right in the head."[76] In addition to poor financial results, Kidder Peabody was wracked by a widely publicized trading scandal that tarnished the reputations of both GE and Kidder Peabody. Welch ended up selling Kidder.

managerial motives
managers acting in their own self-interest rather than to maximize long-term shareholder value.

growth for growth's sake
managers' actions to grow the size of their firms not to increase long-term profitability but to serve managerial self-interest.

egotism
managers' actions to shape their firms' strategies to serve their selfish interests rather than to maximize long-term shareholder value.

The business press has included many stories of how egotism and greed have infiltrated organizations.[77] Some incidents are considered rather astonishing, such as Tyco's former (and now convicted) CEO Dennis Kozlowski's well-chronicled purchase of a $6,000 shower curtain and vodka-spewing, full-size replica of Michaelangelo's David.[78] Other well-known examples of power grabs and extraordinary consumption of compensation and perks include executives at Enron, the Rigas family who were convicted of defrauding Adelphia of roughly $1 billion, former CEO Bernie Ebbers's $408 million loan from WorldCom, and so on.

A more recent example of excess and greed was exhibited by John Thain.[79] On January 22, 2009, he was ousted as head of Merrill Lynch by Bank of America's CEO, Ken Lewis:

> Thain embarrassingly doled out $4 billion in discretionary year-end bonuses to favored employees just before Bank of America's rescue purchase of failing Merrill. The bonuses amounted to about 10 percent of Merrill's 2008 losses.
>
> Obviously, John Thain believed that he was entitled. When he took over ailing Merrill in early 2008, he began planning major cuts, but he also ordered that his office be redecorated. He spent $1.22 million of company funds to make it "livable," which, in part, included $87,000 for a rug, $87,000 for a pair of guest chairs, $68,000 for a 19th-century credenza, and (what really got the attention of the press) $35,000 for a "commode with legs."
>
> He later agreed to repay the decorating costs. However, one might still ask: What kind of person treats other people's money like this? And who needs a commode that costs as much as a new Lexus? Finally, a comment by Bob O'Brien, stock editor at Barrons.com clearly applies: "The sense of entitlement that's been engendered in this group of people has clearly not been beaten out of them by the brutal performance of the financial sector over the course of the last year."

Antitakeover Tactics

Unfriendly or hostile takeovers can occur when a company's stock becomes undervalued. A competing organization can buy the outstanding stock of a takeover candidate in sufficient quantity to become a large shareholder. Then it makes a tender offer to gain full control of the company. If the shareholders accept the offer, the hostile firm buys the target company and either fires the target firm's management team or strips them of their power. Thus, antitakeover tactics are common, including greenmail, golden parachutes, and poison pills.[80]

The first, **greenmail,** is an effort by the target firm to prevent an impending takeover. When a hostile firm buys a large block of outstanding target company stock and the target firm's management feels that a tender offer is impending, they offer to buy the stock back from the hostile company at a higher price than the unfriendly company paid for it. Although this often prevents a hostile takeover, the same price is not offered to preexisting shareholders. However, it protects the jobs of the target firm's management.

Second, a **golden parachute** is a prearranged contract with managers specifying that, in the event of a hostile takeover, the target firm's managers will be paid a significant severance package. Although top managers lose their jobs, the golden parachute provisions protect their income.

Third, **poison pills** are used by a company to give shareholders certain rights in the event of a takeover by another firm. They are also known as shareholder rights plans.

Clearly, antitakeover tactics can often raise some interesting ethical—and legal—issues. Strategy Spotlight 6.6 addresses how antitakeover measures can benefit multiple stakeholders—not just management.

HOW ANTITAKEOVER MEASURES MAY BENEFIT MULTIPLE STAKEHOLDERS, NOT JUST MANAGEMENT

Antitakeover defenses represent a gray area, because management can often legitimately argue that such actions are not there solely to benefit themselves. Rather, they can benefit other stakeholders, such as employees, customers, and the community.

In the late 1980s, takeovers were very popular. The Dayton Hudson Corporation (now Target) even appealed to the Minnesota legislature to pass an antitakeover bill to help Dayton Hudson in its struggle with Hafts—the former owners of Dart, a drug store chain on the East Coast. History had shown that the Dayton Hudson management in place at the time was much better able to manage Dayton Hudson in the long run. In addition to Minnesota, many states now have laws that allow firms to take the interests of all stakeholders into account when considering a takeover bid.

In the summer of 2003, Oracle launched a hostile bid for PeopleSoft. Many charged that the tactics of Oracle CEO Larry Ellison had been unfair, and many of PeopleSoft's customers took its side, indicating that Oracle ownership would not be of benefit to them. PeopleSoft was concerned that Oracle was merely seeking to buy PeopleSoft for its lucrative base of application software and was not interested in supporting the company's products. Oracle, on the other hand, sued PeopleSoft in an attempt to have the latter's so-called poison pill takeover defense removed.

In December 2004, Oracle struck a deal to buy PeopleSoft—ending a bitter 18-month hostile takeover battle. Oracle's $10.3 billion acquisition valued the firm at $26.50 a share—an increase of 66 percent over its initial offer of $16 a share. Noted analyst John DiFucci: "This is a financial acquisition primarily. Oracle is buying PeopleSoft for its maintenance stream." And, worth noting, PeopleSoft executives, including CEO and company founder David Duffield, did not join Oracle during the conference call announcing the acquisition. Oracle dropped its suit against PeopleSoft in which the former charged that PeopleSoft's "poison pill" takeover defense should be dismissed.

On moral grounds, some antitakeover defenses are not undertaken to entrench and protect management, but often they are. When such defenses are used simply to keep management in power, they are wrong. However, when they are used to defend the long-term financial health of the company and to protect broader stakeholder interests, they will be morally permissible.

Sources: Bowie, N. E. & Werhane, P. H. 2005. *Management Ethics*. Malden, MA: Blackwell Publishing; and La Monica, P. R. 2004. Finally, Oracle to Buy PeopleSoft. *CNNMoney.com*, December 13: np.

ISSUE FOR DEBATE

Is Microsoft finally becoming a vertically integrated company?

By Tom McNamara and Helena Gonzalez

Over 40 years ago, Microsoft made a bet that the future of computing was going to be in the software that ran computers and not the computers themselves. And for decades it seemed like a prescient move. As the cost of computing plummeted, PCs became mostly a commodity item. Software and services, on the other hand, remained an extremely lucrative business.

Critics, however, complained Microsoft had not only stifled competition, it stifled innovation as well. Its dominant position, they argued, was a barrier to new products and new services. But who cared? Microsoft had its billions and the world's consumers had PCs that, for the most part, did what they wanted them to do.

Unfortunately for Microsoft, it now appears that the naysayers might be finally having their day in the sun. Since the renaissance of Apple, starting in the late 1990s with the return of its co-founder Steve Jobs, it increasingly looks like Microsoft's view of the future is a bit more clouded. A plethora of new products, devices, and services from companies like Google, Samsung, Facebook, as well as Apple, are changing how we look at computers (and what we even think a computer is). Another challenge is the rise of "open source"

(continued)

(continued)

software that is basically free for anyone to use. Google's Android operating system for smart-phones has a near 80 percent market share.

All of this has not been lost on Microsoft. The company has recently been making moves to get more exposure to the hardware side of the business. In September 2013 it announced the $7 billion acquisition of Nokia's smart-phone. Many analysts take this as a sign that Microsoft is serious about competing head to head against Apple and Google in a fast changing market where the line between a PC and a mobile phone is fading.

By expanding its presence on the "physical" side of the business, Microsoft is hoping to extend its perceived competitive advantage from software to hardware. The Nokia move allows the company to have direct control over both the hardware and the software in its devices. The argument is that this direct control will improve the performance of the phones themselves, making them easier to market and sell. Strategically, the move will make Microsoft more of a vertically integrated company, something it has steadfastly avoided in the past.

But will this move to a more vertically integrated company work? The move can be seen as a sea change for Microsoft in that it will now be operating in an environment that it might not be fully comfortable with. Historically, the company created and sold software that could be used to operate a multitude of different computers from different manufacturers. Now, it will be competing similarly to the way Apple does, selling a proprietary device using propriety software. This sounds oddly like the ecosystem of "i" devices and apps that has made Apple hugely successful. It also sounds like Microsoft plans on keeping one foot in the software side of the business and one foot in the hardware side.

Discussion Questions

1. Do you think Microsoft's competitive advantage in software will help it to compete in hardware and electronic devices?
2. What are the risks and challenges facing Microsoft as it competes more and more directly with Google and Apple?

Sources: Microsoft, September 3 2013 "Accelerating Growth: Microsoft's strategic rationale for deal announced with Nokia"; Farhad Manjoo, Slate, September 3 2013 "R.I.P. Windows".

Reflecting on Career Implications . . .

▣ **Corporate-Level Strategy:** Is your current employer a single business firm or a diversified firm? If it is diversified, does it pursue related or unrelated diversification? Does its diversification provide you with career opportunities, especially lateral moves? What organizational policies are in place to either encourage or discourage you from moving from one business unit to another?

▣ **Core Competencies:** What do you see as your core competencies? How can you leverage them both within your business unit as well as across other business units?

▣ **Sharing Infrastructures:** Identify what infrastructure activities and resources (e.g., information systems, legal) are available in the corporate office that is shared by various business units in the firm. How often do you take advantage of these shared resources? Identify ways in which you can enhance your performance by taking advantage of these shared infrastructures resources.

▣ **Diversification:** From your career perspective, what actions can you take to diversify your employment risk (e.g., coursework at a local university, obtain professional certification such as a C.P.A., networking through professional affiliation, etc.)? In periods of retrenchment, such actions will provide you with a greater number of career options.

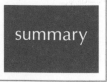

summary

A key challenge for today's managers is to create "synergy" when engaging in diversification activities. As we discussed in this chapter, corporate managers do not, in general, have a very good track record in creating value in such endeavors when it comes to mergers and acquisitions. Among the factors that serve to erode shareholder values are paying an excessive premium for the target firm, failing to integrate the activities of the newly acquired businesses into the corporate family, and undertaking diversification initiatives that are too easily imitated by the competition.

We addressed two major types of corporate-level strategy: related and unrelated diversification. With *related diversification* the corporation strives to enter into areas in which key resources and capabilities of the corporation can be shared or leveraged. Synergies come from horizontal relationships between business units. Cost savings and enhanced revenues can be derived from two major sources. First, economies of scope can be achieved from the leveraging of core competencies and the sharing of activities. Second, market power can be attained from greater, or pooled, negotiating power and from vertical integration.

When firms undergo *unrelated diversification* they enter product markets that are dissimilar to their present businesses. Thus, there is generally little opportunity to either leverage core competencies or share activities across business units. Here, synergies are created from vertical relationships between the corporate office and the individual business units. With unrelated diversification, the primary ways to create value are corporate restructuring and parenting, as well as the use of portfolio analysis techniques.

Corporations have three primary means of diversifying their product markets—mergers and acquisitions, joint ventures/strategic alliances, and internal development. There are key trade-offs associated with each of these. For example, mergers and acquisitions are typically the quickest means to enter new markets and provide the corporation with a high level of control over the acquired business. However, with the expensive premiums that often need to be paid to the shareholders of the target firm and the challenges associated with integrating acquisitions, they can also be quite expensive. Not surprisingly, many poorly performing acquisitions are subsequently divested. At times, however, divestitures can help firms refocus their efforts and generate resources. Strategic alliances and joint ventures between two or more firms, on the other hand, may be a means of reducing risk since they involve the sharing and combining of resources. But such joint initiatives also provide a firm with less control (than it would have with an acquisition) since governance is shared between two independent entities. Also, there is a limit to the potential upside for each partner because returns must be shared as well. Finally, with internal development, a firm is able to capture all of the value from its initiatives (as opposed to sharing it with a merger or alliance partner). However, diversification by means of internal development can be very time-consuming—a disadvantage that becomes even more important in fast-paced competitive environments.

Finally, some managerial behaviors may serve to erode shareholder returns. Among these are "growth for growth's sake," egotism, and antitakeover tactics. As we discussed, some of these issues—particularly antitakeover tactics—raise ethical considerations because the managers of the firm are not acting in the best interests of the shareholders.

SUMMARY REVIEW QUESTIONS

1. Discuss how managers can create value for their firm through diversification efforts.

2. What are some of the reasons that many diversification efforts fail to achieve desired outcomes?

3. How can companies benefit from related diversification? Unrelated diversification? What are some of the key concepts that can explain such success?

4. What are some of the important ways in which a firm can restructure a business?

5. Discuss some of the various means that firms can use to diversify. What are the pros and cons associated with each of these?

6. Discuss some of the actions that managers may engage in to erode shareholder value.

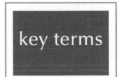

key terms

corporate-level
   strategy 180
diversification 181
related diversification 182
economies of scope 182
core competencies 183
sharing activities 184
market power 185
pooled negotiating power 185
vertical integration 186
transaction cost
   perspective 188
unrelated diversification 189

parenting advantage 189
restructuring 189
portfolio
   management 190
acquisitions 193
mergers 193
divestment 196
strategic alliance 199
joint ventures 199
internal development 200
managerial motives 201
growth for growth's
   sake 201
egotism 201
antitakeover tactics 202
greenmail 202
golden parachute 202
poison pill 202

application questions & exercises

1. What were some of the largest mergers and acquisitions over the last two years? What was the rationale for these actions? Do you think they will be successful? Explain.

2. Discuss some examples from business practice in which an executive's actions appear to be in his or her self-interest rather than the corporation's well-being.

3. Discuss some of the challenges that managers must overcome in making strategic alliances successful. What are some strategic alliances with which you are familiar? Were they successful or not? Explain.

4. Use the Internet and select a company that has recently undertaken diversification into new product markets. What do you feel were some of the reasons for this diversification (e.g., leveraging core competencies, sharing infrastructures)?

ethics questions

1. In recent years there has been a rash of corporate downsizing and layoffs. Do you feel that such actions raise ethical considerations? Why or why not?
2. What are some of the ethical issues that arise when managers act in a manner that is counter to their firm's best interests? What are the long-term implications for both the firms and the managers themselves?

experiential exercise

Time Warner (formerly AOL Time Warner) is a firm that follows a strategy of related diversification. Evaluate its success (or lack thereof) with regard to how well it has: (1) built on core competencies, (2) shared infrastructures, and (3) increased market power. (Fill answers in table below.)

Rationale for Related Diversification	Successful/Unsuccessful?	Why?
1. Build on core competencies		
2. Share infrastructures		
3. Increase market power		

references

1. Grobart, S. & Rusli, E. 2011. For Flip video camera, four years from hot start-up to obsolete. *NYTimes.com.*, April 4: np; Chen, B. 2011. Why Cisco's Flip flopped in the camera business. *Wired.com*, April 11: np; Rose, C. 2012. Charlie Rose talks to Cisco's John Chambers. *Bloomberg Businessweek,* April 24: 41; and *www.cisco.com.*

2. Insights on measuring M&A performance are addressed in: Zollo, M. & Meier, D. 2008. What is M&A performance? *BusinessWeek,* 22(3): 55–77.

3. Insights on how and why firms may overpay for acquisitions are addressed in: Malhotra, D., Ku, G., & Murnighan, J. K. 2008. When winning is everything. *Harvard Business Review,* 66(5): 78–86.

4. Dr. G. William Schwert, University of Rochester study cited in Pare, T. P. 1994. The new merger boom. *Fortune.* November 28: 96.

5. Lipin, S. & Deogun, N. 2000. Big mergers of the 1990's prove disappointing to shareholders. *The Wall Street Journal.* October 30: C1.

6. Rothenbuecher, J. & Schrottke, J. 2008. To get value from a merger, grow sales. *Harvard Business Review,* 86(5): 24–25; and Rothenbuecher, J. 2008. Personal communication, October 1.

7. Kyriazis, D. 2010. The long-term post acquisition performance of Greek acquiring firms. *International Research Journal of Finance and Economics.* 43: 69–79.

8. Pare, T. P. 1994. The new merger boom. *Fortune,* November 28: 96.

9. A discussion of the effects of director experience and acquisition performance is in: McDonald, M. L. & Westphal, J. D. 2008. What do they know? The effects of outside director acquisition experience on firm acquisition performance. *Strategic Management Journal,* 29(11): 1155–1177.

10. Finance and economics: Snoopy sniffs an opportunity; MetLife buys Alico. 2010. *Economist.com,* March 13: np.

11. For a study that investigates several predictors of corporate diversification, read: Wiersema, M. F. & Bowen, H. P. 2008. Corporate diversification: The impact of foreign competition, industry globalization, and product diversification. *Strategic Management Journal,* 29(2): 114–132.

12. Kumar, M. V. S. 2011. Are joint ventures positive sum games? The relative effects of cooperative and non-cooperative behavior. *Strategic Management Journal,* 32(1): 32–54.

13. Makri, M., Hitt, M. A., & Lane, P. J. 2010. Complementary technologies, knowledge relatedness, and invention outcomes in high technology mergers and acquisitions. *Strategic Management Journal,* 31(6): 602–628.

14. A discussion of Tyco's unrelated diversification strategy is in: Hindo, B. 2008. Solving Tyco's identity crisis. *BusinessWeek,* February 18: 62.

15. Our framework draws upon a variety of sources, including Goold, M. & Campbell, A. 1998. Desperately seeking synergy. *Harvard Business Review,* 76(5): 131–143; Porter, M. E. 1987. From advantage to corporate strategy. *Harvard Business Review,* 65(3): 43–59; and Hitt, M. A., Ireland, R. D., & Hoskisson, R. E. 2001. *Strategic management: competitiveness and globalization* (4th ed.). Cincinnati, OH: South-Western.

16. This imagery of the corporation as a tree and related discussion draws on Prahalad, C. K. & Hamel, G. 1990. The core competence of the corporation. *Harvard Business Review,* 68(3): 79–91. Parts of this section also draw on Picken, J. C. & Dess, G. G. 1997. *Mission critical:* chap. 5. Burr Ridge, IL: Irwin Professional Publishing.

17. Graebner, M. E., Eisenhardt, K. M. & Roundy, P. T. 2010. Success and failure in technology acquisitions: Lessons for buyers and sellers. *The Academy of Management Perspectives,* 24(3): 73–92.

18. This section draws on Prahalad & Hamel, op. cit.; and Porter, op. cit.

19. A recent study that investigates the relationship between a firm's technology resources, diversification, and performance can be found in Miller, D. J. 2004. Firms' technological resources and the performance effects of diversification. A longitudinal study. *Strategic Management Journal,* 25: 1097–1119.

20. Chesbrough, H. 2011. Bringing open innovation to services. *MIT Sloan Management Review,* 52(2): 85–90.

21. Fisher, A. 2008. America's most admired companies. *Fortune,* March 17: 74.

22. Choi, C. Starbucks buys bakery to improve food offerings. *Finance. yahoo.com.,* June 4: np.

23. This section draws on Hrebiniak, L. G. & Joyce, W. F. 1984. *Implementing strategy.* New York: MacMillan; and Oster, S. M. 1994. *Modern competitive analysis.* New York: Oxford University Press.

24. The discussion of the benefits and costs of vertical integration draws on Hax, A. C. & Majluf, N. S. 1991. *The strategy concept and process: A pragmatic approach:* 139. Englewood Cliffs, NJ: Prentice Hall.

25. Fahey, J. 2005. Gray winds. *Forbes.* January 10: 143.

26. This discussion draws on Oster, op. cit.; and Harrigan, K. 1986. Matching vertical integration strategies to competitive conditions. *Strategic Management Journal,* 7(6): 535–556.

27. For a scholarly explanation on how transaction costs determine the boundaries of a firm, see Oliver E. Williamson's pioneering books *Markets and Hierarchies: Analysis and Antitrust Implications* (New York: Free Press, 1975) and *The Economic Institutions of Capitalism* (New York: Free Press, 1985).

28. Campbell, A., Goold, M., & Alexander, M. 1995. Corporate strategy: The quest for parenting advantage. *Harvard Business Review,* 73(2): 120–132; and Picken & Dess, op. cit.

29. Anslinger, P. A. & Copeland, T. E. 1996. Growth through acquisition: A fresh look. *Harvard Business Review,* 74(1): 126–135.

30. This section draws on Porter, op. cit.; and Hambrick, D. C. 1985. Turnaround strategies. In Guth, W. D. (Ed.). *Handbook of business strategy:* 10-1–10-32. Boston: Warren, Gorham & Lamont.

31. There is an important delineation between companies that are operated for a long-term profit and those that are bought and sold for short-term gains. The latter are sometimes referred to as "holding companies" and are generally more concerned about financial issues than strategic issues.

32. Lenzner, R. 2007. High on Loews. *Forbes,* February 26: 98–102.

33. Casico. W. F. 2002. Strategies for responsible restructuring. *Academy of Management Executive,* 16(3): 80–91; and Singh, H. 1993. Challenges in researching corporate restructuring. *Journal of Management Studies,* 30(1): 147–172.

34. Hax & Majluf, op. cit. By 1979, 45 percent of Fortune 500 companies employed some form of portfolio analysis, according to Haspelagh, P. 1982. Portfolio planning: Uses and limits. *Harvard Busines Review,* 60: 58–73. A later study conducted in 1993 found that over 40 percent of the respondents used portfolio analysis techniques, but the level of usage was expected to increase to more than 60 percent in the near future: Rigby, D. K. 1994. Managing the management tools. *Planning Review,* September–October: 20–24.

35. Goold, M. & Luchs, K. 1993. Why diversify? Four decades of management thinking. *Academy of Management Executive,* 7(3): 7–25.

36. Other approaches include the industry attractiveness–business strength matrix developed jointly by General Electric and McKinsey and Company, the life-cycle matrix developed by Arthur D. Little, and the profitability matrix proposed by Marakon. For an extensive review, refer to Hax & Majluf, op. cit.: 182–194.

37. Porter, op. cit.: 49–52.

38. Picken & Dess, op. cit.; Cabot Corporation. 2001. 10-Q filing, Securities and Exchange Commission, May 14.

39. Insights on the performance of serial acquirers is found in: Laamanen, T. & Keil, T. 2008. Performance of serial acquirers: Toward an acquisition program perspective. *Strategic Management Journal,* 29(6): 663–672.

40. Some insights from Lazard's CEO on mergers and acquisitions are addressed in: Stewart, T. A. & Morse, G. 2008. Giving great advice. *Harvard Business Review,* 66(1): 106–113.

41. Coy, P., Thornton, E., Arndt, M., & Grow, B. 2005. Shake, rattle, and merge. *BusinessWeek,* January 10: 32–35; and Anonymous. 2005. Love is in the air. *Economist,* February 5: 9.

42. Hill, A. 2011. Mergers indicate market optimism. *www.marketplace.org,* March 21: np.

43. For an interesting study of the relationship between mergers and a firm's product-market strategies, refer to Krisnan, R. A., Joshi, S., & Krishnan, H. 2004. The influence of mergers on firms' product-mix strategies. *Strategic Management Journal,* 25: 587–611.

44. Like many high-tech firms during the economic slump that began in mid-2000, Cisco Systems experienced declining performance. On April 16, 2001, it announced that its revenues for the quarter closing April 30 would drop 5 percent from a year earlier—and a stunning 30 percent from the previous three months—to about $4.7 billion. Furthermore, Cisco announced that it would lay off 8,500 employees and take an enormous $2.5 billion charge to write down inventory. By late October 2002, its stock was trading at around $10, down significantly from its 52-week high of $70. Elstrom, op. cit.: 39.

45. Ignatius, A. 2011. How eBay developed a culture of experimentation. *Harvard Business Review,* 89(3): 92–97;

46. Martinez, J. 2011. eBay's recent acquisitions drive ridiculous m-commerce numbers. *Dmnews.com.,* December 6: np.

47. For a discussion of the trend toward consolidation of the steel industry and how Lakshmi Mittal is becoming a dominant player, read Reed, S. & Arndt, M. 2004. The Raja of steel. *BusinessWeek,* December 20: 50–52.

48. Colvin, G. 2011. Airline king. *Fortune,* May 2: 50–57.

49. This discussion draws upon Rappaport, A. & Sirower, M. L. 1999. Stock or cash? The trade-offs for buyers and sellers in mergers and acquisitions. *Harvard Business Review,* 77(6): 147–158; and Lipin, S. & Deogun, N. 2000. Big mergers of 90s prove disappointing to shareholders. *The Wall Street Journal,* October 30: C1.

50. The downside of mergers in the airline industry is found in: Gimbel, B. 2008. Why airline mergers don't fly. *BusinessWeek,* March 17: 26.

51. Mouio, A. (Ed.). 1998. Unit of one. *Fast Company,* September: 82.

52. Porter, M. E. 1987. From competitive advantage to corporate strategy. *Harvard Business Review,* 65(3): 43.

53. The divestiture of a business which is undertaken in order to enable managers to better focus on its core business has been termed "downscoping." Refer to Hitt, M. A., Harrison, J. S., & Ireland, R. D. 2001. *Mergers and acquisitions: A guide to creating value for stakeholders.* Oxford Press: New York.

54. Sirmon, D. G., Hitt, M. A., & Ireland, R. D. 2007. Managing firm resources in dynamic environments to create value: Looking inside the black box. *Academy of Management Review,* 32(1): 273–292.

55. Kengelbach, J., Klemmer, D., & Roos, A. 2012. Plant and prune: How M&A can grow portfolio value. *BCG Report,* September: 1–38.

56. Berry, J., Brigham, B., Bynum, A., Leu, C., & McLaughlin, R. 2012. Creating value through divestitures— Deans Foods: Theory in practice. *Unpublished manuscript.*

57. A study that investigates alliance performance is: Lunnan, R. & Haugland, S. A. 2008. Predicting and measuring alliance performance: A multidimensional analysis. *Strategic Management Journal,* 29(5): 545–556.

58. For scholarly perspectives on the role of learning in creating value in strategic alliances, refer to Anard, B. N. & Khanna, T. 2000. Do firms learn to create value? *Strategic Management Journal,* 12(3): 295–317; and Vermeulen, F. & Barkema, H. P. 2001. Learning through acquisitions. *Academy of Management Journal,* 44(3): 457–476.

59. For a detailed discussion of transaction cost economics in strategic alliances, read Reuer, J. J. & Arno, A. 2007. Strategic alliance contracts: Dimensions and determinants of contractual complexity. *Strategic Management Journal,* 28(3): 313–330.

60. This section draws on Hutt, M. D., Stafford, E. R., Walker, B. A., & Reingen, P. H. 2000. Case study: Defining the strategic alliance. *Sloan Management Review,* 41(2): 51–62; and Walters, B. A., Peters, S., & Dess, G. G. 1994. Strategic alliances and joint ventures: Making them work. *Business Horizons,* 4: 5–10.

61. A study that investigates strategic alliances and networks is: Tiwana, A. 2008. Do bridging ties complement strong ties? An empirical examination of alliance ambidexterity. *Strategic Management Journal,* 29(3): 251–272.

62. Fashion chain Zara opens its first Indian store. 2010. *bbc.co.uk/news/,* May 31: np.

63. Martin, A. 2007. Merger for SABMiller and Molson Coors. *nytimes.com,* October 10: np.

64. Phelps, C. 2010. A longitudinal study of the influence of alliance network structure and composition on firm exploratory innovation. *Academy of Management Journal,* 53(4): 890–913.

65. ILS Technology supplies deviceWISE M2M to Verizon Wireless. 2011. *automation.com,* March 23: np.

66. For an institutional theory perspective on strategic alliances, read: Dacin, M. T., Oliver, C., & Roy, J. P. 2007. The legitimacy of strategic alliances: An institutional perspective. *Strategic Management Journal,* 28(2): 169–187.

67. A study investigating factors that determine partner selection in strategic alliances is found in: Shah, R. H. & Swaminathan, V. 2008. *Strategic Management Journal,* 29(5): 471–494.

68. Arino, A. & Ring, P. S. 2010. The role of fairness in alliance formation. *Strategic Management Journal,* 31(6): 1054–1087.

69. Greve, H. R., Baum, J. A. C., Mitsuhashi, H. & Rowley, T. J. 2010. Built to last but falling apart: Cohesion, friction, and withdrawal from interfirm alliances. *Academy of Management Journal,* 53(4): 302–322.

70. Narayan, A. 2011. From brewing, an Indian biotech is born. *Bloomberg Businessweek,* February 28: 19–20.

71. For an insightful perspective on how to manage conflict between innovation and ongoing operations in an organization, read: Govindarajan, V. & Trimble, C. 2010. *The other side of innovation: Solving the execution challenge.* Boston, MA: Harvard Business School Press.

72. Dunlap-Hinkler, D., Kotabe, M. & Mudambi, R. 2010. A story of breakthrough versus incremental innovation: Corporate entrepreneurship in the global pharmaceutical industry. *Strategic Entrepreneurship Journal.* 4(2): 106–127.

73. Porter, op. cit.: 43–59.

74. Angwin, J. S. & Wingfield, N. 2000. How Jay Walker built WebHouse on a theory that he couldn't prove. *The Wall Street Journal,* October 16: A1, A8.

75. The fallen. 2003. *BusinessWeek,* January 13: 80–82.

76. The Jack Welch example draws upon Sellers, P. 2001. Get over yourself. *Fortune,* April 30: 76–88.

77. Li, J. & Tang, Y. 2010. CEO hubris and firm risk taking in China: The moderating role of managerial discretion. *Academy of Management Journal,* 53(1): 45–68.

78. Polek, D. 2002. The rise and fall of Dennis Kozlowski. *BusinessWeek,* December 23: 64–77.

79. John Thain and his golden commode. 2009. Editorial. *Dallasnews.com,* January 26: np; Task, A. 2009. Wall Street's $18.4B bonus: The sense of entitlement has not been beaten out. *finance.yahoo.com,* January 29: np; and Exit Thain. 2009. *Newsfinancialcareers.com,* January 22: np.

80. This section draws on Weston, J. F., Besley, S., & Brigham, E. F. 1996. *Essentials of managerial finance* (11th ed.): 18–20. Fort Worth, TX: Dryden Press, Harcourt Brace.

chapter 7

International Strategy:

Creating Value in Global Markets

After reading this chapter, you should have a good understanding of the following learning objectives:

LO7.1 The importance of international expansion as a viable diversification strategy.

LO7.2 The sources of national advantage; that is, why an industry in a given country is more (or less) successful than the same industry in another country.

LO7.3 The motivations (or benefits) and the risks associated with international expansion, including the emerging trend for greater offshoring and outsourcing activity.

LO7.4 The two opposing forces—cost reduction and adaptation to local markets—that firms face when entering international markets.

LO7.5 The advantages and disadvantages associated with each of the four basic strategies: international, global, multidomestic, and transnational.

LO7.6 The difference between regional companies and truly global companies.

LO7.7 The four basic types of entry strategies and the relative benefits and risks associated with each of them.

Learning from Mistakes

Tesco's failure in the US

Tesco PLC, one of the world's leading retailers, has 1,897 stores in the United Kingdom, it employs 250,000 people and has 600 overseas outlets. Tesco was hoping to conquer the United States and challenge the American giant WalMart in its own backyard but instead it has had to write off £1.2 billion and has reported its first fall in profits in 20 years. Tesco is now trying to find a buyer for the whole US business or at least some of its stores.

When Tesco opened its first store to great fanfare in the US under the brand name Fresh & Easy in 2007 there was talk of revolutionizing the way Americans shop and to make fresh and wholesome food available to the rich and poor. This was to be the first of 1,000 shop-more-often convenience stores and the idea was to bring British supermarket shopping to US consumers. At the time three booming states, California, Arizona, and Nevada were chosen to start this ambitious plan but unfortunately within two years they were the worst hit by the sub-prime mortgage crisis and the recession which sent US consumers back to familiar brands. This was unfortunate timing for Tesco as no one could have predicted the sub-prime crisis and its

consequences and even though Tesco spent over £1 billion, it only opened 199 stores and never made a profit in its five years of trading.

One of the problems Tesco faced was positioning; consumers were not able to ascertain whether the chain was aiming for budget shopping or a place for high quality food and drink. The chain did not give out vouchers and coupons which eliminated price-sensitive shoppers and consumers were put off by the stark aisles, plastic wrapped fruit and veg, ready meals that were not compatible with local tastes; and self-service check-outs which were out of place in a country where bagging up groceries is part of basic customer service. Critics say the chain miscalculated the market and failed to cater to American tastes; this has been an expensive mistake since Tesco lost more than £850 million.

The US is a difficult market to crack and what works in Europe does not work in the US. American shoppers go to stores less frequently then their European counterparts and when they go, they buy in bulk. In addition, it is difficult to enter an established category; consumers who have chosen a grocery store will only be motivated to change if the concept is dramatically different. However the similarity with Europe is that the US should not be treated as one country; the different states should be treated according to their different markets and should therefore be correctly targeted. Tesco made some fundamental mistakes in terms of location, marketing, positioning, and products but maybe US retailers also had their part to play since Tesco was also a huge long-term threat to them.

Lessons to be learnt from the US experiment? Maybe, since the US is not the only international failure Tesco is facing; it also has problems with trading and expansion in Poland, Turkey, and the Czech Republic.

By Asha Moore-Mangin and Sarah Hudson

Discussion Questions

1. What are the main reasons for Tesco's failure in the US?
2. Do you think that the choice of location could have made a difference?

In this chapter we discuss how firms create value and achieve competitive advantage in the global marketplace. Multinational firms are constantly faced with the dilemma of choosing between local adaptation—in product offerings, locations, advertising, and pricing—and global integration. We discuss how firms can avoid pitfalls such as those experienced by Tesco, a major international retailer. In addition, we address factors that can influence a nation's success in a particular industry. In our view, this is an important context in determining how well firms might eventually do when they compete beyond their nation's boundaries.

The Global Economy: A Brief Overview

Managers face many opportunities and risks when they diversify abroad.[2] The trade among nations has increased dramatically in recent years and it is estimated that by 2015, the trade *across* nations will exceed the trade within nations. In a variety of industries such as semiconductors, automobiles, commercial aircraft, telecommunications, computers, and consumer electronics, it is almost impossible to survive unless firms scan the world for competitors, customers, human resources, suppliers, and technology.[3]

GE's wind energy business benefits by tapping into talent around the world. The firm has built research centers in China, Germany, India, and the U.S. "We did it," says CEO Jeffrey Immelt, "to access the best brains everywhere in the world." All four centers have played a key role in GE's development of huge 92-ton turbines:[4]

- Chinese researchers in Shanghai designed the microprocessors that control the pitch of the blade.
- Mechanical engineers from India (Bangalore) devised mathematical models to maximize the efficiency of materials in the turbine.
- Power-systems experts in the U.S. (Niskayuna, New York), which has researchers from 55 countries, do the design work.
- Technicians in Munich, Germany, have created a "smart" turbine that can calculate wind speeds and signal sensors in other turbines to produce maximum electricity.

globalization

has two meanings. One is the increase in international exchange, including trade in goods and services as well as exchange of money, ideas, and information. Two is the growing similarity of laws, rules, norms, values, and ideas across countries.

The rise of **globalization**—meaning the rise of market capitalism around the world—has undeniably created tremendous business opportunities for multinational corporations. For example, mobile handset manufacturers sold over 700 million cell phones in emerging markets in 2012.[5]

This rapid rise in global capitalism has had dramatic effects on the growth in different economic zones. As shown in Exhibit 7.1, the growth experienced by developed economies in the first decade of the 2000s was anemic, while the growth in developing economies was robust.[6] This trend is continuing, with emerging markets growing 4 percent faster than developed markets in 2011 and 2012. This has resulted in a dramatic shift in the structure of the global economy. As of 2013, over half the world's output will come from emerging markets. This is leading to a convergence of living standards across the globe and is changing the face of business. One example of this is the shift in the global automobile market. China supplanted the United States as the largest market for automobiles in 2009.

One of the challenges with globalization is determining how to meet the needs of customers at very different income levels. In many developing economies, distributions of income remain much wider than they do in the developed world, leaving many impoverished even as the economies grow. Strategy Spotlight 7.1 provides an interesting perspective on global trade—marketing to the "bottom of the pyramid."[7] This refers to the practice of a multinational firm targeting its goods and services to the nearly 5 billion poor people in the world who inhabit developing countries. Collectively, this represents a very large market with $14 trillion in purchasing power.

MEETING THE NEEDS AT THE "BOTTOM OF THE PYRAMID"

Unilever, the Anglo-Dutch maker of such brands as Dove, Lipton, and Vaseline, has found a vast market selling to poor consumers in emerging markets by upending some of the basic rules of marketing. Their efforts allow them to exploit vast opportunities that exist at "the bottom of the pyramid."

Unilever's strategy was forged about 25 years ago when its Indian subsidiary, Hindustan Lever (HL), found its products out of reach for millions of Indians. HL came up with a strategy to lower the price while making a profit: single-use packets for everything from shampoo to laundry detergent, costing pennies a pack. A bargain? Maybe not, but it put marquee brands within reach. Instead of focusing on value for money, it shrunk packages to set a price even consumers living on $2.50 a day could afford. HL also trained rural women to sell products to their neighbors. "What Unilever does well is get inside these communities, understand their needs, and adapt its business model accordingly," notes a professor at Barcelona's IESE Business School. "It's not about doing good, but about tapping new markets," says Chief Executive Patrick Cescau.

The potential goes well beyond personal products, such as shampoo and soap. Firms in a range of industries are seeing potential with the BOP market. For example, DataWind, a British firm, has developed a tablet computer in partnership with the Indian government that only costs $35. Similarly, Vodafone offers a cell phone in India for $15. These firms view the poor as a bold frontier of opportunity for those who can meet their needs.

Firms need to actively manage the risks that accompany BOP strategies. These include concerns about the image of the firm if they are perceived as exploiting underprivileged customers by providing them with substandard products or selling them something they don't need or can't afford. Second, there is a risk that a low-end version of a brand may detract from the overall attractiveness of the brand. Third, the new low-cost products they develop may cannibalize the sales of their core products. Finally, firms employing a BOP strategy need to be aware of the entrenched competitors they may face. For example, over 90 percent of India's juice market is run by small players, many of whom do not conform to quality or safety standards.

Sources: Karamchandani, A., Kubzansky, M. & Lalwani, N. 2011. Is the bottom of the pyramid really for you? *Harvard Business Review*, 89(3). 107; Now for some good news. 2012. *Economist*, March 3: 80; McGregor, J. 2008. The world's most influential companies. *BusinessWeek*, December 22: 43–53; and Prahalad, C. K. 2005. *The Fortune at the Bottom of the Pyramid: Eradicating Poverty through Profits*. Philadelphia: Wharton School Publishing.

EXHIBIT 7.1 Growth in GDP per Person from 2001-2011 by Region

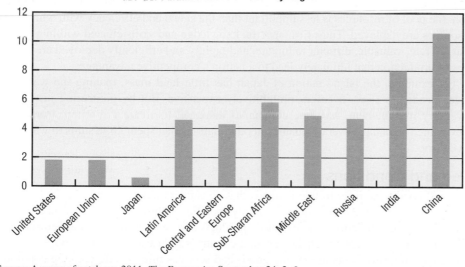

Source: A game of catch-up. 2011. *The Economist*, September 24: 3–6

Next, we will address in more detail the question of why some nations and their industries are more competitive.[8] This establishes an important context or setting for the remainder of the chapter. After we discuss why some *nations and their industries* outperform others, we will be better able to address the various strategies that *firms* can take to create competitive advantage when they expand internationally.

LO7.2

The sources of national advantage; that is, why an industry in a given country is more (or less) successful than the same industry in another country.

Factors Affecting a Nation's Competitiveness

Michael Porter of Harvard University conducted a four-year study in which he and a team of 30 researchers looked at the patterns of competitive success in 10 leading trading nations. He concluded that there are four broad attributes of nations that individually, and as a system, constitute what is termed **the diamond of national advantage**. In effect, these attributes jointly determine the playing field that each nation establishes and operates for its industries. These factors are:

- *Factor endowments.* The nation's position in factors of production, such as skilled labor or infrastructure, necessary to compete in a given industry.
- *Demand conditions.* The nature of home-market demand for the industry's product or service.
- *Related and supporting industries.* The presence or absence in the nation of supplier industries and other related industries that are internationally competitive.
- *Firm strategy, structure, and rivalry.* The conditions in the nation governing how companies are created, organized, and managed, as well as the nature of domestic rivalry.

Factor Endowments[9,10]

Classical economics suggests that factors of production such as land, labor, and capital are the building blocks that create usable consumer goods and services.[11] However, companies in advanced nations seeking competitive advantage over firms in other nations *create* many of the factors of production. For example, a country or industry dependent on scientific innovation must have a skilled human resource pool to draw upon. This resource pool is not inherited; it is created through investment in industry-specific knowledge and talent. The supporting infrastructure of a country—that is, its transportation and communication systems as well as its banking system—are also critical.

Factors of production must be developed that are industry and firm specific. In addition, the pool of resources is less important than the speed and efficiency with which these resources are deployed. Thus, firm-specific knowledge and skills created within a country that are rare, valuable, difficult to imitate, and rapidly and efficiently deployed are the factors of production that ultimately lead to a nation's competitive advantage.

For example, the island nation of Japan has little land mass, making the warehouse space needed to store inventory prohibitively expensive. But by pioneering just-in-time inventory management, Japanese companies managed to create a resource from which they gained advantage over companies in other nations that spent large sums to warehouse inventory.

Demand Conditions

Demand conditions refer to the demands that consumers place on an industry for goods and services. Consumers who demand highly specific, sophisticated products and services force firms to create innovative, advanced products and services to meet the demand. This consumer pressure presents challenges to a country's industries. But in response to these challenges, improvements to existing goods and services often result, creating conditions necessary for competitive advantage over firms in other countries.

Countries with demanding consumers drive firms in that country to meet high standards, upgrade existing products and services, and create innovative products and services. The conditions of consumer demand influence how firms view a market. This, in turn, helps a nation's industries to better anticipate future global demand conditions and proactively respond to product and service requirements.

Denmark, for instance, is known for its environmental awareness. Demand from consumers for environmentally safe products has spurred Danish manufacturers to become leaders in water pollution control equipment—products it successfully exported.

Related and Supporting Industries

Related and supporting industries enable firms to manage inputs more effectively. For example, countries with a strong supplier base benefit by adding efficiency to downstream activities. A competitive supplier base helps a firm obtain inputs using cost-effective, timely methods, thus reducing manufacturing costs. Also, close working relationships with suppliers provide the potential to develop competitive advantages through joint research and development and the ongoing exchange of knowledge.

Related industries offer similar opportunities through joint efforts among firms. In addition, related industries create the probability that new companies will enter the market, increasing competition and forcing existing firms to become more competitive through efforts such as cost control, product innovation, and novel approaches to distribution. Combined, these give the home country's industries a source of competitive advantage.

In the Italian footwear industry the supporting industries enhance national competitive advantage. In Italy, shoe manufacturers are geographically located near their suppliers. The manufacturers have ongoing interactions with leather suppliers and learn about new textures, colors, and manufacturing techniques while a shoe is still in the prototype stage. The manufacturers are able to project future demand and gear their factories for new products long before companies in other nations become aware of the new styles.

related and supporting industries (national advantage) the presence, absence, and quality in the nation of supplier industries and other related industries that supply services, support, or technology to firms in the industry value chain.

Firm Strategy, Structure, and Rivalry

Rivalry is particularly intense in nations with conditions of strong consumer demand, strong supplier bases, and high new entrant potential from related industries. This competitive rivalry in turn increases the efficiency with which firms develop, market, and distribute products and services within the home country. Domestic rivalry thus provides a strong impetus for firms to innovate and find new sources of competitive advantage.

This intense rivalry forces firms to look outside their national boundaries for new markets, setting up the conditions necessary for global competitiveness. Among all the points on Porter's diamond of national advantage, domestic rivalry is perhaps the strongest indicator of global competitive success. Firms that have experienced intense domestic competition are more likely to have designed strategies and structures that allow them to successfully compete in world markets.

In the European grocery retail industry, intense rivalry has led firms such as Aldi and Tesco to tighten their supply chains and improve store efficiency. Thus, it is no surprise that these firms are also strong global players.

The Indian software industry offers a clear example of how the attributes in Porter's "diamond" interact to lead to the conditions for a strong industry to grow. Exhibit 7.2 illustrates India's "software diamond," and Strategy Spotlight 7.2 further discusses the mutually reinforcing elements at work in this market.

firm strategy, structure, and rivalry (national advantage) the conditions in the nation governing how companies are created, organized, and managed, as well as the nature of domestic rivalry.

Concluding Comment on Factors Affecting a Nation's Competitiveness

Porter drew his conclusions based on case histories of firms in more than 100 industries. Despite the differences in strategies employed by successful global competitors, a common theme emerged: Firms that succeeded in global markets had first succeeded in intensely competitive home markets. We can conclude that competitive advantage for global firms typically grows out of relentless, continuing improvement, and innovation.[12]

INDIA AND THE DIAMOND OF NATIONAL ADVANTAGE

The Indian software industry has become one of the leading global markets for software. The industry has grown to over $60 billion, and Indian IT firms provide software and services to over half the Fortune 500 firms. What are the factors driving this success? Porter's diamond of national advantage helps clarify this question. See Exhibit 7.2.

First, *factor endowments* are conducive to the rise of India's software industry. Through investment in human resource development with a focus on industry-specific knowledge, India's universities and software firms have literally created this essential factor of production. For example, India produces the second largest annual output of scientists and engineers in the world, behind only the United States. In a knowledge-intensive industry such as software, development of human resources is fundamental to both domestic and global success.

Second, *demand conditions* require that software firms stay on the cutting edge of technological innovation. India has already moved toward globalization of its software industry; consumer demand conditions in developed nations such as Germany, Denmark, parts of Southeast Asia, and the United States created the consumer demand necessary to propel India's software makers toward sophisticated software solutions.*

Third, India has the *supplier base as well as the related industries* needed to drive competitive rivalry and enhance competitiveness. In particular, information technology (IT) hardware prices declined rapidly in the 1990s. Furthermore, rapid technological change in IT hardware meant that latecomers like India were not locked into older-generation technologies. Thus, both the IT hardware and software industries could "leapfrog" older technologies. In addition, relationships among knowledge workers in these IT hardware and software industries offer the social structure for ongoing knowledge exchange, promoting further enhancement of existing products. Further infrastructure improvements are occurring rapidly.

Fourth, with over 800 firms in the software services industry in India, *intense rivalry forces firms to develop competitive strategies and structures.* Although firms like TCS, Infosys, and Wipro have become large, they still face strong competition from dozens of small and midsized companies aspiring to catch them. This intense rivalry is one of the primary factors driving Indian software firms to develop overseas distribution channels, as predicted by Porter's diamond of national advantage.

It is interesting to note that the cost advantage of Indian firms may be eroding. For example, TCS's engineers' compensation soared 13 percent in 2010. Further, IBM and Accenture

EXHIBIT 7.2 India's Diamond in Software

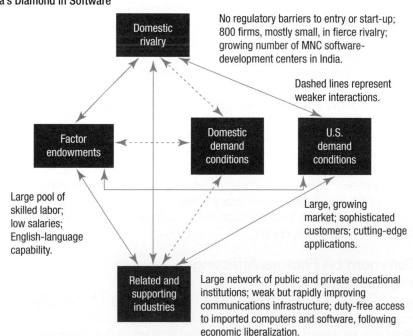

Source: From Kampur D. and Ramamurti R., "India's Emerging Competition Advantage in Services," *Academy of Management Executive: The Thinking Manager's Source.* Copyright © 2001 by Academy of Management. Reproduced with permission of Academy of Management via Copyright Clearance Center.

are aggressively building up their Indian operations, hiring tens of thousands of sought-after Indians by paying them more, thereby lowering their costs while raising those of TCS. Finally, many low labor-cost countries, such as China, Philippines, and Vietnam, are emerging as threats to the Indian competitors.

*Although India's success cannot be explained in terms of its home market demand (according to Porter's model), the nature of the industry enables software to be transferred among different locations simultaneously by way of communications links. Thus, competitiveness of markets outside India can be enhanced without a physical presence in those markets.

Sources: Sachitanand, R. 2010. The New Face of IT. *Business Today,* 19:62; Anonymous. 2010. Training to Lead. *www.Dqindia.com.* October 5: np; Nagaraju, B.2011. India's Software Exports Seen Up 16–18 pct.in Fy12. *www.reuters .com.* February 2: np; Ghemawat, P. & Hout, T. 2008. Tomorrow's Global Giants. *Harvard Business Review,* 86(11): 80–88; Mathur, S. K. 2007. Indian IT Industry: A Performance Analysis and a Model for Possible Adoption. *ideas.repec.org,* January 1: np; Kripalani, M. 2002. Calling Bangalore: Multinationals Are Making It a Hub for High-Tech Research *BusinessWeek,* November 25: 52–54; Kapur, D. & Ramamurti, R. 2001. India's Emerging Competitive Advantage in Services. 2001. *Academy of Management Executive,* 15(2): 20–33; World Bank. *World Development Report:* 6. New York: Oxford University Press. Reuters. 2001. Oracle in India Push, Taps Software Talent. *Washington Post Online,* July 3.

International Expansion: A Company's Motivations and Risks

Motivations for International Expansion

Increase Market Size   There are many motivations for a company to pursue international expansion. The most obvious one is to *increase the size of potential markets* for a firm's products and services.[13] The world's population passed the 7 billion level in early 2013, with the U.S. representing less than 5 percent.

Many **multinational firms** are intensifying their efforts to market their products and services to countries such as India and China as the ranks of their middle class have increased over the past decade. The potential is great. An OECD study predicts that consumption by middle-class consumers in Asian markets with grow from $4.9 trillion in 2009 to over $30 trillion by 2020. At that point, Asia will make up 60 percent of global middle-class consumption, up from 20 percent in 2009.[14]

Expanding a firm's global presence also automatically increases its scale of operations, providing it with a larger revenue and asset base.[15] As we noted in Chapter 5 in discussing overall cost leadership strategies, such an increase in revenues and asset base potentially enables a firm to *attain economies of scale.* This provides multiple benefits. One advantage is the spreading of fixed costs such as R&D over a larger volume of production. Examples include the sale of Boeing's commercial aircraft and Microsoft's operating systems in many foreign countries.

Filmmaking is another industry in which international sales can help amortize huge developmental costs.[16] For example, 71 percent of the $1 billion box office take for the James Bond thriller *Skyfall* came from overseas moviegoers. Similarly, the market for kids' movies is largely outside of the U. S., with 82 percent of the ticket sales for *Ice Age 4* being overseas.

Take Advantage of Arbitrage   *Taking advantage of arbitrage opportunities* is a second advantage of international expansion. In its simplest form, arbitrage involves buying something from where it is cheap and selling it somewhere where it commands a higher price. A big part of Walmart's success can be attributed to the company's expertise in arbitrage. The possibilities for arbitrage are not necessarily confined to simple trading opportunities. It can be applied to virtually any factor of production and every stage of the value chain. For example, a firm may locate its call centers in India, its manufacturing plants in China, and its R&D in Europe, where the specific types of talented personnel may be available at the lowest possible price. In today's integrated global financial markets, a firm can borrow anywhere in the world where capital is cheap and use it to fund a project in a country where capital is expensive. Such arbitrage opportunities are even more attractive to global corporations because their larger size enables them to buy in huge volume, thus increasing their bargaining power with suppliers.

Enhancing a Product's Growth Potential   *Enhancing the growth rate of a product* that is in its maturity stage in a firm's home country but that has greater demand potential

L07.3
The motivations (or benefits) and the risks associated with international expansion, including the emerging trend for greater offshoring and outsourcing activity.

multinational firms
firms that manage operations in more than one country.

arbitrage opportunities
an opportunity to profit by buying and selling the same good in different markets.

elsewhere is another benefit of international expansion. As we noted in Chapter 5, products (and industries) generally go through a four-stage life cycle of introduction, growth, maturity, and decline. In recent decades, U.S. soft-drink producers such as Coca-Cola and PepsiCo have aggressively pursued international markets to attain levels of growth that simply would not be available in the United States. The differences in market growth potential has even led some firms to restructure their operations. For example, Procter & Gamble relocated its global skin, cosmetics, and personal-care unit headquarters from Cincinnati to Singapore to be closer to the fast-growing Asian market.[17]

Optimize the Location of Value-Chain Activities   *Optimizing the physical location for every activity in its value chain* is another benefit. Recall from our discussions in Chapters 3 and 5 that the value chain represents the various activities in which all firms must engage to produce products and services. They include primary activities, such as inbound logistics, operations, and marketing, as well as support activities, such as procurement, R&D, and human resource management. All firms have to make critical decisions as to where each activity will take place.[18] Optimizing the location for every activity in the value chain can yield one or more of three strategic advantages: performance enhancement, cost reduction, and risk reduction. We will now discuss each of these.

Performance Enhancement   Microsoft's decision to establish a corporate research laboratory in Cambridge, England, is an example of a location decision that was guided mainly by the goal of building and sustaining world-class excellence in selected value-creating activities.[19] This strategic decision provided Microsoft with access to outstanding technical and professional talent. Location decisions can affect the quality with which any activity is performed in terms of the availability of needed talent, speed of learning, and the quality of external and internal coordination.

Cost Reduction   Two location decisions founded largely on cost-reduction considerations are (1) Nike's decision to source the manufacture of athletic shoes from Asian countries such as China, Vietnam, and Indonesia, and (2) the decision of Volkswagen to locate a new auto production plant in Chattanooga, Tennessee, to leverage the relatively low labor costs in the area as well as low shipping costs due to Chattanooga's close proximity to both rail and river transportation. Such location decisions can affect the cost structure in terms of local manpower and other resources, transportation and logistics, and government incentives and the local tax structure.

Performance enhancement and cost-reduction benefits parallel the business-level strategies (discussed in Chapter 5) of differentiation and overall cost leadership. They can at times be attained simultaneously. Consider our example in the previous section on the Indian software industry. When Oracle set up a development operation in that country, the company benefited both from lower labor costs and operational expenses as well as from performance enhancements realized through the hiring of superbly talented professionals.

Risk Reduction   Given the erratic swings in the exchange ratios between the U.S. dollar and the Japanese yen (in relation to each other and to other major currencies), an important basis for cost competition between Ford and Toyota has been their relative ingenuity at managing currency risks. One way for such rivals to manage currency risks has been to spread the high-cost elements of their manufacturing operations across a few select and carefully chosen locations around the world. Location decisions such as these can affect the overall risk profile of the firm with respect to currency, economic, and political risks.[20]

reverse innovation
new products developed
by developed country
multination firms for
emerging markets
that have adequate
functionality at a low cost.

Explore Reverse Innovation   Finally, *exploring possibilities for reverse innovation* has become a major motivation for international expansion. Many leading companies are discovering that developing products specifically for emerging markets can pay off in a big way.

EMPLOYING 'EMERGING MARKET' STRATEGIES IN DEVELOPED MARKETS

By Cyrlene Claasen and Helena Gonzalez

In the aftermath of the 2008 recession some of the larger consumer goods companies were forced to shift marketing strategies. They target poverty-stricken Europeans' demand for cheaper goods in the midst of an economic crisis. Here are some examples of firms who have leveraged "reverse innovation:"

- Unilever, the world's third-largest consumer goods company which owns brand such as Flora margarine and Persil laundry detergent, markets its products as if to customers in Third World countries. The company sells more laundry detergent to cash-strapped consumers by offering smaller, cheaper packages, a strategy long employed in Asian countries such as Indonesia, where average monthly wages are less than $400.

  In Greece, the country hardest hit by the crisis affecting the euro single currency, Unilever now offers mashed potatoes and mayonnaise in small bargain packages, and markets tea, olive oil, and other basic products under cheaper generic brand labels. In Spain, it sells its "Surf" detergent in packages that are good for five loads. And in Great Britain it's implementing the same strategy because people are running out of money.

- E.Leclerc, the number one retailer in France with a market share of 18 percent and 556 semi-independent hypermarkets, supermarkets, and speciality stores similarly employs reverse innovation. The retailer is also present in Italy, Spain, Portugal, and other countries. In Italy, for example, where the stores used to sell yoghurt only in multipacks, they have started to sell them as single items.

- L'Oréal, the world's largest cosmetics and beauty products firm, decided to build on "innovation and added value," which would allow the company to raise prices over time, "but reasonably." CEO Jean-Paul Agon said that, unlike others, the company would not adjust its products around the growing poverty in Europe. The race to the lowest price was "not our strategy." Instead of smaller packages, it tries heavy discounting to adjust its strategy to the environment—namely the poor economic state of Europe.

Sources: Braun, S., Apostolou, N., and Mir, M. 2012. Companies target European poor with Third World marketing, CNBC www.cnbc.com August 24: np; RT. 2012. Poverty is back in Europe: Brands adapt sales for record unemployment, rt.com August 12: np; Richter, W. 2012. The "Pauperization of Europe," www.testosteronepit.com August 29: np

In the past, multinational companies typically developed products for their rich home markets and then tried to sell them in developing countries with minor adaptations. However, as growth slows in rich nations and demand grows rapidly in developing countries such as India and China, this approach becomes increasingly inadequate. Instead, companies like GE have committed significant resources to developing products that meet the needs of developing nations, products that deliver adequate functionality at a fraction of the cost. Interestingly, these products have subsequently found considerable success in value segments in wealthy countries as well. Hence, this process is referred to as reverse innovation, a new motivation for international expansion.

As $3,000 cars, $300 computers, and $30 mobile phones bring what were previously considered as luxuries within the reach of the middle class of emerging markets, it is important to understand the motivations and implications of reverse innovation. *First,* it is impossible to sell first-world versions of products with minor adaptations in countries where the average income per person is between $1,000 and $4,000, as is the case in most developing countries. To sell in these markets, entirely new products must be designed and developed by local technical talent and manufactured with local components. *Second,* although these countries are relatively poor, they are growing rapidly. *Third,* if the innovation does not come from first-world multinationals, there are any number of local firms that are ready to grab the market with low-cost products. *Fourth,* as the consumers and governments of many first-world countries are rediscovering the virtues of frugality and are trying to cut down expenses, these products and services originally developed for the first world may gain significant market shares in developing countries as well.

Strategy Spotlight 7.3 describes some examples of reverse innovation.

Potential Risks of International Expansion

When a company expands its international operations, it does so to increase its profits or revenues. As with any other investment, however, there are also potential risks.[21] To help companies assess the risk of entering foreign markets, rating systems have been developed to evaluate political, economic, as well as financial and credit risks.[22] *Euromoney* magazine publishes a semiannual "Country Risk Rating" that evaluates political, economic, and other risks that entrants potentially face.[23] Exhibit 7.3 presents a sample of country risk ratings, published by the World Bank, from the 178 countries that *Euromoney* evaluates. Note that the lower the score, the higher the country's expected level of risk.[24]

Next we will discuss the four main types of risk: political risk, economic risk, currency risk, and management risk.

Political and Economic Risk   Generally speaking, the business climate in the United States is very favorable. However, some countries around the globe may be hazardous to the health of corporate initiatives because of **political risk**.[25] Forces such as social unrest, military turmoil, demonstrations, and even violent conflict and terrorism can pose serious threats.[26] Consider, for example, the ongoing tension and violence in the Middle East associated with the revolutions and civil wars in Egypt, Libya, Syria, and other countries. Such conditions increase the likelihood of destruction of property and disruption of operations as well as nonpayment for goods and services. Thus, countries that are viewed as high risk are less attractive for most types of business.[27]

Another source of political risk in many countries is the absence of the **rule of law.** The absence of rules or the lack of uniform enforcement of existing rules leads to what might often seem to be arbitrary and inconsistent decisions by government officials. This can make it difficult for foreign firms to conduct business.

For example, consider Renault's experience in Russia. Renault paid $1 billion to acquire a 25 percent ownership stake in the Russian automaker AutoVAZ in 2008. Just one year later, Russian Prime Minister Vladimir Putin threatened to dilute Renault's ownership stake unless it contributed more money to prop up AutoVAZ, which was then experiencing a significant slide in sales. Renault realized their ownership claim may not have held up in the corrupt Russian court system. Therefore, they were forced to negotiate and eventually agreed to transfer over $300 million in technology and expertise to the Russian firm to ensure its ownership stake would stay at 25 percent.[28]

Strategy Spotlight 7.4 discusses ways firms can reduce the political risk they face in countries with weak rules of law.

The laws, and the enforcement of laws, associated with the protection of intellectual property rights can be a major potential **economic risk** in entering new countries.[29] Microsoft, for example, has lost billions of dollars in potential revenue through piracy of its software products in many countries, including China. Other areas of the globe, such as the former Soviet Union and some eastern European nations, have piracy problems as well.[30] Firms rich in intellectual property have encountered financial losses as imitations of their products have grown due to a lack of law enforcement of intellectual property rights.[31]

Counterfeiting, a direct form of theft of intellectual property rights, is a significant and growing problem. The International Chamber of Commerce estimates that the value of counterfeit goods will exceed $1.7 trillion by 2015. "The whole business has just exploded," said Jeffrey Hardy, head of the anticounterfeiting program at ICC. "And it goes way beyond music and Gucci bags." Counterfeiting has moved well beyond handbags and shoes to include chemicals, pharmaceuticals, and aircraft parts. According to a University of Florida study, 25 percent of the pesticide market in some parts of Europe is estimated to be counterfeit. This is especially troubling since these chemicals are often toxic.[32] In Strategy Spotlight 7.5, we discuss the challenge of fighting counterfeiting in the pharmaceuticals business and how Pfizer is attempting to fight this threat to their business.

---

political risk
potential threat to a firm's operations in a country due to ineffectiveness of the domestic political system.

rule of law
a characteristic of legal systems where behavior is governed by rules that are uniformly enforced.

economic risk
potential threat to a firm's operations in a country due to economic policies and conditions, including property rights laws and enforcement of those laws.

counterfeiting
selling of trademarked goods without the consent of the trademark holder.

MANAGING POLITICAL RISK

Political instability and adverse actions by governments are two of the greatest risks that firms face in developing markets. However, there are a number of actions firms can take to lessen these risks.

- **Market diversification.** Competing in a range of geographic markets lessens the risk of actions by a single government or turmoil in a single nation. For example, BP has oil and natural gas exploration and drilling activities in 30 countries. As a result, when political instability struck in Algeria, this did not significantly hamper their global natural gas production.

- **Developing stakeholder coalitions.** Firms concerned about risks they face can develop stakeholder coalitions. Firms can develop coalitions with other multinationals investing in the country, local supplier and distributor firms, nongovernmental organizations, and governmental units to help reduce risk. These coalition partners can help a firm

detect potential problems early so they can try to head them off and build contingency plans. These coalition partners can also help foreign firms navigate bureaucracies and foster relationships with power brokers.

- **Wooing the influential.** Smart firms identify the key influencers, such as legislative leaders, regulators, and local key officials, such as mayors or tribal heads. They further make the effort to identify which players are their supporters, which are indifferent but potentially could be influenced to support their case, and which are antagonistic. They then work to cultivate the first two groups and work around the third group.

- **Putting key stakeholders on their boards.** Inviting key public and private sector stakeholders to join a country board aligns their incentives with the company's. It gives the locals a stake in the company's success.

Source: Chironga, M. Leke, A., Lund, S, & van Wamelen, A. 2011. Cracking the next growth market: Africa. *Harvard Business Review,* May: 117–122.

EXHIBIT 7.3 A Sample of Country Risk Ratings, January 2013

Rank	Country	Overall Score	Economic Risk	Political Risk	Structural Risk	Debt Indicators	Access to Capital
1	Norway	89.87	86.82	91.50	81.64	85.00	97.00
2	Luxembourg	87.29	78.71	91.05	84.11	84.50	95.00
3	Singapore	86.84	77.73	89.32	84.32	94.20	88.80
4	Sweden	86.81	79.20	90.27	82.33	81.80	95.50
5	Switzerland	86.78	83.01	89.12	86.39	69.00	90.00
10	Canada	81.82	73.93	87.15	78.70	60.60	95.60
12	Germany	80.88	71.75	83.75	77.49	67.30	97.50
15	United States	74.68	56.64	81.19	78.55	60.00	97.10
32	Japan	65.69	50.56	72.76	66.34	62.30	79.20
39	China	59.88	64.08	49.26	54.63	54.90	70.00
60	Russia	52.68	58.32	42.34	45.96	45.00	81.70
90	Vietnam	38.89	45.14	37.43	47.50	45.50	27.50
112	Argentina	33.72	39.97	29.71	50.38	45.20	22.50
138	Libya	28.11	44.00	27.07	38.00	0.00	30.00
175	North Korea	12.38	13.25	13.24	14.31	0.00	30.00

Source: euromoneycountryrisk.com.

COUNTERFEIT DRUGS: A DANGEROUS AND GROWING PROBLEM

Brian Donnelly has an interesting background. He's both a cop and a pharmacist. He worked as a special agent for the FBI for 21 years, but he also has a PhD in pharmacology. Now he's on the front lines of an important fight: keeping counterfeit drugs from the market. He works as an investigator for Pfizer, one of the world's largest pharmaceutical companies, putting both his pharmacology and law enforcement skills at work to blunt the growing flow of counterfeit drugs. He is one of a small army of former law enforcement officers employed by the pharmaceutical companies working for the same aim.

This is an important fight for two reasons. First, it is of economic consequence for the pharmaceutical companies. Counterfeit drugs are big business. In the United States alone, counterfeit drugs generated around $75 billion in revenue in 2010. They are enticing to customers. For example, while Pfizer's erectile dysfunction pill, Viagra, sells for $15 per tablet, fake versions sold online can be gotten for as little as $1 a pill. The sales of counterfeit drugs cut into the sales and profits of Pfizer and the other pharmaceutical firms. Second and more importantly, these fake drugs are potentially dangerous. The danger comes both from what they contain and also what they don't contain. Fake pills have been found to contain chalk, brick dust, paint, and even pesticides. Thus, they may be toxic, and ingesting them may cause significant health problems. On the other side, they may not contain the correct dose or even any of the active ingredients they are supposed to have. This may lead to severe health consequences. For example, fake Zithromax, an antibiotic, may contain none of the necessary chemical components, leaving the patient unable to fight their infection. According to one estimate, counterfeit drugs contribute to the death of upward of 100,000 people a year globally.

The pharmaceutical firms are fighting back with Donnelly and his colleagues. They use a common law enforcement technique. The fake drugs are sold by local dealers in the United States, who typically sell through websites, such as hardtofindrx.com and even Craigslist. These local dealers, called drop dealers, are the easiest to catch. From there, the investigators try to gain information on the major dealers from whom the drop dealers order. If they can get to these folks, they try to take it back to the kingpins manufacturing the drugs. This typically takes them through multiple law enforcement agencies in multiple countries, often back to manufacturing plants in China and India. To find the source, the pharmaceutical companies also use advanced technology. They determine the chemical composition of fake drugs they seize to search for common chemical signatures that point to the possible sourcing plant.

Pfizer is also fighting the fight from another angle. They are now tagging every bottle of Viagra and many other pharmaceuticals with radio-frequency identification (RFID) tags. Pharmacies can read these tags and input the data into Pfizer's system to confirm that these bottles are legitimate Pfizer drugs. This won't stop shady websites from delivering counterfeit drugs, but they will help keep the counterfeits out of legitimate pharmacies.

Sources: O'Connor, M. 2006. Pfizer using RFID to fight fake Viagra. *RFIDjournal .com*, January 6: np; and Gillette, F. 2013. Inside Pfizer's fight against counterfeit drugs. *Bloomberg BusinessWeek*, January 17: np.

Currency Risks   Currency fluctuations can pose substantial risks. A company with operations in several countries must constantly monitor the exchange rate between its own currency and that of the host country to minimize **currency risks.** Even a small change in the exchange rate can result in a significant difference in the cost of production or net profit when doing business overseas. When the U.S. dollar appreciates against other currencies, for example, U.S. goods can be more expensive to consumers in foreign countries. At the same time, however, appreciation of the U.S. dollar can have negative implications for American companies that have branch operations overseas. The reason for this is that profits from abroad must be exchanged for dollars at a more expensive rate of exchange, reducing the amount of profit when measured in dollars. For example, consider an American firm doing business in Italy. If this firm had a 20 percent profit in euros at its Italian center of operations, this profit would be totally wiped out when converted into U.S. dollars if the euro had depreciated 20 percent against the U.S. dollar. (U.S. multinationals typically engage in sophisticated "hedging strategies" to minimize currency risk. The discussion of this is beyond the scope of this section.)

currency risk
potential threat to a firm's operations in a country due to fluctuations in the local currency's exchange rate.

Below, we discuss how Israel's strong currency—the shekel—forced a firm to reevaluate its strategy.

For years O.R.T. Technologies resisted moving any operations outside of Israel. However, when faced with a sharp rise in the value of the shekel, the maker of specialized software for managing gas stations froze all local hiring and decided to transfer some developmental work to Eastern Europe. Laments CEO Alex Milner, "I never thought I'd see the day when we would have to move R&D outside of Israel, but the strong shekel has forced us to do so."[33]

Management Risks   **Management risks** may be considered the challenges and risks that managers face when they must respond to the inevitable differences that they encounter in foreign markets. These take a variety of forms: culture, customs, language, income levels, customer preferences, distribution systems, and so on.[34] As we will note later in the chapter, even in the case of apparently standard products, some degree of local adaptation will become necessary.[35]

Differences in cultures across countries can also pose unique challenges for managers.[36] Cultural symbols can evoke deep feelings.[37] For example, in a series of advertisements aimed at Italian vacationers, Coca-Cola executives turned the Eiffel Tower, Empire State Building, and the Tower of Pisa into the familiar Coke bottle. So far, so good. However, when the white marble columns of the Parthenon that crowns the Acropolis in Athens were turned into Coke bottles, the Greeks became outraged. Why? Greeks refer to the Acropolis as the "holy rock," and a government official said the Parthenon is an "international symbol of excellence" and that "whoever insults the Parthenon insults international culture." Coca-Cola apologized. Below are some cultural tips for conducting business in HongKong:

- Handshakes when greeting and before leaving are customary.
- After the initial handshake, business cards are presented with both hands on the card. Carefully read the card before putting it away.
- In Hong Kong, Chinese people should be addressed by their professional title (or Mr., Mrs., Miss) followed by their surname.
- Appointments should be made as far in advance as possible.
- Punctuality is very important and demonstrates respect.
- Negotiations in Hong Kong are normally very slow with much attention to detail. The same negotiating team should be kept throughout the proceedings.
- Tea will be served during the negotiations. Always accept and wait for the host to begin drinking before you partake.
- Be aware that "yes" may just be an indication that the person heard you rather than indicating agreement. A Hong Kong Chinese businessperson will have a difficult time saying "no" directly.

Below, we discuss a rather humorous example of how a local custom can affect operations at a manufacturing plant in Singapore.

> Larry Henderson, plant manager, and John Lichthental, manager of human resources, were faced with a rather unique problem. They were assigned by Celanese Chemical Corp. to build a plant in Singapore, and the plant was completed in July. However, according to local custom, a plant should only be christened on "lucky" days. Unfortunately, the next lucky day was not until September 3.
>
> The managers had to convince executives at Celanese's Dallas headquarters to delay the plant opening. As one might expect, it wasn't easy. But after many heated telephone conversations and flaming emails, the president agreed to open the new plant on a lucky day—September 3.[38]

Global Dispersion of Value Chains: Outsourcing and Offshoring

A major recent trend has been the dispersion of the value chains of multinational corporations across different countries; that is, the various activities that constitute the value chain of a firm are now spread across several countries and continents. Such dispersion of value occurs mainly through increasing offshoring and outsourcing.

A report issued by the World Trade Organization describes the production of a particular U.S. car as follows: "30 percent of the car's value goes to Korea for assembly, 17.5 percent to Japan for components and advanced technology, 7.5 percent to Germany for design, 4 percent to Taiwan and Singapore for minor parts, 2.5 percent to U.K. for advertising and marketing services, and 1.5 percent to Ireland and Barbados for data processing. This means that only 37 percent of the production value is generated in the U.S."[39] In today's economy, we are increasingly witnessing two interrelated trends: outsourcing and offshoring.

outsourcing
using other firms to perform value-creating activities that were previously performed in-house.

Outsourcing occurs when a firm decides to utilize other firms to perform value-creating activities that were previously performed in-house.[40] It may be a new activity that the firm is perfectly capable of doing but chooses to have someone else perform for cost or quality reasons. Outsourcing can be to either a domestic or foreign firm.

offshoring
shifting a value-creating activity from a domestic location to a foreign location.

Offshoring takes place when a firm decides to shift an activity that they were performing in a domestic location to a foreign location.[41] For example, both Microsoft and Intel now have R&D facilities in India, employing a large number of Indian scientists and engineers. Often, offshoring and outsourcing go together; that is, a firm may outsource an activity to a foreign supplier, thereby causing the work to be offshored as well.[42]

The recent explosion in the volume of outsourcing and offshoring is due to a variety of factors. Up until the 1960s, for most companies, the entire value chain was in one location. Further, the production took place close to where the customers were in order to keep transportation costs under control. In the case of service industries, it was generally believed that offshoring was not possible because the producer and consumer had to be present at the same place at the same time. After all, a haircut could not be performed if the barber and the client were separated!

For manufacturing industries, the rapid decline in transportation and coordination costs has enabled firms to disperse their value chains over different locations. For example, Nike's R&D takes place in the U.S., raw materials are procured from a multitude of countries, actual manufacturing takes place in China, Indonesia, or Vietnam, advertising is produced in the U.S., and sales and service take place in practically all the countries. Each value-creating activity is performed in the location where the cost is the lowest or the quality is the best. Without finding optimal locations for each activity, Nike could not have attained its position as the world's largest shoe company.

The experience of the manufacturing sector was also repeated in the service sector by the mid-1990s. A trend that began with the outsourcing of low-level programming and data entry work to countries such as India and Ireland suddenly grew manyfold, encompassing a variety of white collar and professional activities ranging from call-centers to R&D. The cost of a long distance call from the U.S. to India has decreased from about $3 to $0.03 in the last 25 years, thereby making it possible to have call centers located in countries like India, where a combination of low labor costs and English proficiency presents an ideal mix of factor conditions.

Bangalore, India, in recent years, has emerged as a location where more and more U.S. tax returns are prepared. In India, U.S.–trained and licensed radiologists interpret chest X-rays and CT scans from U.S. hospitals for half the cost. The advantages from offshoring go beyond mere cost savings today. In many specialized occupations in science and engineering, there is a shortage of qualified professionals in developed countries, whereas countries like India, China, and Singapore have what seems like an inexhaustible supply.[43]

While offshoring offers the potential to cut costs in corporations across a wide range of industries, many firms are finding the benefits of offshoring to be more elusive and the costs greater than they anticipated.[44] A study by AMR research found that 56 percent of companies moving production offshore experienced an increase in total costs, contrary to their expectations of cost savings. In a more focused study, 70 percent of managers said sourcing in China is more costly than they initially estimated.

The cause of this contrary outcome is actually not all that surprising. Common savings from offshoring, such as lower wages, benefits, energy costs, regulatory costs, and taxes, are all easily visible and immediate. In contrast, there are a host of hidden costs that arise over time and often overwhelm the cost savings of offshoring. These hidden costs include:

- **Total wage costs.** Labor cost per hour may be significantly lower in developing markets, but this may not translate into lower overall costs. If workers in these markets are less productive or less skilled, firms end up with a higher number of hours needed to produce the same quantity of product. This necessitates hiring more workers and having employees work longer hours.

- **Indirect costs.** In addition to higher labor costs, there are also a number of indirect costs that pop up. If there are problems with the skill level of workers, the firm will find the need for more training and supervision of workers, more raw material and greater scrap due to the lower skill level, and greater rework to fix quality problems. They may also experience greater need for security staff in their facilities.

- **Increased inventory.** Due to the longer delivery times, firms often need to tie up more capital in work in progress and inventory.

- **Reduced market responsiveness.** The long supply lines from low-cost countries may leave firms less responsive to shifts in customer demands. This may damage their brand image and also increase product obsolescence costs, as they may have to scrap or sell at a steep discount products that fail to meet quickly changing technology standards or customer tastes.

- **Coordination costs.** Coordinating product development and manufacturing can be difficult with operations undertaking different tasks in different countries. This may hamper innovation. It may also trigger unexpected costs, such as paying overtime in some markets so that staff across multiple time zones can meet to coordinate their activities.

- **Intellectual property rights.** Firms operating in countries with weak IP protection can wind up losing their trade secrets or taking costly measures to protect these secrets.

- **Wage inflation.** In moving overseas, firms often assume some level of wage stability, but wages in developing markets can be volatile and spike unexpectedly. For example, the wages of a typical line production worker in Shanghai increased by 125 percent between 2006 and 2011. As Roger Meiners, chairman of the Department of Economics at the University of Texas at Arlington stated, "The U.S. is more competitive on a wage basis because average wages have come down, especially for entry-level workers, and wages in China have been increasing."

Firms need to take into account all of these costs in determining whether or not to move their operations offshore. Strategy Spotlight 7.6 discusses the experience of a small firm that wrestled with this issue and decided to "reshore" its manufacturing.

Achieving Competitive Advantage in Global Markets

L07.4

The two opposing forces—cost reduction and adaptation to local markets—that firms face when entering international markets.

We now discuss the two opposing forces that firms face when they expand into global markets: cost reduction and adaptation to local markets. Then we address the four basic types of international strategies that they may pursue: international, global, multidomestic, and transnational. The selection of one of these four types of strategies is largely dependent on a firm's relative pressure to address each of the two forces.

Two Opposing Pressures: Reducing Costs and Adapting to Local Markets

Many years ago, the famed marketing strategist Theodore Levitt advocated strategies that favored global products and brands. He suggested that firms should standardize all of their products and services for all of their worldwide markets. Such an approach would

RESHORING OPERATIONS: LIGHTSAVER'S EXPERIENCE

LightSaver Technologies is a small firm that produces emergency lights for homes. Much like the emergency lights on planes that direct you to an exit in an emergency, LightSaver's product guides people to a home's exits, which may not be visible during a fire, a blackout, or other emergencies. When they started the firm in 2009, Sonja Zozula and Jerry Anderson decided to outsource their manufacturing to factories in China to minimize costs. They changed course and in 2011 moved their manufacturing back to a facility in Carlsbad, California, only 30 miles from their headquarters in San Clemente.

Why did they move manufacturing to the United States? For LightSaver, the decision was easy. They found that time, language, and cultural differences made communicating with Chinese suppliers difficult. They also had serious logistical challenges, with components shipped from the U.S. to China often stuck in customs for weeks. Tweaking designs was also difficult and often required hours of phone conversations with the factories. As Anderson concluded, "It's probably 30 percent cheaper to manufacture in China, but factor in shipping and all the other B.S. that you have to endure." Once

he factored in all of the costs, Anderson estimated that it is 2 to 5 percent cheaper to manufacture in the U.S. than in China.

Many other firms are reaching the same conclusion. Unilife, a medical device manufacturer, moved their manufacturing back to the United States to facilitate quicker FDA approval for their products. Pigtronix, a manufacturer of pedals that create electric guitar sound effects, moved its production to New York to improve quality and reduce its inventory levels. Bruce Chochrane moved furniture production back from China into a factory in North Carolina that his family's firm abandoned over 15 years ago. In a survey by Tobias Schoenherr, a professor at Michigan State University, 40 percent of manufacturing firm managers believe there is an increase in the reshoring of manufacturing to the United States. To date, the numbers are fairly modest. From its low point in 2010 to the end of 2012, the United States gained just over 500,000 manufacturing jobs, but the Boston Consulting Group concluded that reshoring could result in a gain of 2.5 to 5 million jobs.

Sources: Rocks, D. & Leiber, N. 2012. Made in China? Not worth the trouble. *Bloomberg Businessweek*, June 25: 49–50; Cohen, S. 2012. Some industries ripe for reshoring. *Dallas Morning News*, April 8: 1D–5D; Minter, S. 2012. Evidence for U.S. manufacturing reshoring builds. *Industryweek.com*, October 8: np; and Jean, S. & Alcott, K., 2013. Manufacturing jobs have slid steadily as work has moved offshore. *Dallas Morning News*, Jan 14: 1D.

help a firm lower its overall costs by spreading its investments over as large a market as possible. Levitt's approach rested on three key assumptions:

1. Customer needs and interests are becoming increasingly homogeneous worldwide.
2. People around the world are willing to sacrifice preferences in product features, functions, design, and the like for lower prices at high quality.
3. Substantial economies of scale in production and marketing can be achieved through supplying global markets.[45]

However, there is ample evidence to refute these assumptions.[46] Regarding the first assumption—the increasing worldwide homogeneity of customer needs and interests—consider the number of product markets, ranging from watches and handbags to soft drinks and fast foods. Companies have identified global customer segments and developed global products and brands targeted to those segments. Also, many other companies adapt lines to idiosyncratic country preferences and develop local brands targeted to local market segments. For example, Nestlé's line of pizzas marketed in the United Kingdom includes cheese with ham and pineapple topping on a French bread crust. Similarly, Coca-Cola in Japan markets Georgia (a tonic drink) as well as Classic Coke and Hi-C.

Consider the second assumption—the sacrifice of product attributes for lower prices. While there is invariably a price-sensitive segment in many product markets, there is no indication that this is increasing. In contrast, in many product and service markets—ranging from watches, personal computers, and household appliances, to banking and insurance—there is a growing interest in multiple product features, product quality, and service.

Finally, the third assumption is that significant economies of scale in production and marketing could be achieved for global products and services. Although standardization may lower manufacturing costs, such a perspective does not consider three critical and interrelated points. First, as we discussed in Chapter 5, technological developments in flexible factory automation enable economies of scale to be attained at lower levels of output and do not require production of a single standardized product. Second, the cost of production is only one component, and often not the critical one, in determining the total cost of a product. Third, a firm's strategy should not be product-driven. It should also consider other activities in the firm's value chain, such as marketing, sales, and distribution.

Based on the above, we would have a hard time arguing that it is wise to develop the same product or service for all markets throughout the world. While there are some exceptions, such as Boeing airplanes and some of Coca-Cola's soft-drink products, managers must also strive to tailor their products to the culture of the country in which they are attempting to do business. Few would argue that "one size fits all" generally applies.

The opposing pressures that managers face place conflicting demands on firms as they strive to be competitive.[47] On the one hand, competitive pressures require that firms do what they can to *lower unit costs* so that consumers will not perceive their product and service offerings as too expensive. This may lead them to consider locating manufacturing facilities where labor costs are low and developing products that are highly standardized across multiple countries.

In addition to responding to pressures to lower costs, managers also must strive to be *responsive to local pressures* in order to tailor their products to the demand of the local market in which they do business. This requires differentiating their offerings and strategies from country to country to reflect consumer tastes and preferences and making changes to reflect differences in distribution channels, human resource practices, and governmental regulations. However, since the strategies and tactics to differentiate products and services to local markets can involve additional expenses, a firm's costs will tend to rise.

The two opposing pressures result in four different basic strategies that companies can use to compete in the global marketplace: international, global, multidomestic, and transnational. The strategy that a firm selects depends on the degree of pressure that it is facing for cost reductions and the importance of adapting to local markets. Exhibit 7.4 shows the conditions under which each of these strategies would be most appropriate.

It is important to note that we consider these four strategies to be "basic" or "pure"; that is, in practice, all firms will tend to have some elements of each strategy.

EXHIBIT 7.4 Opposing Pressures and Four Strategies

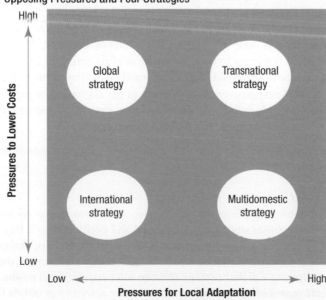

international strategy
a strategy based on firms' diffusion and adaptation of the parent companies' knowledge and expertise to foreign markets, used in industries where the pressures for both local adaptation and lowering costs are low.

International Strategy

There are a small number of industries in which pressures for both local adaptation and lowering costs are rather low. An extreme example of such an industry is the "orphan" drug industry. These are medicines for diseases that are severe but affect only a small number of people. Diseases such as the Gaucher disease and Fabry disease fit into this category. Companies such as Genzyme and Oxford GlycoSciences are active in this segment of the drug industry. There is virtually no need to adapt their products to the local markets. And the pressures to reduce costs are low; even though only a few thousand patients are affected, the revenues and margins are significant, because patients are charged up to $100,000 per year. Legislation has made this industry even more attractive. The 1983 Orphan Drug Act provides various tax credits and exclusive marketing rights for any drug developed to treat a disease that afflicts fewer than 200,000 patients. Since 1983, more than 280 orphan drugs have been licensed and used to treat 14 million patients.[48]

An international strategy is based on diffusion and adaptation of the parent company's knowledge and expertise to foreign markets. Country units are allowed to make some minor adaptations to products and ideas coming from the head office, but they have far less independence and autonomy compared to multidomestic companies. The primary goal of the strategy is worldwide exploitation of the parent firm's knowledge and capabilities. All sources of core competencies are centralized.

The majority of large U.S. multinationals pursued the international strategy in the decades following World War II. These companies centralized R&D and product development but established manufacturing facilities as well as marketing organizations abroad. Companies such as McDonald's and Kellogg are examples of firms following such a strategy. Although these companies do make some local adaptations, they are of a very limited nature. With increasing pressures to reduce costs due to global competition, especially from low-cost countries, opportunities to successfully employ international strategy are becoming more limited. This strategy is most suitable in situations where a firm has distinctive competencies that local companies in foreign markets lack.

Risks and Challenges   Below are some of the risks and challenges associated with an international strategy.

- Different activities in the value chain typically have different optimal locations. That is, R&D may be optimally located in a country with an abundant supply of scientists and engineers, whereas assembly may be better conducted in a low-cost location. Nike, for example, designs its shoes in the United States, but all the manufacturing is done in countries like China or Thailand. The international strategy, with its tendency to concentrate most of its activities in one location, fails to take advantage of the benefits of an optimally distributed value chain.
- The lack of local responsiveness may result in the alienation of local customers. Worse still, the firm's inability to be receptive to new ideas and innovation from its foreign subsidiaries may lead to missed opportunities.

Exhibit 7.5 summarizes the strengths and weaknesses of international strategies in the global marketplace.

Global Strategy

global strategy
a strategy based on firms' centralization and control by the corporate office, with the primary emphasis on controlling costs, and used in industries where the pressure for local adaptation is low and the pressure for lowering costs is high.

As indicated in Exhibit 7.4, a firm whose emphasis is on lowering costs tends to follow a global strategy. Competitive strategy is centralized and controlled to a large extent by the corporate office. Since the primary emphasis is on controlling costs, the corporate office strives to achieve a strong level of coordination and integration across the various businesses.[49] Firms following a global strategy strive to offer standardized products and services as well as to locate manufacturing, R&D, and marketing activities in only a few locations.[50]

EXHIBIT 7.5 Strengths and Limitations of International Strategies in the Global Marketplace

Strengths	Limitations
• Leverage and diffusion of a parent firm's knowledge and core competencies. • Lower costs because of less need to tailor products and services.	• Limited ability to adapt to local markets. • Inability to take advantage of new ideas and innovations occurring in local markets.

A global strategy emphasizes economies of scale due to the standardization of products and services, and the centralization of operations in a few locations. As such, one advantage may be that innovations that come about through efforts of either a business unit or the corporate office can be transferred more easily to other locations. Although costs may be lower, the firm following a global strategy may, in general, have to forgo opportunities for revenue growth since it does not invest extensive resources in adapting product offerings from one market to another.

A global strategy is most appropriate when there are strong pressures for reducing costs and comparatively weak pressures for adaptation to local markets. Economies of scale becomes an important consideration.[51] Advantages to increased volume may come from larger production plants or runs as well as from more efficient logistics and distribution networks. Worldwide volume is also especially important in supporting high levels of investment in research and development. As we would expect, many industries requiring high levels of R&D, such as pharmaceuticals, semiconductors, and jet aircraft, follow global strategies.

Another advantage of a global strategy is that it can enable a firm to create a standard level of quality throughout the world. Let's look at what Tom Siebel, former chairman of Siebel Systems (now part of Oracle), the $2 billion developer of e-business application software, has to say about global standardization.

> Our customers—global companies like IBM, Zurich Financial Services, and Citicorp—expect the same high level of service and quality, and the same licensing policies, no matter where we do business with them around the world. Our human resources and legal departments help us create policies that respect local cultures and requirements worldwide, while at the same time maintaining the highest standards. We have one brand, one image, one set of corporate colors, and one set of messages, across every place on the planet. An organization needs central quality control to avoid surprises.[52]

Risks and Challenges   There are, of course, some risks associated with a global strategy.[53]

- A firm can enjoy scale economies only by concentrating scale-sensitive resources and activities in one or few locations. Such concentration, however, becomes a "double-edged sword." For example, if a firm has only one manufacturing facility, it must export its output (e.g., components, subsystems, or finished products) to other markets, some of which may be a great distance from the operation. Thus, decisions about locating facilities must weigh the potential benefits from concentrating operations in a single location against the higher transportation and tariff costs that result from such concentration.

- The geographic concentration of any activity may also tend to isolate that activity from the targeted markets. Such isolation may be risky since it may hamper the facility's ability to quickly respond to changes in market conditions and needs.

- Concentrating an activity in a single location also makes the rest of the firm dependent on that location. Such dependency implies that, unless the location has world-class competencies, the firm's competitive position can be eroded if problems arise. A European Ford executive, reflecting on the firm's concentration of activities during a global integration program in the mid-1990s, lamented, "Now if you misjudge the market, you are wrong in 15 countries rather than only one."

Many firms have learned through experience that products that work in one market may not be well received in other markets. For example, even Apple has found it a challenge to leverage their global products in some markets.[54] Of their $108 billion in sales in 2011, only 12 percent came from sales in China. Apple, with its global focus, has not developed low-end smartphones to sell in developing markets. As a result, it has had some difficulty competing with Samsung in these markets, because Samsung has a much wider product range that effectively meets the needs of different markets. Wei Jinping, a potential Apple customer in China, outlined the challenge when he stated, "I like the IPhone. It's very cool. But it is a bit out of my price range."

Exhibit 7.6 summarizes the strengths and weaknesses of global strategies.

Multidomestic Strategy

According to Exhibit 7.4, a firm whose emphasis is on differentiating its product and service offerings to adapt to local markets follows a multidomestic strategy.[55] Decisions evolving from a multidomestic strategy tend to be decentralized to permit the firm to tailor its products and respond rapidly to changes in demand. This enables a firm to expand its market and to charge different prices in different markets. For firms following this strategy, differences in language, culture, income levels, customer preferences, and distribution systems are only a few of the many factors that must be considered. Even in the case of relatively standardized products, at least some level of local adaptation is often necessary.

Consider, for example, the Oreo cookie.[56] Kraft has tailored the iconic cookie to better meet the tastes and preferences in different markets. For example, Kraft has created green tea Oreos in China, chocolate and peanut butter Oreos for Indonesia, and banana and dulce de leche Oreos for Argentina. Kraft has also lowered the sweetness of the cookie for China and reduced the bitterness of the cookie for India. The shape is also on the table for change. Kraft has even created wafer-stick style Oreos.

Kraft has tailored other products to meet local market needs. For example, with their Tang drink product, they developed local flavors, such as a lime and cinnamon flavor for Mexico and mango Tang for the Philippines. They also looked to the nutritional needs in different countries. True to the heritage of the brand, they have kept the theme that Tang is a good source of Vitamin C. But in Brazil, where children often have iron deficiencies, they added iron as well as other vitamins and minerals. The local focus strategy has worked well, with Tang's sales almost doubling in five years.

To meet the needs of local markets, companies need to go beyond just product designs. One of the simple ways firms have worked to meet market needs is by finding appropriate names for their products. For example, in China, the names of products imbue them with strong meanings and can be significant drivers of their success. As a result, firms have been careful with how they translate their brands. For example, Reebok became Rui bu, which means "quick steps." Lay's snack foods became Le shi, which means "happy things." And Coca Cola's Chinese name, Ke Kou Ke Le, translates to "tasty fun."

Strategy Spotlight 7.7 discusses how Procter & Gamble has undertaken a range of actions across their value chain to meet the needs of the Vietnamese market.

EXHIBIT 7.6 Strengths and Limitations of Global Strategies

Strengths	Limitations
• Strong integration across various businesses.	• Limited ability to adapt to local markets.
• Standardization leads to higher economies of scale, which lowers costs.	• Concentration of activities may increase dependence on a single facility.
• Helps create uniform standards of quality throughout the world.	• Single locations may lead to higher tariffs and transportation costs.

PROCTER & GAMBLE WORKS TO WIN THE HEARTS AND MINDS OF CUSTOMERS IN VIETNAM

Like many companies with product lines that are mature and seeing slow growth in developed economies, Procter & Gamble is focusing a great deal of energy on growing their business in developing economies. To effectively grow in these markets, P&G looks to tailor their product designs, packaging, and promotion efforts to meet the conditions of the markets they are entering.

In Vietnam, P&G has undertaken a range of efforts to meet the needs of the market and to grow their business. As done by firms for decades, they have developed lower-cost brands that can be sold to consumers with modest incomes, in the hopes that they will trade up to the premium brands P&G produces later. They have also found market-specific uses for their products in Vietnam, such as marketing their deodorizing spray, Ambi Pur (sold as Febreeze in the U.S.), as a means to deodorize motorcycle helmets that tend to be less than fresh smelling when worn in the hot and humid climate in Vietnam. This product is now one of P&G's fastest-growing products in Vietnam. They have also changed the packaging of their products, moving from large bottles and containers to small, cheap one-use packages that are popular in the traditional small stores most customers use. They have also forward integrated into the sales business and operate a boat in the Mekong Delta area to sell to rural customers who live along the water. They also got involved in TV production and had employees travel the country in a van covered in advertisements for their products to recruit contestants for *Vietnam's Got Talent,* a show for which P&G is the sole sponsor. Finally, they have leveraged social activism to build their market presence. They have established a charitable unit that brings needed health, educational, and community services to poor regions. They use these actions as a means to promote P&G brands. For example, employees of P&G raised 80 percent of the funds needed to open a new school in a poor village 80 miles from Hanoi. Each room in the school has a plaque advertising a P&G product.

These efforts to find new ways to design, promote, and distribute P&G products that match the economic and social environment of Vietnam and other developing markets have been effective for P&G. These markets accounted for 37 percent of P&G's sales in 2012, up from 27 percent five years ago.

Source: Coleman-Lochner, L. 2012. P&G woos the hearts, minds, and schools of Vietnam. *Bloomberg Businessweek,* June 5, 19–21; and Rexrode, C. 2012. As U.S. slows, P&G turns to developing markets. *Associated Press,* February 2, np.

Risks and Challenges   As you might expect, there are some risks associated with a multidomestic strategy. Among these are the following:

- Typically, local adaptation of products and services will increase a company's cost structure. In many industries, competition is so intense that most firms can ill afford any competitive disadvantages on the dimension of cost. A key challenge of managers is to determine the trade-off between local adaptation and its cost structure. For example, cost considerations led Procter & Gamble to standardize its diaper design across all European markets. This was done despite research data indicating that Italian mothers, unlike those in other countries, preferred diapers that covered the baby's navel. Later, however, P&G recognized that this feature was critical to these mothers, so the company decided to incorporate this feature for the Italian market despite its adverse cost implications.

- At times, local adaptations, even when well intentioned, may backfire. When the American restaurant chain TGI Fridays entered the South Korean market, it purposely incorporated many local dishes, such as kimchi (hot, spicy cabbage), in its menu. This responsiveness, however, was not well received. Company analysis of the weak market acceptance indicated that Korean customers anticipated a visit to TGI Fridays as a visit to America. Thus, finding Korean dishes was inconsistent with their expectations.

- The optimal degree of local adaptation evolves over time. In many industry segments, a variety of factors, such as the influence of global media, greater international travel, and declining income disparities across countries, may lead to increasing global standardization. On the other hand, in other industry segments, especially where the product or service can be delivered over the Internet (such as music), the need for

EXHIBIT 7.7 Strengths and Limitations of Multidomestic Strategies

Strengths	Limitations
• Ability to adapt products and services to local market conditions. • Ability to detect potential opportunities for attractive niches in a given market, enhancing revenue.	• Decreased ability to realize cost savings through scale economies. • Greater difficulty in transferring knowledge across countries. • May lead to "overadaptation" as conditions change.

even greater customization and local adaptation may increase over time. Firms must recalibrate the need for local adaptation on an ongoing basis; excessive adaptation extracts a price as surely as underadaptation.

Exhibit 7.7 summarizes the strengths and limitations of multidomestic strategies.

Transnational Strategy

transnational strategy
a strategy based on firms' optimizing the trade-offs associated with efficiency, local adaptation, and learning, used in industries where the pressures for both local adaptation and lowering costs are high.

A *transnational strategy* strives to optimize the trade-offs associated with efficiency, local adaptation, and learning.[57] It seeks efficiency not for its own sake, but as a means to achieve global competitiveness.[58] It recognizes the importance of local responsiveness but as a tool for flexibility in international operations.[59] Innovations are regarded as an outcome of a larger process of organizational learning that includes the contributions of everyone in the firm.[60] Also, a core tenet of the transnational model is that a firm's assets and capabilities are dispersed according to the most beneficial location for each activity. Thus, managers avoid the tendency to either concentrate activities in a central location (a global strategy) or disperse them across many locations to enhance adaptation (a multidomestic strategy). Peter Brabeck, former chairman of Nestlé, the giant food company, provides such a perspective.

> We believe strongly that there isn't a so-called global consumer, at least not when it comes to food and beverages. People have local tastes based on their unique cultures and traditions—a good candy bar in Brazil is not the same as a good candy bar in China. Therefore, decision making needs to be pushed down as low as possible in the organization, out close to the markets. Otherwise, how can you make good brand decisions? That said, decentralization has its limits. If you are too decentralized, you can become too complicated—you get too much complexity in your production system. The closer we come to the consumer, in branding, pricing, communication, and product adaptation, the more we decentralize. The more we are dealing with production, logistics, and supply-chain management, the more centralized decision making becomes. After all, we want to leverage Nestlé's size, not be hampered by it.[61]

The Nestlé example illustrates a common approach in determining whether or not to centralize or decentralize a value-chain activity. Typically, primary activities that are "downstream" (e.g., marketing and sales, and service), or closer to the customer, tend to require more decentralization in order to adapt to local market conditions. On the other hand, primary activities that are "upstream" (e.g., logistics and operations), or further away from the customer, tend to be centralized. This is because there is less need for adapting these activities to local markets and the firm can benefit from economies of scale. Additionally, many support activities, such as information systems and procurement, tend to be centralized in order to increase the potential for economies of scale.

A central philosophy of the transnational organization is enhanced adaptation to all competitive situations as well as flexibility by capitalizing on communication and knowledge flows throughout the organization.[62] A principal characteristic is the integration of unique contributions of all units into worldwide operations. Thus, a joint innovation by headquarters and by one of the overseas units can lead potentially to the development of relatively standardized and yet flexible products and services that are suitable for multiple markets.

Asea Brown Boveri (ABB) is a firm that successfully follows a transnational strategy. ABB, with its home bases in Sweden and Switzerland, illustrates the trend toward cross-national mergers that lead firms to consider multiple headquarters in the future. It is managed as a flexible network of units, and one of management's main functions is the facilitation of information and knowledge flows between units. ABB's subsidiaries have complete responsibility for product categories on a worldwide basis. Such a transnational strategy enables ABB to benefit from access to new markets and the opportunity to utilize and develop resources wherever they may be located.

Risks and Challenges   As with the other strategies, there are some unique risks and challenges associated with a transnational strategy.

- *The choice of a seemingly optimal location cannot guarantee that the quality and cost of factor inputs (i.e., labor, materials) will be optimal.* Managers must ensure that the relative advantage of a location is actually realized, not squandered because of weaknesses in productivity and the quality of internal operations. Ford Motor Co., for example, has benefited from having some of its manufacturing operations in Mexico. While some have argued that the benefits of lower wage rates will be partly offset by lower productivity, this does not always have to be the case. Since unemployment in Mexico is higher than in the United States, Ford can be more selective in its hiring practices for its Mexican operations. And, given the lower turnover among its Mexican employees, Ford can justify a high level of investment in training and development. Thus, the net result can be not only lower wage rates but also higher productivity than in the United States.

- *Although knowledge transfer can be a key source of competitive advantage, it does not take place "automatically."* For knowledge transfer to take place from one subsidiary to another, it is important for the source of the knowledge, the target units, and the corporate headquarters to recognize the potential value of such unique know-how. Given that there can be significant geographic, linguistic, and cultural distances that typically separate subsidiaries, the potential for knowledge transfer can become very difficult to realize. Firms must create mechanisms to systematically and routinely uncover the opportunities for knowledge transfer.

Exhibit 7.8 summarizes the relative advantages and disadvantages of transnational strategies.

Global or Regional? A Second Look at Globalization

LO7.6

The difference between regional companies and truly global companies.

Thus far, we have suggested four possible strategies from which a firm must choose once it has decided to compete in the global marketplace. In recent years, many writers have asserted that the process of globalization has caused national borders to become increasingly irrelevant.[63] However, some scholars have recently questioned this perspective, and they have argued that it is unwise for companies to rush into full scale globalization.[64]

Before answering questions about the extent of firms' globalization, let's try to clarify what "globalization" means. Traditionally, a firm's globalization is measured in terms of its foreign sales as a percentage of total sales. However, this measure can be misleading. For example, consider a U.S. firm that has expanded its activities into Canada. Clearly, this initiative is qualitatively different from achieving the same sales volume in a distant country such as China. Similarly, if a Malaysian firm expands into Singapore or a German firm

EXHIBIT 7.8 Strengths and Limitations of Transnational Strategies

Strengths	Limitations
• Ability to attain economies of scale.	• Unique challenges in determining optimal locations of activities to ensure cost and quality.
• Ability to adapt to local markets.	
• Ability to locate activities in optimal locations.	• Unique managerial challenges in fostering knowledge transfer.
• Ability to increase knowledge flows and learning.	

starts selling its products in Austria, this would represent an expansion into a geographically adjacent country. Such nearby countries would often share many common characteristics in terms of language, culture, infrastructure, and customer preferences. In other words, this is more a case of regionalization than globalization.

Extensive analysis of the distribution data of sales across different countries and regions led Alan Rugman and Alain Verbeke to conclude that there is a stronger case to be made in favor of **regionalization** than globalization. According to their study, a company would have to have at least 20 percent of its sales in each of the three major economic regions—North America, Europe, and Asia—to be considered a global firm. However, they found that only nine of the world's 500 largest firms met this standard! Even when they relaxed the criterion to 20 percent of sales each in at least two of the three regions, the number only increased to 25. *Thus, most companies are regional or, at best, biregional—not global—even today.*

In a world of instant communication, rapid transportation, and governments that are increasingly willing to open up their markets to trade and investment, why are so few firms "global"? The most obvious answer is that distance still matters. After all, it is easier to do business in a neighboring country than in a far away country, all else being equal. Distance, in the final analysis, may be viewed as a concept with many dimensions, not just a measure of geographical distance. For example, both Canada and Mexico are the same distance from the U.S. However, U.S. companies find it easier to expand operations into Canada than into Mexico. Why? Canada and the U.S. share many commonalities in terms of language, culture, economic development, legal and political systems, and infrastructure development. Thus, if we view distance as having many dimensions, the U.S. and Canada are very close, whereas there is greater distance between the U.S. and Mexico. Similarly, when we look at what we might call the "true" distance between the U.S. and China, the effects of geographic distance are multiplied by distance in terms of culture, language, religion, and legal and political systems between the two countries. On the other hand, although U.S. and Australia are geographically distant, the "true" distance is somewhat less when one considers distance along the other dimensions.

Another reason for regional expansion is the rise of the **trading blocs** and free trade zones. A number of regional agreements have been created that facilitate the growth of business within these regions by easing trade restrictions and taxes and tariffs. These have included the European Union (EU), North American Free Trade Agreement (NAFTA), Association of Southeast Asian Nations (ASEAN), and MERCOSUR (a South American trading block).

Regional economic integration has progressed at a faster pace than global economic integration and the trade and investment patterns of the largest companies reflect this reality. After all, regions represent the outcomes of centuries of political and cultural history that results not only in commonalities but also mutual affinity. For example, stretching from Algeria and Morocco in the West to Oman and Yemen in the East, more than 30 countries share the Arabic language and the Muslim religion, making these countries a natural regional bloc. Similarly, the countries of South and Central America share the Spanish language (except Brazil), Catholic religion, and a shared history of Spanish colonialism. No wonder firms find it easier and less risky to expand within their region than to other regions.

Entry Modes of International Expansion

A firm has many options available to it when it decides to expand into international markets. Given the challenges associated with such entry, many firms first start on a small scale and then increase their level of investment and risk as they gain greater experience with the overseas market in question.[65]

---

regionalization
increasing international exchange of goods, services, money, people, ideas, and information; and the increasing similarity of culture, laws, rules, and norms within a region such as Europe, North America, or Asia.

trading blocs
groups of countries agreeing to increase trade between them by lowering trade barries.

L07.7
The four basic types of entry strategies and the relative benefits and risks associated with each of them.

EXHIBIT 7.9 Entry Modes for International Expansion

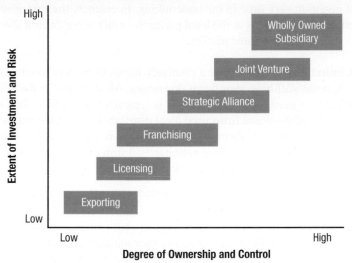

Exhibit 7.9 illustrates a wide variety of modes of foreign entry, including exporting, licensing, franchising, joint ventures, strategic alliances, and wholly owned subsidiaries.[66] As the exhibit indicates, the various types of entry form a continuum ranging from exporting (low investment and risk, low control) to a wholly owned subsidiary (high investment and risk, high control).[67]

There can be frustrations and setbacks as a firm evolves its international entry strategy from exporting to more expensive types, including wholly owned subsidiaries. For example, according to the CEO of a large U.S. specialty chemical company:

> In the end, we always do a better job with our own subsidiaries; sales improve, and we have greater control over the business. But we still need local distributors for entry, and we are still searching for strategies to get us through the transitions without battles over control and performance.[68]

Exporting

Exporting consists of producing goods in one country to sell in another.[69] This entry strategy enables a firm to invest the least amount of resources in terms of its product, its organization, and its overall corporate strategy. Many host countries dislike this entry strategy because it provides less local employment than other modes of entry.[70]

Multinationals often stumble onto a stepwise strategy for penetrating markets, beginning with the exporting of products. This often results in a series of unplanned actions to increase sales revenues. As the pattern recurs with entries into subsequent markets, this approach, named a "beachhead strategy," often becomes official policy.[71]

Benefits Such an approach definitely has its advantages. After all, firms start from scratch in sales and distribution when they enter new markets. Because many foreign markets are nationally regulated and dominated by networks of local intermediaries, firms need to partner with local distributors to benefit from their valuable expertise and knowledge of their own markets. Multinationals, after all, recognize that they cannot master local business practices, meet regulatory requirements, hire and manage local personnel, or gain access to potential customers without some form of local partnership.

exporting
producing goods in one country to sell to residents of another country.

Multinationals also want to minimize their own risk. They do this by hiring local distributors and investing very little in the undertaking. In essence, the firm gives up control of strategic marketing decisions to the local partners—much more control than they would be willing to give up in their home market.

Risks and Limitations Exporting is a relatively inexpensive way to enter foreign markets. However, it can still have significant downsides. Most centrally, the ability to tailor the firm's products to meet local market needs is typically very limited. In a study of 250 instances in which multinational firms used local distributors to implement their exporting entry strategy, the results were dismal. In the vast majority of the cases, the distributors were bought (to increase control) by the multinational firm or fired. In contrast, successful distributors shared two common characteristics:

- They carried product lines that complemented, rather than competed with, the multinational's products.
- They behaved as if they were business partners with the multinationals. They shared market information with the corporations, they initiated projects with distributors in neighboring countries, and they suggested initiatives in their own or nearby markets. Additionally, these distributors took on risk themselves by investing in areas such as training, information systems, and advertising and promotion in order to increase the business of their multinational partners.

The key point is the importance of developing collaborative, win–win relationships.

To ensure more control over operations without incurring significant risks, many firms have used licensing and franchising as a mode of entry. Let's now discuss these and their relative advantages and disadvantages.

Licensing and Franchising

Licensing and franchising are both forms of contractual arrangements. **Licensing** enables a company to receive a royalty or fee in exchange for the right to use its trademark, patent, trade secret, or other valuable item of intellectual property.[72]

Franchising contracts generally include a broader range of factors in an operation and have a longer time period during which the agreement is in effect. Franchising remains a primary form of American business. According to a recent survey, more than 400 U.S. franchisers have international exposure.[73] This is greater than the combined totals of the next four largest franchiser home countries—France, the United Kingdom, Mexico, and Austria.

Benefits In international markets, an advantage of licensing is that the firm granting a license incurs little risk, since it does not have to invest any significant resources into the country itself. In turn, the licensee (the firm receiving the license) gains access to the trademark, patent, and so on, and is able to potentially create competitive advantages. In many cases, the country also benefits from the product being manufactured locally. For example, Yoplait yogurt is licensed by General Mills from Sodima, a French cooperative, for sale in the United States. The logos of college and professional athletic teams in the United States are another source of trademarks that generate significant royalty income domestically and internationally.

Franchising has the advantage of limiting the risk exposure that a firm has in overseas markets. At the same time, the firm is able to expand the revenue base of the company.

Risks and Limitations The licensor gives up control of its product and forgoes potential revenues and profits. Furthermore, the licensee may eventually become so familiar with

licensing
a contractual arrangement in which a company receives a royalty or fee in exchange for the right to use its trademark, patent, trade secret, or other valuable intellectual property.

franchising
a contractual arrangement in which a company receives a royalty or fee in exchange for the right to use its intellectual property; it usually involves a longer time period than licensing and includes other factors, such as monitoring of operations, training, and advertising.

the patent and trade secrets that it may become a competitor; that is, the licensee may make some modifications to the product and manufacture and sell it independently of the licensor without having to pay a royalty fee. This potential situation is aggravated in countries that have relatively weak laws to protect intellectual property. Additionally, if the licensee selected by the multinational firm turns out to be a poor choice, the brand name and reputation of the product may be tarnished.[74]

With franchising, the multinational firm receives only a portion of the revenues, in the form of franchise fees. Had the firm set up the operation itself (e.g., a restaurant through direct investment), it would have had the entire revenue to itself.

Companies often desire a closer collaboration with other firms in order to increase revenue, reduce costs, and enhance their learning—often through the diffusion of technology. To achieve such objectives, they enter into strategic alliances or joint ventures, two entry modes we will discuss next.

Strategic Alliances and Joint Ventures

Joint ventures and strategic alliances have recently become increasingly popular.[75] These two forms of partnership differ in that joint ventures entail the creation of a third-party legal entity, whereas strategic alliances do not. In addition, strategic alliances generally focus on initiatives that are smaller in scope than joint ventures.[76]

Benefits As we discussed in Chapter 6, these strategies have been effective in helping firms increase revenues and reduce costs as well as enhance learning and diffuse technologies.[77] These partnerships enable firms to share the risks as well as the potential revenues and profits. Also, by gaining exposure to new sources of knowledge and technologies, such partnerships can help firms develop core competencies that can lead to competitive advantages in the marketplace.[78] Finally, entering into partnerships with host country firms can provide very useful information on local market tastes, competitive conditions, legal matters, and cultural nuances.[79]

Risks and Limitations Managers must be aware of the risks associated with strategic alliances and joint ventures and how they can be minimized.[80] First, there needs to be a clearly defined strategy that is strongly supported by the organizations that are party to the partnership. Otherwise, the firms may work at cross-purposes and not achieve any of their goals. Second, and closely allied to the first issue, there must be a clear understanding of capabilities and resources that will be central to the partnership. Without such clarification, there will be fewer opportunities for learning and developing competencies that could lead to competitive advantages. Third, trust is a vital element. Phasing in the relationship between alliance partners permits them to get to know each other better and develop trust. Without trust, one party may take advantage of the other by, for example, withholding its fair share of resources and gaining access to privileged information through unethical (or illegal) means. Fourth, cultural issues that can potentially lead to conflict and dysfunctional behaviors need to be addressed. An organization's culture is the set of values, beliefs, and attitudes that influence the behavior and goals of its employees.[81] Thus, recognizing cultural differences as well as striving to develop elements of a "common culture" for the partnership is vital. Without a unifying culture, it will become difficult to combine and leverage resources that are increasingly important in knowledge-intensive organizations (discussed in Chapter 4).[82]

Finally, the success of a firm's alliance should not be left to chance.[83] To improve their odds of success, many companies have carefully documented alliance-management knowledge by creating guidelines and manuals to help them manage specific aspects of the entire alliance life cycle (e.g., partner selection and alliance negotiation and contracting).

For example, Lotus Corp. (part of IBM) created what it calls its "35 rules of thumb" to manage each phase of an alliance from formation to termination. Hewlett-Packard developed 60 different tools and templates, which it placed in a 300-page manual for guiding decision making. The manual included such tools as a template for making the business case for an alliance, a partner evaluation form, a negotiation template outlining the roles and responsibilities of different departments, a list of the ways to measure alliance performance, and an alliance termination checklist.

When a firm desires the highest level of control, it develops wholly owned subsidiaries. Although wholly owned subsidiaries can generate the greatest returns, they also have the highest levels of investment and risk. We will now discuss them.

Wholly Owned Subsidiaries

wholly owned subsidiary
a business in which a multinational company owns 100 percent of the stock.

A **wholly owned subsidiary** is a business in which a multinational company owns 100 percent of the stock. Two ways a firm can establish a wholly owned subsidiary are to (1) acquire an existing company in the home country or (2) develop a totally new operation (often referred to as a "greenfield venture").

Benefits Establishing a wholly owned subsidiary is the most expensive and risky of the various entry modes. However, it can also yield the highest returns. In addition, it provides the multinational company with the greatest degree of control of all activities, including manufacturing, marketing, distribution, and technology development.[84]

Wholly owned subsidiaries are most appropriate where a firm already has the appropriate knowledge and capabilities that it can leverage rather easily through multiple locations. Examples range from restaurants to semiconductor manufacturers. To lower costs, for example, Intel Corporation builds semiconductor plants throughout the world—all of which use virtually the same blueprint. Knowledge can be further leveraged by hiring managers and professionals from the firm's home country, often through hiring talent from competitors.

Risks and Limitations As noted, wholly owned subsidiaries are typically the most expensive and risky entry mode. With franchising, joint ventures, or strategic alliances, the risk is shared with the firm's partners. With wholly owned subsidiaries, the entire risk is assumed by the parent company. The risks associated with doing business in a new country (e.g., political, cultural, and legal) can be lessened by hiring local talent.

For example, Wendy's avoided committing two blunders in Germany by hiring locals to its advertising staff.[85] In one case, the firm wanted to promote its "old-fashioned" qualities. However, a literal translation would have resulted in the company promoting itself as "outdated." In another situation, Wendy's wanted to emphasize that its hamburgers could be prepared 256 ways. The problem? The German word that Wendy's wanted to use for "ways" usually meant "highways" or "roads." Although such errors may sometimes be entertaining to the public, it is certainly preferable to catch these mistakes before they confuse the consumer or embarrass the company.

We have addressed entry strategies as a progression from exporting through the creation of wholly owned subsidiaries. However, we must point out that many firms do not follow such an evolutionary approach. For example, because of political and regulatory reasons, Pepsi entered India through a joint venture with two Indian firms in 1998. As discussed in Strategy Spotlight 7.8, this provided Pepsi with a first-mover advantage within the Indian market, where it remains well ahead of its archrival, Coca-Cola.

PEPSI'S FIRST-MOVER ADVANTAGE IN INDIA HAS PAID OFF

Pepsi (pronounced "Pay-psee") became a common synonym for cola in India's most widely spoken language after having the market to itself in the early 1990s. PepsiCo's linguistic advantage translates into higher sales for its namesake product. Although Atlanta-based Coke has larger total beverage sales in India because it owns several non-cola drink brands, Pepsi's 4.5 percent of the soft drink market outshines Coke's 2.6 percent, according to Euromonitor. That's a notable exception to much of the rest of the world, where Coke's cola soundly beats its main rival.

What explains Pepsi's success in India? Coke pulled out of the market in 1977 after new government regulations forced it to partner with an Indian company and share the drink's secret formula. In contrast, Pepsi formed a joint venture in 1988 with two Indian companies and introduced products under the Lehar brand. (Lehar Pepsi was introduced in 1990.) Coke then re-entered the market in 1993 after Indian regulations were changed to permit foreign brands to operate without Indian partners.

Coke's time out of India cost it dearly. "Pepsi got here sooner, and got to India just as it was starting to engage with the West

and with Western products," said Lalita Desai, a linguist at Jadavpur University who studies how English words enter Indian languages. "And with no real international competition, 'Pepsi' became the catch-all for anything that was bottled, fizzy, and from abroad."

PepsiCo has also been very successful in promoting water conservation in India. Its Indian operation became the first of its global units (and probably the only one in the beverage industry) to conserve and replenish more water that it consumed in 2009. Its rival, Coca Cola, on the other hand, is facing a serious situation in India as it has been fined Rs 216 crore ($4.7 million) as compensation for groundwater pollution and depletion.

As of 2012, PepsiCo was experiencing a double-digit rate of growth in India and had staked out a position as the country's fourth largest consumer products company. The firm also has invested more than $1 billion in India, created direct and indirect employment to almost 200,000 people in the country, and has 13 company-owned bottling plants, according to its website.

Source: Srivastava, M. 2010. For India's Consumers, Pepsi Is the Real Thing. *Bloomberg Businessweek.* September 20–26: 26–27; Bhushan, R. 2010. Pepsi India Touches Eco Watershed, First Unit to Achieve Positive Water Balance. *www.indiatimes.com.* May 27: np; and *www.pepsicoindia.*

ISSUE FOR DEBATE

Samsung and the growing trend of "in-sourcing"

By Sarah Hudson and Asha Moore-Mangin

For current generations of young managers, outsourcing production or services to specialized suppliers and/or countries with cheaper labor is a no-brainer. Not only do you cut costs, but you improve employee motivation by concentrating on core value-adding activities. Everyone in the company is directly concerned with the same aims, and can follow a career to the top, unlike those companies that provide in-house services unconnected with the main activity, such as catering, or IT. It seems, however, that the tide is turning. In a recent survey, Deloitte has found that 48 percent of respondents say they have stopped outsourcing contracts early, and that 34 percent stated that they had taken the decision to bring the work back to be done by their own business units. Apple, for example, has recently "in-sourced" its iPad and iPhone A5 chip production to its Austin, Texas facility. Even more spectacularly, Samsung has now started producing many of the

(continued)

(continued)

key components of its Galaxy S4 smartphone in-house. The cost of producing the S4 was estimated to be about $237, substantially more than its competitors' the Apple iphone 5 at around $205 and Nokia's Lumia 900 costing $209. This analysis shows that in-sourcing can and does incur direct costs. Obviously, the attractions of in-sourcing lie elsewhere. The fact that a giant such as Samsung is in-sourcing production of components at higher costs is sending a very strong signal to the business world about a new bottom line.

Discussion Questions

1. What do you think are the reasons behind this small but growing trend for in-sourcing?
2. What dilemmas can you see for businesses in the decision to in-source services or production?

Sources: Hesseldahl, A. May 2013 "Inside Samsung Phone: Samsung Parts" allthingsd.com/20130508/samsung-galaxy-s4-costs-237-to-build-teardown-analysis-shows/; Anon, March 2013 "Is insourcing gaining ground?" www.abs-cbnnews.com/business/03/29/13/insourcing-gaining-ground; Wartzman, R. February, 2010 "Insourcing and outsourcing: the right mix" www.businessweek.com/managing/content/feb2010/ca2010024_507452.htm

Reflecting on Career Implications . . .

▣ **International Strategy:** Be aware of your organization's international strategy. What percentage of the total firm activity is international? What skills are needed to enhance your company's international efforts? How can you get more involved in your organization's international strategy? For your career, what conditions in your home country might cause you to seek careers abroad?

▣ **Outsourcing and Offshoring:** More and more organizations have resorted to outsourcing and offshoring in recent years. To what extent has your firm engaged in either? What activities in your organization can/should be outsourced or offshored? Be aware that you are competing in the global marketplace for employment and professional advancement. What is the likelihood that your own job may be outsourced or off-shored? In what ways can you enhance your talents, skills, and competencies to reduce the odds that your job may be offshored or outsourced?

▣ **International Career Opportunities:** Taking on overseas assignments in other countries can often provide a career boost. There are a number of ways in which you can improve your odds of being selected for an overseas assignment. Studying abroad for a semester or doing an overseas internship are two obvious strategies. Learning a foreign language can also greatly help. Anticipate how such opportunities will advance your short- and long-term career aspirations.

▣ **Management Risks:** Explore ways in which you can develop cultural sensitivity. Interacting with people from other cultures, foreign travel, reading about foreign countries, watching foreign movies, and similar activities can increase your cultural sensitivity. Identify ways in which your perceptions and behaviors have changed as a result of increased cultural sensitivity.

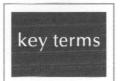

summary

We live in a highly interconnected global community where many of the best opportunities for growth and profitability lie beyond the boundaries of a company's home country. Along with the opportunities, of course, there are many risks associated with diversification into global markets.

The first section of the chapter addressed the factors that determine a nation's competitiveness in a particular industry. The framework was developed by Professor Michael Porter of Harvard University and was based on a four-year study that explored the competitive success of 10 leading trading nations. The four factors, collectively termed the "diamond of national advantage," were factor conditions, demand characteristics, related and supporting industries, and firm strategy, structure, and rivalry.

The discussion of Porter's "diamond" helped, in essence, to set the broader context for exploring competitive advantage at the firm level. In the second section, we discussed the primary motivations and the potential risks associated with international expansion. The primary motivations included increasing the size of the potential market for the firm's products and services, achieving economies of scale, extending the life cycle of the firm's products, and optimizing the location for every activity in the value chain. On the other hand, the key risks included political and economic risks, currency risks, and management risks. Management risks are the challenges associated with responding to the inevitable differences that exist across countries such as customs, culture, language, customer preferences, and distribution systems. We also addressed some of the managerial challenges and opportunities associated with offshoring and outsourcing.

Next, we addressed how firms can go about attaining competitive advantage in global markets. We began by discussing the two opposing forces—cost reduction and adaptation to local markets—that managers must contend with when entering global markets. The relative importance of these two factors plays a major part in determining which of the four basic types of strategies to select: international, global, multidomestic, or transnational. The chapter covered the benefits and risks associated with each type of strategy.

The final section discussed the four types of entry strategies that managers may undertake when entering international markets. The key trade-off in each of these strategies is the level of investment or risk versus the level of control. In order of their progressively greater investment/risk and control, the strategies range from exporting to licensing and franchising, to strategic alliances and joint ventures, to wholly owned subsidiaries. The relative benefits and risks associated with each of these strategies were addressed.

SUMMARY REVIEW QUESTIONS

1. What are some of the advantages and disadvantages associated with a firm's expansion into international markets?

2. What are the four factors described in Porter's diamond of national advantage? How do the four factors explain why some industries in a given country are more successful than others?

3. Explain the two opposing forces—cost reduction and adaptation to local markets—that firms must deal with when they go global.

4. There are four basic strategies—international, global, multidomestic, and transnational. What are the advantages and disadvantages associated with each?

5. What is the basis of Alan Rugman's argument that most multinationals are still more regional than global? What factors inhibit firms from becoming truly global?

6. Describe the basic entry strategies that firms have available when they enter international markets. What are the relative advantages and disadvantages of each?

key terms

globalization 212
diamond of national
   advantage 213
factor endowments (national
   advantage) 214
demand conditions (national
   advantage) 214
related and supporting
   industries (national
   advantage) 215
firm strategy structure
   and rivalry (national
   advantage) 215
multinational firms 217

arbitrage opportunities 217
reverse innovation 218
political risk 220
rule of law 220
economic risk 220
counterfeiting 220
currency risk 222
management risk 223
outsourcing 224
offshoring 224
international strategy 228
global strategy 228
multidomestic strategy 230
transnational strategy 232
regionalization 234
trading blocs 234
exporting 235
licensing 236
franchising 236
wholly owned subsidiary 238

experiential exercise

The United States is considered a world leader in the motion picture industry. Using Porter's diamond framework for national competitiveness, explain the success of this industry.

application questions & exercises

1. Data on the "competitiveness of nations" can be found at *www.imd.org/research/publications/wcy/index.cfm*. This website provides a ranking on

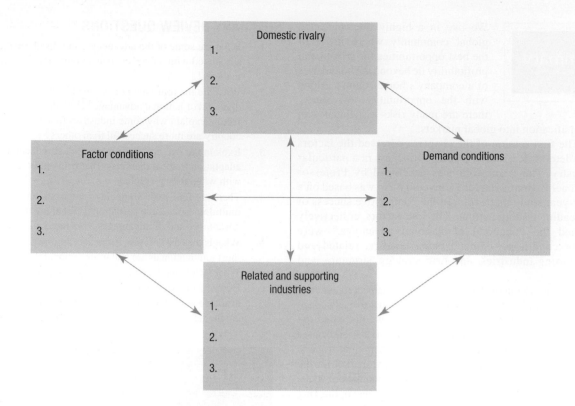

Domestic rivalry
1.
2.
3.

Factor conditions
1.
2.
3.

Demand conditions
1.
2.
3.

Related and supporting industries
1.
2.
3.

329 criteria for 59 countries. How might Porter's diamond of national advantage help to explain the rankings for some of these countries for certain industries that interest you?

2. The Internet has lowered the entry barriers for smaller firms that wish to diversify into international markets. Why is this so? Provide an example.

3. Many firms fail when they enter into strategic alliances with firms that link up with companies based in other countries. What are some reasons for this failure? Provide an example.

4. Many large U.S.–based management consulting companies such as McKinsey and Company and the BCG Group have been very successful in the international marketplace. How can Porter's diamond explain their success?

ethics questions

1. Over the past few decades, many American firms have relocated most or all of their operations from the United States to countries such as Mexico and China that pay lower wages. What are some of the ethical issues that such actions may raise?

2. Business practices and customs vary throughout the world. What are some of the ethical issues concerning payments that must be made in a foreign country to obtain business opportunities?

references

1. Williamson, P. & Raman, A. 2011. How China reset its global acquisition agenda. *Harvard Business Review,* April: 109-114; and SAIC under pressure to help save SsangYong. 2009. *Nytimes.com,* January 12: np.

2. For a recent discussion on globalization by one of international business's most respected authors, read Ohmae, K. 2005. *The next global stage: Challenges and opportunities in our borderless world.* Philadelphia: Wharton School Publishing.

3. Our discussion of globalization draws upon Engardio, P. & Belton, C. 2000. Global capitalism: Can it be made to work better? *BusinessWeek,* November 6: 72–98.

4. Sellers, P. 2005. Blowing in the wind. *Fortune,* July 25: 63.

5. Worldwide mobile phone growth expected to drop to 1.4% in 2012 despite continued growth of smartphones, according to IDC. 2012. *idc.com,* December 4: np.

6. A game of catch-up. 2011. *The Economist,* September 24: 3–6.

7. A recent discussion of the "bottom of the pyramid" is: Akula, V. 2008. Business basics at the bottom of the pyramid. *Harvard Business Review,* 86(6): 53–59.

8. Some insights into how winners are evolving in emerging markets are

addressed in: Ghemawat, P. & Hout, T. 2008. Tomorrow's global giants: Not the usual suspects. *Harvard Business Review,* 66(11): 80–88.

9. For another interesting discussion on a country perspective, refer to Makino, S. 1999. MITI Minister Kaora Yosano on reviving Japan's competitive advantages. *Academy of Management Executive,* 13(4): 8–28.

10. The following discussion draws heavily upon Porter, M. E. 1990. The competitive advantage of nations. *Harvard Business Review,* March–April: 73–93.

11. Landes, D. S. 1998. *The wealth and poverty of nations.* New York: W. W. Norton.

12. A recent study that investigates the relationship between international diversification and firm performance is Lu, J. W. & Beamish, P. W. 2004. International diversification and firm performance: The s-curve hypothesis. *Academy of Management Journal,* 47(4): 598–609.

13. Part of our discussion of the motivations and risks of international expansion draws upon Gregg, F. M. 1999. International strategy. In Helms, M. M. (Ed.), *Encyclopedia of management:* 434–438. Detroit: Gale Group.

14. Anthony, S. 2012. Singapore sessions. *Harvard Business Review.* 90(4): np.

15. Eyring, M. J., Johnson, M. W. & Nair, H. 2011. New business models in emerging markets. *Harvard Business Review,* 89 (1/2): 88–98.

16. Cieply, M. & Barnes, B. 2010. After rants, skepticism over Gibson bankability grows in non-U.S. markets. *International Herald Tribune,* July 23: 1.

17. Glazer, E. 2012. P&G unit bids goodbye to Cincinnati, hello to Asia. *wsj.com,* May 10: np.

18. This discussion draws upon Gupta, A. K. & Govindarajan, V. 2001. Converting global presence into global competitive advantage. *Academy of Management Executive,* 15(2): 45–56.

19. Stross, R. E. 1997. Mr. Gates builds his brain trust. *Fortune,* December 8: 84–98.

20. For a good summary of the benefits and risks of international expansion, refer to Bartlett, C. A. & Ghoshal, S. 1987. Managing across borders: New strategic responses. *Sloan Management Review,* 28(5): 45–53; and Brown, R. H. 1994. *Competing to win in a global economy.* Washington, DC: U.S. Department of Commerce.

21. For an interesting insight into rivalry in global markets, refer to MacMillan, I. C., van Putten, A. B., & McGrath, R. G. 2003. Global gamesmanship. *Harvard Business Review,* 81(5): 62–73.

22. It is important for firms to spread their foreign operations and outsourcing relationships with a broad, well-balanced mix of regions and countries to reduce risk and increase potential reward. For example, refer to Vestring, T., Rouse, T., & Reinert, U. 2005. Hedge your offshoring bets. *MIT Sloan Management Review,* 46(3): 27–29.

23. An interesting discussion of risks faced by Lukoil, Russia's largest oil firm is in: Gimbel, B. 2009. Russia's king of crude. *Fortune,* February 2: 88–92.

24. Some insights on how Africa has improved as a potential source of investment is in: Collier, P. & Warnholz, J-L. 2009. Now's the time to invest in Africa. *Harvard Business Review,* 87(2): 23.

25. For a discussion of some of the challenges associated with government corruption regarding entry strategies in foreign markets, read Rodriguez, P., Uhlenbruck, K., & Eden, L. 2005. Government corruption and entry strategies of multinationals. *Academy of Management Review,* 30(2): 383–396.

26. For a discussion of the political risks in China for United States companies, refer to Garten, J. E. 1998. Opening the doors for business in China. *Harvard Business Review,* 76(3): 167–175.

27. Insights on how forensic economics can be used to investigate crimes and wrongdoing are in: Fisman, R. 2009. The rise of forensic economics. *Harvard Business Review,* 87(2): 26.

28. Iosebashvili, I. 2012. Renault-Nissan buy into Russia's aged auto giant. *wsj.com,* May 3: np.

29. For an interesting perspective on the relationship between diversification and the development of a nation's institutional environment, read Chakrabarti, A., Singh, K., & Mahmood, I. 2007. Diversification and performance: Evidence from East Asian firms. *Strategic Management Journal,* 28(2): 101–120.

30. A study looking into corruption and foreign direct investment is: Brouthers, L. E., Gao, Y., & McNicol, J. P. 2008. *Strategic Management Journal,* 29(6): 673–680.

31. Gikkas, N. S. 1996. International licensing of intellectual property: The promise and the peril. *Journal of Technology Law & Policy,* 1(1): 1–26.

32. Hargreaves, S. 2012. Counterfeit goods becoming more dangerous. *Cnnmoney.com,* September 27: np.

33. Sandler, N. 2008. Israel: Attack of the super-shekel. *BusinessWeek,* Februrary 25: 38.

34. For an excellent theoretical discussion of how cultural factors can affect knowledge transfer across national boundaries, refer to Bhagat, R. S., Kedia, B. L., Harveston, P. D., & Triandis, H. C. 2002. Cultural variations in the cross-border transfer of organizational knowledge: An integrative framework. *Academy of Management Review,* 27(2): 204–221.

35. An interesting discussion on how local companies compete effectively with large multinationals is in: Bhatacharya, A. K. & Michael, D. C. 2008. *Harvard Business Review,* 66(3): 84–95.

36. To gain insights on the role of national and regional cultures on knowledge management models and frameworks, read Pauleen, D. J. & Murphy, P. 2005. In praise of cultural bias. *MIT Sloan Management Review,* 46(2): 21–22.

37. Berkowitz, E. N. 2000. *Marketing* (6th ed.). New York: McGraw-Hill.

38. Harvey, M. & Buckley, M. R. 2002. Assessing the "conventional wisdoms" of management for the 21st century organization. *Organization Dynamics,* 30 (4): 368–378.

39. World Trade Organization. *Annual Report 1998.* Geneva: World Trade Organization.

40. Lei, D. 2005. Outsourcing. In Hitt, M. A. & Ireland, R. D. (Eds.). *The Blackwell encyclopedia of management.* Entrepreneurship: 196–199. Malden, MA: Blackwell.

41. Future trends in offshoring are addressed in: Manning, S., Massini, S., & Lewin, A. Y. 2008. A dynamic perspective on next-generation offshoring: The global sourcing of science and engineering talent. *Academy of Management Perspectives,* 22(3): 35–54.

42. An interesting perspective on the controversial issue regarding the offshoring of airplane maintenance is in: Smith, G. & Bachman, J. 2008. Flying in for a tune-up overseas. *Business Week.* April 21: 26–27.

43. The discussion draws from Colvin, J. 2004. Think your job can't be sent to India? Just watch. *Fortune,* December 13: 80; Schwartz, N. D. 2004. Down and out in white collar America. *Fortune,* June 23: 321–325; Hagel, J. 2004. Outsourcing is not just about cost cutting. *The Wall Street Journal,* March 18: A3.

44. Porter, M. & Rivkin, J. 2012 Choosing the United States. *Harvard Business Review,* 90(3): 80–93; Bussey, J. 2012. U.S. manufacturing, defying naysayers. *wsj.com,* April 19: np; and Jean, S. & Alcott, K., 2013. Manufacturing jobs have slid steadily as work has moved offshore. *Dallas Morning News,* Jan 14: 1D.

45. Levitt, T. 1983. The globalization of markets. *Harvard Business Review,* 61(3): 92–102.

46. Our discussion of these assumptions draws upon Douglas, S. P. & Wind, Y. 1987. The myth of globalization. *Columbia Journal of World Business,* Winter: 19–29.

47. Ghoshal, S. 1987. Global strategy: An organizing framework. *Strategic Management Journal,* 8: 425–440.

48. Huber, P. 2009. Who pays for a cancer drug? *Forbes,* January 12: 72.

49. For insights on global branding, refer to Aaker, D. A. & Joachimsthaler, E. 1999. The lure of global branding. *Harvard Business Review,* 77(6): 137–146.

50. For an interesting perspective on how small firms can compete in their home markets, refer to Dawar & Frost, op. cit.: 119–129.

51. Hout, T., Porter, M. E., & Rudden, E. 1982. How global companies win out. *Harvard Business Review,* 60(5): 98–107.

52. Fryer, B. 2001. Tom Siebel of Siebel Systems: High tech the old-fashioned way. *Harvard Business Review,* 79(3): 118–130.

53. The risks that are discussed for the global, multidomestic, and transnational strategies draw upon Gupta & Govindarajan, op. cit.

54. Powell, B. 2012. Can Apple win over China? *Fortune,* October 29: 107-116.

55. A discussion on how McDonald's adapts its products to overseas markets is in: Gumbel, P. 2008. Big Mac's local flavor. *Fortune,* May 5: 115–121.

56. Einhorn, B. & Winter, C. 2012. Want some milk with your green tea Oreos? *Bloomberg Businessweek,* May 7: 25–26; Khosla, S. & Sawhney, M. 2012. Blank checks: Unleashing the potential of people and business. *Strategy-Business.com,* Autumn: np; and In China, brands more than symbolic. 2012. *Dallas Morning News,* November 27: 3D.

57. Prahalad, C. K. & Doz, Y. L. 1987. *The multinational mission: Balancing local demands and global vision.* New York: Free Press.

58. For an insightful discussion on knowledge flows in multinational corporations, refer to: Yang, Q., Mudambi, R., & Meyer, K. E. 2008. Conventional and reverse knowledge flows in multinational corporations. *Journal of Management,* 34(5): 882–902.

59. Kidd, J. B. & Teramoto, Y. 1995. The learning organization: The case of Japanese RHQs in Europe. *Management International Review,* 35 (Special Issue): 39–56.

60. Gupta, A. K. & Govindarajan, V. 2000. Knowledge flows within multinational corporations. *Strategic Management Journal,* 21(4): 473–496.

61. Wetlaufer, S. 2001. The business case against revolution: An interview with Nestlé's Peter Brabeck. *Harvard Business Review,* 79(2): 112–121.

62. Nobel, R. & Birkinshaw, J. 1998. Innovation in multinational corporations: Control and communication patterns in international R&D operations. *Strategic Management Journal,* 19(5): 461–478.

63. Chan, C. M., Makino, S., & Isobe, T. 2010. Does subnational region matter? Foreign affiliate performance in the United States and China. *Strategic Management Journal,* 31 (11): 1226–1243.

64. This section draws upon Ghemawat, P. 2005. Regional strategies for global leadership. *Harvard Business Review.* 84(12): 98–108; Ghemawat, P. 2006. Apocalypse now? *Harvard Business Review.* 84(12): 32; Ghemawat, P. 2001. Distance still matters: The hard reality of global expansion. *Harvard Business Review,* 79(8): 137–147; Peng, M.W. 2006. *Global strategy:* 387. Mason, OH: Thomson Southwestern; and Rugman, A. M. & Verbeke, A. 2004. A perspective on regional and global strategies of multinational enterprises. *Journal of International Business Studies.* 35: 3–18.

65. For a rigorous analysis of performance implications of entry strategies, refer to Zahra, S. A., Ireland, R. D., & Hitt, M. A. 2000. International expansion by new venture firms: International diversity, modes of entry, technological learning, and performance. *Academy of Management Journal,* 43(6): 925–950.

66. Li, J. T. 1995. Foreign entry and survival: The effects of strategic choices on performance in international markets. *Strategic Management Journal,* 16: 333–351.

67. For a discussion of how home-country environments can affect diversification strategies, refer to Wan, W. P. & Hoskisson, R. E. 2003. Home country environments, corporate diversification strategies, and firm performance. *Academy of Management Journal,* 46(1): 27–45.

68. Arnold, D. 2000. Seven rules of international distribution. *Harvard Business Review,* 78(6): 131–137.

69. Sharma, A. 1998. Mode of entry and ex-post performance. *Strategic Management Journal,* 19(9): 879–900.

70. This section draws upon Arnold, op. cit.: 131–137; and Berkowitz, op. cit.

71. Salomon, R. & Jin, B. 2010. Do leading or lagging firms learn more from exporting? *Strategic Management Journal,* 31(6): 1088–1113.

72. Kline, D. 2003. Strategic licensing. *MIT Sloan Management Review,* 44(3): 89–93.

73. Martin, J. 1999. Franchising in the Middle East. *Management Review.* June: 38–42.

74. Arnold, op. cit.; and Berkowitz, op. cit.

75. An in-depth case study of alliance dynamics is found in: Faems, D., Janssens, M., Madhok, A., & Van Looy, B. 2008. Toward an integrative perspective on alliance governance: Connecting contract design, trust dynamics, and contract application. *Academy of Management Journal,* 51(6): 1053–1078.

76. Knowledge transfer in international joint ventures is addressed in: Inkpen, A. 2008. Knowledge transfer and international joint ventures. *Strategic Management Journal,* 29(4): 447–453.

77. Wen, S. H. & Chuang, C.-M. 2010. To teach or to compete? A strategic dilemma of knowledge owners in

international alliances. *Asia Pacific Journal of Management,* 27(4): 697–726.

78. Manufacturer–supplier relationships can be very effective in global industries such as automobile manufacturing. Refer to Kotabe, M., Martin, X., & Domoto, H. 2003. Gaining from vertical partnerships: Knowledge transfer, relationship duration, and supplier performance improvement in the U.S. and Japanese automotive industries. *Strategic Management Journal,* 24(4): 293–316.

79. For a good discussion, refer to Merchant, H. & Schendel, D. 2000. How do international joint ventures create shareholder value? *Strategic Management Journal,* 21(7): 723–738.

80. This discussion draws upon Walters, B. A., Peters, S., & Dess, G. G. 1994. Strategic alliances and joint ventures: Making them work. *Business Horizons,* 37(4): 5–11.

81. Some insights on partnering in the global area are discussed in: MacCormack, A. & Forbath, T. 2008. *Harvard Business Review,* 66(1): 24, 26.

82. For a rigorous discussion of the importance of information access in international joint ventures, refer to Reuer, J. J. & Koza, M. P. 2000. Asymmetric information and joint venture performance: Theory and evidence for domestic and international joint ventures. *Strategic Management Journal,* 21(1): 81–88.

83. Dyer, J. H., Kale, P., & Singh, H. 2001. How to make strategic alliances work. *MIT Sloan Management Review,* 42(4): 37–43.

84. For a discussion of some of the challenges in managing subsidiaries, refer to O'Donnell, S. W. 2000. Managing foreign subsidiaries: Agents of headquarters, or an independent network? *Strategic Management Journal,* 21(5): 525–548.

85. Ricks, D. 2006. *Blunders in international business* (4th ed.). Malden, MA: Blackwell Publishing.

chapter 8

Entrepreneurial Strategy and Competitive Dynamics

After reading this chapter, you should have a good understanding of the following learning objectives:

LO8.1 The role of opportunities, resources, and entrepreneurs in successfully pursuing new ventures.

LO8.2 Three types of entry strategies—pioneering, imitative, and adaptive—commonly used to launch a new venture.

LO8.3 How the generic strategies of overall cost leadership, differentiation, and focus are used by new ventures and small businesses.

LO8.4 How competitive actions, such as the entry of new competitors into a marketplace, may launch a cycle of actions and reactions among close competitors.

LO8.5 The components of competitive dynamics analysis—new competitive action, threat analysis, motivation and capability to respond, types of competitive actions, and likelihood of competitive reaction.

Learning from Mistakes

Klout: the frustration of trying to get a start-up to reach its full potential

Joe Fernandez came up with the idea for Klout whilst recovering from jaw surgery. He had been using the social network sites to communicate and he realized how much information people provided about themselves on social media platforms. His idea was to measure the data and use it. Today, the start-up collects data for half a billion people from the different social media sites, it analyzes the information and it generates a score for everyone between 1 and 100, the higher the score the more influence the person has. Marketers then use this score to target their ads.

From the beginning, Fernandez's algorithm was controversial with people wanting to have higher scores than their friends and/or competitors. In 2011, when Justin Bieber got the perfect score of 100, ahead of President Obama, people started to doubt how the algorithm worked. Klout had to improve the algorithm and give a clear and detailed description of how these scores were measured. This seemed to calm the skeptics and venture capitalists including Microsoft poured $30 million into Klout. Then Klout disappeared from the headlines.

In 2007, Fred Wilson, a partner at Union Square Ventures and a firm that invested in Twitter, Foursquare, and Etsy,

compared a start-up to a teenager. He said that "Startups come out of the womb with the same bright shiny hopeful optimism as kids do . . . then they hit their ugly adolescent period, they start to doubt themselves, they get zits, they get distracted with other things . . . [To survive adolescence] you have to face the doubts, you have to admit that some of the things you've done were wrong, you often have to cut back the ambition and focus on the little things that are working. That takes leadership," Some start-ups like Twitter and Facebook handle their adolescence well; others have more difficulty finding their place in the business world. So when a start-up disappears from the headlines this means two things: either it has got its head down and is working or it has died.

As an adolescent, Klout seems to be having difficulties since it is two businesses in one. First of all a consumer business that filters and prioritizes people through their scores and second a product that can be used by company clients as a customer relationship tool to target influential people through "perks." So although Klout has enormous business potential, it needs to focus and decide which one to pursue first with the risk of frustrating some investors.

By Asha Moore-Mangin and Sarah Hudson

Discussion Questions

1. Do all start-ups have difficulties making it through adolescence?
2. Why do you think that Klout's CEO Fernandez says that the Klout Score is the company's "best asset and worst enemy"?

By offering a service that rated individuals' influence and impact in the Internet and social media, Klout seemed to have identified an attractive opportunity. But the start-up's faltering progress shows what can go wrong when—even though a good opportunity and the investment of Microsoft are brought together—a business opportunity can disappear as quickly as it appeared.

The Klout case illustrates how important it is for new entrepreneurial entrants—whether they are start-ups or incumbents—to think and act strategically. Even with a strong initial resource base, entrepreneurs are unlikely to succeed if their business ideas lack focus or the execution of the strategy falls short.

In this chapter we address entrepreneurial strategies. The previous three chapters have focused primarily on the business-level, corporate-level, and international strategies of incumbent firms. Here we ask: What about the strategies of those entering into a market or industry for the first time? Whether it's a fast-growing start-up such as Klout or an existing company seeking growth opportunities, new entrants need effective strategies.

Companies wishing to launch new ventures must also be aware that, consistent with the five forces model in Chapter 2, new entrants are a threat to existing firms in an industry. Entry into a new market arena is intensely competitive from the perspective of incumbents in that arena. Therefore, new entrants can nearly always expect a competitive response from other companies in the industry it is entering. Knowledge of the competitive dynamics that are at work in the business environment is an aspect of entrepreneurial new entry that will be addressed later in this chapter.

Before moving on, it is important to highlight the role that entrepreneurial start-ups and small businesses play in entrepreneurial value creation. Small businesses, those defined as having 500 employees or fewer, create about 65 percent of all new jobs in the United States and also generate 13 times as many new patents per employee as larger firms.[3]

Recognizing Entrepreneurial Opportunities

entrepreneurship
the creation of new value by an existing organization or new venture that involves the assumption of risk.

Defined broadly, **entrepreneurship** refers to new value creation. Even though entrepreneurial activity is usually associated with start-up companies, new value can be created in many different contexts including:

- Start-up ventures
- Major corporations
- Family-owned businesses
- Non-profit organizations
- Established institutions

LO8.1

The role of opportunities, resources, and entrepreneurs in successfully pursuing new ventures.

For an entrepreneurial venture to create new value, three factors must be present—an entrepreneurial opportunity, the resources to pursue the opportunity, and an entrepreneur or entrepreneurial team willing and able to undertake the opportunity.[4] The entrepreneurial strategy that an organization uses will depend on these three factors. Thus, beyond merely identifying a venture concept, the opportunity recognition process also involves organizing the key people and resources that are needed to go forward. Exhibit 8.1 depicts the three factors that are needed to successfully proceed—opportunity, resources, and entrepreneur(s). In the sections that follow, we address each of these factors.

Entrepreneurial Opportunities

The starting point for any new venture is the presence of an entrepreneurial opportunity. Where do opportunities come from? For new business start-ups, opportunities come from many sources—current or past work experiences, hobbies that grow into businesses or lead to inventions, suggestions by friends or family, or a chance event that makes an entrepreneur aware of an unmet need. Terry Tietzen, founder and CEO of Edatanetworks puts it this way, "You get ideas through watching the world and through relationships. You get ideas from looking down the road."[5] For established firms, new business opportunities come from the needs of existing customers, suggestions by suppliers, or technological developments that lead to new advances.[6] For all firms, there is a major, overarching factor behind all viable opportunities that emerge in the business landscape: change. Change creates opportunities. Entrepreneurial firms make the most of changes brought about by new technology, sociocultural trends, and shifts in consumer demand.

EXHIBIT 8.1 Opportunity Analysis Framework

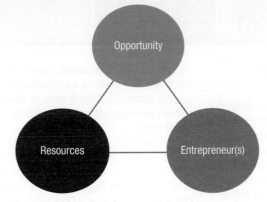

Sources: Based on Timmons, J. A. & Spinelli, S. 2004. *New Venture Creation* (6th ed.). New York: McGraw-Hill/Irwin; and Bygrave, W. D. 1997. The Entrepreneurial Process. In W. D. Bygrave (Ed.), *The Portable MBA in Entrepreneurship* (2nd ed.). New York: Wiley.

How do changes in the external environment lead to new business creation? They spark creative new ideas and innovation. Businesspeople often have ideas for entrepreneurial ventures. However, not all such ideas are good ideas—that is, viable business opportunities. To determine which ideas are strong enough to become new ventures, entrepreneurs must go through a process of identifying, selecting, and developing potential opportunities. This is the process of **opportunity recognition.**[7]

Opportunity recognition refers to more than just the "Eureka!" feeling that people sometimes experience at the moment they identify a new idea. Although such insights are often very important, the opportunity recognition process involves two phases of activity—discovery and evaluation—that lead to viable new venture opportunities.[8]

The discovery phase refers to the process of becoming aware of a new business concept.[9] Many entrepreneurs report that their idea for a new venture occurred to them in an instant, as a sort of "Aha!" experience—that is, they had some insight or epiphany, often based on their prior knowledge, that gave them an idea for a new business. The discovery of new opportunities is often spontaneous and unexpected. For example, Howard Schultz, CEO of Starbucks, was in Milan, Italy, when he suddenly realized that the coffee-and-conversation café model that was common in Europe would work in the U.S. as well. According to Schultz, he didn't need to do research to find out if Americans would pay $3 for a cup of coffee—he just *knew.* Starbucks was just a small business at the time but Schultz began literally shaking with excitement about growing it into a bigger business.[10] Strategy Spotlight 8.1 tells how one entrepreneur combined her heritage with the desire for a healthy lifestyle to build a successful food business.

Opportunity discovery also may occur as the result of a deliberate search for new venture opportunities or creative solutions to business problems. Viable opportunities often emerge only after a concerted effort. It is very similar to a creative process, which may be unstructured and "chaotic" at first but eventually leads to a practical solution or business innovation. To stimulate the discovery of new opportunities, companies often encourage creativity, out-of-the-box thinking, and brainstorming.

Opportunity evaluation, which occurs after an opportunity has been identified, involves analyzing an opportunity to determine whether it is viable and strong enough to be developed into a full-fledged new venture. Ideas developed by new-product groups or in brainstorming sessions are tested by various methods, including talking to potential target customers and discussing operational requirements with production or logistics managers. A technique known as feasibility analysis is used to evaluate these and other critical

opportunity recognition
the process of discovering and evaluating changes in the business environment, such as a new technology, sociocultural trends, or shifts in consumer demand, that can be exploited.

HOW AN ENTREPRENEUR'S BACKGROUND DRIVES HER VISION

Susana Cabrera has a rich background and a full plate. Growing up in Venezuela, she learned about what it means to run your own business by observing her entrepreneur father. Trained as an attorney, she moved to the United States. As a wife and mother, she was interested in maintaining a healthy lifestyle and offering her children healthy food and was appalled by the high sodium content, fat level, and preservatives in major Latin American food brands. Finally, she had a desire to give back to her adopted country.

Her background and interests led her to launch Delicious Bite, a company that makes Latin American appetizers and meals. Drawing on her background and interests, she set the vision of the firm to be the leading provider of easy to prepare, healthy, and authentic Hispanic foods. She emphasizes the freshness of inputs,

no transfats in her ingredients, and no preservatives. In her words, she wants to provide "a treat without the guilt." To support her adopted home, she also decided to source her inputs from U.S. growers and suppliers and manufacture all of her products in the United States.

She launched the firm in 2005 and outgrew her initial 1300 square foot facility and moved into a 17,000 square foot building in 2009. She now has over 15 employees and sells her products through 700 stores in 20 states. The success of Delicious Bite led CNNMoney to name her a "kick butt entrepreneur" in 2012.

Cabrera's story shows that entrepreneurial vision often arises out of an individual's experience and can encompass both a business idea and a vehicle to provide a social benefit.

Sources: Anonymous. 2012. Be a kick butt entrepreneur. *Cnnmoney.com*, January 26: np; *http://www.youtube.com/watch?v=zrN2ENqpmTs*; and *www.delicious-bite.com*.

---

success factors. This type of analysis often leads to the decision that a new venture project should be discontinued. If the venture concept continues to seem viable, a more formal business plan may be developed.[11]

Among the most important factors to evaluate is the market potential for the product or service. Established firms tend to operate in established markets. They have to adjust to market trends and to shifts in consumer demand, of course, but they usually have a customer base for which they are already filling a marketplace need. New ventures, in contrast, must first determine whether a market exists for the product or service they are contemplating. Thus, a critical element of opportunity recognition is assessing to what extent the opportunity is viable *in the marketplace.*

For an opportunity to be viable, it needs to have four qualities.[12]

- *Attractive.* The opportunity must be attractive in the marketplace; that is, there must be market demand for the new product or service.
- *Achievable.* The opportunity must be practical and physically possible.
- *Durable.* The opportunity must be attractive long enough for the development and deployment to be successful; that is, the window of opportunity must be open long enough for it to be worthwhile.
- *Value creating.* The opportunity must be potentially profitable; that is, the benefits must surpass the cost of development by a significant margin.

If a new business concept meets these criteria, two other factors must be considered before the opportunity is launched as a business: the resources available to undertake it, and the characteristics of the entrepreneur(s) pursuing it. In the next section, we address the issue of entrepreneurial resources; following that, we address the importance of entrepreneurial leaders and teams. But first, consider the opportunities that have been created by the recent surge in interest in environmental sustainability. Strategy Spotlight 8.2 discusses how an entrepreneurial firm is working to develop and sell a line of biodegradable plastics.

GREEN PLASTICS

Despite an increasing emphasis on recycling, only 7 percent of the plastic used by Americans is currently recycled. The remainder goes into landfills or ends up in lakes and oceans, where the plastic poisons fish that consume it. One vivid place to find the consequences of plastic use is in the middle of the ocean over a thousand miles off the California coast. It is the Great Pacific Garbage Patch, a collection of mostly plastic trash that has been estimated to be up to twice the size of France, formed as ocean currents pull plastic trash from coastal areas.

How do we reduce our reliance on nonbiodegradable plastics that clog our landfills and oceans? Metabolix, a small firm based in Cambridge, Massachusetts, is stepping up with an innovative solution—environmentally friendly biodegradable plastics. Plastic is typically made from petroleum, and the products made from petroleum-based plastic can take hundreds of years to decompose in landfills. Metabolix has developed a process to make plastics out of plant materials—the first 100 percent bioplastic product that is both biodegradable and durable enough to stand up to heat and use. The firm uses a genetically engineered microbe that consumes the sugar in corn, producing a plastic molecule called PHA. Plastic products made from PHA will decompose in water or soil in a few months.

The challenge for Metabolix is to build a viable market position in the short term and work to make the product widely economically feasible in the long run. For now, Metabolix is aiming at markets that especially benefit from the biodegradable properties of their product and are willing to absorb the higher cost relative to petroleum-based plastics. Their core focus for now is organic waste handling. Specifically, they are striving to sell to municipalities that separate organic waste and send it to composting facilities. This market finds Mirel, Metabolix's product, valuable since it is so pure that consumers can toss them into their compost piles and still use the resulting mulch in vegetable gardens or around their fruit trees.

In the long run, Metabolix is aiming to improve the cost efficiency of their product to be able to compete with other plastics by developing genetically engineered nonfood crops, such as switchgrass and oilseeds, that will produce the PHA polymer within the plant and require less processing to extract into usable plastics. If they are successful, they will reduce the need for petroleum and landfill space and, hopefully, begin to reduce the size of the Great Pacific Garbage Patch.

Sources: Dumaine, B. 2010. Feel-good plastic. *Fortune*, May 3: 36; Ziegler, J. 2009. Metabolix defies skeptics with plastic from plants. *Bloomberg*, May 7: np; Anonymous. 2009. Drowning in plastic. The Great Pacific Garbage Patch is twice the size of France. *telegraph.co.uk*, April 24: np; Bomgardner, M. 2012. Metabolix: The post-ADM update. *Cenblog.org*, July 10: np; Verespej, M. 2012. Metabolix finds new partner to make biopolymer Mirel. *Plasticnews.com*, July 27: np.

Entrepreneurial Resources

As Exhibit 8.1 indicates, resources are an essential component of a successful entrepreneurial launch. For start-ups, the most important resource is usually money because a new firm typically has to expend substantial sums just to start the business. However, financial resources are not the only kind of resource a new venture needs. Human capital and social capital are also important. Many firms also rely on government resources to help them thrive.[13]

Financial Resources Hand-in-hand with the importance of markets (and marketing) to new-venture creation, entrepreneurial firms must also have financing. In fact, the level of available financing is often a strong determinant of how the business is launched and its eventual success. Cash finances are, of course, highly important. But access to capital, such as a line of credit or favorable payment terms with a supplier, can also help a new venture succeed.

The types of financial resources that may be needed depend on two factors: the stage of venture development and the scale of the venture.[14] Entrepreneurial firms that are starting from scratch—start-ups—are at the earliest stage of development. Most start-ups also begin on a relatively small scale. The funding available to young and small firms tends to be quite limited. In fact, the majority of new firms are low-budget start-ups launched with personal savings and the contributions of family and friends.[15] Among firms included in the *Entrepreneur* list of the 100 fastest-growing new businesses in a recent year, 61 percent reported that their start-up funds came from personal savings.[16]

angel investors private individuals who provide equity investments for seed capital during the early stages of a new venture.

venture capitalists companies organized to place their investors' finds in lucrative business opportunities.

Although bank financing, public financing, and venture capital are important sources of small business finance, these types of financial support are typically available only after a company has started to conduct business and generate sales. Even **angel investors**—private individuals who provide equity investments for seed capital during the early stages of a new venture—favor companies that already have a winning business model and dominance in a market niche.[17] According to Cal Simmons, coauthor of *Every Business Needs an Angel,* "I would much rather talk to an entrepreneur who has already put his money and his effort into proving the concept."[18]

Thus, while the press commonly talks about the role of **venture capitalists** and angel investors in start-up firms, the majority of external funding for young and small firms comes from informal sources such as family and friends. Based on a Kaufmann Foundation survey of entrepreneurial firms, Exhibit 8.2 identifies the source of funding used by start-up businesses and by ongoing firms that are five years old. The survey shows that most start-up funding, about 70 percent, comes from either equity investments by the entrepreneur and the entrepreneur's family and friends or personal loans taken out by the entrepreneur.

Once a venture has established itself as a going concern, other sources of financing become readily available. Banks, for example, are more likely to provide later-stage financing to companies with a track record of sales or other cash-generating activity. According to the Kauffman Foundation study, after five years of operation, the largest source of funding is from loans taken out by the business.

At both stages, 5 percent or less of the funding comes from outside investors, such as angel investors or venture capitalists. In fact, few firms ever receive venture capital investments—only 7 of 2606 firms in the Kaufmann study received money from outside investors. But when they do, these firms receive a substantial level of investment—over $1 million on average in the survey—because they tend to be the firms that are the most innovative and have the greatest growth potential. These start-ups typically involve large capital investments or extensive development costs—such as manufacturing or engineering firms trying to commercialize an innovative product—and have high cash requirements soon after they are founded. Since these investments are typically well beyond the capability of the entrepreneur or even a local bank to fund, entrepreneurs running these firms turn to the venture capital market. Other firms turn to venture capitalists when they are on the brink of rapid growth.

EXHIBIT 8.2
Sources of Capital for Start-Up Firms

	Capital Invested in Their First Year	Percentage of Capital Invested in Their First Year	Capital Invested in Their Fifth Year	Percentage of Capital Invested in Their Fifth Year
Insider equity	$33,034	41.1	$13,914	17.9
Investor equity	$ 4,108	5.1	$ 3,108	4.0
Personal debt of owners	$23,353	29.1	$21,754	28.0
Business debt	$19,867	24.7	$39,009	50.1
Total average capital invested	$80,362		$77,785	

Source: From Robb, A., Reedy, E. J., Ballou, J., DesRoches, D., Potter, F., & Zhao, A. 2010. An Overview of the Kauffman Firm Survey. Reproduced with permission from the Ewing Marion Kauffman Foundation.

Venture capital is a form of private equity financing through which entrepreneurs raise money by selling shares in the new venture. In contrast to angel investors, who invest their own money, venture capital companies are organized to place the funds of private investors into lucrative business opportunities. Venture capitalists nearly always have high performance expectations from the companies they invest in, but they also provide important managerial advice and links to key contacts in an industry.[19]

In recent years, a new source of funding, **crowdfunding,** has emerged as a means for start-ups to amass significant pools of capital.[20] In these peer-to-peer investment systems, individuals striving to grow their business post their business ideas on a crowdfunding website. Potential investors who go to the site evaluate the proposals listed and decide which, if any, to fund. Typically, no individual makes a very sizable funding allotment. Most investors contribute up to a few hundred dollars to any investment, but the power of the crowd is at work. If a few thousand investors sign up for a venture, it can potentially raise over a million dollars.

crowdfunding funding a venture by pooling small investments from a large number of investors, often raised on the internet.

The crowdfunding market has taken off since the term was first coined in 2006. There are over 500 crowdfunding websites, and the total value of crowdfunding investments approached $3 billion in 2012. Some crowdfunding websites allow investors to own actual equity in the firms they fund. Others, such as Kickstarter, don't offer investors equity. Instead, they get a reward from the entrepreneurial firm. For example, Mystery Brewing Company gave its investors logoed bottle openers, tulip-shaped beer glasses, T-shirts, posters, and home-brew recipes.

To foster growth and establish stability in this market, the United States Congress included guidelines and rules for this market as part of the Jumpstart Our Business Startups (JOBS) Act, which was passed into law in April 2012. This act allows start-ups to go to the crowdfunding market without going through the expense of filing with the Securities and Exchange Commission. If a firm is trying to raise $100,000 or less, all the entrepreneur needs to do is attest to the validity of the firm's financial statements and provide his or her tax returns. Firms raising $100,000 to $500,000 have to have their financial statements reviewed by a CPA. Financial statements have to be fully audited if the firm is trying to raise over $500,000.

While crowdfunding offers a new avenue for corporations to raise funding, there are some potential downsides. First, the crowdfunding sites take a slice of the funds raised—typically 4 to 9 percent. Second, while crowdfunding offers a marketplace in which to raise funds, it also puts additional pressure on entrepreneurs. The social-network savvy investors who fund these ventures are quick to comment on their social media websites if the firm misses deadlines or falls short of their revenue projections. Finally, entrepreneurs can struggle with how much information to share about their business ideas. They want to share enough information without releasing critical information that competitors trolling these sites can benefit from. They also may be concerned about posting their financials, since these statements give their suppliers and customers access to sensitive information about margins and earnings.

There are also some concerns that the loose rules included in the JOBS Act could lead to significant fraud by firms soliciting investment. According to Stephen Goodman, an attorney with Pryor Cashman LLP, "The SEC has been extremely skeptical of this [crowdfunding] process." Others have faith in the wisdom of the crowd to catch fraud. They point to the experience with Little Monster Productions, a video game developer. Little Monsters was set to raise funds on Kickstarter, but the fund call was closed by Kickstarter when potential investors noticed and commented that Little Monsters had stolen some of the images they were using in their game from another game site. Strategy Spotlight 8.3 provides a checklist for investors considering participating in a crowdfunding effort. Regardless of their source, financial resources are essential for entrepreneurial ventures.[21]

EVALUATING CROWDFUNDING OPPORTUNITIES

Because the requirements for firms raising funds through crowdfunding are lax, investors need to do their homework. Here are some simple recommendations to keep from getting burned.

- **Financial statements**—Be sure to closely review the corporate tax returns that firms are required to post. Better yet, have your accountant review them to see if anything looks fishy.

- **Licenses and registrations**—You should check to see if the company has current licenses and registrations needed to operate in their chosen industry. This can often be done with online checks with the Secretary of State's office or the state's corporation department. Sometimes, it will take a phone call or two. This provides a simple check to see if the company is legitimate.

- **Litigation**—Check to see if the company has been sued. You can search online at the free site justia.com and the law-oriented information sites Westlaw and Lexis. Be sure to check under current and former names of the firm and its principals (top managers).

- **Better Business Bureau**—Check the firm's BBB report. Does the firm appear to exist? What is the grade the BBB gives them? Are they BBB members? All of these give insight into the firm's current operations and their customer relations.

- **Employment and educational history**—This is a bit tricky because of privacy issues, but you can typically contact colleges listed on the filing forms and inquire if the principals of the firm attended and graduated from the schools they list. You can also search employment histories on the websites of the companies the principals used to work at as well as social network sites, such as LinkedIn and Facebook.

- **Required disclosures**—Read all of the documentation carefully. This includes the shareholder rights statement. This statement will provide information on how much of a stake in the firm you get and how this will be diluted by future offerings. Also, read statements on the company's competition and risks it faces.

Sources: Wasik, J. 2012. The brilliance (and madness) of crowdfunding. *Forbes*, June 25: 144–146; Burke, A. 2012. Crowdfunding set to explode with passage of Entrepreneur Access to Capital Act. *Forbes.com*, February 29: np.

Human Capital Bankers, venture capitalists, and angel investors agree that the most important asset an entrepreneurial firm can have is strong and skilled management.[22] According to Stephen Gaal, founding member of Walnut Venture Associates, venture investors do not invest in businesses; instead "We invest in people . . . very smart people with very high integrity." Managers need to have a strong base of experience and extensive domain knowledge, as well as an ability to make rapid decisions and change direction as shifting circumstances may require. In the case of start-ups, more is better. New ventures that are started by teams of three, four, or five entrepreneurs are more likely to succeed in the long run than are ventures launched by "lone wolf" entrepreneurs.[23]

Social Capital New ventures founded by entrepreneurs who have extensive social contacts are more likely to succeed than are ventures started without the support of a social network.[24] Even though a venture may be new, if the founders have contacts who will vouch for them, they gain exposure and build legitimacy faster.[25] This support can come from several sources: prior jobs, industry organizations, and local business groups such as the chamber of commerce. These contacts can all contribute to a growing network that provides support for the entrepreneurial firm. Janina Pawlowski, co-founder of the online lending company E-Loan, attributes part of her success to the strong advisors she persuaded to serve on her board of directors, including Tim Koogle, former CEO of Yahoo![26]

Strategic alliances represent a type of social capital that can be especially important to young and small firms.[27] Strategic alliances can provide a key avenue for growth by entrepreneurial firms.[28] By partnering with other companies, young or small firms can expand or give the appearance of entering numerous markets or handling a range of operations. According to the National Federation of Independent Business (NFIB), nearly two-thirds of small businesses currently hold or have held some type of alliance. Here are a few types of alliances that have been used to extend or strengthen entrepreneurial firms:

- **Technology alliances**—Tech-savvy entrepreneurial firms often benefit from forming alliances with older incumbents. The alliance allows the larger firm to enhance its technological capabilities and expands the revenue and reach of the smaller firm.
- **Manufacturing alliances**—The use of outsourcing and other manufacturing alliances by small firms has grown dramatically in recent years. Internet-enabled capabilities such as collaborating online about delivery and design specifications have greatly simplified doing business, even with foreign manufacturers.
- **Retail alliances**—Licensing agreements allow one company to sell the products and services of another in different markets, including overseas. Specialty products—the types sometimes made by entrepreneurial firms—often seem more exotic when sold in another country.

Although such alliances often sound good, there are also potential pitfalls. Lack of oversight and control is one danger of partnering with foreign firms. Problems with product quality, timely delivery, and receiving payments can also sour an alliance relationship if it is not carefully managed. With technology alliances, there is a risk that big firms may take advantage of the technological know-how of their entrepreneurial partners. However, even with these potential problems, strategic alliances provide a good means for entrepreneurial firms to develop and grow.

Government Resources   In the U.S., the federal government provides support for entrepreneurial firms in two key arenas—financing and government contracting. The Small Business Administration (SBA) has several loan guarantee programs designed to support the growth and development of entrepreneurial firms. The government itself does not typically lend money but underwrites loans made by banks to small businesses, thus reducing the risk associated with lending to firms with unproven records. The SBA also offers training, counseling, and support services through its local offices and Small Business Development Centers.[29] State and local governments also have hundreds of programs to provide funding, contracts, and other support for new ventures and small businesses. These programs are often designed to grow the economy of a region.

Another key area of support is in government contracting. Programs sponsored by the SBA and other government agencies ensure that small businesses have the opportunity to bid on contracts to provide goods and services to the government. Although working with the government sometimes has its drawbacks in terms of issues of regulation and time-consuming decision making, programs to support small businesses and entrepreneurial activity constitute an important resource for entrepreneurial firms.

Entrepreneurial Leadership

Whether a venture is launched by an individual entrepreneur or an entrepreneurial team, effective leadership is needed. Launching a new venture requires a special kind of leadership.[30] It involves courage, belief in one's convictions, and the energy to work hard even in difficult circumstances. Yet these are the very challenges that motivate most business owners. Entrepreneurs put themselves to the test and get their satisfaction from acting independently, overcoming obstacles, and thriving financially. To do so, they must embody

entrepreneurial leadership
leadership appropriate for new ventures that requires courage, belief in ones convictions, and the energy to work hard even in difficult circumstances; and embody vision, dedication and drive, and commit to excellence.

three characteristics of leadership—vision, dedication and drive, and commitment to excellence—and pass these on to all those who work with them:

- *Vision.* This may be an entrepreneur's most important asset. Entrepreneurs envision realities that do not yet exist. But without a vision, most entrepreneurs would never even get their venture off the ground. With vision, entrepreneurs are able to exercise a kind of transformational leadership that creates something new and, in some way, changes the world. Just having a vision, however, is not enough. To develop support, get financial backing, and attract employees, entrepreneurial leaders must share their vision with others.

- *Dedication and drive.* Dedication and drive are reflected in hard work. Drive involves internal motivation; dedication calls for an intellectual commitment that keeps an entrepreneur going even in the face of bad news or poor luck. They both require patience, stamina, and a willingness to work long hours. However, a business built on the heroic efforts of one person may suffer in the long run. That's why the dedicated entrepreneur's enthusiasm is also important—like a magnet, it attracts others to the business to help with the work.[31]

- *Commitment to excellence.* Excellence requires entrepreneurs to commit to knowing the customer, providing quality goods and services, paying attention to details, and continuously learning. Entrepreneurs who achieve excellence are sensitive to how these factors work together. However, entrepreneurs may flounder if they think they are the only ones who can create excellent results. The most successful, by contrast, often report that they owe their success to hiring people smarter than themselves.

In his book *Good to Great,* Jim Collins makes another important point about entrepreneurial leadership: Ventures built on the charisma of a single person may have trouble growing "from good to great" once that person leaves.[32] Thus, the leadership that is needed to build a great organization is usually exercised by a team of dedicated people working together rather than a single leader. Another aspect of this team approach is attracting team members who fit with the company's culture, goals, and work ethic. Thus, for a venture's leadership to be a valuable resource and not a liability it must be cohesive in its vision, drive and dedication, and commitment to excellence.

Once an opportunity has been recognized, and an entrepreneurial team and resources have been assembled, a new venture must craft a strategy. Prior chapters have addressed the strategies of incumbent firms. In the next section, we highlight the types of strategies and strategic considerations faced by new entrants.

Entrepreneurial Strategy

entrepreneurial strategy
a strategy that enables a skilled and dedicated entrepreneur, with a viable opportunity and access to sufficient resources, to successfully launch a new venture.

Successfully creating new ventures requires several ingredients. As indicated in Exhibit 8.1, three factors are necessary—a viable opportunity, sufficient resources, and a skilled and dedicated entrepreneur or entrepreneurial team. Once these elements are in place, the new venture needs a strategy. In this section, we consider several different strategic factors that are unique to new ventures and also how the generic strategies introduced in Chapter 5 can be applied to entrepreneurial firms. We also indicate how combination strategies might benefit entrepreneurial firms and address the potential pitfalls associated with launching new venture strategies.

To be successful, new ventures must evaluate industry conditions, the competitive environment, and market opportunities in order to position themselves strategically. However, a traditional strategic analysis may have to be altered somewhat to fit the entrepreneurial situation. For example, five-forces analysis (as discussed in Chapter 2) is typically used by established firms. It can also be applied to the analysis of new ventures to assess the impact of industry and competitive forces. But you may ask: How does a new entrant evaluate the threat of other new entrants?

First, the new entrant needs to examine barriers to entry. If the barriers are too high, the potential entrant may decide not to enter or to gather more resources before attempting to do so. Compared to an older firm with an established reputation and available resources, the barriers to entry may be insurmountable for an entrepreneurial start-up. Therefore, understanding the force of these barriers is critical in making a decision to launch.

A second factor that may be especially important to a young venture is the threat of retaliation by incumbents. In many cases, entrepreneurial ventures *are* the new entrants that pose a threat to incumbent firms. Therefore, in applying the five-forces model to new ventures, the threat of retaliation by established firms needs to be considered.

Part of any decision about what opportunity to pursue is a consideration of how a new entrant will actually enter a new market. The concept of entry strategies provides a useful means of addressing the types of choices that new ventures have.

Entry Strategies

LO8.2

Three types of entry strategies—pioneering, imitative, and adaptive—commonly used to launch a new venture.

One of the most challenging aspects of launching a new venture is finding a way to begin doing business that quickly generates cash flow, builds credibility, attracts good employees, and overcomes the liability of newness. The idea of an entry strategy or "entry wedge" describes several approaches that firms may take to get a foothold in a market.[33] Several factors will affect this decision.

- Is the product/service high-tech or low-tech?
- What resources are available for the initial launch?
- What are the industry and competitive conditions?
- What is the overall market potential?
- Does the venture founder prefer to control the business or to grow it?

In some respects, any type of entry into a market for the first time may be considered entrepreneurial. But the entry strategy will vary depending on how risky and innovative the new business concept is.[34] New-entry strategies typically fall into one of three categories—pioneering new entry, imitative new entry, or adaptive new entry.[35]

Pioneering New Entry   New entrants with a radical new product or highly innovative service may change the way business is conducted in an industry. This kind of breakthrough—creating new ways to solve old problems or meeting customers' needs in a unique new way—is referred to as a **pioneering new entry.** If the product or service is unique enough, a pioneering new entrant may actually have little direct competition. The first personal computer was a pioneering product; there had never been anything quite like it and it revolutionized computing. The first Internet browser provided a type of pioneering service. These breakthroughs created whole new industries and changed the competitive landscape. And breakthrough innovations continue to inspire pioneering entrepreneurial efforts. Strategy Spotlight 8.4 discusses Pandora, a firm that pioneered a new way to broadcast music.

pioneering new entry
a firm's entry into an industry with a radical new product or highly innovative service that changes the way business is conducted.

The pitfalls associated with a pioneering new entry are numerous. For one thing, there is a strong risk that the product or service will not be accepted by consumers. The history of entrepreneurship is littered with new ideas that never got off the launching pad. Take, for example, Smell-O-Vision, an invention designed to pump odors into movie theatres from the projection room at preestablished moments in a film. It was tried only once (for the film *Scent of a Mystery*) before it was declared a major flop. Innovative? Definitely. But hardly a good idea at the time.[36]

A pioneering new entry is disruptive to the status quo of an industry. It is likely based on a technological breakthrough. If it is successful, other competitors will rush in to copy it. This can create issues of sustainability for an entrepreneurial firm, especially if a larger

PANDORA ROCKS THE MUSIC BUSINESS

Whether the music was transmitted over FM radio signals, streamed over the web, or from a satellite, the musical choices radio listeners had were fairly standardized until Pandora arrived. Radio stations determined their play list based on a combination of interest evident in music sales and listener surveys along with the format of their stations. Listeners in a given market could decide if they wanted to listen to a top 40, adult contemporary, country, or classic rock station, but they couldn't custom design a station to meet their eclectic musical tastes.

Tim Westergren completely changed the radio business when he created Pandora. In 1999 he developed the Music Genome Project—a system that analyzes music for its underlying traits, including melody, rhythm, lyrics, instrumentation, and many other traits. Each song is measured on approximately 400 musical "genes" and given a vector or list of attributes. The vectors of multiple songs can be compared to assess the "distance" between the two songs. Using the Music Genome Project, Westergren launched Pandora in 2000. Users input bands or songs they like, and Pandora creates a customized station that plays music that meets the users' tastes. Users can then tweak the station by giving input on whether or not they like the songs Pandora plays for them.

Pandora radically changes the radio business in multiple ways. First, users create their own customized stations. Second, users can access their personal radio stations wherever they go through any Internet-connected device. Third, the playing of songs is driven by their musical traits, not how popular a band is. If an unsigned garage band has musical traits similar to Pearl Jam, their music will get play on a user's Pearl Jam station. This offers great exposure to aspiring musicians not available on commercial radio. It also offers an avenue for record labels to get exposure for newly signed bands that don't yet get air play on traditional radio.

Pandora has grown in 10 years from a bold new idea to become the largest "radio" station in the world, with 150 million registered users. Pandora faces a number of competitors, such as Spotify, Rdio, and Songza, but it continues to grow and change the music business.

Sources: Copeland, M. V. 2010. Pandora's Founder Rocks the Music Business. *Fortune,* July 5: 27–28; Levy, A. 2010. Pandora's Next Frontier: Your Wheels. *BusinessWeek.com,* October 14: np; *www.pandora.com;* and Kessler, S. 2012. Spotify who? Pandora surges past 150 million registered users. *mashable.com,* May 8: np.

---

company with greater resources introduces a similar product. For a new entrant to sustain its pioneering advantage, it may be necessary to protect its intellectual property, advertise heavily to build brand recognition, form alliances with businesses that will adopt its products or services, and offer exceptional customer service.

Imitative New Entry   Whereas pioneers are often inventors or tinkerers with new technology, imitators usually have a strong marketing orientation. They look for opportunities to capitalize on proven market successes. An **imitative new entry** strategy is used by entrepreneurs who see products or business concepts that have been successful in one market niche or physical locale and introduce the same basic product or service in another segment of the market.

Sometimes the key to success with an imitative strategy is to fill a market space where the need had previously been filled inadequately. Entrepreneurs are also prompted to be imitators when they realize that they have the resources or skills to do a job better than an existing competitor. This can actually be a serious problem for entrepreneurial start-ups if the imitator is an established company. Consider the example of Square.[37] Founded in 2010, Square provides a means for small businesses to process credit and debit card sales without signing up for a traditional credit card arrangement that typically includes monthly fees and minimum charges. Square provides a small credit card reader that plugs into a smartphone to users who sign up for their service. Swipe the card and input the charge amount. Square does the rest for a 2.75 percent transaction fee. By the middle of 2012, Square had signed up over two million users. But success triggers imitation. A host of both upstart and established firms have moved into this new segment. While Square has quickly established itself in the market, it now faces strong competition from major competitors, including Intuit and PayPal. Sensing that they may have difficulty going head to head with

imitative new entry
a firm's entry into an industry with products or services that capitalize on proven market successes and that usually has a strong marketing orientation.

these larger imitators, Square is looking to further innovate and is now offering an app, called Pay with Square, that will allow users to pay by credit straight from their smartphone without ever taking out a credit card.

Adaptive New Entry   Most new entrants use a strategy somewhere between "pure" imitation and "pure" pioneering. That is, they offer a product or service that is somewhat new and sufficiently different to create new value for customers and capture market share. Such firms are adaptive in the sense that they are aware of marketplace conditions and conceive entry strategies to capitalize on current trends.

According to business creativity coach Tom Monahan, "Every new idea is merely a spin of an old idea. [Knowing that] takes the pressure off from thinking [you] have to be totally creative. You don't. Sometimes it's one slight twist to an old idea that makes all the difference."[38] An **adaptive new entry** approach does not involve "reinventing the wheel," nor is it merely imitative either. It involves taking an existing idea and adapting it to a particular situation. Exhibit 8.3 presents examples of four young companies that successfully modified or adapted existing products to create new value.

There are several pitfalls that might limit the success of an adaptive new entrant. First, the value proposition must be perceived as unique. Unless potential customers believe a new product or service does a superior job of meeting their needs, they will have little motivation to try it. Second, there is nothing to prevent a close competitor from mimicking the new firm's adaptation as a way to hold on to its customers. Third, once an adaptive entrant achieves initial success, the challenge is to keep the idea fresh. If the attractive features of the new business are copied, the entrepreneurial firm must find ways to adapt and improve the product or service offering.

Considering these choices, an entrepreneur or entrepreneurial team might ask, Which new entry strategy is best? The choice depends on many competitive, financial, and marketplace considerations. Nevertheless, research indicates that the greatest opportunities

> **adaptive new entry**
> a firm's entry into an industry by offering a product or service that is somewhat new and sufficiently different to create value for customers by capitalizing on current market trends.

EXHIBIT 8.3 Examples of Adaptive New Entrants

Company Name	Product	Adaptation	Result
Under Armour, Inc. Founded in 1995	Undershirts and other athletic gear	Used moisture-wicking fabric to create better gear for sweaty sports.	Under Armour generated over $1.4 billion in sales in 2012 and was number 51 in *Fortune Magazine's* list of fastest-growing firms.
Mint.com Founded in 2005	Comprehensive online money management	Created software that tells users what they are spending by aggregating financial information from online bank and credit card accounts.	Mint has over 10 million users and is helping them manage over $1 billion in assets.
Plum Organics Founded in 2005	Organic baby food and snack foods for children	Made convenient line of baby food using organic ingredients.	Plum now has over 20 products and is listed at number 63 on the *Inc* 500 list of fastest-growing private companies.
Spanx Founded in 2000	Footless pantyhose and other undergarments for women	Combined nylon and Lycra® to create a new type of undergarment that is comfortable and eliminates panty lines.	Now produces over 200 products sold in 3,000 stores to over 6 million customers.

Sources: Bryan, M. 2007. Spanx Me, Baby! *www.observer.com,* December 10, np.; Carey, J. 2006. Perspiration Inspiration. *BusinessWeek,* June 5: 64; Palanjian, A. 2008. A Planner Plumbs for a Niche. *www.wsj.com,* September 30, np.; Worrell, D. 2008. Making Mint. *Entrepreneur,* September: 55; *www.mint.com; www.spanx.com; www.underarmour.com;* Buss, D. 2010. The Mothers of Invention. *Wall Street Journal,* February 8: R7; Crook, J. 2012. Mint.com Tops 10 Million Registered Users, 70% Use Mobile. *techcrunch.com,* August 29: np; and *www.plumorganics.com.*

may stem from being willing to enter new markets rather than seeking growth only in existing markets. One study found that companies that ventured into arenas that were new to the world or new to the company earned total profits of 61 percent. In contrast, companies that made only incremental improvements, such as extending an existing product line, grew total profits by only 39 percent.[39]

However, whether to be pioneering, imitative, or adaptive when entering markets is only one question the entrepreneur faces. A new entrant must also decide what type of strategic positioning will work best as the business goes forward. Those strategic choices can be informed by the guidelines suggested for the generic strategies. We turn to that subject next.

Generic Strategies

Typically, a new entrant begins with a single business model that is equivalent in scope to a business-level strategy (Chapter 5). In this section we address how overall low cost, differentiation, and focus strategies can be used to achieve competitive advantages.

Overall Cost Leadership   One of the ways entrepreneurial firms achieve success is by doing more with less. By holding down costs or making more efficient use of resources than larger competitors, new ventures are often able to offer lower prices and still be profitable. Thus, under the right circumstances, a low-cost leader strategy is a viable alternative for some new ventures. The way most companies achieve low-cost leadership, however, is typically different for young or small firms.

Recall from Chapter 5 that three of the features of a low-cost approach included operating at a large enough scale to spread costs over many units of production (economies of scale), making substantial capital investments in order to increase scale economies, and using knowledge gained from experience to make cost-saving improvements. These elements of a cost-leadership strategy may be unavailable to new ventures. Because new ventures are typically small, they usually don't have high economies of scale relative to competitors. Because they are usually cash strapped, they can't make large capital investments to increase their scale advantages. And because many are young, they often don't have a wealth of accumulated experience to draw on to achieve cost reductions.

Given these constraints, how can new ventures successfully deploy cost-leader strategies? Compared to large firms, new ventures often have simple organizational structures that make decision making both easier and faster. The smaller size also helps young firms change more quickly when upgrades in technology or feedback from the marketplace indicate that improvements are needed. They are also able to make decisions at the time they are founded that help them deal with the issue of controlling costs. For example, they may source materials from a supplier that provides them more cheaply or set up manufacturing facilities in another country where labor costs are especially low. Thus, new firms have several avenues for achieving low cost leadership. Strategy Spotlight 8.5 highlights the success of Vizio, Inc., a new entrant with an overall cost leadership strategy. Whatever methods young firms use to achieve a low-cost advantage, this has always been a way that entrepreneurial firms take business away from incumbents—by offering a comparable product or service at a lower price.

Differentiation   Both pioneering and adaptive entry strategies involve some degree of differentiation. That is, the new entry is based on being able to offer a differentiated value proposition. In the case of pioneers, the new venture is attempting to do something strikingly different, either by using a new technology or deploying resources in a way that radically alters the way business is conducted. Often, entrepreneurs do both.

Amazon founder Jeff Bezos set out to use Internet technology to revolutionize the way books are sold. He garnered the ire of other booksellers and the attention of the public by making bold claims about being the "earth's largest bookseller." As a bookseller,

LOW-COST IMITATOR VIZIO, INC. TAKES OFF

When flat-panel TVs were first introduced in the late 1990s, major manufacturers such as Samsung, Sony, and Matsushita (maker of Panasonic) made heavy investments in R&D in a competition for technological leadership. As a result, the early flat-panel TVs were expensive. Even as technological advances drove prices down, the TVs were growing larger and flatter, and they continued to command premium prices. By 2002, 50-inch plasma TVs were still selling for $8,000–$10,000. But by then, panel technology had also become somewhat commoditized. That's when William Wang, a former marketer of computer monitors, realized he could use existing technologies to create a high-quality TV. Wang discovered he could keep operations lean and outsource everything from tech support to R&D, so he founded Vizio, Inc.

In January 2003, Wang pitched Costco Wholesale Corp. on a 46-inch flat-panel plasma TV for $3,800—half the price of the competition. Although Costco executives laughed when Wang said he wanted to become the next Sony, they decided to give him a chance. By March 2003, the TVs were being offered in over 300 of Costco's U.S. warehouse stores. Today, Vizio is one of Costco's largest suppliers of TVs.

Vizio's success is due not only to enlightened imitation and low-cost operations, but also to Wang's unique approach to financing growth. Although he initially mortgaged his home and borrowed from family and friends, when he needed additional funding, he targeted the manufacturing partners who were supplying him parts. In 2004, Taiwan-based contract manufacturer AmTran Technology Co. purchased an 8 percent stake in Vizio for $1 million; today, AmTran owns 23 percent of Vizio and supplies over 80 percent of its TVs. "Unlike many PC companies who try to make their money by squeezing the vendor," says Wang, "we try to work with our vendor."

Vizio has found success focusing on LCD TVs, staying lean, and working with their suppliers. This has allowed them to grow from an upstart firm to a position of market leadership. Vizio shipped 18.5 percent of the LCD TVs sold in the first quarter of 2012, leading the number two firm, Samsung, which had 17.6 percent of the market. Their status as a major player in consumer electronics is reinforced by their status as the title sponsor of the 2014 Vizio BCS National Championship college football game.

Sources: Lawton, C., Kane, Y. I., & Dean, J. 2008. U.S. upstart takes on TV giants in price war. *www.wsj.com*, April 15, np.; Taub, E. A. 2008. Flat-panel TV prices plummet. *www.nytimes.com*, December 2, np.; Wilson, S. 2008. Picture it. *Entrepreneur*, July: 43; *www.wikipedia.com*; Edwards, C. 2010. How Vizio beat Sony in high-def TV. *Bloomberg Businessweek*, April 26: 51–52; and Morrod, T. 2012. Vizio retakes lead in U.S. LCD TV market; Samsung maintains overall TV dominance. *www.isuppli.com*, July 12: np.

Bezos was not doing anything that had not been done before. But two key differentiating features—doing it on the Internet and offering extraordinary customer service—have made Amazon a differentiated success.

There are several factors that make it more difficult for new ventures to be successful as differentiators. For one thing, the strategy is generally thought to be expensive to enact. Differentiation is often associated with strong brand identity, and establishing a brand is usually considered to be expensive because of the cost of advertising and promotion, paid endorsements, exceptional customer service, etc. Differentiation successes are sometimes built on superior innovation or use of technology. These are also factors where it may be challenging for young firms to excel relative to established competitors.

Nevertheless all of these areas—innovation, technology, customer service, distinctive branding—are also arenas where new ventures have sometimes made a name for themselves even though they must operate with limited resources and experience. To be successful, according to Garry Ridge, CEO of the WD-40 Company, "You need to have a great product, make the end user aware of it, and make it easy to buy."[40] It sounds simple, but it is a difficult challenge for new ventures with differentiation strategies.

Focus   Focus strategies are often associated with small businesses because there is a natural fit between the narrow scope of the strategy and the small size of the firm. A focus strategy may include elements of differentiation and overall cost leadership, as well as combinations of these approaches. But to be successful within a market niche, the key strategic requirement is to stay focused. Here's why:

Despite all the attention given to fast-growing new industries, most start-ups enter industries that are mature.[41] In mature industries, growth in demand tends to be slow and there are often many competitors. Therefore, if a start-up wants to get a piece of the action, it often has to take business away from an existing competitor. If a start-up enters a market with a broad or aggressive strategy, it is likely to evoke retaliation from a more powerful competitor. Young firms can often succeed best by finding a market niche where they can get a foothold and make small advances that erode the position of existing competitors.[42] From this position, they can build a name for themselves and grow.

Consider, for example, the "Miniature Editions" line of books launched by Running Press, a small Philadelphia publisher. The books are palm-sized minibooks positioned at bookstore cash registers as point-of-sale impulse items costing about $4.95. Beginning with just 10 titles in 1993, Running Press grew rapidly and within 10 years had sold over 20 million copies. Even though these books represent just a tiny fraction of total sales in the $23 billion publishing industry, they have been a mainstay for Running Press.[43] As the Running Press example indicates, many new ventures are successful even though their share of the market is quite small.

Combination Strategies

One of the best ways for young and small businesses to achieve success is by pursuing combination strategies. By combining the best features of low-cost, differentiation, and focus strategies, new ventures can often achieve something truly distinctive.

Entrepreneurial firms are often in a strong position to offer a combination strategy because they have the flexibility to approach situations uniquely. For example, holding down expenses can be difficult for big firms because each layer of bureaucracy adds to the cost of doing business across the boundaries of a large organization.[44]

A similar argument could be made about entrepreneurial firms that differentiate. Large firms often find it difficult to offer highly specialized products or superior customer services. Entrepreneurial firms, by contrast, can often create high-value products and services through their unique differentiating efforts. Strategy Spotlight 8.6 shows how two entrepreneurs found a recipe to sell fashionable eyeglasses to demanding customers while also cutting costs and serving a social mission.

For nearly all new entrants, one of the major dangers is that a large firm with more resources will copy what they are doing. Well-established incumbents that observe the success of a new entrant's product or service will copy it and use their market power to overwhelm the smaller firm. The threat may be lessened for firms that use combination strategies. Because of the flexibility of entrepreneurial firms, they can often enact combination strategies in ways that the large firms cannot copy. This makes the new entrant's strategies much more sustainable.

Perhaps more threatening than large competitors are close competitors, because they have similar structural features that help them adjust quickly and be flexible in decision making. Here again, a carefully crafted and executed combination strategy may be the best way for an entrepreneurial firm to thrive in a competitive environment. Nevertheless, competition among rivals is a key determinant of new venture success. To address this, we turn next to the topic of competitive dynamics.

LO8.4

How competitive actions, such as the entry of new competitors into a marketplace, may launch a cycle of actions and reactions among close competitors.

Competitive Dynamics

New entry into markets, whether by start-ups or by incumbent firms, nearly always threatens existing competitors. This is true in part because, except in very new markets, nearly every market need is already being met, either directly or indirectly, by existing firms. As a result, the competitive actions of a new entrant are very likely to provoke a competitive response from companies that feel threatened. This, in turn, is likely to evoke a reaction to

WARBY PARKER SEES VALUE IN A COMBINATION STRATEGY

Wharton School of Business graduates Neil Blumenthal and Dave Gilboa wondered why a pair of eyeglass frames, a simple and mass-produced product, often costs as much as an iPhone. Blumenthal concluded that he knew why. "The optical industry is an oligopoly. A few companies are making outrageous margins and screwing you and me." One of the firms dominating the $16 billion eyeglass industry is Luxottica, which owns LensCrafters, Pearle Vision, Sunglass Hut, and the eyeglass clinics in Target and Sears stores. By owning multiple stores and producing over 25 brands of glasses, Gilboa argues that Luxottica has "created the illusion of choice" in an uncompetitive and high-profit industry.

Blumenthal and Gilboa are striking out to offer real choice to eyeglass wearers. They have developed a simple formula to offer customers new ways to buy glasses. They developed an online system where customers can upload a picture and virtually "try on" a range of glasses. Customers can then order and test try up to five frames at a time in their own home.

Warby Parker keeps its costs low in a number of ways. First, it outsources to low-cost manufacturers. Second, it developed its own brand, leaving out the cost of licensing a fashion brand, which can often add 15 percent to the cost of a pair of glasses. Third,

they don't work through retailers, whose markups can double the cost of glasses. They also rely on low-cost marketing. For example, they use a "brand ambassador" program where unpaid promoters get a free pair of glasses and are asked to share a discount code with friends and family. As a result, they are able to offer their frames at one-third to one-half the cost of their brand name competitors.

Warby Parker also has a social mission. For every pair of glasses the firm sells, it provides a free pair of eyeglasses to a needy person. In 2011, they helped distribute over 100,000 free pairs of glasses. They are also focused on sustainability and are certified as a zero net carbon emissions business.

So far, the firm's balance of fashion, cost consciousness, and social responsibility has led to remarkable success. They have grown from the two founders to over 100 employees in two and a half years. They have also attracted the interest of investors, receiving $37 million in venture capitalist funding in 2012. With this business model, Blumenthal and Gilboa see a bright future.

Sources: Berfield, S. 2011. A startup's new prescription for eyewear. *Bloomberg Businessweek,* July 4, 49–51; Mitroff, S. 2012. With $37M, Warby Parker sets its sights on more than just eyeglasses. *Wired.com,* September 10. Np; and Kim, R. 2012. Warby Parker raises $36.8M to expand fashion eyewear brand. *Gigaom.com,* September 10, np.

---

the response. As a result, a competitive dynamic—action and response—begins among the firms competing for the same customers in a given marketplace.

Competitive dynamics—intense rivalry among similar competitors—has the potential to alter a company's strategy. New entrants may be forced to change their strategies or develop new ones to survive competitive challenges by incumbent rivals. New entry is among the most common reasons why a cycle of competitive actions and reactions gets started. It might also occur because of threatening actions among existing competitors, such as aggressive cost cutting. Thus, studying competitive dynamics helps explain why strategies evolve and reveals how, why, and when to respond to the actions of close competitors. Exhibit 8.4 identifies the factors that competitors need to consider when determining how to respond to a competitive act.

New Competitive Action

Entry into a market by a new competitor is a good starting point to begin describing the cycle of actions and responses characteristic of a competitive dynamic process.[45] However, new entry is only one type of competitive action. Price cutting, imitating successful products, or expanding production capacity are other examples of competitive acts that might provoke competitors to react.

Why do companies launch new competitive actions? There are several reasons:

- Improve market position
- Capitalize on growing demand

competitive dynamics
intense rivalry, involving actions and responses, among similar competitors vying for the same customers in a marketplace

LO8.5

The components of competitive dynamics analysis—new competitive action, threat analysis, motivation and capability to respond, types of competitive actions, and likelihood of competitive reaction.

EXHIBIT 8.4 Model of Competitive Dynamics

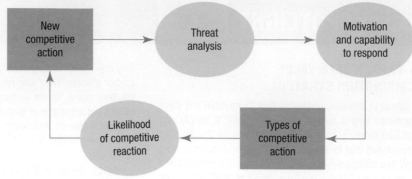

Sources: Adapted from Chen, M. J. 1996. Competitor Analysis and Interfirm Rivalry: Toward a Theoretical Integration. *Academy of Management Review,* 21(1): 100–134; Ketchen, D. J., Snow, C. C., & Hoover, V. L. 2004. Research on competitive dynamics: Recent Accomplishments and Future Challenges. *Journal of Management,* 30(6): 779–804; and Smith, K. G., Ferrier, W. J., & Grimm, C. M. 2001. King of the Hill: Dethroning the Industry Leader. *Academy of Management Executive,* 15(2): 59–70.

- Expand production capacity
- Provide an innovative new solution
- Obtain first mover advantages

Underlying all of these reasons is a desire to strengthen financial outcomes, capture some of the extraordinary profits that industry leaders enjoy, and grow the business. Some companies are also motivated to launch competitive challenges because they want to build their reputation for innovativeness or efficiency. For example, Toyota's success with the Prius signaled to its competitors the potential value of high-fuel-economy cars, and these firms have responded with their own hybrids, electric cars, high-efficiency diesel engines, and even more fuel-efficient traditional gasoline engines. This is indicative of the competitive dynamic cycle. As former Intel Chairman Andy Grove stated, "Business success contains the seeds of its own destruction. The more successful you are, the more people want a chunk of your business and then another chunk and then another until there is nothing left."[46]

When a company enters into a market for the first time, it is an attack on existing competitors. As indicated earlier in the chapter, any of the entry strategies can be used to take competitive action. But competitive attacks come from many sources besides new entrants. Some of the most intense competition is among incumbent rivals intent on gaining strategic advantages. "Winners in business play rough and don't apologize for it," according to Boston Consulting Group authors George Stalk, Jr., and Rob Lachenauer in their book *Hardball: Are You Playing to Play or Playing to Win?*[47] Exhibit 8.5 outlines their five strategies.

The likelihood that a competitor will launch an attack depends on many factors.[48] In the remaining sections, we discuss factors such as competitor analysis, market conditions, types of strategic actions, and the resource endowments and capabilities companies need to take competitive action.

Threat Analysis

Prior to actually observing a competitive action, companies may need to become aware of potential competitive threats. That is, companies need to have a keen sense of who their closest competitors are and the kinds of competitive actions they might be planning.[49] This may require some environmental scanning and monitoring of the sort described in Chapter 2. Awareness of the threats posed by industry rivals allows a firm to understand what type of competitive response, if any, may be necessary.

new competitive action
acts that might provoke competitors to react, such as new market entry, price cutting, imitating successful products, and expanding production capacity.

threat analysis
a firm's awareness of its closest competitors and the kinds of competitive actions they might be planning.

EXHIBIT 8.5 Five "Hardball" Strategies

Strategy	Description	Examples
Devastate rivals' profit sanctuaries	Not all business segments generate the same level of profits for a company. Through focused attacks on a rival's most profitable segments, a company can generate maximum leverage with relatively smaller-scale attacks. Recognize, however, that companies closely guard the information needed to determine just what their profit sanctuaries are.	In 2005, Walmart began offering low-priced extended warranties on home electronics after learning that its rivals such as Best Buy derived most of their profits from extended warranties.
Plagiarize with pride	Just because a close competitor comes up with an idea first does not mean it cannot be successfully imitated. Second movers, in fact, can see how customers respond, make improvements, and launch a better version without all the market development costs. Successful imitation is harder than it may appear and requires the imitating firm to keep its ego in check.	In designing their smartphones, Samsung copied the look, feel, and technological attributes of Apple's IPhone. Samsung lost a patent infringement lawsuit to Apple, but by copying Apple, Samsung was able to improve its market position.
Deceive the competition	A good gambit sends the competition off in the wrong direction. This may cause the rivals to miss strategic shifts, spend money pursuing dead ends, or slow their responses. Any of these outcomes support the deceiving firms' competitive advantage. Companies must be sure not to cross ethical lines during these actions.	Max Muir knew that Australian farmers liked to buy from family-firm suppliers but also wanted efficient suppliers. To meet both needs, he quietly bought a number of small firms to build economies of scale but didn't consolidate brands or his sales force so that, to his customers and rivals, they still looked like independent family firms.
Unleash massive and overwhelming force	While many hardball strategies are subtle and indirect, this one is not. This is a full-frontal attack where a firm commits significant resources to a major campaign to weaken rivals' positions in certain markets. Firms must be sure they have the mass and stamina required to win before they declare war against a rival.	Unilever has taken a dominant position, with 65 percent market share, in the Vietnamese laundry detergent market by employing a massive investment and marketing campaign. In doing so, they decimated the market position of the local, incumbent competitors.
Raise competitors' costs	If a company has superior insight into the complex cost and profit structure of the industry, it can compete in a way that steers its rivals into relatively higher cost/lower profit arenas. This strategy uses deception to make the rivals think they are winning, when in fact they are not. Again, companies using this strategy must be confident that they understand the industry better than their rivals.	Ecolab, a company that sells cleaning supplies to businesses, encouraged a leading competitor, Diversity, to adopt a strategy to go after the low-volume, high-margin customers. What Ecolab knew that Diversity didn't is that the high servicing costs involved with this segment make the segment unprofitable—a situation Ecolab assured by bidding high enough to lose the contracts to Diversity but low enough to ensure the business lost money for Diversity.

Sources: Berner, R. 2005. Watch Out, Best Buy and Circuit City. *BusinessWeek*, November 10; Stalk, G. Jr. 2006. Curveball Strategies to Fool the Competition. *Harvard Business Review*, 84(9): 114–121; and Stalk, Jr., G. & Lachenauer, R. 2004. *Hardball: Are You Playing to Play or Playing to Win?* Cambridge, MA: Harvard Business School Press. Reprinted by permission of Harvard Business School Press from G. Stalk, Jr. and R. Lachenauer. Copyright 2004 by the Harvard Business School Publishing Corporation; all rights reserved; Lam, Y. 2013. FDI companies dominate Vietnam's detergent market. *www.saigon-gpdaily.com.vn*, January 22: np; Vascellaro, J. 2012. Apple wins big in patent case. *www.wsj.com*, August 25: np; and Pech, R. & Stamboulidis, G. 2010. How strategies of deception facilitate business growth. *Journal of Business Strategy*, 31(6): 37–45.

Being aware of competitors and cognizant of whatever threats they might pose is the first step in assessing the level of competitive threat. Once a new competitive action becomes apparent, companies must determine how threatening it is to their business. Competitive dynamics are likely to be most intense among companies that are competing for the same customers or who have highly similar sets of resources.[50] Two factors are used to assess whether or not companies are close competitors:

market commonality
the extent to which competitors are vying for the same customers in the same markets.

resource similarity
the extent to which rivals draw from the same types of strategic resources.

- **Market commonality**—Whether or not competitors are vying for the same customers and how many markets they share in common. For example, aircraft manufacturers Boeing and Airbus have a high degree of market commonality because they make very similar products and have many buyers in common.
- **Resource similarity**—The degree to which rivals draw on the same types of resources to compete. For example, the home pages of Google and Yahoo! may look very different, but behind the scenes, they both rely on the talent pool of high-caliber software engineers to create the cutting-edge innovations that help them compete.

When any two firms have both a high degree of market commonality and highly similar resource bases, a stronger competitive threat is present. Such a threat, however, may not lead to competitive action. On the one hand, a market rival may be hesitant to attack a company that it shares a high degree of market commonality with because it could lead to an intense battle. On the other hand, once attacked, rivals with high market commonality will be much more motivated to launch a competitive response. This is especially true in cases where the shared market is an important part of a company's overall business.

How strong a response an attacked rival can mount will be determined by their strategic resource endowments. In general, the same set of conditions holds true with regard to resource similarity. Companies that have highly similar resource bases will be hesitant to launch an initial attack but pose a serious threat if required to mount a competitive response.[51] Greater strategic resources increase a firm's capability to respond.

Motivation and Capability to Respond

Once attacked, competitors are faced with deciding how to respond. Before deciding, however, they need to evaluate not only how they will respond, but also their reasons for responding and their capability to respond. Companies need to be clear about what problems a competitive response is expected to address and what types of problems it might create.[52] There are several factors to consider.

First, how serious is the impact of the competitive attack to which they are responding? For example, a large company with a strong reputation that is challenged by a small or unknown company may elect to simply keep an eye on the new competitor rather than quickly react or overreact. Part of the story of online retailer Amazon's early success is attributed to Barnes & Noble's overreaction to Amazon's claim that it was "earth's biggest bookstore." Because Barnes & Noble was already using the phrase "world's largest bookstore," it sued Amazon, but lost. The confrontation made it to the front pages of *The Wall Street Journal* and Amazon was on its way to becoming a household name.[53]

Companies planning to respond to a competitive challenge must also understand their motivation for responding. What is the intent of the competitive response? Is it merely to blunt the attack of the competitor or is it an opportunity to enhance its competitive position? Sometimes the most a company can hope for is to minimize the damage caused by a competitive action.

A company that seeks to improve its competitive advantage may be motivated to launch an attack rather than merely respond to one. For example, a few years ago, the *Wall Street Journal (WSJ)* attacked the *New York Times* by adding a local news section to the New York edition of the *WSJ*. Their aim was to become a more direct competitor of the *Times*.

The publishers of the *WSJ* undertook this attack when they realized the *Times* was in a weakened financial condition and would be unable to respond to the attack.[54] A company must also assess its capability to respond. What strategic resources can be deployed to fend off a competitive attack? Does the company have an array of internal strengths it can draw on, or is it operating from a position of weakness?

Consider, the role of firm age and size in calculating a company's ability to respond. Most entrepreneurial new ventures start out small. The smaller size makes them more nimble compared to large firms so they can respond quickly to competitive attacks. Because they are not well-known, start-ups also have the advantage of the element of surprise in how and when they attack. Innovative uses of technology, for example, allow small firms to deploy resources in unique ways.

Because they are young, however, start-ups may not have the financial resources needed to follow through with a competitive response.[55] In contrast, older and larger firms may have more resources and a repertoire of competitive techniques they can use in a counterattack. Large firms, however, tend to be slower to respond. Older firms tend to be predictable in their responses because they often lose touch with the competitive environment and rely on strategies and actions that have worked in the past.

Other resources may also play a role in whether a company is equipped to retaliate. For example, one avenue of counterattack may be launching product enhancements or new product/service innovations. For that approach to be successful, it requires a company to have both the intellectual capital to put forward viable innovations and the teamwork skills to prepare a new product or service and get it to market. Resources such as cross-functional teams and the social capital that makes teamwork production effective and efficient represent the type of human capital resources that enhance a company's capability to respond.

Types of Competitive Actions

Once an organization determines whether it is willing and able to launch a competitive action, it must determine what type of action is appropriate. The actions taken will be determined by both its resource capabilities and its motivation for responding. There are also marketplace considerations. What types of actions are likely to be most effective given a company's internal strengths and weaknesses as well as market conditions?

Two broadly defined types of competitive action include strategic actions and tactical actions. **Strategic actions** represent major commitments of distinctive and specific resources. Examples include launching a breakthrough innovation, building a new production facility, or merging with another company. Such actions require significant planning and resources and, once initiated, are difficult to reverse.

Tactical actions include refinements or extensions of strategies. Examples of tactical actions include cutting prices, improving gaps in service, or strengthening marketing efforts. Such actions typically draw on general resources and can be implemented quickly. Exhibit 8.6 identifies several types of strategic and tactical competitive actions, and Strategy Spotlight 8.7 shows the range of actions that can occur in a rivalrous relationship.

Some competitive actions take the form of frontal assaults, that is, actions aimed directly at taking business from another company or capitalizing on industry weaknesses. This can be especially effective when firms use a low-cost strategy. The airline industry provides a good example of this head-on approach. When Southwest Airlines began its no-frills, no-meals, strategy in the late-1960s, it represented a direct assault on the major carriers of the day. In Europe, Ryanair has similarly directly challenged the traditional carriers with an overall cost leadership strategy.

Guerilla offensives and selective attacks provide an alternative for firms with fewer resources.[56] These draw attention to products or services by creating buzz or generating

strategic actions
major commitments of distinctive and specific resources to strategic initiatives.

tactical actions
refinements or extensions of strategies usually involving minor resource commitments.

EXHIBIT 8.6
Strategic and Tactical Competitive Actions

	Actions	Examples
Strategic Actions	• Entering new markets	• Make geographical expansions
		• Expand into neglected markets
		• Target rivals' markets
		• Target new demographics
	• New product introductions	• Imitate rivals' products
		• Address gaps in quality
		• Leverage new technologies
		• Leverage brand name with related products
		• Protect innovation with patents
	• Changing production capacity	• Create overcapacity
		• Tie up raw materials sources
		• Tie up preferred suppliers and distributors
		• Stimulate demand by limiting capacity
	• Mergers/Alliances	• Acquire/partner with competitors to reduce competition
		• Tie up key suppliers through alliances
		• Obtain new technology/intellectual property
		• Facilitate new market entry
Tactical Actions	• Price cutting (or increases)	• Maintain low price dominance
		• Offer discounts and rebates
		• Offer incentives (e.g., frequent flyer miles)
		• Enhance offering to move upscale
	• Product/service enhancements	• Address gaps in service
		• Expand warranties
		• Make incremetal product improvements
	• Increased marketing efforts	• Use guerilla marketing
		• Conduct selective attacks
		• Change product packaging
		• Use new marketing channels
	• New distribution channels	• Access suppliers directly
		• Access customers directly
		• Develop multiple points of contact with customers
		• Expand Internet presence

Sources: Chen, M. J. & Hambrick, D. 1995. Speed, Stealth, and Selective Attack: How Small Firms Differ from Large Firms in Competitive Behavior. *Academy of Management Journal,* 38: 453–482; Davies, M. 1992. Sales Promotions as a Competitive Strategy. *Management Decision,* 30(7): 5–10; Ferrier, W., Smith, K., & Grimm, C. 1999. The Role of Competitive Action in Market Share Erosion and Industry Dethronement: A Study of Industry Leaders and Challengers. *Academy of Management Journal,* 42(4): 372–388; and Garda, R. A. 1991. Use Tactical Pricing to Uncover Hidden Profits. *Journal of Business Strategy,* 12(5): 17–23.

enough shock value to get some free publicity. TOMS shoes has found a way to generate interest in its products without a large advertising budget to match Nike. Their policy of donating one pair of shoes to those in need for every pair of shoes purchased by customers has generated a lot of buzz on the internet.[57] Over 2 million people have given a "like" rating on TOMS's Facebook page. The policy has a real impact as well, with over 2 million shoes donated as of January 2013.[58]

AMAZON AND APPLE: COLLIDING GIANTS

Amazon and Apple come from very different backgrounds. Amazon's roots are as an online retailer. Apple is the quintessential technology firm. But now they find themselves taking each other on in a multifronted battle. Their battle is an intriguing one since they come from different backgrounds but share similar traits. They are both known for the tight control they keep on their software, secretive cultures, the range of consumer data they collect, and their drive to win. However, their business models are very different. Apple generates the bulk of its profits by selling high-margin hardware. In contrast, Amazon earns razor-thin margins on its hardware but generates the majority of its profits by channeling buyers to its e-commerce businesses.

Today, they compete in two major arenas: tablet computers, and music downloading and electronic books. Interestingly, they are each the leader in one of those markets, but the other has signaled they are willing to fight for each of those markets. Apple was first to the tablet market, but Amazon has aggressively attacked this market with its Kindle Fire. In the fourth quarter of 2012, Apple had 44 percent of the tablet market, while Amazon had a 12 percent market share. As the underdog in this market, Amazon directly compares the utility of its products to the iPad. For example, when it launched the Kindle Fire, Jeff Bezos, Amazon's CEO, directly noted the ability of the Kindle Fire to wirelessly back up media on the tablet without having to sync it to a computer—a step an iPad user had to do. In doing so, Amazon leverages its strong capabilities in cloud computing storage. While Apple doesn't acknowledge Amazon as a key competitor in this market, some analysts believe the development of the mini-iPad was a move to respond to the smaller Kindle Fire.

In their other current area of competition, Amazon and Apple both sell e-books. Amazon dominates this market, with a 60 percent market share in 2012. Apple, with less than 10 percent of this market, is the aggressive upstart. To better compete with Amazon in the e-book market, Apple has developed a platform where users can build interactive e-books.

Amazon is also positioning itself to challenge Apple in some of its other product areas. Amazon has developed its own smartphone, which it will launch in 2013. As part of this launch, Amazon will borrow from its recipe that it used to launch the Kindle Fire and employ a disruptive pricing scheme. Reports indicate they will price their phone much lower than the iPhone and competing high-end smartphones. Amazon is also building up its capabilities in mobile communication software. To better compete on the apps available for its hardware, Amazon has acquired two software firms, Yap and UpNext, giving it capabilities to develop mobile apps, mapping software, and voice recognition software. One example of their action here is Amazon's launch of the Amazon Cloud Player, an app that allows users to purchase music and store it on the cloud to be accessed on a mobile or Internet-connected device whenever and wherever the user wants.

While they compete in many ways, they also complement each other in some ways. For example, one of the most widely downloaded apps for the iPad is the Amazon Kindle app, and some of the most popular items sold on amazon.com are iPads and iPhones.

In their competitive battle, these firms have employed and will continue to employ both strategic and tactical actions as they strive to improve their own competitive position and unsettle the competitive position of their rival. The rivalry between Amazon and Apple is pushing the firms to continue to improve their products and services while also finding ways to provide solutions for their customers at attractive prices.

Sources: Vascellaro, J. & Bensinger, G. 2012. Apple-Amazon war heats up. *Wsj .com*, July 26: np; Krause, R. 2013. Amazon.com smartphone with disruptive pricing. *Investors.com*, January 3: np; and Scarpello, L. 2013. Apple vs. Amazon: Amazon opens mobile MP3 store. *Popai.com*, January 21: np.

Some companies limit their competitive response to defensive actions. Such actions rarely improve a company's competitive advantage, but a credible defensive action can lower the risk of being attacked and deter new entry.

Several of the factors discussed earlier in the chapter, such as types of entry strategies and the use of cost leadership versus differentiation strategies, can guide the decision about what types of competitive actions to take. Before launching a given strategy, however, assessing the likely response of competitors is a vital step.[59]

Likelihood of Competitive Reaction

The final step before initiating a competitive response is to evaluate what a competitor's reaction is likely to be. The logic of competitive dynamics suggests that once competitive actions are initiated, it is likely they will be met with competitive responses.[60] The last step before mounting an attack is to evaluate how competitors are likely to respond. Evaluating potential competitive reactions helps companies plan for future counterattacks. It may also lead to a decision to hold off—that is, not to take any competitive action at all because of the possibility that a misguided or poorly planned response will generate a devastating competitive reaction.

How a competitor is likely to respond will depend on three factors: market dependence, competitor's resources, and the reputation of the firm that initiates the action (actor's reputation). The implications of each of these is described briefly in the following sections.

Market Dependence   If a company has a high concentration of its business in a particular industry, it has more at stake because it must depend on that industry's market for its sales. Single-industry businesses or those where one industry dominates are more likely to mount a competitive response. Young and small firms with a high degree of **market dependence** may be limited in how they respond due to resource constraints.

Competitor's Resources   Previously, we examined the internal resource endowments that a company must evaluate when assessing its capability to respond. Here, it is the competitor's resources that need to be considered. For example, a small firm may be unable to mount a serious attack due to lack of resources. As a result, it is more likely to react to tactical actions such as incentive pricing or enhanced service offerings because they are less costly to attack than large-scale strategic actions. In contrast, a firm with financial "deep pockets" may be able to mount and sustain a costly counterattack.

Actor's Reputation   Whether a company should respond to a competitive challenge will also depend on who launched the attack against it. Compared to relatively smaller firms with less market power, competitors are more likely to respond to competitive moves by market leaders. Another consideration is how successful prior attacks have been. For example, price-cutting by the big automakers usually has the desired result—increased sales to price-sensitive buyers—at least in the short run. Given that history, when GM offers discounts or incentives, rivals Ford and Chrysler cannot afford to ignore the challenge and quickly follow suit.

Choosing Not to React: Forbearance and Co-opetition

The above discussion suggests that there may be many circumstances in which the best reaction is no reaction at all. This is known as **forbearance**—refraining from reacting at all as well as holding back from initiating an attack. The decision of whether a firm should respond or show forbearance is not always clear.

Related to forbearance is the concept of **co-opetition.** This is a term that was coined by network software company Novell's founder and former CEO Raymond Noorda to suggest that companies often benefit most from a combination of competing and cooperating.[61] Close competitors that differentiate themselves in the eyes of consumers may work together behind the scenes to achieve industrywide efficiencies.[62] For example, breweries in Sweden cooperate in recycling used bottles but still compete for customers on the basis of taste and variety. As long as the benefits of cooperating are enjoyed by all participants in a co-opetition system, the practice can aid companies in avoiding intense and damaging competition.[63]

Despite the potential benefits of co-opetition, companies need to guard against cooperating to such a great extent that their actions are perceived as collusion, a practice that has legal ramifications in the United States. In Strategy Spotlight 8.8, we see an example of crossing the line into illegal cooperation.

Once a company has evaluated a competitor's likelihood of responding to a competitive challenge, it can decide what type of action is most appropriate. Competitive actions can take many forms: the entry of a start-up into a market for the first time, an attack by a lower-ranked incumbent on an industry leader, or the launch of a breakthrough innovation that disrupts the industry structure. Such actions forever change the competitive dynamics of a marketplace. Thus, the cycle of actions and reactions that occur in business every day is a vital aspect of entrepreneurial strategy that leads to continual new value creation and the ongoing advancement of economic well-being.

CLEANING UP IN THE SOAP BUSINESS

Consumer product companies Colgate-Palmolive, Unilever, Procter & Gamble (P&G), and Henkel compete with each other globally in the soap business. But as regulators found after a long investigation, this wasn't true in France. The firms in this market had colluded to fix prices for nearly a decade. In the words of a Henkel executive, the detergent makers wanted "to limit the intensity of competition between them and clean up the market." The Autorite de la Concurrance, the French antitrust watchdog, hit these four firms with fines totaling $484 million after completing its investigation.

The firms started sharing pricing information in the 1980s, but by the 1990s their cooperation got bolder, morphing into behavior that sounds like something out of a spy novel. In 1996, four brand directors secretly met in a restaurant in a suburb of Paris and agreed to coordinate the pricing of their soap products. They agreed to prearranged prices at which they would sell to retailers and to notify each other of any planned special offers. They gave each firm a secret alias: Pierre for Procter & Gamble,

Laurence for Unilever, Hugues for Henkel, and Christian for Colgate-Palmolive. From that point forward, they allegedly scheduled clandestine meetings four times a year. The meetings, which they called "store checks" in their schedules to limit any questioning they may have received, often lasted an entire afternoon. They would set complex pricing schemes. For example, P&G sold its Ariel brand as an upscale product and coordinated with Unilever to keep Ariel at a 3 percent markup over Unilever's Skip brand. At these meetings, they would also hash out any complaints about whether and how any of the participants had been bending the rules.

The collusion lasted for almost 10 years until it broke down in 2004. Unilever was the first to defect, offering a 10 percent "D-Day" price cut without negotiating it with the three other firms. Other competitors quickly responded with actions that violated the pricing norms they had set.

Sources: Colchester, M. & Passariello, C. 2011. Dirty secrets in soap prices. *Wsj.com*, December 9: np; Smith, H. & White, A. 2011. P&G, Colgate fined by France in $484 million detergent cartel. *Bloomberg.com*, December 11: np.

ISSUE FOR DEBATE

Rebranding the city of Košice: From industrial eyesore to hotbed of creativity?

By Irena Descubes and Tom McNamara

Košice used to be just a small Slovakian town with about 150,000 visitors a year, mostly Slovaks and the handful of foreigners who were on their way either to or from neighboring Ukraine. Since the era of Communism, the town had the reputation of being a drab, polluted, industrial hub.

But all of that is starting to change. Thanks to Košice's mayor, Mr. Richard Rasi, the town of roughly 250,000 inhabitants has made a substantial effort to rebrand itself and come up with a new image. A major turning point came in 2011, when the city organized the International Ice Hockey Federation World Championships. This created some much needed "buzz" and took advantage of the fact that the city is the birthplace of several famous National Hockey League (NHL) players. But what really helped Košice with its rebranding efforts was the town being selected as one of the European Capitals of Culture (ECOC) in 2013. This played a key part in Košice's "destination management and marketing strategy." Perhaps even more helpful than the ECOC nomination was the fact that the Cable News Network (CNN) called Košice the third most interesting place to visit worldwide, right after Scotland and the city of Rabat in Morocco.

(continued)

(continued)

Leaving nothing to chance in its desire to renew itself, Košice began to reinvent itself. One method was to adopt the "Creative City Index." This is a tool that quantifies and measures the imagination and creativity of a city, providing a benchmark that can be measured against other cities. Another idea was to create a company whose sole purpose would be the promotion and development of Košice.

Unfortunately, Košice still has one big problem with its image. Racism. The city is home to almost 23,000 ethnic Roma, a group with a long history of unfair treatment in Europe. Many local Roma live in desperate poverty and suffer rates of illness and illiteracy higher than the national average. Since 2009, eight consecutive "separation walls" had been built in Košice, illegally and without the necessary permits, in order to isolate the Roma community from the rest of the city. In August 2013, local authorities took legal action to remove all of the walls. Hopefully, this will go a long way in promoting the image of Košice as an enlightened "Capital of Culture."

Discussion Questions

1. What different factors should be taken into account by a country or city wishing to engage in rebranding?
2. What do you think successful "destination branding" depends on? Explain.

Reflecting on Career Implications . . .

◾ **Opportunity Recognition:** What ideas for new business activities are actively discussed in your work environment? Could you apply the four characteristics of an opportunity to determine whether they are viable opportunities? If no one in your organization is excited about or even considering new opportunities, you may want to ask yourself if you want to continue with your current firm.

◾ **Entrepreneurial New Entry:** Are there opportunities to launch new products or services that might add value to the organization? What are the best ways for you to bring these opportunities to the attention of key managers? Or might this provide an opportunity for you to launch your own entrepreneurial venture?

◾ **Entrepreneurial Resources:** Evaluate your resources in terms of financial resources, human capital, and social capital. Are these enough to launch your own venture? If you are deficient in one area, are there ways to compensate for it? Even if you are not interested in starting a new venture, can you use your entrepreneurial resources to advance your career within your firm?

◾ **Competitive Dynamics:** There is always internal competition within organizations: among business units and sometimes even individuals within the same unit. What types of strategic and tactical actions are employed in these internal rivalries? What steps have you taken to strengthen your own position given the "competitive dynamics" within your organization?

summary

New ventures and entrepreneurial firms that capitalize on marketplace opportunities make an important contribution to the U.S. economy. They are leaders in terms of implementing new technologies and introducing innovative products and services. Yet entrepreneurial firms face unique challenges if they are going to survive and grow.

To successfully launch new ventures or implement new technologies, three factors must be present: an entrepreneurial opportunity, the resources to pursue the opportunity, and an entrepreneur or entrepreneurial team willing and able to undertake the venture. Firms must develop a strong ability to recognize viable opportunities.

Opportunity recognition is a process of determining which venture ideas are, in fact, promising business opportunities.

In addition to strong opportunities, entrepreneurial firms need resources and entrepreneurial leadership to thrive. The resources that start-ups need include financial resources as well as human and social capital. Many firms also benefit from government programs that support new venture development and growth. New ventures thrive best when they are led by founders or owners who have vision, drive and dedication, and a commitment to excellence.

Once the necessary opportunities, resources, and entrepreneur skills are in place, new ventures still face numerous strategic challenges. Decisions about the strategic positioning of new entrants can benefit from conducting strategic analyses and evaluating the requirements of niche markets. Entry strategies used by new ventures take several forms, including pioneering new entry, imitative new entry, and adaptive new entry. Entrepreneurial firms can benefit from using overall low cost, differentiation, and focus strategies although each of these approaches has pitfalls that are unique to young and small firms. Entrepreneurial firms are also in a strong position to benefit from combination strategies.

The entry of a new company into a competitive arena is like a competitive attack on incumbents in that arena. Such actions often provoke a competitive response, which may, in turn, trigger a reaction to the response. As a result, a competitive dynamic—action and response—begins among close competitors. In deciding whether to attack or counterattack, companies must analyze the seriousness of the competitive threat, their ability to mount a competitive response, and the type of action—strategic or tactical—that the situation requires. At times, competitors find it is better not to respond at all or to find avenues to cooperate with, rather than challenge, close competitors.

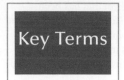

Key Terms

entrepreneurship 248
opportunity
    recognition 249
angel investors 252
venture capitalists 252
crowdfunding 253
entrepreneurial
    leadership 255
entrepreneurial
    strategy 256

pioneering new entry 257
imitative new entry 258
adaptive new entry 259
competitive
    dynamics 263
new competitive
    action 264
threat analysis 264
market commonality 266
resource similarity 266
strategic actions 267
tactical actions 267
market dependence 270
forbearance 270
co-opetition 270

SUMMARY REVIEW QUESTIONS

1. Explain how the combination of opportunities, resources, and entrepreneurs helps determine the character and strategic direction of an entrepreneurial firm.

2. What is the difference between discovery and evaluation in the process of opportunity recognition? Give an example of each.

3. Describe the three characteristics of entrepreneurial leadership: vision, dedication and drive, and commitment to excellence.

4. Briefly describe the three types of entrepreneurial entry strategies: pioneering, imitative, and adaptive.

5. Explain why entrepreneurial firms are often in a strong position to use combination strategies.

6. What does the term *competitive dynamics* mean?

7. Explain the difference between strategic actions and tactical actions and provide examples of each.

applications questions & answers

1. E-Loan and Lending Tree are two entrepreneurial firms that offer lending services over the Internet. Evaluate the features of these two companies and, for each company:

    a. Evaluate their characteristics and assess the extent to which they are comparable in terms of market commonality and resource similarity.

    b. Based on your analysis, what strategic and/or tactical actions might these companies take to improve their competitive position? Could E-Loan and Lending Tree improve their performance more through co-opetition rather than competition? Explain your rationale.

2. Using the Internet, research the Small Business Administration's website (*www.sba.gov*). What different types of financing are available to small firms? Besides financing, what other programs are available to support the growth and development of small businesses?

Company	Market Commonality	Resource Similarity
E-Loan		
Lending Tree		

Company	Strategic Actions	Tectical Actions
E-Loan		
Lending Tree		

3. Think of an entrepreneurial firm that has been successfully launched in the last 10 years. What kind of entry strategy did it use—pioneering, imitative, or adaptive? Since the firm's initial entry, how has it used or combined overall low-cost, differentiation and/or focus strategies?

4. Select an entrepreneurial firm you are familiar with in your local community. Research the company and discuss how it has positioned itself relative to its close competitors. Does it have a unique strategic advantage? Disadvantage? Explain.

ethics questions

1. Imitation strategies are based on the idea of copying another firm's idea and using it for your own purposes. Is this unethical or simply a smart business practice? Discuss the ethical implications of this practice (if any).

2. Intense competition such as price wars are an accepted practice in the United States, but cooperation between companies has legal ramifications because of antitrust laws. Should price wars that drive small businesses or new entrants out of business be illegal? What ethical considerations are raised (if any)?

references

1. Pepitone, J. 2012. Digg sold to Betaworks for pocket change. *CNNmoney.com*, July 12: np.

2. Ante, S. & Walker, J. 2012. Digg admits missteps. *Wsj.com*, July 16: np.

3. *http://web.sba.gov.*

4. Timmons, J. A. & Spinelli, S. 2004. *New venture creation* (6th ed.). New York: McGraw-Hill/Irwin; and Bygrave, W. D. 1997. The entrepreneurial process. In W. D. Bygrave (Ed.), *The portable MBA in entrepreneurship,* 2nd ed. New York: Wiley.

5. Bryant, A. 2012. Want to innovate? Feed a cookie to the monster. *nytimes.com*, March 24: np.

6. Fromartz, S. 1998. How to get your first great idea. *Inc. Magazine,* April 1: 91–94; and, Vesper, K. H. 1990. *New venture strategies,* 2nd ed. Englewood Cliffs, NJ: Prentice-Hall.

7. For an interesting perspective on the nature of the opportunity recognition process, see Baron, R. A. 2006. Opportunity recognition as pattern recognition: How entrepreneurs "connect the dots" to identify new business opportunities. *Academy of Management Perspectives,* February: 104–119.

8. Gaglio, C. M. 1997. Opportunity identification: Review, critique and suggested research directions. In J. A. Katz, ed. *Advances in entrepreneurship, firm emergence and growth,* vol. 3. Greenwich, CT: JAI Press: 139–202; Lumpkin, G. T., Hills, G. E., & Shrader, R. C. 2004. Opportunity recognition. In Harold L. Welsch, (Ed.), *Entrepreneurship: The road ahead,* pp. 73–90. London: Routledge; and Long, W. & McMullan, W. E. 1984. Mapping the new venture opportunity identification process. *Frontiers of entrepreneurship research, 1984.* Wellesley, MA: Babson College: 567–90.

9. For an interesting discussion of different aspects of opportunity discovery, see Shepherd, D. A. & De Tienne, D. R. 2005. Prior knowledge, potential financial reward, and opportunity identification. *Entrepreneurship theory & practice,* 29(1): 91–112; and Gaglio, C. M. 2004. The role of mental simulations and counterfactual thinking in the opportunity identification process. *Entrepreneurship theory & practice,* 28(6): 533–552.

10. Stewart, T. A. 2002. How to think with your gut. *Business 2.0,* November: 99–104.

11. For more on the opportunity recognition process, see Smith, B. R., Matthews, C. H., & Schenkel, M. T. 2009. Differences in entrepreneurial opportunities: The role of tacitness and codification in opportunity identification. *Journal of Small Business Management,* 47(1): 38–57.

12. Timmons, J. A. 1997. Opportunity recognition. In W. D. Bygrave, ed. *The portable MBA in entrepreneurship,* 2nd ed. New York: John Wiley: 26–54.

13. Social networking is also proving to be an increasingly important type of entrepreneurial resource. For an interesting discussion, see Aldrich, H. E. & Kim, P. H. 2007. Small worlds, infinite possibilities? How social networks affect entrepreneurial team formation and search. *Strategic Entrepreneurship Journal,* 1(1): 147–166.

14. Bhide, A. V. 2000. *The origin and evolution of new businesses.* New York: Oxford University Press.

15. Small Business 2001: Where are we now? 2001. *Inc. Magazine,* May 29: 18–19; and Zacharakis, A. L., Bygrave, W. D., & Shepherd, D. A. 2000. *Global entrepreneurship monitor—National entrepreneurship assessment: United States of America 2000 Executive Report.* Kansas City, MO: Kauffman Center for Entrepreneurial Leadership.

16. Cooper, S. 2003. Cash cows. *Entrepreneur,* June: 36.

17. Seglin, J. L. 1998. What angels want. *Inc. Magazine,* 20(7): 43–44.

18. Torres, N. L. 2002. Playing an angel. *Entrepreneur,* May: 130–138.

19. For an interesting discussion of how venture capital practices vary across different sectors of the economy, see Gaba, V. & Meyer, A. D. 2008. Crossing the organizational species barrier: How venture capital practices infiltrated the information technology sector. *Academy of Management Journal,* 51(5): 391–412.

20. Our discussion of crowdfunding draws on Wasik, J. 2012. The brilliance (and madness) of crowdfunding. *Forbes,* June 25: 144–146; Anonymous. 2012. Why crowdfunding may not be path to riches. *Finance.yahoo.com,* October 23: np; and Espinoza, J. 2012. Doing equity crowd funding right. *Wall Street Journal,* May 21: R3.

21. For more on how different forms of organizing entrepreneurial firms as well as different stages of new firm growth and development affect financing, see Cassar, G. 2004. The financing of business start-ups. *Journal of Business Venturing,* 19(2): 261–283.

22. Kroll, M., Walters, B., & Wright, P. 2010. The impact of insider control and environment on post-IPO performance. *Academy of Management Journal,* 53: 693–725.

23. Eisenhardt, K. M. & Schoonhoven, C. B. 1990. Organizational growth: Linking founding team, strategy, environment, and growth among U.S. semiconductor ventures, 1978–1988. *Administrative Science Quarterly,* 35: 504–529.

24. Dubini, P. & Aldrich, H. 1991. Personal and extended networks are central to the entrepreneurship process. *Journal of Business Venturing,* 6(5): 305–333.

25. For more on the role of social contacts in helping young firms build legitimacy, see Chrisman, J. J. & McMullan, W. E. 2004. Outside assistance as a knowledge resource for new venture survival. *Journal of Small Business Management,* 42(3): 229–244.

26. Vogel, C. 2000. Janina Pawlowski. *Working woman,* June: 70.

27. For a recent perspective on entrepreneurship and strategic alliances, see Rothaermel, F. T. & Deeds, D. L. 2006. Alliance types, alliance experience and alliance management capability in high-technology ventures. *Journal of Business Venturing,* 21(4): 429–460; and Lu, J. W. & Beamish, P. W. 2006. Partnering strategies and performance of SMEs' international joint ventures. *Journal of Business Venturing,* 21(4): 461–486.

28. Monahan, J. 2005. All Systems Grow. *Entrepreneur,* March: 78–82; Weaver, K. M. & Dickson, P. 2004. Strategic Alliances. In W. J. Dennis, Jr. (Ed.), *NFIB National Small Business Poll.* Washington, DC: National Federation of Independent Business; and Copeland, M. V. & Tilin, A. 2005. Get Someone to Build It. *Business 2.0,* 6(5): 88.

29. For more information, go to the Small Business Administration website at *www.sba.gov.*

30. Simsek, Z., Heavey, C., & Veiga, J. 2009. The Impact of CEO core self-evaluations on entrepreneurial orientation. *Strategic Management Journal,* 31: 110–119.

31. For an interesting study of the role of passion in entrepreneurial success, see Chen, X-P., Yao, X., & Kotha, S. 2009 Entrepreneur passion and preparedness in business plan presentations: A persuasion analysis of venture capitalists' funding decisions. *Academy of Management Journal,* 52(1): 101–120.

32. Collins, J. 2001. *Good to great.* New York: HarperCollins.

33. The idea of entry wedges was discussed by Vesper, K. 1990. *New venture strategies* (2nd ed.). Englewood Cliffs, NJ: Prentice-Hall; and Drucker, P. F. 1985. *Innovation and entrepreneurship.* New York: HarperBusiness.

34. See Dowell, G. & Swaminathan, A. 2006. Entry timing, exploration, and firm survival in the early U.S. bicycle industry. *Strategic Management Journal,* 27: 1159–1182, for a recent study of the timing of entrepreneurial new entry.

35. Dunlap-Hinkler, D., Kotabe, M., & Mudambi, R. 2010. A story of breakthrough vs. incremental innovation: Corporate entrepreneurship in the global pharmaceutical industry. *Strategic Entrepreneurship Journal,* 4: 106–127.

36. Maiello, M. 2002. They almost changed the world. *Forbes,* December 22: 217–220.

37. Pogue, D. 2012. Pay by app: No cash or card needed. *International Herald Tribune,* July 19: 18.

38. Williams, G. 2002. Looks like rain. *Entrepreneur,* September: 104–111.

39. Pedroza, G. M. 2002. Tech tutors. *Entrepreneur,* September: 120.

40. Romanelli, E. 1989. Environments and strategies of organization start-up: Effects on early survival. *Administrative Science Quarterly,* 34(3): 369–87.

41. Wallace, B. 2000. Brothers. *Philadelphia Magazine,* April: 66–75.

42. Buchanan, L. 2003. The innovation factor: A field guide to innovation. *Forbes,* April 21, *www.forbes.com.*

43. Kim, W. C. & Mauborgne, R. 2005. *Blue ocean strategy.* Boston: Harvard Business School Press.

44. For more on how unique organizational combinations can contribute to competitive advantages of entrepreneurial firms, see Steffens, P., Davidsson, P., & Fitzsimmons, J. Performance configurations over times: Implications for growth- and profit-oriented strategies. *Entrepreneurship Theory & Practice,* 33(1): 125–148.

45. Smith, K. G., Ferrier, W. J., & Grimm, C. M. 2001. King of the hill: Dethroning the industry leader. *Academy of Management Executive,* 15(2): 59–70.

46. Grove, A. 1999. *Only the paranoid survive: How to exploit the crises points that challenge every company.* New York: Random House.

47. Stalk, Jr., G. & Lachenauer, R. 2004. *Hardball: Are you playing to play or playing to win?* Cambridge, MA: Harvard Business School Press.

48. Chen, M. J., Lin, H. C, & Michel, J. G. 2010. Navigating in a hypercompetitive environment: The roles of action aggressiveness and TMT integration. *Strategic Management Journal,* 31: 1410–1430.

49. Peteraf, M. A. & Bergen, M. A. 2003. Scanning competitive landscapes: A market-based and resource-based framework. *Strategic Management Journal,* 24: 1027–1045.

50. Chen, M. J. 1996. Competitor analysis and interfirm rivalry: Toward a theoretical integration. *Academy of Management Review,* 21(1): 100–134.

51. Chen, 1996, op.cit.

52. Chen, M. J., Su, K. H, & Tsai, W. 2007. Competitive tension: The awareness-motivation-capability perspective. *Academy of Management Journal,* 50(1): 101–118.

53. St. John, W. 1999. Barnes & Noble's Epiphany. *Wired, www.wired.com,* June.

54. Anonymous. 2010. Is the *Times* ready for a newspaper war? *Bloomberg Businessweek,* April 26: 30–31.

55. Souder, D. & Shaver, J. M. 2010. Constraints and incentives for making long horizon corporate investments. *Strategic Management Journal,* 31: 1316–1336.

56. Chen, M. J. & Hambrick, D. 1995. Speed, stealth, and selective attack: How small firms differ from large firms in competitive behavior. *Academy of Management Journal,* 38: 453–482.

57. Tenner, L. 2009. TOMS shoes donates one pair of shoes for every pair purchased. *America.gov,* October 19: np.

58. *www.facebook.com/tomsshoes.*

59. For a discussion of how the strategic actions of Apple Computer contribute to changes in the competitive dynamics in both the cellular phone and music industries, see Burgelman, R. A. & Grove, A. S. 2008. Cross-boundary disruptors: Powerful interindustry entrepreneurial change agents. *Strategic Entrepreneurship Journal,* 1(1): 315–327,

60. Smith, K. G., Ferrier, W. J., & Ndofor, H. 2001. Competitive dynamics research: Critique and future directions. In M. A. Hitt, R. E. Freeman, & J. S. Harrison (Eds.), *The Blackwell handbook of strategic management,* pp. 315–361. Oxford, UK: Blackwell.

61. Gee, P. 2000. Co-opetition: The new market milieu. *Journal of Healthcare Management,* 45: 359–363.

62. Ketchen, D. J., Snow, C. C., & Hoover, V. L. 2004. Research on competitive dynamics: Recent accomplishments and future challenges. *Journal of Management,* 30(6): 779–804.

63. Khanna, T., Gulati, R., & Nohria, N. 2000. The economic modeling of strategy process: Clean models and dirty hands. *Strategic Management Journal,* 21: 781–790.

chapter 9

Strategic Control and Corporate Governance

After reading this chapter, you should have a good understanding of the following learning objectives:

LO9.1 The value of effective strategic control systems in strategy implementation.

LO9.2 The key difference between "traditional" and "contemporary" control systems.

LO9.3 The imperative for "contemporary" control systems in today's complex and rapidly changing competitive and general environments.

LO9.4 The benefits of having the proper balance among the three levers of behavioral control: culture, rewards and incentives, and boundaries.

LO9.5 The three key participants in corporate governance: shareholders, management (led by the CEO), and the board of directors.

LO9.6 The role of corporate governance mechanisms in ensuring that the interests of managers are aligned with those of shareholders from both the United States and international perspectives.

Learning from Mistakes

Hewlett-Packard (HP) is one of the largest firms in the world and also one of the most dysfunctional. Sitting #10 on the Fortune 500 list with $120 billion in sales in 2012, it is a titan in the computer hardware market.[1] However, it is a struggling titan that lost $12.6 billion in 2012, in contrast to earnings of almost $9 billion only two years earlier. But HP's struggles go back much farther than the last two years. Their inability to effectively respond to the dramatic shifts that have transformed the computing industry in the last several years has been, at least partly, driven by their toxic corporate governance culture.

The dynamics in the board of directors has resembled a soap opera for over 10 years. Going back to 2002, HP's CEO, Carly Fiorina, was pushing hard for HP to acquire one of its main rivals, Compaq. Standing in her way to get this deal done was Walter Hewitt, the son of one of the firm's founders. The members of the board took sides in this debate and started leaking corporate secrets to the press to bolster their side of the argument. HP eventually did acquire Compaq, but the toxic culture in the boardroom was set.

Fiorina stayed at the helm of HP until early 2005, when she was forced out by the board—but only after board

members leaked documents damaging to Fiorina in the press. She was replaced by Mark Hurd, but the troubles with the board continued. The chairwoman of the board was accused in 2006 of hiring private investigators to obtain the phone records of board members and reporters to try to get at the root of leaks from the board. The scandal was investigated by both the State of California and the U.S. Congress and resulted in Patricia Dunn, the chairwoman, being forced from her position. Hurd, the firm's CEO, was fired in 2010 when it came to light that he had an inappropriate affair with a subordinate and had charged expenses related to his affair to the firm. His departure only served to exacerbate the tension on the board. He had been dismissed on a 6–4 vote by the board, and the tension between the pro- and anti-Hurd factions on the board spilled over to the search for his replacement. It got so bad that some board members refused to be in the same room with other directors. The board settled on Leo Apotheker to replace Hurd, but only after the search firm vetting Apotheker didn't fully disclose issues related to Apotheker that led to his firing from his position of co-CEO at SAP, an enterprise software firm. Apotheker lasted all of 11 months as CEO at HP before he was fired, receiving a $13.2 million dollar severance package from the board. He was replaced by Meg Whitman, the former CEO of eBay, in 2011.

All of the drama in the boardroom has had a devastating effect on HP's businesses. The strategic direction of the firm has been inconsistent over time, moving from traditional hardware, to mobile devices, to computing services, and finally to cloud computing. HP announced it was planning to spin off its PC business only to quickly move away from that plan once the market reacted to the announcement by pummeling the firm's stock. The drama also infested the rest of the company. Both Apotheker and Whitman have had to deal with employees leaking important and damaging information to the press, much like the board has done for years. As a result, there has been very little information sharing within the organization, because no one knows who they can trust and who will leak important information to the press.

Discussion Questions

1. What are the most significant problems with HP's board?
2. How do we see the problems with the board of directors damaging HP's ability to compete in its markets?

strategic control
the process of monitoring and correcting a firm's strategy and performance.

We first explore two central aspects of **strategic control:**[2] (1) *informational control,* which is the ability to respond effectively to environmental change, and (2) *behavioral control,* which is the appropriate balance and alignment among a firm's culture, rewards, and boundaries. In the final section of this chapter, we focus on strategic control from a much broader perspective—what is referred to as *corporate governance.*[3] Here, we direct our attention to the need for a firm's shareholders (the owners) and their elected representatives (the board of directors) to ensure that the firm's executives (the management team) strive to fulfill their fiduciary duty of maximizing long-term shareholder value. As we just saw in the HP example, poor corporate governance can result in significant loss of managerial attention and of the ability to manage major strategic issues.

LO9.1
The value of effective strategic control systems in strategy implementation.

Ensuring Informational Control: Responding Effectively to Environmental Change

We discuss two broad types of control systems: "traditional" and "contemporary." As both general and competitive environments become more unpredictable and complex, the need for contemporary systems increases.

A Traditional Approach to Strategic Control

traditional approach to strategic control
a sequential method of organizational control in which (1) strategies are formulated and top management sets goals, (2) strategies are implemented, and (3) performance is measured against the predetermined goal set.

The **traditional approach to strategic control** is sequential: (1) strategies are formulated and top management sets goals, (2) strategies are implemented, and (3) performance is measured against the predetermined goal set, as illustrated in Exhibit 9.1.

Control is based on a feedback loop from performance measurement to strategy formulation. This process typically involves lengthy time lags, often tied to a firm's annual planning cycle. Such traditional control systems, termed "single-loop" learning by Harvard's Chris Argyris, simply compare actual performance to a predetermined goal.[4] They are most appropriate when the environment is stable and relatively simple, goals and objectives can be measured with a high level of certainty, and there is little need for complex measures of performance. Sales quotas, operating budgets, production schedules, and similar quantitative control mechanisms are typical. The appropriateness of the business strategy or standards of performance is seldom questioned.[5]

LO9.2
The key difference between "traditional" and "contemporary" control systems.

James Brian Quinn of Dartmouth College has argued that grand designs with precise and carefully integrated plans seldom work.[6] Rather, most strategic change proceeds incrementally—one step at a time. Leaders should introduce some sense of direction, some logic in incremental steps.[7] Similarly, McGill University's Henry Mintzberg has written about leaders "crafting" a strategy.[8] Drawing on the parallel between the potter at her wheel and the strategist, Mintzberg pointed out that the potter begins work with some general idea of the artifact she wishes to create, but the details of design—even possibilities for a different design—emerge as the work progresses. For businesses facing complex and turbulent business environments, the craftsperson's method helps us deal with the uncertainty about how a design will work out in practice and allows for a creative element.

EXHIBIT 9.1 Traditional Approach to Strategic Control

Mintzberg's argument, like Quinn's, questions the value of rigid planning and goal-setting processes. Fixed strategic goals also become dysfunctional for firms competing in highly unpredictable competitive environments. Strategies need to change frequently and opportunistically. An inflexible commitment to predetermined goals and milestones can prevent the very adaptability that is required of a good strategy.

A Contemporary Approach to Strategic Control

Adapting to and anticipating both internal and external environmental change is an integral part of strategic control. The relationships between strategy formulation, implementation, and control are highly interactive, as suggested by Exhibit 9.2. It also illustrates two different types of strategic control: informational control and behavioral control. **Informational control** is primarily concerned with whether or not the organization is "doing the right things." **Behavioral control,** on the other hand, asks if the organization is "doing things right" in the implementation of its strategy. Both the informational and behavioral components of strategic control are necessary, but not sufficient, conditions for success. What good is a well-conceived strategy that cannot be implemented? Or what use is an energetic and committed workforce if it is focused on the wrong strategic target?

John Weston is the former CEO of ADP Corporation, the largest payroll and tax-filing processor in the world. He captures the essence of contemporary control systems.

> At ADP, 39 plus 1 adds up to more than 40 plus 0. The 40-plus-0 employee is the harried worker who at 40 hours a week just tries to keep up with what's in the "in" basket. . . . Because he works with his head down, he takes zero hours to think about what he's doing, why he's doing it, and how he's doing it. . . . On the other hand, the 39-plus-1 employee takes at least 1 of those 40 hours to think about what he's doing and why he's doing it. That's why the other 39 hours are far more productive.[9]

Informational control deals with the internal environment as well as the external strategic context. It addresses the assumptions and premises that provide the foundation for an organization's strategy. Do the organization's goals and strategies still "fit" within the context of the current strategic environment? Depending on the type of business, such assumptions may relate to changes in technology, customer tastes, government regulation, and industry competition.

This involves two key issues. First, managers must scan and monitor the external environment, as we discussed in Chapter 2. Also, conditions can change in the internal environment of the firm, as we discussed in Chapter 3, requiring changes in the strategic direction of the firm. These may include, for example, the resignation of key executives or delays in the completion of major production facilities.

In the contemporary approach, information control is part of an ongoing process of organizational learning that continuously updates and challenges the assumptions that underlie the organization's strategy. In such "double-loop" learning, the organization's assumptions, premises, goals, and strategies are continuously monitored, tested, and reviewed. The benefits of continuous monitoring are evident—time lags are dramatically shortened,

LO9.3

The imperative for "contemporary" control systems in today's complex and rapidly changing competitive and general environments.

informational control
a method of organizational control in which a firm gathers and analyzes information from the internal and external environment in order to obtain the best fit between the organization's goals and strategies and the strategic environment.

behavioral control
a method of organizational control in which a firm influences the actions of employees through culture, rewards, and boundaries.

EXHIBIT 9.2 Contemporary Approach to Strategic Control

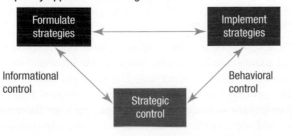

HOW DO MANAGERS AND EMPLOYEES VIEW THEIR FIRM'S CONTROL SYSTEM?

Top executives of organizations often assert that they are pushing for more contemporary control systems. The centralized, periodic setting of objectives and rules with top-down implementation processes is ineffective for organizations facing heterogeneous and dynamic environments. For example, Walmart has, in recent years, realized its top-down, rule-based leadership system was too rigid for a firm emphasizing globalization and technological change. Like many other firms, Walmart is moving to a more decentralized, values-based leadership system where lower-level managers make key decisions, keeping the values of the firm in mind as they do so.

Managers of firms see the need to make this transition, but do lower-level managers and workers see a change in the control systems at their organizations? To get at this question, the Boston Research Group conducted a study of 36,000 managers and employees to get their views on their firm's control systems. Their findings are enlightening. Only 3 percent of employees saw their firm's culture as "self-governing," in which decision making is driven by a "set of core principles and values." In contrast, 43 percent of employees saw their firm as operating using a top-down, command-and-control decision process, what the authors of the study labeled as the "blind obedience" model. 53 percent of employees saw their firm following an "informed acquiescence" model where the overall style is top-down but with skilled management that used a mix of rewards and rules to get the desired behavior. In total, 97 percent of employees saw their firm's culture and decision style as being top-down.

Interestingly, managers had a different view. 24 percent of managers believed their organizations used the values-driven, decentralized "self-governing" model. Thus, managers were eight times more likely than employees to see the firm employing a contemporary, values-driven control system. Similarly, while 41 percent of managers said that their firm rewarded performance based on values and not just financial outcomes, only 14 percent of employees saw this.

The cynicism employees expressed regarding the control systems in their firms had important consequences for the firm. Almost half of the employees who had described their firms as "blind obedience" firms had witnessed unethical behavior in the firm within the last year. Only one in four employees in firms with the other two control types said they had witnessed unethical behavior. Additionally, only one-fourth of the employees in "blind obedience" firms would blow the whistle on unethical behavior, but this rate went up to nine in ten if the firm relied on "self-governance." Finally, the impressions of employees influence the ability of the firm to be responsive and innovative. 90 percent of employees in "self-governing" and 67 percent of employees in "informed acquiescence" firms agreed with the statement that "good ideas are readily adopted by my company." Less than 20 percent of employees in "blind obedience" firms agreed with the same statement.

These findings indicate that managers need to be aware of how the actions they take to improve the control systems in their firms are being received by employees. If the employees see the pronouncements of management regarding moving toward a decentralized, culture-centered control system as simply propaganda, the firm is unlikely to experience the positive changes they desire.

Sources: Anonymous. 2011. The view from the top and bottom. *Economist,* September 24: 76; and Levit, A. 2012. Your employees aren't wearing your rose colored glasses. *Openforum.com,* November 12: np.

changes in the competitive environment are detected earlier, and the organization's ability to respond with speed and flexibility is enhanced.

Contemporary control systems must have four characteristics to be effective.[10]

1. Focus on constantly changing information that has potential strategic importance.
2. The information is important enough to demand frequent and regular attention from all levels of the organization.
3. The data and information generated are best interpreted and discussed in face-to-face meetings.
4. The control system is a key catalyst for an ongoing debate about underlying data, assumptions, and action plans.

An executive's decision to use the control system interactively—in other words, to invest the time and attention to review and evaluate new information—sends a clear signal to the organization about what is important. The dialogue and debate that emerge from such an interactive process can often lead to new strategies and innovations. Strategy Spotlight 9.1 discusses how managers and employees each see the control systems at work in their companies and some of the consequences of those impressions.

Attaining Behavioral Control: Balancing Culture, Rewards, and Boundaries

LO9.4

The benefits of having the proper balance among the three levers of behavioral control: culture, rewards and incentives, and boundaries.

Behavioral control is focused on implementation—doing things right. Effectively implementing strategy requires manipulating three key control "levers": culture, rewards, and boundaries (see Exhibit 9.3). There are two compelling reasons for an increased emphasis on culture and rewards in a system of behavioral controls.[11]

First, the competitive environment is increasingly complex and unpredictable, demanding both flexibility and quick response to its challenges. As firms simultaneously downsize and face the need for increased coordination across organizational boundaries, a control system based primarily on rigid strategies, rules, and regulations is dysfunctional. The use of rewards and culture to align individual and organizational goals becomes increasingly important.

Second, the implicit long-term contract between the organization and its key employees has been eroded.[12] Today's younger managers have been conditioned to see themselves as "free agents" and view a career as a series of opportunistic challenges. As managers are advised to "specialize, market yourself, and have work, if not a job," the importance of culture and rewards in building organizational loyalty claims greater importance.

Each of the three levers—culture, rewards, and boundaries—must work in a balanced and consistent manner. Let's consider the role of each.

Building a Strong and Effective Culture

Organizational culture is a system of shared values (what is important) and beliefs (how things work) that shape a company's people, organizational structures, and control systems to produce behavioral norms (the way we do things around here).[13] How important is culture? Very. Over the years, numerous best sellers, such as *Theory Z, Corporate Cultures, In Search of Excellence,* and *Good to Great,*[14] have emphasized the powerful influence of culture on what goes on within organizations and how they perform.

Collins and Porras argued in *Built to Last* that the key factor in sustained exceptional performance is a cultlike culture.[15] You can't touch it or write it down, but it's there in every organization; its influence is pervasive; it can work for you or against you.[16] Effective leaders understand its importance and strive to shape and use it as one of their important levers of strategic control.[17]

organizational culture
a system of shared values and beliefs that shape a company's people, organizational structures, and control systems to produce behavioral norms.

EXHIBIT 9.3 Essential Elements of Behavioral Control

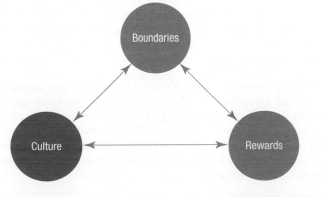

The Role of Culture Culture wears many different hats, each woven from the fabric of those values that sustain the organization's primary source of competitive advantage. Some examples are:

- FedEx and Amazon focus on customer service.
- Lexus (a division of Toyota) and Apple emphasize product quality.
- Google and 3M place a high value on innovation.
- Nucor (steel) and Walmart are concerned, above all, with operational efficiency.

Culture sets implicit boundaries—unwritten standards of acceptable behavior—in dress, ethical matters, and the way an organization conducts its business.[18] By creating a framework of shared values, culture encourages individual identification with the organization and its objectives. Culture acts as a means of reducing monitoring costs.[19]

Strong culture can lead to greater employee engagement and provide a common purpose and identity. Firms have typically relied on economic incentives for workers, using a combination of rewards (carrots) and rules and threats (sticks) to get employees to act in desired ways. But these systems rely on the assumption that individuals are fundamentally self-interested and selfish. However, research suggests that this assumption is overstated.[20] When given a chance to act selfishly or cooperatively with others, over half choose to cooperate, while only 30 percent consistently choose to act selfishly. Thus, cultural systems that build engagement, communication, and a sense of common purpose and identity would allow firms to leverage these collaborative workers.

Sustaining an Effective Culture Powerful organizational cultures just don't happen overnight, and they don't remain in place without a strong commitment—both in terms of words and deeds—by leaders throughout the organization.[21] A viable and productive organizational culture can be strengthened and sustained. However, it cannot be "built" or "assembled"; instead, it must be cultivated, encouraged, and "fertilized."[22]

Storytelling is one way effective cultures are maintained. Many are familiar with the story of how Art Fry's failure to develop a strong adhesive led to 3M's enormously successful Post-it Notes. Perhaps less familiar is the story of Francis G. Okie.[23] In 1922 Okie came up with the idea of selling sandpaper to men as a replacement for razor blades. The idea obviously didn't pan out, but Okie was allowed to remain at 3M. Interestingly, the technology developed by Okie led 3M to develop its first blockbuster product: a waterproof sandpaper that became a staple of the automobile industry. Such stories foster the importance of risk taking, experimentation, freedom to fail, and innovation—all vital elements of 3M's culture.

Rallies or "pep talks" by top executives also serve to reinforce a firm's culture. The late Sam Walton was known for his pep rallies at local Walmart stores. Four times a year, the founders of Home Depot—former CEO Bernard Marcus and Arthur Blank—used to don orange aprons and stage Breakfast with Bernie and Arthur, a 6:30 a.m. pep rally, broadcast live over the firm's closed-circuit TV network to most of its 45,000 employees.[24]

Southwest Airlines' "Culture Committee" is a unique vehicle designed to perpetuate the company's highly successful culture. The following excerpt from an internal company publication describes its objectives:

> The goal of the Committee is simple—to ensure that our unique Corporate Culture stays alive. . . . Culture Committee members represent all regions and departments across our system and they are selected based upon their exemplary display of the "Positively Outrageous Service" that won us the first-ever Triple Crown; their continual exhibition of the "Southwest Spirit" to our Customers and to their fellow workers; and their high energy level, boundless enthusiasm, unique creativity, and constant demonstration of teamwork and love for their fellow workers.[25]

Motivating with Rewards and Incentives

Reward and incentive systems represent a powerful means of influencing an organization's culture, focusing efforts on high-priority tasks, and motivating individual and collective task performance.[26] Just as culture deals with influencing beliefs, behaviors, and attitudes of people within an organization, the **reward system**—by specifying who gets rewarded and why—is an effective motivator and control mechanism.[27] The managers at Not Your Average Joe's, a Massachusett's-based restaurant chain, changed their staffing procedures both to let their servers better understand their performance and to better motivate them.[28] The chain uses sophisticated software to track server performance—both in per customer sales and customer satisfaction as seen in tips. Highly rated servers are given more tables and preferred schedules. In shifting more work and better schedules to the best workers, the chain hopes to improve profitability and motivate all workers.

reward system
policies that specify who gets rewarded and why.

The Potential Downside   While they can be powerful motivators, reward and incentive policies can also result in undesirable outcomes in organizations. At the individual level, incentives can go wrong for multiple reasons. First, if individual workers don't see how their actions relate to how they are compensated, they can be demotivating. For example, if the rewards are related to the firm's stock price, workers may feel that their efforts have little if any impact and won't perceive any benefit from working harder. On the other hand, if the incentives are so closely tied to their individual work, they may lead to dysfunctional outcomes. For example, if a sales representative is rewarded for sales volume, she will be incentivized to sell at all costs. This may lead her to accept unprofitable sales or push sales through distribution channels the firm would rather avoid. Thus, the collective sum of individual behaviors of an organization's employees does not always result in what is best for the organization; individual rationality is no guarantee of organizational rationality.

Reward and incentive systems can also cause problems across organizational units. As corporations grow and evolve, they often develop different business units with multiple reward systems. They may differ based on industry contexts, business situations, stage of product life cycles, and so on. Subcultures within organizations may reflect differences among functional areas, products, services, and divisions. To the extent that reward systems reinforce such behavioral norms, attitudes, and belief systems, cohesiveness is reduced; important information is hoarded rather than shared, individuals begin working at cross-purposes, and they lose sight of overall goals.

Such conflicts are commonplace in many organizations. For example, sales and marketing personnel promise unrealistically quick delivery times to bring in business, much to the dismay of operations and logistics; overengineering by R&D creates headaches for manufacturing; and so on. Conflicts also arise across divisions when divisional profits become a key compensation criterion. As ill will and anger escalate, personal relationships and performance may suffer.

Creating Effective Reward and Incentive Programs   To be effective, incentive and reward systems need to reinforce basic core values, enhance cohesion and commitment to goals and objectives, and meet with the organization's overall mission and purpose.[29]

At General Mills, to ensure a manager's interest in the overall performance of his or her unit, half of a manager's annual bonus is linked to business-unit results and half to individual performance.[30] For example, if a manager simply matches a rival manufacturer's performance, his or her salary is roughly 5 percent lower. However, if a manager's product ranks in the industry's top 10 percent in earnings growth and return on capital, the manager's total pay can rise to nearly 30 percent beyond the industry norm.

Effective reward and incentive systems share a number of common characteristics.[31] (see Exhibit 9.4). The perception that a plan is "fair and equitable" is critically important.

EXHIBIT 9.4

Characteristics of
Effective Reward and
Evaluation Systems

- Objectives are clear, well understood, and broadly accepted.
- Rewards are clearly linked to performance and desired behaviors.
- Performance measures are clear and highly visible.
- Feedback is prompt, clear, and unambiguous.
- The compensation "system" is perceived as fair and equitable.
- The structure is flexible; it can adapt to changing circumstances.

The firm must have the flexibility to respond to changing requirements as its direction and objectives change. In recent years many companies have begun to place more emphasis on growth. Emerson Electric has shifted its emphasis from cost cutting to growth. To ensure that changes take hold, the management compensation formula has been changed from a largely bottom-line focus to one that emphasizes growth, new products, acquisitions, and international expansion. Discussions about profits are handled separately, and a culture of risk taking is encouraged.[32] Finally, incentive and reward systems don't all have to be about financial rewards. Recognition can be a powerful motivator. For example, at Mars Central Europe, they hold an event twice a year in which they celebrate innovative ideas generated by employees. Recognition at the "Make a Difference" event is designed to motivate the winners and also other employees who want to receive the same recognition.[33]

The key is for managers to find a mix of incentives that motivates employees. Gordon Bethune, the former CEO of Continental Airlines used the following analogy.[34]

> "I own a twelve-hundred-acre ranch, and it's got a seventy-acre lake. It's wonderful. And do you know, in spite of all that, I still have to use bait when I fish? Can you believe it? The point is there's got to be something in it for the fish, and it's up to me to know what the fish like. It's not up to them. So maybe if I learn enough about the fish and what they like, they might be easier to get in the boat and provide me a little recreation."

Setting Boundaries and Constraints

In an ideal world, a strong culture and effective rewards should be sufficient to ensure that all individuals and subunits work toward the common goals and objectives of the whole organization.[35] However, this is not usually the case. Counterproductive behavior can arise because of motivated self-interest, lack of a clear understanding of goals and objectives, or outright malfeasance. **Boundaries and constraints** can serve many useful purposes for organizations, including:

boundaries and constraints
rules that specify
behaviors that are
acceptable and
unacceptable.

- Focusing individual efforts on strategic priorities.
- Providing short-term objectives and action plans to channel efforts.
- Improving efficiency and effectiveness.
- Minimizing improper and unethical conduct.

Focusing Efforts on Strategic Priorities   Boundaries and constraints play a valuable role in focusing a company's strategic priorities. For example, several years ago, IBM sold off its PC business as part of its desire to focus its business on computing services. Similarly, Pfizer sold its infant formula business as it refocused its attention on core pharmaceutical products.[36] This concentration of effort and resources provides the firm with greater strategic focus and the potential for stronger competitive advantages in the remaining areas.

Steve Jobs would use white boards to set priorities and focus attention at Apple. For example, he would take his "top 100" people on a retreat each year. One year, he asked the group what 10 things Apple should do next. The group identified ideas. Ideas went up on the board, then got erased or revised; new ones were added, revised, and erased. The group argued about it for a while and finally identified their list of top 10 initiatives. Jobs proceeded to slash the bottom seven, stating, "We can only do three."[37]

Boundaries also have a place in the nonprofit sector. For example, a British relief organization uses a system to monitor strategic boundaries by maintaining a list of companies whose contributions it will neither solicit nor accept. Such boundaries are essential for maintaining legitimacy with existing and potential benefactors.

Providing Short-Term Objectives and Action Plans In Chapter 1 we discussed the importance of a firm having a vision, mission, and strategic objectives that are internally consistent and that provide strategic direction. In addition, short-term objectives and action plans provide similar benefits. That is, they represent boundaries that help to allocate resources in an optimal manner and to channel the efforts of employees at all levels throughout the organization.[38] To be effective, short-term objectives must have several attributes. They should:

- Be specific and measurable.
- Include a specific time horizon for their attainment.
- Be achievable, yet challenging enough to motivate managers who must strive to accomplish them.

Research has found that performance is enhanced when individuals are encouraged to attain specific, difficult, yet achievable, goals (as opposed to vague "do your best" goals).[39]

Short-term objectives must provide proper direction and also provide enough flexibility for the firm to keep pace with and anticipate changes in the external environment, new government regulations, a competitor introducing a substitute product, or changes in consumer taste. Unexpected events within a firm may require a firm to make important adjustments in both strategic and short-term objectives. The emergence of new industries can have a drastic effect on the demand for products and services in more traditional industries.

Action plans are critical to the implementation of chosen strategies. Unless action plans are specific, there may be little assurance that managers have thought through all of the resource requirements for implementing their strategies. In addition, unless plans are specific, managers may not understand what needs to be implemented or have a clear time frame for completion. This is essential for the scheduling of key activities that must be implemented. Finally, individual managers must be held accountable for the implementation. This helps to provide the necessary motivation and "sense of ownership" to implement action plans on a timely basis. Strategy Spotlight 9.2 illustrates how Marks and Spencer puts its sustainability mission into action by creating clear, measurable goals.

Improving Operational Efficiency and Effectiveness Rule-based controls are most appropriate in organizations with the following characteristics:

- Environments are stable and predictable.
- Employees are largely unskilled and interchangeable.
- Consistency in product and service is critical.
- The risk of malfeasance is extremely high (e.g., in banking or casino operations).[40]

McDonald's Corp. has extensive rules and regulations that regulate the operation of its franchises.[41] Its policy manual from a number of years ago stated, "Cooks must turn, never flip, hamburgers. If they haven't been purchased, Big Macs must be discarded in 10 minutes after being cooked and French fries in 7 minutes. Cashiers must make eye contact with and smile at every customer."

Guidelines can also be effective in setting spending limits and the range of discretion for employees and managers, such as the $2,500 limit that hotelier Ritz-Carlton uses to empower employees to placate dissatisfied customers. Regulations also can be initiated to improve the use of an employee's time at work.[42] CA Technologies restricts the use of email during the hours of 10 a.m. to noon and 2 p.m. to 4 p.m. each day.[43]

BREAKING DOWN SUSTAINABILITY INTO MEASURABLE GOALS

Marks & Spencer (M&S) laid out an ambitious goal in early 2010 to become "the world's most sustainable retailer" by 2015. To meet this goal, M&S needed to substantially change how it undertook nearly all of its business operations. To make this process more tractable and to provide opportunities to identify a range of actions managers could take, M&S developed an overarching plan for its sustainability efforts, dubbed Plan A. They called it Plan A because, as M&S managers put it, when it comes to building environmental sustainability, there is no Plan B. Everyone in the firm needed to be committed to the one vision. In this plan, M&S identified three broad themes.

- Aim for all M&S products to have at least one Plan A quality.
- Help our customers make a difference to the social and environmental causes that matter to them.
- Help our customers live a more sustainable life.

Thus, M&S aimed not only to improve its own operations but also to change the lives of its customers and the operations of its suppliers and other partners. Marc Bolland, M&S's CEO, fleshed out the general Plan A goal with 180 environmental commitments. These commitments all had time targets associated with them, some short term and some longer term. For example, one commitment was to make the company carbon neutral by 2012. To meet its goal, M&S estimated it needed to achieve a 25 percent reduction in energy use in its stores by 2012 and extended it to 35 percent by 2015. This provided clear targets for store managers

to work toward. Similarly, M&S set a goal to improve its water use efficiency in stores by 25 percent by the year 2015. Additionally, M&S set out to design new stores that used 35 percent less water than current stores. These targets provided clear metrics for store managers as well as architects and designers working on new stores.

In working with its suppliers, M&S similarly rolled out a series of time-based commitments. For example, it conducted a review with all suppliers on the Plan A initiatives in the first year of the plan. M&S required all suppliers of fresh meat, dairy, produce, and flowers to engage in a sustainable agriculture program by 2012. All clothing suppliers were required to install energy efficient lighting and improved insulation by 2015 to attain a 10 percent reduction in energy usage. These types of efforts spanned across the firm and its supply chain.

With its Plan A, M&S broke down a huge initiative into clear targets that were actionable by managers across the firm and in its partner firms. Interestingly, while this initiative was hatched as a means to achieve environmental sustainability gains, it has also turned out to be an economic win for M&S. In the first year of the plan, the firm experienced an $80 million profit on the actions it undertook. The surplus has resulted from gains in energy efficiency, lower packaging costs, lower waste bills, and profit from a sustainable energy business it set up that relies on burning biowaste to generate electricity.

Sources: Felsted, A. 2011. Marks and Spencer's green blueprint. *Ft.com,* March 17: np; Anonymous. 2012. Marks & Spencer's ambitious sustainability goals. *Sustainablebusiness.com,* March 3: np; and plana.marksandspencer.com.

Minimizing Improper and Unethical Conduct Guidelines can be useful in specifying proper relationships with a company's customers and suppliers.[44] Many companies have explicit rules regarding commercial practices, including the prohibition of any form of payment, bribe, or kickback. For example, Singapore Airlines has a 17-page policy outlining its anticorruption and antibribery policies.[45]

Regulations backed up with strong sanctions can also help an organization avoid conducting business in an unethical manner. After the passing of the Sarbanes-Oxley Act (which provides for stiffer penalties for financial reporting misdeeds), many chief financial officers (CFOs) have taken steps to ensure ethical behavior in the preparation of financial statements. For example, Home Depot's CFO, Carol B. Tome, strengthened the firm's code of ethics and developed stricter guidelines. Now all 25 of her subordinates must sign personal statements that all of their financial statements are correct—just as she and her CEO have to do.[46]

Behavioral Control in Organizations: Situational Factors

Here, the focus is on ensuring that the behavior of individuals at all levels of an organization is directed toward achieving organizational goals and objectives. The three fundamental types of control are culture, rewards and incentives, and boundaries and constraints. An organization may pursue one or a combination of them on the basis of a variety of internal and external factors.

Not all organizations place the same emphasis on each type of control.[47] In high-technology firms engaged in basic research, members may work under high levels of autonomy. An individual's performance is generally quite difficult to measure accurately because of the long lead times involved in R&D activities. Thus, internalized norms and values become very important.

When the measurement of an individual's output or performance is quite straightforward, control depends primarily on granting or withholding rewards. Frequently, a sales manager's compensation is in the form of a commission and bonus tied directly to his or her sales volume, which is relatively easy to determine. Here, behavior is influenced more strongly by the attractiveness of the compensation than by the norms and values implicit in the organization's culture. The measurability of output precludes the need for an elaborate system of rules to control behavior.[48]

Control in bureaucratic organizations is dependent on members following a highly formalized set of rules and regulations. Most activities are routine and the desired behavior can be specified in a detailed manner because there is generally little need for innovative or creative activity. Managing an assembly plant requires strict adherence to many rules as well as exacting sequences of assembly operations. In the public sector, the Department of Motor Vehicles in most states must follow clearly prescribed procedures when issuing or renewing driver licenses.

Exhibit 9.5 provides alternate approaches to behavioral control and some of the situational factors associated with them.

Evolving from Boundaries to Rewards and Culture

In most environments, organizations should strive to provide a system of rewards and incentives, coupled with a culture strong enough that boundaries become internalized. This reduces the need for external controls such as rules and regulations.

First, hire the right people—individuals who already identify with the organization's dominant values and have attributes consistent with them. Kroger, a supermarket chain, uses a pre-employment test to assess the degree to which potential employees will be friendly and communicate well with customers.[49] Microsoft's David Pritchard is well aware of the consequences of failing to hire properly.

> If I hire a bunch of bozos, it will hurt us, because it takes time to get rid of them. They start infiltrating the organization and then they themselves start hiring people of lower quality. At Microsoft, we are always looking for people who are better than we are.

EXHIBIT 9.5

Organizational Control:
Alternative Approaches

Approach	Some Situational Factors
Culture: A system of unwritten rules that forms an internalized influence over behavior.	• Often found in professional organizations. • Associated with high autonomy. • Norms are the basis for behavior.
Rules: Written and explicit guidelines that provide external constraints on behavior.	• Associated with standardized output. • Tasks are generally repetitive and routine. • Little need for innovation or creative activity.
Rewards: The use of performance-based incentive systems to motivate.	• Measurement of output and performance is rather straightforward. • Most appropriate in organizations pursuing unrelated diversification strategies. • Rewards may be used to reinforce other means of control.

Second, training plays a key role. For example, in elite military units such as the Green Berets and Navy SEALs, the training regimen so thoroughly internalizes the culture that individuals, in effect, lose their identity. The group becomes the overriding concern and focal point of their energies. At firms such as FedEx, training not only builds skills, but also plays a significant role in building a strong culture on the foundation of each organization's dominant values.

Third, managerial role models are vital. Andy Grove, former CEO and co-founder of Intel, didn't need (or want) a large number of bureaucratic rules to determine who is responsible for what, who is supposed to talk to whom, and who gets to fly first class (no one does). He encouraged openness by not having many of the trappings of success—he worked in a cubicle like all the other professionals. Can you imagine any new manager asking whether or not he can fly first class? Grove's personal example eliminated such a need.

Fourth, reward systems must be clearly aligned with the organizational goals and objectives. For example, as part of its efforts to drive sustainability efforts down through its suppliers, Marks and Spencer pushes the suppliers to develop employee rewards systems that support a living wage and team collaboration.

LO9.5

The three key participants in corporate governance: shareholders, management (led by the CEO), and the board of directors.

corporate governance
the relationship among various participants in determining the direction and performance of corporations. The primary participants are (1) the share-holders, (2) the management, and (3) the board of directors.

The Role of Corporate Governance

We now address the issue of strategic control in a broader perspective, typically referred to as "corporate governance." Here we focus on the need for both shareholders (the owners of the corporation) and their elected representatives, the board of directors, to actively ensure that management fulfills its overriding purpose of increasing long-term shareholder value.[50]

Robert Monks and Nell Minow, two leading scholars in **corporate governance,** define it as "the relationship among various participants in determining the direction and performance of corporations. The primary participants are (1) the shareholders, (2) the management (led by the CEO), and (3) the board of directors."* Our discussion will center on how corporations can succeed (or fail) in aligning managerial motives with the interests of the shareholders and their elected representatives, the board of directors.[51] As you will recall from Chapter 1, we discussed the important role of boards of directors and provided some examples of effective and ineffective boards.[52]

Good corporate governance plays an important role in the investment decisions of major institutions, and a premium is often reflected in the price of securities of companies that practice it. The corporate governance premium is larger for firms in countries with sound corporate governance practices compared to countries with weaker corporate governance standards.[53]

Sound governance practices often lead to superior financial performance. However, this is not always the case. For example, practices such as independent directors (directors who are not part of the firm's management) and stock options are generally assumed to result in better performance. But in many cases, independent directors may not have the necessary expertise or involvement, and the granting of stock options to the CEO may lead to decisions and actions calculated to prop up share price only in the short term. Strategy Spotlight 9.3 presents some research evidence on governance practices and firm performance.

---

*Management cannot ignore the demands of other important firm stakeholders such as creditors, suppliers, customers, employees, and government regulators. At times of financial duress, powerful creditors can exert strong and legitimate pressures on managerial decisions. In general, however, the attention to stakeholders other than the owners of the corporation must be addressed in a manner that is still consistent with maximizing long-term shareholder returns. For a seminal discussion on stakeholder management, refer to Freeman, R. E. 1984. *Strategic Management: A Stakeholder Approach.* Boston: Pitman.

THE RELATIONSHIP BETWEEN RECOMMENDED CORPORATE GOVERNANCE PRACTICES AND FIRM PERFORMANCE

A significant amount of research has examined the effect of corporate governance on firm performance. Some research has shown that implementing good corporate governance structures yields superior financial performance. Other research has not found a positive relationship between governance and performance. Results of a few of these studies are summarized below.

1. *A positive correlation between corporate governance and different measures of corporate performance.* Recent studies show that there is a strong positive correlation between effective corporate governance and different indicators of corporate performance such as growth, profitability, and customer satisfaction. Over a recent three-year period, the average return of large capitalized firms with the best governance practices was more than five times higher than the performance of firms in the bottom corporate governance quartile.

2. *Compliance with international best practices leads to superior performance.* Studies of European companies show that greater compliance with international corporate governance best practices concerning board structure and function has significant and positive relationships with return on assets (ROA). In 10 of 11 Asian and Latin American markets, companies in the top corporate governance quartile for their respective regions averaged 10 percent greater return on capital employed (ROCE) than their peers.

In a study of 12 emerging markets, companies in the lowest corporate governance quartile had a much lower ROCE than their peers.

3. *Many recommended corporate governance practices do not have a positive relationship with firm performance.* In contrast to these studies, there is also a body of research suggesting that corporate governance practices do not have a positive influence on firm performance. With corporate boards, there is no evidence that including more external directors on the board of directors of U.S. corporations has led to substantially higher firm performance. Also, giving more stock options to CEOs to align their interests with stakeholders may lead them to take high-risk bets in firm investments that have a low probability to improve firm performance. Rather than making good decisions, CEOs may "swing for the fences" with these high-risk investments. Additionally, motivating CEOs with large numbers of stock options appears to increase the likelihood of unethical accounting violations by the firm as the CEO tries to increase the firm's stock price.

Sources: Dalton, D. R., Daily, C. M., Ellstrand, A. E., & Johnson, J. L., 1998. Meta-analytic reviews of board composition, leadership structure, and financial performance. *Strategic Management Journal,* 19(3): 269–290; Sanders, W. G. & Hambrick, D. C. 2007. Swinging for the fences: The effects of CEO stock options on company risk-taking and performance. *Academy of Management Journal,* 50(5): 1055–1078; Harris, J. & Bromiley, P. 2007. Incentives to cheat: The influence of executive compensation and firm performance on financial misrepresentation. *Organization Science,* 18(3). 350–367; Bauwhede, H. V. 2009. On the relation between corporate governance compliance and operating performance. *Accounting and Business Research.* 39(5); 497–513; Gill, A. 2001. Credit Lyonnais Securities (Asia). *Corporate governance in emerging markets: Saints and sinners,* April; and Low, C. K. 2002. *Corporate governance: An Asia-Pacific critique.* Hong Kong: Sweet & Maxwell Asia.

At the same time, few topics in the business press are generating as much interest (and disdain!) as corporate governance.

Some recent notable examples of flawed corporate governance include:[54]

- In 2012 Japanese camera and medical equipment maker Olympus Corporation and three of its former executives pleaded guilty to charges that they falsified accounting records over a five-year period to inflate the financial performance of the firm. The total value of the accounting irregularities came to $1.7 billion.[55]
- In October 2010, Angelo Mozilo, the co-founder of Countrywide Financial, agreed to pay $67.5 million to the Securities and Exchange Commission (SEC) to settle fraud charges. He was charged with deceiving the home loan company's investors while reaping a personal windfall. He was accused of hiding risks about Countrywide's loan portfolio as the real estate market soured. Former Countrywide President David Sambol and former Chief Financial Officer Eric Sieracki were also charged with fraud, as they failed to disclose the true state of Countrywide's deteriorating mortgage portfolio. The SEC accused Mozilo of insider trading, alleging that he sold millions of dollars worth of Countrywide stock after he knew the company was doomed.

- In 2008, former Brocade CEO Gregory Reyes was sentenced to 21 months in prison and fined $15 million for his involvement in backdating stock option grants. Mr. Reyes was the first executive to go on trial and be convicted over the improper dating of stock-option awards, which dozens of companies have acknowledged since the practice came to light.

Because of the many lapses in corporate governance, we can see the benefits associated with effective practices.[56] However, corporate managers may behave in their own self-interest, often to the detriment of shareholders. Next we address the implications of the separation of ownership and management in the modern corporation, and some mechanisms that can be used to ensure consistency (or alignment) between the interests of shareholders and those of the managers to minimize potential conflicts.

The Modern Corporation:
The Separation of Owners (Shareholders) and Management

Some of the proposed definitions for a *corporation* include:

- "The business corporation is an instrument through which capital is assembled for the activities of producing and distributing goods and services and making investments. Accordingly, a basic premise of corporation law is that a business corporation should have as its objective the conduct of such activities with a view to enhancing the corporation's profit and the gains of the corporation's owners, that is, the shareholders." (Melvin Aron Eisenberg, *The Structure of Corporation Law*)
- "A body of persons granted a charter legally recognizing them as a separate entity having its own rights, privileges, and liabilities distinct from those of its members." (*American Heritage Dictionary*)
- "An ingenious device for obtaining individual profit without individual responsibility." (Ambrose Bierce, *The Devil's Dictionary*)[57]

All of these definitions have some validity and each one reflects a key feature of the corporate form of business organization—its ability to draw resources from a variety of groups and establish and maintain its own persona that is separate from all of them. As Henry Ford once said, "A great business is really too big to be human."

Simply put, a **corporation** is a mechanism created to allow different parties to contribute capital, expertise, and labor for the maximum benefit of each party.[58] The shareholders (investors) are able to participate in the profits of the enterprise without taking direct responsibility for the operations. The management can run the company without the responsibility of personally providing the funds. The shareholders have limited liability as well as rather limited involvement in the company's affairs. However, they reserve the right to elect directors who have the fiduciary obligation to protect their interests.

Over 75 years ago, Columbia University professors Adolf Berle and Gardiner C. Means addressed the divergence of the interests of the owners of the corporation from the professional managers who are hired to run it. They warned that widely dispersed ownership "released management from the overriding requirement that it serve stockholders." The separation of ownership from management has given rise to a set of ideas called "agency theory." Central to agency theory is the relationship between two primary players—the *principals* who are the owners of the firm (stockholders) and the *agents,* who are the people paid by principals to perform a job on their behalf (management). The stockholders elect and are represented by a board of directors that has a fiduciary responsibility to ensure that management acts in the best interests of stockholders to ensure long-term financial returns for the firm.

Agency theory is concerned with resolving two problems that can occur in agency relationships.[59] *The first is the agency problem that arises (1) when the goals of the principals*

---

corporation
a mechanism created to allow different parties to contribute capital, expertise, and labor for the maximum benefit of each party.

agency theory
a theory of the relationship between principals and their agents, with emphasis on two problems: (1) the conflicting goals of principals and agents, along with the difficulty of principals to monitor the agents, and (2) the different attitudes and preferences toward risk of principals and agents.

and agents conflict, and (2) when it is difficult or expensive for the principal to verify what the agent is actually doing.[60] The board of directors would be unable to confirm that the managers were actually acting in the shareholders' interests because managers are "insiders" with regard to the businesses they operate and thus are better informed than the principals. Thus, managers may act "opportunistically" in pursuing their own interests—to the detriment of the corporation.[61] Managers may spend corporate funds on expensive perquisites (e.g., company jets and expensive art), devote time and resources to pet projects (initiatives in which they have a personal interest but that have limited market potential), engage in power struggles (where they may fight over resources for their own betterment and to the detriment of the firm), and negate (or sabotage) attractive merger offers because they may result in increased employment risk.[62]

The second issue is the problem of risk sharing. This arises when the principal and the agent have different attitudes and preferences toward risk. The executives in a firm may favor additional diversification initiatives because, by their very nature, they increase the size of the firm and thus the level of executive compensation.[63] At the same time, such diversification initiatives may erode shareholder value because they fail to achieve some synergies that we discussed in Chapter 6 (e.g., building on core competencies, sharing activities, or enhancing market power). Agents (executives) may have a stronger preference toward diversification than shareholders because it reduces their personal level of risk from potential loss of employment. Executives who have large holdings of stock in their firms were more likely to have diversification strategies that were more consistent with shareholder interests—increasing long-term returns.[64]

At times, top-level managers engage in actions that reflect their self-interest rather than the interests of shareholders. We provide two examples below:

- Steve Wynn, the CEO of Wynn Resorts, had a great year in 2011, even though his stockholders barely broke even. He received a starting salary of $3.9 million. On top of that, he received two bonuses, one worth $2 million and another for $9 million. In addition to cash compensation, he received over $900,000 worth of personal flying time on the corporate jet and over $500,000 worth of use of the company's villa.[65]
- John Sperling retired as chairman emeritus of Apollo Group in early 2013. He founded Apollo, the for-profit education company best known for its University of Phoenix unit, in 1973. Even though he already owns stock in Apollo worth in excess of $200 million, the board of directors, which includes his son as a member, granted him a "special retirement bonus" of $5 million, gave him two cars, and awarded him a lifetime annuity of $71,000 a month. He received all of these benefits even though Apollo's stock at the time of his retirement was worth one-fourth of its value in early 2009.[66]

Governance Mechanisms: Aligning the Interests of Owners and Managers

LO9.6

The role of corporate governance mechanisms in ensuring that the interests of managers are aligned with those of shareholders from both the United States and international perspectives.

As noted above, a key characteristic of the modern corporation is the separation of ownership from control. To minimize the potential for managers to act in their own self-interest, or "opportunistically," the owners can implement some governance mechanisms.[67] First, there are two primary means of monitoring the behavior of managers. These include (1) a committed and involved *board of directors* that acts in the best interests of the shareholders to create long-term value and (2) *shareholder activism,* wherein the owners view themselves as share*owners* instead of share*holders* and become actively engaged in the governance of the corporation. Finally, there are managerial incentives, sometimes called "contract-based outcomes," which consist of *reward and compensation agreements.* Here the goal is to carefully craft managerial incentive packages to align the interests of management with those of the stockholders.[68]

We close this section with a brief discussion of one of the most controversial issues in corporate governance—duality. Here, the question becomes: Should the CEO also be chairman of the board of directors? In many Fortune 500 firms, the same individual serves in both roles. However, in recent years, we have seen a trend toward separating these two positions. The key issue is what implications CEO duality has for firm governance and performance.

A Committed and Involved Board of Directors The **board of directors** acts as a fulcrum between the owners and controllers of a corporation. They are the intermediaries who provide a balance between a small group of key managers in the firm based at the corporate headquarters and a sometimes vast group of shareholders.[69] In the United States, the law imposes on the board a strict and absolute fiduciary duty to ensure that a company is run consistent with the long-term interests of the owners—the shareholders. The reality, as we have seen, is somewhat more ambiguous.[70]

The Business Roundtable, representing the largest U.S. corporations, describes the duties of the board as follows:

1. Select, regularly evaluate, and, if necessary, replace the CEO. Determine management compensation. Review succession planning.
2. Review and, where appropriate, approve the financial objectives, major strategies, and plans of the corporation.
3. Provide advice and counsel to top management.
4. Select and recommend to shareholders for election an appropriate slate of candidates for the board of directors; evaluate board processes and performance.
5. Review the adequacy of the systems to comply with all applicable laws/regulations.[71]

Given these principles, what makes for a good board of directors?[72] According to the Business Roundtable, the most important quality is a board of directors who are active, critical participants in determining a company's strategies.[73] That does not mean board members should micromanage or circumvent the CEO. Rather, they should provide strong oversight going beyond simply approving the CEO's plans. A board's primary responsibilities are to ensure that strategic plans undergo rigorous scrutiny, evaluate managers against high performance standards, and take control of the succession process.[74]

Although boards in the past were often dismissed as CEO's rubber stamps, increasingly they are playing a more active role by forcing out CEOs who cannot deliver on performance.[75] According to the consulting firm Booz Allen Hamilton, the rate of CEO departures for performance reasons more than tripled, from 1.3 percent to 4.2 percent, between 1995 and 2002.[76] And today's CEOs are not immune to termination.

- In September 2010, Jonathan Klein, the president of the CNN/U.S. cable channel, was fired because CNN's ratings had suffered.[77]
- Don Blankenship, CEO of coal mining giant Massey Energy, resigned in December 2010 after a deadly explosion in Massey's Upper Big Branch mine in West Virginia, a mine that had received numerous citations for safety violations in the last few years. The blast was the worst mining disaster in the United States in 40 years and resulted in criminal as well as civil investigations and lawsuits.
- Tony Hayward, CEO of oil and energy company British Petroleum (BP), was forced to step down in October 2010 after the Deepwater Horizon oil spill in the Gulf of Mexico led to an environmental disaster and a $20 billion recovery fund financed by BP.
- Carol Bartz was ousted as the CEO of Yahoo after two and a half years when the board observed limited improvement in the firm's market position, turmoil over job cuts and secrecy during her leadership, and a flat stock price. Similarly, Vikram Pandit was pressured to resign from his position as CEO of Citigroup after five tumultuous years and increasing investor unhappiness over the performance of the firm.

board of directors
a group that has a fiduciary duty to ensure that the company is run consistently with the long-term interests of the owners, or shareholders, of a corporation and that acts as an intermediary between the shareholders and management.

Increasing CEO turnover could, however, pose a major problem for many organizations. Why? It appears that boards of directors are not typically engaged in effective succession planning. For example, only 35 percent of 1,318 executives surveyed by Korn/Ferry International in December 2010 said their companies had a succession plan. And 61 percent of respondents to a survey (conducted by Heidrick & Struggles and Stanford University's Rock Center for Corporate Governance) claimed their companies had *no* viable internal candidates. This issue is also true in private companies. Only 23 percent of private firms surveyed by the National Association of Corporate Directors indicated they had developed formal succession plans.[78]

Another key component of top-ranked boards is director independence.[79] Governance experts believe that a majority of directors should be free of all ties to either the CEO or the company.[80] That means a minimum of "insiders" (past or present members of the management team) should serve on the board, and that directors and their firms should be barred from doing consulting, legal, or other work for the company.[81] Interlocking directorships—in which CEOs and other top managers serve on each other's boards—are not desirable. But perhaps the best guarantee that directors act in the best interests of shareholders is the simplest: Most good companies now insist that directors own significant stock in the company they oversee.[82]

Taking it one step further, research and simple observations of boards indicate that simple prescriptions, such as having a majority of outside directors, are insufficient to lead to effective board operations. Firms need to cultivate engaged and committed boards. There are several actions that can have a positive influence on board dynamics as the board works to both oversee and advise management.[83]

1. **Build in the right expertise on the board.** Outside directors can bring in experience that the management team is missing. For example, corporations that are considering expanding into a new region of the globe may want to add a board member who brings expertise on and connections in that region. Similarly, research suggests that firms who are focusing on improving their operational efficiency benefit from having an external board member whose full time position is as a chief operating officer, a position that typically focuses on operational activities.

2. **Keep your board size manageable.** Small, focused boards, generally with 5 to 11 members, are preferable to larger ones. As boards grow in size, the ability for them to function as a team declines. The members of the board feel less connected with each other, and decision making can become unwieldy.

3. **Choose directors who can participate fully.** The time demands on directors have increased as their responsibilities have grown to include overseeing management, verifying the firm's financial statements, setting executive compensation, and advising on the strategic direction of the firm. As a result, the average number of hours per year spent on board duties has increased to over 350 hours for directors of large firms. Directors have to dedicate significant time to their roles—not just for scheduled meetings, but also to review materials between meetings and to respond to time-sensitive challenges. Thus, firms should strive to include directors who are not currently overburdened by their core occupation or involvement on other boards.

4. **Balance the need to focus on the past, the present, and the future.** Boards have a three-tiered role. They need to focus on the recent performance of the firm, how the firm is meeting current milestones and operational targets, and what the strategic direction of the firm will be moving forward. Under current regulations, boards are required to spend a great amount of time on the past as they vet the firm's financials. However, effective boards balance this time and ensure that they give adequate consideration to the present and the future.

5. **Consider management talent development.** As part of their future-oriented focus, effective boards develop succession plans for the CEO but also focus on talent development at other upper echelons of the organization. In a range of industries, human capital is an increasingly important driver of firm success, and boards should be involved in evaluating and developing the top management core.

6. **Get a broad view.** In order to better understand the firm and make contact with key managers, the meetings of the board should rotate to different operating units and sites of the firm.

7. **Maintain norms of transparency and trust.** Highly functioning boards maintain open, team-oriented dialogue where information flows freely and questions are asked openly. Directors respect each other and trust that they are all working in the best interests of the corporation.

With financial crises and corporate scandals, regulators and investors have pushed for significant changes in the structure and actions of boards. Exhibit 9.6 highlights some of the changes seen among firms in the S&P 500.

EXHIBIT 9.6

The Changing Face of the Board of Firms in the S&P 500

Issue	Then and Now		Explanation
	1987	2011	
Percentage of boards that have an average age of 64 or older	3	37	Fewer sitting CEOs are willing to serve on the boards of other firms. As a result, companies are raising the retirement age for directors and pulling in retired executives to their boards.
Average pay for directors	$36,667	$95,262	Board work has taken greater time and commitment. Additionally, the personal liability directors face has increased. As a result, compensation has increased to attract and retain board members.
Percentage of board members who are female	9	16.2	While the number of boards with women and minorities has increased, these groups are still underrepresented. Still, companies have emphasized including female directors in key roles. For example, over half the audit and compensation committees of S&P 500 firms have at least one female member.
Percentage of boards with 12 or fewer members	22	83	As the strategic role and the legal requirements of the board have increased, firms have opted for smaller boards since these smaller boards better operate as true decision-making groups.
Percentage of the directors that are independent	68	84	The Sarbanes-Oxley Act and pressure from investors have led to an increase in the number of independent directors. In fact, over half the S&P 500 firms now have no insiders other than the CEO on the board.

Sources: Anonymous. 2011. Corporate boards: Now and then. *Harvard Business Review,* 89(11): 38–39; and Dalton, D. & Dalton, C. 2010. Women and corporate boards of directors: The promise of increased, and substantive participation in the post Sarbanes-Oxley era. *Business Horizons,* 53: 257–268.

Shareholder Activism As a practical matter, there are so many owners of the largest American corporations that it makes little sense to refer to them as "owners" in the sense of individuals becoming informed and involved in corporate affairs.[84] However, even an individual shareholder has several rights, including (1) the right to sell the stock, (2) the right to vote the proxy (which includes the election of board members), (3) the right to bring suit for damages if the corporation's directors or managers fail to meet their obligations, (4) the right to certain information from the company, and (5) certain residual rights following the company's liquidation (or its filing for reorganization under bankruptcy laws), once creditors and other claimants are paid off.[85]

Collectively, shareholders have the power to direct the course of corporations.[86] This may involve acts such as being party to shareholder action suits and demanding that key issues be brought up for proxy votes at annual board meetings.[87] The power of shareholders has intensified in recent years because of the increasing influence of large institutional investors such as mutual funds (e.g., T. Rowe Price and Fidelity Investments) and retirement systems such as TIAA-CREF (for university faculty members and school administrative staff).[88] Institutional investors hold approximately 50 percent of all listed corporate stock in the United States.[89]

Shareholder activism refers to actions by large shareholders, both institutions and individuals, to protect their interests when they feel that managerial actions diverge from shareholder value maximization.

> **shareholder activism**
> actions by large shareholders to protect their interests when they feel that managerial actions of a corporation diverge from shareholder value maximization.

Many institutional investors are aggressive in protecting and enhancing their investments. They are shifting from traders to owners. They are assuming the role of permanent shareholders and rigorously analyzing issues of corporate governance. In the process they are reinventing systems of corporate monitoring and accountability.[90]

Consider the proactive behavior of CalPERS, the California Public Employees' Retirement System, which manages over $240 billion in assets and is the third largest pension fund in the world. Every year CalPERS reviews the performance of the 1,000 firms in which it retains a sizable investment.[91] They review each firm's short- and long-term performance, its governance characteristics, its financial status, and market expectations for the firm. CalPERS then meets with selected companies to better understand their governance and business strategy. If needed, CalPERS requests changes in the firm's governance structure and works to ensure shareholders' rights. If CalPERS does not believe that the firm is responsive to its concerns, they consider filing proxy actions at the firm's next shareholders meeting and possibly even court actions. CalPERS's research suggests that these actions lead to superior performance. The portfolio of firms they have included in their review program produced a cumulative return that was 11.59 percent higher than a respective set of benchmark firms over a three-year period. Thus, CalPERS has seen a real benefit of acting as an interested owner, rather than as a passive investor.

Perhaps no discussion of shareholder activism would be complete without mention of Carl Icahn, a famed activist with a personal net worth of about $13 billion:

> The bogeyman I am now chasing is the structure of American corporations, which permit managements and boards to rule arbitrarily and too often receive egregious compensation even after doing a subpar job. Yet they remain accountable to no one.[92]

The market appears to value the actions of activist investors. On the day it became publicly known that Icahn had taken a 10 percent ownership in Netflix, the stock price of Netflix soared 14 percent.[93]

Managerial Rewards and Incentives As we discussed earlier in the chapter, incentive systems must be designed to help a company achieve its goals.[94] From the perspective of governance, one of the most critical roles of the board of directors is to create incentives that align the interests of the CEO and top executives with the interests of owners of the corporation—long-term shareholder returns.[95] Shareholders rely on CEOs to adopt policies and strategies that maximize the value of their shares.[96] A combination of three basic policies may create the right monetary incentives for CEOs to maximize the value of their companies:[97]

1. Boards can require that the CEOs become substantial owners of company stock.
2. Salaries, bonuses, and stock options can be structured so as to provide rewards for superior performance and penalties for poor performance.
3. Dismissal for poor performance should be a realistic threat.

In recent years the granting of stock options has enabled top executives of publicly held corporations to earn enormous levels of compensation. In 2011, the average CEO in the Standard & Poor's 500 stock index took home 380 times the pay of the average worker—up from 40 times the average in 1980. The counterargument, that the ratio is down from the 514 multiple in 2000, doesn't get much traction.[98]

Many boards have awarded huge option grants despite poor executive performance, and others have made performance goals easier to reach. However, stock options can be a valuable governance mechanism to align the CEO's interests with those of the shareholders. The extraordinarily high level of compensation can, at times, be grounded in sound governance principles.[99] Research by Steven Kaplan at the University of Chicago found that firms with CEOs in the top quintile of pay generated stock returns 60 percent higher than their direct competitors, while firms with CEOs in the bottom quintile of pay saw their stock underperform their rivals by almost 20 percent.[100] For example, David Zaslav CEO of Discovery Communications, took home $37.8 million in 2011, but his firm's stock appreciated by 57 percent over the 2011-2012 period.[101]

That doesn't mean that executive compensation systems can't or shouldn't be improved. Exhibit 9.7 outlines a number of ways to build effective compensation packages for executives.[102]

EXHIBIT 9.7

Six Policies for Effective Top-Management Compensation

Boards need to be diligent in building executive compensation packages that will incentivize executives to build long-term shareholder value and to address the concerns that regulators and the public have about excessive compensation. The key is to have open, fair, and consistent pay plans. Here are five policies to achieve that.

1. **Increase transparency.** Principles and pay policies should be consistent over time and fully disclosed in company documents. For example, Novartis has emphasized making their compensation policies fully transparent and not altering the targets used for incentive compensation in midstream.

2. **Build long-term performance with long-term pay.** The timing of compensation can be structured to force executives to think about the long-term success of the organization. For example, ExxonMobil times two-thirds of its senior executives' incentive compensation so that they don't receive it until they retire or for 10 years, whichever is longer. Similarly, in 2009, Goldman Sachs replaced its annual bonuses for its top managers with restricted stock grants that executives could sell in three to five years.

3. **Reward executives for performance, not simply for changes in the company's stock price.** To keep them from focusing only on stock price, Target includes a component in its executives' compensation plan for same-store sales performance over time.

4. **Have executives put some "skin in the game."** Firms should create some downside risk for managers. Relying more on restricted stock, rather than stock options, can achieve this. But some experts suggest that top executives should purchase sizable blocks of the firm's stock with their own money.

5. **Avoid overreliance on simple metrics.** Rather than rewarding for short-term financial performance metrics, firms should include future-oriented qualitative measures to incentivize managers to build for the future. Companies could include criteria such as customer retention rates, innovation and new product launch milestones, and leadership development criteria. For example, IBM added bonuses for executives who evidenced actions fostering global cooperation.

6. **Increase equity between workers and executives.** Top executives, with their greater responsibilities, should and will continue to make more than front-line employees, but firms can signal equity by dropping special perks, plans, and benefits for top managers. Additionally, companies can give employees the opportunity to share in the success of the firm by establishing employee stock ownership plans.

Sources: George, B. 2010. Executive pay: Rebuilding trust in an era of rage. *Bloomberg Businessweek,* September 13: 56; and Barton, D. 2011. Capitalism for the long term. *Harvard Business Review,* 89(3): 85.

CEO Duality: Is It Good or Bad?

CEO duality is one of the most controversial issues in corporate governance. It refers to the dual leadership structure where the CEO acts simultaneously as the chair of the board of directors.[103] Scholars, consultants, and executives who are interested in determining the best way to manage a corporation are divided on the issue of the roles and responsibilities of a CEO. Two schools of thought represent the alternative positions:

Unity of Command   Advocates of the unity of command perspective believe when one person holds both roles, he or she is able to act more efficiently and effectively. CEO duality provides firms with a clear focus on both objectives and operations as well as eliminates confusion and conflict between the CEO and the chairman. Thus, it enables smoother, more effective strategic decision making. Holding dual roles as CEO/chairman creates unity across a company's managers and board of directors and ultimately allows the CEO to serve the shareholders even better. Having leadership focused in a single individual also enhances a firm's responsiveness and ability to secure critical resources. This perspective maintains that separating the two jobs—that of a CEO and that of the chairperson of the board of directors—may produce all types of undesirable consequences. CEOs may find it harder to make quick decisions. Ego-driven chief executives and chairmen may squabble over who is ultimately in charge. The shortage of first-class business talent may mean that bosses find themselves second-guessed by people who know little about the business.[104] Companies like Coca-Cola, JPMorgan Chase, and Time Warner have refused to divide the CEO's and chairman's jobs and support this duality structure.

Agency Theory   Supporters of agency theory argue that the positions of CEO and chairman should be separate. The case for separation is based on the simple principle of the separation of power. How can boards discharge their basic duty—monitoring the boss—if the boss is chairing its meetings and setting its agenda? How can a board act as a safeguard against corruption or incompetence when the possible source of that corruption and incompetence is sitting at the head of the table? CEO duality can create a conflict of interest that could negatively affect the interests of the shareholders.

Duality also complicates the issue of CEO succession. In some cases, a CEO/chairman may choose to retire as CEO but keep his or her role as the chairman. Although this splits up the roles, which appeases an agency perspective, it nonetheless puts the new CEO in a difficult position. The chairman is bound to question some of the new changes put in place, and the board as a whole might take sides with the chairman they trust and with whom they have a history. This conflict of interest would make it difficult for the new CEO to institute any changes, as the power and influence would still remain with the former CEO.[105]

Duality also serves to reinforce popular doubts about the legitimacy of the system as a whole and evokes images of bosses writing their own performance reviews and setting their own salaries. One of the first things that some of America's troubled banks, including Citigroup, Washington Mutual, Wachovia, and Wells Fargo, did when the financial crisis hit in 2007–2008 was to separate the two jobs. Firms like Siebel Systems, Disney, Oracle, and Microsoft have also decided to divide the roles between the CEO and chairman and eliminate duality. Finally, more than 90 percent of S&P 500 companies with CEOs who also serve as chairman of the board have appointed "lead" or "presiding" directors to act as a counterweight to a combined chairman and chief executive.

Research suggests that the effects of going from having a joint CEO/Chairman to separating the two positions is contingent on how the firm is doing. When the positions are broken apart, there is a clear shift in the firm's performance. If the firm has been performing well, its performance declines after the separation. If the firm has been doing poorly, it experiences improvement after separating the two roles. This research suggests that there is no one correct answer on duality, but that firms should consider its current position and performance trends when deciding whether to keep the CEO and Chairman position in the hands of one person.[106]

External Governance Control Mechanisms

Thus far, we've discussed internal governance mechanisms. Internal controls, however, are not always enough to ensure good governance. The separation of ownership and control that we discussed earlier requires multiple control mechanisms, some internal and some external, to ensure that managerial actions lead to shareholder value maximization. Further, society-at-large wants some assurance that this goal is met without harming other stakeholder groups. Now we discuss several **external governance control mechanisms** that have developed in most modern economies. These include the market for corporate control, auditors, governmental regulatory bodies, banks and analysts, media, and public activists.

The Market for Corporate Control Let us assume for a moment that internal control mechanisms in a company are failing. This means that the board is ineffective in monitoring managers and is not exercising the oversight required of them and that shareholders are passive and are not taking any actions to monitor or discipline managers. Under these circumstances managers may behave opportunistically.[107] Opportunistic behavior can take many forms. First, they can *shirk* their responsibilities. Shirking means that managers fail to exert themselves fully, as is required of them. Second, they can engage in *on the job consumption*. Examples of on the job consumption include private jets, club memberships, expensive artwork in the offices, and so on. Each of these represents consumption by managers that does not in any way increase shareholder value. Instead, they actually diminish shareholder value. Third, managers may engage in *excessive product-market diversification*.[108] As we discussed in Chapter 6, such diversification serves to reduce only the employment risk of the managers rather than the financial risk of the shareholders, who can more cheaply diversify their risk by owning a portfolio of investments. Is there any external mechanism to stop managers from shirking, consumption on the job, and excessive diversification?

The **market for corporate control** is one external mechanism that provides at least some partial solution to the problems described. If internal control mechanisms fail and the management is behaving opportunistically, the likely response of most shareholders will be to sell their stock rather than engage in activism.[109] As more stockholders vote with their feet, the value of the stock begins to decline. As the decline continues, at some point the market value of the firm becomes less than the book value. A corporate raider can take over the company for a price less than the book value of the assets of the company. The first thing that the raider may do on assuming control over the company will be to fire the underperforming management. The risk of being acquired by a hostile raider is often referred to as the **takeover constraint.** The takeover constraint deters management from engaging in opportunistic behavior.[110]

Although in theory the takeover constraint is supposed to limit managerial opportunism, in recent years its effectiveness has become diluted as a result of a number of defense tactics adopted by incumbent management (see Chapter 6). Foremost among them are poison pills, greenmail, and golden parachutes. Poison pills are provisions adopted by the company to reduce its worth to the acquirer. An example would be payment of a huge one-time dividend, typically financed by debt. Greenmail involves buying back the stock from the acquirer, usually at an attractive premium. Golden parachutes are employment contracts that cause the company to pay lucrative severance packages to top managers fired as a result of a takeover, often running to several million dollars.

external governance control mechanisms
methods that ensure that managerial actions lead to shareholder value maximization and do not harm other stakeholder groups that are outside the control of the corporate governance system.

market for corporate control
an external control mechanism in which shareholders dissatisfied with a firm's management sell their shares.

takeover constraint
the risk to management of the firm being acquired by a hostile raider.

Auditors   Even when there are stringent disclosure requirements, there is no guarantee that the information disclosed will be accurate. Managers may deliberately disclose false information or withhold negative financial information as well as use accounting methods that distort results based on highly subjective interpretations. Therefore, all accounting statements are required to be audited and certified to be accurate by external auditors. These auditing firms are independent organizations staffed by certified professionals who verify the firm's books of accounts. Audits can unearth financial irregularities and ensure that financial reporting by the firm conforms to standard accounting practices.

However, these audits often fail to catch accounting irregularities. In the past, auditing failures played an important part in the failures of firms such as Enron and WorldCom. A recent study by the Public Company Accounting Oversight Board (PCAOB) found that audits conducted by the Big 4 accounting firms were often deficient. For example, 20 percent of the Ernst & Young audits examined by the PCAOB failed. And this was the best of the Big 4! The PCAOB found fault with 45 percent of the Deloitte audits it examined. Why do these reputable firms fail to find all of the issues in audits they conduct? First, auditors are appointed by the firm being audited. The desire to continue that business relationship sometimes makes them overlook financial irregularities. Second, most auditing firms also do consulting work and often have lucrative consulting contracts with the firms that they audit. Understandably, some of them tend not to ask too many difficult questions, because they fear jeopardizing the consulting business, which is often more profitable than the auditing work.

Banks and Analysts   Commercial and investment banks have lent money to corporations and therefore have to ensure that the borrowing firm's finances are in order and that the loan covenants are being followed. Stock analysts conduct ongoing in-depth studies of the firms that they follow and make recommendations to their clients to buy, hold, or sell. Their rewards and reputation depend on the quality of these recommendations. Their access to information, knowledge of the industry and the firm, and the insights they gain from interactions with the management of the company enable them to alert the investing community of both positive and negative developments relating to a company.

It is generally observed that analyst recommendations are often more optimistic than warranted by facts. "Sell" recommendations tend to be exceptions rather than the norm. Many analysts failed to grasp the gravity of the problems surrounding failed companies such as Lehman Brothers and Countrywide till the very end. Part of the explanation may lie in the fact that most analysts work for firms that also have investment banking relationships with the companies they follow. Negative recommendations by analysts can displease the management, who may decide to take their investment banking business to a rival firm. Otherwise independent and competent analysts may be pressured to overlook negative information or tone down their criticism.

Regulatory Bodies   The extent of government regulation is often a function of the type of industry. Banks, utilities, and pharmaceuticals are subject to more regulatory oversight because of their importance to society. Public corporations are subject to more regulatory requirements than private corporations.[111]

All public corporations are required to disclose a substantial amount of financial information by bodies such as the Securities and Exchange Commission. These include quarterly and annual filings of financial performance, stock trading by insiders, and details of executive compensation packages. There are two primary reasons behind such requirements. First, markets can operate efficiently only when the investing public has faith in the market system. In the absence of disclosure requirements, the average investor suffers from a lack of reliable information and therefore may completely stay away from the capital market. This will negatively impact an economy's ability to grow. Second, disclosure of information such as insider trading protects the small investor to some extent from the negative consequences of information asymmetry. The insiders and large investors typically have more information than the small investor and can therefore use that information to buy or sell before the information becomes public knowledge.

The failure of a variety of external control mechanisms led the U.S. Congress to pass the Sarbanes-Oxley Act in 2002. This act calls for many stringent measures that would ensure better governance of U.S. corporations. Some of these measures include:[112]

- *Auditors* are barred from certain types of nonaudit work. They are not allowed to destroy records for five years. Lead partners auditing a client should be changed at least every five years.
- *CEOs* and *CFOs* must fully reveal off-balance-sheet finances and vouch for the accuracy of the information revealed.
- *Executives* must promptly reveal the sale of shares in firms they manage and are not allowed to sell when other employees cannot.
- *Corporate lawyers* must report to senior managers any violations of securities law lower down.

Media and Public Activists   The press is not usually recognized as an external control mechanism in the literature on corporate governance. There is no denying that in all developed capitalist economies, the financial press and media play an important indirect role in monitoring the management of public corporations. In the United States, business magazines such as *Bloomberg Businessweek* and *Fortune,* financial newspapers such as *The Wall Street Journal* and *Investors Business Daily,* as well as television networks like Fox Business Network and CNBC are constantly reporting on companies. Public perceptions about a company's financial prospects and the quality of its management are greatly influenced by the media. Food Lion's reputation was sullied when ABC's *Prime Time Live* in 1992 charged the company with employee exploitation, false package dating, and unsanitary meat handling practices. Bethany McLean of *Fortune* magazine is often credited as the first to raise questions about Enron's long-term financial viability.[113]

Similarly, consumer groups and activist individuals often take a crusading role in exposing corporate malfeasance.[114] Well-known examples include Ralph Nader and Erin Brockovich, who played important roles in bringing to light the safety issues related to GM's Corvair and environmental pollution issues concerning Pacific Gas and Electric Company, respectively. Ralph Nader has created over 30 watchdog groups, including:[115]

- *Aviation Consumer Action Project.* Works to propose new rules to prevent flight delays, impose penalties for deceiving passengers about problems, and push for higher compensation for lost luggage.
- *Center for Auto Safety.* Helps consumers find plaintiff lawyers and agitate for vehicle recalls, increased highway safety standards, and lemon laws.
- *Center for Study of Responsive Law.* This is Nader's headquarters. Home of a consumer project on technology, this group sponsored seminars on Microsoft remedies and pushed for tougher Internet privacy rules. It also took on the drug industry over costs.
- *Pension Rights Center.* This center helped employees of IBM, General Electric, and other companies to organize themselves against cash-balance pension plans.

As we have noted above, some public activists and watchdog groups can exert a strong force on organizations and influence decisions that they may make. Strategy Spotlight 9.4 provides an example of this phenomenon.

RADICAL ACTIVISM AND NESTLÉ: HOW THE COMPANY IS BEING FORCED TO RE-THINK ITS STRATEGY AND POLICIES

By Asha Moore-Mangin and Tom McNamara

Nestlé is the world's largest food company and one of the most multinational. It has more than 450 manufacturing facilities in over 80 countries spread over six continents. The company seems determined to feed the entire human race and likes to call itself the "world's leading nutrition, health and wellness company." However, it is also one of the world's most controversial corporations.

Today, there are many places around the world where Nestlé operations are being challenged by workers and local communities for numerous reasons; some to do with bottled water (US, Brazil, Canada), misrepresenting products (horsemeat in beef products in Europe), labeling in English in foreign countries (Mozambique), using suppliers that violate human rights (buying cocoa that uses child slaves), destroying the environment (palm oil from the rainforest), and denying the rights of workers to collective bargain to name but a few, and a lot to do with formula baby milk, which activists have been campaigning about for the past 36 years. Outrage started against Nestlé in 1970 when activists brought into the open its exploitative practices and it was accused of getting third world mothers hooked on formula milk which is less healthy and more expensive than breast milk.

Nestlé's marketing practices included showing posters of healthy bottle fed babies and hiring "sales girls in nurses uniforms" (who were not necessarily qualified) to drop in on mothers and explain the benefits of formula milk. Nestlé was accused of creating a need where there was none, convincing the consumers that the products were indispensable and linking the products with the most desirable and unattainable, and then giving a sample. Nestlé did not take these allegations lightly and sued activists for libel.

It won its suit in 1976 but with a caveat: the judge warned Nestlé to modify its publicity methods fundamentally if it did not want to face accusations of causing death and illness. *Time* magazine declared this a "moral victory for consumers" and as a result, new standards were defined for the industry that states among other things that baby food companies are no longer allowed to: promote products in hospitals, shops or to the public; give samples to mothers; give gifts to health workers or mothers; or give misleading information. However, the bad publicity sparked a global boycott of Nestlé which was suspended in 1984 but restarted in the late 1980s in Ireland, Australia, Mexico, Sweden, and the UK.

When the laws do not exist or fail to hold a global company like Nestlé accountable, public action has been able to force Nestlé to change its policies. Public action can take many forms including boycotting brands but the aim of public action is to spread the word about Nestlé's unethical business practices and put pressure on international organizations and governments to pass legislation that prevents Nestlé from doing something that puts people, animals, and the environment at risk.

Recent studies from Kellogg School of Management suggest that activists serve a real social purpose because companies are concerned about their reputation and spend a lot of time and money engaging in reputation enhancing activities. An activist that puts pressure on a company's reputation keeps it motivated to do more good deeds than it would otherwise do. To this day, Nestlé is scrutinized by NGOs, activists, and citizens alike.

Sources: Tim Worstall, Forbes.com, April 9 2013 "Google Might Have Walked Into A Nestlé Boycott Problem With Android KitKat"; Mike Muller, Theguardian.com, February 13 2013 "Nestlé baby milk scandal has grown up but not gone away"; Jill Kransny, Businessinsider.com, June 25 2012 "Every parent should know the scandalous history of infant formula"; Phillip Marrera, www.corp-research.org/nestle "Nestlé: Corporate Rap Sheet", July 1 2013; insight.kellogg.northwestern.edu/article/the_games_companies_and_activists_play/#ixzz2gJzu3HfB "Companies With Great Reputations Are The Best Targets For Activists."

Corporate Governance: An International Perspective

The topic of corporate governance has long been dominated by agency theory and based on the explicit assumption of the separation of ownership and control.[116] The central conflicts are principal–agent conflicts between shareholders and management. However, such an underlying assumption seldom applies outside of the United States and the United Kingdom. This is particularly true in emerging economies and continental Europe. Here, there is often concentrated ownership, along with extensive family ownership and control, business group structures, and weak legal protection for minority shareholders. Serious conflicts tend to exist between two classes of principals: controlling shareholders and minority shareholders. Such conflicts can be called **principal–principal (PP) conflicts,** as opposed to *principal–agent* conflicts (see Exhibits 9.8 and 9.9).

Strong family control is one of the leading indicators of concentrated ownership. In East Asia (excluding China), approximately 57 percent of the corporations have board chairmen and CEOs from the controlling families. In continental Europe, this number is 68 percent. A very common practice is the appointment of family members as board chairmen, CEOs, and other top executives. This happens because the families are controlling (not

principal–principal conflicts
conflicts between two classes of principals—controlling shareholders and minority shareholders—within the context of a corporate governance system.

EXHIBIT 9.8

Traditional Principal–Agent Conflicts versus Principal–Principal Conflicts: How They Differ along Dimensions

	Principal–Agent Conflicts	Principal–Principal Conflicts
Goal Incongruence	Between shareholders and professional managers who own a relatively small portion of the firm's equity.	Between controlling shareholders and minority shareholders.
Ownership Pattern	Dispersed—5%–20% is considered "concentrated ownership."	Concentrated—Often greater than 50% of equity is controlled by controlling shareholders.
Manifestations	Strategies that benefit entrenched managers at the expense of shareholders in general (e.g., shirking, pet projects, excessive compensation, and empire building).	Strategies that benefit controlling shareholders at the expense of minority shareholders (e.g., minority shareholder expropriation, nepotism, and cronyism).
Institutional Protection of Minority Shareholders	Formal constraints (e.g., judicial reviews and courts) set an upper boundary on potential expropriation by majority shareholders. Informal norms generally adhere to shareholder wealth maximization.	Formal institutional protection is often lacking, corrupted, or un-enforced. Informal norms are typically in favor of the interests of controlling shareholders ahead of those of minority investors.

Source: Adapted from Young, M., Peng, M. W., Ahlstrom, D., & Bruton, G. 2002. Governing the Corporation in Emerging Economies: A Principal–Principal Perspective. *Academy of Management Best Papers Proceedings,* Denver.

EXHIBIT 9.9 Principal–Agent Conflicts and Principal–Principal Conflicts: A Diagram

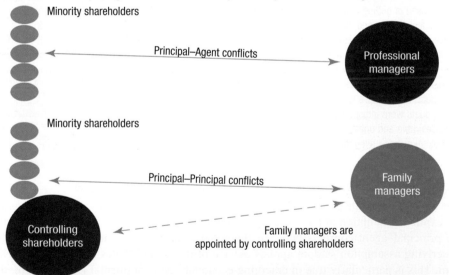

Source: Young, M. N., Peng, M. W., Ahlstrom, D., Bruton, G. D., & Jiang, 2008. Principal–Principal Conflicts in Corporate Governance. *Journal of Management Studies* 45(1):196–220; and Peng, M. V. 2006. *Global Strategy.* Cincinnati: Thomson South-Western. We are very appreciative of the helpful comments of Mike Young of Hong Kong Baptist University and Mike Peng of the University of Texas at Dallas.

necessarily majority) shareholders. In 2003, 30-year-old James Murdoch was appointed CEO of British Sky Broadcasting (BSkyB), Europe's largest satellite broadcaster. There was very vocal resistance by minority shareholders. Why was he appointed in the first place? James's father just happened to be Rupert Murdoch, who controlled 35 percent of BSkyB and chaired the board. Clearly, this is a case of a PP conflict.

In general, three conditions must be met for PP conflicts to occur:

- A dominant owner or group of owners who have interests that are distinct from minority shareholders.
- Motivation for the controlling shareholders to exercise their dominant positions to their advantage.
- Few formal (such as legislation or regulatory bodies) or informal constraints that would discourage or prevent the controlling shareholders from exploiting their advantageous positions.

The result is often that family managers, who represent (or actually are) the controlling shareholders, engage in **expropriation of minority shareholders,** which is defined as activities that enrich the controlling shareholders at the expense of minority shareholders. What is their motive? After all, controlling shareholders have incentives to maintain firm value. But controlling shareholders may take actions that decrease aggregate firm performance if their personal gains from expropriation exceed their personal losses from their firm's lowered performance.

Another ubiquitous feature of corporate life outside of the United States and United Kingdom are *business groups* such as the keiretsus of Japan and the chaebols of South Korea. This is particularly dominant in emerging economies. A **business group** is "a set of firms that, though legally independent, are bound together by a constellation of formal and informal ties and are accustomed to taking coordinated action."[117] Business groups are especially common in emerging economies, and they differ from other organizational forms in that they are communities of firms without clear boundaries.

Business groups have many advantages that can enhance the value of a firm. They often facilitate technology transfer or intergroup capital allocation that otherwise might be impossible because of inadequate institutional infrastructure such as excellent financial services firms. On the other hand, informal ties—such as cross-holdings, board interlocks, and coordinated actions—can often result in intragroup activities and transactions, often at very favorable terms to member firms. Expropriation can be legally done through *related transactions,* which can occur when controlling owners sell firm assets to another firm they own at below market prices or spin off the most profitable part of a public firm and merge it with another of their private firms.

expropriation of minority shareholders
activities that enrich the controlling shareholders at the expense of the minority shareholders.

business groups
a set of firms that, though legally independent, are bound together by a constellation of formal and informal ties and are accustomed to taking coordinated action.

ISSUE FOR DEBATE

Better Corporate Governance: If CEOs can't do it, shareholders will

By Helena Gonzalez and Tom McNamara

In the aftermath of the economic crisis of 2008, firms have witnessed an increase in shareholder involvement, with several factors contributing to this change. Public exposure of executives' pay and the consequential outrage over their excesses, new regulations that give shareholders more say, and an increase in shareholder scrutiny are just a few of the elements that have forced many companies to rethink their corporate governance policies. And increasingly, companies are finding that their policies are not up to standards.

In the past, shareholders used to intervene and actively participate only in cases where firms had very poor performance. What is more, this activism was rare. In most cases, shareholders would simply walk away from poorly run companies by selling their shares. Nowadays things are different, and shareholders are playing a much more active role, even in cases where a company's performance is good.

(continued)

(continued)

Walt Disney is a major example of this new trend. After an exceptionally good year of increased profits, having successfully acquired Lucasfilm and benefitted from several ongoing cash generating projects, shareholder activists almost succeeded in depriving Bob Iger of one of his titles, voting to separate the chairman and chief executive officer roles (the measure didn't pass).

In a similar move, Apple shareholders wanted to introduce majority voting for the election of directors, even though the firm's share price was rising. When the shares started to fall in 2013, Apple ended up offering new voting rules at its annual meeting.

The case of JP Morgan Chase is another striking example. In May 2013, shareholders were encouraged to vote on two decisions: 1) whether or not to let Jamie Dimon continue serving as both chief executive officer and chairman of the board, and 2) if three members of the risk policy committee should be voted out.

Some shareholders of Walmart in Mexico wanted to unseat members of the audit committee who were in office when alleged bribes were paid out.

Shareholders of Dell were resistant to Michael Dell's idea of taking the computer-maker private without increasing the offering price. The reported acquisition of a 6 percent stake in the company by Carl Icahn, a well-known activist investor, is proof of this growing trend.

What these cases illustrate is the enormous power that shareholders have gradually acquired and are using. Activists are attacking boards despite the growing criticism that their actions are receiving. Critics mainly accuse activist shareholders, like some hedge funds, of wanting quick and easy short-term profits, while disregarding the long-term consequences of their actions on the firm. Proxy Monitor, a conservative think-tank, issued a report analyzing shareholder activity and found that during the 2011–12 period, 36 percent of shareholder resolutions came from trade union pension funds. Another 31 percent came from three wealthy individual trusts, and 22 percent came from so-called "socially responsible" funds having an explicit religious or public policy objective.

It is debatable as to whether or not the main goal of activist investors is to better align a firm's long-term goals more closely with those of its shareholders. But what is clear is that the days of rubber stamping corporate boards are over. The time for lively board meetings and debate has arrived. If not, shareholders might have something to say about it.

Discussion Questions

1. Do you think that shareholder involvement contributes to a firm's organic growth? Explain.
2. What are the risks and challenges facing a firm that has shareholders who are becoming more active?

Sources: The Economist, March 9 2013 "Corporate governance: Shareholders at the gates"; Simon Johnson, Economix, The New York Times, May 9 2013 "The Problem With Corporate Governance at JPMorgan Chase."

Reflecting on Career Implications . . .

◼ **Behavioral Control:** What types of behavioral control does your organization employ? Do you find these behavioral controls helping or hindering you from doing a good job? Some individuals are comfortable with and even desire rules and procedures for everything. Others find that they inhibit creativity and stifle initiative. Evaluate your own level of comfort with the level of behavioral control and then assess the match between your own optimum level of control and the level and type of control used by your organization. If the gap is significant, you might want to consider other career opportunities.

◼ **Setting Boundaries and Constraints:** Your career success depends to a great extent on you monitoring and regulating your own behavior. Setting boundaries and constraints on yourself can help you focus on strategic priorities, generate short-term objectives and action plans, improve efficiency and effectiveness, and minimize improper conduct. Identify the boundaries and constraints you have placed on yourself and evaluate how each of those contributes to your personal growth and career development. If you do not have boundaries and constraints, consider developing them.

◼ **Rewards and Incentives:** Is your organization's reward structure fair and equitable? On what criteria do you base your conclusions? How does the firm define outstanding performance and reward it? Are these financial or nonfinancial rewards? The absence of rewards that are seen as fair and equitable can result in the long-term erosion of morale, which may have long-term adverse career implications for you.

◼ **Culture:** Given your career goals, what type of organizational culture would provide the best work environment? How does your organization's culture deviate from this concept? Does your organization have a strong and effective culture? In the long run, how likely are you to internalize the culture of your organization? If you believe that there is a strong misfit between your values and the organization's culture, you may want to reconsider your relationship with the organization.

For firms to be successful, they must practice effective strategic control and corporate governance. Without such controls, the firm will not be able to achieve competitive advantages and outperform rivals in the marketplace.

We began the chapter with the key role of informational control. We contrasted two types of control systems: what we termed "traditional" and "contemporary" information control systems. Whereas traditional control systems may have their place in placid, simple competitive environments, there are fewer of those in today's economy. Instead, we advocated the contemporary approach wherein the internal and external environment are constantly monitored so that when surprises emerge, the firm can modify its strategies, goals, and objectives.

Behavioral controls are also a vital part of effective control systems. We argued that firms must develop the proper balance between culture, rewards and incentives, and boundaries and constraints. Where there are strong and positive cultures and rewards, employees tend to internalize the organization's strategies and objectives. This permits a firm to spend fewer resources on monitoring behavior, and assures the firm that the efforts and initiatives of employees are more consistent with the overall objectives of the organization.

In the final section of this chapter, we addressed corporate governance, which can be defined as the relationship between various participants in determining the direction and performance of the corporation. The primary participants include shareholders, management (led by the chief executive officer), and the board of directors. We reviewed studies that indicated a consistent relationship between effective corporate governance and financial performance. There are also several internal and external control mechanisms that can serve to align managerial interests and shareholder interests. The internal mechanisms include a committed and involved board of directors, shareholder activism, and effective managerial incentives and rewards. The external mechanisms include the market for corporate control, banks and analysts, regulators, the media, and public activists. We also addressed corporate governance from both a United States and an international perspective.

SUMMARY REVIEW QUESTIONS

1. Why are effective strategic control systems so important in today's economy?
2. What are the main advantages of "contemporary" control systems over "traditional" control systems? What are the main differences between these two systems?
3. Why is it important to have a balance between the three elements of behavioral control—culture; rewards and incentives; and, boundaries?
4. Discuss the relationship between types of organizations and their primary means of behavioral control.
5. Boundaries become less important as a firm develops a strong culture and reward system. Explain.
6. Why is it important to avoid a "one best way" mentality concerning control systems? What are the consequences of applying the same type of control system to all types of environments?
7. What is the role of effective corporate governance in improving a firm's performance? What are some of the key governance mechanisms that are used to ensure that managerial and shareholder interests are aligned?
8. Define principal–principal (PP) conflicts. What are the implications for corporate governance?

strategic control 278
traditional approach to
    strategic control 278
informational control 279
behavioral control 279
organizational culture 281
reward system 283
boundaries and
    constraints 284

corporate governance 288
corporation 290
agency theory 290
board of directors 292
shareholder activism 295
external governance control
    mechanisms 298
market for corporate
    control 298
takeover constraint 298
principal–principal
    conflicts 301
expropriation of minority
    shareholders 303
business groups 303

experiential exercise

McDonald's Corporation, the world's largest fast-food restaurant chain, with 2012 revenues of $28 billion, has recently been on a "roll." Its shareholder value rose by over 50% from May 2010 to May 2013. Using the Internet or library sources, evaluate the quality of the corporation in terms of management, the board of directors, and shareholder activism. Are the issues you list favorable or unfavorable for sound corporate governance?

application questions & exercises

1. The problems of many firms may be attributed to a "traditional" control system that failed to continuously monitor the environment and make necessary changes in their strategy and objectives.

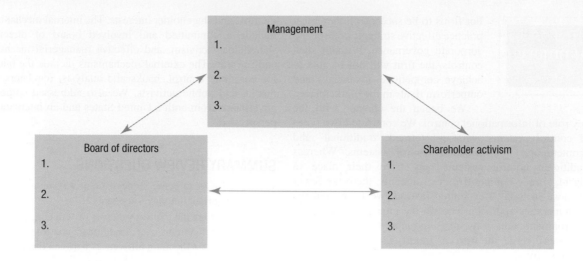

What companies are you familiar with that responded appropriately (or inappropriately) to environmental change?

2. How can a strong, positive culture enhance a firm's competitive advantage? How can a weak, negative culture erode competitive advantages? Explain and provide examples.

3. Use the Internet to research a firm that has an excellent culture and/or reward and incentive system. What are this firm's main financial and nonfinancial benefits?

4. Using the Internet, go to the website of a large, publicly held corporation in which you are interested. What evidence do you see of effective (or ineffective) corporate governance?

ethics questions

1. Strong cultures can have powerful effects on employee behavior. How does this create inadvertent control mechanisms? That is, are strong cultures an ethical way to control behavior?

2. Rules and regulations can help reduce unethical behavior in organizations. To be effective, however, what other systems, mechanisms, and processes are necessary?

references

1. Bandler, J. 2012. How HP lost its way. *Fortune,* May 21: 147–164; and Task, A. 2010. Another corporate outrage: 'Golden parachutes' for failed CEOs. *Finance.yahoo.com,* December 12: np.

2. This chapter draws upon Picken, J. C. & Dess, G. G. 1997. *Mission critical.* Burr Ridge, IL: Irwin Professional Publishing.

3. For a unique perspective on governance, refer to: Carmeli, A. & Markman, G. D. 2011. Capture, governance, and resilience: Strategy implications from the history of Rome. *Strategic Management Journal,* 32(3):332–341.

4. Argyris, C. 1977. Double-loop learning in organizations. *Harvard Business Review,* 55: 115–125.

5. Simons, R. 1995. Control in an age of empowerment. *Harvard Business Review,* 73: 80–88. This chapter draws on this source in the discussion of informational control.

6. Goold, M. & Quinn, J. B. 1990. The paradox of strategic controls. *Strategic Management Journal,* 11: 43–57.

7. Quinn, J. B. 1980. *Strategies for change.* Homewood, IL: Richard D. Irwin.

8. Mintzberg, H. 1987. Crafting strategy. *Harvard Business Review,* 65: 66–75.

9. Weston, J. S. 1992. Soft stuff matters. *Financial Executive,* July–August: 52–53.

10. This discussion of control systems draws upon Simons, op. cit.

11. Ryan, M. K., Haslam, S. A., & Renneboog, L. D. R. 2011. Who gets the carrot and who gets the stick? Evidence of gender discrimination in executive remuneration. *Strategic Management Journal,* 32(3): 301–321.

12. For an interesting perspective on this issue and how a downturn in the economy can reduce the tendency toward "free agency" by managers and professionals, refer to Morris, B. 2001. White collar blues. *Fortune,* July 23: 98–110.

13. For a colorful example of behavioral control in an organization, see: Beller, P. C. 2009. Activision's unlikely hero. *Forbes.* February 2: 52–58.

14. Ouchi, W. 1981. *Theory Z.* Reading, MA: Addison-Wesley; Deal, T. E. & Kennedy, A. A. 1982. *Corporate cultures.* Reading, MA: Addison-Wesley; Peters, T. J. & Waterman, R. H. 1982. *In search of excellence.* New York: Random House; Collins, J. 2001. *Good to great.* New York: HarperCollins.

15. Collins, J. C. & Porras, J. I. 1994. *Built to last: Successful habits of visionary companies.* New York: Harper Business.

16. Lee, J. & Miller, D. 1999. People matter: Commitment to employees, strategy, and performance in Korean firms. *Strategic Management Journal,* 6: 579–594.

17. For an insightful discussion of IKEA's unique culture, see Kling, K. & Goteman, I. 2003. IKEA CEO Anders Dahlvig on international growth and IKEA's unique corporate culture and brand identity. *Academy of Management Executive,* 17(1): 31–37.

18. For a discussion of how professionals inculcate values, refer to Uhl-Bien, M. & Graen, G. B. 1998. Individual self-management: Analysis of professionals' self-managing activities in functional and cross-functional work teams. *Academy of Management Journal,* 41(3): 340–350.

19. A perspective on how antisocial behavior can erode a firm's culture can be found in Robinson, S. L. & O'Leary-Kelly, A. M. 1998. Monkey see, monkey do: The influence of work groups on the antisocial behavior of employees. *Academy of Management Journal,* 41(6): 658–672.

20. Benkler, Y. 2011. The unselfish gene. *Harvard Business Review,* 89(7): 76–85.

21. An interesting perspective on organizational culture is in: Mehta, S. N. 2009. UnderArmour reboots. *Fortune,* February 2: 29–33.

22. For insights on social pressure as a means for control, refer to: Goldstein, N. J. 2009. Harnessing social pressure. *Harvard Business Review,* 87(2): 25.

23. Mitchell, R. 1989. Masters of innovation. *BusinessWeek,* April 10: 58–63.

24. Sellers, P. 1993. Companies that serve you best. *Fortune,* May 31: 88.

25. Southwest Airlines Culture Committee. 1993. *Luv Lines* (company publication), March April: 17–18; for an interesting perspective on the "downside" of strong "cultlike" organizational cultures, refer to Arnott, D. A. 2000. *Corporate cults.* New York: AMACOM.

26. Kerr, J. & Slocum, J. W., Jr. 1987. Managing corporate culture through reward systems. *Academy of Management Executive,* 1(2): 99–107.

27. For a unique perspective on leader challenges in managing wealthy professionals, refer to Wetlaufer, S. 2000. Who wants to manage a millionaire? *Harvard Business Review,* 78(4): 53–60.

28. Netessine, S. & Yakubovich, V. 2012. The darwinian workplace. *Harvard Business Review,* 90(5): 25–28.

29. For a discussion of the benefits of stock options as executive compensation, refer to Hall, B. J. 2000. What you need to know about stock options. *Harvard Business Review,* 78(2): 121–129.

30. Tully, S. 1993. Your paycheck gets exciting. *Fortune,* November 13: 89.

31. Carter, N. M. & Silva, C. 2010. Why men still get more promotions than women. *Harvard Business Review,* 88(9): 80–86.

32. Zellner, W., Hof, R. D., Brandt, R., Baker, S., & Greising, D. 1995. Go-go goliaths. *BusinessWeek,* February 13: 64–70.

33. Birkinshaw, J., Bouquet, C., & Barsoux, J. 2011. The 5 myths of innovation. *MIT Sloan Management Review,* Winter: 43–50.

34. Bryant, A. 2011. *The corner office.* New York: St. Martin's Griffin: 173.

35. This section draws on Dess & Picken, op. cit.: chap. 5.

36. Anonymous. 2012. Nestle set to buy Pfizer unit. *Dallas Morning News,* April 19: 10D.

37. Isaacson, W. 2012. The real leadership lessons of Steve Jobs. *Harvard Business Review,* 90(4): 93–101.

38. This section draws upon Dess, G. G. & Miller, A. 1993. *Strategic management.* New York: McGraw-Hill.

39. For a good review of the goal-setting literature, refer to Locke, E. A. & Latham, G. P. 1990. *A theory of goal setting and task performance.* Englewood Cliffs, NJ: Prentice Hall.

40. For an interesting perspective on the use of rules and regulations that is counter to this industry's (software) norms, refer to Fryer, B. 2001. Tom Siebel of Siebel Systems: High tech the old fashioned way. *Harvard Business Review,* 79(3): 118–130.

41. Thompson, A. A. Jr. & Strickland, A. J., III. 1998. *Strategic management: Concepts and cases* (10th ed.): 313. New York: McGraw-Hill.

42. Ibid.

43. Teitelbaum, R. 1997. Tough guys finish first. *Fortune,* July 21: 82–84.

44. Weaver, G. R., Trevino, L. K., & Cochran, P. L. 1999. Corporate ethics programs as control systems: Influences of executive commitment and environmental factors. *Academy of Management Journal,* 42(1): 41–57.

45. www.singaporeair.com/pdf/media-centre/anti-corruption-policy-procedures.pdf.

46. Weber, J. 2003. CFOs on the hot seat. *BusinessWeek,* March 17: 66–70.

47. William Ouchi has written extensively about the use of clan control (which is viewed as an alternate to bureaucratic or market control). Here, a powerful culture results in people aligning their individual interests with those of the firm. Refer to Ouchi, op. cit. This section also draws on Hall, R. H. 2002. *Organizations: Structures, processes, and outcomes* (8th ed.).

Upper Saddle River, NJ: Prentice Hall.

48. Poundstone, W. 2003. *How would you move Mount Fuji?* New York: Little, Brown: 59.

49. Abby, E. 2012. Woman sues over personality test job rejection. *abcnews.go.com,* October 1: np.

50. Interesting insights on corporate governance are in: Kroll, M., Walters, B. A., & Wright, P. 2008. Board vigilance, director experience, and corporate outcomes. *Strategic Management Journal,* 29(4): 363–382.

51. For a brief review of some central issues in corporate governance research, see: Hambrick, D. C., Werder, A. V., & Zajac, E. J. 2008. New directions in corporate governance research. *Organization Science,* 19(3): 381–385.

52. Monks, R. & Minow, N. 2001. *Corporate governance* (2nd ed.). Malden, MA: Blackwell.

53. Pound, J. 1995. The promise of the governed corporation. *Harvard Business Review,* 73(2): 89–98.

54. Maurer, H. & Linblad, C. 2009. Scandal at Satyam. *BusinessWeek,* January 19: 8; Scheck, J. & Stecklow, S. 2008. Brocade ex-CEO gets 21 months in prison. *The Wall Street Journal,* January 17: A3; Levine, D. & Graybow, M. 2010. Mozilo to pay millions in Countrywide settlement. *finance.yahoo.com.* October 15: np; Ellis, B. 2010. Countrywide's Mozilo to pay $67.5 million settlement. *cnnmoney.com.* October 15: np; Frank, R., Efrati, A., Lucchetti, A. & Bray, C. 2009. Madoff jailed after admitting epic scam. *The Wall Street Journal.* March 13: A1; and Henriques, D. B. 2009. Madoff is sentenced to 150 years for Ponzi scheme. *www.nytimes.com.* June 29: np.

55. Anonymous. 2012. Olympus and ex-executives plead guilty in accounting fraud. *nytimes.com,* September 25: np.

56. Corporate governance and social networks are discussed in: McDonald, M. L., Khanna, P., & Westphal, J. D. 2008. *Academy of Management Journal.* 51(3): 453–475.

57. This discussion draws upon Monks & Minow, op. cit.

58. For an interesting perspective on the politicization of the corporation, read: Palazzo, G. & Scherer, A. G. 2008. Corporate social responsibility, democracy, and the politicization of the corporation. *Academy of Management Review,* 33(3): 773–774.

59. Eisenhardt, K. M. 1989. Agency theory: An assessment and review. *Academy of Management Review,* 14(1): 57–74. Some of the seminal contributions to agency theory include Jensen, M. & Meckling, W. 1976. Theory of the firm: Managerial behavior, agency costs, and ownership structure. *Journal of Financial Economics,* 3: 305–360; Fama, E. & Jensen, M. 1983. Separation of ownership and control. *Journal of Law and Economics,* 26: 301, 325; and Fama, E. 1980. Agency problems and the theory of the firm. *Journal of Political Economy,* 88: 288–307.

60. Nyberg, A. J., Fulmer, I. S., Gerhart, B. & Carpenter, M. 2010. Agency theory revisited: CEO return and shareholder interest alignment. *Academy of Management Journal,* 53(5): 1029–1049.

61. Managers may also engage in " shirking"—that is, reducing or withholding their efforts. See, for example, Kidwell, R. E., Jr. & Bennett, N. 1993. Employee propensity to withhold effort: A conceptual model to intersect three avenues of research. *Academy of Management Review,* 18(3): 429–456.

62. For an interesting perspective on agency and clarification of many related concepts and terms, visit *www.encycogov.com.*

63. The relationship between corporate ownership structure and export intensity in Chinese firms is discussed in: Filatotchev, I., Stephan, J., & Jindra, B. 2008. Ownership structure, strategic controls and export intensity of foreign-invested firms in transition economies. *Journal of International Business,* 39(7): 1133–1148.

64. Argawal, A. & Mandelker, G. 1987. Managerial incentives and corporate investment and financing decisions. *Journal of Finance,* 42: 823–837.

65. Gross. D. 2012. Outrageous CEO compensation: Wynn, Adelson, Dell and Abercrombie shockers. *finance .yahoo.com,* June 7: np.

66. Anonymous. 2013. Too early for the worst footnote of 2013? *footnoted .com,* January 18: np.

67. For an insightful, recent discussion of the academic research on corporate governance, and in particular the role of boards of directors, refer to Chatterjee, S. & Harrison, J. S. 2001. Corporate governance. In Hitt, M. A., Freeman, R. E., & Harrison, J. S. (Eds.). *Handbook of strategic management:* 543–563. Malden, MA: Blackwell.

68. For an interesting theoretical discussion on corporate governance in Russia, see: McCarthy, D. J. & Puffer, S. M. 2008. Interpreting the ethicality of corporate governance decisions in Russia: Utilizing integrative social contracts theory to evaluate the relevance of agency theory norms. *Academy of Management Review,* 33(1): 11–31.

69. Haynes, K. T. & Hillman, A. 2010. The effect of board capital and CEO power on strategic change. *Strategic Management Journal,* 31(110): 1145–1163.

70. This opening discussion draws on Monks & Minow, op. cit. 164, 169; see also Pound, op. cit.

71. Business Roundtable. 1990. *Corporate governance and American competitiveness,* March: 7.

72. The director role in acquisition performance is addressed in: Westphal, J. D. & Graebner, M. E. 2008. What do they know? The effects of outside director acquisition experience on firm acquisition performance. *Strategic Management Journal,* 29(11): 1155–1178.

73. Byrne, J. A., Grover, R., & Melcher, R. A. 1997. The best and worst boards. *BusinessWeek,* November 26: 35–47. The three key roles of boards of directors are monitoring the actions of executives, providing advice, and providing links to the external environment to provide resources. See Johnson, J. L., Daily, C. M., & Ellstrand, A. E. 1996. Boards of directors: A review and research agenda. *Academy of Management Review,* 37: 409–438.

74. Pozen, R. C. 2010. The case for professional boards. *Harvard Business Review,* 88(12): 50–58.

75. The role of outside directors is discussed in: Lester, R. H., Hillman, A., Zardkoohi, A., & Cannella, A. A. Jr. 2008. Former government officials as outside directors: The role of human and social capital. *Academy of Management Journal,* 51(5): 999–1013.

76. McGeehan, P. 2003. More chief executives shown the door, study says. *New York Times,* May 12: C2.

77. The examples in this paragraph draw upon Helyar, J. & Hymowitz, C. 2011. The recession is gone, and the CEO could be next. *Bloomberg Businessweek.* Februrary 7–February 13: 24–26; Stelter, B. 2010. Jonathan Klein to leave CNN. *mediadecoder. blogs.nytimes.com.* September 24: np; Silver, A. 2010. Milestones. *TIME Magazine.* December 20: 28; *www. bp.com* and Mouawad, J. & Krauss, C. 2010. BP is expected to replace Hayward as chief with American. *The New York Times.* July 26: A1.

78. Stoever, H. 2012. NACD highlights growing need for succession planning and diversity in the boardroom. *nacdonline.org,* March 22: np.

79. For an analysis of the effects of outside directors' compensation on acquisition decisions, refer to Deutsch, T., Keil, T., & Laamanen, T. 2007. Decision making in acquisitions: The effect of outside directors' compensation on acquisition patterns. *Journal of Management,* 33(1): 30–56.

80. Director interlocks are addressed in: Kang, E. 2008. Director interlocks and spillover effects of reputational penalties from financial reporting fraud. *Academy of Management Journal,* 51(3): 537–556.

81. There are benefits, of course, to having some insiders on the board of directors. Inside directors would be more aware of the firm's strategies. Additionally, outsiders may rely too often on financial performance indicators because of information asymmetries. For an interesting discussion, see Baysinger, B. D. & Hoskisson, R. E. 1990. The composition of boards of directors and strategic control: Effects on corporate strategy. *Academy of Management Review,* 15: 72–87.

82. Hambrick, D. C. & Jackson, E. M. 2000. Outside directors with a stake: The linchpin in improving governance. *California Management Review,* 42(4): 108–127.

83. Corsi, C, Dale, G., Daum, J, Mumm, J, & Schoppen, W. 2010. 5 things board directors should be thinking about. *spencerstuart.com,* December: np; Evans, B. 2007. Six steps to building an effective board. *Inc.com,* np; Beatty, D. 2009. New challenges for corporate governance. *Rotman Magazine,* Fall: 58-63; and Krause, R., Semadeni, M., & Cannella, A. 2013. External COO/presidents as expert directors: A new look at the service role of boards. *Strategic Management Journal.* In press.

84. A discussion on the shareholder approval process in executive compensation is presented in: Brandes, P., Goranova, M., & Hall, S. 2008. Navigating shareholder influence: Compensation plans and the shareholder approval process. *Academy of Management Perspectives,* 22(1): 41–57.

85. Monks and Minow, op. cit.: 93.

86. A discussion of the factors that lead to shareholder activism is found in Ryan, L. V. & Schneider, M. 2002. The antecedents of institutional investor activism. *Academy of Management Review,* 27(4): 554–573.

87. For an insightful discussion of investor activism, refer to David, P., Bloom, M., & Hillman, A. 2007. Investor activism, managerial responsiveness, and corporate social performance. *Strategic Management Journal,* 28(1): 91–100.

88. There is strong research support for the idea that the presence of large block shareholders is associated with value-maximizing decisions. For example, refer to Johnson, R. A., Hoskisson, R. E., & Hitt, M. A. 1993. Board of director involvement in restructuring: The effects of board versus managerial controls and characteristics. *Strategic Management Journal,* 14: 33–50.

89. For a discussion of institutional activism and its link to CEO compensation, refer to: Chowdhury, S. D. & Wang, E. Z. 2009. Institutional activism types and CEO compensation. *Journal of Management,* 35(1): 5–36.

90. For an interesting perspective on the impact of institutional ownership on a firm's innovation strategies, see Hoskisson, R. E., Hitt, M. A., Johnson, R. A., & Grossman, W. 2002. *Academy of Management Journal,* 45(4): 697–716.

91. *www.calpers-governance.org.*

92. Icahn, C. 2007. Icahn: On activist investors and private equity run wild. *BusinessWeek,* March 12: 21–22. For an interesting perspective on Carl Icahn's transition (?) from corporate raider to shareholder activist, read Grover, R. 2007. Just don't call him a raider. *BusinessWeek,* March 5: 68–69. The quote in the text is part of Icahn's response to the article by R. Grover.

93. Bond, P. 2012. Netflix stock climbs after Carl Icahn takes a position. *hollywoodreporter.com,* October 31: np.

94. For a study of the relationship between ownership and diversification, refer to Goranova, M., Alessandri, T. M., Brandes, P., & Dharwadkar, R. 2007. Managerial ownership and corporate diversification: A longitudinal view. *Strategic Management Journal,* 28(3): 211–226.

95. Jensen, M. C. & Murphy, K. J. 1990. CEO incentives—It's not how much you pay, but how. *Harvard Business Review,* 68(3): 138–149.

96. For a perspective on the relative advantages and disadvantages of "duality"—that is, one individual serving as both Chief Executive Office and Chairman of the Board, see Lorsch, J. W. & Zelleke, A. 2005. Should the CEO be the chairman?

MIT Sloan Management Review, 46(2): 71–74.

97. A discussion of knowledge sharing is addressed in: Fey, C. F. & Furu, P. 2008. Top management incentive compensation and knowledge sharing in multinational corporations. *Strategic Management Journal,* 29(12): 1301–1324.

98. Sasseen, J. 2007. A better look at the boss's pay. *BusinessWeek,* February 26: 44–45; and Weinberg, N., Maiello, M., & Randall, D. 2008. Paying for failure. *Forbes,* May 19: 114, 116.

99. Research has found that executive compensation is more closely aligned with firm performance in companies with compensation committees and boards dominated by outside directors. See, for example, Conyon, M. J. & Peck, S. I. 1998. Board control, remuneration committees, and top management compensation. *Academy of Management Journal,* 41: 146–157.

100. Anonymous. 2012. American chief executives are not overpaid. *The Economist,* September 8: 67.

101. Caldwell, D. & Francolla, G. 2012. Highest paid CEOs. *cnbc.com,* November 19: np.

102. George, B. 2010. Executive pay: Rebuilding trust in an era of rage. *Bloomberg Businessweek,* September 13: 56.

103. Chahine, S. & Tohme, N. S. 2009. Is CEO duality always negative? An exploration of CEO duality and ownership structure in the Arab IPO context. *Corporate Governance: An International Review.* 17(2): 123–141; and McGrath, J. 2009. How CEOs work. *HowStuffWorks.com.* January 28: np.

104. Anonymous. 2009. Someone to watch over them. *The Economist.* October 17: 78; Anonymous. 2004. Splitting up the roles of CEO and Chairman: Reform or red herring? *Knowledge@Wharton.* June 2: np; and Kim, J. 2010. Shareholders reject split of CEO and chairman jobs at JPMorgan. *FierceFinance.com.* May 18: np.

105. Tuggle, C. S., Sirmon, D. G., Reutzel, C. R. & Bierman, L. 2010. Commanding board of director attention: Investigating how organizational performance and CEO duality affect board members' attention to monitoring. *Strategic Management Journal.* 31: 946–968; Weinberg, N. 2010. No more lapdogs. *Forbes.* May 10: 34–36; and Anonymous. 2010. Corporate constitutions. *The Economist.* October 30: 74.

106. Semadeni, M. & Krause, R. 2012. Splitting the CEO and chairman roles: It's complicated . . . *businessweek.com,* November 1: np.

107. Such opportunistic behavior is common in all principal-agent relationships. For a description of agency problems, especially in the context of the relationship between shareholders and managers, see Jensen, M. C. & Meckling, W. H. 1976. Theory of the firm: Managerial behavior, agency costs, and ownership structure. *Journal of Financial Economics,* 3: 305–360.

108. Hoskisson, R. E. & Turk, T. A. 1990. Corporate restructuring: Governance and control limits of the internal market. *Academy of Management Review,* 15: 459–477.

109. For an insightful perspective on the market for corporate control and how it is influenced by knowledge intensity, see Coff, R. 2003. Bidding wars over R&D-intensive firms: Knowledge, opportunism, and the market for corporate control. *Academy of Management Journal,* 46(1): 74–85.

110. Walsh, J. P. & Kosnik, R. D. 1993. Corporate raiders and their disciplinary role in the market for corporate control. *Academy of Management Journal,* 36: 671–700.

111. The role of regulatory bodies in the banking industry is addressed in: Bhide, A. 2009. Why bankers got so reckless. *BusinessWeek,* February 9: 30–31.

112. Wishy-washy: The SEC pulls its punches on corporate-governance rules. 2003. *Economist,* February 1: 60.

113. McLean, B. 2001. Is Enron overpriced? *Fortune,* March 5: 122–125.

114. Swartz, J. 2010. Timberland's CEO on standing up to 65,000 angry activists. *Harvard Business Review,* 88 (9): 39–43.

115. Bernstein, A. 2000. Too much corporate power. *BusinessWeek,* September 11: 35–37.

116. This section draws upon Young, M. N., Peng, M. W., Ahlstrom, D., Bruton, G. D., & Jiang, Y. 2005. Principal–principal conflicts in corporate governance (un-published manuscript); and, Peng, M. W. 2006. *Globalstrategy.* Cincinnati: Thomson South-Western. We appreciate the helpful comments of Mike Young of Hong Kong Baptist University and Mike Peng of the University of Texas at Dallas.

117. Khanna, T. & Rivkin, J. 2001. Estimating the performance effects of business groups in emerging markets. *Strategic Management Journal,* 22: 45–74.

chapter 10

Creating Effective Organizational Designs

After reading this chapter, you should have a good understanding of the following learning objectives:

LO10.1 The growth patterns of major corporations and the relationship between a firm's strategy and its structure.

LO10.2 Each of the traditional types of organizational structure: simple, functional, divisional, and matrix.

LO10.3 The implications of a firm's international operations for organizational structure.

LO10.4 The different types of boundaryless organizations—barrier-free, modular, and virtual—and their relative advantages and disadvantages.

LO10.5 The need for creating ambidextrous organizational designs that enable firms to explore new opportunities and effectively integrate existing operations.

Learning from Mistakes

Organizational Structure: Is Siemens too big to manage?

Siemens AG is the largest Europe-based electronics and electrical engineering company. Its principal activities are in industry, energy, transportation, and healthcare. Its subsidiaries employ approximately 360,000 people across nearly 190 countries. However, the company has been the subject of considerable controversy in recent years.

Fresh concerns spun out of control in 2012 when new orders had dropped in almost every division, compared with the year before, most dramatically in energy, infrastructure, and cities (which includes high-speed trains). Orders from within Germany and from India had fallen by over 40 percent. Even China ordered 11 percent less. Much of this was due to the economic slowdown, especially in Europe, and returned to normal after some big orders in 2011, Siemens's best year ever. Currently revenues are up despite the falling orders. But the declines reflect some strategic errors.

First, Siemens bet on a global recovery in 2012. That didn't happen, especially in Europe. Second, Siemens overreached in wind parks and particle therapy, an

experimental cancer treatment. In both cases it launched too many ground-breaking projects at once and hit unexpected problems and costs: bad planning again.

As a result, CEO Peter Löscher, an Austrian, was fired. It had been assumed that, as he was recruited from outside of the company, he would be better placed to clean up Siemens after a bribery scandal which had led to large fines in America and Germany. He joined in 2007 and, initially, it was thought he was doing well polishing up both the company's image and its operations, and he enjoyed a good reputation. However, as the setbacks mounted, his outsider status made it easier to sack him.

Peter Löscher was replaced by Joe Kaeser, chief financial officer at the time. Kaeser insisted that the company is "certainly not in crisis, nor is it in need of major restructuring." But there is plenty that needs fixing. Shortly before being forced out Löscher admitted that his target of a 12 percent profit margin by 2014 would not be met. His critics said the focus on size was a distraction from the more important profit target. But Siemens's problems cannot be blamed entirely on the former CEO. The company may simply be too diverse to run well.

Löscher simplified Siemens's structure, leaving just four main divisions: energy, industry, health care, and a new infrastructure-and-cities division. But it still has too many weak subdivisions. It made a costly mistake with the 2009 purchase of Solel, a solar-power company that depended on state subsidies which later evaporated. Siemens quit that business in 2012, having lost a total of €606 million in 2011 and 2012.

The question now is whether Kaeser will be more ruthless with underperforming businesses. According to an industry analysts, he recognizes Siemens's sprawling portfolio as its main problem. That would be good news for those investors seeking a leaner Siemens.

Conglomerates are hard to slim down. In the case of Siemens which has 130,000 employees in Germany, one of the solutions is to shed jobs. However, this is rather difficult. In 2008 it struck an agreement, renewed in 2010, to safeguard German jobs and plants in the long term. Recently it has even been adding to its workforce. But some relocation is likely. Its subsidiary Osram, a lighting manufacturer, has been shifting jobs away from making obsolescent light bulbs.

Siemens is in it for the long haul but it is learning that it cannot wholly ignore investors, nor the analysts who sway them. The firm aims to beat its great rival, GE, and to hit annual revenues of €100 billion (2012's were €74 billion). Sensibly, it hasn't specified when.

By Cyrlene Claasen and Helena Gonzalez

Discussion Questions

1. Why is it so difficult for Siemens to cut jobs even though it seems like a good strategy to make the firm leaner?
2. Should Kaeser continue with Löscher's strategy of simplifying Siemens's structure?

One of the central concepts in this chapter is the importance of boundaryless organizations. Successful organizations create permeable boundaries among the internal activities as well as between the organization and its external customers, suppliers, and alliance partners. We introduced this idea in Chapter 3 in our discussion of the value-chain concept, which consisted of several primary (e.g., inbound logistics, marketing and sales) and support activities (e.g., procurement, human resource management). There are a number of possible benefits to outsourcing activities as part of becoming an effective boundaryless organization. However, outsourcing can also create challenges. As in the case of Siemens, the firm lost a large amount of control due to it focusing on its complicated organizational structure rather than hitting profit targets.

Today's managers are faced with two ongoing and vital activities in structuring and designing their organizations.[2] First, they must decide on the most appropriate type of organizational structure. Second, they need to assess what mechanisms, processes, and techniques are most helpful in enhancing the permeability of both internal and external boundaries.

Traditional Forms of Organizational Structure

organizational structure
the formalized patterns of interactions that link a firm's tasks, technologies, and people.

Organizational structure refers to the formalized patterns of interactions that link a firm's tasks, technologies, and people.[3] Structures help to ensure that resources are used effectively in accomplishing an organization's mission. Structure provides a means of balancing two conflicting forces: a need for the division of tasks into meaningful groupings and the need to integrate such groupings in order to ensure efficiency and effectiveness.[4] Structure identifies the executive, managerial, and administrative organization of a firm and indicates responsibilities and hierarchical relationships. It also influences the flow of information as well as the context and nature of human interactions.[5]

Most organizations begin very small and either die or remain small. Those that survive and prosper embark on strategies designed to increase the overall scope of operations and enable them to enter new product-market domains. Such growth places additional pressure on executives to control and coordinate the firm's increasing size and diversity. The most appropriate type of structure depends on the nature and magnitude of growth.

LO10.1
The growth patterns of major corporations and the relationship between a firm's strategy and its structure.

Patterns of Growth of Large Corporations:
Strategy-Structure Relationships

A firm's strategy and structure change as it increases in size, diversifies into new product markets, and expands its geographic scope.[6] Exhibit 10.1 illustrates common growth patterns of firms.

EXHIBIT 10.1 Dominant Growth Patterns of Large Corporations

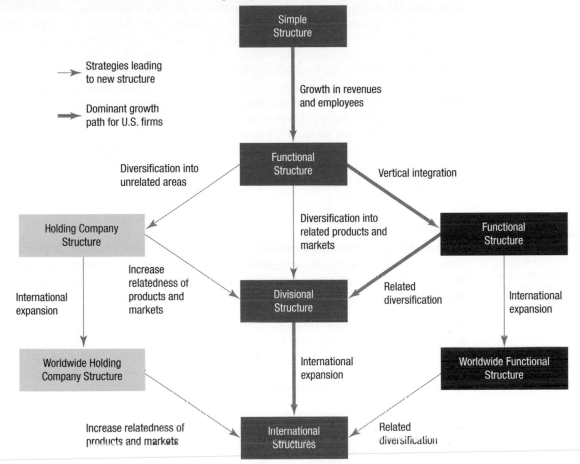

Source: Adapted from J. R. Galbraith and R. K Kazanjian. *Strategy Implementation: Structure, Systems and Process,* 2nd ed. Copyright © 1986.

A new firm with a *simple structure* typically increases its sales revenue and volume of outputs over time. It may also engage in some vertical integration to secure sources of supply (backward integration) as well as channels of distribution (forward integration). The simple-structure firm then implements a *functional structure* to concentrate efforts on both increasing efficiency and enhancing its operations and products. This structure enables the firm to group its operations into either functions, departments, or geographic areas. As its initial markets mature, a firm looks beyond its present products and markets for possible expansion.

A strategy of related diversification requires a need to reorganize around product lines or geographic markets. This leads to a *divisional structure.* As the business expands in terms of sales revenues, and domestic growth opportunities become somewhat limited, a firm may seek opportunities in international markets. A firm has a wide variety of structures to choose from. These include *international division, geographic area, worldwide product division, worldwide functional,* and *worldwide matrix.* Deciding upon the most appropriate structure when a firm has international operations depends on three primary factors: the extent of international expansion, type of strategy (global, multidomestic, or transnational), and the degree of product diversity.[7]

Some firms may find it advantageous to diversify into several product lines rather than focus their efforts on strengthening distributor and supplier relationships through vertical integration. They would organize themselves according to product lines by implementing a divisional structure. Also, some firms may choose to move into unrelated product areas, typically by acquiring existing businesses. Frequently, their rationale is that acquiring assets and competencies is more economical or expedient than developing them internally. Such an unrelated, or conglomerate, strategy requires relatively little integration across businesses and sharing of resources. Thus, a *holding company structure* becomes appropriate. There are many other growth patterns, but these are the most common.*

Now we will discuss some of the most common types of organizational structures—simple, functional, divisional (including two variants: *strategic business unit* and *holding company*), and matrix and their advantages and disadvantages. We will close the section with a discussion of the structural implications when a firm expands its operations into international markets.[8]

> **LO10.2**
>
> Each of the traditional types of organizational structure: simple, functional, divisional, and matrix.

Simple Structure

The **simple organizational structure** is the oldest, and most common, organizational form. Most organizations are very small and have a single or very narrow product line in which the owner-manager (or top executive) makes most of the decisions. The owner-manager controls all activities, and the staff serves as an extension of the top executive.

simple organizational structure
an organizational form in which the owner-manager makes most of the decisions and controls activities, and the staff serves as an extension of the top executive.

Advantages   The simple structure is highly informal and the coordination of tasks is accomplished by direct supervision. Decision making is highly centralized, there is little specialization of tasks, few rules and regulations, and an informal evaluation and reward system. Although the owner-manager is intimately involved in almost all phases of the business, a manager is often employed to oversee day-to-day operations.

Disadvantages   A simple structure may foster creativity and individualism since there are generally few rules and regulations. However, such "informality" may lead to problems. Employees may not clearly understand their responsibilities, which can lead to conflict and confusion. Employees may take advantage of the lack of regulations, act in their own self-interest, which can erode motivation and satisfaction and lead to the possible misuse of organizational resources. Small organizations have flat structures that limit opportunities for upward mobility. Without the potential for future advancement, recruiting and retaining talent may become very difficult.

Functional Structure

When an organization is small (15 employees or less), it is not necessary to have a variety of formal arrangements and groupings of activities. However, as firms grow, excessive demands may be placed on the owner-manager in order to obtain and process all of the information necessary to run the business. Chances are the owner will not be skilled in all specialties (e.g., accounting, engineering, production, marketing). Thus, he or she will need to hire specialists in the various functional areas. Such growth in the overall scope and complexity of the business necessitates a **functional organizational structure** wherein the major functions of the firm are grouped internally. The coordination and integration of the functional areas becomes one of the most important responsibilities of the chief executive of the firm (see Exhibit 10.2).

functional organizational structure
an organizational form in which the major functions of the firm, such as production, marketing, R&D, and accounting, are grouped internally.

---

*The lowering of transaction costs and globalization have led to some changes in the common historical patterns that we have discussed. Some firms are, in effect, bypassing the vertical integration stage. Instead, they focus on core competencies and outsource other value-creation activities. Also, even relatively young firms are going global early in their history because of lower communication and transportation costs. For an interesting perspective on global start-ups, see McDougall, P. P. & Oviatt, B. M. 1996. New Venture Internationalization, Strategic Change and Performance: A Follow-Up Study. *Journal of Business Venturing,* 11: 23–40; and McDougall, P. P. & Oviatt, B. M. (Eds.). 2000. The Special Research Forum on International Entrepreneurship. *Academy of Management Journal,* October: 902–1003.

EXHIBIT 10.2 Functional Organizational Structure

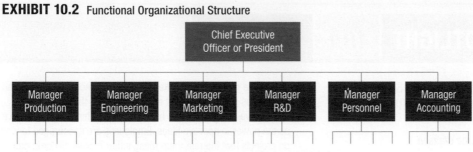

Lower-level managers, specialists, and operating personnel

Functional structures are generally found in organizations in which there is a single or closely related product or service, high production volume, and some vertical integration. Initially, firms tend to expand the overall scope of their operations by penetrating existing markets, introducing similar products in additional markets, or increasing the level of vertical integration. Such expansion activities clearly increase the scope and complexity of the operations. The functional structure provides for a high level of centralization that helps to ensure integration and control over the related product-market activities or multiple primary activities (from inbound logistics to operations to marketing, sales, and service) in the value chain (addressed in Chapters 3 and 4). Strategy Spotlight 10.1 provides an example of an unusual but effective functional organization structure.

Advantages   By bringing together specialists into functional departments, a firm is able to enhance its coordination and control within each of the functional areas. Decision making in the firm will be centralized at the top of the organization. This enhances the organizational-level (as opposed to functional area) perspective across the various functions in the organization. In addition, the functional structure provides for a more efficient use of managerial and technical talent since functional area expertise is pooled in a single department (e.g., marketing) instead of being spread across a variety of product-market areas. Finally, career paths and professional development in specialized areas are facilitated.

Disadvantages   The differences in values and orientations among functional areas may impede communication and coordination. Edgar Schein of MIT has argued that shared assumptions, often based on similar backgrounds and experiences of members, form around functional units in an organization. This leads to what are often called "stove pipes" or "silos," in which departments view themselves as isolated, self-contained units with little need for interaction and coordination with other departments. This erodes communication because functional groups may have not only different goals but also differing meanings of words and concepts. According to Schein:

> The word "marketing" will mean product development to the engineer, studying customers through market research to the product manager, merchandising to the salesperson, and constant change in design to the manufacturing manager. When they try to work together, they will often attribute disagreements to personalities and fail to notice the deeper, shared assumptions that color how each function thinks.[9]

Such narrow functional orientations also may lead to short-term thinking based largely upon what is best for the functional area, not the entire organization. In a manufacturing firm, sales may want to offer a wide range of customized products to appeal to the firm's customers; R&D may overdesign products and components to achieve technical elegance; and manufacturing may favor no-frills products that can be produced at low cost by means

"YOU WANT TO SPEAK TO THE BOSS? SORRY, THERE IS NONE." CORPORATE STRUCTURE AT VALVE SOFTWARE

By Helena Gonzalez and Cyrlene Claasen

Valve Software is very good at developing first-person shooter games such as *Half-Life* and *Counter-Strike,* but it is unique at managing people. With 300 employees, there are no managers or bosses at Valve Software. Not even Gabe Newell, Valve co-founder, is directly in charge of anyone.

It is not only the lack of managers that is particular to Valve. The company does not have a traditional marketing or sales organization either. As a result, each developer is in charge of creating ways to measure and optimize customer satisfaction. Although at first glance this may look difficult to achieve, Valve believes that having the right people makes all the difference. Even if it means sometimes getting the most expensive talent there is.

At Valve, every employee has the power to hire someone, as well as the power to approve ideas. Employees are encouraged to work on projects that interest them most, either individually or in groups. This results in employees working on multiple projects and having the opportunity to work on anything they want to. In order to promote "project jumping," Valve employees' desks are even equipped with wheels to facilitate the movement of their workstations.

As a result of this particular structure, Valve has a high degree of success with its projects and produces superior video games in the highly competitive world of hi-tech.

Sources: "Why There Are No Bosses at Valve" by Claire Suddath, Bloomberg Business Week, April 27 2012; "What Makes Valve Software the Best Office Ever?" by Claire Suddath, Bloomberg Business Week, April 25 2012

of long production runs. Functional structures may overburden the top executives in the firm because conflicts have a tendency to be "pushed up" to the top of the organization since there are no managers who are responsible for the specific product lines. Functional structures make it difficult to establish uniform performance standards across the entire organization. It may be relatively easy to evaluate production managers on the basis of production volume and cost control, but establishing performance measures for engineering, R&D, and accounting become more problematic.

Divisional Structure

divisional organizational structure
an organizational form in which products, projects, or product markets are grouped internally.

The **divisional organizational structure** (sometimes called the multidivisional structure or M-Form) is organized around products, projects, or markets. Each of the divisions, in turn, includes its own functional specialists who are typically organized into departments.[10] A divisional structure encompasses a set of relatively autonomous units governed by a central corporate office. The operating divisions are relatively independent and consist of products and services that are different from those of the other divisions.[11] Operational decision making in a large business places excessive demands on the firm's top management. In order to attend to broader, longer-term organizational issues, top-level managers must delegate decision making to lower-level managers. Divisional executives play a key role: they help to determine the product-market and financial objectives for the division as well as their division's contribution to overall corporate performance.[12] The rewards are based largely on measures of financial performance such as net income and revenue. Exhibit 10.3 illustrates a divisional structure.

General Motors was among the earliest firms to adopt the divisional organizational structure.[13] In the 1920s the company formed five major product divisions (Cadillac, Buick, Oldsmobile, Pontiac, and Chevrolet) as well as several industrial divisions. Since then, many firms have discovered that as they diversified into new product-market activities, functional structures—with their emphasis on single functional departments—were unable to manage the increased complexity of the entire business.

Advantages By creating separate divisions to manage individual product markets, there is a separation of strategic and operating control. Divisional managers can focus

EXHIBIT 10.3 Divisional Organizational Structure

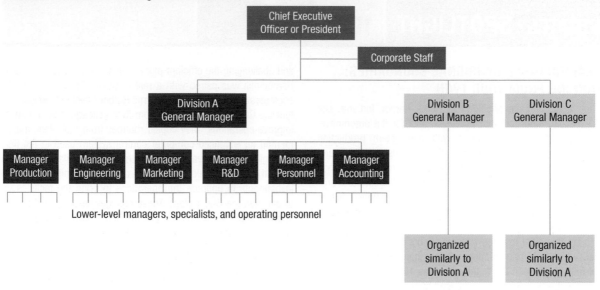

Lower-level managers, specialists, and operating personnel

their efforts on improving operations in the product markets for which they are responsible, and corporate officers can devote their time to overall strategic issues for the entire corporation. The focus on a division's products and markets—by the divisional executives—provides the corporation with an enhanced ability to respond quickly to important changes. Since there are functional departments within each division of the corporation, the problems associated with sharing resources across functional departments are minimized. Because there are multiple levels of general managers (executives responsible for integrating and coordinating all functional areas), the development of general management talent is enhanced.

Disadvantages   It can be very expensive; there can be increased costs due to the duplication of personnel, operations, and investment since each division must staff multiple functional departments. There also can be dysfunctional competition among divisions since each division tends to become concerned solely about its own operations. Divisional managers are often evaluated on common measures such as return on assets and sales growth. If goals are conflicting, there can be a sense of a "zero-sum" game that would discourage sharing ideas and resources among the divisions for the common good of the corporation. Ghoshal and Bartlett, two leading strategy scholars, note:

> As their label clearly warns, divisions divide. The divisional model fragmented companies' resources; it created vertical communication channels that insulated business units and prevented them from sharing their strengths with one another. Consequently, the whole of the corporation was often less than the sum of its parts.[14]

With many divisions providing different products and services, there is the chance that differences in image and quality may occur across divisions. One division may offer no-frills products of lower quality that may erode the brand reputation of another division that has top quality, highly differentiated offerings. Since each division is evaluated in terms of financial measures such as return on investment and revenue growth, there is often an urge to focus on short-term performance. If corporate management uses quarterly profits as the key performance indicator, divisional management may tend to put significant emphasis

BREAKING DOWN DIVISIONAL BOUNDARIES: LEARNING FROM YOUR TWIN

On the edge of Lake Michigan in Burns Harbor, Indiana, sits a 50-year-old steel mill that produces steel for the automotive, appliance, and other industries with midwestern production plants. The steel mill struggled through the 1980s and 1990s and went bankrupt in 2002. It was bought out of bankruptcy and has been owned by ArcelorMittal Steel, the world's largest steel producer, since 2005. However, the plant faced a another crisis in 2007 when it was threatened with closure unless it became more productive and efficient.

Today, this plant requires 1.32 man hours per ton of steel produced, which is 34 percent more efficient than the average in U.S. steel mills. Further, in 2011, the plant was 19 percent more efficient than it was in 2007 and produced twice the quantity of steel it produced in 2009. Its future as a productive steel plant is now secure.

How did ArcelorMittal achieve these gains and rejuvenate an old steel mill? It did it by breaking down the barriers between organization units to facilitate knowledge transfer and learning. One of the disadvantages of a divisional structure is that the divisions often perceive themselves as being in competition with each other and are therefore unwilling to share information to help other divisions improve. ArcelorMittal has overcome this by "twinning" different steel mills, one efficient and one struggling,

and challenging the efficient plant to help out its twin. The Burns Harbor mill was paired with a mill in Ghent, Belgium. Over 100 engineers and managers from Burns Harbor traveled to Belgium to tour the Ghent plant and learn from their colleagues there how to improve operations. They copied routines from that plant, implemented an advanced computer control system used in the Belgian mill, and employed automated machines similar to the ones used in Belgium. ArcelorMittal also provided $150 million in capital investments to upgrade the operations to bring the facilities up to par with the Ghent plant. These changes resulted in dramatic improvements in the efficiency of the Burns Harbor mill. The Belgians take pride in the improvements in Burns Harbor and now find themselves striving to improve their own operations to stay ahead of the Americans. The Ghent plant now produces 950 tons of steel per employee each year, only 50 tons per employee more than Burns Harbor, but the Ghent managers boast they will soon increase productivity to 1100 tons per employee. Thus, Ghent cooperates and is willing to help Burns Harbor, but the managers and employees at Ghent have a competitive streak as well.

The experience of ArcelorMittal demonstrates how firms can act to overcome the typical disadvantages of their divisional structure.

Source: Miller, J. 2012. Indiana steel mill revived with lessons from abroad. *WSJ .com*, May 21: np; *www.nishp.org/bh-history.htm;* and Markovich, S. 2012. Morning brief: Foreign investment revives Indiana steel mill. *blogs.cfr.org,* May 21: np.

on "making the numbers" and minimizing activities, such as advertising, maintenance, and capital investments, which would detract from short-term performance measures. Strategy Spotlight 10.2 discusses how ArcelorMittal works to overcome some of the disadvantages of the divisional structure by "twinning" its plants.

We'll discuss two variations of the divisional form: the strategic business unit (SBU) and holding company structures.

Strategic Business Unit (SBU) Structure Highly diversified corporations such as ConAgra, a $13 billion food producer, may consist of dozens of different divisions.[15] If ConAgra were to use a purely divisional structure, it would be nearly impossible for the corporate office to plan and coordinate activities, because the span of control would be too large. To attain synergies, ConAgra has put its diverse businesses into three primary SBUs: food service (restaurants), retail (grocery stores), and agricultural products.

strategic business unit (SBU) structure an organizational form in which products, projects, or product market divisions are grouped into homogeneous units.

With an **SBU structure,** divisions with similar products, markets, and/or technologies are grouped into homogeneous units to achieve some synergies. These include those discussed in Chapter 6 for related diversification, such as leveraging core competencies, sharing infrastructures, and market power. Generally the more related businesses are within a corporation, the fewer SBUs will be required. Each of the SBUs in the corporation operates as a profit center.

Advantages   The SBU structure makes the task of planning and control by the corporate office more manageable. Also, with greater decentralization of authority, individual businesses can react more quickly to important changes in the environment than if all divisions had to report directly to the corporate office.

Disadvantages   Since the divisions are grouped into SBUs, it may become difficult to achieve synergies across SBUs. If divisions in different SBUs have potential sources of synergy, it may become difficult for them to be realized. The additional level of management increases the number of personnel and overhead expenses, while the additional hierarchical level removes the corporate office further from the individual divisions. The corporate office may become unaware of key developments that could have a major impact on the corporation.

Holding Company Structure   The **holding company structure** (sometimes referred to as a *conglomerate*) is also a variation of the divisional structure. Whereas the SBU structure is often used when similarities exist between the individual businesses (or divisions), the holding company structure is appropriate when the businesses in a corporation's portfolio do not have much in common. Thus, the potential for synergies is limited.

Holding company structures are most appropriate for firms with a strategy of unrelated diversification. Companies such as Berkshire Hathaway and Loews use a holding company structure to implement their unrelated diversification strategies. Since there are few similarities across the businesses, the corporate offices in these companies provide a great deal of autonomy to operating divisions and rely on financial controls and incentive programs to obtain high levels of performance from the individual businesses. Corporate staffs at these firms tend to be small because of their limited involvement in the overall operation of their various businesses.[16]

Advantages   The holding company structure has the cost savings associated with fewer personnel and the lower overhead resulting from a small corporate office and fewer hierarchical levels. The autonomy of the holding company structure increases the motivational level of divisional executives and enables them to respond quickly to market opportunities and threats.

Disadvantages   There is an inherent lack of control and dependence that corporate-level executives have on divisional executives. Major problems could arise if key divisional executives leave the firm, because the corporate office has very little "bench strength"—additional managerial talent ready to quickly fill key positions. If problems arise in a division, it may become very difficult to turn around individual businesses because of limited staff support in the corporate office.

Matrix Structure

One approach that tries to overcome the inadequacies inherent in the other structures is the **matrix organizational structure.** It is a combination of the functional and divisional structures. Most commonly, functional departments are combined with product groups on a project basis. For example, a product group may want to develop a new addition to its line; for this project, it obtains personnel from functional departments such as marketing, production, and engineering. These personnel work under the manager of the product group for the duration of the project, which can vary from a few weeks to an open-ended period of time. The individuals who work in a matrix organization become responsible to two managers: the project manager and the manager of their functional area. Exhibit 10.4 illustrates a matrix structure.

Some large multinational corporations rely on a matrix structure to combine product groups and geographical units. Product managers have global responsibility for the

holding company structure
an organizational form that is a variation of the divisional organizational structure in which the divisions have a high degree of autonomy both from other divisions and from corporate headquarters.

matrix organizational structure
an organizational form in which there are multiple lines of authority and some individuals report to at least two managers.

EXHIBIT 10.4 Matrix Organizational Structure

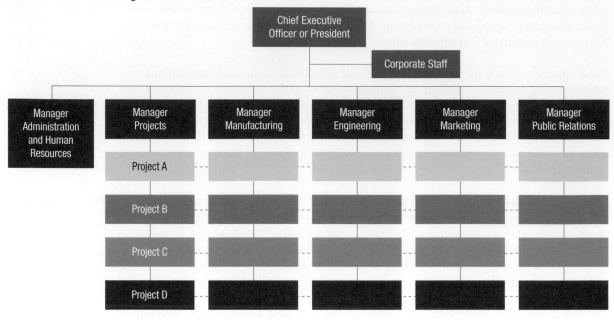

development, manufacturing, and distribution of their own line, while managers of geographical regions have responsibility for the profitability of the businesses in their regions. In the mid-1990s, Caterpillar, Inc., implemented this type of structure.

Other organizations, such as Cisco, use a matrix structure to try to maintain flexibility. In these firms, individual workers have a permanent functional home but also are assigned to and work within temporary project teams.[17]

Advantages   The matrix structure facilitates the use of specialized personnel, equipment, and facilities. Instead of duplicating functions, as would be the case in a divisional structure based on products, the resources are shared. Individuals with high expertise can divide their time among multiple projects. Such resource sharing and collaboration enable a firm to use resources more efficiently and to respond more quickly and effectively to changes in the competitive environment. The flexibility inherent in a matrix structure provides professionals with a broader range of responsibility. Such experience enables them to develop their skills and competencies.

Disadvantages   The dual-reporting structures can result in uncertainty and lead to intense power struggles and conflict over the allocation of personnel and other resources. Working relationships become more complicated. This may result in excessive reliance on group processes and teamwork, along with a diffusion of responsibility, which in turn may erode timely decision making.

Let's look at Procter & Gamble (P&G) to see some of the disadvantages associated with a matrix structure:

> After 50 years with a divisional structure, P&G went to a matrix structure in 1987. In this structure, they had product categories, such as soaps and detergents, on one dimension and functional managers on the other dimension. Within each product category, country managers reported to regional managers who then reported to product managers. The structure became complex to manage, with 13 layers of management and significant power struggles as the functional managers developed their own strategic agendas that often were

EXHIBIT 10.5 Functional, Divisional, and Matrix Organizational Structures: Advantages and Disadvantages

Functional Structure	
Advantages	**Disadvantages**
• Pooling of specialists enhances coordination and control.	• Differences in functional area orientation impede communication and coordination.
• Centralized decision making enhances an organizational perspective across functions.	• Tendency for specialists to develop short-term perspective and narrow functional orientation.
• Efficient use of managerial and technical talent.	• Functional area conflicts may overburden top-level decision makers.
• Facilitates career paths and professional development in specialized areas.	• Difficult to establish uniform performance standards.

Divisional Structure	
Advantages	**Disadvantages**
• Increases strategic and operational control, permitting corporate-level executives to address strategic issues.	• Increased costs incurred through duplication of personnel, operations, and investment.
• Quick response to environmental changes.	• Dysfunctional competition among divisions may detract from overall corporate performance.
• Increases focus on products and markets.	• Difficult to maintain uniform corporate image.
• Minimizes problems associated with sharing resources across functional areas.	• Overemphasis on short-term performance.
• Facilitates development of general managers.	

Matrix Structure	
Advantages	**Disadvantages**
• Increases market responsiveness through collaboration and synergies among professional colleagues.	• Dual-reporting relationships can result in uncertainty regarding accountability.
• Allows more efficient utilization of resources.	• Intense power struggles may lead to increased levels of conflict.
• Improves flexibility, coordination, and communication.	• Working relationships may be more complicated and human resources duplicated
• Increases professional development through a broader range of responsibility.	• Excessive reliance on group processes and teamwork may impede timely decision making.

at odds with the product managers' agendas. After seeing their growth rate decline from 8.5 percent in the 1980s to 2.6 percent in the late 1990s, P&G scrapped the matrix structure to go to a global product structure with three major product categories to offer unity in direction and more responsive decision making.[18]

Exhibit 10.5 briefly summarizes the advantages and disadvantages of the functional, divisional, and matrix organizational structures.

International Operations: Implications for Organizational Structure

Today's managers must maintain an international outlook on their firm's businesses and competitive strategies. In the global marketplace, managers must ensure consistency between their strategies (at the business, corporate, and international levels) and the structure of their organization. As firms expand into foreign markets, they generally follow

LO10.3

The implications of a firm's international operations for organizational structure.

a pattern of change in structure that parallels the changes in their strategies.[19] Three major contingencies that influence the chosen structure are (1) the type of strategy that is driving a firm's foreign operations, (2) product diversity, and (3) the extent to which a firm is dependent on foreign sales.[20]

As international operations become an important part of a firm's overall operations, managers must make changes that are consistent with their firm's structure. The primary types of structures used to manage a firm's international operations are:[21]

- International division
- Geographic-area division
- Worldwide functional
- Worldwide product division
- Worldwide matrix

Multidomestic strategies are driven by political and cultural imperatives requiring managers within each country to respond to local conditions. The structures consistent with such a strategic orientation are the **international division** and **geographic-area division structures.** Here local managers are provided with a high level of autonomy to manage their operations within the constraints and demands of their geographic market. As a firm's foreign sales increase as a percentage of its total sales, it will likely change from an international division to a geographic-area division structure. And, as a firm's product and/or market diversity becomes large, it is likely to benefit from a **worldwide matrix structure.**

Global strategies are driven by economic pressures that require managers to view operations in different geographic areas to be managed for overall efficiency. The structures consistent with the efficiency perspective are the **worldwide functional** and **worldwide product division structures.** Here, division managers view the marketplace as homogeneous and devote relatively little attention to local market, political, and economic factors. The choice between these two types of structures is guided largely by the extent of product diversity. Firms with relatively low levels of product diversity may opt for a worldwide product division structure. However, if significant product–market diversity results from highly unrelated international acquisitions, a worldwide holding company structure should be implemented. Such firms have very little commonality among products, markets, or technologies, and have little need for integration.

Global Start-Ups: A Recent Phenomenon

International expansion occurs rather late for most corporations, typically after possibilities of domestic growth are exhausted. Increasingly, we are seeing two interrelated phenomena. First, many firms now expand internationally relatively early in their history. Second, some firms are "born global"—that is, from the very beginning, many start-ups are global in their activities. For example, Logitech Inc., a leading producer of personal computer accessories, was global from day one. Founded in 1982 by a Swiss national and two Italians, the company was headquartered both in California and Switzerland. R&D and manufacturing were also conducted in both locations and, subsequently, in Taiwan and Ireland.[22]

The success of companies such as Logitech challenges the conventional wisdom that a company must first build up assets, internal processes, and experience before venturing into faraway lands. It also raises a number of questions: What exactly is a global start-up? Under what conditions should a company start out as a global start-up? What does it take to succeed as a global start-up?

A **global start-up** has been defined as a business organization that, from inception, seeks to derive significant competitive advantage from the use of resources and the sale of outputs in multiple countries. Right from the beginning, it uses in-puts from around the world and sells its products and services to customers around the world. Geographical boundaries of nation-states are irrelevant for a global start-up.

international division structure

an organizational form in which international operations are in a separate, autonomous division. Most domestic operations are kept in other parts of the organization.

geographic-area division structure

a type of divisional organizational structure in which operations in geographical regions are grouped internally.

worldwide matrix structure

a type of matrix organizational structure that has one line of authority for geographic-area divisions and another line of authority for worldwide product divisions.

worldwide functional structure

a functional structure in which all departments have worldwide reponsibilities.

worldwide product division structure

a product division structure in which all divisions have worldwide responsibilities.

global start-up

a business organization that, from inception, seeks to derive significant advantage from the use of resources and the sale of outputs in multiple countries.

GLOBAL START-UP AIMING TO BRING A CHARGE TO THE WORLD

Buffalo Grid is a firm that has yet to fully roll out its service offerings, but it has already positioned itself as a truly global firm. Buffalo Grid aims to bring inexpensive electrical charging stations to rural markets in Africa and India. In these markets, millions of individuals have mobile phones and other portable electronic devices but live off the grid and have no electrical service in their homes. They charge up their devices in convenience stores, restaurants, and bars, often at very high prices. Buffalo Grid aims to address this issue with an environmentally sustainable and cost-effective solution.

Buffalo Grid has developed zero carbon emission microgenerators for the developing world that can be used for pennies an hour. The generators are mounted on bikes and run on pedal power. Thus, they are environmentally friendly and can easily move through the neighborhoods they serve.

The global orientation of Buffalo Grid is evident in its management core, the geographic spread of its operations, and the location of its partners. Looking at its management core, we see the foundation of its global mindset. The business is the brainchild of six entrepreneurs who have diverse global backgrounds. The founders of the firm include an individual who spent his early childhood years in Kenya and helped run a business that works with suppliers in Africa. Another of the founders grew up in Mexico. Another has lived in Guatemala and Peru. A fourth founder lived in a number of developing countries in his youth. A fifth of the founders grew up in Northern Ireland but also spent time living in India. The geographic scope of the firm is also notable. Its headquarters is set in in Britain, but the firm aims to serve customers thousands of miles away in India and Africa. The firm has also enlisted a global partner and has signed an agreement with Infosys, the Indian IT firm. Infosys will provide a mentor to Buffalo Grid who will support them and provide contacts and business advice to exploit opportunities in India.

Sources: Anonymous. 2013. Infosys to mentor 16 British start-ups locally in the UK. *Economictimes.indiatimes.com*, February 12: np; and *Buffalogrid.com*.

There is no reason for every start-up to be global. Being global necessarily involves higher communication, coordination, and transportation costs. Therefore, it is important to identify the circumstances under which going global from the beginning is advantageous.[23] First, if the required human resources are globally dispersed, going global may be the best way to access those resources. For example, Italians are masters in fine leather and Europeans in ergonomics. Second, in many cases foreign financing may be easier to obtain and more suitable. Traditionally, U.S. venture capitalists have shown greater willingness to bear risk, but they have shorter time horizons in their expectations for return. If a U.S. start-up is looking for patient capital, it may be better off looking overseas. Third, the target customers in many specialized industries are located in other parts of the world. Fourth, in many industries a gradual move from domestic markets to foreign markets is no longer possible because, if a product is successful, foreign competitors may immediately imitate it. Therefore, preemptive entry into foreign markets may be the only option. Finally, because of high up-front development costs, a global market is often necessary to recover the costs. This is particularly true for start-ups from smaller nations that do not have access to large domestic markets.

Successful management of a global start-up presents many challenges. Communication and coordination across time zones and cultures are always problematic. Since most global start-ups have far less resources than well-established corporations, one key for success is to internalize few activities and outsource the rest. Managers of such firms must have considerable prior international experience so that they can successfully handle the inevitable communication problems and cultural conflicts. Another key for success is to keep the communication and coordination costs low. The only way to achieve this is by creating less costly administrative mechanisms. The boundaryless organizational designs that we discuss in the next section are particularly suitable for global start-ups because of their flexibility and low cost.

Strategy Spotlight 10.3 discusses a British start-up with a global vision and scope of operations.

How an Organization's Structure Can Influence Strategy Formulation

Discussions of the relationship between strategy and structure usually strongly imply that structure follows strategy. The strategy that a firm chooses (e.g., related diversification) dictates such structural elements as the division of tasks, the need for integration of activities, and authority relationships within the organization. However, an existing structure can influence strategy formulation. Once a firm's structure is in place, it is very difficult and expensive to change.[24] Executives may not be able to modify their duties and responsibilities greatly, or may not welcome the disruption associated with a transfer to a new location. There are costs associated with hiring, training, and replacing executive, managerial, and operating personnel. Strategy cannot be formulated without considering structural elements.

An organization's structure can also have an important influence on how it competes in the marketplace. It can also strongly influence a firm's strategy, day-to-day operations, and performance.[25]

boundaryless organizational designs
organizations in which the boundaries, including vertical, horizontal, external, and geographic boundaries, are permeable.

Boundaryless Organizational Designs

The term *boundaryless* may bring to mind a chaotic organizational reality in which "anything goes." This is not the case. As Jack Welch, GE's former CEO, has suggested, boundaryless does not imply that all internal and external boundaries vanish completely, but that they become more open and permeable.[26] Strategy Spotlight 10.4 discusses four types of boundaries.

We are not suggesting that **boundaryless organizational designs** replace the traditional forms of organizational structure, but they should complement them. Sharp Corp. has implemented a functional structure to attain economies of scale with its applied research and manufacturing skills. However, to bring about this key objective, Sharp has relied on several integrating mechanisms and processes:

> To prevent functional groups from becoming vertical chimneys that obstruct product development, Sharp's product managers have responsibility—but not authority— for coordinating the entire set of value-chain activities. And the company convenes enormous numbers of cross-unit and corporate committees to ensure that shared activities, including the corporate R&D unit and sales forces, are optimally configured and allocated among the different product lines. Sharp invests in such time-intensive coordination to minimize the inevitable conflicts that arise when units share important activities.[27]

We will discuss three approaches to making boundaries more permeable, that help to facilitate the widespread sharing of knowledge and information across both the internal and external boundaries of the organization. The *barrier-free* type involves making all organizational boundaries—internal and external—more permeable. Teams are a central building block for implementing the boundaryless organization. The *modular* and *virtual* types of organizations focus on the need to create seamless relationships with external organizations such as customers or suppliers. While the modular type emphasizes the outsourcing of noncore activities, the virtual (or network) organization focuses on alliances among independent entities formed to exploit specific market opportunities.

The Barrier-Free Organization

The "boundary" mind-set is ingrained deeply into bureaucracies. It is evidenced by such clichés as "That's not my job," "I'm here from corporate to help," or endless battles over transfer pricing. In the traditional company, boundaries are clearly delineated in the design

BOUNDARY TYPES

There are primarily four types of boundaries that place limits on organizations. In today's dynamic business environment, different types of boundaries are needed to foster high degrees of interaction with outside influences and varying levels of permeability.

1. *Vertical boundaries between levels in the organization's hierarchy.* SmithKline Beecham asks employees at different hierarchical levels to brainstorm ideas for managing clinical trial data. The ideas are incorporated into action plans that significantly cut the new product approval time of its pharmaceuticals. This would not have been possible if the barriers between levels of individuals in the organization had been too high.

2. *Horizontal boundaries between functional areas.* Fidelity Investments makes the functional barriers more porous and flexible among divisions, such as marketing, operations, and customer service, in order to offer customers a more integrated experience when conducting business with the company. Customers can take their questions to one person, reducing the chance that customers will "get the run-around" from employees who feel customer service is not their responsibility. At Fidelity, customer service is everyone's business, regardless of functional area.

3. *External boundaries between the firm and its customers, suppliers, and regulators.* GE Lighting, by working closely with retailers, functions throughout the value chain as a single operation. This allows GE to track point-of-sale purchases, giving it better control over inventory management.

4. *Geographic boundaries between locations, cultures, and markets.* The global nature of today's business environment spurred PricewaterhouseCoopers to use a global groupware system. This allows the company to instantly connect to its 26 worldwide offices.

Source: Ashkenas, R. 1997. The organization's New Clothes. In Hesselbein, F., Goldsmith, M., and Beckhard, R. (Eds.). *The Organization of the Future:* 104–106. San Francisco: Jossey Bass.

---

of an organization's structure. Their basic advantage is that the roles of managers and employees are simple, clear, well-defined, and long-lived. A major shortcoming was pointed out to the authors during an interview with a high-tech executive: "Structure tends to be divisive; it leads to territorial fights."

Such structures are being replaced by fluid, ambiguous, and deliberately ill-defined tasks and roles. Just because work roles are no longer clearly defined, however, does not mean that differences in skills, authority, and talent disappear. A **barrier-free organization** enables a firm to bridge real differences in culture, function, and goals to find common ground that facilitates information sharing and other forms of cooperative behavior. Eliminating the multiple boundaries that stifle productivity and innovation can enhance the potential of the entire organization.

barrier-free organization
an organizational design in which firms bridge real differences in culture, function, and goals to find common ground that facilitates information sharing and other forms of cooperative behavior.

Creating Permeable Internal Boundaries For barrier-free organizations to work effectively, the level of trust and shared interests among all parts of the organization must be raised.[28] The organization needs to develop among its employees the skill level needed to work in a more democratic organization. Barrier-free organizations also require a shift in the organization's philosophy from executive to organizational development, and from investments in high-potential individuals to investments in leveraging the talents of all individuals.

Teams can be an important aspect of barrier-free structures.[29] Jeffrey Pfeffer, author of several insightful books, including *The Human Equation,* suggests that teams have three primary advantages.[30] First, teams substitute peer-based control for hierarchical control of work activities. Employees control themselves, reducing the time and energy management needs to devote to control. Second, teams frequently develop more creative solutions to problems because they encourage the sharing of the tacit knowledge held by individuals.[31]

Brainstorming, or group problem solving, involves the pooling of ideas and expertise to enhance the chances that at least one group member will think of a way to solve the problems at hand. Third, by substituting peer control for hierarchical control, teams permit the removal of layers of hierarchy and absorption of administrative tasks previously performed by specialists. This avoids the costs of having people whose sole job is to watch the people who watch other people do the work.

Effective barrier-free organizations must go beyond achieving close integration and coordination within divisions in a corporation. Research on multidivisional organizations has stressed the importance of interdivisional coordination and resource sharing.[32] This requires interdivisional task forces and committees, reward and incentive systems that emphasize interdivisional cooperation, and common training programs.

Frank Carruba (former head of Hewlett-Packard's labs) found that the difference between mediocre teams and good teams was generally varying levels of motivation and talent.[33] But what explained the difference between good teams and truly superior teams? The key difference—and this explained a 40 percent overall difference in performance— was the way members treated each other: the degree to which they believed in one another and created an atmosphere of encouragement rather than competition. Vision, talent, and motivation could carry a team only so far. What clearly stood out in the "super" teams were higher levels of authenticity and caring, which allowed the full synergy of their individual talents, motivation, and vision.

Developing Effective Relationships with External Constituencies In barrier-free organizations, managers must also create flexible, porous organizational boundaries and establish communication flows and mutually beneficial relationships with internal (e.g., employees) and external (e.g., customers) constituencies.[34] IBM has worked to develop a long-standing cooperative relationship with the Mayo Clinic. The clinic is a customer but more importantly a research partner. IBM has placed staff at the Mayo Clinic, and the two organizations have worked together on technology for the early identification of aneurysms, the mining of data in electronic health records to develop customized treatment plans for patients, and other medical issues. Having worked collaboratively for over a dozen years, the IBM and Mayo researchers have built strong relationships.[35]

Barrier-free organizations create successful relationships between both internal and external constituencies, but there is one additional constituency—competitors—with whom some organizations have benefited as they developed cooperative relationships. For example, after struggling on their own to develop the technology, Ford, Renault-Nissan, and Daimler have agreed to cooperate with each other to develop zero emission, hydrogen fuel cell systems to power automobiles.[36]

By joining and actively participating in the Business Roundtable—an organization consisting of CEOs of leading U.S. corporations—Walmart has been able to learn about cutting-edge sustainable initiatives of other major firms. This free flow of information has enabled Walmart to undertake a number of steps that increased the energy efficiency of its operations.

Risks, Challenges, and Potential Downsides Many firms find that creating and managing a barrier-free organization can be frustrating.[37] Puritan-Bennett Corporation, a manufacturer of respiratory equipment, found that its product development time more than doubled after it adopted team management. Roger J. Dolida, director of R&D, attributed this failure to a lack of top management commitment, high turnover among team members, and infrequent meetings. Often, managers trained in rigid hierarchies find it difficult to make the transition to the more democratic, participative style that teamwork requires.

Christopher Barnes, a consultant with PricewaterhouseCoopers, previously worked as an industrial engineer for Challenger Electrical Distribution (a subsidiary of Westinghouse,

NATIONAL GEOGRAPHIC: SAVING THE PLANET IS ITS STRATEGY

By Irena Descubes and Tom McNamara

Throughout its 125-year long history, the National Geographic Society (NGS) has encouraged the conservation of natural resources, as well as raising the public's awareness regarding the importance of natural habitats and the plants and wildlife that they support. Another goal has been to make people aware of the environmental problems threatening these natural habitats, especially over the past 50 years.

National Geographic has a large and diversified audience that it reaches through print, television and online by way of National Geographic Magazine, National Geographic Traveler magazine, National Geographic Kids magazine, National Geographic Little Kids magazine, National Geographic Newsstand Specials, the National Geographic TV Channel and the Nat Geo Wild TV Channel. All in all, the National Geographic magazine comes in 33 different languages in addition to English.

Since 1888, the National Geographic Society has been documenting the exploration of the planet, supporting expeditions and promoting the research of brilliant minds such as polar explorer Robert Peary, mountain gorilla expert Dian Fossey, and underwater explorer (and discoverer of the sunken remains of the Titanic) Robert Ballard. The Society has also encouraged the environmentally responsible stewardship of the planet through education initiatives.

National Geographic's editors, journalists, and photographers are excellent storytellers who are able to establish a meaningful dialog with readers through their images, testimonials, and comprehensive coverage of complex issues. The Society makes its audience think about their role in the world and how they should act regarding the planet's preservation.

The editors at National Geographic believe that people react more strongly and passionately to striking pictures than they do from even the most compelling experts' testimony. It recently released an online interactive map with the provocative title "Rising Seas: If All the Ice Melted." The map shows the world as it is now, and how it would look with sea levels increased by 216 feet due to the melting of the polar ice caps, resulting in new shore-lines for all of the continents and inland seas.

The campaign to celebrate the 125th anniversary of National Geographic clearly illustrated its mission to inspire people to care about the planet: "If you are, you breathe. If you breathe, you talk. If you talk, you ask. If you ask, you think. If you think, you search. If you search, you experience. If you experience, you learn. If you learn, you grow. If you grow, you wish. If you wish, you find. And if you find, you doubt. If you doubt, you question. If you question, you understand and if you understand, you know. If you know, you want to know more. If you want to know more you are alive."

Since 1900, global sea levels have risen by about 8 inches, and are now rising at a rate of about an eighth of an inch a year, with average temperatures for the planet increasing as well. We should be fine, but what about the next generation? National Geographic is doing its best to ensure that it will have an audience for a long time to come.

Sources: National Geographic Milestones. press.nationalgeographic.com/about-national-geographic/milestones/[accessed online November 11 2013]; Rising Seas—Interactive: If All the Ice Melted. /ngm.nationalgeographic.com/2013/09/rising-seas/if-ice-melted-map [accessed online November 11 2013]; National Geographic 2013 Preview by Editorial Topic www.nationalgeographic.com/mediakit/pdf/ng-magazine/NGM_Media_Kit_2013.pdf [accessed online November 1 2013]; Taking a look at National Geographic's thought provoking fracking primer news.enersciences.com/blog/fracking-fluids/taking-a-look-at-national-geographics-thought-provoking-fracking-primer/ [accessed online November 5 2013].

now part of CBS) at a plant which produced circuit-breaker boxes. His assignment was to lead a team of workers from the plant's troubled final-assembly operation with the mission: "Make things better." That vague notion set the team up for failure. After a year of futility, the team was disbanded. In retrospect, Barnes identified several reasons for the debacle: (1) limited personal credibility—he was viewed as an "outsider"; (2) a lack of commitment to the team—everyone involved was forced to be on the team; (3) poor communications—nobody was told why the team was important; (4) limited autonomy—line managers refused to give up control over team members; and (5) misaligned incentives—the culture rewarded individual performance over team performance. Barnes's experience has implications for all types of teams, whether they are composed of managerial, professional, clerical, or production personnel.[38] The pros and cons of barrier-free structures are summarized in Exhibit 10.6.

EXHIBIT 10.6 Pros and Cons of Barrier-Free Structures

Pros	Cons
• Leverages the talents of all employees. • Enhances cooperation, coordination, and information sharing among functions, divisions, SBUs, and external constituencies. • Enables a quicker response to market changes through a single-goal focus. • Can lead to coordinated win–win initiatives with key suppliers, customers, and alliance partners.	• Difficult to overcome political and authority boundaries inside and outside the organization. • Lacks strong leadership and common vision, which can lead to coordination problems. • Time-consuming and difficult-to-manage democratic processes. • Lacks high levels of trust, which can impede performance.

The Modular Organization

As Charles Handy, author of *The Age of Unreason,* has noted:

> While it may be convenient to have everyone around all the time, having all of your workforce's time at your command is an extravagant way of marshaling the necessary resources. It is cheaper to keep them outside the organization . . . and to buy their services when you need them.[39]

modular organization
an organization in which nonvital functions are outsourced, which uses the knowledge and expertise of outside suppliers while retaining strategic control.

The **modular organization** outsources nonvital functions, tapping into the knowledge and expertise of "best in class" suppliers, but retains strategic control. Outsiders may be used to manufacture parts, handle logistics, or perform accounting activities.[40] The value chain can be used to identify the key primary and support activities performed by a firm to create value: Which activities do we keep "in-house" and which activities do we outsource to suppliers?[41] The organization becomes a central hub surrounded by networks of outside suppliers and specialists and parts can be added or taken away. Both manufacturing and service units may be modular.[42]

Apparel is an industry in which the modular type has been widely adopted. Nike and Reebok, for example, concentrate on their strengths: designing and marketing high-tech, fashionable footwear. Nike has few production facilities and Reebok owns no plants. These two companies contract virtually all their footwear production to suppliers in China, Vietnam, and other countries with low-cost labor. Avoiding large investments in fixed assets helps them derive large profits on minor sales increases. Nike and Reebok can keep pace with changing tastes in the marketplace because their suppliers have become expert at rapidly retooling to produce new products.[43]

In a modular company, outsourcing the noncore functions offers three advantages.

1. A firm can decrease overall costs, stimulate new product development by hiring suppliers with superior talent to that of in-house personnel, avoid idle capacity, reduce inventories, and avoid being locked into a particular technology.
2. A company can focus scarce resources on the areas where it holds a competitive advantage. These benefits can translate into more funding for R&D hiring the best engineers, and providing continuous training for sales and service staff.
3. An organization can tap into the knowledge and expertise of its specialized supply-chain partners, adding critical skills and accelerating organizational learning.[44]

The modular type enables a company to leverage relatively small amounts of capital and a small management team to achieve seemingly unattainable strategic objectives.[45] Certain preconditions are necessary before the modular approach can be successful. First, the company must work closely with suppliers to ensure that the interests of each party are being fulfilled. Companies need to find loyal, reliable vendors who can be trusted with trade secrets. They also need assurances that suppliers will dedicate their financial, physical, and human resources to satisfy strategic objectives such as lowering costs or being first to market.

Second, the modular company must be sure that it selects the proper competencies to keep in-house. For Nike and Reebok, the core competencies are design and marketing, not shoe manufacturing; for Honda, the core competence is engine technology. An organization must avoid outsourcing components that may compromise its long-term competitive advantages.

Strategic Risks of Outsourcing The main strategic concerns are (1) loss of critical skills or developing the wrong skills, (2) loss of cross-functional skills, and (3) loss of control over a supplier.[46]

Too much outsourcing can result in a firm "giving away" too much skill and control.[47] Outsourcing relieves companies of the requirement to maintain skill levels needed to manufacture essential components.[48] At one time, semiconductor chips seemed like a simple technology to outsource, but they have now become a critical component of a wide variety of products. Companies that have outsourced the manufacture of these chips run the risk of losing the ability to manufacture them as the technology escalates. They become more dependent upon their suppliers.

Cross-functional skills refer to the skills acquired through the interaction of individuals in various departments within a company.[49] Such interaction assists a department in solving problems as employees interface with others across functional units. However, if a firm outsources key functional responsibilities, such as manufacturing, communication across departments can become more difficult. A firm and its employees must now integrate their activities with a new, outside supplier.

The outsourced products may give suppliers too much power over the manufacturer. Suppliers that are key to a manufacturer's success can, in essence, hold the manufacturer "hostage." Nike manages this potential problem by sending full-time "product expatriates" to work at the plants of its suppliers. Also, Nike often brings top members of supplier management and technical teams to its headquarters. This way, Nike keeps close tabs on the pulse of new developments, builds rapport and trust with suppliers, and develops long-term relationships with suppliers to prevent hostage situations.

Exhibit 10.7 summarizes the pros and cons of modular structures.[50]

The Virtual Organization

In contrast to the "self-reliant" thinking that guided traditional organizational designs, the strategic challenge today has become doing more with less and looking outside the firm for opportunities and solutions to problems. The virtual organization provides a new means of leveraging resources and exploiting opportunities.[51]

The **virtual organization** can be viewed as a continually evolving network of independent companies—suppliers, customers, even competitors—linked together to share skills, costs, and access to one another's markets.[52] The members of a virtual organization, by pooling and sharing the knowledge and expertise of each of the component organizations, simultaneously "know" more and can "do" more than any one member of the group could do alone. By working closely together, each gains in the long run from individual and organizational learning.[53] The term *virtual,* meaning "being in effect but not actually so," is commonly used in the computer industry. A computer's ability to appear to have more storage capacity than it really possesses is called virtual memory. Similarly, by assembling resources from a variety of entities, a virtual organization may seem to have more capabilities than it really possesses.[54]

Virtual organizations need not be permanent and participating firms may be involved in multiple alliances. Virtual organizations may involve different firms performing complementary value activities, or different firms involved jointly in the same value activities,

virtual organization
a continually evolving network of independent companies that are linked together to share skills, costs, and access to one another's markets.

EXHIBIT 10.7 Pros and Cons of Modular Structures

Pros	Cons
• Directs a firm's managerial and technical talent to the most critical activities.	• Inhibits common vision through reliance on outsiders.
• Maintains full strategic control over most critical activities—core competencies.	• Diminishes future competitive advantages if critical technologies or other competencies are outsourced.
• Achieves "best in class" performance at each link in the value chain.	• Increases the difficulty of bringing back into the firm activities that now add value due to market shifts
• Leverages core competencies by outsourcing with smaller capital commitment.	• Leads to an erosion of cross-functional skills.
• Encourages information sharing and accelerates organizational learning.	• Decreases operational control and potential loss of control over a supplier.

such as production, R&D, and distribution. The percentage of activities that are jointly performed with partners may vary significantly from alliance to alliance.[55]

How does the virtual type of structure differ from the modular type? Unlike the modular type, in which the focal firm maintains full strategic control, the virtual organization is characterized by participating firms that give up part of their control and accept interdependent destinies. Participating firms pursue a collective strategy that enables them to cope with uncertainty through cooperative efforts. The benefit is that, just as virtual memory increases storage capacity, the virtual organizations enhance the capacity or competitive advantage of participating firms.

Strategy Spotlight 10.6 discusses the collaboration between firms from apparently unrelated industries to develop a technology that could potentially affect all products that use plastic as a component, a container, or a package.

Each company that links up with others to create a virtual organization contributes only what it considers its core competencies. It will mix and match what it does best with the best of other firms by identifying its critical capabilities and the necessary links to other capabilities.[56]

Challenges and Risks   Such alliances often fail to meet expectations: In the 1980s, several competing U.S. computing firms set up a consortium, US Memories, to design and manufacture memory chips for computers. The purpose of the consortium was to allow the firms to better compete with Japanese and Taiwanese competitors. But the consortium collapsed as a result of differences in the interests and objectives of the firms involved.

The virtual organization demands that managers build relationships with other companies, negotiate win–win deals for all parties find the right partners with compatible goals and values, and provide the right balance of freedom and control. Information systems must be designed and integrated to facilitate communication with current and potential partners.

Managers must be clear about the strategic objectives while forming alliances. Some objectives are time bound, and those alliances need to be dissolved once the objective is fulfilled. Some alliances may have relatively long-term objectives and will need to be clearly monitored and nurtured to produce mutual commitment and avoid bitter fights for control. The highly dynamic personal computer industry is characterized by multiple temporary alliances among hardware, operating systems, and software producers.[57] But alliances in the more stable automobile industry, such as those involving Nissan and Volkswagen have long-term objectives and tend to be relatively stable.

PLANT PLASTICS 2.0: A COLLABORATIVE INITIATIVE AMONG 5 GLOBAL FIRMS

Coca-Cola, Ford Motor Company, H.J. Heinz, Nike, and Procter & Gamble are five firms that are typically neither competitors, suppliers, or customers, but they have come together to address a joint concern. They are working together to develop plant-based plastics. Coca-Cola has been at the forefront of this technology and has developed a plastic bottle that includes 30 percent plant-based plastic. Heinz had already licensed this technology, but these two firms, along with the other three partners, have created the Plant PET Technology Collaborative (PTC) to jointly develop the plant-based plastic technology further, with the goal of creating 100 percent plant-based plastics that can be used in a range of products across a number of industries. As the spokesperson of the PTC stated, "PTC members are committed to supporting and championing research, expanding knowledge and accelerating technology development to enable commercially viable, more sustainably sourced, 100 percent plant-based PET plastic while reducing the use of fossil fuels."

This cooperative is important for these firms to achieve the sustainability goals that they have laid out. For example, P&G has targeted a 25 percent reduction in the amount of petroleum-based products the firm uses by 2020, with a long-term goal of completely replacing petroleum-based materials with sustainable sources. Ed Sawiki, associate director of global business development, asserted that the collaborative R&D effort is important since it allows P&G to "work with others to advance the pace of technical learning and commercial availability of 100 percent plant-based PET faster than any one party can do alone. This enables us to deliver products and packages that consumers want in a sustainable fashion. It creates a win-win situation for the company, consumers, and the environment." The members of the PTC hope to have a marketable 100 percent plant-based plastic by 2016 or 2017.

The collaborative also serves a second goal for the firms. That is the development of common methods, standards, and terminology for sustainable plastics. The brands will then promote these standards to facilitate both customer acceptance and preference and use worldwide by other corporations. These standards could also be used in regulatory efforts by governments to incentivize the use of sustainable packaging.

Sources: Caliendo, H. 2012. Five major brands collaborating on plant-based PET. *Plasticstoday.com*, June 5: np; and Siemers, E. 2012. Nike joins Coke, Ford, Heinz, and P&G to develop plant-based plastics. *Sustainablebusinessoregon.com*, June 5: np.

The virtual organization is a logical culmination of joint-venture strategies of the past. Shared risks, costs, and rewards are the facts of life in a virtual organization.[58] When virtual organizations are formed, they involve tremendous challenges for strategic planning. As with the modular corporation, it is essential to identify core competencies. However, for virtual structures to be successful, a strategic plan is also needed to determine the effectiveness of combining core competencies.

The strategic plan must address the diminished operational control and overwhelming need for trust and common vision among the partners. This new structure may be appropriate for firms whose strategies require merging technologies (e.g., computing and communication) or for firms exploiting shrinking product life cycles that require simultaneous entry into multiple geographical markets. It may be effective for firms that desire to be quick to the market with a new product or service. The recent profusion of alliances among airlines was primarily motivated by the need to provide seamless travel demanded by the full-fare paying business traveler. Exhibit 10.8 summarizes the advantages and disadvantages.

Boundaryless Organizations: Making Them Work

Designing an organization that simultaneously supports the requirements of an organization's strategy, is consistent with the demands of the environment, and can be effectively implemented by the people around the manager is a tall order for any manager.[59] The most effective solution is usually a combination of organizational types. That is, a firm may outsource many parts of its value chain to reduce costs and increase quality, engage simultaneously in multiple alliances to take advantage of technological developments or penetrate new markets, and break down barriers within the organization to enhance flexibility.

EXHIBIT 10.8 Pros and Cons of Virtual Structures

Pros	Cons
• Enables the sharing of costs and skills. • Enhances access to global markets. • Increases market responsiveness. • Creates a "best of everything" organization since each partner brings core competencies to the alliance. • Encourages both individual and organizational knowledge sharing and accelerates organizational learning.	• Harder to determine where one company ends and another begins, due to close interdependencies among players. • Leads to potential loss of operational control among partners. • Results in loss of strategic control over emerging technology. • Requires new and difficult-to-acquire managerial skills.

Source: Miles, R. E., & Snow, C. C. 1986. Organizations: New Concepts for New Forms. *California Management Review,* Spring: 62–73; Miles & Snow. 1999. Causes of Failure in Network Organizations. *California Management Review,* Summer: 53–72; and Bahrami, H. 1991. The Emerging Flexible Organization: Perspectives from Silicon Valley. *California Management Review,* Summer: 33–52.

When an organization faces external pressures, resource scarcity, and declining performance, it tends to become more internally focused, rather than directing its efforts toward managing and enhancing relationships with existing and potential external stakeholders. This may be the most opportune time for managers to carefully analyze their value-chain activities and evaluate the potential for adopting elements of modular, virtual, and barrier-free organizational types.

In this section, we will address two issues managers need to be aware of as they work to design an effective boundaryless organization. First, managers need to develop mechanisms to ensure effective coordination and integration. Second, managers need to be aware of the benefits and costs of developing strong and long-term relationships with both internal and external stakeholders.

Facilitating Coordination and Integration   Achieving the coordination and integration necessary to maximize the potential of an organization's human capital involves much more than just creating a new structure. Techniques and processes to ensure the coordination and integration of an organization's key value-chain activities are critical. Teams are key building blocks of the new organizational forms, and teamwork requires new and flexible approaches to coordination and integration.

Managers trained in rigid hierarchies may find it difficult to make the transition to the more democratic, participative style that teamwork requires. As Douglas K. Smith, co-author of *The Wisdom of Teams,* pointed out, "A completely diverse group must agree on a goal, put the notion of individual accountability aside and figure out how to work with each other. Most of all, they must learn that if the team fails, it's everyone's fault."[60] Within the framework of an appropriate organizational design, managers must select a mix and balance of tools and techniques to facilitate the effective coordination and integration of key activities. Some of the factors that must be considered include:

- Common culture and shared values.
- Horizontal organizational structures.
- Horizontal systems and processes.
- Communications and information technologies.
- Human resource practices.

Common Culture and Shared Values   Shared goals, mutual objectives, and a high degree of trust are essential to the success of boundaryless organizations. In the fluid and flexible environments of the new organizational architectures, common cultures, shared values, and carefully aligned incentives are often less expensive to implement and are often a more effective means of strategic control than rules, boundaries, and formal procedures. Tony Hsieh, the founder of Zappos, echoes this need for a shared culture and values when as he describes his role this way. "I think of myself less as a leader and more of being an architect of an environment that enables employees to come up with their own ideas."[61]

Horizontal Organizational Structures   These structures, which group similar or related business units under common management control, facilitate sharing resources and infrastructures to exploit synergies among operating units and help to create a sense of common purpose. Consistency in training and the development of similar structures across business units facilitates job rotation and cross training and enhances understanding of common problems and opportunities. Cross-functional teams and inter-divisional committees and task groups represent important opportunities to improve understanding and foster cooperation among operating units.

horizontal organizational structures organizational forms that group similar or related business units under common management control and facilitate sharing resources and infrastructures to exploit synergies among operating units and help to create a sense of common purpose.

Horizontal Systems and Processes   Organizational systems, policies, and procedures are the traditional mechanisms for achieving integration among functional units. Existing policies and procedures often do little more than institutionalize the barriers that exist from years of managing within the framework of the traditional model. Beginning with an understanding of basic business processes in the context of "a collection of activities that takes one or more kinds of input and creates an output that is of value to the customer," Michael Hammer and James Champy's 1993 best-selling *Reengineering the Corporation* outlined a methodology for redesigning internal systems and procedures that has been embraced by many organizations.[62] Successful reengineering lowers costs, reduces inventories and cycle times, improves quality, speeds response times, and enhances organizational flexibility. Others advocate similar benefits through the reduction of cycle times, total quality management, and the like.

Communications and Information Technologies (IT)   The effective use of IT can play an important role in bridging gaps and breaking down barriers between organizations. Electronic mail and videoconferencing can improve lateral communications across long distances and multiple time zones and circumvent many of the barriers of the traditional model. IT can be a powerful ally in the redesign and streamlining of internal business processes and in improving coordination and integration between suppliers and customers. Internet technologies have eliminated the paperwork in many buyer–supplier relationships, enabling cooperating organizations to reduce inventories, shorten delivery cycles, and reduce operating costs. IT must be viewed more as a prime component of an organization's overall strategy than simply in terms of administrative support.

Human Resource Practices   Change always involves and affects the human dimension of organizations. The attraction, development, and retention of human capital are vital to value creation. As boundaryless structures are implemented, processes are reengineered, and organizations become increasingly dependent on sophisticated ITs, the skills of workers and managers alike must be upgraded to realize the full benefits.

Strategy Spotlight 10.7 discusses Procter & Gamble's successful introduction of Crest Whitestrips. This example shows how P&G's tools and techniques, such as communities of practice, information technology, and human resource practices, help to achieve effective collaboration and integration across the firm's different business units.

The Benefits and Costs of Developing Lasting Internal and External Relationships
Successful boundaryless organizations rely heavily on the relational aspects of organizations. Rather than relying on strict hierarchical and bureaucratic systems, these firms are flexible and coordinate action by leveraging shared social norms and strong social

CREST'S WHITESTRIPS: AN EXAMPLE OF HOW P&G CREATES AND DERIVES BENEFITS FROM A BOUNDARYLESS ORGANIZATION

Given its breadth of products—soaps, diapers, toothpaste, potato chips, lotions, detergent—Procter & Gamble (P&G) has an enormous pool of resources it can integrate in various ways to launch exciting new products. For example, the company created a new category, teeth-whitening systems, with Crest Whitestrips. Teeth whitening done at a dentist's office can brighten one's smile in as little as one visit, but it can cost hundreds of dollars. On the other hand, over-the-counter home whitening kits like Crest Whitestrips cost far less and are nearly equally effective.

Whitestrip was created through a combined effort of product developers from three different units in P&G. People at the oral-care division provided teeth-whitening expertise; experts from the fabric and home-care division supplied bleach expertise; and scientists at corporate research and development provided a novel film technology. Three separate units, by collaborating and combining their technologies, succeeded in developing an affordable product to brighten smiles and, according to the website, bring "greater success in work and love." With $300 million in annual retail sales, the launch of the Whitestrips product has been a big success for P&G, one that would not have been possible without the firm's collaborative ability.

Such collaborations are the outcome of well-established organizational mechanisms. P&G has created more than 20 communities of practice, with 8,000 participants. Each group comprises volunteers from different parts of the company and focuses on an area of expertise (fragrance, packaging, polymer chemistry, skin science, and so on). The groups solve specific problems that are brought to them, and they meet to share best practices. The company also has posted an "ask me" feature on its intranet, where employees can describe a business problem, which is directed to those people with appropriate expertise. At a more fundamental level, P&G promotes from within and rotates people across countries and business units. As a result, its employees build powerful cross-unit networks.

Sources: Hansen, M. T. 2009. *Collaboration: How Leaders Avoid the Traps, Create Unity, and Reap Big Results.* Boston: Harvard Business Press, 24–25; Anonymous. 2004. At P&G, It's 360-Degree Innovation. *www.businessweek.com*, October 11: np; *www.whitestrips.com*; Anonymous. 2009. The Price of a Whiter, Brighter Smile. *www.washingtonpost.com*, July 21: np; Hansen, M. T. & Birkinshaw, J. 2007. The Innovation Value Chain. *Harvard Business Review*, June: 85(6): 121–130.

---

relationships between both internal and external stakeholders.[63] At the same time, it is important to acknowledge that relying on relationships can have both positive and negative effects. To successfully move to a more boundaryless organization, managers need to acknowledge and attend to both the costs and benefits of relying on relationships and social norms to guide behavior.

There are three primary benefits that organizations accrue when relying on relationships.

- *Agency costs within the firm can be dramatically cut through the use of relational systems.* Managers and employees in relationship-oriented firms are guided by social norms and relationships they have with other managers and employees. As a result, the firm can reduce the degree to which it relies on monitoring, rules and regulations, and financial incentives to ensure that workers put in a strong effort and work in the firm's interests. A relational view leads managers and employees to act in a supportive manner and makes them more willing to step out of their formal roles when needed to accomplish tasks for others and for the organization. They are also less likely to shirk their responsibilities.

- *There is also likely to be a reduction in the transaction costs between a firm and its suppliers and customers.* If firms have built strong relationships with partnering firms, they are more likely to work cooperatively with these firms and build trust that their partners will work in the best interests of the alliance. This will reduce the need for the firms to write detailed contracts and set up strict bureaucratic rules to outline the responsibilities and define the behavior of each firm. Additionally, partnering firms with strong relationships are more likely to invest in assets that specifically support the partnership. Finally, they will have much less fear that their partner will try to take advantage of them or seize the bulk of the benefits from the partnership.

- *Since they feel a sense of shared ownership and goals, individuals within the firm as well as partnering firms will be more likely to search for win-win rather than win-lose solutions.* When taking a relational view, individuals are less likely to look out solely for their personal best interests. They will also be considerate of the benefits and costs to other individuals in the firm and to the overall firm. The same is true at the organizational level. Firms with strong relationships with their partners are going to look for solutions that not only benefit themselves but also provide equitable benefits and limited downside for the partnering firms. Such a situation was evident with a number of German firms during the economic crisis of 2008–2010. The German government, corporations, and unions worked together to find the fairest way to respond to the crisis. The firms agreed not to lay off workers. The unions agreed to reduced workweeks. The government kicked in a subsidy to make up for some of the lost wages. In other words, they negotiated a shared sacrifice to address the challenge. This positioned the German firms to bounce back quickly once the crisis passed.

While there are a number of benefits with using a relational view, there can also be some substantial costs.

- *As the relationships between individuals and firms strengthen, they are also more likely to fall prey to suboptimal lock-in effects.* The problem here is that as decisions become driven by concerns about relationships, economic factors become less important. As a result, firms become less likely to make decisions that could benefit the firm since those decisions may harm employees or partnering firms. For example, firms may see the economic logic in exiting a market, but the ties they feel with employees that work in that division and partnering firms in that market may reduce their willingness to make the hard decision to exit the market. This can be debilitating to firms in rapidly changing markets where successful firms add, reorganize, and sometimes exit operations and relationships regularly.
- *Since there are no formal guidelines, conflicts between individuals and units within firms as well as between partnering firms are typically resolved through ad hoc negotiations and processes.* In these circumstances, there are no legal means or bureaucratic rules to guide decision making. Thus, when firms face a difficult decision where there are differences of opinion about the best course of action, the ultimate choices made are often driven by the inherent power of the individuals or firms involved. This power use may be unintentional and subconscious, but it can result in outcomes that are deemed unfair by one or more of the parties.
- *The social capital of individuals and firms can drive their opportunities.* Thus, rather than identifying the best person to put in a leadership role or the optimal supplier to contract with, these choices are more strongly driven by the level of social connection the person or supplier has. This also increases the entry barriers for potential new suppliers or employees with whom a firm can contract since new firms likely don't have the social connections needed to be chosen as a worthy partner with whom to contract. This also may limit the likelihood that new innovative ideas will enter into the conversations at the firm.

As mentioned earlier in the chapter, the solution may be to effectively integrate elements of formal structure and reward systems with stronger relationships. This may influence specific relationships so that a manager will want employees to build relationships while still maintaining some managerial oversight and reward systems that motivate the desired behavior. This may also result in different emphases with different relationships. For example, there may be some units, such as accounting, where a stronger role for traditional structures and forms of evaluation may be optimal. However, in new product development units, a greater emphasis on relational systems may be more appropriate.

Creating Ambidextrous Organizational Designs

In Chapter 1, we introduced the concept of "ambidexterity," which incorporates two contradictory challenges faced by today's managers.[64] First, managers must explore new opportunities and adjust to volatile markets in order to avoid complacency. They must ensure that they maintain **adaptability** and remain proactive in expanding and/or modifying their product–market scope to anticipate and satisfy market conditions. Such competencies are especially challenging when change is rapid and unpredictable.

Second, managers must also effectively exploit the value of their existing assets and competencies. They need to have **alignment,** which is a clear sense of how value is being created in the short term and how activities are integrated and properly coordinated. Firms that achieve both adaptability and alignment are considered *ambidextrous organizations*— aligned and efficient in how they manage today's business but flexible enough to changes in the environment so that they will prosper tomorrow.

Handling such opposing demands is difficult because there will always be some degree of conflict. Firms often suffer when they place too strong a priority on either adaptability or alignment. If it places too much focus on adaptability, the firm will suffer low profitability in the short term. If managers direct their efforts primarily at alignment, they will likely miss out on promising business opportunities.

Ambidextrous Organizations: Key Design Attributes

A study by Charles O'Reilly and Michael Tushman[65] provides some insights into how some firms were able to create successful **ambidextrous organizational designs.** They investigated companies that attempted to simultaneously pursue modest, incremental innovations as well as more dramatic, breakthrough innovations. The team investigated 35 attempts to launch breakthrough innovations undertaken by 15 business units in nine different industries. They studied the organizational designs and the processes, systems, and cultures associated with the breakthrough projects as well as their impact on the operations and performance of the traditional businesses.

Companies structured their breakthrough projects in one of four primary ways:

- Seven were carried out within existing *functional organizational structures.* The projects were completely integrated into the regular organizational and management structure.
- Nine were organized as *cross-functional teams.* The groups operated within the established organization but outside of the existing management structure.
- Four were organized as *unsupported teams.* Here, they became independent units set up outside the established organization and management hierarchy.
- Fifteen were conducted within *ambidextrous organizations.* Here, the breakthrough efforts were organized within structurally independent units, each having its own processes, structures, and cultures. However, they were integrated into the existing senior management structure.

The performance results of the 35 initiatives were tracked along two dimensions:

- Their success in creating desired innovations was measured by either the actual commercial results of the new product or the application of practical market or technical learning.
- The performance of the existing business was evaluated.

The study found that the organizational structure and management practices employed had a direct and significant impact on the performance of both the breakthrough initiative and the traditional business. The ambidextrous organizational designs were more effective than the other three designs on both dimensions: launching breakthrough products or services (i.e., adaptation) and improving the performance of the existing business (i.e., alignment).

Why Was the Ambidextrous Organization the Most Effective Structure?

The study found that there were many factors. A clear and compelling vision, consistently communicated by the company's senior management team was critical in building the ambidextrous designs. The structure enabled cross-fertilization while avoiding cross-contamination. The tight coordination and integration at the managerial levels enabled the newer units to share important resources from the traditional units such as cash, talent, and expertise. Such sharing was encouraged and facilitated by effective reward systems that emphasized overall company goals. The organizational separation ensured that the new units' distinctive processes, structures, and cultures were not overwhelmed by the forces of "business as usual." The established units were shielded from the distractions of launching new businesses, and they continued to focus all of their attention and energy on refining their operations, enhancing their products, and serving their customers.

ISSUE FOR DEBATE

Supercell has the world's weakest CEO. On purpose.

By Tom McNamara and Asha Moore-Mangin

"Games are a form of art," says Ilkka Paananen, the CEO of Supercell, a Finnish gaming startup. He could have also added, "And so are strategic business decisions." And one thing that is certain—Mr. Paananen is not afraid to take unorthodox decisions.

Supercell operates in the highly competitive market of developing games for portable electronic devices. And while the company only started creating games in 2011, it already enjoys profit margins in the neighborhood of 70 percent.

The key to success in this dynamic industry is to consistently come up with new and exciting games that people want (which are usually downloaded onto smart-phones as "apps"). Creativity and imagination, as well as a supportive organizational structure, are vital. It appears that Supercell has all of these things in abundance.

Supercell believes in hiring talented people and then giving them the freedom and autonomy to succeed. Hire the best people and "good things will happen," says Mr. Paananen. And apparently the best way for good things to happen is by having people work in small teams or "cells," comprised of about five people each. All of these cells working on their own projects, together, make up one great big cell—a kind of "Supercell." Hence the company's name.

It is the individual cells that are responsible for coming up with new ideas for games or developing new features for existing games. Workers are free to organize themselves and their work as they see fit, with Mr. Paananen claiming to have absolutely no creative control over the teams once they are established.

What does this mean for the role of the CEO? Basically, it's a very lonely position at Supercell. Telling people how to do their jobs is not the CEO's job, according to Mr. Paananen. Every day, all employees receive an email updating them on key statistics about the company's performance. After that, there is really nothing more for a CEO to say,

(continued)

(continued)

argues Mr. Paananen. He calls himself "the "world's least powerful CEO," something that not too many chief executives would be proud of.

But the strategy and organizational structure at Supercell appear to be working. The company was recently valued at $770 million, and makes about $2.4 million a day with an estimated 8.5 million daily users. Impressively, it has been described as "the fastest growing company ever." With its nimble, lean, and flat structure, the fun and games at Supercell should continue for some time to come.

Discussion Questions

1. What is it about Supercell's organizational structure that might give it a competitive advantage over rivals?
2. As the company grows, do you think that it will be able to maintain this structure, as well as advantage? Explain.

Sources: Erik Kain, Forbes, May 6 2013 "Clash Of Kings: Zynga Struggles As Supercell Soars"; Walter Chen , Business Insider, April 20 2013 "Finnish CEO Made Himself Weak On Purpose"; supercell.net; Kim-Mai Cutler, Tech Crunch, November 21 2012 "Why Culture Matters: Supercell's Calculated Path To The Top Of The App Store."

Reflecting on Career Implications . . .

▣ **Boundaryless Organizational Designs:** Does your firm have structural mechanisms (e.g., culture, human resources practices) that facilitate sharing information across boundaries? Regardless of the level of boundarylessness of your organization, a key issue for your career is the extent to which you are able to cut across boundaries within your organization. Such boundaryless behavior on your part will enable you to enhance and leverage your human capital. Evaluate how boundaryless you are within your organizational context. What actions can you take to become even more boundaryless?

▣ **Horizontal Systems and Processes:** One of the approaches suggested in the chapter to improve boundarylessness

within organizations is *reengineering.* Analyze the work you are currently doing and think of ways in which it can be reengineered to improve quality, accelerate response time, and lower cost. Consider presenting the results of your analysis to your immediate superiors. Do you think they will be receptive to your suggestions?

▣ **Ambidextrous Organizations:** Firms that achieve *adaptability* and *alignment* are considered ambidextrous. As an individual, you can also strive to be ambidextrous. Evaluate your own ambidexterity by assessing your adaptability (your ability to change in response to changes around you) and alignment (how good you are at exploiting your existing competencies). What steps can you take to improve your ambidexterity?

summary

Successful organizations must ensure that they have the proper type of organizational structure. Furthermore, they must ensure that their firms incorporate the necessary integration and processes so that the internal and external boundaries of their firms are flexible and permeable. Such a need is increasingly important as the environments of firms become more complex, rapidly changing, and unpredictable.

In the first section of the chapter, we discussed the growth patterns of large corporations. Although most organizations remain small or die, some firms continue to grow in terms of revenues, vertical integration, and diversity of products and services. In addition, their geographical scope may increase to include international operations. We traced the dominant pattern of growth, which evolves from a simple structure to a functional structure as a firm grows in terms of size and increases its level of vertical integration. After a firm expands into related products and services, its structure changes from a functional to a divisional form of organization. Finally, when the firm enters international markets, its structure again changes to accommodate the change in strategy.

We also addressed the different types of organizational structure—simple, functional, divisional (including two variations—strategic business unit and holding company), and matrix—as well as their relative advantages and disadvantages. We closed the section with a discussion of the implications for structure when a firm enters international markets. The three primary factors to take into account when determining the appropriate structure are type of international strategy, product diversity, and the extent to which a firm is dependent on foreign sales.

The second section of the chapter introduced the concept of the boundaryless organization. We did not suggest that the concept of the boundaryless organization replaces the traditional forms of organizational structure. Rather, it should complement them. This is necessary to cope with the increasing complexity and change in the competitive environment. We addressed three types of boundaryless organizations. The barrier-free type focuses on the need for the internal and external boundaries of a firm to be more flexible and permeable. The modular type emphasizes the strategic outsourcing of noncore activities. The virtual type centers on the strategic benefits of alliances and the forming of network organizations. We discussed both the advantages and disadvantages of each type of boundaryless organization as well as suggested some techniques and processes that are necessary to successfully implement them. These are common culture and values, horizontal organizational structures, horizontal systems and processes, communications and information technologies, and human resource practices.

The final section addresses the need for managers to develop ambidextrous organizations. In today's rapidly changing global environment, managers must be responsive and proactive in order to take advantage of new opportunities. At the same time, they must effectively integrate and coordinate existing operations. Such requirements call for organizational designs that establish project teams that are structurally independent units, with each having its own processes, structures, and cultures. But, at the same time, each unit needs to be effectively integrated into the existing management hierarchy.

SUMMARY REVIEW QUESTIONS

1. Why is it important for managers to carefully consider the type of organizational structure that they use to implement their strategies?

2. Briefly trace the dominant growth pattern of major corporations from simple structure to functional structure to divisional structure. Discuss the relationship between a firm's strategy and its structure.

3. What are the relative advantages and disadvantages of the types of organizational structure—simple, functional, divisional, matrix—discussed in the chapter?

4. When a firm expands its operations into foreign markets, what are the three most important factors to take into account in deciding what type of structure is most appropriate? What are the types of international structures discussed in the text and

what are the relationships between strategy and structure?

5. Briefly describe the three different types of boundaryless organizations: barrier-free, modular, and virtual.

6. What are some of the key attributes of effective groups? Ineffective groups?

7. What are the advantages and disadvantages of the three types of boundaryless organizations: barrier-free, modular, and virtual?

8. When are ambidextrous organizational designs necessary? What are some of their key attributes?

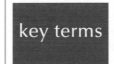
key terms

organizational structure 312
simple organizational structure 314
functional organizational structure 314
divisional organizational structure 316
strategic business unit (SBU) structure 318
holding company structure 319
matrix organizational structure 319
international division structure 322
geographic-area division structure 322
worldwide matrix structure 322
worldwide functional structure 322
worldwide product division structure 322
global start-up 322
boundaryless organizational designs 324
barrier-free organization 325
modular organization 328
virtual organization 329
horizontal organizational structures 333
adaptability 336
alignment 336
ambidextrous organizational designs 336

experiential exercise

Many firms have recently moved toward a modular structure. For example, they have increasingly outsourced many of their information technology (IT) activities. Identify three such organizations. Using secondary sources, evaluate (1) the firm's rationale for IT outsourcing and (2) the implications for performance.

	Firm	Rationale	Implication(s) for Performance
1.			
2.			
3.			

application questions & exercises

1. Select an organization that competes in an industry in which you are particularly interested. Go on the Internet and determine what type of organizational structure this organization has. In your view, is it consistent with the strategy that it has chosen to implement? Why? Why not?

2. Choose an article from *Bloomberg Businessweek, Fortune, Forbes, Fast Company,* or any other well-known publication that deals with a corporation that has undergone a significant change in its strategic direction. What are the implications for the structure of this organization?

3. Go on the Internet and look up some of the public statements or speeches of an executive in a major corporation about a significant initiative such as entering into a joint venture or launching a new product line. What do you feel are the implications for making the internal and external barriers of the firm more flexible and permeable? Does the executive discuss processes, procedures, integrating mechanisms, or cultural issues that should serve this purpose? Or are other issues discussed that enable a firm to become more boundaryless?

4. Look up a recent article in the publications listed in question 2 above that addresses a firm's involvement in outsourcing (modular organization) or in strategic alliance or network organizations (virtual organization). Was the firm successful or unsuccessful in this endeavor? Why? Why not?

ethics questions

1. If a firm has a divisional structure and places extreme pressures on its divisional executives to meet short-term profitability goals (e.g., quarterly income), could this raise some ethical considerations? Why? Why not?

2. If a firm enters into a strategic alliance but does not exercise appropriate behavioral control of its employees (in terms of culture, rewards and incentives, and boundaries—as discussed in Chapter 9) that are involved in the alliance, what ethical issues could arise? What could be the potential long-term and short-term downside for the firm?

references

1. Wilson, K. & Doz, Y. 2012. 10 rules for managing global innovation. *Harvard Business Review,* 90(10): 84–92; Wallace, J. 2007. Update on problems joining 787 fuselage sections. *Seattlepi.com,* June 7: np; Peterson, K. 2011. Special report: A wing and a prayer: Outsourcing at Boeing. *Reuters.com,* January 20: np; Hiltzik, M. 2011. 787 Dreamliner teaches Boeing costly lesson on outsourcing. *Latimes. com,* February 15: np; and Gates, D. 2013. Boeing 787's problems blamed on outsourcing, lack of oversight. *Seattletimes.com,* February 2: np.

2. For a unique perspective on organization design, see: Rao, R. 2010. What 17th century pirates can teach us about job design. *Harvard Business Review,* 88(10): 44.

3. This introductory discussion draws upon Hall, R. H. 2002. *Organizations: Structures, processes, and outcomes* (8th ed.). Upper Saddle River, NJ: Prentice Hall; and Duncan, R. E. 1979. What is the right organization structure? Decision-tree analysis provides the right answer. *Organizational Dynamics,* 7(3): 59–80. For an insightful discussion of strategy-structure relationships in the organization theory and strategic management literatures, refer to Keats, B. & O'Neill, H. M. 2001.

Organization structure: Looking through a strategy lens. In Hitt, M. A., Freeman, R. E., & Harrison, J. S. 2001. *The Blackwell handbook of strategic management:* 520–542. Malden, MA: Blackwell.

4. Gratton, L. 2011. The end of the middle manager. *Harvard Business Review,* 89(1/2): 36.

5. An interesting discussion on the role of organizational design in strategy execution is in: Neilson, G. L., Martin, K. L., & Powers, E. 2009. The secrets to successful strategy execution. *Harvard Business Review,* 87(2): 60–70.

6. This discussion draws upon Chandler, A. D. 1962. *Strategy and structure.* Cambridge, MA: MIT Press; Galbraith J. R. & Kazanjian, R. K. 1986. *Strategy implementation: The role of structure and process.* St. Paul, MN: West Publishing; and Scott, B. R. 1971. Stages of corporate development. Intercollegiate Case Clearing House, 9-371-294, BP 998. Harvard Business School.

7. Our discussion of the different types of organizational structures draws on a variety of sources, including Galbraith & Kazanjian, op. cit.; Hrebiniak, L. G. & Joyce, W. F. 1984. *Implementing strategy.* New York: Macmillan;

Distelzweig, H. 2000. Organizational structure. In Helms, M. M. (Ed.). *Encyclopedia of management:* 692–699. Farmington Hills, MI: Gale; and Dess, G. G. & Miller, A. 1993. *Strategic management.* New York: McGraw-Hill.

8. A discussion of an innovative organizational design is in: Garvin, D. A. & Levesque, L. C. 2009. The multiunit enterprise. Harvard Business Review, 87(2): 106–117.

9. Schein, E. H. 1996. Three cultures of management: The key to organizational learning. *Sloan Management Review,* 38(1): 9–20.

10. Insights on governance implications for multidivisional forms are in: Verbeke, A. & Kenworthy, T. P. 2008. Multidivisional vs. metanational governance. *Journal of International Business,* 39(6): 940–956.

11. Martin, J. A. & Eisenhardt, K. 2010. Rewiring: Cross-business-unit collaborations in multibusiness organizations. *Academy of Management Journal,* 53(2): 265–301.

12. For a discussion of performance implications, refer to Hoskisson, R. E. 1987. Multidivisional structure and performance: The contingency of diversification strategy. *Academy of Management Journal,* 29: 625–644.

13. For a thorough and seminal discussion of the evolution toward the divisional form of organizational structure in the United States, refer to Chandler, op. cit. A rigorous empirical study of the strategy and structure relationship is found in Rumelt, R. P. 1974. *Strategy, structure, and economic performance.* Cambridge, MA: Harvard Business School Press.

14. Ghoshal S. & Bartlett, C. A. 1995. Changing the role of management: Beyond structure to processes. *Harvard Business Review,* 73(1): 88.

15. Koppel, B. 2000. Synergy in ketchup? Forbes, February 7: 68–69; and Hitt, M. A., Ireland, R. D., & Hoskisson, R. E. 2001. *Strategic management: Competitiveness and globalization* (4th ed.). Cincinnati, OH: Southwestern Publishing.

16. Pitts, R. A. 1977. Strategies and structures for diversification. *Academy of Management Journal,* 20(2): 197–208.

17. Silvestri, L. 2012. The evolution of organizational structure. *footnote 1 .com,* June 6: np.

18. Andersen, M. M., Froholdt, M., Poulfelt, F. 2010. *Return on strategy. How to achieve it.* New York: Routledge.

19. Haas, M. R. 2010. The double-edged swords of autonomy and external knowledge: Analyzing team effectiveness in a multinational organization. *Academy of Management Journal,* 53(5): 989–1008.

20. Daniels, J. D., Pitts, R. A., & Tretter, M. J. 1984. Strategy and structure of U.S. multinationals: An exploratory study. *Academy of Management Journal,* 27(2): 292–307.

21. Habib, M. M. & Victor, B. 1991. Strategy, structure, and performance of U.S. manufacturing and service MNCs: A comparative analysis. *Strategic Management Journal,* 12(8): 589–606.

22. Our discussion of global start-ups draws from Oviatt, B. M. & McDougall, P. P. 2005. The internationalization of entrepreneurship. *Journal of International Business Studies,* 36(1): 2–8; Oviatt, B. M. & McDougall, P. P. 1994. Toward a theory of international new ventures. *Journal of International Business Studies,* 25(1): 45–64; and Oviatt, B. M. & McDougall, P. P. 1995. Global start-ups: Entrepreneurs on a worldwide stage. *Academy of Management Executive,* 9(2): 30–43.

23. Some useful guidelines for global start-ups are provided in Kuemmerle, W. 2005. The entrepreneur's path for global expansion. *MIT Sloan Management Review,* 46(2): 42–50.

24. See, for example, Miller, D. & Friesen, P. H. 1980. Momentum and revolution in organizational structure. *Administrative Science Quarterly,* 13: 65–91.

25. Many authors have argued that a firm's structure can influence its strategy and performance. These include Amburgey, T. L. & Dacin, T. 1995. As the left foot follows the right? The dynamics of strategic and structural change. *Academy of Management Journal,* 37: 1427–1452; Dawn, K. & Amburgey, T. L. 1991. Organizational inertia and momentum: A dynamic model of strategic change. *Academy of Management Journal,* 34: 591–612; Fredrickson, J. W. 1986. The strategic decision process and organization structure. *Academy of Management Review,* 11: 280–297; Hall, D. J. & Saias, M. A. 1980. Strategy follows structure! *Strategic Management Journal,* 1: 149–164; and Burgelman, R. A. 1983. A model of the interaction of strategic behavior, corporate context, and the concept of strategy. *Academy of Management Review,* 8: 61–70.

26. An interesting discussion on how the Internet has affected the boundaries of firms can be found in Afuah, A. 2003. Redefining firm boundaries in the face of the Internet: Are firms really shrinking? *Academy of Management Review,* 28(1): 34–53.

27. Collis & Montgomery, op. cit.

28. Govindarajan, V. G. & Trimble, C. 2010. Stop the innovation wars. *Harvard Business Review,* 88(7/8): 76–83.

29. For a discussion of the role of coaching on developing high performance teams, refer to Kets de Vries, M. F. R. 2005. Leadership group coaching in action: The zen of creating high performance teams. *Academy of Management Executive,* 19(1): 77–89.

30. Pfeffer, J. 1998. *The human equation: Building profits by putting people first.* Cambridge, MA: Harvard Business School Press.

31. For a discussion on how functional area diversity affects performance, see Bunderson, J. S. & Sutcliffe, K. M. 2002. *Academy of Management Journal,* 45(5): 875–893.

32. See, for example, Hoskisson, R. E., Hill, C. W. L., & Kim, H. 1993. The multidivisional structure: Organizational fossil or source of value? *Journal of Management,* 19(2): 269–298.

33. Pottruck, D. A. 1997. Speech delivered by the co-CEO of Charles Schwab Co., Inc., to the Retail Leadership Meeting, San Francisco, CA, January 30; and Miller, W. 1999. Building the ultimate resource. *Management Review,* January: 42–45.

34. Public-private partnerships are addressed in: Engardio, P. 2009. State capitalism. *BusinessWeek,* February 9: 38–43.

35. Aller, R., Weiner, H., & Weilart, M. 2005. IBM and Mayo collaborating to customize patient treatment plans. *cap.org,* January: np; and McGee, M. 2010. IBM, Mayo partner on aneurysm diagnostics. *informationweek.com,* January 25: np.

36. Anonymous. 2013. Automakers in alliance to speed fuel-cell development. *latimes.com,* January 29: np.

37. Dess, G. G., Rasheed, A. M. A., McLaughlin, K. J., & Priem, R. 1995. The new corporate architecture. *Academy of Management Executive,* 9(3): 7–20.

38. Barnes, C. 1998. A fatal case. *Fast Company,* February–March: 173.

39. Handy, C. 1989. The age of unreason. Boston: Harvard Business School Press; Ramstead, E. 1997. APC maker's low-tech formula: Start with the box. *The Wall Street Journal,* December 29: B1; Mussberg, W. 1997. Thin screen PCs are looking good but still fall flat. *The Wall Street Journal,* January 2: 9; Brown, E. 1997. Monorail: Low cost PCs. *Fortune,* July 7: 106–108; and Young, M. 1996. Ex-Compaq executives start new company. *Computer Reseller News,* November 11: 181.

40. An original discussion on how open-sourcing could help the Big 3 automobile companies is in: Jarvis, J 2009. How the Google model could help Detroit. *BusinessWeek,* February 9: 32–36.

41. For a discussion of some of the downsides of outsourcing, refer to Rossetti, C. & Choi, T. Y. 2005. On the dark side of strategic sourcing: Experiences from the aerospace industry. *Academy of Management Executive,* 19(1): 46–60.

42. Tully, S. 1993. The modular corporation. *Fortune,* February 8: 196.

43. Offshoring in manufacturing firms is addressed in: Coucke, K. & Sleuwaegen, L. 2008. Offshoring as a survival strategy: Evidence from manufacturing firms in Belgium. *Journal of International Business Studies,* 39(8): 1261–1277.

44. Quinn, J. B. 1992. *Intelligent enterprise: A knowledge and service based paradigm for industry.* New York: Free Press.

45. For an insightful perspective on outsourcing and its role in developing capabilities, read Gottfredson, M., Puryear, R., & Phillips, C. 2005. Strategic sourcing: From periphery to the core. *Harvard Business Review,* 83(4): 132–139.

46. This discussion draws upon Quinn, J. B. & Hilmer, F. C. 1994. Strategic outsourcing. *Sloan Management Review,* 35(4): 43–55.

47. Reitzig, M. & Wagner, S. 2010. The hidden costs of outsourcing: Evidence from patent data. *Strategic Management Journal.* 31(11): 1183–1201.

48. Insights on outsourcing and private branding can be found in: Cehn, S-F. S. 2009. A transaction cost rationale for private branding and its implications for the choice of domestic vs. offshore outsourcing. *Journal of International Business Strategy,* 40(1): 156–175.

49. For an insightful perspective on the use of outsourcing for decision analysis, read: Davenport, T. H. & Iyer, B. 2009. Should you outsource your brain? *Harvard Business Review,* 87(2): 38.

50. See also Stuckey, J. & White, D. 1993. When and when not to vertically integrate. *Sloan Management Review,* Spring: 71–81; Harrar, G. 1993. Outsource tales. *Forbes ASAP,* June 7: 37–39, 42; and Davis, E. W. 1992. Global outsourcing: Have U.S. managers thrown the baby out with the bath water? *Business Horizons,* July–August: 58–64.

51. For a discussion of knowledge creation through alliances, refer to Inkpen, A. C. 1996. Creating knowledge through collaboration. *California Management Review,* 39(1): 123–140; and Mowery, D. C., Oxley, J. E., & Silverman, B. S.

1996. Strategic alliances and interfirm knowledge transfer. *Strategic Management Journal,* 17 (Special Issue, Winter): 77–92.

52. Doz, Y. & Hamel, G. 1998. *Alliance advantage: The art of creating value through partnering.* Boston: Harvard Business School Press.

53. DeSanctis, G., Glass, J. T., & Ensing, I. M. 2002. Organizational designs for R&D. *Academy of Management Executive,* 16(3): 55–66.

54. Barringer, B. R. & Harrison, J. S. 2000. Walking a tightrope: Creating value through interorganizational alliances. *Journal of Management,* 26: 367–403.

55. One contemporary example of virtual organizations is R&D consortia. For an insightful discussion, refer to Sakaibara, M. 2002. Formation of R&D consortia: Industry and company effects. *Strategic Management Journal,* 23(11): 1033–1050.

56. Bartness, A. & Cerny, K. 1993. Building competitive advantage through a global network of capabilities. *California Management Review,* Winter: 78–103. For an insightful historical discussion of the usefulness of alliances in the computer industry, see Moore, J. F. 1993. Predators and prey: A new ecology of competition. *Harvard Business Review,* 71(3): 75–86.

57. See Lorange, P. & Roos, J. 1991. Why some strategic alliances succeed and others fail. *Journal of Business Strategy,* January–February: 25–30; and Slowinski, G. 1992. The human touch in strategic alliances. *Mergers and Acquisitions,* July–August: 44–47. A compelling argument for strategic alliances is provided by Ohmae, K. 1989. The global logic of strategic alliances. *Harvard Business Review,* 67(2): 143–154.

58. Some of the downsides of alliances are discussed in Das, T. K. & Teng, B. S. 2000. Instabilities of strategic alliances: An internal tensions perspective. *Organization Science,* 11: 77–106.

59. This section draws upon Dess, G. G. & Picken, J. C. 1997. *Mission critical.* Burr Ridge, IL: Irwin Professional Publishing.

60. Katzenbach, J. R. & Smith, D. K. 1994. *The wisdom of teams: Creating the high performance organization.* New York: HarperBusiness.

61. Bryant, A. 2011. *The corner office.* New York: St. Martin's Griffin, 230.

62. Hammer, M. & Champy, J. 1993. *Reengineering the corporation: A manifesto for business revolution.* New York: HarperCollins.

63. Gupta, A. 2011. The relational perspective and east meets west. *Academy of Management Perspectives,* 25(3): 19–27.

64. This section draws on Birkinshaw, J. & Gibson, C. 2004. Building ambidexterity into an organization. *MIT Sloan Management Review,* 45(4): 47–55; and Gibson, C. B. & Birkinshaw, J. 2004. The antecedents, consequences, and mediating role of organizational ambidexterity. *Academy of Management Journal,* 47(2): 209–226. Robert Duncan is generally credited with being the first to coin the term "ambidextrous organizations" in his article entitled: Designing dual structures for innovation. In Kilmann, R. H., Pondy, L. R., & Slevin, D. (Eds.). 1976. *The management of organizations,* vol. 1: 167–188. For a seminal academic discussion of the concept of exploration and exploitation, which parallels adaptation and alignment, refer to: March, J. G. 1991. Exploration and exploitation in organizational learning. *Organization Science,* 2: 71–86.

65. This section is based on O'Reilly, C. A. & Tushman, M. L. 2004. The ambidextrous organization. *Harvard Business Review,* 82(4): 74–81.

chapter 11

Strategic Leadership:

Creating a Learning Organization and an Ethical Organization

After reading this chapter, you should have a good understanding of the following learning objectives:

LO11.1 The three key interdependent activities in which all successful leaders must be continually engaged.

LO11.2 Two elements of effective leadership: overcoming barriers to change and the effective use of power.

LO11.3 The crucial role of emotional intelligence (EI) in successful leadership as well as its potential drawbacks.

LO11.4 The importance of developing competency companions and creating a learning organization.

LO11.5 The leader's role in establishing an ethical organization.

LO11.6 The difference between integrity-based and compliance-based approaches to organizational ethics.

LO11.7 Several key elements that organizations must have to become an ethical organization.

Learning from Mistakes

GlaxoSmithKline's problems in China: Not what the doctor ordered

GlaxoSmithKline (GSK) is a global pharmaceutical and healthcare giant, with turnover in third quarter 2013 alone of over £6.5 billion. Headquartered in the UK, the company has offices in over 115 countries, with millions of people using its products every day. The company primarily develops and produces vaccines, as well as prescription drugs and over-the-counter medicine, and has three main business units: 1) pharmaceuticals, 2) vaccines, and 3) consumer healthcare.

While priding itself on being a good corporate citizen, providing products that allow people to live longer and better lives, reports of disturbing behaviour have emerged. In July 2013, government officials in China made allegations that GSK had bribed hospitals, doctors, and health officials, all in an effort to get them to prescribe the company's drugs to patients. The alleged sums involved are substantial—a reported $490 million. As a result, four employees of GSK's operations in China, including a

senior executive, were detained. The company reported that its finance director in China was barred from leaving the country but was not being held.

Almost immediately, GSK went into damage control mode, issuing a statement that said "Certain senior executives of GSK China who know our systems well appear to have acted outside of our processes and controls, which breaches Chinese law." The company, to its credit, quickly acknowledged and admitted illegal behaviour on the part of some of its employees, but it went to great lengths to stress that this was not how GSK operated and that these reported bribes were a deviation from normal operating procedures. Chinese police alleged that GSK employees transferred the bribe money to recipients through travel agencies and consulting firms, all in an attempt to hide the source and true nature of the funds.

In defense of the pharmaceutical company, even Chinese officials acknowledged that the amount of subterfuge employed in the schemes showed the great lengths that the employees had to go to in order to evade and undermine GSK's internal anti-bribery controls. And the company emphatically stated its desire to fully cooperate with and help the Chinese government get to the bottom of the corruption scandal.

A GSK executive said that the company will "actively look at our business model to ensure we make a significant contribution to meeting the economic, healthcare, and environmental needs of China and its citizens." It was not clear what the immediate, if any, strategic challenges would be for the company, or if any reorganization or rethink in strategy would be required.

There are reports that GSK had the unfortunate bad luck of being caught up in an overall crackdown by the Chinese government on the pharmaceutical market in general. And the company has clearly stated that it had no prior knowledge of the alleged improper behavior and that safeguards were in place (statements by investigators would appear to corroborate this). That said, the company realizes the gravity of the situation. During the drug scandal, sales in China dropped by 61 percent. But the CEO of GSK was emphatic in his denials that the company would quit China any time soon. It can't. China is a vital component to the company's strategy, with the Chinese market expected to be the largest for pharmaceuticals by 2020. It is imperative that GSK convinces the Chinese government that its internal controls are rigorous and that the chances of something like this occurring again are highly unlikely.

Shortly after the allegations came to light, the CEO of GSK said that he was commissioning an independent review into the company's operations in China. It was announced that the law firm of Ropes & Gray was hired to conduct the review. Undoubtedly, GSK will incorporate any suggestions that the law firm comes up with for making its internal controls even more stringent.

By Tom McNamara and Irena Descubes

Discussion Questions

1. What could GlaxoSmithKline have done differently, if anything, to avoid this scandal?
2. Do you think this scandal will have a negative impact on the company's future operations in China?

Clearly, in the end, GlaxoSmithKline (GSK) paid a high price for the unethical and illegal actions that took place—fines, a loss of reputation, and a massive fall in sales. In this instance, the GSK CEO can be said to have handled the situation well in acknowledging the problems face on and commissioning an independent review into the behavior of his company. Effective leaders play an important and often pivotal role in creating an organizational culture that pursues excellence while adhering to high standards of ethical behavior.

This chapter provides insights into the role of strategic leadership in managing, adapting, and coping in the face of increased environmental complexity and uncertainty. First, we define leadership and its three interdependent activities—setting a direction, designing the organization, and nurturing a culture dedicated to excellence and ethical behavior. Then, we identify two elements of leadership that contribute to success—overcoming barriers to change and the effective use of power. The third section focuses on emotional intelligence, a trait that is increasingly acknowledged to be critical to successful leadership. Next, we emphasize the importance of leaders developing competency companions and creating a learning organization. Here, we focus on empowerment wherein employees and managers throughout an organization develop a sense of self-determination, competence, meaning, and impact that is centrally important to learning. Finally, we address the leader's role in building an ethical organization and the elements of an ethical culture that contribute to firm effectiveness.

Leadership: Three Interdependent Activities

In today's chaotic world, few would argue against the need for leadership, but how do we go about encouraging it? Is it enough to merely keep an organization afloat, or is it essential to make steady progress toward some well-defined objective? We believe custodial management is not leadership. Leadership is proactive, goal-oriented, and focused on the creation and implementation of a creative vision. **Leadership** is the process of transforming organizations from what they are to what the leader would have them become. This definition implies a lot: *dissatisfaction* with the status quo, a *vision* of what should be, and a *process* for bringing about change. An insurance company executive shared the following insight: "I lead by the Noah Principle: It's all right to know when it's going to rain, but, by God, you had better build the ark."

Doing the right thing is becoming increasingly important. Many industries are declining; the global village is becoming increasingly complex, interconnected, and unpredictable; and product and market life cycles are becoming increasingly compressed. When asked to describe the life cycle of his company's products, the CEO of a supplier of

leadership
the process of transforming organizations from what they are to what the leader would have them become.

EXHIBIT 11.1 Three Interdependent Leadership Activities

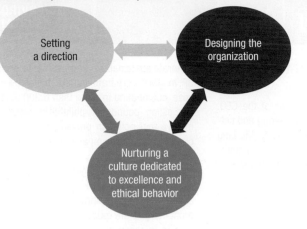

computer components replied, "Seven months from cradle to grave—and that includes three months to design the product and get it into production!" Richard D'Aveni, author of *Hypercompetition,* argued that in a world where all dimensions of competition appear to be compressed in time and heightened in complexity, *sustainable* competitive advantages are no longer possible.

Despite the importance of doing the "right thing," leaders must also be concerned about "doing things right." Charan and Colvin strongly believe that execution, that is, the implementation of strategy, is also essential to success.

> Mastering execution turns out to be the odds-on best way for a CEO to keep his job. So what's the right way to think about that sexier obsession, strategy? It's vitally important—obviously. The problem is that our age's fascination feeds the mistaken belief that developing exactly the right strategy will enable a company to rocket past competitors. In reality, that's less than half the battle.[2]

Thus, leaders are change agents whose success is measured by how effectively they formulate *and* implement a strategic vision and mission.[3]

Many authors contend that successful leaders must recognize three interdependent activities that must be continually reassessed for organizations to succeed. As shown in Exhibit 11.1, these are: (1) setting a direction, (2) designing the organization, and (3) nurturing a culture dedicated to excellence and ethical behavior.[4]

The interdependent nature of these three activities is self-evident. Consider an organization with a great mission and a superb organizational structure, but a culture that implicitly encourages shirking and unethical behavior. Or one with a sound direction and strong culture, but counterproductive teams and a "zero-sum" reward system that leads to the dysfunctional situation in which one party's gain is viewed as another party's loss, and collaboration and sharing are severely hampered. Clearly, such combinations would be ineffective.

Often, failure of today's organizations can be attributed to a lack of equal consideration of these three activities. The imagery of a three-legged stool is instructive: It will collapse if one leg is missing or broken. Let's briefly look at each of these activities as well as the value of an ambicultural approach to leadership.

Setting a Direction

A holistic understanding of an organization's stakeholders requires an ability to scan the environment to develop a knowledge of all of the company's stakeholders and other salient environmental trends and events. Managers must integrate this knowledge into a vision of

L011.1

The three key interdependent activities in which all successful leaders must be continually engaged.

setting a direction
a strategic leadership activity of strategy analysis and strategy formulation.

A VISION OF ENVIRONMENTAL SUSTAINABILITY HELPS 3M TO STAY COMPETITIVE

Vision and creative change are not solely domains of the CEO. Take former vice president of environmental engineering and pollution control at 3M Joe Ling as an example. In 1975 Mr. Ling oversaw 3M's efforts to comply with new legal pollution requirements. Years ago, 3M focused on lowering its environmental impact through, for instance, placing scrubbers on smokestacks, treating effluence before releasing wastewater, and segregating solid waste. While this prevention strategy allowed 3M to comply with legal requirements, Mr. Ling's vision went much further. Instead of seeing environmental concerns as a necessary evil, he asked whether 3M could prevent pollution altogether and profit from doing so. He thought 3M could, and he started 3M's famous Pollution Prevention Pays (or 3P) program that survives to this day.

While it is challenging to introduce creative change into any organization, Mr. Ling did not shy away from setting challenging goals. Any idea that would reduce pollution must also save money for 3M. Executives at 3M stick to this ideal and reiterate that "anything not a product is considered a cost." This sustainability strategy is firmly grounded in the 3P philosophy that everything that increases 3M's footprint is not just pollution or waste, but also a sign of operational inefficiency.

3P not only encourages top executives to rethink products and processes, but also empowers lower-level employees to generate sustainability improvements. Mr. Ling's vision to embed 3P in 3M's corporate culture has grown to phenomenal success, culminating in more than 6,300 sustainability projects and 2.6 billion pounds of pollutants saved. Consistent with 3P's mantra that pollution prevention is instrumental to 3M's financial success, the company achieved over $1 billion in first-year project savings.

3P has been an integral part of 3M's corporate strategy in an increasingly global marketplace. One could imagine that sustainability cost savings show up in increased profitability, yet 3M's profit margins are roughly the same as 30 years ago. Yet 3M operates in increasingly competitive industrial businesses, reducing operating margins and making operational efficiency programs such as 3P crucial to 3M's long-term success. Therefore, it comes as no surprise that 3M continues to challenge its employees with high sustainability standards. Over the past two decades, 3M has slashed toxic releases by 99 percent and greenhouse gas emissions by 72 percent. This makes 3M the only company that has won the EPA's Energy Star Award every year since the prize has been awarded, and they have saved costs and stayed competitive while doing so.

Sources: Esty, D.C. & Winston, A.S. 2009. *Green to Gold.* Hoboken, NJ: Wiley: 106–110; Anonymous. 2012. 2015 Sustainability goals: Sometimes our toughest challenges are the ones we put on ourselves. *www.3m.com,* June 10: np; and Winston, A.S. 2012. 3M's sustainability innovation machine. *www.businessweek.com,* May 15: np.

what the organization could become.[5] It necessitates the capacity to solve increasingly complex problems, become proactive in approach, and develop viable strategic options. A strategic vision provides many benefits: a clear future direction; a framework for the organization's mission and goals; and enhanced employee communication, participation, and commitment.

At times the creative process involves what the CEO of Yokogawa, GE's Japanese partner in the Medical Systems business, called "bullet train" thinking.[6] That is, if you want to increase the speed by 10 miles per hour, you look for incremental advances. However, if you want to double the speed, you've got to think "out of the box" (e.g., widen the track, change the overall suspension system). Leaders need more creative solutions than just keeping the same train with a few minor tweaks. Instead, they must come up with more revolutionary visions.

Strategy Spotlight 11.1 discusses Joe Ling's visionary approach to 3M's sustainability strategy. This example illustrates that visionary leadership is not just the domain of the CEO.

Designing the Organization

designing the organization
a strategic leadership activity of building structures, teams, systems, and organizational processes that facilitate the implementation of the leader's vision and strategies.

At times, almost all leaders have difficulty implementing their vision and strategies.[7] Such problems may stem from a variety of sources:

- Lack of understanding of responsibility and accountability among managers.
- Reward systems that do not motivate individuals (or collectives such as groups and divisions) toward desired organizational goals.

- Inadequate or inappropriate budgeting and control systems.
- Insufficient mechanisms to integrate activities across the organization.

Successful leaders are actively involved in building structures, teams, systems, and organizational processes that facilitate the implementation of their vision and strategies. Without appropriately structuring organizational activities, a firm would generally be unable to attain an overall low-cost advantage by closely monitoring its costs through detailed and formalized cost and financial control procedures. With regard to corporate-level strategy, a related diversification strategy would necessitate reward systems that emphasize behavioral measures because interdependence among business units tends to be very important. In contrast, reward systems associated with an unrelated diversification strategy should rely more on financial indicators of performance because business units are relatively autonomous.

These examples illustrate the important role of leadership in creating systems and structures to achieve desired ends. As Jim Collins says about the importance of designing the organization, "Along with figuring out what the company stands for and pushing it to understand what it's really good at, building mechanisms is the CEO's role—the leader as architect."[8]

Nurturing a Culture Committed to Excellence and Ethical Behavior

excellent and ethical organizational culture an organizational culture focused on core competencies and high ethical standards.

Organizational culture can be an effective means of organizational control.[9] Leaders play a key role in changing, developing, and sustaining an organization's culture. Consider a Chinese firm, Huawei, a highly successful producer of communication network solutions and services.[10] In 2012, it achieved revenues of $35.4 billion and net profits of $2.5 billion. Its strong culture can be attributed to its founder, Ren Zhengfei, and his background in the People's Liberation Army. It is a culture which eliminates individualism and promotes collectivism and the idea of hunting in packs. It is the "wolf culture" of Huawei:

> The culture of Huawei is built on a sense of patriotism, with Mr. Zhengfei frequently citing Mao Zedong's thoughts in his speeches and internal publications such as the employee magazine *Huawei People*. Sales teams are referred to as "Market Guerrillas," and battlefield tactics, such as "occupy rural areas first to surround cities," are used internally. In addition to Mao Zedong, Mr. Zhengfei has urged his employees to look to the Japanese and Germans for inspiration on how to conduct themselves. This is exemplified by the words written in a letter to new hires that states, "I hope you abandon the mentality of achieving quick results, learn from the Japanese down-to-earth attitude and the German's spirit of being scrupulous to every detail."
>
> The notion of "wolf culture" stems from the fact that Huawei workers are encouraged to learn from the behavior of wolves, which have a keen sense of smell, are aggressive, and, most important of all, hunt in packs. It is this collective and aggressive spirit that is the center of the Huawei culture. Combining the behavior of wolves with military-style training has been instrumental in building the culture of the company, which, in turn, is widely thought to be instrumental in the company's success.

In sharp contrast, leaders can also have a very detrimental effect on a firm's culture and ethics. Imagine the negative impact that Todd Berman's illegal activities have had on a firm that he cofounded—New York's private equity firm Chartwell Investments.[11] He stole more than $3.6 million from the firm and its investors. Berman pleaded guilty to fraud charges brought by the Justice Department. For 18 months he misled Chartwell's investors concerning the financial condition of one of the firm's portfolio companies by falsely claiming it needed to borrow funds to meet operating expenses. Instead, Berman transferred the money to his personal bank account, along with fees paid by portfolio companies.

Clearly, a leader's behavior and values can make a strong impact on an organization—for good or for bad. Strategy Spotlight 11.2 provides a positive example. It discusses how the chairman of Infosys create an ethical culture by "walking the talk."

INSTILLING ETHICS AND A FIRM'S VALUES: WALKING THE TALK

Firms often draft elaborate value statements and codes of conduct, yet many firms do not to live up to their own standards—or in other words, fail to "walk the talk." Take the positive example of N. R. Narayana Murthy, chairman and one of the founders of Infosys (a giant Indian technology company). In February 1984, shortly after the firm was founded, Infosys decided to import a super minicomputer so that it could start developing software for overseas clients. When the machine landed at Bangalore Airport, the local customs official refused to clear it unless the company "took care of him"—the Indian euphemism for demanding a bribe. A delay at customs could have threatened the project. Yet, instead of caving into the

unethical customs official's demands, Mr. Murthy kept true to his values and took the more expensive formal route of paying a customs duty of 135 percent with dim chances of successfully appealing the duty and receiving a refund.

Reflecting on these events, Mr. Murthy reasons, "We didn't have enough money to pay the duty and had to borrow it. However, because we had decided to do business ethically, we didn't have a choice. We would not pay bribes. We effectively paid twice for the machine and had only a slim chance of recovering our money. But a clear conscience is the softest pillow on which you can lay your head down at night. . . . It took a few years for corrupt officials to stop approaching us for favors."

Source: Raman, A. P. 2011. "Why don't we try to be India's most respected company?" *Harvard Business Review,* 89(11): 82.

Managers and top executives must accept personal responsibility for developing and strengthening ethical behavior throughout the organization. They must consistently demonstrate that such behavior is central to the vision and mission of the organization. Several elements must be present and reinforced for a firm to become highly ethical, including role models, corporate credos and codes of conduct, reward and evaluation systems, and policies and procedures. Given the importance of these elements, we address them in detail in the last section of this chapter.

Getting Things Done: Overcoming Barriers and Using Power

LO11.2

Two elements of effective leadership: overcoming barriers to change and the effective use of power.

The demands on leaders in today's business environment require them to perform a variety of functions. The success of their organizations often depends on how they as individuals meet challenges and deliver on promises. What practices and skills are needed to get the job done effectively? In this section, we focus on two capabilities that are marks of successful leadership—overcoming barriers to change and the effective use of power. Then, in the next section, we will examine an important human trait that helps leaders be more effective—emotional intelligence.

Overcoming Barriers to Change

barriers to change
characteristics of individuals and organizations that prevent a leader from transforming an organization.

What are the **barriers to change** that leaders often encounter, and how can they best bring about organizational change?[12] After all, people generally have some level of choice about how strongly they support or resist a leader's change initiatives. Why is there often so much resistance? Organizations at all levels are prone to inertia and are slow to learn, adapt, and change because:

vested interest in the status quo
a barrier to change that stems from people's risk aversion.

1. Many people have **vested interests in the status quo.** People tend to be risk averse and resistant to change. There is a broad stream of research on "escalation," wherein certain individuals continue to throw "good money at bad decisions" despite negative performance feedback.[13]

2. There are **systemic barriers.** The design of the organization's structure, information processing, reporting relationships, and so forth impede the proper flow and evaluation of information. A bureaucratic structure with multiple layers, onerous requirements for documentation, and rigid rules and procedures will often "inoculate" the organization against change.

3. **Behavioral barriers** cause managers to look at issues from a biased or limited perspective due to their education, training, work experiences, and so forth. Consider an incident shared by David Lieberman, marketing director at GVO, an innovation consulting firm:

> A company's creative type had come up with a great idea for a new product. Nearly everybody loved it. However, it was shot down by a high-ranking manufacturing representative who exploded: "A new color? Do you have any idea of the spare-parts problem that it will create?" This was not a dimwit exasperated at having to build a few storage racks at the warehouse. He'd been hearing for years about cost cutting, lean inventories, and "focus." Lieberman's comment: "Good concepts, but not always good for innovation."

4. **Political barriers** refer to conflicts arising from power relationships. This can be the outcome of a myriad of symptoms such as vested interests, refusal to share information, conflicts over resources, conflicts between departments and divisions, and petty interpersonal differences.

5. **Personal time constraints** bring to mind the old saying about "not having enough time to drain the swamp when you are up to your neck in alligators." Gresham's law of planning states that operational decisions will drive out the time necessary for strategic thinking and reflection. This tendency is accentuated in organizations experiencing severe price competition or retrenchment wherein managers and employees are spread rather thin.

Strategy Spotlight 11.3 discusses how Microsoft and Natura Cosméticos were able to overcome political barriers to change through creating a more collaborative environment.

Leaders must draw on a range of personal skills as well as organizational mechanisms to move their organizations forward in the face of such barriers. Two factors mentioned earlier—building a learning organization and ethical organization— provide the kind of climate within which a leader can advance the organization's aims and make progress toward its goals.

One of the most important tools a leader has for overcoming barriers to change is their personal and organizational power. On the one hand, good leaders must be on guard not to abuse power. On the other hand, successful leadership requires the measured exercise of power. We turn to that topic next.

The Effective Use of Power

Successful leadership requires the effective use of power in overcoming barriers to change.[14] As humorously noted by Mark Twain, "I'm all for progress. It's change I object to." **Power** refers to a leader's ability to get things done in a way he or she wants them to be done. It is the ability to influence other people's behavior, to persuade them to do things that they otherwise would not do, and to overcome resistance and opposition. Effective exercise of power is essential for successful leadership.[15]

A leader derives his or her power from several sources or bases. The simplest way to understand the bases of power is by classifying them as organizational and personal, as shown in Exhibit 11.2.

Organizational bases of power refer to the power that a person wields because of her formal management position.[16] These include legitimate, reward, coercive, and information power. *Legitimate power* is derived from organizationally conferred decision-making

systemic barriers
barriers to change that stem from an organizational design that impedes the proper flow and evaluation of information.

behavioral barriers
barriers to change associated with the tendency for managers to look at issues from a biased or limited perspective based on their prior education and experience.

political barriers
barriers to change related to conflicts arising from power relationships.

personal time constraints
a barrier to change that stems from people's not having sufficient time for strategic thinking and reflection.

power
a leader's ability to get things done in a way he or she wants them to be done.

organizational bases of power
a formal management position that is the basis of a leader's power.

OVERCOMING POLITICAL BARRIERS TO CHANGE

To overcome barriers to organizational change, companies today work more collaboratively than ever before, inside their own organizations and with outsiders. While virtual team meetings and other technology gadgets such as Facebook and Twitter facilitate discussions and employee empowerment, it is not enough for leaders to rely on technology. Instead, top management must lead by example and be good collaborators themselves. One obstacle to effective collaboration is higher-level political battles. Take Microsoft as an example. Before Apple released its tablet smash hit iPad, Microsoft had developed a viable tablet more than a decade earlier. However, entrenched interests and turf fights between competing Microsoft divisions eventually killed the project. Microsoft since then appears to be focusing on closer managerial collaboration, as the recent acquisition of Skype illustrates. The voice and video conferencing provider will become a Microsoft business unit that is required to collaborate closely with other Microsoft divisions in an effort to realize the anticipated synergies of the acquisition.

Brazil's Natura Cosméticos provides another example of overcoming barriers to change by addressing political barriers. Alessandro Carlucci, CEO of the large manufacturer and marketer of beauty products, has implemented a comprehensive "engagement process" that promotes a collaborative mindset at all levels of the organization. As part of this process, Mr. Carlucci made it a priority to unify his top executives behind common goals and stop internal power struggles that became increasingly evident after Natura became a public company in 2004. He asked top managers to invest in self-development as part of their stewardship of the company. So each executive embarked on a "personal journey" with a dedicated coach, who met with everyone individually and with the team as a whole. Carlucci explains that "it is a different type of coaching. It's not just talking to your boss or subordinates but talking about a person's life history, with their families; it is more holistic, broader, integrating all the different roles of a human being." Different from other developmental processes, this coaching approach emphasizes the human side of top team members, with all their distinct strengths but also their weaknesses. This coaching experience effectively illustrates that no top manager at Natura alone has all the answers and that collaboration is not only possible but also essential for long-term success. Carlucci's efforts to create a collaborative mindset have started to get recognized by outsiders and have helped the firm win a top spot on *Fortune*'s list of best companies for leaders.

Source: Ibarra, H. and Hansen, M.T. 2011. Are you a collaborative leader? *Harvard Business Review*, 89(7/8): 68–75; Anonymous. 2011. Analysis: What does Microsoft's Skype acquisition mean for businesses? *www.computerweekly.com*, May 13: np; Hansen, M.T. and Ibarra, H. 2011. Getting collaboration right. *blogs .hbr.org*, May 16: np.

EXHIBIT 11.2 A Leader's Bases of Power

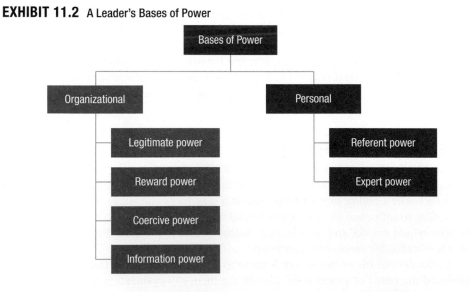

authority and is exercised by virtue of a manager's position in the organization. *Reward power* depends on the ability of the leader or manager to confer rewards for positive behaviors or outcomes. *Coercive power* is the power a manager exercises over employees using

THE USE OF "SOFT" POWER AT SIEMENS

Until 1999, paying bribes in international markets was not only legally allowed in Germany, German corporations could also deduct bribes from taxable income. However, once those laws changed, German industrial powerhouse Siemens found it hard to break its bribing habit in its sprawling global operations. Eventually a major scandal forced many top executives out of the firm, including CEO Klaus Kleinfeld. As the successor to Mr. Kleinfeld, Peter Löscher became the first outside CEO in the more than 160-year history of Siemens in 2007. As an outsider Mr. Löscher found it challenging to establish himself as a strong leader inside the bureaucratic Siemens organization. However, he eventually found a way to successfully transition into his new position.

Naturally, in the early stage of his tenure, he lacked internal connections and the bases of power associated with inside knowledge of people and processes. Yet Siemens faced tremendous challenges, such as a lack of customer orientation, and required a strong leader with the ability to change the status quo. Absent a more formal power base, he turned to more informal means to accomplish his mandate of organizational change and increasing customer orientation.

Once a year, all 700 of Siemens top managers come together for a leadership conference in Berlin. Given the historical lack of customer focus, Löscher used peer pressure as an informal (or soft) form of power in order to challenge and eventually change the lack of customer orientation. As he recalls from his first leadership conference as CEO, "I collected the Outlook calendars for the previous year from all my division CEOs and board members. Then I mapped how much time they had spent with customers and I ranked them. There was a big debate in my inner circle over whether I should use names. Some felt we would embarrass people, but I decided to put the names on the screen anyway."

The results of this exercise were quite remarkable: Mr. Löscher spent around 50 percent of his time with customers, more than any other top executive. Clearly, the people who were running the business divisions should rank higher on customer interaction than the CEO. This confirmed the lack of customer orientation in the organization. This ranking has been repeated at every Siemens leadership conference since Löscher took office. Over time, customer orientation has improved because nobody wants to fall short on this metric and endure potential ridicule. Löscher's leadership style and use of soft power during his early time in office seemed to have paid off, as the Siemens board extended his contract as CEO of the German industry icon a year early.

Source: Löscher, P. 2012. The CEO of Siemens on using a scandal to drive change. *Harvard Business Review*, 90(11): 42; and Anonymous. 2011. Löscher soll Vorstandschef bleiben. *www.manager-magazin.de*, July 25: np.

---

fear of punishment for errors of omission or commission. *Information power* arises from a manager's access, control, and distribution of information that is not freely available to everyone in an organization.

A leader might also be able to influence subordinates because of his or her personality characteristics and behavior. These would be considered the **personal bases of power,** including *referent power* and *expert power*. The source of *referent power* is a subordinate's identification with the leader. A leader's personal attributes or charisma might influence subordinates and make them devoted to that leader. The source of *expert power* is the leader's expertise and knowledge. The leader is the expert on whom subordinates depend for information that they need to do their jobs successfully.

Successful leaders use the different bases of power, and often a combination of them, as appropriate to meet the demands of a situation, such as the nature of the task, the personality characteristics of the subordinates, and the urgency of the issue.[17] Persuasion and developing consensus are often essential, but so is pressing for action. At some point stragglers must be prodded into line.[18] Peter Georgescu, who recently retired as CEO of Young & Rubicam (an advertising and media subsidiary of the UK-based WPP Group), summarized a leader's dilemma brilliantly (and humorously), "I have knee pads and a .45. I get down and beg a lot, but I shoot people too."[19]

Strategy Spotlight 11.4 addresses some of the subtleties of power. Here, the CEO of Siemens successfully brought about organizational change by the effective use of peer pressure.

personal bases of power
a leader's personality characteristics and behavior that are the basis of the leader's power.

LO11.3

The crucial role of emotional intelligence (EI) in successful leadership as well as its potential drawbacks.

Emotional Intelligence: A Key Leadership Trait

In the previous sections, we discussed skills and activities of strategic leadership. The focus was on "what leaders do and how they do it." Now, the issue becomes "who leaders *are*," that is, what leadership traits are the most important. Clearly, these two issues are related, because successful leaders possess the valuable traits that enable them to perform effectively in order to create value for their organization.[20]

There has been a vast amount of literature on the successful traits of leaders.[21] These traits include integrity, maturity, energy, judgment, motivation, intelligence, expertise, and so on. For simplicity, these traits may be grouped into three broad sets of capabilities:

- Purely technical skills (like accounting or operations research).
- Cognitive abilities (like analytical reasoning or quantitative analysis).
- Emotional intelligence (like self-management and managing relationships).

"Emotional intelligence (EI)" has become popular in both the literature and management practice in recent years.[22] *Harvard Business Review* articles published in 1998 and 2000 by psychologist/journalist Daniel Goleman, who is most closely associated with the concept, have become *HBR*'s most highly requested reprint articles. And two of Goleman's recent books, *Emotional Intelligence* and *Working with Emotional Intelligence,* were both on the *New York Times*'s best-seller lists. Goleman defines **emotional intelligence** as the capacity for recognizing one's own emotions and those of others.[23]

Recent studies of successful managers have found that effective leaders consistently have a high level of EI.[24] Findings indicate that EI is a better predictor of life success (economic well-being, satisfaction with life, friendship, family life), including occupational attainments, than IQ. Evidence is consistent with the catchy phrase: "IQ gets you hired, but EQ (Emotional Quotient) gets you promoted." Human resource managers believe this statement to be true, even for highly technical jobs such as those of scientists and engineers.

This is not to say that IQ and technical skills are irrelevant, but they become "threshold capabilities." They are the necessary requirements for attaining higher-level managerial positions. EI, on the other hand, is essential for leadership success. Without it, Goleman claims, a manager can have excellent training, an incisive analytical mind, and many smart ideas but will still not be a great leader.

Exhibit 11.3 identifies the five components of EI: self-awareness, self-regulation, motivation, empathy, and social skill.

emotional intelligence (EI) an individual's capacity for recognizing his or her own emotions and those of others, including the five components of self-awareness, self-regulation, motivation, empathy, and social skills.

Self-Awareness

Self-awareness is the first component of EI and brings to mind that Delphic oracle who gave the advice "know thyself" thousands of years ago. Self-awareness involves a person having a deep understanding of his or her emotions, strengths, weaknesses, and drives. People with strong self-awareness are neither overly critical nor unrealistically optimistic. Instead, they are honest with themselves and others.

People generally admire and respect candor. Leaders are constantly required to make judgment calls that require a candid assessment of capabilities—their own and those of others. People who assess themselves honestly (i.e., self-aware people) are well suited to do the same for the organizations they run.[25]

Self-Regulation

Biological impulses drive our emotions. Although we cannot do away with them, we can strive to manage them. Self-regulation, which is akin to an ongoing inner conversation, frees us from being prisoners of our feelings.[26] People engaged in such conversation feel bad moods and emotional impulses just as everyone else does. However, they find ways to control them and even channel them in useful ways.

EXHIBIT 11.3 The Five Components of Emotional Intelligence at Work

	Definition	Hallmarks
Self-management skills:		
Self-awareness	• The ability to recognize and understand your moods, emotions, and drives, as well as their effect on others.	• Self-confidence • Realistic self-assessment • Self-deprecating sense of humor
Self-regulation	• The ability to control or redirect disruptive impulses and moods. • The propensity to suspend judgment—to think before acting.	• Trustworthiness and integrity • Comfort with ambiguity • Openness to change
Motivation	• A passion to work for reasons that go beyond money or status. • A propensity to pursue goals with energy and persistence.	• Strong drive to achieve • Optimism, even in the face of failure • Organizational commitment
Managing relationships:		
Empathy	• The ability to understand the emotional makeup of other people. • Skill in treating people according to their emotional reactions.	• Expertise in building and retaining talent • Cross-cultural sensitivity • Service to clients and customers
Social skill	• Proficiency in managing relationships and building networks. • An ability to find common ground and build rapport.	• Effectiveness in leading change • Persuasiveness • Expertise in building and leading teams

Source: Reprinted by permission of *Harvard Business Review.* Exhibit from "What Makes a Leader," by D. Goleman, January 2004. Copyright © 2004 by the Harvard Business School Publishing Corporation; all rights reserved.

Self-regulated people are able to create an environment of trust and fairness where political behavior and infighting are sharply reduced and productivity tends to be high. People who have mastered their emotions are better able to bring about and implement change in an organization. When a new initiative is announced, they are less likely to panic; they are able to suspend judgment, seek out information, and listen to executives explain the new program.

Motivation

Successful executives are driven to achieve beyond expectations—their own and everyone else's. Although many people are driven by external factors, such as money and prestige, those with leadership potential are driven by a deeply embedded desire to achieve for the sake of achievement.

Motivated people show a passion for the work itself, such as seeking out creative challenges, a love of learning, and taking pride in a job well done. They also have a high level of energy to do things better as well as a restlessness with the status quo. They are eager to explore new approaches to their work.

Empathy

Empathy is probably the most easily recognized component of EI. Empathy means thoughtfully considering an employee's feelings, along with other factors, in the process of making intelligent decisions. Empathy is particularly important in today's business

EMPATHY IN A PEDIATRIC DENTAL PRACTICE

A key strength of effective leaders is to see situations from another person's perspective—or in other words, to show empathy. Empathy is especially important when dealing with customers who may not always be able to articulate their preferences. Take dental practices for children. Children's dental offices often look, smell, and sound remarkably similar to regular dental practices for the simple reason that the owners design their offices in terms of what they produce (i.e., dental services) instead of what would be best for their customers.

While even many parents have negative feelings toward dental offices, it is naturally quite challenging to create some excitement or at least lower the anxieties children experience. That's where a healthy portion of empathy enters the picture. Let's try to view your dental practice from a child's point of view. How to best accomplish this? Forget conventional wisdom, and experience your dental practice from your knees! Several interesting insights may emerge just by emulating a child's experience. First, what is the first thing that you see when you enter the practice?

Chances are, not much, as the reception area is conveniently set at eye level—*adult* eye level. Even the most wonderful receptionist remains invisible for children coming into the practice. Second, what do you hear? Again, chances are that you will hear the all-too-familiar sound of dental equipment, something that may sound to children like torturing mice in the next room. Third, what do you smell? Frankly, doctor's offices have a distinct smell that equals panic for children and even many adults.

So what is the major takeaway from putting yourself into a kid's shoes? Seeing the world from your customer's point of view may lead you to lower the reception desk so children can see the sweet receptionist. You may also play some one-beat-per-second music to evoke the sense of a heartbeat. Finally, you could sound-proof the examination rooms so that dental drilling noise is reduced. Overall, this example demonstrates that empathy—or the ability to see situations from another person's perspective—may allow business owners to tailor their service and product offerings to specific customer segments.

Source: Burrus, D. 2011. *Flash foresight.* New York: Harper Business: xxii–xxiv.

---

environment for at least three reasons: the increasing use of teams, the rapid pace of globalization, and the growing need to retain talent.[27]

When leading a team, a manager is often charged with arriving at a consensus—often in the face of a high level of emotions. Empathy enables a manager to sense and understand the viewpoints of everyone around the table.

Globalization typically involves cross-cultural dialogue that can easily lead to miscues. Empathetic people are attuned to the subtleties of body language; they can hear the message beneath the words being spoken. They have a deep understanding of the existence and importance of cultural and ethnic differences.

Empathy also plays a key role in retaining talent. Human capital is particularly important to a firm in the knowledge economy when it comes to creating advantages that are sustainable. Leaders need empathy to develop and keep top talent, because when high performers leave, they take their tacit knowledge with them.

Strategy Spotlight 11.5 shows that empathy can pay off in a wide variety of settings. Here it helps a pediatric dental practice to view its business through the eyes of a child.

Social Skill

While the first three components of EI are all self-management skills, the last two—empathy and social skill—concern a person's ability to manage relationships with others. Social skill may be viewed as friendliness with a purpose: moving people in the direction you desire, whether that's agreement on a new marketing strategy or enthusiasm about a new product.

Socially skilled people tend to have a wide circle of acquaintances as well as a knack for finding common ground and building rapport. They recognize that nothing gets done alone, and they have a network in place when the time for action comes.

Social skill can be viewed as the culmination of the other dimensions of EI. People will be effective at managing relationships when they can understand and control their own emotions and empathize with others' feelings. Motivation also contributes to social skill. People who are driven to achieve tend to be optimistic, even when confronted with setbacks. And when people are upbeat, their "glow" is cast upon conversations and other social encounters. They are popular, and for good reason.

A key to developing social skill is to become a good listener—a skill that many executives find to be quite challenging. Teresa Taylor, chief operating officer at Quest Communications, says:[28]

> "Over the years, something I really try to focus on is truly listening. When I say that, I mean sometimes people act like they're listening but they're really formulating their own thoughts in their heads. I'm trying to put myself into someone else's shoes, trying to figure out what's motivating them, and why they are in the spot they are in."

Emotional Intelligence: Some Potential Drawbacks and Cautionary Notes

Many great leaders have great reserves of empathy, interpersonal astuteness, awareness of their own feelings, and an awareness of their impact on others.[29] More importantly, they know how to apply these capabilities judiciously as best benefits the situation. Having some minimum level of EI will help a person be effective as a leader as long as it is channeled appropriately. However, if a person has a high level of these capabilities it may become "too much of a good thing" if he or she is allowed to drive inappropriate behaviors. Some additional potential drawbacks of EI can be gleaned by considering the flip side of its benefits.

Effective Leaders Have Empathy for Others   However, they also must be able to make the "tough decisions." Leaders must be able to appeal to logic and reason and acknowledge others' feelings so that people feel the decisions are correct. However, it is easy to overidentify with others or confuse empathy with sympathy. This can make it more difficult to make the tough decisions.

Effective Leaders Are Astute Judges of People   A danger is that leaders may become judgmental and overly critical about the shortcomings they perceive in others. They are likely to dismiss other people's insights, making them feel undervalued.

Effective Leaders Are Passionate about What They Do, and They Show It   This doesn't mean that they are always cheerleaders. Rather, they may express their passion as persistence in pursuing an objective or a relentless focus on a valued principle. However, there is a fine line between being excited about something and letting your passion close your mind to other possibilities or cause you to ignore realities that others may see.

Effective Leaders Create Personal Connections with Their People   Most effective leaders take time to engage employees individually and in groups, listening to their ideas, suggestions and concerns, and responding in ways that make people feel that their ideas are respected and appreciated. However, if the leader makes too many unannounced visits, it may create a culture of fear and micromanagement. Clearly, striking a correct balance is essential.

From a moral standpoint, emotional leadership is neither good nor bad. On the one hand, emotional leaders can be altruistic, focused on the general welfare of the company and its employees, and highly principled. On the other hand, they can be manipulative, selfish, and dishonest. For example, if a person is using leadership solely to gain power, that is not leadership at all.[30] Rather, they are using their EI to grasp what people want and pander to those desires in order to gain authority and influence. After all, easy answers sell.

LO11.4

The importance
of developing
competency
companions
and creating
a learning
organization.

Developing Competency Companions and Creating a Learning Organization

Leaders at all levels of the organization need to reflect on the skills that they have and how they can build and extend their skill set. [31] Too often leaders get stuck extending the competencies they already have. However, the most promising path for an individual to learn and grow may be to develop new competencies that complement the skills and abilities they already have. For example, a leader who has great competency in developing innovative ideas can extend the value of that competency by developing strong communication skills. Such a leader would benefit from an interaction effect, a situation where the combination of two skills can generate an outcome that is significantly greater than either skill can produce on its own. By enhancing communication skills, this highly innovative leader is more likely to be able to communicate the value of both innovative ideas she has developed and also the necessity to push innovative learning and development throughout the organization.

Strategy Spotlight 11.6 provides useful insights on the benefits of developing competency companions and how to go about it.

Once leaders have reflected on and enhanced their own competencies, they can turn their attention to building a learning organization. Such an organization is capable of adapting to change, fostering creativity, and succeeding in highly competitive markets.

To introduce the concept of a learning organization, we'll draw on Charles Handy, one of today's most respected business visionaries. He is author of *The Age of Unreason* and *The Age of Paradox* and he shared an amusing story several years ago:

> The other day, a courier could not find my family's remote cottage. He called his base on his radio, and the base called us to ask directions. He was just around the corner, but his base managed to omit a vital part of the directions. So he called them again, and they called us again. Then the courier repeated the cycle a third time to ask whether we had a dangerous dog. When he eventually arrived, we asked whether it would not have been simpler and less aggravating to everyone if he had called us directly from the roadside telephone booth where he had been parked. "I can't do that," he said, "because they won't refund any money I spend." "But it's only pennies!" I exclaimed. "I know," he said, "but that only shows how little they trust us!"[32]

At first glance, it would appear that the story epitomizes the lack of empowerment and trust granted to the hapless courier: Don't ask questions! Do as you're told![33] However, implicit in this scenario is also the message that learning, information sharing, adaptation, decision making, and so on are *not* shared throughout the organization. In contrast, leading-edge organizations recognize the importance of having everyone involved in the process of actively learning and adapting. As noted by today's leading expert on learning organizations, MIT's Peter Senge, the days when Henry Ford, Alfred Sloan, and Tom Watson *"learned for the organization"* are gone.

> In an increasingly dynamic, interdependent, and unpredictable world, it is simply no longer possible for anyone to "figure it all out at the top." The old model, "the top thinks and the local acts," must now give way to integrating thinking and acting at all levels. While the challenge is great, so is the potential payoff. "The person who figures out how to harness the collective genius of the people in his or her organization," according to former Citibank CEO Walter Wriston, "is going to blow the competition away."[34]

Learning and change typically involve the ongoing questioning of an organization's status quo or method of procedure. This means that all individuals throughout the organization must be reflective.[35] Many organizations get so caught up in carrying out their

COMPETENCY COMPANIONS: LEVERAGING A LEADER'S STRENGTHS

Leaders who want to take the next step in their career can follow a straightforward four-step cross-training process. The basic idea behind this cross-training approach is simple yet effective. While the most effective leaders have at least one competency that makes them great and eventually indispensable, it makes little sense to continually work on already great qualities. Instead, leaders can benefit from identifying and developing complementary strengths. Building complementary strengths—or competency companions—may lead to substantially greater leadership effectiveness than finding increasingly rare opportunities to improve an already outstanding competency.

First, leaders must identify their strengths in areas that usually fall into five categories: character, personal capability, getting results, interpersonal skills, and leading change. While this task can be done in multiple ways, it is important to realize that your own view is less important than how others see you, making a 360-degree evaluation the method of choice.

Second, choose a strength to focus on. Most people find it easy to identify weaknesses and focus their attention on improving them. Unless a competence is extremely underdeveloped (i.e., in the 10th percentile), however, it may pay to focus on an already strong yet not outstanding competency. Developing a competency from strong to outstanding often can raise the perceived leadership effectiveness dramatically. However, choosing between multiple strong competencies is easier said than done, because most people lack clear selection criteria. To engage effectively in this process, leaders should focus on a strong competency that is important to the organization. Moreover, leaders should choose a competency they feel passionate about.

Third, select a companion behavior. While developing a great or outstanding competency is an important step on the journey to becoming an indispensable leader, it may increasingly pay to also focus on a mediocre competency that can be developed in an interacting (or complementary) fashion. As before, this companion competency should be valued by the organization and also be something the leader feels passionate about.

Lastly, develop your companion behavior. Once you have settled on an organizationally valued and personally engaging competency, you should now work on improving the basic skills in this area. Practically speaking, you could look for as many opportunities as possible to develop this competency, both inside and outside of work. For instance, you could take courses or practice informally with friends and coworkers. Volunteer to engage in activities that allow you to practice this skill, and ask for continuous feedback.

Extensive research by Zenger Folkman, a leadership development consultancy, provides solid evidence of the benefits of pairing leader attributes. Such findings were based on an analysis of their database of more than a quarter million 360-degree surveys of some 30,000 developing leaders. Take, for example, the competencies "focuses on results" and "builds relationships." Only 14 percent of leaders who were reasonably strong (that is, scored in the 75th percentile) in focusing on results but less so in building relationships reached the extraordinary leadership level: the 90th percentile in overall leadership effectiveness. Similarly, only 12 percent of those who were reasonably strong in building relationships but less so in focusing on results reached that level. However, when an individual performed well in both categories, something dramatic happened: Fully 72 percent of those in the 75th percentile in both categories reached the 90th percentile on overall leadership effectiveness.

Source: Zenger, J. H., Folkman, J. R., & Edinger, S. K. 2011. Making yourself indispensable. *Harvard Business Review,* 89(10): 84–92.

day-to-day work that they rarely, if ever, stop to think objectively about themselves and their businesses. They often fail to ask the probing questions that might lead them to call into question their basic assumptions, to refresh their strategies, or to reengineer their work processes. According to Michael Hammer and Steven Stanton, the pioneer consultants who touched off the reengineering movement:

> Reflection entails awareness of self, of competitors, of customers. It means thinking without preconception. It means questioning cherished assumptions and replacing them with new approaches. It is the only way in which a winning company can maintain its leadership position, by which a company with great assets can ensure that they continue to be well deployed.[36]

To adapt to change, foster creativity, and remain competitive, leaders must build learning organizations. Exhibit 11.4 lists the five elements of a learning organization.

EXHIBIT 11.4

Key Elements of a
Learning Organization

These are the five key elements of a learning organization. Each of these items should be viewed as *necessary, but not sufficient.* That is, successful learning organizations need all five elements.

1. Inspiring and motivating people with a mission or purpose.
2. Empowering employees at all levels.
3. Accumulating and sharing internal knowledge.
4. Gathering and integrating external information.
5. Challenging the status quo and enabling creativity.

Inspiring and Motivating People with a Mission or Purpose

learning organizations
organizations that create a proactive, creative approach to the unknown, characterized by (1) inspiring and motivating people with a mission and purpose, (2) empowering employees at all levels, (3) accumulating and sharing internal knowledge, (4) gathering and integrating external information, and (5) challenging the status quo and enabling creativity.

Successful **learning organizations** create a proactive, creative approach to the unknown, actively solicit the involvement of employees at all levels, and enable all employees to use their intelligence and apply their imagination. Higher-level skills are required of everyone, not just those at the top.[37] A learning environment involves organizationwide commitment to change, an action orientation, and applicable tools and methods.[38] It must be viewed by everyone as a guiding philosophy and not simply as another change program.

A critical requirement of all learning organizations is that everyone feels and supports a compelling purpose. In the words of William O'Brien, CEO of Hanover Insurance, "Before there can be meaningful participation, people must share certain values and pictures about where we are trying to go. We discovered that people have a real need to feel that they're part of an enabling mission."[39] Such a perspective is consistent with an intensive study by Kouzes and Posner, authors of *The Leadership Challenge.*[40] They recently analyzed data from nearly one million respondents who were leaders at various levels in many organizations throughout the world. A major finding was that what leaders struggle with most is communicating an image of the future that draws others in, that is, it speaks to what others see and feel. To illustrate:

> Buddy Blanton, a principal program manager at Rockwell Collins, learned this lesson firsthand. He asked his team for feedback on his leadership, and the vast majority of it was positive. However, he got some strong advice from his team about how he could be more effective in inspiring a shared vision. "You would benefit by helping us, as a team, to understand how you go to your vision. We want to walk with you while you create the goals and vision, so we all get to the end of the vision together."[41]

Inspiring and motivating people with a mission or purpose is a necessary but not sufficient condition for developing an organization that can learn and adapt to a rapidly changing, complex, and interconnected environment.

Empowering Employees at All Levels

"The great leader is a great servant," asserted Ken Melrose, CEO of Toro Company and author of *Making the Grass Greener on Your Side.*[42] A manager's role becomes one of creating an environment where employees can achieve their potential as they help move the organization toward its goals. Instead of viewing themselves as resource controllers and power brokers, leaders must envision themselves as flexible resources willing to assume numerous roles as coaches, information providers, teachers, decision makers, facilitators, supporters, or listeners, depending on the needs of their employees.[43]

The central key to empowerment is effective leadership. Empowerment can't occur in a leadership vacuum. According to Melrose, "You best lead by serving the needs of your people. You don't do their jobs for them; you enable them to learn and progress on the job."

Leading-edge organizations recognize the need for trust, cultural control, and expertise at all levels instead of the extensive and cumbersome rules and regulations inherent

EMPLOYEE EMPOWERMENT AT GE

By Tom McNamara and Irena Descubes

General Electric (GE) is a global power house of a company, involved in everything from providing financial services to making locomotives. With 300,000 employees working in over 140 countries, GE says that it is the productivity, creativity, and innovation of these people that provides it with a competitive advantage. But exactly how does GE ensure that its workers, spread out across a multitude of continents, remain productive, creative, and innovative? That's easy—empowerment.

GE likes to consider itself a "We Company" and not a "Me Company." Having motivated, independent, and free thinking employees, who can still collaborate and work in teams, is critical. The best way to do this, GE believes, is by using a six-point employee empowerment program:

- Health & Safety: The health and well being of GE's 300,000 employees is of utmost concern. Multiple programs are in place to ensure the highest workplace standards.

- Soliciting Opinions: Every two years a targeted survey is carried out on 20,000 employees worldwide to determine what the critical issues affecting the work environment at GE are.

- Inclusivity: GE is committed to hiring the best people in the world and having a diversified workforce representative of the diverse regions that it does business in.

- Integrity and Privacy: GE believes in strict confidentiality and integrity when it comes to information about its employees, customers, suppliers, and operations.

- Labor Relations: GE treats all of its employees with respect and adheres to all of the relevant labor laws of the different countries that it operates in.

- Learning and Development: Every year GE spends more than $1 billion on learning and development initiatives, ensuring a well trained and qualified workforce.

Another part of this empowerment program involves using what are called "affinity networks." These are groups of GE employees who are drawn together and driven to collectively work on some issue or problem. As a result, a large number of specialized employee organizations have been created, making it easy for colleagues who share similar interests and backgrounds to connect. The aim is to ensure that "all voices are listened to and all backgrounds are respected."

GE does its best to provide opportunities at all levels of the organization that will hopefully allow people to express and exercise their creativity, while at the same time developing themselves and their careers. The results can be seen in just how successful GE's performance has been and just how many CEOs of Fortune 500 companies once worked for GE.

Sources: ge.com; Knowledge@Wharton September 2010 "Orchestrating leadership strategies in a reset economy."

---

in hierarchical control.[44] Some have argued that too often organizations fall prey to the "heroes-and-drones syndrome," wherein the value of those in powerful positions is exalted and the value of those who fail to achieve top rank is diminished. Such an attitude is implicit in phrases such as "Lead, follow, or get out of the way" or, even less appealing, "Unless you're the lead horse, the view never changes." Few will ever reach the top hierarchical positions in organizations, but in the information economy, the strongest organizations are those that effectively use the talents of all the players on the team.

Empowering individuals by soliciting their input helps an organization to enjoy better employee morale. It also helps create a culture in which middle- and lower-level employees feel that their ideas and initiatives will be valued, and enhance firm performance as explained in Strategy Spotlight 11.7.

Accumulating and Sharing Internal Knowledge

Effective organizations must also *redistribute information, knowledge* (skills to act on the information), and *rewards*.[45] A company might give frontline employees the power to act as "customer advocates," doing whatever is necessary to satisfy customers. The company needs to disseminate information by sharing customer expectations and feedback as well as financial information. The employees must know about the goals of the business as well as how key value-creating activities in the organization are related to each other. Finally, organizations should allocate rewards on how effectively employees use information, knowledge, and power to improve customer service quality and the company's overall performance.[46]

Let's take a look at Whole Foods Market, Inc., the largest natural foods grocer in the United States.[47] An important benefit of the sharing of internal information at Whole Foods becomes the active process of *internal benchmarking*. Competition is intense at Whole Foods. Teams compete against their own goals for sales, growth, and productivity; they compete against different teams in their stores; and they compete against similar teams at different stores and regions. There is an elaborate system of peer reviews through which teams benchmark each other. The "Store Tour" is the most intense. On a periodic schedule, each Whole Foods store is toured by a group of as many as 40 visitors from another region. Lateral learning—discovering what your colleagues are doing right and carrying those practices into your organization—has become a driving force at Whole Foods.

In addition to enhancing the sharing of company information both up and down as well as across the organization, leaders also have to develop means to tap into some of the more informal sources of internal information. In a recent survey of presidents, CEOs, board members, and top executives in a variety of nonprofit organizations, respondents were asked what differentiated the successful candidates for promotion. The consensus: The executive was seen as a person who listens. According to Peter Meyer, the author of the study, "The value of listening is clear: You cannot succeed in running a company if you do not hear what your people, customers, and suppliers are telling you. . . . Listening and understanding well are key to making good decisions."[48]

Gathering and Integrating External Information

Recognizing opportunities, as well as threats, in the external environment is vital to a firm's success. As organizations *and* environments become more complex and evolve rapidly, it is far more critical for employees and managers to become more aware of environmental trends and events—both general and industry-specific—and more knowledgeable about their firm's competitors and customers. Next, we will discuss some ideas on how to do it.

First, the Internet has dramatically accelerated the speed with which anyone can track down useful information or locate people who might have useful information. Prior to the Net, locating someone who used to work at a company—always a good source of information—was quite a challenge. However, today people post their résumés on the web; they participate in discussion groups and talk openly about where they work.

Marc Friedman, manager of market research at $1 billion Andrew Corporation, a fast-growing manufacturer of wireless communications products provides an example of effective Internet use.[49] One of Friedman's preferred sites to visit is Corptech's website, which provides information on 45,000 high-tech companies and more than 170,000 executives. One of his firm's product lines consisted of antennae for air-traffic control systems. He got a request to provide a country-by-country breakdown of upgrade plans for various airports. He knew nothing about air-traffic control at the time. However, he found a site on the Internet for the International Civil Aviation Organization. Fortunately, it had a great deal of useful data, including several research companies working in his area of interest.

Second, company employees at all levels can use "garden variety" traditional sources to acquire external information. Much can be gleaned by reading trade and professional journals, books, and popular business magazines. Other venues for gathering external information include membership in professional or trade organizations, attendance at meetings and conventions, and networking among colleagues inside and outside of your industry. Intel's Andy Grove gathered information from people like DreamWorks SKG's Steven Spielberg and Tele-Communications Inc.'s John Malone.[50] He believed that such interaction provides insights into how to make personal computers more entertaining and better at communicating. Internally, Grove spent time with the young engineers who run Intel Architecture labs, an Oregon-based facility that Grove hoped to become the de facto R&D lab for the entire PC industry.

benchmarking
managers seeking out best examples of a particular practice as part of an ongoing effort to improve the corresponding practice in their own organization.

Third, benchmarking can be a useful means of employing external information. Here managers seek out the best examples of a particular practice as part of an ongoing effort to improve the corresponding practice in their own organization.[51] There are two primary types of benchmarking. **Competitive benchmarking** restricts the search for best practices to competitors, while **functional benchmarking** endeavors to determine best practices regardless of industry. Industry-specific standards (e.g., response times required to repair power outages in the electric utility industry) are typically best handled through competitive benchmarking, whereas more generic processes (e.g., answering 1-800 calls) lend themselves to functional benchmarking because the function is essentially the same in any industry.

competitive benchmarking
benchmarking where the examples are drawn from competitors in the industry.

functional benchmarking
benchmarking where the examples are drawn from any organization, even those outside the industry.

Ford Motor Company used benchmarking to study Mazda's accounts payable operations.[52] Its initial goal of a 20 percent cut in its 500-employee accounts payable staff was ratcheted up to 75 percent—and met. Ford found that staff spent most of their time trying to match conflicting data in a mass of paper, including purchase orders, invoices, and receipts. Following Mazda's example, Ford created an "invoiceless system" in which invoices no longer trigger payments to suppliers. The receipt does the job.

Fourth, focus directly on customers for information. For example, William McKnight, head of 3M's Chicago sales office, required that salesmen of abrasives products talk directly to the workers in the shop to find out what they needed, instead of calling on only front-office executives.[53] This was very innovative at the time—1909! But it illustrates the need to get to the end user of a product or service. (McKnight went on to become 3M's president from 1929 to 1949 and chairman from 1949 to 1969.) More recently, James Taylor, senior vice president for global marketing at Gateway 2000, discussed the value of customer input in reducing response time, a critical success factor in the PC industry.

> We talk to 100,000 people a day—people calling to order a computer, shopping around, looking for tech support. Our website gets 1.1 million hits per day. The time it takes for an idea to enter this organization, get processed, and then go to customers for feedback is down to minutes. We've designed the company around speed and feedback.[54]

Challenging the Status Quo and Enabling Creativity

Earlier in this chapter we discussed some of the barriers that leaders face when trying to bring about change in an organization: vested interests in the status quo, systemic barriers, behavioral barriers, political barriers, and personal time constraints. For a firm to become a learning organization, it must overcome such barriers in order to foster creativity and enable it to permeate the firm. This becomes quite a challenge if the firm is entrenched in a status quo mentality.

Perhaps the best way to challenge the status quo is for the leader to forcefully create a sense of urgency. For example, when Tom Kasten was vice president of Levi Strauss, he had a direct approach to initiating change.

> You create a compelling picture of the risks of *not* changing. We let our people hear directly from customers. We videotaped interviews with customers and played excerpts. One big customer said, "We trust many of your competitors implicitly. We sample their deliveries. We open *all* Levi's deliveries." Another said, "Your lead times are the worst. If you weren't Levi's, you'd be gone." It was powerful. I wish we had done more of it.[55]

Such initiative, if sincere and credible, establishes a shared mission and the need for major transformations. It can channel energies to bring about both change and creative endeavors.

Establishing a "culture of dissent" can be another effective means of questioning the status quo and serving as a spur toward creativity. Here norms are established whereby dissenters can openly question a superior's perspective without fear of retaliation or retribution. Consider the perspective of Steven Balmer, Microsoft's CEO, in discussing the firm's former chairman, Bill Gates.

> Bill [Gates] brings to the company the idea that conflict can be a good thing. . . . Bill knows it's important to avoid that gentle civility that keeps you from getting to the heart of an issue quickly. He likes it when anyone, even a junior employee, challenges him, and you know he respects you when he starts shouting back.[56]

Closely related to the culture of dissent is the fostering of a culture that encourages risk taking. "If you're not making mistakes, you're not taking risks, and that means you're not going anywhere," claimed John Holt, coauthor of *Celebrate Your Mistakes*.[57] "The key is to make errors faster than the competition, so you have more chances to learn and win."

Companies that cultivate cultures of experimentation and curiosity make sure that *failure* is not, in essence, an obscene word. They encourage mistakes as a key part of their competitive advantage. It has been said that innovation has a great paradox: Success— that is, true breakthroughs—usually come through failure. Below are some approaches to encourage risk taking and learning from mistakes in an organization:[58]

- **Formalize Forums for Failure**   To keep failures and the important lessons that they offer from getting swept under the rug, carve out time for reflection. GE recently began sharing lessons from failure by bringing together managers whose "Imagination Breakthrough" efforts were put on the shelf.
- **Move the Goalposts**   Innovation requires flexibility in meeting goals, since early predictions are often little more than educated guesses. Intuit's Scott Cook even goes so far as to suggest that teams developing new products ignore forecasts in the early days. "For every one of our failures, we had spreadsheets that looked awesome," he claims.
- **Bring in Outsiders**   Outsiders can help neutralize the emotions and biases that prop up a flop. Customers can be the most valuable. After its DNA chip failed, Corning brought pharmaceutical companies in early to test its new drug-discovery technology, Epic.
- **Prove Yourself Wrong, Not Right**   Development teams tend to look for supporting, rather than countervailing, evidence. "You have to reframe what you're seeking in the early days," says Innosight's Scott Anthony. "You're not really seeking proof that you have the right answer. It's more about testing to prove yourself wrong."

Finally, failure can play an important and positive role in one's professional development. John Donahue, eBay's CEO, draws on the sport of baseball in recalling the insight (and inspiration!) one of his former bosses shared with him:[59]

> "The best hitters in Major League Baseball, world class, they can strike out six times out of ten and still be the greatest hitters of all time. That's my philosophy—the key is to get up in that batter's box and take a swing. And all you have to do is hit one single, a couple of doubles, and an occasional home run out of every ten at-bats, and you're going to be the best hitter or the best business leader around. You can't play in the major leagues without having a lot of failures."

LO11.5

The leader's role in establishing an ethical organization.

ethics

a system of right and wrong that assists individuals in deciding when an act is moral or immoral and/or socially desirable or not.

Creating an Ethical Organization

Ethics may be defined as a system of right and wrong.[60] Ethics assists individuals in deciding when an act is moral or immoral, socially desirable or not. The sources for an individual's ethics include religious beliefs, national and ethnic heritage, family practices, community standards, educational experiences, and friends and neighbors. Business ethics is the application of ethical standards to commercial enterprise.

Individual Ethics versus Organizational Ethics

Many leaders think of ethics as a question of personal scruples, a confidential matter between employees and their consciences. Such leaders are quick to describe any wrongdoing as an isolated incident, the work of a rogue employee. They assume the company should not bear any responsibility for individual misdeeds. In their view, ethics has nothing to do with leadership.

Ethics has everything to do with leadership. Seldom does the character flaw of a lone actor completely explain corporate misconduct. Instead, unethical business practices typically involve the tacit, if not explicit, cooperation of others and reflect the values, attitudes, and behavior patterns that define an organization's operating culture. Ethics is as much an organizational as a personal issue. Leaders who fail to provide proper leadership to institute proper systems and controls that facilitate ethical conduct share responsibility with those who conceive, execute, and knowingly benefit from corporate misdeeds.[61]

The **ethical orientation** of a leader is a key factor in promoting ethical behavior. Ethical leaders must take personal, ethical responsibility for their actions and decision making. Leaders who exhibit high ethical standards become role models for others and raise an organization's overall level of ethical behavior. Ethical behavior must start with the leader before the employees can be expected to perform accordingly.

There has been a growing interest in corporate ethical performance. Some reasons for this trend may be the increasing lack of confidence regarding corporate activities, the growing emphasis on quality of life issues, and a spate of recent corporate scandals. Without a strong ethical culture, the chance of ethical crises occurring is enhanced. Ethical crises can be very expensive—both in terms of financial costs and in the erosion of human capital and overall firm reputation. Merely adhering to the minimum regulatory standards may not be enough to remain competitive in a world that is becoming more socially conscious. Strategy Spotlight 11.8 highlights some of the delicate issues companies must deal with when exploring new means of producing cheaper, yet still "clean," energy.

The past several years have been characterized by numerous examples of unethical and illegal behavior by many top-level corporate executives. These include executives of firms such as Enron, Tyco, WorldCom, Inc., Adelphia, and Healthsouth Corp., who were all forced to resign and are facing (or have been convicted of) criminal charges. Perhaps the most glaring example is Bernie Madoff, whose Ponzi scheme, which unraveled in 2008, defrauded investors of $50 billion in assets they had set aside for retirement and charitable donations.

The ethical organization is characterized by a conception of ethical values and integrity as a driving force of the enterprise.[62] Ethical values shape the search for opportunities, the design of organizational systems, and the decision-making process used by individuals and groups. They provide a common frame of reference that serves as a unifying force across different functions, lines of business, and employee groups. Organizational ethics helps to define what a company is and what it stands for.

There are many potential benefits of an ethical organization, but they are often indirect. Research has found somewhat inconsistent results concerning the overall relationship between ethical performance and measures of financial performance.[63] However, positive relationships have generally been found between ethical performance and strong organizational culture, increased employee efforts, lower turnover, higher organizational commitment, and enhanced social responsibility.

The advantages of a strong ethical orientation can have a positive effect on employee commitment and motivation to excel. This is particularly important in today's knowledge-intensive organizations, where human capital is critical in creating value and competitive advantages. Positive, constructive relationships among individuals (i.e., social capital) are vital in leveraging human capital and other resources in an organization. Drawing on the

---

organizational ethics the values, attitudes, and behavioral patterns that define an organization's operating culture and that determine what an organization holds as acceptable behavior.

ethical orientation the practices that firms use to promote an ethical business culture, including ethical role models, corporate credos and codes of conduct, ethically-based reward and evaluation systems, and consistently enforced ethical policies and procedures.

THE FRACKING INDUSTRY: IS IT REALLY CLEAN ENERGY?

By Tom McNamara and Erika Marsillac

What if I told you that there was an almost unlimited supply of natural gas that burned cleaner than other fossil fuels, produced less CO_2, and was better for the environment? Sounds too good to be true, right? Well, that's exactly how the proponents of the shale gas industry are promoting their product.

Recently, there has been an explosion in the exploration and development of natural gas that is "trapped" in shale rock formations (shale gas). The gas is released through a process known as fracturing or "fracking." Fracking involves pumping vast amounts of water and sand (as well as industrial chemicals) into wells under high pressure. This pressurized mixture cracks or "fractures" the shale rock, allowing the natural gas to be collected, processed and then sold on the open market. In the United States, reserves are believed to be so enormous that the country is now being called the new Saudi Arabia.

Industry experts talk optimistically of energy independence from unstable oil producing countries, a boom to economies, and the creation of good paying jobs. In the US, shale gas now makes up 25 percent of the natural gas produced (it was only 1 percent in 2000), with an increase in supply resulting in dramatically falling prices. In 2012 the price of gas in the US was just a quarter of that in Europe (and only a sixth of that in Asia).

But people are starting to question the benefits (as well as supposed "green credentials") of shale gas. For one thing, several European countries have banned its exploration and commercial development, mostly out of concern that the chemicals used in fracking (some of which are toxic and carcinogenic) could contaminate aquifers. Some researchers now believe that fracking releases huge amounts of methane, a known greenhouse gas. There have also been reports of fracking operations resulting in earthquakes in nearby towns.

Many industry experts believe that all of these concerns can be addressed with better technology and sensible regulations. But it remains to be seen if shale gas can deliver on its many promises.

Sources: Steve Hargreaves, CNNMoney.com, October 28th 2010 "Can shale gas be produced safely?"; Mark Fischetti, Scientific American, January 20 2012 "Fracking Would Emit Large Quantities of Greenhouse Gases"; T.W., The Economist, August 19 2013 "How safe is fracking?"; The Economist, March 11 2010 "Natural gas"; George Monbiot, The Guardian, August 31 2011 "The UK's lack of fracking regulation is insane."

concept of stakeholder management, an ethically sound organization can also strengthen its bonds among its suppliers, customers, and governmental agencies.

Integrity-Based versus Compliance-Based Approaches to Organizational Ethics

LO11.6

The difference between integrity-based and compliance-based approaches to organizational ethics.

Before discussing the key elements of an ethical organization, one must understand the links between organizational integrity and the personal integrity of an organization's members.[64] There cannot be high-integrity organizations without high-integrity individuals. However, individual integrity is rarely self-sustaining. Even good people can lose their bearings when faced with pressures, temptations, and heightened performance expectations in the absence of organizational support systems and ethical boundaries. Organizational integrity rests on a concept of purpose, responsibility, and ideals for an organization as a whole. An important responsibility of leadership is to create this ethical framework and develop the organizational capabilities to make it operational.[65]

Lynn Paine, an ethics scholar at Harvard, identifies two approaches: the compliance-based approach and the integrity-based approach. (See Exhibit 11.5 for a comparison of compliance-based and integrity-based strategies.) Faced with the prospect of litigation, several organizations reactively implement **compliance-based ethics programs.** Such programs are typically designed by a corporate counsel with the goal of preventing, detecting, and punishing legal violations. But being ethical is much more than being legal, and an integrity-based approach addresses the issue of ethics in a more comprehensive manner.

compliance-based ethics programs programs for building ethical organizations that have the goal of preventing, detecting, and punishing legal violations.

Integrity-based ethics programs combine a concern for law with an emphasis on managerial responsibility for ethical behavior. It is broader, deeper, and more demanding

EXHIBIT 11.5 Approaches to Ethics Management

Characteristics	Compliance-Based Approach	Integrity-Based Approach
Ethos	Conformity with externally imposed standards	Self-governance according to chosen standards
Objective	Prevent criminal misconduct	Enable responsible conduct
Leadership	Lawyer-driven	Management-driven with aid of lawyers, HR, and others
Methods	Education, reduced discretion, auditing and controls, penalties	Education, leadership, accountability, organizational systems and decision processes, auditing and controls, penalties
Behavioral Assumptions	Autonomous beings guided by material self-interest	Social beings guided by material self-interest, values, ideals, peers

Source: Reprinted by permission of *Harvard Business Review*. Exhibit from "Managing Organizational Integrity," by L. S. Paine. Copyright © 1994 by the Harvard Business School Publishing Corporation; all rights reserved.

than a legal compliance initiative. It is broader in that it seeks to enable responsible conduct. It is deeper in that it cuts to the ethos and operating systems of an organization and its members, their core guiding values, thoughts, and actions. It is more demanding because it requires an active effort to define the responsibilities that constitute an organization's ethical compass. Most importantly, organizational ethics is seen as the responsibility of management.

A corporate counsel may play a role in designing and implementing integrity strategies, but it is managers at all levels and across all functions that are involved in the process. Once integrated into the day-to-day operations, such strategies can prevent damaging ethical lapses, while tapping into powerful human impulses for moral thought and action. Ethics becomes the governing ethos of an organization and not burdensome constraints. Here is an example of an organization that goes beyond mere compliance to laws in building an ethical organization:

> In teaching ethics to its employees, Texas Instruments, the $13 billion chip and electronics manufacturer, asks them to run an issue through the following steps: Is it legal? Is it consistent with the company's stated values? Will the employee feel bad doing it? What will the public think if the action is reported in the press? Does the employee think it is wrong? If the employees are not sure of the ethicality of the issue, they are encouraged to ask someone until they are clear about it. In the process, employees can approach high-level personnel and even the company's lawyers. At TI, the question of ethics goes much beyond merely being legal. It is no surprise, that this company is a benchmark for corporate ethics and has been a recipient of three ethics awards: the David C. Lincoln Award for Ethics and Excellence in Business, American Business Ethics Award, and Bentley College Center for Business Ethics Award.[66]

integrity-based ethics programs programs for building ethical organizations that combine a concern for law with an emphasis on managerial responsibility for ethical behavior, including (1) enabling ethical conduct; (2) examining the organization's and members' core guiding values, thoughts, and actions; and (3) defining the responsibilities and aspirations that constitute an organization's ethical compass.

Compliance-based approaches are externally motivated—that is, based on the fear of punishment for doing something unlawful. On the other hand, integrity-based approaches are driven by a personal and organizational commitment to ethical behavior.

A firm must have several key elements to become a highly ethical organization:

- Role models.
- Corporate credos and codes of conduct.
- Reward and evaluation systems.
- Policies and procedures.

These elements are highly interrelated. Reward structures and policies will be useless if leaders are not sound role models. That is, leaders who implicitly say, "Do as I say, not as

LO11.7

Several key elements that organizations must have to become an ethical organization.

I do," will quickly have their credibility eroded and such actions will sabotage other elements that are essential to building an ethical organization.

Role Models

For good or for bad, leaders are role models in their organizations. Perhaps few executives can share an experience that better illustrates this than Linda Hudson, president of General Dynamics.[67] Right after she was promoted to become her firm's first female president, she went to Nordstrom and bought some new suits to wear to work. A lady at the store showed her how to tie a scarf in a very unique way. The day after she wore it to work, guess what: no fewer than a dozen women in the organization were wearing scarves tied exactly the same way! She reflects:

> "And that's when I realized that life was never going to be the way it had been before, that people were watching everything I did. And it wasn't just going to be about how I dressed. It was about my behavior, the example I set, the tone I set, the way I carried myself, and how confident I was—all those kinds of things. . . . As the leader, people are looking at you in a way you could not have imagined in other roles."

Clearly, leaders must "walk the talk"; they must be consistent in their words and deeds. The values as well as the character of leaders become transparent to an organization's employees through their behaviors. When leaders do not believe in the ethical standards that they are trying to inspire, they will not be effective as good role models. Being an effective leader often includes taking responsibility for ethical lapses within the organization—even though the executives themselves are not directly involved. Consider the perspective of Dennis Bakke, CEO of AES, the $18 billion global electricity company based in Arlington, Virginia.

> There was a major breach (in 1992) of the AES values. Nine members of the water treatment team in Oklahoma lied to the EPA about water quality at the plant. There was no environmental damage, but they lied about the test results. A new, young chemist at the plant discovered it, told a team leader, and we then were notified. Now, you could argue that the people who lied were responsible and were accountable, but the senior management team also took responsibility by taking pay cuts. My reduction was about 30 percent.[68]

Such action enhances the loyalty and commitment of employees throughout the organization. Many would believe that it would have been much easier (and personally less expensive!) for Bakke and his management team to merely take strong punitive action against the nine individuals who were acting contrary to the behavior expected in AES's ethical culture. However, by sharing responsibility for the misdeeds, the top executives—through their highly visible action—made it clear that responsibility and penalties for ethical lapses go well beyond the "guilty" parties. Such courageous behavior by leaders helps to strengthen an organization's ethical environment.

Corporate Credos and Codes of Conduct

corporate credo
a statement of the beliefs typically held by managers in a corporation.

Corporate credos and codes of conduct are mechanisms that provide statements of norms and beliefs as well as guidelines for decision making. They provide employees with a clear understanding of the organization's policies and ethical position. Such guidelines also provide the basis for employees to refuse to commit unethical acts and help to make them aware of issues before they are faced with the situation. For such codes to be truly effective, organization members must be aware of them and what behavioral guidelines they contain.[69] Strategy Spotlight 11.9 examines how furniture retailer IKEA maintains a strong corporate identity and manages its stakeholder alignment through a program called "The IKEA Way."

THE IKEA WAY OR THE IWAY

By Tom McNamara and Irena Descubes

IKEA is mainly known for its Scandinavian designed modern furniture and accessories, and its desire "To create a better everyday life for the many people." The company is also known for making you go find the item that you want yourself, drag it to the checkout counter, get it home, and then put it together with wordless directions.

What is less known is how IKEA excels at maintaining a strong corporate identity and culture. It has been able to achieve what brand consultant Denise Lee Yohn calls "horizontal alignment." This means that all of the partners in IKEA's entire stakeholder ecosystem, both internal (executives and employees) and external (suppliers, distributors, agencies, etc.), share a common understanding of the company's brand and business.

One way IKEA has achieved this stakeholder alignment is through a program called "The IKEA Way" or IWAY. It is a list of standards, principles, international laws, and accepted protocols that people must respect and adhere to if they wish to work for, or work with, IKEA. The goal is to ensure that IKEA "shall have an overall positive impact on people and the environment."

Social and environmental issues are given a prominent place in IWAY, particularly people's working conditions. IKEA argues that it can "do good business" while at the same time "being a good business." It believes that this is a key component that defines who it is as a company and will be a key determinant of its future growth.

Sources: Denise Lee Yohn, Business Insider, June 10 2013 "Change happens"; IKEA website: ikea.com.

Large corporations are not the only ones to develop and use codes of conduct. Consider the example of Wetherill Associates (WAI), a small, privately held supplier of electrical parts to the automotive market.

> Rather than a conventional code of conduct, WAI has a Quality Assurance Manual—a combination of philosophy text, conduct guide, technical manual, and company profile—that describes the company's commitment to honesty, ethical action, and integrity. WAI doesn't have a corporate ethics officer, because the company's corporate ethics officer is Marie Bothe, WAI's CEO. She sees her main function as keeping the 350-employee company on the path of ethical behavior and looking for opportunities to help the community. She delegates the "technical" aspects of the business—marketing, finance, personnel, and operations—to other members of the organization.[70]

Reward and Evaluation Systems

It is entirely possible for a highly ethical leader to preside over an organization that commits several unethical acts. How? A flaw in the organization's reward structure may inadvertently cause individuals to act in an inappropriate manner if rewards are seen as being distributed on the basis of outcomes rather than the means by which goals and objectives are achieved.[71]

Generally speaking, unethical (or illegal) behaviors are also more likely to take place when competition is intense. Some have called this the "dark side of competition." Consider a couple of examples:[72]

- Competition among educational institutions for the best student is becoming stiffer. A senior admissions officer at Claremont McKenna College resigned after admitting to inflating SAT scores of the incoming classes for six years. The motive, of course, was to boost the school's rankings in the *U.S. News and World Report's* annual listing of top colleges and universities in the United States. Carmen Nobel, who reported the incident in *Working Knowledge* (a Harvard Business School publication), suggested that the scandal "questions the value of competitive rankings."

- A study of 11,000 New York vehicle emission test facilities found that companies with a greater number of local competitors passed cars with considerably high emission rates, and lost customers when they failed to pass the tests. The authors of the study concluded, "In contexts when pricing is restricted, firms use illicit quality as a business strategy."

Many companies have developed reward and evaluation systems that evaluate whether a manager is acting in an ethical manner. For example, Raytheon, a $24 billion defense contractor, incorporates the following items in its "Leadership Assessment Instrument":[73]

- Maintains unequivocal commitment to honesty, truth, and ethics in every facet of behavior.
- Conforms with the letter and intent of company policies while working to affect any necessary policy changes.
- Actions are consistent with words; follows through on commitments; readily admits mistakes.
- Is trusted and inspires others to be trusted.

As noted by Dan Burnham, Raytheon's former CEO: "What do we look for in a leadership candidate with respect to integrity? What we're really looking for are people who have developed an inner gyroscope of ethical principles. We look for people for whom ethical thinking is part of what they do—no different from 'strategic thinking' or 'tactical thinking.' "

Policies and Procedures

Many situations that a firm faces have regular, identifiable patterns. Leaders tend to handle such routine by establishing a policy or procedure to be followed that can be applied uniformly to each occurrence. Such guidelines can be useful in specifying the proper relationships with a firm's customers and suppliers. For example, Levi Strauss has developed stringent global sourcing guidelines and Chemical Bank (part of J. P. Morgan Chase Bank) has a policy of forbidding any review that would determine if suppliers are Chemical customers when the bank awards contracts.

Carefully developed policies and procedures guide behavior so that all employees will be encouraged to behave in an ethical manner. However, they must be reinforced with effective communication, enforcement, and monitoring, as well as sound corporate governance practices. In addition, the Sarbanes-Oxley Act of 2002 provides considerable legal protection to employees of publicly traded companies who report unethical or illegal practices. Provisions in the Act coauthored by Senator Grassley include:[74]

- Make it unlawful to "discharge, demote, suspend, threaten, harass, or in any manner discriminate against 'a whistleblower.' "
- Establish criminal penalties of up to 10 years in jail for executives who retaliate against whistleblowers.
- Require board audit committees to establish procedures for hearing whistleblower complaints.
- Allow the Secretary of Labor to order a company to rehire a terminated whistleblower with no court hearings whatsoever.
- Give a whistleblower the right to a jury trial, bypassing months or years of cumbersome administrative hearings.

Ethically made clothing. You wear it but how do you really know it's been made ethically?

By Tom McNamara and Irena Descubes

The global fashion industry is a $1 trillion business. But "ethically made" clothing, i.e. clothing made in factories that ensure safe working conditions and that respect workers' rights, makes up less than 1 percent of this market. Why so small?

One reason, to put it bluntly, is that some retailers just don't care. They don't see the demand for ethically made clothing as being sufficiently large to justify a strategic initiative to meet it. Furthermore, thanks to longer and more complex supply chains, it can be extremely difficult to verify that every single link in that chain is operating ethically. Many major clothing retailers use suppliers who then turn around and contract the work out to other companies. This can mean that the retailers themselves don't always know the origin of the clothes they are selling. It's even more difficult to figure out if the clothes you are buying were made in safe factories if you're shopping at retailers that don't specifically market their clothes as ethically made.

But in light of recent tragedies that have occurred in factories (fires, building collapses, suicides, etc.) located in emerging markets and the developing world, this could all change. As consumers become more socially aware they are starting to ask, "Exactly how was the item I am buying made and was it made ethically?"

When it comes to clothing, that question is a lot harder to answer than you might think. Walter Loeb, a New York-based retail consultant, says he has visited many clothing factories and that it can be very difficult to regularly monitor whether or not they are safe and operating in an ethical manner.

One country that is notorious for its poor working conditions is Bangladesh, where a factory collapse in April 2013 killed more than 1,000 people. Safety standards are rarely enforced by the government and deadly worker accidents are a common event.

Unfortunately (or fortunately if you are a worker in one of these factories) the Bangladesh tragedy shined an unwelcomed spotlight on H&M, Walmart, Benetton, GAP, and Zara, to name just a few. These companies pride themselves as being responsible corporate citizens, and yet they all sourced clothing from that country.

Discussion Questions

1. What can companies do to ensure that their clothing suppliers are operating ethically?
2. Do you think the market for ethically made clothing will become an important one in the future?

Sources: Pamela Engel, Business Insider, May 13 2013 "Here Are Some Of The Biggest Brands That Make Clothes In Bangladesh"; Anne d'Innocenzio, Associated Press, from Business Insider, May 1 2013 "It's Incredibly Difficult To Prove That Clothing Is 'Ethically Made.'"

Reflecting on Career Implications . . .

▣ **Strategic Leadership:** The chapter identifies three interdependent activities that are central to strategic leadership; namely, setting direction, designing the organization, and nurturing a culture dedicated to excellence and ethical behavior. Both during your life as a student and in organizations you work, you have often assumed leadership positions. To what extent have you consciously and successfully engaged in each of these activities? Observe the leaders in your organizations and assess to what extent you can learn from them the qualities of strategic leadership that you can use to advance your own careers.

▣ **Power:** Identify the sources of power used by your superior at work. How do his or her primary source of power and the way he/she uses it affect your own creativity, morale, and willingness to stay with the organization? In addition, identify approaches you will use to enhance your power as

(continued)

you move up your career ladder. Explain why you chose these approaches.

◻ **Emotional Intelligence:** The chapter identifies the five components of Emotional Intelligence (self-awareness, self-regulation, motivation, empathy, and social skills). How do you rate yourself on each of these components? What steps can you take to improve your Emotional Intelligence and achieve greater career success?

◻ **Creating an Ethical Organization:** Identify an ethical dilemma that you personally faced in the course of your work. How did you respond to it? Was your response compliance-based, integrity-based, or even unethical? If your behavior was compliance-based, speculate on how it would have been different if it were integrity-based. What have you learned from your experience that would make you a more ethical leader in the future?

summary

Strategic leadership is vital in ensuring that strategies are formulated and implemented in an effective manner. Leaders must play a central role in performing three critical and interdependent activities: setting the direction, designing the organization, and nurturing a culture committed to excellence and ethical behavior. If leaders ignore or are ineffective at performing any one of the three, the organization will not be very successful. We also identified two elements of leadership that contribute to success—overcoming barriers to change and the effective use of power.

For leaders to effectively fulfill their activities, emotional intelligence (EI) is very important. Five elements that contribute to EI are self-awareness, self-regulation, motivation, empathy, and social skill. The first three elements pertain to self-management skills, whereas the last two are associated with a person's ability to manage relationships with others. We also addressed some of the potential drawbacks from the ineffective use of EI. These include the dysfunctional use of power as well as a tendency to become overly empathetic, which may result in unreasonably lowered performance expectations.

Leaders need to develop competency companions and play a central role in creating a learning organization. Gone are the days when the top-level managers "think" and everyone else in the organization "does." With rapidly changing, unpredictable, and complex competitive environments, leaders must engage everyone in the ideas and energies of people throughout the organization. Great ideas can come from anywhere in the organization—from the executive suite to the factory floor. The five elements that we discussed as central to a learning organization are inspiring and motivating people with a mission or purpose, empowering people at all levels throughout the organization, accumulating and sharing internal knowledge, gathering external information, and challenging the status quo to stimulate creativity.

In the final section of the chapter, we addressed a leader's central role in instilling ethical behavior in the organization. We discussed the enormous costs that firms face when ethical crises arise—costs in terms of financial and reputational loss as well as the erosion of human capital and relationships with suppliers, customers, society at large, and governmental agencies. And, as we would expect, the benefits of having a strong ethical organization are also numerous. We contrasted compliance-based and integrity-based approaches to organizational ethics. Compliance-based approaches are largely externally motivated; that is, they are motivated by the fear of punishment for doing something that is unlawful. Integrity-based approaches, on the other hand, are driven by a personal and organizational commitment to ethical behavior. We also addressed the four key elements of an ethical organization: role models, corporate credos and codes of conduct, reward and evaluation systems, and policies and procedures.

SUMMARY REVIEW QUESTIONS

1. Three key activities—setting a direction, designing the organization, and nurturing a culture and ethics—are all part of what effective leaders do on a regular basis. Explain how these three activities are interrelated.

2. Define emotional intelligence (EI). What are the key elements of EI? Why is EI so important to successful strategic leadership? Address potential "downsides."

3. The knowledge a firm possesses can be a source of competitive advantage. Describe ways that a firm can continuously learn to maintain its competitive position.

4. How can the five central elements of "learning organizations" be incorporated into global companies?

5. What are the benefits to firms and their shareholders of conducting business in an ethical manner?

6. Firms that fail to behave in an ethical manner can incur high costs. What are these costs and what is their source?

7. What are the most important differences between an "integrity organization" and a "compliance organization" in a firm's approach to organizational ethics?

8. What are some of the important mechanisms for promoting ethics in a firm?

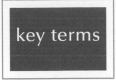

key terms

leadership 346
setting a direction 347
designing the organization 348

excellent and ethical
    organizational culture 349
barriers to change 350
vested interest in the status
    quo 350
systemic barriers 351
behavioral barriers 351
political barriers 351
personal time constraints 351

power 351
organizational bases of
    power 351
personal bases of power 353
emotional intelligence (EI) 354
learning organizations 360
benchmarking 362
competitive
    benchmarking 363

functional benchmarking 363
ethics 364
organizational ethics 365
ethical orientation 365
compliance-based ethics
    programs 366
integrity-based ethics
    programs 367
corporate credo 368

experiential exercise

Select two well-known business leaders—one you admire and one you do not. Evaluate each of them on the five characteristics of emotional intelligence.

Emotional Intelligence Characteristics	Admired Leader	Leader Not Admired
Self-awareness		
Self-regulation		
Motivation		
Empathy		
Social skills		

application questions & exercises

1. Identify two CEOs whose leadership you admire. What is it about their skills, attributes, and effective use of power that causes you to admire them?

2. Founders have an important role in developing their organization's culture and values. At times, their influence persists for many years. Identify and describe two organizations in which the cultures and values established by the founder(s) continue to flourish. You may find research on the Internet helpful in answering these questions.

3. Some leaders place a great emphasis on developing superior human capital. In what ways does this help a firm to develop and sustain competitive advantages?

4. In this chapter we discussed the five elements of a "learning organization." Select a firm with which you are familiar and discuss whether or not it epitomizes some (or all) of these elements.

ethics questions

1. Sometimes organizations must go outside the firm to hire talent, thus bypassing employees already working for the firm. Are there conditions under which this might raise ethical considerations?

2. Ethical crises can occur in virtually any organization. Describe some of the systems, procedures, and processes that can help to prevent such crises.

references

1. Kimes, M. 2012. Bad to the bone. *Forbes,* October 12:140-154; Loftus, P. 2011. 4 former Synthes executives sentenced to prison time for unapproved bone cement study. *www.orthostreams.com*, December 13: np; Lotus, P. 2011. Corporate News: Former Synthes officers receive prison sentences. *Wall Street Journal,* November 22: B4; and Synthes Annual Report, 2011.

2. Charan, R. & Colvin, G. 1999. Why CEOs fail. *Fortune,* June 21: 68–78.

3. Yukl, G. 2008. How leaders influence organizational effectiveness. *Leadership Quarterly,* 19(6): 708–722.

4. These three activities and our discussion draw from Kotter, J. P. 1990. What leaders really do. *Harvard Business Review,* 68(3): 103–111; Pearson, A. E. 1990. Six basics for general managers. *Harvard Business Review,* 67(4): 94–101; and Covey, S. R. 1996. Three roles of the leader in the new paradigm. In

The leader of the future: 149–160. Hesselbein, F., Goldsmith, M., & Beckhard, R. (Eds.). San Francisco: Jossey-Bass. Some of the discussion of each of the three leadership activity concepts draws on Dess, G. G. & Miller, A. 1993. *Strategic management:* 320–325. New York: McGraw-Hill.

5. García-Morales, V. J., Lloréns-Montes, F. J., & Verdú-Jover, A. J. 2008. The effects of transformational leadership on organizational

performance through knowledge and innovation. *British Journal of Management,* 19(4): 299–319.

6. Day, C., Jr. & LaBarre, P. 1994. GE: Just your average everyday $60 billion family grocery store. *Industry Week,* May 2: 13–18.

7. Martin, R. 2010. The execution trap. *Harvard Business Review,* 88(7/8): 64–71.

8. Collins, J. 1997. What comes next? *Inc. Magazine.* October: 34–45.

9. Hsieh, T. 2010. Zappos's CEO on going to extremes for customers. *Harvard Business Review,* 88(7/8): 41–44.

10. Andersen, M. M., Froholdt, M. & Poulfelt, F. 2010. *Return on strategy.* New York: Routledge; and 2009 Huawei Annual Report.

11. Anonymous. 2006. Looking out for number one. *BusinessWeek,* October 30: 66.

12. Schaffer, R. H. 2010. Mistakes leaders keep making. *Harvard Business Review,* 88(9): 86–91.

13. For insightful perspectives on escalation, refer to Brockner, J. 1992. The escalation of commitment to a failing course of action. *Academy of Management Review,* 17(1): 39–61; and Staw, B. M. 1976. Knee-deep in the big muddy: A study of commitment to a chosen course of action. *Organizational Behavior and Human Decision Processes,* 16: 27–44. The discussion of systemic, behavioral, and political barriers draws on Lorange, P. & Murphy, D. 1984. Considerations in implementing strategic control. *Journal of Business Strategy,* 5: 27–35. In a similar vein, Noel M. Tichy has addressed three types of resistance to change in the context of General Electric: technical resistance, political resistance, and cultural resistance. See Tichy, N. M. 1993. Revolutionalize your company. *Fortune,* December 13: 114–118. Examples draw from O'Reilly, B. 1997. The secrets of America's most admired corporations: New ideas and new products. *Fortune,* March 3: 60–64.

14. This section draws on Champoux, J. E. 2000. *Organizational behavior: Essential tenets for a new millennium.* London: South-Western; and The mature use of power in organizations. 2003. *RHR International-Executive Insights,* May 29, *12.19.168.197/ execinsights/8-3.htm.*

15. An insightful perspective on the role of power and politics in organizations is provided in Ciampa, K. 2005. Almost ready: How leaders move up. *Harvard Business Review,* 83(1): 46–53.

16. Pfeffer, J. 2010. Power play. *Harvard Business Review,* 88(7/8): 84–92.

17. Westphal, J. D., & Graebner, M. E. 2010. A matter of appearances: How corporate leaders manage the impressions of financial analysts about the conduct of their boards. *Academy of Management Journal,* 53(4): 15–44.

18. A discussion of the importance of persuasion in bringing about change can be found in Garvin, D. A. & Roberto, M. A. 2005. Change through persuasion. *Harvard Business Review,* 83(4): 104–113.

19. Lorsch, J. W. & Tierney, T. J. 2002. *Aligning the stars: How to succeed when professionals drive results.* Boston: Harvard Business School Press.

20. Some consider EI to be a "trait," that is, an attribute that is stable over time. However, many authors, including Daniel Goleman, have argued that it can be developed through motivation, extended practice, and feedback. For example, in D. Goleman, 1998, What makes a leader? *Harvard Business Review,* 76(5): 97, Goleman addresses this issue in a sidebar: "Can emotional intelligence be learned?"

21. For a review of this literature, see Daft, R. 1999. *Leadership: Theory and practice.* Fort Worth, TX: Dryden Press.

22. This section draws on Luthans, F. 2002. Positive organizational behavior: Developing and managing psychological strengths. *Academy of Management Executive,* 16(1): 57–72; and Goleman, D. 1998. What makes a leader? *Harvard Business Review,* 76(6): 92–105.

23. EI has its roots in the concept of "social intelligence" that was first identified by E. L. Thorndike in 1920 (Intelligence and its uses. *Harper's Magazine,* 140: 227–235). Psychologists have been uncovering other intelligences for some time now and have grouped them into such clusters as abstract intelligence (the ability to understand and manipulate verbal and mathematical symbols), concrete intelligence (the ability to understand and manipulate objects), and social intelligence (the ability to understand and relate to people). See Ruisel, I. 1992. Social intelligence: Conception and methodological problems. *Studia Psychologica,* 34(4–5): 281–296.

Refer to *trochim.human.cornell.edu/ gallery.*

24. See, for example, Luthans, op. cit.; Mayer, J. D., Salvoney, P., & Caruso, D. 2000. Models of emotional intelligence. In Sternberg, R. J. (Ed.). *Handbook of intelligence.* Cambridge, UK: Cambridge University Press; and Cameron, K. 1999. Developing emotional intelligence at the Weatherhead School of Management. *Strategy: The Magazine of the Weatherhead School of Management,* Winter: 2–3.

25. Tate, B. 2008. A longitudinal study of the relationships among self-monitoring, authentic leadership, and perceptions of leadership. *Journal of Leadership & Organizational Studies,* 15(1): 16–29.

26. Moss, S. A., Dowling, N., & Callanan, J. 2009. Towards an integrated model of leadership and self-regulation. *Leadership Quarterly,* 20(2): 162–176.

27. An insightful perspective on leadership, which involves discovering, developing and celebrating what is unique about each individual, is found in Buckingham, M. 2005. What great managers do. *Harvard Business Review,* 83(3): 70–79.

28. Bryant, A. 2011. *The corner office.* New York: St. Martin's Griffin, 197.

29. This section draws upon Klemp. G. 2005. *Emotional intelligence and leadership: What really matters.* Cambria Consulting, Inc., *www. cambriaconsulting.com.*

30. Heifetz, R. 2004. Question authority. *Harvard Business Review,* 82(1): 37.

31. Our discussion of competency companions draws on: Zenger, J. H., Folkman, J. R., & Edinger, S. K. 2011. Making yourself indispensable. *Harvard Business Review,* 89(10): 84–92.

32. Handy, C. 1995. Trust and the virtual organization. *Harvard Business Review,* 73(3): 40–50.

33. This section draws upon Dess, G. G. & Picken, J. C. 1999. *Beyond productivity.* New York: AMACOM. The elements of the learning organization in this section are consistent with the work of Dorothy Leonard-Barton. See, for example, Leonard-Barton, D. 1992. The factory as a learning laboratory. *Sloan Management Review,* 11: 23–38.

34. Senge, P. M. 1990. The leader's new work: Building learning organizations. *Sloan Management Review,* 32(1): 7–23.

35. Bernoff, J. & Schandler, T. 2010. Empowered. *Harvard Business Review,* 88(7/8): 94–101.

36. Hammer, M. & Stanton, S. A. 1997. The power of reflection. *Fortune,* November 24: 291–296.

37. Hannah, S. T. & Lester, P. B. 2009. A multilevel approach to building and leading learning organizations. *Leadership Quarterly,* 20(1): 34–48.

38. For some guidance on how to effectively bring about change in organizations, refer to Wall, S. J. 2005. The protean organization: Learning to love change. *Organizational Dynamics,* 34(1): 37–46.

39. Covey, S. R. 1989. *The seven habits of highly effective people: Powerful lessons in personal change.* New York: Simon & Schuster.

40. Kouzes, J. M. & Posner, B. Z. 2009. To lead, create a shared vision. *Harvard Business Review,* 87(1): 20–21.

41. Kouzes and Posner, op. cit.

42. Melrose, K. 1995. *Making the grass greener on your side: A CEO's journey to leading by servicing.* San Francisco: Barrett-Koehler.

43. Tekleab, A. G., Sims Jr., H. P., Yun, S., Tesluk, P. E., & Cox, J. 2008. Are we on the same page? Effects of self-awareness of empowering and transformational leadership. *Journal of Leadership & Organizational Studies,* 14(3): 185–201.

44. Helgesen, S. 1996. Leading from the grass roots. In *Leader of the future:* 19–24 Hesselbein et al.

45. Bowen, D. E. & Lawler, E. E., III. 1995. Empowering service employees. *Sloan Management Review,* 37: 73–84.

46. Easterby-Smith, M. & Prieto, I. M. 2008. Dynamic capabilities and knowledge management: An integrative role for learning? *British Journal of Management,* 19(3): 235–249.

47. Schafer, S. 1997. Battling a labor shortage? It's all in your imagination. *Inc.,* August: 24.

48. Meyer, P. 1998. So you want the president's job . . . *Business Horizons,* January–February: 2–8.

49. Imperato, G. 1998. Competitive intelligence: Get smart! *Fast Company,* May: 268–279.

50. Novicki, C. 1998. The best brains in business. *Fast Company,* April: 125.

51. The introductory discussion of benchmarking draws on Miller, A. 1998. *Strategic management:* 142–143. New York: McGraw-Hill.

52. Port, O. & Smith, G. 1992. Beg, borrow—and benchmark. *BusinessWeek,* November 30: 74–75.

53. Main, J. 1992. How to steal the best ideas around. *Fortune,* October 19: 102–106.

54. Taylor, J. T. 1997. What happens after what comes next? *Fast Company,* December–January: 84–85.

55. Sheff, D. 1996. Levi's changes everything. *Fast Company,* June–July: 65–74.

56. Isaacson, W. 1997. In search of the real Bill Gates. *Time,* January 13: 44–57.

57. Holt, J. W. 1996. *Celebrate your mistakes.* New York: McGraw-Hill.

58. McGregor, J. 2006. How failure breeds success. *Bloomberg Businessweek,* July 10: 42–52.

59. Bryant, A. 2011. *The Corner Office.* New York: St. Martin's Griffin, 34.

60. This opening discussion draws upon Conley, J. H. 2000. Ethics in business. In Helms, M. M. (Ed.). *Encyclopedia of management* (4th ed.): 281–285; Farmington Hills, MI: Gale Group; Paine, L. S. 1994. Managing for organizational integrity. *Harvard Business Review,* 72(2): 106–117; and Carlson, D. S. & Perrewe, P. L. 1995. Institutionalization of organizational ethics through transformational leadership. *Journal of Business Ethics,* 14: 829–838.

61. Pinto, J., Leana, C. R., & Pil, F. K. 2008. Corrupt organizations or organizations of corrupt individuals? Two types of organization-level corruption. *Academy of Management Review,* 33(3): 685–709.

62. Soule, E. 2002. Managerial moral strategies—in search of a few good principles. *Academy of Management Review,* 27(1): 114–124.

63. Carlson & Perrewe, op. cit.

64. This discussion is based upon Paine. Managing for organizational integrity; Paine, L. S. 1997. *Cases in leadership, ethics, and organizational integrity: A Strategic approach.* Burr Ridge, IL: Irwin; and Fontrodona, J. 2002. Business ethics across the Atlantic. Business Ethics Direct, *www.ethicsa.org/BED_art_ fontrodone.html.*

65. For more on operationalizing capabilities to sustain an ethical framework, see Largay III, J. A. & Zhang, R. 2008. Do CEOs worry about being fired when making investment decisions. *Academy of Management Perspectives,* 22(1): 60–61.

66. See *www.ti.com/corp/docs/ company/citizen/ethics/benchmark. shtml;* and *www.ti.com/corp/docs/ company/citizen/ethics/quicktest. shtml.*

67. Bryant, A. 2011. *The corner office.* New York: St. Martin's Griffin, 91.

68. Wetlaufer, S. 1999. Organizing for empowerment: An interview with AES's Roger Sant and Dennis Bakke. *Harvard Business Review,* 77(1): 110–126.

69. For an insightful, academic perspective on the impact of ethics codes on executive decision making, refer to Stevens, J. M., Steensma, H. K., Harrison, D. A., & Cochran, P. S. 2005. Symbolic or substantive document? The influence of ethics code on financial executives' decisions. *Strategic Management Journal,* 26(2): 181–195.

70. Paine. Managing for organizational integrity.

71. For a recent study on the effects of goal setting on unethical behavior, read Schweitzer, M. E., Ordonez, L., & Douma, B. 2004. Goal setting as a motivator of unethical behavior. *Academy of Management Journal,* 47(3): 422–432.

72. Williams, R. 2012. How competition can encourage unethical business practices. *business.financialpost. com,* July 31: np.

73. Fulmer, R. M. 2004. The challenge of ethical leadership. *Organizational Dynamics,* 33 (3): 307–317.

74. *www.sarbanes-oxley.com.*

chapter 12

Managing Innovation and Fostering Corporate Entrepreneurship

After reading this chapter, you should have a good understanding of the following learning objectives:

LO12.1 The importance of implementing strategies and practices that foster innovation.

LO12.2 The challenges and pitfalls of managing corporate innovation processes.

LO12.3 How corporations use new venture teams, business incubators, and product champions to create an internal environment and culture that promote entrepreneurial development.

LO12.4 How corporate entrepreneurship achieves both financial goals and strategic goals.

LO12.5 The benefits and potential drawbacks of real options analysis in making resource deployment decisions in corporate entrepreneurship contexts.

LO12.6 How an entrepreneurial orientation can enhance a firm's efforts to develop promising corporate venture initiatives.

Learning from Mistakes

If you ask a group of students to name a successful company, Google is likely to be one of the first firms mentioned. It dominates online search and advertising, has developed a successful browser, and developed the operating system that powers 75 percent of the smartphones sold in 2012.[1] Its success is evident in its stock price, which rose from about $350 at the beginning of 2009 to near $800 a share in early 2013. But that doesn't mean that Google has been successful at all it has tried. One of Google's most notable failures occurred when it tried to venture outside the online and wireless markets. In 2006, Google decided to expand its advertising business to radio advertising. After spending several hundred million dollars on their entrepreneurial effort in the radio advertising market, Google pulled the plug on this business in 2009.

Google saw great potential in applying its business model to the radio advertising industry. In the traditional radio advertising model, companies that wished to advertise their products and services contracted with an advertising agency to develop a set of radio spots (commercials). They then bought blocks of advertising time from radio stations.

Advertisers paid based on the number of listeners on each station. Google believed that they could develop a stronger model. Their design was to purchase large blocks of advertising time from stations. They would then sell the time in a competitive auction to companies who wished to advertise. Google believed they could sell ad time to advertisers at a higher rate if they could identify what ads on what stations had the greatest impact for advertisers. Thus, rather than charging based on audience size, Google would follow the model they used on the Web and charge based on ad effectiveness. To develop the competency to measure ad effectiveness, Google purchased dMarc, a company that developed technology to manage and measure radio ads, for $102 million.

Google's overall vision was even broader. They also planned to enter print and TV advertising. They could then provide a "dashboard" to marketing executives at firms that would provide information on the effectiveness of advertising on the Web, TV, print, and radio. Google would then sell them a range of advertising space among all four to maximize a firm's ad expenditures.

However, Google found that their attempt to innovate the radio market bumped up against two core challenges. First, the radio advertising model was based much more on relationships than online advertising was. Radio stations, advertising firms, and advertising agencies had long-standing relationships that limited Google's ability to break into the market. In fact, few radio stations were willing to sell advertising time to Google. Also, advertising agencies saw Google as a threat to their business model and were unwilling to buy time from Google. Second, Google found that their ability to measure the effectiveness of radio ads was limited. Unlike online markets, where they could measure if people clicked on ads, they found it difficult to measure whether listeners responded to ads. They tried ads that mentioned specific websites that listeners could go to, but they found few people accessed these sites. In the end, Google was able to sell radio time at only a fraction of what radio stations could get from working their traditional advertising deals. This led stations to abandon Google's radio business.

Google found that they had the initiative to innovate the radio market, but they didn't have the knowledge, experience, or social connections needed to win in this market.

Discussion Questions

1. Why didn't the lessons Google learned in the online advertising market apply to the radio market?
2. Radio is increasingly moving to satellite and streaming systems. Is this a new opportunity for Google, or should they steer clear of radio altogether?

LO12.1

The importance of implementing strategies and practices that foster innovation.

Managing change is one of the most important functions performed by strategic leaders. There are two major avenues through which companies can expand or improve their business—innovation and corporate entrepreneurship. These two activities go hand-in-hand because they both have similar aims. The first is strategic renewal. Innovations help an organization stay fresh and reinvent itself as conditions in the business environment change. This is why managing innovation is such an important strategic implementation issue. The second is the pursuit of venture opportunities. Innovative breakthroughs, as well as new product concepts, evolving technologies, and shifting demand, create opportunities for corporate venturing. In this chapter we will explore these topics—how change and innovation can stimulate strategic renewal and foster corporate entrepreneurship.

Managing Innovation

innovation
the use of new knowledge to transform organizational processes or create commercially viable products and services.

One of the most important sources of growth opportunities is innovation. **Innovation** involves using new knowledge to transform organizational processes or create commercially viable products and services. The sources of new knowledge may include the latest technology, the results of experiments, creative insights, or competitive information. However it comes about, innovation occurs when new combinations of ideas and information bring about positive change.

The emphasis on newness is a key point. For example, for a patent application to have any chance of success, one of the most important attributes it must possess is novelty. You can't patent an idea that has been copied. This is a central idea. In fact, the root of the word *innovation* is the Latin *novus,* which means new. Innovation involves introducing or changing to something new.[2]

Among the most important sources of new ideas is new technology. Technology creates new possibilities. Technology provides the raw material that firms use to make innovative products and services. But technology is not the only source of innovations. There can be innovations in human resources, firm infrastructure, marketing, service, or in many other value-adding areas that have little to do with anything "high-tech." Strategy Spotlight 12.1 highlights a simple but effective innovation by Dutch Boy paints. As the Dutch Boy example suggests, innovation can take many forms.

Types of Innovation

Although innovations are not always high-tech, changes in technology can be an important source of change and growth. When an innovation is based on a sweeping new technology, it often has a more far-reaching impact. Sometimes even a small innovation can add value and create competitive advantages. Innovation can and should occur throughout an organization—in every department and all aspects of the value chain.

product innovation
efforts to create product designs and applications of technology to develop new products for end users.

One distinction that is often used when discussing innovation is between process innovation and product innovation.[3] **Product innovation** refers to efforts to create product designs and applications of technology to develop new products for end users. Recall

DUTCH BOY'S SIMPLE PAINT CAN INNOVATION

Sometimes a simple change can make a vast improvement in a product. Any painter knows that getting the paint can open and pouring out paint without drips are two of the challenges of painting. Dutch Boy addressed this issue by developing a twist and pour paint container. The all-plastic container has a large, easy-to-use twist-off top and a handle on the side. The result was a consumer-friendly product that made painting easier and less messy. The handle also reduces the need for a paint stirring stick since you can mix the paint by shaking the container. Even though Dutch Boy's innovation was simple, nontechnological, and had nothing to do with the core product, the launch of the new packaging led to articles in 30 national consumer magazines and 60 major newspapers as well as a story on *Good Morning America*. The Twist and Pour can was also named "Product of the Year" by *USA Today, Bloomberg Businessweek,* and *Better Homes & Gardens.* It was also named a winner of the 2011 Good Housekeeping VIP Awards, which commemorate the most innovative products from the past decade.

Sources: 11 Innovative Products from the Past Decade. 2011 *The Good Housekeeping Research Institute;* and *www.fallscommunications.com.*

---

from Chapter 5 how generic strategies were typically different depending on the stage of the industry life cycle. Product innovations tend to be more common during the earlier stages of an industry's life cycle. Product innovations are also commonly associated with a differentiation strategy. Firms that differentiate by providing customers with new products or services that offer unique features or quality enhancements often engage in product innovation.

Process innovation, by contrast, is typically associated with improving the efficiency of an organizational process, especially manufacturing systems and operations. By drawing on new technologies and an organization's accumulated experience (Chapter 5), firms can often improve materials utilization, shorten cycle time, and increase quality. Process innovations are more likely to occur in the later stages of an industry's life cycle as companies seek ways to remain viable in markets where demand has flattened out and competition is more intense. As a result, process innovations are often associated with overall cost leader strategies, because the aim of many process improvements is to lower the costs of operations.

Another way to view the impact of an innovation is in terms of its degree of innovativeness, which falls somewhere on a continuum that extends from incremental to radical.[4]

> **process innovation**
> efforts to improve the efficiency of organizational processes, especially manufacturing systems and operations.

- *Radical innovations* produce fundamental changes by evoking major departures from existing practices. These breakthrough innovations usually occur because of technological change. They tend to be highly disruptive and can transform a company or even revolutionize a whole industry. They may lead to products or processes that can be patented, giving a firm a strong competitive advantage. Examples include electricity, the telephone, the transistor, desktop computers, fiber optics, artificial intelligence, and genetically engineered drugs.

> **radical innovation**
> an innovation that fundamentally changes existing practices.

- *Incremental innovations* enhance existing practices or make small improvements in products and processes. They may represent evolutionary applications within existing paradigms of earlier, more radical innovations. Because they often sustain a company by extending or expanding its product line or manufacturing skills, incremental innovations can be a source of competitive advantage by providing new capabilities that minimize expenses or speed productivity. Examples include frozen food, sports drinks, steel-belted radial tires, electronic bookkeeping, shatterproof glass, and digital thermometers.

> **incremental innovation**
> an innovation that enhances existing practices or makes small improvements in products and processes.

Some innovations are highly radical; others are only slightly incremental. But most innovations fall somewhere between these two extremes (see Exhibit 12.1).

EXHIBIT 12.1 Continuum of Radical and Incremental Innovations

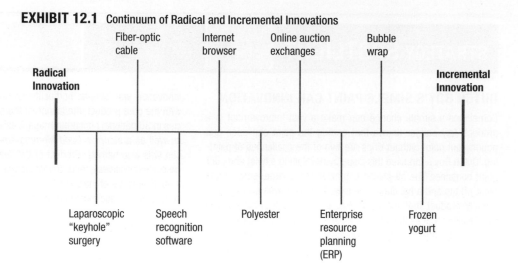

Harvard Business School Professor Clayton M. Christensen identified another useful approach to characterize types of innovations.[5] Christensen draws a distinction between sustaining and disruptive innovations. *Sustaining innovations* are those that extend sales in an existing market, usually by enabling new products or services to be sold at higher margins. Such innovations may include either incremental or radical innovations. For example, the Internet was a breakthrough technology that transformed retail selling. But rather than disrupting the activities of catalog companies such as Lands' End and L.L. Bean, the Internet energized their existing business by extending their reach and making their operations more efficient.

By contrast, *disruptive innovations* are those that overturn markets by providing an altogether new approach to meeting customer needs. The features of a disruptive innovation make it somewhat counterintuitive. Disruptive innovations:

- Are technologically simpler and less sophisticated than currently available products or services.
- Appeal to less demanding customers who are seeking more convenient, less expensive solutions.
- Take time to take effect and only become disruptive once they have taken root in a new market or low-end part of an existing market.

Christensen cites Walmart and Southwest Airlines as two disruptive examples. Walmart started with a single store, Southwest with a few flights. But because they both represented major departures from existing practices and tapped into unmet needs, they steadily grew into ventures that appealed to a new category of customers and eventually overturned the status quo. "Instead of sustaining the trajectory of improvement that has been established in a market," says Christensen, a disruptive innovation "disrupts it and redefines it by bringing to the market something that is simpler."[6]

Innovation is a force in both the external environment (technology, competition) and also a factor affecting a firm's internal choices (generic strategy, value-adding activities).[7] Nevertheless, innovation can be quite difficult for some firms to manage, especially those that have become comfortable with the status quo.

BANKING ON THE UNBANKED

By Sarah Hudson and Asha Moore-Mangin

African nations have long been viewed as cash-based economies whose populations have little truck with traditional banking services, preferring to keep their wealth firmly within physical reach. Recently, this has started to change with the large-scale deployment of mobile phone networks extending over the whole continent which has led to a massive rise in the use of mobile phones as a means of cash transfer. The most striking example of this phenomenon is that of Safaricom, the leading Kenyan integrated communications company with 18 million subscribers in a population of 43 million. Safaricom started out in 1993 as a department of Kenya Posts & Telecommunications Corporation, 40 percent of which was acquired by the UK firm Vodaphone in 2000.

Safaricom's success has come from its thriving mobile banking service called M-PESA, which enables Kenyans to transfer money via SMS without requiring them to have bank accounts. The M-PESA subscriber buys digital funds at one of over 40,000 outlets in the country and transfers them to another subscriber who can cash them in at another outlet anywhere in Kenya. It is estimated that a quarter of Kenya's GNP flows through M-PESA.

The company then decided to extend this service to provide a cheap and easy banking service named M-Shwari from the Swahili word for "calm" or "cool." The service is operated jointly with the Commercial Bank of Africa, and no other bank. Unlike the traditional banking sector, no physical branch facilities are available, and there is almost no person-to-person communication. It can be set up and accessed immediately with no minimum balance required. A small overdraft is offered with a single 7.5 percent fee, and the penalty for defaulters is a possibility of losing their phone number which is an extremely strong deterrent in a country where dependence on mobile phones is total. Take-up of the service rocketed. Some 2.3 million M-PESA customers opted in to M-Shwari; 900,000 with active accounts. Before the year was out, deposits totaled $47 million and one-third of users had applied for small loans, averaging around $12.

The CEO of Safaricom, Bob Collymore, believes that there is potentially $34 billion in unbanked savings which could enter the banking system. Another effect of taking up M-Shwari services could be to pull more of the Kenyan population into the formal, tax-paying economy.

A similar trend is taking place in other African countries. The firm EMP (Emerging Markets Payments) wants to take advantage of the fact that only 15–20 percent of Africans have bank accounts but 60–70 percent have mobile phones, and is building systems throughout the continent to ensure that e-payments can flow rapidly and safely through mobile phone networks. If EMP manages to roll out its services throughout Africa, this will translate into economies of scale and easier cross-border payments. For banks, such pan-continental systems would mean that they could offer their services in several countries at the same time.

With innovative business models such as Safaricom's, and platforms such as those of EMP, it looks like the African continent is set to skip the bricks and mortar stage of traditional banking and move directly from a cash-based economy to a lightweight, virtual service.

Sources: Anon (March 2013) "Safaricom widens its banking services from payments to savings and loans," The Economist www.economist.com/news/finance-and-economics/21574520-safaricom-widens-its-banking-services-payments-savings-and-loans-it; Anon (September 2013) "Paul Edwards took pay TV and mobile phones to Africa. Now it's e-payments," The Economist www.economist.com/news/finance-and-economics/21586309-paul-edwards-took-pay-tv-and-mobile-phones-afri; http://www.safaricom.co.ke/.

Challenges of Innovation

> **LO12.2**
>
> The challenges and pitfalls of managing corporate innovation processes.

Innovation is essential to sustaining competitive advantages. Recall from Chapter 3 that one of the four elements of the Balanced Scorecard is the innovation and learning perspective. The extent and success of a company's innovation efforts are indicators of its overall performance. As management guru Peter Drucker warned, "An established company which, in an age demanding innovation, is not capable of innovation is doomed to decline and extinction."[8] In today's competitive environment, most firms have only one choice: "Innovate or die."

As with change, however, firms are often resistant to innovation. Only those companies that actively pursue innovation, even though it is often difficult and uncertain, will get a payoff from their innovation efforts. But managing innovation is challenging.[9] As former Pfizer chairman and CEO William Steere puts it: "In some ways, managing innovation is analogous to breaking in a spirited horse. You are never sure of success until you achieve your goal. In the meantime, everyone takes a few lumps."[10]

What is it that makes innovation so difficult? The uncertainty about outcomes is one factor. Companies are often reluctant to invest time and resources into activities with an unknown future. Another factor is that the innovation process involves so many choices. These choices present five dilemmas that companies must wrestle with when pursuing innovation.[11]

- **Seeds versus Weeds.** Most companies have an abundance of innovative ideas. They must decide which of these is most likely to bear fruit—the "Seeds"—and which should be cast aside—the "Weeds." This is complicated by the fact that some innovation projects require a considerable level of investment before a firm can fully evaluate whether they are worth pursuing. Firms need a mechanism with which they can choose among various innovation projects.
- **Experience versus Initiative.** Companies must decide who will lead an innovation project. Senior managers may have experience and credibility but tend to be more risk averse. Midlevel employees, who may be the innovators themselves, may have more enthusiasm because they can see firsthand how an innovation would address specific problems. Firms need to support and reward organizational members who bring new ideas to light.
- **Internal versus External Staffing.** Innovation projects need competent staffs to succeed. People drawn from inside the company may have greater social capital and know the organization's culture and routines. But this knowledge may actually inhibit them from thinking outside the box. Staffing innovation projects with external personnel requires that project managers justify the hiring and spend time recruiting, training, and relationship building. Firms need to streamline and support the process of staffing innovation efforts.
- **Building Capabilities versus Collaborating.** Innovation projects often require new sets of skills. Firms can seek help from other departments and/or partner with other companies that bring resources and experience as well as share costs of development. However, such arrangements can create dependencies and inhibit internal skills development. Further, struggles over who contributed the most or how the benefits of the project are to be allocated may arise. Firms need a mechanism for forging links with outside parties to the innovation process.
- **Incremental versus Preemptive Launch.** Companies must manage the timing and scale of new innovation projects. An incremental launch is less risky because it requires fewer resources and serves as a market test. But a launch that is too tentative can undermine the project's credibility. It also opens the door for a competitive response. A large-scale launch requires more resources, but it can effectively preempt a competitive response. Firms need to make funding and management arrangements that allow for projects to hit the ground running and be responsive to market feedback.

These dilemmas highlight why the innovation process can be daunting even for highly successful firms. Strategy Spotlight 12.3 discusses how Procter & Gamble has been struggling with these challenges to improve its innovativeness. Next, we consider five steps that firms can take to improve the innovation process within the firm.[12]

Cultivating Innovation Skills

Some firms, such as Apple, Google, and Amazon, regularly produce innovative products and services, while other firms struggle to generate new, marketable products. What separates these innovative firms from the rest of the pack? Jeff Dyer, Hal Gregersen, and Clayton Christensen argue it is the Innovative DNA of the leaders of these firms.[13] The leaders of these firms have exhibited "discovery skills" that allow them to see the potential in innovations and to move the organization forward in leveraging the value of those innovations.[14] These leaders spend 50 percent more time on these discovery activities than the leaders of less innovative firms. To improve their innovative processes, firms need to cultivate the innovation skills of their managers.

The key attribute that firms need to develop in their managers in order to improve their innovative potential is creative intelligence. Creative intelligence is driven by a core skill

PROCTER & GAMBLE STRIVES TO REMAIN INNOVATIVE

From the development of Ivory Soap in 1879; to Crisco Oil, the first all-vegetable shortening, in 1911; to Crest, the first fluoridated toothpaste in 1955; to the stackable Pringles chips in 1968; to the Swiffer mop in 1998, Procter & Gamble (P&G) has long been known as a successful innovative firm. It led the market with these products and used these innovative products to build up its position as a differentiated consumer products firm. By all measures, P&G is a very successful company and was honored as the Fifth Most Admired Company by *Fortune* magazine in 2012. Still, P&G has found it challenging to remain innovative. The last major innovative blockbuster product P&G launched was Crest Whitestrips, and this product was introduced in 2001. Instead, in recent years, their new products have been extensions of current products, such as adding whitening flecks to Crest toothpaste, or derivatives of current products, such as taking the antihistamine in Nyquil and using it as a sleeping aid, labeled ZzzQuil. With ZzzQuil, P&G is not an innovator in this market, since there were a number of earlier entrants in the sleep market, such as Johnson & Johnson with its Tylenol PM product. One portfolio manager at a mutual fund manager derided the ZzzQuil product, saying, "It's a sign of what passes for innovation at P&G. It's not enough. It's incremental, derivative."

The factors leading to P&G's struggles to remain innovative should not be surprising. They largely grow out of the success the firm has had. First, with its wide range of products, P&G has a wide range of potential new product extensions and derivatives from which to choose. Though these are unlikely to be blockbusters, they look much safer than truly new innovative ideas. Second, while lower-level managers at P&G may be excited about new, innovative ideas, the division heads of P&G units, who are responsible for developing new products, are likely to shy away from big-bet product launches. These unit heads are also responsible for and rewarded on current division performance, a metric that will be negatively affected by the large costs associated with developing and marketing truly innovative new products. Third, due to its large size, P&G moved R&D responsibilities down to the divisions. While this enhances the divisions' abilities to quickly launch incrementally new products, it doesn't facilitate the collaboration across units often needed to develop boldly new products.

P&G is trying to address these issues by centralizing 20 to 30 percent of its research efforts within a new corporate-level business creation and innovation unit. Having a corporate effort at innovation separates the budget for product development from divisional profit numbers, enhancing the firm's willingness to invest in long-term product development efforts. Also, the corporate unit will be able to foster collaboration between units to develop blockbuster products.

Sources: Coleman-Lochner, L. & Hymowitz, C. 2012. At P&G, the innovation well runs dry. *Bloomberg Businessweek*, September 10: 24–26; and Bussey, J. 2012. The innovator's enigma. *wsj.com*, October 4: np.

---

of associating—the ability to see patterns in data and integrating different questions, information, and insights—and four patterns of action: questioning, observing, experimenting, and networking. As managers practice the four patterns of action, they will begin to develop the skill of association. Dyer and his colleagues offer the following illustration to demonstrate that individuals using these skills are going to develop more creative, higher-potential innovations.

> Imagine that you have an identical twin, endowed with the same brains and natural talents that you have. You're both given one week to come up with a creative new business-venture idea. During that week, you come up with ideas alone in your room. In contrast, your twin (1) talks with 10 people—including an engineer, a musician, a stay-at-home dad, and a designer—about the venture, (2) visits three innovative start-ups to observe what they do, (3) samples five "new to the market" products, (4) shows a prototype he's built to five people, and (5) asks the questions "What if I tried this?" and "Why do you do that?" at least 10 times each day during these networking, observing, and experimenting activities. Who do you bet will come up with the more innovative (and doable) ideas?

The point is that by questioning, observing, experimenting, and networking as part of the innovative process, managers will both make better innovation decisions now but, more importantly, start to build the innovative DNA needed to be more successful innovators in the future. As they get into the practice of these habits, decision makers will see opportunities and be more creative as they associate information from different parts of their life, different people they come in contact with, and different parts of their organizations. The ability to innovate is not hard-wired into our brains at birth. Research suggests that only one-third of our ability to think creatively is genetic. The other two-thirds is developed over time. Neuroscience research indicates that the brain is "plastic," meaning it changes over time due to experiences. As managers build up the ability to ask creative questions, develop a wealth of experiences from diverse settings, and link together insights from different arenas of their lives, their brains will follow suit and will build the ability to easily see situations creatively and draw upon a wide range of experiences and knowledge to identify creative solutions. The five traits of the effective innovator are described and examples of each trait are presented in Exhibit 12.2.

Defining the Scope of Innovation

Firms must have a means to focus their innovation efforts. By defining the "strategic envelope"—the scope of a firm's innovation efforts—firms ensure that their innovation efforts are not wasted on projects that are outside the firm's domain of interest. Strategic

EXHIBIT 12.2 The Innovator's DNA

Trait	Description	Example
Associating	Innovators have the ability to connect seemingly unrelated questions, problems, and ideas from different fields. This allows them to creatively see opportunities that others miss.	Pierre Omidyar saw the opportunity that led to eBay when he linked three items: (1) a personal fascination with creating more efficient markets, (2) his fiancee's desire to locate hard to find collectible Pez dispensers, and (3) the ineffectiveness of local classified ads in locating such items.
Questioning	Innovators constantly ask questions that challenge common wisdom. Rather than accept the status quo, they ask "Why not?" or "What if?" This gets others around them to challenge the assumptions that limit the possible range of actions the firm can take.	After witnessing the emergence of eBay and Amazon, Marc Benioff questioned why computer software was still sold in boxes rather than leased with a subscription and downloaded through the Internet. This was the genesis of Salesforce.com, a firm with over $2.2 billion in sales in 2012.
Observing	Discovery-driven executives produce innovative business ideas by observing regular behavior of individuals, especially customers and potential customers. Such observations often identify challenges customers face and previously unidentified opportunities.	From watching his wife struggle to keep track of the family's finances, Intuit founder Scott Cook identified the need for easy-to-use financial software that provided a single place for managing bills, bank accounts, and investments.
Experimenting	Thomas Edison once said, "I haven't failed. I've simply found 10,000 ways that do not work." Innovators regularly experiment with new possibilities, accepting that many of their ideas will fail. Experimentation can include new jobs, living in different countries, and new ideas for their businesses.	Founders Larry Page and Sergey Brin provide time and resources for Google employees to experiment. Some, such as the Android cell phone platform, have been big winners. Others, such as the Orkut and Buzz social networking systems, have failed. But Google will continue to experiment with new products and services.
Networking	Innovators develop broad personal networks. They use this diverse set of individuals to find and test radical ideas. This can be done by developing a diverse set of friends. It can also be done by attending idea conferences where individuals from a broad set of backgrounds come together to share their perspectives and ideas, such as the Technology, Entertainment, and Design (TED) Conference or the Aspen Ideas Festival.	Michael Lazaridis got the idea for a wireless, email device that led him to found Research in Motion, now called Blackberry, from a conference he attended. At the conference, a speaker was discussing a wireless system Coca-Cola was using that allowed vending machines to send a signal when they needed refilling. Lazaridis saw the opportunity to use the same concept with email communications, and the idea for the Blackberry was hatched.

enveloping defines the range of acceptable projects. A **strategic envelope** creates a firm-specific view of innovation that defines how a firm can create new knowledge and learn from an innovation initiative even if the project fails. It also gives direction to a firm's innovation efforts, which helps separate seeds from weeds and builds internal capabilities.

strategic envelope
a firm-specific view of innovation that defines how a firm can create new knowledge and learn from an innovation initiative even if the project fails.

One way to determine which projects to work on is to focus on a common technology. Then, innovation efforts across the firm can aim at developing skills and expertise in a given technical area. Another potential focus is on a market theme. Consider how DuPont responded to a growing concern for environmentally sensitive products:

> In the early 1990s, DuPont sought to use its knowledge of plastics to identify products to meet a growing market demand for biodegradable products. It conducted numerous experiments with a biodegradable polyester resin it named Biomax. By trying different applications and formulations demanded by potential customers, the company was finally able to create a product that could be produced economically and had market appeal. DuPont has continued to extend the Biomax brand and now produces a large line of environmentally sensitive plastics.[15]

Companies must be clear not only about the kinds of innovation they are looking for but also the expected results. Each company needs to develop a set of questions to ask itself about its innovation efforts:

- How much will the innovation initiative cost?
- How likely is it to actually become commercially viable?
- How much value will it add; that is, what will it be worth if it works?
- What will be learned if it does not pan out?

However a firm envisions its innovation goals, it needs to develop a systematic approach to evaluating its results and learning from its innovation initiatives. Viewing innovation from this perspective helps firms manage the process.[16]

Managing the Pace of Innovation

Along with clarifying the scope of an innovation by defining a strategic envelope, firms also need to regulate the pace of innovation. How long will it take for an innovation initiative to realistically come to fruition? The project time line of an incremental innovation may be 6 months to 2 years, whereas a more radical innovation is typically long term—10 years or more.[17] Radical innovations often begin with a long period of exploration in which experimentation makes strict timelines unrealistic. In contrast, firms that are innovating incrementally in order to exploit a window of opportunity may use a milestone approach that is more stringently driven by goals and deadlines. This kind of sensitivity to realistic time frames helps companies separate dilemmas temporally so they are easier to manage.

Time pacing can also be a source of competitive advantage because it helps a company manage transitions and develop an internal rhythm.[18] Time pacing does not mean the company ignores the demands of market timing; instead, companies have a sense of their own internal clock in a way that allows them to thwart competitors by controlling the innovation process. With time pacing, the firm works to develop an internal rhythm that matches the buying practices of customers. For example, for years, Intel worked to develop new microprocessor chips every 18 months. They would have three chips in process at any point in time—one they were producing and selling, one they were currently developing, and one that was just on the drawing board. This pacing also matched the market, because most corporate customers bought new computers about every three years. Thus, customers were then two generations behind in their computing technology, leading them to feel the need to upgrade at the three-year point. In the post-PC era, Apple has developed a similar but faster internal cycle, allowing them to launch a new generation of the iPad on an annual basis.

This doesn't mean the aim is always to be faster when innovating. Some projects can't be rushed. Companies that hurry up their research efforts or go to market before they are ready can damage their ability to innovate—and their reputation. Thus, managing the pace of innovation can be an important factor in long-term success.

Staffing to Capture Value from Innovation

People are central to the processes of identifying, developing, and commercializing innovations effectively. They need broad sets of skills as well as experience—experience working with teams and experience working on successful innovation projects. To capture value from innovation activities, companies must provide strategic decision makers with staff members who make it possible.

This insight led strategy experts Rita Gunther McGrath and Thomas Keil to research the types of human resource management practices that effective firms use to capture value from their innovation efforts.[19] Four practices are especially important:

- Create innovation teams with experienced players who know what it is like to deal with uncertainty and can help new staff members learn venture management skills.
- Require that employees seeking to advance their career with the organization serve in the new venture group as part of their career climb.
- Once people have experience with the new venture group, transfer them to mainstream management positions where they can use their skills and knowledge to revitalize the company's core business.
- Separate the performance of individuals from the performance of the innovation. Otherwise, strong players may feel stigmatized if the innovation effort they worked on fails.

There are other staffing practices that may sound as if they would benefit a firm's innovation activities but may, in fact, be counterproductive:

- Creating a staff that consists only of strong players whose primary experience is related to the company's core business. This provides too few people to deal with the uncertainty of innovation projects and may cause good ideas to be dismissed because they do not appear to fit with the core business.
- Creating a staff that consists only of volunteers who want to work on projects they find interesting. Such players are often overzealous about new technologies or overly attached to product concepts, which can lead to poor decisions about which projects to pursue or drop.
- Creating a climate where innovation team members are considered second-class citizens. In companies where achievements are rewarded, the brightest and most ambitious players may avoid innovation projects with uncertain outcomes.

Unless an organization can align its key players into effective new venture teams, it is unlikely to create any differentiating advantages from its innovation efforts.[20] An enlightened approach to staffing a company's innovation efforts provides one of the best ways to ensure that the challenges of innovation will be effectively met. Strategy Spotlight 12.4 describes the approach Apple is using to enhance its innovation efforts.

Collaborating with Innovation Partners

It is rare for any one organization to have all the information it needs to carry an innovation from concept to commercialization. Even a company that is highly competent with its current operations usually needs new capabilities to achieve new results. Innovation partners provide the skills and insights that are needed to make innovation projects succeed.[21]

Innovation partners may come from many sources, including research universities and the federal government. Each year the federal government issues requests for proposals (RFPs) asking private companies for assistance in improving services or finding solutions

APPLE FINALLY GIVES IN TO PERKS TO ATTRACT AND RETAIN EMPLOYEES WITH ITS "BLUE SKY" INITIATIVE

By Asha Moore-Mangin and Sarah Hudson

Silicon Valley perks were long shunned by former Apple CEO Steve Jobs who believed that having employees work at the company and on its products was enough to retain employees. With employees on the move from Apple, the new leader Tim Cook has had to think about how to retain existing employees and attract new ones. His response has been to introduce perks into the company, something that many existing employees are not familiar with.

These perks include new discounts on Apple products or matching employees' contributions to charities, stock grants, and a "Blue Sky" initiative which allows a select and small group of employees to spend time on their favorite engineering projects. He is also working on making his employees feel more valued by praising them at public events and giving counter-offers to retain employees that are being offered jobs from competitors.

The "Blue Sky" initiative mirrors a key Google work arrangement "20% time" that gives employees one day a week to work on projects of their choice. These work arrangements are very valuable to employees who are innovative and initiative-taking. The company is giving a clear signal to employees that it values them as creators and innovators and they also stand to benefit from these projects. However, the downside of this kind of perk is that the company has to hire more people to do the normal workload, otherwise employees will not be able to take advantage of the perk. However perks alone are not enough to attract and retain employees, the company culture also has to adapt to allow employees to benefit from the perks.

Sources: Jessica Lessin, 12 November 2012, online.wsj.com/article/SB10001424 127887324073504578115071154910456.html?KEYWORDS=tim+cook+and+ap ple+perks "Apple Gives In to Employee Perks; CEO Tim Cook Pushes Employee-Friendly Benefits Long Shunned by Steve Jobs;" 20 November 2012 www. knowledgeatwharton.com.cn/index.cfm?fa=article&articleid=2706&language=1 "iPerks: Apple, Like Others, Takes Steps to Woo Employees"; Trevor Mogg, 12 November 2012 www.digitaltrends.com/apple/apple-introduces-blue-sky-program to-give-select-employees-time-for-personal-projects/ "Apple introduces 'Blue Sky' program to give select employees time for personal projects."

to public problems. Universities are another type of innovation partner. Chip-maker Intel, for example, has benefited from underwriting substantial amounts of university research. Rather than hand universities a blank check, Intel bargains for rights to patents that emerge from Intel-sponsored research. The university retains ownership of the patent, but Intel gets royalty-free use of it.[22]

Strategic partnering requires firms to identify their strengths and weaknesses and make choices about which capabilities to leverage, which need further development, and which are outside the firm's current or projected scope of operations.

To choose partners, firms need to ask what competencies they are looking for and what the innovation partner will contribute.[23] These might include knowledge of markets, technology expertise, or contacts with key players in an industry. Innovation partnerships also typically need to specify how the rewards of the innovation will be shared and who will own the intellectual property that is developed.[24] Strategy Spotlight 12.5 discusses how Coke and Deka found that they each had only some of the resources needed to take on a bold global initiative, but together they had all the resources needed.

Innovation efforts that involve multiple partners and the speed and ease with which partners can network and collaborate are changing the way innovation is conducted.[25] Strategy Spotlight 12.6 outlines how IBM is using crowdsourcing technologies to foster collaboration between employees, customers, suppliers, and other stakeholders to enhance its innovation efforts.

Corporate Entrepreneurship

Corporate entrepreneurship (CE) has two primary aims: the pursuit of new venture opportunities and strategic renewal.[26] The innovation process keeps firms alert by exposing them to new technologies, making them aware of marketplace trends, and helping them evaluate new possibilities. CE uses the fruits of the innovation process to help firms

corporate entrepreneurship
the creation of new value for a corporation, through investments that create either new sources of competitive advantage or renewal of the value proposition.

COKE AND DEKA: PARTNERS TO SOLVE THE NEED FOR CLEAN WATER

Coca-Cola and DEKA each have an innovative vision. Apart, they are unlikely to reach their visions. Together, they just may make it happen. Coca-Cola set a goal of replenishing 100 percent of the water used in the production of its beverages by the year 2020. To get there, they have worked to improve the water efficiency of their plants and invested in a number of water projects. This has gotten them 35 percent of the way to their goal, but they need to find ways to add fresh water into the equation. DEKA Research has a vision to provide clean drinking water to areas of the developing world where clean water is a scarce commodity, but they don't have the financial resources to make it happen.

While we take drinking water for granted in the developed world, 20 percent of the world's population does not have access to clean water. Governments and nongovernmental organizations (NGOs) have invested billions of dollars in major public water projects to take available water from rivers, lakes, and oceans and treat it to provide drinkable water. But this effort still hasn't met the need of many. DEKA Research has an innovative solution to this issue, a water purification system called the Slingshot that is simple, portable, and affordable. Rather than relying on major, multimillion dollar water projects, this is a low-cost system (about $2,000 each) that can produce 250 gallons of drinkable water each day, enough for about 300 people, using less electricity than needed to run a blow dryer. The Slingshot is about the size of a dormitory refrigerator and its technology borrows from a desalination process used to generate drinking water on naval ships. Using a vapor compression distillation process, the system heats water through multiple cycles. This process removes minerals, heavy metals, and other contaminants by evaporating the water away from the contaminants. It also kills bacteria and viruses through pasteurization of the water. Still, DEKA faced a major challenge bringing this technology to market. DEKA needed millions of dollars to build a manufacturing facility to produce the Slingshots.

That is where Coke enters the picture. Coke's CEO, Muhtar Kent, has pledged to become water neutral as a firm. "Water is the lifeblood of our business, and our commitment is to ensure we're doing our part to replenish the water we use and give it back to communities around the world," Kent said. Coke sees DEKA as a great partner to reach their target. Coke has the financial resources to make it happen, but they didn't have the technology to generate water in the way that DEKA does. Coke has pledged "tens of millions of dollars" to help DEKA build their plant and to begin to produce Slingshots. In addition to their financial investment, Coke also has the operational resources to deliver the Slingshots to areas around the world that have no other access to fresh water. They have already begun field testing the machines in rural areas in South Africa, Mexico, and Paraguay. They hope to ramp up mass production of the machines by the middle of 2013. Combined, these two firms appear to have all the resources needed to make the Slingshot an innovative and valuable solution in the quest for clean water.

Sources: Copeland, M. V. 2010. Dean Kamen (Still) wants to save the world. *Fortune,* May 3: 61–62; Nasr, S. L. 2009. How the Slingshot water purifier works. *HowStuffWorks.com*, July 27: np; Solomon, D. 2012. Dean Kaman's Slingshot heard 'round the world. *unionleader.com*, October 7: np; and Geller, M. 2012. Coke, Segway inventor team up on clean water project. *reuters.com*, September 25: np.

build new sources of competitive advantage and renew their value propositions. Just as the innovation process helps firms to make positive improvements, corporate entrepreneurship helps firms identify opportunities and launch new ventures.

Corporate new venture creation was labeled "intrapreneuring" by Gifford Pinchot because it refers to building entrepreneurial businesses within existing corporations.[27] However, to engage in corporate entrepreneurship that yields above-average returns and contributes to sustainable advantages, it must be done effectively. In this section we will examine the sources of entrepreneurial activity within established firms and the methods large corporations use to stimulate entrepreneurial behavior.

In a typical corporation, what determines how entrepreneurial projects will be pursued? That depends on many factors, including:

- Corporate culture.
- Leadership.
- Structural features that guide and constrain action.
- Organizational systems that foster learning and manage rewards.

IBM'S INNOVATION JAM

IBM is one of the best known corporations in the world, but their CEO, Samuel Palmisano, saw a major challenge for the firm. Though IBM had great ability to do basic scientific research and owned the rights to over 40,000 patents, they had struggled to translate their patented knowledge into marketable products. Also, they had built a reputation with investors as a firm with incremental product development, not the reputation needed in dynamic technological markets. Palmisano saw crowdsourcing as a means to move IBM forward in a bold way.

In 2006, IBM hosted an Innovation Jam, an open event that involved 150,000 IBM employees, family members, business partners, clients, and university researchers. The jam took place over two 72-hour sessions. Participants from over 100 countries jammed for 24 hours a day over three days. The discussions were organized around 25 technologies in six broad categories. While the jam discussions were rich in content, it was a challenge for IBM to pull meaningful data from them. The 24-hour format meant that no single moderator could follow any discussion, and the volume of posts to the discussion threads left IBM with a huge amount of data to wade through. The discussions yielded 46,000 potential business ideas. To make sense of the data, IBM organized the discussion threads using sophisticated text analysis software and had a team of 50 managers read through the organized data. Using data from the first session, the managers identified 31 "big ideas." They further explored these 31 ideas in the second jam session. IBM then used another set of 50 global managers to review the discussions from the jam. Teams of managers focused on related groups of ideas, such as health care and the environment.

IBM's managers saw the jam as serving three purposes. First, it gave individuals both inside and outside IBM who already had big ideas a forum in which to share their vision with top managers. Second, it gave individuals with smaller ideas a venue to link up with others with related ideas, resulting in larger major initiatives. For example, individuals who had ideas about better local weather forecasting, sensing devices for water utilities, and long-term climate forecasting came together to create "Predictive Water Management," a comprehensive solution for water authorities to manage their resources, a business solution no one at IBM had thought of before the jam. Third, the global structure of the jam allowed IBM, early on, to see how employees, partners, and customers from different regions had different goals and concerns about possible new businesses. For example, what customers wanted from systems to manage health care records varied greatly across regions.

Based on the jam sessions, IBM launched 10 new businesses using $100 million in funding. One, the Intelligent Transportation System, a system that gathers, manages, and disseminates real-time information about metropolitan transportation systems to optimize traffic flow, has been sold to transportation authorities in Sweden, the UK, Singapore, Dubai, and Australia. Another, Intelligent Utility Networks, became a core product in IBM's public utility business. A third, Big Green, became part of the largest initiative in IBM's history, a billion-dollar project on better managing energy and other resources.

Sources: Bjelland, O. M. & Wood, R. C. 2008. An Inside View of IBM's Innovation Jam. *Sloan Management Review.* Fall: 32–40; Hempel, J. 2006. Big Blue Brainstorm. *BusinessWeek,* August 7: 70; Takahashi, D. 2008. IBM's Innovation Jam 2008 Shows How Far Crowdsourcing Has Come. *Businessweek.com,* October 9: np.

All of the factors that influence the strategy implementation process will also shape how corporations engage in internal venturing.

Other factors will also affect how entrepreneurial ventures will be pursued.

- The use of teams in strategic decision making.
- Whether the company is product or service oriented.
- Whether its innovation efforts are aimed at product or process improvements.
- The extent to which it is high-tech or low-tech.

Because these factors are different in every organization, some companies may be more involved than others in identifying and developing new venture opportunities.[28] These factors will also influence the nature of the CE process.

Successful CE typically requires firms to reach beyond their current operations and markets in the pursuit of new opportunities. It is often the breakthrough opportunities that provide the greatest returns. Such strategies are not without risks, however. In the sections that follow, we will address some of the strategic choice and implementation issues that influence the success or failure of CE activities.

focused approaches to corporate entrepreneurship
corporate entrepreneurship in which the venturing entity is seperated from the other ongoing operations of the firm.

new venture group
a group of individuals, or a division within a corporation, that identifies, evaluates, and cultivates venture opportunities.

business incubator
a corporate new venture group that supports and nurtures fledgling entrepreneurial ventures until they can thrive on their own as stand-alone businesses.

Two distinct approaches to corporate venturing are found among firms that pursue entrepreneurial aims. The first is *focused* corporate venturing, in which CE activities are isolated from a firm's existing operations and worked on by independent work units. The second approach is *dispersed*, in which all parts of the organization and every organization member are engaged in intrapreneurial activities.

Focused Approaches to Corporate Entrepreneurship

Firms using a focused approach typically separate the corporate venturing activity from the other ongoing operations of the firm. CE is usually the domain of autonomous work groups that pursue entrepreneurial aims independent of the rest of the firm. The advantage of this approach is that it frees entrepreneurial team members to think and act without the constraints imposed by existing organizational norms and routines. This independence is often necessary for the kind of open-minded creativity that leads to strategic breakthroughs. The disadvantage is that, because of their isolation from the corporate mainstream, the work groups that concentrate on internal ventures may fail to obtain the resources or support needed to carry an entrepreneurial project through to completion. Two forms—new venture groups (NVGs) and business incubators—are among the most common types of focused approaches.

New Venture Groups (NVGs)   Corporations often form NVGs whose goal is to identify, evaluate, and cultivate venture opportunities. These groups typically function as semi-autonomous units with little formal structure. The **new venture group** may simply be a committee that reports to the president on potential new ventures. Or it may be organized as a corporate division with its own staff and budget. The aims of the NVG may be open-ended in terms of what ventures it may consider. Alternatively, some corporations use them to promote concentrated effort on a specific problem. In both cases, they usually have a substantial amount of freedom to take risks and a supply of resources to do it with.[29]

NVGs usually have a larger mandate than a typical R&D department. Their involvement extends beyond innovation and experimentation to coordinating with other corporate divisions, identifying potential venture partners, gathering resources, and actually launching the venture.

Business Incubators   The term *incubator* was originally used to describe a device in which eggs are hatched. **Business incubators** are designed to "hatch" new businesses. They are a type of corporate NVG with a somewhat more specialized purpose—to support and nurture fledgling entrepreneurial ventures until they can thrive on their own as stand-alone businesses. Corporations use incubators as a way to grow businesses identified by the NVG. Although they often receive support from many parts of the corporation, they still operate independently until they are strong enough to go it alone. Depending on the type of business, they are either integrated into an existing corporate division or continue to operate as a subsidiary of the parent firm.

Incubators typically provide some or all of the following five functions.[30]

- *Funding.* Includes capital investments as well as in-kind investments and loans.
- *Physical space.* Incubators in which several start-ups share space often provide fertile ground for new ideas and collaboration.
- *Business services.* Along with office space, young ventures need basic services and infrastructure; may include anything from phone systems and computer networks to public relations and personnel management.

TOO MUCH INNOVATION? HOW LEGO'S INNOVATIVE CULTURE ALMOST DESTROYED THE COMPANY.

By Helena Gonzalez and Cyrlene Claasen

In 2003, 56 years after having developed the first plastic-injection molding machine and positioning itself as one of the leading toy companies in the world, Lego realized that innovation and thinking "out of the box" was the cause for its almost going out of business.

Lego's first success came in 1949, after it developed its now famous toy building blocks. These blocks allowed children to connect different pieces into a multitude of shapes, a revolutionary advancement over traditional wooden blocks that were usually just stacked one on top of the other.

In 1978, with its second great idea—the mini-figure—sales really took off. But by 1993, thanks to Chinese competition, sales at Lego started to slow (the Chinese could manufacture similar items at a fraction of the cost). To face this new challenge, Lego expanded its product line. But while costs went up, sales didn't. Moreover, with the arrival of electronic toys, children started to get interested in sophisticated devices at an earlier age, giving up their Legos sooner, thus putting a squeeze on the size of the company's potential market.

Lego again faced up to its challenges, this time by starting an aggressive and multifaceted innovation campaign. By following the advice of experts and customers alike, it developed a plethora of new products and businesses. But by 2003, Lego was virtually out of cash. By trying to be too creative, Lego lost control of its own innovation and got away from what it was good at and what it was recognized for.

In 2003, Lego made the decision to regain control of its innovation process. A first step was to slash costs by selling a majority stake in its "Legoland" parks. It also moved its Danish headquarters to a nearby factory and outsourced the production of its plastic bricks to cheaper facilities. Lego then created a more organized structure to control innovation. Now, every employee in the company is encouraged to propose new ideas for growth. But their ideas, before they are further developed, need to be proven as being consistent with Lego's goal of being recognized as the best company for family products.

As a result, Lego has shown that controlled innovation works.

Sources: "Innovation Almost Bankrupted Lego—Until It Rebuilt with a Better Blueprint" by Knowledge@Wharton, Time, July 23 2012; "How Lego Clawed Its Way Out Of Near Bankruptcy" Knowledge@Wharton, July 1 2013.

- *Mentoring.* Senior executives and skilled technical personnel often provide coaching and experience-based advice.
- *Networking.* Contact with other parts of the firm and external resources such as suppliers, industry experts, and potential customers facilitates problem solving and knowledge sharing.

Because Microsoft has struggled to reinvigorate its entrepreneurial capabilities, the company has created a business incubator to enhance corporate entrepreneurship efforts.

To encourage entrepreneurship, corporations sometimes need to do more than create independent work groups or venture incubators to generate new enterprises. In some firms, the entrepreneurial spirit is spread throughout the organization.

Dispersed Approaches to Corporate Entrepreneurship

The second type of CE is dispersed. For some companies, a dedication to the principles and practices of entrepreneurship is spread throughout the organization. One advantage of this approach is that organizational members don't have to be reminded to think entrepreneurially or be willing to change. The ability to change is considered to be a core capability. This leads to a second advantage: Because of the firm's entrepreneurial reputation, stakeholders such as vendors, customers, or alliance partners can bring new ideas or venture opportunities to anyone in the organization and expect them to be well-received. Such opportunities make it possible for the firm to stay ahead of the competition. However, there are disadvantages as well. Firms that are overzealous about CE sometimes feel they must change for the sake of change, causing them to lose vital competencies or spend heavily on

> **dispersed approaches to corporate entrepreneurship**
> corporate entrepreunership in which a dedication to the principles and policies of entrepreunership is spread throughout the organization.

R&D and innovation to the detriment of the bottom line. Three related aspects of dispersed entrepreneurship include entrepreneurial cultures that have an overarching commitment to CE activities, resource allotments to support entrepreneurial actions, and the use of product champions in promoting entrepreneurial behaviors.

entrepreneurial culture
corporate culture in which change and renewal are a constant focus of attention.

Entrepreneurial Culture   In some large corporations, the corporate culture embodies the spirit of entrepreneurship. A culture of entrepreneurship is one in which the search for venture opportunities permeates every part of the organization. The key to creating value successfully is viewing every value-chain activity as a source of competitive advantage. The effect of CE on a firm's strategic success is strongest when it animates all parts of an organization. It is found in companies where the strategic leaders and the culture together generate a strong impetus to innovate, take risks, and seek out new venture opportunities.[31]

In companies with an entrepreneurial culture, everyone in the organization is attuned to opportunities to help create new businesses. Many such firms use a top-down approach to stimulate entrepreneurial activity. The top leaders of the organization support programs and incentives that foster a climate of entrepreneurship. Many of the best ideas for new corporate ventures, however, come from the bottom up. Catherine Winder, president of Rainmaker Entertainment, discussed how she welcomes any employee to generate and pitch innovative ideas this way[32]:

> We have an open-door policy for anyone in the company to pitch ideas . . . to describe their ideas in 15 to 30 seconds. If we like the core idea, we'll work with them. If you can be concise and come up with your idea in a really clear way, it means you're on to something.

An entrepreneurial culture is one in which change and renewal are on everybody's mind. Amazon, 3M, Intel, and Cisco are among the corporations best known for their corporate venturing activities. Many fast-growing young corporations also attribute much of their success to an entrepreneurial culture. But other successful firms struggle in their efforts to remain entrepreneurial. For example, Sony was very successful in their corporate venturing efforts for many years, but more recently they have had great difficulty maintaining their position as an entrepreneurial leader in consumer electronics and computers.

Resource Allotments   CE requires the willingness of the firm to invest in the generation and execution of innovative ideas. On the generation side, employees are much more likely to develop these ideas if they have the time to do so. For decades, 3M allowed its engineers free time, up to 15 percent of their work schedule, to work on developing new products.[33] Google has followed a similar path with its 70-20-10 rule. Google expects its employees to spend 70 percent of their time on the company's core, existing product lines. Employees can spend 20 percent of their time on related product spheres in which the company can look to extend its product line. The remaining 10 percent of the time is open. This is time the employees can use to think up bold new ideas. According to Larry Page, Google's CEO, this last 10 percent is "important to let people really be creative and think outside the box." In addition to time, firms can foster CE by providing monetary investment to fund entrepreneurial ideas. Johnson & Johnson (J&J) uses its Internal Ventures Group to support entrepreneurial ideas developed inside the firm. Entrepreneurs within J&J submit proposals to the group. The review board decides which proposals to fund and then solicits further investments from J&J's operating divisions. Nike's Sustainable Business and Innovation Lab and Google's Ventures Group have a similar charter to review and fund promising corporate entrepreneurship activities. The availability of these time and financing sources can enhance the likelihood of successful entrepreneurial activities within the firm.

Product Champions   CE does not always involve making large investments in start-ups or establishing incubators to spawn new divisions. Often, innovative ideas emerge in the normal course of business and are brought forth and become part of the way of doing business. Entrepreneurial champions are often needed to take charge of internally generated ventures. **Product** (or project) **champions** are those individuals working within a corporation who bring entrepreneurial ideas forward, identify what kind of market exists for the product or service, find resources to support the venture, and promote the venture concept to upper management.[34]

product champion
an individual working within a corporation who brings entrepreneurial ideas forward, identifies what kind of market exists for the product or service, finds resources to support the venture, and promotes the venture concept to upper management.

When lower-level employees identify a product idea or novel solution, they will take it to their supervisor or someone in authority. A new idea that is generated in a technology lab may be introduced to others by its inventor. If the idea has merit, it gains support and builds momentum across the organization.[35] Even though the corporation may not be looking for new ideas or have a program for cultivating internal ventures, the independent behaviors of a few organizational members can have important strategic consequences.

No matter how an entrepreneurial idea comes to light, however, a new venture concept must pass through two critical stages or it may never get off the ground:

1. *Project definition.* An opportunity has to be justified in terms of its attractiveness in the marketplace and how well it fits with the corporation's other strategic objectives.
2. *Project impetus.* For a project to gain impetus, its strategic and economic impact must be supported by senior managers who have experience with similar projects. It then becomes an embryonic business with its own organization and budget.

For a project to advance through these stages of definition and impetus, a product champion is often needed to generate support and encouragement. Champions are especially important during the time after a new project has been defined but before it gains momentum. They form a link between the definition and impetus stages of internal development, which they do by procuring resources and stimulating interest for the product among potential customers.[36] Often, they must work quietly and alone. Consider the example of Ken Kutaragi, the Sony engineer who championed the PlayStation.

Even though Sony had made the processor that powered the first Nintendo video games, no one at Sony in the mid-1980s saw any future in such products. "It was a kind of snobbery," Kutaragi recalled. "For Sony people, the Nintendo product would have been very embarrassing to make because it was only a toy." But Kutaragi was convinced he could make a better product. He began working secretly on a video game. Kutaragi said, "I realized that if it was visible, it would be killed." He quietly began enlisting the support of senior executives, such as the head of R&D. He made a case that Sony could use his project to develop capabilities in digital technologies that would be important in the future. It was not until 1994, after years of "underground" development and quiet building of support, that Sony introduced the PlayStation. By the year 2000, Sony had sold 55 million of them, and Kutaragi became CEO of Sony Computer Entertainment. By 2005, Kutagari was Sony's Chief Operating Officer, and was supervising efforts to launch PS3, the next generation version of the market-leading PlayStation video game console.[37]

Product champions play an important entrepreneurial role in a corporate setting by encouraging others to take a chance on promising new ideas.[38]

Measuring the Success of Corporate Entrepreneurship Activities

At this point in the discussion, it is reasonable to ask whether CE is successful. Corporate venturing, like the innovation process, usually requires a tremendous effort. Is it worth it? We consider factors that corporations need to take into consideration when evaluating the success of CE programs. We also examine techniques that companies can use to limit the expense of venturing or to cut their losses when CE initiatives appear doomed.

LO12.4

How corporate
entrepreneurship
achieves both
financial goals and
strategic goals.

Comparing Strategic and Financial CE Goals   Not all corporate venturing efforts are financially rewarding. In terms of financial performance, slightly more than 50 percent of corporate venturing efforts reach profitability (measured by ROI) within six years of their launch.[39] If this were the only criterion for success, it would seem to be a rather poor return. On the one hand, these results should be expected, because CE is riskier than other investments such as expanding ongoing operations. On the other hand, corporations expect a higher return from corporate venturing projects than from normal operations. Thus, in terms of the risk–return trade-off, it seems that CE often falls short of expectations.[40]

There are several other important criteria, however, for judging the success of a corporate venture initiative. Most CE programs have strategic goals.[41] The strategic reasons for undertaking a corporate venture include strengthening competitive position, entering into new markets, expanding capabilities by learning and acquiring new knowledge, and building the corporation's base of resources and experience. Three questions should be used to assess the effectiveness of a corporation's venturing initiatives:[42]

1. *Are the products or services offered by the venture accepted in the marketplace?* Is the venture considered to be a market success? If so, the financial returns are likely to be satisfactory. The venture may also open doors into other markets and suggest avenues for other venture projects.
2. *Are the contributions of the venture to the corporation's internal competencies and experience valuable?* Does the venture add to the worth of the firm internally? If so, strategic goals such as leveraging existing assets, building new knowledge, and enhancing firm capabilities are likely to be met.[43]
3. *Is the venture able to sustain its basis of competitive advantage?* Does the value proposition offered by the venture insulate it from competitive attack? If so, it is likely to place the corporation in a stronger position relative to competitors and provide a base from which to build other advantages.

These criteria include both strategic and financial goals of CE. Another way to evaluate a corporate venture is in terms of the four criteria from the Balanced Scorecard (Chapter 3). In a successful venture, not only are financial and market acceptance (customer) goals met but so are the internal business and innovation and learning goals. Thus, when assessing the success of corporate venturing, it is important to look beyond simple financial returns and consider a well-rounded set of criteria.[44]

Exit Champions   Although a culture of championing venture projects is advantageous for stimulating an ongoing stream of entrepreneurial initiatives, many—in fact, most—of the ideas will not work out. At some point in the process, a majority of initiatives will be abandoned. Sometimes, however, companies wait too long to terminate a new venture and do so only after large sums of resources are used up or, worse, result in a marketplace failure. Motorola's costly global satellite telecom project known as Iridium provides a useful illustration. Even though problems with the project existed during the lengthy development process, Motorola refused to pull the plug. Only after investing $5 billion and years of effort was the project abandoned.[45]

One way to avoid these costly and discouraging defeats is to support a key role in the CE process: **exit champions.** In contrast to product champions and other entrepreneurial enthusiasts within the corporation, exit champions are willing to question the viability of a venture project.[46] By demanding hard evidence and challenging the belief system that is carrying an idea forward, exit champions hold the line on ventures that appear shaky.

exit champion
an individual working
within a corporation who
is willing to question
the viability of a venture
project by demanding
hard evidence of venture
success and challenging
the belief system that
carries a venture forward.

Both product champions and exit champions must be willing to energetically stand up for what they believe. Both put their reputations on the line. But they also differ in important ways.[47] Product champions deal in uncertainty and ambiguity. Exit champions reduce ambiguity by gathering hard data and developing a strong case for why a project should be killed. Product champions are often thought to be willing to violate procedures and operate outside normal channels. Exit champions often have to reinstate procedures and re-assert the decision-making criteria that are supposed to guide venture decisions. Whereas product champions often emerge as heroes, exit champions run the risk of losing status by opposing popular projects.

The role of exit champion may seem unappealing. But it is one that could save a corporation both financially and in terms of its reputation in the marketplace. It is especially important because one measure of the success of a firm's CE efforts is the extent to which it knows when to cut its losses and move on.

Real Options Analysis: A Useful Tool

LO12.5

The benefits and potential drawbacks of real options analysis in making resource deployment decisions in corporate entrepreneurship contexts.

One way firms can minimize failure and avoid losses from pursuing faulty ideas is to apply the logic of real options. **Real options analysis** (ROA) is an investment analysis tool from the field of finance. It has been slowly, but increasingly, adopted by consultants and executives to support strategic decision making in firms. What does ROA consist of and how can it be appropriately applied to the investments required to initiate strategic decisions? To understand *real* options it is first necessary to have a basic understanding of what *options* are.

Options exist when the owner of the option has the right but not the obligation to engage in certain types of transactions. The most common are stock options. A stock option grants the holder the right to buy (call option) or sell (put option) shares of the stock at a fixed price (strike price) at some time in the future.[48] The investment to be made immediately is small, whereas the investment to be made in the future is generally larger. An option to buy a rapidly rising stock currently priced at $50 might cost as little as $.50.[49] Owners of such a stock option have limited their losses to $.50 per share, while the upside potential is unlimited. This aspect of options is attractive, because options offer the prospect of high gains with relatively small up-front investments that represent limited losses.

real options analysis an investment analysis tool that looks at an investment or activity as a series of sequential steps, and for each step the investor has the option of (a) investing additional funds to grow or accelerate, (b) delaying, (c) shrinking the scale of, or (d) abandoning the activity.

The phrase "real options" applies to situations where options theory and valuation techniques are applied to real assets or physical things as opposed to financial assets. Applied to entrepreneurship, real options suggest a path that companies can use to manage the uncertainty associated with launching new ventures. Some of the most common applications of real options are with property and insurance. A real estate option grants the holder the right to buy or sell a piece of property at an established price some time in the future. The actual market price of the property may rise above the established (or strike) price—or the market value may sink below the strike price. If the price of the property goes up, the owner of the option is likely to buy it. If the market value of the property drops below the strike price, the option holder is unlikely to execute the purchase. In the latter circumstance, the option holder has limited his or her loss to the cost of the option, but during the life of the option retains the right to participate in whatever the upside potential might be.

Applications of Real Options Analysis to Strategic Decisions

The concept of options can also be applied to strategic decisions where management has flexibility. Situations arise where management must decide whether to invest additional funds to grow or accelerate the activity, perhaps delay in order to learn more, shrink the scale of the activity, or even abandon it. Decisions to invest in new ventures or other business activities such as R&D, motion pictures, exploration and production of oil wells, and the opening and closing of copper mines often have this flexibility.[50] Important issues to note are:

- ROA is appropriate to use when investments can be staged; a smaller investment up front can be followed by subsequent investments. Real options can be applied to an investment decision that gives the company the right, but not the obligation, to make follow-on investments.
- Strategic decision makers have "tollgates," or key points at which they can decide whether to continue, delay, or abandon the project. Executives have flexibility. There are opportunities to make other go or no-go decisions associated with each phase.
- It is expected that there will be increased knowledge about outcomes at the time of the next investment and that additional knowledge will help inform the decision makers about whether to make additional investments (i.e., whether the option is in the money or out of the money).

Many strategic decisions have the characteristic of containing a series of options. The phenomenon is called "embedded options," a series of investments in which at each stage of the investment there is a go/no–go decision. Consider the real options logic that Johnson Controls, a maker of car seats, instrument panels, and interior control systems uses to advance or eliminate entrepreneurial ideas.[51] Johnson options each new innovative idea by making a small investment in it. To decide whether to exercise an option, the idea must continue to prove itself at each stage of development. Here's how Jim Geschke, vice president and general manager of electronics integration at Johnson, describes the process:

> Think of Johnson as an innovation machine. The front end has a robust series of gates that each idea must pass through. Early on, we'll have many ideas and spend a little money on each of them. As they get more fleshed out, the ideas go through a gate where a go or no-go decision is made. A lot of ideas get filtered out, so there are far fewer items, and the spending on each goes up. . . . Several months later each idea will face another gate. If it passes, that means it's a serious idea that we are going to develop. Then the spending goes way up, and the number of ideas goes way down. By the time you reach the final gate, you need to have a credible business case in order to be accepted. At a certain point in the development process, we take our idea to customers and ask them what they think. Sometimes they say, "That's a terrible idea. Forget it." Other times they say, "That's fabulous. I want a million of them."

This process of evaluating ideas by separating winning ideas from losing ones in a way that keeps investments low has helped Johnson Controls grow its revenues to over $42 billion a year. Using real options logic to advance the development process is a key way that firms reduce uncertainty and minimize innovation-related failures.[52] Real options logic can also be used with other types of strategic decisions. Strategy Spotlight 12.8 discusses how Intel uses real options logic in making capacity expansion decisions.

Potential Pitfalls of Real Options Analysis

Despite the many benefits that can be gained from using ROA, managers must be aware of its potential limitations or pitfalls. Below we will address three major issues.[53]

back-solver dilemma
problem with investment decisions in which managers scheme to have a project meet investment approval criteria, even though the investment may not enhance firm value.

Agency Theory and the Back-Solver Dilemma Let's assume that companies adopting a real-options perspective invest heavily in training and that their people understand how to effectively estimate variance—the amount of dispersion or range that is estimated for potential outcomes. Such training can help them use ROA. However, it does not solve another inherent problem: managers may have an incentive and the know-how to "game the system." Most electronic spreadsheets permit users to simply back-solve any formula; that is, you can type in the answer you want and ask what values are needed in a formula to get that answer. If managers know that a certain option value must be met in order for the

SAVING MILLIONS WITH REAL OPTIONS AT INTEL

The semiconductor business is complex and dynamic. This makes it a difficult one to manage. On the one hand, both the technology in the chips and the consumer demand for chips are highly volatile. This makes planning for the future as far as chip designs and the production plants needed difficult. On the other hand, it is incredibly expensive to build new chip plants, about $5 billion each, and chip manufacturing equipment needs to be ordered well ahead of when it is needed. The lead time for ordering new equipment can be up to three years. This creates a great challenge. Firms have to decide how much and what type of equipment to purchase long before they have a good handle on what the demand for semiconductor chips will be. Guessing wrong leaves the firm with too much or too little capacity.

Intel has figured out a way to limit the risk it faces by using option contracts. Intel pays an up-front fee for the right to purchase key pieces of equipment at a specific future date. At that point, Intel either purchases the equipment or releases the supplier from the contract. In these cases, the supplier is then free to sell the equipment to someone else. This all seems fairly simple. A number of commodities, such as wheat and sugar, have robust option markets. The challenge isn't in setting up the contracts. It is in pricing those contracts. Unlike wheat and sugar, where a large number of suppliers and buyers results in an efficient market that sets the prices of standard commodity products, there are few buyers and suppliers of chip manufacturing equipment. Further,

the equipment is not a standard commodity. As a result, prices for equipment options are the outcome of difficult negotiations.

Karl Kempf, a mathematician with Intel, has figured out how to make this process smoother. Along with a group of mathematicians at Stanford, Kempf has developed a computing logic for calculating the price of options. He and his colleagues create a forecasting model for potential demand. They calculate the likelihood of a range of potential demand levels. They also set up a computer simulation of a production plant. They then use the possible demand levels to predict how many pieces of production equipment they will need in the plant to meet the demand. They run this over and over again, thousands of times, to generate predictions about the likelihood they will need to purchase a specific piece of equipment. They use this information to identify what equipment they definitely need to order. Where there is significant uncertainty about the need for equipment, they use the simulation results to identify the specific equipment for which they need option contracts and the value of those options to Intel. This helps with the pricing.

Intel estimates that since 2008, the use of options in equipment purchases has saved the firm in excess of $125 million and provided the firm with at least $2 billion in revenue upside for expansions they could have quickly made using optioned equipment.

Sources: Kempf, K., Erhun, F., Hertzler, E., Rosenberg, T., & Peng, C. 2013. Optimizing capital investment decisions at Intel Corporation, *Interfaces*, 43(1): 62–78; and King, I. 2012. A chipmaker's model mathematician. *Bloomberg Businessweek*, June 4: 35.

proposal to get approved, they can back-solve the model to find a variance estimate needed to arrive at the answer that upper management desires.

Agency problems are typically inherent in investment decisions. They may occur when the managers of a firm are separated from its owners—when managers act as "agents" rather than "principals" (owners). A manager may have something to gain by not acting in the owner's best interests, or the interests of managers and owners are not co-aligned. Agency theory suggests that as managerial and owner interests diverge, managers will follow the path of their own self-interests. Sometimes this is to secure better compensation: Managers who propose projects may believe that if their projects are approved, they stand a much better chance of getting promoted. So while managers have an incentive to propose projects that *should* be successful, they also have an incentive to propose projects that *might* be successful. And because of the subjectivity involved in formally modeling a real option, managers may have an incentive to choose variance values that increase the likelihood of approval.

Managerial Conceit: Overconfidence and the Illusion of Control   Often, poor decisions are the result of such traps as biases, blind spots, and other human frailties. Much of this literature falls under the concept of **managerial conceit.**[54]

First, managerial conceit occurs when decision makers who have made successful choices in the past come to believe that they possess superior expertise for managing uncertainty. They believe that their abilities can reduce the risks inherent in decision

managerial conceit biases, blind spots, and other human frailties that lead to poor managerial decisions.

making to a much greater extent than they actually can. Such managers are more likely to shift away from analysis to trusting their own judgment. In the case of real options, they can simply declare that any given decision is a real option and proceed as before. If asked to formally model their decision, they are more likely to employ variance estimates that support their viewpoint.

Second, employing the real-options perspective can encourage decision makers toward a bias for action. Such a bias may lead to carelessness. Managerial conceit is as much a problem (if not more so) for small decisions as for big ones. Why? The cost to write the first stage of an option is much smaller than the cost of full commitment, and managers pay less attention to small decisions than to large ones. Because real options are designed to minimize potential losses while preserving potential gains, any problems that arise are likely to be smaller at first, causing less concern for the manager. Managerial conceit could suggest that managers will assume that those problems are the easiest to solve and control—a concern referred to as the illusion of control. Managers may fail to respond appropriately because they overlook the problem or believe that since it is small, they can easily resolve it. Thus, managers may approach each real-option decision with less care and diligence than if they had made a full commitment to a larger investment.

escalation of commitment
the tendency for managers to irrationally stick with an investment, even one that is broken down into a sequential series of decisions, when investment criteria are not be met.

Managerial Conceit: Irrational Escalation of Commitment   A strength of a real options perspective is also one of its Achilles heels. Both real options and decisions involving escalation of commitment require specific environments with sequential decisions.[55] As the escalation-of-commitment literature indicates, simply separating a decision into multiple parts does not guarantee that decisions made will turn out well. This condition is potentially present whenever the exercise decision retains some uncertainty, which most still do. The decision to abandon also has strong psychological factors associated with it that affect the ability of managers to make correct exercise decisions.[56]

An option to exit requires reversing an initial decision made by someone in the organization. Organizations typically encourage managers to "own their decisions" in order to motivate them. As managers invest themselves in their decision, it proves harder for them to lose face by reversing course. For managers making the decision, it feels as if they made the wrong decision in the first place, even if it was initially a good decision. The more specific the manager's human capital becomes, the harder it is to transfer it to other organizations. Hence, there is a greater likelihood that managers will stick around and try to make an existing decision work. They are more likely to continue an existing project even if it should perhaps be ended.[57]

Despite the potential pitfalls of a real options approach, many of the strategic decisions that product champions and top managers must make are enhanced when decision makers have an entrepreneurial mind-set.

L012.6

How an entrepreneurial orientation can enhance a firm's efforts to develop promising corporate venture initiatives.

Entrepreneurial Orientation

Firms that want to engage in successful CE need to have an entrepreneurial orientation (EO).[58] EO refers to the strategy-making practices that businesses use in identifying and launching corporate ventures. It represents a frame of mind and a perspective toward entrepreneurship that is reflected in a firm's ongoing processes and corporate culture.[59]

An EO has five dimensions that permeate the decision-making styles and practices of the firm's members: autonomy, innovativeness, proactiveness, competitive aggressiveness, and risk taking. These factors work together to enhance a firm's entrepreneurial performance. But even those firms that are strong in only a few aspects of EO can be very successful.[60] Exhibit 12.3 summarizes the dimensions of **entrepreneurial orientation.** Below, we discuss the five dimensions of EO and how they have been used to enhance internal venture development.

entrepreneurial orientation
the practices that businesses us in identifying and launching corporate ventures.

Dimension	Definition
Autonomy	Independent action by an individual or team aimed at bringing forth a business concept or vision and carrying it through to completion.
Innovativeness	A willingness to introduce novelty through experimentation and creative processes aimed at developing new products and services as well as new processes.
Proactiveness	A forward-looking perspective characteristic of a market-place leader that has the foresight to seize opportunities in anticipation of future demand.
Competitive aggressiveness	An intense effort to outperform industry rivals characterized by a combative posture or an aggressive response aimed at improving position or overcoming a threat in a competitive marketplace.
Risk taking	Making decisions and taking action without certain knowledge of probable outcomes; some undertakings may also involve making substantial resource commitments in the process of venturing forward.

EXHIBIT 12.3

Dimensions of Entrepreneurial Orientation

Sources: Dess, G. G. & Lumpkin, G. T. 2005. The Role of Entrepreneurial Orientation in Stimulating Effective Corporate Entrepreneurship. *Academy of Management Executive,* 19(1): 147–156; Covin, J. G. & Slevin, D. P. 1991. A Conceptual Model of Entrepreneurship as Firm Behavior. *Entrepreneurship Theory & Practice,* Fall: 7–25; Lumpkin, G. T. and Dess, G. G. 1996. Clarifying the Entrepreneurial Orientation Construct and Linking It to Performance. *Academy of Management Review,* 21: 135–172; Miller, D. 1983. The Correlates of Entrepreneurship in Three Types of Firms. *Management Science,* 29: 770–791.

Autonomy

Autonomy refers to a willingness to act independently in order to carry forward an entrepreneurial vision or opportunity. It applies to both individuals and teams that operate outside an organization's existing norms and strategies. In the context of corporate entrepreneurship, autonomous work units are often used to leverage existing strengths in new arenas, identify opportunities that are beyond the organization's current capabilities, and encourage development of new ventures or improved business practices.[61]

The need for autonomy may apply to either dispersed or focused entrepreneurial efforts. Because of the emphasis on venture projects that are being developed outside of the normal flow of business, a focused approach suggests a working environment that is relatively autonomous. But autonomy may also be important in an organization where entrepreneurship is part of the corporate culture. Everything from the methods of group interaction to the firm's reward system must make organizational members feel as if they can think freely about venture opportunities, take time to investigate them, and act without fear of condemnation. This implies a respect for the autonomy of each individual and an openness to the independent thinking that goes into championing a corporate venture idea. Thus, autonomy represents a type of empowerment (see Chapter 11) that is directed at identifying and leveraging entrepreneurial opportunities. Exhibit 12.4 identifies two techniques that organizations often use to promote autonomy.

Creating autonomous work units and encouraging independent action may have pitfalls that can jeopardize their effectiveness. Autonomous teams often lack coordination. Excessive decentralization has a strong potential to create inefficiencies, such as duplication of effort and wasting resources on projects with questionable feasibility. For example, Chris Galvin, former CEO of Motorola, scrapped the skunkworks approach the company had been using to develop new wireless phones. Fifteen teams had created 128 different phones, which led to spiraling costs and overly complex operations.[62]

For autonomous work units and independent projects to be effective, such efforts have to be measured and monitored. This requires a delicate balance: companies must have the patience and budget to tolerate the explorations of autonomous groups and the strength to cut back efforts that are not bearing fruit. It must be undertaken with a clear sense of purpose—namely, to generate new sources of competitive advantage.

autonomy
independent action by an individual or team aimed at bringing forth a business concept or vision and carrying it through to completion.

EXHIBIT 12.4 Autonomy Techniques

Autonomy		
Technique	**Description/Purpose**	**Example**
Use skunkworks to foster entrepreneurial thinking	Skunkworks are independent work units, often physically separate from corporate headquarters. They allow employees to get out from under the pressures of their daily routines to engage in creative problem solving.	Overstock.com created a skunkworks to address the problem of returned merchandise. The solution was a business within a business: Overstock auctions. The unit has grown by selling products returned to Overstock and offers fees 30 percent lower than eBay's auction service.
Design organizational structures that support independent action	Established companies with traditional structures often need to break out of such old forms to compete more effectively.	Deloitte Consulting, a division of Deloitte Touche Tohmatsu, found it difficult to compete against young agile firms. So it broke the firm into small autonomous units called "chip-aways" that operate with the flexibility of a start-up. In its first year, revenues were $40 million—10 percent higher than its projections.

Sources: Conlin, M. 2006. Square Feet. Oh How Square! *BusinessWeek, www.businessweek.com*, July 3; Cross, K. 2001. Bang the Drum Quickly. *Business 2.0*, May: 28–30; Sweeney, J. 2004. A Firm for All Reasons. *Consulting Magazine, www.consultingmag.com*; and Wagner, M. 2005. Out of the Skunkworks. *Internet Retailer*, January, *www.internetretailer.com*.

Innovativeness

innovativeness
a willingness to introduce novelty through experimentation and creative processes aimed at developing new products and services as well as new processes.

Innovativeness refers to a firm's efforts to find new opportunities and novel solutions. In the beginning of this chapter we discussed innovation; here the focus is on innovativeness—a firm's attitude toward innovation and willingness to innovate. It involves creativity and experimentation that result in new products, new services, or improved technological processes.[63] Innovativeness is one of the major components of an entrepreneurial strategy. As indicated at the beginning of the chapter, however, the job of managing innovativeness can be very challenging.

Innovativeness requires that firms depart from existing technologies and practices and venture beyond the current state of the art. Inventions and new ideas need to be nurtured even when their benefits are unclear. However, in today's climate of rapid change, effectively producing, assimilating, and exploiting innovations can be an important avenue for achieving competitive advantages. Interest in global warming and other ecological concerns has led many corporations to focus their innovativeness efforts on solving environmental problems.

As our earlier discussion of CE indicated, many corporations owe their success to an active program of innovation-based corporate venturing.[64] Exhibit 12.5 highlights two of the methods companies can use to enhance their competitive position through innovativeness.

Innovativeness can be a source of great progress and strong corporate growth, but there are also major pitfalls for firms that invest in innovation. Expenditures on R&D aimed at identifying new products or processes can be a waste of resources if the effort does not yield results. Another danger is related to the competitive climate. Even if a company innovates a new capability or successfully applies a technological breakthrough, another company may develop a similar innovation or find a use for it that is more profitable. Finally R&D and other innovation efforts are among the first to be cut back during an economic downturn.

Even though innovativeness is an important means of internal corporate venturing, it also involves major risks, because investments in innovations may not pay off. For strategic managers of entrepreneurial firms, successfully developing and adopting innovations can generate competitive advantages and provide a major source of growth for the firm.

EXHIBIT 12.5 Innovativeness Techniques

Innovativeness		
Technique	**Description/Purpose**	**Example**
Foster creativity and experimentation	Companies that support idea exploration and allow employees to express themselves creatively enhance innovation outcomes.	To tap into its reserves of innovative talent, Royal Dutch/Shell created "GameChanger" to help employees develop promising ideas. The process provides funding up to $600,000 for would-be entrepreneurs to pursue innovative projects and conduct experiments.
Invest in new technology, R&D, and continuous improvement	The latest technologies often provide sources of new competitive advantages. To extract value from a new technology, companies must invest in it.	Dell Computer Corporation's OptiPlex manufacturing system revolutionized the traditional assembly line. Hundreds of custom-built computers can be made in an eight-hour shift using state of the art automation techniques that increased productivity per person by 160 percent.

Sources: Breen, B. 2004. Living in Dell Time. *Fast Company,* November: 88–92: Hammonds, K. H. 2002. Size Is Not a Strategy. *Fast Company,* August: 78–83; Perman, S. 2001. Automate or Die. *eCompanyNow.com,* July; Dell, M. 1999. *Direct from Dell.* New York: HarperBusiness; and Watson, R. 2006. Expand Your Innovation Horizons. *Fast Company, www.fastcompany.com,* May.

Proactiveness

Proactiveness refers to a firm's efforts to seize new opportunities. Proactive organizations monitor trends, identify the future needs of existing customers, and anticipate changes in demand or emerging problems that can lead to new venture opportunities. Proactiveness involves not only recognizing changes but also being willing to act on those insights ahead of the competition.[65] Strategic managers who practice proactiveness have their eye on the future in a search for new possibilities for growth and development. Such a forward-looking perspective is important for companies that seek to be industry leaders. Many proactive firms seek out ways not only to be future oriented but also to change the very nature of competition in their industry.

Proactiveness puts competitors in the position of having to respond to successful initiatives. The benefit gained by firms that are the first to enter new markets, establish brand identity, implement administrative techniques, or adopt new operating technologies in an industry is called first mover advantage.[66]

First movers usually have several advantages. First, industry pioneers, especially in new industries, often capture unusually high profits because there are no competitors to drive prices down. Second, first movers that establish brand recognition are usually able to retain their image and hold on to the market share gains they earned by being first. Sometimes these benefits also accrue to other early movers in an industry, but, generally speaking, first movers have an advantage that can be sustained until firms enter the maturity phase of an industry's life cycle.[67]

First movers are not always successful. The customers of companies that introduce novel products or embrace breakthrough technologies may be reluctant to commit to a new way of doing things. In his book *Crossing the Chasm,* Geoffrey A. Moore noted that most firms seek evolution, not revolution, in their operations. This makes it difficult for a first mover to sell promising new technologies.[68]

Even with these caveats, however, companies that are first movers can enhance their competitive position. Exhibit 12.6 illustrates two methods firms can use to act proactively.

Being an industry leader does not always lead to competitive advantages. Some firms that have launched pioneering new products or staked their reputation on new brands have

proactiveness
a forward-looking perspective characteristic of a marketplace leader that has the foresight to seize opportunities in anticipation of future demand.

EXHIBIT 12.6 Proactiveness Techniques

Proactiveness		
Technique	**Description/Purpose**	**Example**
Introduce new products or technological capabilities ahead of the competition.	Being a first mover provides companies with an ability to shape the playing field and shift competitive advantages in their favor.	Amazon was able to define the online bookselling market by entering the market early and defining the user experience. They further leveraged their position as an early mover when moving into other retailing ventures and later into cloud computing.
Continuously seek out new product or service offerings.	Firms that provide new resources or sources of supply can benefit from a proactive stance.	Costco seized a chance to leverage its success as a warehouse club that sells premium brands when it introduced Costco Home Stores. The home stores are usually located near its warehouse stores and its rapid inventory turnover gives it a cost advantage of 15 to 25 percent over close competitors such as Bassett Furniture and the Bombay Company.

Sources: Bryce, D. J. & Dyer, J. H. 2007. Strategies to Crack Well-Guarded Markets. *Harvard Business Review,* May: 84–92; Collins, J. C. & Porras, J. I. 1997. *Built to Last.* New York: HarperBusiness; Robinson, D. 2005. Sony Pushes Reliability in Vaio Laptops. *IT Week, www.itweek.co.uk*, October 12; and *www.sony.com.*

failed to get the hoped-for payoff. Coca-Cola and PepsiCo invested $75 million to launch sodas that would capitalize on the low-carb diet trend. But with half the carbohydrates taken out, neither *C2,* Coke's entry, nor *Pepsi Edge* tasted very good. The two new brands combined never achieved more than one percent market share. PepsiCo halted production in 2005 and Coca-Cola followed suit in 2007.[69] Such missteps are indicative of the dangers of trying to proactively anticipate demand. Another danger for opportunity-seeking companies is that they will take their proactiveness efforts too far. For example, Porsche has tried to extend its brand images outside of the automotive arena. While some efforts have worked, such as Porsche-designed T-shirts and sunglasses, other efforts have failed, such as the Porsche-branded golf clubs.

Careful monitoring and scanning of the environment, as well as extensive feasibility research, are needed for a proactive strategy to lead to competitive advantages. Firms that do it well usually have substantial growth and internal development to show for it. Many of them have been able to sustain the advantages of proactiveness for years.

Competitive Aggressiveness

competitive aggressiveness
an intense effort to outperform industry rivals characterized by a combative posture or an aggressive response aimed at improving position or overcoming a threat in a competitive marketplace.

Competitive aggressiveness refers to a firm's efforts to outperform its industry rivals. Companies with an aggressive orientation are willing to "do battle" with competitors. They might slash prices and sacrifice profitability to gain market share or spend aggressively to obtain manufacturing capacity. As an avenue of firm development and growth, competitive aggressiveness may involve being very assertive in leveraging the results of other entrepreneurial activities such as innovativeness or proactiveness.

Competitive aggressiveness is directed toward competitors. The SWOT analysis discussed in Chapters 2 and 3 provides a useful way to distinguish between these different approaches to CE. Proactiveness, as we saw in the last section, is a response to opportunities—the O in SWOT. Competitive aggressiveness, by contrast, is a response to threats—the T in SWOT. A competitively aggressive posture is important for firms that seek to enter new markets in the face of intense rivalry.

Strategic managers can use competitive aggressiveness to combat industry trends that threaten their survival or market position. Sometimes firms need to be forceful in defending

EXHIBIT 12.7 Competitive Aggressiveness Techniques

Competitive Aggressiveness		
Technique	**Description/Purpose**	**Example**
Enter markets with drastically lower prices.	Narrow operating margins make companies vulnerable to extended price competition.	Using open-source software, California-based Zimbra, Inc. has become a leader in messaging and collaboration software. Its product costs about one-third less than its direct competitor Microsoft Exchange. Zimbra generated $4.3 billion in sales in 2012.
Find successful business models and copy them.	As long as a practice is not protected by intellectual property laws, it's probably okay to imitate it. Finding solutions to existing problems is generally quicker and cheaper than inventing them.	Best Practices LLC is a North Carolina consulting group that seeks out best practices and then repackages and resells them. With annual revenues in excess of $8 million, Best Practices has become a leader in continuous improvement and benchmarking strategies.

Sources: Guth, R. A. 2006. Trolling the Web for Free Labor, Software Upstarts Are New Force. *The Wall Street Journal,* November 12: 1; Mochari, I. 2001. Steal This Strategy. *Inc.,* July: 62–67; *www.best-in-class.com*; and *www.zimbra.com*.

the competitive position that has made them an industry leader. Firms often need to be aggressive to ensure their advantage by capitalizing on new technologies or serving new market needs. Exhibit 12.7 suggests two of the ways competitively aggressive firms enhance their entrepreneurial position.

Another practice companies use to overcome the competition is to make preannouncements of new products or technologies. This type of signaling is aimed not only at potential customers but also at competitors to see how they will react or to discourage them from launching similar initiatives. Sometimes the preannouncements are made just to scare off competitors, an action that has potential ethical implications.

Competitive aggressiveness may not always lead to competitive advantages. Some companies (or their CEOs) have severely damaged their reputations by being overly aggressive. Although it continues to be a dominant player, Microsoft's highly aggressive profile makes it the subject of scorn by some businesses and individuals. Efforts to find viable replacements for the Microsoft products have helped fuel interest in alternative options provided by Google, Apple, and the open-source software movement.[70]

Competitive aggressiveness is a strategy that is best used in moderation. Companies that aggressively establish their competitive position and vigorously exploit opportunities to achieve profitability may, over the long run, be better able to sustain their competitive advantages if their goal is to defeat, rather than decimate, their competitors.

Risk Taking

Risk taking refers to a firm's willingness to seize a venture opportunity even though it does not know whether the venture will be successful—to act boldly without knowing the consequences. To be successful through corporate entrepreneurship, firms usually have to take on riskier alternatives, even if it means forgoing the methods or products that have worked in the past. To obtain high financial returns, firms take such risks as assuming high levels of debt, committing large amounts of firm resources, introducing new products into new markets, and investing in unexplored technologies.

All of the approaches to internal development that we have discussed are potentially risky. Whether they are being aggressive, proactive, or innovative, firms on the path of CE must act without knowing how their actions will turn out. Before launching their strategies, corporate entrepreneurs must know their firm's appetite for risk.[71]

risk taking
making decisions and taking action without certain knowledge of probable outcomes. Some undertakings may also involve making substantial resource commitments in the process of venturing forward.

Three types of risk that organizations and their executives face are business risk, financial risk, and personal risk:

- *Business risk taking* involves venturing into the unknown without knowing the probability of success. This is the risk associated with entering untested markets or committing to unproven technologies.
- *Financial risk taking* requires that a company borrow heavily or commit a large portion of its resources in order to grow. In this context, risk is used to refer to the risk/return trade-off that is familiar in financial analysis.
- *Personal risk taking* refers to the risks that an executive assumes in taking a stand in favor of a strategic course of action. Executives who take such risks stand to influence the course of their whole company, and their decisions also can have significant implications for their careers.

Even though risk taking involves taking chances, it is not gambling. The best-run companies investigate the consequences of various opportunities and create scenarios of likely outcomes. A key to managing entrepreneurial risks is to evaluate new venture opportunities thoroughly enough to reduce the uncertainty surrounding them. Exhibit 12.8 indicates two methods companies can use to strengthen their competitive position through risk taking.

Risk taking, by its nature, involves potential dangers and pitfalls. Only carefully managed risk is likely to lead to competitive advantages. Actions that are taken without sufficient forethought, research, and planning may prove to be very costly. Therefore, strategic managers must always remain mindful of potential risks. In his book *Innovation and Entrepreneurship*, Peter Drucker argued that successful entrepreneurs are typically not risk takers. Instead, they take steps to minimize risks by carefully understanding them. That is how they avoid focusing on risk and remain focused on opportunity.[72] Risk taking is a good place to close this chapter on corporate entrepreneurship. Companies that choose to grow through internal corporate venturing must remember that entrepreneurship always involves embracing what is new and uncertain.

EXHIBIT 12.8 Risk-Taking Techniques

Risk Taking		
Technique	**Description/Purpose**	**Example**
Research and assess risk factors to minimize uncertainty	Companies that "do their homework"—that is, carefully evaluate the implications of bold actions—reduce the likelihood of failure.	Graybar Electric Co. took a risk when it invested $144 million to revamp its distribution system. It consolidated 231 small centers into 16 supply warehouses and installed the latest communications network. Graybar is now considered a leader in facility redesign and its sales have increased steadily since the consolidation, topping $5 billion in sales in a recent year.
Use techniques that have worked in other domains	Risky methods that other companies have tried may provide an avenue for advancing company goals.	Autobytel.com, one of the first companies to sell cars online, decided on an approach that worked well for others—advertising during the Super Bowl. It was the first dot-com ever to do so and its $1.2 million 30-second ad paid off well by generating weeks of free publicity and favorable business press.

Sources: Anonymous. 2006. Graybar Offers Data Center Redesign Seminars. *Cabling Installation and Maintenance, www.cim.pennnet.com*, September 1; Keenan, F. & Mullaney, T. J. 2001. Clicking at Graybar. *BusinessWeek,* June 18: 132–34; Weintraub, A. 2001. Make or break for Autobytel. *BusinessWeek e.biz,* July 9: EB30-EB32; *www.autobytel.com*; and *www.graybar.com*.

Citizen-riders speak up and crowd source the Pibal

By Irena Descubes and Tom McNamara

Cycling has become more and more popular. Concerns about physical fitness, the rising costs of running a car, and gridlocked city streets would be just a few of the reasons that an increasing number of people are turning to biking. But whereas once considered the "poor man's means of transport" or something for children, cycling has now become a symbol of ecologically friendly, and socially aware, citizens. Proof of this can be found in a report showing that in 2011, bicycle sales exceeded those for new cars in 19 out of 23 European countries surveyed.

Many cities are trying to ride this green trend by developing bike-sharing schemes. The principle is simple. Just like hiring a taxi, a person picks up a bicycle where and when it is needed and then leaves it at a select destination when done. Paris, London, New York, Montreal, Taipei, Seoul, and Adelaide are just a few of the major metropolitan areas that have introduced bike sharing schemes. Often operated by a "for profit" company, the bicycles tend to have a similar look and feel, and are not always well adapted to the specific landscapes or climates where they will be used. Complaints by the people who use them that the bikes are "heavy" and "difficult-to-maneuver" are not uncommon.

The city of Bordeaux (approximately 215,000 inhabitants) has had a bike-sharing scheme in place since 2003. But due to growing criticism concerning the hefty bicycle fleet, city officials decided in late 2011 to change it. What was different about the project was that the people who actually used the bikes were asked to take part in the system's redesign.

In early 2012, locals were invited to come up with an ideal bike for both riding long distances and maneuvering through heavy traffic in the city center. More than 300 design ideas were solicited through an online crowdsourcing platform called "jeparticipe. bordeaux.fr." The submissions were then refined by the famous French designer Philippe Starck, who agreed to offer his services to the city free of charge. Previously, Mr. Starck was known for having been involved in several Earth-friendly projects.

The end result was something called Pibal. The name is a play on words due to the fact that the bikes have a slight resemblance to a serpent-like eel called a *pibale* in French. The Pibal is half-bike and half-scooter and has several innovations. Bright yellow rims, mudguards and tires with reflective strips for increased visibility, built-in lighting, a two-speed integrated gear hub to allow for comfortable riding both downhill and uphill, a foot platform that allows you to push the bike just like a scooter, support for a U shaped anti-theft locker, adjustable seat and handlebars to accommodate different sized riders, and robust shock absorbers were all advanced features that were incorporated into the bike's design. "Just like the Eel *(pibale)*, undulating and playing in a stream, Pibal is an answer to new urban ergonomics," says Mr. Starck.

Peugeot, the famous French bike manufacturer with over 125 years of experience in production and design, has agreed to team up with Mr. Stark and the city of Bordeaux. The first 300 bikes are expected to be delivered in February 2014.

Discussion Questions

1. In groups, discuss the comparative advantages and disadvantages of the bike sharing systems used in New York City (http://citibikenyc.com) and in Paris (http://en.velib.paris.fr/).
2. Smart cities are populated more and more with smart citizens. In your opinion, what are the key success factors for the crowdsourcing of ideas?

Sources: Boyer M. (2013). "Philippe Starck and Peugeot Design 'Pibal' Scooter-Cycle for Bike-Sharing Program in Bordeaux"; "Recession transport: bike sales overtake cars" by Mona Chalabi, The Guardian, September 17 2013; Un vélo-trotinette: le vélo-Bordeaux par Philippe Starck, et les Bordelais; Dessine-moi un vélo urbain.

summary

To remain competitive in today's economy, established firms must find new avenues for development and growth. This chapter has addressed how innovation and corporate entrepreneurship can be a means of internal venture creation and strategic renewal, and how an entrepreneurial orientation can help corporations enhance their competitive position.

Innovation is one of the primary means by which corporations grow and strengthen their strategic position. Innovations can take several forms, ranging from radical breakthrough innovations to incremental improvement innovations. Innovations are often used to update products and services or for improving organizational processes. Managing the innovation process is often challenging, because it involves a great deal of uncertainty and there are many choices to be made about the extent and type of innovations to pursue. By cultivating innovation skills, defining the scope of innovation, managing the pace of innovation, staffing to capture value from innovation, and collaborating with innovation partners, firms can more effectively manage the innovation process.

We also discussed the role of corporate entrepreneurship in venture development and strategic renewal. Corporations usually take either a focused or dispersed approach to corporate venturing. Firms with a focused approach usually separate the corporate venturing activity from the ongoing operations of the firm in order to foster independent thinking and encourage entrepreneurial team members to think and act without the constraints imposed by the corporation. In corporations where venturing activities are dispersed, a culture of entrepreneurship permeates all parts of the company in order to induce strategic behaviors by all organizational members. In measuring the success of corporate venturing activities, both financial and strategic objectives should be considered. Real options analysis is often used to make better quality decisions in uncertain entrepreneurial situations. However, a real options approach has potential drawbacks.

Most entrepreneurial firms need to have an entrepreneurial orientation: the methods, practices, and decision-making styles that strategic managers use to act entrepreneurially. Five dimensions of entrepreneurial orientation are found in firms that pursue corporate venture strategies. Autonomy, innovativeness, proactiveness, competitive aggressiveness, and risk taking each make a unique contribution to the pursuit of new opportunities. When deployed effectively, the methods and practices of an entrepreneurial orientation can be used to engage successfully in corporate entrepreneurship and new venture creation. However, strategic managers must remain mindful of the pitfalls associated with each of these approaches.

SUMMARY REVIEW QUESTIONS

1. What is meant by the concept of a continuum of radical and incremental innovations?

2. What are the dilemmas that organizations face when deciding what innovation projects to pursue? What steps can organizations take to effectively manage the innovation process?

3. What is the difference between focused and dispersed approaches to corporate entrepreneurship?

4. How are business incubators used to foster internal corporate venturing?

5. What is the role of the product champion in bringing a new product or service into existence in a corporation? How can companies use product champions to enhance their venture development efforts?

6. Explain the difference between proactiveness and competitive aggressiveness in terms of achieving and sustaining competitive advantage.

7. Describe how the entrepreneurial orientation (EO) dimensions of innovativeness, proactiveness, and risk taking can be combined to create competitive advantages for entrepreneurial firms.

Entrepreneurial Orientation	Company A	Company B
Autonomy		
Innovativeness		
Proactiveness		
Competitive Aggressiveness		
Risk Taking		

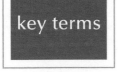

key terms

innovation 378
product innovation 378
process innovation 379
radical innovation 379
incremental innovation 379
strategic envelope 385

corporate
  entrepreneurship 387
focused approaches
  to corporate
  entrepreneurship 390
new venture group 390
business incubator 390
dispersed approaches
  to corporate
  entrepreneurship 391

entrepreneurial
  culture 392
product champion 393
exit champion 394
real options
  analysis 395
back-solver dilemma 396
managerial conceit 397
escalation of
  commitment 398

entrepreneurial
  orientation 398
autonomy 399
innovativeness 400
proactiveness 401
competitive
  aggressiveness 402
risk taking 403

experiential exercise

Select two different major corporations from two different industries (you might use Fortune 500 companies to make your selection). Compare and contrast these organizations in terms of their entrepreneurial orientation.

BASED ON YOUR COMPARISON:

1. How is the corporation's entrepreneurial orientation reflected in its strategy?
2. Which corporation would you say has the stronger entrepreneurial orientation?
3. Is the corporation with the stronger entrepreneurial orientation also stronger in terms of financial performance?

application questions & exercises

1. Select a firm known for its corporate entrepreneurship activities. Research the company and discuss how it has positioned itself relative to its close competitors. Does it have a unique strategic advantage? Disadvantage? Explain.
2. Explain the difference between product innovations and process innovations. Provide examples of firms that have recently introduced each type of

innovation. What are the types of innovations related to the strategies of each firm?

3. Using the Internet, select a company that is listed on the NASDAQ or New York Stock Exchange. Research the extent to which the company has an entrepreneurial culture. Does the company use product champions? Does it have a corporate venture capital fund? Do you believe its entrepreneurial efforts are sufficient to generate sustainable advantages?
4. How can an established firm use an entrepreneurial orientation to enhance its overall strategic position? Provide examples.

ethics questions

1. Innovation activities are often aimed at making a discovery or commercializing a technology ahead of the competition. What are some of the unethical practices that companies could engage in during the innovation process? What are the potential long-term consequences of such actions?
2. Discuss the ethical implications of using entrepreneurial policies and practices to pursue corporate social responsibility goals. Are these efforts authentic and genuine or just an attempt to attract more customers?

references

1. Yarow, J. 2012. It's official: Apple is just a niche player in smartphones now. *businessinsider.com,* November 2: np; Vascellaro, J. 2009. Radio tunes out Google in rare miss for web titan. *wsj.com*, May 12: np; and McGrath, R. 2011. Failing by design. *Harvard Business Review*, 89(4): 76–83.

2. For an interesting discussion, see Johannessen, J. A., Olsen, B., & Lumpkin, G. T. 2001. Innovation as newness: What is new, how new, and new to whom? *European Journal of Innovation Management,* 4(1): 20–31.

3. The discussion of product and process innovation is based on Roberts, E. B. (Ed.). 2002. *Innovation: Driving product, process, and market change.* San Francisco: Jossey-Bass; Hayes, R. & Wheelwright, S. 1985. Competing through manufacturing. *Harvard Business Review,* 63(1): 99–109; and Hayes, R. & Wheelwright, S. 1979. Dynamics of product–process life cycles. *Harvard Business Review,* 57(2): 127–136.

4. The discussion of radical and incremental innovations draws from Leifer, R., McDermott, C. M., Colarelli, G., O'Connor, G. C., Peters, L. S., Rice, M. P., & Veryzer, R. W. 2000. *Radical innovation: How mature companies can outsmart upstarts.* Boston: Harvard Business School Press; Damanpour, F. 1996. Organizational complexity and innovation: Developing and testing multiple contingency models. *Management Science,* 42(5): 693–716; and Hage, J. 1980. *Theories of organizations.* New York: Wiley.

5. Christensen, C. M. & Raynor, M. E. 2003. *The innovator's solution.* Boston: Harvard Business School Press.

6. Dressner, H. 2004. The Gartner Fellows interview: Clayton M. Christensen. *www.gartner.com*, April 26.

7. For another perspective on how different types of innovation affect organizational choices, see Wolter, C. & Veloso, F. M. 2008. The effects of innovation on vertical structure: Perspectives on transactions costs and competences. *Academy of Management Review,* 33(3): 586–605.

8. Drucker, P. F. 1985. *Innovation and entrepreneurship: 2000* New York: Harper & Row.

9. Birkinshaw, J., Hamel, G., & Mol, M. J. 2008. Management innovation. *Academy of Management Review,* 33(4): 825–845.

10. Steere, W. C., Jr. & Niblack, J. 1997. Pfizer, Inc. In Kanter, R. M., Kao, J., & Wiersema, F. (Eds.), *Innovation: Breakthrough thinking at 3M, DuPont, GE, Pfizer, and Rubbermaid:* 123–145. New York: HarperCollins.

11. Morrissey, C. A. 2000. Managing innovation through corporate venturing. *Graziadio Business Report,* Spring, *gbr.pepperdine.edu*; and Sharma, A. 1999. Central dilemmas of managing innovation in large firms. *California Management Review,* 41(3): 147–164.

12. Sharma, op. cit.

13. Dyer, J. H., Gregerson, H. B., & Christensen, C. M. 2009. The innovator's DNA. *Harvard Business Review,* December: 61-67.

14. Eggers, J. P., & Kaplan, S. 2009. Cognition and renewal: Comparing CEO and organizational effects on incumbent adaptation to technical change. *Organization Science,* 20: 461–477.

15. Biodegradable Products Institute. 2003. "Compostable Logo" of the Biodegradable Products Institute gains momentum with approval of DuPont Biomax resin, *www.bpiworld.org*, June 12; Leifer et al., op. cit.

16. For more on defining the scope of innovation, see Valikangas, L. & Gibbert, M. 2005. Boundary-setting strategies for escaping innovation traps. *MIT Sloan Management Review,* 46(3): 58–65.

17. Leifer et al., op. cit.

18. Bhide, A. V. 2000. *The origin and evolution of new businesses.* New York: Oxford University Press; Brown, S. L. & Eisenhardt, K. M. 1998. *Competing on the edge: Strategy as structured chaos.* Cambridge, MA: Harvard Business School Press.

19. McGrath, R. G. & Keil, T. 2007. The value captor's process: Getting the most out of your new business ventures. *Harvard Business Review,* May: 128–136.

20. For an interesting discussion of how sharing technology knowledge with different divisions in an organization can contribute to innovation processes, see Miller, D. J., Fern, M. J., & Cardinal, L. B. 2007. The use of knowledge for technological innovation within diversified firms. *Academy of Management Journal,* 50(2): 308–326.

21. Ketchen Jr., D. J., Ireland, R. D., & Snow, C. C. 2007 Strategic entrepreneurship, collaborative innovation, and wealth creation. *Strategic Entrepreneurship Journal,* 1(3–4): 371–385.

22. Chesbrough, H. 2003. *Open innovation: The new imperative for creating and profiting from technology.* Boston: Harvard Business School Press.

23. For a recent study of what makes alliance partnerships successful, see Sampson, R. C. 2007. R&D alliances and firm performance: The impact of technological diversity and alliance organization on innovation. *Academy of Management Journal,* 50(2): 364–386.

24. For an interesting perspective on the role of collaboration among multinational corporations see Hansen, M. T. & Nohria, N. 2004. How to build collaborative advantage. *MIT Sloan Management Review,* 46(1): 22–30.

25. Wells, R. M. J. 2008. The product innovation process: Are managing information flows and cross-functional collaboration key? *Academy of Management Perspectives,* 22(1): 58–60. Dougherty, D., & Dunne, D. D. 2011. Organizing ecologies of complex innovation. *Organization Science,* forthcoming. Kim, H. E., Pennings, J. M. 2009. Innovation and strategic renewal in mature markets: A study of the tennis racket industry. *Organization Science,* 20: 368–383.

26. Guth, W. D. & Ginsberg, A. 1990. Guest editor's introduction: Corporate entrepreneurship. *Strategic Management Journal,* 11: 5–15.

27. Pinchot, G. 1985. *Intrapreneuring.* New York: Harper & Row.

28. For an interesting perspective on the role of context on the discovery and creation of opportunities, see Zahra, S. A. 2008. The virtuous cycle of discovery and creation of entrepreneurial opportunities. *Strategic Entrepreneurship Journal,* 2(3): 243–257.

29. Birkinshaw, J. 1997. Entrepreneurship in multinational corporations: The characteristics of subsidiary initiatives. *Strategic Management Journal,* 18(3): 207–229; and Kanter, R. M. 1985. *The change masters.* New York: Simon & Schuster.

30. Hansen, M. T., Chesbrough, H. W., Nohria, N., & Sull, D. 2000. Networked incubators: Hothouses of the new economy. *Harvard Business Review,* 78(5): 74–84.

31. For more on the importance of leadership in fostering a climate of entrepreneurship, see Ling, Y., Simsek, Z., Lubatkin, M. H., & Veiga, J. F. 2008. Transformational leadership's role in promoting corporate entrepreneurship: Examining the CEO-TMT interface. Academy of Management Journal, 51(3): 557–576.

32. Bryant, A. 2011. Got an idea? Sell it to me in 30 seconds. *nytimes.com,* January 1: np.

33. Gunther, M. 2010. 3M's innovation revival. *Cnnmoney.com,* September 24: np; Byrne, J. 2012. The 12 greatest entrepreneurs of our time. *Fortune,* April 9: 76; and Anonymous. 2007. Johnson & Johnson turns to internal venturing. *silico.wordpress.com,* July 16. np.

34. For an interesting discussion, see Davenport, T. H., Prusak, L., & Wilson, H. J. 2003. Who's bringing you hot ideas and how are you responding? *Harvard Business Review,* 80(1): 58–64.

35. Howell, J. M. 2005. The right stuff. Identifying and developing effective champions of innovation. *Academy of Management Executive,* 19(2): 108–119. See also Greene, P., Brush, C., & Hart, M. 1999. The corporate venture champion: A resource-based approach to role and process. *Entrepreneurship Theory & Practice,* 23(3): 103–122; and Markham, S. K. & Aiman-Smith, L. 2001. Product champions: Truths, myths and management. Research Technology Management, May–June. 44–50.

36. Burgelman, R. A. 1983. A process model of internal corporate venturing in the diversified major firm. *Administrative Science Quarterly,* 28: 223–244.

37. Hamel, G. 2000. *Leading the revolution.* Boston: Harvard Business School Press.

38. Greene, Brush, & Hart, op. cit.; and Shane, S. 1994. Are champions different from non-champions? Journal of Business Venturing, 9(5): 397–421.

39. Block, Z. & MacMillan, I. C. 1993. *Corporate venturing—Creating new businesses with the firm.* Cambridge, MA: Harvard Business School Press.

40. For an interesting discussion of these trade-offs, see Stringer, R. 2000. How to manage radical innovation. *California Management Review,* 42(4): 70–88; and Gompers, P. A. & Lerner, J. 1999. *The venture capital cycle.* Cambridge, MA: MIT Press.

41. Cardinal, L. B., Turner, S. F., Fern, M. J., & Burton, R. M. 2011. Organizing for product development across technological environments: Performance trade-offs and priorities. *Organization Science,* Forthcoming.

42. Albrinck, J., Hornery, J., Kletter, D., & Neilson, G. 2001. Adventures in corporate venturing. *Strategy + Business,* 22: 119–129; and McGrath, R. G. & MacMillan, I. C. 2000. *The entrepreneurial mind-set.* Cambridge, MA: Harvard Business School Press.

43. Kiel, T., McGrath, R. G., Tukiainen, T., 2009. Gems from the ashes: Capability creation and transforming in internal corporate venturing. *Organization Science,* 20: 601–620.

44. For an interesting discussion of how different outcome goals affect organizational learning and employee motivation, see Seijts, G. H. & Latham, G. P. 2005. Learning versus performance goals: When should each be used? *Academy of Management Executive,* 19(1): 124–131.

45. Crockett, R. O. 2001. Motorola. *BusinessWeek,* July 15: 72–78.

46. The ideas in this section are drawn from Royer, I. 2003. Why bad projects are so hard to kill. *Harvard Business Review,* 80(1): 48–56.

47. For an interesting perspective on the different roles that individuals play in the entrepreneurial process, see Baron, R. A. 2008. The role of affect in the entrepreneurial process. *Academy of Management Review,* 33(2): 328–340.

48. Hoskin, R. E. 1994. *Financial accounting.* New York: Wiley.

49. We know stock options as derivative assets—that is, "an asset whose value depends on or is derived from the value of another, the underlying asset": Amram, M. & Kulatilaka, N. 1999. *Real options: Managing strategic investment in an uncertain world: 34.* Boston: Harvard Business School Press.

50. For an interesting discussion on why it is difficult to "kill options," refer to Royer, I. 2003. Why bad projects are so hard to kill. *Harvard Business Review,* 81(2): 48–57.

51. Slywotzky, A. & Wise, R. 2003. Double-digit growth in no-growth times. Fast Company, April: 66–72; *www.hoovers.com;* and *www.johnsoncontrols.com.*

52. For more on the role of real options in entrepreneurial decision making, see Folta, T. B. & O'Brien, J. P. 2004. Entry in the presence of dueling options. *Strategic Management Journal,* 25: 121–138.

53. This section draws on Janney, J. J. & Dess, G. G. 2004. Can real options analysis improve decision-making? Promises and pitfalls. *Academy of Management Executive,* 18(4): 60–75. For additional insights on pitfalls of real options, consider McGrath, R. G. 1997. A real options logic for initiating technology positioning investment. *Academy of Management Review,* 22(4): 974–994; Coff, R. W. & Laverty, K. J. 2001. Real options on knowledge assets: Panacea or Pandora's box. *Business Horizons,* 73: 79, McGrath, R. G. 1999. Falling forward: Real options reasoning and entrepreneurial failure. *Academy of Management Review,* 24(1): 13–30; and, Zardkoohi, A. 2004.

54. For an understanding of the differences between how managers say they approach decisions and how they actually do, March and Shapira's discussion is perhaps the best. March, J. G. & Shapira, Z. 1987. Managerial perspectives on risk and risk-taking. *Management Science,* 33(11): 1404–1418.

55. A discussion of some factors that may lead to escalation in decision making is included in Choo, C. W. 2005. Information failures and organizational disasters. *MIT Sloan Management Review,* 46(3): 8–10.

56. For an interesting discussion of the use of real options analysis in the application of wireless communications, which helped to lower the potential for escalation, refer to McGrath, R. G., Ferrier, W. J., & Mendelow, A. L. 2004. Real options as engines of choice and heterogeneity. *Academy of Management Review,* 29(1): 86–101.

57. One very useful solution for reducing the effects of managerial conceit is to incorporate an "exit champion" into the decision process. Exit champions provide arguments for killing off the firm's commitment to a decision. For a very insightful discussion on exit champions, refer to Royer, I. 2003. Why bad projects are so hard to kill. *Harvard Business Review,* 81(2): 49–56.

58. For more on how entrepreneurial orientation influences organizational performance, see Wang, L. 2008. Entrepreneurial orientation, learning orientation, and firm performance. *Entrepreneurship Theory & Practice,* 32(4): 635–657; and Runyan, R., Droge, C., & Swinney, J. 2008. Entrepreneurial orientation versus small business orientation: What are their relationships to firm performance? *Journal of Small Business Management,* 46(4): 567–588.

59. Covin, J. G. & Slevin, D. P. 1991. A conceptual model of entrepreneurship as firm behavior. *Entrepreneurship Theory and Practice,* 16(1): 7–24; Lumpkin, G. T. & Dess, G. G. 1996. Clarifying the entrepreneurial orientation construct and linking it to performance. *Academy of Management Review,* 21(1): 135–172; and McGrath, R. G. & MacMillan, I. C. 2000. *The entrepreneurial mind-set.* Cambridge, MA: Harvard Business School Press.

60. Lumpkin, G. T. & Dess, G. G. 2001. Linking two dimensions of entrepreneurial orientation to firm performance: The moderating role of environment and life cycle. *Journal of Business Venturing,* 16: 429–451.

61. For an interesting discussion, see Day, J. D., Mang, P. Y., Richter, A., & Roberts, J. 2001. The innovative organization: Why new ventures need more than a room of their own, *McKinsey Quarterly,* 2: 21–31.

62. Crockett, R. O. 2001. Chris Galvin shakes things up—again. *BusinessWeek,* May 28: 38–39.

63. For insights into the role of information technology in innovativeness, see Dibrell, C., Davis, P. S., & Craig, J. 2008. Fueling innovation through information technology in SMEs. *Journal of Small Business Management,* 46(2): 203–218.

64. For an interesting discussion of the impact of innovativeness on organizational outcomes see Cho, H. J. & Pucik, V. 2005. Relationship between innovativeness, quality, growth, profitability, and market value. *Strategic Management Journal,* 26(6): 555–575.

65. Danneels, E., & Sethi, R. 2011. New product exploration under environmental turbulence. *Organization Science,* forthcoming.

66. Lieberman, M. B. & Montgomery, D. B. 1988. First mover advantages. *Strategic Management Journal,* 9 (Special Issue): 41–58.

67. The discussion of first mover advantages is based on several articles, including Lambkin, M. 1988. Order of entry and performance in new markets. *Strategic Management Journal,* 9: 127–140; Lieberman & Montgomery, op. cit.: 41–58; and Miller, A. & Camp, B. 1985. Exploring determinants of success in corporate ventures. *Journal of Business Venturing,* 1(2): 87–105.

68. Moore, G. A. 1999. *Crossing the chasm* (2nd ed.). New York: HarperBusiness.

69. Mallas, S. 2005. PepsiCo loses its Edge. Motley Fool, June 1, *www.fool.com.*

70. Lyons, D. 2006. The cheap revolution. Forbes, September 18: 102–111.

71. Miller, K. D. 2007. Risk and rationality in entrepreneurial processes. *Strategic Entrepreneurship Journal,* 1(1–2): 57–74.

72. Drucker, op. cit., pp. 109–110.

chapter 13

Analyzing Strategic Management Cases

After reading this chapter, you should have a good understanding of the following learning objectives:

LO13.1 How strategic case analysis is used to simulate real-world experiences.

LO13.2 How analyzing strategic management cases can help develop the ability to differentiate, speculate, and integrate when evaluating complex business problems.

LO13.3 The steps involved in conducting a strategic management case analysis.

LO13.4 How to get the most out of case analysis.

LO13.5 How integrative thinking and conflict-inducing discussion techniques can lead to better decisions.

LO13.6 How to use the strategic insights and material from each of the 12 previous chapters in the text to analyze issues posed by strategic management cases.

Why Analyze Strategic Management Cases?

"If you don't ask the right questions, then you're never going to get the right solution. I spent too much of my career feeling like I'd done a really good job answering the wrong question. And that was because I was letting other people give me the question. One of the things that I've tried to do more and more and I obviously have the opportunity to do as a leader—is to take ownership of the question. And so I'm much more interested these days in having debates about what the questions should be than I necessarily am about the solutions."[1]

—Tim Brown, CEO of IDEO (a leading design consulting firm)

It is often said that the key to finding good answers is to ask good questions. Strategic managers and business leaders are required to evaluate options, make choices, and find solutions to the challenges they face every day. To do so, they must learn to ask the right questions. The study of strategic management poses the same challenge. The process of analyzing, decision making, and implementing strategic actions raises many good questions.

- Why do some firms succeed and others fail?
- Why are some companies higher performers than others?
- What information is needed in the strategic planning process?
- How do competing values and beliefs affect strategic decision making?
- What skills and capabilities are needed to implement a strategy effectively?

How does a student of strategic management answer these questions? By strategic case analysis. **Case analysis** simulates the real-world experience that strategic managers and company leaders face as they try to determine how best to run their companies. It places students in the middle of an actual situation and challenges them to figure out what to do.[2]

case analysis
a method of learning complex strategic management concepts—such as environmental analysis, the process of decision making, and implementing strategic actions—through placing students in the middle of an actual situation and challenging them to figure out what to do.

Asking the right questions is just the beginning of case analysis. In the previous chapters we have discussed issues and challenges that managers face and provided analytical frameworks for understanding the situation. But once the analysis is complete, decisions have to be made. Case analysis forces you to choose among different options and set forth a plan of action based on your choices. But even then the job is not done. Strategic case analysis also requires that you address how you will implement the plan and the implications of choosing one course of action over another.

A strategic management case is a detailed description of a challenging situation faced by an organization.[3] It usually includes a chronology of events and extensive support materials, such as financial statements, product lists, and transcripts of interviews with employees. Although names or locations are sometimes changed to provide anonymity, cases usually report the facts of a situation as authentically as possible.

One of the main reasons to analyze strategic management cases is to develop an ability to evaluate business situations critically. In case analysis, memorizing key terms and conceptual frameworks is not enough. To analyze a case, it is important that you go beyond textbook prescriptions and quick answers. It requires you to look deeply into the information that is provided and root out the essential issues and causes of a company's problems.

The types of skills that are required to prepare an effective strategic case analysis can benefit you in actual business situations. Case analysis adds to the overall learning experience by helping you acquire or improve skills that may not be taught in a typical lecture course. Three capabilities that can be learned by conducting case analysis are especially useful to strategic managers—the ability to differentiate, speculate, and integrate.[4] Here's how case analysis can enhance those skills.

1. *Differentiate.* Effective strategic management requires that many different elements of a situation be evaluated at once. This is also true in case analysis. When analyzing cases, it is important to isolate critical facts, evaluate whether assumptions are useful or faulty, and distinguish between good and bad information. Differentiating between the factors that are influencing the situation presented by a case is necessary for making a good analysis. Strategic management also involves understanding that problems are often complex and multilayered. This applies to case analysis as well. Ask whether the case deals with operational, business-level, or corporate issues. Do the problems stem from weaknesses in the internal value chain or threats in the external environment? Dig deep. Being too quick to accept the easiest or least controversial answer will usually fail to get to the heart of the problem.

2. *Speculate.* Strategic managers need to be able to use their imagination to envision an explanation or solution that might not readily be apparent. The same is true with case analysis. Being able to imagine different scenarios or contemplate the outcome of a decision can aid the analysis. Managers also have to deal with uncertainty since most decisions are made without complete knowledge of the circumstances. This is also true in case analysis. Case materials often seem to be missing data or the information provided is contradictory. The ability to speculate about details that are unknown or the consequences of an action can be helpful.

3. *Integrate.* Strategy involves looking at the big picture and having an organization-wide perspective. Strategic case analysis is no different. Even though the chapters in this textbook divide the material into various topics that may apply to different parts of an organization, all of this information must be integrated into one set of recommendations that will affect the whole company. A strategic manager needs to comprehend how all the factors that influence the organization will interact. This also applies to case analysis. Changes made in one part of the organization affect other parts. Thus, a holistic perspective that integrates the impact of various decisions and environmental influences on all parts of the organization is needed.

In business, these three activities sometimes "compete" with each other for your attention. For example, some decision makers may have a natural ability to differentiate among elements of a problem but are not able to integrate them very well. Others have enough innate creativity to imagine solutions or fill in the blanks when information is missing. But they may have a difficult time when faced with hard numbers or cold facts. Even so, each of these skills is important. The mark of a good strategic manager is the ability to simultaneously make distinctions and envision the whole, and to imagine a future scenario while staying focused on the present. Thus, another reason to conduct case analysis is to help you develop and exercise your ability to differentiate, speculate, and integrate. David C. Novak, the CEO of Young Brands, provides a useful insight on this matter:[5]

> "I think what we need in our leaders, the people who ultimately run our companies and run our functions, is whole-brained people—people who can be analytical but also have the creativity, the right-brain side of the equation. There's more and more of a premium on that today than ever before."

Case analysis takes the student through the whole cycle of activity that a manager would face. Beyond the textbook descriptions of concepts and examples, case analysis asks you to "walk a mile in the shoes" of the strategic decision maker and learn to evaluate situations critically. Executives and owners must make decisions every day with limited information and a swirl of business activity going on around them. Consider the example of Sapient Health Network, an Internet start-up that had to undergo some analysis and problem solving just to survive. Strategy Spotlight 13.1 describes how this company transformed itself after a serious self-examination during a time of crisis.

As you can see from the experience of Sapient Health Network, businesses are often faced with immediate challenges that threaten their lives. The Sapient case illustrates how the strategic management process helped it survive. First, the company realistically assessed the environment, evaluated the marketplace, and analyzed its resources. Then it made tough decisions, which included shifting its market focus, hiring and firing, and redeploying its assets. Finally, it took action. The result was not only firm survival, but also a quick turnaround leading to rapid success.

How to Conduct a Case Analysis

LO13.3

The steps involved in conducting a strategic management case analysis.

The process of analyzing strategic management cases involves several steps. In this section we will review the mechanics of preparing a case analysis. Before beginning, there are two things to keep in mind that will clarify your understanding of the process and make the results of the process more meaningful.

First, unless you prepare for a case discussion, there is little you can gain from the discussion and even less that you can offer. Effective strategic managers don't enter into problem-solving situations without doing some homework—investigating the situation, analyzing and researching possible solutions, and sometimes gathering the advice of others. Good problem solving often requires that decision makers be immersed in the facts, options, and implications surrounding the problem. In case analysis, this means reading and thoroughly comprehending the case materials before trying to make an analysis.

The second point is related to the first. To get the most out of a case analysis you must place yourself "inside" the case—that is, think like an actual participant in the case situation. However, there are several positions you can take. These are discussed in the following paragraphs:

- **Strategic decision maker.** This is the position of the senior executive responsible for resolving the situation described in the case. It may be the CEO, the business owner, or a strategic manager in a key executive position.

ANALYSIS, DECISION MAKING, AND CHANGE AT SAPIENT HEALTH NETWORK

Sapient Health Network (SHN) had gotten off to a good start. CEO Jim Kean and his two cofounders had raised $5 million in investor capital to launch their vision: an Internet-based health care information subscription service. The idea was to create an Internet community for people suffering from chronic diseases. It would provide members with expert information, resources, a message board, and chat rooms so that people suffering from the same ailments could provide each other with information and support. "Who would be more voracious consumers of information than people who are faced with life-changing, life-threatening illnesses?" thought Bill Kelly, one of SHN's cofounders. Initial market research and beta tests had supported that view.

During the beta tests, however, the service had been offered for free. The troubles began when SHN tried to convert its trial subscribers into paying ones. Fewer than 5 percent signed on, far less than the 15 percent the company had projected. Sapient hired a vice president of marketing who launched an aggressive promotion, but after three months of campaigning SHN still had only 500 members. SHN was now burning through $400,000 per month, with little revenue to show for it.

At that point, according to SHN board member Susan Clymer, "there was a lot of scrambling around trying to figure out how we could wring value out of what we'd already accomplished." One thing SHN had created was an expert software system which had two components: an "intelligent profile engine" (IPE) and an "intelligent query engine" (IQE). SHN used this system to collect detailed information from its subscribers.

SHN was sure that the expert system was its biggest selling point. But how could they use it? Then the founders remembered that the original business plan had suggested there might be a market for aggregate data about patient populations gathered from the website. Could they turn the business around by selling patient data? To analyze the possibility, Kean tried out the idea on the market research arm of a huge East Coast health care conglomerate. The officials were intrigued. SHN realized that its expert system could become a market research tool.

Once the analysis was completed, the founders made the decision: They would still create Internet communities for chronically ill patients, but the service would be free. And they would transform SHN from a company that processed subscriptions to one that sold market research.

Finally, they enacted the changes. Some of it was painful, including laying off 18 employees. Instead, SHN needed more health care industry expertise. It even hired an interim CEO, Craig Davenport, a 25-year veteran of the industry, to steer the company in its new direction. Finally, SHN had to communicate a new message to its members. It began by reimbursing the $10,000 of subscription fees they had paid.

All of this paid off dramatically in a matter of just two years. Revenues jumped to $1.9 million and early in the third year, SHN was purchased by WebMD. Less than a year after that, WebMD merged with Healtheon. The combined company still operates a thriving office out of SHN's original location in Portland, Oregon.

Sources: Ferguson, S. 2007. Health Care Gets a Better IT Prescription. *Baseline, www.baselinemag.com,* May 24. Brenneman, K. 2000. Healtheon/WebMD's Local Office Is Thriving. *Business Journal of Portland,* June 2; Raths, D. 1998. Reversal of Fortune. *Inc. Technology,* 2: 52–62.

- **Board of directors.** Since the board of directors represents the owners of a corporation, it has a responsibility to step in when a management crisis threatens the company. As a board member, you may be in a unique position to solve problems.

- **Outside consultant.** Either the board or top management may decide to bring in outsiders. Consultants often have an advantage because they can look at a situation objectively. But they also may be at a disadvantage since they have no power to enforce changes.

Before beginning the analysis, it may be helpful to envision yourself assuming one of these roles. Then, as you study and analyze the case materials, you can make a diagnosis and recommend solutions in a way that is consistent with your position. Try different perspectives. You may find that your view of the situation changes depending on the role you play. As an outside consultant, for example, it may be easy for you to conclude that certain individuals should be replaced in order to solve a problem presented in the case. However, if you take the role of the CEO who knows the individuals and the challenges they have been facing, you may be reluctant to fire them and will seek another solution instead.

The idea of assuming a particular role is similar to the real world in various ways. In your career, you may work in an organization where outside accountants, bankers,

USING A BUSINESS PLAN FRAMEWORK TO ANALYZE STRATEGIC CASES

Established businesses often have to change what they are doing in order to improve their competitive position or sometimes simply to survive. To make the changes effectively, businesses usually need a plan. Business plans are no longer just for entrepreneurs. The kind of market analysis, decision making, and action planning that is considered standard practice among new ventures can also benefit going concerns that want to make changes, seize an opportunity, or head in a new direction.

The best business plans, however, are not those loaded with decades of month-by-month financial projections or that depend on rigid adherence to a schedule of events that is impossible to predict. The good ones are focused on four factors that are critical to new-venture success. These same factors are important in case analysis as well because they get to the heart of many of the problems found in strategic cases.

1. *The People.* "When I receive a business plan, I always read the résumé section first," says Harvard Professor William Sahlman. The people questions that are critically important to investors include: What are their skills? How much experience do they have? What is their reputation? Have they worked together as a team? These same questions also may be used in case analysis to evaluate the role of individuals in the strategic case.

2. *The Opportunity.* Business opportunities come in many forms. They are not limited to new ventures. The chance to enter new markets, introduce new products, or merge with a competitor provides many of the challenges that are found in strategic management cases. What are the consequences of such actions? Will the proposed changes affect the firm's business concept? What factors might stand in the way of success? The same issues are also present in most strategic cases.

3. *The Context.* Things happen in contexts that cannot be controlled by a firm's managers. This is particularly true of the general environment where social trends, economic changes, or events such as the September 11, 2001, terrorist attacks can change business overnight. When evaluating strategic cases, ask: Is the company aware of the impact of context on the business? What will it do if the context changes? Can it influence the context in a way that favors the company?

4. *Risk and Reward.* With a new venture, the entrepreneurs and investors take the risks and get the rewards. In strategic cases, the risks and rewards often extend to many other stakeholders, such as employees, customers, and suppliers. When analyzing a case, ask: Are the managers making choices that will pay off in the future? Are the rewards evenly distributed? Will some stakeholders be put at risk if the situation in the case changes? What if the situation remains the same? Could that be even riskier?

Whether a business is growing or shrinking, large or small, industrial or service oriented, the issues of people, opportunities, context, and risks and rewards will have a large impact on its performance. Therefore, you should always consider these four factors when evaluating strategic management cases.

Sources: Wasserman, E. 2003. A Simple Plan. *MBA Jungle,* February: 50–55; DeKluyver, C. A. 2000. *Strategic Thinking: An Executive Perspective.* Upper Saddle River, NJ: Prentice Hall; and Sahlman, W. A. 1997. How to Write a Great Business Plan. *Harvard Business Review,* 75(4): 98–108.

---

lawyers, or other professionals are advising you about how to resolve business situations or improve your practices. Their perspective will be different from yours but it is useful to understand things from their point of view. Conversely, you may work as a member of the audit team of an accounting firm or the loan committee of a bank. In those situations, it would be helpful if you understood the situation from the perspective of the business leader who must weigh your views against all the other advice that he or she receives. Case analysis can help develop an ability to appreciate such multiple perspectives.

One of the most challenging roles to play in business is as a business founder or owner. For small businesses or entrepreneurial start-ups, the founder may wear all hats at once— key decision maker, primary stockholder, and CEO. Hiring an outside consultant may not be an option. However, the issues faced by young firms and established firms are often not that different, especially when it comes to formulating a plan of action. Business plans that entrepreneurial firms use to raise money or propose a business expansion typically revolve around a few key issues that must be addressed no matter what the size or age of the business. Strategy Spotlight 13.2 reviews business planning issues that are most important to consider when evaluating any case, especially from the perspective of the business founder or owner.

Next we will review five steps to follow when conducting a strategic management case analysis: becoming familiar with the material, identifying the problems, analyzing the strategic issues using the tools and insights of strategic management, proposing alternative solutions, and making recommendations.[6]

Become Familiar with the Material

Written cases often include a lot of material. They may be complex and include detailed financials or long passages. Even so, to understand a case and its implications, you must become familiar with its content. Sometimes key information is not immediately apparent. It may be contained in the footnotes to an exhibit or an interview with a lower-level employee. In other cases the important points may be difficult to grasp because the subject matter is so unfamiliar. When you approach a strategic case try the following technique to enhance comprehension:

- Read quickly through the case one time to get an overall sense of the material.
- Use the initial read-through to assess possible links to strategic concepts.
- Read through the case again, in depth. Make written notes as you read.
- Evaluate how strategic concepts might inform key decisions or suggest alternative solutions.
- After formulating an initial recommendation, thumb through the case again quickly to help assess the consequences of the actions you propose.

Identify Problems

When conducting case analysis, one of your most important tasks is to identify the problem. Earlier we noted that one of the main reasons to conduct case analysis was to find solutions. But you cannot find a solution unless you know the problem. Another saying you may have heard is, "A good diagnosis is half the cure." In other words, once you have determined what the problem is, you are well on your way to identifying a reasonable solution.

Some cases have more than one problem. But the problems are usually related. For a hypothetical example, consider the following: Company A was losing customers to a new competitor. Upon analysis, it was determined that the competitor had a 50 percent faster delivery time even though its product was of lower quality. The managers of company A could not understand why customers would settle for an inferior product. It turns out that no one was marketing to company A's customers that its product was superior. A second problem was that falling sales resulted in cuts in company A's sales force. Thus, there were two related problems: inferior delivery technology and insufficient sales effort.

When trying to determine the problem, avoid getting hung up on symptoms. Zero in on the problem. For example, in the company A example above, the symptom was losing customers. But the problems were an underfunded, understaffed sales force combined with an outdated delivery technology. Try to see beyond the immediate symptoms to the more fundamental problems.

Another tip when preparing a case analysis is to articulate the problem.[7] Writing down a problem statement gives you a reference point to turn to as you proceed through the case analysis. This is important because the process of formulating strategies or evaluating implementation methods may lead you away from the initial problem. Make sure your recommendation actually addresses the problems you have identified.

One more thing about identifying problems: Sometimes problems are not apparent until *after* you do the analysis. In some cases the problem will be presented plainly, perhaps in the opening paragraph or on the last page of the case. But in other cases the problem does not emerge until after the issues in the case have been analyzed. We turn next to the subject of strategic case analysis.

Conduct Strategic Analyses

This textbook has presented numerous analytical tools (e.g., five-forces analysis and value-chain analysis), contingency frameworks (e.g., when to use related rather than unrelated diversification strategies), and other techniques that can be used to evaluate strategic situations. The previous 12 chapters have addressed practices that are common in strategic management, but only so much can be learned by studying the practices and concepts. The best way to understand these methods is to apply them by conducting analyses of specific cases.

The first step is to determine which strategic issues are involved. Is there a problem in the company's competitive environment? Or is it an internal problem? If it is internal, does it have to do with organizational structure? Strategic controls? Uses of technology? Or perhaps the company has overworked its employees or underutilized its intellectual capital. Has the company mishandled a merger? Chosen the wrong diversification strategy? Botched a new product introduction? Each of these issues is linked to one or more of the concepts discussed earlier in the text. Determine what strategic issues are associated with the problems you have identified. Remember also that most real-life case situations involve issues that are highly interrelated. Even in cases where there is only one major problem, the strategic processes required to solve it may involve several parts of the organization.

Once you have identified the issues that apply to the case, conduct the analysis. For example, you may need to conduct a five-forces analysis or dissect the company's competitive strategy. Perhaps you need to evaluate whether its resources are rare, valuable, difficult to imitate, or difficult to substitute. Financial analysis may be needed to assess the company's economic prospects. Perhaps the international entry mode needs to be reevaluated because of changing conditions in the host country. Employee empowerment techniques may need to be improved to enhance organizational learning. Whatever the case, all the strategic concepts introduced in the text include insights for assessing their effectiveness. Determining how well a company is doing these things is central to the case analysis process.

Financial ratio analysis is one of the primary tools used to conduct case analysis. Appendix 1 to Chapter 13 includes a discussion and examples of the financial ratios that are often used to evaluate a company's performance and financial well-being. Exhibit 13.1 provides a summary of the financial ratios presented in Appendix 1 to this chapter.

In this part of the overall strategic analysis process, it is also important to test your own assumptions about the case.[8] First, what assumptions are you making about the case materials? It may be that you have interpreted the case content differently than your team members or classmates. Being clear about these assumptions will be important in determining how to analyze the case. Second, what assumptions have you made about the best way to resolve the problems? Ask yourself why you have chosen one type of analysis over another. This process of assumption checking can also help determine if you have gotten to the heart of the problem or are still just dealing with symptoms.

As mentioned earlier, sometimes the critical diagnosis in a case can only be made after the analysis is conducted. However, by the end of this stage in the process, you should know the problems and have completed a thorough analysis of them. You can now move to the next step: finding solutions.

> **financial ratio analysis**
> a method of evaluating a company's performance and financial well-being through ratios of accounting values, including short-term solvency, long-term solvency, asset utilization, profitability, and market value ratios.

Propose Alternative Solutions

It is important to remember that in strategic management case analysis, there is rarely one right answer or one best way. Even when members of a class or a team agree on what the problem is, they may not agree upon how to solve the problem. Therefore, it is helpful to consider several different solutions.

EXHIBIT 13.1 Summary of Financial Ratio Analysis Techniques

Ratio	What It Measures
Short-term solvency, or liquidity, ratios:	
Current ratio	Ability to use assets to pay off liabilities.
Quick ratio	Ability to use liquid assets to pay off liabilities quickly.
Cash ratio	Ability to pay off liabilities with cash on hand.
Long-term solvency, or financial leverage, ratios:	
Total debt ratio	How much of a company's total assets are financed by debt.
Debt-equity ratio	Compares how much a company is financed by debt with how much it is financed by equity.
Equity multiplier	How much debt is being used to finance assets.
Times interest earned ratio	How well a company has its interest obligations covered.
Cash coverage ratio	A company's ability to generate cash from operations.
Asset utilization, or turnover, ratios:	
Inventory turnover	How many times each year a company sells its entire inventory.
Days' sales in inventory	How many days on average inventory is on hand before it is sold.
Receivables turnover	How frequently each year a company collects on its credit sales.
Days' sales in receivables	How many days on average it takes to collect on credit sales (average collection period).
Total asset turnover	How much of sales is generated for every dollar in assets.
Capital intensity	The dollar investment in assets needed to generate $1 in sales.
Profitability ratios:	
Profit margin	How much profit is generated by every dollar of sales.
Return on assets (ROA)	How effectively assets are being used to generate a return.
Return on equity (ROE)	How effectively amounts invested in the business by its owners are being used to generate a return.
Market value ratios:	
Price-earnings ratio	How much investors are willing to pay per dollar of current earnings.
Market-to-book ratio	Compares market value of the company's investments to the cost of those investments.

After conducting strategic analysis and identifying the problem, develop a list of options. What are the possible solutions? What are the alternatives? First, generate a list of all the options you can think of without prejudging any one of them. Remember that not all cases call for dramatic decisions or sweeping changes. Some companies just need to make small adjustments. In fact, "Do nothing" may be a reasonable alternative in some cases. Although that is rare, it might be useful to consider what will happen if the company does nothing. This point illustrates the purpose of developing alternatives: to evaluate what will happen if a company chooses one solution over another.

Thus, during this step of a case analysis, you will evaluate choices and the implications of those choices. One aspect of any business that is likely to be highlighted in this part of the analysis is strategy implementation. Ask how the choices made will be implemented. It may be that what seems like an obvious choice for solving a problem creates an even bigger problem when implemented. But remember also that no strategy or strategic "fix" is going to work if it cannot be implemented. Once a list of alternatives is generated, ask:

- Can the company afford it? How will it affect the bottom line?
- Is the solution likely to evoke a competitive response?
- Will employees throughout the company accept the changes? What impact will the solution have on morale?
- How will the decision affect other stakeholders? Will customers, suppliers, and others buy into it?
- How does this solution fit with the company's vision, mission, and objectives?
- Will the culture or values of the company be changed by the solution? Is it a positive change?

The point of this step in the case analysis process is to find a solution that both solves the problem and is realistic. A consideration of the implications of various alternative solutions will generally lead you to a final recommendation that is more thoughtful and complete.

Make Recommendations

The basic aim of case analysis is to find solutions. Your analysis is not complete until you have recommended a course of action. In this step the task is to make a set of recommendations that your analysis supports. Describe exactly what needs to be done. Explain why this course of action will solve the problem. The recommendation should also include suggestions for how best to implement the proposed solution because the recommended actions and their implications for the performance and future of the firm are interrelated.

Recall that the solution you propose must solve the problem you identified. This point cannot be overemphasized; too often students make recommendations that treat only symptoms or fail to tackle the central problems in the case. Make a logical argument that shows how the problem led to the analysis and the analysis led to the recommendations you are proposing. Remember, an analysis is not an end in itself; it is useful only if it leads to a solution.

The actions you propose should describe the very next steps that the company needs to take. Don't say, for example, "If the company does more market research, then I would recommend the following course of action. . . ." Instead, make conducting the research part of your recommendation. Taking the example a step further, if you also want to suggest subsequent actions that may be different *depending* on the outcome of the market research, that's OK. But don't make your initial recommendation conditional on actions the company may or may not take.

In summary, case analysis can be a very rewarding process but, as you might imagine, it can also be frustrating and challenging. If you will follow the steps described above, you will address the different elements of a thorough analysis. This approach can give your analysis a solid footing. Then, even if there are differences of opinion about how to interpret the facts, analyze the situation, or solve the problems, you can feel confident that you have not missed any important steps in finding the best course of action.

Students are often asked to prepare oral presentations of the information in a case and their analysis of the best remedies. This is frequently assigned as a group project. Or you may be called upon in class to present your ideas about the circumstances or solutions for a case the class is discussing. Exhibit 13.2 provides some tips for preparing an oral case presentation.

EXHIBIT 13.2 Preparing an Oral Case Presentation

Rule	Description
Organize your thoughts.	Begin by becoming familiar with the material. If you are working with a team, compare notes about the key points of the case and share insights that other team members may have gleaned from tables and exhibits. Then make an outline. This is one of the best ways to organize the flow and content of the presentation.
Emphasize strategic analysis.	The purpose of case analysis is to diagnose problems and find solutions. In the process, you may need to unravel the case material as presented and reconfigure it in a fashion that can be more effectively analyzed. Present the material in a way that lends itself to analysis—don't simply restate what is in the case. This involves three major categories with the following emphasis: Background/Problem Statement — 10–20% Strategic Analysis/Options — 60–75% Recommendations/Action Plan — 10–20% As you can see, the emphasis of your presentation should be on analysis. This will probably require you to reorganize the material so that the tools of strategic analysis can be applied.
Be logical and consistent.	A presentation that is rambling and hard to follow may confuse the listener and fail to evoke a good discussion. Present your arguments and explanations in a logical sequence. Support your claims with facts. Include financial analysis where appropriate. Be sure that the solutions you recommend address the problems you have identified.
Defend your position.	Usually an oral presentation is followed by a class discussion. Anticipate what others might disagree with and be prepared to defend your views. This means being aware of the choices you made and the implications of your recommendations. Be clear about your assumptions. Be able to expand on your analysis.
Share presentation responsibilities.	Strategic management case analyses are often conducted by teams. Each member of the team should have a clear role in the oral presentation, preferably a speaking role. It's also important to coordinate the different parts of the presentation into a logical, smooth-flowing whole. How well a team works together is usually very apparent during an oral presentation.

LO13.4

How to get the most out of case analysis.

How to Get the Most from Case Analysis

One of the reasons case analysis is so enriching as a learning tool is that it draws on many resources and skills besides just what is in the textbook. This is especially true in the study of strategy. Why? Because strategic management itself is a highly integrative task that draws many areas of specialization at several levels, from the individual to the whole of society. Therefore, to get the most out of case analysis, expand your horizons beyond the concepts in this text and seek insights from your own reservoir of knowledge. Here are some tips for how to do that.[9]

- ***Keep an open mind.*** Like any good discussion, a case analysis discussion often evokes strong opinions and high emotions. But it's the variety of perspectives that makes case analysis so valuable: Many viewpoints usually lead to a more complete analysis. Therefore, avoid letting an emotional response to another person's style or opinion keep you from hearing what he or she has to say. Once you evaluate what is said, you may disagree with it or dismiss it as faulty. But unless you keep an open mind in the first place, you may miss the importance of the other person's contribution. Also, people often place a higher value on the opinions of those they consider to be good listeners.

- ***Take a stand for what you believe.*** Although it is vital to keep an open mind, it is also important to state your views proactively. Don't try to figure out what your friends or the instructor wants to hear. Analyze the case from the perspective of your own background and belief system. For example, perhaps you feel that a decision is unethical or that the managers in a case have misinterpreted the facts. Don't be afraid to assert that in the discussion. For one thing, when a person takes a strong stand, it often encourages others to evaluate the issues more closely. This can lead to a more thorough investigation and a more meaningful class discussion.

- ***Draw on your personal experience.*** You may have experiences from work or as a customer that shed light on some of the issues in a case. Even though one of the purposes of case analysis is to apply the analytical tools from this text, you may be able to add to the discussion by drawing on your outside experiences and background. Of course, you need to guard against carrying that to extremes. In other words, don't think that your perspective is the only viewpoint that matters! Simply recognize that firsthand experience usually represents a welcome contribution to the overall quality of case discussions.

- ***Participate and persuade.*** Have you heard the phrase, "Vote early . . . and often"? Among loyal members of certain political parties, it has become rather a joke. Why? Because a democratic system is built on the concept of one person, one vote. Even though some voters may want to vote often enough to get their candidate elected, it is against the law. Not so in a case discussion. People who are persuasive and speak their mind can often influence the views of others. But to do so, you have to be prepared and convincing. Being persuasive is more than being loud or long-winded. It involves understanding all sides of an argument and being able to overcome objections to your own point of view. These efforts can make a case discussion more lively. And they parallel what happens in the real world; in business, people frequently share their opinions and attempt to persuade others to see things their way.

- ***Be concise and to the point.*** In the previous point, we encouraged you to speak up and "sell" your ideas to others in a case discussion. But you must be clear about what you are selling. Make your arguments in a way that is explicit and direct. Zero in on the most important points. Be brief. Don't try to make a lot of points at once by jumping around between topics. Avoid trying to explain the whole case situation at once. Remember, other students usually resent classmates who go on and on, take up a lot of "airtime," or repeat themselves unnecessarily. The best way to avoid this is to stay focused and be specific.

- ***Think out of the box.*** It's OK to be a little provocative; sometimes that is the consequence of taking a stand on issues. But it may be equally important to be imaginative and creative when making a recommendation or determining how to implement a solution. Albert Einstein once stated, "Imagination is more important than knowledge." The reason is that managing strategically requires more than memorizing concepts. Strategic management insights must be applied to each case differently—just knowing the principles is not enough. Imagination and out-of-the-box thinking help to apply strategic knowledge in novel and unique ways.

- ***Learn from the insights of others.*** Before you make up your mind about a case, hear what other students have to say. Get a second opinion, and a third, and so forth. Of course, in a situation where you have to put your analysis in writing, you may not be able to learn from others ahead of time. But in a case discussion, observe how various students attack the issues and engage in problem solving.

Such observation skills also may be a key to finding answers within the case. For example, people tend to believe authority figures, so they would place a higher value on what a company president says. In some cases, however, the statements of middle managers may represent a point of view that is even more helpful for finding a solution to the problems presented by the case.

- *Apply insights from other case analyses.* Throughout the text, we have used examples of actual businesses to illustrate strategy concepts. The aim has been to show you how firms think about and deal with business problems. During the course, you may be asked to conduct several case analyses as part of the learning experience. Once you have performed a few case analyses, you will see how the concepts from the text apply in real-life business situations. Incorporate the insights learned from the text examples and your own previous case discussions into each new case that you analyze.

- *Critically analyze your own performance.* Performance appraisals are a standard part of many workplace situations. They are used to determine promotions, raises, and work assignments. In some organizations, everyone from the top executive down is subject to such reviews. Even in situations where the owner or CEO is not evaluated by others, they often find it useful to ask themselves regularly, Am I being effective? The same can be applied to your performance in a case analysis situation. Ask yourself, Were my comments insightful? Did I make a good contribution? How might I improve next time? Use the same criteria on yourself that you use to evaluate others. What grade would you give yourself? This technique will not only make you more fair in your assessment of others but also will indicate how your own performance can improve.

- *Conduct outside research.* Many times, you can enhance your understanding of a case situation by investigating sources outside the case materials. For example, you may want to study an industry more closely or research a company's close competitors. Recent moves such as mergers and acquisitions or product introductions may be reported in the business press. The company itself may provide useful information on its website or in its annual reports. Such information can usually spur additional discussion and enrich the case analysis. (*Caution:* It is best to check with your instructor in advance to be sure this kind of additional research is encouraged. Bringing in outside research may conflict with the instructor's learning objectives.)

Several of the points suggested above for how to get the most out of case analysis apply only to an open discussion of a case, like that in a classroom setting. Exhibit 13.3 provides some additional guidelines for preparing a written case analysis.

Useful Decision-Making Techniques in Case Analysis

LO13.5

How integrative thinking and conflict-inducing discussion techniques can lead to better decisions.

The demands on today's business leaders require them to perform a wide variety of functions. The success of their organizations often depends on how they as individuals—and as part of groups—meet the challenges and deliver on promises. In this section we address two different techniques that can help managers make better decisions and, in turn, enable their organizations to achieve higher performance.

First, we discuss integrative thinking, a technique that helps managers make better decisions through the resolution of competing demands on resources, multiple contingencies, and diverse opportunities. Second, we introduce devil's advocacy and dialectical inquiry. Both of these approaches to decision making involve the effective use of conflict in the decision-making process.

EXHIBIT 13.3 Preparing a Written Case Analysis

Rule	Description
Be thorough.	Many of the ideas presented in Exhibit 13.2 about oral presentations also apply to written case analysis. However, a written analysis typically has to be more complete. This means writing out the problem statement and articulating assumptions. It is also important to provide support for your arguments and reference case materials or other facts more specifically.
Coordinate team efforts.	Written cases are often prepared by small groups. Within a group, just as in a class discussion, you may disagree about the diagnosis or the recommended plan of action. This can be healthy if it leads to a richer understanding of the case material. But before committing your ideas to writing, make sure you have coordinated your responses. Don't prepare a written analysis that appears contradictory or looks like a patchwork of disconnected thoughts.
Avoid restating the obvious.	There is no reason to restate material that everyone is familiar with already, namely, the case content. It is too easy for students to use up space in a written analysis with a recapitulation of the details of the case—this accomplishes very little. Stay focused on the key points. Only restate the information that is most central to your analysis.
Present information graphically.	Tables, graphs, and other exhibits are usually one of the best ways to present factual material that supports your arguments. For example, financial calculations such as break-even analysis, sensitivity analysis, or return on investment are best presented graphically. Even qualitative information such as product lists or rosters of employees can be summarized effectively and viewed quickly by using a table or graph.
Exercise quality control.	When presenting a case analysis in writing, it is especially important to use good grammar, avoid misspelling words, and eliminate typos and other visual distractions. Mistakes that can be glossed over in an oral presentation or class discussion are often highlighted when they appear in writing. Make your written presentation appear as professional as possible. Don't let the appearance of your written case keep the reader from recognizing the importance and quality of your analysis.

The challenges facing today's leaders require them to confront a host of opposing forces. As the previous section indicated, maintaining consistency across a company's culture, vision, and organizational design can be difficult, especially if the three activities are out of alignment.

How does a leader make good strategic decisions in the face of multiple contingencies and diverse opportunities? A recent study by Roger L. Martin reveals that executives who have a capability known as **integrative thinking** are among the most effective leaders. In his book *The Opposable Mind,* Martin contends that people who can consider two conflicting ideas simultaneously, without dismissing one of the ideas or becoming discouraged about reconciling them, often make the best problem solvers because of their ability to creatively synthesize the opposing thoughts. In explaining the source of his title, Martin quotes F. Scott Fitzgerald, who observed, "The test of a first-rate intelligence is the ability to hold two opposing ideas in mind at the same time and still retain the ability to function. One should, for example, be able to see that things are hopeless yet be determined to make them otherwise."[10]

In contrast to conventional thinking, which tends to focus on making choices between competing ideas from a limited set of alternatives, integrative thinking is the process by which people reconcile opposing thoughts to identify creative solutions that provide them with more options and new alternatives. Exhibit 13.4 outlines the

integrative thinking
a process of reconciling opposing thoughts by generating new alternatives and creative solutions rather than rejecting one thought in favor of another.

EXHIBIT 13.4 Integrative Thinking: The Process of Thinking and Deciding

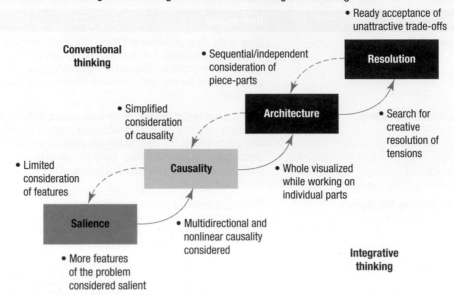

four stages of the integrative thinking and deciding process. Martin uses the admittedly simple example of deciding where to go on vacation to illustrate the stages:

- *Salience*—Take stock of what features of the decision you consider relevant and important. For example: Where will you go? What will you see? Where will you stay? What will it cost? Is it safe? Other features may be less important, but try to think of everything that may matter.
- *Causality*—Make a mental map of the causal relationships between the features, that is, how the various features are related to one another. For example, is it worth it to invite friends to share expenses? Will an exotic destination be less safe?
- *Architecture*—Use the mental map to arrange a sequence of decisions that will lead to a specific outcome. For example, will you make the hotel and flight arrangements first, or focus on which sightseeing tours are available? No particular decision path is right or wrong, but considering multiple options simultaneously may lead to a better decision.
- *Resolution*—Make your selection. For example, choose which destination, which flight, and so forth. You final resolution is linked to how you evaluated the first three stages; if you are dissatisfied with your choices, the dotted arrows in the diagram (Exhibit 13.4) suggest you can go back through the process and revisit your assumptions.

Applied to business, an integrative thinking approach enables decision makers to consider situations not as forced trade-offs—either decrease costs or invest more; either satisfy shareholders or please the community—but as a method for synthesizing opposing ideas into a creative solution. The key is to think in terms of "both-and" rather than "either-or." "Integrative thinking," says Martin, "shows us that there's a way to integrate the advantages of one solution without canceling out the advantages of an alternative solution."

LINKEDIN AND PROCESS REENGINEERING: BETTER PERFORMANCE THAN GOOGLE OR FACEBOOK

By Tom McNamara and Helena Gonzalez

In the competitive world of hi-tech, not only do you need to come up with an excellent product or service, you also need to provide constant availability and stellar customer service. Consumers expect your website to be "always on" and functioning perfectly.

It was in this challenging environment that the computer programmers of LinkedIn found themselves working. Founded in 2003, LinkedIn is a social networking site geared towards business professionals, similar to a Facebook for business people.

Unfortunately for LinkedIn, as the site became more and more popular, its problems became more and more numerous. Internal systems would constantly fail, and for the computer programmers and engineers whose job it was to keep everything running, the task was a nightmare. Workers needed huge lead times just to add new features to the site, and fixing even small technical glitches took forever. Jay Kreps, an engineer at the company, talks about all of the long hours and hard work required to hold everything together. "You were there well past midnight trying to deal with the things going wrong," said Kreps.

LinkedIn was not alone. Engineers talk infamously about how Mark Zuckerberg, co-founder of Facebook, once requested that all of the image icons on their site have rounded corners. The engineers complied, but the solution resulted in the site running 10 percent slower. A couple of months later Zuckerberg had them go back to the old system.

In 2011, LinkedIn had decided that enough was enough. There had to be a better way to run the systems. That's where "Project Inversion" came in. A team of engineers got together and decided that all work on new features would be stopped. Instead, the company's programmers would focus on completely overhauling LinkedIn's infrastructure. It was a monumental—as well as risky—task, the success of which was not assured.

Redesigning their internal processes and systems took two months. The company incorporated updated database technology into the core of its computing systems, as well as developing new tools and software to help create computer code for the site.

The results were impressive. Before, it could take several weeks to add a new feature to the site. Now, thanks to a new series of automated verification systems and algorithms, updates can be added to the site "live." This gives the company a huge advantage over its competitors and other websites.

At Google and Facebook, quite often a team of specialized engineers must be assembled to examine vast amounts of computer code (sometimes running into millions of lines) before a new feature can be added, an extremely time consuming and tedious activity. Not at LinkedIn. The beauty of its system is that people have largely been removed from the verification process. This frees them up to work on more exciting, and value adding, propositions.

Since the Project Inversion initiative, LinkedIn has been able to make major upgrades to its site three times a day. Facebook, by comparison, can update its site once a day (occasionally twice). Google, surprisingly, appears to be the laggard, updating its site once a week.

All of this allows LinkedIn to simultaneously run thousands of different tests on the site, trying out different looks and features to see which one works best before making them permanent. As for the engineers, while they might miss the cameradery of the old late night sessions, they don't miss the long hours.

Sources: Max Nisen, April 29 2013 Business Insider "How LinkedIn Saved Its Engineers From Marathon Late-Night Coding Sessions"; Ashlee Vance, Bloomberg Business Week, April 29 2013 "LinkedIn: A Story About Silicon Valley's Possibly Unhealthy Need for Speed."

Although Martin found that integrative thinking comes naturally to some people, he also believes it can be taught. But it may be difficult to learn, in part because it requires people to *un*learn old patterns and become aware of how they think. For executives willing to take a deep look at their habits of thought, integrative thinking can be developed into a valuable skill. Strategy Spotlight 13.3 shows how LinkedIn used integrative thinking to redesign its troublesome internal processes and systems and now out performs its closest rivals, including Facebook and Google.

Conflict Inducing Techniques

Next we address some techniques often used to improve case analyses that involve the constructive use of conflict. In the classroom—as well as in the business world—you will frequently be analyzing cases or solving problems in groups. While the word *conflict* often has a negative connotation (e.g., rude behavior, personal affronts), it can be very helpful in arriving at better solutions to cases. It can provide an effective means for new insights as well as for rigorously questioning and analyzing assumptions and strategic alternatives. In fact, if you don't have constructive conflict, you may only get consensus. When this happens, decisions tend to be based on compromise rather than collaboration.

In your organizational behavior classes, you probably learned the concept of "groupthink."[11] Groupthink, a term coined by Irving Janis after he conducted numerous studies on executive decision making, is a condition in which group members strive to reach agreement or consensus without realistically considering other viable alternatives. In effect, group norms bolster morale at the expense of critical thinking and decision making is impaired.[12]

Many of us have probably been "victims" of groupthink at one time or another in our life. We may be confronted with situations when social pressure, politics, or "not wanting to stand out" may prevent us from voicing our concerns about a chosen course of action. Nevertheless, decision making in groups is a common practice in the management of many businesses. Most companies, especially large ones, rely on input from various top managers to provide valuable information and experience from their specialty area as well as their unique perspectives. Organizations need to develop cultures and reward systems that encourage people to express their perspectives and create open dialogues. Constructive conflict can be very helpful in that it emphasizes the need for managers to consider other people's perspectives and not simply become a strong advocate for positions that they may prefer.

Chapter 11 emphasized the importance of empowering individuals at all levels to participate in decision-making processes. After all, many of us have experienced situations where there is not a perfect correlation between one's rank and the viability of their ideas! In terms of this course, case analysis involves a type of decision making that is often conducted in groups. Strategy Spotlight 13.4 provides guidelines for making team-based approaches to case analysis more effective.

Clearly, understanding how to work in groups and the potential problems associated with group decision processes can benefit the case analysis process. Therefore, let's first look at some of the symptoms of groupthink and suggest ways of preventing it. Then, we will suggest some conflict-inducing decision-making techniques—devil's advocacy and dialectical inquiry—that can help to prevent groupthink and lead to better decisions.

Symptoms of Groupthink and How to Prevent It   Irving Janis identified several symptoms of groupthink, including:

- *An illusion of invulnerability.* This reassures people about possible dangers and leads to overoptimism and failure to heed warnings of danger.
- *A belief in the inherent morality of the group.* Because individuals think that what they are doing is right, they tend to ignore ethical or moral consequences of their decisions.
- *Stereotyped views of members of opposing groups.* Members of other groups are viewed as weak or not intelligent.
- *The application of pressure to members who express doubts about the group's shared illusions or question the validity of arguments proposed.*
- *The practice of self-censorship.* Members keep silent about their opposing views and downplay to themselves the value of their perspectives.
- *An illusion of unanimity.* People assume that judgments expressed by members are shared by all.
- *The appointment of mindguards.* People sometimes appoint themselves as mindguards to protect the group from adverse information that might break the climate of consensus (or agreement).

MAKING CASE ANALYSIS TEAMS MORE EFFECTIVE

Working in teams can be very challenging. Not all team members have the same skills, interests, or motivations. Some team members just want to get the work done. Others see teams as an opportunity to socialize. Occasionally, there are team members who think they should be in charge and make all the decisions; other teams have freeloaders—team members who don't want to do anything except get credit for the team's work.

One consequence of these various styles is that team meetings can become time wasters. Disagreements about how to proceed, how to share the work, or what to do at the next meeting tend to slow down teams and impede progress toward the goal. While the dynamics of case analysis teams are likely to always be challenging depending on the personalities involved, one thing nearly all members realize is that, ultimately, the team's work must be completed. Most team members also aim to do the highest quality work possible. The following guidelines provide some useful insights about how to get the work of a team done more effectively.

Spend More Time Together

One of the factors that prevents teams from doing a good job with case analysis is their failure to put in the necessary time. Unless teams really tackle the issues surrounding case analysis—both the issues in the case itself and organizing how the work is to be conducted—the end result will probably be lacking because decisions that are made too quickly are unlikely to get to the heart of the problem(s) in the case. "Meetings should be a precious resource, but they're treated like a necessary evil," says Kenneth Sole, a consultant who specializes in organizational behavior. As a result, teams that care more about finishing the analysis than getting the analysis right often make poor decisions.

Therefore, expect to have a few meetings that run long, especially at the beginning of the project when the work is being organized and the issues in the case are being sorted out, and again at the end when the team must coordinate the components of the case analysis that will be presented. Without spending this kind of time together, it is doubtful that the analysis will be comprehensive and the presentation is likely to be choppy and incomplete.

Make a Focused and Disciplined Agenda

To complete tasks and avoid wasting time, meetings need to have a clear purpose. To accomplish this at Roche, the Swiss drug and diagnostic product maker, CEO Franz Humer implemented a "decision agenda." The agenda focuses only on Roche's highest value issues and discussions are limited to these major topics. In terms of case analysis, the major topics include sorting out the

issues of the case, linking elements of the case to the strategic issues presented in class or the text, and assigning roles to various team members. Such objectives help keep team members on track.

Agendas also can be used to address issues such as the time line for accomplishing work. Otherwise the purpose of meetings may only be to manage the "crisis" of getting the case analysis finished on time. One solution is to assign a team member to manage the agenda. That person could make sure the team stays focused on the tasks at hand and remains mindful of time constraints. Another role could be to link the team's efforts to the steps presented in Exhibits 13.2 and Exhibit 13.3 on how to prepare a case analysis.

Pay More Attention to Strategy

Teams often waste time by focusing on unimportant aspects of a case. These may include details that are interesting but irrelevant or operational issues rather than strategic issues. It is true that useful clues to the issues in the case are sometimes embedded in the conversations of key managers or the trends evident in a financial statement. But once such insights are discovered, teams need to focus on the underlying strategic problems in the case. To solve such problems, major corporations such as Cadbury Schweppes and Boeing hold meetings just to generate strategic alternatives for solving their problems. This gives managers time to consider the implications of various courses of action. Separate meetings are held to evaluate alternatives, make strategic decisions, and approve an action plan.

Once the strategic solutions or "course corrections" are identified—as is common in most cases assigned—the operational implications and details of implementation will flow from the strategic decisions that companies make. Therefore, focusing primarily on strategic issues will provide teams with insights for making recommendations that are based on a deeper understanding of the issues in the case.

Produce Real Decisions

Too often, meetings are about discussing rather than deciding. Teams often spend a lot of time talking without reaching any conclusions. As Raymond Sanchez, CEO of Florida-based Security Mortgage Group, says, meetings are often used to "rehash the hash that's already been hashed." To be efficient and productive, team meetings need to be about more than just information sharing and group input. For example, an initial meeting may result in the team realizing that it needs to study the case in greater depth and examine links to strategic issues more carefully. Once more analysis is conducted, the team needs to reach a consensus so that the decisions that are made will last once the meeting is

(continued)

(continued)

over. Lasting decisions are more actionable because it frees team members to take the next steps.

One technique for making progress in this way is recapping each meeting with a five-minute synthesis report. According to Pamela Schindler, director of the Center for Applied Management at Wittenberg University, it's important to think through the implications of the meeting before ending it. "The real joy of synthesis," says Schindler, "is realizing how many meetings you won't need."

Not only are these guidelines useful for helping teams finish their work, but they can also help resolve some of the difficulties that teams often face. By involving every team member, using a meeting agenda, and focusing on the strategic issues that are critical to nearly every case, the discussion is limited and the criteria for making decisions become clearer. This allows the task to dominate rather than any one personality. And if the team finishes its work faster, this frees up time to focus on other projects or put the finishing touches on a case analysis presentation.

Sources: Mankins, M. C. 2004. Stop Wasting Valuable Time. *Harvard Business Review,* September: 58–65; and Sauer, P. J. 2004. Escape from Meeting Hell. *Inc. Magazine,* May, *www.inc.com.*

Clearly, groupthink is an undesirable and negative phenomenon that can lead to poor decisions. Irving Janis considers it to be a key contributor to such faulty decisions as the failure to prepare for the attack on Pearl Harbor, the escalation of the Vietnam conflict, and the failure to prepare for the consequences of the Iraqi invasion. Many of the same sorts of flawed decision making occur in business organizations. Janis has provided several suggestions for preventing groupthink that can be used as valuable guides in decision making and problem solving:

- Leaders must encourage group members to address their concerns and objectives.
- When higher-level managers assign a problem for a group to solve, they should adopt an impartial stance and not mention their preferences.
- Before a group reaches its final decision, the leader should encourage members to discuss their deliberations with trusted associates and then report the perspectives back to the group.
- The group should invite outside experts and encourage them to challenge the group's viewpoints and positions.
- The group should divide into subgroups, meet at various times under different chairpersons, and then get together to resolve differences.
- After reaching a preliminary agreement, the group should hold a "second chance" meeting which provides members a forum to express any remaining concerns and rethink the issue prior to making a final decision.

Using Conflict to Improve Decision Making   In addition to the above suggestions, the effective use of conflict can be a means of improving decision making. Although conflict can have negative outcomes, such as ill will, anger, tension, and lowered motivation, both leaders and group members must strive to assure that it is managed properly and used in a constructive manner.

devil's advocacy
a method of introducing conflict into a decision-making process by having specific individuals or groups act as a critic to an analysis or planned solution.

Two conflict-inducing decision-making approaches that have become quite popular are *devil's advocacy* and *dialectical inquiry.* Both approaches incorporate conflict into the decision-making process through formalized debate. A group charged with making a decision or solving a problem is divided into two subgroups and each will be involved in the analysis and solution.

With **devil's advocacy,** one of the groups (or individuals) acts as a critic to the plan. The devil's advocate tries to come up with problems with the proposed alternative and suggest reasons why it should not be adopted. The role of the devil's advocate is to create dissonance. This ensures that the group will take a hard look at its original proposal or alternative. By having a group (or individual) assigned the role of devil's advocate, it becomes clear that such an adversarial stance is legitimized. It brings out criticisms that might otherwise not be made.

Some authors have suggested that the use of a devil's advocate can be very helpful in helping boards of directors to ensure that decisions are addressed comprehensively and to avoid groupthink.[13] And Charles Elson, a director of Sunbeam Corporation, has argued that:

> Devil's advocates are terrific in any situation because they help you to figure a decision's numerous implications. . . . The better you think out the implications prior to making the decision, the better the decision ultimately turns out to be. That's why a devil's advocate is always a great person, irritating sometimes, but a great person.

As one might expect, there can be some potential problems with using the devil's advocate approach. If one's views are constantly criticized, one may become demoralized. Thus, that person may come up with "safe solutions" in order to minimize embarrassment or personal risk and become less subject to criticism. Additionally, even if the devil's advocate is successful with finding problems with the proposed course of action, there may be no new ideas or counterproposals to take its place. Thus, the approach sometimes may simply focus on what is wrong without suggesting other ideas.

Dialectical inquiry attempts to accomplish the goals of the devil's advocate in a more constructive manner. It is a technique whereby a problem is approached from two alternative points of view. The idea is that out of a critique of the opposing perspectives—a thesis and an antithesis—a creative synthesis will occur. Dialectical inquiry involves the following steps:

1. Identify a proposal and the information that was used to derive it.
2. State the underlying assumptions of the proposal.
3. Identify a counterplan (antithesis) that is believed to be feasible, politically viable, and generally credible. However, it rests on assumptions that are opposite to the original proposal.
4. Engage in a debate in which individuals favoring each plan provide their arguments and support.
5. Identify a synthesis which, hopefully, includes the best components of each alternative.

There are some potential downsides associated with dialectical inquiry. It can be quite time consuming and involve a good deal of training. Further, it may result in a series of compromises between the initial proposal and the counterplan. In cases where the original proposal was the best approach, this would be unfortunate.

Despite some possible limitations associated with these conflict-inducing decision-making techniques, they have many benefits. Both techniques force debate about underlying assumptions, data, and recommendations between subgroups. Such debate tends to prevent the uncritical acceptance of a plan that may seem to be satisfactory after a cursory analysis. The approach serves to tap the knowledge and perspectives of group members and continues until group members agree on both assumptions and recommended actions. Given that both approaches serve to use, rather than minimize or suppress, conflict, higher quality decisions should result. Exhibit 13.5 briefly summarizes these techniques.

dialectical inquiry
a method of introducing conflict into a decision-making process by devising different proposals that are feasible, politically viable, and credible, but rely on different assumptions; and debating the merits of each.

EXHIBIT 13.5   Two Conflict-Inducing Decision-Making Processes

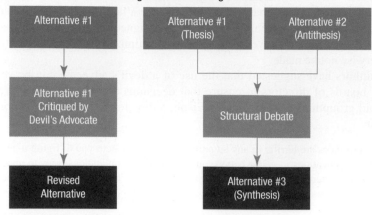

Following the Analysis-Decision-Action Cycle in Case Analysis

LO13.6

How to use the strategic insights and material from each of the 12 previous chapters in the text to analyze issues posed by strategic management cases.

In Chapter 1 we defined strategic management as the analysis, decisions, and actions that organizations undertake to create and sustain competitive advantages. It is no accident that we chose that sequence of words because it corresponds to the sequence of events that typically occurs in the strategic management process. In case analysis, as in the real world, this cycle of events can provide a useful framework. First, an analysis of the case in terms of the business environment and current events is needed. To make such an analysis, the case background must be considered. Next, based on that analysis, decisions must be made. This may involve formulating a strategy, choosing between difficult options, moving forward aggressively, or retreating from a bad situation. There are many possible decisions, depending on the case situation. Finally, action is required. Once decisions are made and plans are set, the action begins. The recommended action steps and the consequences of implementing these actions are the final stage.

Each of the previous 12 chapters of this book includes techniques and information that may be useful in a case analysis. However, not all of the issues presented will be important in every case. As noted earlier, one of the challenges of case analysis is to identify the most critical points and sort through material that may be ambiguous or unimportant.

In this section we draw on the material presented in each of the 12 chapters to show how it informs the case analysis process. The ideas are linked sequentially and in terms of an overarching strategic perspective. One of your jobs when conducting case analysis is to see how the parts of a case fit together and how the insights from the study of strategy can help you understand the case situation.

1. *Analyzing organizational goals and objectives.* A company's vision, mission, and objectives keep organization members focused on a common purpose. They also influence how an organization deploys its resources, relates to its stakeholders, and matches its short-term objectives with its long-term goals. The goals may even impact how a company formulates and implements strategies. When exploring issues of goals and objectives, you might ask:

   • Has the company developed short-term objectives that are inconsistent with its long-term mission? If so, how can management realign its vision, mission, and objectives?
   • Has the company considered all of its stakeholders equally in making critical decisions? If not, should the views of all stakeholders be treated the same or are some stakeholders more important than others?

- Is the company being faced with an issue that conflicts with one of its long-standing policies? If so, how should it compare its existing policies to the potential new situation?

2. *Analyzing the external environment.* The business environment has two components. The general environment consists of demographic, sociocultural, political/legal, technological, economic, and global conditions. The competitive environment includes rivals, suppliers, customers, and other factors that may directly affect a company's success. Strategic managers must monitor the environment to identify opportunities and threats that may have an impact on performance. When investigating a firm's external environment, you might ask:

- Does the company follow trends and events in the general environment? If not, how can these influences be made part of the company's strategic analysis process?
- Is the company effectively scanning and monitoring the competitive environment? If so, how is it using the competitive intelligence it is gathering to enhance its competitive advantage?
- Has the company correctly analyzed the impact of the competitive forces in its industry on profitability? If so, how can it improve its competitive position relative to these forces?

3. *Analyzing the internal environment.* A firm's internal environment consists of its resources and other value-adding capabilities. Value-chain analysis and a resource-based approach to analysis can be used to identify a company's strengths and weaknesses and determine how they are contributing to its competitive advantages. Evaluating firm performance can also help make meaningful comparisons with competitors. When researching a company's internal analysis, you might ask:

- Does the company know how the various components of its value chain are adding value to the firm? If not, what internal analysis is needed to determine its strengths and weakness?
- Has the company accurately analyzed the source and vitality of its resources? If so, is it deploying its resources in a way that contributes to competitive advantages?
- Is the company's financial performance as good as or better than that of its close competitors? If so, has it balanced its financial success with the performance criteria of other stakeholders such as customers and employees?

4. *Assessing a firm's intellectual assets.* Human capital is a major resource in today's knowledge economy. As a result, attracting, developing, and retaining talented workers is a key strategic challenge. Other assets such as patents and trademarks are also critical. How companies leverage their intellectual assets through social networks and strategic alliances, and how technology is used to manage knowledge may be a major influence on a firm's competitive advantage. When analyzing a firm's intellectual assets, you might ask:

- Does the company have underutilized human capital? If so, what steps are needed to develop and leverage its intellectual assets?
- Is the company missing opportunities to forge strategic alliances? If so, how can it use its social capital to network more effectively?
- Has the company developed knowledge-management systems that capture what it learns? If not, what technologies can it employ to retain new knowledge?

5. *Formulating business-level strategies.* Firms use the competitive strategies of differentiation, focus, and overall cost leadership as a basis for overcoming the five competitive forces and developing sustainable competitive advantages.

Combinations of these strategies may work best in some competitive environments. Additionally, an industry's life cycle is an important contingency that may affect a company's choice of business-level strategies. When assessing business-level strategies, you might ask:

- Has the company chosen the correct competitive strategy given its industry environment and competitive situation? If not, how should it use its strengths and resources to improve its performance?
- Does the company use combination strategies effectively? If so, what capabilities can it cultivate to further enhance profitability?
- Is the company using a strategy that is appropriate for the industry life cycle in which it is competing? If not, how can it realign itself to match its efforts to the current stage of industry growth?

6. ***Formulating corporate-level strategies.*** Large firms often own and manage portfolios of businesses. Corporate strategies address methods for achieving synergies among these businesses. Related and unrelated diversification techniques are alternative approaches to deciding which business should be added to or removed from a portfolio. Companies can diversify by means of mergers, acquisitions, joint ventures, strategic alliances, and internal development. When analyzing corporate-level strategies, you might ask:

- Is the company competing in the right businesses given the opportunities and threats that are present in the environment? If not, how can it realign its diversification strategy to achieve competitive advantages?
- Is the corporation managing its portfolio of businesses in a way that creates synergies among the businesses? If so, what additional business should it consider adding to its portfolio?
- Are the motives of the top corporate executives who are pushing diversification strategies appropriate? If not, what action can be taken to curb their activities or align them with the best interests of all stakeholders?

7. ***Formulating international-level strategies.*** Foreign markets provide both opportunities and potential dangers for companies that want to expand globally. To decide which entry strategy is most appropriate, companies have to evaluate the trade-offs between two factors that firms face when entering foreign markets: cost reduction and local adaptation. To achieve competitive advantages, firms will typically choose one of three strategies: global, multidomestic, or transnational. When evaluating international-level strategies, you might ask:

- Is the company's entry into an international marketplace threatened by the actions of local competitors? If so, how can cultural differences be minimized to give the firm a better chance of succeeding?
- Has the company made the appropriate choices between cost reduction and local adaptation to foreign markets? If not, how can it adjust its strategy to achieve competitive advantages?
- Can the company improve its effectiveness by embracing one international strategy over another? If so, how should it choose between a global, multidomestic, or transnational strategy?

8. ***Formulating entrepreneurial strategies.*** New ventures add jobs and create new wealth. To do so, they must identify opportunities that will be viable in the marketplace as well as gather resources and assemble an entrepreneurial team to enact the opportunity. New entrants often evoke a strong competitive response from incumbent firms in a given marketplace. When examining the role of strategic

thinking on the success of entrepreneurial ventures and the role of competitive dynamics, you might ask:

- Is the company engaged in an ongoing process of opportunity recognition? If not, how can it enhance its ability to recognize opportunities?
- Do the entrepreneurs who are launching new ventures have vision, dedication and drive, and a commitment to excellence? If so, how have these affected the performance and dedication of other employees involved in the venture?
- Have strategic principles been used in the process of developing strategies to pursue the entrepreneurial opportunity? If not, how can the venture apply tools such as five-forces analysis and value-chain analysis to improve its competitive position and performance?

9. *Achieving effective strategic control.* Strategic controls enable a firm to implement strategies effectively. Informational controls involve comparing performance to stated goals and scanning, monitoring, and being responsive to the environment. Behavioral controls emerge from a company's culture, reward systems, and organizational boundaries. When assessing the impact of strategic controls on implementation, you might ask:

- Is the company employing the appropriate informational control systems? If not, how can it implement a more interactive approach to enhance learning and minimize response times?
- Does the company have a strong and effective culture? If not, what steps can it take to align its values and rewards system with its goals and objectives?
- Has the company implemented control systems that match its strategies? If so, what additional steps can be taken to improve performance?

10. *Creating effective organizational designs.* Organizational designs that align with competitive strategies can enhance performance. As companies grow and change, their structures must also evolve to meet new demands. In today's economy, firm boundaries must be flexible and permeable to facilitate smoother interactions with external parties such as customers, suppliers, and alliance partners. New forms of organizing are becoming more common. When evaluating the role of organizational structure on strategy implementation, you might ask:

- Has the company implemented organizational structures that are suited to the type of business it is in? If not, how can it alter the design in ways that enhance its competitiveness?
- Is the company employing boundaryless organizational designs where appropriate? If so, how are senior managers maintaining control of lower-level employees?
- Does the company use outsourcing to achieve the best possible results? If not, what criteria should it use to decide which functions can be outsourced?

11. *Creating a learning organization and an ethical organization.* Strong leadership is essential for achieving competitive advantages. Two leadership roles are especially important. The first is creating a learning organization by harnessing talent and encouraging the development of new knowledge. Second, leaders play a vital role in motivating employees to excellence and inspiring ethical behavior. When exploring the impact of effective strategic leadership, you might ask:

- Do company leaders promote excellence as part of the overall culture? If so, how has this influenced the performance of the firm and the individuals in it?
- Is the company committed to being a learning organization? If not, what can it do to capitalize on the individual and collective talents of organizational members?

- Have company leaders exhibited an ethical attitude in their own behavior? If not, how has their behavior influenced the actions of other employees?

12. ***Fostering corporate entrepreneurship.*** Many firms continually seek new growth opportunities and avenues for strategic renewal. In some corporations, autonomous work units such as business incubators and new-venture groups are used to focus corporate venturing activities. In other corporate settings, product champions and other firm members provide companies with the impetus to expand into new areas. When investigating the impact of entrepreneurship on strategic effectiveness, you might ask:

- Has the company resolved the dilemmas associated with managing innovation? If so, is it effectively defining and pacing its innovation efforts?
- Has the company developed autonomous work units that have the freedom to bring forth new product ideas? If so, has it used product champions to implement new venture initiatives?
- Does the company have an entrepreneurial orientation? If not, what can it do to encourage entrepreneurial attitudes in the strategic behavior of its organizational members?

summary

Strategic management case analysis provides an effective method of learning how companies analyze problems, make decisions, and resolve challenges. Strategic cases include detailed accounts of actual business situations. The purpose of analyzing such cases is to gain exposure to a wide variety of organizational and managerial situations. By putting yourself in the place of a strategic decision maker, you can gain an appreciation of the difficulty and complexity of many strategic situations. In the process you can learn how to ask good strategic questions and enhance your analytical skills. Presenting case analyses can also help develop oral and written communication skills.

In this chapter we have discussed the importance of strategic case analysis and described the five steps involved in conducting a case analysis: becoming familiar with the material, identifying problems, analyzing strategic issues, proposing alternative solutions, and making recommendations. We have also discussed how to get the most from case analysis. Finally, we have described how the case analysis process follows the analysis-decision-action cycle of strategic management and outlined issues and questions that are associated with each of the previous 12 chapters of the text.

key terms

case analysis 413
financial ratio
    analysis 419
integrative
    thinking 425
devil's advocacy 431
dialectical inquiry 431

references

1. Bryant, A. 2011. *The corner office.* New York: St. Martin's, 15.

2. The material in this chapter is based on several sources, including Barnes, L. A., Nelson, A. J., & Christensen, C. R. 1994. *Teaching and the case method: Text, cases and readings.* Boston: Harvard Business School Press: Guth, W. D. 1985. Central concepts of business unit and corporate strategy. In W. D. Guth (Ed.). *Handbook of business strategy:* 1–9. Boston: Warren, Gorham & Lamont; Lundberg, C. C., & Enz, C. 1993. A framework for student case preparation. *Case Research Journal,* 13 (Summer): 129–140; and Ronstadt, R. 1980. *The art of case analysis: A guide to the diagnosis of business situations.* Dover, MA: Lord Publishing.

3. Edge, A. G. & Coleman, D. R. 1986. *The guide to case analysis and reporting* (3rd ed.). Honolulu, HI: System Logistics.

4. Morris, E. 1987. Vision and strategy: A focus for the future. *Journal of Business Strategy* 8: 51–58.

5. Bryant, A. 2011. *The corner office.* New York: St. Martin's, 18.

6. This section is based on Lundberg & Enz, op. cit., and Ronstadt, op. cit.

7. The importance of problem definition was emphasized in Mintzberg, H., Raisinghani, D. & Theoret, A. 1976. The structure of "unstructured" decision processes. *Administrative Science Quarterly,* 21(2): 246–275.

8. Drucker, P. F. 1994. The theory of the business. *Harvard Business Review,* 72(5): 95–104.

9. This section draws on Edge & Coleman, op. cit.

10. Evans, R. 2007. The either/or dilemma. *www.ft.com*, December 19; np; and Martin, R. L. 2007. *The opposable mind.* Boston: Harvard Business School Press.

11. Irving Janis is credited with coining the term *groupthink,* and he applied it primarily to fiascos in government (such as the Bay of Pigs incident in 1961). Refer to Janis, I. L. 1982. *Victims of groupthink* (2nd ed.). Boston: Houghton Mifflin.

12. Much of our discussion is based upon Finkelstein, S. & Mooney, A. C. 2003. Not the usual suspects: How to use board process to make boards better. *Academy of Management Executive,* 17(2): 101–113; Schweiger, D. M., Sandberg, W. R., & Rechner, P. L. 1989. Experiential effects of dialectical inquiry, devil's advocacy, and consensus approaches to strategic decision making. *Academy of Management Journal,* 32(4): 745–772; and Aldag, R. J. & Stearns, T. M. 1987. *Management.* Cincinnati: South-Western Publishing.

13. Finkelstein and Mooney, op. cit.

APPENDIX 1 TO CHAPTER 13

Financial Ratio Analysis*

Standard Financial Statements

One obvious thing we might want to do with a company's financial statements is to compare them to those of other, similar companies. We would immediately have a problem, however. It's almost impossible to directly compare the financial statements for two companies because of differences in size.

For example, Oracle and IBM are obviously serious rivals in the computer software market, but IBM is much larger (in terms of assets), so it is difficult to compare them directly. For that matter, it's difficult to even compare financial statements from different points in time for the same company if the company's size has changed. The size problem is compounded if we try to compare IBM and, say, SAP (of Germany). If SAP's financial statements are denominated in Euros, then we have a size *and* a currency difference.

To start making comparisons, one obvious thing we might try to do is to somehow standardize the financial statements. One very common and useful way of doing this is to work with percentages instead of total dollars. The resulting financial statements are called *common-size statements.* We consider these next.

Common-Size Balance Sheets

For easy reference, Prufrock Corporation's 2012 and 2013 balance sheets are provided in Exhibit 13A.1. Using these, we construct common-size balance sheets by expressing each item as a percentage of total assets. Prufrock's 2012 and 2013 common-size balance sheets are shown in Exhibit 13A.2.

Notice that some of the totals don't check exactly because of rounding errors. Also notice that the total change has to be zero since the beginning and ending numbers must add up to 100 percent.

In this form, financial statements are relatively easy to read and compare. For example, just looking at the two balance sheets for Prufrock, we see that current assets were 19.7 percent of total assets in 2013, up from 19.1 percent in 2012. Current liabilities declined from 16.0 percent to 15.1 percent of total liabilities and equity over that same time. Similarly, total equity rose from 68.1 percent of total liabilities and equity to 72.2 percent.

Overall, Prufrock's liquidity, as measured by current assets compared to current liabilities, increased over the year. Simultaneously, Prufrock's indebtedness diminished as a percentage of total assets. We might be tempted to conclude that the balance sheet has grown "stronger."

---

*This entire Appendix is adapted from Rows, S. A., Westerfield, R. W., & Jordan, B. D. 1999. *Essentials of Corporate Finance* (2nd ed.). chap. 3. NewYork: McGraw-Hill.

EXHIBIT 13A.1
Prufrock Corporation

	2012	2013
Assets		
Current assets		
Cash	$ 84	$ 98
Accounts receivable	165	188
Inventory	393	422
Total	$ 642	$ 708
Fixed assets		
Net plant and equipment	$2,731	$2,880
Total assets	$3,373	$3,588
Liabilities and Owners' Equity		
Current liabilities		
Accounts payable	$ 312	$ 344
Notes payable	231	196
Total	$ 543	$ 540
Long-term debt	$ 531	$ 457
Owners' equity		
Common stock and paid-in surplus	$ 500	$ 550
Retained earnings	1,799	2,041
Total	$2,299	$2,591
Total liabilities and owners' equity	$3,373	$3,588

Balance Sheets as of December 31, 2012 and 2013 ($ in millions)

Common-Size Income Statements

A useful way of standardizing the income statement, shown in Exhibit 13A.3, is to express each item as a percentage of total sales, as illustrated for Prufrock in Exhibit 13A.4.

This income statement tells us what happens to each dollar in sales. For Prufrock, interest expense eats up $.061 out of every sales dollar and taxes take another $.081. When all is said and done, $.157 of each dollar flows through to the bottom line (net income), and that amount is split into $.105 retained in the business and $.052 paid out in dividends.

These percentages are very useful in comparisons. For example, a relevant figure is the cost percentage. For Prufrock, $.582 of each $1.00 in sales goes to pay for goods sold. It would be interesting to compute the same percentage for Prufrock's main competitors to see how Prufrock stacks up in terms of cost control.

Ratio Analysis

Another way of avoiding the problems involved in comparing companies of different sizes is to calculate and compare *financial ratios*. Such ratios are ways of comparing and investigating the relationships between different pieces of financial information. We cover some of the more common ratios next, but there are many others that we don't touch on.

One problem with ratios is that different people and different sources frequently don't compute them in exactly the same way, and this leads to much confusion. The specific definitions

	2012	2013	Change
Assets			
Current assets			
Cash	2.5%	2.7%	+ .2%
Accounts receivable	4.9	5.2	+ .3
Inventory	11.7	11.8	+ .1
Total	19.1	19.7	+ .6
Fixed assets			
Net plant and equipment	80.9	80.3	− .6
Total assets	100.0%	100.0%	.0%
Liabilities and Owners' Equity			
Current liabilities			
Accounts payable	9.2%	9.6%	+ .4%
Notes payable	6.8	5.5	−1.3
Total	16.0	15.1	− .9
Long-term debt	15.7	12.7	−3.0
Owners' equity			
Common stock and paid-in surplus	14.8	15.3	+ .5
Retained earnings	53.3	56.9	+3.6
Total	68.1	72.2	+4.1
Total liabilities and owners' equities	100.0%	100.0%	.0%

EXHIBIT 13A.2
Prufrock Corporation

Common-Size Balance Sheets as of December 31, 2012 and 2013 (%)

Note: Numbers may not add up to 100.0% due to rounding.

Sales		$2,311
Cost of goods sold		1,344
Depreciation		276
Earnings before interest and taxes		$ 691
Interest paid		141
Taxable income		$ 550
Taxes (34%)		187
Net income		$ 363
Dividends	$121	
Addition to retained earnings	242	

EXHIBIT 13A.3
Prufrock Corporation

2013 Income Statement ($ in millions)

EXHIBIT 13A.4

Prufrock Corporation

Sales	100.0%
Cost of goods sold	58.2
Depreciation	11.9
Earnings before interest and taxes	29.9
Interest paid	6.1
Taxable income	23.8
Taxes (34%)	8.1
Net income	15.7%
Dividends	5.2%
Addition to retained earnings	10.5

2013 Common-Size Income Statement (%)

we use here may or may not be the same as others you have seen or will see elsewhere. If you ever use ratios as a tool for analysis, you should be careful to document how you calculate each one, and, if you are comparing your numbers to those of another source, be sure you know how its numbers are computed.

For each of the ratios we discuss, several questions come to mind:

1. How is it computed?
2. What is it intended to measure, and why might we be interested?
3. What is the unit of measurement?
4. What might a high or low value be telling us? How might such values be misleading?
5. How could this measure be improved?

Financial ratios are traditionally grouped into the following categories:

1. Short-term solvency, or liquidity, ratios.
2. Long-term solvency, or financial leverage, ratios.
3. Asset management, or turnover, ratios.
4. Profitability ratios.
5. Market value ratios.

We will consider each of these in turn. In calculating these numbers for Prufrock, we will use the ending balance sheet (2013) figures unless we explicitly say otherwise. The numbers for the various ratios come from the income statement and the balance sheet.

Short-Term Solvency, or Liquidity, Measures

As the name suggests, short-term solvency ratios as a group are intended to provide information about a firm's liquidity, and these ratios are sometimes called *liquidity measures*. The primary concern is the firm's ability to pay its bills over the short run without undue stress. Consequently, these ratios focus on current assets and current liabilities.

For obvious reasons, liquidity ratios are particularly interesting to short-term creditors. Since financial managers are constantly working with banks and other short-term lenders, an understanding of these ratios is essential.

One advantage of looking at current assets and liabilities is that their book values and market values are likely to be similar. Often (though not always), these assets and liabilities just don't live long enough for the two to get seriously out of step. On the other hand, like any type of near cash, current assets and liabilities can and do change fairly rapidly, so today's amounts may not be a reliable guide to the future.

Current Ratio One of the best-known and most widely used ratios is the *current ratio*. As you might guess, the current ratio is defined as:

$$\text{Current ratio} = \frac{\text{Current assets}}{\text{Current liabilities}}$$

For Prufrock, the 2011 current ratio is:

$$\text{Current ratio} = \frac{\$708}{\$540} = 1.31 \text{ times}$$

Because current assets and liabilities are, in principle, converted to cash over the following 12 months, the current ratio is a measure of short-term liquidity. The unit of measurement is either dollars or times. So, we could say Prufrock has $1.31 in current assets for every $1 in current liabilities, or we could say Prufrock has its current liabilities covered 1.31 times over.

To a creditor, particularly a short-term creditor such as a supplier, the higher the current ratio, the better. To the firm, a high current ratio indicates liquidity, but it also may indicate an inefficient use of cash and other short-term assets. Absent some extraordinary circumstances, we would expect to see a current ratio of at least 1, because a current ratio of less than 1 would mean that net working capital (current assets less current liabilities) is negative. This would be unusual in a healthy firm, at least for most types of businesses.

The current ratio, like any ratio, is affected by various types of transactions. For example, suppose the firm borrows over the long term to raise money. The short-run effect would be an increase in cash from the issue proceeds and an increase in long-term debt. Current liabilities would not be affected, so the current ratio would rise.

Finally, note that an apparently low current ratio may not be a bad sign for a company with a large reserve of untapped borrowing power.

Quick (or Acid-Test) Ratio Inventory is often the least liquid current asset. It's also the one for which the book values are least reliable as measures of market value, since the quality of the inventory isn't considered. Some of the inventory may later turn out to be damaged, obsolete, or lost.

More to the point, relatively large inventories are often a sign of short-term trouble. The firm may have overestimated sales and overbought or overproduced as a result. In this case, the firm may have a substantial portion of its liquidity tied up in slow-moving inventory.

To further evaluate liquidity, the *quick,* or *acid-test, ratio* is computed just like the current ratio, except inventory is omitted:

$$\text{Quick ratio} = \frac{\text{Current assets} - \text{Inventory}}{\text{Current liabilities}}$$

Notice that using cash to buy inventory does not affect the current ratio, but it reduces the quick ratio. Again, the idea is that inventory is relatively illiquid compared to cash.

For Prufrock, this ratio in 2011 was:

$$\text{Quick ratio} = \frac{\$708 - 422}{\$540} = .53 \text{ times}$$

The quick ratio here tells a somewhat different story than the current ratio, because inventory accounts for more than half of Prufrock's current assets. To exaggerate the point, if this inventory consisted of, say, unsold nuclear power plants, then this would be a cause for concern.

Cash Ratio   A very short-term creditor might be interested in the *cash ratio:*

$$\text{Cash ratio} = \frac{\text{Cash}}{\text{Current liabilities}}$$

You can verify that this works out to be .18 times for Prufrock.

Long-Term Solvency Measures

Long-term solvency ratios are intended to address the firm's long-run ability to meet its obligations, or, more generally, its financial leverage. These ratios are sometimes called *financial leverage ratios* or just *leverage ratios.* We consider three commonly used measures and some variations.

Total Debt Ratio   The *total debt ratio* takes into account all debts of all maturities to all creditors. It can be defined in several ways, the easiest of which is:

$$\text{Total debt ratio} = \frac{\text{Total assets} - \text{Total equity}}{\text{Total assets}}$$

$$= \frac{\$3,588 - 2,591}{\$3,588} = .28 \text{ times}$$

In this case, an analyst might say that Prufrock uses 28 percent debt.[1] Whether this is high or low or whether it even makes any difference depends on whether or not capital structure matters.

Prufrock has $.28 in debt for every $1 in assets. Therefore, there is $.72 in equity ($1 − .28) for every $.28 in debt. With this in mind, we can define two useful variations on the total debt ratio, the *debt-equity ratio* and the *equity multiplier:*

$$\text{Debt-equity ratio} = \text{Total debt/Total equity}$$
$$= \$.28/\$.72 = .39 \text{ times}$$
$$\text{Equity multiplier} = \text{Total assets/Total equity}$$
$$= \$1/\$.72 = 1.39 \text{ times}$$

The fact that the equity multiplier is 1 plus the debt-equity ratio is not a coincidence:

$$\text{Equity multiplier} = \text{Total assets/Total equity} = \$1/\$.72 = 1.39$$
$$= (\text{Total equity} + \text{Total debt})/\text{Total equity}$$
$$= 1 + \text{Debt-equity ratio} = 1.39 \text{ times}$$

The thing to notice here is that given any one of these three ratios, you can immediately calculate the other two, so they all say exactly the same thing.

Times Interest Earned   Another common measure of long-term solvency is the *times interest earned* (TIE) *ratio.* Once again, there are several possible (and common) definitions, but we'll stick with the most traditional:

$$\text{Times interest earned ratio} = \frac{\text{EBIT}}{\text{Interest}}$$

$$= \frac{\$691}{\$141} = 4.9 \text{ times}$$

As the name suggests, this ratio measures how well a company has its interest obligations covered, and it is often called the interest coverage ratio. For Prufrock, the interest bill is covered 4.9 times over.

---

[1]Total equity here includes preferred stock, if there is any. An equivalent numerator in this ratio would be (Current liabilities + Long-term debt).

Cash Coverage A problem with the TIE ratio is that it is based on earnings before interest and taxes (EBIT), which is not really a measure of cash available to pay interest. The reason is that depreciation, a noncash expense, has been deducted. Since interest is most definitely a cash outflow (to creditors), one way to define the *cash coverage ratio* is:

$$\text{Cash coverage ratio} = \frac{\text{EBIT} + \text{Depreciation}}{\text{Interest}}$$

$$= \frac{\$691 + 276}{\$141} = \frac{\$967}{\$141} = 6.9 \text{ times}$$

The numerator here, EBIT plus depreciation, is often abbreviated EBDIT (earnings before depreciation, interest, and taxes). It is a basic measure of the firm's ability to generate cash from operations, and it is frequently used as a measure of cash flow available to meet financial obligations.

Asset Management, or Turnover, Measures

We next turn our attention to the efficiency with which Prufrock uses its assets. The measures in this section are sometimes called *asset utilization ratios*. The specific ratios we discuss can all be interpreted as measures of turnover. What they are intended to describe is how efficiently, or intensively, a firm uses its assets to generate sales. We first look at two important current assets: inventory and receivables.

Inventory Turnover and Days' Sales in Inventory During the year, Prufrock had a cost of goods sold of $1,344. Inventory at the end of the year was $422. With these numbers, *inventory turnover* can be calculated as:

$$\text{Inventory turnover} = \frac{\text{Cost of goods sold}}{\text{Inventory}}$$

$$= \frac{\$1,344}{\$422} = 3.2 \text{ times}$$

In a sense, we sold off, or turned over, the entire inventory 3.2 times. As long as we are not running out of stock and thereby forgoing sales, the higher this ratio is, the more efficiently we are managing inventory.

If we know that we turned our inventory over 3.2 times during the year, then we can immediately figure out how long it took us to turn it over on average. The result is the average *days' sales in inventory:*

$$\text{Days' sales in inventory} = \frac{365 \text{ days}}{\text{Inventory turnover}}$$

$$= \frac{365}{3.2} = 114 \text{ days}$$

This tells us that, on average, inventory sits 114 days before it is sold. Alternatively, assuming we used the most recent inventory and cost figures, it will take about 114 days to work off our current inventory.

For example, we frequently hear things like "Majestic Motors has a 60 days' supply of cars." This means that, at current daily sales, it would take 60 days to deplete the available inventory. We could also say that Majestic has 60 days of sales in inventory.

Receivables Turnover and Days' Sales in Receivables Our inventory measures give some indication of how fast we can sell products. We now look at how fast we collect on those sales. The *receivables turnover* is defined in the same way as inventory turnover:

$$\text{Receivables turnover} = \frac{\text{Sales}}{\text{Accounts receivable}}$$

$$= \frac{\$2,311}{\$188} = 12.3 \text{ times}$$

Loosely speaking, we collected our outstanding credit accounts and reloaned the money 12.3 times during the year.[2]

This ratio makes more sense if we convert it to days, so the *days' sales in receivables* is:

$$\text{Days' sales in receivables} = \frac{365 \text{ days}}{\text{Receivables turnover}}$$

$$= \frac{365}{12.3} = 30 \text{ days}$$

Therefore, on average, we collect on our credit sales in 30 days. For obvious reasons, this ratio is very frequently called the *average collection period* (ACP).

Also note that if we are using the most recent figures, we can also say that we have 30 days' worth of sales currently uncollected.

Total Asset Turnover Moving away from specific accounts like inventory or receivables, we can consider an important "big picture" ratio, the *total asset turnover ratio*. As the name suggests, total asset turnover is:

$$\text{Total asset turnover} = \frac{\text{Sales}}{\text{Total assets}}$$

$$= \frac{\$2,311}{\$3,588} = .64 \text{ times}$$

In other words, for every dollar in assets, we generated $.64 in sales.

A closely related ratio, the *capital intensity ratio,* is simply the reciprocal of (i.e., 1 divided by) total asset turnover. It can be interpreted as the dollar investment in assets needed to generate $1 in sales. High values correspond to capital intensive industries (e.g., public utilities). For Prufrock, total asset turnover is .64, so, if we flip this over, we get that capital intensity is $1/.64 = \$1.56$. That is, it takes Prufrock $1.56 in assets to create $1 in sales.

Profitability Measures

The three measures we discuss in this section are probably the best known and most widely used of all financial ratios. In one form or another, they are intended to measure how efficiently the firm uses its assets and how efficiently the firm manages its operations. The focus in this group is on the bottom line, net income.

Profit Margin Companies pay a great deal of attention to their *profit margin:*

$$\text{Profit margin} = \frac{\text{Net income}}{\text{Sales}}$$

$$= \frac{\$363}{\$2,311} = 15.7\%$$

This tells us that Prufrock, in an accounting sense, generates a little less than 16 cents in profit for every dollar in sales.

---

[2]Here we have implicitly assumed that all sales are credit sales. If they were not, then we would simply use total credit sales in these calculations, not total sales.

All other things being equal, a relatively high profit margin is obviously desirable. This situation corresponds to low expense ratios relative to sales. However, we hasten to add that other things are often not equal.

For example, lowering our sales price will usually increase unit volume, but will normally cause profit margins to shrink. Total profit (or, more importantly, operating cash flow) may go up or down; so the fact that margins are smaller isn't necessarily bad. After all, isn't it possible that, as the saying goes, "Our prices are so low that we lose money on everything we sell, but we make it up in volume!"[3]

Return on Assets   *Return on assets* (ROA) is a measure of profit per dollar of assets. It can be defined several ways, but the most common is:

$$\text{Return on assets} = \frac{\text{Net income}}{\text{Total assets}}$$

$$= \frac{\$363}{\$3,588} = 10.12\%$$

Return on Equity   *Return on equity* (ROE) is a measure of how the stockholders fared during the year. Since benefiting shareholders is our goal, ROE is, in an accounting sense, the true bottom-line measure of performance. ROE is usually measured as:

$$\text{Return on equity} = \frac{\text{Net income}}{\text{Total equity}}$$

$$= \frac{\$363}{\$2,591} = 14\%$$

For every dollar in equity, therefore, Prufrock generated 14 cents in profit, but, again, this is only correct in accounting terms.

Because ROA and ROE are such commonly cited numbers, we stress that it is important to remember they are accounting rates of return. For this reason, these measures should properly be called *return on book assets* and *return on book equity*. In addition, ROE is sometimes called *return on net worth*. Whatever it's called, it would be inappropriate to compare the results to, for example, an interest rate observed in the financial markets.

The fact that ROE exceeds ROA reflects Prufrock's use of financial leverage. We will examine the relationship between these two measures in more detail below.

Market Value Measures

Our final group of measures is based, in part, on information not necessarily contained in financial statements—the market price per share of the stock. Obviously, these measures can only be calculated directly for publicly traded companies.

We assume that Prufrock has 33 million shares outstanding and the stock sold for $88 per share at the end of the year. If we recall that Prufrock's net income was $363 million, then we can calculate that its earnings per share were:

$$\text{EPS} = \frac{\text{Net income}}{\text{Shares outstanding}} = \frac{\$363}{33} = \$11$$

Price-Earnings Ratio   The first of our market value measures, the *price-earnings,* or PE, *ratio* (or multiple), is defined as:

$$\text{PE ratio} = \frac{\text{Price per share}}{\text{Earnings per share}}$$

$$= \frac{\$88}{\$11} = 8 \text{ times}$$

---

[3]No, it's not; margins can be small, but they do need to be positive!

In the vernacular, we would say that Prufrock shares sell for eight times earnings, or we might say that Prufrock shares have, or "carry," a PE multiple of 8.

Since the PE ratio measures how much investors are willing to pay per dollar of current earnings, higher PEs are often taken to mean that the firm has significant prospects for future growth. Of course, if a firm had no or almost no earnings, its PE would probably be quite large; so, as always, be careful when interpreting this ratio.

Market-to-Book Ratio   A second commonly quoted measure is the *market-to-book ratio:*

$$\text{Market-to-book ratio} = \frac{\text{Market value per share}}{\text{Book value per share}}$$

$$= \frac{\$88}{(\$2,591/33)} = \frac{\$88}{\$78.5} = 1.12 \text{ times}$$

Notice that book value per share is total equity (not just common stock) divided by the number of shares outstanding.

Since book value per share is an accounting number, it reflects historical costs. In a loose sense, the market-to-book ratio therefore compares the market value of the firm's investments to their cost. A value less than 1 could mean that the firm has not been successful overall in creating value for its stockholders.

Conclusion

This completes our definition of some common ratios. Exhibit 13A.5 summarizes the ratios we've discussed.

EXHIBIT 13A.5 A Summary of Five Types of Financial Ratios

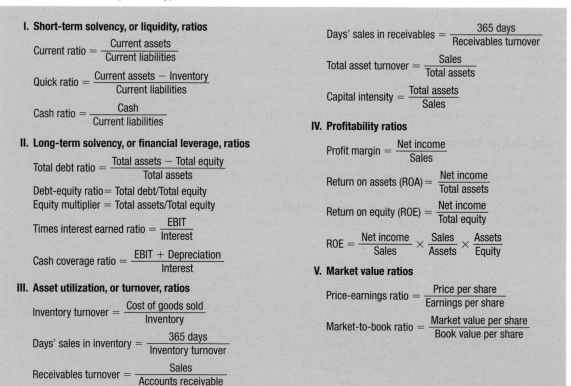

Sources of Company and Industry Information*

In order for business executives to make the best decisions when developing corporate strategy, it is critical for them to be knowledgeable about their competitors and about the industries in which they compete. The process used by corporations to learn as much as possible about competitors is often called "competitive intelligence." This appendix provides an overview of important and widely available sources of information that may be useful in conducting basic competitive intelligence. Much information of this nature is available in libraries in article databases, business reference books, and on websites. This list will recommend a variety of them. Ask a librarian for assistance, because library collections and resources vary.

The information sources are organized into 10 categories:

Competitive Intelligence
Public or Private—Subsidiary or Division—U.S. or Foreign?
Finding Public Company Information
Guides and Tutorials
SEC Filings/EDGAR—Company Disclosure Reports
Company Rankings
Business Websites
Strategic and Competitive Analysis—Information Sources
Sources for Industry Research and Analysis
Search Engines

Competitive Intelligence

Students and other researchers who want to learn more about the value and process of competitive intelligence should see four recent books on this subject. Ask a librarian about electronic (ebook) versions of the following titles.

Michaeli Rainer. *Competitive Intelligence: Competitive Advantage through Analysis of Competition, Markets and Technologies.* London: Springer-Verlag, 2012.

John J. McGonagle and Carolyn M. Vella. *Proactive Intelligence: The Successful Executive's Guide to Intelligence.* London: Springer-Verlag, 2012.

Hans Hedin, Irmeli Hirvensalo, and Markko Vaarnas. *Handbook of Market Intelligence: Understand, Compete and Grow in Global Markets.* Chichester, West Sussex, U.K.: John Wiley & Sons, 2011.

Benjamin Gilad. *Early Warning: Using Competitive Intelligence to Anticipate Market Shifts, Control Risk, and Create Powerful Strategies.* New York: American Management Association, 2004.

Public or Private—Subsidiary or Division—U.S. or Foreign?

Companies traded on stock exchanges in the United States are required to file a variety of reports that disclose information about the company. This begins the process that produces a wealth of data on public companies and at the same time distinguishes them from private companies, which often lack available data. Similarly, financial data of subsidiaries and divisions are typically filed in a consolidated financial statement by the parent company, rather

---

*This information was compiled by Ruthie Brock and Carol Byrne, Business Librarians at The University of Texas at Arlington. We greatly appreciate their valuable contribution.

than treated independently, thus limiting the kind of data available on them. On the other hand, foreign companies that trade on U.S. stock exchanges are required to file 20F reports, similar to the 10-K for U.S. companies, the most comprehensive of the required reports. The following directories provide brief facts about companies, including whether they are public or private, subsidiary or division, U.S. or foreign.

The *Corporate Directory* provides company profiles of more than 9,000 publicly traded companies in the United States, including foreign companies trading on the U.S. exchanges (ADRs). Some libraries may subscribe to an alternative online version at *www.walkersresearch.com*.

Corporate Affiliations. New Providence, NJ: LexisNexis, 2011.

This 8-volume directory features brief profiles of major U.S. and foreign corporations, both public and private, as well as their subsidiaries, divisions, and affiliates. The directory also indicates hierarchies of corporate relationships. An online version of the directory allows retrieval of a list of companies that meet specific criteria. Results can be downloaded to a spreadsheet. The online version requires a subscription, available in some libraries.

ReferenceUSA. Omaha, NE: Infogroup.Inc.

ReferenceUSA is an online directory of more than 14 million businesses located in the United States. One of the unique features is that it includes public and private companies, both large and small. Custom and Guided search tabs are available. Also, results can be analyzed using Quick, the data summary feature, which allows for a snapshot of how the industry breaks down by size, geographic location, etc. Other subscription modules are available using the ReferenceUSA interface and may be available in some libraries.

Ward's Business Directory lists brief profiles on more than 112,000 public and private companies and indicates whether they are public or private, a subsidiary or division. Two volumes of the set are arranged using the Standard Industrial Classifications (SIC) and the North American Industry Classification System (NAICS) and feature company rankings within industries. Some libraries may offer this business directory as part of a database called *Gale Directory Library*.

Finding Public Company Information

Most companies have their annual report to shareholders and other financial reports available on their corporate website. Note that some companies use a variation of their company name in their Web address, such as Procter & Gamble: *www.pg.com*. A few "aggregators" have also conveniently provided an accumulation of links to many reports of U.S. and international corporations or include a PDF document as part of their database, although these generally do not attempt to be comprehensive.

The Public Register Online. Woodstock Valley, CT: Bay Tact Corp.

Public Register Online includes over 5,000 public company shareholder annual reports and 10-K filings for online viewing. Links are provided to reports on individual companies' websites, official filings from the Securities and Exchange Commission website, stock information from the NYSE Euronext exchange, or some combination of these sources. A link is also provided on this website for ordering personal copies of hard copy annual reports.

http://www.annualreportservice.com/

Mergent Online. New York: Mergent, Inc.

Mergent Online is a database that provides company reports and financial statements for both U.S. and foreign public companies. Mergent's database has up to 25 years of quarterly and annual financial data that can be downloaded into a spreadsheet for analysis across time or across companies. Students should check with a librarian to determine the availability of this database at their college or university library.

http://mergentonline.com

Guides & Tutorials for Researching Companies and Industries

Researching Companies Online. Debbie Flanagan. Fort Lauderdale, FL

This site provides a step-by-step process for finding free company and industry information on the web.

www.learnwebskills.com/company/

Guide to Financial Statements and *How to Read Annual Reports.* Armonk, NY: IBM

These two educational guides, located on IBM's website, provide basic information on how to read and make sense of financial statements and other information in 10-K and shareholder annual reports for companies in general, not IBM specifically.

www.ibm.com/investor/help/guide/introduction.wss

www.ibm.com/investor/help/reports/introduction.wss

EDGAR Full-Text Search Frequently Asked Questions (FAQ). Washington DC: U.S. Securities and Exchange Commission

The capability to search full-text SEC filings (popularly known as EDGAR filings), was vastly improved when the SEC launched its new search form in late 2006. Features are explained at the FAQ page.

www.sec.gov/edgar/searchedgar/edgarfulltextfaq.htm

Locating Company Information. Tutorial. William and Joan Schreyer Business Library, Penn State University, University Park, PA

Created by librarians at Penn State, this outstanding tutorial provides suggestions for online and print resources for company information. Click on "how to" links for each item to view a brief instruction vignette.

www.libraries.psu.edu/psul/researchguides/business.html

Ten Steps to Industry Intelligence. Industry Tutorial. George A. Smathers Libraries, University of Florida, Gainesville, FL

Provides a step-by-step approach for finding information about industries, with embedded links to recommended sources.

http://businesslibrary.uflib.ufl.edu/industryresearch

Conducting Business Research. This tutorial provides a step-by-step process for business research. http://www.lib.utexas.edu/services/instruction/learningmodules/businessresearch/intro.html

SEC Filings/EDGAR—Company Disclosure Reports

SEC Filings are the various reports that publicly traded companies must file with the Securities and Exchange Commission to disclose information about their corporation. These are often referred to as "EDGAR" filings, an acronym for the Electronic Data Gathering, Analysis and Retrieval System. Some websites and commercial databases improve access to these reports by offering additional retrieval features not available on the official (*www.sec.gov*) website.

EDGAR Database Full-Text Search. U.S. Securities and Exchange Commission (SEC), Washington, DC

10-K reports and other required corporate documents are made available in the SEC's EDGAR database within 24 hours after being filed. Annual reports, on the other hand, are typically sent directly to shareholders and are not required as part of EDGAR by the SEC, although some companies voluntarily include them. Both 10-Ks and shareholder's annual reports are considered basic sources of company research. The SEC offers a search interface for full-text searching of the content and exhibits of EDGAR SEC filings. The advanced search is recommended to locate "hard-to-find" information within documents filed by corporations and their competitors. Searches for specific types of reports or certain industries can also be performed.

http://searchwww.sec.gov/EDGARFSClient/jsp/EDGAR_MainAccess.jsp

LexisNexis Academic—SEC Filings & Reports. Bethesda, MD: LexisNexis.

Company Securities Exchange Commission filings and reports are available through a database called LexisNexis Academic. These reports and filings can be retrieved by company name, industry code, or ticker symbol for a particular time period or by a specific report. Proxy, 10-K, prospectus, and registration filings are also available.

Mergent Online—EDGAR Search. New York: Mergent, Inc.

As an alternative to *sec.gov*, the Securities and Exchange Commission website, it is possible to use the *Mergent Online* database to search for official company filings. Check to be sure if your library subscribes to the *Mergent Online* database. Select the "Filings" tab and then click on the "EDGAR Search" link. Next, Mergent's Government Filings search allows searching by company name, ticker, CIK (Central Index Key) number, or industry SIC number. The search can be limited by date and by type of SEC filing. The URL below should also work if your library subscribes to the Mergent Online database.

http://www.mergentonline.com/filingsearch.php?type=edgar&criteriatype=findall&submitvalues

Company Rankings

Fortune 500. New York: Time Inc.

The *Fortune 500* list and other company rankings are published in the printed edition of *Fortune* magazine and are also available online.

http://money.cnn.com/magazines/fortune/fortune500/2012/full_list/index.html

Forbes Global 2000. Forbes, Inc.

The companies listed on The Forbes Global 2000 are the biggest and most powerful in the world.

http://www.forbes.com/global2000/

Business Websites

Big Charts. San Francisco: MarketWatch, Inc.

BigCharts is a comprehensive and easy-to-use investment research website, providing access to professional-level research tools such as interactive charts, current and historical quotes, industry analysis, and intraday stock screeners, as well as market news and commentary.

MarketWatch operates this website, a service of Dow Jones & Company. Supported by site sponsors, it is free to self-directed investors.

http://bigcharts.marketwatch.com/

GlobalEdge. East Lansing, MI: Michigan State University

GlobalEdge is a web portal providing a significant amount of information about international business, countries around the globe, the U.S. states, industries, and news.

http://globaledge.msu.edu/

Yahoo Finance. Sunnyvale, CA: Yahoo! Inc.

This website links to information on U.S. markets, world markets, data sources, finance references, investment editorials, financial news, and other helpful websites.

http://finance.yahoo.com

Strategic and Competitive Analysis—Information Sources

Analyzing a company can take the form of examining its internal and external environment. In the process, it is useful to identify the company's strengths, weaknesses, opportunities, and threats (SWOT). Sources for this kind of analysis are varied, but perhaps the best would be to locate articles from *The Wall Street Journal,* business magazines and industry trade publications. Publications such as these can be found in the following databases available at many public and academic libraries. When using a database that is structured to allow it, try searching the company name combined with one or more keywords, such as "IBM and competition" or

"Microsoft and lawsuits" or "AMR and fuel costs" to retrieve articles relating to the external environment.

ABI/INFORM Complete. Ann Arbor, MI: ProQuest LLC.

ABI/INFORM Complete provides abstracts and full-text articles covering disciplines such as management, law, taxation, economics, health care, and information technology from more than 6,800 scholarly, business, and trade publications. Other types of resources include company and industry reports, case studies, market research reports, and a variety of downloadable economic data.

Business Insights: Essentials. Farmington Hills, MI: Gale CENGAGE Learning.

Business Insights provides company and industry intelligence for a selection of public and private companies. Company profiles include parent-subsidiary relationships, industry rankings, products and brands, industry statistics, and financial ratios. Selections of SWOT analysis reports are also available. The Company and Industry comparison tool allows a researcher to compare up to six companies' revenues, employees, and sales data over time. Results are available as an image, chart, or spreadsheet.

Business Source Complete. Ipswich, MA: EBSCO Publishing

Business Source Complete is a full-text database with over 3,800 scholarly business journals covering management, economics, finance, accounting, international business, and more. The database also includes detailed company profiles for the world's 10,000 largest companies, as well as selected country economic reports provided by the Economist Intelligence Unit (EIU). The database includes case studies, investment and market research reports, SWOT analyses, and more. *Business Source Complete* contains over 2,400 peer-reviewed business journals.

Thomson ONE Research.

Thomson ONE Research offers full-text analytical reports on more than 65,000 companies worldwide. The research reports are excellent sources for strategic and financial profiles of a company and its competitors and of industry trends. Developed by a global roster of brokerage, investment banking, and research firms, these full-text investment reports include a wealth of current and historical information useful for evaluating a company or industry over time.

International Directory of Company Histories. Detroit, MI: St. James Press, 1988–present. 141 volumes to date.

This directory covers more than 11,000 multinational companies, and the series is still adding volumes. Each company history is approximately three to five pages in length and provides a summary of the company's mission, goals, and ideals, followed by company milestones, principal subsidiaries, and competitors. Strategic decisions made during the company's period of existence are usually noted. This series covers public and private companies and nonprofit entities. Entry information includes a company's legal name, headquarters information, URL, incorporation date, ticker symbol, stock exchange, sales figures, and the primary North American Industry Classification System (NAICS) code. Further reading selections complete the entry information. Volume 59 to current date, is available electronically in the Gale Virtual Reference Library database from Gale CENGAGE Learning.

LexisNexis Academic. Bethesda, MD: LexisNexis

This advanced search provides access to major business publications, broadcast transcripts, and industry news. Industry and market information cover over 25 industries. The Companies section provides access to company dossiers, company profiles and SEC filings. The Company Dossier research tool allows a researcher to compare up to five companies' financial statements at one time with download capabilities.

The Wall Street Journal. New York: Dow Jones & Co.

This respected business newspaper is available in searchable full-text from 1984 to the present in the *Factiva* database. The "News Pages" link provides access to current articles and issues of *The Wall Street Journal.* Dow Jones, publisher of the print version of the *Wall*

Street Journal, also has an online subscription available at wsj.com. Some libraries provide access to *The Wall Street Journal* through the ProQuest Newspapers database.

Sources for Industry Research and Analysis

Factiva. New York: Dow Jones & Co.

The *Factiva* database has several options for researching an industry. One would be to search the database for articles in the business magazines and industry trade publications. A second option in *Factiva* would be to search in the Companies/Markets category for company/industry comparison reports.

Mergent Online. New York: Mergent Inc.

Mergent Online is a searchable database of over 60,000 global public companies. The database offers worldwide industry reports, U.S. and global competitors, and executive biographical information. *Mergent*'s Basic Search option permits searching by primary industry codes (either SIC or NAICS). Once the search is executed, companies in that industry should be listed. A comparison or standard peer group analysis can be created to analyze companies in the same industry on various criteria. The Advanced Search allows the user to search a wider range of financial and textual information. Results, including ratios for a company and its competitors, can be downloaded to a spreadsheet.

North American Industry Classification System (NAICS)

The North American Industry Classification System has officially replaced the Standard Industrial Classification (SIC) as the numerical structure used to define and analyze industries, although some publications and databases offer both classification systems. The NAICS codes are used in Canada, the United States, and Mexico. In the United States, the NAICS codes are used to conduct an Economic Census every five years providing a snapshot of the U.S. economy at a given moment in time.

NAICS: *www.census.gov/eos/www/naics/*

Economic Census: *www.census.gov/econ/census07/*

NetAdvantage. New York: S & P Capital IQ

The database includes company, financial, and investment information as well as the well-known publication called *Industry Surveys.* Each industry report includes information on the current environment, industry trends, key industry ratios and statistics, and comparative company financial analysis. Available in HTML, PDF, or Excel formats.

Business Insights: Essentials. Farmington Hills, MI: Gale CENGAGE Learning.

Business Insights provides company and industry intelligence for a selection of public and private companies. Company profiles include parent-subsidiary relationships, industry rankings, products and brands, industry statistics, and financial ratios. Selections of SWOT analysis reports are also available. The Company and Industry comparison tool allows a researcher to compare up to six companies' revenues, employees, and sales data over time. Results are available as an image, chart, or spreadsheet.

Plunkett Research Online. Houston, TX: Plunkett Research, Ltd.

Plunkett's provides industry-specific market research, trends analysis, and business intelligence for 34 industries.

Search Engines

Google. Mountain View, CA: Google, Inc.

Recognized for its advanced technology, quality of results, and simplicity, the search engine Google is highly recommended by librarians and other expert Web surfers.

www.google.com

Dogpile. Bellevue, WA: InfoSpace, Inc.

Dogpile is a metasearch engine that searches and compiles the most relevant results from more than 12 individual search engines.

http://www.dogpile.com/

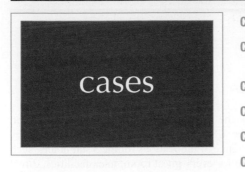

cases

CASE 1   Reinventing Accor C2

CASE 2   Apple and the Retail Industry for Specialist Consumer
Electronics in the United Kingdom C10

CASE 3   Robin Hood C15

CASE 4   eBay: Expanding into China C16

CASE 5   Microfinance Banks: Going Global . . . and Going Public? C27

CASE 6   McDonald's C30

CASE 7   Whirlpool and the Built-in Appliance Industry in India C36

CASE 8   The Best-Laid Incentive Plans C41

CASE 9   Johnson & Johnson C45

CASE 10   Proctor & Gamble C52

CASE 11   Studio 100: A Showcase in Show Business C57

CASE 12   Rhino Capture in Kruger National Park C67

CASE 13   HTC Corporation: A Smartphone Pioneer
From Taiwan C79

CASE 14   Innovative Tata Inc.—India's Pride! C92

CASE 15   Dating at Ikea China: An Unexpected
Management Challenge C101

CASE 16   Google Ventures: Disrupting Corporate
Venture Capital? C103

CASE 17   Heineken C109

CASE 18   Yahoo! C114

CASE 19   Netflix: Can it Recover from its Strategy Mistakes? C120

CASE 20   Building the New Bosco-Zeta Pharma (A) C138

CASE 21   Silence is Not Golden: Golden Agri-Resources,
Greenpeace and Sustainable Palm Oil C149

CASE 22   Going Flat: Pursuit of a Democratic
Organizational Structure C153

CASE 23   Pixar C157

CASE 24   Apple Inc.: Still Taking a Bite Out of the Competition? C161

CASE 1
REINVENTING ACCOR

Alex Janes
University of Exeter

Denis Hennequin became chief executive officer (CEO) of the Accor Group in December 2010 with the vision to make the firm one of the world's top three leading hotel groups by 2015. The group had decided to focus on its hotel brands in 2009, but it had taken over a year to demerge this part of the business from its prepaid business services division, Accor Services (re-named Edenred in 2010). The stage was now set for a new strategy to take the hotel group to 2015. An initial announcement had been promised for September 2011 with further details to follow as Hennequin's vision was fleshed out by the other senior executives in the firm.[1]

The Accor Group had a 2.9 per cent share of the global hotel market in 2010[2] with revenues of $7.9 billion (€5.9 billion)[3] (see Exhibit 1 for selected financial data on Accor), but this put the firm some way behind the top three in the industry, US based groups Marriot International and Hilton Worldwide, and InterContinental Hotels whose headquarters were in London. There were also other challengers in the industry vying to break into the top group. Starwood Hotels & Resorts and Wyndham Worldwide had both achieved significant growth between 2005 and 2010 (see Exhibit 2 for Global Hotel figures).

Accor were well positioned to achieve a leading position in the industry. They were the leading hotel group in Western Europe, the Middle East and Africa and had a strong position in Eastern Europe and in many emerging markets in Asia-Pacific and South America. The group had 145000 employees and over 4200 hotels in 90 countries in August 2010.[4] Accor's portfolio of hotels offered substantial breadth as well as depth, from luxury brands, such as Sofitel, through mid-market chains such as Novotel and Mercure, to economy and no-frills offerings such as Ibis and Motel6 (see Exhibit 3 for details of Accor's portfolio of brands).

History of Accor

The Accor Group was created in 1983 and brought together the various hotel brands that Paul Dubrule and Gerard Pelisson had developed or acquired since starting the Novotel hotel chain in the 1960s. The two entrepreneurs, neither of whom had a background in hospitality, opened their first Novotel in 1967 adjacent to Lille airport. Their formula for success was very different from the established strategies followed by hotels in the 1960s and 1970s.

Novotel took the idea of the standardised hotel concept, popular in the USA and transported it to Europe. They introduced a range of innovations for the 3 star hotels, such as a bathroom for every guest room, telex facilities, direct dial telephones in guest bedrooms and outdoor amenities such as swimming pools, children's play areas and free car parking, all of which quickly became standard in the new breed of out of town hotels. The hotel chain also treated its staff very differently with much less hierarchy and job specialisation, employees were encouraged to move location and learn a range of functions to maximise flexibility. The group created its own corporate university in 1985, the Academie Accor.

Pelisson and Dubrule expanded their business by building new hotels and then acquiring other chains. During the 1970s Novotel was growing by an average of one hotel per month. The company began its international growth in 1973 with its first hotel outside France in Warsaw, Poland. In 1974 the firm launched a new 2 star hotel brand with the first Ibis hotel, which opened in Bordeaux. This was followed in 1975 by the acquisition of rival 3 star operator, Mercure. 1980 saw the firm make its most dramatic acquisition yet, with the purchase of 4 star deluxe hotel chain, Sofitel.[5] They now had nearly 200 hotels in 22 countries.[6]

The group then expanded into related businesses. In 1982, the acquisition of Jacques Borel International took them into the catering and food services sector with the Ticket Restaurant concept. By the time the Accor group was formally created in 1983, they had 440 hotels, 1500 restaurants and 35000 employees in 45 countries. The group's growth continued throughout the rest of the 1980s and 1990s. Accor entered the budget end of the market in 1985 with the creation of Formule 1, a one star motel brand and in 1990 it acquired the Motel6 chain which gave it a larger presence in the USA. The firm also expanded in Asia with developments in China and Thailand. The early 1990s were a tough time for the group in the aftermath of the First Gulf War with the subsequent reduction in travel. However, Accor proved it was capable of reinventing itself and in 1993 completed a comprehensive overhaul of the Novotel brand and its business model, which had become rather tired and much imitated. They also launched a new economy brand of hotel, Etap, in 1991 in response to the tough economic conditions.

In 2001, Accor started to move into a wider range of businesses with the acquisition of Employee Advisory Resource Ltd in the UK, which specialized in employee assistance programmes. The following year it acquired

EXHIBIT 1

Selected financial data on Accor SA

In € millions	2009	2010	2011
Revenue	5490	5948	6100
Operating expense	(3972)	(4134)	(4177)
EBITDAR	1518	1814	1923
Rental expense	(854)	(934)	(995)
EBITDA	664	880	928
Operating profit before tax	(263)	(12)	326
Profits after taxes	(295)	(404)	52
Assets			
Assets held for sale	144	813	386
Non-current assets	7290	5555	5038
Current assets	4312	2310	2576
Total assets	11 746	8678	8000
Equity/Liabilities			
Equity	3254	3949	3768
Long-term liabilities	2818	2015	1850
Current liabilities	5670	2336	2293
Liability on assets held for sale	4	378	89
Total liabilities and equity	11 746	8678	8000

Sources: Accor (2012) *New Frontiers in Hospitality: 2011 Annual Report*, Paris, Accor; Accor (2012) *New Frontiers in Hospitality: 2011 Registration Document and Annual Financial Report*, Paris, Accor.

EXHIBIT 2 Global hotel industry key figures

Company	2005 % value share	2010 % value share	2010 value sales, US$ mn	% growth 2005/2010	% CAGR 2005–2010
Marriott International Inc	4.6	4.8	19 812.5	24.4	4.5
Hilton Worldwide	–	4.1	17 029.8	–	–
InterContinental Hotels Group Plc	3.4	3.7	15 130.1	27.7	5.0
Accor Group	2.6	2.9	11 740.5	31.2	5.6
Starwood Hotels & Resorts Worldwide	2.2	2.5	10 103.6	31.9	5.7
Wyndham Worldwide Corp	–	1.9	7620.0	–	–
Choice Hotels International Inc	1.6	1.5	6262.0	9.5	1.8
Best Western International Inc	1.7	1.5	6030.4	0.5	0.1
Hyatt Hotels Corp	–	0.9	3764.7	–	–
Carlson Cos Inc	0.8	0.7	2998.9	12.0	2.3

Source: Euromonitor International (2011) *Passport—Global Hotels: Reshaping Hotel Experiences*, London, Euromonitor International, p.16.

Davidson Trahaire, Australia's leading human resources (HR) consulting firm. The services business had grown from the pre-paid ticket restaurants part of the business and in 2005 it launched services in Mexico and later India. This part of Accor's business continued to expand with the acquisition of a controlling stake in Motivano in 2008, an employee benefits firm in the UK and Quasar which offered similar programmes in Germany. In 2009 Accor

EXHIBIT 3 Accor's brands in 2011/12

Adagio—was a European brand offering apartments, but with some hotel-type features. The apartments ranged from economy to upscale and the services on offer could be tailored to the needs of individual guests—but each apartment was fully equipped. There were 99 Adagio 'Aparthotels' in nine countries at the end of 2011.

All Seasons—was one of the economy products offered by Accor. All Seasons hotels were located in business areas of towns and cities and were non-standardized, despite being all-inclusive. The hotels were rebranded as Ibis Styles during 2011 and consisted of 149 hotels in 14 countries.

Etap—was another of the firm's economy brands. The no-frills brand was renamed as Ibis Budget (which also replaced Hotel Formule 1 outside Europe) in 2011 and had 522 hotels in 18 countries. The brand mainly appealed to business travellers.

Grand Mercure (or Mei Jue)—was launched in 2011/12 and aimed specifically at the upscale market in China. By the end of 2011 there were nine hotels.

HotelF1- was a no-frills brand with 243 hotels in France

Ibis—as noted above, Ibis was revamped to become the umbrella brand for most of Accor's economy brands in 2011. However, the Ibis hotels continued to operate alongside Ibis Styles and Ibis Budget. Ibis Hotels was the largest element of the Ibis brand in 2011 with 933 hotels in 53 countries. The hotels offered as standardized product appealing to both business and leisure travellers.

Mercure—offered a boutique hotel-style experience to mid-scale travellers and was aimed at both leisure and business travellers. Locations were city and rurally based. There were 716 hotels in 49 countries at the end of 2011.

MGallery—had grown rapidly since its launch in 2009 with 49 hotels in 19 countries by the end of 2011. These hotels were upscale and intended to appeal to both business and leisure travellers. The brand's appeal was similar to that of many boutique hotels with distinctive identities in each location and less of a chain hotel feel.

Motel 6—was another one of Accor's regional hotel chains, operating only in the USA and Canada. In 2011 the 1028 economy motels attracted mainly leisure travellers, although it was rumoured that Accor had plans to sell off the brand.

Novotel—probably the best known of Accor's brands, there were 394 hotels in 56 countries at the end of 2011. The mid-scale chain was intended to appeal to both leisure and business travellers, with dual purpose rooms and meeting spaces, restaurants and so on. The hotels were located in major city centres throughout the globe. The Suite Novotel was a separate product offering long-stay, flexible room spaces for business and leisure guests.

Pullman—was an upscale brand, mainly aimed at business travellers. These hotels were mainly located in regional/international hub cities. There were 20 Pullman hotels in 20 countries in 2011.

Sofitel—was Accor's luxury hotel brand, consisting of non-standardized accommodation, which were generally sited in prestigious city centre locations and were reflective of the local culture as well as the group's French roots. There were 112 Sofitels in 39 countries in 2011.

Studio6—was a North American brand of extended-stay budget accommodation, with hotel facilities. This could be seen as an economy version of Adagio. Accor had 66 of these hotels in 2011, but as with Motel6, appeared to be looking for a buyer for the brand.

Sources: Accor (2012) *New Frontiers in Hospitality: 2011 Annual Report*, Paris, Accor; Accor (2012) *New Frontiers in Hospitality: 2011 Registration Document and Annual Financial Report*, Paris, Accor.

Note: Accor announced the sale of the Motel6 and Studio6 brands to Blackstone Real Estate for $1.9 billion in May 2012.

further consolidated their position as a provider of pre-pay services through a joint venture with MasterCard to offer service throughout Europe.

Meanwhile the firm's hotel and leisure business was also showing significant growth. Accor created a long stay hotel brand aimed at executive customers, Suite Novotel in 1999. This provided 30 sq.m. suites in city centre location for more flexible accommodation with lounge and catering facilities as well as meeting spaces. Accor continued to refresh and expand their existing brands, installing WiFi into both their economy and luxury ranges from 2003 and renaming their Formule 1 brand hotelF1 in 2008. They opened their first Ibis hotel in China in 2003 and continued to expand rapidly in Asia. The group also opened a series of Ibis and Formule 1 hotels in Brazil from 2008 onwards. Accor also launched a new business hotel brand, Pullman, and a new chain of individual economy hotels, All Seasons in 2007. Their non-standardized offering was also extended to the upscale sector of the industry with the launch of MGallery hotels in 2008. Accor had even made a move into casinos and gambling with the creation of Groupe Lucien Barrière as a joint venture with Colony Capital in 2004.

The group divested hotels that were not performing and also sold them to property firms and investment companies to release the capital in the asset. Some of the hotels sold were leased back. Accor released €518 million in 2007 with the sale of 57 hotels in France and Switzerland to a consortium of real estate investment companies. This release of capital could support the two brands launched that year.[7] In 2009 Accor sold 158 of its hotelF1 properties in France for €272 million. The capital generated by sales of real estate and divestment of underperforming hotels also supported the firm's expansion in new faster growing markets such as China, India and Brazil. In 2009 the group opened more luxury hotels under its Sofitel brand in China.

Demerger

The rapid growth of the services and hotel businesses coupled with a poor performance in 2009 which saw the hospitality operations record a net loss of €262 million prompted Gilles Pelisson, the group Chairman and CEO, to start the process of demerging the two elements of the business. The board of directors and other stakeholders finally agreed the separation of the services and hotel businesses in February 2010 with the actual demerger taking place in June. The firm's rationale for the split centred on the view that the businesses now operated in very different business environments and needed very different resources and skills to excel in their contrasting environments.[8] Each business was also very capital intensive and as separate entities they would be better placed to attract a larger number of investors. The demerger left the majority of the group's €1.6 billion consolidated debt with the new hotel company, Accor SA, with Edenred, the renamed services company taking on €0.4 billion and Accor €1.2 billion. The hotel business had a substantially larger tangible asset base against which to offset debt. Both firms would be able to increase their level of equity funds by appealing to investors with different goals. There would be no capital ties between the firms. The demerger was also sold to stakeholders on the basis of its impact on partnerships and strategic alliances. Each of the new firms would be free to pursue different partners without the baggage of the other's business model or capital structure limitations.

The Global Hotel Industry

History

Offering hospitality and accommodation to travellers for payment dates back to antiquity and there are many examples of spas, inns and taverns in the Greek and Roman worlds as well as outside Europe. In fact, the oldest hotel in the world is the Hoshi ryokan in Komatsu, Japan, which has been run by the same family for 46 generations and dates back to 717.[9] However, the growth of the global industry is a much more recent phenomenon. Most hotels were and still are individual enterprises or family run businesses centring on a single location. It was in the nineteenth century that large scale hotels were constructed in Europe as railways replaced the stagecoach as the dominant form of transport. A further boom in hotel construction occurred in the 1920s, particularly in North America,

but the real genesis of the global industry began in the 1950s and 1960s when franchising and branded chain hotels allowed rapid expansion and the development of operationally effective, standardised offerings at a national and international level.[10, 11]

The 1970s marked the start of another key phase in the global industry, driven by middle- eastern states and their oil revenues, the growth of mass tourism and the opening up of China and other Asian countries. This led to a 1980s' boom as hotels were built in increasing numbers next to airports, and in a wide range of new resort destinations, catering for both tourists on vacation and commercial audiences as the conference trade grew and business became more globalized.[12] The 1980s also marked the start of the consolidation of the industry through a series of high profile mergers and acquisitions.[13] If the 1980s were the boom, then the 1990s were the bust. The First Gulf War in 1991 created uncertainty in world travel markets and led to a decline in revenues for many hotel based businesses. The decade also saw the beginning of a greater emphasis on environmental issues for the industry as well as a range of new strategies and business models. Some hotel operators ceased to own their hotels and moved to a management company role, leasing or renting their premises, others invested heavily in customer loyalty schemes and brand extensions to cater for a wider range of tastes and wallets. Technology also had a profound effect through the introduction of the Internet, electronic reservation systems and a range of computerized systems, from stock ordering to point of sales facilities in restaurants and bars.

In the last 10 years, many of these trends have accelerated as the industry becomes more competitive and technology more pervasive. The advent of web 2.0 has meant that consumers have far more access to information about hotels, from prices to reviews, and a stronger voice in the marketplace. Guests expected to be able to use their laptops in their rooms, have access to a range of satellite channels on the TV, access a wide choice of dining styles from fast food to á la carte, keep fit in the in-house gym or indulge in a range of beauty and wellness therapies. Like other travel sector companies, hotel firms have also found that there are many advantages in partnerships both within the industry and with a wide range of other organizations.

Current Trends

Globally, the hotel sector was valued at between $415 billion and $544 billion in 2010.[14, 15] There is agreement that the sector has bounced back from the recession after it contracted by some 2.8 per cent worldwide in 2009. Growth of between 4 and 7.8 per cent CAGR (Compound Annual Growth Rate) was being forecast for the period 2010–15. Commentators were predicting that most of this growth would come from the Asia Pacific market which had been increasing at more than 7 per cent as opposed to Europe, where growth was less than 1 per cent in 2010. The leisure part of the hotel industry was still dominant in 2010, accounting for over three-quarters of the market value, with business making up the remainder. Europe and the Americas were the most valuable element of the global market, making up 39 per cent and 31 per cent of the total value of the industry in 2010.[16] Asia Pacific accounted for just over a quarter of the global industry's value with the remainder of the market (4.2 per cent) in the Middle East and Africa.

Brands continued to be an important element in the global hotel industry and after the 2009 dip many of the biggest chains began upgrading and refreshing their different lines. The US market was particularly sensitive to this sort of activity due to the fact that 70 per cent of hotels are branded chain outlets. Re-branding in the hotel sector is far more than just a new advertising campaign. Refreshing a hotel brand often involves new interior design schemes for lobbies, communal and dining areas as well as guest rooms. New furniture is often part of the package and new amenities in the hotel itself, from gym and fitness facilities to spa and health and beauty treatments. The staffing profile in hotels may also be altered as a result. In some cases it will result in the disposal of hotel properties that no longer fit the new brand and development of new properties in new locations that do. This makes this element of strategy implementation one of the most expensive for firms in the industry. In 2010/1 most of the key players were moving away from a traditional look and feel—even in their no-frills offerings—to a minimalist, contemporary atmosphere.

Despite the investment in brands and the growth of loyalty schemes, such as Hilton's HHonours and IHG's Priority Club Rewards,[17] it cost consumers very little to switch providers and this led to an increasingly competitive marketplace. Few of the major players competed on price alone, despite the fact that many consumers were price sensitive in the light of the global downturn. As part of their branding, hotel chains also adopted a highly segmented approach to marketing their ranges of hotels. Innovation also played a key role in attracting and retaining customers and many of the hotel firms were focused on extending their offer and reducing costs in all but the premium sector of the market.

In terms of geographic expansion, most of the main hotel chains were focusing on Asia Pacific as their main growth market. North America and Europe were considered mature markets where growth was difficult to achieve without potential retaliation from other incumbents, although there was some scope for consolidation in Europe are most hotels remained independently owned. The top players in the global industry all had plans to significantly increase their penetration of the Indian and Chinese markets. Starwood announced plans to double their number of hotels in China from 150 to 300 by 2012 and Marriott were planning to develop a further 100 hotels in India and China between 2010 and 2015 to add to their existing stock of 131. However, most hotel firms have focused on the larger cities in each country and this has meant that real estate prices and local taxes have risen in response to demand/opportunity in cities such as Mumbai and Shanghai. Second and third tier destinations, such as Huangshan and Wuzhen are becoming increasingly popular because demand is still outstripping supply and there is significant potential for growth.[18]

Spas have long provided destinations for travellers interested in improving their health and social changes to people's attitudes towards health and fitness are providing a new lease of life for this style of hotel and destination.[19] Investment in facilities to cater for the growing interest in wellness has taken place in a wide range of hotels. This can include indoor and outdoor exercise facilities, and spaces for a range of therapies, from use of special muds and minerals to traditional geo-thermal and sea water based cures. Hilton launched the first of 80 planned in-house spas in October 2010. Globally, the largest growth in this sector is predicted for India, Vietnam and the Philippines.[20] Hotels are also increasingly developing holistic packages to include food, room features, and wellness classes. As consumers become more interested in how and where their food is produced and demand more healthy options, such as anti-energy or relaxation drinks, hotels have had to respond. Westin Hotels announced a $30 million investment in promoting and delivering well-being throughout their chain of hotels in 2011–2.[21]

Consumers' environmental concerns were also driving change in the hotel industry, with a number of the main players using ISO14001 or LEED (Leadership in Energy and Environmental Design) certification as the basis for improving their sustainability. Hotel firms had then found that the changes they made improved operational effectiveness, InterContinental Hotel Group (IHG) found that their Green Engage programme not only gained them LEED certification in January 2011, but it also produced 20 per cent savings due to reduced energy use in their premises. Hilton's LightStay system, launched in 2010, produced similar savings in energy and water use, which helped to reduce operating costs. Extensive re-branding activities have enabled firms such as Marriott and Starwood to change menus and make use of low energy lighting, green bedding and beauty/personal care products.[22]

The Internet and a range of other technologies have had a profound effect on the global hotel industry. The rise of online booking websites such as Lastminute.com, Expedia.com and TripAdvisor.co.uk which also carry reviews meant customers had access to much more information about hotels and the deals they could offer. However, this also made social media an increasingly important tool for marketing. The major chains now had access to much more information about their customers and could make use of advocates with large followings on Facebook or Twitter to help spread positive messages about their hotels and resorts. Marriott ran this sort of campaign for its SpringHill Suites chain by offering a variety of incentives to guests willing to enthuse their friends about the hotel.[23]

The hotel industry had always been a capital intensive industry, because of the amount of equipment and furniture needed to run a full-service establishment and the cost of the real estate in the first place. Increasing reliance on and need for technology had increased this in the last few years. Hotels now had a whole range of procurement and reservation systems, databases and associated networks, plus a whole host of expert suppliers that provided these products and services.[24] In 2011 several hotel chains were experimenting with digital concierges—especially in midmarket and economy hotels. Further changes were being seen from the growth in the use of mobile technology for everything from booking and checking in to providing special maps and even, like IHG, allowing guests to use their smartphones in place of room keys.[25]

Accor's Strategy

Since its separation from the services business, Accor SA had followed an ambitious expansions strategy, mainly focusing on emerging markets in the Asia Pacific region. In October 2011, the firm announced[26] plans to add more than 200 hotels to its existing portfolio of 450 by 2014. The expansion would mainly focus on China, India and Indonesia, with some more limited growth in Australia and Vietnam. Accor's strategy was to seek to increase its level of activity in fast-growing emerging country economies outside Europe. Within Europe, where the company remained the largest player in the market, expansion would be in the economy segment of the industry.[27] Europe still accounted for over 70 per cent of the group's revenue in 2010.

Like most of its competitors, Accor needed to find funds to pay for their expansion into faster growth segments and regions. The decision to focus on hotels following the demerger, led to the sale of some of the group's related businesses, such as casinos and catering.[28] Accor sold its rail catering business Compagnie des Wagon-lit in 2010 and its 49 per cent stake in casino group Lucien Barriere in March 2011. Its gourmet dining brand, Lenôtre, was sold for €75 million the same year. However, most of the capital for expansion was raised by the sale and leaseback of the group's owned hotel properties in Europe and North America. One of the key aims of Accor's strategy under Denis Hennequin was to reduce their proportion of owned hotels and those on fixed leases from 60 per cent to between 20 and 30 per cent of the total.[29] Again, this was becoming a common trend in the industry as firm's sought to avoid taking on a high burden of debt, through what was becoming known as an 'asset light' approach. Rather than owning hotels, firms would use franchise contracts or manage the hotel under contract to the owners or rent the property through a variable lease. Accor felt that this approach to managing its existing portfolio and developing new hotels through franchise agreements and management contracts

would allow it to grow rapidly and take advantage of the new markets in emerging economies. Accor's expansion in Australia and New Zealand in 2011 was mainly facilitated through the purchase of hotel management firm, Mirvac, rather than the acquisition or development of hotel real estate.[30]

Hennequin also recognized that the effective management of Accor's portfolio of brands would be critical to the firm's success. The group covered a wide range of segments with their 14 hotel brands. Much of their strength lay in their economy and no-frills brands such as Ibis, hotelF1 and Motel 6. The firm's roots were in the midmarket brands, such as Novotel and Mercure, but they also had the capabilities to manage and create upscale brands such as Pullman and MGallery and succeed with luxury establishments such as their Sofitel chain. Accor's brands combined regional offerings (Motel 6 was specific to the USA) with global hotels such as Ibis. The firm also covered the extended stay segment with an economy brand in the USA, Studio 6, and Suite Novotel, internationally.

However, it was the economy brands that were the best performers in the firm's portfolio showing year on year growth of +6.3 per cent at the end of 2011 compared with +5.0 per cent growth in the upscale and midscale hotels.[31] Accor's strategy was to focus on the Ibis megabrand and align the other international no-frills brands, Etap and Hotel Formula 1 under the Ibis Budget brand and its other economy brand, All Seasons, under the Ibis Style brand. The positioning for the Ibis umbrella brand would be captured by the concepts of 'modernity, simplicity and well-being'.[32]

Another aspect of Accor's strategy was its focus on sustainable initiatives. The group's Earth Guest programme covers a range of activities from encouraging the procurement of fair trade goods for use in hotels, to recycling glass, cardboard and paper. By 2011, 495 of Accor's hotels had achieved ISO14001 and over 90 per cent subscribed to the Hotel Operator's Environmental Charter. Accor was listed on the four main international indexes: Ethibel, FTSE4Good, Dow Jones Sustainability and ASPI Eurozone.[33]

Key Players in the Global Hotel Industry

Marriott Corporation entered the hotel business a decade before Accor and by 2011 was the leading global hotel company. They had flagship J.W. Marriott and Ritz-Carlton hotels with deluxe accommodation for business travellers and holidaymakers; its Courtyard by Marriott and SpringHill Suites brands catered to business travellers looking for moderately priced lodging; and the Marriott Residence Inns and TownePlace Suites were designed as a 'home away from home' for travellers staying five or more nights. The company operated in 70 countries and had over 3500 hotels in 2011, using both an owned and a franchised business model. Marriott also operated over 2000 rental houses and condominiums for corporates. The corporation recorded revenues of $11.7 billion for the financial year ending December 2010 and employed 129 000 staff.[34]

Hilton Worldwide was also headquartered in the USA and employed a similar number of staff to Marriott (130 000 in 2011). Hilton operated 3750 hotels in 84 countries world-wide. The firm was originally known as the Hilton Hotel Corporation until it was acquired by Blackstone and taken private in 2007. Founded by Conrad Hilton in 1919, the firm owns, manages and franchises a wide range of hotels. Its portfolio of brands ranged from luxury hotels such as the Waldorf Astoria and the Conrad, through mid-priced accommodation such as Hilton and Doubletree, to value brands such as Hampton. Hilton also catered for the extended stay, executive sector through its Homewood and Home2 Suites.[35]

InterContinental Hotel Group (IHG) had adopted a different approach to most of its rivals and although its company revenues were substantially lower than the other players at the top of the market, it had more hotels than Hilton, Marriott or Accor. However, most of the hotels were operated under franchise agreements. InterContinental had 4520 hotels globally in 2011 operating in 100 countries under the Intercontinental, Crowne Plaza, Hotel Indigo, Holiday Inn, Staybridge and Candlewood brands. Their portfolio covered both business and leisure sectors and offered everything from economy brands, such as Holdiay Inn Express to the medium stay suite products such as Candlewood. Based in the UK, the group directly employed just over 7000 staff and generated revenues of $1.6 billion in 2010 and an operating profit of $459 million. The vast majority of their hotels were operated under franchise agreements (over 3700 properties fell into this category), so the group had strong skills in working with hotel owners. About 15 per cent of their hotels were operated on a managed basis and the group only owned 15 hotels itself in 2010.[36]

Starwood was one of the fastest growing hotel and leisure groups in the world in 2010/11. The firm's headquarters were on the US East coast in New York. Starwood employed 145 000 staff in 2010 and had revenues in excess of $5 billion. The company's main focus was in the luxury end of the market and they operated hotels and resorts. Brands included, Sheraton, Le Meridien, Westin, St Regis, Element and Aloft. About half of the firm's hotels are franchised and the rest managed on behalf of property owners or owned outright by Starwood. The company has been a relatively late entrant to a number of emerging markets, such as India and China. It opened its first hotel in Russia in 2011. Starwood was founded in 1969 and incorporated in 1980. The company has plans for significant expansion in the Middle East, South America and India over the next few years.[37]

Becoming one of the top 3 It was clear from their end of year figures for December 2011 that Accor was back on track after their demerger and the losses of 2009.

However, with other strong competitors in its market and new trends in the industry there were no guarantees that its strategy would be capable of providing a sustainable competitive advantage. Accor's greatest successes had often been achieved by adopting a different approach to the rest of the hotel trade. Was Accor's current strategy distinctive enough to take it the next step and join the best in the world?

ENDNOTES

1. Accor (2011a) 'Accor's strategic vision'. Available online at www.accor.com/en/group/accor-strategic-vision.html (accessed 1 February 2012).

2. Euromonitor (2011) *Global Hotels: Shaping Hotel Experiences*, August, Euromonitor.com, London.

3. Datamonitor (2011a) *Global Hotels and Motels*, October 2011, Datamonitor.com, London.

4. Accor (2011b) 'Accor in brief'. Available online at www.accor.com/fileadmin/user_upload/Contenus_Accor/Franchise_Management/Documents_utiles/General_information/accor_in_brief__uk_dec_2011.pdf (accessed 1 February 2012).

5. Accor (2011c) 'Chronology'. Available online at www.accor.com/en/group/history/chronology.html (accessed 1 February 2012).

6. Datamonitor (2011b) *Accor SA Company Profile*, June, Datamonitor.com, London.

7. Ibid.

8. Accor (2010) 'Demerging the two businesses and details of the demerger process', 24 February, press release. Available online at www.accor.com/fileadmin/user_upload/Contenus_Accor/Finance/Pressreleases/2010/EN/20100224_CPScission_EN.pdf (accessed 1 February 2012).

9. The most famous hotels in the world (2010) 'Hoshi Ryokan: the world's oldest guest house', 17 April 2010. Available online at www.famoushotels.org/article/1013 (accessed 1 February 2012).

10. IRS (2007) 'Hotel industry overview', August. Available online at www.irs.gov/businesses/article/0,,id=174494,00.html (accessed 1 February 2012).

11. Levy-Bonvin, J. (2003) 'Hotels: a brief history'. Available online at www.hospitalitynet.org/news/4017990.search (accessed 1 February 2012).

12. Ibid.

13. IRS (2007) op. cit.

14. Euromonitor (2011) op. cit.

15. Datamonitor (2011a) op. cit.

16. Ibid.

17. Euromonitor (2011) op. cit.

18. Ibid.

19. Crook, Y. and Stevens, T. (2009) 'Wellness tourism: back to basics', *Health Tourism Magazine*. Available online at www.healthtourismmagazine.com/article/Back-Basics.html (available 1 February 2012).

20. Euromonitor (2011) op. cit.

21. Ibid.

22. Ibid.

23. Ibid.

24. Datamonitor (2011a) op. cit.

25. Euromonitor (2011) op. cit.

26. Saminather, N. (2011) 'Accor plans Asia-Pacific expansion with 200 hotels in pipeline', *Bloomberg Business Week*, 14 October.

27. Accor (2012) 'Sustained revenue growth in 2011', press release, 17 January. Available online at www.accor.com/fileadmin/user_upload/Contenus_Accor/Finance/Pressreleases/2012/EN/20120117_pr_ca_t4_2011.pdf (accessed 1 February 2012).

28. Kenna, A. (2011) 'Accor buys Mirvac Hotels for $254 million to grow in Australia' *Bloomberg Business Week*, 16 December.

29. Saminather, N. (2011) op. cit.

30. Kenna, A. (2011) op. cit.

31. Accor (2012) op. cit.

32. Ibid.

33. Accor (2011b) op. cit.

34. Datamonitor (2011c) *Marriott International, Inc. company profile*, July, datamonitor.com, London.

35. Datamonitor (2011d) *Hilton Worldwide company profile*, October, datamonitor.com, London.

36. Datamonitor (2011e) *InterContinetal Hotel Group plc. company profile*, October, datamonitor.com, London.

37. Datamonitor (2011f) *Starwood Hotels and Resorts Worldwide, Inc. company profile*, August, datamonitor.com, London.

CASE 2

APPLE AND THE RETAIL INDUSTRY FOR SPECIALIST CONSUMER ELECTRONICS IN THE UNITED KINGDOM

Dr John Sanders
Heriot-Watt University

Background

In general the retail industry for consumer electronics (brown goods) sells personal computers, telephones, MP3 players, audio equipment, televisions, digital cameras, camcorders and DVD players. In 2011 UK consumers spent £21.5 billion on consumer electronics in general, which was a fall of 4 per cent from the previous year (source: Mintel). This decline in consumer spending arose from the global credit crisis and subsequent recession in 2008.

Prior to the recession the retail sales of brown goods had been relatively static for many years. Static sales meant the rivalry between UK retailers was intense as they jostled to maintain or grow profitability. Falling sales due to the recession heightened the already intense rivalry among UK retailers.

Apart from the recession there are two other elements that shape the retail industry for brown goods. First, the leading UK retailers find it difficult to differentiate themselves from each other. The lack of differentiation arises because leading UK retailers of brown goods generally sell products from the same manufacturers. As a consequence, UK customers in general base their purchase choices on price alone. The major winners from price competition have been UK supermarkets and online retailers like Amazon, because they are perceived as being cheaper. For example, Amazon has been gradually increasing its share of industry sales at the expense of leading retailers. Leading brown good retailers have also been guilty of neglecting their customer service activities.

Second, technological convergence is affecting the ability of many specialist retail chains or independent stores to maintain or continue to emphasize differences in their services and activities compared to mainstream stores. For example, specialist camera stores are struggling, because the benefits of purchasing a standalone camera from them are being eroded by the widespread inclusion of digital cameras within other products like mobile phones, tablets, personal computers, laptop computers and other devices at increasingly low prices.

The major electrical and computing competitors and their share of the specialist brown goods market in 2011 are shown in Exhibit 1. In the main industry competitors try to serve the mass market for consumer electronics.

EXHIBIT 1 Leading electrical and computing competitors' market share of the specialist consumer electronic market in 2011.

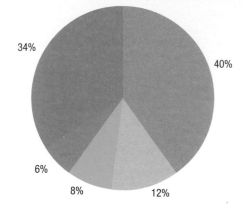

34%
40%
6%
8%
12%

■ DSGi ■ Comet ■ Euronics ■ Apple retail ■ Other

Source: Mintel.

Major Industry Participants

DSGi

DSGi (Dixons Store Group International) operates three retail chains in the UK known as Currys, Currys.digital and PC World. The

company has extensive overseas interests in electrical retailing, and therefore has strong buying power due to its broad geographical coverage. In the UK the company operates a total of 519 Currys and Currys.digital stores, while it has 161 PC World stores. Its broad range of good quality international branded products attracts a wide cross-section of consumers from different ages and economic backgrounds. The company also sells some superior quality and value brands at premium and low budget prices respectively. However, the vast majority of the branded products are sold at prices around the industry average. The Group also run e-commerce operations to support the Currys and PC World brands. Currys and Currys.digital stores differ in regard to size and location. Currys.digital stores are smaller outlets located in high street locations and offer a small selection of popular consumer electronics, telephones and photographic equipment. On the contrary, Currys stores are larger, positioned in retail parks and offer a large selection of consumer electronics, telephones, photographic equipment and household appliances (white goods). PC World stores concentrate on selling computing and photographic equipment although large screen televisions, home cinema systems and DVD players are increasingly prominent in these stores. The company also operates two online retail web sites under the Dixons and Pixmania brand names. Dixons focuses on selling consumer electronics and white goods, while Pixmania retails consumer electronics as well as a wide range of other products such as home and garden products, jewellery, watches, toys, and health and beauty products. Both of these operations focus on low price to compete with online retailers.

For many years across all three store formats (PC World, Currys and Currys.digital) poor-quality customer service has been a major problem for DSGi. Certainly, annual customer satisfaction surveys conducted by 'Which? Magazine'[1] have demonstrated that UK customers find the service at all these stores to be below standard on an annual basis. These stores achieve scores in the forties and fifties out of a total possible score of 100 per cent. In contrast, superior UK retail stores in the same annual surveys score in the seventies and eighties like Apple Retail, John Lewis Partnership and IKEA.

To better survive lower consumer spending and rectify its poor customer service record, DSGi implemented three major changes across its retail stores and web sites. First, across all of its branded web sites major improvements were made to the product information provided and services offered such as instant or three hour delivery and installation. Second, the level of customer support was increased to aid customer installation issues, improved in-store, home and telephone technical advice, reduced repair times and the introduction of a loyalty club. Third, the appearance and layout of its retail branded stores (Currys, Currys.digital and PC World) were renewed and larger store formats introduced. The layout and design of Currys and PC World stores were made visually more appealing and easier to navigate for customers to find products. As far as larger store formats, Currys' branded stores began a gradual movement into larger-sized outlets called megastores, so a much deeper assortment of

branded products can be displayed. The company has also launched a small number of 'Currys/PC World' retail stores. These stores combine the range of products usually sold separately by Currys and PC World stores into one convenient location. The Megastores and combined stores are part of DSGi's long-term strategy to have fewer, but larger outlets in cheaper out-of-town retail parks. Under-performing stores have also been closed. These changes attempt to enhance the customer experience by offering improved stores, better online selling processes and support activities.

Vitally DSGi has built strong relationships with suppliers of branded products so it is able to rapidly and efficiently replenish stock. It has managed to gain growing support from a number of premium brand suppliers as well.

Comet

After spending several months in administration, it was announced November 2012 that Comet would be

closing the doors to its 250 stores in the UK. Until November 2011, Comet had been owned by Kesa Electricals who decided to sell it after suffering losses of £9 million in 2010/11. The new owners were a London-based private investment firm called OpCapita, who ultimately failed to halt its decline.

Due to the company's large network of stores it always had some power over the manufacturers of consumer electronics, and continually liaised with them to maintain good working relationships. Comet targeted a wide array of customers with a broad choice of good quality products from mainstream international brands. Like DSGi, Comet sold some superior quality and value brands at premium and budget prices respectively, but in the main it sold branded products priced around the industry average.

Comet stores were regularly criticised for poor customer service issues and inadequately trained sales staff in a similar vein to DSGi. Indeed, under Kesa Electricals, Comet did try to remedy its customer service issues by enhancing the customer experience. The company's efforts to enhance the customer experience had included improvements in their home delivery service, more installation options, customer credit, a 24 hour helpline, and a free 30-day telephone helpline on TVs and home cinema systems. Comet had also improved its web site for customers by revamping its appearance, improving navigation, including product videos, providing customer reviews and offering online delivery tracking. Interestingly a survey commissioned by Mintel Group, a market research company, found that UK consumers perceived Currys and Comet as being impossible to tell apart. Retail experts state that Comet outlets looked dull and drab compared to refurbished Currys and Currys.digital stores (source: Mintel).

Independents

Besides these large retail chains there are over 5000 small independent consumer electronics retailers in the UK. These independent retailers are often family-run with less than 10 employees. Independent retailers have been having a tough time competing with the large retail chains on price and product range. The disadvantages of less space, narrow ranges and above industry prices are eroding their market position over time. Internet use is generally unsophisticated as most independents do not employ a transactional web site. In its place, independent web sites tend to be for informational purposes only.

Euronics

Some small UK independents have attempted to bolster their position by joining together with other European independents to form  a cooperative buying group called EURONICS. EURONICS is the largest electrical buying group in Europe with nearly 9000 members across 25 European countries. Over 600 small UK independent stores have joined the buying group, but membership numbers are volatile. Joining the EURONICS buying group enables independent stores to obtain industry competitive prices from international suppliers. EURONICS source a narrower assortment of good quality brands from far fewer suppliers than the industry leaders, but this increases its buying power. EURONICS has also undertaken advertising on behalf of its members, in order to boost public awareness of the brand. The group operates on behalf of its members an e-commerce web site as well. Independents belonging to the EURONICS group charge prices around the industry average.

Apart from the above independents, a small number of them charge premium prices and focus on a few unique or specialize products and services to survive like high-end audio and/or visual products (i.e. home cinema systems). These specialized independent retailers argue that they can offer better service through in-depth personal knowledge of their products, understanding their local customer base more thoroughly, exclusive availability of certain upmarket or superior quality brands and retaining staff for longer to provide product familiarity.

Apple Retail

While most of the previous companies have struggled in the downturn of consumer spending, one company has thrived and achieved impressive sales growth. This company is Apple Incorporated via its UK retail operations. Since November 2004, Apple Incorporated, the iconic US multinational company that designs and markets consumer electronics (e.g. iPhones, iPods, iPod accessories, iPads and Apple TV), computer software and personal computers, has rapidly strengthened its retail presence in the UK. Particularly between 2007 and 2009, the company's retail outlet numbers doubled, while its revenues tripled. At present Apple have 28 stores in the UK. It operates a mixture of flagship stores (stand-alone stores located in high profile locations such as London's Covent Garden) and small retail outlets, which are inside shopping malls. In spite of this increase in retail outlets, it is worth mentioning that Apple generates a large proportion of its turnover from online sales in the UK as well.

Despite selling just its own narrow product range, Apple's turnover has proven to be exceptionally resilient during the downturn. This resilience is due to the strong loyalty of its customers. The company is well known for its passionate and dedicated customer base. Apple's foray into the UK retail sector has not disrupted its activities as a supplier of its products to other third party retailers like DSGi, Comet, Tesco, Asda and Amazon. The company stores sell the entire Apple product range, while its retail customers usually stock a much narrower selection. Apple's products are perceived as being of superior quality than other brands. This perception of superiority enables Apple to charge premium prices. Apple's retail stores also provide product presentations, repairs, expert advice and support. Without doubt Apple stores are perceived by loyalty customers as a haven for sharing their passion with other users, they also give them a sense of belonging to an exclusive, technological astute community that appreciates innovative design, style and quality. The stores reflect the aforementioned attributes as they are modern and spacious. In particular, the flagship stores have gained design awards for their stunning interiors and exteriors. Regardless of Apple products being available from other retailers discussed, Apple customers are known to travel long distances to visit Apple retail stores to make their purchases. No matter the retail location, Apple's range of products attracts a premium price.

Many industry analysts were sceptical of Apple's move into retailing. Certainly, when the first Apple store opened in the USA in 2001 it was viewed as a strategic mistake, because Dell's avoidance of retail stores and its online selling of computers had been extremely successful at that time.[2] Moreover, Gateway, the US-based computer designer, manufacturer and marketer was closing stores at that time as well. However, by the late 2000s, Apple stores had become an iconic presence in stylish high street locations and represented a key element of Apple's marketing strategy.

When Apple was developing its retail strategy, the company wanted to offer their customers an experience unlike those of other companies within the computer industry. Certainly, the customer shopping experience at an Apple retail store contrasts sharply with those previously described at DSGi and Comet Group stores. Visitors to an Apple store are greeted by numerous well-trained and enthusiastic employees wearing colourful Apple T-shirts.[3] The recruitment of Apple store personnel is undertaken very carefully by the company. Getting a job in an Apple retail store requires six

An Interior example of an Apple retail store.

to eight interviews.[4] Ron Johnson, who created and developed the Apple store format, states that the intensive staff selection process means people who are hired feel honoured to be part of the team.[5] This is a very different philosophy than trying to recruit somebody at the lowest possible cost.

An important ingredient of the Apple store experience is the Genius Bar. Genius Bars attempt to replicate a five star hotel's concierge desk where face-to-face support, information and advice can be readily obtained.[6] The employees or 'Geniuses' staffing the bar will look at any Apple product for free, regardless of whether it was bought at one of its stores.[7] They even offer advice about non-technical support issues like how to use Apple software or attempt to fix non-Apple software issues. The Genius Bars are now so popular that Apple uses a reservation system to manage the demand. No charges are made for this support, customers just pay for repairs for out-of-warranty goods.[8] 'Geniuses' also have latitude to waiver these fees. Genius Bars are a loss leader for the company as it believes customers will probably invest in other Apple products before they leave the store.[9] The company believes customers prefer face-to-face contact offered by Genius Bars rather than telephone and web support, which are often frustrating and ineffective. Apple's retail strategy is also about restoring and enhancing customer relationships that may have been damaged by product problems. The essence of Apple retail stores is to really build a face-to-face relationship that deepens a connection and trust with its customers.[10]

Apple's retail stores provide it with invaluable product information as well. The sales data obtained from its physical and online stores enable Apple to track demand and adjust production accordingly. Certainly if component shortages become apparent the company can rapidly deploy resources to get around any bottlenecks.

Apple Suppliers

Most Apple components are manufactured in Korea, Japan and Taiwan.[11] Generally, Apple wields immense power and influence over its key suppliers. This influence results from Apple's ability to prepay its key suppliers. Prepayment ensures availability and low prices for Apple—and sometimes limits the component options for its competitors. For instance, before the release of the iPhone 4 in June 2010, rivals such as HTC couldn't buy screens they needed because contract manufacturers were using available stock to fill Apple orders.[12]

Due to high volumes, suppliers have done very well from their relationship with Apple, but it is a demanding purchaser. The company requires very detailed breakdowns of its suppliers' material and labour costs, and projected profit levels.[13] Apple's bargaining tactics tend to exert downward pressure on prices, leading to lower profits and margins. In addition, Apple requires many key suppliers to keep two weeks of inventory within a mile of Apple's assembly plants in Asia.[14]

Nevertheless, Apple is not always in a powerful position versus its suppliers. Some key components are obtained from single or limited sources, which subject it to significant supply and pricing risks.

Apple's control over suppliers reaches its pinnacle in the lead-up to product launches. For weeks in advance of a product launch, factories work overtime to build hundreds of thousands of devices. Apple engineers closely monitor suppliers and manufacturers, helping refine processes that transform prototypes into mass-produced devices. For new designs such as the MacBook's unibody shell, cut from a single piece of aluminium, Apple's designers worked with suppliers to create new tooling equipment.[15]

Apple's effort to tightly control its suppliers payoffs as its gross margins are estimated to be around 40 per cent per product, compared with 10 to 20 per cent for most other hardware companies. Those margins increase markedly when Apple sells the products via its website or stores.[16]

Others

Competition from non-specialists such as supermarkets and Internet-based only compa-  nies has put pressure on prices particularly as the current economic outlook encourages consumers to focus on low prices. Without doubt an increasing number of consumers are using the Internet to research products and use price comparison services. Greater use of the Internet is inevitably leading consumers to the price-led online companies, which makes it very difficult for Currys and PC World to show the added value they can offer via customer service. The largest online retailer of consumer electronics in the UK is Amazon. The company sells some superior quality and value brands at premium and low budget prices, respectively, but in the main it sells a broad range of good quality consumer electronics at prices below or around the industry average. Retail experts estimate its sales of consumer electronics was around £400 million in 2009 (source: Mintel). Amazon has considerable purchasing power due to the scale of its global operation.

Taking advantage of their customer loyalty, supermarkets have aggressively moved into the retailing of consumer electronics both in their stores and online. Prices are generally low or below the industry average with a moderate range of consumer electronics compared to the industry leaders. Tesco is without doubt the most important supermarket to enter the industry. The company is the UK's biggest supermarket chain and Europe's second largest retailer. The company has the largest customer base in the UK, strong brand loyalty and recognition, and high purchasing power due to its size. It has recently set a target of becoming the second largest retailer of consumer electronics in the UK. Tesco operates 2306 stores in the UK. Asda, the UK's second largest supermarket, is also strong in consumer electronics. The company has 340 supermarkets of various sizes and layouts. US retailer Wal-Mart, the largest retailer in the world, owns Asda. As a subsidiary of Wal-Mart, Asda has higher purchasing power than most of the other incumbents in the industry. Other notable participants in the industry are John Lewis Department store and Argos Catalogue Company. US multinational retailer, Best Buy, opened its first store in the UK in April 2010 and by November 2011 had established 11 stores. However, due to substantial losses during that period decided to close these stores. Best Buy's business strategy for consumer electronics was very similar to DGSi and Comet.

In summary, the leading industry participants' look and behave the same, with the notable exception of Apple. The inability of rivals to differentiate themselves has left customers with nothing but price as a basis for their choice. In consequence, the retail industry for brown goods is dominated by price competition. UK supermarkets and online retailers have benefited from this price competition as they are perceived as being cheaper.

Apple's modest share places it in fourth place. However, Apple store sales are expected to grow due to the anticipated release of more innovative, must-have gadgets. Apple unlike the other leading retailers has created superior value for its customers by performing activities in a different way and also by offering activities that competitors don't perform. For example, its products are stylish and innovative. While a visit to any Apple store demonstrates a very different customer service experience compared to other retailers. The physical appearance and layout of Apple retail stores is inspired. The customer service experience also allows customers to interact with the products and ask questions of enthusiastic and knowledgeable staff. The Genius Bars located in every Apple store provides customers with free assistance as well. What happens within the Apple stores demonstrates that it is possible to counter the trend towards price competition within the retail industry of brown goods.

ENDNOTES

1. *Which*? magazine is a well-known consumer watchdog organization in the UK.
2. Helft, M. (2011) 'Steve Jobs' real legacy: Apple Inc', *Fortune* (cited 4 April 2012). Available online at www.tech.fortune.cnn.com/2011/09/08/steve-jobs-real-legacy-apple-inc/.
3. Ibid.
4. Morse, G. (2011) 'Retail isn't broken, stores are', Interview with Ron Johnson, *Harvard Business Review*, 79: 78–82.
5. Ibid.
6. Manjoo, F. (2010) 'Apple nation', *Fast Company*, Issue 147, July/August (cited 9 April 2012). Available online at www.fastcompany.com/magazine/147/apple-nation.html.
7. Ibid.
8. Ibid.
9. Ibid.
10. Morse, op, cit.
11. Wright, A. (2012) 'Analyzing apple products', *Communications of the ACM*, January, 55(1).
12. Satariano, A. and Burrows, P. (November 7–November 13, 2011) 'Apple's supply-chain secret? Hoard lasers', *Bloomberg Business Week: Technology* (cited 9 April 2012). Available online at www.businessweek.com/magazine/apples-supplychain-secret-hoard-lasers-11032011.html.
13. Ibid.
14. Ibid.
15. Ibid.
16. Ibid.

Apple retail store in London's Regent Street.

CASE 3
ROBIN HOOD*

It was in the spring of the second year of his insurrection against the High Sheriff of Nottingham that Robin Hood took a walk in Sherwood Forest. As he walked he pondered the progress of the campaign, the disposition of his forces, the Sheriff's recent moves, and the options that confronted him.

The revolt against the Sheriff had begun as a personal crusade, erupting out of Robin's conflict with the Sheriff and his administration. Alone, however, Robin Hood could do little. He therefore sought allies, men with grievances and a deep sense of justice. Later he welcomed all who came, asking few questions, and only demanding a willingness to serve. Strength, he believed, lay in numbers.

He spent the first year forging the group into a disciplined band, united in enmity against the Sheriff, and willing to live outside the law. The band's organization was simple. Robin ruled supreme, making all important decisions. He delegated specific tasks to his lieutenants. Will Scarlett was in charge of intelligence and scouting. His main job was to shadow the Sheriff and his men, always alert to their next move. He also collected information on the travel plans of rich merchants and tax collectors. Little John kept discipline among the men, and saw to it that their archery was at the high peak that their profession demanded. Scarlock took care of the finances, converting loot into cash, paying shares of the take, and finding suitable hiding places for the surplus. Finally, Much the Miller's son had the difficult task of provisioning the ever-increasing band of Merrymen.

The increasing size of the band was a source of satisfaction for Robin, but also a source of concern. The fame of his Merrymen was spreading, and new recruits poured in from every corner of England. As the band grew larger, their small bivouac became a major encampment. Between raids the men milled about, talking and playing games. Vigilance was in decline, and discipline was becoming harder to enforce. "Why," Robin reflected, "I don't know half the men I run into these days."

The growing band was also beginning to exceed the food capacity of the forest. Game was becoming scarce, and supplies had to be obtained from outlying villages. The cost of buying food was beginning to drain the band's financial reserves at the very moment when revenues were in decline. Travelers, especially those with the most to lose, were now giving the forest a wide berth. This was costly and inconvenient to them, but it was preferable to having all their goods confiscated.

Robin believed that the time had come for the Merrymen to change their policy of outright confiscation of goods to one of a fixed transit tax. His lieutenants strongly resisted this idea. They were proud of the Merrymen's famous motto: "Rob the rich and give to the poor." "The farmers and the townspeople," they argued, "are our most important allies. How can we tax them, and still hope for their help in our fight against the Sheriff?"

Robin wondered how long the Merrymen could keep to the ways and methods of their early days. The Sheriff was growing stronger and better organized. He now had the money and the men, and was beginning to harass the band, probing for its weaknesses.

The tide of events was beginning to turn against the Merrymen. Robin felt that the campaign must be decisively concluded before the Sheriff had a chance to deliver a mortal blow. "But how," he wondered, "could this be done?"

Robin had often entertained the possibility of killing the Sheriff, but the chances for this seemed increasingly remote. Besides, while killing the Sheriff might satisfy his personal thirst for revenge, it would not improve the situation. Robin had hoped that the perpetual state of unrest, and the Sheriff's failure to collect taxes, would lead to his removal from office. Instead, the Sheriff used his political connections to obtain reinforcement. He had powerful friends at court, and was well regarded by the regent, Prince John.

Prince John was vicious and volatile. He was consumed by his unpopularity among the people, who wanted the imprisoned King Richard back. He also lived in constant fear of the barons, who had first given him the regency, but were now beginning to dispute his claim to the throne. Several of these barons had set out to collect the ransom that would release King Richard the Lionheart from his jail in Austria. Robin was invited to join the conspiracy in return for future amnesty. It was a dangerous proposition. Provincial banditry was one thing, court intrigue another. Prince John's spies were everywhere. If the plan failed, the pursuit would be relentless and retribution swift.

The sound of the supper horn startled Robin from his thoughts. There was the smell of roasting venison in the air. Nothing was resolved or settled. Robin headed for camp promising himself that he would give these problems his utmost attention after tomorrow's raid.

CASE 4

EBAY

*Expanding into China**

Like many U.S. Internet companies, eBay has repeatedly tried to broaden its reach by entering new appealing sectors, such as mobile commerce, and expanding into other geographical sectors, especially in Asia, where local rivals had strong ties to users. With Asia's population exceeding 4 billion, more than half the world's population, and Internet usage in the region skyrocketing at 620 percent,[1] eBay needed to develop a strategy that would successfully adapt to Asian local markets and compete with local competitors such as Taobao, China's top auction site.

In 2012 Xiu.com and eBay partnered up to launch an online shopping platform, named eBay Style, that aimed to "bring the very best of eBay to Chinese consumers, particularly in fashion." Xiu.com focuses on the sale of products from overseas to Chinese customers in a way that they are comfortable with. The company is based in Shenzhen and has roughly 800 employees. With the new partnership in place, Chinese consumers are able to access the global collection of products on eBay's platform, while Xiu.com took control of managing all sales, logistics, and customer service. Xiu.com also took responsibility for curating and translating the inventory and implementing a product search function suitable for Chinese customers. The new eBay Style included only new items from a collection of 5,000 brands across all categories, including apparel, handbags, shoes, accessories, health and beauty products, and other lifestyle categories. At the time of the deal's fruition, Xiu said it employed almost 1,500 people in China and mentioned new smartphone and tablet apps that were in the making.[2] Even with this new deal, eBay Style faced unyielding competition, especially Alibaba's Taobao.com, the largest Chinese online retailer. Also, Alipay, a payment processing company and another unit of the Alibaba Group, had 300 million users, three times as many as PayPal in China.[3]

Taobao, eBay Style's largest threat, consciously portrays itself as a Chinese company. For example, online moderators use screen names imitative of popular characters from Chinese kung-fu novels.[4] Taobao also strived to implement a more interactive and user-friendly customer service initiative. In 2003 Taobao began using an instant communication tool called Aliwangwang to help buyers

and sellers interact with one another. Alipay, an online payment system, was started a year later. By 2010 Taobao assisted over 80 percent of the e-commerce market in China, with roughly 170 million registered users.[5] At the same time, eBay decided to concentrate its focus on cross-border e-commerce, where Chinese consumers sell to consumers overseas. It currently operates as the leader in that segment.

eBay

Since its inception in 1995, eBay has enjoyed strong revenue growth and been a dominant player in the online auction industry. The company posted net income of $3.2 billion and revenue of $11.65 billion for 2011 (see Exhibit 1).

eBay's founder, Pierre Omidyar, envisioned a community built on commerce, sustained by trust, and inspired by opportunity. The company's mission was to "enable individual self-empowerment on a global scale" and employ "business as a tool for social good." Omidyar cited "trust between strangers" as the social impact tied to eBay's ability to remain profitable.

The company's unique business model, which united buyers and sellers in an online marketplace, attracted over 221 million registered users. eBay has enabled e-commerce at multiple levels (local, national, and international) through an array of websites, including eBay Marketplaces, PayPal, Rent.com, Shopping.com, and its newest addition, eBay Style. The company's range of products and services evolved from collectibles to household products, customer services, automobiles, and the mobile industry. The variety of products attracted a range of users that included students, small businesses, independent sellers, major corporations, and government agencies.

Despite eBay's outstanding growth performance, the company still faced a number of challenges in both domestic and international markets. The low entry barriers in the online marketplace attracted a number of large dot-com competitors, including Amazon, Yahoo, uBid, and Overstock. Historically, the company had acquired other online competitors, such as Stubhub (tickets), but established players such as Yahoo and Amazon posed a major threat to eBay's market share and ability to sustain profitability. Still, eBay's top management felt that the company would end up as a specialty business, an idea suggesting that it would face little threat from these major competitors. The company had no plans for further big acquisitions but intended to expand and identify synergies within existing business lines.

*This case was prepared by Professor Alan B. Eisner and graduate students David J. Morates and Shruti Shrestha of Pace University. This case was solely based on library research and was developed for class discussion rather than to illustrate either effective or ineffective handling of an administrative situation. Copyright © 2013 Alan B. Eisner.

EXHIBIT 1 Income Statements (in millions, except per-share amounts; year-end December 31)

	2009	2010	2011	2012
Net revenues	$8,727	$9,156	$11,652	$14,072
Cost of net revenues	2,480	2,565	3,460	4,216
Gross profit	6,248	6,592	8,191	9,856
Operating expenses:				
Sales and marketing	1,886	1,947	2,435	2,913
Product development	803	908	1,235	1,573
General and administrative	1,418	1,079	1,364	1,567
Provision for transaction and loan losses	383	392	517	580
Amortization of acquired intangible assets	263	190	267	335
Restructuring	38,187	21,437	(489)	—
Total operating expenses	4,791	4,538	5,817	6,968
Income from operations	1,457	2,054	2,373	2,888
Interest and other income, net	1,422	45	1,537	196
Income before income taxes	2,879	2,098	3,910	3,084
Provision for income taxes	(490)	(297)	(681)	(475)
Net income	$2,389	$1,801	$3,229	$2,609
Net income per share:				
Basic	$1.85	$1.38	$2.50	$2.02
Diluted	$1.83	$1.36	2.46	1.99
Weighted average shares:				
Basic	1,289	1,305	1,292	1,292
Diluted	1,304	1,327	1,312	1,313

eBay did however acknowledge its inability to grow and compete in certain international markets. The company created localized sites in 24 countries and established a presence in Latin America through its investment in MercadoLibre.com. However, eBay's numerous attempts to penetrate the Asia Pacific market, specifically China and Japan, ended in failure, with the company pulling out of Japan and buying out Chinese start-up Eachnet, essentially canceling years of invested work. According to many analysts, the company's recent interest in its South Korean rival Gmarket Inc. and joint venture with Beijing-based Tom Online were further indications that eBay couldn't compete in these countries. To remain successful and enjoy the same financial performance as it had in the past, eBay needed to develop an effective strategy to compete in major Asian markets and mitigate the risk of existing local competitors.

Evolution of Auctions
Traditional Auctions

According to Greek scribes, the first known auctions occurred in Babylon in 500 BC. At that time, women were sold on the condition of marriage, and it was considered illegal for daughters to be sold outside auctions. Auctions evolved during the French Revolution and throughout the American Civil War, where colonels auctioned goods that were seized by armies.[6] Although there were various types of auctions, they all provided a forum where sellers could find buyers. Auctions were considered one of the purest markets, because buyers paid what they were willing to spend for an item, thereby determining the true market value of the item. Over time, auction formats evolved, and through technological advances and improved communication they found a new home—the Internet.

Online Auctions

The primary difference between traditional and online auctions is that the online auction process occurs over the Internet as opposed to at a specific location where both buyers and sellers were present. Online auctions offer strategic advantages to both parties that are not typically available in traditional auctions. Buyers can select from millions of products and engage in multiple auctions simultaneously. Given the massive inventory of an online auction market, items are usually available in multiple auctions, allowing buyers to compare starting bid prices and search for better prices. Sellers are exposed to millions of buyers, since more buyers have access to the Internet and feel comfortable making purchases online. Thus, the Internet gave buyers and sellers access to a marketplace that spanned the world.

Online auctions also offer the following strategic advantages:

1. *No time constraints.* A bid can be placed at any time.
2. *No geographic constraints.* Sellers and buyers can participate from any location with Internet access.
3. *Network economies.* The large number of bidders attracts more sellers, which attracts more bidders, and so on. This creates a large system that has more value for both parties. Online auctions also allow businesses to easily sell off excess inventory or discontinued items. This is done through either business-to-business (B2B) or business-to-consumer (B2C) auctions. Offering products and services in an online auction helps small businesses build their brand and reputation by establishing a devoted customer base. Finally, some businesses use the online marketplace as an inexpensive yet effective way to test-market for upcoming products.

E-Commerce

Although Vannevar Bush originally conceived the idea of the Internet in 1945, it wasn't until the 1990s that the Internet became overwhelmingly popular. According to Internet World Stats, in June 2012 there were over 2.4 billion Internet users in over 150 countries. Exhibit 2 shows world Internet usage and population as of June 30, 2012, and Internet usage growth between 2000 and 2012.

As of 2012, North America was the region most penetrated by the Internet, with approximately 78.6 percent of the population already online. However, Internet usage growth between 2000 and 2012 was considerably less in North America than in other regions. Internet usage growth was highest in developing regions, such as Africa, the Middle East, Latin America, and Asia, where penetration was low. Considering that close to 80 percent of the world's population resides in these areas, it is inevitable that Internet usage growth will continue to increase dramatically in these regions.

Although Asia constituted approximately 56 percent of the world's population, its penetration rate was only 27.5 percent. Compared to other regions with high usage growth rates, such as Africa and the Middle East, Asia invested more in its technology infrastructure and contained by far the most current Internet users, making it a more attractive market.

As the usage growth of the Internet increased, so did the popularity of e-commerce. E-commerce, or electronic commerce, is the concept of conducting business transactions over the Internet. Like online auctions, e-commerce eliminates boundaries such as time and geography, allowing businesses and customers to interact with one another constantly. As more users were exposed to the Internet, they became comfortable with the idea of conducting transactions online. In correlation with Internet growth usage, revenue generated through e-commerce has increased dramatically since the 1990s.

EXHIBIT 2 World Internet Usage and Population Statistics, as of June 30, 2012

World Regions	Population (millions)	Internet Usage (millions)	Percentage of Population Penetrated	Usage as Percentage of World Total	Usage Growth, 2000–2012 (%)
Africa	1,073,380,925	167.3	15.6	7.0	3,606.7
Asia	3,922,066,987	1076.7	27.5	44.8	841.9
Europe	820,918,446	518.5	63.2	21.5	393.4
Middle East	223,608,203	90.0	40.2	3.7	2,639.9
North America	348,280,154	273.8	78.6	11.4	153.3
Latin America	593,688,638	254.9	42.9	10.6	1,310.8
Australia	35,903,569	24.3	67.6	1.0	218.7
Total	**7,017,846,922**	**2405.5**	**34.3**	**100.0**	**566.4**

Source: Internet World Stats. 2012. Usage and Population Statistics, *www.internetworldstats.com/*.

In Asia, e-commerce has grown rapidly since China's admission into the World Trade Organization (WTO) on December 11, 2001. Induction into the WTO allowed China to conduct business with other nations more freely by reducing tariffs and eliminating market and government impediments.

Company Background

Computer programmer Pierre Omidyar founded the online auction website in San Jose, California, on September 3, 1995. Omidyar was born in Paris, France, and moved to Maryland with his family when his father took on a residency at Johns Hopkins University Medical Center. Omidyar became fascinated with computers and later graduated from Tufts University with a degree in computer science. While living and working in the San Francisco Bay area, he met his current wife, Pamela Wesley, a management consultant, who later became a driving force in launching the auction website. The couple's vision was to establish an online marketplace where people could share the same passion and interest as Pamela had for her hobby of collecting and trading Pez candy dispensers.[7] Omidyar also envisioned an online auction format that would create a fair and open marketplace, where the market truly determined an item's value. To ensure trust in the open forum, Omidyar based the site on five main values:

1. People are basically good.
2. Everyone has something to contribute.
3. An honest, open environment can bring out the best in people.
4. Everyone deserves recognition and respect as a unique individual.
5. You should treat others the way you want to be treated.

On Labor Day weekend in 1995, Omidyar launched Auction Web, an online trading platform. After the business exploded, Omidyar decided to dedicate more attention to his new enterprise and work as a consultant under the name Echo Bay Technology Group. When he tried to register a website for his company, Omidyar discovered Echo Bay was unavailable, so he decided to use the abbreviated version *eBay,* which also stood for "electronic bay area." The company's name was also selected to attract San Francisco residents to the site and prompt them to buy and sell items.

Initially, the company did not charge fees to either buyers or sellers, but as traffic grew rapidly, Omidyar was forced to charge buyers a listing fee to cover Internet service provider costs. When Omidyar noticed that the fees had no effect on the level of bids, he realized the potential for profitability of his business. To handle and manage the company's day-to-day operations, Omidyar hired Jeffrey Skoll (B.A.Sc. University of Toronto, MBA Stanford University). Skoll was hired as the company's first president, and he wrote the business plan that eBay later followed from its emergence as a start-up to its maturity as a financial success. The two worked out of Skoll's living room and various Silicon Valley facilities until they eventually settled in the company's current location in San Jose, California.

By the middle of 1997, after less than a year under the name eBay, the company was hosting nearly 800,000 auctions a day.[8] Although the rapid expansion of eBay's traffic caused the company to suffer a number of service interruptions, the site remained successful and continued to gain the confidence of its strong customer base. Skoll remained president until early 1998, when the company hired Meg Whitman as president and CEO. At the time, the company had only 30 employees and was solely located in the United States; in a decade the number of employees went up to over 15,000. In September 1998 eBay launched a successful public offering, making both Omidyar and Skoll instant billionaires. By the time eBay went public, less than three years after Omidyar had created the company, the site had more than a million registered users. The company grew exponentially in the late 1990s and, based on its 2011 performance, indicated no sign of stopping. Exhibit 3 highlights the company's recent growth performance by segments.

Whitman stepped down as the president and CEO of the company on March 31, 2008, but remained on the board of directors. Omidyar, the chairman of the board, said this

EXHIBIT 3 eBay Growth (in millions, year-end December 31)

Supplemental Operating Data	2010	2011	2012
Marketplace Segment:			
Gross merchandise volume*	$61,819	$60,332	$67,763
Payments Segment:			
Net total payment volume†	$91,956	$118,758	$144,937

*Total value of all successfully closed items between users on eBay Marketplaces trading platforms during the period, regardless of whether the buyer and seller actually consummated the transaction.
†Total dollar volume of payments, net of payment reversals, successfully completed through eBay payments network or on Bill Me Later accounts during the period, excluding the payment gateway business.

Source: eBay Inc., *www.ebayinc.com/.*

about Whitman, "With humor, smarts and unflappable determination, Meg took a small, barely known online auction site and helped it become an integral part of our lives."[9] Both Omidyar and Whitman were confident that the new CEO, John Donahoe, was a good choice to lead eBay. Donahoe joined the company in 2005 as president of eBay's largest division, Marketplaces, and within three years managed to double the revenues and profits for this business unit. Before joining eBay, Donahoe served as the CEO of Bain & Company, an international consulting firm based in Boston.[10] "I'm extremely confident in John's skills and the abilities of John's veteran management team," Meg Whitman commented on the transition.[11]

Whitman's confidence appears to have been well-founded. In 2012, after 4 years on the job as CEO, Donahoe had helped eBay make impressive progress. Although eBay's financial outlook was not dreadful when Donahoe took over in March 2008, there was a growing perception that its growth was beginning to decline and that its run as the leader of the e-commerce industry was behind it, as Amazon began to make strides toward becoming the next best thing. During the global financial crisis, eBay's stock had fallen to almost $10 per share in February 2009, far below the optimistic price of $58 that it reached in 2004. Since 2009, however, the stock has been on a stable uptrend, more than doubling during a 12-month period from 2011 to 2012 and closing at almost $49 in November 2012. "What John Donahoe has accomplished over the past few years is one of the most remarkable feats in the valley's history," said Gil Luria, an analyst at Wedbush Securities. So what has the new CEO done to spur this turnaround? Luria noted that eBay began investing more in technology and was willing to take risks regarding altering the look and feel of the platform's shopping experience.[12]

eBay Now was also implemented to offer same-day delivery of products from online and offline merchants in San Francisco. ThinkEquity analyst Ron Josey wrote, "We view eBay Now as one of the most innovative products eBay has launched in some time." The new service functions as a mobile app, one representation of Donahoe's vision for eBay to begin embracing the increasing trend of mobile and offline shopping. "We've gone from competing in a $500 billion e-commerce market to now a $10 trillion retail market," Donahoe recently told analysts.[13]

eBay Platforms

eBay's overall strategy comprised three primary components: products, sense of community, and aggressive expansion. All three components evolved around the various geographic and specialty platforms the company introduced.

Product Categories

eBay had an array of product categories and trading platforms that offered a range of pricing formats, such as fixed pricing. Relatively new for the company, establishing a fixed-price format allowed eBay to compete directly with major competitors such as Amazon.com and penetrate new market space. Before fixed pricing, selling prices were solely determined by the highest auction bid, and this took days or weeks, depending on the length of the auction. eBay's different trading platforms also offered distinct services and target-specific market niches, which allowed eBay to broaden its customer base. The platforms included:

- *PayPal:* Founded in 1998 and acquired by eBay in 2002, PayPal enabled individuals to securely send payments quickly and easily online. PayPal was considered the global leader in online payments, with tens of millions of registered users. In 2011 Paypal's president, Scott Thompson, expected revenue to double to $6 billion to $7 billion by 2013. He also predicted that 75 percent to 80 percent of eBay transactions will be done through PayPal by 2013, up from 69 percent in 2010.[14]

- *Rent.com:* Acquired by eBay in February 2005, Rent.com was the most visited online apartment listing service in the United States, with more than 20,000 properties listed.

- *Online classifieds:* By 2009, eBay had the world-leading portfolio of online classifieds sites, including Kijiji, Intoko, Gumtree, LoQUo.com, Marktplaats.nl, and mobile.de. CEO John Donahoe said, "We are the global leader in classifieds, with top positions in Canada, Australia, Germany, Japan and the United Kingdom, and sites in more than 1,000 cities across 20 countries."[15]

- *Shopping.com:* With thousands of merchants and millions of products and reviews, Shopping.com empowered consumers to make informed choices, which drove value for merchants.

- *Stubhub.com:* StubHub was an online marketplace for selling and purchasing tickets for sports events, concerts, and other live entertainment events.

- *eBay Express:* eBay Express behaved like a standard Internet shopping site but gave sellers access to over 200 million buyers worldwide. Sellers could design product categories within minutes, and buyers could purchase from multiple sellers by using a single shopping cart.

- *eBay Motors:* This specialty site was considered the largest marketplace for automobile buyers and sellers. Buyers could purchase anything from automobile parts to new or antique vehicles.

- *Skype:* Acquired by eBay in October 2005, Skype was the world's fastest-growing online communication solution, allowing free video and audio communication between users of Skype software. By November 2009, Skype connected more than 480 million registered users.[16]

Sale of Skype: eBay's acquisition of Skype was expected to enhance the customer experience by improving communication between buyers and sellers. When it acquired Skype, eBay said it hoped the service would support its auctions and its PayPal payment service by letting buyers and sellers discuss transactions. But eBay users were not so chatty. In November 2009 eBay sold Skype to a group led by Silver Lake Partners, a private equity firm in Silicon Valley. The deal was made at $2.75 billion, with eBay retaining a 30 percent stake. Mr. Donahoe said eBay did not regret having bought Skype when company executives believed eBay was in a mortal struggle with Google, which was also pursuing the service. He said the spinoff would allow eBay to focus on its core e-commerce and online payment businesses and avoid extra distractions. "We don't regret having done this at all. We compete in a dynamic market, and you have to move quickly and take risks," Mr. Donahoe said. "When we bought Skype we thought it had synergies with our other two businesses, and it turns out it did not. But it also turned out that it's a great stand-alone business."[17]

In May 2011, Microsoft agreed to buy Skype for $8.5 billion from Silver Lake. eBay said it will earn more than a 50 percent return from the firm's initial investment of $2.6 billion in Skype six years earlier. "With this sale, we have realized a total return of $1.4 billion on our original investment in Skype," said John Pluhowski, a spokesman for eBay. Considering that eBay had bought Skype in a heavily criticized deal in 2005 and that it was considered a failed acquisition, the latest Microsoft agreement turned out to be good news for eBay, making eBay one of the big winners in the Microsoft and Skype deal.

Sense of Community

The underlying key to all eBay sites and trading platforms was creating trust between sellers and buyers. The company created "community values," and this was why eBay users were willing to send money to strangers across the country. The Feedback Forum was created in February 1996 and encouraged users to post comments about trading partners. Originally, Omidyar handled disputes between buyers and sellers via email by putting the disputing parties in touch with each other to resolve the issue themselves. He soon realized that an open forum where users could post opinions and feedback about one another would create the trust and sense of community the site required. Buyers and sellers were encouraged to post comments (positive, negative, or neutral) about each other at the completion of each transaction. The individual feedback was recorded and amended to a user profile, which ultimately established a rating and reputation for each buyer and seller. eBay users could view this information before engaging in a transaction. The company believed that the feedback forum was critical for creating initial user acceptance for purchasing and selling over the Internet and that it contributed more than anything else to eBay's success.

Aggressive Expansion

To compete effectively and create a global trading platform, the company continued to develop in U.S. and international markets that utilized the Internet. With intense competition in the online auction industry, eBay aimed to increase market share and revenue through acquisitions and partnerships in related and unrelated businesses. For example:

- In June 2000 eBay acquired Half.com for $318 million.
- In August 2001 eBay acquired MercadoLibre, Lokau, and iBazar, Latin American auction sites.
- On August 13, 2004, eBay took a 25 percent stake in Craigslist, an online network of urban communities.
- In September 2005 eBay invested $ 2 million in the Meetup social networking site.
- In August 2006 eBay announced international cooperation with Google.
- In January 2007 eBay acquired online ticket marketplace Stubhub for $310 million.
- In June 2010 eBay acquired RedLaser, a mobile application that would let customers scan bar codes to list items faster on its online auction site and to compare prices.[18]
- In December 2010 eBay acquired Milo, a leading local shopping engine that provides consumers access to accurate, real-time, local store inventory and pricing, giving them even more choices and flexibility when shopping online.[19]
- In December 2010 eBay acquired Critical Path Software Inc., a developer of smartphone applications, to accelerate its lead in mobile commerce.[20]

Company Business Model

eBay's business model was based on a person-to-person marketplace on the Internet, where sellers conveniently listed items for sale and interested buyers bid on these items. The objective was to create a forum that allowed buyers and sellers to come together in an efficient and effective manner. The business model overcame the inefficiencies of traditional fragmented marketplaces, which tended to offer a limited variety of goods. According to former CEO Meg Whitman, the company started with commerce and what grew out of that was a community, essentially creating a community-commerce model.[21] The company's success relied primarily on establishing a trustworthy environment that attracted a large number of buyers and sellers. As eBay's reputation grew, so did the number of buyers and sellers, keeping the company in line with Omidyar's original vision. However, as new competitors entered the online auction business and the popularity of the Internet increased, eBay tweaked its business model to accommodate changes in the fast-paced environment.

The company was aggressively expanding globally and looking for new products and services to offer to customers. It was also looking closely at the kind of merchants who sold on eBay. In the beginning, eBay focused on a consumer-to-consumer business model, but since some of the individuals became small dealers, the model changed to a mix of consumer-to-consumer and business-to-consumer. The sellers wanted to maintain their business on eBay, since it was their most profitable distribution channel. eBay wanted new ways to generate revenue as a result of more small dealers and businesses selling their products through the company's website.

eBay generated revenue through three main channels: marketplaces, payments, and, until 2009, communications. Marketplaces, which generated revenue by charging sellers a fee for every item they sold, accounted for over 65 percent of the company's revenue. As of December 2011 marketplace revenue was approximately $6.6 billion of the company's $11.65 billion total revenue. Another $4.4 billion of the company's revenue came from fees charged

through electronic payments made through the company website, primarily via PayPal. The newest source of revenue, until November 2009, was communications (Skype), which produced $620 million of the company's revenue for that year. Although free, Skype generated revenue through its premium offerings, such as making and receiving calls to and from landline and mobile phones, as well as voice mail, ring tones, and call forwarding. Exhibit 4 shows the company's recent revenue performance by type.

In addition to the primary revenue sources, there were specific elements of eBay's business model that made the company a success. eBay's dominance of the online auction market and the large number of buyers, sellers, and listed items were primary reasons for eBay's tremendous growth. The trust and safety programs, such as the Feedback Forum, continued to attract and retain new and current eBay users. The cost-effective and convenient trading, coupled with the strong sense of

EXHIBIT 4 Net Revenues by Type (in millions, except percentage changes)

	Year Ended December 31, 2010	Year Ended December 31, 2011	Year Ended December 31, 2012
Net Revenues by Type:			
Net transaction revenues			
Marketplaces	4,800	5,431	6,078
Payments	3,261	4,123	5,146
GSI	—	460	850
Total net transaction revenues	8,061	10,014	12,074
Marketing services and other revenues			
Marketplaces	921	1,211	1,320
Payments	174	289	428
GSI	—	130	233
Total marketing services and other revenues	1,095	1,638	2,020
Total net revenues	$9,156	$11,652	$14,072
Net Revenues by Segment:			
Marketplaces	$5,721	6,642	7,398
Payments	3,436	4,412	5,574
GSI	—	598	1,730
Total net revenues	$9,157	$11,652	$14,072
Net Revenues by Geography:			
U.S.	$4,214	5,484	6,778
International	4,942	6,168	7,294
Total net revenues	$9,156	$11,652	$14,072

Source: eBay Inc., www.ebayinc.com/.

community, added further value to the company's business model. However, as the company continued to grow and new trends evolved, eBay had to continue to adjust its model to remain competitive.

International Expansion

As competition intensified in the online auction industry, eBay expanded its international presence in an effort to create an online global marketplace. Gradually, eBay localized sites in the following countries:

- *Asia Pacific:* Australia, China, Hong Kong, India, Malaysia, New Zealand, Philippines, Singapore, South Korea, and Taiwan.
- *Europe:* Austria, Belgium, Denmark, France, Germany, Ireland, Italy, Netherlands, Poland, Spain, Sweden, Switzerland, and the United Kingdom.
- *North America:* Canada and the United States.

In many of the international websites, eBay provided local language and currency options to gain popularity and ensure the sense-of-community feeling. In most cases, eBay expanded its business by either acquiring or forming a partnership with a local company, as it recently has done with Xiu.com in its re-entry into the Chinese market. This strategy helped eBay better understand local cultures and ensure that the company was meeting specific local needs. This approach proved successful with the company's equity investment in MercadoLibre.com, which targeted Argentina, Brazil, Chile, Colombia, Costa Rica, the Dominican Republic, Ecuador, Mexico, Panama, Peru, Uruguay, and Venezuela. At the end of 2006, MercadoLibre.com reported 18 million registered users who performed 15.8 million transactions worth $1.1 billion.[22] Other notable international growth acquisitions are listed below.

Asia Pacific

- Acquired China-based Eachnet for approximately $150 million. eBay's failure to manage the company resulted in its recent partnership with communications company Tom Online.
- Acquired all outstanding shares of India's Baazee.com, which later became eBay India.
- Acquired Korean rival Internet Auction Co. by purchasing nearly 3 million shares. Acquisition has not proved successful due to intense competition from top Korean auction site Gmarket.

Europe

- Acquired Alando auction house for $43 million, a company that later became eBay Germany. Alando was previously considered Germany's leading online trading company. Germany became eBay's second-largest market, accounting for 21 percent of the company's total listings.

- Acquired Dutch competitor Marktplaats.nl, which had 80 percent of the Netherlands market share.
- Acquired Sweden's leading online auction company, Tradera.com, for $48 million.
- Acquired Denmark's leading online classifieds businesses, Den Bla Avis and BilBasen, for $390 million.[23]

For the most part, eBay was successful in expanding in Europe and Latin America, where it was able to quickly adapt to local needs through its partners. The company was also successful in countries it expanded to from the ground up, such as Canada and the United Kingdom. In 2007 the United Kingdom accounted for 15.5 percent of eBay's total listings. By engaging the local community in these countries, eBay customized its sites to meet specific local needs while providing access to the online global community.

eBay was considered the leader in each of its markets with the exception of Japan and China, in which it struggled repeatedly to gain market share. In 2002 eBay was forced to pull out of Japan due to rising costs and intense competition by rival Yahoo Japan. eBay also faced fierce competition in Korea, where Gmarket, another investment of Yahoo, dominated the market.

Despite its lack of success in local Asian markets, eBay continued its attempts to expand into the region, recognizing the tremendous growth potential that was available. In June 2006 eBay formed a joint venture with PChome Online in Taiwan. PChome Online was an Internet service provider in Taiwan, with more than 10 million members.[24] The company offered services such as Internet portal, e-commerce platform, and telecommunications. The move was expected to provide eBay with the local e-commerce expertise it needed to launch a new trading website that catered to the needs of Taiwan's Internet users.

In 2006 eBay emphasized its commitment to the Chinese e-commerce market by announcing a new joint venture with Beijing-based Tom Online Inc. Tom Online, which primarily sold cell phone add-on services, such as ring tones and avatars, put in $20 million for a 51 percent share and management control of eBay's online China site, Eachnet.[25] In 2002 eBay had purchased a 30 percent stake in Eachnet and within a year bought out local investors. Central management control of Eachnet was maintained in eBay's San Jose, California, location. Many believed the move to partner with Tom Online was a result of eBay's failure to adapt to local needs and successfully compete with China's online auction market leader, Taobao, which controlled approximately 70 percent of the market. Jack Ma, the chief executive of Alibaba.com, Taobao's parent company, believed eBay's failure in China was due to an inability to build a community effect in the country, which, according to Ma, begins with customer satisfaction. Ma also felt that since eBay had to adhere to a global platform, meeting specific local needs was difficult because changes at a global level had to be approved in the United States, which further limited the company's ability to produce a website tailored to the Chinese market.[26]

In April 2009 eBay secured agreements to buy a 67 percent stake of South Korea's Gmarket in a deal estimated to be worth $1.2 billon. The move was part of Donahoe's effort to increase revenue in coming years. It was expected that Gmarket would help eBay's push into Asia.[27]

Competitors

As eBay's product offerings and pricing formats evolved, so did its range of competitors. Originally, the company faced competition from alternative auctions or other venues for collectors, such as flea markets and garage sales. However, as the company grew and introduced fixed pricing, the range of competitors included large companies like Walmart and Kmart that also had retail websites. eBay's product platforms, like eBay Motors, put the company in direct competition with auto dealers and other online auto sites, such as Autobytes. Still, eBay faced the harshest competition from major online companies, including Yahoo and Amazon, which also had online auctions that rivaled eBay's.

Yahoo!

eBay's larger online competitor was Yahoo, which also had a strong global presence, particularly in Asian markets. Yahoo originally started as a search engine and quickly evolved to include additional products and services, such as Yahoo! Mail, Yahoo! Maps, and Yahoo! Messenger. The company also offered e-commerce services through Yahoo! Shopping, Yahoo! Autos, Yahoo! Auctions, and Yahoo! Travel. Like eBay, Yahoo's e-commerce sites allowed users to obtain relevant information and make transactions and purchases online. However, Yahoo's business model primarily focused on generating revenue through search advertising. In the United States, in response to potential threats from web giant Google, Yahoo and eBay formed an alliance in which Yahoo utilized eBay's payment system, PayPal, and eBay gained additional advertising through Yahoo searches. Still, Yahoo posed a major competitive threat in foreign markets, particularly the Asia Pacific area, through its partnerships with Gmarket and Taobao.

Gmarket

Yahoo's stake in Korean auction site Gmarket proved successful, with more than 17.2 million unique visitors. Founded in 2000, Gmarket was a Korean online auction and shopping-mall website that generated its revenue by charging a fee based on selling price.[28] Like Taobao, Gmarket offered fixed prices and provided an option to negotiate prices with sellers on an exclusive basis. This allowed buyers to conduct deals instantly instead of waiting until bids were completed. Gmarket also offered cheaper listings. These options, along with constant new features, allowed Gmarket to dominate the Korean online auction industry.[29]

Gmarket frequently introduced new marketing initiatives to provide sellers with various options to attract new customers. Gmarket grew financially powerful in 2006 when it launched its IPO, and Yahoo purchased a 9 percent stake in the company.

In 2009 eBay decided to secure an interest in its rival and was granted approval to purchase a combined 67 percent stake in Gmarket from Interpark Corp. and its chairman. In May 2010 eBay announced that it intended to work with Gmarket's founder to expand Gmarket's presence in Japan and Singapore. Lorie Norrington, president of eBay Marketplaces commented, "This joint venture is a sign of our continued commitment to help grow and lead ecommerce across Asia by offering more opportunities for sellers and extraordinary buying experiences for consumers."[30]

Taobao

In 2005 Yahoo entered a strategic partnership with Alibaba.com, Taobao's parent company, which created an instant threat in the Chinese market. The move created one of the largest Internet companies in China, one with a leading position in business-to-business e-commerce, consumer e-commerce, and online payments. Like Gmarket, Taobao offered buyers and sellers quick and convenient ways to conduct business. Its instant messaging and fixed price arrangements allowed transactions to be conducted quickly. In 2006 the company partnered with Intel to offer customers a wireless platform. This further improved communication and convenience when customers were conducting transactions. In 2011 Taobao was eBay's largest competitor in China, controlling over 80 percent of the Chinese online auction market.[31]

In early 2010 eBay announced the partnership of Paypal with China UnionPay, a local intrabank card system operator, which would make it accessible for customers to make online purchases from overseas. This move was made to challenge Alipay, a unit of Alibaba Group, which controlled about 50 percent of the market. This partnership would allow international retailers to sell to a large base of Chinese customers, who, combined, held 2.1 billon China UnionPay cards.[32] "After years of being the export hub for the world, now China is open for business as an import e-commerce market," said Scott Thompson, president of PayPal. "PayPal's partnership with China UnionPay removes an important friction point that exists across borders, and we are thrilled to eliminate the payments barrier so merchants can welcome millions of new Chinese customers to their sites."[33]

Amazon

Despite not having a huge presence in the online auction industry, Amazon was still considered a fierce online global competitor. Amazon started as Earth's biggest bookstore and rapidly evolved to selling everything, including toys, electronics, home furnishings, apparel, health and beauty aids, groceries, and so on. Still, books, CDs, and DVDs accounted for more than 65 percent of the firm's sales. Although Amazon had a large international presence, the company's linkage to brick-and-mortar shops in the United States made it a greater threat locally than in foreign markets. Amazon's international local sites were in Canada, the United Kingdom, Germany, Japan, France, and China. Despite its large online presence, Amazon scaled back its online auction business, cutting staff and shutting down Livebid, as part of an overall corporate restructuring.

The Future of eBay

eBay had a number of opportunities in which it had already taken action. By 2011, eBay had made a number of strategic acquisitions that included Rent.com, international classified websites, Stubhub.com, and Shopping.com. These acquisitions added to and complemented eBay's product offerings and further diversified the company's targeted market. With increased competition from Google and other major online companies, eBay had to continue to diversify and provide depth in its product offerings to remain competitive. Creating options and targeting distinct market niches would enable eBay to distinguish itself from competitors. This was particularly important because, as e-commerce and Internet usage rates continued to grow, so would the market opportunity for eBay. Because of its market-leading brand, eBay was in a unique position to capture a significant share of the market at an early stage.

eBay could also expand its existing products and services, such as PayPal. The product was relatively new and had the potential to grow and attract new customers, especially in international markets. Expanding PayPal into international markets would enable eBay to provide a simple way to conduct transactions across market borders. Considering the growth potential in developing markets, such as those in Africa, Asia, and the Middle East, expanding PayPal would attract many new customers, thus increasing eBay's revenue base. In line with e-commerce growth, as more customers felt comfortable with conducting transactions online, PayPal had the potential to be the preferred form of payment over the Internet.

However, for eBay to capitalize on these opportunities, the company would have to overcome the challenges of expanding into large foreign markets such as China and Japan. With almost 79 percent of the North American population using the Internet and only a 27.5 percent usage rate in the Asia Pacific area, eBay had a tremendous opportunity to expand and gain new customers. Considering that the Asia Pacific region had more than 50 percent of the world's population and was experiencing some of the largest online usage growth percentages in the world, tapping into this market was critical for eBay to expand.

eBay's operations in China remained small compared to Alibaba Group and other Chinese e-commerce companies, but the company had refocused its energies on export-oriented merchants in China who wanted to reach overseas buyers on its international websites.[34] Experts viewed eBay's strategy of forming a partnership with former rival Alibaba Group as the best way to generate sales from China. All hopes were on Paypal's acceptance by Chinese partners who were looking to expand international sales. It was critical for eBay to partner with local Chinese companies rather than going alone in the world's biggest Internet market in order to proceed in the local market.

ENDNOTES

1. Internet World Stats. 2010. Internet Usage Statistics. *www.internetworldstats.com/stats.htm.*

2. Wauters, Robin. 2012, eBay Style: Ecommerce giant inks deal with Chinese fashion site Xiu.com, The Next Web, http://thenextweb.com/asia/2012/11/12/ebay-style-ecommerce-giant-inks-deal-with-chinese-fashion-site-xiu-com/.

3. Galante, J. 2010. PayPal teams with China UnionPay to challenge Alipay. *Bloomberg News,* March 17, *www.bloomberg.com/apps/news?pid=newsarchive&sid=au4i5vaUlMNQ.*

4. Mark Greeven, Shengyun Yang, Tao Yue, Eric van Heck and Barbara Krug. March 12, 2012. How Taobao bested Ebay in China. Financial Times, http://www.ft.com/intl/cms/s/0/52670084-6c2c-11e1-b00f-00144feab49a.html#axzz2E2E0o7wP.

5. Mark Greeven, Shengyun Yang, Tao Yue, Eric van Heck and Barbara Krug. March 12, 2012. How Taobao bested Ebay in China. Financial Times, http://www.ft.com/intl/cms/s/0/52670084-6c2c-11e1-b00f-00144feab49a.html#axzz2E2E0o7wP.

6. Doyle, R. A. 2002. The history of auctions. *Auctioneer,* November 1, *www.absoluteauctionrealty.com/history_detail.php?id=5094.*

7. *Internet Based Moms.* 2007. Pierre Omidyar—the man behind eBay. April.

8. Academy of Achievement. 2005. Biography—Pierre Omidyar. November 9, *www.achievement.org.*

9. eBay Inc. 2008. Meg Whitman to step down.

10. eBay corporate website, *ebayinc.com.*

11. eBay Inc. 2008. Meg Whitman to step down.

12. O'Brien, Chris. November, 4 2012. Is eBay's John Donahoe the best CEO in Silicon Valley?. Mercurynews.com, http://www.mercurynews.com/chris-obrien/ci_21908264/obrien-is-ebays-john-donahoe-best-ceo-silicon

13. O'Brien, Chris. November, 4 2012. Is eBay's John Donahoe the best CEO in Silicon Valley? Mercurynews.com, http://www.mercurynews.com/chris-obrien/ci_21908264/obrien-is-ebays-john-donahoe-best-ceo-silicon

14. Galante, J. 2011. PayPal's revenue will double by 2013, Thompson says. *Bloomberg News,* February 10, *www.businessweek.com/news/2011-02-10/paypal-s-revenue-will-double-by-2013-thompson-says.html.*

15. eBay Inc. 2008. eBay Inc. buys leading payments and classifieds businesses, streamlines existing organization to improve growth. Press release, October 6, *www.ebayinc.com/content/press_release/20081006005605.*

16. eBay Inc. 2009. *Annual report.*

17. Stone, B. 2009. In a sale, Skype wins a chance to prosper. *New York Times,* September 1, *www.nytimes.com/2009/09/02/technology/companies/02ebay.html?_r=1.*

18. MacMillan, D. 2010. EBay buys bar-code app. *Bloomberg Businessweek,* June 23, *www.businessweek.com/technology/content/jun2010/tc20100623_901174.htm.*

19. eBay Inc. 2010. eBay acquires Milo, a leading local shopping engine. Press release, December 2, *www.ebayinc.com/content/press_release/20101202006358.*

20. eBay Inc. 2010. eBay acquires industry leading mobile application developer. Press release, December 15, *www.ebayinc.com/content/press_release/20101215006520.*

21. Himelstein, L., & Whitman, M. 1999. Q&A with eBay's Meg Whitman. *BusinessWeek Online,* May 31, *www.businessweek .com/1999/99_22/b3631008.htm.*

22. *IT Digest.* 2007. Argentina: MercadoLibre has 18mil registered users. January 25, *www.infobae.com.*

23. eBay Inc. 2008. eBay acquires leading classifieds sites in Denmark.

24. eBay Inc. 2006. eBay and PChome Online to form joint venture in Taiwan. Press release, June 5, *www.ebayinc.com/content/ press_release/20060605199313.*

25. Knowledge@Wharton. 2007. ebay's deal with Tom Online offers some timely lessons for managers of global online companies. February 14, *www.knowledgeatwharton.com.cn/index.cfm?fa5view Article&articleID51562&languageid51.*

26. Ma, J. 2005. Alibaba CEO says Taobao will dominate China online auctions. *Forbes.com,* May 5, *www.forbes.com/feeds/afx/2005/05/20/ afx2043109.html.*

27. Cho, K., & Galante, J. 2009. EBay offers to buy Korea's Gmarket for $1.2 billion. *Bloomberg.com,* April 16, *www.bloomberg.com/apps/ news?pid=newsarchive&sid=asyO3.3yVdnE&refer=home.*

28. Ihlwan, M. 2006. Gmarket eclipses eBay in Asia. *BusinessWeek Online,* June 28, *www.businessweek.com/globalbiz/content/jun2006/ gb20060628_910393.htm.*

29. *BusinessWeek Online.* 2006. Out-eBaying eBay in Korea. July 17, *www.businessweek.com/magazine/content/06_29/b3993080.htm.*

30. Caverly, D. 2010. eBay announces new joint venture in Asia. *WebProNews.com,* May 7, *www.webpronews.com/ ebay-announces-new-joint-venture-in-asia-2010-05.*

31. Epstein, G. 2010. eBay chief visits his Chinese conqueror. *Blogs .Forbes.com,* September 9, *blogs.forbes.com/gadyepstein/2010/09/09/ ebay-chief-visits-his-chinese-conqueror/.*

32. *China Tech News.* 2010. PayPal works with China UnionPay for online payment services. March 23, *www.chinatechnews. com/2010/03/23/11777-paypal-works-with-china-unionpay-for- online-payment-services.*

33. *BusinessWire.com.* 2010. PayPal and China UnionPay open the global marketplace to Chinese consumers. March 17, *www.businesswire.com/news/home/20100317005661/en/ PayPal-China-UnionPay-Open-Global-Marketplace-Chinese.*

34. Chao, L. 2010. EBay sees a market in China yet. *ChinaRealtimeReport,* May 19. *blogs.wsj.com/ chinarealtime/2010/05/19/ebay-sees-a-market-in-china-yet/.*

CASE 5

MICROFINANCE BANKS

*Going Global . . . and Going Public?**

In the world of development, if one mixes the poor and nonpoor in a program, the nonpoor will always drive out the poor, and the less poor will drive out the more poor, unless protective measures are instituted right at the beginning.

–Dr. Muhammad Yunus, founder of the Grameen Bank[1]

More than 2.5 billion people in the world earn less than $2.50 a day. None of the developmental economics theories have helped change this situation. Less than $2.50 a day means that these unfortunate people have been living without clean water, sanitation, or sufficient food to eat, or a proper place to sleep. In Southeast Asia alone, more than 500 million people live under these circumstances. In the past, almost every effort to help the very poor has been either a complete failure or at best partially successful. As Dr. Yunus argues, in every one of these instances, the poor will push the very poor out!

In 1972 Dr. Muhammad Yunus, a young economics professor trained at Vanderbilt, returned home to Bangladesh to take a position at Chittagong University. Upon his arrival, he was struck by the stark contrast between the developmental economics he taught in the classroom and the abject poverty of the villages surrounding the university. Dr. Yunus witnessed more suffering of the poor when, in 1974, inclement weather wiped out food crops and resulted in a widespread and prolonged famine. The theories of developmental economics and the traditional banking institutions, he concluded, were completely ineffectual for lessening the hunger and homelessness among the very poor of that region.

In 1976 Dr. Yunus and his students were visiting the poorest people in the village of Jobra to see whether they could directly help them in any way. They met a group of craftswomen making simple bamboo stools. After paying for their raw materials and financing, the women were left with a profit of just two cents per day. From his own pocket, Dr. Yunus gave $27 to be distributed among 42 craftswomen and *rickshaw* (human-driven transport) drivers. Little did he know that this simple act of generosity was the beginning of a global revolution in microfinance that would eventually help millions of impoverished and poor begin a transition from destitution to economic self-sufficiency. Dr. Yunus was convinced that a nontraditional approach to financing is the only way to help the very poor to help themselves.

The Grameen Project would soon follow—it officially became a bank under the law in 1983. The poor borrowers own 95 percent of the bank, and the rest is owned by the Bangladeshi government. Loans are financed through deposits only, and there are 8.35 million borrowers, of which 97 percent are women. There are over 2,500 branches serving around 81,000 villages in Bangladesh with a staff of more than 22,000 people. Since its inception, the bank has dispersed more than $10 billion, with a cumulative loan recovery rate of 97.38 percent. The Grameen Bank has been profitable every year since 1976 except three years and pays returns on deposits up to 100 percent to its members.[2] In 2006 Dr. Yunus and the Grameen Bank shared the Nobel Peace Prize for the concept and methodology of microfinance, also known as micro-credit or microloans.[3]

What Is Microfinance?

Microfinance involves a small loan (US $20–$750) with a high rate of interest (0 to 200 percent), typically provided to poor or destitute entrepreneurs without collateral.[4] A traditional loan has two basic components captured by interest rates: (1) risk of future payment, and (2) present value (given the time value of money). Risk of future payments is particularly high when dealing with the poor, who are unlikely to have familiarity with credit. To reduce this uncertainty, many microfinance banks refuse to lend to individuals and only lend to groups. Groups have proven to be an effective source of "social collateral" in the micro-loan process.

In addition to the risk and time value of money, the value of a loan must also include the transaction costs associated with administering the loan. A transaction cost is the cost associated with an economic exchange and is often considered the cost of doing business.[5] For banks like the Grameen Bank, the cost of administering ($125) a small loan may exceed the amount of the small loan itself ($120). These transaction costs have been one of the major deterrents for traditional banks.

Consider a bank with $10,000 to lend. If broken into small loans ($120), the available $10,000 can provide about 83 transactions. If the cost to administer a small loan ($120) is $125, its cost per unit is about 104 percent (!),

*This case was developed by Brian C. Pinkham, LL.M., and Dr. Padmakumar Nair, both from the University of Texas at Dallas. Material has been drawn from published sources to be used for class discussion. Copyright © 2011 Brian C. Pinkham and Padmakumar Nair.

while the cost of one $10,000 loan is only 1.25 percent. Because of the high cost per unit and the high risk of future payment, the rate of interest assigned to the smaller loan is much higher than the larger loan.

Finally, after these costs are accounted for, there must be some margin (or profit). In the case of microfinance banks, these margins are split between funding the growth of the bank (adding extra branches) and returns on deposits for bank members. This provides even the poorest bank member a feeling of "ownership."

Microfinance and Initial Public Offerings

With the global success of the microfinance concept, the number of private microfinance institutions exploded. Today there are more than 7,000 microfinance institutions, and their profitability has led many of the larger institutions to consider whether or not to "go public." Many microfinance banks redistribute profits to bank members (the poor) through returns on deposits. Once the bank goes public through an initial public offering (IPO), however, there is a transfer of control to public buyers (typically investors from developed economies). This transfer creates a fiduciary duty of the bank's management to maximize value for the shareholders.[6]

For example, Banco Compartamos (Banco) of Mexico raised $467 million in its IPO in 2007. The majority of buyers were leading investment companies from the United States and United Kingdom—the geographic breakdown of the investors was 52 percent U.S., 33 percent Europe, 5 percent Mexico, and 10 percent other Latin American countries. Similarly, Bank Rakyat Indonesia (BRI) raised $480 million in its IPO by listing on multiple stock exchanges in 2003; with the majority of investors who purchased the available 30 percent interest in the bank were from the United States and United Kingdom. The Indonesian government controls the remaining 70 percent stake in BRI. In Kenya, Equity Bank raised $88 million in its IPO in late 2006. Because of the small scale of Equity Bank's initial listing on the Nairobi Stock Exchange, the majority of the investors were from Eastern Africa.[7] About one-third of the investors were from the European Union and United States.[8]

Banco Compartamos[9]

Banco started in 1990 as a nongovernmental organization (NGO). At the time, population growth in Latin America and Mexico outpaced job growth. This left few job opportunities within the largest population group in Mexico— the low-income. Banco recognized that the payoffs for high-income opportunities were much larger (dollars a day), relative to low-income opportunities that may only return pennies a day. Over the next 10 years, Banco offered larger loans to groups and individuals to help bridge the gap between these low-income and high-income opportunities. However, their focus is to serve low-income individuals and groups, particularly the women who make up 98 percent of Banco's members.

The bank offers two microfinance options available to women only. The first is the *credito mujer* (women's credit). This loan ranges from $115–$2,075, available to groups (12–50) of women. Maturity is four months, and payments are weekly or biweekly.

If a group of women demonstrates the ability to manage credit through the *credito mujer,* they have access to credito mejora tu casa (home-improvement loans). This loan ranges from $230–$2,300 with a 6- to 24-month maturity. Payments are either biweekly or monthly.

The average interest rate on these loans is 80 percent. Banco focuses on loans to *groups* of women and requires the guarantee of the group—*every* individual in the group is held liable for the payment of the loan. This provides a social reinforcement mechanism for loan payments typically absent in traditional loans. The bank also prefers groups because they are more likely to take larger loans. This has proven effective even in times of economic downturn, when banks typically expect higher demand for loans and lower recovery of loans.

In 2009, with Mexico still reeling from the economic recession of 2008, Banco provided financing to 1.5 million Mexican households. This represented a growth of 30 percent from 2008. The core of the financing was credito mujer, emphasizing the bank's focus on providing services for the low-income groups. The average loan was 4.6 percent of GDP per capita ($440), compared with an average loan of 54 percent of GDP per capita ($347) at the Grameen Bank in Bangladesh.[10] With pressure from the economic downturn, Banco also reduced its cost per client by more than 5 percent, and continues (in late 2010) to have a cost per client under $125.

Consider two examples of how these microloans are used. Julia González Cueto, who started selling candy door-to-door in 1983, used her first loan to purchase accessories to broaden the image of her business. This provided a stepping stone for her decision to cultivate mushrooms and nopales (prickly pear leaves) to supplement her candy business. She now exports wild mushrooms to an Italian restaurant chain. Leocadia Cruz Gómez has had 16 loans, the first in April 2006. She invested in looms and thread to expand her textile business. Today, her workshop has grown, she is able to travel and give classes, and her work is widely recognized.

Beyond the Grameen Bank

These are just a few examples of how capitalistic free-market enterprises have helped the world to progress. It is generally accepted that charitable contributions and government programs alone cannot alleviate poverty. More resources and professional management are essential for microfinance institutions to grow further and sustain their mission. An IPO is one way to achieve this goal when deposits alone cannot sustain the demand for loans. At the same time, investors expect a decent return on their investment, and this expectation might work against the most important goal of microfinancing, namely, to help the very poor. Dr. Yunus has recently reemphasized his concern of the nonpoor driving out the poor, and talks about microfinance institutions seeking investments from "social-objective-driven" investors with a need to create a separate "social stock market."[11]

The Grameen Bank story, and that of microfinancing, and the current enthusiasm in going public raise several concerns. Institutions like the Grameen Bank have to grow and sustain a long-run perspective. The Grameen Bank has not accepted donor money since 1998 and does not foresee a need for donor money or other sources of external capital. The Grameen Bank charges four interest rates, depending on who is borrowing and for what purpose the money is being used: 20 percent for income-generating loans, 8 percent for housing loans, 5 percent for student loans, and interest-free loans for struggling members (unsympathetically called beggars). (Although these rates would appear to be close to what U.S. banks charge, we must point out that the terms of these loans are typically three or four months. Thus, the annualized interest rates would be four or five times the aforementioned rates.)

The Grameen Bank's "Beggars-As-Members" program is a stark contrast to what has been theorized and practiced in contemporary financial markets—traditional banking would assign high-risk borrowers (like beggars) the highest interest rate compared to more reliable borrowers who are using the borrowed money for generating income. Interestingly, the loan recovery rate is 79 percent from the "Beggars-As-Members" program, and about 20,000 members (out of 110,000) have left begging completely.[12] However, it is difficult to predict the future, and it is possible that the Grameen Bank might consider expanding its capital base by going public just like its Mexican counterpart.

Most developmental economists question the wisdom of going public, because publicly traded enterprises are likely to struggle to find a balance between fiduciary responsibilities and social good.[13] The three large IPOs mentioned above (Banco, BRI, and Equity First) all resulted in improved transparency and reporting for stockholders. However, the profits, which were originally distributed to bank members as returns on deposits, are now split between bank members (poor) and stockholders (made up of mostly EU and U.S. investors). Many of these microfinance banks are feeling the pressure of NGOs and bank members requesting lower interest rates.[14] This trend could potentially erode the large profit margins these banks currently enjoy. When faced with falling profits, publicly traded microfinance institutions will have to decide how best to provide financial services for the very poor and struggling members of the society without undermining their fiduciary duties to stockholders.

ENDNOTES

1. Yunus, M. 2007. *Banker to the poor: Micro-lending and the battle against world poverty.* New York: PublicAffairs.

2. The Grameen Bank removes funding for administration and branch growth from the initial profits and redistributes the remaining profits to bank members. This means that a poor bank member who deposits $1 in January may receive up to $1 on December 31! Grameen Bank, *www.grameen-info.org.*

3. Grameen Bank, *www.grameen-info.org.*

4. Microfinance banks vary to the extent that the rates of interest are annualized or specified to the term. Grameen Bank, for instance, annualizes the interest on its microloans. However, many other banks set a periodic rate where, in extreme cases, interest may accrue daily. Grameen Bank, *www.grameen-info.org.*

5. Chapter 6, pages 213–214.

6. Khavul, S. 2010. Microfinance: Creating opportunities for the poor? Academy of Management Perspectives, 24(3): 58–72.

7. Equity Bank, *www.equitybank.co.ke.*

8. Rhyne, E., & Guimon, A. 2007. The Banco Compartamos initial public offering, Accion: InSight, no. 23: 1–17. *resources. centerforfinancialinclusion.org/insight/IS23en.pdf.*

9. Unless otherwise noted, this section uses information from Banco Compartamos, *www.compartamos.com.*

10. We calculated all GDP per capita information as normalized to current (as of 2010) U.S. dollars using the International Monetary Fund (IMF) website, *www.imf.org.* The estimated percentages are from Banco Compartamos, *www.compartamos.com.*

11. Yunus. 2007. *Banker to the poor.*

12. Grameen Bank, *www.grameen-info.org.*

13. Khavul. 2010. Microfinance.

14. Rhyne & Guimon. 2007. The Banco Compartamos initial public offering.

CASE 6

MCDONALD'S*

Although McDonald's earnings for the fourth quarter of 2012 beat expectations, the world's largest restaurant chain stated that it will continue to face considerable challenges in 2013. During 2012, the firm reported the first monthly same-store sales decline in nine years, reflecting the effect of the shaky global economy (see Exhibits 1 and 2). On January 23, 2013, Chief Executive Don Thompson, who had stepped into the job just six months before, told investors, "More specifically, growth in the informal eating-out industry has been relatively flat to declining around the world and we expect that to continue."[1]

The dip in sales figures came as a surprise to most analysts, because McDonald's had managed to show consistent performance since 2003, leading to a surge in operating profits and stock price over almost a decade. Most of this could be attributed to the "Plan to Win," which was first outlined by James R. Cantalupo, who came out of retirement to guide McDonald's after overexpansion had caused the chain to lose focus. The core of the plan was to increase sales at existing locations by improving the menu, refurbishing the outlets, and extending hours.

In spite of management changes, McDonald's has remained committed to pushing on various aspects of this

*Case developed by Professor Jamal Shamsie, Michigan State University, with the assistance of Professor Alan B. Eisner, Pace University. Material has been drawn from published sources to be used for purposes of class discussion. Copyright © 2013 Jamal Shamsie and Alan B. Eisner.

plan. The chain has continued to expand its menu over the years, with more sandwiches and salads. It also started to add snacks and drinks, two of the few areas where restaurant sales have still been growing in spite of the economic downturn. Its addition of specialty coffee, ice-cold frappes, and fruit smoothies in its newly added McCafes has helped boosted the average spent by each customer and lured them to its outlets for snacks during slower parts of the day.

Nevertheless, McDonald's is aware that it is facing a rapidly fragmenting market, where consumers are looking for healthier and even more exotic foods. The chain is facing tougher competition from Burger King and Wendy's, both of which have been adding to their menus and remodeling their outlets. At the same time, McDonald's is also losing customers to chains such as Subway, Chipotle, and Taco Bell, which had not previously been viewed as strong competitors. Many analysts therefore believe that the chain must continue to work on its turnaround strategy in order to meet these challenges.

Thompson has been monitoring pricing in order to make sure the menu stays affordable even though commodity prices have been rising. He believes that the chain was hurt by its increased emphasis on the Extra Value Menu that included items priced higher than a dollar. It has since shifted its focus back to the Dollar Menu, which has continued to generate almost 15 percent of total sales. Steven Kron, an analyst with Goldman Sachs, emphasized the attractiveness of the firm's

EXHIBIT 1

Income Statements

Go to library tab in Connect to access Case Financials.

A	B	C	D
	Year Ending*		
	Dec. 31, 2012	Dec. 31, 2011	Dec. 31, 2010
Total revenue	27,567	27,006	24,075
Gross profit	10,816	10,687	9,637
Operating income	8,605	8,528	7,473
EBIT	8,596	8,505	7,451
Net income	5,465	5,503	4,946

*Figures in millions of U.S. dollars.

Source: McDonald's.

EXHIBIT 2

Balance Sheets*

Go to library tab in Connect to access Case Financials.

A	B	C	D
	Year Ending*		
	Dec 31, 2012	Dec 31, 2011	Dec 31, 2010
Current assets	4,922	4,403	4,368
Total assets	35,386	32,990	31,975
Current liabilities	3,403	3,509	2,925
Total liabilities	20,093	18,600	17,341
Stockholder equity	15,294	14,390	14,634

*Figures in millions of U.S. dollars.

Source: McDonald's.

affordable Dollar Menu: "When people are seeking value, these guys have a very powerful component."[2]

Experiencing a Downward Spiral

Since it was founded more than 50 years ago, McDonald's has been defining the fast-food business. It provided millions of Americans their first jobs even as it changed their eating habits. It rose from a single outlet in a Chicago suburb to become one of the largest chains of outlets spread around the globe. But it gradually began to run into various problems which began to slow down its sales growth (see Exhibit 3).

EXHIBIT 3 McDonald's Milestones

1948	Brothers Richard and Maurice McDonald open the first restaurant in San Bernadino, California, that sells hamburgers, fries, and milk shakes.
1955	Ray A.Kroc, 52, opens his first McDonald's in Des Plaines, Illinois. Kroc, a distributor of milk shake mixers, figures he can sell a bundle of them if he franchises the McDonald's business and installs his mixers in the new stores.
1961	Kroc buys out the McDonald brothers for $2.7 million.
1963	Ronald McDonald makes his debut as corporate spokesclown, using future NBC-TV weatherman Willard Scott. During the year, the company also sells its 1 billionth burger.
1965	McDonald's stock goes public at $22.50 a share. It will split 12 times in the next 35 years.
1967	The first McDonald's restaurant outside the U.S. opens in Richmond, British Columbia. Today there are 31,108 McDonald's in 118 countries.
1968	The Big Mac, the first extension of McDonald's basic burger, makes its debut and is an immediate hit.
1972	McDonald's switches to the frozen variety for its successful french fries.
1974	Fred L. Turner succeeds Kroc as CEO. In the midst of a recession, the minimum wage rises to $2 per hour, a big cost increase for McDonald's, which is built around a model of young, low-wage workers.
1975	The first drive-through window is opened in Sierra Vista, Arizona.
1979	McDonald's responds to the needs of working women by introducing Happy Meals. A burger, some fries, a soda, and a toy give working moms a break.
1987	Michael R. Quinlan becomes chief executive.
1991	Responding to the public's desire for healthier foods, McDonald's introduces the low-fat McLean Deluxe burger. It flops and is withdrawn from the market. Over the next few years, the chain stumbles several times trying to spruce up its menu.
1992	The company sells its 90 billionth burger and stops counting.
1996	To attract more adult customers, the company launches its Arch Deluxe, a "grownup" burger with an idiosyncratic taste. As with the low-fat burger, it falls flat.
1997	McDonald's launches Campaign 55, which cuts the cost of a Big Mac to $0.55. It is a response to discounting by Burger King and Taco Bell. The move, which prefigures similar price wars in 2002, is widely considered a failure.
1998	Jack M. Greenberg becomes McDonald's fourth chief executive. A 16-year company veteran, he vows to spruce up the restaurants and their menu.
1999	For the first time, sales from international operations outstrip domestic revenues. In search of other concepts, the company acquires Aroma Cafe, Chipotle, Donatos, and, later, Boston Market.
2000	McDonald's sales in the U.S. peak at an average of $1.6 million annually per restaurant, a figure that has not changed since. It is, however, still more than at any other fast-food chain.
2001	Subway surpasses McDonald's as the fast-food chain with the most U.S. outlets. At the end of the year it had 13,247 stores, 148 more than McDonald's.
2002	McDonald's posts its first-ever quarterly loss, of $343.8 million. The stock drops to around $13.50, down 40% from five years earlier.
2003	James R. Cantalupo returns to McDonald's in January as CEO. He immediately pulls back from the company's 10%–15% forecast for per-share earnings growth.
2004	Charles H. Bell takes over the firm after the sudden death of Cantalupo. He states that he will continue with the strategies developed by his predecessor.
2005	Jim Skinner takes over as CEO after Bell retires for health reasons.
2006	McDonald's launches specialty beverages, including coffee-based drinks.
2008	McDonald's plans to add McCafes to each of its outlets.
2012	Don Thompson succeeds Jim Skinner as CEO of the chain.

Source: McDonald's.

This decline could be attributed in large part to a drop in McDonald's once-vaunted service and quality since its expansion in the 1990s, when headquarters stopped grading franchises for cleanliness, speed, and service. By the end of the decade, the chain ran into more problems because of the tighter labor market. McDonald's began to cut back on training as it struggled to find new recruits, leading to a dramatic falloff in the skills of its employees. According to a 2002 survey by market researcher Global Growth Group, McDonald's came in third in average service time behind Wendy's and sandwich shop Chick-fil-A Inc.

McDonald's also began to fail consistently with its new product introductions, such as the low-fat McLean Deluxe and Arch Deluxe burgers, both of which were meant to appeal to adults. It did no better with its attempts to diversify beyond burgers, often because of problems with the product development process. Consultant Michael Seid, who managed a franchise consulting firm in West Hartford, pointed out that McDonald's offered a pizza that didn't fit through the drive-through window and salad shakers that were packed so tightly that dressing couldn't flow through them.

In 1998, after McDonald's posted its first-ever decline in annual earnings, CEO Michael R. Quinlan was forced out and replaced by Jack M. Greenberg, a 16-year veteran of the firm. Greenberg cut back on McDonald's expansion as he tried to deal with some of the growing problems. But his efforts to deal with the decline of McDonald's were slowed down by his acquisition of other fast-food chains such as Chipotle Mexican Grill and Boston Market.

On December 5, 2002, after watching McDonald's stock slide 60 percent in three years, the board ousted Greenberg. He had lasted little more than two years. His short tenure had been marked by the introduction of 40 new menu items, none of which caught on big, and the purchase of a handful of nonburger chains, none of which helped the firm to sell more burgers. Indeed, his critics say that by trying so many different things and executing them poorly, Greenberg allowed the burger business to continue with its decline. According to Los Angeles franchisee Reggie Webb, "We would have been better off trying fewer things and making them work."[3]

Pushing for a Turnaround

By the beginning of 2003, consumer surveys were indicating that McDonald's was headed for serious trouble.

Measures for the service and quality of the chain were continuing to fall, dropping far behind those of its rivals. In order to deal with its deteriorating performance, the firm decided to bring back retired Vice chairman James R. Cantalupo, 59, who had overseen McDonald's successful international expansion in the 1980s and 1990s. Cantalupo, who had retired only a year earlier, was perceived to be the only candidate with the necessary qualifications, despite shareholder sentiment for an outsider. The board felt that it needed someone who knew the company well and could move quickly to turn things around.

Cantalupo realized that McDonald's often tended to miss the mark on delivering the critical aspects of consistent, fast, and friendly service and an all-around enjoyable experience for the whole family. He understood that its franchisees and employees alike needed to be inspired as well as retrained on their role in putting the smile back into the McDonald's experience. When Cantalupo and his team laid out their turnaround plan in 2003, they stressed getting the basics of service and quality right, in part by reinstituting a tough "up or out" grading system that would kick out underperforming franchisees. "We have to rebuild the foundation. It's fruitless to add growth if the foundation is weak," said Cantalupo.[4]

To begin with, Cantalupo cut back on the opening of new outlets, focusing instead on generating more sales from its existing outlets. He shifted the company's emphasis to obtaining most of its revenue growth from increasing sales in the over 30,000 outlets that were already operating around the world (see Exhibits 4 through 6). In part, McDonalds tried to draw more customers by introducing new products. And it seemed to be working. The chain had a positive response to its increased emphasis on healthier foods, led by a revamped line of fancier salads. The revamped menu was promoted through a worldwide ad slogan, "I'm loving it," which was delivered by pop idol Justin Timberlake through a set of MTV-style commercials.

But the biggest success for the firm came in the form of the McGriddles breakfast sandwich, which was launched nationwide in June 2003. The popular new offering consisted of a couple of syrup-drenched pancakes, stamped with the Golden Arches, which acted as the top and bottom of the sandwich to hold eggs, cheese, sausage, and bacon in three different combinations.

EXHIBIT 4

Number of Outlets

Go to library tab in Connect to access Case Financials.

	A	B	C	D
1		**Number of Outlets**		
2		Total	Company Owned	Franchised
3	2012	34,480	6,598	**27,882**
4	2011	33,510	6,435	27,075
5	2010	32,737	6,399	26,338
6	2009	32,478	6,262	26,216
7	2008	31,967	6,502	25,465

Source: McDonald's.

EXHIBIT 5

Distribution of Outlets

Go to library tab in
Connect to access
Case Financials.

	A	B	C	D	E	F
1		**Distribution of Outlets**				
2		2012	2011	2010	2009	2008
3	U.S.	14,157	14,098	14,027	13,980	13,918
4	Europe	7,368	7,156	6,969	6,785	6,628
5	Asia Pacific	9,454	8,865	8,424	8,488	8,255
6	Americas*	3,501	3,391	3,317	3,225	3,166

*Canada & Latin America.

Source: McDonald's.

EXHIBIT 6

Breakdown of Revenues*

Go to library tab in
Connect to access
Case Financials.

	A	B	C	D	E	F
1		**Breakdown of Revenues***				
2		2012	2011	2010	2009	2008
3	U.S.	8,814	8,529	8,116	7,043	8,048
4	Europe	10,827	10,886	9,569	9,273	9,923
5	Asia Pacific	6,391	6,019	5,065	4,337	4,231
6	Americas†	1,535	1,572	1,328	1,190	1,290

*Figures in millions of U.S. dollars.
†Canada & Latin America.

Source: McDonald's.

McDonald's has estimated that the new breakfast addition has been bringing in about one million new customers every day.

With his efforts largely directed at a turnaround strategy for McDonald's, Cantalupo decided to divest the nonburger chains that his predecessor had acquired. Collectively lumped under the Partner Brands, these have consisted of Chipotle Mexican Grill and Boston Market. The purpose of these acquisitions had been to find new growth and to offer the best franchises new expansion opportunities. But these acquired businesses had not fuelled much growth and had actually posted considerable losses in recent years.

Striving for Healthier Offerings

When Jim Skinner took over from Cantalupo in 2004, he felt that one of his top priorities was to deal with the growing concerns about the unhealthy image of McDonald's, given the rise of obesity in the U.S. These concerns were highlighted in the popular documentary *Super Size Me,* made by Morgan Spurlock. Spurlock vividly displayed the health risks that were posed by a steady diet of food from the fast-food chain. With a rise in awareness of the high fat content of most of the products offered by McDonald's, the firm was also beginning to face lawsuits from some of its loyal customers.

In response to the growing health concerns, one of the first steps taken by McDonald's was to phase out supersizing by the end of 2004. The supersizing option allowed customers to get a larger order of French fries and a bigger soft drink by paying a little extra. McDonald's also announced that it intended to start providing nutrition information on the packaging of its products to inform customers about the calories, fat, protein, carbohydrates, and sodium that are in each product. Finally, McDonald's also began to remove the artery-clogging trans fatty acids from the oil that it used to make its french fries and announced plans to reduce the sodium content in all of its products by 15 percent.

At the same time, Skinner was also putting out more offerings that customers were likely to perceive to be healthier. McDonalds has continued to build upon its white-meat chicken offerings with products such as Chicken Selects. It has also emphasized its new salad offerings. McDonald's has carried out extensive experiments and tests with these, deciding to use higher quality ingredients, from a variety of lettuces and tasty cherry tomatoes to sharper cheeses and better cuts of meat. It offered a choice of *Newman's Own* dressings, a well-known higher-end brand. "Salads have changed the way people think of our brand," said Wade Thoma, vice president for menu development in the U.S. "It tells people that we are very serious about offering things people feel comfortable eating."[5]

McDonald's has also been trying to include more fruits and vegetables in its popular Happy Meals. It announced in 2011 that it would reduce the amount of French fries and phase out the caramel dipping sauce that accompanied the apple slices in these meals. The addition of fruits and vegetables has raised the firm's operating costs, as these are more expensive to ship and store because of their more perishable nature. "We are doing what we can," said Danya Proud, a spokesperson for the firm. "We have to evolve with the times."[6]

The current rollout of new beverages, highlighted by new coffee-based drinks, represents the chain's biggest menu expansion in almost three decades. Under a plan to add a McCafe section to all of its nearly 14,000 U.S. outlets, McDonald's has been offering lattes, cappuccinos, ice-blended frappes, and fruit-based smoothies to its customers. "In many cases, they're now coming for the beverage, whereas before they were coming for the meal," said Lee Renz, an executive who was responsible for the rollout.[7]

Revamping the Outlets

As part of its turnaround strategy, McDonald's has also been selling off the outlets that it owned. More than 75 percent of its outlets are now in the hands of franchisees and other affiliates. Skinner is now working with the franchisees to address the look and feel of many of the chain's aging stores. Without any changes to their décor, the firm is likely to be left behind by other more savvy fast-food and drink retailers. The firm is pushing harder to refurbish—or reimage—all of its outlets around the world. "People eat with their eyes first," said Thompson. "If you have a restaurant that is appealing, contemporary, and relevant both from the street and interior, the food tastes better."[8]

The reimaging concept was first tried in France in 1996 by Dennis Hennequin, an executive in charge of the chain's European operations, who felt that the effort was essential to revive the firm's sagging sales. "We were hip 15 years ago, but I think we lost that," he said.[9] McDonald's has been applying the reimaging concept to its outlets around the world, with a budget of more than half of its total annual capital expenditures. In the U.S., the changes cost an average of $150,000 per restaurant, a cost that is shared with the franchisees when the outlet is not company owned.

One of the prototype interiors being tested out by McDonald's has curved counters with surfaces painted in bright colors. In one corner, a touch-activated screen allows customers to punch in orders without queuing. The interiors can feature armchairs and sofas, modern lighting, large television screens, and wireless Internet access. The firm is also developing new features for its drive-through customers, which account for 65 percent of all transactions in the U.S. They include music aimed at queuing vehicles and a wall of windows on the drive-through side of the restaurant, allowing customers to see meals being prepared from their cars.

The chain has even been developing McCafes inside its outlets next to the usual fast-food counter. The McCafe concept originated in Australia in 1993 and has been rolled out in many restaurants around the world. McDonald's has just begun to introduce the concept to the U.S. as it refurbishes many of its existing outlets. In fact, part of the refurbishment has focused on installing a specialty beverage platform across all U.S. outlets. The cost of installing this equipment is running at about $100,000 per outlet, with McDonald's subsidizing part of this expense.

Eventually, all McCafes will offer espresso-based coffee, gourmet coffee blends, fresh baked muffins, and high-end desserts. Customers will be able to consume these while they relax in soft leather chairs listening to jazz, big band, or blues music. Commenting on this significant expansion of offerings, Marty Brochstein, executive editor of *The Licensing Letter,* said, "McDonald's wants to be seen as a lifestyle brand, not just a place to go to have a burger."[10]

More Gold in These Arches?

Even though McDonald's recovered from the drop in monthly same-store sales, there were questions about the future of the fast-food chain. The firm was trying out a variety of strategies to increase its appeal to different segments of the market. Through a mix of outlet décor and menu items, McDonald's attempted to target young adults, teenagers, children, and families. In so doing, it had to ensure that it did not alienate any one of these groups in its efforts to reach out to the other.

Its marketing campaign anchored around the catchy phrase "I'm loving it," took on different forms in order to target each of the groups that it was seeking. Larry Light, who was the head of global marketing at McDonald's that pushed for this new campaign, insisted that the firm had to exploit its brand through pushing it in many different directions. The brand could be positioned differently in different locations, at different times of the day and to target different customer segments. In large urban centers, McDonald's could target young adults for breakfast with its gourmet coffee, egg sandwiches, and fat-free muffins. Light explained the adoption of such a multiformat strategy by saying, "The days of mass-media marketing are over."[11]

McDonald's continued to expand its menu through offerings that performed well in test markets. Its introduction of Cheddar Bacon Onion sandwiches represented an alternative to its traditional line-up of hamburger and chicken items. More recently, the chain tried out Fish McBites, using the same Alaskan Pollock as in its fish sandwiches. Nevertheless, the expansion of the menu beyond the staple of burgers and fries does raise some fundamental questions. Most significantly, it is not clear just how far McDonald's can stretch its brand while keeping all of its outlets under the traditional symbol of its golden arches.

The long-term success of the firm may well depend on its ability to compete with rival burger chains. "The burger category has great strength," said David C. Novak, chairman and CEO of Yum! Brands, parent of KFC and Taco Bell. "That's America's food. People love hamburgers."[12] But Thompson was under pressure to take more aggressive action to reenergize the world's largest fast-food chain. Scott Rothbort, president of an asset management firm that had invested heavily in McDonald's, said that the verdict on Thompson's performance was still pending: "What will be the deciding factor is how he deals with some of these short-term setbacks."[13]

ENDNOTES

1. Jargon, J. 2013. McDonald's issues cautious forecast. *Wall Street Journal,* January 24: B4.
2. Adamy, J. 2009. McDonald's to expand, posting strong results. *Wall Street Journal,* January 27: B1.
3. Gogoi, P., & Arndt, M. 2003. Hamburger hell. *BusinessWeek,* March 3: 106.
4. Gogoi & Arndt. 2003. Hamburger hell: 105.
5. Warner, M. 2005. You want any fruit with that Big Mac? *New York Times,* February 20: 8.
6. Strom, S. 2011. McDonald's trims its Happy Meal. July 27: B7.
7. Adamy, J. 2008. McDonald's coffee strategy is tough sell. *Wall Street Journal,* October 27: B3.
8. Paynter. B. 2010. Super style me. *Fast Company,* October: 107.
9. Grant, J. 2006. McDonald's to revamp UK outlets. *Financial Times,* February 2: 14
10. Horovitz, B. 2003. McDonald's ventures beyond burgers to duds, toys. *USA Today,* November 14: 6B.
11. *Economist.* 2004. Big Mac's makeover. October 16: 65.
12. Gogoi & Arndt. 2003. Hamburger hell: 108.
13. Jargon, J. 2012. McDonald's is feeling fried. *Wall Street Journal,* November 9: B2.

CASE 7

WHIRLPOOL AND THE BUILT-IN APPLIANCE INDUSTRY IN INDIA[1]

IVEY | Publishing

Indian customers have wondered why they did not have sophisticated, western-style kitchens. Appliances were built only into the cabinets of modular kitchens, found mostly in contemporary houses. Built-in appliances gave kitchens a modern look, besides maximizing kitchen space: people in India started realizing the importance of having a built-in kitchen.

In India, increasing GDP growth rate, consumer buying power and middle class aspirations towards brands led to the entry of foreign brands such as Faber, Miele and Kaff. This was an impetus for the established consumer durable brands of India to foray into this growing market. Strangely, until the end of 2012, no player from the Indian durables industry—worth INR350 billion (US$6.39 billion)—had a marked presence in the built-in appliance market.

Whirlpool, a U.S. corporation, had an opportunity to reinforce its dominance in the Indian consumer durables market over its competitors. Shantanu Dasgupta, vice-president of corporate affairs and strategy, remarked, "Whirlpool of India plans to focus on water purifiers and built-in kitchen appliances over the next three years to maximize growth."[2]

Capturing and capitalizing on the built-in appliance market would give it an edge. Whirlpool planned to invest over INR7.5 billion (US$1.5 million) in India over three years, with more than half earmarked for innovation (as it targeted market leadership in the country).[3] The key issue was whether to go ahead and gain the prime mover advantage or wait for the other players to cultivate the market and reap the benefits later.

Company Overview

Whirlpool, the first commercial manufacturer of motorized washers and the world's number one manufacturer and marketer of major home appliances as of December 1, 2012, had a global presence involving 170 countries, with manufacturing operations in 13 countries. It had always set industry milestones and benchmarks. Whirlpool was started in 1911, with its U.S. headquarters in Benton Harbor, Michigan. It began its global expansion in 1958 by entering Brazil, and in the 1980s, it forayed into the Indian market under a joint venture with the TVS Group.

Whirlpool of India, formerly known as Kelvinator India, was started in 1960 by J. R. Desai in collaboration with Kelvinator International Corporation, USA. Whirlpool Incorporation, USA, and Sundaram Clayton Ltd. started TVS Whirlpool Ltd. as a joint venture. In 1996, Kelvinator and TVS acquisitions were merged to create the Indian home appliance leader of the future, Whirlpool India.[4] The company's portfolio ranges from washing machines, refrigerators and microwave ovens to air conditioners. The company owned three state-of-the-art manufacturing facilities, one each in Faridabad, Puducherry and Pune. Whirlpool engineered its products to suit the requirements of "intelligent, accomplished and confident" Indian homemakers. The product range employed unique technology and offered consumer-relevant solutions specific to the needs of Indian home environments. In the financial year ending March 2012, the annual turnover of Whirlpool India was INR27.04 billion (US$537 million; see Exhibit 1). Whirlpool, with a market share of more than 25 per cent (as of March 2012), was among the leading brands in the home appliance industry in India.[5]

Industry Overview

The consumer durables industry consisted of durable goods and appliances for domestic use, such as televisions, air conditioners, refrigerators and washing machines, and

EXHIBIT 1 Financials of Whirlpool India

Year End: March 2012	FY2009	FY2010	FY2011
Sales (INR in millions)	22,192	17,192	27,041
Growth	−5%	29%	22%
EBITDA margin	7.6%	10.6%	9.8%
PAT (INR in millions)	705	1,450	1,660
PAT margin	4%	7%	6%
EPS (INR in millions)	4.2	10.0	12.2
RoE (return on equity)	51%	86%	60%
RoCE (return on capital employed)	35%	68%	62%

Source: Adapted from company data, Bloomberg, BSE, GEPL Capital Research, www.geplcapital.com/reports/ConsumerDurables_vJuly_15v1.pdf, accessed October, 2012.

kitchen appliances such as microwaves and ovens. The market size of the consumer durables industry was estimated to grow to approximately US$12.5 billion by the end of 2015.[6] Further, the consumer durables could be classified as brown goods and white goods. White goods appliances were air conditioners, refrigerators, washing machines and sewing machines, while brown goods appliances were microwave ovens, cooking ranges, chimneys, mixers and electronic fans (see Exhibits 2 and 3).

The home appliance industry witnessed a slowdown in market growth in financial year 2011–2012 as there was an adverse impact on the sales of refrigerators and air conditioners. Air conditioners especially, for the first time in the past five years, registered a negative growth of 15 per cent.[7] Though microwaves showed a 10 per cent market growth, it was much lower than the compound annual growth rate registered over the last few years.[8] Even though sales have declined, a positive opportunity exists at the low income level of appliance ownership. The penetration of home appliances into the rural market also contributed to that market's enormous untapped potential, which many market players viewed as ideal for investment.

The white goods industry was growing at a fast pace in the Indian markets as the consumption pattern was moving towards the western style. Single-door refrigerators and semiautomatic washing machines were the dominant formats in their categories. Consumer interest was growing at a much faster rate and shifting from window air conditioners towards split air conditioners. The increase in working women improved the standard of living and thus stimulated the need for high-end cooking appliances. Some of the most sought after high-end cooking appliances were built-in hobs,[9] hoods, ovens and dishwashers. Finish and design became very important for the customers in the age group below 30 years as they looked for stylish lifestyle products. Increase in demand for modern housing was also driving the demand for modern modular kitchen appliances like hoods and hobs. At the premium end, built-in suites of ovens, microwaves and dishwashers presented an interesting opportunity.

As the modular kitchen market witnessed strong growth, many international players were looking forward to venturing into the Indian market. Until 2010, this market in India was unorganized and primarily dominated by local and small players. The potential for growth was more likely present in urban India as the adoption rate was chiefly driven by consumers' lifestyle evolution. Even though the built-in appliance industry was nascent in India in 2012, the market was growing at 25 to 30 per cent, and 10 years down the line, it would mean a big business opportunity in India.[10]

Major Competitors for Whirlpool in India

Though the industry was very unorganized, some companies like Miele, Fisher & Paykel, and Foster were trying to dominate its premium category. Further, many companies,

---

EXHIBIT 2 Key Dynamics of Consumer-Durable Industry

Industry Size	INR350 billion
Key Categories	white goods, brown goods and consumer electronics
Competitive Landscape	dominated by South Korean majors like LG and Samsung in most segments
Margin Profile	low margin, dependent on volumes
Growth Opportunities	lower penetration coupled with increasing disposable income

Source: Adapted from Report on Consumer Durable Market in India, March 2012, www.cci.in/pdf/surveys_reports/Consumer-Durables-Industry-in-India.pdf, accessed October, 2012.

EXHIBIT 3 Classification of Consumer Durables

White Goods	Brown Goods	Consumer Electronics
• air conditioners	• microwave ovens	• TVs
• refrigerators	• cooking range	• audio and video systems
• sewing machines	• chimneys	• electronic accessories
• watches and clocks	• mixers	• pcs
• cleaning equipment	• grinders	• mobile phones
• other domestic appliances	• electronic fans	• digital cameras
	• irons	• DVDs

Source: Adapted from Report on Consumer Durable Market in India, March 2012, www.cci.in/pdf/surveys_reports/Consumer-Durables-Industry-in-India.pdf, accessed October, 2012.

including Faber, Sunflame and Kaff, were trying to establish a position for themselves in the organized sector while battling to make their presence felt in the market. The following are brief descriptions of the major players trying to capture the market share in the white goods space in India.

Miele

Based in Gutersloh, Germany, and founded in 1899, Miele had been a family-owned and -run company since its inception. As of 2012, the company had 16,700 employees, with an annual turnover of US$4.07 billion.[11] The company specialized in manufacturing high-end domestic appliances, fitted kitchens and commercial equipment.

The company had its manufacturing facilities in Germany, Romania, Austria, China and the Czech Republic and had a presence in about 97 countries, of which 47 were with company-owned subsidiaries; the remaining 50 were through independent importers. The company entered the Indian subcontinent in the 2009 and had its operations based in New Delhi, the nation's capital. Markus Miele, managing director of Miele, said, "In absolute terms, there are more potential Miele customers in India than in most countries worldwide."[12]

Fisher & Paykel

With close to 3,300 employees, Fisher & Paykel, a publically listed company, was founded by Maurice Paykel and Sir Woolf Fisher in 1935.[13] Headquartered in Auckland, New Zealand, the company operated in more than 50 countries and five continents. With revenue of US$748 million in the fiscal year ending March 2012, the company had again proven its ability to impress customers.[14]

The company's competitive advantage lay in its flair for technology. In a recent takeover, Chinese appliance maker Haier had acquired more than 90 per cent of the shares of Fisher & Paykel Appliances Holdings Ltd.[15] This acquisition provided Haier with Fisher & Paykel's technological innovations in dish drawers and direct-drive washing machine motors (with a 10-year warranty).[16] The company entered the Indian retail space in December, 2011.[17]

Faber

Hoods or electrical chimneys were the only product in the company's portfolio. Established in 1955 in Fabriano, Italy, the company had grown into the coveted market leader position, with almost 50 per cent market share in the country's premium kitchen-ventilation systems in 2012.[18] The company had a presence in 13 countries across three continents, with six manufacturing facilities.

Faber managed its leading local brands such as the Spar in Argentina, Mepamsa in Spain and Roblin in France.[19] Faber entered the Indian market in 1997 as a joint venture with Heatkraft Industries Ltd.[20] Faber owned a 75 per cent stake in the Indian joint venture.[21] The company aimed to expand its global operations though organic and inorganic growth.

Sunflame

Sunflame grew to become a respectable and trusted brand among Indian consumers. Headquartered in Faridabad, India, the company planned to reposition itself from mere kitchen appliance maker to high-end equipment designer. Sunflame assured its customers dependability and quality.[22]

As a next step, Sunflame partnered with Elica Italy to introduce the latter's technologically superior product range for the Indian consumer.

Kaff

Kaff, a major built-in appliance dealer in India, imported most of their product lines from almost 40 vendors in Germany and Italy. It also had its manufacturing facility in Rajasthan, India, and in Sri Lanka. The company offered its products in four verticals: kitchen appliances, modular kitchen accessories, ventilating fans and hardware. In 2011, the company made arrangements to make refrigerators in Turkey and also planned to venture into the room air-conditioner sector.[23]

Hometown and EVOK

Hometown and EVOK were two of the leading companies in the specialty home interior business. These were the two most sought after companies when it came to building either a modular or a semi-modular kitchen.

The EVOK group was a subsidiary of Hindware Home Retail Private Ltd., which had a vision of being a total home solutions enterprise. In 2010, the company planned to invest over INR2.5 billion in the next five years to open 50 large-format stores in the country. The company catered to the needs of both business-to-business (B2B) and business-to-consumer (B2C) segments.[24]

Hometown, a subsidiary of Future Group, offered its customers an array of products and the services of skilled technicians. The company website claimed, "We provide consumers all that goes into building a house and everything to make it a 'Home', all under one roof."[25]

India's Evolving Preferences

According to a report from real estate consulting firm Knight Frank, during 2010 and 2011, 533,954 residential units were launched in the top seven cities, including Mumbai, NCR, Pune, Kolkata, Bengaluru, Chennai and Hyderabad.[26] According to the India Brand Equity Foundation report, the Indian real estate market size was expected to grow and reach US$180 billion by 2020.[27] As the market evolved and demands increased, investments and improvements in infrastructure, software, education, work force, installation, after-sales service and logistics were bound to happen. This would in turn kick off a strong cycle of profitable growth. Besides this, non-resident Indians were also looking forward to investing in real estate, owing to the dollar's appreciation in value terms in recent times.

India's GDP was expected to grow by 5.5 per cent in 2012–2013.[28] From January to March 2012, the Indian economy grew by a mere 5.3 per cent, the slowest annual quarterly growth in the last nine years. Nevertheless, India slowly picked up in the next quarter, with GDP growth rate pegged at 5.5 per cent and the economy showing other signs of recovery. Analysts averred that the 1.2 billion people in India had started moving towards a western-style consumer-spending pattern.[29] India's rapid economic growth during the past few years had set the stage for a fundamental change among the country's consumers. The burgeoning middle class, coupled with the increase in affluent customers, had pushed India into the league of countries with tech-savvy, educated customers. These customers dreamed big and were fully determined to translate their aspirations into reality, even if it meant overspending. In particular, the youth of India had become progressively inclined towards lifestyle products (see Exhibit 4).

A study by McKinsey Global Institute showed that aggregate consumer spending could more than quadruple, eventually reaching 70 trillion rupees, by 2025.[30] The increase in consumption was also supported by higher private incomes, and to a lesser extent by population growth. There were enough opportunities available as millions of new buyers would come forward to improve their lifestyles and get products to make themselves feel more comfortable, or even to change their lifestyles completely. Still, it might be too hasty to decide the kind of products or companies that might be successful in cashing in on these evolving opportunities. Total spending had risen tremendously, spreading to millions of households earning a modest income, compared to the developed world. On the other hand, bureaucratic hurdles, political blockages and shortcomings in infrastructure might cause some setbacks for those who try to exploit the source of wealth.

In Indian society, a kitchen that used to be a very small place to perform domestic chores started assuming importance as a social room and a central hub for gathering in the house. With the onset of globalization, the kitchen came a long way from being simple and small. Modern built-in appliances were being installed at a fast pace. Consumers were looking for designers who could arrange perfect marriages between furniture and appliances. Marketing expert and Future Brands CEO Santosh Desai said, "The kitchen is becoming a sign of who you are today and reflects success. These so-called ritual spaces of the home are becoming the new desire for consumers and becoming a social space for family and friends."[31]

The emerging opportunity in the built-in appliance segment was recognized by the European kitchen makers, who in turn were attracted by the huge nascent market that India offered and were making a beeline for Indian shores. Established European kitchen manufacturing companies sought partners who could interpret their brand philosophy in the right way without diluting it and who had a sound financial background.

Whirlpool's View of the Indian Market

Whirlpool has been a strong player in the refrigerator and washing machine categories in the Indian market, yet it intended to expand its market share by offering new formats, capacities and price points. Its plans included adding an additional layer of sales force and service personnel to improve focus in this principal category, followed by launching a new range of products with excellent features, aesthetics and high energy efficiency, as well as reaching out to customers with comprehensive promotional activities. Shantanu Das Gupta observed that the Indian market was clearly inclined towards better technology, while energy efficiency was a new purchasing consideration. Moreover, technology and energy efficiency, design and aesthetics were also increasingly important factors in purchasers' decision-making process. Whirlpool viewed India as a market with strong, sustained demand for home appliances. Thus, Whirlpool might intend to leverage their strong brand presence—coupled with its product-innovation

EXHIBIT 4 Per Capita Expenditure on Furniture, Furnishings and Appliances in India (In Inr)

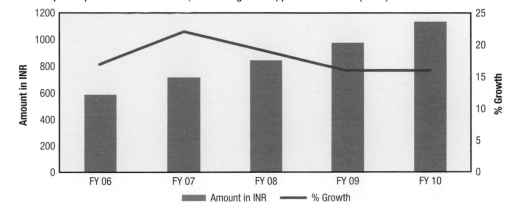

Source: Adapted from CEAMA, MOSPI, GEPL Capital Research, www.geplcapital.com/reports/ConsumerDurables_vJuly_15v1.pdf, accessed October, 2012.

capabilities, cost control and vast distribution network—to beat its competitors in the Indian market.[32]

Although, the market for high-value built-in appliances had just opened up in India, the concept of built-in products was not yet fully appreciated by the Indian consumers. Before setting foot in the market, Whirlpool had to ensure its strategies were correct, considering the market's growth. It might also be imperative for Whirlpool to tweak its product design to suit the requirements of the Indian consumers. Indian customers understood the importance of having a modular kitchen with modern appliances, though modern built-in appliances were definitely expensive, compared to those in the traditional kitchen.

Conclusion

With the current improvement trends in the industry and the scenario described above, should Whirlpool attempt to tap this emerging market? If yes, what could be the strategic objectives and the positioning strategies of Whirlpool to hold its own amidst the competition?

ENDNOTES

1. This case has been written on the basis of published sources only. Consequently, the interpretation and perspectives presented in this case are not necessarily those of Whirlpool or any of its employees.
2. "Whirlpool to Focus on Water Purifiers, Built-In Appliances," Business Standard, September 19, 2012.
3. "Whirlpool Eyes Top Slot in Home Appliances Market," The Economic Times, September 20, 2012.
4. www.whirlpoolindia.com/corp-india.php, accessed November 13, 2012.
5. "A Brief Report on Consumer Durable Industry in India," Corporate Catalyst India, March 2012.
6. "Consumer Durables November 2011,"Indian Brand Equity Foundation website, www.ibef.org/download/consumer_durables50112.pdf, accessed October 2012.
7. Whirlpool of India Limited, 2012, p. 27, www.whirlpoolindia.com/Annual%20Report_2011-12_complete.pdf, accessed October 23, 2012.
8. Ibid.
9. A flat metal shelf at the side or back of a fireplace, having its surface level with the top of the grate and used especially for heating pans.
10. "Built-In Appliance Business in India Is at a Nascent Stage: Electrolux," EFYTimes.com, April 23, 2012.
11. www.miele-presse.de/de/en/press/8412_8441.htm, accessed October 12, 2012.
12. "Our Biggest Challenge Is India's Geography: Markus Miele, MD Miele," The Economic Times, May 14, 2012.
13. www.fisherpaykel.in/global/company/parent_company.cfm, accessed October 21, 2012.
14. Ibid.
15. "Haier Obtains More Than 90% of Fisher & Paykel Shares," The Wall Street Journal, November 5, 2012.
16. www.fisherpaykel.com/customer-care/smart-drive-warranty/, accessed October 23, 2012.
17. www.indiaretailing.com/News.aspx?Topic=1&Id=6311, accessed October 5, 2012.
18. www.faberonline.com/aboutfaber.html, accessed October 15, 2012.
19. www.faberspa.com/it/en/home/azienda/azienda-faber-nel-mondo.html, accessed October 12, 2012.
20. www.faberspa.com/it/en/home/azienda/azienda-la-nostra-storia.html, accessed October 2012.
21. "Faber Spa Hikes Stake in JV to 75% to Infuse Another Rs 8 Cr," The Economic Times, January 25, 2004.
22. www.sunflame.com/Corporate.asp, accessed October 2012.
23. "KAFF Appliances to Expand," The Hindu, October 19, 2011.
24. www.evok.in/about_us.asp, accessed October 13, 2012.
25. www.pantaloonretail.in/businesses/home-town-retail-format.html, accessed October 21, 2012.
26. www.sourcinghardware.net/node/229, accessed October 19, 2012.
27. www.ibef.org/industry/realestate.aspx, accessed October 21, 2012.
28. https://www.crisilresearch.com/CuttingEdge/economyView.jspx#; accessed October 23, 2012.
29. "Slowdown Bites: Consumer Spending at 7 Yr Lows," Hindustan Times, August 7, 2012.
30. "Tracking the Growth of India's Middle Class," McKinsey Quarterly, November 2007, accessed October 2012, www.relooney.info/00_New_2016.pdf.
31. "Rich Indians Spending up to Rupees 1 Crore on Kitchens," The Economic Times, July 6, 2011.
32. www.indiainfoline.com/Research/LeaderSpeak/Mr.-Shantanu-Das-Gupta-Vice-President-Corporate-Affairs-and-Strategy-Asia-South-Whirlpool-of-India/7100401, accessed June 5, 2013.

CASE 8

THE BEST-LAID INCENTIVE PLANS*

Hiram Phillips finished tying his bow tie and glanced in the mirror. Frowning, he tugged on the left side, then caught sight of his watch in the mirror. Time to get going. Moments later, he was down the stairs, whistling cheerfully and heading toward the coffeemaker.

"You're in a good mood," his wife said, looking up from the newspaper and smiling. "What's that tune? 'Accentuate the Positive'?"

"Well done!" Hiram called out. "You know, I do believe you're picking up some pop culture in spite of yourself." It was a running joke with them. She was a classically trained cellist and on the board of the local symphony. He was the one with the Sinatra and Bing Crosby albums and the taste for standards. "You're getting better at naming that tune."

"Or else you're getting better at whistling." She looked over her reading glasses and met his eye. They let a beat pass before they said in unison: "Naaah." Then, with a wink, Hiram shrugged on his trench coat, grabbed his travel mug, and went out the door.

Fat and Happy

It was true. Hiram Phillips, CFO and chief administrative officer of Rainbarrel Products, a diversified consumer-durables manufacturer, was in a particularly good mood. He was heading into a breakfast meeting that would bring nothing but good news. Sally Hamilton and Frank Ormondy from Felding & Company would no doubt already be at the office when he arrived and would have with them the all-important numbers—the statistics that would demonstrate the positive results of the performance management system he'd put in place a year ago. Hiram had already seen many of the figures in bits and pieces. He'd retained the consultants to establish baselines on the metrics he wanted to watch and had seen various interim reports from them since. But today's meeting would be the impressive summation capping off a year's worth of effort. Merging into the congestion of Route 45, he thought about the upbeat presentation he would spend the rest of

Harvard Business Review's cases, which are fictional, present common managerial dilemmas and offer concrete solutions from experts.

* Steven Kerr is the chief learning officer at Goldman Sachs in New York. Prior to joining Goldman Sachs in 2001, he spent seven years as the chief learning officer and head of leadership development at General Electric. He was responsible for GE's leadership development center at Crotonville.

the morning preparing for tomorrow's meeting of the corporate executive council.

It was obvious enough what his introduction should be. He would start at the beginning—or, anyway, his own beginning at Rainbarrel Products a year ago. At the time, the company had just come off a couple of awful quarters. It wasn't alone. The sudden slowdown in consumer spending, after a decade-long boom, had taken the whole industry by surprise. But what had quickly become clear was that Rainbarrel was adjusting to the new reality far less rapidly than its biggest competitors.

Keith Randall, CEO of Rainbarrel, was known for being an inspiring leader who focused on innovation. Even outside the industry, he had a name as a marketing visionary. But over the course of the ten-year economic boom, he had allowed his organization to become a little lax.

Take corporate budgeting. Hiram still smiled when he recalled his first day of interviews with Rainbarrel's executives. It immediately became obvious that the place had no budget integrity whatsoever. One unit head had said outright, "Look, none of us fights very hard at budget time, because after three or four months, nobody looks at the budget anyway." Barely concealing his shock, Hiram asked how that could be; what did they look at, then? The answer was that they operated according to one simple rule: "If it's a good idea, we say yes to it. If it's a bad idea, we say no."

"And what happens," Hiram had pressed, "when you run out of money halfway through the year?" The fellow rubbed his chin and took a moment to think before answering. "I guess we've always run out of good ideas before we've run out of money." Unbelievable!

"Fat and happy" was how Hiram characterized Rainbarrel in a conversation with the headhunter who had recruited him. Of course, he wouldn't use those words in the CEC meeting. That would sound too disparaging. In fact, he'd quickly fallen in love with Rainbarrel and the opportunities it presented. Here was a company that had the potential for greatness but that was held back by a lack of discipline. It was like a racehorse that had the potential to be a Secretariat but lacked a structured training regimen. Or a Ferrari engine that needed the touch of an expert mechanic to get it back in trim. In other words, the only thing Rainbarrel was missing was what someone like Hiram Phillips could bring to the table. The allure was irresistible; this was the assignment that would define his career. And now, a year later, he was ready to declare a turnaround.

Lean and Mean

Sure enough, as Hiram steered toward the entrance to the parking garage, he saw Sally and Frank in a visitor parking space, pulling their bulky file bags out of the trunk of Sally's sedan. He caught up to them at the security checkpoint in the lobby and took a heavy satchel from Sally's hand.

Moments later, they were at a conference table, each of them poring over a copy of the consultants' spiral-bound report. "This is great," Hiram said. "I can hand this out just as it is. But what I want to do while you're here is to really nail down what the highlights are. I have the floor for 40 minutes, but I guess I'd better leave ten for questions. There's no way I can plow through all of this."

"If I were you," Sally advised, "I would lead off with the best numbers. I mean, none of them are bad. You hit practically every target. But some of these, where you even exceeded the stretch goal. . . ."

Hiram glanced at the line Sally was underscoring with her fingernail. It was an impressive achievement: a reduction in labor costs. This had been one of the first moves he'd made, and he'd tried to do it gently. He'd come up with the idea of identifying the bottom quartile of performers throughout the company and offering them fairly generous buyout packages. But when that hadn't attracted enough takers, he'd gone the surer route. He'd imposed an across-the-board headcount reduction of 10% on all the units. In that round, the affected people were given no financial assistance beyond the normal severance.

"It made a big difference," he nodded. "But it wasn't exactly the world's most popular move." Hiram was well aware that a certain segment of the Rainbarrel workforce currently referred to him as "Fire 'em." He pointed to another number on the spreadsheet. "Now, that one tells a happier story: lower costs as a result of higher productivity."

"And better customer service to boot," Frank chimed in. They were talking about the transformation of Rainbarrel's call center—where phone representatives took orders and handled questions and complaints from both trade and retail customers. The spreadsheet indicated a dramatic uptick in productivity: The number of calls each service rep was handling per day had gone up 50%. A year earlier, reps were spending up to six minutes per call, whereas now the average was less than four minutes. "I guess you decided to go for that new automated switching system?" Frank asked.

"No!" Hiram answered. "That's the beauty of it. We got that improvement without any capital investment. You know what we did? We just announced the new targets, let everyone know we were going to monitor them, and put the names of the worst offenders on a great big 'wall of shame' right outside the cafeteria. Never underestimate the power of peer pressure!"

Sally, meanwhile, was already circling another banner achievement: an increase in on-time shipments. "You should talk about this, given that it's something that wasn't even being watched before you came."

It was true. As much as Rainbarrel liked to emphasize customer service in its values and mission statement, no reliable metric had been in place to track it. And getting a metric in place hadn't been as straightforward as it might've seemed—people had haggled about what constituted "on time" and even what constituted "shipped." Finally, Hiram had put his foot down and insisted on the most objective of measures. On time meant when the goods were promised to ship. And nothing was counted as shipped till it left company property. Period. "And once again," Hiram announced, "not a dollar of capital expenditure. I simply let people know that, from now on, if they made commitments and didn't keep them, we'd have their number."

"Seems to have done the trick," Sally observed. "The percentage of goods shipped by promise date has gone up steadily for the last six months. It's now at 92%."

Scanning the report, Hiram noticed another huge percentage gain, but he couldn't recall what the acronym stood for. "What's this? Looks like a good one: a 50% cost reduction?"

Sally studied the item. "Oh, that. It's a pretty small change, actually. Remember we separated out the commissions on sales to employees?" It came back to Hiram immediately. Rainbarrel had a policy that allowed current and retired employees to buy products at a substantial discount. But the salespeople who served them earned commissions based on the full retail value, not the actual price paid. So, in effect, employee purchases were jacking up the commission expenses. Hiram had created a new policy in which the commission reflected the actual purchase price. On its own, the change didn't amount to a lot, but it reminded Hiram of a larger point he wanted to make in his presentation: the importance of straightforward rules—and rewards—in driving superior performance.

"I know you guys don't have impact data for me, but I'm definitely going to talk about the changes to the commission structure and sales incentives. There's no question they must be making a difference."

"Right," Sally nodded. "A classic case of 'keep it simple,' isn't it?" She turned to Frank to explain. "The old way they calculated commissions was by using this really complicated formula that factored in, I can't remember, at least five different things."

"Including sales, I hope?" Frank smirked.

"I'm still not sure!" Hiram answered. "No, seriously, sales were the most important single variable, but they also mixed in all kinds of targets around mentoring, prospecting new clients, even keeping the account information current. It was all way too subjective, and salespeople were getting very mixed signals. I just clarified the message so they don't have to wonder what they're getting paid for. Same with the sales contests. It's simple now: If you sell the most product in a given quarter, you win."

With Sally and Frank nodding enthusiastically, Hiram again looked down at the report. Row after row of numbers attested to Rainbarrel's improved performance. It wouldn't be easy to choose the rest of the highlights, but what a problem to have! He invited the consultants to weigh in again and leaned back to bask in the superlatives. And his smile grew wider.

Cause for Concern

The next morning, a well-rested Hiram Phillips strode into the building, flashed his ID badge at Charlie, the guard, and joined the throng in the lobby. In the crowd waiting for the elevator, he recognized two young women from Rainbarrel, lattes in hand and headphones around their necks. One was grimacing melodramatically as she turned to her friend. "I'm so dreading getting to my desk," she said. "Right when I was leaving last night, an e-mail showed up from the buyer at Sullivan. I just know it's going to be some big, hairy problem to sort out. I couldn't bring myself to open it, with the day I'd had. But I'm going to be sweating it today trying to respond by five o'clock. I can't rack up any more late responses, or my bonus is seriously history."

Her friend had slung her backpack onto the floor and was rooting through it, barely listening. But she glanced up to set her friend straight in the most casual way. "No, see, all they check is whether you responded to an e-mail within 24 hours of opening it. So that's the key. Just don't open it. You know, till you've got time to deal with it."

Then a belltone announced the arrival of the elevator, and they were gone.

More Cause for Concern

An hour later, Keith Randall was calling to order the quarterly meeting of the corporate executive council. First, he said, the group would hear the results of the annual employee survey, courtesy of human resources VP Lew Hart. Next would come a demonstration by the chief marketing officer of a practice the CEO hoped to incorporate into all future meetings. It was a "quick market intelligence," or QMI, scan, engaging a few of Rainbarrel's valued customers in a prearranged—but not predigested—conference call, to collect raw data on customer service concerns and ideas. "And finally," Keith concluded, "Hiram's going to give us some very good news about cost reductions and operating efficiencies, all due to the changes he's designed and implemented this past year."

Hiram nodded to acknowledge the compliment. He heard little of the next ten minutes' proceedings, thinking instead about how he should phrase certain points for maximum effect. Lew Hart had lost him in the first moments of his presentation on the "people survey" by beginning with an overview of "purpose, methodology, and historical trends." Deadly.

It was the phrase "mindlessly counting patents" that finally turned Hiram's attention back to his colleague. Lew, it seemed, was now into the "findings" section of his remarks. Hiram pieced together that he was reporting on

an unprecedented level of negativity in the responses from Rainbarrel's R&D department and was quoting the complaints people had scribbled on their surveys. "Another one put it this way," Lew said. "We're now highly focused on who's getting the most patents, who's getting the most copyrights, who's submitting the most grant proposals, etc. But are we more creative? It's not that simple."

"You know," Rainbarrel's chief counsel noted, "I have thought lately that we're filing for a lot of patents for products that will never be commercially viable."

"But the thing that's really got these guys frustrated seems to be their 'Innovation X' project," Lew continued. "They're all saying it's the best thing since sliced bread, a generational leap on the product line, but they're getting no uptake."

Eyes in the room turned to the products division president, who promptly threw up his hands. "What can I say, gang? We never expected that breakthrough to happen in this fiscal year. It's not in the budget to bring it to market."

Lew Hart silenced the rising voices, reminding the group he had more findings to share. Unfortunately, it didn't get much better. Both current and retired employees were complaining about being treated poorly by sales personnel when they sought to place orders or obtain information about company products. There was a lot of residual unhappiness about the layoffs, and not simply because those who remained had more work to do. Some people had noted that, because the reduction was based on headcount, not costs, managers had tended to fire low-level people, crippling the company without saving much money. And because the reduction was across the board, the highest performing departments had been forced to lay off some of the company's best employees. Others had heard about inequities in the severance deals: "As far as I can tell, we gave our lowest performers a better package than our good ones," he quoted one employee as saying.

And then there was a chorus of complaints from the sales organization. "No role models." "No mentoring." "No chance to pick the veterans' brains." "No knowledge sharing about accounts." More than ever, salespeople were dissatisfied with their territories and clamoring for the more affluent, high-volume districts. "It didn't help that all the sales-contest winners this year were from places like Scarsdale, Shaker Heights, and Beverly Hills," a salesperson was quoted as saying. Lew concluded with a promise to look further into the apparent decline in morale to determine whether it was an aberration.

The Ugly Truth

But if the group thought the mood would improve in the meeting's next segment—the QMI chat with the folks at longtime customer Brenton Brothers—they soon found out otherwise. Booming out of the speakerphone in the middle of the table came the Southern-tinged voices of Billy Brenton and three of his employees representing various parts of his organization.

"What's up with your shipping department?" Billy called out. "My people are telling me it's taking forever to get the stock replenished."

Hiram sat up straight, then leaned toward the speakerphone. "Excuse me, Mr. Brenton. This is Hiram Phillips—I don't believe we've met. But are you saying we are not shipping by our promise date?"

A cough—or was it a guffaw?—came back across the wire. "Well, son. Let me tell you about that. First of all, what y'all promise is not always what we are saying we require—and what we believe we deserve. Annie, isn't that right?"

"Yes, Mr. Brenton," said the buyer. "In some cases, I've been told to take a late date or otherwise forgo the purchase. That becomes the promise date, I guess, but it's not the date I asked for."

"And second," Billy continued, "I can't figure out how you fellas define 'shipped.' We were told last Tuesday an order had been shipped, and come to find out, the stuff was sitting on a railroad siding across the street from your plant."

"That's an important order for us," another Brenton voice piped up. "I sent an e-mail to try to sort it out, but I haven't heard back about it." Hiram winced, recalling the conversation in the lobby that morning. The voice persisted: "I thought that might be the better way to contact your service people these days? They always seem in such an all-fired hurry to get off the phone when I call. Sometimes it takes two or three calls to get something squared away."

The call didn't end there—a few more shortcomings were discussed. Then Keith Randall, to his credit, pulled the conversation onto more positive ground by reaffirming the great regard Rainbarrel had for Brenton Brothers and the mutual value of that enduring relationship. Promises were made and hearty thanks extended for the frank feedback. Meanwhile, Hiram felt the eyes of his colleagues on him. Finally, the call ended and the CEO announced that he, for one, needed a break before the last agenda item.

Dazed and Confused

Hiram considered following his boss out of the room and asking him to table the whole discussion of the new metrics and incentives. The climate was suddenly bad for the news he had looked forward to sharing. But he knew that delaying the discussion would be weak and wrong. After all, he had plenty of evidence to show he was on the right track. The problems the group had just been hearing about were side effects, but surely they didn't outweigh the cure.

He moved to the side table and poured a glass of ice water, then leaned against the wall to collect his thoughts. Perhaps he should reframe his opening comments in light of the employee and customer feedback. As he considered how he might do so, Keith Randall appeared at his side.

"Looks like we have our work cut out for us, eh, Hiram?" he said quietly—and charitably enough. "Some of those metrics taking hold, um, a little too strongly?" Hiram started to object but saw the seriousness in his boss's eyes.

He lifted the stack of reports Felding & Company had prepared for him and turned to the conference table. "Well, I guess that's something for the group to talk about."

Should Rainbarrel revisit its approach to performance management?

CASE 9

JOHNSON & JOHNSON*

Information presented on January 25, 2013, during an ongoing trial, revealed that executives from health care conglomerate Johnson & Johnson had known about a critical design flaw with an artificial hip but decided to conceal this information from physicians and patients. Johnson & Johnson's DePuy Orthopaedics unit kept selling the hip replacement, called the Articular Surface Replacement, although its design flaw caused it to shed large quantities of metallic debris after implantation. The firm finally recalled the unit in 2010, almost five years after problems had begun to surface. Johnson & Johnson may now face more than 10,000 lawsuits in the U.S. as a result of one of the largest medical failures in recent history.

The problems with the artificial hip represented yet another problem for Johnson & Johnson, which has struggled to emerge from a swarm of product recalls, manufacturing lapses, and government inquiries that have tarnished the name of one of the nation's most trusted brands.

*Case developed by Professor Jamal Shamsie, Michigan State University, with the assistance of Professor Alan B. Eisner, Pace University. Material has been drawn from published sources to be used for purposes of class discussion. Copyright © 2013 Jamal Shamsie and Alan B. Eisner.

Serious problems surfaced a couple of years ago at McNeil Consumer Healthcare, which has had to recall many of its products—including the biggest children's drug recall of all time—that were potentially contaminated with dark particles. The Food and Drug Administration also slapped one of McNeil's plants with a scalding inspection report, causing the company to close down the factory to bring it up to federal standards.

Much of the blame for Johnson & Johnson's stumbles fell on William C. Weldon, who stepped down as CEO in April 2012 after presiding over one of the most tumultuous decades in the firm's history (See Exhibits 1 and 2). Critics said the company's once vaunted attention to quality had slipped under his watch. Weldon, who had started out as a sales representative at the firm, was believed to have been obsessed with meeting tough performance targets, even by cutting costs that might affect quality. Erik Gordon, who teaches business at the University of Michigan, elaborated on this philosophy: "We will make our numbers for the analysts, period."[1]

Weldon was replaced by Alex Gorsky, who had headed the medical devices and diagnostics unit. The division generates the largest amount of sales for

EXHIBIT 1
Income
Statement*

Go to library tab in
Connect to access
Case Financials.

	A	B	C	D
1	Income Statement*			
2			Year Ending	
3		Dec. 30, 2012	Dec. 31, 2011	Jan. 1, 2011
4	Total Revenue	67,224	65,030	61,587
5	Cost of Revenue	21,658	20,360	18,792
6	Gross Profit	45,566	44,670	42,795
7	Operating Expenses			
8	Research & development	7,665	7,548	6,844
9	Selling, general, and administrative	20,869	20,969	19,424
10	Nonrecurring	1,163	569	–
11	Operating Income or Loss	15,869	15,584	16,527
12	Income from Continuing Operations			
13	Total other income/expenses net	(1,562)	(2,652)	875
14	Earnings before interest and taxes	14,307	12,932	17,402
15	Interest expense	532	571	455
16	Income before tax	13,775	12,361	16,947
17	Income tax expense	3,261	2,689	3,613
18	Minority interest	339	–	–
19	Net Income	10,853	9,672	13,334
20	Net Income Applicable to Common Shares	10,853	9,672	13,334

*Figures in millions of dollars.

Source: *finance.yahoo.com.*

EXHIBIT 2
Balance Sheets*

Go to library tab in Connect to access Case Financials.

	A	B	C	D
1	**Balance Sheets***			
2			Year Ending	
3		Dec. 30, 2012	Dec. 31, 2011	Jan. 1, 2011
4	Assets			
5	Current Assets			
6	Cash and cash equivalents	14,911	24,542	19,355
7	Short-term investments	6,178	7,719	8,303
8	Net receivables	14,448	13,137	11,998
9	Inventory	7,495	6,285	5,378
10	Other current assets	3,084	2,633	2,273
11	**Total Current Assets**	**46,116**	**54,316**	**47,307**
12	Property plant and equipment	16,097	14,739	14,553
13	Goodwill	22,424	16,138	15,294
14	Intangible assets	28,752	18,138	16,716
15	Other assets	3,417	3,773	3,942
16	Deferred long-term asset charges	4,541	6,540	5,096
17	**Total Assets**	**121,347**	**113,644**	**102,908**
18	Liabilities			
19	Current liabilities			
20	Accounts payable	19,586	16,153	15,455
21	Short/current long-term debt	4,676	6,658	7,617
22	**Total Current Liabilities**	**24,262**	**22,811**	**23,072**
23	Long-term debt	11,489	12,969	9,156
24	Other liabilities	17,634	18,984	12,654
25	Deferred long-term liability charges	3,136	1,800	1,447
26	**Total Liabilities**	**56,521**	**56,564**	**46,329**
27	Stockholders' Equity			
28	Common stock	3,120	3,120	3,120
29	Retained earnings	85,992	81,251	77,773
30	Treasury stock	(18,476)	(21,659)	(20,783)
31	Other stockholder equity	(5,810)	(5,632)	(3,531)
32	**Total Stockholder Equity**	**64,826**	**57,080**	**56,579**
33	**Net Tangible Assets**	**13,650**	**22,804**	**24,569**

*Figures in millions of dollars.

Source: *finance.yahoo.com.*

Johnson & Johnson and is expected to grow further with the acquisition in 2012 of Synthes, a Swiss-American medical-device maker. Like his predecessor, Gorsky worked his way up by meeting tough performance targets as a sales representative and continues the firm's 126-year tradition of hiring leaders from within. "The future of Johnson & Johnson is in very capable hands," said Weldon.[2]

At the same time, the decision to hire another insider may indicate that Johnson & Johnson was not serious about changing the corporate culture that had created so many of its recent problems. "As somebody steeped in J.&J. culture, I would be very surprised to see big changes," said Les Funtleyder, a portfolio manager at a firm that owns the firm's stock. Furthermore, even if Gorsky attempted to make changes that would address the growing list of problems, it would be a daunting task. "It's so big that it would take a very long time to move a big battleship like that," added Funtleyder.[3]

Cultivating Entrepreneurship

Johnson & Johnson has relied heavily upon acquisitions to enter and to expand in a wide range of businesses that fall broadly under the category of health care. It has purchased more than 70 different firms over the past decade. In 2008 it paid $1.1 billion to acquire Mentor Corporation, a leading supplier of products for the global aesthetic market. It topped this last year with a $20 billion purchase of Synthes, a leading player in trauma surgery. A person familiar with the industry remarked that this latest acquisition of a maker of orthopedic devices was "a good match for them."[4]

As it has grown, Johnson & Johnson has developed into an astonishingly complex enterprise, made up of over 250 different businesses that have been broken down into three different divisions. The most widely known of these is the division that makes consumer products, such as *Johnson & Johnson* baby care products, *Band-Aid* adhesive strips, and *Visine* eye drops. The division grew substantially after J&J acquired the consumer health unit of Pfizer in 2006 for $16.6 billion, the biggest in its 120-year history. The acquisition allowed the firm to add well-known products to its line up such as *Listerine* mouthwash and *Benadryl* cough syrup.

But Johnson & Johnson has reaped far more sales and profits from its other two divisions. Its pharmaceuticals division sells several blockbuster drugs, such as anemia drug *Procit* and schizophrenia drug *Risperdal*. A new drug, named *Zytiga*, prescribed to treat prostate cancer has been selling well. Its medical devices division is responsible for best-selling products such as *Depuy* orthopedic joint replacements and *Cyper* coronary stents. These two divisions tend to generate operating profit margins of around 30 percent, almost double those generated by the consumer business.

To a large extent, however, Johnson & Johnson's success across its three divisions and many different businesses has hinged on its unique structure and culture. Most of its far-flung business units were acquired because of the potential demonstrated by some promising new products in its pipeline. Each of these units was therefore granted near-total autonomy to develop and expand upon their best-selling products (See Exhibit 3). That independence has fostered an entrepreneurial attitude that has kept J&J intensely competitive as others around it have faltered. The relative autonomy that is accorded to the business units has also provided the firm with the ability to respond swiftly to emerging opportunities.

Johnson & Johnson has been quite proud of the considerable freedom that it has given to its different business units to develop and execute their own strategies. Besides developing their strategies, these units have also been allowed to work with their own resources. Many of the businesses even have their own finance and human resources departments. While this degree of decentralization has led to relatively high overhead costs, none of the executives that have run J&J, Weldon included, had ever thought that this was too high a price to pay. "J&J is a huge company, but you didn't feel like you were in a big company," recalled a scientist who used to work there.[5]

Pushing for More Collaboration

The entrepreneurial culture that Johnson & Johnson has developed over the years has allowed it to be successful with its various businesses. Indeed, Johnson & Johnson has top-notch products in each of the areas in which it operates (see Exhibit 4). It has been spending heavily on research and development for many years, taking its position among the world's top spenders (see Exhibit 5). It currently spends about 12 percent of its sales on about 9,000 scientists working in research laboratories around the world. This allows each of the three divisions to continually introduce promising new products.

In spite of the benefits that Johnson & Johnson has derived from giving its various enterprises considerable autonomy, there have been growing concerns that they can

no longer be allowed to operate in near isolation. Weldon had begun to realize that J&J is in a strong position to exploit new opportunities by drawing on the diverse skills of its various business units across the three divisions. In particular, he was aware that his firm could benefit from the combination of its knowledge in drugs, devices, and diagnostics, since few companies were able to match its reach and strength in these basic areas.

This required him to find ways to make its fiercely independent businesses work together. In his own words: "There is a convergence that will allow us to do things we haven't done before."[6] Through pushing the various far-flung units of the firm to pool their resources, Weldon believed that the firm could become one of the few that may actually be able to attain that often-promised, rarely delivered idea of synergy. He created a corporate office that would get business units to work together on promising new opportunities. "It's a recognition that there's a way to treat disease that's not in silos," Weldon stated, referring to the need for collaboration between J&J's largely independent businesses.[7]

For the most part, Weldon confined himself to fostering better communication and more frequent collaboration among Johnson & Johnson's disparate operations. But the company had to take care that these attempts to achieve synergy through collaboration among the business units did not quash the entrepreneurial spirit that has spearheaded most of the firm's growth to date. Jerry Caccott, managing director of consulting firm Strategic Decisions Group, emphasized that cultivating those alliances "would be challenging in any organization, but particularly in an organization that has been so successful because of its decentralized culture."[8]

These collaborative efforts have led to the introduction of some highly successful products. Even the company's fabled consumer brands have been starting to show growth as a result of increased collaboration between the consumer products and pharmaceutical divisions. Its new liquid *Band-Aid* is based on a material used in a wound-closing product sold by one of J&J's hospital-supply businesses. And J&J has used its prescription antifungal treatment, *Nizoral*, to develop a dandruff shampoo. In fact, products that have developed in large part out of such a form of cross-fertilization have allowed the firm's consumer business to experience considerable internal growth.

Confronting Quality Issues

Even as Johnson & Johnson has been trying to get more involved with the efforts of its business units, it ran into problems with quality control with several over-the-counter drugs made by McNeil Consumer Healthcare. Since 2008, FDA inspectors have found significant violations of manufacturing standards at two McNeil plants, leading to the temporary closure of one of these. These problems have forced the firm to make several recalls of some of its best-selling products. Weldon admitted that problems

EXHIBIT 3 Sales and Profits by Segment and Region*

Johnson & Johnson is made up of over 250 different companies. These individual companies have been assigned to three different divisions: Consumer, Pharmaceutical, and Medical Devices and Diagnostics.

Go to library tab in Connect to access Case Financials.

	A	B	C	D
1	Sales and Profits by Segment and Region*			
2		Sales to Customers		
3		2012	2011	2010
4	Consumer –			
5	United States	$ 5,046	5,151	5,519
6	International	9,401	9,732	9,071
7	Total	14,447	14,883	14,590
8	Pharmaceutical –			
9	United States	12,421	12,386	12,519
10	International	12,930	11,982	9,877
11	Total	25,351	24,368	22,396
12	Medical Devices and Diagnostics –			
13	United States	12,363	11,371	11,412
14	International	15,063	14,408	13,189
15	Total	27,426	25,779	24,601
16	Worldwide total	$ 67,224	65,030	61,587
17		Pre-Tax Profit		
18		2012	2011	2010
19	Consumer	$ 1,693	2,096	2,342
20	Pharmaceutical	6,075	6,406	7,086
21	Medical Devices and Diagnostics	7,187	5,263	8,272
22	Total	14,955	13,765	17,700
23	Less: Expanse not allocated to Segments	1,180	1,404	753
24	Worldwide total	$ 13,775	12,361	16,947

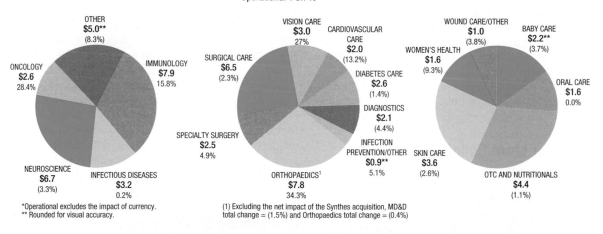

Pharmaceutical Segment Sales
Sales by Therapeutic Area (in billions of dollars)
2012 Sales: $25.4 billion
Sales Change:
    Total: 4.0%
    Operational*: 6.8%

OTHER $5.0** (8.3%)
ONCOLOGY $2.6 28.4%
IMMUNOLOGY $7.9 15.8%
NEUROSCIENCE $6.7 (3.3%)
INFECTIOUS DISEASES $3.2 0.2%

*Operational excludes the impact of currency.
** Rounded for visual accuracy.

Medical Devices and Diagnostics Segment Sales
Sales by Major Franchise (in billions of dollars)
2012 Sales: $27.4 billion
Sales Change:[1]
    Total: 6.4%
    Operational*: 8.7%

VISION CARE $3.0 27%
CARDIOVASCULAR CARE $2.0 (13.2%)
SURGICAL CARE $6.5 (2.3%)
DIABETES CARE $2.6 (1.4%)
DIAGNOSTICS $2.1 (4.4%)
SPECIALTY SURGERY $2.5 4.9%
INFECTION PREVENTION/OTHER $0.9** 5.1%
ORTHOPAEDICS[1] $7.8 34.3%

(1) Excluding the net impact of the Synthes acquisition, MD&D total change = (1.5%) and Orthopaedics total change = (0.4%)

Consumer Segment Sales
Sales by Major Franchise (in billions of dollars)
2012 Sales: $14.4 billion
Sales Change:
    Total: (2.9%)
    Operational*: 0.5%

WOUND CARE/OTHER $1.0 (3.8%)
BABY CARE $2.2** (3.7%)
WOMEN'S HEALTH $1.6 (9.3%)
ORAL CARE $1.6 0.0%
SKIN CARE $3.6 (2.6%)
OTC AND NUTRITIONALS $4.4 (1.1%)

*Figures in millions of dollars.

Source: Johnson & Johnson.

had surfaced, but he insisted that these were confined to McNeil. In a recent interview he stated, "This is one of the most difficult situations I've ever had to personally deal with. It hits at the core of who J&J is. Our first responsibility is to the people who use our products. We've let them down."[9]

Quality problems have arisen before, but they were usually fixed on a regular basis. Analysts suggest that the problems at McNeil may have been exacerbated in 2006 when J&J decided to combine it with the newly acquired consumer health care unit from Pfizer. The firm believed that it could achieve $500 to $600 million in annual savings

EXHIBIT 4 Key Brands

PHARMACEUTICALS

RISPERDAL for schizophrenia

PROCRIT for anemia

REMICADE for rheumatoid arthritis

TOPAMIX for epilepsy

DURAGESIC for chronic pain

DOXIL for ovarian cancer

HALDOL for psychosis

NATRECOR for heart failure

ELMIRON for bladder pain

MEDICAL DEVICES

DEPUY orthopedic joint reconstruction products

CORDIS CYPHER stents

ETHICON surgery products

LIFESCAN diabetic testing products

VERIDEX diagnostic devices

ANIMAS insulin pumps

ACUVUE contact lenses

CONSUMER PRODUCTS

BAND AID bandages

JOHNSON & JOHNSON baby care products

NEUTROGENA skin and hair care products

LISTERINE oral health care

TYLENOL pain killers

ROLAIDS antacids

BENADRYL cold and cough syrups

BEN GAY pain relief ointments

TUCK'S hemorrhoidal ointments

VISINE eye drops

ROGAINE hair regrowth treatments

STAY FREE women's health products

SPLENDA sweeteners

Source: Johnson & Johnson.

EXHIBIT 5 Research Expenditures*

Go to library tab in Connect to access Case Financials.

	A	B
1	**Research Expenditures***	
2	2012	$ 7,665
3	2011	7,548
4	2010	6,844
5	2009	6,986
6	2008	7,577
7	2007	7,680
8	2006	7,125
9	2005	6,462

*Figures in millions of dollars.

Source: Johnson & Johnson.

by merging the two units. After the merger, McNeil was also transferred from the heavily regulated pharmaceutical division to the marketing-driven consumer products division, headed by Collen Goggins. Because these consumer executives lacked pharmaceutical experience, they began to demand several changes at McNeil that led to a reduced emphasis on quality control.

Weldon was aware of the threat faced by Johnson & Johnson as a result of its problems with quality. He was especially concerned about the allegation by the FDA that the firm initially tried to hide the problems that it found with Motrin in 2009, hiring a contractor to quietly go around from store to store, buying all of the packets off the shelves. McNeil's conduct surrounding the recalls led to an inquiry by both the House Committee on Oversight and Investigations and by the FDA's office of criminal investigations.

Various changes were made at McNeil to resolve these quality issues. Goggins was pushed out of her post as senior executive in charge of all consumer businesses. Weldon allocated more than $100 million to upgrade McNeil's plants and equipment, appoint new manufacturing executives, and hire a third-party consulting firm to improve procedures and systems. Bonnie Jacobs, a McNeil spokeswoman, wrote in a recent email, "We will invest the necessary resources and make whatever changes are needed to do so, and we will take the time to do it right."[10]

The problems at McNeil, coupled with growing problems with its artificial hips and contact lenses, led Johnson & Johnson to make changes to its corporate oversight of its supply chain and manufacturing. In August 2010, the firm appointed Ajit Shetty, a longtime executive, to oversee a new system of companywide quality control that involves a single framework for quality across all of the operating units and a new reporting system. The need for these changes was highlighted by Erik Gordon, a professor at the Ross School of Business at the University of Michigan: "Nothing is more valuable to Johnson & Johnson than the brand bond of trust with consumers."[11]

Addressing New Problems

In April 2013, Johnson & Johnson appointed Alex Gorsky to lead the health care conglomerate out of the difficulties that it has faced over the past few years. He had been with the firm since 1988, holding positions in its pharmaceutical businesses across Europe, Africa, and the Middle East before leaving for a few years to work at Novartis. Shortly after his return to Johnson & Johnson in 2008, he took over its medical device and diagnostic group. Because of his extensive background with the firm, and with the division that was being investigated about its faulty hip replacements, Gorsky might have been regarded as the ideal person to take over the job.

When he took over, DePuy, the firm's orthopedic unit was already running into trouble with its newest artificial hip. It was facing resistance from the Food and Drug Administration even as complaints about the device were mounting from doctors and regulators around the world. Gorsky moved quickly to phase out the defective hip replacements, although he did not publicly disclose the problems that it had been experiencing with the FDA over the sale of these. The decision not to publicize the agency's findings to doctors, patients, and others while continuing to market the device has exposed Johnson & Johnson to the lawsuits that can tarnish its reputation.

DePuy finally recalled the artificial hip in August 2010, amid growing concerns about its failure among those who had received the implant. Until then, however, executives from the firm had repeatedly insisted that the device was safe. Gorsky continued to state publicly that Johnson & Johnson had decided to drop it because of declining sales rather than out of safety concerns. Andrew Ekdahl, the president of DePuy, recently reiterated that position. "This was purely a business decision," he said.[12]

In the trial in Los Angeles Superior Court regarding the defective hip replacement, however, Michael A. Kelly, the lawyer making the case against Johnson & Johnson, suggested that company executives might have concealed information out of concern for firm profits. DePuy officials, for example, never told doctors that the device had failed an internal performance test. "They changed the test and tested it against other things until they found one it could beat," he stated.[13]

In spite of all these issues, Johnson & Johnson has not attempted to clarify what information Gorsky may have had about the problems associated with the artificial hip. Under these circumstances, his promotion to lead the firm surprised Dr. Robert Hauser, a cardiologist and an advocate for improved safety of medical devices. "He's been overseeing one of the major J.&J. quality issues and the board of J.&J. sees fit to name him the new C.E.O.?" he questioned.[14]

Is There a Cure Ahead?

Moving forward, Gorsky must try to maintain a balance at Johnson & Johnson between the controls throughout the firm that are necessary to protect its reputation and the freedom for the business units that can allow it to keep growing. Quality problems have persisted, as the firm announced in early 2012 that it would recall about a half-million bottles of liquid Infants' Tylenol because of a faulty dosing system. Additionally, McNeil is still working with the FDA to bring the plant that was the source of many of the over-the-counter recalls up to federal standards.

In order to repair the damage to its consumer brands from the recalls, Johnson & Johnson recently announced that it would remove a host of potentially harmful chemicals, like formaldehyde, from its line of consumer products by the end of 2015. It is the first major consumer products company to make such a widespread commitment. "We've never really seen a major personal care product company take the kind of move that they are taking with this," said Kenneth A. Cook, president of the Environmental Working Group.[15]

Even as its DePuy unit is trying to recover from its problems with the faulty artificial hips, Johnson & Johnson is completing its biggest ever acquisition that would reinvigorate its device business. Its $20 billion purchase of Synthes would make the firm a dominant player in a major segment of the medical device market. Synthes, a maker of equipment used in trauma surgery, accounts for nearly 50 percent of sales of plates and screws that are used to treat broken bones. The $5.5 billion trauma category grew 8 percent last year, according to estimates by Wells Fargo Securities.

Even as he tries to provide more direction and assert more control, Gorksy is also aware that much of its success has resulted from the relative autonomy that Johnson & Johnson has granted to each of its business units. Like others before him, Gorsky knows that even as he pushes for more control and direction, he does not want to threaten the entrepreneurial spirit that has served his firm so well. But he must also decide how much to push on its business units to try to work more closely together than they have done in the past. Johnson & Johnson must be able to tap into many more opportunities when it tries to bring together the various skills that it has managed to develop across different divisions.

But it is clear that the health care giant has to rethink the process by which it manages its diversified portfolio of companies in order to ensure that there are no further threats to its reputation. "This is a company that was purer than Caesar's wife, this was the gold standard, and all of a sudden it just seems like things are breaking down," said William Trombetta, a professor of pharmaceutical marketing at Saint Joseph's University in Philadephia.[16]

ENDNOTES

1. Thomas, K. 2012. J.&J.'s next chief is steeped in sales culture. *New York Times,* February 24: B6.
2. Thomas, K., & Abelson, R. 2012. J.&J. chief to resign one role. *New York Times,* February 22: B8.
3. Thomas. 2012. J.&J.'s next chief: B1.
4. Rockoff, J. D. 2011. J&J, Synthes hold talks. *Wall Street Journal,* April 18: B1.
5. Loftus, P., & Wang, S. S. 2009. J&J sales show health care feels the pinch. *Wall Street Journal,* January 21: B1.

6. Johnson, A. 2007. J&J's consumer play paces growth. *Wall Street Journal,* January 24: A3.

7. Preston, H. H. 2005. Drug giant provides a model of consistency. *Herald Tribune,* March 12–13: 12.

8. Barrett, A. 2003. Staying on top. *BusinessWeek,* May 5: 62.

9. Ibid.

10. Singer, N., & Abelson, R. 2011. Can Johnson & Johnson get its act together? *New York Times,* January 16: B4.

11. Ibid.

12. Thomas & Abelson. 2012. J.&J. chief to resign one role.

13. Meier, B. 2013. Maker hid data about design flaw in hip implant, records show. *New York Times,* January 26.

14. Thomas. 2012. J.&J.'s next chief: B6.

15. Thomas, K. 2012. Johnson & Johnson to remove questionable chemicals in products. *New York Times,* August 16: B1.

16. Singer, N. 2010. Hip implants are recalled by J&J unit. *New York Times,* August 27: B1.

CASE 10

PROCTER & GAMBLE*

There was a visible sign of relief in the voice of Bob McDonald, the embattled CEO of Procter & Gamble, when he announced the firm's quarterly numbers on January 25, 2013. Sales had actually risen by 3 percent, beating analysts' expectations. This was a rare moment of achievement for McDonald, who has struggled to show results for P&G since he took over in 2009. Back then, he had boldly announced that the company's sales would rise from $75 billion in 2009 to over $100 billion by 2013. Instead, the firm had only managed to raise sales to about $84 billion, while its net income had dropped by as much as 20 percent.

Since its founding 175 years ago, P&G had risen to the status of an American icon with well-known consumer products such as *Pampers, Tide, Downy,* and *Crest.* In fact, the firm has long been admired for its superior products, its marketing brilliance, and the intense loyalty of its employees, who have respectfully come to be known as Proctoids. With 25 brands that each generate more than $1 billion in sales, P&G has become the largest consumer products company in the world.

It was therefore clear to McDonald that he was taking on the mantle of one of the biggest companies in the world, one that had shown consistent growth for most of its existence. Beyond this, he was succeeding Alan G. Lafley, who had resurrected P&G after its last major downturn. Lafley had electrified a then-demoralized organization by shaking things up. He shepherded products such as *Swiffer* and *Febreze* to megahit status and acquired Gillette to provide P&G with a major presence in the men's market for the first time. Finally, by relaunching Olay and acquiring Clairol, Lafley had pushed the firm into higher-margin beauty products (see Exhibit 1).

Under McDonald, however, P&G's growth has stalled, as it has been losing market share in two-thirds of its markets. Recession-battered consumers have abandoned the firm's premium-priced products for cheaper alternatives even as the company's efforts to build market share in the developing world have been stymied by newly nimble rivals such as Unilever and Colgate-Palmolive. New products that have targeted lower-income consumers have not generated sufficient sales to make up for the loss of sales to the struggling middle-class segment (see

*Case developed by Professor Jamal Shamsie, Michigan State University, with the assistance of Professor Alan B. Eisner, Pace University. Material has been drawn from published sources to be used for purposes of class discussion. Copyright © 2013 Jamal Shamsie and Alan B. Eisner.

EXHIBIT 1 Business Segments

	Key Products	Billion Dollar Brands
Fabric care & home care	Air care Batteries Dish care Fabric care Pet care	Ace Ariel Dawn Downy Duracell Febreze Gain Tide Iams
Beauty	Cosmetics Deodorants Hair Care Personal Cleansing Fragrances Skin Care	Head & Shoulders Olay Pantene Wella SK-II
Baby care & family care	Baby wipes Bath & facial tissue Diapers Paper towels	Bounty Charmin Pampers
Health care	Feminine care Oral care Rapid diagnostics Personal health care	Always Crest Oral B Vicks
Grooming	Blades and Razors Face and Shave Products Hair care appliances	Braun Fusion Gillette Mach 3

Source: P&G.

Exhibits 2 to 4). More significantly, the firm's vaunted innovation machine has stalled, with no major product success over the last five years.

P&G's woes have eroded morale among employees, with many managers taking early retirement or bolting to competitors. Says Ed Artzt, who was CEO from 1990 to 1995, "The most unfortunate aspect of this whole thing is the brain drain. The loss of good people is almost irreparable when you depend on promotion from within to continue building the company."[1] Critics claim that the current turmoil may have serious implications for the long-term prospects for the firm. Ali Dibadj, a senior analyst at San Bernstein expanded on this view: "The next six months may be the most crucial in P&G's 175-year history."[2]

EXHIBIT 2

Income Statement

Go to library tab in
Connect to access
Case Financials.

	A	B	C	D	E	F
1				Income Statement		
2		2012	2011	2010	2009	2008
3	Total revenue	83,680	82,559	78,938	76,694	83,503
4	Gross profit	41,595	41,245	41,019	38,004	42,808
5	Operating income	13,292	15,495	16,021	15,374	17,083
6	Ebit	12,785	14,997	15,993	15,771	17,545
7	Net income	10,756	11,797	12,736	13,436	12,075

Note: Figures in $ millions. Years ending June 30.

Source: P&G

EXHIBIT 3

Balance Sheet

Go to library tab in
Connect to access
Case Financials.

	A	B	C	D	E	F
1				Balance Sheet		
2		2012	2011	2010	2009	2008
3	Current assets	21,910	21,970	18,782	21,905	24,515
4	Total assets	132,244	138,354	128,172	134,833	143,992
5	Current liabilities	24,907	27,293	24,282	30,901	30,958
6	Total liabilities	68,805	70,714	67,057	71,734	74,498
7	Stockholder equity	63,439	67,640	61,439	63,382	69,494

Note: Figures in $ millions. Years ending June 30.

Source: P&G.

EXHIBIT 4

Financial Breakdown

Fabric Care & Home Care			
Net Sales:	2012: $27.3 Billion	*Net Earnings:*	2012: $2.9 Billion
	2011: $26.5 Billion		2011: $3.1 Billion
	2009: $23.1 Billion		2009: $3.0 Billion
Beauty			
Net Sales:	2012: $20.3 Billion	*Net Earnings:*	2012: $2.4 Billion
	2011: $19.9 Billion		2011: $2.5 Billion
	2009: $18.9 Billion		2009: $2.6 Billion
Health Care			
Net Sales:	2012: $12.4 Billion	*Net Earnings:*	2012: $1.8 Billion
	2011: $12.0 Billion		2011: $1.8 Billion
	2009: $11.3 Billion		2009: $1.8 Billion
Baby Care & Family Care			
Net Sales:	2012: $16.5 Billion	*Net Earnings:*	2012: $2.1 Billion
	2011: $15.6 Billion		2011: $2.0 Billion
	2009: $14.1 Billion		2009: $1.8 Billion
Grooming			
Net Sales:	2012: $8.3 Billion	*Net Earnings:*	2012: $1.8 billion
	2011: $8.2 billion		2011: $1.8 billion
	2009: $7.4 billion		2009: $1.4 billion

Source: P&G.

Fighting Off a Decline

For most of its long history, P&G has been one of America's preeminent companies. The firm has developed several well-known brands such as *Tide,* one of the pioneers in laundry detergents, which was launched in 1946, and *Pampers,* the first disposable diaper, which was introduced in 1961. P&G also built its brands through its innovative marketing techniques. In the 1880s, it was one of the first companies to advertise nationally. Later on, P&G invented the soap opera by sponsoring *Ma Perkins* when radio caught on and *Guiding Light* when television took hold. In the 1930s, P&G was the first firm to develop the idea of brand management, setting up marketing teams for each brand and urging them to compete against each other.

But by the 1990s, P&G was in danger of becoming another Eastman Kodak or Xerox, a once-great company that might have lost its way. Sales on most of its 18 top brands were slowing, as it was being outhustled by more focused rivals such as Kimberly-Clark and Colgate-Palmolive. The only way P&G kept profits growing was by cutting costs, which would hardly work as a strategy for the long term. At the same time, the dynamics of the industry were changing as power shifted from manufacturers to massive retailers. Retailers such as Walmart were starting to use their size to negotiate better deals from P&G, further squeezing its profits.

In 1999, P&G decided to bring in Durk I. Jager to try and make the big changes that were obviously needed to get P&G back on track. But the moves that he made generally misfired, sinking the firm into deeper trouble. He introduced expensive new products that never caught on, while letting existing brands drift. He also put in place a company-wide reorganization that left many employees perplexed and preoccupied. During the fiscal year when he was in charge, earnings per share showed an anemic rise of just 3.5 percent, much lower than in previous years. And during that time, the share price slid 52 percent, cutting P&G's total market capitalization by $85 billion.

But Jager's greatest failing was his scorn for the family. Jager, a Dutchman who had joined P&G overseas and worked his way to corporate headquarters, pitted himself against the P&G culture. Susan E. Arnold, president of P&G's previous beauty and feminine care division, said that Jager tried to make the employees turn against the prevailing culture, contending that it was burdensome and insufferable. Some go-ahead employees even wore buttons that read "Old World/New World" to express disdain for P&G's past.

In 2000, Alan G. Lafley received a call from John Pepper, a former CEO who was a board member. He was asked to take over the reins of P&G from Jager, representing a boardroom coup unprecedented in the firm's history. In a sense, Lafley, who had risen up through the ranks of P&G, had been preparing for this job his entire adult life. By the time he took charge, Lafley had developed a reputation as a boss who steps back to give his staff plenty of responsibility and who helped shape decisions by asking a series of keen questions. As CEO, Lafley refrained from making any grand pronouncements on the future of P&G. Instead, he spent an inordinate amount of time patiently communicating to his employees about the types of changes that he wanted to see at P&G.

Restructuring the Organization

Lafley began his tenure by breaking down the walls between management and the employees. Since the 1950s, all of the senior executives at P&G used to be located on the 11th floor at the firm's corporate headquarters. Lafley changed this setup, moving all five division presidents to the same floors as their staff. Then he turned some of the emptied space into a leadership training center. On the rest of the floor, he knocked down the walls so that the remaining executives, including himself, would share open offices.

Indeed, Lafley's charm offensive so disarmed most P&G employees that he was able to make drastic changes within the company. He replaced more than half of the company's top 30 managers, more than any P&G boss in memory, and trimmed its workforce by as many as 9,600 jobs. He also moved more women into senior positions. In fact, Lafley skipped over 78 general managers with more seniority to name 42-year-old Deborah A. Henretta to head P&G's then-troubled North American baby-care division.

In fact, Lafley was simply acknowledging the importance of developing people, particularly those in managerial roles at P&G. For years, the firm has been known to dispatch line managers rather than human resource staffers to do much of its recruiting. For the few that get hired, their work life becomes a career-long development process. At every level, P&G has a different "college" to train individuals, and every department has its own "university." The general manager's college holds a weeklong school term once a year when there are a handful of newly promoted managers.

One of the most important items on Lafley's agenda was a weekly meeting with Dick Antoine, his head of human resources. At each meeting, the two of them discussed the potential assignments for various P&G employees. For those who demonstrated that they had the potential to rise to the executive ranks, P&G tried to give them as broad an experience as possible. "If you train people to work in different countries and businesses, you develop a deep bench," said the current human resource executive, Moheet Nagrath.[3]

Under Lafley, P&G also continued its efforts to maintain a comprehensive data base of all of its more than 130,000 employees, each of whom is tracked carefully through monthly and annual talent reviews. All managers are reviewed not only by their bosses but also by lateral managers who have worked with them, as well as on their own direct reports. Every February, one entire board meeting is devoted to reviewing the high-level executives, with the goal of coming up with at least three potential candidates for each of the 35 to 40 jobs at the top of the firm.

Pushing for Consumer-Driven Ideas

Above all, however, Lafley was intent on shifting the focus of P&G back to its consumers. At every opportunity, he tried to drill his managers and employees to not lose sight of the consumer. He felt that P&G had often let technology dictate its new products rather than consumer needs. He wanted to see the firm work more closely with retailers, the place where consumers first see the product on the shelf. And he placed a lot of emphasis on getting a better sense of the consumer's experience with P&G products when they actually use them at home.

Over the decade of Lafley's leadership, P&G managed to update all of its 200 brands by adding innovative new products. It began to offer devices that built on its core brands, such as *Tide StainBrush,* a battery-powered brush for removing stains, and *Mr. Clean AutoDry,* a water-pressure-powered car cleaning system that dries without streaking. P&G also began to approach its brands more creatively (see Exhibit 5). *Crest,* for example, which used to be marketed as a toothpaste brand, is now defined as an oral care brand. The firm now sells *Crest*-branded toothbrushes and tooth whiteners.

In order to ensure that P&G continued to come up with innovative ideas, Lafley also confronted head-on the stubbornly held notion that everything must be invented within P&G, asserting that half of its new products should come from the outside. Under the new "Connect and Develop" model of innovation, the firm began to get almost 50 percent of its new product ideas from outside the firm. This can be compared to the 10 percent figure that existed at P&G when Lafley had taken charge.

A key element of P&G's strategy, however, was to move the firm away from basic consumer products such as laundry detergents, which can be knocked off by private labels, to higher-margin products. Under Lafley, P&G made costly acquisitions of Clairol, Wella, and Gillette to complement its *Cover Girl* and *Oil of Olay* brands. The firm even moved into prestige fragrances through licenses with Hugo Boss, Gucci, and Dolce & Gabbana. When Lafley stepped down, beauty products had risen to account for about one-third of the firm's total revenues.

But P&G's riskiest moves were in its expansion into services, starting with car washes and dry cleaning. The car washes build on *Mr. Clean,* P&G's popular cleaning product. In expanding the brand to car washes, the firm expected to distinguish its outlets from others by offering additional services, such as *Febreze* odor eliminators, lounges with Wi-Fi and big screen televisions, and spray guns that children can aim at cars passing through the wash. Similarly, P&G's dry cleaning outlets are named after *Tide,* its best-selling laundry detergent. The stores will include drive-through services, 24-hour pickup, and environmentally benign cleaning methods.

Pinning Hopes on a New Leader

On July 1, 2009, Lafley passed the leadership of P&G to McDonald, who had joined P&G in 1980 and worked his way up through posts in Canada, Japan, the Philippines, and Belgium to become chief operating officer. Known for being earnest and friendly, McDonald remembers names of people who work under him and likes to lunch with lower-level employees at every stop he makes around the world. At heart, however, he is an engineer, who is fanatical about processes that he has tried to introduce to P&G.

McDonald took over from Lafley after the start of a calamitous recession and had to deal with various emerging problems. The "Connect and Develop" program that had been started by Lafley to bring in new ideas from outsiders had reduced expenses but had failed to produce any blockbusters. After 2006, most of P&G's growth had come from line extensions of existing brands or from costly acquisitions. Furthermore, Lafley's push to expand the firm's operations in emerging markets was also yielding few results in the face of stiff competition from Unilever and Colgate-Palmolive, who already had a strong presence. Finally, commodity prices were surging, even as P&G's products were already too expensive for the struggling middle-class that it was targeting everywhere.

EXHIBIT 5 Significant Innovations

- Tide was the first heavy-duty laundry detergent.
- Crest was the first fluoride toothpaste clinically proven to prevent tooth decay.
- Downy was the first ultra-concentrated rinse-add fabric softener.
- Pert Plus was the first 2-in-1 shampoo and conditioner.
- Head & Shoulders was the first pleasant-to-use shampoo effective against dandruff.
- Pampers was the first affordable, mass-marketed disposable diaper.
- Bounty was the first three-dimensional paper towel.
- Always was the first feminine protection pad with an innovative, dry-weave topsheet.
- Febreze was the first fabric and air care product that actually removes odors from fabrics and the air.
- Crest White Strips was the first patented in-home teeth-whitening technology.

Source: P&G.

Perhaps the most serious challenge stemmed from Lafley's design of a complex matrix organizational system that shared power among executives in charge of functions such as HR, marketing, and finance; executives overseeing different geographic regions; and executives for various product categories such as health care and beauty care. The groups served as checks and balances on one another so that no one person or group had complete responsibility for any product or area. But under McDonald, the system became more cumbersome, leading to a decline in the influence of brand and country managers. "The organizational structure may not be right for today," said former P&G executive Jim Stengel. "It's complex and accountability has become more diffuse."[4]

In order to deal with all of these challenges, McDonald replaced Lafley's clear motto of "The consumer is boss" with his own slogan of "Purpose-inspired growth." In his own words, this meant that P&G was "touching and improving more consumers' lives, in more parts of the world, more completely." "Purpose" was an undeniably laudable ambition, but many employees simply could not fathom how to translate this rhetoric into action. Dick Antoine, P&G's head of HR from 1998 to 2008, commented, "'Purpose-inspired growth' is a wonderful slogan, but it doesn't help allocate assets."[5]

The new focus seemed to fit well with McDonald, who seemed more comfortable engaging on a broad or abstract level, showing less interest in digging into the specific details of a troubled unit. At the same time, he began to institute various procedures throughout the firm that were designed to increase efficiency. For example, he authorized an efficiency study that assessed every act and function performed by every employee and then reduced the number of specific procedures to be used across the entire firm to 88. Sonsoles Gonzalez, a manager who recently left, said, "There was a lot of concern for productivity, but little interest in winning the consumer."[6]

Fighting for Its Iconic Status

By the middle of 2012, it was becoming obvious that P&G was struggling under McDonald's leadership. Known for its reliable performance, the firm was forced to lower its profit guidelines three times in six months, frustrating analysts and investors alike. A large part of the firm's problems may stem from the difficulties that McDonald has experienced in establishing priorities for P&G. Given the wide range of problems that he faced, McDonald has been trying to address all of them at the same time. Dibadj, the analyst

at Sanford Bernstein, commented on this multipronged effort: "The strategic problem was that they decided to go after everything. But they ran out of ammo too quickly."[7]

There are some signs, however, that P&G may be recovering as a result of a series of bold new initiatives that have recently been announced by McDonald. In June 2012, he unveiled what he called "40/20/10," which will narrow the firm's focus to its 40 biggest category/country combinations, its 20 largest innovations, and its 10 most lucrative developing markets. McDonald has also recentralized innovation efforts under one executive and named another to head a council focused on creating a "culture of productivity." He has not yet provided enough details about how each of these will work.

Although it is still in its early stages, McDonald's recent moves have led to a significant improvement in P&G's performance in the last quarter, the first in a long time. The firm has also managed to revive its product development efforts with a successful line extension for *Tide* detergent packaged in "pods." To complement these moves, McDonald has also announced another set of layoffs that will eliminate 2 to 4 percent of employees each year through fiscal 2016. He claims that this will eventually lead to $10 billion in cost savings, which will help the firm's bottom line.

All of these developments have managed to ease the pressure on McDonald for a while as critics wait to see whether the firm can continue to build on its recent improvements. Nevertheless, many analysts are questioning whether P&G may need to make more radical changes to get back on a sound footing. Even within the firm, many executives believe that McDonald has not been able to take the bold moves that may allow the firm to recover from its slump. Activist investor Bill Ackerman has made clear his disappointment with McDonald's poor performance: "We're delighted to see the company's made some progress," he said. "But P&G deserves to be led by one of the best CEO's in the world."[8]

ENDNOTES

1. Reingold, J., & Burke, D. 2013. Can P&G's CEO hang on? *Fortune,* February 25: 69.
2. Ibid.
3. Kimes, M. 2009. P&G's leadership machine. *Fortune,* April 13: 22.
4. Reingold & Burke. 2013. Can P&G's CEO hang on?: 75.
5. Ibid., 70.
6. Ibid., 71.
7. Ibid., 70.
8. Ibid., 75.

CASE 11
STUDIO 100: A SHOWCASE IN SHOW BUSINESS*

Kurt Verweire
Vlerick Business School

Studio 100 is an international family entertainment group founded in 1996 in Belgium. Some years earlier, Hans Bourlon, Gert Verhulst, and Danny Verbiest had made a production called *'Samson & Gert'* for the national Belgian television station (BRT), which was very successful in Flanders, the northern part of Belgium. Samson's success led to TV and theatre shows. The three programme makers decided to leave the BRT to create their own production house so that they could build a business around the characters they had created. They started the company without any help from investors and bought an office in Schelle, a town close to Antwerp (Belgium) where they created new characters, recorded television shows and rehearsed for the theatre shows. The company started with five people in an office building that was much too large.

Fifteen years later, Studio 100 has more than 1000 employees and dozens of popular characters, it is the owner of one of the largest independent catalogues of children's TV series in the world, and distributes TV series in more than 120 countries.[1] The company's revenues have increased from 5.6 million euro in 1996 to 170.2 million euro in 2011 (see Exhibit 1 for an overview of key financial figures). How has the company been able to achieve this phenomenal growth?

Studio 100's Early Years
New Characters
Soon after the company was founded, Studio 100 created a new format called *'Plop the Gnome'*. This format was broadcast on the Flemish commercial television station and was a big success too. In the years that followed, Studio 100 created other formats, such as *'Pirate Pete', 'Bumba',* and *'Big & Betsy'* (see Exhibit 2) which were broadcast in Flanders and the Netherlands on the most important TV channels.[2] Studio 100 also created stage shows and movies. Studio 100 became the market leader in theatre shows for children and families in Belgium and the Netherlands. These shows are based on the Studio 100 characters or on a classic fairy tale

---

* This case study is based on a Vlerick publication 'Studio 100: a showcase in show business', written by Kurt Verweire and MBA students Kristoff Lievens, Nicolas Van Boven, and Pascal Vercruysse in 2009, and a report written by MBA students Annick Bolland, Leonardo Fininzola e Silva, Stefan Keereman, Jef Laurijssen, Werner Roelandt, and Alex Waterinkx (2009) 'Studio 100—growth strategy' for the Vlerick strategy course.

such as *'Pinocchio', 'Robin Hood',* or *'Snow White'*. In addition, Studio 100 has released on average two or three movies per year. Every movie is an original adventure related to one of the well-known Studio 100 characters.

Even today, the characters that were introduced on television more than 10 years ago are still on prime time in Belgium and the Netherlands. The success of Studio 100's characters can be attributed to the fact that the characters are timeless: it is the good versus the bad and there is always the happy end. Another reason for the success is the omnipresence of the Studio 100 characters. They record songs, they appear in books, newspapers and magazines, and they go live on stage in theatres, concerts, or musicals. This means that the characters of Studio 100 are part of the daily life of the Belgian and Dutch children and their (grand)parents. A final element is that Studio 100's characters are very Flemish and Dutch. This provides the company with a significant advantage over many international production companies, since many audiences prefer local TV programming.[3]

Theme Parks
The end of the previous decade saw some new initiatives from Studio 100. One of those new initiatives was the opening of a theme park, called *'Plopsaland'* (see Exhibit 3). Studio 100 bought the old 'Meli-Park', a theme park near the town of De Panne on the Belgian coast. The Meli-Park was originally created by a honey company and based on a bee theme. However, during the 1990s the theme park lost much of its appeal and the number of visitors dropped drastically. Hans Bourlon and Gert Verhulst decided to buy this park and thematize it around the popular Studio 100 characters. Studio 100 invested a lot in extra catering and parking and added new attractions every year.

Looking back at this move, Hans Bourlon admits the creation of Plopsaland was a crazy idea. It was a risky move but it was an immediate success. Studio 100 opened the park in April 2000. In the first year, it attracted 575 000 visitors. In 2004, that number had increased to 781 000. In 2010, with some 35 attractions and more than 1,1 million visitors per year, Plopsaland is one of the most frequented parks in Belgium, the Netherlands, and Luxembourg. Hans Bourlon comments on this strategic move:

To be honest, none of the plans about Plopsaland made any sense. We had never imagined that we would have so many visitors . . . and three other theme parks some 8 years later . . . But that is how it goes within our company. We are always open to new things.

EXHIBIT 1 (A) Studio 100's revenue evolution (million euro).

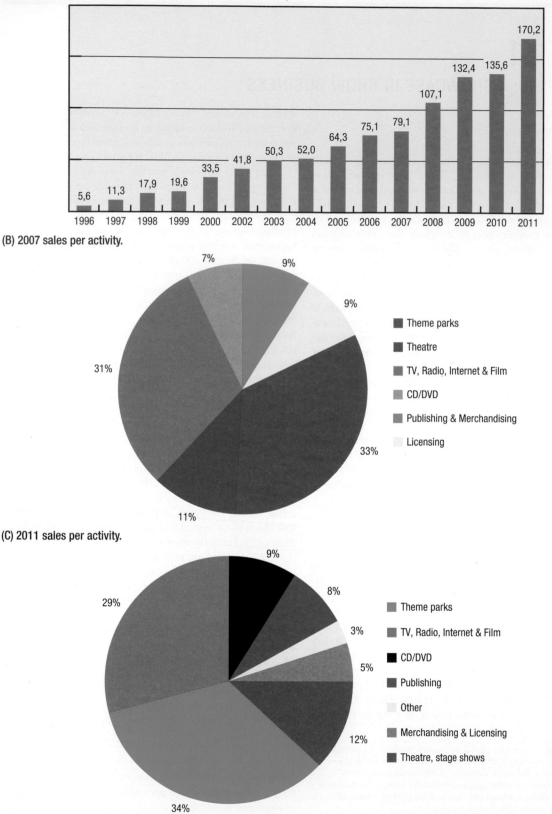

(B) 2007 sales per activity.

Theme parks
Theatre
TV, Radio, Internet & Film
CD/DVD
Publishing & Merchandising
Licensing

(C) 2011 sales per activity.

Theme parks
TV, Radio, Internet & Film
CD/DVD
Publishing
Other
Merchandising & Licensing
Theatre, stage shows

EXHIBIT 2

Some early Studio 100 formats

Samson & Gert · Big & Betsy · Plop · Pirate Pete · Bumba

EXHIBIT 3

Plopsaland De Panne

The success of Plopsaland De Panne led to the creation of other theme parks. In 2005 Studio 100 opened the first indoor theme park in Flanders: *'Plopsa Indoor'*. This park is open 300 days per year and offers some 20 attractions. A third park has been added to the list: *'Plopsa Coo'*, located at the Coo waterfalls, a popular tourist attraction in the southern part of Belgium. Besides the spectacular falls, Plopsa Coo also offers 15 attractions and a wildlife park. In April 2010, Studio 100 opened its first theme park in the Netherlands in Coevoorden. And in that same year, the company bought Holiday Park in Germany as well.

A Girl's Band

In 2002, Studio 100 acquired *'K3'*, a Flemish girl's band. K3 was founded in 1999 but when they became fully part of Studio 100 in 2002, K3 exploded. The three girls of K3 are solely responsible for creating a new phenomenon in the Belgian and Dutch market: toddler pop. The girls released 35 singles and with the constant rotation of their music videos, six successful feature films and many sold out concerts, the girls are unstoppable. *'The world of K3'*, a weekly magazine show, has towering ratings and the girls are superstars, adored by the public and feted by the media. What is more, K3 have their own line of clothing and accessories. There are comic books, magazines, posters, and daily newspaper adventures. MP3 players come pre-loaded with K3 songs. There are K3 cookies for the peckish K3 mega fan, K3 lunchboxes to put the cookies in, and K3 backpacks to put the lunchboxes in.

Merchandising and Licensing

Merchandising and licensing is extremely important for Studio 100. In 2010, 15 per cent of the 135,6 million euro turnover came from these activities. The company has developed a multi-track merchandising strategy aimed at maximizing revenue streams while keeping a tight control on image and brand. A significant part of the revenues comes from merchandising. Merchandising lines are developed and designed in-house and sold to wholesalers and retailers. Depending on the character, one or two merchandising lines are developed each year.[4] Local teams of in total about 20 people manage the contracts with the licence holders in Belgium, the Netherlands, France, and Germany. Every activity that connects Studio 100 with the outside world and that could affect the company's image is formalized and controlled. The company receives many requests to licence their characters. The reputation of the characters results in significant extra sales for the licence holders. But obviously, Studio 100 wins too. Tom Grymonprez, commercial director, explains:

We ask ourselves a series of questions. Is there a fit with our company? What about the quality of the product? Where is the product sold? And last but not least: does the product fit in the world of our target audience? You won't see Bumba toy guns in the product assortment.[5]

More Formats

Studio 100 has continuously added new formats to its product portfolio. In 2002, the company introduced *'Spring'* targeting the 'older tweens'. In the years that followed, Studio 100 further expanded and created *'TopStars'*, *'Mega Mindy'*, *'Anubis House'*, *'Amika'*, *'Galaxy Park'*, *'Rox'*, *'Dobus'*, *'Bobo'*, and *'Hotel 13'* (see Exhibit 4 for some examples). And after the TV series came the CDs, games, merchandizing, movies, and musicals. In this way, Studio 100 has become the largest provider of family and children entertainment in the Benelux. Common features

to all of these programmes have been the high production quality, the clear focus on the target audience of children—segmented by age and gender (see Exhibit 5)—and the family-friendly entertaining value.[6]

Studio 100 is not afraid to apply some radical changes to existing formats. This has helped to create a boost in the formats that had reached the saturation phase. A great example is how the musical 'The Three Piglets' gave a new boost to K3's career. Hans Bourlon reflects:

One day, we were searching for a way to boost the career of K3, our girl band. One of our employees, who was sitting at the conference table, said: 'Turn them into piglets and make them the main characters in a new musical called 'The 3 Piglets'. We couldn't stop laughing. But one year later, the musical 'The 3 Piglets' was completely sold out. It was a major success. You don't get such ideas out of a market study. If we had asked the public via market research to say what they expected the next K3 show to be like, we would simply have ended up with a 'greatest hits' extravaganza.

Some Challenges

Despite the many successes of the firm, Studio 100 has faced significant challenges over the years. New initiatives have not always been successful. *'Radio Bembem'*, the radio station project for children, was stopped. And sometimes key people leave. In December 2004, Danny Verbiest, the founder who had lent his voice to Samson for 15 years, decided to retire and sell his shares of Studio 100. In 2009, Belgium was shocked when Kathleen—the 'blonde' singer of K3—decided to quit the band. The company turned a problem into an opportunity and set up a reality show *'K2 searching for K3'*, where they found a new, Dutch K3 member.

International Exploration and Exploitation
Expansion to French-speaking Belgium

In 2005, Studio 100 set another milestone. For the first time TV content was made in a different language than Dutch, namely French, for the market of southern Belgium (Wallonia). In that year, the company did remakes of the Plop shows which were aired on the Wallonian TV. The shows were now called 'Le Lutin Plop' and featured characters such as 'Lutin Dordebou' ('Lazy'), 'Lutin Pipolette'

EXHIBIT 4
Some later Studio 100 formats

Spring   TopStars   Mega Mindy   Amika   Anubis House

EXHIBIT 5 Market segmentation of Studio 100

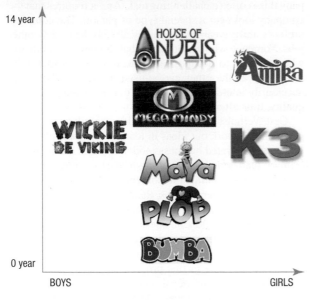

network; EM delivered children programmes to more than 120 countries. It would have taken decades for Studio 100 to build such a distribution network. But what was more: EM Entertainment also has an impressive independent catalogue of content with characters such as *Maya the Bee*, *Vicky the Viking*, *Heidi*, *Lassie*, and *Pippi Longstocking*. What if Studio 100 could use its competences to revitalize and commercialize these well-known international characters?

Studio 100 Animation

With the acquisition of EM Entertainment Studio 100 also became the owner of Flying Bark, an Australian animation studio. In that same year, Studio 100 opened an animation studio in Paris. Studio 100 Animation develops, finances, and produces series and feature films in 2D or 3D. The Paris studio produces mainly TV series while feature films are the mainstay of production in Sydney.[8] Studio 100 is working on remakes of classics such as Maya the Bee and Heidi.

Germany is now the spearhead for Studio 100's international expansion as the company purchased in November 2010 the German leisure park *Holiday Park*. Studio 100 transformed this park into a theme park where German children can meet their favorite characters such as Tabaluga, Maya the Bee, and Vicky the Viking, much like what happened in Belgium with Plopsaland.

Further Internationalization

Studio 100 internationalized in other markets as well. It started a coproduction, called *'Big & Small'* with Kindle Entertainment, 3J's Productions, the BBC and Treehouse TV. The show is a live action comedy filmed in the UK with British actors. Because of the high quality of the show, Studio 100 has managed to get a foot in the door with the BBC, a distribution channel that is envied by many competitors. In the meantime, Studio 100 has set up another coproduction with the BBC, called *'Kerwhizz'*.

Studio 100 also has expanded in the US. The company remade *'The House of Anubis'*, originally a teen drama mystery TV series for the Belgian and Dutch market. The company sold the series to Nickelodeon, a US children's channel, which made a very successful German remake of the series, and later a US remake. Again, the series was a success both in Germany and in the UK and US and this helped to boost merchandizing and publishing revenues in those countries significantly.

Studio 100's Special Dna

The success rate of many of Studio 100's initiatives is high. This is because the two managing directors (and founders), Gert Verhulst and Hans Bourlon, have not only focused on creating new characters and exploiting that content in many different ways, but also because the two managers have been able to build a very specific organizational culture. The two managers have been awarded 'Managers of

('Chatter'), and 'Lutin Bric' ('Chore'). Studio 100 also did remakes of every Samson & Gert show, which in French were translated as *'Fred & Samson'*. The main driver for offering TV shows in French was to convince the Belgian national retail chains to distribute the merchandized material. But since Wallonia is rather small, the revenues and profits of this expansion were rather limited. Would they be able to expand internationally? Studio 100 has always been successful because its characters were Dutch and Flemish. Could they just export these characters to different markets?

Expansion into Germany

Studio 100 decided to bet high on international expansion and they recruited Jo Daris as Director of International Business. The company also looked for additional funding and founded Studio 100 Media in Munich in 2007. This unit distributes TV series worldwide and was the first entry of Studio 100 in the German market. But Jo Daris discovered soon that the international TV stations were hardly interested in the stories of Plop the Gnome, Pirate Pete, and Mega Mindy. Jo Daris comments:

The people at Studio 100 are used to having everything they touch turn into gold. This time, however, many eggs were touched, but none of them turned to gold. It was very difficult to convince the buyers at the television stations that our characters could be successful in other countries than Belgium and the Netherlands.[7]

Nevertheless, the company continued with the internationalization. In 2008 the international expansion process was accelerated by the acquisition of the German EM Entertainment Group. Studio 100 paid 41 million euro for EM Entertainment and got an enormous distribution

the Year' in 2008 and the company was named 'Company of the Year' in 2009 in Belgium. But Hans Bourlon hates the word 'management':

A company starts to get in trouble when it only organizes, plans and structures what is already there—which is what I call 'management'. That is why I am more afraid that we will lose that creative drive. If we start to do 'more of the same' and exploit rather than explore, then that is the end of Studio 100.

Creativity, Entrepreneurship, and Innovation

The DNA of Studio 100 can be described as 'boundless creativity and innovation'. The essence of Studio 100 is about discovery: creating new ideas, every day, over and over again, starting from a white piece of paper. What makes Studio 100 unique is the fact that the shareholders and founders of the company are still involved in the conceptual and creative side of the business. This does not often happen in media companies: the creative minds usually stay as far away as possible from the business brains. But in Studio 100, doing business and being creative are inextricably linked, and therein lies the company's success. But there is a clear understanding that creativity comes first, because it is these creative impulses which keep pushing the company forward.[9]

Creativity helps the company to cope with difficult times. Expanding a business is full of unexpected changes and indefinite opportunities. When the company was founded, the CD sale was its biggest success. Ten years later, the audio market had collapsed. But by then, the shows in the theme parks and in theatres have become the money makers.

Gert Verhulst and Hans Bourlon see it as their major task to push creativity down in the organization. Although both managers are still heavily involved with the new projects they 'manage' new ideas rather than 'developing and creating' the ideas themselves. This means challenging the people, providing feedback, giving advice, and coaching. Leading a creative environment means detecting and recognizing strong ideas and promoting them within the company.

It goes without saying that we are always open to new ideas, although it is obvious that in first instance people are expected to do what we pay them for.[10] But overall I think that people with great ideas have the opportunity to develop them. For example, our cost controller has developed a new quiz program. And the guy who develops our websites has produced a board game.

From Ideas to Business

Generating ideas however is only a first step. Equally important is to make everyone in the organization believe in a great idea and go for it. This implies for many people forgetting about their own ideas. In a creative media company this is often a challenging task. And it requires that the company looks for a special type of person. The company prefers a thirty-year-old, who has already had a few other jobs. Someone who understands that drawing is a craft and who is happy to do his best to draw Plop in exactly the same way as the other cartoonists. Someone who is not necessarily interested in 'standing out' but wants to deliver quality, time after time.

Gert Verhulst and Hans Bourlon stimulate people to generate and work out ideas in team. The power of Studio 100 is its integrated business model. TV and music are the primary platforms for launching new characters. Then the company further builds the content and characters in multimedia such as theme parks, theatre shows, movies, CDs, books, merchandising, and licensing. All elements are crucial in Studio 100's business model. And this requires that teams from different departments work together seamlessly. The marketing department of Studio 100 plays a very important role in this process. In many media companies, the marketing department is a separate entity, cut off from the creative process. At Studio 100, the two sides have to work together. Creative ideas are only supported when they can be commercialized. Studio 100 is business-driven and no-nonsense. The company has clear goals. That makes it different from many other creative companies, who do not make plans and just carry on, relying on a hazy form of artistry . . .

Managing People through an Appropriate Organizational Climate

Stimulating creativity is above all providing the people with a warm nest, an environment that gives them the possibility to slowly rise and shine. The management team of Studio 100 sees this as one of their major tasks: 'We, as an employer, have to create that environment and above all, need to mingle with them.' There's a lot of energy going round at Studio 100. Very often, you can hear music in the corridors: an orchestra is rehearsing, there are ballet lessons or some of the characters are learning new songs.

According to Jo Daris, 'most synergy is created when employees—whatever is their function or their department—meet each other continuously. An open workspace promotes all that'. Indeed, there are some offices in the Studio 100 building, but most of the space goes to studios, rehearsal rooms, ballet rooms, and the clothing department where the costumes are made. That is where the employees write songs, create new shows, invent new attractions for the theme parks and make sceneries. On the tables, you will find models of the theme park attractions or sceneries. And rhyming dictionaries are more commonly used than calculators. At noon, the restaurant looks like carnival: pirates, gnomes, piglets, and mermaids are all sitting at one table. And while they are having lunch, new ideas bubble up. The food is provided for free.

Studio 100 pays a lot of attention to attracting the right people. In a fast-growing company, the question whether you have the right people is a vivid one. The company looks for energized and engaged people. There is a deliberate choice not to attract famous actors for a particular character. The total picture should be right. You just can't play Pirate Pete for one year, earn a lot of money, and then leave the company.

Everybody in Studio 100 gets a fixed pay, even the sales people. This is a quite conservative rewarding system, yet it focuses on the equal importance of all factors in the creation and sale of qualitative products. When somebody, e.g. an actor, asks for more than a fair pay, this might be a reason to change the format and exclude the actor. These discussions occur from time to time. In order to counter these problems, Studio 100 tries to create a group feeling, where everybody feels at home and earns well. The company offers people a long-term perspective, although some people feel they should receive part of the income of their successful project. But Studio 100 is very strict here. Employees might get an extra fee only if they perform *more*; you do not get a bonus for contributing to a successful project. Motivated, creative, and committed employees obviously get more promotion opportunities. In 2009 Studio 100 introduced an option plan for all employees, but Hans Bourlon doubts whether this was really necessary. He wonders whether money really drives commitment.

The company has no trade unions because there have never been candidates. Studio 100 has flexible working hours and does whatever possible to create an energizing and positive environment. The company organizes power yoga sessions, there are quiz teams, and so on. The real writing often takes place late in the evening, in groups and certainly not in suits. In short, the classic 9 to 5 clerk is not around at Studio 100.[11]

Control

In Studio 100, the command-and-control style has given way to a 'softer control' with more emphasis on output control. Although the firm uses clear performance measures to track the progress of specific projects, most attention is paid to a more personal form of control and coaching. Some projects are monitored extensively by the top managers, for others there is the confidence that the organization will bring the projects to a good end. One could say that control is primarily done through creating an appropriate culture in the organization, a culture built around creativity, entrepreneurship, and informality.[12]

A Structured Approach

Creativity and entrepreneurship are core in Studio 100. That does not mean that the company thrives on chaos. In the earlier years, the two managers were entrepreneurial and made decisions without business plans. But today, the company underpins its new strategic ideas with business plans that are used flexibly.

The creative process has become more structured as well and tends to follow a certain process. For example, the creation of a new character takes three phases. The first phase is the development of the baseline for the character. Gert Verhulst and Hans Bourlon are involved frequently in this phase. In a second phase, the characters are further fed into small creative cells to be elaborated upon. Here, the deepening of the characters takes place. The small cells are also responsible for the creation of the derivatives that are based on the core character like games, publishing, shows, movies, etc. The last phase is the development of the character. In this phase the characters are stable, have proven themselves and are simply further developed through, for instance, licensing and merchandising. At this point in time, every employee can contribute ideas or concepts. Though in phase 1 and 2 this is also welcomed it is noticed that in the early phases creativity experts are in place. (Exhibit 6 provides an overview of these phases for 'Plop the Gnome'.)

Portfolio Management

Over the years, Studio 100 has developed strong competences in portfolio management. The different characters have their own strategy and life cycle. Formats targeted to older children, such as *The House of Anubis* or *Mega Mindy* are more prone to hypes and have the potential to generate substantial cash flows in short time frames. Formats direct towards younger children, such as Bumba or Plop have longer life cycles and the potential to generate steady cash flows over longer periods (see Exhibit 7). The goal of portfolio management is to create the right mix of formats and characters that generate shorter-term, potentially more volatile cash flows, counterbalanced with concepts generating longer-term steady cash flows.[13]

Communication

In a fast-growing company, it is important to keep employees informed about the strategic projects and key challenges of the organization. Studio 100 organizes 'strategy meetings' every 2 to 3 months. These meetings can take an entire afternoon. The management presents what and how well the company is doing. It also formulates questions, and presents where it has doubts. Furthermore, people are asked to present in about 15 minutes what they are doing. And of course, this is also the forum where new commercial projects are presented. If an employee at home sees a commercial on TV for a new show of Studio 100, then it is important that (s)he can explain to his/her family what it is about.

We are very open in this company. There is no hidden agenda. Some people are sceptical about all that. But I feel this leads to involvement and motivation. A good idea can come from anyone and anywhere.

Apart from these formal meetings, both Gert Verhulst and Hans Bourlon provide employees with a lot of input and market information. Says Hans Bourlon:

EXHIBIT 6 The 'product development process' in Studio 100—example: Plop the Gnome

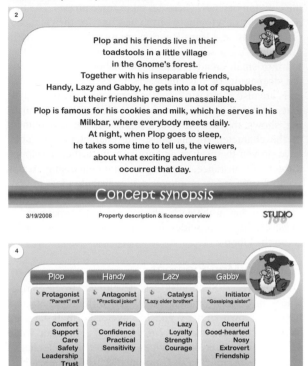

Concept synopsis

Character signature

Target focus

Every morning, I search on the websites of a few newspapers for articles that are related to Studio 100 in one way or another. And I forward these articles to employees that can use them. Everything you see in the world can be a source of inspiration for a story, a new concept or project. Our

employees need to know what is on television these days, what are big hits and what interests' people have at this moment. Information should be available to the people who need it.

Creativity Embedded in the Organization Structure

Creative companies stimulate imagination and out-of the box thinking, which implies a certain chaos in the organization. Studio 100 is no exception. It has quite a flexible and fluid organization. The company has set up creative cells that create new characters and monitor the correct interpretation of and alignment with the character over all different departments, such as the TV department, the merchandising department, the theatre department, and the marketing department.

Both the creative cells and the departments have a direct link to the executive management team. This makes decision lines very short. And it results in a balanced organization. This structure also offers the best guarantees that the main ideas and philosophies of the top are transferred to every part of the organization.

Expanding the DNA Abroad

The internationalization of Studio 100 from 2007 onwards necessitated a change in the company's organization structure. The company has created a new organization structure since December 2010 with four main business units: Studio 100 Benelux, Studio 100 Plopsa (theme parks), Studio 100 Media, and Studio 100 Animation (see Exhibit 8). All these units have their own executive teams.

The theme park business was always considered a separate activity. The activities and the risks associated with running this business are very different from the rest of the Studio 100 activities. The theme park business is not a very creative business. There are many temporary workers and the culture of a theme park is very different from the culture of the other business units within the Group.

For the other three business units there are many overlapping activities. Content is created in Studio 100 Benelux. Studio 100 Benelux represents the original, fully integrated business model where characters show up in live action shows and are then exploited through different channels (stage shows, DVD, audio, publishing, website, merchandising, and licensing).

Studio 100 Media focuses on selling and distributing Studio 100 programmes to TV broadcasters. No content is created in this unit. The managers of Studio 100 tried to export the organizational climate of the Belgian unit to the German unit but that did not work well. In 2012, about 40 people work on the sales and marketing of the international portfolio and is responsible for 15 per cent of the company's revenues.

Studio 100 Animation is a rather new activity in the group's portfolio as it develops, finances, and produces

EXHIBIT 7 Illustrative life cycles of characters

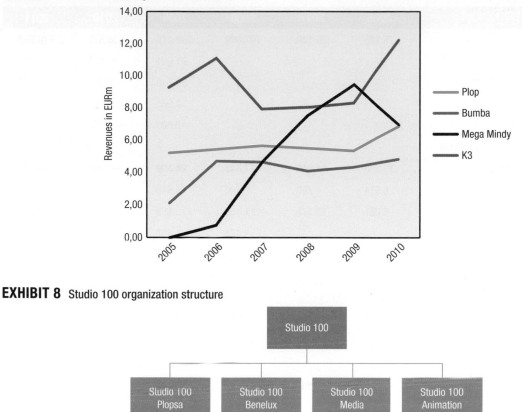

EXHIBIT 8 Studio 100 organization structure

```
                        Studio 100
                            |
     ┌──────────────┬───────────┬──────────────┐
 Studio 100     Studio 100   Studio 100    Studio 100
  Plopsa         Benelux       Media        Animation
```

animated series and feature films. This unit operates from Paris and Sydney (because of more favourable financing conditions in those countries). The development of new series and concepts is undertaken in close collaboration with Studio 100 Benelux. But the business model of Animation is different than the traditional Studio 100 business model. The business model of Animation is more complex, more global, and the process to bring a character to TV takes much longer. On average, it takes one year to get the financing for a movie and making the movie adds another two years. This means that it takes a few years before the first productions go to market. An important advantage of animations is that these can be truly international products that need little tailoring for local markets. They allow for proper exploitation of economies of scale and can be sold in very large volumes once successful.[14]

Studio 100 realized that its traditional model with live action shows is rather unique in the world. And Jo Daris,

the International Business Director (now Director Business Development), could convince the management team of Studio 100 to enter the market of animations. Jo Daris and Koen Peeters, the Chief Financial Officers (CFOs) of the company, believe that this animation silo offers great potential and might very well become the biggest driver of profits in the long run. As Exhibit 9 indicates, this is not yet the case.

Over the years, Studio 100 has developed a clear and winning business model in Belgium and the Netherlands, built around 'boundless creativity and innovation'. The company has been able to leverage its competences in an international context, but Jo Daris and Koen Peeters agree that the international expansion is a challenging task. You cannot just copy a successful business model from one country to another. Nevertheless, Studio 100 is determined to further enlarge the international business in its corporate portfolio.

EXHIBIT 9 Financial figures of different business units

	2006	2007	2008	2009	2010	2011
Revenues (k EUR)	75.125	79.128	107.099	132.419	135.572	170.205
Benelux				71.091	67.548	83.500
Plopsa				38.749	43.681	58.300
Media				14.965	19.484	22.700
Animation				7.609	4.859	5.500
Business development and corporate				5	0	
Recurring EBITDA (k EUR)	13.995	14.846	17.842	28.199	30.090	38.085
Benelux	6.914	4.750	7.420	10.645	7.177	6.150
Plopsa	8.081	10.276	11.488	15.889	17.168	24.571
Media			3.474	4.652	5.820	6.493
Animation			−1.973	−226	2.659	4.350
Business development and corporate	−1.000	−422	−2.567	−2.761	−2.735	−3.478
EBITDA in % of sales	18,6%	18,8%	16,7%	31,1%	29,9%	22,4%
Net result (k EUR)	6.159	2.036	55	7.316	4.611	329
Profit margin	8,2%	2,6%	0,1%	5,5%	3,4%	0,0%

Source: Company information.

ENDNOTES

1. Corporate Overview Studio 100. Available online at www.studio100.tv/sites/default/files/pdf/corporate_overview.pdf, accessed 25 May 2012.
2. People in Flanders and the Netherlands speak Dutch. That is why Studio 100 has quickly reached out to the Dutch market. In the southern part of Belgian, the main language is French.
3. Ghemawat, P. (2001) 'Distance still matters: the hard reality of global expansion', *Harvard Business Review*, September, pp. 137–147.
4. Studio 100 (2011) *Preliminary Offering Memorandum*, Studio 100, p. 60.
5. Petitjean, F. (2009) 'De nv Kristel, Karen en Kathleen', *De Standaard*, 28 March.
6. Bolland, A., Fininzola e Silva, L., Keereman, S., Laurijssen, J., Roelandt, W. and Waterinckx, A. (2009) 'Studio 100—growth strategy', *Assignment Strategic Management Part-Time MBA Vlerick Leuven Gent Management School*, Gent/Leuven.
7. Ibid., p. 9.
8. Studio 100 (2011) *Preliminary Offering Memorandum*, Studio 100, p. 68.
9. Schelfout, S. And Spyns, P. (2009) 'Combining business and creativity, therein lies the success of Studio 100: an interview with Hans Bourlon', Manager of the Year and co-founder of Studio 100', *EWI Review (Periodical of the Department of Economy, Science, and Innovation)*, September, p. 41.
10. Ibid., p. 43.
11. Bourlon, H. (2009), Speech for the International Full-time MBA students of Vlerick Leuven Gent Management School, 12 March.
12. Bontinck, W., Conings, L., Devisch, S., Leirman, L., Loeckx, D., Pelemans, E. and Vandecruys, A. (2008) 'Studio 100 case', *Assignment Strategic Management Part-Time MBA Vlerick Leuven Gent Management School*, Gent/Leuven.
13. Studio 100 (2011) *Preliminary Offering Memorandum*, Studio 100, pp. 55–6.
14. Bolland, A., Fininzola e Silva, L., Keereman, S., Laurijssen, J., Roelandt, W. and Waterinckx, A. (2009) 'Studio 100—growth strategy', *Assignment Strategic Management Part-Time MBA Vlerick Leuven Gent Management School*, Gent/Leuven.

CASE 12

RHINO CAPTURE IN KRUGER NATIONAL PARK

A. J. Strickland
University of Alabama

William E. Mixon
University of Alabama
MBA Candidate

EXHIBIT 2 Rhino population in South Africa

	2007	2010
White rhinos	15 000	17 500
Black rhinos	1500	4200

Dr. Markus Hofmeyr, head of Veterinary Wildlife Services for South African National Parks (SANParks), returned from another rhino capture with his team. They had captured their 252nd rhino for the year before the rainy season set in, with heat and rain making it almost impossible to continue the capture program. As Hofmeyr and his team were winding down another successful year, given that each rhino was worth between $30 000 and $35 000,[1] he began to reflect on next year's game capture. Hofmeyr faced the daunting question of how to continue to supplement the funding for SANParks' Park Development Fund. Over the years, the budget for his unit had been reduced, and pressure for self-funding of SANParks was increasing.

Some of the funding for SANParks' operations had long been provided by the South African national government in the form of an annual grant. That began to change in 2010, however, when a budget shortfall forced the government to initiate the removal of the grant over three years. The South African government shifted its strategy toward building a new South Africa, focused on providing additional funds for education, job creation through infrastructure expansions, better health care for all South Africans, and economic prosperity. Funding cuts outside of these priority areas threatened the ability of SANParks' Veterinary Wildlife Services to continue delivering normal veterinary and operational services— services that were beneficial to all SANParks wildlife and the habitat in which the wildlife had roamed for centuries. SANParks' budget allocation is shown in Exhibit 1.

Kruger National Park

Kruger National Park was established in South Africa in 1898 to protect the nation's fast-dwindling wildlife areas. By the turn of that century, it was estimated that white

EXHIBIT 1 SANParks budget allocation (in U.S. Dollars)

Kruger National Park Budget	$4 951 900
Poaching	$275 100
Infrastructure	$275 100

rhinos were extinct in Kruger. The first translocation of white rhinos to Kruger National Park occurred in 1961, and a total of 345 white rhinos had been relocated from the parks in Kwa Zulu Natal by the mid-1970s. In 2007, an assessment by the African Rhino Specialist Group estimated that 15 000 white rhinos and 1500 black rhinos existed in South Africa. As of 2009, research indicated that 10 000 white rhinos and 500 black rhinos existed within Kruger National Park, making it home to the largest rhino population in the world. Population estimates for rhinos in South Africa are shown in Exhibit 2.[*]

Kruger National Park covered 7722 square miles (20 000 square kilometers) of conservation area, with eight gates that controlled the flow of unauthorized traffic into the park. Since its establishment, it had become known for its unrivaled wildlife diversity and easy viewing and for its world leadership in advanced environmental management techniques, research, and policies. Many viewed Kruger as the best national park in all of Africa in all aspects— management, infrastructure, and, of course, biodiversity. The flagship of South Africa's 22 national parks, Kruger held a variety of species: 336 trees, 49 fish, 34 amphibians, 114 reptiles, 507 birds, and 147 mammals. Over time, the park had developed into a tourist attraction because of the wildlife and the beautiful scenery, which was representative of South Africa's Lowveld region. (The Lowveld consisted of areas around the eastern part of the country where the altitude was about 1000 feet.)

Tourist operations at Kruger were quite large, with the park offering 21 rest camps, 7 private lodge concessions, and 11 private safari lodges. Lodges that previously had been private were operated in partnership between communities and private companies, which provided concessions for parcels of land. The concessions were placed on tender, and areas were allocated for 25- to 30-year leases, during which operational activities linked with tourism were allowed. At the end of the period, the fixed assets became the property of SANParks, which could decide to extend the lease or retender the concession. An integral part of Kruger National Park's conservation effort was game capture. Traditionally, capturing game allowed Kruger to reintroduce certain species to previously uninhabited areas of the park, as well as to introduce rhino to the other national parks in South Africa and neighboring countries.

Game capture also enabled the park to better manage rare species by placing them in breeding enclosures. In some instances, game capture was used to reduce populations where that goal was impeded by natural regulatory mechanisms. Traditional game capture evolved into an income-generating operation as the demand for rhinos increased.

Income Generation from Game Capture

The sale of wildlife for income generation was accepted and supported by South Africa's National Environmental Management Act (2004). SANParks maximized income from wildlife sales by concentrating on selling high-value species. The two species sold without clearly required ecological reasons for their sale were white rhinos from Kruger National Park and disease-free buffalos from other parks. The only condition required when an animal was sold was that its removal could not negatively impact the populations from which it came. In 2009, 500 rhinos were sold in South Africa. Kruger National Park claimed 252 of these transactions; the others were sold from provincial parks and the private sector. A flow chart of sales transactions is shown in Exhibit 3. The average selling price for a white rhino was $30 300. Many wildlife biologists and other experts feared that these rhinos would eventually fall into the hands of private game hunters. Rhino hunting and rhino breeding for future sales or hunting were driving up the price for a rhino. SANParks accepted hunting as a legal form of wildlife utilization but did not support unethical put-and-take hunting practices because it was very difficult to determine what happened to a rhino after leaving SANParks. SANParks was not responsible for enforcing hunting regulations on wildlife; instead, this responsibility was passed on to each respective South African province. However, many provinces were understaffed, which weakened the regulation of hunting activities.

The most common method for selling rhinos outside Kruger National Park was through provincial and private-sector auctions. In 2009, 45 auctions accounted for most rhino sales outside SANParks. During that year, 252 rhinos on a direct tender were captured in the bush and sold at three auctions held by SANParks. The revenue generated from rhino sales in 2009 totaled $7 033 400. These revenue sales supplemented the conservation budget for SANParks' Park Development Fund. The buyers of the live rhinos were dealers who specialized in wild game or private owners who bought directly from SANParks. Rhinos were typically sold to a private game reserve for either tourist viewing or hunting. Rhinos were also sold or donated by SANParks to neighboring countries. Rhinos purchased in the private sector were sometimes sold internationally to zoos or to buyers who dealt in wild game.

Typically, white rhinos were sold more often than black rhinos, since black rhinos were rarer and much more aggressive. SANParks had sold only two black rhino bulls; the other black rhinos moved from Kruger were donated as part of conservation efforts to reestablish them in countries where they had gone extinct. The private sector bought black rhinos from Kwa Zulu Natal Wildlife, where the remaining black rhinos survived with white rhinos at the turn of the twentieth century. Kwa Zulu Natal moved from completely selling black rhinos to retaining full ownership of the adults and partial ownership of the offspring. Offspring were placed into a custodianship program that split the rights between two or more parties. North West Province sold black rhinos, as did the private sector. Compared with white rhinos, black rhinos were more difficult to introduce and had a higher intraspecies mortality rate from fighting. The tendency to fight made black rhinos a riskier investment than white rhinos, which bred and coexisted much better than black rhinos. The majority of white rhinos were purchased in cow/calf combinations, which were not hunted. White rhino bulls were much more likely than white rhino cows to be purchased for hunting. However, most provinces had

EXHIBIT 3

Flow chart of sales transactions

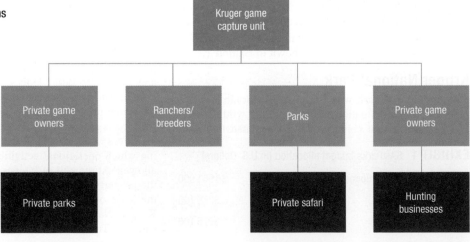

regulations that limited the number of rhinos eligible to be hunted. Before a rhino was killed, it had to have lived on the current property for more than two years; however, this regulation was very difficult to enforce. Park Services was a critical component of conservation for rhinos and other animals within the park.

Park Services

Veterinary Wildlife Services (VWS) offered a variety of operational and veterinary services for Kruger National Park. Veterinarian operations were critical to the conservation of wildlife within and outside the park. The service's operations included wildlife capture, holding, and translocation; park development; species conservation management; wildlife sales; animal exchanges and contractual commitments; regional cooperation; and research. VWS's aims and objectives and responsibilities are shown in Exhibit 4. Game capture operations began in the 1980s for Kruger National Park; Kruger had also operated game capture in other parks. In the 1990s, a second unit was established for operations outside Kruger. Both units were combined to form VWS in 2002, ensuring that

EXHIBIT 4 Aims, objectives, and responsibilities of sanparks' Veterinary Wildlife Services

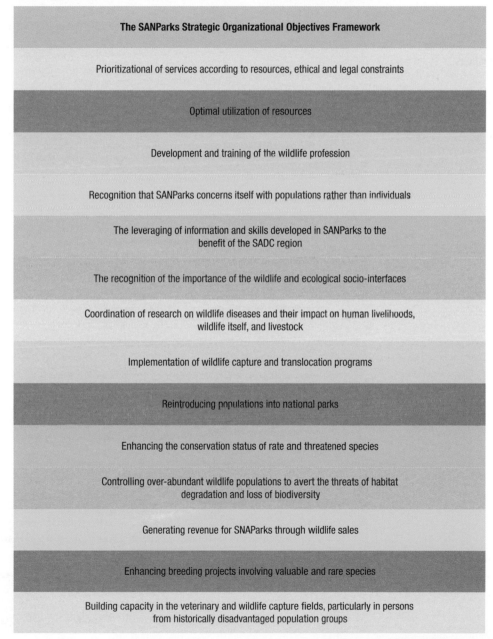

The SANParks Strategic Organizational Objectives Framework

Prioritizational of services according to resources, ethical and legal constraints

Optimal utilization of resources

Development and training of the wildlife profession

Recognition that SANParks concerns itself with populations rather than individuals

The leveraging of information and skills developed in SANParks to the benefit of the SADC region

The recognition of the importance of the wildlife and ecological socio-interfaces

Coordination of research on wildlife diseases and their impact on human livelihoods, wildlife itself, and livestock

Implementation of wildlife capture and translocation programs

Reintroducing populations into national parks

Enhancing the conservation status of rate and threatened species

Controlling over-abundant wildlife populations to avert the threats of habitat degradation and loss of biodiversity

Generating revenue for SNAParks through wildlife sales

Enhancing breeding projects involving valuable and rare species

Building capacity in the veterinary and wildlife capture fields, particularly in persons from historically disadvantaged population groups

the service was serving SANParks' objectives and not just those of Kruger. Kruger aimed for VWS to 'provide ethical and professional services relating to capture, holding, translocation and research pertaining to wildlife.'[2] Some of the values and functions associated with VWS are shown in Exhibit 5.

SANParks' Game Capture Unit

SANParks' game capture unit had branch offices in three locations in South Africa: Kruger, Kimberley, and Port Elizabeth. The capture, translocation and reestablishment functions of SANParks' Veterinary Wildlife Services are shown in Exhibit 6.

Population growth, sex and age structure, spatial use, natural dispersal, resource distribution, and population dynamics were considered when making the decision to sell an animal to a private buyer. According to SANParks' chief executive officer, Dr. David Mabunda, 'SANParks, by selling or donating rhino, is assisting in the process of recolonization of the range in the country and outside. It should be noted that it would be foolhardy if South Africa were to have its only rhino population residing in the Kruger, because we run the danger of losing them should there be a major outbreak of disease or rampant poaching. We would be sitting ducks.' Bovine tuberculosis and anthrax were two diseases being monitored by VWS in efforts to

EXHIBIT 5

Veterinary Wildlife Services' values and functions

Veterinary Wildlife Values

VWS is a service delivery department for SANParks, providing specialist veterinary and wildlife handling and translocation support

The SANParks strategic organizational objectives framework of biodiversity, balancing, people and enabling systems will guide these services

The resource, ethical, and legal constraints as well as other drivers will make it necessary to prioritize the services that can be delivered. (Guided by the Wildlife Management Commitee recommendations.)

Optimal utilitization of resources

The leveraging of information and skills developed in SANParks to the benefit of the SADEC region, particularly in SANParks TFC involment

Development and training of the wildlife profession

The recognition of the importance of wildlife and ecological and diagnostic test development

Veterinary Wildlife Functions

Service to scientific services and park managment with regard to implementing veterinary aspects of removals and introductions into our parks, collar fitting, sample taking and any other activities that require handling of wildlife

Disease monitoring, management and surveillance (including sample taking, storing and distribution aid research)

Development of current veterinary aspects of capture, translocation and animal husbandry techniques

Veterinary support to special species management related to approved plans (e.g., predator management plans)

Conservation medicine (implementing and integrating disease and ecological principles in our function)

Veterinary research relevant to the service delivery component of VWS

Liaison and education at the appropriate national and international level

EXHIBIT 6

The capture, translocation and reestablishment functions of SANParks' Veterinary Wildlife Services

Capture, Translocation and Reestablishment Functions

Operational capture, care and translocation of wildlife species aligned with SANParks requirements

Import species and disease-free breeding projects

Coordination of game sales

Transfrontier development

International translocations

Coordination of capture by external entities

EXHIBIT 7

Veterinary Wildlife Service's disease management services

Disease Management Services

BTB monitoring in Buffalo and Lion within Kruger

Monitoring in all parks when opportunities arise

Sarcoid research in Mountain Zebra in Bontebok NP

Disease prevention principles applied to animal movements and quarantine facilities both in Kruger and Kimberley

better understand how to contain them, which in turn would lead to better decisions about disease management where required. Intervention was not always needed in wildlife populations, but an understanding of how a disease influenced population dynamics was. VWS disease management services are shown in Exhibit 7. In addition to these issues, SANParks concerned itself with Kruger National Park's capability to assess and evaluate financial implications and the risks imposed to its white rhino population by intense localized removals and emerging diseases.[3]

Capturing a Rhino

The rhino capture process involved the use of state-of-the-art equipment accompanied by a team of experts. A game capture team included a helicopter pilot, a veterinarian, an operational coordinator, a veterinary technician, five capture staff personnel, and two drivers for the translocation and crane trucks. Selected operating expenses of a rhino capture are shown in Exhibit 8.

Once a rhino was located, the capture process consisted of darting it with a drug combination from a helicopter.

EXHIBIT 8 Selected operating expenses of rhino capture

Game capture operating expenses	Cost per rhino	Cost per hour	Cost per day	Cost per year	Unit cost
Helicopter	N/A	$800	N/A	N/A	N/A
Transportation of rhino	$300	N/A	N/A	$11 000	N/A
Truck	N/A	N/A	$300	N/A	N/A
Boom	N/A	N/A	$300	N/A	N/A
Capture team	N/A	$200	$1400	N/A	N/A
RFID microchip	$50	N/A	N/A	N/A	$17

The fast-acting drug combination made the whole capture process less dangerous to the capture unit by rendering the rhino unconscious for evaluation before relocation. Once the rhino was unconscious, a team from the game capture unit moved in to examine it. The game capture unit conducted a medical examination of the rhino by taking blood samples to test for any signs of disease. At this point in the game capture process, three radio-frequency identification (RFID) microchips were tagged on the rhino for identification purposes. Inserting an RFID microchip involved drilling into the horn, which is made of keratin, a material similar to that which human hair and fingernails are composed of. Photos of the game capture process are shown in Exhibit 9.

Park officials used tagging as a method to better understand the rhinos' movement within their landscape. South African law mandated the tagging of any rhino darted as well. Park services were also looking at ways to place tracking devices on rhinos to increase the capability of understanding rhino movements within their landscape. Prevention was the main emphasis of the rhino poaching counteroffensive in Kruger. It was thought that these potential tracking devices would help deter poaching, but the main deterrent was gaining information from informants on possible plans for rhino poaching.

After the evaluation and tagging process, a partial antidote was administered to partially wake up the rhino but keep it in a semi-anesthetized state. Partial antidotes were necessary to protect the game capture team while walking the rhino into the transportation crate. After the rhino was successfully loaded into a transportation crate, a boom truck lifted the crate onto the translocation truck. A boom truck was needed since an average rhino weighed 3300 pounds (1500 kilograms). Typically, the average distance traveled by a rhino captured from Kruger National Park was 50 miles (80 kilometers), at a cost of $300 per rhino per 16

EXHIBIT 9
The game capture process

The game capture unit follows the helicopter in pursuit of a rhino.

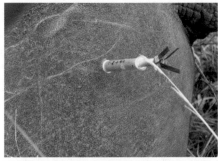

The dart shot from the helicopter is inspected by game capture personnel.

Game capture unit personnel inspect the sedated rhino.

Game capture personnel drill a hole in the rhino's horn to insert the RFID microchip.

Game capture personnel inspect the sedated rhino.

Boom trucks are needed to load the rhino.

After the antidote is given, the staff helps the rhino stand up.

EXHIBIT 10 Dr. Markus Hofmeyr standing above several *Bomas* (holding pens)

miles. The next translocation process was maintenance in holding facilities (see Exhibit 10). Rhinos were placed in *bomas* (holding pens). *Bomas* allowed a rhino to become accustomed to a new habitat by slowly facilitating a passive

release. Once released, the rhino was typically still confined to a larger pen or fenced-in area, depending on the buyer's intentions. It was estimated that 50 percent of the bulls transferred to private hunting companies were killed within two years, at a price of $2800 per inch of rhino horn.

Rhino Hunting

A typical rhino hunt could cost $82 400 per hunter. In 2009, South Africa generated an estimated $6.9 billion in revenues from tourist attractions; of that amount, hunting accounted for about 70 percent, or about $4.8 billion.[4] The cost of booking a rhino hunt varied depending on the safari company, as detailed in Exhibit 11. Most safari companies required a deposit of 50 percent of the basic cost of a safari, which was fully refundable until within three months of the contracted safari date. Accommodations varied according to packages offered by each safari company and were considered comparable to those of any other tourist attraction in the world. Some safari companies offered photo safaris and wedding packages, in addition to hunting services, to further generate revenue for operations.

Typically, each safari company recommended certain equipment and clothing for hunters to bring along with

EXHIBIT 11 Selected company safari expenses and trip details

Africa Sport Hunting Safaris

Services offered
- First-class rifle and bow hunting
- Ethical, professional hunters
- Personal attention to all our clients
- Family and photographic tours
- Specialized, well-maintained vehicles
- Luxury accommodation
- Excellent cuisine
- Dedicated staff

Firearms and calibers
- Rhino legal minimum .375 caliber and 3–9 × 40 variable-power telescope
- Ammunition recommended minimum of 40 full metal jacket/solids in addition to soft point bullets

Travel information
- Valid passport required

Trophy handling
- All animals will be skinned by our very experienced skinners, as well as marked, salted, and dried prior to being sent to a taxidermist. All documentation will be handled by Africa Sport Hunting Safaris

Clothing and other requirements
- Three sets of hunting clothing: long pants (zip-offs), long-sleeve shirts, socks, and underwear
- Hunting boots/shoes— comfortable
- Casual/running shoes
- Sweater/warm jacket
- Flip flops/sweat suit
- Cap/wide-brimmed hat
- Casual clothes
- Adjust your clothing to the time of year your hunt takes place.
- Winter May–August (35–70°F)
- Summer September–April (50–90°F)

(continued)

EXHIBIT 11 Selected company safari expenses and trip details (*continued*)

Personal
- Personal medical kit
- Sunblock— minimum 30 SPF
- Mosquito repellent
- Pair of sunglasses
- Toiletries

Additional equipment
- Small day pack
- Flashlight with spare batteries
- Binoculars
- Camera with spare film and batteries
- Pocket knife

Accommodation: luxury thatched chalets with a true African ambience

- Private rooms with ensuite bathrooms
- Running hot and cold water
- Electricity with converters
- Flush toilets

Food and beverages
- Traditional South African cuisine. For dietary requirements such as diabetes and high cholesterol, please make arrangements on booking of the safari

Additional services
- Facials and full body massages
- Manicures and pedicures
- Day excursions

South African hunting areas price list Limpopo Province 2010

- White Rhino	$45 000
- White Rhino (Green-Hunt)	$13 000

Daily rate: South Africa

- Dangerous Game	$800
- Plains Game	
- 1 Hunter × 1 Professional Hunter:	$400
- 2 Hunters × 1 Professional Hunter:	$300
- All non-hunters are welcome at:	$200

Included in daily rate
- Pick up and drop off at Polokwane International Airport
- Hunting licenses and fees
- Transportation to and from hunting concessions
- Field preparation of trophies
- Professional hunters, trackers, skinners, and camp staff
- Fully equipped hunting vehicles
- Luxury accommodation and meals
- Drinks and beverages in moderation
- Daily laundry services

Excluded from daily rates
- Flights: international and domestic
- Charter flights where applicable
- All animals shot and wounded will be charged per price list
- Dipping, packing, taxidermy cost
- Non-hunting, traveling days at $150 per day
- Accommodation before and after hunt
- Any additional tours or excursions

(*continued*)

EXHIBIT 11 Selected company safari expenses and trip details   (*continued*)

Methods of payment accepted
− U.S. currency
− Traveler's checks
− Wire transfers
− Credit cards
− Personal checks with prior approval

Members of:
− Professional Hunters Association South Africa
− Accredited Tour Guides
− Safari Club International
− North American Hunters Association
− National Rifle Association

Chattaronga Safaris	
Daily fees hunter	
1	$400
2	$350
3	$300
4	$300
Observer	$200

Included tariffs
− Accommodation including full board
− Liquor and beverages served in camp
− Full-time service of experienced professional hunter.
− Trained staff
− Trackers
− Skinners
− Field preparation of trophies
− All transportation within hunting areas
− All hunting licenses
− Pickup and drop-off at international airport: Limpopo-Polokwane, Kwa-Zulu Natal-Johannesburg, Mpumalanga-Johannesburg

Excluded tariffs
− International and domestic flights
− Traveling day (non-hunting days) at $180 per day
− Trophy fees of animal shot or wounded
− Rifle hire (firearms may be rented at $80 per day)
− Ammunition is available at cost
− Dipping, packing, taxidermy, and shipping
− Air charters and accommodation before and after safari
− Tips for staff, telephone calls, and curio purchases

Rhino safari	
7 Day 1 × 1	$60 000
Includes representative 20' fake horn (because it is not standard practice to cut off the horn of a rhino).	

Dumukwa	
Daily rates	
1 hunter/1 professional hunter	$400
2 hunters/1 professional hunter	$300
Non-hunters/observers	$200
Rhino dart	$8500
5 day 1 × 1 Hunt	

(*continued*)

EXHIBIT 11 Selected company safari expenses and trip details   *(continued)*

Included in daily rates
- Full accommodation, meals, and use of camp facilities
- All liquid refreshments including wine, beer, bottled water, and sodas
- Daily laundry
- Service of professional hunter with his team of skinners and trackers
- Field preparation of trophies
- Transport of raw trophies to local taxidermist for the area you in hunt in
- All transportation during the safari including from and to the airport
- 14 percent value added tax (VAT) on all packages

Excluded in daily rates
- Internet, faxes, and telephone calls
- Airfare
- Hotel accommodation before and after the contracted safari
- Dipping and packing or mounting of trophies
- Shipping of trophies back to your country
- Optional hire of firearms

Zingeli Safaris

Included in daily rates
- Full board and lodging with traditional catering
- South African wines and beer in moderation, and soft drinks
- Experienced professional hunter and trained staff
- Trackers and skinners
- Field preparation, salting and packing
- Transportation of trophies to reliable and qualified taxidermist who will follow your instructions and fulfill the necessary requirements
- Use of hunting vehicle
- Laundry services
- Transportation to the ranch and return to Johannesburg International Airport or charter plane

Excluded in daily rates
- Air travel before, during and after the contracted period of the safari
- Accommodation and travel charges incurred before and after the contracted period of the safari
- Trophy fees for animals taken or wounded
- Value added tax (VAT) 14 percent on daily rates
- Air charters
- Gratuities to professional hunters and staff
- Preparation, packing, documentation, and export of trophies from South Africa

them. This list varied by season, since temperatures could range between 30°F (low) in the winter and 90°F (high) in the wet summer season. Expenses also varied according to the specific details of a trip such as length of stay, trophy fees, number of hunters and observers, and the daily rate charged per hunter. Airfare to and from South Africa also varied depending on how far in advance travel arrangements were made and whether the flight was direct. Typically, coach seating ranged from $800 to $1100, whereas first-class price ranges easily approached $3000. Rifles, bows, and darting weapons were offered in some packages, but rifles could be imported into South Africa under strict guidelines and regulations. However, hunters were not allowed to import automatic or semiautomatic weapons.

Some companies charged high trophy fees and low daily rates, in contrast to low trophy fees and high daily rates. Trophy fees varied according to the specific animal wounded or

killed and were typically not paid until the end of the safari. Daily rates depended on the services offered and could include or exclude a number of amenities necessary to hunt in South Africa. In general, some safari companies offered a lower daily rate as a marketing tool to increase their customer base; a large trophy fee reflected the fact that a safari company's profits depended on a successful hunt by the customer. As Zingeli Safaris stated in its brochure, 'If you don't get your animal we lose; this is your guarantee that we will do our best to find you your dream trophy!' Customers incurred taxidermist fees, in addition to trophy fees, if they desired to have something tangible to take home.

Poaching

Demand for rhino horn in emerging markets such as Asia and India made rhino poaching highly profitable. In 2009, rhino horn was sold on the black market at $3600 per pound, but by 2010 the price was reported to be $7200 per pound. An average rhino horn weighed six to eight pounds. Businesses with ties to political insiders were entering the market to supply and sell rhino horn as wealth creation resulted from the growth of Asia's and India's economies.

The market for raw rhino horn was mainly driven by demand in China and Vietnam. Cultural beliefs, combined with increasing wealth, were creating a strong foundation for the demand of rhino horn. Asians believed that rhino horn was a very beneficial aphrodisiac, and Indians desired rhino horn daggers. These beliefs and desires were strong enough to produce enough capital to entice the illegal killing of rhinos without regard to law enforcers such as the SANParks Environmental Crimes Unit, South African Police Service, and park rangers.

Poachers were well equipped with highly sophisticated transportation such as helicopters and the latest military weaponry available in the region. They were able to strike fast within even the most protected game conservation areas. Poaching was even a problem in Kruger National Park, home to what some considered the best antipoaching unit in South Africa. In 2006, two rhinos were even poached by staff members employed by SANParks. In 2009 alone, there were about 50 rhinos poached in Kruger and 100 poached in South Africa as a whole. As of January 22, 2010, poachers had killed 14 rhinos in Kruger National Park as well.

Poachers were ruthless in the slaughtering of rhinos. They typically cut off the rhino's horns after darting it with a deadly poison (see Exhibit 12). Poachers also darted rhinos with an immobilizing antidote that sometimes left the rhino helpless in the wild to be eaten by other game. SANParks' CEO, Dr. David Mabunda, described poachers as 'dangerous criminals.' Their exploits were not limited to killing rhinos, but also included human trafficking, arms smuggling, prostitution, and drug trafficking.

'Poachers must beware,' Mabunda said in a statement announcing a $250 000 funding boost, in addition to the $5.2 million allocated to train and prepare the SANParks Environmental Crimes Unit and South African Police

Service. Fifty-seven rangers equipped with night vision goggles and high-powered motorbikes had been dispatched to guard highly poached areas of the park day and night. Said Mabunda, 'This war we plan on winning.' In addition to the funding boost, plans were considered to guard the porous border near Kruger National Park with military personnel. Elisabeth McLellan, a species expert with the World Wildlife Foundation (WWF), was quoted as saying, 'The situation is bad for rhino worldwide, in terms of poaching.' Conservationists were facing an environment that had evolved into an industry, as world trade had reached a 15-year high for illegal rhino horn trading.

Kenyan authorities at Jomo Kenyatta International Airport had seized a 662-pound load of elephant tusk and rhino horn believed to have come from South Africa. It was speculated that the load, valued at approximately $1 million, was destined for China. Industry experts suggested that the high value placed on elephant tusk and rhino horn by consumers was driving the demand for both substances.

Animal Supermarket

Kruger National Park was determined to win the war against poaching, but determination alone wasn't enough to protect the rhino. Primary-market transactions involved buyers that protected the rhino— such as other national parks, private game farms, game dealers, and photography safari business owners— but secondary markets from the sale of captured rhinos had also developed. Hunters had become the most numerous buyers in the secondary market, which wasn't aligned with Kruger National Park's mission. Animal rights activists dubbed the sale of animals at Kruger National Park an 'animal supermarket.' Many believed that the commercial trade posed a greater threat than poaching did. Many also felt it was fundamentally wrong to herd animals from a popular wildlife reserve and sell them in efforts at 'conservation.' Wildlife activists accused SANParks of misusing the park by serving as nothing more than a private game breeder, and experts feared that the vast majority of the rhinos sold by SANParks would fall into the hands of private hunters.

SANParks' Justification

SANParks was guided in its decision to sell wildlife by Clause 55(2)(b) of the Protected Areas Act No. 57 of 2003 (as amended), which stated that 'SANParks may, in managing national parks, sell, exchange or donate any animal, plant, or other organism occurring in a park, or purchase, exchange or otherwise acquire any indigenous species which it may consider desirable to reintroduce into a specific park.' SANParks believed that it was critical to its conservation efforts to maintain the sale of animals to private entities. For years, SANParks had sold animals to fund conservation efforts, and in many cases the park had traded animals to obtain other species. Also, SANParks screened animals and buyers to ensure that animals were released not arbitrarily, but to buyers with the proper permits and

EXHIBIT 12 Rhino left to die after poachers cut off horn

EXHIBIT 13

Responsibilities of conservation biologists

Identify key research themes necessary for national parks to achieve their conservation objectives

Conduct research on key themes

Coordinating research projects conducted by external scientific institutions in national parks.

Integrating best available biodiversity data into park management through interactions with external researchers and research institutions

Maintaining inventories of biodiversity in national parks, including species checklists for vertebrates and higher plants and the mapping of landscape. Geology, soil and vegetation

Identifying and averting threats to biodiversity in national parks, including overabundance of certain wildlife populations, invasive alien plant and animal species, pollutants, human development, excessive resource exploitation or other factors

Ensuring that development within parks takes place in a manner that does not compromise biodiversity conservation

Conservation for rare and threatened species

Provide scientific inputs on the rehabilitation of degraded landscapes

Providing scientific inputs on biodiversity aspects of park management plans and activities

Building capacity in conservation biology and related sciences, particularly in persons from historically disadvantaged population groups

---

intentions. Decisions to sell or donate wildlife were scientifically determined according to population dynamics, sex and age structure, spatial use, natural dispersal, and resource distribution.

SANParks' strategy was informed by the following objectives: population control, broadening of the range for populations, spreading the risk of managing wildlife, making the populations more resilient and viable, and fund-raising for specific conservation and land-expansion programs. The responsibilities of SANParks' conservation biologists are shown in Exhibit 13. The challenge facing SANParks was how to effectively communicate that selling rhinos was for the greater good.

ENDNOTES

* © 2010 by A.J. Strickland. All rights reserved.
1. All monetary amounts in this case are in U.S. dollars.
2. *Wildlife Research Magazine.*
3. Sam Ferreira & Travis Smith Scientific Services, SANParks, Skukuza, South Africa.
4. *Wildlife Research Magazine.*

CASE 13

HTC CORPORATION: A SMARTPHONE PIONEER FROM TAIWAN*

In February 2010, Peter Chou, chief executive officer (CEO) of HTC Corporation, the pioneer of smartphone manufacturing in Taiwan, was attending an annual industry festival, the Mobile World Congress in Barcelona. At a press conference at the event, at which members of his global team were also present, Chou unveiled the company's "quietly brilliant" advertising campaign, aimed at reinforcing the spirit of the HTC brand. He also introduced three new smartphone models made by the company—of which two were based on the Android platform of Google Inc. (Google) and one on the Windows Mobile 6.5 platform of Microsoft Corporation (Microsoft). Although HTC products had gained credibility among mobile phone subscribers worldwide, Chou and his team faced a rapidly changing competitive landscape, in which the smartphone segment was getting more crowded and new categories (such as e-reader and tablet devices) were also emerging.

Company Background

HTC Corporation (known as High Tech Computer Corporation before 2008) was founded in Taiwan in May 1997 by two entrepreneurs: Cher Wang and H T Cho. Wang, who was from a well-known business family in Taiwan, had ventured out on her own path at a young age to create a successful enterprise that made computer chipsets. Cho was an engineer with Digital Equipment Corp (DEC), a U.S. mini-computer manufacturer that had a plant in Taiwan. HTC's start-up team also consisted of nine other engineers, including Chou, who joined HTC as vice president of Research and Development (R&D) and was named its CEO in 2004.

* Professor Lien-Ti Bei (College of Commerce, National Chengchi University) and Professor Shih-Fen Chen (Richard Ivey School of Business, University of Western Ontario) co-authored this case solely to provide material for class discussion. The authors do not intend to illustrate either effective or ineffective handling of a managerial situation. The authors may have disguised certain names and other identifying information to protect confidentiality.

HTC was created on an investment of NT$5 million (roughly US$172,000) as a subcontractor of hand-held devices for Western buyers. The company's first client was Compaq Computers (Compaq) which, in January 1998, acquired DEC in what was considered a blockbuster deal, worth $9.6 billion.[1] Compaq was searching for a product to compete with the Palm Pilot, a personal data assistant (PDA) launched by Palm Computing Inc. (Palm) in 1996. Within weeks of launch in the United States, the Palm Pilot had sparked a mobile-computing revolution.

Chou, as vice president of HTC's R&D, had heard about the nascent mobile technology as early as February 1998, at the 3GSM World Congress in Cannes. After joining HTC, he formed a team to work on the idea of combining the data-processing ability of a PDA and the communication ability of a mobile phone.

HTC developed a PDA prototype for Compaq based on two innovations: a coloured screen (in 1999) and a Windows software platform (in 2000). This PDA was the only coloured handheld personal computer (PC) at that time—the first successful innovation by the fledgling startup. The software platform, called Windows CE, was originally developed by Microsoft for large consumer electronic products. HTC paid a licence fee of over US$1 million for the right to adapt it to PDA. This adaptation allowed HTC's PDA to communicate with PCs and run other Windows applications.

After signing up HTC as an original design manufacturer (ODM), Compaq marketed the new PDA under its own brand, iPAQ, which was introduced in April 2000. This pocket device caught on with business professionals because it used the Windows CE operating system and could run Microsoft Pocket Office applications. Eventually, HTC made 2.5 million PDAs per annum for Compaq and also supplied it under the ODM arrangement for other computer companies like HP and Dell.

In 2002, HTC expanded its ability to make white-label PDAs to two new customer segments: mobile phone manufacturers and mobile network operators. The trigger was provided by the close partnership HTC had fostered with Microsoft. Gaining early access to Microsoft's mobile platform technologies, HTC had eventually developed a smartphone using Windows compatible applications.

HTC's smartphone was marketed by O2 (a British network operator) under its XDA brand, by Orange (a French network operator) under its SPV name and by T-Mobile under its Pocket PC Phone label, all in 2002. All these network operators saw an increase in their average revenue per subscriber. This introduction of the smartphone line opened up an opportunity for HTC to become an ODM not only for other network operators (like Vodafone) but also for branded handset makers (such as Palm). Chou described the move from PDA to smartphone for the company: "Switching our business to smartphone starts a new era for HTC. We used to focus on cost-cutting, but now we have to be innovative. We hope that one day, when people think about Taiwan, they think about HTC."

In 2006, HTC launched a new smartphone line under its own name (see Exhibit 1). The company was now firmly on the path to becoming an own-brand manufacture (OBM) company. Up to the end of 2010, it had developed more than 50 models of smartphones. Each was a world-class product designed to deliver a unique and customized wireless telecommunication solution to the customer. Such a smooth transition from a subcontractor to a brand marketer surprised many investors, given that the initial launch of the HTC brand triggered a sharp drop in its stock price by approximately US$1 billion in total value.

For the year ending December 2009, HTC had revenues of NT$144.5 billion and a gross profit of NT$24.62 billion (see Exhibits 2A and 2B). HTC sold 24.7 million devices in 2010, up from 10.8 million smartphones in 2009. Its 2010 annual sales were NT$275 billion (about US$9.49 billion), which nearly doubled the figure of 2009. HTC was ranked fifth among smartphone manufacturers worldwide and ninth in the overall mobile market by share in 2010.

Mobile Telecom Industry

Globally, there were 4.9 billion mobile subscribers at the end of 2009. The number was forecasted to reach 5.3 billion by the end of 2010.[2] The year 2009 had, however, witnessed a 4.8 percent fall over the previous year in the total sales of mobile phones (regular and smart).[3] The fall was largely due to recessionary trends worldwide.

Contrastingly, the global sales of smartphones grew by 14.6 percent over 2008, topping 173.5 million units in 2009. Recession had not affected the appeal of smartphones, which acquired, in a short span, the status of a lifestyle accessory. The product life cycle was becoming shorter, between six and nine months, creating its own demand.

The smartphone had its origins at IBM, which showcased it as a concept in 1992.[4] While the mobile phone provided voice communications and text messaging through the wireless medium, a smartphone integrated mobile phone capabilities with the more advanced features of a handheld computer. It enabled web browsing and e-mail.

The technology of smartphones was Internet compatible. It was evolving even while incorporating progressively more advanced features like high-speed data transfer and directional services through GPS. Consumers saw the smartphone as both a productivity enhancement and entertainment tool, beyond the basic function of voice communication provided by the regular mobile phone.

Mobile Phone History

The concept of a mobile phone was a century old. It had its tentative beginnings in the concept of a "car phone" as early as 1910 when Lars Magnus Ericsson, the founder of the eponymous Swedish telephone company, attempted to build a telephone into his vehicle and connect it to the overhead telephone lines. The technology was based on the idea that the voice of the speaker at either end could be transformed into radio waves, which could journey through the air; once they hit a receiver at a nearby base station, the latter used the mainline telephone network to re-route the call. However, the major requirement for this transmission was the radio spectrum, which was limited. As a result, there was no further development of the concept for the next four decades.

In 1947, Bell Laboratories in the United States devised a system by which a particular geographic territory could be divided into a number of cells, each serving as a base station with its own transmitter and receiver. The application ensured that the spectrum was not wasted. This was the beginning of modern cellular technology. In 1973, Motorola displayed the first portable phone, which weighed two kilograms. In 1979, NTT launched car phones on a pilot commercial scale in Tokyo.

The technology platform of the mobile phone went through three sequential phases. The first phase was known as 1G (first generation), characterized by analog transmission of voice communication. It was launched by Nordic Mobile Telephone (NMT) in 1981 in four countries simultaneously: Denmark, Finland, Norway and Sweden. The major limitations of 1G were low transmission capacity and poor quality of voice flow.[5]

EXHIBIT 1 HTC – Timeline

- 1997: HTC established
- 1998: First Windows PDA
- 1999: First colour palm-size PC
- 2000: First Microsoft Pocket PC
- 2002: First Microsoft wireless Pocket PC
- 2002: First Microsoft-powered smartphone
- 2004: First Microsoft Smart Music Phone—Large 2.8" TFT touch-screen LCD display
- 2005: First Microsoft 3G Phone
- 2005: First Microsoft Windows Mobile 5.0 Platform Phone
- 2005: First tri-band UMTS 3G device on the Microsoft Windows Mobile platform
- 2006: First Microsoft Windows 5.0 smartphone
- 2007: First tri-band UMTS PDA; first intuitive touch screen to allow finger tip navigation
- 2008: First Google Android smartphone
- 2010: First Nexus One smartphone for Google

Source: HTC company records.

EXHIBIT 2A HTC – Income Statement

	2010	2009	2008	2007	2006	2005	2004	2003	2002	2001
Operating revenues	275,046,954	144,880,715	152,558,766	118,579,953	104,816,548	72,768,522	36,397,166	21,821,605	20,644,316	15,550,363
Cost of sales	(195,489,982)	(99,018,232)	(101,916,912)	(72,880,172)	(70,779,066)	(54,758,040)	(28,493,144)	(17,938,644)	(17,041,738)	(13,429,918)
Gross profit	79,556,972	45,862,483	50,641,854	45,699,786	34,037,482	18,010,482	7,904,022	3,882,961	3,602,578	2,120,445
Operating expenses	(37,024,324)	(21,713,430)	(20,426,453)	(14,665,297)	(7,336,582)	(5,161,215)	(3,594,554)	(2,056,260)	(1,484,059)	(935,505)
Operating income	42,295,343	24,174,994	30,256,385	31,023,425	26,551,966	12,840,479	4,310,420	1,819,460	2,118,519	1,184,940
Non-operating income	2,536,080	1,623,362	2,300,018	1,810,908	1,234,336	217,975	312,956	482,678	421,980	255,943
Non-operating expenses	(340,114)	(585,892)	(965,924)	(683,036)	(828,424)	(902,515)	(662,848)	(342,293)	(1,032,470)	(450,632)
Income before income tax	44,491,309	25,212,464	31,590,479	32,151,297	26,957,878	12,155,939	3,960,528	1,959,845	1,508,029	990,251
Income tax expense	(4,957,709)	(2,603,562)	(2,955,130)	(3,212,435)	(1,710,551)	(373,995)	(105,182)	(109,113)	(43,575)	(27,523)
Net income	39,533,600	22,608,902	28,635,349	28,938,862	25,247,327	11,781,944	3,855,346	1,850,732	1,464,454	962,728

Note 1. All figures are in thousand NT dollars.

Note 2. US$1 is equal to NT$29 by the end of 2010.

EXHIBIT 2B HTC – Balance Sheet

	2010	2009	2008	2007	2006	2005	2004	2003	2002	2001	2000
Assets											
Current assets	156,908,107	101,503,673	101,271,990	83,172,719	61,810,772	36,616,174	19,391,836	13,118,636	6,787,550	4,402,907	3,369,442
Long-term investment	10,708,420	6,506,194	5,160,891	2,899,109	824,481	325,533	352,000	111,187	88,169	9,007	11,126
Fixed assets	10,941,230	8,314,177	7,375,651	3,715,901	2,909,624	2,495,256	2,518,942	2,234,005	2,288,487	2,220,442	1,005,116
Other assets	5,284,115	3,297,898	1,417,830	656,817	449,300	484,309	278,298	398,343	376,172	419,127	92,444
Total	184,050,453	119,621,942	115,226,362	90,444,546	65,994,177	39,921,272	22,541,076	15,862,171	9,540,378	7,051,483	4,478,128
Liabilities and Stockholders' Equity											
Current liabilities	109,335,331	53,980,282	54,558,470	34,368,139	23,421,319	16,935,170	9,421,405	8,184,249	5,097,949	3,877,586	2,660,285
Long-term liabilities	0	0	0	0	0	0	1,477,171	0	57,164	87,638	120,859
Other liabilities	628	1,210	6,406	628	640	561	273,078	32,174	19,835	12,675	13,294
Total liabilities	109,335,959	53,981,492	54,564,876	34,368,767	23,421,959	16,935,731	11,171,654	8,216,423	5,174,948	3,977,899	2,794,438
Stockholders' equity	74,714,494	65,640,450	60,661,486	56,075,779	42,572,218	22,985,541	11,369,422	7,645,748	4,365,430	3,073,584	1,683,690
Total	184,050,453	119,621,942	115,226,362	90,444,546	65,994,177	39,921,272	22,541,076	15,862,171	9,540,378	7,051,483	4,478,128

Note 1. All figures are in thousand NT dollars.

Note 2. US$1 is equal to NT$29 by the end of 2010.

The second phase was known as 2G (second generation). The transmission of voice was digital, which was a technological leap. 2G was available in several countries during the early 1990s. The medium of communication was clearer than 1G, the transmission had fewer interruptions and the transmission capacity was also higher. The global system for mobile communication (GSM) deployed by 2G went on to become a popular mobile digital standard in subsequent years.

The third phase was known as 3G (third generation), characterized by digital transmission of both voice and data through the medium of the Internet. The technology was pioneered by NTT DoCoMo in 2001. 3G facilitated applications requiring higher bandwidth, such as video-conferencing. The 3G market did not grow as quickly as system operators expected because handset makers could not keep pace with the progress in technology. By 2009, the penetration of 3G handsets was still only 15 percent.[6]

Even though 3G had still not covered all the markets, 4G was being developed simultaneously. The chief improvements of 4G over 3G were mobile ultra-broadband access (gigabit speed) and multi-carrier transmission.

Market Growth

The mobile market exploded in the 1990s largely because of two factors: the operators were awarded licences by their governments and the mobile phone became portable. Until 2008, the penetration rate of mobile phones was 42 percent worldwide (see Exhibit 3). The penetration rate in Europe was the highest, exceeding 100 percent in countries such as Greece. In North and South America, the rate was 90 percent in Argentina, Bahamas, Brazil, Chile,

Jamaica and the United States. Both Canada and Mexico had a penetration rate of 60 percent.

The mobile communication markets in Australia and New Zealand were also mature, with penetration rates of 100.8 percent and 94 percent, respectively, in 2008. Countries in the Asia-Pacific region such as Hong Kong, Macau, Malaysia, Singapore and Taiwan had a penetration rate of 100 percent, and in Indonesia, Japan and South Korea, it was over 90 percent. China and India were two big markets with tremendous growth potential, where the penetration rate was about 50 percent. With their enormous populations, the two markets had become hot spots for both operators and manufacturers.

The African market was still under-developed. Nigeria had 16.5 percent penetration, making it the largest single market in Africa. Egypt (14.15 percent) and South Africa (13 percent) were in second and third place, respectively.

Worldwide, the mobile telecom industry consisted of two players: network operators and handset makers, which were sharply differentiated.

Network Operators

The world's largest network operator was China Mobile. It had 500 million mobile phone subscribers in 2009. More than 50 mobile operators in the world had 10 million plus subscribers each. More than 150 mobile operators had at least one million subscribers by the end of 2009.

The business of networks was characterized by scale and consolidation. Customers did not have a wide choice as far as network operators were concerned. In the United States, for example, over 90 percent of the networks market was confined to four major players: Verizon, AT&T,

EXHIBIT 3 Worldwide Mobile Subscription Penetration – Actuals & Forecast

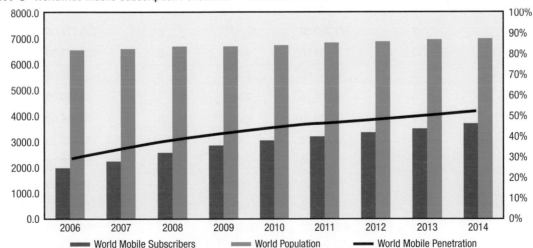

Source: Frost & Sullivan (*http://www.frost.com/prod/servlet/frost-home.pag*).

Sprint and Deutsche Telekom (now T-Mobile). In Canada, the market was also divided among four operators (Rogers Wireless, Bell Mobility, TELUS Mobility and Wind Mobile). Vodafone, Orange, Telefónica, Deutsche Telekom and O2 were the major European players. Another major market, Japan, had only three players (NTT DoCoMo, KDDI and Softbank Mobile). Other key operators in Asia included CMCC (China), China Unicom, China Telecom and CSL (Hong Kong). The primary operator in Australia was Telstra.

The networks business had high entry barriers because investments in fixed assets like cables, stations and towers were capital-intensive. Entry was also restricted to those holding a licence issued by the government. A licence was considered an asset in its own right. In each country, the telecom industry had a designated official regulator exercising control over competitive conduct.

In spite of the national level consolidation, the networks market was fragmented by region (e.g., Asia, Europe, etc.). National players competed in each country as a distinct market within the region. They also cooperated with their counterparts in other nations inside or outside the same region so that home consumers could make calls via international roaming while traveling to other countries.

Network operators wielded strong power over phone makers because they influenced the choice of handsets by customers. This was particularly true in the United States. A Verizon subscriber, for example, could buy only a handset that was approved by Verizon. Carriers subsidized the purchase of a handset as an incentive to subscribers. Europe was an exception to this rule, where carriers did not usually lock in their handset providers.

Handset Makers

By 2010, the top five handset makers were Nokia, Samsung, LG, Research in Motion (RIM) and Apple (see Exhibit 4). Motorola lost its first mover advantage to Nokia during the 3G era, as did Sony Ericsson. The maturity of 3G devices reshuffled the ranks of mobile phone makers and pushed RIM and Apple into the top five list.

Nokia, a Finnish multinational, was driven by the vision of connecting people. Its competitive advantages included brand equity, scale, distribution capability, product portfolio and leadership in many individual markets. Its mobile devices covered many segments and price points. In its global expansion, the company was customizing its products to suit local conditions, as in emerging markets like India.

Samsung and LG were multinational conglomerates headquartered in South Korea. They both had a strong foundation in electronics on which they built their mobile phones business. Samsung's focus was on simplifying the way consumers work and play, while LG focused on manufacturing mobile phones that consumers would want to take everywhere, matching style with function.

Sony Ericsson was a 50/50 joint venture, established in 2001, by the Japanese consumer electronics company Sony and the Swedish telecommunications company

EXHIBIT 4 Worldwide Top Mobile Devices: Unit Sales and Market Share

Company Name	2010			2009		
	Rank	Sales	Share	Rank	Sales	Share
Nokia	1	461,318.20	28.89%	1	440,881.60	36.40%
Samsung	2	281,065.80	17.60	2	235,772.00	19.47
LG	3	114,154.60	9.42	3	121,972.10	10.07
Research In Motion	4	47,451.60	2.97	6	34,346.60	2.84
Apple	5	46,598.30	2.92	7	24,889.70	2.05
Sony Ericsson	6	41,819.20	2.62	5	54,956.60	4.54
Motorola	7	38,553.70	2.41	4	58,475.20	4.83
ZTE	8	28,768.70	1.80	8	16,026.10	1.32
HTC	9	24,688.40	1.55	10	10,811.90	0.89
Huawei Technologies	10	23,814.70	1.49	9	13,490.60	1.11
Others		488,569.33	30.60		199,617.20	16.48
Total		1,596,802.40			1,211,239.60	

Note 1: Sales unit in thousands.

Source: Gartner, (February 2011).

EXHIBIT 5 Smartphone Operation System Vendors – Global Market Shares

OS vendor	2010		2009		2008	
	Shipments	Share	Shipments	Share	Shipments	Share
Symbian	112,918,570	37.7%	78,511,980	47.2%	74,926,550	52.4%
RIM	48,897,460	16.3	34,544,100	20.8	23,562,650	16.5
Apple	47,506,160	15.9	25,103,770	15.1	13,727,740	9.6
Microsoft	12,310,150	4.1	14,679,720	8.8	19,945,530	13.9
Google (Android)	69,102,300	23.4	7,786,870	4.7	663,550	0.5
Others	7,984,440	2.7	5,644,610	3.4	10,241,510	7.2
Total	299,716,880	100.0	166,271,050	100.0	143,067,530	100.0

Source: Canalys estimates, May 2011.

Ericsson. Combining Sony's consumer electronics expertise with Ericsson's communication technology, this venture was aimed at providing experiences that blurred the lines between communication and entertainment.

Many players, like Sanyo, Siemens, Sagem, NEC, Sharp and Alcatel, owned less than one percent of the market. Over a dozen players held less than 0.1 percent of the global share. Mobile operators, such as T-Mobile and mmO2, also bought mobile phones from subcontractors and sold them under their own brand name. Some were co-branding with the manufacturer's brand.

Unlike network operators who operated locally, major mobile phone manufacturers usually shipped their products to the global market. For example, Nokia mobile phones were available in more than 160 countries. Handset makers produced mobile phones that could generally fit operators with GSM 900 MHz or 1800 MHz systems in most areas of the world before the 3G era.

The Rise of Smartphones

The main technological milestone that distinguished 2G from 3G environments was the use of packet-switching rather than circuit-switching for data transmission. The advanced development of data transmission allowed new application services, such as mobile Internet access, video calls and mobile television, plus traditional wireless voice telephone.

These new applications required technologies related to computers and the Internet. This suggested that new phones had to combine a phone and a hand-held computer into a single portable device—a device that was later dubbed the smartphone. Until the early 2000s, all major handset makers did not have enough technological ability to integrate the two functions, which opened a window for new players, such as RIM, HTC and Apple.

The key to the function of a smartphone was its operating system. The top five operating systems included BlackBerry (used by RIM), Windows mobile (introduced by Microsoft), Symbian (used by Nokia), iOS (used by Apple) and Android (introduced by Google).

Android, released in 2008, had originally been developed by Android Inc., a firm acquired by Google. The Android team at Google went on to create the Open Handset Alliance, a group of 79 handset makers and mobile network operators committed to an open source platform and to "accelerating innovation in mobile and offering consumers a richer, less expensive and a better mobile experience."[7]

The major smartphone manufacturers were HTC, Apple and RIM. As a member of the Android alliance, HTC was the first handset maker to use the Android system in its HTC Dream, a smartphone line distributed by T-Mobile in 2008. Unlike RIM, which incorporated a keyboard into its phones, HTC and Apple both pursued the development of finger-optimized touch screens, which was considered the trend of the future (see Exhibit 6).

Apple was a relative late-comer to the smartphone market but had quickly seized the initiative to lead the smartphone segment. In 2007, the company introduced its first iPhone, which had a touch screen. Customers who were familiar with the brand and its Macintosh range of computers had been highly anticipating the new features promised by the iPhone.

Under the 3G system, the software in smartphones needed to be customized to fit each operator's system in order to deliver Internet-related services and videos. Because manufacturers needed the assistance of operators to design and test new smartphones, the entry barriers for developing and making smartphones were higher than for designing a PC or other information technology products.

Network-Handset Interactions

Consumers had to buy a mobile phone and also subscribe to a system in order to use the mobile medium. The mobile phone was a one-time purchase, but the subscription would extend for the period of contract. The two were commonly

EXHIBIT 6 Touch-Screen Smartphones – Global Market Shares

| Vendor | 2009 | | 2008 | | Growth |
	Shipments	Share	Shipments	Share	2009/2008
Apple	25,103,770	33.1%	13,727,740	37.8%	82.9%
Nokia	22,364,000	29.5%	536,210	1.5%	4,070.8%
HTC	7,726,770	10.2%	7,270,630	20.0%	6.3%
Samsung	4,840,750	6.4%	2,290,110	6.3%	111.4%
Others	15,815,510	20.9%	12,484,660	34.4%	26.7%
Total	75,850,800	100.0%	36,309,350	100.0%	108.9%

Source: Press release by Canalys estimates, February 8, 2010, *http://www.canalys.com/pr/2010/r2010021.html*.

bundled together as a promotional package to attract consumers. The bundle was usually provided by the network operator who was the retail face of handsets to the customer. A lock-in operator would buy phones in bulk from handset makers at a discount and offer a package, at a bargain price, to the end-user.

A network operator would also try to entice end-users to switch from competitors. There were often switching costs to the customer (i.e., a locked-up handset), which were subsidized by the operator in some form. The switches would happen with the launch of a new phone model or the introduction of a new variant of the existing model. A network operator would provide special deals wherein end-users could own the most advanced phone with almost zero payment, for example. In this way, mobile phones were a promotional tool for network operators.

The nature of network-handset interactions might lead to some confusion over who was accountable for the ultimate quality of mobile phone service. Consumers had no information about who, between two vendors, played what role over a wide range of issues that mattered to them most, such as speed of transmission, quality of communication, connectivity, access to multimedia and the functionality of the mobile device.

Network-Handset Gaps in Technology

Network operators and mobile phone manufacturers had to work in harmony to deliver full service to consumers; however, there was a performance gap between the two in terms of technological development, where handset makers tended to fall behind network operators. While the latter had developed 3G technologies, for instance, the former were not keeping up. Their products could not upload, download or display pictures or video smoothly or quickly enough to fulfill consumers' needs.

There were several reasons for this dissonance. Most governments issued 1G, 2G and 3G licences separately. Network operators would wait until the government issued the licence to establish their operating systems, followed by manufacturers introducing a new model to meet operators'

needs. Additionally, 3G models had to be altered model by model and operator by operator. Manufacturers were unwilling to undertake small orders of customized phones for each operator in each market. To gain the benefits of scale, they would wait to identify the operators who would attract enough subscribers.

Furthermore, phone makers of the 2G era were not adept at digital information processing. For example, Motorola, Nokia and Ericsson were voice communication players with R&D ability in communication, not in data transmission. Initially, the content and applications for 3G phones were insufficient and consumers had reservations about buying the new 3G phones. Eventually, it was the popularity of the iPhone that attracted the attention of software developers who quickly provided application programs for iPhones and, subsequently, for other smartphones.

HTC Smartphone

The growth of HTC's smartphone business could be divided into three phases: ODM of PDA, ODM of mobile phones and own-brand manufacture (OBM) of smartphones.

ODM of PDA

The first phase of HTC's growth, as mentioned earlier, consisted of making PDAs as a subcontractor for computer manufacturers. Like most high-tech startups in Taiwan at the time, HTC sought subcontracting opportunities where its team had the necessary R&D experience and was confident of delivering end products with a reasonable value-to-price ratio to clients. Designing handheld devices was one of the areas of competence of its founding team of engineers, which could be traced to their days at DEC where they had worked together. Between 2000 and 2002, the PDA business was HTC's primary source of income, generating 13.64 percent of gross profits in 2001 and 17.45 percent in 2002.

The flipside of HTC's ODM business strategy was that the client seemed to have an inordinate amount of control. Even if Compaq accounted for 86 percent of HTC's revenue—and the iPAQs made by HTC accounted for

80 percent of Compaq's annual shipments—Compaq had no hesitation in looking for alternate sources of supply, such as LG Electronics. HTC had to diversify its revenue streams.

ODM of Mobile Phones

The second phase of HTC's growth was triggered by a collaboration opportunity with Palm to manufacture wireless PDAs: Palm VII in 1999. This gave HTC an opportunity to develop competencies in wireless technology, which would later provide growth momentum.

As a late-comer in handset design and manufacture, HTC faced barriers in securing subcontracting orders from established mobile phone makers (such as Nokia, Motorola and Sony Ericsson). These phone makers already had long-term subcontracting partners that competed with one another based largely on price. However, HTC was able to secure business from network operators and its mobile phone business was able to begin after obtaining an ODM order from O2. The focal handset in this deal had a touch colour screen and was sold under the XDA label, a brand name owned by O2.

Later, XDA was remodeled as the T-Mobile Pocket PC Phone Edition for introduction in the U.S. market. In seeking business from network operators, HTC was also fulfilling a market segment that had been under-served. Major handset manufacturers were less willing to supply phones to network operators because the order size was invariably small in relation to their global sales.

It was also in 2002 that HTC decided to gradually give up its PDA ODM business and concentrate on designing and producing smartphones. Chou explained this decision by saying:

> The decision did not go well with our investors. However, we, at the management, had two strong grounds. First, we knew that we simply didn't have enough resources to handle both businesses. Second, the PDA business was becoming competitive because there were too many new entrants. We wanted to move on to the next-generation product. We had set our minds on a business that could not be easily replicated by others. The business of smartphones seemed logical.

The success of XDA, which was HTC's first 2.5G mobile phone, had attracted the attention of other network operators like AT&T, Rogers, France Telecom and Deutsche Telekom AG. In early 2005, HTC started supplying 3G phones to British Telecom (BT), as a direct result of a joint development project initiated by the parties to bridge the network-handset gaps in technology. This joint project represented a milestone in the second phase of HTC's mobile phone business.

British Telecom Project

Being an ODM of mobile phones differed from being an ODM of PDAs in certain aspects. Subcontractors of smartphones not only designed and built the phones based on customer specifications but also tested them in a live operating environment. For instance, the data transmission function of a phone (such as email, instant news, word processing, etc.) had to be customized before delivery. There were incentive misalignments between handset makers and network operators on grounds of technology gaps and order sizes.

British Telecom (BT), a network operator in the United Kingdom, found a willing partner in HTC to bridge the network-handset gap. As an ODM supplier of wireless PDAs, HTC had established a relationship with BT, which was eager to demonstrate its leadership in 3G technologies in Europe. In 1998, Chou presented his idea of combining wireless and computing technologies together for the 2.5G mobile phones to BT. It was a fresh idea to BT, which had already spent over £5 billion (about US$3 billion) on 2.5G and 3G technologies but had yet to make any major breakthroughs. BT appreciated the idea of allying with a supplier that was adept at wireless data transmission in order to break the technological barrier and quickly offered HTC a platform to "co-develop" a smartphone.

HTC secured this co-development project partly because the opportunity was less attractive to major phone manufacturers. The initial order size from BT was relatively small, which did not appeal to major handset manufacturers such as Nokia and Motorola. Furthermore, traditional handset makers, like Nokia, did not seriously consider the offer from Microsoft to promote its platform for smartphones.

HTC's first joint research project with BT began in 1999 and lasted for three and half years, during which the R&D teams of both sides worked in close proximity. BT invested almost US$20 million in the joint project, which involved six sites in three continents, including HTC in Taiwan, BT in London, Microsoft in Seattle and several offices of Texas Instruments (TI) in the United States, France and Germany. BT promised to buy a minimum of 500,000 smartphones from HTC upon its launch.

HTC's relationship with BT had given it the credibility and momentum that would take the company to a premier market position in smartphones. It soon established subcontracting relationships with major network operators worldwide, including the five leading players in Europe (Orange, mmO2, T-Mobile, TeliaSonera and Vodafone), the top four in the United States (AT&T, Sprint, T-Mobile and Verizon) and many Asian operators (such as NTT DoCoMo of Japan). An increase in its customer base gave HTC a greater organizational focus on developing smartphones.

Limits of Subcontracting

Throughout its history, HTC developed products based on extensive R&D but without its own brand name. The company was therefore unable to communicate the attributes of its products directly to end-users. Simultaneously, ODM clients (network operators) were unlikely to emphasize the role of HTC as a designer and manufacturer of a brand that they owned.

Another problem that HTC faced as a subcontractor was that it did not have sufficient protection for its innovation. Some network operators would transfer HTC's designs to other subcontractors without compensating HTC. This issue had troubled HTC since its beginnings in selling PDAs to Compaq, which had once transferred the manufacturing of a model developed by HTC to LG Electronics, a leading South Korean company. "We can't blame Compaq for seeking more subcontractors," recalled Chou, "If I were to put myself in their shoes, I would make the same decision."

Subcontracting had its limits for network operators as well. Some were discovering that selling mobile phones with their own private brand had a negative side. They had to take responsibility for after-sales and repair services, which was costly. Indeed, some of them did not mind letting HTC co-brand the product and share part of the burden. BT, for example, allowed HTC to co-brand its first clamshell smartphone with a new label called Qtek. Consumers selected HTC's Qtek line largely due to BT's endorsement, which helped the brand to be recognized by the end-users in its own right.

In spite of launching the Qtek line in the European market, the management team at HTC believed that in order to support its corporate brand, the company must build a reservoir of capabilities in product design and brand marketing. HTC did not complete the last mile on the branding road until 2006, eight years after its founding as a PDA subcontractor. The year 2006 marked the beginning of the third phase of growth for HTC.

The HTC Brand

HTC had long known that the company should have its own brand; it was only a matter of time before the company began to move in that direction. When HTC made the first coloured screen smartphone for O2 in February 2002, O2 encouraged HTC to use its own brand but Chou did not think the timing was right. Although HTC had invested in Qtek in Europe in 2001, this line was only a small test of running a brand.

The HTC management team carefully evaluated the branding decision for five years and the board of directors discussed it for three years. In the middle of its internal deliberations over introducing its own brand, HTC established an R&D team in 2005 to develop a finger-optimized touch-screen smartphone. This initiative was unknown to anyone outside the company.

The right time for OBM came in 2006, when the secretive touch-screen project had reached major breakthroughs. In the meantime, HTC's revenue, margin and net profit all reached record highs. The arrival of this new generation of smartphones with an innovative touch-screen experience seemed like the perfect product with which to go solo. In 2006, the company formally triggered the process of launching a new mobile phone line under the HTC brand. "We should now be the one making the call and no longer the one waiting for the call," Chou stated.

Chou persuaded the board of directors at HTC to accept the branding idea by pointing out the nature of its ODM business, where profits would be vanishing eventually. Most investors and financial analysts, however, were not supportive because of apprehensions about the financial outlay. Furthermore, they felt that the branding decision might endanger the ODM business, where current clients might retaliate. Given the technological advantage that HTC enjoyed at the time, Chou firmly believed that the company should take the branding road. "We wanted to control our own destiny and we had the advantage to build a brand," said Chou, "HTC was the leader in many communication technologies. We had the technological advantage to support the brand."

Chou learned from earlier brand marketers in Asia (Acer Group in Taiwan, Samsung Electronics in Korea and Sony Corporation in Japan) that global marketing expertise was critical to the success of the HTC brand worldwide. Nevertheless, global managers were hesitant to work for unknown Asian companies. HTC would have to reshape its internal culture in order to project a successful global working environment and attract and keep managers recruited outside Taiwan.

It took HTC a year to shape an international culture for its new branding strategy. The company's management team carefully reexamined and rebuilt every step of its internal communications channels so that no cultural barriers would hinder information flow across managers of different nationalities. It sent engineers abroad to work with top-tier R&D teams worldwide. These efforts transformed HTC from a local Taiwanese firm into a multinational enterprise, which allowed Chou to persuade a variety of talents in hardware and software design to join the company.

The Brand

The introduction of the HTC brand to the world finally came in 2006. The first popular model line sold under the new HTC logo was the HTC Touch (June 2007), the first smartphone with a touch-screen experience that preempted the need for a keyboard.

Before choosing HTC as the new brand name, the company considered using Qtek, the existing brand introduced earlier in Europe, or Dopod, another established trademark that was relatively recognizable in Asia. However, neither brand had premium and high-technology appeal that could compete effectively with major players in the global market. Chou believed that the HTC brand would best symbolize all that the company stood for. "We thought about Qtek or Dopod," said Chou, "They had enough brand awareness in certain regional markets but a local image was also tied to the names. We needed a fresh start even though it meant that we had to invest in rebuilding brand awareness and brand image."

Following the introduction of the HTC brand, Chou made the surprising decision to drop the ODM business altogether. This decision caused some internal and external debates. Many people suggested that HTC should keep both the ODM and branded businesses simultaneously and perhaps assign them to two separate companies. The ODM business represented easy money and constituted a large segment of the company's profit before 2006. Nevertheless, limited resources did not allow HTC to cover both businesses and Chou argued that if branding was the company's future, then all resources should be devoted to it.

A Distraction on the Branding Road

HTC initially planned to launch the new phone line during 2007, after more than two years of development and preparation. In January 2007, however, Apple made a dramatic announcement that necessitated immediate reaction from HTC.

On June 12, 2007, the HTC Touch, as the new brand was called, was formally launched in Asia and Europe—17 days before Apple shipped out its first iPhone in the United States. HTC intentionally held the announcement until the shipping day to attract the attention of venders and consumers. Following the introduction of the HTC Touch, the company launched another new product in May 2008, the HTC Touch Diamond.

From 2007 to 2008, HTC and Apple were the only two companies in the world selling smartphones with a finger-optimized touch screen. Based on their experience with PDAs, major handset makers (e.g., Nokia, Motorola, Samsung, LG and Sony Ericsson) believed that touch-screens were not on the right track, since consumers did not prefer to write directly on the screen. The iPhone's popularity threw other handset makers off balance, opening a window for HTC. In the United States, for example, HTC was happy to align with Verizon, T-Mobile and Sprint, while iPhone was bundled exclusively with AT&T's services.

Reactions of ODM Clients

One major concern for many ODM subcontractors who introduced their own brands was that their current clients might retaliate. Before the introduction of its own brand name, HTC estimated that most network operators would not object to its new branding strategy. Focusing on a particular geographic area, network operators were not competing with HTC in the handset market.

HTC launched its brand softly in that it did not insist on attaching the HTC logo to its products. The HTC brand was only an option for its operator clients. HTC's strategy was to promote the brand value to the consumer. Once the value of the HTC brand was recognized by the market, its operator clients would have no hesitation in accepting the logo and co-branding with it.

Before mid-2007, few operator customers had enough confidence in the HTC logo to display it on the product. For example, T-Mobile would rather use its own "T-Mobile MDA Touch" logo without showing the HTC label and Sprint called the model "Sprint Touch by HTC." Operator customers did not believe that the HTC logo could provide add-on value for the phone. Their attitude towards the brand changed only after the HTC Touch became a hit product that was heavily discussed in trade magazines and on the Internet. From that point, more operator customers allowed HTC to co-brand its products.

However, some handset makers that were subcontracting to HTC remained concerned about the introduction of the HTC brand. For instance, a firm called i-mate (based in Dubai) shifted part of its orders to Inventec Corporation, a Taiwanese competitor of HTC, although i-mate used to outsource handsets exclusively from HTC for sales in Armenia, Australia, Italy, India, South Africa, and the United Kingdom, etc. Arguably, HTC might have lost these orders even if it did not take the branding road, since placing orders with multiple subcontractors to reduce risk was a general policy among many ODM clients.

Brand Performance

HTC continued to co-brand with network operators. In 2010, over 90 percent of HTC smartphones were sold via operators' stores, such as Verizon and AT&T stores in the United States. In Europe, more than half of its products were distributed through stores owned by network operators, including Vodafone, T-Mobile and Orange. In addition, HTC began to distribute its branded products through retail chains, such as Best Buy and Radio Shack in the United States and Carphone Warehouse in Europe. In Asia, most HTC smartphones were distributed through retail stores with the HTC logo on the products

Since 2007, HTC has released over 100 smartphone models under the HTC logo. The market response has been very positive. HTC also launched co-branded products with its network operator customers. In 2010, for example, it had designed the Nexus One for Google and co-branded this new line. It also sold a few models under private brands owned by network operators.

The new branding strategy had led to some changes in HTC's operations—particularly the reduction in its ODM business. In 2003, for instance, HP was the dominant client, constituting 90 percent of the ODM business. In 2007, however, subcontract orders accounted for only 10 percent of HTC's revenue, with the HTC brand making up the remaining 90 percent. By the end of 2009, the company's subcontracting business had dropped almost to zero. The last regular ODM order was placed by T-Mobile in 2009. Since then, HTC chose to work only on special ODM projects (e.g., developing a digital mobile television project for Qualcomm).

In July 2006 (prior to the introduction of its HTC brand), HTC had secured the third spot in *BusinessWeek's* list of InfoTech-100 companies in Asia. In August 2007, it was rated second-best among the magazine's list of top-performing technology companies. In 2008, HTC was the first handset maker that used Google's Android operating system to develop a smartphone. It was named the 2010 Technology Brand of the Year at T3's prestigious Gadget Awards. The award was given to the most innovative, functional, visible and stylish gadgets and technology of the past 12 months by more than 750,000 readers and a panel of expert judges.

More Developments

The transformation of HTC's business from PDAs to smartphones might have seemed smooth to outsiders but those who were involved knew that it was not an easy task. After the transformation, HTC had built a strong management team at the strategy and execution levels. It had also built an impressive R&D group. Yet the move from contractual manufacturing to brand marketing posed new challenges. Both brand building and global marketing were new territory for the company.

The Quietly Brilliant Campaign

In late 2009, HTC debuted its first global advertising campaign: "quietly brilliant." In the campaign, HTC was portrayed as a company that did "great things in a humble way with the belief that the best things in life are experienced, not explained." This brand positioning not only fit its corporate culture very well but also reflected the shared personality of its employees (see Exhibit 7).

Compared to the other tag lines under consideration by HTC, "quietly brilliant" was not a brand position that was easy to explain or understand, yet the management team at HTC believed that the company embodied the attitude expressed in the slogan and could own the "quietly brilliant" position exclusively. Results of an internal survey revealed that the tag line was ownable, inspirational and honest. Since the fundamental attitude of humility behind this position fit HTC well, the marketing team did not need to make significant extra efforts to communicate this brand concept to its employees.

Initially, HTC was not sure whether this "quietly brilliant" concept, which seemed to work well in the Asian context, would succeed in the global arena. The company ran focus groups in major markets and the conclusion was that many individuals around the world had some friends who were "quietly brilliant." The tagline was culturally universal and was expected to connect well with the target audience.

The main theme of this global advertising campaign was expressed as: "You don't need to get a phone. You need a phone that gets you." The brand promise was, "It's all about YOU, the consumer, not the device." The "YOU" in HTC's "quietly brilliant" campaign emphasized that HTC put the user at the centre of its focus (see Exhibit 8).

R&D Ability

HTC had set aside sufficient funds for R&D since day one. Financial support from Chairwoman Wang and other investors was unwavering. The company made a strong commitment to the spirit of innovation among its employees. "Innovation is the value of HTC," Chou stated repeatedly.

In 2005, HTC set up an R&D team dubbed MAGIC Labs, aimed at generating novel product concepts and breakthrough ideas. MAGIC stood for Mobility Advancement Group & Innovation Centre and consisted of a group of labs working together to ensure that new products launched by HTC would precede a competitor launch by 6 to 12 months. The members of the MAGIC Labs had various backgrounds, ranging from electronic engineering to psychology to jewelry design. One of the MAGIC Labs' early projects was the touch-screen phone.

HTC also established a design centre in Seattle, focusing on user interface design. It had also acquired a design

EXHIBIT 8 Advertisement Sample

EXHIBIT 7 The HTC Logo and Tag Line

EXHIBIT 9 HTC – R&D Intensity

Year	R&D Expenditure (1,000 billion NT$)	Revenue (1,000 billion NT$)	R&D Intensity (%)	R&D People
1998	1.49	3.62	41.20	119
1999	1.94	14.89	13.00	154
2000	3.11	43.35	7.20	222
2001	4.84	151.18	3.20	330
2002	6.99	199.74	3.50	424
2003	10.48	211.35	5.00	600
2004	19.94	355.98	5.60	840
2005	23.99	731.45	3.30	950
2006	29.74	1,053.58	2.80	1,140
2007	37.05	1,182.18	3.10	2,342
2008	93.51	1,523.53	6.10	2,718
2009	83.73	1,444.93	5.80	2,732
2010	129.40	2,787.61	4.60	2,978

Note 1. R&D Intensity equals R&D Expenditure divided by Revenue.

Note 2. US$1 is equal to NT$29 by the end of 2010.

company in San Francisco. One of the cornerstones of its R&D strategy was the concurrent execution of multiple projects. While ongoing projects were still being executed, dedicated teams would be working on future ideas. The company's R&D team had grown from 70 engineers in 1999 to 1,800 in 2010, accounting for 25 percent of HTC's total employee base. HTC had so far obtained more than 800 patents worldwide (see Exhibit 9).

Next Step

The competitive context for HTC was changing. Chou estimated that 3G products would continuously and quickly expand in 2011, while 4G products would be ready by 2011 and popular in 2012. At the same time, the smartphone segment would be getting more and more crowded. The company had to move faster than competitors, including Apple, which was seeing HTC as a threat. In addition, more traditional handset makers such as Samsung had invaded its territory by launching smartphones based on Windows Mobile.

Another notable development was the emergence of new product categories (e.g., e-readers and tablet devices). By the end of 2009, Amazon's Kindle and Barnes & Noble's Nook were both available with wireless Internet capacity. Apple had also embedded wireless Internet on its iPad, whose introduction in early 2010 caught the attention of the worldwide market. HTC had considered several projects on e-readers and tablet PCs and determined its product concepts had to be just as innovative as the current offerings by competitors.

"No me-too products" was one ground rule at HTC since its founding. The founding team had refused to introduce "me-too products" and be part of the price war in the PC market, which was why HTC had turned to handheld devices in the early days of the company. In response to the emerging trend of mobile computing a decade later, it had to join the tablet PC bandwagon. The question at hand was whether or not HTC could sustain this "no me-too" rule in an ever-evolving competitive landscape.

ENDNOTES

1. Randy Schultz, "Compaq to Buy DEC," CNNMoney, January 26, 1998.
2. *www.itu.int/ITU-D/ict/statistics/material/graphs/2010/Global_mobile_cellular_00-10.jpg*, accessed November 20, 2010.
3. HTC annual report for the year ending December 2009, p. 32.
4. J. Schneidawind, "Big Blue Unveiling," USA Today, November 23, 1992, p. 2B.
5. *www.westlake.co.uk/Mobile_Phone_Glossary.htm*, accessed October 26, 2010.
6. *www.morganstanley.com/institutional/techresearch*, accessed November 20, 2010.
7. *www.openhandsetalliance.com/*, accessed November 20, 2010.

CASE 14

INNOVATIVE TATA INC.—INDIA'S PRIDE!

"The world will always need innovators and innovations; it is not a destination but an endless journey and the spirit of entrepreneurship will continue to be a great enabler."[1]

–Syamal Gupta, Director, Tata Sons.

"If you can imagine it, you can do it."[2]

–Walt Disney, Visionary Filmmaker.

"We are very pleased at the prospect of Jaguar and Land Rover being a significant part of our automotive business."[3]

–Ratan Tata, Chairman of Tata Sons and Tata Motors.

Companies across the globe are emerging as top-notch innovators. Tata Motors' innovation metrics not only include a number of patents, but also importance to increase their revenue and something valuable for the betterment of the society. The Tata Group has once again proved its determination as it ranked sixth on the list of top 25 'most innovative' companies of the world.[4] Tata has earned this position for designing the common man's car 'Nano' at an extremely affordable price. Apart from this, Tata's acquisition of the Anglo-Dutch steelmaker 'Corus' is considered as the largest Indian takeover of a foreign company and created the world's fifth-largest steel group. Another strategic and innovative move from Tata was the acquisition of the Jaguar and the Land Rover. This initiative is expected to give Tata the opportunity to expand its presence in the passenger car market beyond India and give it the clout necessary to compete with international players.

Tata Inc.: Growth through Innovation

The Tata Company was founded by Jamsetji Tata in 1868; the Tata Group's ventures in its early years were marked by the spirit of nationalism. The Tata Group pioneered a number of industries of national importance in

www.ibscdc.org

India–like steel, power, hospitality and airlines. Tata is a rapidly growing business group based in India with significant international operations. It is one of India's oldest, largest and most respected business conglomerates. The Group's businesses are spread over seven business sectors (Annexure I). Revenues in 2007–2008 are estimated in excess of $55 billion,[5] of which 65% is from business outside India. It's comprised of 98 companies and operates in six continents.[6] Tata Group's pioneering spirit has been showcased by companies like Tata Consultancy Services, India's first software company,[7] which pioneered the international delivery model, Tata Steel, Tata Power, Tata Chemicals, Tata Tea, Indian Hotels and Tata Communications. The group employs around 350,000 people worldwide.[8] The Tata name has earned respect for its devotion to strong values and business ethics and maintained its image for the last 140 years in India. The business operations of the Tata Group are divided into seven sectors: communications and information technology, engineering, materials, services, energy, consumer products and chemicals. As of July 3, 2008, Tata Group's 27 publicly listed ventures are among the most valued Indian business houses; they have a collective market capitalisation of $49.56 billion and a shareholder base of 2.9 million.[9]

Internationally, the Tata Group is recognised as a major player after their acquisition of Corus, the largest acquisition abroad by an Indian company.[10] This acquisition was a turning point for Tata Steel, after which it became the fifth largest steel maker in the world.[11] Corus was Europe's second largest steel producer with revenue of 9.2 billion in 2005,[12] and crude steel production of 18.2 million[13] tons primarily in the UK and Netherlands. This company was primarily engaged in the manufacture of semi-finished and finished carbon steel products. Its activities are divided into three main divisions: strip products, and the distribution and building systems division, which operates as a link between Corus's manufacturing operation and its customers. It has a global network of sales offices and service centers. The acquisition was made by Tata Steel UK, a wholly owned indirect subsidiary[14] of Tata Steel, incorporated in the UK for the purpose of completing the acquisition. The acquisition was funded through its own cash resources and loans raised by Tata Steel and its subsidiary companies formed for the purpose of this acquisition.

The acquisition of Corus by Tata Steel is in consonance with Tata Steel's stated objective of growth and globalisation. Growth at Tata Steel is focusing towards new, higher end-markets and a more sophisticated customer base. Tata

ANNEXURE I Seven Business Sectors of Tata Group

Sl. No	Business Ventures	Details of the Business
1	Engineering	**Automotive** Tata AutoComp Systems-Subsidiaries / associates / joint ventures: Automotive Composite Systems International, Automotive Stampings and Assemblies, JBM Sung woo, Knorr-Bremse Systems for Commercial Vehicles, TACO Faurecia Design Center, TACO MobiApps Telematics, Tata Autoplastic Systems, Tata Ficosa, Tata Johnson Controls, Tata Nifco Fasteners, Tata Toyo Radiator, Tata Yazaki AutoComp, Tata Yutaka, TC Springs **Tata Motors** Subsidiaries / associates / joint ventures: Concorde Motors, HV Axels, HV Transmissions, Nita Company, TAL Manufacturing Solutions, Tata Cummins, Tata Daewoo Commercial Vehicles Company, Tata Engineering Services, Tata Finance, Tata Holset, Tata Precision Industries, Tata Technologies, Telco Construction Equipment Company **Engineering Services** Tata Projects, TCE Consulting Engineers, Voltas **Engineering Products** TAL Manufacturing Solutions, Telco Construction Equipment Company, TRF
2	Materials	**Composites** Tata Advanced Materials **Metals** **Tata Steel** Subsidiaries / associates / joint ventures: Jamshedpur Injection Powder (Jamipol), Lanka Special Steel, Metaljunction Services Ltd., Sila Eastern Company, Tata Metaliks, Tata Pigments, Tata Ryerson, Tata Sponge Iron, The Tinplate Company of India, Tata Refractories, Tayo Rolls, The Indian Steel and Wire Products, Wires Division
3	Energy	Transmission Tower **Power** **Tata BP Solar India, Tata Power** Subsidiaries / associates / joint ventures: Tata Ceramics, Tata Power Trading, Tata Petrodyne
4	Chemicals	Rallis India, Tata Chemicals, Tata Pigments
5	Services	**Hotels and Realty** **Indian Hotels (Taj group)** Subsidiaries / associates / joint ventures: Taj Air **THDC** **Financial Services** Tata-AIG General Insurance, Tata-AIG Life Insurance, Tata Asset Management, Tata Financial Services, Tata Investment Corporation, Tata Share Registry **Other Services** Tata Economic Consultancy Services, Tata Quality Management Services, Tata Services, Tata Strategic Management Group
6	Consumer Products	**Tata Tea** Subsidiaries / associates / joint ventures: Tetley Group, Tata Coffee, Tata Tetley, Tata Tea Inc. **Tata Ceramics, Tata McGraw-Hill Publishing Company, Titan Industries, Trent**
7	Information Systems And Communications	**Information Systems** **Nelito Systems,** **Tata Consultancy Services** Subsidiaries / associates / joint ventures: APONLINE, Airline Financial Support Services, Aviation Software Development Consultancy, CMC, CMC Americas Inc., Conscripti, HOTV, TCS Business Transformation Solutions, Tata America International Corporation, TCS Business Transformation Solutions, WTI Advanced Technology. Tata Elxsi, Tata InfoTech, Tata Interactive Systems, Tata Technologies **Communications** **Idea Cellular, Tata Teleservices** Subsidiaries / associates / joint ventures: Tata Teleservices (Maharashtra), Tata Internet Services **VSNL, Tatanet** **Industrial Automation** **Nelco** Subsidiaries / associates / joint ventures: Tatanet

Compiled by the authors from: "Tata Group," http://www.managementparadise.com/forums/archive/index.php/t-153.html, August 23, 2005.

Steel saw a number of prospects behind the acquisition of Corus. Its improved scale positioned the combined group as the sixth largest steel company in the world by production, with a presence in both Europe and Asia. The powerful combination of low cost upstream production in India with the high end downstream processing facilities of Corus improved the competitiveness of the European operations of Corus significantly. This combination of both the companies allows the cross-fertilisation of research and development capabilities in the automotive, packaging and construction sectors and there is a transfer of technology, best practices and expertise of senior Corus management, from Europe to India. In addition, Tata Steel retained access to low cost raw materials and slabs for the enlarged group, and exposure to high growth in emerging markets, whilst gaining price stability in developed markets. Between the two companies, there exists a high degree of cultural compatibility, which would facilitate an effective integration of the businesses. Tata Steel leads the enlarged group with a combined management team. Manufacturing will be organised so as to produce slabs/primary steel in low-cost facilities and produce high end products in proximity to client bases—in both Europe and India.

Tata Motors is India's largest automobile company, with revenues of $8.8 billion in 2007–2008.[15] This company is among the top five[16] commercial vehicle manufacturers and top three[17] in passenger vehicles manufacturers in the world. It is the world's fourth largest[18] truck manufacturer and the second largest[19] bus manufacturer. Tata cars, buses and trucks are being marketed in several countries in Europe, Africa, the Middle East, South Asia, South East Asia and South America. Tata Motors operates in South Korea, Thailand and Spain through its subsidiaries and associate companies. It also has a strategic alliance with Fiat for creation and establishment of an industrial joint venture in India. Tata Motors acquired Jaguar and Land Rover for $2.3 billion.[20] The main motive behind this acquisition is to own Jaguar and Land Rover for perpetual royalty-free licenses of all necessary Intellectual Property Rights, manufacturing plants, two advanced design centers in the UK, and worldwide network of National Sales Companies. Ratan Tata stated that, "Jaguar and Land Rover are two iconic British brands with worldwide growth prospects. Tata is looking forward to extending their full support to the Jaguar Land Rover team to realise their competitive potential. Jaguar and Land Rover will retain their distinctive identities and continue to pursue their respective business plans as before. Tata Motors recognises the significant improvement in the performance of the two brands and looks forward to this trend continuing in the coming years too (Exhibit 1). It is their intention to work closely to support the Jaguar Land Rover team in building the success and supremacy of the two brands."[21]

The latest to strike the ever-growing Asian and European markets is the sensational Tata Nano, the no-fuss, fuel-efficient energy car that has fueled every Indian's dream to own a car. The Nano, the prototype of which was launched in January 2008, is the biggest innovation from Tata Motors (Exhibit 2). In India, this car is labeled as the "People's Car."[22] The manner in which the Nano has been built and the features that are included, for the declared price, show Tata's innovative strategy and vision.

EXHIBIT 1 Performance of Tata Motors from April–March 2008

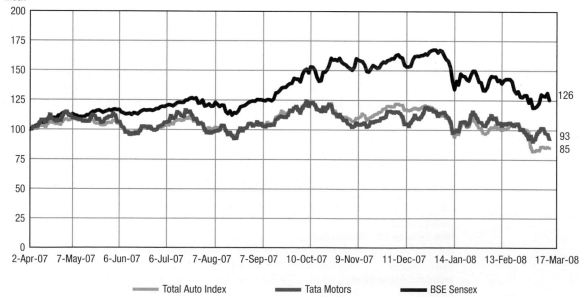

Source: "Annual Report of Tata Motors," *http://ir.tatamotors.com/performance/a_reports/pdf/2008/TML-2007-08.pdf*.

Note: All figures rebased to April 2, 2007 = 10.

EXHIBIT 2 Tata Nano "People's Car" and Its Features

Features of this car:

- Affordable for all income groups
- Four-seater capacity designed to meet the need of a small family
- Meets safety requirements and emission norms
- Is fuel efficient
- Uniquely combines space and maneuverability on busy Indian roads
- First car in the world which uses two-cylinder gasoline engine with single balancer shaft
- Its performance is controlled by a specially designed electronic engine management system aimed at delivering high fuel efficiency.
- Safety features of the Nano's performance are expected to exceed modern regulatory requirements
- Offering the double benefits of an inexpensive transportation solution with a low carbon footprint

Compiled by the authors from: "Nano Car," http://www.mytatanano.co.in/nano-car-pic.html.

According to the analysts, the impact of this venture is huge, and everyone is excited at the prospect of owning a car that is only INR 1 lakh ($2500).[23] The car is the result of about five years of research and input from designers across the world. But it is considered by industry watchers as a step ahead in innovation—right from using aerospace adhesives instead of welding, and a clean and efficient fuel-burning technology, to the concept, distribution strategy and marketing—and has succeeded in catching the attention of the world.

TATA: The Pride of India

The founder of Tata Group Jamsetji Tata's creative thinking and foresight were established way back in the 19th century. He imagined hydroelectric power as a clean source of energy; a hundred years on, the world continues its debate on the Kyoto protocol sustainable development and clean development mechanism. His concept of welfare and community development around a steel plant was far ahead of his times. The Tata Group has raised innovative ideas and displayed entrepreneurial spirit in venturing into new geographies, market segments, and product areas (Exhibit 3).

BUSINESSWEEK magazine, issue dated April 28, 2008 has published its list of the world's 50 most innovative companies. The two Indian industrial groups, included in the list for the first time, are the Tatas and the Mukesh Ambani's Reliance Group (Exhibit 4), where the Tata Group is ranked 6th and Reliance bagged the 19th position (Annexure II). To achieve this position the Tata Group has taken up this challenge of innovation anticipating the need of the Indian community. Tata has faced challenges in many of its innovations but yet has been able to overcome those successfully. For instance, when Tata Indica was launched, it did not take off and was touted as a failure but after a thorough analysis of the cause for failure, Tata Motors was able to put the car on the right path. According to the Boston Consulting Group (BCG) list, this group ranks well above IBM, BMW, Honda Motor, General Motors, Boeing, Audi and Daimler.

The group is focusing on new technologies and innovation to drive its business in India and around the globe. Nano is one such example, which ranked the world's fourth fastest,[24] developed by one of its companies. The group aims to build a series of world class, world scale businesses in selected sectors. Headquartered in India and linked to its traditional values and strong ethics, the group is building a multinational business which will achieve growth through excellence and innovation with corresponding benefits to its shareholders, its employees and wider society.

EXHIBIT 3 Innovative / Novel Endeavor by the Tata Group

SI.No	Company Name	Innovation
1	Tata Motors	• An exciting project is the 'People's Car,' which would sell for around $2,200 (about Rs 1 lakh). A number of incremental innovations mark the project, like the possible use of bolted or glued panels instead of welded bodies. • Indigo—the first sedan designed and manufactured in India. This technology (as is used the world over) allows Tata Motors to meet customer needs in different segments with a single base model.
2	Titan	• Edge from Titan—the ultra slim wristwatch that is only 3.5mm thick and 30mm water-resistant is a path-breaking design concept. No other company selling mass produced watch is slimmer than this.
3	Tata Steel	• Developed low phosphorus steel from high phosphorus ore.
4	Tata BP Solar	• The sun, sand and sea (water) are all inexhaustible sources of renewable and clean energy. It will play a significant role in the years ahead in terms of innovative harnessing and applications of solar energy for the benefit of the larger mankind.

Compiled by the authors from: Gupta Syamal, "Innovation and entrepreneurship," http://www.tata.com/0_media/features/speakers_forum/20060321_syamal_gupta.htm.

EXHIBIT 4 Top Most 50 Innovative Countries in the World (As per BCG Listing 2008)

Country	Number of Innovative Companies
USA	31
Britain	4
Germany	4
Japan	4
India	2
Canada	1
Finland	1
Netherlands	1
Singapore	1
South Korea	1
Total	50

Compiled by the authors from: "SAJA FORUM," http://www.sajaforum.org/2008/04/index.html, April 30, 2008.

Tata Group has accelerated its R&D, as many executives of the company continue to believe that enhanced innovation is required to fuel their future growth. R&D spending by Tata Group in the country is very huge and growing rapidly. The ongoing innovation in their products helps them gain competitive advantage. Tata Group is opening up a new era to develop and promote new business models in response to emerging market needs. A post of 'Chief Innovation Officer' was created to guide and promote the group's overall R&D strategy while working closely with each business group. Tata has taken steps to evaluate new opportunities and to bring about a match between innovation and market needs.

Tata is facing a challenging task ahead of becoming globally competitive in terms of cost and quality. They realise the need of the hour is to recognise and pursue innovation as a tool for sustainable advantage in products, processes, business models and organisations. They believe that innovation has to be integrally woven into a firm's strategy and has to drive and sustain competitiveness. Entrepreneurs are first and foremost change makers, achievers and not just visionaries. This thought has been echoed by visionaries such as Mahatma Gandhi[25] and J. R. D. Tata, who were enterprising in all their efforts and approaches. Tata BP Solar, a division of Tata Group, has developed various novel applications of solar photovoltaic and thermals with a view to serving the larger community and rural needs. The impact of innovative applications has a great role to play in enhancing the quality of life of the people in a developing country like India.

For instance, Tata Steel's acquisition of Corus has changed the steel industry, presenting a greater need for technically trained employees and engineers. The deal, which analysts say could still face a counter bid from rival steelmakers, illustrates the drive by low-cost producers to expand their global reach and add more high-technology products. Tata Group has a lot of challenges to face in the post-acquisition period of Corus. Their primary concern was to pay no more than reasonable compensation for Corus in order to result in a profitable combination. Second was to deal with the successful integration between the companies, timely execution of Greenfield projects in India and securing quality raw materials. Though Tata Steel's indigenous iron ore mines in India may be sufficient to meet the current requirements of its Indian operations at Jamshedpur (a city in India), Tata imports about 40% of the coal requirement for its Jamshedpur operations. Finally, it has started evaluating the strategic options for iron ore and coal to vertically integrate their operations and maintain profitability.

ANNEXURE II 50 Top Most Innovative Companies in the World

Rank	Company	HQ Country	HQ Continent	Revenue Growth 2004–07* (in %)	Margin Growth 2004–07* (in %)	Stock Returns 2004–07** (in %)	Most Known for Its Innovative ... (% who think so)
1	Apple	USA	North America	47	69	83	Products (52%)
2	Google	USA	North America	73	5	53	Customer Experience (26%)
3	Toyota Motor	Japan	Asia	12	1	15	Processes (36%)
4	General Electric	USA	North America	9	1	3	Processes (43%)
5	Microsoft	USA	North America	16	8	12	Products (26%)
6	Tata Group	India	Asia	Private	Private	Private	Products (58%)
7	Nintendo	Japan	Asia	37	4	77	Products (63%)
8	Procter & Gamble	USA	North America	16	4	12	Processes (30%)
9	Sony	Japan	Asia	8	13	17	Products (56%)
10	Nokia	Finland	Europe	20	2	35	Products (36%)
11	Amazon.com	USA	North America	29	−11	28	Customer Experience (33%)
12	IBM	USA	North America	1	11	4	Processes (31%)
13	Research In Motion	Canada	North America	56	−1	51	Products (37%)
14	BMW	Germany	Europe	6	−5	11	Customer Experience (40%)
15	Hewlett-Packard	USA	North America	10	17	35	Processes, Business Models, and Customer Experience (27% each)
16	Honda Motor	Japan	Asia	12	6	14	Products (40%)
17	Walt Disney	USA	North America	6	14	7	Customer Experience (63%)
18	General Motors	USA	North America	−2	NA***	−11	Products (55%)
19	Reliance Industries	India	Asia	31	−7	94	Business Models (31%)
20	Boeing	USA	North America	9	32	21	Products (63%)
21	Goldman Sachs Group	USA	North America	30	6	28	Processes and Business Models (33% each)
22	3M	USA	North America	7	5	3	Products (45%)
23	Wal-Mart Stores	USA	North America	10	−2	−2	Processes (48%)

(continued)

Rank	Company	HQ Country	HQ Continent	Revenue Growth 2004-07* (in %)	Margin Growth 2004-07* (in %)	Stock Returns 2004-07** (in %)	Most Known for Its Innovative … (% who think so)
24	Target	USA	North America	11	3	0	Customer Experience (67%)
25	Facebook	USA	North America	Private	Private	Private	Customer Experience (51%)
26	Samsung Electronics	South Korea	Asia	2	−14	8	Products (42%)
27	AT&T	USA	North America	43	6	23	Customer Experience (33%)
28	Virgin Group	Britain	Europe	Private	Private	Private	Customer Experience (47%)
29	Audi	Germany	Europe	11	11	41	Products (50%)
30	McDonald's	USA	North America	7	−7	25	Customer Experience (42%)
31	Daimler	Germany	Europe	−11	37	28	Products (35%)
32	Starbucks	USA	North America	23	−2	−13	Customer Experience (60%)
33	Ebay	USA	North America	33	−37	−17	Business Models (28%)
34	Verizon Communications	USA	North America	12	0	9	Services (41%)
35	Cisco Systems	USA	North America	20	−5	12	Products (35%)
36	Ing Group	Netherlands	Europe	7	4	11	Services (41%)
37	Singapore Airlines	Singapore	Asia	9	5	20	Customer Experience (55%)
38	Siemens	Germany	Europe	1	21	22	Products (41%)
39	Costco Wholesale	USA	North America	11	−5	14	Customer Experience (46%)
40	HSBC	Britain	Europe	12	−1	4	Services (39%)
41	Bank of America	USA	North America	12	0	0	Customer Experience and Services (23% each)
42	Exxon Mobil	USA	North America	11	7	25	Processes (50%)
43	News Corp.	USA	North America	4	4	4	Business Models (47%)

(*continued*)

Rank	Company	HQ Country	HQ Continent	Revenue Growth 2004-07* (in %)	Margin Growth 2004-07* (in %)	Stock Returns 2004-07** (in %)	Most Known for Its Innovative ... (% who think so)
44	BP	Britain	Europe	14	−5	11	Processes (42%)
45	Nike	USA	North America	8	−1	14	Customer Experience (43%)
46	Dell	USA	North America	7	−12	−17	Business Models (37%)
47	Vodafone Group	Britain	Europe	7	−21	15	Business Models (33%)
48	Intel	USA	North America	4	−10	6	Products (53%)
49	Southwest Airlines	USA	North America	15	9	−9	Customer Experience (50%)
50	American Express	USA	North America	3	1	3	Customer Experience (35%)

Source: "The World's 50 Most Innovative Companies," http://bwnt.businessweek.com/interactive_reports/innovative_companies/.

Notes. Analysis and data provided in collaboration with the innovation practice of the Boston Consulting Group and BCG-ValueScience. Reuters and Compustat were used for financial and industry data and Bloomberg for total shareholder returns.

*Compound growth rates for revenue and operating margins are based on 2004–07 fiscal year data as originally stated. Operating margin is earnings before interest and taxes, as a percentage of revenue. Where possible, quarterly and semiannual data were used to bring performance for pre-June year-ends closer to December, 2007. Financial figures were calculated in local currency.

**Stock returns are annualized, 12/31/04 to 12/31/07, and account for price appreciation and dividends.

***Calculating three-year compound annual growth rate for operating margins was not possible when either figure was negative.

Another major challenge in the integration process is the cultural difference. But Tata Group has managed this situation by sharing very similar work ethics and culture, which is basic to the success of any post-acquisition integration process. They opted for a coordinated solution through collaboration which has led to the potential for greater gains for both. Tata Steel's integration process puts pressure on constant and seamless communication between not only the top management of both the companies but also between the operating units, to inculcate respect for each other's culture. This strategy will help in developing appropriate 'performance culture' and 'operating models' of the enlarged entity. Tata has retained the management structure in all their group of companies. The task that lies ahead of them is to continue to successfully execute the integration of operations. Tata stated that, "Together we will be even better equipped to remain at the leading edge of the fast changing steel industry."[26] Tata took extreme care and consideration to ensure that they fully understand the national and corporate cultures of the companies they have bought. At the time of the Jaguar acquisition, Tata also had issues of cultural and communication barriers.

Tata was familiar with British business culture following the recent acquisition of steel producer Corus, but here also Tata worked hard to understand Jaguar and Land Rover's unique motoring heritage and business culture. Key to their success was their ability to maintain clear and open channels of communication with all Jaguar and Land Rover employees.

In the making of Nano, Tata is faced with challenges in meeting cost and time targets. The Nano is being produced entirely at Tata's Singur plant, West Bengal (a state in India), which is to have an annual capacity of 250,000–350,000 units. As part of the cost-cutting exercise, 35 parts suppliers have moved into the same complex, reducing transport costs and time delays dramatically. Some of the other challenges are from the rise in the fuel price and Singur being in a flood-prone area. At this stage, Tata has had to work on new variants of the world's cheapest car Nano, to overcome the challenge posed by high fuel prices, which could negatively impact vehicle sales. Tata Motors has also started developing alternative models of Nano to meet environmental and fuel price challenges, as well as market requirements of several international markets. Though fraught with a lot of challenges in achieving a place in the list of topmost innovative companies in the world, at the time of launch of Nano in January 2008, Ratan Tata stated that "The year ahead will be no more daunting than the challenges [we] have faced in difficult years in the past." [27]

ENDNOTES

1. "The world will always need innovators and innovations," *http://www.tata.com/media/Speeches/inside.aspx?artid=rp1fqgVFrmg=*, March 21, 2006.

2. Gupta, Syamal, "Innovation and entrepreneurship," http://www.tata.com/0_media/features/speakers_forum/20060321_syamal_gupta.htm.

3. "Tata buys Jaguar in £1.15bn deal," *http://news.bbc.co.uk/2/hi/business/7313380.stm*, March 26, 2008.

4. Nussbaum, Bruce, "50 of the Most Innovative Companies in the World. Tata, General Motors, Facebook Are Big Surprises," *http://www.businessweek.com/innovate/NussbaumOnDesign/archives/2008/04/50_most_innovat.html*, April 18, 2008.

5. "Tata Group profile," *http://www.tata.com/0_about_us/group_profile.htm*.

6. Ibid.

7. "Tata Consultancy Services—India's first global billion-dollar software organisation," *http://goliath.ecnext.com/coms2/gi_0199-2894756/Tata-Consultancy-Services-India-s.html*.

8. "Tata Group profile," op. cit.

9. "Tata Group profile," op. cit.

10. "Tata's 100 years of steeling the thunder," *http://www.tata.com/tata_steel/media/20070827_3.htm*, August 26, 2007.

11. Ibid.

12. "Tata Steel completes £6.2bn acquisition of Corus Group plc," *http://www.corusgroup.com/en/company/financial_information/tata_steel_offer/2007_tata_steel_acquisition_complete*, April 2, 2007.

13. Ibid.

14. Wholly owned subsidiaries are indirectly controlled by the parent company e.g. the parent company has a significant share/stake in the company to influence decision-making but they do not wholly own or directly control the company. A joint ventures is a good example of an indirect subsidiary.

15. "Tata Motors completes acquisition of Jaguar Land Rover," *http://www.tatamotors.com/our_world/press_releases.php?ID=370&action=Pull*.

16. Ibid.

17. Ibid.

18. Ibid.

19. Ibid.

20. "Tata acquires Jaguar, Land Rover for $2.30 bn," *http://timesofindia.indiatimes.com/Business/India_Business/Tata_acquires_Jaguar_Land_Rover_for_230_bn/rssarticleshow/2902216.cms*, March 26, 2008.

21. "Tata Motors completes acquisition of Jaguar Land Rover," op. cit.

22. "Tata Motors unveils the People's Car," *http://www.tatamotors.com/our_world/press_releases.php?ID=340&action=Pull*, January 10, 2008.

23. Ibid.

24. "Tata Group profile," op. cit.

25. Mohandas Karamchand Gandhi, commonly known around the world as Mahatma Gandhi, was a major political and spiritual leader of India and the Indian independence movement, which led India to independence and inspired movements for civil rights and freedom across the world. He is officially honoured in India as the 'Father of the Nation.'

26. "Tata to take over Corus," *http://www.financialexpress.com/old/latest_full_story.php?content_id=144037*, October 20, 2006.

27. "New Nano model underway to mitigate fuel price challenges: Tata," *http://economictimes.indiatimes.com/News/News_By_Industry/Auto/Automobiles/New_Nano_model_underway_to_mitigate_fuel_price_challengesTata/rssarticleshow/3184422.cms*, July 1, 2008.

CASE 15

DATING AT IKEA CHINA: AN UNEXPECTED MANAGEMENT CHALLENGE*

Jerome Deloix, the manager of IKEA's Xu Hui store in Shanghai, could not quite believe either the noise or the scene before his eyes. One of the store's security guards had summoned him urgently to the restaurant. It was 2.30pm on a Tuesday and, ever since the store had opened at 9am, a stream of middle-aged and older people had been filling up the restaurant. By this time, nearly 500 of them had gathered to socialize and spend the day drinking the free coffee to which they were entitled as IKEA Family Member cardholders. Not only were they drinking many cups of coffee and taking all the sugar, they were also eating food they had brought with them—instead of enjoying the tasty meals available for purchase from the counter—and were playing radios, calling out to each other, and generally behaving as though they were in their own homes. They were also checking out members of the opposite sex. A seniors' dating club had adopted the IKEA Xu Hui restaurant as the location for its meetings.

Arguments sometimes broke out between dating club members, and one man had thrown hot coffee over the security guard who had tried to intervene. If they were asked not to eat food brought from home, club members just yelled and carried on as before. Ordinary IKEA customers were getting upset that every Tuesday and Thursday, the days that the club met, there was no space for them to relax and eat in the restaurant. IKEA co-workers[1] were unhappy at what was going on. The ambiance of the store was disrupted and sales suffered on the dating club days—none of the club members bought things from the store and each might spend only RMB 10 on food. The problem had been growing over the last 18 months, as club meetings became more and more popular. At first, in 2009, when there were under 250 seniors participating, IKEA co-workers felt they could cope, but when numbers climbed in 2011 to around 700 the situation got beyond a joke.

Enough was enough. Something had to be done to stop this disruptive behaviour. *"We want to be nice, but there are limits!"* remarked Deloix to his fellow managers. Ruefully he reflected: *"If you have a weakness, people will find it immediately."* But what measures could he take against the seniors' activities that would

be respectful of ordinary customers' needs while also remaining true to IKEA's deeply-held customer service concepts? Being a good member of the community was just as important to IKEA as its commitment to customers and co-workers. Was it fair that his co-workers—all Chinese—had to bear the brunt of dating club members' bad behaviour? How far did the store's concept of community engagement require it to go?

A Very Different Culture: IKEA In China

As in every IKEA outlet worldwide, the Xu Hui store's restaurant lay at its centre, halfway along the path mapped out for visitors through the enormous display of furniture and home interior furnishings. The Xu Hui store stocked 8,500 different items in its 35,000 m² floor space, so it was bigger than the typical 25,000–30,000 m² IKEA outlets in Europe. Still, it was the smallest of IKEA's 11 stores in China, which averaged around 45,000 m² in size. The Xu Hui store was also unusual in that it occupied a city centre site and 60 percent of its visitors arrived by public transport. With well over 5 million visitors per year, the store ranked in IKEA's top 10 worldwide revenue-generators although the average spend per customer was relatively low. An indication of its popularity was that 80,000 people visited on the opening day in 2003, even though it was the middle of the SARS epidemic. IKEA's Shanghai Beicai store was newer, its largest in Asia, and had plenty of car-parking space, so most people arrived with their own transport. An even bigger third store was scheduled to open in 2013. Compared with both of these stores, by mid-2012 the Xu Hui branch was beginning to look a little tired.

Part of the IKEA concept is to provide a spacious, clean location where customers can rest and eat Swedish-inspired meals and snacks, as a means of encouraging them to stay longer in the store. The restaurant did not operate as a profit centre but as a marketing tool, to support the customer service ethos. Because many women came to shop there, the Xu Hui store restaurant offered breakfast deals from 9am for mothers who had dropped their children off at school, lunch sets that varied from day to day, 'happy hour' snacks during the afternoon, and other special offers right up until the store closed at 11pm each evening. Customers who had IKEA Family Member cards (which they could get by simply filling in a form) were entitled to free coffee, as was the case in IKEA worldwide. People who did not have a Family Member card paid RMB 5 for a cup of coffee—far cheaper than in coffee shop chains like

Starbucks or Costa Coffee—and could have a free refill. In China, drinking coffee was still a rather exotic pastime even 30 years after the country began to embrace western ideas. After the scandal over adulterated milk in 2008, good milk was expensive but was offered freely to IKEA coffee-drinkers.

While the IKEA vision was 'to create a better life for the many people'[2]—comprising customers, co-workers and the community—determining who the 'many people' were in China was very different than in Sweden which, after all, had only 9 million citizens. Shanghai's population alone was 23 million. During his 10 years with IKEA in China, Deloix had seen many things he had never experienced at IKEA France, his previous posting. At the store in Dalian, which he had opened and managed before coming to Shanghai, families had sat at tables in the dining room display area to eat food that they had brought with them and then walked away leaving a mess. He had seen ayis (nannies) put small children to sleep in the cots during the morning, wake them for lunch in the restaurant, and put them down again for a nap in the afternoon. On hot days in Shanghai, the sofas and beds were attractive places to stretch out and sleep for a while.

Sometimes long-distance tour buses arrived too early for hotels to be ready, so the drivers would drop their passengers off to rest in the conveniently located Xu Hui store. IKEA co-workers did their best to respond sensitively to all this, for example waking people who were sleeping too long or had sprawled inappropriately, or explaining to nannies that other people wanted to look at the children's rooms.

Deloix admired some of the entrepreneurial spirit he encountered. One company organized tours of the Xu Hui store, complete with tour guide wearing a microphone—but very often participants bought something afterwards. He knew that people in distant parts of China, where IKEA was not present, commissioned contacts to buy items and despatch them for an extra fee. And after a special offer had ended, it was not uncommon to see those products offered for sale on the online retailing site TaoBao.com or in another province at the higher price. There was nothing IKEA could do about that. On the other hand, informal taxi drivers hassling customers inside the store could be dealt with by the police.

"It's not so much a question of whether something is good or bad," said Deloix, *"but whether we accept it. And if the answer is yes, then how?"*

The Free Coffee Dating club (as IKEA co-workers dubbed it) was also making money for its organizer by charging membership fees of RMB 10 per person when they signed up online. Dating clubs had become a big business in China, and huge 'marriage markets' occurred regularly in many cities where young people paid a fee and, often with their mothers, gathered to post their own mini-CV, scan other CVs for promising members of the opposite sex and—for the brave ones (or even their mothers!)—get up on a podium to "sell" their virtues to the passing crowds. The differences in IKEA's case were the age group the Free Coffee Dating club catered to and the location it chose for its meetings.

Deloix tried but failed to identify the Free Coffee Dating club organizer. Concerned that the reputation of IKEA would be damaged by customers' negative comments on social networking sites, he took the unusual step of inviting journalists to come and see the problem for themselves. The story appeared in a variety of Chinese and English-language newspapers and on Chinese TV—which believed it was the government's duty to halt the group's activities because it was responsible for people's behaviour.

The store's co-workers debated what to do. Deloix proposed cancelling the free coffee for IKEA Family Members and instead giving them a free drink with a set meal, but the IKEA China head office told him, "Don't touch the free coffee!" It was too important a part of IKEA's culture worldwide to abandon. Chinese co-workers were protective of the company and highly critical of the Free Coffee Daters. Some even said that the group demonstrated the attitude typical of the over-45 generation, which had no sense of civic behavior—they only took and never gave. Deloix wanted to look through his customers' eyes and see what could be learned. *"It's nice that older people like to date."*

IKEA believed in being socially responsible within its local community; it wanted to be close to people and part of their lives. Maybe it should go into the dating club business itself? Or should Deloix simply crack down and ban the group?

Eventually Deloix and his team defined a specific area in the restaurant where the group could meet and provided them with special green cups for their coffee. Extra security guards were posted to keep order and notices were posted at the entrance asking for good behaviour and banning shouting, radio-playing, and knitting. Says Deloix: *"We can't solve this problem, so we have to manage it in the right way. It takes time to change people's habits."*

In early 2013 Deloix was going to begin a phased renovation of the store. Maybe he should start with the restaurant? Perhaps, by the time the remodelled store fully re-opened in 2014, the senior dating club would have gone to look for romance elsewhere.

ENDNOTES

1. All IKEA employees were called co-workers, no matter what their job was, reflecting the company's core values of openness and equality.
2. http://www.ikea.com/ms/en_CN/about_ikea/the_ikea_way/our_business_idea/index.html

CASE 16

GOOGLE VENTURES: DISRUPTING CORPORATE VENTURE CAPITAL?

"The success of Google's venturing efforts will hinge, to a large extent, on finding the right balance between entrepreneurial finance and organizational realities."[1]

–Gary Dushnitsky[2]

The venture capital (VC) industry in the US, which had fuelled the growth of the technology industry, had witnessed a trend among companies for establishing their own VC arms. Though still small in comparison to traditional or independent VC firms, in terms of dollars invested or number of deals implemented, corporate VC arms were beginning to make a mark in the VC industry. Google, one of the world's leading internet companies, launched its venture capital (VC) arm, Google Ventures, in March 2009. Google had set up GV with a view to finding and helping to develop highly promising start-ups in a number of areas, such as consumer internet, software, clean-tech, bio-tech, and health care, through early-stage investments. Besides finance, GV offered entrepreneurs several add-on services, including space on its campus to operate. There was general apprehension among start-ups about the conditionalities involved in accessing corporate VC. Corporate venture capitalists were known to have bought out start-ups quite soon after the initial round of funding—a practice generally not witnessed among independent VC firms. GV, with its strong offering of finance and a number of start-up support services, showed the potential to chart new paths in the VC industry. The case study discusses the concept of corporate venture capital, Google's entry into the venture capital market through GV, GV's business strategy, and the challenges and potential for GV in the VC industry.

Corporate Venture Capital: A Background Note

Venture capital was a type of equity investment that focused on investing in start-ups and emerging companies that had potential for high growth. While most VC was directed towards start-ups, a significant portion of it was also invested at different stages of a company's growth cycle. In return for the investment, the venture capitalist received an ownership stake in the enterprise. Most venture capitalists focused mainly on start-ups that were involved in developing significant innovations. The nature of VC usually made it a high risk-high return proposition. The venture capitalist would mitigate the investment risk by developing a portfolio of emerging companies in a single fund. In addition to finance, the venture capitalist usually possessed expertise and experience in business planning, industry knowledge, and taking a company public. Venture capitalists supported the growth of companies, but eventually exited their ventures—in the case of an early stage investment, the exit was usually after seven or 10 years. The goal of a venture capitalist was to facilitate the growth of a company to a point where he could take it public, or sell it to a large company at a considerable profit.[3]

Professionally managed venture capital firms (VCFs) generally were in the form of private partnerships or closely-held corporations funded by private and public pension funds, endowment funds, foundations, corporations, wealthy individuals, foreign investors, and venture capitalists themselves (Exhibit 1). The venture capital fund was structured as a limited partnership—with the investors in the fund as limited partners—while the VCF, which managed the venture capital fund, was the general partner who received a management fee from the fund as well as a share in its profits.[4]

In contrast to such VC, also referred to as "private VC" or independent VC there were also "corporate VC investments," made in start-ups. Corporate VC referred to investments made by a company out of its reserve funds directly into start-ups. Corporate VC did not include investments in new internal ventures, which legally remained within the company's fold.[5]

The defining features of a corporate VC investment were: a) its objective, and b) the extent to which the operations of the investing company and the start-up company were linked.[6] The objective of a corporate VC investment was either strategic—looking for synergies between the company's business and the new venture—or financial—looking for attractive returns.[7] The key task for a corporate VC unit was to identify highly profitable new projects and promising technologies before the competition, and collaborate with the best minds in the field.[8]

Among the most successful corporate VC investments were the ones made by Intel[9] in enterprises such as Red Hat,[10] a software distributor in North Carolina, and WebMD,[11] an online medical information company.[12]

A study conducted by Gary Dushnitsky, Professor of Management at the Wharton School, University of Pennsylvania,

This case was written by S. Rajagopalan, Amity Research Centers Headquarters, Bangalore. It is intended to be used as the basis for class discussion rather than to illustrate either effective or ineffective handling of a management situation. The case was compiled from published sources.

EXHIBIT 1 Investors in Venture Capital Funds

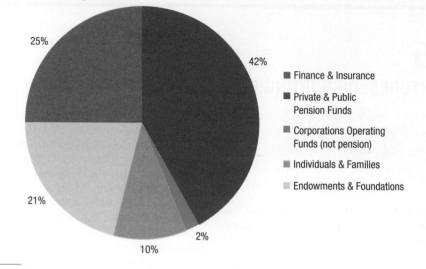

- Finance & Insurance
- Private & Public Pension Funds
- Corporations Operating Funds (not pension)
- Individuals & Families
- Endowments & Foundations

42%
25%
21%
10%
2%

Source: "Venture Capital 101: What is Venture Capital?," http://www.nvca.org/index.php?option=com_content&view=article&id=141&Itemid=133

and Zur Shapira, Professor of Management at the Stern School of Business, revealed that corporate venture capitalists had a higher rate of successful portfolio exits than independent venture capitalists, which they attributed to the access that corporate venture capitalists had to their parent company's resources, industry knowledge, and customer and supplier networks.[13] Dushnitsky also pointed out the connectedness between independent VC and corporate VC and said, "You cannot disconnect corporate VCs from independent VCs. They invest in the same kinds of ventures and often do so together. They are dependent on each other for deal flow. Corporations need to be aware of the implications

of what they are doing. They may be hindering their corporate VC units from fulfilling their full potential."[14]

Independent VC dominated the VC market. According to the National Venture Capital Association (of the US), the share of corporate VC in VC dollars invested in US companies was 8.5 percent in 2010, up from 7.4 percent in 2009 (Exhibit 2). The share in number of VC deals reflected a better picture for corporate VC: 13.9 percent of the deals in 2010 had corporate VC involvement, up from 12.7 percent in 2009.[15] The average amount of all VC deals in 2010 was $6.75 million, while the average amount of corporate VC participation was $4.15 million.[16]

EXHIBIT 2 Independent Venture Capital and Corporate Venture Capital: A Comparison

Year	Total number of VC deals	Number of deals with corporate VC involvement	Percentage of VC deals with corporate VC involvement	Average amount of all VC deals (in $ million)	Average amount of corporate VC participation (in $ million)	Percentage of dollars coming from corporate VC
2001	4579	963	21.0	8.31	4.86	12.3
2002	3177	533	16.8	6.56	3.53	9.0
2003	3000	433	14.4	6.29	2.93	6.7
2004	3157	510	16.2	6.91	2.92	6.8
2005	3232	512	15.8	7.02	2.88	6.5
2006	3787	623	16.5	6.91	3.19	7.6
2007	4085	729	17.8	7.43	3.33	8.0
2008	4082	757	18.5	7.02	2.81	7.4
2009	3041	387	12.7	6.37	3.71	7.4
2010	3447	478	13.9	6.75	4.15	8.5

Source: Compiled by the author from: "Corporate VC Stats as of 3/31/2011," http://www.nvca.org/index.php?option=com_docman&task=cat_view&gid=99&Itemid=317

Google Ventures: Google's Foray into Venture Capital

Google was a US-based multinational company with internet search technologies as its main business. Founded by Larry Page and Sergey Brin, two Stanford University graduate students, Google was incorporated on September 4 1998. Google hosted and developed a number of internet-based services and products, and generated revenues mainly from advertising. The company's mission was: "To organise the world's information and make it universally accessible and useful."[17] Google's flagship product was its internet search engine "Google". Over time, the company had expanded its product line beyond the search engine, introducing products such as Gmail, the email service; Google Toolbar; Orkut, a social networking site; Google Talk, a chat program; Google Chrome, an Internet browser; Google Books; Google News Archive; Google Buzz, a social networking facility embedded in Gmail, and several others. In June 2011, the company launched Google Plus, another social networking forum. The number of users of Google Plus had reached 25 million by the end of July 2011, 20 times faster than any other social networking website.[18]

Google's major revenue source was its advertising software's, Google AdWords and Google AdSense. Google AdWords allowed advertisers to display their advertisements in the Google content network, through either a cost-per-click or cost-per-view scheme, and Google AdSense, enabled website owners to display these advertisements on their website, and earn money every time ads were clicked.[19] Google had gained recognition in the technology sector for its considerable innovation capabilities.

In March 2009, Google launched a VC fund to identify and help develop promising start-ups in the fields of software, clean technology, biotechnology, health care, and consumer internet.[20] The VC fund was named "Google Ventures" (GV).[21] GV's main focus was on investing in the early stage of a new venture. At the time of its launch, Rich Miner and Bill Maris, Managing Partners of Google Ventures, wrote, "Central to our effort will be our fellow Googlers, whom we view as a critically important resource to help educate us about potential investments areas and evaluate specific companies. Economically, times are tough, but great ideas come when they will. If anything, we think the current downturn is an ideal time to invest in nascent companies that have the chance to be the 'next big thing,' and we'll be working hard to find them."[22] GV was expected to take over the investment operation that was pursued by its Google.org, Google's philanthropic arm, which had supported companies that were interested in clean energy and international healthcare.[23]

There were a number of areas in which GV offered to support entrepreneurs (Exhibit 3).

GV invited all Google employees to participate in the search for promising start-ups by launching a referral programme that provided an award of $10,000 for the employee if GV invested in the referred start-up.[24] All that an employee was required to do was to fill in a form on the company's internal website stating why he liked the start-up and provide an introduction to a key employee at the start-up.[25]

Initially, GV aimed at investing about $100 million a year in varied deal sizes, which ranged from a small amount of a hundred thousand dollars in a seed investment to a late-stage investment of tens of millions of dollars.[26] Over two years after its founding, GV was planning to double its annual investment plan to $200 million, and also increase its office space and staff strength.[27] The companies that GV had invested since 2009 were diverse in their business profiles (Exhibit 4). However, Miner pointed out

EXHIBIT 3 GV's Support to Entrepreneurs

Recruiting
GV helped entrepreneurs recruit their first five employees and then trained them on further recruitment, with inputs on relevant matters such as compensation package.

Design
Entrepreneurs could get support from GV in designing their products. GV facilitated them in answering product design questions, such as: Who were the users? How would they use the product? How could the user experience be made seamless and fun?

Engineering
GV could also provide the expertise of Google's engineers to entrepreneurs. This could be particularly useful for entrepreneurs where products needed to be scaled up to cater to a large number of users.

Start-up University
GV also set up a facility to provide inputs to entrepreneurs in a classroom mode. Instructors came from GV, Google, and the industry.

Start-up Lab
A start-up lab was established by GV near its headquarters which could be used by start-ups financed by GV.

Support of Googlers
Entrepreneurs could draw upon the support of thousands of Googlers—scientists, engineers, product marketers, product managers, former CEOs and founders, statisticians, human capital managers, and others.

Source: Compiled by the author from: "Google Ventures—How we can help," http://www.googleventures.com/how-we-can-help.html

EXHIBIT 4 GV's Investments

	Name of Company	Area of Business
1	Adimab	Fully integrated, yeast-based antibody discovery platform.
2	Airy Labs	Creates social learning games for kids aged between 5 and 13 years.
3	Astrid	Mobile social to-do list that helps individuals and groups stay organized, get more done, and have fun in the process.
4	Cool Planet Bio Fuels	Development of negative carbon and carbon neutral fuels based on plant photosynthesis, which absorb carbon from the air.
5	Copious	A marketplace to buy from and sell to people, not strangers.
6	Corduro	Payment services for internet, mobile, and traditional retail transactions.
7	Crittercism	Infrastructure for mobile applications.
8	Dasient	Anti-malware technology.
9	English Central	Interactive web video based English learning facility.
10	Firespotter Labs	A company creation shop that generates ideas, builds products, and launches the most promising ones as independent companies.
11	Hipster	Helping to find information on real world locations not yet available online.
12	HubSpot	Marketing software platform for small and medium-sized businesses.
13	iPierian	Creating new therapeutics discovered using cellular reprogramming and directed differentiation of patient cells.
14	Kabam	Publishes Massively Multiplayer Social Games.
15	LawPivot	Legal Q & A website enabling companies, especially startups, to confidentially receive crowdsourced legal answers from highly qualified lawyers at a very low cost.
16	Luminate	A platform for image applications that transforms static images into a canvas for shopping, sharing, and exploring.
17	Miso	A social platform to enhance TV viewing experience.
18	Miso Media	Educational software for easy and enjoyable ways of learning instruments.
19	Next Autoworks	Car manufacturer that will introduce a safe, high-quality, fuel-efficient car for the US market at a very competitive price.
20	OpenCandy	Solution provider for distribution, monetization, and discovery problems in the consumer application space.
21	Parse	Provides cloud services for mobile phone applications.
22	Read it Later	Saving facility for reading/viewing material from the Web on any device.
23	Recorded Future	Allows extraction of time and event information from the Web offering customers new ways to analyze the past, present, and the predicted future.
24	RelayRides	Neighbor-to-neighbor car sharing service.
25	Rocket Lawyer	Legal service on the internet.
26	Schematic Labs	Provides social entertainment mobile applications for the real world.
27	SCVNGR	Part game, part gaming platform.
28	Shopobot	Tracking of price changes at popular stores, and helping people decide the best time and place to buy.
29	Signpost	Community-powered deal site that helps people find attractive local deals.

(continued)

EXHIBIT 4 GV's Investments *(continued)*

	Name of Company	Area of Business
30	Silver Spring Networks	Smart grid solutions provider that helps utilities reduce carbon emissions, operate more efficiently, and empower their customers with new ways to monitor and manage their energy consumption.
31	Smarterer	Skill measurement platform.
32	ThinkNear	Yield management solution.
33	Trada	Crowdsourced paid search marketplace.
34	Transphorm	Makes ultra-efficient power modules.
35	VigLink	Tool for publishers to make monetization of their outbound links effortless, transparent, and honest.
36	23andMe	Personal genetics company that helps people to understand their own genetic information through DNA analysis technologies and web-based interactive tools.
37	Weather Bill	Helping people and businesses to adapt to climate change through technologically advanced weather insurance products.
38	WhaleShark Media	Coupon and deal websites.

Source: "Meet the companies in our portfolio," http://www.googleventures.com/portfolio.html

that "[GV] won't invest in a company that we don't think we can properly vet and understand."[28]

Road Ahead

GV had made significant strides investing in start-ups with diverse businesses. Since it started operations, GV had had two successful exits, while one was in the process of exit. Ngmoco, the smartphone social games publisher, was acquired by DeNA, a leading Japanese gaming company in November 2010, while HomeAway Inc., the online marketplace for vacation rentals and bed and breakfasts, became a public company in June 2010.[29] Another expected exit was from Silver Spring Networks which had filed for an IPO (initial public offering) in July 2011.[30] However, there was no clear picture on the overall profitability of GV since the company did not disclose the amount of its investments.[31] Going forward, GV faced some challenges, while it also exhibited the potential to open up new dimensions in the VC industry.

One challenge emanated from the kind of VC—corporate VC—that GV represented. A number of start-ups were apprehensive about the conditionalities that corporate VC could involve, such as giving the corporate VC firm the right to acquire the start-up at a later date.[32] A partner at an independent VC firm remarked that the practice among corporate VC funds to buy out a start-up shortly after investing in it was inconsistent with the general convention in the VC industry to make several rounds of investments and provide guidance to a start-up.[33] This, they feared, would put off other potential investors.[34] Other experts pointed to the higher risk involved in corporate VC than independent VC. Companies such as Intel, which had made VC investments, had made huge losses after a tech

market crash, whereas other majors such as Boeing and Dell exited the VC business.[35] Mark Heeson, President of the National Venture Capital Association, remarked that, "They got burned after the bubble, probably even more than the traditional VCs."[36]

A criticism about corporate VC was that its goal was not always to maximize returns.[37] Corporate VC had often invested in start-ups for strategic reasons, but not all the investments made money.[38]

Given Google's track record of questioning conventional wisdom and developing new approaches to new businesses, there was speculation about how GV would impact the venture capital industry. Bradford Coffey, Director of Strategy and Corporate Development at HubSpot,[39] argued that GV was attempting to disrupt the VC industry.[40] The thrust of his argument was that GV had several advantages that gave it a strong edge over traditional VC firms. According to Coffey, unlike traditional VC firms which lent their expertise in business models and professional networking to start-ups, GV had an engineering-focused support system to offer to entrepreneurs, which worked as a competitive differentiator for GV and held tremendous value for entrepreneurs.[41] Besides, Google had strong brand recognition that it could effectively leverage with the small businesses that constituted the majority of America's economy.[42] Coffey further pointed out that with the millions of resumes that Google received every year, it was well-placed to provide talented human resources to the technology companies in its portfolio.[43] Therefore, besides infusing cash, GV was in a good position to ensure that the cash secured good talent as well. With GV, entrepreneurs could access the rest of Google's services as well.[44] While GV did not tout this as a major plus for entrepreneurs, there was at least one example of a GV-supported start-up—SCVNGR—having benefited from the larger Google set-up. SCVNGR launched in integration with Google Places API,[45] which allowed the firm to scale internationally.[46]

It remains to be seen whether GV could succeed as a corporate VC enterprise with its innovative and differentiated offering to entrepreneurs and create a new business model for the VC industry.

ENDNOTES

1. "Want to Crank Up Corporate Venture Capital Performance? Consider Matching Independent VC Pay Packages," http://knowledge.wharton.upenn.edu/article.cfm?articleid=2102, November 26 2008.
2. Assistant Professor of Management at Wharton School, University of Pennsylvania.
3. "VC Industry Overview," http://www.nvca.org/index.php?option=com_content&view=article&id=141&Itemid=589
4. Christofidis, C. and Debande, D., "Financing Innovative Firms Through Venture Capital," http://www.eib.org/attachments/pj/vencap.pdf, February 2001.
5. Chesbrough, H., "Making Sense of Corporate Venture Capital", http://hbswk.hbs.edu/archive/2854.html, March 25 2002.
6. Ibid.
7. Ibid.
8. See note 1.
9. Intel is a US-based multinational technology company and one of the world's leading semiconductor chip makers.
10. Red Hat was founded in 1993 and is a leading provider of enterprise Linux and open source technology.
11. WebMD is an online medical information company that provides information, supportive communities, and in-depth reference material about health subjects.
12. See note 1.
13. See note 1.
14. See note 1.
15. "Corporate VC Stats as of 3/31/2011," http://www.nvca.org/index.php?option=com_docman&task=cat_view&gid=99&Itemid=317
16. Ibid.
17. "Company", http://www.google.com/corporate/index.html
18. Young, R., "Google Plus Reaches 25 Million Users, Activity Declines," http://www.searchenginejournal.com/google-plus-reaches-25-million-users-activity-declines/31500/, August 3 2001.
19. See note 17.
20. Miner, R. and Maris B., "Google's newest venture," http://googleblog.blogspot.com/2009/03/googles-newest-venture.html, March 30 2009.
21. Ibid.
22. Ibid.
23. Harvey Mike, "Google Ventures looks to invest in startups," http://business.timesonline.co.uk/tol/business/industry_sectors/technology/article6012139.ece, March 31 2009.
24. Arrington Michael, "Google Ventures Launches $10,000 Startup Referral Program For Employees," http://techcrunch.com/2011/03/18/google-ventures-launches-10000-startup-referral-program-for-employees/, March 18 2011.
25. Ibid.
26. "Where we invest," http://www.googleventures.com/where-we-invest.html
27. Chapman, L., "Google Ventures Scaling Up With More Cash, 'Googlers in Residence'," http://blogs.wsj.com/venturecapital/2011/07/11/google-ventures-scaling-up-with-more-cash-googlers-in-residence/, July 11 2011.
28. Schonfeld Erick, "The Google Ventures Cheat Sheet," http://techcrunch.com/2009/04/04/the-google-ventures-cheat-sheet/, April 4 2009.
29. See note 27.
30. See note 27.
31. See note 27.
32. Vascellaro, J. E., "Google to Extend Reach With Venture-Capital Arm," http://online.wsj.com/article/SB121747323523899779.html, July 31 2008.
33. Ricadela, A., "Google's New Role: Venture Capitalist," http://www.businessweek.com/technology/content/sep2007/tc20070831_697591.htm, September 4 2007.
34. See note 32.
35. See note 33.
36. See note 33.
37. Schonfeld, E., "Google Ventures Almost Ready To Launch, But It Is A Bad Idea," http://techcrunch.com/2009/03/20/google-ventures-almost-ready-to-launch-but-it-is-a-bad-idea/, March 20 2009.
38. Ibid.
39. HubSpot is an internet marketing software producer.
40. Coffey, B., "Will Google disrupt venture capital?," http://finance.fortune.cnn.com/2011/06/22/will-google-ventures-disrupt-venture-capital/", June 22 2011.
41. Ibid.
42. Ibid.
43. Ibid.
44. Ibid.
45. The Google Places API is a service that returns information about Places—defined within this API as establishments, geographic locations, or prominent points of interest—using HTTP requests.
46. See note 40.

CASE 17

HEINEKEN*

At the start of 2013, Dutch brewer Heineken had strengthened its position as the world's third largest brewer by securing a stronger foothold in the lucrative Asian beer market. It had recently paid over $6 billion to secure control of Asian Pacific Breweries, the owner of *Tiger* beer, *Bintang* lager, and other popular Asian brands. Listed in Singapore, Asia Pacific Breweries operates 30 breweries across the region, with operations in Cambodia, China, Indonesia, Malaysia, New Zealand, Singapore, Thailand, and Vietnam. CEO Francois van Boxmeer stated that the firm had wanted to make "a bold move in the region, which will be a growth market for decades to come."[1]

The move came on the heels of acquisitions and capacity investments that Heineken has been making in other developing markets. In 2011, it purchased five breweries in Nigeria to increase its presence in Africa, which is becoming one of the world's fastest-growing beer markets. The previous year, it had acquired Mexican brewer FEMSA Cervesa, producer of *Dos Equis, Sol,* and *Tecate* beers, to become a stronger, more competitive player in Latin America. With its purchase of Asia Pacific Breweries, Heineken expects that around 55 percent of its operating profits will come from such high-growth markets.

At the same time, Heineken has maintained its leading position across Europe. It made a high-profile acquisition of Scottish-based brewer Scottish & Newcastle, the brewer of well-known brands such as *Newcastle Brown Ale* and *Kronenbourg 1664.* Although the purchase had been made in partnership with Carlsberg, Heineken was able to gain control of Scottish & Newcastle's operations in several crucial European markets, such as the United Kingdom, Ireland, Portugal, Finland, and Belgium.

These decisions to acquire brewers that operate in different parts of the world have been a part of a series of changes that the Dutch brewer has been making to raise its stature in the various markets and to respond to changes that are occurring in the global market for beer. Beer consumption has been declining in the U.S. and Europe as a result of tougher drunk-driving laws and a growing appreciation for wine. At the same time, the beer industry has become ever more competitive, as the largest brewers have been expanding across the globe through acquisitions of smaller regional and national players (see Exhibits 1 and 2).

---

* Case developed by Professor Jamal Shamsie, Michigan State University, with the assistance of Professor Alan B. Eisner, Pace University. Material has been drawn from published sources to be used for purposes of class discussion. Copyright © 2013 Jamal Shamsie and Alan B. Eisner.

EXHIBIT 1 Income Statements*

Go to library tab in Connect to access Case Financials.

	A	B	C	D	E	F	G
1		Income Statements*					
2		2012	2011	2010	2009	2008	2007
3	Revenue	18,383	17,123	16,133	14,701	14,319	12,564
4	EBIT	3,904	2,455	2,476	1,757	1,080	1,528
5	Net Profit	2,949	1,430	1,436	1,018	347	807

*Figures in millions of Euros.

Source: Heineken.

EXHIBIT 2 Balance Sheets*

Go to library tab in Connect to access Case Financials.

	A	B	C	D	E	F	G
1		Balance Sheets*					
2		2012	2011	2010	2009	2008	2007
3	Assets	35,979	27,127	26,549	20,180	20,563	12,968
4	Liabilities	23,217	17,035	16,321	14,533	15,811	7,022
5	Equity	12,762	10,092	10,228	5,647	4,752	5,946

*Figures in millions of Euros.

Source: Heineken.

The need for change was clearly reflected in the appointment in October 2005 of Jean-Francois van Boxmeer as Heineken's first non-Dutch CEO. He was brought in to replace Thorny Ruys, who had decided to resign 18 months ahead of schedule because of his failure to significantly improve Heineken's performance. Prior to the appointment of Ruys in 2002, Heineken had been run by three generations of Heineken ancestors, whose portraits still adorn the dark-paneled office of the CEO in its Amsterdam headquarters. Like Ruys, van Boxmeer faces the challenge of preserving the firm's family-driven traditions, while trying to deal with threats that have never been faced before.

Confronting a Globalizing Industry

Heineken was one of the pioneers of an international strategy, using cross-border deals to expand its distribution of its *Heineken, Amstel,* and about 250 other beer brands in more than 175 countries around the globe. For years, it has been picking up small brewers from several countries to add more brands and to get better access to new markets. From its roots on the outskirts of Amsterdam, the firm has evolved into one of the world's largest brewers, operating more than 125 breweries in over 70 countries in the world, claiming about 10 percent of the global market for beer (see Exhibits 3 and 4).

EXHIBIT 3 Geographical Breakdown of Sales*

Go to library tab in Connect to access Case Financials.

	A	B	C	D	E	E	F
1		Balance Sheets*					
2		2012	2011	2010	2009	2008	2007
3	Western Europe	7,785	7,752	7,894	8,432	7,661	5,450
4	Central & Eastern Europe	3,280	3,229	3,143	3,200	3,687	3,686
5	Africa & Middle East	2,639	2,223	1,988	1,541	1,566	2,043
6	Americas	4,523	4,029	3,296	1,817	1,774	1,416
7	Asia Pacific	527	216	206	305	279	597

*Figures in millions of Euros.

Source: Heineken.

EXHIBIT 4 Significant Heineken Brands in Various Markets

Country	Brands
U.S.	Heineken, Amstel Light, Paulaner,* Moretti
Netherlands	Heineken, Amstel, Lingen's Blond, Murphy's Irish Red
France	Heineken, Amstel, Buckler,[†] Desperados[‡]
Italy	Heineken, Amstel, Birra Moretti
Spain	Heineken, Amstel, Cruzcampo, Buckler
Poland	Heineken, Krolewskie, Kujawiak, Zywiec
China	Heineken, Tiger, Reeb[§]
Singapore	Heineken, Tiger, Anchor, Baron's
India	Heineken, Arlem, Kingfisher
Indonesia	Heineken, Bintang, Guinness
Kazakhstan	Heineken, Amstel, Tian Shan
Egypt	Heineken, Birell, Meister, Fayrouz[†]
Israel	Heineken, Maccabee, Gold Star[§]
Nigeria	Heineken, Amstel Malta, Maltina, Gulder
South Africa	Heineken, Amstel, Windhoek, Strongbow
Panama	Heineken, Soberana, Crystal, Panama
Chile	Heineken, Cristal, Escudo, Royal

*Wheat beer.
[†]Nonalcoholic beer.
[‡]Tequila-flavored beer.
[§] Minority interest.

Source: Heineken.

In fact, the firm's flagship *Heineken* brand ranked second only to *Budweiser* in a global brand survey jointly undertaken by *BusinessWeek* and Interbrand a couple of years ago. The premier brand has achieved worldwide recognition according to Kevin Baker, director of alcoholic beverages at British market researcher Canadean Ltd. A U.S. wholesaler recently asked a group of marketing students to identify an assortment of beer bottles that had been stripped of their labels. The stubby green *Heineken* container was the only one that incited instant recognition among the group.

But the beer industry has been undergoing significant change due to a furious wave of consolidation. Most of the bigger brewers have begun to acquire or merge with their competitors in foreign markets in order to become global players. Over the past decade, South African Breweries Plc acquired U.S.-based Miller Brewing and then Fosters, the largest Australian brewer, to become a major global brewer. U.S.-based Coors linked with Canada-based Molson in 2005, with their combined operations allowing it to rise to a leading position among the world's biggest brewers. More recently, Belguim's Interbrew, Brazil's AmBev, and U.S.-based Anheuser-Busch merged to become the largest global brewer with operations across most of the continents (see Exhibit 5).

Many brewers have also expanded their operations without the use of such acquisitions. For example, Anheuser-Busch had brought equity stakes in and struck partnership deals with Mexico's Grupo Modelo, China's Tsingtao, and Chile's CCU. Such cross-border deals have provided significant benefits to the brewing giants. To begin with, it has given them ownership of local brands that has propelled them into a dominant position in various markets around the world. Beyond this, acquisitions of and partnerships with foreign brewers can provide the firm with the manufacturing and distribution capabilities that they could use to develop a few global brands. "The era of global brands is coming," said Alan Clark, Budapest-based managing director of SABMiller Europe.[2]

Since its acquisition of Anheuser-Busch, InBev is planning to include *Budweiser* in its existing efforts to develop *Stella Artois, Brahma,* and *Becks* as global flagship brands. Each of these brands originated in different locations, with *Budweiser* coming from the U.S., *Stella Artois* from Belgium, *Brahma* from Brazil, and *Becks* from Germany. Similarly, the newly formed SAB Miller has been attempting to develop the Czech brand *Pilsner Urquell* into a global brand. Exports of this pilsner have doubled since SAB acquired it in 1999. John Brock, the CEO of InBev, commented: "Global brands sell at significantly higher prices, and the margins are much better than with local beers."[3]

Wrestling with Change

Although the management of Heineken has moved away from the family for the first time, they are certainly aware of the long-standing and well-established family traditions that would be difficult to change. Even with the appointment of non-family members to manage the firm, a little over half of the shares of Heineken are still owned by a holding company controlled by the family. With the death of Freddy Heineken, the last family member to head the Dutch brewer, control passed to his only child and heir, Charlene de Carvalho, who has insisted on having a say in all of the major decisions.

And the family members were behind some of changes that were announced at the time of van Boxmeer's appointment, changes to support its next phase of growth as a global organization. As part of the plan, dubbed Fit 2 Fight, the executive board was cut down from five members to three, all of whom are relatively young. Along with van Boxmeer, the board is made up of the firm's chief operating officer and chief financial officer. Later, this board was further cut down to two members. The change is expected to assist the firm in thinking about the steps that it needs to take to win over younger customers across different markets whose tastes are still developing.

Heineken has also created management positions that would be responsible for five different operating regions and nine different functional areas. These positions were created to more clearly define different spheres of responsibility. Van Boxmeer argues that the new structure also provides incentives for people to be accountable for their performance: "There is more pressure for results, for

EXHIBIT 5 Leading Brewers

Brewer	2012 Market Share*
1. Anheuser-Busch InBev, Leuven, Belgium	20%
2. SAB Miller, London, UK	12%
3. Heineken, Amsterdam, Netherlands	10%
4. Carlsberg, Copenhagen, Denmark	6%
5. Molson Coors Brewing, Denver, USA	4%

*Market share based on annual sales, in US dollars.

Source: Beverage World.

achievement."[4] He claims the new structure has already encouraged more risk taking and boosted the level of energy within the firm.

The executive committee of Heineken was also cut down from 36 to 13 members in order to speed up the decision-making process. Besides the two members of the executive board, this management group consists of the managers who are responsible for the five different operating regions and six of the key functional areas. Van Boxmeer hopes that the reduction in the size of this group will allow the firm to combat the cumbersome consensus culture that has made it difficult for Heineken to respond swiftly to various challenges even as its industry has been experiencing considerable change.

Finally, all of the activities of Heineken have been overseen by a supervisory board, which currently consists of 10 members. Individuals that make up this board are drawn from different countries and cover a wide range of expertise and experience. They set up policies for the firm to use in making major decisions in its overall operations. Members of the supervisory board are rotated on a regular basis.

Maintaining a Premium Position

For decades, Heineken has been able to rely upon the success of its flagship *Heineken* brand, which has enjoyed a leading position among premium beers in many markets around the world. It had been the best-selling imported beer in the U.S. for several decades, giving it a steady source of revenues and profits from the world's biggest market. But by the late 1990s, *Heineken* had lost its 65-year-old leadership among imported beers in the U.S. to Group Modelo's *Corona*. The Mexican beer has been able to reach out to the growing population of Hispanic Americans, who represent one of the fastest-growing segments of beer drinkers.

Furthermore, the firm was also concerned that *Heineken* was being perceived as an obsolete brand by many young drinkers. John A. Quelch, a professor at Harvard Business School who has studied the beer industry, said of Heineken: "It's in danger of becoming a tired, reliable, but unexciting brand."[5] The firm has therefore been working hard to increase awareness of their flagship brand among younger drinkers. It has been running commercials on websites such as YouTube and Facebook. Two recent videos showed a young man on a wild date and a man's show-stopping arrival at a wild party. Through such efforts, the firm has managed to reduce the average age of the Heineken drinker from about 40 years old in the mid-1990s to about 30 years old.

Heineken recently introduced a light beer, *Heineken Premium Light,* to target the growing market for such beers in the U.S. It has also rolled out a new design for the Heineken bottle that will be used across all of the countries where it is sold. The firm has also introduced *Heineken* in other new forms of packaging. It has achieved some success with a portable draught beer system called DraughtKeg. About 20 glasses of beer can be dispensed from this mini keg. A BeerTender system, which keeps kegs fresh for several weeks once they have been tapped, also continues to grow in sales.

At the same time, Heineken has also been pushing on other brands that would reduce its reliance on its core *Heineken* brand. It has already achieved considerable success with *Amstel Light,* which has become the leading imported light beer in the U.S. and has been selling well in many other countries. But many of the other brands that it carries are strong local brands that it has added through its string of acquisitions of smaller breweries around the globe. It has managed to develop a relatively small but loyal base of consumers by promoting some of these as specialty brands, such as *Murphy's Irish Red* and *Moretti.*

Finally, Heineken has been stepping up its efforts to target Hispanics, who account for one-quarter of U.S. sales. Besides developing specific marketing campaigns for them, it added popular Mexican beers such as *Tecate* and *Dos Equis* to its line of offerings. For years, these had been marketed and distributed by Heineken in the U.S. under a license from FEMSA Cerveza. In 2010, Heineken decided to acquire the two firms, giving them full control over all of their brands. Benj Steinman, publisher and editor of *Beer Marketer's Insight* newsletter, believes their relationship with FEMSA has been quite beneficial: "This gives Heineken a commanding share of the U.S. import business and . . . gives them a bigger presence in the Southwest . . . and better access to Hispanic consumers."[6]

Above all, Heineken wants to maintain its leadership in the premium beer category, which represents the most profitable segment of the beer business. In this category, the firm's brands face competition in the U.S. from domestic beers such as Anheuser's *Budweiser Select* and imported beers such as InBev's *Stella Artois*. Although premium brews often have slightly higher alcohol content than standard beers, they are developed through a more exclusive positioning of the brand. This allows the firm to charge a higher price for these brands. A six-pack of *Heineken,* for example, costs $10, versus around $7 for a six-pack of *Budweiser.* Furthermore, Just-drinks.com, a London-based online research service, estimates that the market for premium beer will continue to expand over the next decade.

Building a Global Presence

Van Boxmeer is well aware of the need for Heineken to use its brands to build upon its existing stature across global markets. In spite of its formidable presence in markets around the world, Heineken has failed to match the recent moves of formidable competitors such as Belgium's InBev and U.K.'s SABMiller, which have grown significantly through mega-acquisitions. Many industry watchers assume that the firm has been reluctant to make such acquisitions in large part because of the dilution of family control.

For many years, Heineken had limited itself to snapping up small national brewers such as Italy's Moretti and Spain's Cruzcampo, which have provided it with small, but profitable avenues for growth. In 1996, for example,

Heineken acquired Fischer, a small French brewer, whose *Desperados* brand has been quite successful in niche markets. Similarly, *Paulaner,* a wheat beer that the firm picked up in Germany a few years ago, has been making inroads into the U.S. market.

But as other brewers have been reaching out to make acquisitions from all over the globe, Heineken has been running the risk of falling behind its more aggressive rivals. To deal with this growing challenge, the firm has broken out of its play-it-safe corporate culture to make a few big deals. In 2003, Heineken spent $2.1 billion to acquire BBAG, a family-owned company based in Linz, Austria. Because of BBAG's extensive presence in Central Europe, Heineken has become the biggest beer maker in seven countries across Eastern Europe. The acquisition of Scottish & Newcastle in 2008 similarly reinforced the firm's dominance in Western Europe.

At the same time, Heineken has made major acquisitions in other parts of the world. Its recent acquisitions in Singapore, Nigeria, and Mexico have allowed it to build its position in these growing markets. The firm has also made an aggressive push into Russia with the acquisition of mid-sized brewing concerns. Through several acquisitions since 2002, Russia has become one of Heineken's largest markets by volume. Heineken now ranks as the third-largest brewer in Russia, behind Sweden's Baltic Beverages Holding and InBev.

Rene Hooft Graafland, the company's chief financial officer, has stated that Heineken will continue to participate in the consolidation of the $460 billion global retail beer industry by targeting many different markets around the world. During the last decade, the firm has added several more labels to Heineken's shelf, pouncing on brewers in far-flung places like Belarus, Panama, Egypt, and Kazakhstan. In Egypt, Ruys bought a majority stake in Al Ahram Beverages Co. and hopes to use the Cairo-based brewer's fruit-flavored, nonalcoholic malts as an avenue into other Muslim countries.

A Break from the Past?

The recent acquisitions in different parts of the world—Asia, Africa, Latin America, and Europe—represent an important step in Heineken's quest to build upon its existing global stature. In fact, most analysts expected that van Boxmeer and his team would continue to build Heineken into a powerful global competitor. Without providing any specific details, Graafland, the firm's CFO made it clear that the firm's management would take initiatives that would drive long-term growth. In his own words: "We are positive that the momentum in the company and trends will continue."[7]

Upon taking over the helm of Heineken, van Boxmeer also announced that he would have to work on the company's culture in order to accelerate the speed of decision making. This led many people both inside and outside the firm to expect that the new management would try to break loose from the conservative style that has resulted from the family's tight control. Instead, the affable 46-year-old Belgian has indicated that he is focusing on changing the firm's decision-making process rather than making any drastic shifts in its existing culture.

Van Boxmeer's devotion to the firm is quite evident. Heineken's first non-Dutch CEO spent 20 years working his way up within the firm. Even his cufflinks are silver miniatures of a Heineken bottle cap and opener. "We are in the logical flow of history," he recently explained. "Every time you have a new leader, you have a new kind of vision. It is not radically different, because you are defined by what your company is and what your brands are."[8]

Furthermore, van Boxmeer seems quite comfortable working with the family-controlled structure. "Since 1952 history has proved it is the right concept," he stated about the current ownership structure. "The whole business about family restraint on us is absolutely untrue. Without its spirit and guidance, the company would not have been able to build a world leader."[9]

ENDNOTES

1. Sterling, T. 2012. Heineken pays $6.1 billion as it nets Tiger Beer. Associated Press, September 28.
2. Ewing. J., & Khermouch, G. 2003. Waking up Heineken. *BusinessWeek,* September 8: 68.
3. Tomlinson, R. 2004. The new king of beers. *Fortune,* October 18: 238.
4. Bickerton, I., & Wiggins, J. 2006. Change is brewing at Heineken. *Financial Times,* May 9: 12.
5. Ewing & Khermouch. 2003. Waking up Heineken: 69.
6. Kaplan, A. 2004. Border crossings. *Beverage World,* July 15: 6.
7. Williams, C. C. 2006. Heineken seeing green. *Barron's,* September 18: 19.
8. Bickerton & Wiggins. 2006. Change is brewing at Heineken: 12.
9. Ibid.

CASE 18

YAHOO!*

On March 25, 2013, Yahoo! announced the acquisition for almost $30 million of Summly, an app that condenses full-length stories into bite-sized nuggets that fit on a smartphone's screen. The British start-up was headed by 17-year-old Nick D'Aloisio, a high school student who created the new language processing technology that drives the app. "My manifesto with Summly was to get our technology into as many user's hands as possible," said D'Alosio, pointing to Yahoo!'s hundreds of millions of users. "With Yahoo!'s reputation as a content portal, we have an opportunity to fundamentally change the way content is consumed."[1]

Summly was just the latest of half a dozen start-ups snapped up by Yahoo! in as many months to help it reboot for a smartphone-obsessed world. The Internet firm had already bought Stamped, Alike, and Jybe, which built apps for personalized recommendations of, among other things, books, food, and music. Marissa Mayer, Yahoo!'s CEO since July 2012, said she was determined to make the company a stronger force on smartphones and tablets. She believed that such personalized content would help her struggling company to make the transition from the desktop to mobile devices.[2]

The appointment of Mayer, who left a senior post at Google, represented a major coup for Yahoo!, which had gone through four chief executives in less than a year, two of which were only intended to be interim appointments. Having spent 13 years at Google, Mayer was responsible for the look and feel of some of Google's most popular products and was behind the search firm's famously unadorned white home page. Consequently, her selection for the top job at Yahoo! kindled a fresh interest in the prospects for the Web-based firm's future.[3]

Despite its pioneering efforts that helped to shape the direction of the Internet during the 1990s, the momentum had shifted away from Yahoo! to newer start-ups such as Google and Facebook, which have created new users. With the appointment of Mayer as CEO, analysts were eager to see whether she could lure back advertisers, reinvigorate a muddled brand, and improve morale at a company that has been marred by executive churn, constant cost-cutting, and mass layoffs. "The sheer attention that they are getting from hiring her will be helpful for a while," said David

Hallerman, an analyst at eMarketer. "But it will only carry them so far" (see Exhibits 1 and 2).

Mayer recognized the challenges that she faced, but believed that she could build on Yahoo!'s strong franchises, including email, news, finances, and sports. Because of these, she asserted that the firm can capitalize on the shift of consumers to mobile devices. Noting that the most frequent use of smartphones was checking news, obtaining sports scores, getting financial information, and sharing photos, she asked: "Does that sound like any particular company that you know?"

Creating a Theme Park

After a period of strong growth in the late 1990s, Yahoo! saw a steep fall in revenues and profits as advertisers cut back on their spending after the dot-com bust. Under Tim Koogle, Yahoo! had developed as a Web portal that relied heavily on advertising revenues for profits. He had been confident that advertisers would continue to pay in order to reach the younger and technologically savvy surfers who were the main users of his portal. As advertising revenues dropped off sharply, leading to a steep decline in the firm's stock price, Koogle was replaced in April 2001 by Terry Semel, an experienced Hollywood media executive who had once controlled Warner Brothers.

Semel worked hard to entice traditional advertisers back to his site. But he also began to push for other sources of revenue by making acquisitions that would allow his site to offer more premium services that consumers would be willing to pay for. One of the first of these was the buyout of HotJobs.com in 2002, which moved the firm into the online job-hunting business. Semel followed up with the acquisition of online music service Musicmatch Inc., hoping to bring more subscribers into the Yahoo! fold. Over the next few years, the firm continued to add to its growing range of services by acquiring firms such as Flickr, a photo-sharing site, and Del.icio.us, a bookmark-sharing site.

By making such smart deals, Semel was able to build Yahoo! into a site that could offer surfers many different services, with several of them requiring the customer to pay a small fee. He wanted to coax Web surfers to spend hard cash on everything from digital music and online games to job listings and premium email accounts with loads of extra storage. With the expansion of services, Semel envisioned building Yahoo! into a digital Disneyland, a souped-up theme park for the Internet Age. The idea was that Web surfers logging on to Yahoo!'s site, like

---

*Case developed by Professor Jamal Shamsie, Michigan State University, with the assistance of Professor Alan B. Eisner, Pace University. Material has been drawn from published sources to be used for purposes of class discussion. Copyright © 2013 Jamal Shamsie and Alan B. Eisner.

EXHIBIT 1

Income Statement*

Go to library tab in Connect to access Case Financials.

	A	B	C	D
1	Income Statement*			
2		Period Ending		
3		Dec. 30, 2012	Dec. 30, 2011	Dec. 30, 2010
4	Total Revenue	4,986,566	4,984,199	6,324,651
5	Cost of Revenue	1,620,566	1,586,997	2,682,074
6	Gross Profit	3,366,000	3,397,202	3,642,577
7	Operating Expenses			
8	Research Development	885,824	919,368	1,028,716
9	Selling General and Administrative	1,641,819	1,619,481	1,751,754
10	Non Recurring	236,170	24,420	57,957
11	Others	35,819	33,592	31,626
12	Total Operating Expenses	2,799,632	2,596,861	2,870,053
13	Operating Income or Loss	566,368	800,341	772,524
14	Income from Continuing Operations			
15	Total Other Income/Expenses Net	4,647,839	27,175	297,869
16	Earnings Before Interest and Taxes	5,214,207	827,516	1,070,393
17	Income Before Tax	5,214,207	827,516	1,070,393
18	Income Tax Expense	1,940,043	241,767	221,523
19	Minority Interest	(5,123)	(13,842)	(12,965)
20	Net Income from Continuing Ops	3,945,479	1,048,827	1,231,663
21	Net Income	3,945,479	1,048,827	1,231,663

*All numbers in thousands.

Source: Yahoo!.

EXHIBIT 2

Balance Sheet*

Go to library tab in Connect to access Case Financials.

	A	B	C	D
1	Balance Sheet*			
2		Period Ending		
3		Dec. 30, 2012	Dec. 30, 2011	Dec. 30, 2010
4	Assets			
5	Current Assets			
6	Cash And Cash Equivalents	2,667,778	1,562,390	1,526,427
7	Short Term Investments	1,516,175	493,189	1,357,661
8	Net Receivables	1,008,448	1,037,474	1,028,900
9	Other Current Assets	460,312	359,483	432,560
10	Total Current Assets	5,652,713	3,452,536	4,345,548
11	Long-Term Investments	4,678,582	5,223,382	4,756,483
12	Property Plant and Equipment	1,685,845	1,730,888	1,653,422
13	Goodwill	3,826,749	3,900,752	3,681,645
14	Intangible Assets	153,973	254,600	255,870
15	Other Assets	1,105,391	220,628	235,136
16	Total Assets	17,103,253	14,782,786	14,928,104
17	Liabilities			
18	Current Liabilities			
19	Accounts Payable	993,306	1,012,639	1,371,216
20	Other Current Liabilities	296,926	194,722	254,656
21	Total Current Liabilities	1,290,232	1,207,361	1,625,872
22	Long Term Debt	124,587	134,905	142,799
23	Deferred Long Term Liability Charges	1,082,831	859,173	563,023
24	Minority Interest	45,403	40,280	38,281
25	Total Liabilities	2,543,053	2,241,719	2,369,975
26	Stockholders' Equity			
27	Common Stock	1,187	1,242	1,306
28	Retained Earnings	5,792,459	2,432,294	1,942,656
29	Treasury Stock	(1,368,043)	(416,237)	-
30	Capital Surplus	9,563,348	9,825,899	10,109,913
31	Other Stockholder Equity	571,249	697,869	504,254
32	Total Stockholder Equity	14,560,200	12,541,067	12,558,129
33	Net Tangible Assets	10,579,478	8,385,715	8,620,614

*All numbers in thousands.

Source: Yahoo!.

customers squeezing through the turnstiles in Anaheim, should find themselves in a self-contained world full of irresistible offerings. Instead of Yahoo! being an impartial tour guide to the Web, it should be able to entice surfers to stay inside its walls as long as possible.

In order to make such a concept work, Semel believed that the firm should establish strong links between its various sites that would allow its consumers to move effortlessly from one of them to another. He demanded that Yahoo!'s myriad of offerings, from email accounts to stock quotes to job listings, interact with each other. Semel called this concept "network optimization" and regarded this as a key goal for his firm. In order to ensure that the various efforts that were being made by managers were tied to each other more closely, he moved swiftly to replace the company's freewheeling culture with a more deliberate sense of order. All ideas had to be formally presented to a group called the Product Council, which consisted of nine managers from different parts of the firm.

Semel's biggest moves, however, were tied to his efforts to strengthen Yahoo!'s position in the search area. Yahoo! had been using Google to provide these services, but with Google's growing strengths in this area, Semel decided Yahoo! should further develop its own search engine. In 2002, he purchased Inktomi, a strong contender in search engines with whom Yahoo! had also worked in the past. A year later, Yahoo! also bought Overture Services, a company that specialized in identifying and ranking the popularity of websites and in helping advertisers find the best sites to advertise on. Finally, Semel spent millions of dollars on further improving its search advertising system in order to stem the continual loss of search related advertising revenues to Google.

Facing an Identity Crisis

In spite of Semel's efforts to direct the growth of Yahoo! into new areas, the push to develop a digital theme park led some analysts to question whether the firm had spread itself too thin. Even some people inside Yahoo! began to question its goal of providing a broad range of services that could attract an audience that could be sold to advertisers. In a scathing internal memo written in the fall of 2006, Brad Garlinghouse, a senior Yahoo! vice president, compared Yahoo!'s strategy to indiscriminately spreading peanut butter across the Internet. "We lack a focused, cohesive vision for our company," he stated in the memo. "We want to do everything and be everything—to everyone. We've known this for years, talked about it incessantly, but done nothing to fundamentally address it."[4]

Garlinghouse's memo was intended to push Yahoo! into establishing a clearer vision for the firm to pursue. He had realized that Yahoo!'s attempts to offer a wide variety of services had led to a proliferation of new executive hires, which eventually contributed to a growth of conflict between various business units. This had made it difficult to move swiftly to make critical decisions, such as making key partnerships and acquisitions to keep up with the changing competitive landscape. The once high-flying Internet pioneer was losing online advertising revenues to search engines such as Google and social networking sites such as Facebook.

More significantly, there was some confusion among Yahoo! employees about the role of content. Semel had brought in several individuals from the entertainment sector to create unique content for the firm. This led to some conflicts with those people in the firm who had been working to develop Yahoo! as a site where other people could place their content. "The age-old question with Yahoo! has been: Is it technology first or is it media and content first?" said David Cohen, a media executive.[5]

Shareholder dissatisfaction with Yahoo!'s financial performance finally led to the resignation of Semel in July 2007. The firm turned to Jerry Yang, one of its cofounders, to improve earnings and profits. He began a 100-day review of every aspect of the firm's operations but could not find ways to define the specific strengths that could be used to narrow its focus. Rob Sanderson, a technology analyst pointed out that Yahoo! had to make some critical choices. "They're relevant, and hold their audience pretty well, but the investor and media perception is that Yahoo! is another AOL—a once-great company in decline," he explained.[6]

One of the biggest challenges faced by Yang was the offer made by Microsoft in early 2008 to buy Yahoo! for $33 a share, or approximately $47.5 billion. Yang refused to sell his company for less than $37 a share, although these shares had been trading for around $20. Shareholders were upset, because they stood to lose about $20 billion by the rejection of Microsoft's offer. "I don't think anything Yahoo! puts out there is going to be comparable with what Microsoft was offering" said Darren Chervitz, comanager of the Jacob Internet Fund, which owned about 150,000 shares of Yahoo!.[7]

Scrambling for a Focus

Less than a year and a half after he had assumed control, Yang decided to give up his role as CEO and once again took up the post of "chief Yahoo!," the strategy position that he had held before. After an extensive search, the board appointed Carol Bartz as the new head of the firm. Bartz had been in charge of Autodesk (a computer-aided software design firm) for 14 years before getting the call from Yahoo!. She was expected to develop a stronger focus for a firm that was perceived to have been drifting, especially during Yang's turbulent leadership. Analysts were generally positive about her appointment, although many suggested that she lacked online media experience.

Bartz was expected to move quickly to reassure investors who were angry with Yahoo!'s board for refusing to accept Microsoft's bid for the firm. Shortly after she took over, Bartz moved to overhaul the company's top executive ranks, consolidating several positions and creating others in an attempt to make the firm more efficient. She combined Yahoo!'s technology and product groups into one unit and created a customer advocacy group to better incorporate customer feedback. The changes were intended to speed up decision making within the company by making it "a lot faster on its feet," Bartz wrote in a Yahoo! public blog. But Ross Sandler, an analyst with RBC Capital Markets, said the restructuring was more promising because it clarified responsibilities. "There has been confusion at the top for so long," he said. "This should solve that problem."[8]

Bartz also managed to refocus Yahoo! on areas such as news, sports, and finance, where it had considerable strengths. While she moved the firm away from other activities she considered to be peripheral, Bartz invested heavily in content during her first year, hiring dozens of editorial employees and buying Associated Content, a freelance news site, to enhance local news coverage. She made some progress with revamping the technology behind the Web portal that would have made it possible to introduce new services much more quickly in the future. At the same time, Bartz managed to achieve an improvement in Yahoo!'s profit margins due to her aggressive moves to cut costs wherever possible.

But Bartz's most questionable move was to hand over its search operations to Microsoft, which had invested heavily in relaunching its search engine and renamed it Bing. The terms of the 10-year agreement gave Microsoft access to search technologies that Yahoo! had helped to pioneer and develop (see Exhibit 3). Yahoo! agreed to transfer many of its talented engineers to Microsoft and lay off 400 employees that ran the search operations. In return, Yahoo! would receive 88 percent of the search-related ad revenue for the first five years of the deal, much higher than is standard in the industry. Nevertheless, some Yahoo! shareholders have expressed concerns that the company would lose its valuable search experience, which would be difficult to recover from.

Even more questions were raised about Bartz's abrasive style and her frequent use of foul language in public. This may have contributed to continual turnover among executives, particularly at the top level. Moreover, some investors lost patience with the slow pace of improvements, leading to demands for Bartz's replacement by the board. Salim Ismail, a former Yahoo! executive elaborated on this: "They're putting on a Band-Aid when what they really need is major surgery."[9] The news that some private equity firms were considering a bid to buy Yahoo! created even more pressure for some form of drastic action, leading to Bartz's ouster in September 2011 (see Exhibit 4).

Pinning Hopes on a Star

In July 2012, after some churning of CEOs, including the resignation of Scott Thompson over alleged discrepancies in his prior record, Yahoo! was finally able to entice Marissa Mayer to defect from long-standing rival Google. With Mayer's appointment, there was hope that her extensive experience would provide some much-needed direction for what had been increasingly viewed as a rudderless ship. "Yahoo! finally has someone who has both business acumen and geek cred at the helm," said Chris Sacca, a venture capitalist who had previously worked with Mayer at Google. "She stands for a product-and-engineering-driven culture, and Yahoo! has been missing that for years."[10]

Soon after she took over, Mayer took steps to try and boost employee morale throughout the firm, which had dropped as a result of its recent struggles. Borrowing from the playbook of Google, she gave employees the option to trade in their BlackBerry phones for new iPhones and Android-powered phones. She also provided free food in the cafeteria to Yahoo! employees. These moves were designed to let people know that the firm was moving away from its recent emphasis on cost cutting and layoffs.

Mayer also began trying to turn around Yahoo!'s drop in display ad revenue, which went from a leading 15.5 percent of all digital ad revenue in the U.S. in 2009 to about 8.4 percent in 2012. She revamped the firm's Web page, which was often cluttered with low-quality ads and irrelevant content, replacing these with a Twitter-like news feed and a stream of content recommended by users' Facebook friends. Beyond this, Mayer revamped Yahoo!'s Mail and Messenger services and redesigned other services like Flickr, the firm's photo-sharing app. "More personalized content and increased product innovation will be key to getting us back to the path for display revenue growth," she stated (see Exhibit 5).[11]

In order to assist her efforts, Mayer also began recruiting more talent in order to make up for employees who had

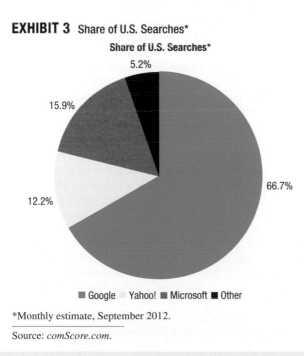

EXHIBIT 3 Share of U.S. Searches*

Share of U.S. Searches*

- 66.7%
- 15.9%
- 12.2%
- 5.2%

■ Google □ Yahoo! ■ Microsoft ■ Other

*Monthly estimate, September 2012.

Source: *comScore.com.*

EXHIBIT 4 Significant Milestones

1994	David Filo and Jerry Yang start the company as "Jerry's guide to the World Wide Web," later renaming it Yahoo!.
1996	Yahoo! goes public, raising $338 million. Filo and Yang ask Tim Koogle, an experienced ex-Motorola executive with an engineering background, to be the new CEO.
1999	Yahoo! begins to make major acquisitions, including GeoCities, the third most visited website at the time.
2001	Koogle departs because of sharp drop in firm's stock price as a result of declining advertising revenue. Yang asks Terry Semel to take over the firm.
2001	Yahoo! acquires more firms, such as HotJobs, a leading Internet job hunting and placement company.
2002	Yahoo! buys Inktomi, a search engine leader.
2003	Yahoo! buys Overture Services, a company that specializes in Web search advertising.
2005	Yahoo! acquires Flickr, a photo-sharing site and announces that it will link several sites together to create a social networking group.
2007	Semel is pushed out because of decline in performance. Yang takes over as CEO.
2009	Yang steps down and Carol Bartz is appointed as the new CEO. Bartz concludes a major deal with Microsoft to cede control of its search business.
2011	Bartz is ousted, leading to a succession of CEOs.
2012	Marissa Mayer is hired as new CEO, reviving hopes for a turnaround.

Source: Yahoo!.

EXHIBIT 5 U.S. Unique Website Visitors*

Google	189 million
Yahoo!	186 million
Microsoft	163 million
Facebook	144 million

*Monthly estimates, February 2013.

Source: *comScore.com*.

left over the past few years. Her most significant achievement was the appointment of another Silicon Valley tech star, Max Levchin, to Yahoo!'s board at the end of 2012. She was having a harder time attracting engineers, but managed to deal with this shortage in part by acquiring the mobile app companies mentioned earlier.

Mayer's most controversial move, as of early 2013, was to abolish Yahoo!'s work-at-home policy and order everyone to come back to work in the office. Drawing lessons from the success of Google's approach to business, she explained that face-to-face interaction among employees fosters a more innovative culture. Recent studies have shown strong support for this link. "If you want innovation, then you need interaction," said John Sullivan, a professor of management at San Francisco State University.[12] The new policy unleashed a storm of criticism from advocates for workplace flexibility, who claimed it that would especially hurt those who care for young children.

Signs of Revival?

Over the first two quarters under the charge of Mayer, Yahoo! showed improved performance: increasing revenue for the first time in four years and beating Wall Street expectations. Mayer attributed the growth to a renewed focus on people and products in a recent call with analysts. "We have a fundamental foundation on which to grow," Mayer said. "We believe Yahoo!'s best days lie ahead."[13]

Although they were glad that Mayer had jolted Yahoo! back to life, investors and analysts were eager to see whether she could deliver sustained growth. The firm's Web page drew one of the largest audiences on the Internet, and more people used their email than any other service. However, advertisers had come under increased financial pressures and were experimenting with other platforms, such as Facebook. Yahoo! took some steps in 2011 to increase its revenues by the forming a partnership with Microsoft and AOL to sell advertising for each other. It also bought the online advertising company Interclick, which allowed marketers to tailor ads demographically.

As Mayer acknowledged, the Internet firm's future may well depend on its mobile strategy. Critics pointed out that without mobile hardware like a tablet computer, a browser, or a social networking platform of its own, Yahoo!'s move into the mobile arena would not be easy. "Yahoo! is mainly a media company," said Hallerman of *eMarketer*. "It doesn't have an operating system. It doesn't have the devices."[14]

Nevertheless, Mayer had managed to do more to move Yahoo! forward in her first eight months as chief executive than any of her five predecessors had done over the previous six years. She produced results by making improvements to the firm's existing services while continuing to search for new ones develop. "Marissa will have to protect Yahoo!'s legacy business while positioning the company for future growth," Colin Gillis, an Internet analyst, said recently. "That is not easy."[15]

ENDNOTES

1. Bradshaw, T. 2013. Teen makes the news with $30m Yahoo deal. *Financial Times,* March 26: 1.
2. Perlroth, N., & Vega, T. 2012. Appointment gets attention, but executive faces a Yahoo identity crisis. *New York Times,* July 19: B3.
3. Perlroth, N. 2012. Earnings report gives Yahoo's new chief a good start. *New York Times,* October 23: B2.
4. Ackerman, E. 2007. Can "Chief Yahoo" Yang make it work this time as CEO? *Knight Ridder Tribune Business News.* June 24: 1.
5. Perlroth & Vega. 2012. Appointment gets attention.
6. Swartz, J. 2008. Yahoo encounters a fork in road toward its future. *USA Today,* January 28: 2B.
7. Helft, M. 2008. Yahoo celebrates (for now). *New York Times,* May 5: C1.
8. Vascellaro, J. E. 2009. Bartz remakes Yahoo's top ranks. *Wall Street Journal,* February 27: B3.
9. Kopytoff, V. G. 2010. Even under new captain, Yahoo seems adrift. *New York Times,* October 18: B4.
10. Sorkin, A. R., & Rusli, E. M. 2012. Silicon Valley pioneer steps onto bigger, if shakier, stage. *New York Times,* July 18: B1.
11. Perlroth, N. 2013. The chief of Yahoo lifts sales, and spirits. *New York Times,* January 29: B7.
12. Miller, C. C., & Rampell, C. 2013. Yahoo orders home workers back to office. *New York Times,* February 26: A1.
13. Perlroth. 2012. Earnings report.
14. Perlroth & Vega. 2012. Appointment gets attention.
15. Perlroth. 2013. The chief of Yahoo lifts sales.

CASE 19

NETFLIX: CAN IT RECOVER FROM ITS STRATEGY MISTAKES?

Arthur A. Thompson,
The University of Alabama

Throughout 2010 and the first 6 months of 2011, Netflix was on a roll. Film enthusiasts were flocking to become Netflix subscribers in unprecedented numbers, and shareholders were exceptionally pleased with Netflix's skyrocketing stock price. During those 18 months from January 1, 2010 through June 30, 2011, the number of Netflix subscribers in the US alone doubled from 12.3 million to 24.6 million, quarterly revenues climbed from $445 million to $770 million, and quarterly operating income climbed from $53 million to $125 million. Netflix's swift growth in the U.S and its promising potential for expanding internationally pushed the company's stock price to an all-time high of $304.79 on July 13, 2011, up from a close of $55.19 on December 31, 2009. Already solidly entrenched as the biggest and best-known Internet subscription service for watching TV shows and movies, the only question in mid-2011 seemed to be how big and pervasive might Netflix's service one day become in the larger world market for renting movies and TV episodes.

Then, over the next 4 months, Netflix announced a series of strategy changes and new initiatives that tarnished the company's reputation and sent the company's stock price into a tailspin:

- In mid-July 2011, Netflix announced a new pricing plan that effectively raised the monthly subscription price by 60 percent for customers who were paying $9.99 per month for the ability to (1) receive an unlimited DVDs each month (delivered and returned by mail 1 title out-at-a-time) and (2) watch an unlimited number of movies and TV episodes streamed over the Internet. The new arrangement called for total separation of unlimited DVDs and unlimited streaming to better reflect the different costs associated with the two delivery methods and to give members a choice: a DVD-only plan, a streaming-only plan, or the option to subscribe to both. The monthly subscription price for the unlimited streaming plan was set at $7.99 a month. The monthly subscription price for DVDs-only, one-out-at-a-time, was also set at $7.99 a month. If customers wanted both unlimited streaming and unlimited DVDs, they had to sign up for both plans and pay a total of $15.98 a month ($7.99 + $7.99)—Netflix said it was discontinuing all plans that included both streaming and DVDs by mail.

For new Netflix members, the changes were effective immediately. For existing members, the new pricing started for charges on or after September 1, 2011.

- Customer reaction was decidedly negative. Unhappy subscribers posted thousands of comments on Netflix's site and Facebook page. Over the next 8 weeks, Netflix's stock price dropped steadily to around $210–$220 per share, partly because of rumors that perhaps as many as 600,000 Netflix customers had cancelled their subscriptions.

- The stock price slide was exacerbated by media reports that Starz, a premium movie channel offered by many multi-channel TV providers, had broken off talks with Netflix regarding renewal of the contract whereby Starz supplied Netflix with certain Starz-controlled movies and TV shows that Netflix could then provide either on DVDs or via streaming to its subscribers. The substance of the breakdown in negotiations centered on the much higher price that Starz was asking Netflix to pay to renew its rights to distribute Starz content to Netflix subscribers—Starz was rumored to have demanded as much as $300 million annually to renew its license with Netflix, versus the $30 million annually that Netflix had been paying.[1] (Netflix's licensing agreement with Starz later expired in March 2012, and the content was removed from its library of offerings to subscribers.)

- On September 18, 2011, in an attempt at damage control, Netflix CEO Reed Hastings in a post on the Netflix blog at *http://blog.netflix.com/* apologetically said that the basis for the new pricing had been poorly communicated and personally took the blame for the miscue. He elaborated on the rationale behind the new pricing plans and then, in something of a bombshell, went on to reveal that Netflix was separating its DVD-by-mail subscription service and its unlimited streaming subscription service into two business operating at different websites. Hastings said the DVD-by-mail service would be renamed Qwikster, with its own website (*www.qwikster.com*) and its own billing. Current Netflix subscribers who wanted DVDs-by-mail would have to go to *www.qwikster.com* and sign up for the plan. He indicated that the Qwikster website would be operational in a matter of weeks—see Exhibit 1 for the full text of Hastings' post.

EXHIBIT 1 Reed Hasting's Blog Posting, September 18, 2011

An Explanation and Some Reflections

Reed Hastings

I messed up. I owe everyone an explanation.

It is clear from the feedback over the past two months that many members felt we lacked respect and humility in the way we announced the separation of DVD and streaming, and the price changes. That was certainly not our intent, and I offer my sincere apology. I'll try to explain how this happened.

For the past five years, my greatest fear at Netflix has been that we wouldn't make the leap from success in DVDs to success in streaming. Most companies that are great at something – like AOL dialup or Borders bookstores – do not become great at new things people want (streaming for us) because they are afraid to hurt their initial business. Eventually these companies realize their error of not focusing enough on the new thing, and then the company fights desperately and hopelessly to recover. Companies rarely die from moving too fast, and they frequently die from moving too slowly.

When Netflix is evolving rapidly, however, I need to be extra-communicative. This is the key thing I got wrong.

In hindsight, I slid into arrogance based upon past success. We have done very well for a long time by steadily improving our service, without doing much CEO communication. Inside Netflix I say, "Actions speak louder than words," and we should just keep improving our service.

But now I see that given the huge changes we have been recently making, I should have personally given a full justification to our members of why we are separating DVD and streaming, and charging for both. It wouldn't have changed the price increase, but it would have been the right thing to do.

So here is what we are doing and why:

Many members love our DVD service, as I do, because nearly every movie ever made is published on DVD, plus lots of TV series. We want to advertise the breadth of our incredible DVD offering so that as many people as possible know it still exists, and it is a great option for those who want the huge and comprehensive selection on DVD. DVD by mail may not last forever, but we want it to last as long as possible.

I also love our streaming service because it is integrated into my TV, and I can watch anytime I want. The benefits of our streaming service are really quite different from the benefits of DVD by mail. We feel we need to focus on rapid improvement as streaming technology and the market evolve, without having to maintain compatibility with our DVD by mail service.

So we realized that streaming and DVD by mail are becoming two quite different businesses, with very different cost structures, different benefits that need to be marketed differently, and we need to let each grow and operate independently. It's hard for me to write this after over 10 years of mailing DVDs with pride, but we think it is necessary and best: In a few weeks, we will rename our DVD by mail service to "Qwikster".

We chose the name Qwikster because it refers to quick delivery. We will keep the name "Netflix" for streaming.

Qwikster will be the same website and DVD service that everyone is used to. It is just a new name, and DVD members will go to qwikster.com to access their DVD queues and choose movies. One improvement we will make at launch is to add a video games upgrade option, similar to our upgrade option for Blu-ray, for those who want to rent Wii, PS3 and Xbox 360 games. Members have been asking for video games for many years, and now that DVD by mail has its own team, we are finally getting it done. Other improvements will follow. Another advantage of separate websites is simplicity for our members. Each website will be focused on just one thing (DVDs or streaming) and will be even easier to use. A negative of the renaming and separation is that the Qwikster.com and Netflix.com websites will not be integrated. So if you subscribe to both services, and if you need to change your credit card or email address, you would need to do it in two places. Similarly, if you rate or review a movie on Qwikster, it doesn't show up on Netflix, and vice-versa.

There are no pricing changes (we're done with that!). Members who subscribe to both services will have two entries on their credit card statements, one for Qwikster and one for Netflix. The total will be the same as the current charges.

Andy Rendich, who has been working on our DVD service for 12 years, and leading it for the last 4 years, will be the CEO of Qwikster. Andy and I made a short welcome video. (You'll probably say we should avoid going into movie making after watching it.) We will let you know in a few weeks when the Qwikster.com website is up and ready. It is merely a renamed version of the Netflix DVD website, but with the addition of video games. You won't have to do anything special if you subscribe to our DVD by mail service.

For me the Netflix red envelope has always been a source of joy. The new envelope is still that distinctive red, but now it will have a Qwikster logo. I know that logo will grow on me over time, but still, it is hard. I imagine it will be the same for many of you. We'll also return to marketing our DVD by mail service, with its amazing selection, now with the Qwikster brand.

Some members will likely feel that we shouldn't split the businesses, and that we shouldn't rename our DVD by mail service. Our view is with this split of the businesses, we will be better at streaming, and we will be better at DVD by mail. It is possible we are moving too fast – it is hard to say. But going forward, Qwikster will continue to run the best DVD by mail service ever, throughout the United States. Netflix will offer the best streaming service for TV shows and movies, hopefully on a global basis. The additional streaming content we have coming in the next few months is substantial, and we are always working to improve our service further.

I want to acknowledge and thank our many members that stuck with us, and to apologize again to those members, both current and former, who felt we treated them thoughtlessly.

Both the Qwikster and Netflix teams will work hard to regain your trust. We know it will not be overnight. Actions speak louder than words. But words help people to understand actions.

Respectfully yours,
Reed Hastings, Co-Founder and CEO, Netflix
Source: Posting at Netflix Blog, http://blog.netflix.com/, September 18, 2011, accessed March 6, 2012.

- Hastings' announcement of Netflix's strategy to split the DVDs-by-mail business from the Internet streaming business and to create Qwikster sparked a second furor from already disgruntled subscribers and further adverse investor reaction (the stock price plunged from around $208 per share to about $115 per share over the next three weeks). Netflix's strategy to split the DVDs-by-mail business from the Internet streaming business drew harsh criticism from Wall Street analysts and business commentators; virtually all knowledgeable industry observers expressed amazement that Netflix executives would even contemplate such a move.

- On October 10, 2011, three weeks after Hastings disclosed the plan to divide Netflix into two standalone businesses, Netflix sent personal e-mails to all U.S. subscribers stating that it was scrapping its Qwikster proposal and that U.S. members would continue to use one website, one account, and one password for their movie and TV watching enjoyment under the Netflix brand. Simultaneously, Netflix issued a press release and posted statements on the Netflix blog at *http://blog.netflix.com/* saying that it was abandoning the Qwikster strategy. In the blog, Reed Hastings said, "It is clear that for many of our members two websites would make things more difficult. So we are going to keep Netflix as one place to go for streaming and DVDs."

- On October 24, 2011, Netflix announced that in early 2012 it would begin offering unlimited TV shows and movies instantly streamed over the Internet to some 26 million households in the United Kingdom and Ireland—20 million of these households had high-speed broadband Internet service and thus could stream movies to their TVs, computers, or other devices. This move represented the third strategic initiative to expand Netflix's international reach. Netflix began streaming to members in Canada in 2010 and, in September 2011, initiated streaming services to 43 countries in Latin America and the Caribbean; there were 4 times as many households with high-speed broadband service in these 43 countries as there were in Canada. In all three cases, Netflix estimated that it would take about two years after initial launch to attract sufficient subscribers to generate a positive "contribution profit"—Netflix defined "contribution profit (loss)" as revenues less cost of revenues and marketing expenses; cost of revenues included subscription costs and order fulfillment costs.

- In announcing the company's entry into Latin America and the Caribbean, Netflix said it was establishing a single low monthly price of 99 pesos for subscribers in Mexico and a price of US$7.99 for customers in the 42 countries in Central America, South America, and the Caribbean. In Brazil, Netflix content was available in Portuguese; in 8 other South American countries and all of the Central America countries, Netflix content was made available in Spanish; in the Caribbean, Netflix was available in English and Spanish. As part of its September entry into Latin America and the Caribbean, Netflix had entered into regional license agreements to obtain movies and TV shows in Spanish and Portuguese from a big variety of major motion picture and television studios, including Walt Disney Studios, Paramount Studios, Sony Pictures Television, NBCUniversal International Television, CBS Television, MGM, Lionsgate, Summit, Relativity, BBC Worldwide, TV Bandeirantes, Televisa, Telemundo, TV Azteca, TV Globo, Caracol, Telefe, and RCTV.

- Also, on October 24, Netflix announced that the number of domestic subscribers dropped by a net of 810,000 during the third quarter of 2011, thus resulting in operating profits, net income and earnings per share that were below Wall Street estimates and investor expectations. Internationally, the company said it had reached 1 million subscribers in Canada and that member counts in Latin America and the Caribbean should exceed 500,000 by year-end 2011. However, Netflix's contribution losses from international operations jumped from ($9.3 million) in the second quarter of 2011 to ($23.3 million) in the third quarter of 2011, owing to increased expenses associated with the startup of operations in Latin America and the Caribbean.

- On the day following the release of Netflix's third quarter financial results, the company's stock price dropped from $118.84 to close at $77.37.

- On November 21, 2011, Netflix announced that it had raised $400 million in new capital by (1) selling 2.86 million shares of common stock to certain mutual funds and accounts managed by T. Rowe Price Associates for $70 per share (which generated proceeds of $200 million) and (2) selling $200 million aggregate principal amount of Zero Coupon Convertible Senior Notes due December 1, 2018 to a private party. Any time after 6 months, Netflix had the option of converting the Zero Coupon Notes into shares of Netflix common stock at an initial conversion rate of 11.6533 shares of common stock per $1,000 principal amount, subject to the satisfaction of certain conditions. Netflix executives said that the company did not intend to spend any of the newly-raised capital. Rather, the company intended to use the capital as a safety-net, since the company's cash on hand and future cash flows from operations would likely be squeezed in upcoming quarters by the ongoing need to:
  - Make cash payments for additions to its library of titles available for streaming.
  - Absorb the expected contribution losses from international operations over the next 5 to 7 quarters.

In the weeks following the announcement of the $400 million in new financing, Netflix's stock price dropped to as low as $62.37 and traded in the range of $65 to $71 for most all of December 2011.

Financial statement data for Netflix for 2000–2011 are shown in Exhibits 2 and 3.

Industry Environment

Since 2000, the introduction of new technologies and electronics products had rapidly multiplied consumer opportunities to view movies. It was commonplace in 2012 for movies to be viewed at theaters, on airline flights, in hotels, from the rear seats of motor vehicles equipped with video consoles, in homes, or most anywhere on a laptop PC or handheld device like an Apple iPhone, iPad, or iPod Touch. Home viewing was possible on PCs, televisions connected to a digital video disc (DVD) player, and video game consoles. As of 2012, more than 90 percent of U.S. households had DVD players connected to their TVs, enabling them to play movie DVDs. Households with big-screen high-definition TVs and a Blu-ray player could rent a Blu-ray DVD and enjoy a significantly higher picture quality. In recent years, millions of households had upgraded to high-speed or broadband Internet service and purchased Blu-ray DVD devices, video game consoles, and/or televisions with built-in connectivity to the Internet, enabling them to view content streamed over the Internet. However, heading into 2012, it was clear that the 134 million U.S. households with high speed Internet service and

EXHIBIT 2 Netflix's Consolidated Statements of Operations, 2000–2011 (in millions, except per share data)

	2000	2005	2007	2009	2010	2011
Revenues	$ 35.9	$682.2	$1,205.3	$1,670.3	$2,162.6	$3,205.6
Cost of Revenues:						
Subscription costs	24.9	393.8	664.4	909.5	1,154.1	1,789.6
Fulfillment expenses	10.2	72.0	121.3	169.8	203.2	250.3
Total cost of revenues	35.1	465.8	786.2	1,079.3	1,357.4	2,039.9
Gross profit	0.8	216.4	419.2	591.0	805.3	1,164.7
Operating expenses						
Technology and development	16.8	35.4	71.0	114.5	163.3	259.0
Marketing	25.7	144.6	218.2	237.7	293.8	402.6
General and administrative	7.0	35.5	52.4	51.3	64.5	117.9
Other	9.7	(2.0)	(14.2)	(4.6)	–	9.0
Total operating expenses	59.2	213.4	327.4	399.1	521.6	788.8
Operating income	(58.4)	3.0	91.8	191.9	283.6	376.1
Interest and other income (expense)	(0.2)	5.3	20.1	0.3	(15.9)	(16.5)
Income before income taxes	–	8.3	110.9	192.2	267.7	359.5
Provision for (benefit from) income taxes	–	(33.7)	44.3	76.3	106.8	133.4
Net income	$(58.5)	$ 42.0	$ 66.7	$ 115.9	160.8	226.1
Net income per share:						
Basic	$(20.61)	$ 0.79	$ 0.99	$ 2.05	$ 3.06	$ 4.28
Diluted	(20.61)	0.64	0.97	1.98	2.96	4.16
Weighted average common shares outstanding:						
Basic	2.8	53.5	67.1	56.6	52.5	52.8
Diluted	2.8	65.5	68.9	58.4	54.3	54.4

Note: Totals may not add due to rounding.

Source: Company 10-K reports for 2003, 2006, and 2009.

EXHIBIT 3 Selected Balance Sheet and Cash Flow Data for Netflix, 2000–2011 (in millions of $)

	2000	2005	2007	2009	2010	2011
Selected Balance Sheet Data						
Cash and cash equivalents	$ 14.9	$212.3	$177.4	$134.2	$194.5	$508.1
Short-term investments	–	–	207.7	186.0	155.9	290.0
Current assets	n.a.	243.7	432.4	416.5	637.2	1,830.9
Net investment in content library	n.a.	57.0	128.4	146.1	362.0	1,966.6
Total assets	52.5	364.7	679.0	679.7	982.1	3,069.2
Current liabilities	n.a.	137.6	208.9	226.4	388.6	1,225.1
Working capital*	(1.7)	106.1	223.5	190.1	248.6	605.8
Stockholders' equity	(73.3)	226.3	429.8	199.1	290.2	642.8
Cash Flow Data						
Net cash provided by operating activities	$(22.7)	$157.5	$277.4	$325.1	$276.4	$317.7
Net cash used in investing activities	(25.0)	(133.2)	(436.0)	(246.1)	(116.1)	(265.8)
Net cash provided by (used in) financing activities	48.4	13.3	(64.4)	(84.6)	(100.0)	261.6

* Defined as current assets minus current liabilities.

Sources: Company 10-K Reports for 2003, 2005, 2007, 2008, 2009, and 2011.

Internet-connected Blu-ray players, video game consoles, TVs, computers, tablets, and/or smartphones were rapidly shifting from renting physical DVDs to watching movies and TV episodes streamed over the Internet.

Increasing numbers of devices had recently appeared in electronics stores (or become available from cable, satellite, and fiber-optic TV providers) that enabled TVs to be connected to the Internet and receive streamed content from online providers with no hassle. These devices made it simple for households to order streamed movies with just a few clicks instead of traveling to a video rental store or waiting for a disk to be delivered through the mail. In 2012, more than 700 different devices were capable of streaming content from Netflix.

Consumers could obtain or view movie DVDs and TV episodes through a wide variety of distribution channels and providers. The options included:

- Watching movies on assorted cable channels included in the TV and entertainment packages provided by traditional cable providers (such as Time Warner, Comcast, Cox, and Charter), direct broadcast satellite providers (such as DirecTV and DISH Network), or fiber-optics providers (like AT&T and Verizon that had installed thousands of miles of fiber-optic cable that enabled them to simultaneously provide TV packages, telephone, and Internet services to customers).
- Subscribing to any of several movie-only channels (such as HBO, Showtime, and Starz) through a cable, satellite, or fiber-optics provider.

- Using a TV remote to order movies instantly streamed directly to a TV on a pay-per-view basis (generally referred to as "video-on-demand" or VOD). Cable, satellite, and fiber-optic providers of multi-channel TV packages were promoting their VOD services and making more movie titles available to their customers. In 2011, about 40 million U.S. households (15 percent) spent about $1.3 billion on VOD movie rentals.[2]

- Purchasing DVDs from such retailers as WalMart, Target, Best Buy, Toy-R-Us, and Amazon.com. DVD sales, however, had declined for the past three years, partially a reflection of growing consumer preferences to rent rather than purchase DVDs of movies and TV episodes.

- Renting DVDs from Blockbuster and other local retail stores or from standalone rental kiosks like Redbox and Blockbuster Express. Physical-disc rentals at traditional brick-and-mortar locations had been trending downward for 5–8 years, but the downward spiral accelerated in 2010–2011. Blockbuster's share of physical disc rentals dropped from 23 percent in 2010 to 17 percent in 2011.[3] The chief beneficiary of declining rentals at brick-and-mortar movie rental locations was Redbox. Since 2007, when Redbox first began deploying its distinctive red vending machine kiosks, Redbox's share of physical-disc DVD and Blu-ray movie rentals in the U.S. had mushroomed to 37 percent as of 2011(up from 25 percent in 2010).

- Renting DVDs online from Netflix, Blockbuster, and several other subscription services that either mailed DVDs directly to subscribers' homes or streamed the content to subscribers via broadband Internet connections. In 2011, Netflix had about a 30 percent share of the physical DVD rental market and about a 56 percent share of streaming rentals.[4]

- Utilizing the rental or download services of such providers as Apple's iTunes store, Amazon Instant Video, Hulu.com, Vudu.com, Best Buy CinemaNow, Sony PlayStation Network, and Google's YouTube.

- Most recently, a new class of user interface apps had become available that enabled subscribers to the services of multi-channel TV providers (like cable or satellite operators) to watch certain TV shows, movies, and other programs at their convenience rather than at scheduled broadcast times. This service—called TV Everywhere—gave subscribers to watch programs on Internet connected TVs and computers, iPads, iPhones, Android phones, and other devices. HBO's TV Everywhere application—called HBO GO—enabled HBO subscribers to have anytime, anywhere access to all HBO shows, hit movies, and other programs through participating multichannel TV providers. In 2012, most multi-channel TV providers and the owners of most channels carried on cable and satellite networks were exploring TV Everywhere options and packages for interested viewers.

- Pirating files of movies and other content from Internet sources via the use of illegal file-sharing software. Piracy was widely thought to be a contributing factor to declining sales of movie DVDs. In 2011–2012, movie studios were becoming increasingly concerned that digital piracy could become a tidal wave.[5] Much of Netflix's streaming library was rumored to be available through online piracy.

In recent years, movie studios had released filmed entertainment content for distribution to movie DVD retailers and to companies renting movie DVDs about 17 weeks after a film first began showing in theaters. After about 3 months in theaters, movie studios usually released first-run films to pay-per-view and video-on-demand (VOD) providers (prior to the last several years, the release window had been about six months). In 2011, a few studios experimented with charging up to $30 for films released to pay-per-view and VOD providers for showing after 8 weeks in theaters, but quickly ceased because of disappointingly small purchase volumes.[6] However, in October 2011, a Kevin Spacey film was released in theaters and through both Netflix and Time Warner Cable on the same day; the movie grossed $3.5 million at theaters and the studio realized more than $5 million each from Netflix and Time Warner Cable.[7] Premium TV channels like HBO, Starz, Cinemax, and Showtime were next in the distribution window, typically getting access to premium films one year after initial theater showings. Movie studios released films for viewing to basic cable and network TV some two to three years after theatrical release. TV episodes were often made available for Internet viewing shortly after the original airing date.

Recently, however, some movie studios had experimented with shortened release periods, including making new release titles available to video-on-demand providers or for online purchase on the same date DVDs could be sold by retailers. Other movie studios had implemented or announced their intention to implement policies preventing movie rental providers from renting movie DVDs until 30 to 60 days following the date DVD titles could be sold by retailers. For example, in January 2012, Warner Home Entertainment increased the availability date for rental DVDs top kiosks and subscription-by-mail services to 58 days. Movie studios and TV networks were expected to continue to experiment with the timing of the releases to various distribution channels and providers, in an ongoing effort to discover how best to maximize revenues.

Market Trends in Home Viewing of Movies

The wave of the future in the market for renting movies and TV content was unquestionably in streaming movies and TV shows to Internet-connected TVs, computers, and mobile devices. Streaming had the advantage of allowing household members to order and instantly watch the movies and TV programs they wanted to see. Renting a streamed movie could be done either by utilizing the services of Netflix, Blockbuster Online, Amazon Instant Video, Apple's iTunes, and other streaming video providers or by using a TV remote to place orders with a cable, satellite, or fiber-optics provider to instantly watch a movie from a list of several hundred selections that changed periodically. With a few exceptions, rental prices for pay-per-view and VOD movies ranged from $1 to $6, but the rental price for popular recently-released movies was usually $3.99 to $5.99. During 2011, several movie studios had experimented with charging up to $30 for films released to pay-per-view and VOD providers for showing after 8 weeks in theaters, but disappointingly small viewer response to such high-priced rentals quickly put an end to this strategy.[8] However, in October 2011, a Kevin Spacey film was released in theaters and through both Netflix and Time Warner Cable on the same day; the movie grossed $3.5 million at theaters and the studio realized more than $5 million each from Netflix and Time Warner Cable.[9] In 2012, many in-home movie viewers saw unlimited Internet streaming from subscription services as a better value than pay-per-view—the rental costs for 2 pay-per-view movies usually exceeded the $7.99 monthly price for unlimited streaming currently being charged by Netflix.

Several strategic initiatives to promote increased use of streaming video were underway in 2012.

- The owners of Hulu—Providence Equity Partners, The Walt Disney Company (owner of the ABC network), News Corp. (the parent of Fox Broadcasting and Fox Entertainment) and Comcast (the owner of NBCUniversal)—had for several years offered a free online video service at (*www.hulu.com*) where viewers could watch a selection of hit TV shows and movies from the libraries of ABC, NBC, Fox Broadcasting, Walt Disney Studios, Universal Studios, Fox Entertainment and a few others; the revenues to support the free Hulu site came from advertisers whose commercials were inserted into all of the free programs. But in mid-2011, three years after creating the Hulu site, the owners became reluctant to continue giving their content away for free and began an effort to sell the venture. In October 2011, the sales process was abandoned; Google, the Dish Network, Amazon, and Yahoo were rumored to have contemplated or made offers to acquire Hulu. Shortly thereafter, Hulu began actively promoting an advertising-supported unlimited streaming service called Hulu Plus where, for $7.99 per month, subscribers could watch a much larger selection of premium movies and primetime TV shows interspersed with commercials.

- Time Warner Cable, Comcast, Charter, Dish Network, DirecTV, HBO, Showtime, and others were in the early stages of promoting their TV Everywhere concept and program offerings that enabled customers to watch certain TV shows free at any time on any Internet-connected device (including computers and such mobile devices as iPads and smart phones) so long as they were paying subscribers. For example, DirecTV had created a device called Nomad to help subscribers watch their recorded programs anywhere; Nomad allowed subscribers to synchronize their smartphone, laptop, or tablet with recorded content on their DVRs and watch the recorded programs anywhere, anytime. Dish Network had introduced a "Sling Adapter" that—in conjunction with an Internet-connected DVR and a free Dish remote access app downloaded onto a mobile device—enabled customers to watch TV programs at their convenience on any Internet-connected device. However, for TV Everywhere to reach its full potential, each cable, satellite, and fiber-optic multi-channel TV provider had to negotiate agreements for online rights to each channel's programming. As of early 2012, just a few multi-channel TV providers had secured online rights to as many as 15 channels, but this was expected to be temporary.

- Google and Apple were rolling out new versions of their Google TV and Apple TV products to try to win traction with consumers. Google had partnered with LG, Vizio, and Samsung to introduce TVs equipped with Google TV and was rapidly expanding its library of apps optimized for Google TV, all in an attempt to facilitate easy consumer discovery of content that was available for streaming to TVs and/or Android devices. In addition, Google had invested in a new subsidiary called Google Fiber that was actively exploring plans to enter the Internet service and/or TV provider marketplaces by offering a one-gigabit-per-second Internet service coupled with an on-demand TV service that enabled customers to watch what they wanted when they wanted without ever having to record anything. In March 2012, Google filed applications with the Missouri Public Service Commission and the Kansas Corporation Commission for approval to offer a video service to subscribers in the Kansas City area—the proposal called for Google to use national and regional programming collection points to send IPTV (a television-over-Internet technology) across its private fiber-optic network (Google Fiber) to subscribers in Kansas City. It remained to be seen whether Google could secure broadcast rights from the owners of various TV channels and Hollywood movie studios to lure customers; however, Google's YouTube was spending hundreds of millions of dollars funding new TV channels that were scheduled to be available online and could be a part of Google's TV package. Time Warner Cable was the dominant TV provider in Kansas City, while Direct TV, Dish Network, and AT&T's Uverse had smaller customer bases.

Apple TV was a tiny box that enabled users to play high-definition content from iTunes, Netflix, YouTube, and live sports events (professional baseball, hockey, and basketball) on TVs, or to stream content to TVs from an iPad, iPhone or iPod touch, or to stream music and photos from computers to TVs. In March 2012, Netflix and Apple implemented an agreement whereby Apple TV users could sign up for Netflix services directly through their Apple TV device, using their iTunes account.

IHS Screen Digest Research had forecast that streaming content would exceed 3.4 billion views in 2012.[10] It also expected that movie viewing online in 2012 would exceed combined viewing on DVDs and Blu-ray devices for the first time.[11]

Competitive Intensity

The movie rental business was intensely competitive in 2012. Local brick-and-mortar stores that rented DVD discs were in the throes of a death spiral, as growing number of their customers switched either to obtaining their DVDs at Redbox vending kiosks or utilizing Internet streaming services of one kind or another. Blockbuster, once a movie rental powerhouse with over $4.5 billion in annual rental revenues and more than 9,000 company-owned and franchised stores in a host of countries, was a shadow of its former self in 2012. After losing over $4 billion during the 2002–2010 period, closing thousands of store locations, and launching several unsuccessful strategic attempts to rejuvenate revenues and return to profitability, Blockbuster filed for Chapter 11 bankruptcy protection in September 2010. Following a bankruptcy court auction, Dish Network emerged in April 2011 as the owner of Blockbuster's operations in the United States and certain foreign countries for a winning bid valued at $321 million. From the acquisition date of April 26, 2011 through December 31, 2011, Blockbuster operations contributed $975 million in revenue and $4 million in net income to Dish Network's consolidated results of operations. Going into 2012, Blockbuster was operating some 1,500 retail stores in the United States, but Dish Network management had announced that it expected to close over 500 domestic Blockbuster stores during the first half of 2012 as a result of weak store-level financial performance and that additional stores might also need to be closed. For the time being, Blockbuster was offering movies and video games for sale and rental through its retail stores, the blockbuster.com website (via a DVDs-by-mail subscription service), and pay-per-view VOD service. In addition, Dish Network subscribers could access Blockbuster@Home to obtain movies, video games, and TV shows through Internet streaming, mail and in-store exchanges, and online downloads.

Movie Gallery, once the second largest movie rental chain, filed for Chapter 11 bankruptcy protection in February 2010 and, shortly thereafter, opted to liquidate its entire movie rental business and close 1,871 Movie Gallery, 545 Hollywood Video, and 250 Game Crazy store locations. Within months, Movie Gallery ceased to exist.

The big winner in renting DVD discs was Redbox. Redbox had entered the movie rental business in 2007 with a vending machine-based strategy whereby Redbox self-service DVD kiosks were placed in leading supermarkets, drug stores, mass merchants like Walmart, convenience stores, and fast-food restaurants (McDonald's). Customers could rent new release movie DVDs for $1 per day (the price was raised to $1.20 per day in Fall 2011). Retailers with Redbox kiosks were paid a percentage of the rental revenues. Going into 2012, Redbox had deployed 35,400 of its vending machine kiosks in 29,300 locations in every state of the United States and in Puerto Rico. In February 2012, Redbox agreed to acquire about 9,000 Blockbuster-branded DVD kiosks operated by NCR Corp. Redbox and Netflix (with its DVDs-by-mail subscription option) were positioned to dominate the physical DVD rental segment for the foreseeable future.

The main battle in the movie rental marketplace was in the VOD and Internet streaming segments where several classes of competitors employing a variety of strategies were maneuvering to win the viewing time of consumers, capture enough revenue to be profitable, and become one of the market leaders. Competitors offering pay-per-view and VOD rentals were popular options for households and individuals that rented movies occasionally (once or at most twice per month), since the rental costs tended to be less than either the monthly subscription prices for unlimited streaming or the monthly fees to access premium movie channels like HBO, Starz, Cinemax, and Showtime. However, competitors offering unlimited Internet streaming plans tended to be the most economical and convenient choice for individuals and households that watched an average of three or more titles per month and for individuals that wanted to be able to watch movies or TV shows on mobile devices.

Netflix was the clear leader in Internet streaming in 2012, with over 23 million streaming subscribers that watched an average of 30 hours of video monthly and some 60,000 titles that could viewed on an Internet-connected device.[12] But Netflix had numerous ambitious rivals that saw huge revenue and profit opportunities in using online technology to provide movies, TV programming, and other entertainment content to all types of Internet-connected devices on an anywhere, anytime basis.

Netflix's two most important subscription-based instant streaming rivals included:

- Hulu Plus—The subscription fee for Hulu Plus was $7.99 per month for unlimited streaming, and new subscribers got a 1-week free trial. All Hulu Plus content included advertisements as a means of helping keep the monthly subscription price low. The Hulu Plus library of offerings included all current season episodes of popular TV shows, over 15,000 back season episodes of 380+ TV shows, and over 425 movies, many in high-definition.

- Amazon Prime Instant Video—This service entailed becoming an Amazon Prime member for a fee of $79 per year (after a 1-month free trial). All Amazon Prime members were entitled to free two-day shipping on *all Amazon orders*, unlimited commercial-free streaming of 17,000 movies and TV programs, one free Kindle book rental each month, and assorted other perks. In March 2012, there were an estimated 3.5 to 5 million Amazon Prime members. New Amazon Prime members were entitled to a 1-month free trial. While Amazon had originally created its Amazon Prime membership program as a means of providing unlimited two-day shipping to customers that frequently ordered merchandise from Amazon and liked to receive their orders quickly, in 2012 it was clear that Amazon was also endeavoring to brand Amazon Prime as a standalone streaming service at a subscription price below that of Netflix. In addition, Amazon competed with Netflix's DVDs-by-mail subscription service and with VOD and pay-per-view providers via its Amazon Instant Video offering, which enabled any visitor to the Amazon Web site to place an online order to instantly watch on a pay-per-view basis any of the 42,000 movies or TV shows in Amazon's rental library.

In February 2010, Wal-Mart Stores announced its intention to distribute movies over the Internet and had acquired Vudu, a leading provider of digital technologies that enabled online delivery of entertainment content. In 2012, Vudu was the largest home entertainment retailer in the United States with the capability to stream about 20,000 movie titles (including some 4,000 HD titles with Dolby Surround Sound) to Internet-connected TVs, Blu-ray players, computers, iPads and other tablets, and video game consoles (XBox 360 and PlayStation 3). Movies were available the same day they were released on DVD or Blu-ray discs and could be purchased or rented without a subscription; the rental fee was $2 per night for 2 nights. First-time users were eligible for free Vudu movie credits that could be used for a one-month trial period. In April 2012, Walmart initiated an exclusive in-store disc-to-digital service powered by Vudu technology which enabled people to bring their DVD and Blu-ray collections from partnering movie studios (Paramount, Sony, Fox, Universal, and Warner Bros.) to a Walmart Photo Center and have digital copies of the DVDs placed in a personal Vudu account. Then Vudu account holders could log on to Vudu.com and view their movies any time, any place on more than 300 different Internet-connected devices.

The growing rush among multi-channel TV providers to offer subscribers attractive TV Everywhere packages signaled a widespread belief that using Internet streaming to enable subscribers to watch certain TV shows or movies free at any time on any Internet-connected device was the best long-term solution for competing effectively with Netflix's Internet streaming service. In 2012, most every major network broadcaster, multi-channel TV provider, and premium movie channel was investing in Internet apps for all types of Internet-connected TVs, laptops, video game consoles, tablets and smart phones and otherwise positioning themselves to offer attractive TV Everywhere packages. HBO with its HBO GO offering (*www.hbogo.com*) and Showtime with its Showtime Anytime offering (*www.showtimeanytime.com*) were both trying to gain more viewing hours with their subscribers. Pricing for TV Everywhere offerings was simple—users just entered an authentication code verifying their subscription status at the appropriate website. Subscribers then clicked on whichever offering interested them to initiate instant streaming to their device.

According to market research done by The NPD Group, 15 percent of U.S. consumers ages 13 and older used pay-TV VOD services from their multi-channel cable, satellite, and fiber-optic providers in the twelve months ending August 2011; this translated into 40 million users and rental revenues of $1.1 billion.[13] However, there were four million fewer VOD users who paid additional fees to watch movies from these same providers in August 2011 compared to August 2010. This was attributed to the growing number of attractive VOD offerings from rival online VOD providers such as iTunes, Amazon Instant Video, Vudu, and others that instantly streamed rentals over the Internet. The NPD Group estimated that Internet streaming accounted for one out of every 6 VOD rentals in 2011 and that the share of Internet-streamed VOD rentals was likely to continue to grow, chiefly because many consumers saw the prices of Internet-streamed rentals as a better value and believed such providers had more movie-title selections.[14]

Netflix's Business Model and Strategy

Since launching the company's online movie rental service in 1999, Reed Hastings, founder and CEO of Netflix, had been the chief architect of Netflix's subscription-based business model and strategy that had transformed Netflix into the world's largest online entertainment subscription service and revolutionized the way that many people rented movies and previously broadcast TV shows. Hastings' goals for Netflix were simple: Build the world's best Internet movie service, keep improving Netflix's offerings and services faster than rivals, attract growing numbers of subscribers every year, and grow long-term earnings per share. Hastings was a strong believer in moving early and fast to initiate strategic changes that would help Netflix outcompete rivals, strengthen its brand image and reputation, and fortify its position as industry leader.

Netflix's Subscription-Based Business Model

Netflix employed a subscription-based business model. Members could choose from a variety of subscription plans whose prices and terms had varied over the years. Originally, all of the subscription plans were based on obtaining and returning DVDs by mail, with monthly prices dependent on the number of titles out at a time. But as more and more households began to have high-speed Internet connections, Netflix began bundling unlimited streaming with each of its DVD-by-mail subscription options, with the long-term intent of encouraging subscribers to switch to watching instantly-streamed movies rather than using DVD discs delivered and returned by mail. The DVDs-by-mail part of the business had order fulfillment costs and postage costs that were bypassed when members opted for instant streaming.

The DVD-by-Mail Option   Subscribers who opted to receive movie and TV episode DVDs by mail went to Netflix's Web site, selected one or more movies from its DVD library of over 120,000 titles, and received the movie DVDs by first-class mail generally within 1 business day—more than 97 percent of Netflix's subscribers lived within 1-day delivery of the company 50 distribution centers (plus 50 other shipping points) located throughout the United States. During the 2004-2010 period, Netflix had aggressively added more distribution centers and shipping points in order to provide members with 1-business-day delivery on DVD orders. Subscribers could keep a DVD for as long as they wished, with no due dates, no late fees, no shipping fees, and no pay-per-view fees. Subscribers returned DVDs via the U.S. Postal Service in a prepaid return envelope that came with each movie order. The address on the return envelope was always the closest distribution center/shipping point so that returned DVDs could quickly be returned to inventory and used to fill incoming orders from subscribers.

Exhibit 4 shows Netflix's various subscription plan options during 2010–2012. The most popular DVD-by-mail plans were those with one, two, or three titles out-at-a-time.

The Streaming Option   Netflix launched its Internet streaming service in January 2007, with instant-watching capability for 2,000 titles on personal computers. Very quickly, Netflix invested aggressively to enable its software to instantly stream content to a growing number of "Netflix-ready" devices, including Sony's PlayStation 3 consoles, Microsoft's Xbox 360, Nintendo's Wii, Internet-connected Blu-ray players and TVs, TiVo DVRs, and special Netflix players made by Roku and several other electronics manufacturers. At the same time, it began licensing increasing amounts of digital content that could be instantly streamed to subscribers. Initially, Netflix took a "metered" approach to streaming, offering, in essence, an hour per month of instant watching on a PC for every dollar of a subscriber's monthly subscription plan. For example, subscribers on the $16.99 per month plan, which provides unlimited DVD rentals with three discs out at a time, received 17 hours a month of movies and

EXHIBIT 4   Netflix's Subscription Plans, 2010–2012

Subscription Plan Choices	Monthly Subscription Price		
	June 2010	November 22, 2010 through June 2011	September 2011 through 2012
Unlimited DVD Plans:			
1 title out at a time	$8.99 plus unlimited streaming	$9.99 plus unlimited streaming	$7.99
2 titles out at a time	$13.99 plus unlimited streaming	$14.99 plus unlimited streaming	$11.99
3 titles out at a time	$16.99 plus unlimited streaming	$19.99 plus unlimited streaming	$15.99
4 titles out at a time	$23.99 plus unlimited streaming	$27.99 plus unlimited streaming	$21.99
5 to 8 titles out at a time	$29.99–$47.99 plus unlimited streaming	$34.99–$53.99 plus unlimited streaming	$27.99–$43.99
Unlimited streaming (no DVDs)	Not available	$7.99	$7.99
Unlimited Streaming plus DVDs			
Unlimited streaming plus 1 DVD title out at a time	–	–	$15.98
Unlimited streaming plus 2 DVD titles out at a time	–	–	$19.98
Unlimited streaming with 3-8 DVDs			$23.98–$51.98
Limited Plan:			
• 1 DVD title out a time	$4.99	$4.99	$4.99
• A maximum of 2 DVD rentals per month			
• 2 hours of video streaming to a PC or Apple Mac per month (this plan did not allow members to stream movies to TVs via a Netflix-ready device)			
• Limited streaming selection			

Source: Company records and postings at *www.netflix.com*.

TV episodes watched instantly on their PCs while those on the $4.99 limited plan were entitled to 5 hours of instant streaming. In January 2009, Netflix switched to an unlimited streaming option on all of its monthly subscription plans for unlimited DVD rentals; the limited plan continued to have a monthly streaming limit. Netflix had about 6,000 movie titles available for streaming as of January 2009 and about 20,000 titles in mid-2010.

Then in July 2011, Netflix announced that effective September 1, 2011 it would no longer offer a single subscription plan including both DVD-by-mail and streaming in the United States. Domestic subscribers who wished to receive DVDs-by-mail and also watch streamed content had to elect both a DVD-by-mail subscription plan and a streaming subscription plan. At December 31, 2011, Netflix had a total of 21.7 million domestic streaming subscribers (including 1.52 million who were in their free-trial period) and 11.2 million domestic DVD-by-mail subscribers (including 210,000 who were in their free-trial period); almost 6.6 million Netflix members had both a streaming subscription and a DVD-by mail subscription.

All new Netflix subscribers received a free 1-month trial. At the end of the free trial period, members automatically began paying the monthly fee, unless they canceled their subscription. All paying subscribers were billed monthly in advance. Payments were made by credit card or debit card. Subscribers could cancel at any time.

Exhibit 5 shows trends in Netflix's subscriber growth in the United States. Exhibit 6 shows quarterly trends in Netflix subscriptions and profitability by market segment.

New subscribers were drawn to try Netflix's online movie rental service because of (1) the wide selection, (2) the extensive information Netflix provided about each movie in its rental library (including critic reviews, member reviews, online trailers, and subscriber ratings), (3) the ease with which they could find and order movies, (4) Netflix's policies of no late fees and no due dates on DVD rentals (which eliminated the hassle of getting DVDs back to local rental stores by the designated due date), (5) the convenience of being provided a postage-paid return envelope for mailing DVDs back to Netflix, and (6) the convenience of ordering and instantly watching movies streamed to their TVs or computers with no additional pay-per-view charge.

Management believed that Netflix's subscriber base consisted of three types of customers: those who liked the convenience of home delivery and/or instant streaming, bargain-hunters who were enthused about being able to watch many movies for an economical monthly price, and movie buffs who wanted the ability to choose from a very wide selection of films and TV shows.

Netflix's Strategy

Netflix had a multi-pronged strategy to build an ever-growing subscriber base that included:

- Providing subscribers with a comprehensive selection of DVD titles.
- Acquiring new content by building and maintaining mutually beneficial relationships with entertainment video providers.

EXHIBIT 5 Domestic Subscriber Data for Netflix, 2000–2011

	2000	2005	2007	2009	2010	January 1–June 30, 2011	July 1–December 31, 2011
Total subscribers at beginning of period	107,000	2,610,000	6,316,000	9,390,000	12,268,000	19,501,000	24,594,000
Gross subscriber additions during period	515,000	3,729,000	5,340,000	9,322,000	15,648,000	11,614,000	9,930,000
Subscriber cancellations during the period	330,000	2,160,000	4,177,000	6,444,000	8,415,000	6,521,000	10,129,000
Total subscribers at end of period	292,000	4,179,000	7,479,000	12,268,000	19,501,000	24,594,000	24,395,000
Net subscriber additions during the period	185,000	1,569,000	1,163,000	2,878,000	7,233,000	5,093,000	(199,000)
Free trial subscribers at end of period	n.a.	153,000	153,000	376,000	1,566,000	1,331,000	1,537,000
Subscriber acquisition cost	$ 49.96	$ 38.78	$ 40.86	$ 25.48	$ 18.21	$ 14.70	$ 15.41
Average monthly revenue per paying subscriber	n.a.	$ 17.94	$ 14.95	$ 13.30	$ 12.20	$ 11.49	$ 12.35

Note: n.a. = not available.

Sources: Netflix's 10-K Reports, 2010, 2009, 2005, and 2003 and Netflix Quarterly Report for the period ending June 30, 2011, posted in the investors relations section at *www.netflix.com*, accessed March 16, 2012.

EXHIBIT 6 Quarterly Trends in Netflix Subscriptions and Profitability, by Market Segment, Quarter 3, 2011 through Quarter 1, 2012 (in 000s)

	Three months ended		
	September 30, 2011	December 31, 2011	March 31, 2012
Domestic Streaming			
Free subscriptions at end of period	937	1,518	
Paid subscriptions at end of period	20,511	20,153	
Total subscriptions at end of period	21,448	21,671	
Revenue	n.a.	$476,334	
Cost of revenues and marketing expenses	n.a.	424,224	
Contribution profit		52,110	
International Streaming			
Free subscriptions at end of period	491	411	
Paid subscriptions at end of period	989	1,447	
Total subscriptions at end of period	1,480	1,858	
Revenue	$ 22,687	$ 28,988	
Cost of revenues and marketing expenses	46,005	88,731	
Contribution profit	$ (23,318)	$ (59,743)	
Domestic DVDs-by-Mail			
Free subscriptions at end of period	115	126	
Paid subscriptions at end of period	13,813	11,039	
Total subscriptions at end of period	13,928	11,039	
Revenue		$370,253	
Cost of revenues and marketing expenses		176,488	
Contribution profit		$193,765	
Consolidated operations			
Free unique subscribers at end of period*	1,437	1,948	
Paid unique subscribers s at end of period*	23,832	24,305	
Total unique subscribers at end of period*	25,269	26,253	
Revenue	$821,839	$875,575	
Cost of revenues and marketing expenses	625,725	689,443	
Contribution profit	196,114	186,132	
Other operating expenses	99,272	124,260	
Operating income	96,842	61,872	
Other income (expense)	(3,219)	(5,037)	
Provision for income taxes	31,163	21,616	
Net income	$ 62,460	$ 35,219	

Note: Netflix defined "contribution profit (loss)" as revenues less cost of revenues and marketing expenses. Cost of revenue includes expenses related to the acquisition and licensing of content (streaming content license agreements, DVD direct purchases and DVD revenue sharing agreements with studios, distributors and other content suppliers), as well as content delivery costs related to providing streaming content and shipping DVDs to subscribers (which includes the postage costs to mail DVDs to and from our paying subscribers, the packaging and label costs for the mailers, all costs associated with streaming content over the Internet, the costs of operating and staffing shipping centers and customer service centers, DVD inventory management expenses, and credit card fees).
*Since some Netflix members in the United States subscribed to both streaming and DVD-by-mail plans, they were counted as a single unique subscriber to avoid double counting the same subscriber.
n.a. = not applicable. During July and August of the third quarter of 2011, Netflix's domestic streaming content and DVD-by-mail operations were combined. Subscribers in the United States were able to receive both streaming content and DVDs under a single hybrid plan. Accordingly, revenues were generated and marketing expenses were incurred in connection with the subscription offerings as a whole. Therefore, the company did not allocate revenues or marketing expenses for the domestic streaming and domestic DVD segments prior to the fourth quarter of 2011.

Source: Netflix records posted in the Financial Statements portion of the investor relations section at *www.newtflix.com*, accessed March 19, 2012.

- Making it easy for subscribers to identify movies and TV shows they were likely to enjoy and to put them in a queue for either instant streaming or delivery by mail.
- Giving subscribers a choice of watching streaming content or receiving quickly delivered DVDs by mail.
- Spending aggressively on marketing to attract subscribers and build widespread awareness of the Netflix brand and service.
- Promoting rapid transition of U.S. subscribers to streaming delivery rather than mail delivery.
- Expanding internationally.

A Comprehensive Library of Movies and TV Episodes Since its early days, Netflix's strategy had been to offer subscribers a large and diverse selection of DVD titles. It had aggressive in seeking out attractive new titles to add to its offerings. Its library of offerings had grown from some 55,000 titles in 2005 to about 120,000 titles in 2012, although the number of titles available for streaming was only about 30,000 as mid-2012 approached. The lineup included everything from the latest available Hollywood releases to releases several decades old to movie classics to independent films to hard-to-locate documentaries to TV shows and how-to videos, as well as a growing collection of cartoons and movies for children 12 and under. Netflix's DVD library far outdistanced the selection available in local brick-and-mortar movie rental stores and the 200 to 400 titles available in Redbox vending machines, but it was on a par with the number of titles available at Amazon. In mid-2012, Netflix's streaming library contained more titles than any other streaming service.

New Content Acquisition Over the years, Netflix had spent considerable time and energy establishing strong ties with various entertainment video providers and leveraging these ties to both expand its content library and gain access to new releases as early as possible—the time frame that Netflix gained access to films after their theatrical release was an important item of negotiation for Netflix (in 2011 Netflix was able to negotiate access to certain films produced by Lionsgate within one year of their initial theatrical release for showing to members in the UK and Ireland). Also, in 2011, Netflix had successfully negotiated *exclusive* rights to show a number of titles produced by several studios.

In August 2011, Netflix introduced a new "Just for Kids" section on its Web site that contained a large selection of kid-friendly movies and TV shows. In March 2012, all of the Just for Kids selections became available for streaming on PlayStation 3 game consoles. As of early March 2012, over 1 billion hours of Just for Kids programming had been streamed to Netflix members.

New content was acquired from movie studios and distributors through direct purchases, revenue-sharing agreements, and licensing agreements to stream content. Netflix acquired many of its new release movie DVDs from studios for a low upfront fee in exchange for a commitment for a defined period of time either to share a percentage of subscription revenues or to pay a fee based on content utilization. After the revenue-sharing period expired for a title, Netflix generally had the option of returning the title to the studio, purchasing the title, or destroying its copies of the title. On occasion, Netflix also purchased DVDs for a fixed fee per disc from various studios, distributors and other suppliers. Netflix had about 140,000 titles in its DVD library as of April 2012.

In the case of movie titles and TV episodes that were delivered to subscribers via the Internet for instant viewing, Netflix generally paid a fee to license the content for a defined period of time, with the total fees spread out over the term of the license agreement (so as to match up content payments with the stream of subscription revenues coming in for that content). Following expiration of the license term, Netflix either removed the content from its library of streamed offerings or negotiated extension or renewal of the license agreement. Netflix greatly accelerated its acquisition of new streaming content in 2010 and 2011, growing its streaming library to around 60,000 titles, up from about 17,000 titles in 2009. Netflix's payments to movie studios for streaming rights in 2010–2011 exceeded its payments for DVD distribution rights—see Exhibit 7. In 2010–2011, Netflix's rapidly growing subscriber base gave movie studios and the network broadcasters of popular TV shows considerably more bargaining power to negotiate higher prices for the new content that Netflix sought to acquire for its content library. Netflix management was fully aware of its weakening bargaining position in new content acquisition, and the higher prices it was having to pay to secure streaming rights largely accounted for why the company's contribution profits from streaming were lower than from DVD rentals—see Exhibit 6. However, Netflix executives expected that long-term growth in the number of streaming subscribers would enable the company to earn attractive profits on its streaming business, despite the increased costs of acquiring attractive new content.

Netflix had incurred obligations to pay $3.91 billion for streaming content as of December 31, 2011, up from $1.12 billion as of December 31, 2010. Some of these obligations did not appear on the company's year-end 2011 balance sheet because they did not meet content library asset recognition criteria (either the fee was not known or reasonably determinable for a specific title or the fee was known but the title was not yet available for streaming to subscribers). Certain of Netflix's new licensing agreements also had variable terms and included renewal provisions that were solely at the option of the content provider. The expected timing of the Netflix's streaming content payments was as follows:[15]

Less than one year	$ 797.6 million
Due after one year and through 3 years	2,384.4
Due after 3 years and through 5 years	650.5
Due after 5 years	74.7
Total streaming obligations	$3,907.2 million

EXHIBIT 7 Netflix's Quarterly Expenditures for Additions to Content Library, 2009–2011

	Expenditures for Additions to DVD Library (in 000s)	Expenditures for Additions to Streaming Content Library (in 000s)	Total Expenditures for New Content (in 000s)
2009			
Quarter 1	$ 46,499	$ 22,091	$ 68,590
Quarter 2	43,224	9,343	52,567
Quarter 3	46,273	9,998	56,271
Quarter 4	57,048	22,785	79,833
Annual Total	$193,044	$ 64,217	$ 257,261
2010			
Quarter 1	$ 36,902	$ 50,475	$ 87,377
Quarter 2	24,191	66,157	90,348
Quarter 3	29,900	115,149	145,049
Quarter 4	32,908	174,429	207,337
Annual Total	$123,901	$ 406,210	$ 530,111
2011			
Quarter 1	$ 22,119	$ 192,307	$ 214,426
Quarter 2	19,065	612,595	631,660
Quarter 3	20,826	539,285	560,111
Quarter 4	23,144	976,545	999,689
Annual Total	$ 85,154	$2,320,732	$2,405,886

Source: Company cash flow data, posted in the investor relations section at *www.netflix.com*, accessed March 16, 2012.

Netflix's Convenient and Easy-to-Use Movie Selection Software Netflix had developed proprietary software technology that allowed members to easily scan a movie's length, appropriateness for various types of audiences (G, PG, or R), primary cast members, genre, and an average of the ratings submitted by other subscribers (based on 1 to 5 stars). With one click, members could watch a short preview if they wished. Most important, perhaps, was a personalized 1- to 5-star recommendation for each title that was based on a subscribers' own ratings of movies previously viewed, movies that the member had placed on a list for future streamed viewing and/or mail delivery), and the overall or average rating of all subscribers.

Subscribers often began their search for movie titles by viewing a list of several hundred personalized movie title "recommendations" that Netflix's software automatically generated for each member. Each member's list of recommended movies was the product of Netflix-created algorithms that organized the company's entire library of titles into clusters of similar movies and then sorted the movies in each cluster from most liked to least liked based on over 3 billion ratings provided by subscribers. In 2010–2011, Netflix added new movie ratings from subscribers to its database at a rate of about 20 million per week. Those subscribers who rated similar movies in similar clusters were categorized as like-minded viewers. When a subscriber was online and browsing through the movie selections, the software was programmed to check the clusters the subscriber had rented/viewed in the past, determine which movies the customer had yet to rent/view in that cluster, and recommended only those movies in the cluster that had been highly rated by viewers. Viewer ratings determined which available titles were displayed to a subscriber and in what order. When streaming members came upon a title they wanted to view, that title could with a single click be put on their "instant queue"—a list for future viewing. A member's instant queue was immediately viewable with one click whenever the member went to Netflix's web site; with one additional click, any title on a member's instant queue could be activated for immediate viewing. In Spring 2011, a number of the world's leading consumer electronics companies began placing a Netflix button on their remotes for operating newly-purchased TVs, Blu-ray disc players, and other devices that had built-in Internet connections—the button provided Netflix subscribers with a one-click connection to their instant queue. Clicking on a remote with a Netflix button resulted in all of the titles in a subscriber's instant queue appearing on the TV screen within a few seconds; streaming was instantly initiated by clicking on whichever title the subscriber wished to watch. In the case of members with DVD-by-mail subscriptions, members browsing the title library on Netflix's Web site could with one click place a title on their list (or queue) to receive by mail. DVD subscribers specified the order in which titles in their personal queue were to be mailed out and could alter the lists or the mailing order at any time. It was also possible to reserve a copy of upcoming releases. Netflix management saw the movie recommendation tool as a quick and personalized means of helping subscribers identify titles they were likely to enjoy.

Netflix management believed that over 50 percent of the titles selected by subscribers came from the recommendations generated by its proprietary software. The software algorithms were thought to be particularly effective in promoting selections of smaller, high-quality films to subscribers who otherwise might not have discovered them in the company's massive and ever-changing collection. On average, about 85 percent of the titles in Netflix's content library were rented each quarter, an indication of the effectiveness of the company's recommendation software in steering subscribers to movies of interest and achieving broader utilization of the company's entire library of titles.

A Choice of Mail Delivery Versus Streaming

Until 2007-2008 when streaming technology had advanced to the point that made providing video-on-demand a viable option, Netflix concentrated its efforts on speeding the time it took to deliver subscriber orders via mail delivery. The strategy was to establish a nationwide network of distribution centers and shipping points with the capability to deliver DVDs ordered by subscribers within one business-day. To achieve quick delivery and return capability, Netflix created sophisticated software to track the location of each DVD title in inventory and determine the fastest way of getting the DVD orders to subscribers. When a subscriber placed an order for a specific DVD, the system first looked for that DVD at the shipping center closest to the customer. If that center didn't have the DVD in stock, the system then checked for availability at the next closest center The search continued until the DVD was found, at which point the regional distribution center with the ordered DVD in inventory was provided with the information needed to initiate the order fulfillment and shipping process. If the DVD was unavailable anywhere in the system, it was wait-listed. The software system then moved to the customer's next choice and the process started all over. And no matter where the DVD was sent from, the system knew to print the return label on the pre-paid envelope to send the DVDs to the shipping center closest to the customer to reduce return mail times and permit more efficient use of Netflix's DVD inventory. No subscriber orders were shipped on holidays or weekends.

By early 2007, Netflix had 50 regional distribution centers and another 50 shipping points scattered across the U.S., giving it one business-day delivery capability for 95 percent of its subscribers and, in most cases, also enabling 1-day return times. As of 2010, additional improvements in Netflix's distribution and shipping network had resulted in one business-day delivery capability for 98 percent of Netflix's subscribers.

In 2007, when entertainment studios became more willing to allow Internet delivery of their content (since recent technological advances prevented streamed movies from being pirated), Netflix moved quickly to better compete with the growing numbers of video-on-demand providers by adding the feature of unlimited streaming to its regular monthly subscription plans. The market for Internet delivery of media content consisted of three segments: the rental of Internet delivered content, the download-to-own segment, and the advertising-supported online delivery segment (mainly, YouTube and Hulu). Netflix's objective was to be the clear leader in the rental segment via its instant watching feature.

Giving subscribers the option of watching DVDs delivered by mail or instantly watching movies streamed to subscribers' computers or TVs had considerable strategic appeal to Netflix in two respects. One, giving subscribers the option to order and instantly watch streamed content put Netflix in position to compete head-to-head with the growing numbers of video-on-demand providers. Second, providing streamed content to subscribers had the attraction of being cheaper than (1) incurring the postage expenses on DVD orders and returns, (2) having to obtain and manage an ever-larger inventory of DVDs, and (3) covering the labor costs of additional distribution center personnel to fill a growing volume of DVD orders and handle increased numbers of returned DVDs. But streaming content to subscribers was not cost-free; it required server capacity, software to authenticate orders from subscribers, and a system of computers containing copies of the content files placed at various points in a network so as to maximize bandwidth and allow subscribers to access a copy of the file on a server near the subscriber. Having subscribers accessing a central server ran the risk of an Internet transmission bottleneck. Netflix also utilized third party content delivery networks to help it efficiently stream movies and TV episodes in high volume to Netflix subscribers over the Internet. According to one report, Netflix incurred a cost of about 5-cents to stream a movie to a subscriber compared to costs of about $1 in roundtrip mailing and labor fees for a DVD.[16]

Netflix executives believed that the strategy of combining streaming and DVDs-by-mail into a single monthly subscription price during the 2007- September 2011period enabled Netflix not only to offer members an attractively large selection of movies for one low monthly price but also to enjoy a competitive advantage vis-à-vis rivals as compared to providing a postal-delivery-only or Internet-delivery-only subscription service. Furthermore, Netflix management believed the company's combination postal-delivery/streaming service delivered compelling customer value and customer satisfaction by eliminating the hassle involved in making trips to local movie rental stores to choose and return rented DVDs.

In March 2012, six months after instituting separate plans for streaming and DVDs-by-mail, Netflix instituted as yet unannounced and somewhat subtle changes at its website. A support page appeared at *www.netflix.com* that sent people registering for a free trial subscription to "dvd.netflix.com" if they wanted to sign up for a DVD-by-mail-only account.[17] In addition, Netflix began redirecting DVD-by-mail customers to a separate Web page when they tried to rate movies on Netflix's main site, and DVD-by-mail-only subscribers that searched for movie titles were only shown titles that were also available for streaming rather than the heretofore full library of DVD titles.[18] Furthermore, ratings and recommendations by DVD and streaming customers were separated.

Marketing and Advertising   Netflix used multiple marketing channels to attract subscribers, including online advertising (paid search listings, banner ads, text on popular sites such as AOL and Yahoo, and permission-based e-mails), radio stations, regional and national television, direct mail, and print ads. The costs of free monthly trials were treated as a marketing expense. It also participated in a variety of cooperative advertising programs with studios through which Netflix received cash consideration in return for featuring a studio's movies in its advertising. In recent years, Netflix had worked closely with the makers of Netflix-ready electronics devices to expand the number of devices on which subscribers could view Netflix-streamed content; these expenses were all considered as marketing expenses and sometimes took the form of payments to various consumer electronics partners for their efforts to produce and distribute these devices.

Management had boosted marketing expenditures of all kinds (including paid advertising) from $25.7 million in 2000 (16.8 percent of revenues) to $142.0 million in 2005 (20.8 percent of revenues) to $218.2 million in 2007 (18.1 percent of revenues). When the recession hit in late 2007 and 2008, management trimmed 2008 marketing expenditures to $199.7 million (14.6 percent of revenues) as a cost containment measure but in 2009 marketing expenditures resumed their upward trend, climbing to $237.7 million (14.2 percent of revenues). Marketing expenses rose to even more dramatically to $298.8 million in 2010 and to $402.6 million in 2011 owing to:

- Increased adverting efforts, particularly in the newly-entered countries of Canada, Latin America, the United Kingdom, and Ireland.
- Increased costs of free trial subscriptions.
- Increased payments to the company's consumer electronics partners.

Advertising campaigns of one type or another were underway more or less continuously, with the lure of 1-month free trials usually being the prominent ad feature. Advertising expenses totaled approximately $205.9 million in 2009, $181.4 million in 2008 and $207.9 million in 2007—ad expenses for 2011 and 2010 were not publicly reported.

Transitioning to Internet Delivery of Content. Netflix's core strategy in 2012 was to grow its streaming subscription business domestically and globally. Since launching streaming to Internet-connected devices in 2007, the company had continuously improved the streaming experience of subscribers in three major ways:

- Expanding the size of its streaming content library, currently about 60,000 titles.
- Working with consumer electronics partners to increase the number of Internet-connected devices that could be used to view Netflix-streamed content.
- Improving the ease with which subscribers could navigate Netflix's Web site to locate and select content they wanted to watch.

The result had been rapidly growing consumer acceptance of and interest in the delivery of TV shows and movies directly over the Internet. Netflix subscribers watched over 2 billion hours of streaming video in the fourth quarter of 2011, an average of approximately 30 hours per member per month (which equated to a cost of $0.27 per hour of viewing, given the current $7.99 subscription price).[19] During this same period, the company realized a contribution profit of $52.1 million on its domestic streaming business segment (see Exhibit 6).

Going forward, Netflix executives expected that the number of members with DVD-by-mail subscriptions would decline, as subscribers migrated from DVD-by-mail plans to Internet streaming plans and as subscribers with both DVD-by-mail and streaming subscriptions opted for streaming-only subscriptions. An ever-smaller fraction of new subscribers was expected to opt for the DVD-by-mail plan. Management saw no need to proactively encourage or try to accelerate the decline in domestic DVD-by-mail subscriptions beyond the actions already taken—rather the strategy was to simply let subscribers choose whichever plan or plans they wished, since the company had ample ability to provide a satisfying experience to both DVD and streaming subscribers. Netflix management projected that the number of domestic DVD subscribers would decline from just over 11.0 million at the end of 2011 to about 9.5 million at the end of March 2012, with smaller sequential declines in future quarters. Early indications were that the number of Netflix streaming subscribers in the United States would rise by about 1.7 million in the first quarter of 2012.

In the near term, the falloff in revenues from declining domestic DVD subscriptions was projected to be offset by revenue gains from ongoing growth in the numbers of domestic streaming subscribers. Domestic DVD contribution margins were expected to remain healthy despite shrinking volume, due to the lower postage costs and order fulfillment costs associated with declines in the number of DVD discs being ordered by DVD-by-mail subscribers.

In March 2012, there were reports that Netflix was in exploratory discussions with multi-channel TV providers about offering its streaming content as an add-on option alongside such premium movie channels as HBO, Showtime, and Starz.[20] One benefit from such a strategic approach was said to be the likelihood that customers who purchased Netflix through a multi-channel TV provider would be more likely to remain a subscriber. Anywhere from 30 percent to 70 percent of Netflix's subscribers canceled their subscriptions each year (see Exhibit 3)—the percentage of existing subscribers that canceled their subscriptions was referred to as the "churn rate." For Netflix to grow its subscriber base in upcoming years, it had to overcome its churn rate by attracting enough new subscribers to more than offset subscriber cancellations. The appeal of offering Netflix through multichannel TV providers was that pay-television channels had a customer churn rate of only 20 to 25 percent. At an investor event in San Francisco in late February 2012, Reed Hastings said partnering with cable companies to offer Netflix streaming as an add-on option was a natural progression for the company.[21]

International Expansion Strategy

Making Netflix's streaming service available to growing numbers of households and individuals outside the United States was a central element of Netflix's long-term strategy to grow revenues and profits. Netflix executives were fully aware that international expansion would temporarily depress overall company profitability since it took roughly 2 years to build a sufficiently large subscriber base in newly-entered country markets to have sufficient revenues to cover all the associated costs. The biggest cost to enter new countries was the expense of obtaining licenses from movie studios and the owners of TV shows to stream their content to subscribers in these countries. The second biggest cost related to the incremental advertising and marketing expenses needed to attract new subscribers and grow subscription revenues fast enough to achieve profitability within the targeted 2-year time frame.

In 2011, Netflix's international streaming segment (Canada and Latin America) reported a contribution loss of $103.1 million. Top management had projected that the added international expenses of expanding service to the UK and Ireland in January 2012 would result in total international contribution losses for Canada, Latin America, United Kingdom, and Ireland of between $108 million and $118 million in Quarter 1 of 2012.

Netflix planned to continue to invest in expanding its streaming content libraries in Latin America, the United Kingdom, and Ireland throughout 2012 and beyond, just as it had done since launching its service in Canada. According to CEO Reed Hastings and CFO David Wells, a bigger content library:[22]

> improves the consumer experience, builds strong word of mouth and positive brand awareness, and drives additional acquisition [of new subscribers], all elements of a strong foundation for long-term success.

Nonetheless, Netflix's entry into Latin America presented unique challenges not encountered in the other international markets. The concept of on-demand streaming video (outside of piracy and YouTube) was not something most Latin American households were familiar with, which required Netflix to do more work in driving consumer understanding and acceptance of the company's streaming service. Moreover, in Latin America, a smaller fraction of households had fewer internet-connected TVs, Bluray players, and other devices that readily connected to Netflix's service, plus in many locations there was an under-developed Internet infrastructure, relatively low credit card usage among households and individual, and consumer payment challenges for ecommerce. Many Latin American banks turned down all ecommerce debit card transactions due to fraud risk.

Netflix's Performance Prospects in 2012

At the time of printing, management's latest forecast for 2012 called for modest quarterly losses throughout 2012 and a loss for the whole year, due entirely to the sizable contribution losses in the international segment. However, continued growth in the number of domestic streaming subscribers was expected to produce contribution margins of 10–12 percent during 2012, comfortably above the company's long-term domestic streaming target of 8 percent and in line with the 10.9 percent domestic streaming contribution margin in the fourth quarter of 2011. Netflix management said that until the company returned to global profitability, it did not intend to launch additional international expansion.

Highlights of Netflix's Performance in the First Quarter of 2012

For the first three months of 2012, Netflix reported revenues of $869.8 million (21.0 percent higher than the revenues of $718.6 million in the first quarter of 2011) and a net loss of $4.6 million (versus net income of $60.2 million in the first quarter of 2011). The net loss for the quarter stemmed from contribution losses of $102.7 million in the international streaming segment; however, Netflix added 1 million more paying international subscribers during Quarter 1 and had another 600,000 international subscribers enrolled in free trials. International streaming revenues were $43.4 million in the first quarter, versus revenues of $29.0 million for the fourth quarter of 2011 and $12.3 million for the first quarter of 2011.

In the United States, the total number of streaming subscribers (including free trial subscribers) rose from 21.7 million at the end of the fourth quarter of 2011 to 23.4 million at the end the first quarter of 2012. Total paying subscribers jumped by 1.85 million during the quarter (from 20.15 million as of December 31, 2011 to 22.0 million as of March 31, 2012). Not surprisingly, the number of domestic DVD subscribers dropped by almost 1.1 million during the quarter to a total of 10.1 million as of March 31; nonetheless, the customer count exceeded management's expectations and contribution profits from this segment were $146.1 million—seven million of the DVD subscribers were also streaming subscribers. Viewing per member was at a record high level during the quarter.

Reed Hastings indicated that Netflix would likely add a net of 7 million domestic streaming subscribers during 2012 (about the same number added in 2010) and end the year with approximately 27.2 million domestic streaming customers. He also said that:

- It would take longer than 8 quarters after initial entry for the company's operations in Latin America, the UK, and Ireland to reach sustained profitability, owing to ongoing investments in content improvements and somewhat slower-than-expected growth in membership.

- The company expected to return to global profitability in the second quarter of 2012 because of increasing contribution profits in domestic streaming, slow erosion of contribution profits in the domestic DVD segment, and narrowing contribution losses in the international streaming segment. Netflix had positive free cash flow of $2 million during the first three months of 2012.

- Given the strong response to the launch of the company's service in the UK, the company planned to enter another European market in Q4 of 2012. Quickly investing the growing profits from the company's domestic business in additional global expansion had two key advantages, One, entering foreign markets ahead of other streaming rivals made it easier for Netflix to build a profitable subscriber base. Two, having growing numbers of subscribers in a growing number of countries enabled Netflix to more quickly reach the global scale needed to license global content rights economically.

Initial investor reaction to all this was decidedly negative. In the week following the April announcement of Netflix's first quarter results, full-year expectations, and future plans, Netflix's stock price—which had climbed to $129 per share in mid-February before falling back to the $105-$110 range in mid-April—dropped about $25 per share and then over the next ten days slid further, trading as low as $72.49.

ENDNOTES

1. Michael Liedtke, "Netflix's Online Gaps Likely to Continue," Associated Press, April 9, 2012, accessed April 16, 2012 at *www.sltrib.com/sltrib/money/538815*.
2. NPD Group press release, February 16, 2012, accessed March 13, 2012 at *www.npd.com*.
3. NPD Group press release, January 19, 2012, accessed March 13, 2012 at *www.npd.com*.
4. Ibid.
5. See Daniel Frankel, "Analyst to Studios: It's Time to Force Early VOD on Theater Chains," posted at *www.paidcontent.org*, accessed March 12, 2012.
6. See, for example, Bret Lang, "Lionsgate Tests Early VOD Waters with Taylor Lautner's 'Abduction,'" The Wrap, posted at *www.thewrap.com*, August 10, 2011, accessed March 12, 2012 and also Frankel, "Analyst to Studios: It's Time to Force Early VOD on Theater Chains."
7. Frankel, "Analyst to Studios: It's Time to Force Early VOD on Theater Chains."
8. See, for example, Bret Lang, "Lionsgate Tests Early VOD Waters with Taylor Lautner's 'Abduction,'" *The Wrap*, posted at *www.thewrap.com*, August 10, 2011, accessed March 12, 2012 and also Frankel, "Analyst to Studios: It's Time to Force Early VOD on Theater Chains."
9. Frankel, "Analyst to Studios: It's Time to Force Early VOD on Theater Chains."
10. According to information in Amanda Alix, "Is Netflix Trying to Pull Another Quikster?" The Motley Fool, posted March 29, 2012 at *www.fool.com* and accessed on March 30, 2012.
11. William Launder, "Online Movie Viewing to Outpace DVD, Blu-ray Views This Year," The Wall Street Journal, posted at *http://online.wsj.com* on March 23, 2012, accessed March 30, 2012.
12. Michael Liedtke, "Netflix's Online Gaps Likely to Continue," Associated Press, April 9, 2012, accessed April 16, 2012 at *www.sltrib.com/sltrib/money/538815*.
13. NPD Group press release, February 16, 2012, accessed March 13, 2012 at *www.npd.com*.
14. Ibid.
15. Netflix's 2011 10-K Report, p. 62.
16. Michael V. Copeland, "Reed Hastings: Leader of the Pack," *Fortune*, December 6, 2010, p. 128.
17. Amanda Alix, "Is Netflix Trying to Pull Another Quikster?" *The Motley Fool*, posted March 29, 2012 at *www.fool.com* and accessed on March 30, 2012.
18. Ibid.
19. Letter to Shareholders, January 25, 2012, p. 1; posted in the investor relations section at *www.netflix.com*, accessed March 28, 2012.
20. Angela Moscaritolo, "Report: Netflix Looking to Partner with Cable Companies," PC Magazine, posted at *www.PCMag.com* on March 7, 2012, accessed March 7, 2012 and John Jannarone, "Netflix Risks Tangle with Cable," *The Wall Street Journal*, March 29, 2012, p. C12.
21. Moscaritolo, "Report: Netflix Looking to Partner with Cable Companies."
22. Letter to Shareholders, January 25, 2012, p. 6; posted in the investor relations section at *www.netflix.com*, accessed March 28, 2012.

CASE 20

BUILDING THE NEW BOSCO-ZETA PHARMA (A)*

Markus Biennel was flustered. Having just announced Bosco Pharmaceutical's acquisition of Zeta AG (Zeta), the Bosco chairman was unsure about whether to follow his instinct to merge the two firms using only internal resources or whether he should accept the help of Deloitte Consulting.

John Powers, the Deloitte partner in charge of the project, advocated a complete overhaul of Bosco's organization in more than 100 countries to accommodate Zeta, which was one-fifth Bosco's size. But Biennel thought that because Zeta had so few complementarities with Bosco—primarily in the oncology sector—he was not sure whether Zeta's worldwide product structure should be adopted by Bosco or whether Zeta should be required to conform to Bosco's more geographic structure.

Bosco was a latecomer to the global M&A consolidation trend in the pharmaceutical industry, and, by relying solely on in-house R&D to generate new products, the company had missed the window of opportunity for "in-licensing" new drugs from biotechnology start-ups. Biennel thought that the Zeta acquisition would provide a way to catch up.

Unfortunately, the market reaction to his announcement of the acquisition was not kind. As he gazed at the Rhine from his office on the 17th floor, he thought about the analysts' statements. Analyst A had said, "We are rather skeptical about the transaction, as the overlap of the therapeutic areas is rather small and because the cost reductions are predominantly planned in R&D, which should be retained to remain competitive." Analyst B had said, "The proposed deal is primarily targeting scale. Apart from the cost synergies, the fit between the two companies is limited." And Analyst C had said, "A choice to maintain their conglomerate structure despite better critical size in health care is negative for the investment case as investors willing to play the turnaround story in health care will be exposed to risks of downturn in material science."

Biennel understood the viewpoints of these analysts because Bosco's history had been bleak. In August 2005, the company had been forced to withdraw its major cholesterol-lowering drug from the market after it was linked to more than 220 deaths. Now, after several years of restructuring and on the heels of the Winthrough merger, the Zeta acquisition was the biggest in Bosco's 110-year history. The integration issues were not trivial, as the combined entity would have more than 40,000 employees in more than 100 countries. (See Exhibit 1 for both firms' financials.)

Deal Background

Despite market reaction, the mood was upbeat at Bosco's headquarters in the industrial town of Weeze, Germany. "At the very least, the merger will restore some luster to Germany's pharma sector," observed Biennel. Bosco was an established, legendary name in the pharmaceutical industry as the discoverer of the pain-killing and fever-reducing wonder drug Colospirin in 1897, and as a leader in the modern drug industry. But Bosco had endured several setbacks during the last two decades of industry consolidation, as it was overshadowed by such companies as America's Pfizer, Britain's GlaxoSmithKline, and Switzerland's Novartis.

* This case was prepared by Nandini Bose (MBA '05), Yogesh Goswami, Sudeep Mathur, John Powers, all from Deloitte Consulting, and Paul M. Hammaker Research Professor L. J. Bourgeois III. It was written as a basis for class discussion rather than to illustrate effective or ineffective handling of an administrative situation. The contribution of Deloitte Consulting is gratefully acknowledged. Copyright © 2008 by the University of Virginia Darden School Foundation, Charlottesville, VA. All rights reserved. *To order copies, send an e-mail to sales@dardenbusinesspublishing.com. No part of this publication may be reproduced, stored in a retrieval system, used in a spreadsheet, or transmitted in any form or by any means—electronic, mechanical, photocopying, recording, or otherwise—without the permission of the Darden School Foundation.*

DARDEN BUSINESS PUBLISHING
UNIVERSITY of VIRGINIA

EXHIBIT 1 Financial Metrics

	Bosco	Zeta
Key Metrics (in EUR millions)		
Total assets	35,000	6,000
Total revenue	25,000	5,000
Operating income	10,000	2,700
Total net income	+5,000	1,350
Margins (%)		
Operating margin	40	54
Net profit margin	20	27
Ratios		
Total debt to equity	0.75	0.08
Current ratio	1.8	2.3

Source: Bosco Investor Presentation.

In the 1980s, Bosco had been one of the top five pharmaceutical and chemicals companies, but by the year 2000, it dropped to the second tier. Like a lot of companies, Bosco believed that sustainability was achieved through internal innovation by increasing its R&D expenditures rather than growing through acquisitions. As a result, when the industry began to consolidate, Bosco passed up some opportunities to participate. In addition, its focus on pharmaceuticals and its neglect of other businesses resulted in its having an unbalanced portfolio. Finally had Bosco's now-withdrawn cholesterol-lowering drug fulfilled its potential, it would have been a $4 billion to $5 billion asset. During the two years after its 2005 withdrawal, Bosco's market value plummeted.

In response, Bosco returned to its traditional, diversified, multimarket approach, participating in consumer and animal health and pharmaceuticals. Within the pharmaceutical sector, it focused on high-margin specialty products, efficient use of its sales force, and licensing as a source of new products.

Bosco also expanded in the consumer-health sector. Traditionally a lower-margin business than brand-name prescription drugs, consumer health had been growing rapidly and offered some often overlooked advantages. For example, there were limits on the synergies available for acquiring prescription pharmaceutical products. A pharmaceutical sales force could, at maximum, promote two products. After a merger, both legacy sales organizations were needed, however, a consumer business somewhat resembled a catalog business because new products could be added to existing sales and marketing organizations.

Driven by that logic, Bosco's consumer healthcare division acquired Winthrough Consumer Health for $2 billion in August 2005. The deal brought Bosco pain relievers, antiseptic creams, and multivitamins, making Bosco the third-largest provider of nonprescription medicines. At the time, analysts thought Bosco had significantly overpaid for Winthrough. But compared with more recent acquisitions in the over-the-counter (OTC) consumer sector, Bosco actually got a bargain and the advantage of being in on the start of the OTC consolidation.

One particularly hard decision Bosco made was to exit a market that had been one of the richest in health care for decades: diagnostics. At the time, the market speculated that this was a high-risk strategy, and yet, 18 months later, just as with the Winthrough acquisition, it was considered a smart move. Letting go of diagnostics not only improved Bosco's profitability but also served as the catalyst that allowed the company to focus more closely on specialty products.

The Deal

On March 24, 2007, Hamburg-based Zeta accepted the (euro) EUR16 billion cash offer from Bosco. The deal merged Zeta, the world's largest maker of birth control pills and cancer drugs, and Bosco, Germany's last remaining pharmaceutical and chemical conglomerate.

The new company could boast a much richer pipeline—with two drugs filed with the U.S. Food and Drug Administration (FDA) and ten in late-stage testing. Investment bankers had predicted that the merger would lead to annual cost savings of EUR700 million by 2010. Biennel hoped to use Zeta's specialist sales force in the United States to market its own potential blockbuster, Nextvarian, which the FDA had approved at the end of 2006 as a treatment for kidney cancer. The drug was also being tested for treatment of liver, skin, and lung cancers.

Prescription drugs, along with OTC standbys such as Once Daily vitamins, accounted for 30% of Bosco's annual revenues of EUR25 billion in 2006. The new company could now focus on treatments for cancer and cardiovascular diseases and a select group of specialized therapeutic markets. Zeta brought Danielle, the world's top-selling contraceptive, and Alphaseron, a treatment for multiple sclerosis, which was expected to bring EUR100 million in annual sales.

After getting the approval of the management and supervisory boards, Bosco outlined the key points of the transaction:

- *Sites*: The headquarters of the consolidated pharmaceuticals business would be Hamburg. The key research locations were Duisburg and Cologne (Germany), as well as Gloucester, Minturn, and West Hartford (United States).
- *Employees*: Possible staff reductions would be equally and fairly allocated between the two companies.
- *Management*: The management of the combined pharmaceuticals business would be chosen on the basis of objective criteria and third-party advice.
- *Name*: To the extent legally possible, the new name for the combined pharmaceutical business would be Bosco-Zeta Pharma.
- *Corporate structure*: Management would report directly to Bosco Healthcare, one of Bosco's three business groups. Integration committees with equal representation of executives from both Zeta and Bosco would be established.

Pharmaceutical Industry[1]

In 2004, the global pharmaceuticals and biotechnology (P&B) industry was valued at EUR503 billion, having expanded at a compound annual growth rate (CAGR) of 9.9% since 2000. Although the pharmaceuticals segment generated revenues of EUR415 billion, the EUR88 billion biotechnology segment had outperformed pharmaceuticals consistently during the previous five years. And during the same period, governments in most of the world's major developed markets exerted significant downward pressure on pharmaceutical pricing. Generic competition had also created major downward price pressure since 2000.

During 2001–02, market growth slowed from 11% per year to 8%. By 2005, growth rates recovered, reflecting companies' efforts to restructure business models to emphasize product development and to improve efficiencies. The U.S. markets for P&B were the largest; U.S. sales were EUR238 billion or 47% of the global market. In comparison, Europe generated 23%, whereas the Asia/Pacific region accounted for a further 17%. By 2010, the global P&B industry was expected to reach a value of EUR807 billion for a CAGR of 9.9% from 2005.

The EUR88 billion biotechnology market was still relatively immature; none of the pure biotech firms were featured as leading players within the overall P&B industry. Instead, the top six players overall were all pharmaceutical giants. Collectively, these top six controlled 29% of the global market. Pfizer was the clear leader, with Sanofi-Aventis and GlaxoSmithKline closely matched for the number two position.

The pharmaceutical industry was one of the most research-intensive industries in the United States. On average, pharmaceutical firms invested as much as 17% to 22% of sales in R&D, compared with 3% for the average U.S. manufacturing firm.

In the last few years, the average return on investment for new drugs had fallen. In addition, spiraling R&D costs and the reduced likelihood of new drugs developing blockbuster status meant players had become more selective in their investments. Despite this, in 2007, there was a greater number of drug molecules approaching the market compared with the previous five years. As a result, companies focused on developing balanced portfolios, rather than on emphasizing blockbusters.

During that time, there had been a significant change in attitude toward private-label OTC products, which often mimicked their branded predecessors but at significantly discounted prices. It was particularly noticeable in Europe and North America, where consumers viewed certain OTC drugs as commodities. With leading brands struggling to differentiate their products in the face of this cheaper competition, companies needed to invest even more intensively in product R&D.

The United States was expected to maintain its position as the world's dominant market for biotechnology products with such players as Amgen, Biogen, and Genentech. Legislation providing a zero capital-gains tax rate for direct investment into the equities of entrepreneurial firms was likely to spur economic growth, create high-wage jobs, and ensure the future competitiveness of U.S. biotech entrepreneurial firms.

With several blockbuster biological products approaching patent expiry and the emergence of new approval pathways, the biotech-generics sector represented an attractive opportunity for companies looking to escape intensifying competition in the generic-pharmaceuticals sector. Despite strong opposition from the biotechnology industry, regulatory bodies were expected to establish approval pathways for generic biotech in the future, driven by the potential cost savings for governments and health care payers with access to lower-cost biotech generics.

Meanwhile, leading genomics[2] companies were restructuring their businesses in a push toward profitability. The market for technology agreements was becoming saturated, and genomics companies had been forced to develop products in-house in order to continue growth. Companies were increasingly investing in product development and marketing initiatives, reducing the number of in-licensing opportunities for pharmaceutical companies.

Bosco AG

Incorporated in 1902, Bosco Aktiengesellschaft (Bosco AG) offered a range of products, including ethical pharmaceuticals; health care products; agricultural products; and polymers. Bosco AG was the management holding company of the Bosco Group, which included approximately 280 consolidated subsidiaries (Exhibit 2). The business operations of the company were organized into the three groups:

- Bosco Healthcare: consumer care, animal health, and pharmaceuticals
- Bosco Crop Care: crop protection, environmental science, and bioscience segments
- Bosco Material Care: specialty materials for the polymers industry

Bosco Healthcare

Bosco Healthcare, in turn, consisted of three divisions: Consumer Care, Animal Care, and "Specialty Care" (pharmaceuticals) (Exhibit 3).

Consumer Care ranked among the largest marketers of OTC medications and nutritional supplements in the world. In January 2005, its acquisition of Winthrough Consumer Care placed Bosco among the top-three OTC consumer-health organizations in the world; it had a presence in more than 100 countries. Bosco Consumer Care operated in North America, Europe, Latin America, and Asia/Pacific. Some of its most recognized global brands were for analgesics for cough and cold, gastrointestinal products, dermatological/topical products, and multivitamins and dietary supplements.

Animal Care researched, developed, and marketed new products for animal health. Of the two business units—food-animal products and companion-animal products—the real growth driver was companion animals, particularly in the United States. This business had above-average profitability in the industry and, in 2006, achieved almost double-digit growth in the United States. The animal health business covered worldwide markets, including China, Vietnam, and others in Southeast Asia.

EXHIBIT 2 Organizational Structure of Bosco AG

1. Business Units include Marketing, R&D, Business Development, and Regulatory Affairs
2. Corporate Functions include Strategy, Investor Relations, Communications, Treasury, Country Coordination and Labor Relations
3. Central Functions include Finance, Human Resources, Information Technology, Manufacturing, Marketing Real-Estate and Procurement
4. Geographic Areas includes Sales and Distribution, have a shared leader between business areas and may be co-located in shared facilities

Source: Bosco Investor Presentation.

EXHIBIT 3 Organizational Structure of Bosco Healthcare

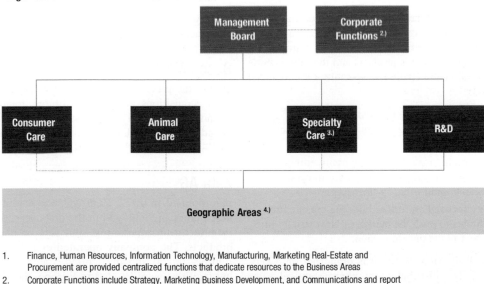

1. Finance, Human Resources, Information Technology, Manufacturing, Marketing Real-Estate and Procurement are provided centralized functions that dedicate resources to the Business Areas
2. Corporate Functions include Strategy, Marketing Business Development, and Communications and report directly to the Management Board, with a dotted line relationship to the Holding Board
3. Specialty Care includes three divisions: Hematology / Cardiology, Primary Care and Oncology
4. Geographic Areas share Management, Sales, and Distribution resources between divisions

Source: Bosco Investor Presentation.

EXHIBIT 4 Bosco-Pharma Product Portfolio

Therapeutic Area	Drug	Drug Description
Hematology/cardiology	Nabalat	Used to treat various types of angina (chest pain) and hypertension (high blood pressure).
	Ruetane	A recombinant factor VIII treatment indicated for the treatment of hemophilia.
	Tralysol	The only product approved by FDA for the prevention of perioperative blood loss and the need for blood transfusion among patients undergoing coronary-artery-bypass graft surgery.
Primary care	Flucoday	Established as the first step in diabetes therapy and reduces cardiovascular risks.
	Genitra	An ED medication that treats erectile dysfunction.
	Hypofloxacin	A prescription antibiotic effective against a broad range of bacteria. It is prescribed for prostatitis, cystitis, bacterial infections, and cancer.
	Ruetane	A recombinant factor VIII treatment indicated for the treatment of hemophilia.
Oncology	Nextvarian	Indicated for the treatment of patients with advanced renal cell carcinoma.
	Vader	Treats the symptoms of advanced prostate cancer.

Source: Bosco Investor Presentation.

TABLE 1 Distribution of Bosco Pharmaceutical Sales

Region	Europe, Middle East, Africa	North America	Latin America	Asia/Pacific
Sales % of total	50%	25%	10%	15%
Growth rates	5%	10%	20%	15%

Specialty Care (pharmaceuticals) focused on the development and marketing of ethical pharmaceuticals, with principal markets in North America, Western Europe, and Asia. A summary of Bosco's products and their therapeutic applications is shown in Exhibit 4. Specialty Care included three divisions:

1. Hematology/cardiology focused on the start of Phase II/Phase III of the formulation of long-acting Kogenate FS.
2. Primary care focused its R&D on maintaining current sales levels for key products, life-cycle management, and further in-licensing.
3. Oncology focused on further building outside the United States to push the launch of Nextvarian—the key product in the oncology area.

Within each division, Bosco was organized on a geographic basis. The distribution of pharmaceutical sales across global regions is shown in Table 1.

Within each region, marketing and distribution (sales) was organized on a country basis. The country's general manager reported to the region as a profit center. Each country was responsible for deciding which set of Bosco pharmaceuticals to promote.

Bosco M&A History

During the previous three years, Bosco made more than eight acquisitions and 11 divestitures, totaling revenues of more than EUR17.5 billion, including the successful integration of the EUR7 billion ACS acquisition and the EUR4.2 billion Winthrough OTC business in 2004.

Zeta AG

Incorporated in 1872, Zeta AG was a global research-based company engaged in the discovery, development, manufacturing, marketing, and sale of pharmaceutical products. The company operated eight R&D centers in Europe, Japan, and the United States. Its manufacturing facilities were located in Europe, the United States, Latin America, and Asia, and marketed and sold in more than 100 countries; Zeta had acquired 11 companies since 2004. Exhibit 5 shows Zeta's organizational structure.

EXHIBIT 5 Zeta's Organizational Structure

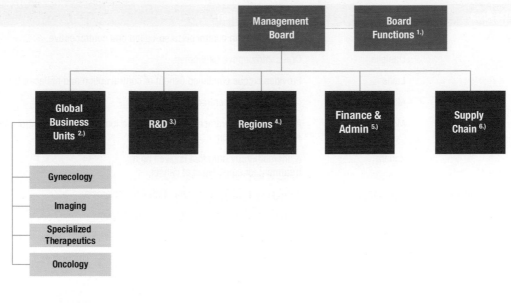

1. Board Functions include Communications, Corporate Marketing, Investor Relations, Labor Relations, Corporate Strategy and Crisis Management
2. Global Business Units include Strategy, Business Development, and Brand Management
3. R&D includes Research, Discovery, Development and Regulatory Affairs
4. Regions include Sales, Marketing and Distribution
5. Finance and Admin includes Planning, Reporting, Accounting, Controlling, Treasury, Accounts Payable, Accounts Receivables, Procurement and Information Technology
6. Supply Chain includes Manufacturing and Product Supply

Source: Bosco Investor Presentation.

Zeta concentrated its R&D and sales in four core business areas. Each business unit was responsible for sales and profits on a worldwide basis.

1. Gynecology and andrology (EUR2 billion sales in 2006, mostly in female contraception and menopause management)
2. Diagnostic imaging (EUR1.5 billion, primarily in X-ray media)
3. Specialized therapeutics (EUR1.2 billion, mostly in central nervous systems)
4. Oncology (EUR400 million, split between hematology and solid tumors)

Approximately 38% of Zeta's 2006 sales came from four key products: Alphaferon, sold in the United States and Canada under the Alphaseron trademark (16% of net sales); Danielle (11%); Angevit (6%); and U-vit (5%).

A list of Zeta's major products and therapeutic applications is shown in Exhibit 6. The global distribution of Zeta sales is shown in Table 2.

Deal Highlights

Bosco planned to merge Zeta into the Bosco Healthcare unit, whose name would be changed to Bosco-Zeta Pharma (BZP). Anticipated sales of this new unit were expected to be more than EUR9 billion, with increased total Healthcare division sales expected to reach EUR15 billion. The deal would allow Bosco to expand its footprint in the faster-growing specialty care business and reduce its exposure to economic cycles. The Bosco Healthcare division would become the largest Bosco subgroup (almost 50% of the overall portfolio).

At a total value of EUR16 billion, this was Bosco's largest acquisition to date, representing a payout of $2.7 \times 2009E$ sales and $11.5 \times 2007E$ EBITDA. EPS would be dilutive for the first two years and accretive only by 2010. The deal was going to be financed through a mix of equity, term debt, and hybrid securities. Bosco would dispose of two noncore units from its other divisions to finance the deal in addition to approximately EUR7.6 billion in debt through Switzbank and Townbank. The rest was expected to come from EUR3 billion in marketable securities with Bosco.

EXHIBIT 6 Zeta Product Portfolio in 2006

Therapeutic Area	Drug	Drug Description
Gynecology	Belaniane	A hormonal birth control pill, a so-called oral contraceptive.
	Danielle	Oral contraceptive for women.
	Laine	Provides unique combined benefit of contraception and antiacne treatment.
	Macrogynine	A combined oral contraceptive pill.
	Meerina	An intrauterine contraception that offers a long- term birth control option without sterilization.
Oncology	Zodara	A chemotherapy drug that is given as a treatment for some types of cancer.
Specialized therapeutics	Alphaferon	A drug provided for treatment of multiple sclerosis.
Diagnostic imaging	U-vit	A nonionic iodinated radiological contrast agent.
	Angevit	A contrast agent used in magnetic resonance imaging (MRI).
	Ropamairion	An X-ray contrast agent.

Source: Bosco Investor Presentation.

TABLE 2 Distribution of Zeta Pharmaceutical Sales

Region	Europe	United States	Japan	Latin America/ Canada	Asia Pacific
Sales % of total	45%	25%	15%	20%	5%
Growth rates	5%	15%	0%	15%	10%

Strategic Rationale

Boost to Health Care Business

The merger would create a global health care company that would rank among the top 12 companies in the world (Exhibit 7). The combined pharmaceuticals business would be characterized by a balanced portfolio whose oncology, cardiology/hematology, and gynecology offerings would generate above-average growth. Bosco expected that the combined size of the future company would make it more attractive as a partner for in-licensing activities in pharmaceuticals.

A key role was envisaged for the future research platform produced by combining the R&D activities of the two companies. Following the acquisition, BZP would have two projects in registration, 10 in Phase III clinical testing, 10 undergoing Phase II trials, and an additional 20 in Phase I development.[3] After the acquisition, sales from the overall life sciences would rise to approximately 70% of total Bosco sales, up from approximately 60% before the deal. In addition, Bosco now could increase the Specialty Care products share of overall pharmaceutical sales from the current level of 25% to nearly 75%, giving the company a leadership position in this highly attractive market.

The combined biotech platform was expected to be the foundation for further growth. The products in this area included Alphaseron, Zeta's top-selling drug for the treatment of multiple sclerosis, and Leukinine, used to boost a patient's immune system during cancer therapy, together with Bosco's genetically engineered Factor VIII Ruetane. These biotech products generated sales of approximately EUR2 billion.

Synergy Potential

The merger of the Bosco and Zeta pharmaceuticals businesses would include the potential for significant revenue and cost synergies. As outlined in Table 3, Bosco anticipated synergy benefits of around EUR700 million annually, starting in year three.

Specific synergy items included:

- Global headcount reduction of approximately 6,000 people (10% of combined Healthcare business)
- Leveraging the combined oncology business
- Procurement and supply-chain optimization
- Production-site rationalization
- Integration of head office and central functions

EXHIBIT 7 Top 20 Pharma Companies by Revenue in 2006

2006 Rank	Company	2006 Global Pharma Sales (in USD billions)
1	Company A	$44.0
2	Company B	$34.0
3	Company C	$32.0
4	Company D	$25.0
5	Company E	$24.0
6	Company F	$22.0
7	Company G	$22.0
8	Company H	$15.0
9	Company I	$15.0
10	Company J	$15.0
11	Company K	$14.70
12	**Bosco-Zeta Pharma**	**$14.0**
12	Company L	$14.0
13	Company M	$12.0
14	Company N	$10.0
15	Company O	$ 8.0
16	Company P	$ 8.0
17	Company Q	$ 7.0
18	**Bosco**	**$ 7.0**
19	Company R	$ 7.0
20	**Zeta AG**	**$ 6.0**

Source: Bosco Investor Presentation

TABLE 3 Sources of Synergy (in EUR millions)

		Year 1	Year 2	Year 3
Synergies:	% of total	250	450	700
• Procurement/manufacturing	10%–15%			
• Marketing and sales	20%–25%			
• R&D, approximately	25%–30%			
• General and administrative, approximately	25%–40%			
One-time costs		(500)	(500)	—
Net synergies		(250)	(50)	700

Source: Bosco Investor Presentation.

- Rationalization of country platforms and commercial infrastructures
- Optimization of R&D activities

Units to Be Divested

Bosco planned to sell two subsidiaries of Bosco Material Science by the end of 2007 to finance the merger and narrow its strategic focus. The subsidiaries were deemed unfit for the core business of Bosco Material Science, which in the future would focus on expanding technology and market leadership in polycarbonate and isocyanate chemistries. The divestitures of these two units would reduce headcount by 4,400 and revenues by EUR1.25 billion.

Organization of Bosco-Zeta Pharma

The new BZP organization was to be based primarily on the existing structure of Bosco Healthcare. The goal was to integrate Zeta functions into the respective "like" functions or divisions in Bosco, and in this way, preserve the Bosco Holding and Bosco Healthcare reporting and management. The proposed distribution of the Zeta Group into the Bosco organization is depicted in Exhibit 8.

The Challenge Ahead

The German takeover code and corporate laws could potentially affect the timing, tone, and sequencing of certain integration activities. German takeover law allowed all shareholders, regardless of the percentage of shares owned, to hold up the close of a merger, pending a lengthy court review and could prevent synergy attainment for as long as a year.

Markus Biennel was aware that due diligence on the transaction was inadequate and that developing a new operating model would be crucial. His thoughts turned into questions: "Should I manage BZP as a regional organization with country managers in control of the entire portfolio of products? Or should I adopt Zeta's product structure throughout our own organization? Or, should we use a matrix structure? In what country or countries should I start the postmerger integration process?" (Exhibit 9) He wondered how the back-office functions of Bosco and Zeta would interact under the new operating model, and he asked himself: "How should I organize and staff the integration team? Have I overcommitted on synergies? What about cultural integration?" The big question, however, was whether he should integrate first and then change the culture or do it the other way around.

EXHIBIT 8 Distribution of Zeta into the Bosco Organization

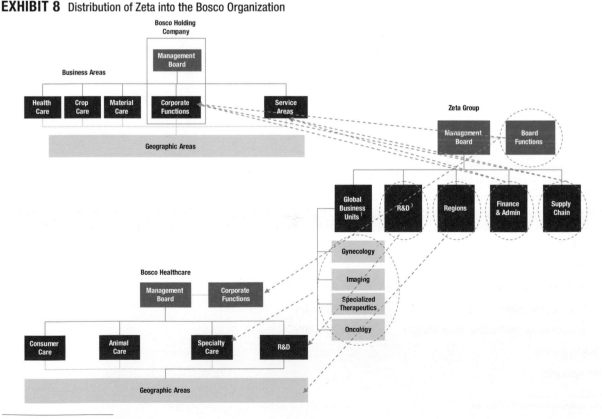

Source: Bosco Investor Presentation.

EXHIBIT 9 Country Operations Overlap

A. Countries where both firms had only marketing and distribution. (Regional designations were Bosco's; differences from Zeta's classification are noted.)

Asia/Pacific: (Bolded countries = Zeta classified as Europe)

Afghanistan	Indonesia	Palau
Bangladesh	Malaysia	Philippine Islands
Bhutan	**Maldive Islands**	Republic of Korea
Cambodia	Marshall Islands	Singapore
Dem Rep. of Korea	**Mongolia**	**Sri Lanka**
Dem Rep. of Laos	Myanmar (Burma)	Taiwan
East Timor	**Nepal**	Vanuatu
Guam	New Zealand	Vietnam
India	**Pakistan**	

EMEA: (EMEA = Europe, Middle East & Africa. Zeta classified all of these as "Europe" except for French Polynesia, which Zeta allocated to Asia/Pacific.)

Albania	Israel	Sao Tome and Principe
Algeria	Italy	Saudi Arabia
Arab Republic	Jordan	Senegal
Bahrain	Kazakhstan	Serbia and Montenegro
Belarus	Kenya	Seychelles
Botswana	Kirgiziya	Sierra Leone
Burundi	Kuwait	Slovakia
Cameroon	Latvia	Slovenia
Canary Islands	Lebanon	Somali
Central African Republic	Lesotho	South Africa
Chad	Liberia	Ssian Federation
Comoro Islands	Libyan Arab	Sweden
Cote D'Ivoire	Jamahiriya	Switzerland
Croatia	Liechtenstein	Syria
Cyprus	Lithuania	Tadzhikistan
Czech Republic	Madagascar	Tangier
Dem Republic of the Congo	Malawi	Tunisia
Denmark	Mali	Turkey

EMEA: (EMEA = Europe, Middle East & Africa. Zeta classified all of these as "Europe" except for French Polynesia, which Zeta allocated to Asia/Pacific.)

Denmark	Mali	Turkey
Egypt	Malta	Turkmenistan
Estonia	Monaco	Uganda
Ethiopia	Mozambique	Ukraine
Faeroe Islands	Namibia	United Arab Emirates
Finland	Netherlands	United Kingdom
French Polynesia	Niger	United Rep. of Tanzania
Georgia	Norway	Uzbekistan
Ghana	Oman	Vatican City
Gibraltar	P. Armenia	West Bank (including Jerusalem)
Greenland	Palestinian Authority	Yemen

(continued)

EXHIBIT 9 Country Operations Overlap (*continued*)

EMEA: (EMEA = Europe, Middle East & Africa. Zeta classified all of these as "Europe" except for French Polynesia, which Zeta allocated to Asia/Pacific.)		
Iceland	Poland	Zambia
Iraq	Qatar	Zimbabwe
Ireland	Republic of the Congo	
Islamic Republic of Iran	San Marino	

Japan		
Latin America: (Zeta classified these as Latin America and Canada)		
Antigua and Barbuda Islands	Cuba	Nicaragua
Argentina	Dominican Republic	Paraguay
Aruba	Ecuador	Peru
Bolivia	El Salvador	Uruguay
Chile	Guatemala	Venezuela
Colombia	Haiti	

North America
Canada (Zeta = Latin America and Canada)
Puerto Rico (Zeta = United States)

B. Countries where either firm had additional facilities (in addition to marketing and distribution):

Region	Country	Bosco Operations	Zeta Operations
Asia/Pacific	Australia	Manufacturing	—
	Hong Kong	—	Manufacturing
	China	Manufacturing	—
EMEA	Belgium	—	Manufacturing
	France	R&D	Manufacturing
	Germany	R&D, manufacturing	R&D, manufacturing
	Hungary	R&D	—
	Portugal	Manufacturing	—
	Spain	R&D	Manufacturing
Latin America	Brazil	R&D, manufacturing	Manufacturing
	Mexico	Manufacturing	—
North America	USA	R&D, manufacturing	Manufacturing

Source: Bosco Investor Presentation.

ENDNOTES

1. "Pharmaceuticals: Global Industry Guide," *Datamonitor*, M2 Communications Ltd., February 2008.

2. Genomics was the study of an organism's entire genome or hereditary information encoded in its DNA. Investigation of single genes, their functions, and roles had become very common in medical and biological research.

3. Clinical trials were conducted in phases. The trials at each phase have different purposes and help scientists answer different questions. In Phase I, researchers test an experimental drug or treatment for the first time in a small group of people (20–80) to evaluate its safety, determine a safe dosage range, and identify side effects. In Phase II, the experimental drug or treatment is given to a larger group of people (100–300) to see if it is effective and to further evaluate its safety. In Phase III, the experimental drug or treatment is given to large groups of people (1,000–3,000) to confirm its effectiveness, monitor side effects, compare it to commonly used treatments, and collect information that will allow the experimental drug or treatment to be used safely. In Phase IV, postmarketing studies delineate additional information, including the drug's risks, benefits, and optimal use.

CASE 21

SILENCE IS NOT GOLDEN: GOLDEN AGRI-RESOURCES, GREENPEACE AND SUSTAINABLE PALM OIL

by Professor David Grayson CBE

Between December 2009 and September 2010, the Singapore listed palm oil company, Golden Agri-Resources (GAR), lost a string of high-profile multinational customers such as Nestlé, Unilever, Burger King, and Carrefour supermarkets; it was suspended from the multi-stakeholder partnership, The Round-table on Sustainable Palm Oil (RSPO);[1] and it was the subject of critical media stories around the world for alleged complicity in the destruction of the rainforests.[2,3] This was all the result of a carefully orchestrated campaign by the international NGO Greenpeace International.[4] The successful campaign against GAR was part of a much wider Greenpeace programme on palm oil which inter alia also saw the NGO produce a spoof Kit-Kat advert for the Nestlé chocolate brand, which was widely viewed on YouTube;[5] a consumer campaign to encourage the Unilever-owned DOVE soap brand to change their supplier of palm oil;[6] and the occupation of the Unilever corporate HQ with activists dressed as Orang-utans.[7]

Greenpeace focused heavily on Indonesia because Indonesia is now one of the world's largest carbon emitters (third behind the US and China) as a result of peat lands being burnt and deforestation. In the past decade land under cultivation for palm oil in Indonesia doubled to almost 8 million hectares, four times the size of Wales. Much of that used to be virgin rainforest, mainly in Borneo and Sumatra. It's the same story in neighbouring Malaysia, which, together with Indonesia, accounts for nearly 90 percent of total palm-oil production. The Indonesian government wants to double the size of the palm oil industry by 2020. Greenpeace alleged that GAR was burning forest for land clearance, clearing forests without environmental impact assessments, developing land for plantation without legal authority, illegally planting on peat, planting on high conservation lands, driving the orang-utan to extinction, having oppressive relations with local peoples, and misrepresenting GAR's involvement with sustainable palm-oil initiatives through selective memberships of RSPO.[8]

GAR is a publicly quoted company registered on the Singapore Stock Exchange but with 49.6 percent of the shares held by the Widjaja Family. GAR is part of the Sinar Mas Group, along with Asian Pulp and Paper. GAR is the world's second largest palm oil plantation owner (427,000 hectares of plantations), and it is Indonesia's largest producer of palm oil. It has a market capitalisation of US$7.5 billion as at 31 December 2010. Palm oil is used widely in cooking oil, margarine and fats, healthcare/cosmetics, and some bio-diesel. GAR is seen as playing a significant role in Indonesia's economic development, providing jobs, tax revenues and contributing to the economic development of less developed parts of the country. In 2010, palm oil accounted for $16 billion in exports, or about 8 percent of Indonesia's trade, and 4.5 million jobs. It is also meeting a critical need for food production. (The availability of foodstuffs and cooking products at affordable prices is a key concern of the Indonesian authorities—particularly given the food riots which have swept many countries in recent years.) Mahendra Siregar, Indonesia's vice-minister of trade, said: "Our obligation is to cut the number of poor. By addressing poverty you address practices that create unnecessary carbon emissions."[9] Indonesia's palm oil boom has led to companies buying up swathes of land from the Congo to Brazil in the hope of cashing in on the market.

Confronted with the Greenpeace campaign and its consequent loss of business and reputation, what should GAR do? Imagine you are called in as an adviser to the Chairman and Chief Executive Officer, Franky Oesman Widjaja, in autumn 2010. What would you recommend GAR to do? Give your recommendations and justification for your recommendations.

ENDNOTES

1. The Round-table on Sustainable Palm Oil (RSPO) was formed in 2004 with the objective of promoting the growth and use of sustainable oil palm products through credible global standards and engagement of stakeholders: www.rspo.org. Just a tenth of the world's palm oil is sustainable. RSPO is an example of a multi-stakeholder initiative. These are non-profit distributing organizations concerned with corporate responsibility in which businesses are involved but are not predominant in membership, funding and/or governance and accountability.

2. http://www.bbc.co.uk/news/world-asia-pacific-10798849

3. http://www.prweek.com/uk/news/992445/Taking-Action---Greenpeace-vs-Nestle

4. http://www.greenpeace.org/international/en/campaigns/forests/asia-pacific/

5. http://www.youtube.com/watch?v=1BCA8dQfGi0

6. http://www.greenpeace.org.uk/blog/forests/dove-leads-the-onslaught-er-20080421

7. http://www.greenpeace.org/usa/Global/usa/report/2010/2/how-unilever-palm-oil-supplier.pdf

8. For further information on the Greenpeace Sustainable Palm Oil campaign, see www.greenpeace.org/international/Global/international/publications/forests/2012/Indonesia/PalmOilScorecard.pdf. See also: Lessons from the palm oil showdown, Guardian Sustainable Business Blog October 27 2010 www.guardian.co.uk/sustainable-business/palm-oil-greenpeace-social-media

9. Sunday Times Business News, August 21 2011.

APPENDICES
INDONESIA IN 2010 FACT-SHEET

Free and fair legislative elections took place in 1999 after decades of repressive rule. Indonesia is now the world's third most populous democracy, the world's largest archipelagic state, and home to the world's largest Muslim population. Current issues include: alleviating poverty, improving education, preventing terrorism, consolidating democracy after four decades of authoritarianism, implementing economic and financial reforms, stemming corruption, holding the military and police accountable for human rights violations, addressing climate change, and controlling infectious diseases, particularly those of global and regional importance.

2010 economic growth returned to 6%

Indonesia still struggles with poverty and unemployment, in adequate infrastructure, corruption, a complex regulatory environment, and unequal resource distribution among regions.

In late 2010, increasing inflation, driven by higher and volatile food prices, posed an increasing challenge to economic policy makers and threatened to push millions of the near-poor below the poverty line.

The government in 2011 faced the on-going challenge of improving Indonesia's infrastructure to remove impediments to growth, while addressing climate change concerns, particularly with regard to conserving Indonesia's forests and peatlands, the focus of a potentially trailblazing $1 billion REDD+ pilot project.

GDP per capita (PPP): $ 4,200 (2010 est.)

GDP per sector:

>   agriculture: 15.3%

>   industry: 47%

>   services: 37.6 % (2010 est.)

Workforce: 116.5 million (2010 est.)

Unemployment: 7.1% (2010 est.)

Population: 245,613,043 (July 2011 est.)—4th largest in world

Median age: 28.2 years

Population below poverty line 13.33% (2010)

Source: CIA World FactBook.

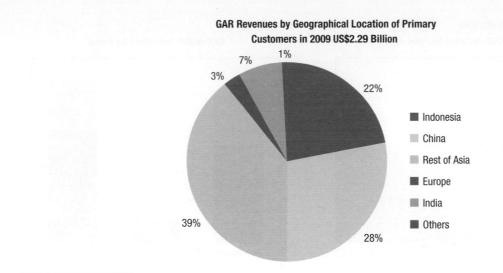

GAR Revenues by Geographical Location of Primary Customers in 2009 US$2.29 Billion

- 22% Indonesia
- 1%
- 7%
- 3%
- 39%
- 28%

Legend:
- Indonesia
- China
- Rest of Asia
- Europe
- India
- Others

Source: GAR Annual Report page 65

NB: GAR mostly sells to brokers/traders and this slide indicates where they are based—not necessarily the product end-users.

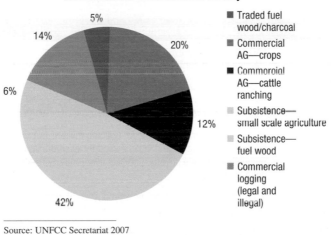

The Main Causes of Deforestation Globally

- 5%
- 14%
- 20%
- 6%
- 12%
- 42%

Legend:
- Traded fuel wood/charcoal
- Commercial AG—crops
- Commercial AG—cattle ranching
- Subsistence—small scale agriculture
- Subsistence—fuel wood
- Commercial logging (legal and illegal)

Source: UNFCC Secretariat 2007

Causes of deforestation in Indonesia

Indonesia has a total land mass of 187.75 million square hectares of which 133.6 million is classified as various forms of forest

No	Types of land and forest	Hectares in Sq Millions	% of total landmass
1.	Land for settlements farming and "other purposes" Legally designated Forest lands	54.09	29
2.	Convertible or degraded forest with some HCV and peat	22.79	12
3.	Permanent production forest with some HCV and peat	36.64	19
4.	Limited production forest with some HCV and peat	22.50	12
5.	Protected forest mainly primary with peat	31.60	17
6.	Natural/conservation forest mainly primary with peat	19.90	11
7.	Hunting Parks	0.23	0
	TOTALS	**187.75**	**100**

Source: The Ministry of Forestry, 2008, Statistic of Forestry 2008, and The Ministry of Agriculture, 2008

The Palm Oil Industry in Indonesia

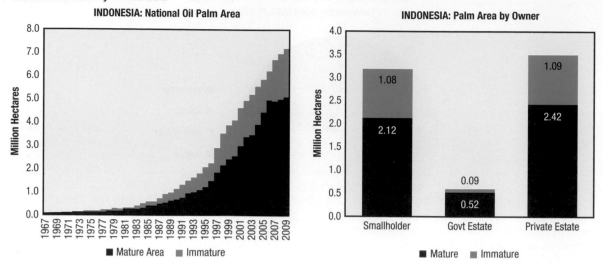

Source: Indonesian Palm Oil Commission (IPOC), Directorate General of Estate Crops, 2009

Greenpeace/NGO Claim	Palm Oil Industry Response
Palm oil is the leading cause for deforestation citing a UNEP report	FAO statistics disprove this myth with bulk of land clearing attributed to poverty—the poor clearing forests for food, shelter, and fuel as well as roads and buildings.
Palm oil endangers the Orang-utan	Poverty and human settlement are far bigger threats. Palm oil was not even identified as a threat to Bornean Orang-utans in the Great Ape Survival Project, i.e. prior to the anti-palm oil campaign. The rebuilding efforts post-Tsunami had a greater impact on Orang-utan habitats.
Palm oil harms the poor and indigenous forest dwellers	Palm oil has been responsible for uplifting millions out of poverty and providing access to education, healthcare and income security. Even the World Bank rated it as the leading means to eradicate poverty. Conflicts over property rights do occur but are not unique to the palm oil industry.
Palm oil is unsustainable	Palm oil is proven to be the most productive of vegetable oils in terms of energy generation/consumption ratio, land yield, and yield over lifecycle.
Indonesia has the highest deforestation	FAO statistics reveal an opposite picture.
Palm oil releases more carbon emissions than burning fossil fuels if deforestation and peat	The IFPR study of EU Biofuels mandate has found that *"even if peat land emissions are considered, palm oil is the most efficient feedstock."*
20 years from now, there could be little or no forest cover left in Malaysia and Indonesia.	Malaysia has 55% of land under forest cover and has pledged not to clear more primary forests. Similarly, Indonesia has designated 60% of land as forests, including primary and production forests.

Source: World Growth, *http://www.worldgrowth.org/*

For a statement of the philosophy of the NGO *World growth,* see: *http://worldgrowth.org/who-we-are/our-philosophy/*

CASE 22

GOING FLAT: PURSUIT OF A DEMOCRATIC ORGANIZATIONAL STRUCTURE

Bella Wilfer graduated from the Darden Graduate School of Business Administration in 2010, ready to become a principled leader in the world of practical affairs. Wilfer had pursued the consulting track while at Darden and had spent her summer internship at a large, prestigious, management consulting firm. After being offered a full-time job and deciding that her summer employer was not a good fit, Wilfer had taken time in the fall of her second year to explore other options for full-time employment after graduation before accepting her offer.

In her off-grounds search, Wilfer had found Ethical Business Company (EBC) through an alumni connection and was instantly intrigued. Not only did the company consult on many of the ethical issues that were important to Wilfer, it also had a flat organizational structure. When she compared it with the other large, hierarchical organizations, she decided she would have a greater impact earlier in her career and more control over it at EBC. Although it was a riskier choice than going with a larger and more established firm, Wilfer was excited about being able to use her skills in direct interaction with clients and senior executives, rather than having them hidden beneath multiple layers of hierarchy. After long consideration, she turned down the offer from her summer employer and signed with EBC.

Company History

John Harmon, the CEO of EBC, had earned a BA in philosophy from Duke in 1986 and his MA in philosophy from Columbia in 1988. He had subsequently graduated from Yale Law School in 1991 and accepted a position at a Boston law firm. After less than a year at the firm, Harmon decided to start his own company. He wanted to help companies prevent the ethical problems that led to lawsuits, rather than having to deal with them after the fact. His firm offered training and a series of workshops to engage and educate employees on ethical issues as well as advisory services related to corporate ethics.

In 2001 and 2002, the scandals at Enron and WorldCom rocked the corporate world. The surge of interest in corporate ethics that resulted created a boom in business for EBC, particularly in advisory services, and the company's

visibility increased when Harmon was interviewed for several articles on corporate ethics. By EBC's 15th anniversary, it had grown to 400 employees in four global offices and included a number of notable *Fortune* 500 companies in its client base. There were only a few small firms that dealt specifically with ethics issues, but EBC still faced competition from larger management consulting firms whose competencies included organizational behavior and change.

Then in 2008, Harmon published *Flat: A New Business Operating System*, a manifesto on the need for change in the business community to more effectively inspire principled performance. Harmon tapped into growing trends toward decentralized organizational structures inspired by an increasingly globalized and interconnected world. Companies such as Semco and Google had been successful by eliminating organizational layers, and hierarchy was declining in companies across industries. Shortly after its publication, Harmon's book was in the top 100 books bought from Amazon.com and one of the top 20 books on business and investing.

In 2009, EBC acquired a 30-person boutique consulting firm called Rokesmith and Handford, LLC, that specialized in addressing human rights issues. The same year, Harmon began restructuring the combined company based on the principles outlined in his book.

Philosophy

Harmon envisioned a business that operated as a democracy, characterized by flat governance, open communication, shared leadership, and radical transparency. In his own company, he had a specific plan to implement this vision. The existing leadership structure of the CEO and several vice presidents would become an executive committee that was aided in its decision making by four committees democratically elected by all personnel. Employees throughout the company would be encouraged to think about their roles differently. Rather than organizing the company hierarchically with titles that reflected seniority, employees would be categorized by work area. Specifically, they would be grouped into three categories of responsibility: "Support," "Seek," and "See."

EBC would make other changes to solidify the new organizational structure and get employees thinking in the new mindset. The company would move into a new office space designed to reflect the flatter organizational structure. Offices for senior-level managers would be replaced by cubicles for all levels of employees and shared office space. Performance reviews that had been based primarily on individual metrics would be replaced by more collective division and company goals.

The Office

The highlight of Wilfer's first day at ECB was her office. Harmon had designed every detail, down to the furniture and wall décor, and loved to give tours to anyone who visited the office. Harmon was clearly very passionate about his work. He struck Wilfer as a cross between a politician and a motivational speaker.

The space into which EBC had moved earlier that year was a physical representation of the flatness and transparency of the company. The office was very open and full of natural light, with a beautiful view overlooking Boston Common. The internal walls were all glass, allowing its occupants to enjoy the light and the view from anywhere in the spacious office. The cubicle walls were low and made of glass, so Wilfer could see clear across the office from where she sat. There were no closed doors, and the space conveyed openness and accessibility. Throughout the office were a variety of shared meeting spaces, all with state-of-the-art technology, as well as movable walls to allow for different types of collaboration.

In each cubicle and meeting space was a copy of the Leadership Charter, a diagram of the traits of a successful leader taken from Harmon's book. The charter not only reinforced the company's values but also supported the idea that everyone in the company was a leader. The meeting spaces were named after such core company values as integrity and trust. Even the artwork reflected the company's vision with depictions of famous philosophers and their notable quotes. Wilfer did not think any of her fellow b-school graduates walked past pictures of Confucius, Gandhi, and Adam Smith on a daily basis.

Settling In

In her first week, Wilfer went through training with four other new employees. Many names were mentioned during the training, and one of Wilfer's fellow hires had asked to see an organizational chart in order to put names with faces. The response: There was no organizational chart because EBC was a flat company. As Wilfer was introduced to new people, she found it confusing not to know where they fit in the company hierarchy. Who were her colleagues? Who would she be managing? Who would be managing her? As part of adjusting to the company culture, she figured she would have to get over her impulse to categorize people hierarchically.

By noon on her second day, Wilfer had been given her laptop and her e-mail had been set up, so she read her first messages. One e-mail introduced five new employees with a brief paragraph about each of their backgrounds. She glanced through the e-mail and noticed that she was not referred to as an associate but as a person who operated with a "Support mindset." She looked at the two other employees hired right out of b-school. One was also listed as "Support," but the other was listed as "See."

During a break in afternoon training, Wilfer asked her cohort what was meant by a mindset. One person had mentioned that "Seek" referred to more senior people who were involved in engaging new clients, "See" referred to those people who were working to find solutions for those clients, and "Support" referred to people who were involved in activities such as HR that enabled other employees. Someone else asked about the categories and got these responses: "See" stood for the more senior people who set company vision and strategy, "Support" stood for people who supported that vision in their daily work with clients, and "Seek" stood for HR because it sought out new talent. But when Wilfer asked another employee to clarify further, he merely shrugged and said the definitions were not firm.

At the end of her second day, Wilfer looked through a stack of papers from that day's training and found a to-do list for new hires. Working her way down the list, she looked for something quick she could finish before she left. Because ordering business cards seemed straightforward, she went to the website and began filling out the form until she came to the place for her title. She was stuck. Should she put associate? Could she hand a client a business card that said "Support mindset"? Since EBC had done away with titles, what other option did she have? With a sigh, she realized she would have to ask someone, although she didn't know who.

Coffee Chat

As she walked to work on Monday morning, her second week of work, Wilfer was excited to be done with training and ready for her first project. She was assigned to help a major electric utility conduct an assessment of its internal transparency and recommend ways to improve communication across the company. At least on the project, it was clear who the manager was. After chatting with her teammates, she was able to figure out who had MBAs versus who had college degrees and how long everyone had been at the company. Wilfer was more comfortable once she had worked out the seniority on her own.

On Tuesday morning, the project manager asked Wilfer to put some survey results into PowerPoint by the end of the day. Looking at her schedule, Wilfer thought she would have plenty of time to complete the task and agreed to do it. The only thing she had on her calendar in the afternoon was a coffee chat with John Harmon. She had scheduled an hour and a half for that, and she assumed it was a social meet and greet to give everyone a chance to talk informally with the CEO. She had hoped to be able to talk more to the charismatic leader of the company.

As an Outlook reminder popped up on her screen to remind her of the coffee chat, she was surprised when everyone started moving toward the lobby. When she made a comment about this to a colleague named Eugene Wrayburn, he said, "Oh, coffee chats are mandatory." Wilfer found this odd but was still looking forward to it. When she reached the crowded lobby, she was surprised when John Harmon began addressing the entire group. Harmon announced that he was aware of the concerns regarding his recent post on his business blog and launched into a speech.

Wilfer was confused as to what this was all about, but she began to understand as she listened to Harmon's speech and was helped by a few whispered comments from Wrayburn. Harmon's blog post had focused on EBC's journey to becoming a flat organization. In the article, he had referenced the company's four democratically elected committees. In reality, the committees had not been elected democratically: Following an initial nomination process for committee members that was open to all employees, Harmon had added more criteria for nomination including number of years at the company and alignment with EBC values. This change in the process effectively narrowed the pool of nominees to members of the senior leadership who had managed the company before its restructuring.

One specific grievance concerned an employee named Jenny Wren. Wren had been nominated by a number of people for the employee excellence committee, which handled EBC's HR functions. Before coming to work at EBC, Wren had spent several years as a human capital consultant. For this reason, her co-workers thought she would be a valuable asset to the committee. But Wren had only a college degree and just two years of work experience at EBC, so her name was removed from the ballot before the election. Many employees believed this action was contrary to the idea of democratic governance. Wilfer agreed.

The larger issue, however, was not the election itself, but how Harmon had portrayed it publicly. Given that one of EBC's service offerings was implementing organizational change, employees thought it was misleading to gloss over the company's own implementation process. Employees argued that although most companies might not be so open and transparent about their internal struggles, EBC was not most companies. EBC claimed to hold itself to a higher standard. Harmon apologized for the article, saying it was an error in wording that should have been caught before publication. He also stated that the elections were part of an ongoing process on EBC's journey toward democratic leadership.

Wilfer left the coffee break concerned about the election and the blog and disappointed in Harmon's response. When she got back to her desk, she was shocked to see that the coffee break had taken two hours. As she scrambled to finish her work before the end of the day, she kept thinking about the coffee break. Her concern was not only about the content of the meeting, but also how many working hours across the organization had been devoted to it.

Leadership Charter

As the week continued, Wilfer was preoccupied with getting up to speed on her project, which had already started. Later in the week, she headed to a conference room for a team meeting. When she arrived, she learned that the project manager was running late and the other recent MBA grad would be calling in from another location. For the moment, she was accompanied only by the more junior employees or, as they called themselves, "the employees formerly known as analysts." While they waited, she became distracted by the conversation going on around her.

The conversation was about the Leadership Charter that took up a large part of one wall of the conference room. The "analysts" were making jokes about the language in the charter, which contrasted the traits of a poor leader with those of a good leader. One example was, "Watches the clock" versus "Time has no meaning," which prompted one person to remark about working in the Twilight Zone, and someone else to comment that some part describing the trait did not even make grammatical sense. Another pairing, "Stops at the minimum" versus "Never stops" had inspired one employee to sketch on the board an Energizer Bunny leading lemmings off a cliff.

Wilfer was not sure how to react. Although she agreed that some of the language in the Leadership Charter was over the top, she felt uncomfortable openly mocking the core principles of the company. But she did not want to say anything because she did not think it was her job to try and instill respect for the charter in her fellow employees. That raised the question of whose job it was, but before she had time to think about that, she saw the project manager heading toward the conference room. The sketch had disappeared, and everyone had their laptops up and ready by the time the manager arrived.

Passion

At the end of the meeting, the project manager asked Wilfer to book a conference room for three hours on the following Monday. Wilfer pulled up Outlook immediately to book the room, but she was not yet familiar with the names and capacities of all of the rooms, so Eugene Wrayburn stayed to help. As she studied the meeting planner, Wilfer realized it was going to be hard to find a room available for three hours. Almost all of those with enough room for their entire team did not show any three-hour gaps. Only the "Passion" room looked available.

"Looks like we can't schedule it on Monday," Wrayburn said. When Wilfer responded that Passion was open, Wrayburn said, "Passion is never available." Not sure what to make of his comment, Wilfer booked Passion for a three-hour block on Monday. Then, heeding Wrayburn's warning, she also booked the "Trust" room for Tuesday just in case. Immediately, she received two automated responses: One confirmed "Trust" for Tuesday, and the other notified her that "Passion" was unavailable. "What's up with 'Passion'?," Wilfer asked.

Wrayburn responded that it was Harmon's office. But Wilfer already thought she knew from the tour where Harmon's cubicle was. Wrayburn explained that, although Harmon had a cubicle, everyone knew that the "Passion" conference room, located directly behind his cubicle, was reserved for his use at all times. Wrayburn said that, in addition to the conference table, it even had a large desk and with pictures of Harmon's family. Wilfer did not have any problem with Harmon having an office like other CEOs did. She just thought it weird that he pretended not to have one. The situation reminded her of a quote in George Orwell's *Animal Farm* in which the animals' new society was created on the principle that "all animals are equal," before the pigs added, "but some animals are more equal than others."

Town Hall Meeting

By Friday, Wilfer was frustrated. She noticed an hour blocked off on her calendar for a town hall meeting in the afternoon. She had other meetings scheduled for client work and other internal projects and was worried about finding time to get it all done. When she asked Wrayburn what a town hall meeting was, he replied that it was a forum for Harmon to respond to employee concerns. "How is it different from a coffee chat?" Wilfer asked. "It isn't," he replied.

The concerns raised at the town hall meeting had to do with the division that had been Rokesmith and Handford, LLC, before its acquisition the previous year. The complaints were focused on goals and hiring. Earlier in the week, Harmon had announced the goals for EBC's upcoming fiscal year, and he had said that no one would be eligible for a bonus unless his or her division met its goal. Overall, the company's goal was to grow by 10 percent. But that growth was very unevenly distributed. The division that had been Rokesmith and Handford was required to double that growth, whereas the rest of the company's requirement was less than 2 percent. The employees of the Rokesmith and Handford division wanted an explanation as to why their growth targets were so much higher, particularly given that the division was not scheduled for a proportionally high staff increase.

In addition, all employees were concerned that it was taking too long to hire new staff. Wilfer had been hired before the council structure had been implemented. Since that time, the hiring process had slowed, and it was now taking more than six months to get people on board. The company had three positions still unfilled since January, and it was now July. Several people had interviewed for each position, and the employee excellence committee had repeatedly said it was in the final stages of the hiring process but gave no further details.

Harmon responded with metaphorical answers to employees' straightforward operational questions. When asked how goals were determined, Harmon talked about the vision of a horizontal organization and then explained how the root of "horizontal" was the word "horizon." He claimed that the horizon was as far as the eye could see and indicated unlimited, unknown possibilities. As Harmon orated, Wilfer realized he was not going to answer the question, and she noticed most of her colleagues in the room had tuned him out.

The Exodus

On Thursday of her third week, Wilfer once again headed to the lobby for an "all hands" meeting. This time, Wilfer was expecting more employee complaints, so she was not prepared for what happened. At the front of the lobby with Harmon were four of the most senior employees at the company. Then, one at a time, all four announced that they were leaving and gave their reasons for departure: "I'm taking some time off to travel," "I've never stayed with any company longer than five years and feel it's time to move on," "After so many years as a consultant, I need to work in industry to gain experience in implementation," and "I'd like to spend more time with my family." The reasons were transparent, and the overall message was clear: Four high-level people were jumping ship.

That afternoon, employees in the Rokesmith and Handford division worried about how they were going to meet their aggressive targets without two of their senior leaders. Everyone worried about how long it was going to take to replace four senior-level people, given the existing hiring backlog. There was speculation as to why the employees were really leaving and worry that qualified people would not want to work at EBC for the same reasons. Some said it was because the flatter organizational structure involved a flatter compensation plan, which was no longer competitive in the industry. Others added that, because collective goals had replaced individual metrics, the bonus plan was also not competitive. And some even said that Harmon was forcing out anyone who did not buy into the restructuring and the ideas in his manifesto.

The next day, Wilfer sat in a meeting with all the project managers, those who represented the next layer of management under the four people who had announced their departures. These managers were worried about how the company was going to attract the new clients necessary for them to meet their performance goals. Everyone contributed to the list of what needed to be done, but no one offered to do anything. Wilfer was surprised that in a room of people with MBAs and years of experience at the firm, most of them concentrated on the problems instead of the solutions. Top people had just stepped down, but no one stepped up. She had thought the problem was that Harmon was not ready to let go of the reins, but maybe the problem was that no one was ready to pick them up. After years of being insulated within a hierarchy, her co-workers were not going to stick their necks out and take on a bigger role in managing the company.

The Dilemma

Wilfer reflected on everything that had happened during her three weeks at EBC. She agreed with the idea of a flat, democratic organization, but now she was not sure just how to achieve it. She wondered if a flat structure was right for all companies and all employees or if there were certain companies and people who fit better in the hierarchy more than others. She tried to decide what she would have done differently if she had been John Harmon. Most of all, Wilfer worried about what she should do about her current situation at EBC.

CASE 23

PIXAR*

On the morning of January 10, 2013, everyone at Pixar Animated Studios was pleased to find that *Brave* had received an Academy Award nomination for best animated feature. After a continuous string of critically acclaimed films running through *Toy Story, Finding Nemo, Ratatouille, Wall-E,* and *Up,* the studio had failed to obtain a single nomination for *Cars 2.* This was a great setback for Pixar, which had already claimed five trophies, more than any other studio, since the category was added in 2001.

Although *Cars 2* made about $560 million in theaters worldwide, matching the success of many of the studio's other hits, the film did not win the critical acclaim that has been accorded to every other Pixar offering (see Exhibit 1). This led many industry observers to question whether the sequel had been developed as a result of pressure from the Walt Disney Company because of the opportunities that it would offer for sales of related merchandise. John Lasseter, Pixar's chief creative officer and the director of *Cars 2,* denied that there was any such pressure: "It's not true. It's people who don't know the facts, rushing to judge."[1]

Pixar had been acquired by Disney in 2006 for the hefty sum of $7.4 billon. The deal had been finalized by the late Steve Jobs, the Apple Computer chief executive who had also served as the head of the computer animation firm. Jobs had previously developed a deal that had allowed Disney to distribute all of Pixar's films and to split the profits. Disney CEO Bob Iger worked hard to eventually acquire Pixar, whose track record had made it one of the world's most successful animation companies.

Both Jobs and Iger had been aware, however, that they must try and protect Pixar's creative culture while they also tried to carry some of this over to Disney's animation efforts. In order to ensure this, Disney has not only allowed Pixar to operate on its own, but also assigned some of the animation studio's key talent to take over the combined activities of both Pixar and Disney. The creative team at Pixar has been trying to use elements of its lengthy process of playfully crafting a film to replace the standard production line approach that had been pursued by Disney. This contrast in culture is best reflected in the Oscars that the employees at Pixar have displayed proudly, but which have been painstakingly dressed in Barbie doll clothing.

Above all, everyone at Pixar remains committed to making films that are original in concept and execution,

---

* Case developed by Professor Jamal Shamsie, Michigan State University, with the assistance of Professor Alan B. Eisner, Pace University. Material has been drawn from published sources to be used for purposes of class discussion. Copyright © 2013 Jamal Shamsie and Alan B. Eisner.

EXHIBIT 1 Pixar Films

All of Pixar's films released to date have ended up among the top animated films of all time based on worldwide box office revenue in millions of U.S. dollars.

Rank	Title	Year	Revenue
1	*Toy Story 3*	2010	$1064
2	*Finding Nemo*	2003	$906
3	*Up*	2009	$731
4	*The Incredibles*	2005	$631
5	*Ratatouille*	2007	$624
6	*Cars 2*	2011	$560
7	*Brave*	2012	$555
8	*Monsters, Inc.*	2002	$525
9	*Wall-E*	2009	$521
10	*Toy Story 2*	1999	$485
11	*Cars*	2006	$462
12	*A Bug's Life*	1998	$363
13	*Toy Story*	1995	$362

Source: IMDb, *Variety.*

despite the risks involved. They make sequels only when they are able to come up with a compelling story that can make use of the old characters. Lasseter claims, however, that because everyone expects Pixar to stick with original films, any sequels that it makes are judged rather harshly. He compared his role as director of *Cars 2* to that of a trapeze artist with a death wish. "Not only is there no net," he said, "you're doing it over spikes with poisoned ends."[2]

Pushing for Computer Animated Films

The roots of Pixar stretch back to 1975 with the founding of a vocational school in Old Westbury, New York, called the New York Institute of Technology. It was there that Edwin E. Catmull, a straitlaced Mormon from Salt Lake City who loved animation but couldn't draw, teamed up with the people who would later form the core of Pixar. "It was artists and technologists from the very start," recalled Alvy Ray Smith, who worked with Catmull during those years. "It was like a fairy tale."[3]

By 1979, Catmull and his team decided to join forces with famous Hollywood director George W. Lucas, Jr. They were hopeful that this would allow them to pursue their dream of making animated films. As part of Lucas's filmmaking facility in San Rafael, California, Catmull's group of aspiring animators was able to make substantial progress in the art of computer animation. But the unit was not able to generate any profits, and Lucas was not willing to let it grow beyond using computer animation for special effects.

Catmull finally turned in 1985 to Jobs, who had just been ousted from Apple. Jobs was reluctant to invest in a firm that wanted to make full-length feature films using computer animation. But a year later, Jobs did decide to buy Catmull's unit for just $10 million, which represented a third of Lucas's asking price. While the newly named Pixar Animation Studios tried to push the boundaries of computer animation over the next five years, Jobs ended up having to invest an additional $50 million—more than 25 percent of his total wealth at the time. "There were times that we all despaired, but fortunately not all at the same time," said Jobs.[4]

Still, Catmull's team did continue to make substantial breakthroughs in the development of computer-generated full-length feature films (see Exhibit 2). In 1991, Disney gave Pixar a three-film contract that started with *Toy Story.* When the movie was finally released in 1995, its success surprised everyone in the film industry. Rather than the nice little film Disney had expected, *Toy Story* became the sensation of 1995. It rose to the rank of the third highest grossing animated film of all time, earning $362 million in worldwide box office revenues.

Within days, Jobs decided to take Pixar public. When the shares, priced at $22, shot past $33, Jobs called his best friend, Oracle CEO Lawrence J. Ellison, to tell him he had company in the billionaire's club. With Pixar's sudden success, Jobs returned to strike a new deal with Disney. Early in 1996, at a lunch with Walt Disney chief Michael D. Eisner, Jobs made his demands: an equal share of the profits, equal billing on merchandise and on-screen credits, and guarantees that Disney would market Pixar films as they did its own.

Boosting the Creative Component

With the success of *Toy Story,* Jobs realized that he had hit something big. He had tapped into his Silicon Valley roots and, with Catmull's team, used computers to forge a unique style of creative moviemaking. In each of their subsequent films, Pixar has continued to develop computer animation that has allowed for more lifelike backgrounds, texture, and movement than ever before. For example, because real leaves are translucent, Pixar's engineers developed special software algorithms that both reflect and absorb light, creating luminous scenes among jungles of clover.

In spite of the significance of these advancements in computer animation, Jobs was well aware that successful feature films would require a strong creative spark. He understood that it would be the marriage of technology with creativity that would allow Pixar to rise above its competition. To get that, Jobs fostered a campuslike environment within the newly formed outfit, similar to the freewheeling, charged atmosphere in the early days of his beloved Apple (where he also returned as acting CEO). "It's not simply the technology that makes Pixar," said Dick Cook, former president of Walt Disney studios.[5]

Even though Jobs did play a crucial supportive role, it is Catmull, now elevated to the position of Pixar's

EXHIBIT 2 Milestones

1986	Steve Jobs buys Lucas's computer group and christens it Pixar. The firm completes a short film, *Luxo Jr.,* which is nominated for an Oscar.
1988	Pixar adds computer-animated ads to its repertoire, making spots for Listerine, Lifesavers, and Tropicana. Another short, *Tin Toy,* wins an Oscar.
1991	Pixar signs a production agreement with Disney. Disney is to invest $26 million; Pixar is to deliver at least three full-length, computer-animated feature films.
1995	Pixar releases *Toy Story,* the first fully digital feature film, which becomes the top-grossing movie of the year and wins an Oscar. A week after release, the company goes public.
1997	Pixar and Disney negotiate a new agreement: a fifty-fifty split of development costs and profits of five feature-length movies. Short *Geri's Game* wins an Oscar.
1998–99	*A Bug's Life* and *Toy Story 2* are released, together pulling in $1.3 billion in box office and video.
2001–04	A string of hits from Pixar: *Monsters, Inc.; Finding Nemo;* and *The Incredibles.*
2006	Disney acquires Pixar and assigns responsibilities for its own animation unit to Pixar's creative brass. *Cars* is released and becomes another box office hit.
2009	*Wall-E* becomes the fourth film from Pixar to receive the Oscar for a feature-length animated film.
2011	*Toy Story 3* receives five Oscar nominations and wins two, including one for best animated film.

Source: Pixar.

president, who has been mainly responsible for ensuring that the firm's technological achievements help to pump up the firm's creative efforts. He has been the keeper of the company's unique innovative culture, which has blended Silicon Valley techies, Hollywood production honchos, and artsy animation experts. In the pursuit of Catmull's vision, this eclectic group has transformed their office cubicles into tiki huts, circus tents, and cardboard castles, with bookshelves stuffed with toys and desks adorned with colorful iMac computers.

Catmull has also worked hard to build upon this pursuit of creative innovation by creating programs to develop the employees. Employees are encouraged to devote up to four hours a week, every week, to further their education at Pixar University. The in-house training program offers 110 different courses that cover subjects such as live improvisation, creative writing, painting, drawing, sculpting, and cinematography. For many years, the school's dean was Randall E. Nelson, a former juggler who has been known to perform his act using chain saws so students in animation classes have something compelling to draw.

It is such an emphasis on the creative use of technology that has kept Pixar on the cutting edge. The firm has turned out ever more lifelike short films, including 1998's Oscar-winning *Geri's Game*, which used a technology called subdivision surfaces. This makes realistic simulation of human skin and clothing possible. "They're absolute geniuses," gushed Jules Roman, cofounder and CEO of rival Tippett Studio. "They're the people who created computer animation really."[6]

Becoming Accomplished Storytellers

A considerable part of the creative energy goes into story development. Jobs had understood that a film works only if its story can move the hearts and minds of families around the world. His goal was to develop Pixar into an animated movie studio that becomes known for the quality of its storytelling above everything else: "We want to create some great stories and characters that endure with each generation."[7]

For story development, Pixar has relied heavily on 43-year-old John Lasseter, who goes by the title of vice president of the creative. Known for his collection of 358 Hawaiian shirts and his irrepressible playfulness with toys, Lasseter has been the key to the appeal of all of Pixar's films. Lasseter gets very passionate about developing great stories and then harnessing computers to tell these stories. Most of Pixar's employees believe it is this passion that has ensured that each of the studio's films has been a commercial hit. In fact, Lasseter is being regarded as the Walt Disney for the 21st century.

When it's time to start a project, Lasseter isolates a group of eight or so writers and directs them to forget about the constraints of technology. The group bounces ideas off each other, taking collective responsibility for developing a story. While many studios try to rush from script to production, Lasseter takes up to two years just to work out all the details.

Once the script has been developed, artists create storyboards that connect the various characters to the developing plot. "No amount of great animation is going to save a bad story," he said. "That's why we go so far to make it right."[8]

Only after the basic story has been set does Lasseter begin to think about what he'll need from Pixar's technologists. And it's always more than the computer animators expect. Lasseter, for example, demanded that the crowds of ants in *A Bug's Life* not be a single mass of look-alike faces. To solve the problem, computer expert William T. Reeves developed software that randomly applied physical and emotional characteristics to each ant. In another instance, writers brought a model of a butterfly named Gypsy to researchers, asking them to write code so that when she rubs her antennae, you can see the hairs press down and pop back up.

At any stage during the process, Lasseter may go back to potential problems that he sees with the story. In *A Bug's Life*, for example, the story was totally revamped after more than a year of work had been completed. Originally, it was about a troupe of circus bugs run by P.T. Flea that tries to rescue a colony of ants from marauding grasshoppers. But because of a flaw in the story—Why would the circus bugs risk their lives to save stranger ants?—codirector Andrew Stanton recast the story to be about Flik, the heroic ant who recruits Flea's troupe to fight the grasshoppers. "You have to rework and rework it," explained Lasseter. "It is not rare for a scene to be rewritten as much as 30 times."[9]

Pumping Out the Hits

In spite of its formidable string of hits, Pixar has had difficulty in stepping up its pace of production. Although they may cost 30 percent less, computer-generated animated films do still take considerable time to develop. Furthermore, because of the emphasis on every single detail, Pixar used to complete most of the work on a film before moving on to the next one. Catmull and Lasseter have since decided to work on several projects at the same time, but the firm has not been able to release more than one movie in a year.

In order to push for an increase in production, Pixar has more than doubled its number of employees over the last decade. It is also turning to a stable of directors to oversee its movies. Lasseter, who directed Pixar's first three films, is supervising other directors who are taking the helm of various films that the studio chooses to develop. *Monsters, Inc., Finding Nemo, The Incredibles, Ratatouille*, and *Brave* were directed by some of this new talent. But there are concerns about the number of directors that Pixar can rely upon to turn out high-quality animated films. Michael Savner of Bane of America Securities commented, "You can't simply double production. There is a finite amount of talent."[10]

To meet the faster production pace, Catmull has also added new divisions, including one to help with the development of new movies and one to oversee movie development shot by shot. The eight-person development team has helped to generate more ideas for new films. "Once more ideas are percolating, we have more options to choose from so no one artist is feeling the weight of the world on their shoulders," said Sarah McArthur, who served as Pixar's vice president of production.[11]

Finally, Catmull keeps pushing on technology in order to improve the quality of animation with no more than 100 animators working on each film. Toward this end, Catmull has been overseeing the development of new animation software, called Luxo, which has allowed him to use fewer people, who can focus on addressing various challenges that come up. During the production of *Brave,* for example, the animators had to make the curly hair of the main character appear to be natural. Claudia Chung, who worked on the film, talked about their reaction to various methods they kept trying: "We'd kind of roll our eyes and say, 'I guess we can do that,' but inside we were all excited, because it's one more stretch we can do."[12]

Catmull is well aware of the dangers of growth for a studio whose successes came out of a lean structure that wagered everything on each film. It remains to be seen whether Pixar can keep drawing on its talent to increase production without compromising the high standards that have been set by Catmull and Lasseter. Jobs was keen to maintain the quality of every one of Pixar's films by ensuring that each one got the best efforts of the firm's animators, storytellers, and technologists. "Quality is more important than quantity," he emphasized. "One home run is better than two doubles."[13]

In order to preserve Pixar's high standards, Catmull has been working hard to retain the company's commitment to quality even as it grows. He has been using Pixar University to encourage collaboration among all employees so that they can develop and retain the key values that are tied to their success. And he has helped devise ways to avoid collective burnout. A masseuse and a doctor now come by Pixar's campus each week, and animators must get permission from their supervisors if they want to work more than 50 hours a week.

To Infinity and Beyond?

The growth in emphasis on sequels has raised concerns about the ability of Pixar to keep turning out movies that generate both box office revenues and critical acclaim, given their reliance on a high degree of creativity. The studio will be releasing a sequel to *Monsters, Inc.* later this year and has a sequel to *Finding Nemo* in the works. At the same time, Lasseter is overseeing work on films with bold new ideas, such as *Inside Out,* based on a story told from the perspective of the emotions inside the mind of a little girl.

Despite the poor reviews that some critics gave to *Cars 2,* it is widely believed that Pixar will continue to maintain its creativity even while it is owned by Disney. In fact, Jobs was convinced that Pixar's links with Disney would be mutually beneficial for both firms. In his own words, "Disney is the only company with animation in their DNA."[14] In fact, the acquisition of Pixar was viewed as an attempt by Disney to boost its own animation efforts by acquiring a group in which the talent of the individuals and the quality of the finished product are valued above everything else.

In order to ensure this, Ed Catmull and John Lasseter have been in charge of the combined animation business of both Pixar and Disney. *Tangled* and *Wreck-It Ralph,* which were both commercial and critical successes, were Disney films that were completed under the supervision of these Pixar heads. For Lasseter, the new responsibilities for Disney have represented a return to his roots. He had been inspired by Disney films as a kid and started his career at Disney before being lured away to Pixar by Catmull. "For many of us at Pixar, it was the magic of Disney that influenced us to pursue our dreams of becoming animators, artists, storytellers and filmmakers," Lasseter stated.[15]

But Catmull and Lasseter continue to face a challenging task. They must ensure that they keep developing hits for Pixar even as they try to turn things around at Disney. Furthermore, it is still too early to tell whether Pixar will be affected by the loss of Jobs, who passed away in 2011. He was an important sounding board for Lasseter, who often relied on the perspective of Jobs in supervising the films that Pixar was developing.

At the same time, everyone at Pixar understands that a large part of their success can be attributed to the talent that the firm is able to recruit and train to work together. This leads to a continuous exchange of ideas and fosters a collective sense of responsibility on all their projects. "We created the studio we want to work in," Lasseter remarked. "We have an environment that's wacky. It's a creative brain trust: It's not a place where I make my movies—it's a place where a group of people make movies."[16]

ENDNOTES

1. Barnes, B. 2011. It wasn't a wreck, not really. *New York Times,* October 18: C4.
2. Ibid.: C1.
3. Burrows, P., & Grover, G. 1998. Steve Jobs: Movie mogul. *BusinessWeek,* November 23: 150.
4. Ibid.: 150.
5. Ibid.: 146.
6. Ibid.: 146.
7. Graser, M. 1999. Pixar run by focused group. *Variety,* December 20: 74.
8. Barnes, op. cit.: C4.
9. Burrows & Grover, op. cit.: 146.
10. Bary, A. 2003. Coy story. *Barron's,* October 13: 21.
11. Terdiman, D. 2012. Bravely going where Pixar animation tech has never gone. *CNET News,* June 16.
12. Tam, P.-W. 2001. Will quantity hurt Pixar's quality? *Wall Street Journal,* February 15: B4.
13. Burrows, P., & Grover, G. 2006. Steve Jobs' magic kingdom. *BusinessWeek,* February 6: 66.
14. Solomon, C. 2006. Pixar creative chief to seek to restore the Disney magic. *New York Times,* January 25: C6.
15. Ibid.
16. Bary, A. 2003. Coy story. *Barron's,* October 13: 21.

CASE 24

APPLE INC.

Still Taking a Bite Out of the Competition?*

On January 25, 2013, just after Apple CEO Tim Cook presented the company's first quarter earnings report, Apple's stock price dropped below $440. For most other public companies, this stock price might seem something to celebrate, but for Apple it was bad news. 2012 had been a year of milestones. In September Apple stock had hit its all-time high of $702.10, making Apple the most valuable company in the world by market capitalization. September 2012 also marked Tim Cook's first full year as CEO, and the first full year since the death of Apple's visionary founder Steve Jobs. Although most Apple watchers mourned Steve Jobs's death on October 5, 2011, most also realized that Jobs's appointed successor, Tim Cook, came to the position as CEO with an impressive track record.

Cook had continued to grow the company, releasing the iPhone 5 and iPad Mini in September, and the 2012 year-end numbers had shown continued financial success across almost all product lines. However, expectations were still very high, and December 2012 rumors of a reduction in Asian supplier component orders for the iPhone for 2013 led investors to worry about a drop off in demand for the company's flagship product. This worry led to a subsequent drop in Apple stock price of nearly 24 percent from its all-time high.[1]

In his first quarter 2013 conference call, CEO Cook attempted to defuse concerns over supply chain issues. That didn't stop analysts and media watchers from writing headlines such as: "Is Apple Losing Its Brand Equity?" Listing issues such as Apple's slipping online satisfaction scores, increasing competition, fewer repeat purchasers, and lower stock valuation, several writers wondered whether Apple was losing its luster.[2] These headlines posed yet again the unavoidable question that now loomed large over 35-year-old Apple: What happens to a modern company whose innovations and inspirations are so closely tied to the vision of one leader when that leader's influence is no longer present?[3]

Cook should have had every reason to be confident. In the 2013 first quarter, Apple had reported $54.5 billion in revenue, up 18 percent from a year before (see Exhibits 1 and 2).[4] The results were excellent by most accounts, but investors were obviously looking for more. Despite Apple's improving profit margins, higher cash reserves, and the first dividend payment to shareholders—plus the assumption of product plans for 2013 and beyond—some analysts believed that without Jobs's stubbornness and obsession about process and product details, Apple would never be the same.

Apple, *Fortune Magazine*'s "world's most admired company" since 2008,[5] had distinguished itself by excelling over the years not only in product innovation but also in revenue and margins (since 2006 Apple had consistently reported gross margins of over 30 percent). Founded as a computer company in 1976 and known early on for its intuitive adaptation of the "graphical user interface" or GUI (via the first mouse and the first on-screen "windows"),[6] Apple had dropped the word *computer* from its corporate name in 2007. Apple Inc. in 2013 was known for having top-selling products not only in desktop (iMac) and notebook (MacBook) personal computers but also in portable digital music players (iPod), online music and "app" services (iTunes and App Store), mobile communication devices (iPhone), digital consumer entertainment (Apple TV), handheld devices able to download third-party applications, including games (iPod Touch via the App Store), and, recently, tablet computers (iPad) and online services (iCloud) (see Exhibit 3).

Although most of those innovations occurred after 1998, when Apple was under Steve Jobs's leadership, there was a 12-year period in which Jobs was not in charge. The company's ongoing stated strategy had been to leverage "its unique ability to design and develop its own operations systems, hardware, application software, and services to provide its customers new products and solutions with superior ease-of-use, seamless integration and innovative industrial design."[7] This strategy required not only product design and marketing expertise but also scrupulous attention to operational details. Given Apple's global growth in multiple product categories, and the associated complexity in strategic execution, would the loss of one man be sufficient to prevent the company from sustaining its competitive advantage? Had Steve Jobs been essential to Apple's success? Was Apple's run of innovation and growth finally over? Could it *still* take a bite out of all competition, or was the competition catching up?

* This case was prepared by Professor Alan B. Eisner of Pace University and Associate Professor Pauline Assenza, Western Connecticut State University. This case was based solely on library research and was developed for class discussion rather than to illustrate either effective or ineffective handling of an administrative situation. Copyright © 2013 Alan B. Eisner.

EXHIBIT 1

Apple Sales

Go to library tab in Connect to access Case Financials.

	A	B	C	D	E	F
1		Net Sales by Product				
2		2012 (in millions)	% Change	2011 (in millions)	% Change	2010 (in millions)
3	Desktops	$6,040	(6)%	$ 6,439	4%	$ 6,201
4	Portables	17,181	12%	15,344	(36)%	11,278
5	iPod	5,615	(25)%	7,453	(10)%	8,274
6	Music*	8,534	35%	6,314	28%	4,948
7	iPhone	80,477	71%	47,057	87%	25,179
8	iPad	32,424	59%	20,358	311%	4,958
9	Peripherals	2,778	19%	2,330	28%	1,814
10	Software, services	3,459	17%	2,954	15%	2,573
11	Total net sales	$ 156,508	45%	$ 108,249	66%	$ 65,225
12	Cost of sales	87,846		64,431		39,541
13	Gross margin	$ 68,662		$ 43,818		$ 25,684
14	Gross margin %	43.9%		40.5%		39.4%
15	Research and development	$ 3,381		$ 2,429		$ 1,782
16	Percentage of net sales	2%		2%		2.7%
17	Selling, general, and administrative	$ 10,040		$ 7,599		$ 5,517
18	Percentage of net sales	6%		7%		8.5%
19	Total operating expenses	$ 13,421		$ 10,028		$ 7,299
20	Net income	$ 41,733		$ 25,922		$ 14,013

	A	B	C	D	E	F
1		Net Sales by Region				
2		2012 (in millions)	% Change	2011 (in millions)	% Change	2010 (in millions)
3	Americas	$ 57,512	50%	$ 38,315	56%	$ 24,498
4	Europe	36,323	31%	27,778	49%	18,692
5	Japan	10,571	94%	5,437	37%	3,981
6	Asia-Pacific	33,274	47%	22,592	174%	8,256
7	Retail Net Sales	18,828	33%	14,127	44%	9,798

*Includes revenue from sales from the iTunes Store, App Store, and iBookstore in addition to sales of iPod services and Apple-branded and third-party iPod accessories.

Source: Apple 10K SEC filing, 2012.

EXHIBIT 2

Apple First Quarter 2013 Sales

Go to library tab in Connect to access Case Financials.

	A	B	C	F
1		Net Sales by Product		
2		1st Quarter 2013 (in millions)	1st Quarter 2012 (in millions)	Percentage Change
3	iPhone*	$ 30,660	$ 23,950	28%
4	iPad*	10,674	8,769	22%
5	Mac*	5,519	6,598	(16)%
6	iPod*	2,143	2,528	(15)%
7	iTunes, Software and Services†	3,687	3,020	22%
8	Accessories‡	1,829	1,468	25%
9	Total net sales	$ 54,512	$ 46,333	18%

	A	B	C	F
1		Net Sales by Region		
2		1st Quarter 2013 (in millions)	1st Quarter 2012 (in millions)	Percentage Change
3	Americas	$ 20,341	$ 17,714	15%
4	Europe	12,464	11,256	11%
5	Greater China§	6,830	4,080	67%
6	Japan	4,443	3,550	25%
7	Asia-Pacific	3,993	3,617	10%
8	Retail	6,441	6,116	5%

*Includes deferrals and amortization of related nonsoftware services and software upgrade rights.
†Includes revenue from sales on the iTunes Store, the App Store, the Mac App Store, and the iBookstore, and revenue from sales of AppleCare, licensing, and other services.
‡Includes sales of hardware peripherals and Apple-branded and third-party accessories for iPhone, iPad, Mac, and iPod.
§Greater China includes China, Hong Kong, and Taiwan.

Source: Apple 10Q SEC filing, 2013.

EXHIBIT 3 Apple Innovation Time Line

Date	Product	Events
1976	Apple I	Steve Jobs, Steve Wozniak, and Ronald Wayne found Apple Computer.
1977	Apple II	Apple logo first used.
1979	Apple II+	Apple employs 250 people; the first personal computer spreadsheet software, *VisiCalc,* is written by Dan Bricklin on an Apple II.
1980	Apple III	Apple goes public with 4.6 million shares; IBM personal computer announced.
1983	Lisa	John Sculley becomes CEO.
1984	Mac 128K, Apple IIc	Super Bowl ad introduces the Mac desktop computer.
1985		**Jobs resigns** and forms NeXT Software; Windows 1.01 released.
1986	Mac Plus	Jobs establishes Pixar.
1987	Mac II, Mac SE	Apple sues Microsoft over GUI.
1989	Mac Portable	Apple sued by Xerox over GUI.
1990	Mac LC	Apple listed on Tokyo Stock Exchange.
1991	PowerBook 100, System 7	System 7 operating-system upgrade released, the first Mac OS to support PowerPC-based computers.
1993	Newton Message Pad (one of the first PDAs)	Sculley resigns; Spindler becomes CEO; PowerBook sales reach 1 million units.
1996		Spindler is out; Amelio becomes CEO; Apple acquires NeXT Software, with Jobs as adviser.
1997		Amelio is out; **Jobs returns** as interim CEO; online retail Apple Store opened.
1998	iMac	iMac colorful design introduced, including USB interface; Newton scrapped.
1999	iMovie, Final Cut Pro (video editing software)	iBook (part of PowerBook line) becomes best-selling retail notebook in October; Apple has 11% share of notebook market.
2000	G4Cube	**Jobs becomes permanent CEO.**
2001	iPod, OS X	First retail store opens, in Virginia.
2002	iMac G4	Apple releases iLife software suite.
2003	iTunes	Apple reaches 25 million iTunes downloads.
2004	iMac G5	**Jobs undergoes successful surgery for pancreatic cancer.**
2005	iPod Nano, iPod Shuffle, Mac Mini	First video iPod released; video downloads available from iTunes.
2006	MacBook Pro	Apple computers use Intel's Core Duo CPU and can run Windows software; iWork software competes with Microsoft Office.
2007	iPhone, Apple TV, iPod Touch	Apple Computer changes name to Apple Inc.; Microsoft Vista released.
2008	iPhone 3G, MacBook Air, App Store	App Store launched for third-party applications for iPhone and iPod Touch and brings in $1million in one day.
2009	17-inch MacBook Pro, iLife, iWork '09	iTunes Plus provides DRM-free music, with variable pricing; **Jobs takes medical leave.**
2010	iPad, iPhone 4	iPhone 4 provides FaceTime feature; iTunes reaches 10 billion songs sold.
2011	iPad2, iPhone 4S, iCloud	iPhone available on Verizon Wireless; **Jobs resigns as CEO, dies on October 5th. Tim Cook becomes CEO.**
2012	iBook Author, iPhone5, iPad Mini	iBook supports textbook creation on iPad. Apple becomes world's most valuable company (market cap).

Source: *Apple.com*; Fried, I. 2009. Celebrating three decades of Apple. CNET News, Special issue: Apple turns 30, March 28. *news.cnet.com/2009-1041-6053869. html*; and Wikipedia. Apple Inc. *en.wikipedia.org/wiki/Apple_inc.*

Company Background

Founder Steve Jobs

Apple Computer was founded in Mountain View, California, on April 1, 1976, by Steve Jobs and Steve Wozniak. Jobs was the visionary and marketer, Wozniak was the technical genius, and A. C. "Mike" Markkula Jr., who had joined the team several months earlier, was the businessman. Jobs set the mission of empowering individuals, one person–one computer, and doing so with elegance of design and fierce attention to detail. In 1977 the first version of the Apple II became the first computer ordinary people could use right out of the box, and its instant success in the home market caused a computing revolution, essentially creating the personal computer industry. By 1980 Apple was the industry leader and went public in December of that year.

In 1983 Wozniak left the firm and Jobs hired John Sculley away from PepsiCo to take the role of CEO at Apple, citing the need for someone to spearhead marketing and operations while Jobs worked on technology. The result of Jobs's creative focus on personal computing was the Macintosh. Introduced in 1984, with the now-famous Super Bowl television ad based on George Orwell's novel *Nineteen Eighty-Four,*[8] the Macintosh was a breakthrough in terms of elegant design and ease of use. Its ability to handle large graphic files quickly made it a favorite with graphic designers, but it had slow performance and limited compatible software was available. That meant the product as designed at the time was unable to significantly help Apple's failing bottom line. In addition, Jobs had given Bill Gates at Microsoft some Macintosh prototypes to use to develop software, and in 1985 Microsoft subsequently came out with the Windows operating system, a version of GUI for use on IBM PCs.

Steve Jobs's famous volatility led to his resignation from Apple in 1985. Jobs then founded NeXT Computer. The NeXT Cube computer proved too costly for the business to become commercially profitable, but its technological contributions could not be ignored. In 1997 then Apple CEO Gilbert Amelio bought out NeXT, hoping to use its Rhapsody, a version of the NeXTStep operating system, to jump-start the Mac OS development, and Jobs was brought back as a part-time adviser.

Under CEOs Sculley, Spindler, and Amelio

John Sculley tried to take advantage of Apple's unique capabilities. Because of this, Macintosh computers became easy to use, with seamless integration (the original plug-and-play) and reliable performance. This premium performance meant Apple could charge a premium price. However, with the price of IBM compatibles dropping, and Apple's costs, especially R&D, way above industry averages (in 1990 Apple spent 9 percent of sales on R&D, compared to 5 percent at Compaq and 1 percent at many manufacturers of IBM clones),[9] this was not a sustainable scenario.

Sculley's innovative efforts were not enough to substantially improve Apple's bottom line, and he was replaced as CEO in 1993 by company president Michael Spindler. Spindler continued the focus on innovation, producing the PowerMac, based on the PowerPC microprocessor, in 1994. Even though this combination produced a significant price-performance edge over both previous Macs and Intel-based machines, the IBM clones continued to undercut Apple's prices. Spindler's response was to allow other companies to manufacture Mac clones, a strategy that ultimately led to clones stealing 20 percent of Macintosh unit sales.

Gilbert Amelio, an Apple director and former semiconductor turnaround expert, was asked to reverse the company's financial direction. Amelio intended to reposition Apple as a premium brand, but his extensive reorganizations and cost-cutting strategies couldn't prevent Apple's stock price from slipping to a new low. However, Amelio's decision to stop work on a brand-new operating system and jump-start development by using NeXTStep brought Steve Jobs back to Apple in 1997.

Steve Jobs's Return

One of Jobs's first strategies on his return was to strengthen Apple's relationships with third-party software developers, including Microsoft. In 1997 Jobs announced an alliance with Microsoft that would allow for the creation of a Mac version of the popular Microsoft Office software. He also made a concerted effort to woo other developers, such as Adobe, to continue to produce Mac-compatible programs.

In late October 2001, Apple released its first major non-computer product, the iPod. This device was an MP3 music player that packed up to 1,000 CD-quality songs into an ultraportable, 6.5-ounce design: "With iPod, Apple has invented a whole new category of digital music player that lets you put your entire music collection in your pocket and listen to it wherever you go," said Steve Jobs. "With iPod, listening to music will never be the same again."[10] This prediction became even truer in 2002, when Apple introduced an iPod that would download from Windows—its first product that didn't require a Macintosh computer and thus opened up the Apple "magic" to everyone. In 2003 all iPod products were sold with a Windows version of iTunes, making it even easier to use the device regardless of computer platform.

In April 2003, Apple opened the online iTunes Music Store to everyone. This software, downloadable on any computer platform, sold individual songs through the iTunes application for 99 cents each. When announced, the iTunes Music Store already had the backing of five major record labels and a catalog of 200,000 songs. Later that year, the iTunes Music Store was selling roughly 500,000 songs a day. In 2003 the iPod was the only portable digital player that could play music purchased from iTunes, and this intended exclusivity helped both products become dominant.

After 30 years of carving a niche for itself as the premier provider of technology solutions for graphic artists, Web designers, and educators, Apple appeared to be reinventing itself as a digital entertainment company, moving beyond the personal computer industry. The announcement in 2007 of the iPhone, a product incorporating a wireless phone, a music and video player, and a mobile Internet browsing device, meant Apple was also competing in the cell phone/smartphone industry.

Also introduced in 2007, the iPod Touch incorporated Wi-Fi connectivity, allowing users to purchase and download music directly from iTunes without a computer. Then, in 2008 Apple opened the App Store. Users could now purchase applications written by third-party developers specifically for the iPhone and iPod Touch. These applications included games, prompting analysts to wonder whether Apple was now becoming a competitor in the gaming market.

In 2010 Apple launched the large-screen touch-based tablet called the iPad and sold over 2 million of these devices in the first two months.[11] That same year, Apple's stock value increased to the extent that the company's market cap exceeded Microsoft's, making it the biggest tech company in the world.[12] In 2011 Steve Jobs made his last product launch appearance to introduce iCloud, an online storage and syncing service. On October 4, 2011, Apple announced the iPhone 4S, which included "Siri," the "intelligent software assistant." The next day, on October 5, came the announcement that Steve Jobs had died.

Apple continued to innovate, however, and on September 21, 2012, Apple had its biggest iPhone launch ever, with the iPhone 5. Over 2 million preorders for this larger and more powerful phone pushed the delivery date back to late October.[13] Later in the fall, Apple released the iPad

Mini with a smaller screen. On September 19, 2012, Apple stock reached $702.10, its highest level to date, which made Apple the most valuable company in the world.

Apple had become a diversified digital entertainment corporation (see Exhibit 4). All the way back in 2005 analysts had believed Apple had "changed the rules of the game for three industries—PCs, consumer electronics, and music . . . and appears to have nothing to fear from major rivals."[14] On top of steady sales increases of its computers of the iPod, and of iTunes, the added categories of iPhone and iPad had shown substantial growth. Apple had taken bites out of the competition on all fronts (see Exhibit 4). However, by 2013, Samsung had outperformed Apple in worldwide smartphone sales,[15] and Google's Android had captured the largest market share of cell phone operating systems. At the same time, both the Amazon Kindle Fire HD and Microsoft's Surface tablet were nipping at the iPad's heels. Was this a warning of things to come?

Apple's Operations

Maintaining a competitive edge required more than innovative product design. Operational execution was also important. For instance, while trying to market its increasingly diverse product line, Apple believed that its own retail stores could serve customers better than could third-party retailers. By the end of 2012, Apple had 390 stores open, including 140 international locations, with average store revenue of about $51.5 million, and had received trademark protection for its retail stores' "distinctive design and layout."[16]

In further operational matters, regarding a head-to-head competition against Dell in the computer market, for instance, while Dell's perceived early dominance might have been partly the result of its efficient supply-chain

EXHIBIT 4 Apple's Product Lines and Major Competitors

Product Category	Apple Products	Major Competitors
Computers	iMac, Mac Pro, Mac mini, MacBook, MacBook Pro, MacBook Air	HP, Dell, Toshiba in the laptop; Acer and Asus in the netbook/ultrabook form factor
Portable music/media players	iPod Shuffle, iPod Nano, iPod Classic, iPod Touch	Samsung, SanDisk Sansa, Archos, Microsoft Zune
Smartphones	iPhone	Nokia, RIM, Samsung, ZTE, LG, Google/Motorola, HTC
Music/media downloads	iTunes, the App Store	Amazon, Google Android apps
Handheld gaming devices	iPod Touch, iPhone	Nintendo, Sony
Software*	Safari web browser, QuickTime	Microsoft IE, Mozilla Firefox, Google Chrome, Windows Media Player, RealNetworks
Home theater downloads	Apple TV	Roku, possibly Tivo
Tablet computers	iPad	Samsung Galaxy Tab, Amazon Kindle Fire, Google Nexus, Windows Surface

*Includes only the software that is sold separately to use on either Windows or Mac computers.

management, Apple had outperformed Dell in inventory and other metrics since 2001.[17] To solidify its own supply chain, Apple entered into multiyear agreements with suppliers of key components. In addition, Apple had historically had the best margins, partly because of its simpler product line, leading to lower manufacturing costs.[18] Also, Apple had been outsourcing manufacturing and final assembly of iMacs, iPods, and iPhones to partners in Asia, paying close attention to scheduling and quality issues.

Outsourcing to Asian manufacturers was not without its problems, however. In 2012, headlines worldwide accompanied the exposure of China's Foxconn manufacturing facility for labor abuses that led to worker suicide threats. Apple, as well as most other technology companies, used Foxconn facilities to assemble products, including the iPad and iPhone. After the story broke, Apple CEO Tim Cook visited the Foxconn plant and reviewed an audit of working conditions that found violations in wages, overtime, and environmental standards. Apple stated that it remained "committed to the highest standards of social responsibility across our worldwide supply chain,"[19] and Cook announced that Apple would be bringing some of the production of Mac computers back to the U.S., starting in 2013. They could do this possibly without affecting the company's profitability, because of automation cost savings. As one supply chain expert said, "Apple's product line is highly standardized, with a very small number of products and very few configurations, and that makes it much easier to do automation."[20]

Supply chain and product design and manufacturing efficiencies were not the only measures of potential competitive superiority. Apple had also historically paid attention to research and development, increasing its R&D investment year after year. In 2012, Apple spent $952 million on R&D, an increase from $647 million in the previous year. Among its current rivals, Apple's R&D investment was beaten only by Microsoft (number 1), Google, Hewlett-Packard, and Amazon.[21]

As one of Steve Jobs's legacies, Apple had traditionally kept the specifics of its research and development a closely guarded secret and fiercely protected its innovative patents. A well-publicized series of lawsuits in 2012 highlighted rifts between Apple and Samsung, both a rival and supplier. Samsung smartphones had captured more market share than Apple's iPhones in the beginning of 2012, and Apple argued that Samsung had succeeded with both its phones and tablets only by copying Apple's designs. Samsung replied by claiming that Apple had infringed on Samsung's patents.[22] U.S. intellectual property courts found in favor of Apple, but Japanese courts found in favor of Samsung. The ongoing battle meant Apple needed to look for other suppliers of chips and displays. In September 2012, supply chain watchers pointed out that Apple had a major challenge ahead finding reliable suppliers for increasingly scarce components. This shortage endangered CEO Cook's historical strategy of cutting tight deals with suppliers and meant Apple could see smaller profit margins ahead, especially for the previously lucrative iPhone.[23]

Status of Apple's Business Units in 2013
The Apple Computer Business

In the computer market, Apple had always refused to compete on price, relying instead on its reliability, design elegance, ease of use, and integrated features to win customers. From the beginning, some analysts had believed Apple had the opportunity to steal PC market share as long as its system was compatible, no longer proprietary, and offered upgrades at a reasonable cost.[24] This opportunity for increased market share was realized when Apple began using Intel processors in the iMac desktop and the MacBook portables, which allowed them to run Microsoft Office and other business software.

Despite the continuing push to convert customers to the Macintosh computing products, Apple's worldwide Mac computer sales during the first quarter of 2013 decreased almost 22 percent over the same quarter in the previous year, to $5.5 billion. Reportedly, this decline was partly because of supply constraints,[25] but sales of desktop computers, especially, were slowing worldwide as the tablet and smartphone markets grew. This caused analysts to wonder if the high-margin Mac sales might be further cannibalized by the iPad, leading to a continued erosion of Apple profit margins.[26] Sales of Apple computers in the United States during the fourth quarter of 2012 did see a decline over the previous year, but not as much as the domestic shipments of Dell (down 16.6 percent). According to market analysis done by IDC, the Mac's domestic market share grew from 10.9 to 11.4 percent, putting it in third place overall in IDC's survey of PC vendor units shipped in 4Q2012 (see Exhibit 5).[27] This is up substantially from 2010, when Apple had only 7.4 percent of the U.S. market.[28]

Personal Digital Entertainment Devices: iPod

Although many analysts at the time had felt the MP3 player market was oversaturated, Apple introduced the iPod Touch in 2007, intending it to be "an iPhone without the phone," a portable media player and Wi-Fi Internet device without the AT&T phone bill.[29] The iPod Touch borrowed most of its features from the iPhone, including the finger-touch interface, but it remained mainly an iPod, with a larger viewing area for videos. Apple released the fifth-generation iPod Touch in September 2012, with upgraded features like support for recording 1080p video and panoramic still photos, and support for Apple's "Siri."

Apple reported selling 12.7 million iPod units during the first quarter of 2013, a decline of 18 percent over the same period in the previous year.[30] As with desktop computer sales, the MP3 player market was contracting overall as smartphone and tablet devices took over many music-related tasks. Even with the decline in iPod sales, Apple was

EXHIBIT 5 Domestic PC Market Share, Fourth Quarter 2012, units in thousands

Company	4Q12 Shipments	4Q12 Market Share (%)	4Q11 Shipments	4Q11 Market Share (%)	4Q12–4Q11 Growth (%)
Hewlett-Packard	4,797	27.0	4,266	23.0	12.4%
Dell	3,475	19.6	4,166	22.4	−16.6
Apple	2,030	11.4	2,033	10.9	−0.2
Lenovo	1,504	8.5	1,348	7.3	11.6
Toshiba	1,256	7.1	1,900	10.2	−33.9
Others	4,685	26.4	4,862	26.2	−3.6
Total	**17,747**	**100.0**	**18,575**	**100.0**	**−6.6**

Note: PCs include desktops, portables, mini notebooks, and workstations. It does not include handhelds, x86 servers, and tablets (i.e., iPad and Android-based tablets). Data for all vendors are reported for calendar periods.

Source: IDC Worldwide Quarterly PC Tracker, January 10, 2013

still leading well over its rivals. According to NPD group, in 2012 the iPod had a 70 percent share of the MP3 player market in the United States.[31] Apple rival Microsoft's entry into this space, the Zune, was discontinued in October 2011. Its market share never exceeded 1 percent.[32]

Mobile Communication Devices: iPhone

In 2007 further competition for the iPod came from the blurring of lines between digital music players and other consumer electronic devices. While others may have seen the computer as central to the future of digital music, telecom companies worked to make the mobile phone a center of the digital world. Apple's entry, the iPhone, combined an Internet-enabled smartphone and video iPod. The iPhone allowed users to access all iPod content and play music and video content purchased from iTunes. More recent smartphone models increased the quality of the photo and video components to make even the digital camera or camcorder appear obsolete. The smartphone market in 2007 was estimated at 10 percent of all mobile phone sales, or 100 million devices a year. Steve Jobs had said he "would like to see the iPhone represent 1 percent of all mobile phone sales by the end of 2008."[33] This proved to be a conservative estimate, and by 2012 Apple had achieved 6.9 percent (see Exhibit 6).

Going into 2013, it appeared that the cell phone landscape was changing yet again, with smartphones becoming the device of choice for most manufacturers—smartphones were also often the electronic data consumers' device of choice, with multiple features, including cameras and the ability to surf the Internet while being held in the hand, rather than taking up the space of a tablet or ultra-thin computer. However, the smartphone market was increasingly turning into a battle between mobile operating systems.

Apple's iPhone, running on iOS, now had considerable competition from Samsung's Galaxy smartphones,

EXHIBIT 6 Worldwide Market Share—Cell Phones, 2nd Quarter 2012

Manufacturer	Market Share 2Q2012	Market Share 2Q2011
Samsung	21.6%	16.3%
Nokia	19.9	22.8
Apple	6.9	4.6
ZTE	4.3	3.0
LG	3.4	5.7
Huawei	2.6	2.1
TLC	2.2	1.9
HTC	2.2	2.6
Motorola	2.2	2.4
Research in Motion	1.9	3.0
Others	32.8	35.7

Source: Gartner 2012.

especially. And this was partly due to Samsung's use of Google's Android operating system. Historical worldwide leader Nokia had stumbled badly with its outdated Symbian operating system and was trying to regain a foothold by partnering with Microsoft, using the Windows Phone operating system. Research in Motion had had problems updating its BlackBerry line of phones, although RIM still had some long-term Blackberry fans awaiting the delayed release of BlackBerry 10. The market share by operating system map was now worth watching, with Android devices expected to continue to capture the majority of market share through 2016 (see Exhibit 7).[34]

EXHIBIT 7 Top Smartphone Operating Systems, Forecast Market Share, and Compound Annual Growth Rate, 2012–2016

Smartphone OS	Market Share 2012	Projected Market Share 2016	CAGR 2012–2016 (%)
Google Android	68.3%	63.8%	16.3%
Apple iOS	18.8	19.1	18.8
RIM BlackBerry OS	4.7	4.1	14.6
Microsoft Windows Phone	2.6	11.4	71.3
Linux	2.0	1.5	10.5
Others	3.6	0.1	−100.0
TOTAL	**100.0**	**100.0**	**18.3%**

Source: IDC. 2012. Worldwide mobile phone growth expected to drop to 1.4 % in 2012 despite continued growth of smartphones, according to IDC. IDC, December 4. www.idc.com/getdoc.jsp?containerId=prUS23818212#.UQSn-_J5V8E.

Apple's growth was projected to continue to slow, partly because its high price relative to other smartphones made it cost prohibitive for some users in the emerging markets of China, India, and Russia. Even though Apple sold more than two million iPhone 5 units in China over the weekend launch in January 2013, a cheaper iPhone might position Apple even better in this developing market.[35] However, this potential move by Apple to reduce prices would go against the company's long-held stance that quality was worth the higher price tag.

Analysts were questioning this strategy, pointing out that "the iPhone and related revenue accounted for about 51% of Apple's revenue in FY12 and will grow to about 54% of revenue in FY13." Therefore, a strategy of "competing on the price-point" rather than competing by creating new technologies that blow the competitors away appeared "to be a sign of slowing innovation."[36] The lower price points would also reduce Apple's profit margins, especially in this iPhone category, traditionally one of Apple's more financially successful operating segments.

In addition, by 2013 it appeared some of the "cool" factor had disappeared from the iPhone. In Asian markets, especially, Apple's shares of mobile devices had fallen sharply in 2012, losing considerable ground to Samsung and HTC smartphones. Younger users, the 20-something college students and fresh graduates, were looking for the next new thing, and that was increasingly an Android-driven device. A social media expert in Singapore noted, "Apple is still viewed as a prestigious brand, but there are just so many other cool smartphones out there now that the competition is just much stiffer." This was a problem, because this Asian market was also where consumers were adopting very quickly, spending 78 percent more on smartphones in 2012 than they did in 2011.[37] In addition, CEO Tim Cook's visit to China in the fall of 2012, presumably to woo China Mobile's chief executive into subsidizing the iPhone, didn't have the expected result. China Mobile's wireless network, the world's largest, wouldn't be adding the iPhone without better terms from Apple. Instead it would be offering its subscribers the Nokia Lumia Windows 8 phone.[38] Given all these challenges, could Apple continue to ride the success of the iPhone to greater profits? Many were skeptical.

Tablet Computer: iPad

In April 2010 Apple released the iPad, a tablet computer, as a platform for audio-visual media, including books, periodicals, movies, music, games, and web content. More than 300,000 iPads were scooped up by eager tech consumers during the device's first day on store shelves. Weighing only 1.5 pounds, this lightweight, portable, and touch-screen device was seen as a gigantic iPod Touch.[39]

Considering that previous tablet computers had failed to catch on in the mass market, Apple made a bold move by introducing the iPad. Upon its release, some users criticized the iPad for a lack of features, such as a physical keyboard, a webcam, USB ports, and Flash support, and for its inability to multitask, share files, and print. However, features like the sleek design, touch screen, multiple apps, and fast and easy-to-navigate software made the iPad popular in business, education, and the entertainment industry. The iPad was selected by *Time* magazine as one of the 50 Best Inventions of the Year 2010.[40]

Up until September 2010, Apple iPads accounted for 95 percent of tablet computer sales, according to research firm Strategy Analytics.[41] But by the end of 2012, that figure had fallen to 78.9 percent. The loss of share was due to the arrival of new tablet devices, such as Samsung's Galaxy, based on Google's open-source Android system. Other platforms and devices had also begun to appear, including Google's Nexus, Amazon's Kindle Fire HD, and Microsoft's Windows 8 Surface tablet.[42]

In October 2012 Apple released the iPad Mini, a 7-inch version of the iPad, pitting it directly against Amazon's popular Kindle Fire. Although analysts were worried that the Mini would cannibalize sales of the standard-size iPad, sales of the Mini over the holidays in 2012 were excellent, exceeding 5 million units.[43] This easily beat the rate of Amazon's sales after the Kindle Fire's launch in 2011, causing one analyst to label the iPad Mini a "game changer" in the market share wars.[44]

The Software Market

Although Apple has always created innovative hardware, software development was also an important goal. Software had increasingly becoming Apple's core strength, especially in its computers, due to its reliability and resistance to virus infections and resulting crashes.[45] The premier piece of Apple software was the operating system. The iOS allowed Apple to develop software applications such as Final Cut Pro, a video-editing program for professionals' digital camcorders, and the simplified version for regular consumers, called iMovie. The iLife software package provided five integrated applications, allowing the computer to become a home studio: iMovie; iDVD, for recording photos, movies, and music onto DVDs; iPhoto, for touching up digital photos; GarageBand, for making and mixing personally created music; and the iTunes digital music jukebox. Also available was iWork, containing a PowerPoint-type program called Keynote and a word-processor/page-layout program called Pages. Both iLife and iWork underwent major upgrades in 2009, further increasing their respective abilities to compete with Microsoft applications.

Apple's Web browser, Safari, was upgraded in 2009 to compete with Windows Internet Explorer, Mozilla Firefox, and the new entrant, Chrome from Google. Apple announced, "Safari 4 is the world's fastest and most innovative browser,"[46] but analysts were quick to point out that Google's Chrome, which debuted six months earlier, was perhaps the first to take the browser interface in a new direction. One commentator called Chrome "a wake-up call for the Safari UI guys. . . . It's not that any particular feature of Chrome is so wonderful, or even that the sum of those features puts Safari back on its heels in the browser wars. It's the idea that someone other than Apple has taken such clear leadership in this area. Google Chrome makes Safari's user interface look conservative; it makes Apple look timid. And when it comes to innovation, overall daring counts for a lot more than individual successes or failures on the long-term graph."[47] Reviews of Apple's Safari upgrade noted, "Whether or not the individual features of Chrome inspired Apple, it's clear that Apple isn't going to let Google have the lead in browser innovation without a fight. And the more innovation that happens, the better it will be for users of Web browsers—which at this point is pretty much everybody with a computer!"[48] Browser market share data at the end of 2012 showed Microsoft with the majority, but Safari was still in second place at around 20 percent, beating out Chrome, Firefox, Android, and others.[49]

In other software development areas, Apple had not been that successful. In 2012 Apple had stumbled badly with its Maps software. Released in iOS6, Apple Maps was meant to replace Google Maps on the iPhone, but instead produced distorted images and gave really bad directions. CEO Tim Cook had to apologize that Apple had fallen short of its commitment to making "world-class products," and suggested customers go back to using its competitor's mapping software.[50]

iTunes

Arguably, Apple's most innovative software product was iTunes, a free downloadable software program for consumers running on either Mac or Windows operating systems. It was bundled with all Mac computers and iPods and connected with the iTunes Music Store for purchasing digital music and movie files that could be downloaded and played by iPods, iPads, and the iPhone, and by iTunes on PCs.

Although the volume was there, iTunes had not necessarily been a profitable venture. Out of the 99 cents Apple charged for a song, about 65 cents went to the music label; 25 cents went for distribution costs, including credit card charges, servers, and bandwidth; and the balance went to marketing, promotion, and the amortized cost of developing the iTunes software.[51] However, if not wildly profitable, iTunes was still considered a media giant, especially with its over 435 million accounts stored in its database as of 2013.[52]

Several competitors had tried to compete with the iTunes service. RealNetworks's Rhapsody subscription service, Yahoo MusicMatch, and AOL music downloads all had tried to compete for the remaining market share, using the potentially buggy Microsoft Windows Media format, and all had subsequently failed.[53] Even though one commentator had said in 2004 that "ultimately someone will build a piece of software that matches iTunes,"[54] as of 2013 the only serious competition was from Amazon.

At the start of 2013, iTunes accounted for over 60 percent of all digital music sales. In second place was Amazon's MP3 store with 16 percent market share. Google Play, eMusic, Zune Music Pass, Rhapsody, and a few others each captured 5 percent or less of the remaining sales. Growth, however, was occurring in the streaming service market, especially with the rising popularity of online radio and Internet streaming provider Pandora. This caused market watchers to wonder whether Apple might be thinking of adding a streaming capability to iTunes.[55]

The App Store

In March 2008, Apple announced that it was releasing the iPhone software development kit (SDK), allowing developers to create applications for the iPhone and iPod Touch and sell these third-party applications via the Apple App Store. The App Store was made available on iTunes, and it was directly available from the iPhone, iPad, and iPod Touch products. This opened the window for another group of Apple customers, the application developers, to collaborate with Apple. Developers could purchase the iPhone Developer Program from Apple for $99, create either free or commercial applications for the iPhone and iPod Touch, and then submit these applications to be sold in the App Store. Developers would be paid 70 percent of the download fee iPhone or iPod Touch customers paid to the App Store, and Apple would get 30 percent of the revenue. The applications ranged from simple audio files that were available for free (e.g., ringtones), to straightforward programs that sold for 99 cents (e.g., a program that turned the iPhone into a simple voice recorder), to full-featured applications that retailed for up to $69.99 (e.g., ForeFlight Mobile, which allowed pilots to get weather and airport information), and included complete games from top developers such as Zynga and Electronic Arts (EA).

As of January 2013, over 40 billion apps had been downloaded from Apple's App Store, but Google Play, the app store for Android users, was gaining ground, indicating that Google might be attracting more top-tier developers and quality titles to its marketplace. However, downloads for both platforms had slowed in 2013, causing market watchers to wonder if a plateau might be coming. This might mean diminishing returns and a less prosperous business model for all concerned.[56]

The Future of Apple

Although Steve Jobs had always been given credit for Apple's ability to innovate and to appeal especially to a certain type of consumer (Jobs had originally estimated Apple's market share in the creative-professional marketplace as over 50 percent),[57] Jobs himself credited his people:

> We hire people who want to make the best things in the world . . . our primary goal is to make the world's best PCs—not to be the biggest or the richest. We have a second goal, which is to always make a profit—both to make some money but also so we can keep making those great products. . . . [Regarding the systemization of innovation,] the system is that there is no system. That doesn't mean we don't have process. Apple is a very disciplined company, and we have great processes. But that's not what it's about. Process makes you more efficient . . . but innovation . . . comes from saying no to 1,000 things to make sure we don't get on the wrong track or try to do too much. We're always thinking about new markets we could enter, but it's only by saying no that you can concentrate on the things that are really important.[58]

Jobs, according to the portrait laid out in countless biographies and articles over the years, was a control freak with a compulsive attention to detail. He routinely sent products back to the lab, killed them in their crib, demanded new features, or euthanized old ones, all while keeping Apple's attention narrowly focused on just a few products with the potential for high returns.[59]

With Jobs's death, the question on everyone's mind was obvious: Could Apple survive with Jobs gone? Most analysts were enthusiastic about the talents of Tim Cook. Cook was an operations genius, keen-minded, demanding, and adept at cutting costs while delivering complex products on time and coping with staggering growth targets. He was also monastic and incredibly devoted to Apple. He had been responsible for oversight of sales, customer support, and logistics—which meant much of the company had already reported to him. Cook had also ably run the company during Jobs's medical absences, so when Jobs gave the CEO job to Cook in 2011, most were satisfied.

However, in the past, Jobs had still remained involved in all major strategic decisions, even throughout his illness. Critics noted that Cook had been a good temporary replacement, but feared he lacked the dynamism and creative vision to see Apple continue its innovative growth.[60] Cook needed to demonstrate that the company's values—true passion for innovation, design excellence, and almost unstoppable momentum around new product development—would continue in Jobs's absence.[61] Cook needed to create a management structure that didn't depend on a single guiding genius like a Steve Jobs.

Since Jobs's death, there has been attrition and restructuring in the top ranks. Ron Johnson, former head of Apple Retail, responsible for the success of Apple Stores, left to try his luck as head of J.C. Penney. This meant Philip Schiller, head of Apple's worldwide marketing, had more on his plate. Scott Forstall, head of software design, was escorted out of the company in October 2012, presumably because of missteps and maverick moves, including the poorly researched Maps software.[62] Jonathan Ive, Apple's design chief, was asked to take on Forstall's software role as well as hardware, a move applauded in some circles. Ive's leadership in industrial design would become critical—with such a small product line, Apple could not afford a single misstep going forward. CEO Cook's leadership and the depth of his upper management team were critical. As one technophile put it, "no other company in the industry puts so much control over product direction and design in the hands of such a tiny number of executives."[63]

During Tim Cook's first year as CEO, he had had to deal with a flat economy, supplier troubles, increasing competition, investor panic, and possibly unrealistic expectations, and yet the company still grew by 60 percent. Under Cook, Apple appeared to be transitioning itself "from being a hypergrowth company to being a premium, branded consumer company." [64] It may be that Apple was becoming "simply a wildly profitable company that continues to be a major (or dominant) player in various product categories," and was that so bad?[65]

ENDNOTES

1. Allsopp, A. 2012. Apple shares drop 6.4% on worst trading day in four years, analysts speculate why. *MacWorld,* December 6, *www.macworld.co.uk/digitallifestyle/news/?newsid=3415160.*

2. Travlos, D. 2013. Is Apple losing its brand equity? *Forbes,* January 19, *www.forbes.com/sites/darcytravlos/2013/01/19/is-apple-losing-its-brand-equity/.*

3. Stone, B., & Burrows, P. 2011. The essence of Apple. *Bloomberg Businessweek,* January 24–30.

4. Apple Inc. 2012/2013. 2012 annual report, 10-K filing; 2013 10Q filing. Available at *www.apple.com/investor*.

5. World's most admired companies. 2012. *Fortune,* 165, no. 4 (March 19): 139–140.

6. Apple was the first firm to have commercial success selling GUI systems, but Xerox developed the first systems in 1973. Xerox PARC researchers built a single-user computer called the Alto that featured a bit-mapped display and a mouse and the world's first what-you-see-is-what-you-get (WYSIWYG) editor. From *www.parc.xerox.com/about/history/default.html*.

7. Apple Inc. 2012. 2012 annual report, 10-K filing. Available at *www.apple.com/investor*.

8. January 24, 2009, was the 25th anniversary of the Macintosh, unveiled by Apple in the "Big Brother" Super Bowl ad in 1984. Watch via YouTube: *www.youtube.com/watch?v=OYecfV3ubP8*. See also the 1983 Apple keynote speech by a young Steve Jobs, introducing this ad: *www.youtube.com/watch?v=lSiQA6KKyJo*.

9. See Mank, D. A., & Nystrom, H. E. 2000. The relationship between R&D spending and shareholder returns in the computer industry. *Engineering Management Society, Proceedings of the 2000 IEEE,* 501–504.

10. Apple Inc. 2001. Ultra-portable MP3 music player puts 1,000 songs in your pocket. October 23. *www.apple.com/pr/library/2001/oct/23ipod.html*.

11. Apple Inc. 2010. Apple sells two million iPads in less than 60 days. Press release. May 31, *www.apple.com/pr/library/2010/05/31Apple-Sells-Two-Million-iPads-in-Less-Than-60-Days.html*.

12. BBC News. 2010. Apple passes Microsoft to be biggest tech company. BBC News, May 27, *www.bbc.co.uk/news/10168684*.

13. Keizer, G. 2012. Apple drains iPhone5 pre-order supplies in an hour. *Computerworld,* September 14. *www.computerworld.com/s/article/9231285/Apple_drains_iPhone_5_pre_order_supplies_in_an_hour*.

14. Schlender, B. 2005. How big can Apple get? *Fortune,* February 21. *money.cnn.com/magazines/fortune/-fortune_archive/2005/02/21/8251769/index.htm*.

15. Tofel, K. C. 2012. Why only Samsung builds phones that outsell iPhones. *GigaOM,* November 9, *www.businessweek.com/articles/2012-11-09/why-only-samsung-builds-phones-that-outsell-iphones*.

16. Apple Inc. 2012. 2012 Annual Report; Palladino, V. 2013. Apple Store receives trademark for "distinctive design and layout." *Wired,* January 30. *www.wired.com/design/2013/01/apple-store-trademark/*.

17. Burrows, P. 2004. The seed of Apple's innovation. *BusinessWeek Online,* October 12, *www.businessweek.com/bwdaily/dnflash/oct2004/nf20041012_4018_db083.htm*.

18. Fox, F. 2008. Mac Pro beats HP and Dell at their own game: Price. LowEndMac.com, May 16, *lowendmac.com/ed/fox/08ff/mac-pro-vs-dell-hp.html*.

19. Lowensohn, J. 2012. Lingering issues found at Foxconn's iPhone factory. *CNET,* December 14, *news.cnet.com/8301-13579_3-57559327-37/lingering-issues-found-at-foxconns-iphone-factory/*.

20. Bennett, D. 2012. Apple's Cook says more Macs will be born in the U.S.A. *Bloomberg Businessweek,* December 10, www.businessweek.com/articles/2012-12-10/apples-cook-says-more-macs-will-be-born-in-the-u-dot-s-dot-a-dot.

21. Apple Inc. 2012. 2012 annual report; King, R. 2011. Inventing the future of computing. *Bloomberg Businessweek,* October 31, www.businessweek.com/technology/inventing-the-future-of-computing-10312011.html.

22. Jones, A., & Vascellaro, J. E. 2012. Apple v. Samsung: The patent trial of the century. Wall Street Journal, July 24, online.wsj.com/article/SB10000872396390443295404577543221814648592.html?mod=wsj_streaming_apple-v-samsung-trial-over-patents.

23. Evans, J. 2012. iPhone 5 component supply challenges could threaten Apple's empire. *Computerworld,* September 6, blogs.computerworld.com/smartphones/20947/iphone-5-component-supply-challenges-could-threaten-apples-empire.

24. *StealingShare.com*. 2006. Growing market share—branding in the computer industry 2006. *www.stealingshare.com/content/1137644625875.htm*.

25. Apple Inc. 2013. Apple's first quarter results, 2013.

26. Sharma, H., & Ghosh, S. Apple shares slide by most in over four years on disappointing iPhone sales. *Reuters,* January 24, news.yahoo.com/apples-weak-results-spark-fresh-round-price-target-115325283--finance.html.

27. IDC. 2013. Soft PC shipments in fourth quarter lead to annual decline as HP holds onto top spot, according to IDC. IDC, January 10, www.idc.com/getdoc.jsp?containerId=prUS23903013#.UQSWjPJ5V8F.

28. *MacWorld Middle East*. 2011. Apple shipments up in US: Market share boosted. January 14, *www.macworldme.net/2011/01/14/apple-shipments-up-in-us-market-share-boosted/*.

29. Elmer-DeWitt, P. 2008. Apple challenges Sony and Nintendo. Apple 2.0—Blogs, December 13, *apple20.blogs.fortune.cnn.com/2008/12/13/apple-challenges-sony-and-nintendo*.

30. Apple Inc. 2013. Apple's first quarter results, 2013.

31. *MacTech*. 2012. iPod still has 70% of MP3 player market. *MacTech,* July 24, *www.mactech.com/2012/07/24/ipod-still-has-70-mp3-player-market*.

32. Rehman, A. 2010. iPod gains 76 percent of mp3 player market in US while Zune is a failure with just 1 percent share after 4 years. *AbdulRehman.net,* July 14, *www.abdulrehman.net/ipod-gains-76-percent-of-mp3-player-market-in-us-while-zune-is-a-failure-with-just-1-percent-share-after-4-years/*.

33. Ogren, E. 2007. Ballmer says iPhone won't succeed. Has Windows Mobile? *InformationWeek,* May 1, *www.informationweek.com/blog/main/archives/2007/05/ballmer_says_ip.html*.

34. IDC. 2012. Worldwide mobile phone growth expected to drop to 1.4 % in 2012 despite continued growth of smartphones, according to IDC. IDC. December 4, *www.idc.com/getdoc.jsp?containerId=prUS23818212#.UQSn-_J5V8E*.

35. Bar, Z. 2013. A cheaper iPhone would confirm a lack of innovation and declining margins at Apple. *Seeking Alpha,* January 9, *seekingalpha.com/article/1102591-a-cheaper-iphone-would-confirm-a-lack-of-innovation-and-declining-margins-at-apple*.

36. Ibid.

37. Wagstaff, J. 2012. In Asia's trend-setting cities, iPhone fatigue sets in. Reuters, January 27, *www.yahoo.com/asias-trend-setting-cities-iphone-fatigue-sets-212849658--finance.html*.

38. Farzad, R. 2012. The autumn of Apple's discontent. *Bloomberg Businessweek,* December 6, *www.businessweek.com/articles/2012-12-06/as-apples-stock-slides-a-lone-analyst-sounds-the-alarm*.

39. Pogue, D. 2010. Looking at the iPad from two angles. *New York Times,* March 31, *www.nytimes.com/2010/04/01/technology/personaltech/01pogue.html?_r=1&pagewanted=all&partner=rss&emc=rss*.

40. McCracken, H. 2010. iPad. *Time,* November 11, *www.time.com/time/specials/packages/article/0,28804,2029497_2030652,00.html*.

41. Cellan-Jones, R. 2011. iPad 2 tablet launched by Apple's Steve Jobs. BBC News, March 2, *www.bbc.co.uk/news/technology-12620077*.

42. Johnson, J. 2013. Kindle Fire, Android tablets chip away at iPad marketshare. *Inquisitr,* January 2, *www.inquisitr.com/465784/kindle-fire-android-tablets-chip-away-at-ipad-marketshare/#Q2bAVTfXbEpu72tB.99*.

43. Saintvilus, R. 2012. iPad Mini proves major for Apple Shares. *Forbes,* November 23, *www.forbes.com/sites/richardsaintvilus/2012/11/23/ipad-mini-proves-major-for-apple-shares/*.

44. Epstein, Z. 2012. iPad mini deemed a "game changer," outgrew Kindle Fire by nearly 50%. BGR, December 13, *bgr.com/2012/12/13/ipad-mini-market-share-2012/*.

45. Schlender. 2005. How big can Apple get?

46. Apple Inc. 2009. Apple announces Safari 4—the world's fastest and most innovative browser. Press release. February 24, *www.apple.com/pr/library/2009/02/24safari.html.*

47. Siracusa, J. 2008. Straight out of Compton: Google Chrome as a paragon of ambition, if not necessarily execution. *ars technica,* September 2, *arstechnica.com/staff/fatbits/2008/09/straight-out-of-compton.ars.*

48. Snell, J. 2009. Google Chrome: A wake-up call for Safari. *PC World,* February 24, *www.pcworld.com/businesscenter/article/160129/google_chrome_a_wakeup_call_for_safari.html.*

49. Jones, C. 2012. Mobile and desktop November web browser market shares. *Forbes,* December 14, *www.forbes.com/sites/chuckjones/2012/12/14/mobile-and-desktop-november-web-browser-market-shares/.*

50. Cheng, R. 2012. Apple CEO: We are "extremely sorry" for Maps flap. CNET, September 28, *news.cnet.com/8301-13579_3-57522196-37/apple-ceo-we-are-extremely-sorry-for-maps-flap/.*

51. Cherry, S. 2004. Selling music for a song. *Spectrum Online,* December, *www.spectrum.ieee.org/dec04/3857.*

52. Lee, E. 2012. Apple's iTunes would be one of world's biggest media companies. *Bloomberg News,* December 3, *go.bloomberg.com/tech-blog/2012-12-03-apple%E2%80%99s-itunes-would-be-one-of-world%E2%80%99s-biggest-media-companies/.*

53. Leonard, D. 2006. The player. *Fortune,* March 8, *money.cnn.com/magazines/fortune/fortune_archive/2006/03/20/8371750/index.htm.*

54. Salkever, A. 2004. It's time for an iPod IPO. *BusinessWeek,* May 5, *www.businessweek.com/technology/content/may2004/tc2004055_8689_tc056.htm.*

55. Archer, R. 2012. iTunes dominates download market & streaming audio grows. *Cepro,* October 10, *www.cepro.com/article/itunes_dominates_download_market_streaming_audio_grows/.*

56. Empson, R. 2013. Report: Market for paid apps hits $8B in 2012, while average revenue per app drops 27%. *TechcrunchI,* January 22, *techcrunch.com/2013/01/22/report-market-for-paid-apps-hits-8b-in-2012-while-average-revenue-per-app-drops-27/.*

57. Goodell, Jeff. 2003. Steve Jobs: *Rolling Stone,* December 25, Issue 938/939, p31-33.

58. Burrows. The seed of Apple's innovation.

59. Stone, B., & Burrows, P. 2011. Apple, with or without Steve Jobs. *Bloomberg Businessweek,* January 19, *www.businessweek.com/magazine/content/11_05/b4213006664366.htm.*

60. Eaton, K. 2011. 8 potential replacements for Steve Jobs at Apple. *Fast Company,* January 21, *www.fastcompany.com/1719458/who-could-replace-steve-jobs-at-apple.*

61. Davey, N. 2011. Apple and Steve Jobs: Can you separate the brand from the man? *MyCustomer.com,* January 24, *www.mycustomer.com/topic/marketing/apple-and-steve-jobs-can-you-separate-brand-man/118964.*

62. Grobart, S. 2012. Steve Jobs's "Sorcerer's Apprentice" is out at Apple. *Bloomberg Businessweek,* October 29, *www.businessweek.com/articles/2012-10-29/steve-jobs-sorcerers-apprentice-is-out-at-apple.*

63. Egan, M. 2012. Why Apple products will now stop failing. *Datamation,* October 31, *www.datamation.com/feature/why-apple-products-will-now-stop-failing-1.html.*

64. Russolillo, S. 2013. Apple losing luster: Is it now a value stock? *Wall Street Journal,* January 14, *blogs.wsj.com/marketbeat/2013/01/14/apple-growth-or-value-stock/.*

65. Grobart, S. 2013. Apple and Google: Slouching toward steady profits. *Bloomberg Businessweek,* January 22, *www.businessweek.com/articles/2013-01-22/apple-and-google-slouching-toward-steady-profits.*

A

ABB; *see* Asea Brown Boveri
Abbott's Frozen Custard, C113
ABC TV, 300, 381, C41
Abercrombie & Fitch, C51, C52, C54
Accenture, 20, 112, 128, 216–217
Access Health, 128–129
Accion, C136
Accor, C2
Ace Hardware, 154
Adam's Mark hotels, 147
Adelphia Communications, 202, 365
Adidas, 17
Adobe Systems, 20, C20
ADP Corporation, 279
Aer Lingus, C149, C152
AES, 368
Ahold USA, C205, C208
AIG; *see* American International Group
Airbus Industrie, 266, C152, C221
Air Products and Chemicals Inc., 386
   staffing for innovation, 387
AirTran Holdings Inc., C137, C142,
   C143, C147
Akami Technologies, 120–121
Al Ahram Beverages Company, C62
Alamo Drafthouse Cinemas, C104
Alberto-Culver, 165
Albertsons, 28, 142
Alchemy & Science, C129
Alcon Inc., C240
Aldi, 143, 145, 215
Alibaba Group, C74, C81, C82, C83
Alico, 181
Alike, C268
All American Specialty Restaurants Inc., C113
Allegheny International, 41
Allergan, C30
Alliance of Automobile Manufacturers, C233
Alliant Energy of Iowa, 366
Allied Signal, 78
ALLtech Inc., C107
Alpha Natural Resources, 303–304
Amazon, 46, 57, 86, 87, 88, 126, 157, 183, 260–
   261, 266, 382, 384, 392, 402, C21, C22, C24,
   C25, C74, C102, C186, C209, C210, C211
   competition with Apple Inc., 269
   competition with eBay, C82–C83
Amazon Prime, 88
Amazon Web Services, 58
AmBev, C60
AMC, C98, C99, C104
American Airlines, C143, C147, C152
American Association of Community
   Organizations, C247
American Business Information, 51
American Cancer Society, C251
American Gaming Association, C15

American Heart Association, C252
American Honda Motor Company Inc., C228
American Institute of Philanthropy, C253
American International Group, 181
American International Group, case
   CEO compensation, C6
   credit default swaps problem, C4
   excess bonus payments, C4–C6
   in financial crisis of 2008, C4
   government bailout, C4
   leadership failure, C5–C6
   lowered credit rating, C4
American Productivity and Quality
   Center, 387
American Suzuki Motor Corporation, C229
America Online, 180, C270, C272
Amgen, 9
Amoco, 181, 187
AMR Corporation, 224, C152
AmTran Technology, 261
Anderson Consulting, 120, 128, C205
Andersen Windows, 154
Andersen Worldwide, 201
Andrew Corporation, 362
Anheuser-Busch InBev, 193, C60, C61, C128,
   C131, C132, C133, C136
   description, C134–C135
Aniboom, 199
Ann Hewitt Associates, 116
ANN Inc., C54
Ann Taylor, case
   in apparel industry, C51–C54
   balance sheet, C50
   brand identity, C55–C56
   brands, C47
   business-level strategy, C48–C49, C53–C54
   cannibalization problem, C55
   cash flow statements, C51
   CEO change, C47, C49
   company history, C48–C49
   competitors, C51–C54
   corporate-level strategy, C54–C55
   customer base, C47
   divisions, C47, C48–C49
   in financial crisis of 2008, C47, C49
   financial performance, C48
   future initiatives, C56
   income statements, C50
   initial public offering, C48
   management turnover, C55–C56
   multichannel sales approach, C54
   operations, C54–C55
   product line expansion, C49
   restructuring plan, C49, C54–C55
   sales 2005–2012, C49
Ann Taylor Factory, C49
Ann Taylor LOFT, C47
AOL Time Warner, 206, C69
Apollo Group, 291

Applegate Inc., C113
Apple Inc., 2, 17, 57, 60, 84, 92, 107, 116, 131,
   132, 147, 155, 181, 183, 194, 230, 282, 284,
   352, 382, 385, 391, 403
   versus Amazon, 269
   and competitors, 61
   market value, 108
Apple Inc., case
   alliance with Microsoft, C20
   breakthrough products, C20
   business units
Apple Stores, 271
APQC (American Productivity
   and Quality Center), 387
aQuantive, 180
Arcelor, 193
ArcelorMittal, divisional boundaries, 318
Arco, 181
Arthur Andersen, 15
Asea Brown Boveri, 232
Arkore International, 199
Atlas Door, creating competitive
   advantage, 158–160
Audi, 171
Autobytel.com, 404
AutoNation, 27
Autonomy, 180
AutoVAZ, 220

B

B. Dalton, 88
Baby Bells, 51
Bain & Company, 112
Bankhaus Metzler, 153
Bank of America, 202
Barnes & Noble, 3, 4, 88, 157, 266
Bassett Furniture, 402
Bath & Body Works, C66
Bear Stearns, 2
Beca Group, 81–82
Beecham Group, 196
Bellagio, C13
Ben & Jerry's, 150
Beneficial Financial, 195
Berkshire Hathaway, 75, 184–185,
   189, 319
Best Buy, 15, 156, 187
Best Practices LLC, 403
Betaworks, 247
Biocon, 200
Black Tooth Brewing, 132
Blissful Yoga, 271
Blockbuster Inc., 36, 157
Blue Bell, C108
Blue Cross of California, 59
Blue Sky Creamery, C113
BMW, 61, 63, 71, 75–76, 147, 152
   Mini cars, 153

BMW-Mini, C227
BNP Paribas, 193
Board Source, C253
Boeing Company, 20, 217, 227, 266, 311–313, 429, C138, C221, C232, C233
Boise Cascade, 188
Bombay Company, 402
Booz Allen Hamilton, 292
Borders, 5, 36
  demise of, 3–4
Boston Consulting Group, 143, 190–191, 198, 226, 242, 264
Boston Research Group, 280
Boston Scientific, 193
Bowls: A Cereal Joint, 151
Brinker International mission statement, 25
British American Tobacco, 64
British Petroleum, 5, 18, 181, 204, 292
British Sky Broadcasting, 302
Brocade, 290
Buffalo Grid, global start-up, 233
Burberry, 163
Burdines, 76
Business Round-table, 292, 326
  and sustainability practices, 327

C

Cable Value Network shopping channel, C64
Cabot Corporation, 192
Cadbury Schweppes, 429
Cadillac, 316
CalPERS, 295
Calvin Klein, 167
Campbell Soup Company, 75, 80
Canadean Ltd., C60
Cannondale, 147, 155
Canon, 24
Cargill, 86
CarMax, 79
  competitive analytics, 80
Carrier Air Conditioning, 39
Casio, 183
Casual Male Retail Group, 44
Catalyst, 114
CA Technologies, 285
Caterpillar, Inc., 147, 165, 320
  value chain analysis, 99–100
Cathay Pacific, 11
CBS, 327, 381
CCU, C60
Celanese Chemical Corporation, 223
Cendant, 91
Center for Applied Management, 430
Center for Automotive Research, 59
Center for Talent Innovation, 114
Center for Work-Life Policy, 112
Cerberus Capital, 180
Cereal Bowl, 151
Cereal Cabinet, 151
Cereality, 151
Challenger Electrical Distribution, 326
Chartwell Investments, 349
Cheesecake Factory, 147–148
Chemical Bank, 370
Chery Automobile Company, 63
Chevrolet, 54, 62, 71, 316
Chico's, C47

Chili's, 25
Choice Hotels, 337
Chrysler Corporation, 2, 15, 63, 147, 169, 180, 195, 270
Ciba-Geigy, 182
Cigar City Brewing, 132
Circuit City, 2, 36
Cisco Systems, 126, 128, 132, 178–180, 194, 320, 392
Citibank, 358
Citicorp, 229
Citigroup, 5, 40, 292, 297
Clayton, Dublilier & Rice, 189, 198
Clearspire.com, 163
Clearwell Systems Inc., 163
Clegg, 112
CNBC, 300
CNET, 58
CNN/Money, 250
CNN/U.S., 292
Coca-Cola Company, 87, 165, 218, 223, 226, 227, 230, 238, 239, 297, 331, 384, 387, 402, C159
  partner with DEKA, 388
Colgate-Palmolive, 271
Comcast, 84
Commerce Bank, breakaway positioning, 167
Compaq Computer, 276
ConAgra, 86, 182, 318
Cone Communications, 18
ConocoPhillips, 203–204
Conseco, 180, 195
Construction Users Anti-Inflation Roundtable, 327
Continental Airlines, 87, 144, 195, 284
Cooper Industries, 181, 182
Cooper Software, Inc., 111
Coors Brewing, 147
Corel, 196
Corning, 364
Corptech, 362
Costco Home Stores, 402
Costco Wholesale Corporation, 261
Countrywide Financial, 289, 299
Craigslist, 222
Custom Research Inc, 149
CVS Pharmacies, 151
Cypress Semiconductor, 23

D

Daily Deal Media, 86
Daimler-Benz, 180, 326
Dart, 203
DataWind, 213
Dayton Hudson Corporation, 203
Deere & Company, 219
DEKA Research, 387, 388
Dell Inc., 85, 116, 152–153, 157, 401
  eroding competitive advantage, 89–90
Deloitte Consulting, 299, 400
Deloitte Touche Tohmatsu, 400
Delphi Corporation, 59
Delta Air Lines, 13, 195
Deschutes Brewery, 132
Destination XL, 44
Diamond Offshore Drilling, 190
Digital Directory Assistance, 51
Digital Equipment Corporation, 40, 125
Discovery Communications, 296

Disneyland, 24
Diversity, 265
dMarc, 377
Dolce & Gabbana, 81
Dollar General, 143
Dow Jones & Company, 450
Dream Works SKG, 362
Dropbox, 58
Drybar, 271
Duke Energy, 113, 193
Duke Power of Indiana, 366
Dun & Bradstreet, 124
DuPont, 385
Duracell, 151
Dutch Boy, 378
  innovation at, 379

E

eBay, 3, 195, 364, 384
Ecolab, 265
Edatanetworks, 248
Eleuria, 155
ElevationLab, C188
Eli Lilly & Company, 55
E-Loan, 254, 273
EMC, 361
Emerson Electric, 284
Encyclopaedia Britannica, 36, 39, 73
Enron Corporation, 15, 201, 202, 299, 365
Epic, 364
Ernst & Young, 299
ExxonMobil, 181, 296

F

Facebook, 120, 126, 152, 247, 254, 352
Fannie Mae, 40
Federal Express, 11, 84, 150, 282, 327
  mission statement, 25
Ferrari, 62, 63, 171
Fiat, 195
Fidelity Investments, 295, 325
Fleet Mortgage, 76
Flickr, 179
Food Lion, 300
Ford Motor Company, 21, 22, 62, 63, 147, 171, 185, 218, 229, 233, 270, 326, 331, 363
  turnaround, 170
Forrester Research, 165
Fortune Brands, 27
Fox Business Network, 300
Fractal Graphics, 49
Freddie Mac, 40
FreeMarkets, 52
Freeport-McMoran, 181
Full Sail Brewing, 132

G

Gateway Computer, 363
Geek Squad, 187
Geely Automotive, 170
General Dynamics, 168, 368
General Electric, 5, 20, 26, 78, 79, 113, 115, 193, 201, 212, 219, 324, 361, 364
General Electric Aerospace, 1668
General Electric Healthcare, 219
General Electric Lighting, 325

General Electric Medical Systems, 111
General Mills, 236, 283
General Motors, 5, 20, 21, 59, 63, 147, 210,
    270, 300
Genzyme, 228
Gerber Products Company, 86
Gibson guitars, 150
Gillette Company, 151, 183
GlaxoSmithKline, 114–115, 344–345
Global Crossing, 201
Gmarket Inc., 195,
Goldcorp, 46
    crowdsourcing by, 49
Goldman Sachs, 296
Goodyear Aerospace, 166
Google Inc., 2, 24, 57, 86, 107, 111, 112, 117, 131,
    152–153, 181, 246, 266, 282, 376–378, 382,
    384, 392, 403
    market value, 108
Graybar Electric Company, 404
Greenpeace, 17
Green Tree Financial, 180, 195
Greylock Partners, 246
Groupon, 86
GSI Commerce, 195
Gucci, 81, 151, 220
Guidant, 193
GVO, 351

H

H. J. Heinz Company, 331
Hamilton, 167
Hanover Insurance, 360
Hardtofindix.com, 222
Harley-Davidson, 84, 145
Harley-Davidson Café, 84
Harry Winston, 167
HCI Direct, 76
    evaluation system, 116
Healtheon, 416
HealthSouth Corporation, 365
Heidrick & Struggles, 293
Hewlett-Packard, 5, 23, 117, 125, 127, 153, 180,
    238, 276–277, 326
Hill & Knowlton/Harris Interactive, 18
Hilton Hotels, 337
Hindustan Unilever, 113, 213
Hitachi, 105
Home Brewers Association, 132
Home Depot, 44, 154, 282, 286
Home Shopping Network, 110
Honda Motor Company, 6, 54, 63, 71, 75, 147
Honeywell ElectroOptics, 168
Honeywell International, Inc., 41, 46, 78
Household International, 195
HTC, 131
Huawei, 349
Hudson Square Research, 88
Hyatt Hotels, 337
Hyundai Motors, 61, 62, 63, 72

I

IBM, 20, 21, 40, 53, 91, 120, 169, 183, 216, 229,
    238, 284, 296, 326, 387, 437, 449
    alliance with WellPoint, 184
    innovation jam, 389
IBM Global, 80

Icos Corporation, 55
IDEO, 22
Ignition Corporation, 120
IKEA, 8, 369
ILS Technology, 200
Imperial Tobacco, 64
Infosys, 216, 233, 349
    ethics and values, 350
ING SRI Index Fund, 20
Institute for Supply Management, 79
Intel Architecture labs, 362
Intel Corporation, 5, 14, 79, 107, 113,
    114, 181, 224, 238, 264, 288, 362, 385,
    387, 392, 397
    market value, 108
International Paper Company, 20, 46, 107
    sustainable business practices, 21
International Public Relations Association, 77
Internet Nonprofit Center, C253
Interstate Bakeries, 140
Intuit, 169, 190, 258, 364, 384
Iowa Beef Processors, 86
Ispionage, 39
iTunes Music Store, 61

J

J. D. Power & Associates, 54, 149, 170
Jaguar, 170, 185
Japan Tobacco International, 64
JCPenney, 62
Johnson & Johnson, 37, 345, 346, 383, 392,
    C161, C162
Johnson Controls, 396
JPMorgan Chase, 15, 297, 370
Juno Online Services, 76

K

Kaufmann Foundation, 252
Kazaa, 61
Kellogg's, 228
Kentucky Fried Chicken, 186
Kia Motors, 62, 63
Kickstarter, 253
Kidder Peabody, 201
KKR, 189
KKR Capstone, 189
Klout, 246–247
Kmart, 61, 165
Korn/Ferry International, 293
Košice, 271–272
KPMG, 112
Kraft Foods Group, 230
Kroger stores, 142, 287

L

L. L. Bean, 380
Labor Law Study Committee, 327
La Boulange, 185
Lacoste, 81
Lamborghini, 62, 63, 171
Land Rover, 170
Lands' End, 155, 380
La Quinta, 337
Lay's, 230
LegalZoom.com, 57
Lego, 40, 391

Lehman Brothers, 299
Lending Tree, 273
Lenscrafters, 263
Levi Strauss, 363, 370
Lexus, 63, 147, 149, 282
LG Electronics, 78
    procurement, 79
Lightsaver Technologies, reshoring operations, 226
LinkedIn, 152, 153, 254, 427
Linksys, 178
Lipton Tea, 150
Little Monster Productions, 253
Litton Industries, 41
LivingSocial, 86
Lockheed Martin, 9, 112, 168, 188
Loews Corporation, 190, C98
Logitech, 322
Longine, 167
Loral Corporation, 188
Lotus Corporation, 238
Lowe's, 44, 154
Luxottica, 263

M

Make Meaning, 272
Mandalay Entertainment, 22
March Group, 327
Marks and Spencer, 285, 288
    measurable goals, 286
Marlin Steel Wire Products, 152–153
Marriott Corporation, 144
Mars Central Europe, 284
Martin guitars, 147
Martin Marietta, 9
Maserati of North America Inc., C229
Massey Energy, 292
Mattel, C68
Maui Brewing, 132
Mayo Clinic, 37, 326
    knowledge organization, 38
McDonald's Corporation, 24, 186, 188–189, 228,
    285, 305
    external control mechanisms, 301
McKesson, 182
McKinsey & Company, 19, 40, 242
Medtronic, 24, 147, 198
Men's Wearhouse, 44
Mercedes-Benz, 61, 63, 70–71, 151, 171
Merck & Company, 94, 107, 115
Merrill Lynch, 2, 5, 104–105, 106, 202
Metabolix, 251
MetLife, 181
Metorex, 7
Microchip Technologies, 132
Microsoft Corporation, 2–4, 39, 45, 73, 78, 107,
    109, 111, 120, 127, 180, 193, 203, 218, 220,
    224, 287, 297, 306, 351, 352, 364, 391, 403,
    427
    market value, 108
Microsoft Exchange, 403
Microsoft Kinect for Xbox 360
    description, C182
Millennium Hotels, 337
Mini Cooper, 71
Mint.com, 259
Mittal Steel, 193
MonsterTRAK, 110
Morgan Stanley, 147

Morgan Street Brewing, 132
Morningstar, 20
Motel 6, 37, 40
Motorola, 24, 394, 399
MRM Worldwide, 199
Music Genome Project, 258
MySimon, 58
Mystery Brewing Company, 253

N

Napster, 61, 131
National Association of Corporate Directors, 293
National Federation of Independent Business, 255
National Geographic, 327
Natura Cosméticos, 351, 352
NBC-TV, 381
NEC, 19
Neiman Marcus, 62
Nestlé SA, 185–186, 226, 232
Netflix, 157, 295
NewPage Corporation, 110
New York Times vs. Wall Street Journal, 266
Nextel, 180
Niagara College, 132
Nike, Inc., 17, 187, 218, 224, 228, 268, 329, 331, 392
    external control mechanisms, 301
Nikeid.com, 155
Nintendo, 60, 393
Nissan Motor Company, 54, 63, 71, 330
Nokia, 119
Nordstrom, 61, 76, 81–82, 147, 368
Norian, 344–345
North Face, 147
Northwest Airlines, 195
Not Your Average Joe's, 283
Novartis, 11, 182
Novell, 196, 270
NPD Group, 179
Nucor Steel Company, 107, 175, 282
    market value, 108
Nynex, 51

O

O. R. T. Technologies, 222–223
Office Depot, 156
Olam Industries, 19
Oldsmobile, 316
Olympus Corporation, 15, 289
Omega watches, 167
1-800-Got-Junk, 126
On the Border, 25
Oracle Corporation, 107, 127, 203, 218, 229, 297, 427, 437
Otis elevator, 39
Outboard Marine Corporation, 24
Overstock.com, 400
Oxford ClycoSciences, 228

P

Pacific Gas and Electric, 300
Pacific Investment Management Company, 371
Paychex, 59
Pearle Vision, 263
Penske Automotive Group, 71
PeopleSoft, 203

PepsiCo, 77, 87, 112, 186, 218, 219, 238, 327, 402
    in India, 239
Pfizer, Inc., 55, 86, 94, 134, 193, 197, 220, 222, 284, 381
Phelps Dodge, 181
Philip Morris, 64
Pier 1 Imports, 37
Pizza Hut, 186
Plant PET Technology Collaboration, 331
Plum Organics, 259
Polaroid, 125
Porsche, 62, 63, 402
PPG Industries, 27
Premier Automotive Group, 170
Priceline.com, 201, 337
PricewaterhouseCoopers, 118, 325, 326
ProCD, 51, 73
Procter & Gamble, 16–17, 19, 27, 36, 46, 113, 165–166, 181, 218, 230, 271, 320–321, 331, 333, 382, 448
    boundaryless organization, 334
    innovativeness, 383
    prosumer concept, 81
    in Vietnam, 231
Progress Energy, 193
Providence Equity Partners, 97
Pryor Cashman LLP, 253
Pure Digital Technologies, 178
Puritan-Bennett Corporation, 326

Q

Quaker Oats, 163, 196
Quora, 39
Qwest Communications, 357

R

Radio Shack, 2, 156
Raimaker Entertainment, 392
Ralphs, 28, 142
Raytheon, 122, 370
Rdio, 258
Reckitt Benckiser, 118
    workplace diversity, 119
Recreational Vehicle Dealer Association, 185
Redbox, 157
Reddit, 246
Reebok, 187, 230, 329
Renault, 145, 220
    low costs, 146
Renault-Nissan, 326
Research in Motion, 384
Ritz-Carlton Hotels, 285
Roche, 429
Rock Center for Corporate Governance, 293
Rockwell Collins, 360
Roomkey.com, 337–338
Royal Dutch Shell, 401
Running Press, 262
Ryanair, 267

S

Saab Cars North America, Inc., C229
Salemi Industries, 34–35
Samsung Electronics, 131, 230, 261, 265
Samsung Group, 24
SAP, 46, 277, 369, 437

knowledge sources, 129
Sapient Health Network, 415
    analysis, decision making and change, 416
Sears, 2, 21, 61, 96, 111, 147
Sears Vision, 263
Security Mortgage Group, 429
Sephora.com, 76
Seventh Generation, 28
Shanghai Automotive Industry Corporation, 210
Shaw Industries, 75, 182, 184–185, 186
    vertical integration, 187
Shell Oil Company, 19, 41, 117
ShopRunner, 88
Siebel Systems, 229, 297
Siemens AG, soft power, 310–311, 353
Sikorsky helicopters, 39
Singapore Airlines, 286
Single Source Systems, 27
Siri Inc., 194
Six Flags, C112
Skype, 128, 193, 352
Slideshare, 39
SmithKline Beecham, 196, 325
Snapple Beverage Corporation, 196
Sodima, 236
Softbank, 180, 193
Solectron, 112–113
Solomon Smith Barney, 180
Songza, 258
Sony Computer Entertainment, 393
Sony Corporation, 6, 19, 200, 261, 393
Southern Alliance for Clean Energy, 366
Southwest Airlines, 5, 8, 79, 86, 87, 107, 111, 267, 282, 380
    market value, 108
Spanx, 259
Sports Authority, 88
Spotify, 258
Sprecher Brewing, 132
Sprint, 20, 180, 193
Sprint Nextel, 180
Square, 258
SsangYong, 211
Starbucks, 185, 249
Standard and Poor's, 4, 15
Studio, 100
Sunbeam Corporation, 201, 431
Sunglass Hut, 263
Sun Microsystems, 127
Supercell, 337–338
Swatch Group, breakaway positioning, 167
Swatch Watches, 70
Sweetwater Brewing, 132

T

T. Rowe Price, 295
Taco Bell, 186
Tandem Computers, 117
Target Corporation, 203
Target Stores, 4, 17, 21, 165, 263, 296
Tata Group, 170, 199
Tata Motors, 63
Taylor Wall & Associates, 49
TCS, 216, 217
TD Bank, 167
Teach for America, 23
Tele-Communications Inc., 362
Tesco, 145, 210–215, 215

Tesoro, 203–204
Texas Instruments, 367
T.G.I. Friday's, 231
Third Millennium Communications, 120
3M Corporation, 87, 182, 200, 282, 363, 392
  environmental sustainability, 348
Time Warner, 180, 206, 297
Timothy's Coffee of the World Inc.,
T-Mobile, 185
Tokyo Electric Power Company, 5
TOMS, 268
Toro Company, 360
Toshiba Corporation, 5
Toyota Motor Company, 6, 54, 63, 71, 73, 75, 147,
    149, 170, 218, 264, 282
Trainer Refinery, 203
Travelocity.com, 337
Triarc, 196
Tribune, 2
True Value, 154
Tumblr, 104–106
Twitter, 161, 352
Tyco International, 15, 197, 202, 365
  divestment by, 198

U

Under Armour, Inc., 259
Unilever, 46, 148, 165–166, 213, 265, 271
  crowdsourcing by, 150
Unilife, 226
United Parcel Service, 11, 46
United Technologies, competitive intelligence, 39
Univision, 381
UpNext, 269
U.S. Memories, 330
U.S. Open Beer Championship, 132

V

Valero, 203–204
Values Technology, 117
Valve Software, 316
Vantage Hospitality, 337

Varian Medical Systems, 27
Verizon Communications, 327
Verizon Wireless, 200
Viewpoint DataLabs International, 90
Virgin Group, 21, 189
Vizio, Inc., 260
  low-cost imitator, 261
Vodafone, 213
Volkswagen, 171, 210, 218, 330
Volvo, 170
Vons, 28
Vought Aircraft, 311

W

Wachovia, 297
Wahaha, 87
Wall Street Journal vs. New York Times, 266
Walmart Stores Inc., 4, 8, 16, 17, 20, 46, 61, 62,
    143, 145, 155, 156, 165, 217, 219, 265, 280,
    282, 326, 327, 380
  sustainable business practices, 21
Walnut Venture Associates, 254
Walt Disney Company, 297
Warby Parker, combination strategy, 263
Washington Mutual, 5, 40, 297
Waste Management, 201
WBG Construction, 361
WD-40 Company, 261, 390
  teams at, 391
WebMD, 416
WellPoint Health Network, 59
  mission and vision, 25
Wells Fargo, 13, 24, 27, 112, 297
Westinghouse, 326
Wetherill Associates, 369
Whirlpool, 22, 327
Whole Foods Market, Inc., 143, 362
Wikipedia, 39, 46
Winnebago, 185
Wipro, 216
WordPerfect, 196
WorldCom, Inc., 201, 202, 299, 365
World Triathlon Corporation, 97

World Wildlife Fund, 17
WPP Group PLC, 126, 353
Wyeth, 193
Wynn Resorts, 291

X

Xerox Corporation, 24

Y

Yahoo!, 104–106, 254, 266, 292, 450
Yakult, 240
Yap, 269
Yokogawa, 348
Young & Rubicam, 353
Young Brands, 415
YouTube, 39, 84, 179
Yugo, 144
Yum! Brands, 186

Z

Zara, 199
Zenger Folkman, 359
Zhejiang Geely Holding Company, 63
Zimbra, Inc., 403
Zong, 195
Zynga, 24

NAME INDEX

A

Aaker, David A., 174, 244
Abby, E., 307
Abelson, J., C57
Abelson, R., C121, C122
Abelson, Reed, C243
Ackerman, Bill, C200
Ackerman, E., C273
Ackerman, Jason, C201, C202, C203
Adams, R., 102
Adams, S., 135
Adamy, J., C93
Adler, Charles, C186, C187, C189, C190
Adler, P. S., 137
Afuah, A., 68, 341
Agins, T., C57
Aguirre, D., 136
Ahlstrom, D., 309
Aiman-Smith, L., 409
Aime, F., 137
Akerson, Daniel, C214, C217, C218, C219
Akula, V., 242
Albanesius, Chloe, C184
Albaugh, Jim, 311
Albrinck, J., 409
Alcott, K., 226, 244
Aldag, R. J., 437
Aldrich, H. E., 274, 275
Alessandri, T. M., 309
Alexander, M., 207
Alexander the Great, C114
Allard, M. J., 137
Allen-MacGregor, Jacqueline, C252
Aller, R., 341
Allsop, A., C26
Alsever, J., 136
Alvarez, S. A., 66
Amabile, T. M., 136
Amburgey, T. L., 341
Amelio, Gilbert, C19, C20
Amit, R., 102
Ammana, Daniel, C218
Amos, Karen, C141
Amram, M., 409
An, J., C189
Anard, B. N., 208
Anders, G., 174
Andersen, M. M., 341, 374
Anderson, Abram, C135
Anderson, E., 101
Anderson, G., C114
Anderson, J. C., 100
Anderson, Jerry, 226
Anderson, M. M., 101, 102
Anderson, P., 135
Anderson, Richard, 13
Anderson, S., C255
Andreessen, Marc, 246

Andre the Giant, C68, C70
Angel, R., 102
Angle, Kurt, C70
Angwin, J. S., 208
Anmuth, Douglas, C67
Anslinger, P. A., 207
Ante, S. E., 180, 274
Anthony, Scott, 243, 364
Antoine, Dick, C198, C200
Apotheker, Leo, 277
Aramony, William, C252
Archer, R., C28
Argawal, A., 308
Argyris, Chris, 278, 306
Arikan, A. M., 31, 101
Arino, A., 208
Armstrong, R. W., 174
Arnaud, Bernard, C167, C170, C171, C176
Arndt, M., 207, C93
Arnold, D., 244
Arnold, Susan E., C198
Arnott, D. A., 307
Arregale, J.-L., 101, 137
Arrfelt, M., 304
Artzt, Ed, C196
Ash, L., 6
Ashkenas, R., 325
Assenza, Pauline, C17, C47
Aston, A., 67
Auerback, John, C190
Augustine, Norman R., 9, 31, 175
Austen, B., 30
Austin, R. D., 31, 174
Austin, Steve, C70, C72

B

Bacani, C., C184
Bachman, J., 243, C144
Back, A., C104
Backs, Melanie, C213
Bader, P., 138
Bahrami, H., 332
Baiao, Andy, C187
Baier, J., 135
Bailey, J., C153
Baker, Kevin, C60
Baker, Stephen, 67, 179, 307
Bakke, Dennis, 368, 375
Ball, B., C73
Ball, Robert M., C143
Ballou, J., 252
Balmer, Steven, 364
Balzar, Harry, C108
Bamford, C. E., 67
Bandler, J., 306
Bansal, P., 135
Ba-Oh, Jorge, C184

Bar, Z., C27
Barbaro, M., C57
Barbora, D., 17
Barger, David, C152
Barkema, H. P., 176, 208
Barkley, Charles, C36
Barman, Emily, C254
Barnes, B., 243, C10
Barnes, Christopher, 326–327, 341
Barnes, L. A., 436
Barnett, M. L., 68
Barnevik, Percy, 32, 136
Barney, J. B., 31, 66, 83, 101, 135, 174
Baron, R. A., 135, 274, 409
Barrera, Luz, C246
Barrett, A., C122
Barrett, Colleen, C137, C140, C141
Barrett, W. P., C254
Barrette, Michael, C107
Barringer, B. R., 342
Barry, Stephanie, 391
Barsoux, J., 307
Bart, C. K., 33
Bartholomew, D., C153
Bartlett, C. A., 175, 243, 317, 341
Bartness, A., 342
Barton, N., C254
Bartz, Carol, 292, C270, C271, C272
Barwise, P., 136
Bary, A., 10
Baugher, Dan, C135
Baum, J. A. C., 208
Baumgardner, M., 251
Baumgarter, P., 68
Bauwhede, H. V., 289
Bay, Michael, 77
Bay, W., C153
Baysinger, B. D., 308
Beamish, P. W., 243, 275
Beamish, Paul W., C155
Bearden, W. O., 175
Beartini, M., 97
Beatty, D., 308
Becht, Ben, 119
Becker, G. S., 135
Beckhard, R., 31, 325, 373
Begley, T. M., 31
Beiersdorf, Paul C., C155
Bell, Charles H., C89
Beller, P. C., 306
Belton, C., 242
Benioff, Marc, 384
Benkler, Y., 307
Bennett, D., C27
Bennett, N., 308
Bennett, Stephen M., 169–170
Benoit, Chris, C69
Benoit, D., 135
Bensaou, B. M., 101

Bensinger, G., 269
Benson, C., 21
Benz, M., 32
Berfield, S., 262, C233
Bergen, M. E., 174
Bergmann, Jens, C165
Berk, C. C., C56
Berkowitz, E. N., 243
Berkowitz, K., 175
Berle, Adolf, 290
Berlusconi, Silvio, 6
Berman, P., 316
Berman, Todd, 349
Bernanke, Ben, 40
Bernardino, Joseph, 201
Berner, R., 265
Berns, Gregory, 124
Bernstein, A., 309
Bernstein, Sanford C., 105
Berrard, Steven, C40
Berry, Halle, C64
Berry, J., 208
Berry, M. A., 32
Bertini, M., 174
Besley, S., 208
Bethune, Gordon, 144
Bettcher, K. E., 369
Bezos, Jeff, 4, 260–261, 269
Bezzera, Luigi, C260
Bhagat, R. S., 243
Bhatia, Arvind, C177
Bhattacharya, A. K., 243
Bhattacharya, C. B., 32
Bhide, A. V., 274, 309, 408
Bhushan, R., 239
Bickerton, L., C62
Bierce, Ambrose, 290
Bierman, L., 309
Bigley, G. A., 31
Bilbao, R., 338
Bindley, K., C189
Birger, Nicolai, C165
Birke, A., 254
Birkinshaw, J., 10, 31, 244, 307, 334, 342, 408
Bjelland, O. M., 389
Blacharski, D., 405
Blake, S., 137
Blanford, Lawrence, C256
Blank, Arthur, 282
Blank, D., C153
Blankenship, Don, 292
Blanton, Buddy, 360
Block, John, C262
Block, Z., 409
Bloom, M., 309
Bloomberg, Michael, C44
Blum, D. E., C255
Blumenthal, Neil, 262
Blumenthal, Richard, C6
Blyler, M., 102
Bodick, N., 174
Bodwell, C., 32
Boehm, Edward Marshall, C3
Boehmer, J., C144
Boehret, K., C184
Boesler, Matthew, C231
Bogner, W. C., 135
Boh, W. F., 137
Bolland, Marc, 286

Bonamici, K., C144
Bond, P., 309
Bonnabeau, E., 174
Boorstin, J., C104
Booth, Lewis, 170
Borders, Louis, 3
Borders, Tom, 3
Boris, C., C190
Bosman, J., C212
Bosse, D. A., 32
Bothe, Marie, 369
Boughner, Bob, C14
Bounds, G., 391
Bouquet, C., 307
Bourbeau, Tina, C210
Bouwer, Marc, C64
Bowen, D. E., 375
Bowen, H. P., 206
Bower, J. L., 10
Bower, Joseph, C220
Bowie, N. E., 203
Boyd, D. P., 31
Doyle, M., 67, C243
Brabeck, Peter, 232, 244
Braddock, Richard, C202, C205
Bradley, D., C73
Bradshaw, T., C273
Brady, D., 371
Brandenburger, A., 59, 60, 68
Brandes, P., 308, 309
Brandt, R., 307
Branson, Richard, 21, 32, 136
Brasher, P., 301
Brass, Dick, 405
Brat, I., C243
Bratzel, Stefan, 171
Brauer, K., C234
Bray, C., 307
Breech, Ernest, C220
Breen, B., 401
Brennan, Terrance, C202
Brenneman, K., 416
Bresser, R. F., 102
Bricklin, Dan, C19
Briggs, Bill, C213
Brigham, B., 208
Brigham, E. F., 208
Brin, Sergey, 384
Brnoff, J., 375
Broache, A., 67
Brock, Ruthie, 447n
Brockner, J., 374
Brockovich, Erin, 300
Brockstein, Marty, C92
Bromiley, P., 289
Brook, John, C60
Brook-Carter, C., C212
Brooker, K., 175
Brouthers, L. E., 243
Brown, E., 341
Brown, J. S., 129
Brown, Jeff, C71
Brown, R. H., 243
Brown, R. L., 67
Brown, S. L., 408
Brown, Tim, 22, 174, 413
Brück, Mario, C165
Bruder, J., C213
Bruno, K., C212

Brush, C., 409
Bruton, G. D., 309
Bryan, M., 259
Bryant, A., 31, 32, 33, 136, 274, 307, 342, 374, 375, 409, 436
Bryant, Clara Jane, C222
Bryant, James, 51
Bryce, D. J., 402
Bryon, E., 67
Buchanan, L., 275
Buckingham, M., 374
Buckley, M. R., 243
Buckman, R. C., 137
Buffett, Warren, 35–36
Bunderson, J. S., 341
Bungay, S., 33
Bunkley, N., C219, C234
Burgelman, R. A., 275, 341, 409
Burke, D., C200
Burke, Michael, C166, C176
Burnham, Dan, 370
Burrill, Greg, 361
Burris, Dan, 37, 38, 67
Burrows, P., 31, C10, C26, C27, C28
Burrus, D., 174, 356
Burt, Ronald S., 122, 137
Burton, R. M., 409
Bush, J., 68
Bush, Vannevar, C76
Buss, D., 259
Bussey, J., 383
Bustillo, M., 301
Butz, H. E., 175
Bygrave, W. D., 249, 274
Bynum, A., 208
Byrne, Carol, 447n
Byrne, J. A., 308
Byrne, James E., C73

C

Cabrera, Susana, 250
Caecelle, Yves, C166
Caho, L., C84
Cain, T., 100
Caldwell, D., 309
Caldwell, Jessica, C219
Callahan, Brian R., C106
Callanan, J., 374
Calliendo, H., 331
Cameron, K., 374
Camillus, J. C., 32, 40
Camp, B., 410
Campbell, A., 206, 207
Campbell, J. T., 101
Campbell, Joseph, C135
Camusi, Paul, C133
Cannella, A. A., Jr., 308
Canning, A., 156
Cantalupo, James R., C88, C89, C90, C91
Caplan, J., 174
Caplinger, D., C46, C57
Cappelli, P., 135, 137
Cappelli, Paul, C13
Carcelle, Yves, C170, C173
Cardin, R., 136
Cardinal, L. B., 408, 409
Cardona, M., C57
Cardoz, Floyd, C210

Carey, J., 68, 259
Carey, S., 204
Cariaga, V., C57
Carley, W. M., 136
Carlson, D. S., 375
Carmelli, A., 306
Carpenter, M., 308
Carr, N. G., 68
Carrey, Jim, C101
Carrott, G. T., 32
Carruba, Frank, 326
Carter, N. M., 307
Caruso, D., 374
Cash, J. I., Jr., 101
Casico, W. F., 207
Cassar, G., 274
Cassidy, J. C., 175
Catmull, Edwin E., C7–C10
Cattani, K., 175
Causey, Julie, 119
Caverly, D., C84
Cehn, S.-F. S., 342
Cellan-Jones, R., C27
Cena, John, C69, C71
Cerny, K., 342
Cescau, Patrick, 213
Cesesa, John, C217
Chahine, S., 309
Chakrabarti, A., 243
Challenger, J., 67
Chambers, John, 179
Champion, David, 151
Champoux, J. E., 374
Champy, James, 333, 342
Chan, C. M., 244
Chan, P., 175
Chandler, Alfred D., 340, 341
Chang, V., 136
Chang Donghoon, C194
Charan, R., 31, 347, 373
Charitou, C. D., 66
Charnovitz, S., 32
Chase, S., 119
Chatman, J., 136
Chatterjee, S., 33, 308
Chen, B., 206
Chen, B. X., C195
Chen, M. J., 264, 268, 275
Chen, Perry, C186, C187, C189, C190
Chen, Winston, 113
Chen, X.-P., 275
Cheng, R., C28
Cherry, S., C28
Chervitz, Darren, C270
Chesbrough, H. W., 207, 386, 408, 409
Chironga, M., 221
Cho, H. J., 410
Cho, K., C84
Chochrane, Bruce, 226
Choi, C., 207
Choi, T. Y., 79, 341
Choo, C. W., 409
Chowdhury, S. D., 309
Chrisman, J. J., 275
Christakis, N. A., 137
Christensen, Clayton M., 380, 383, 384, 408, 436
Chuang, C.-M., 244
Chung, Claudia, C10
Chung, M., 137

Ciampa, K., 374
Cieply, M., 243
Clark, Alan, C60
Clarke, G., 405
Clausen, Sven Oliver, C165
Clay, Eleanor Lowthian, C222
Clayton, Paul E., C40, C42
Clifford, S., 272, C67
Clymer, Susan, 416
Cochran, P. L., 307
Cochran, P. S., 375
Coff, R. W., 102, 309, 409
Cohan, P., C213
Cohen, D., 137
Cohen, David, C270
Cohen, S., 226
Colarelli, G., 408
Colby, S. J., 26
Colchester, M., 271
Cole, David E., 59
Coleman, D. R., 436
Coleman, J. S., 137
Coleman-Lochner, L., 231, 383
Collier, P., 243
Collins, G., C243
Collins, J. C., 281, 402
Collins, Jim, 256, 275, 306, 349, 374
Collins, M., 371
Collis, D. J., 33, 101, 102, 341
Colvin, G., 31, 67, 174, 207, 347, 373
Colvin, J. G., 244
Comarow, A., C32
Conant, Douglas R., C237, C238
Conley, J. G., 138
Conley, J. H., 375
Conlin, M., 400
Constans, John, C166
Conway, Ron, 246
Conyon, M. J., 309
Cook, Dick, C8
Cook, Kenneth A., C121
Cook, Scott, 364, 384
Cook, Tim, C17, C19, C22, C24, C25, C26
Cook, Timothy, 131, 138
Cooper, S., 274
Copeland, M. V., 258, 275, 388
Copeland, T. E., 207
Corcoran, Barbara, C41
Coronado, Julia, 193
Corsi, C., 308
Corstjens, M., 174
Cotte, J., 32
Coucke, K., 341
Courtney, H., 67
Courtney, Peter J., C128
Covey, S. R., 373, 375
Covin, J. G., 384, 410
Cox, J., 375
Cox, T. H., 136, 137
Coy, P., 67, 207
Coyne, E. J., Sr., 175
Coyne, K. P., 175
Coyne, S. T., 175
Craig, J., 410
Craig, S., 135
Crain, K., C233
Crockett, R. O., 409, 410
Crook, J., 259
Cross, R., 67, 136, 137

Crossan, Mary, C166
Cruise, Tom, 76
Csere, C., 68
Cueto, Julia Gonzalez, C86
Cuomo, Andrew, C5, C6
Cupta, A., 342

D

Dacin, M. T., 208, 341
Dae Je Chin, C194
Daft, R., 374
Dagnino, G. B., 175
Dahan, E., 175
Daily, C. M., 289, 308
Dale, G., 308
D'Aloisio, Nick, C268
Dalton, C., 294
Dalton, D. R., 289, 294
Damanpour, F., 408
Damaraju, Naga Lakshmi, C137, C146, C220
Daniels, J. D., 341
Danigelis, A., C212
Danna, D., 102
Danneels, E., 138, 410
D'Arpizio, Claudia, C176
Das, T. K., 342
Daum, J., 308
D'Aveni, Richard A., 175, 347
Davenport, Craig, 416
Davenport, T. H., 136, 174, 342, 361, 409
Davey, N., C28
David, P., 309
Davidson, P., 275
Davies, A., 67
Davies, M., 268
Davis, E. W., 342
Davis, Legroom, 345
Davis, P. S., 175, 410
Davis, S., 174
Davison, L., 129
Dawar, 244
Dawn, K., 341
Day, C., 374
Day, G. S., 66, 101
Day, J. C., 137
Day, J. D., 410
Day, Paul, C64
Deal, T. E., 306
Dean, B. V., 175
Dean, J., 261
Dean, T. J., 67
De Carvalho, Charlene, C60
De Castella, T., 49
Deeds, D. L., 275
Deephouse, D. L., 102
Deering, Mark, C184
DeGeneres, Ellen, C185
DeKluyver, C.A., 417
De La Merced, M. J., C219
Delgrosso, P., 174
Dell, Michael, 89, 116, 401
Delmas, M. A., 32
DeLollis, B., 338
DeLong, T. J., 31
De Meuse, K. P., 176
Dennis, W. J., 275
Deogun, N., 206, 207
De Paula, M., 100

Dergarabedian, Paul, C102
Desal, Lalita, 239
DeSanctis, G., 342
DeSanctis, Kevin, C11
DeSantis, Jake, C5, C6
Despande, R., 369
DesRoches, D., 252
Dess, Gregory G., 31, 73, 101, 130, 135, 137, 174,
    175, 206, 207, 208, 245, 306, 307, 340, 341,
    342, 373, 374, 399, 409, 410, C4, C137, C146
De Tienne, D.R., 274
Deutsch, T., 308
Devers, C., 304
Dharwaskar, R., 309
Dholakia, U., 174
Dias, Fiona, 88
Dibadj, Ali, C196, C200
Dibrell, C., 410
DiChiara, Jennifer M., C29
Dickler, J., C56
Dickson, P. R., 175, 275
DiFucci, John, 203
Dignan, L., C212
Diller, Barry, C64
Dimon, James, 15
Distelzweig, H., 340
Ditkoff, S. W., 26
Dixon, M., 174
Dobson, C., 31
Dodes, R., C105
Doh, J. P., 32
Doherty, D., 240
Dolida, Roger J., 326
Domoto, H., 245
Donahoe, John, C78, C79
Donahue, John, 3, 30, 364
Donlon, J. P., 101
Donnelly, Brian, 222
Donnelly, S., C144
Dorrance, John T., C237
Dorsey, Jack, C186
Dostal, E., C45
Dougherty, D., 408
Douglas, C. A., 136
Douglas, S. P., 244
Douma, B., 375
Doving, E., 138
Dowell, G., 275
Dowling, G. R., 135
Dowling, N., 374
Downing, L., 174
Doyle, R. A., C83
Doz, Yves L., 244, 340, 342
Dragone, Peter, C264
Dranove, D., 68
Dressner, H., 408
Drewnowski, Adam, C242
Driver, M., 32
Droege, Scott, 174
Droge, C., 410
Drucker, Peter F., 35–36, 39, 66, 67, 275, 381, 404,
    408, 410, 436
Druckman, Steve, C211
Dubbs, D., C212
Dubini, P., 275
Duff, Mike, C267
Duffield, David, 203
Duke, Mike, 327
Dumaine, Brian, 251

Duncan, R. E., 340
Duncan, Robert, 342
Dunlap, S., 137
Dunlap-Hinkler, D., 208, 275
Dunn, Patricia, 277
Dunne, D. D., 408
Dunsch, Jürgen, C165
Durbin, D. A., C234
Durnan, K., C37
Dutta, S., 101
Dutton, A., C57
Dutton, G., 135
Duvall, M., C153
Dyer, Jeff H., 100, 135, 245, 382–384, 402, 408
Dykes, B., 197

Earl, M. J., 101
Easterby-Smith, M., 375
Eaton, K., C28
Ebbers, Bernard, 202
Edelman, D. C., 175
Eden, L., 243
Edge, A. G., 436
Edinger, S. K., 359, 374
Edmondson, G., 153
Edvisson, Leif, 135
Edwards, C., 261, C195
Efrati, A., 307
Egan, M., C28
Eggers, J. P., 408
Ehrenfeld, J. R., 32
Eickhoff, Gerald, 120
Eidam, M., 153
Einhorn, B., 244
Einstein, Albert, 423
Eisenberg, Melvin Aron, 290
Eisenhardt, K. M., 138, 206, 274, 308,
    340, 408
Eisner, Alan B., C7, C11, C17, C29, C39, C47,
    C58, C63, C68, C74, C88, C106, C116, C123,
    C128, C135, C137, C146, C177, C191, C196,
    C201, C214, C220, C246, C256, C268
Eisner, Michael D., C8
Ekdahl, Andrew, C121
Elenkov, D. S., 66
Elfenbein, H. A., 32
Elgin, B., 366
Ellinghaus, Uwe, 76
Ellingson, A., C105
Elliot, S., C212
Elliott, H., 171
Elliott, M., 67
Ellis, B., 307
Ellison, Lawrence J., 203, C8
Ellstrand, A. E., 289, 308
Elmer-DeWitt, P., C27
Elson, Charles, 431
Emerson, Ralph Waldo, 40
Emmerich, Toby, C101
Empson, R., C28
Eng, D., 174
Engardio, P., 242, 341, C195
Engelson, Eric S., C123, C128, C177, C185
Ensing, I. M., 342
Entner, Roger, C195
Enz, C., 436
Epstein, G., C84

Epstein, Z., C27
Erhun, F., 397
Erickson, T. J., 135, 136
Espinoza, J., 274
Esty, D. C., 17, 32, 348
Ethiraj, S. K., 101
Evans, J., C27
Evans, P. B., 67
Evans, R., 437
Ewing, J., 31, C62
Eyring, M. J., 31, 243

F

Faems, D., 244
Fahey, E., 174
Fahey, J., 207
Fahey, L., 66, 67
Fahlander, A., 135
Fairbanks, B., C114
Fairclough, G., 68
Fake, Caterina, C186
Fama, Eugene, 308
Farley, Jim, 170
Farrel, J., C189, C190
Farzad, R., C27
Fatone, Joey, C112
Fedele, Joseph, C201, C202
Feeny, D., 101
Feinberg, ric, C63
Felberbaum, M., 80
Feld, Peter, C157, C164
Feldman, Alan, C15
Felps. W., 31
Felsted, A., 286
Felton, M., 135
Fenner, L., 275
Ferguson, G., 67
Ferguson, S., 416
Fern, M. J., 408, 409
Ferrarini, E., 391
Ferrier, W. J., 264, 268, 275, 409
Fey, C. F., 309
Fickenscher, L., C212, C213
Fickling, D., 64
Field, D., C153
Field, J. M., 101
Filatochev, I., 308
Filo, David, C272
Finch, Jacqueline, 271
Finegold, D., 32
Finkelstein, Ben, 84
Finkelstein, S., 135, 437
Finnigan, D., C73
Fiorina, Carly, 5, 276–277
Firestone, Harvey S., C222
Firestone, Martha Parke, C222
Fischer, Scott, C106, C111
Fisher, A., 136, 207
Fisher, L. M., C212
Fisher, M. L., 100
Fisman, R., 243
Fitzsimmons, J., 275
Fjeldstad, O. D., 100
Flay, Bobbie, C203
Flint, J., 174
Flint, P., C144
Florian, E., C37
Foley, A., 153

Folkman, J. R., 359, 374
Folliard, Tom, 80
Folta, T. B., 409
Fontana, Dominic, C112
Fontrodona, J., 375
Forbath, T., 245
Forbush, T., 31
Ford, Alfred Brush, C222
Ford, Benson, Jr., C222
Ford, Benson, Sr., C222
Ford, Charlotte M., C222
Ford, Cleanor Clay (Sullivan), C222
Ford, Edsel B., II, C222
Ford, Edsel Bryant, C222
Ford, Elena Anne, C222
Ford, Elizabeth Hudson (Kontulis), C222
Ford, George, C222
Ford, Henry, 21, 358, C222
Ford, Henry, II, C220, C222
Ford, Isaac, C222
Ford, Jane, C222
Ford, John, C222
Ford, Josephine Clay, C222
Ford, Josephine Clay (Ingle), C222
Ford, Lynn (alandt), C222
Ford, Margaret, C222
Ford, Martha Parke "Muffy" (Morse), C222
Ford, Mary, C222
Ford, Nancy, C222
Ford, Rebecca, C222
Ford, Robert, C222
Ford, Samuel, C222
Ford, Samuel, II, C222
Ford, Sheila Firestone (Hamp), C222
Ford, Walter Buhl, II, C222
Ford, Walter Buhl, III, C222
Ford, William, C222
Ford, William, II, C222
Ford, William, III, C222
Ford, William Clay, C222
Ford, William Clay "Bill," Jr., C220, C221, C222,
    C223, C232, C233
Forest-Cummings, Heather, 114
Forstall, Scott, C26
Foster, A. C., 28
Foust, D., 67, 68
Fowler, G. A., 88
Fowler, S. W., 101
Fowler, T., 204
Fox, F., C27
Fox, M. A., C212
Franco, T. C., 198
Francolla, G., 309
Frank, Barney, 40
Frank, Oren, 199
Frank, R., 307
Fredrickson, J. W., 341
Freeman, K., 174
Freeman, R. E., 31, 32, 137, 275, 288n, 308, 340
Freiberg, J., C144
Freiberg, K., C144
Frey, B. S., 32
Friedman, Marc, 362
Frier, S., 184
Friesen, P. H., 341
Friess, S., C16
Fritz, B., C104
Froholdt, M., 101, 102, 341, 374
Fromartz, S., 274

Frost, 244
Fry, Art, 282
Fryer, B., 67, 244, 307
Fulmer, I. S., 308
Fulmer, R. M., 375
Funtleyder, Les, C117
Furbush, Dean, C202, C206
Furu, P., 309

G

Gaal, Stephen, 254
Gaba, V., 274
Gabarro, J. J., 31
Gabriel, Mike, C102
Gadiesh, O., 174, 175
Gaglio, C. M., 274
Gaines-Ross, L., 101
Gajilan, A. T., C153
Galante, J., C83, C84
Galbraith, J. R., 313, 340
Galcin, Chris, 399
Gallagher, Brian A., C247, C249, C251, C253,
    C254, C255
Gallagher, L., 136
Galvin, Chris, 410
Gao, Y., 243
Garcia-Morales, V. J., 373
Garda, R. A., 268
Garg, V., 136
Garlinghouse, Brad, C270
Garnier, J.-P., 101
Garten, J. E., 243
Garvin, D. A., 31, 340, 374
Gasparro, A., 174
Gates, Bill, 109, 364, 375, C20, C246, C247
Gates, D., 340
Gates, Melinda, C247
Gee, P., 275
Gee Sung Choi, C194
Geithner, Timothy, C5
Geller, M., 388
Gelman, S. R., C255
George, B., 296, 309
George, Michael, C67
Georgescu, Peter, 353
Gerdes, L., 136
Gerhart, B., 308
Geschke, Jim, 396
Ghemawat, Pankaj, 67, 217, 243, 244
Ghosh, S., C27
Ghoshal, Sumantra, 66, 135, 175, 243, 244, 317,
    341
Ghosn, Carlos, 146, C220
Gibbert, M., 408
Gibelman, M., C255
Gibney, F., C195
Gibson, C. B., 138, 342
Gibson, David, C183
Gibson, J., 10
Gikkas, N. S., 243
Gilad, Benjamin, 447
Gilbert, J. L., 174, 175
Gilboa, Dave, 262
Giligan, E., C67
Gillis, Colin, C273
Gilmartin, Ray, 115
Gilmore, J., 175
Gimbel, B., 174, 207, 243, C144

Ginsberg, A., 408
Girsky, Stephen J., C218
Gladwell, Malcolm, 120
Glass, J. T., 342
Glazer, E., 243
Glimcher, Michael, 271–272
Glover, K., 301
Goddard, J., 31
Goffee, R., 135
Goggins, Colleen, C120
Gogoi, P., C93
Golbin, Pamela, C176
Goldsmith, Marshall, 31, 126, 138, 325, 373
Goldstein, N. J., 307
Goldstein, P., C104
Goleman, Daniel, 354, 355, 374
Golisano, Tom, 59
Goll, I., 67
Golvin, Charles, C191, C193
Gomer, Gregory, C184
Gomez, Leocardia Cruz, C86
Gompers, P. A., 409
Gonzalez, Sonsoles, C200
Goode, Mary, 120
Goodell, Jeff, C28
Gooderham, P. N., 138
Goodman, Stephen, 253
Goodstein, L. D., 175
Goold, M., 206, 207, 306
Goranova, M., 308, 309
Gordon, Erik, C116, C120
Gorge, Michael, C64
Gorsky, Alex, C116, C117, C120–C121
Gosier, C., C255
Goteman, I., 306
Gottfredson, M., 342
Goudreau, Jenna, C243, C245
Gould, James, C39
Gourville, J. T., 97
Govan, F., 6
Gove, Steve, C94
Govindarajan, V. G., 208, 243, 244, 341, 391
Gower, T., C38
Graafland, Rene Hooft, C62
Graddy-Gamel, A., C254
Graebner, M. E., 206, 308, 374
Graen, G. B., 307
Graham, Ben, 135
Grant, J., C93
Grant, R. M., 83, 102
Graser, M., 10
Grassley, Chuck, 370
Gratton, L., 136, 340
Graves, T., C243
Graves, Tom, C15
Graybow, M., 307
Green, J., 304
Green, S., 101
Greenberg, Jack M., C89, C90
Greenblatt, Drew, 152
Greene, I., 67
Greene, P., 409
Greenfield, Bob, C100
Greenhouse, S., 301
Greenspan, Alan, 138
Greenwald, B., 67
Greenwald, W., C184
Greenwell, M., C255
Greenwood, R., 32

Greeven, Mark, C83
Gregersen, Hal B., 382–384, 408
Gregg, F. M., 243
Greising, D., 307
Greve, H. R., 208
Grimm, C. M., 264, 268, 275
Grobart, S., 206, C28
Groenfeldt, T., 184
Gronbjerg, Kirsten, C253–C254
Gross, Bill, 371
Gross, D., 308
Grossman, Kerr, C133
Grossman, Mindy, 110, 136
Grossman, W., 309
Grove, Andrew S., 5, 79, 113, 114, 136, 264, 275, 288, 362
Grover, C. M., 308
Grover, G., 10
Grover, R., 309
Grow, B., 67, 101, 207
Gruber, Peter, 22
Guimon, A., C87
Guinan, P. J., 138
Gulati, R., 275
Gumbel, P., 244
Gunther, M., 30, 409
Gupta, A. K., 243, 244
Gupta, N. J., 21
Gupta, P., 180
Gusko, Ralph, C157, C164
Guterman, J., 67
Guth, R. A., 403
Guth, W. D., 175, 207, 408, 436

H

Haas, M. R., 135, 341
Haber, P., 244
Habib, M. M., 341
Haddad, C., 101
Hagel, J., 129, 244, 408
Hagerty, J., 174
Haleblian, J., 197
Halkias, M., 88
Hall, Brian J., 117, 307
Hall, D. J., 341
Hall, H., C254
Hall, J., 66
Hall, R. H., 307, 340
Hall, S., 308
Hall, W. K., 175
Hallerman, David, C268, C272
Hambrick, D. C., 176, 268, 275, 289, 307, 308
Hamel, Gary, 32, 35, 66, 106, 135, 206, 207, 342, 408, 409
Hammer, Michael, 333, 342, 359, 375
Hammonds, K. H., 31, 401
Hamstra, M., C212
Handy, Charles, 32, 328, 341, 358, 374
Hannah, S. T., 375
Hansen, M. T., 116, 119, 135, 137, 138, 334, 352, 408, 409
Hardy, Jeffrey, 220
Hardy, Q., 33
Hargreaves, S., 204, 243
Harnish, V., 33, 138
Harrigan, K., 207
Harris, J., 136, 289
Harrison, D. A., 375

Harrison, J. S., 31, 32, 137, 208, 275, 308, 340, 342
Hart, Bret, C70
Hart, M., 409
Hart, Stuart L., 19, 32
Hartley, S. W., 175
Harveston, P. D., 243
Harvey, C. P., 137
Harvey, M., 243
Hasan, F., 101
Haslam, S. A., 306
Haspelagh, P., 207
Hasse, Vanessa, C155
Hatch, N. W., 135
Haughton, K., 68
Haugland, S. A., 208
Hauser, Robert, C121
Haveri, Mikael, C177
Hawkins, Asher, 52
Hax, A. C., 207
Hayashi, A. M., 124
Hayek, Nicholas, 70
Hayes, R., 408
Haynes, K. T., 308
Hayward, Tony, 18, 292
Heavey, C., 275
Hedin, Hans, 447
Heeg, Thiemo, C165
Heidenreich, Stefan F., C155, C157, C165
Heiferman, Scott, C186
Heifetz, R., 374
Heina, Ku, 68
Heineken, Freddy, C60
Helft, M., C273
Helgesen, S., 375
Heller, A., C213
Hellmich, N., C38
Helms, M. M., 32, 175, 243, 340, 375
Helper, S., 68
Helyar, J., 308
Hemp, P., 31
Hempel, J., 389
Hemrajani, Abhishek, C137
Henderson, Frederick A., C217
Henderson, Larry, 223
Henkoff, R., 101, 136
Hennequin, Dennis, C92
Henretta, Deborah A., C198
Henriques, D. B., 307
Henry, J., C234
Heracleous, L., 175
Hertzler, E., 397
Herz, Michael, C157
Herz family, C157–C158, C164
Herzlinger, R., C255
Hessel, E., 32
Hesselbein, F., 31, 325, 373
Hesseldahl, A., 61
Hewitt, Walter, 276
Hewlett, Sylvia Ann, 114, 137
Hill, A. D., 137, 207
Hill, C. W. L., 341
Hill, K., 67
Hillman, A., 308, 309
Hills, G. E., 274
Hilmer, F. C., 342
Hiltzik, M., 340
Himelstein, L., C84
Hindo, B., 206
Hines, Brenda, C225

Hintz, Brad, 105
Hirvensalo, Irmeli, 447
Hitt, M. A., 32, 83, 101, 102, 135, 137, 176, 197, 206, 208, 243, 244, 275, 308, 309, 340, 341
Ho, E., C153
Hoch, Jason, C71
Hoetker, G., 101
Hof, R. D., 307
Hogan, Hulk, C68, C69, C70
Hogan, M., C38
Holcomb, T. R., 176
Holden, D., 366
Hollande, François, 6
Hollender, J., 32
Holme, C., 150
Holmes, S., C233, C234
Holt, John W., 364, 375
Hoover, V. L., 264, 275
Hopkins, M. S, 327
Hopkins, M. S., 68
Horn, J., C105
Hornery, J., 409
Horovitz, B., C93
Hoskin, R. E., 409
Hoskisson, R. E., 83, 206, 244, 308, 309, 340, 341
Hotard, D., 175
Hout, T. M., 67, 217, 243, 244
Howe, Jeff, 46, 67
Howell, J. M., 409
Howell, Robert A., 107
Hrebiniak, L. G., 31, 207, 340
Hsieh, Tony, 149, 333, 374
Hudson, Jennifer, C36
Hudson, Linda, 368
Hughes, J., C144
Hugo, M., C143
Hult, T. M., 68
Humer, Franz, 429
Hurd, Mark, 5, 23, 277
Hutt, M. D., 208
Huy, Q. H., 32
Hymowitz, C., 308, 383

I

Ibarra, H., 33, 116, 119, 137, 352
Icahn, Carl, 295, 309
Iger, Bob, C7
Ignatius, A., 207
Ihlwan, M., 79, C84, C195
Immelt, Jeffrey, 20, 78, 101, 212
Imperato, G., 101, 375
Ingram, T. N., 175
Ingrassia, P., C234
Inkpen, A. C., 244, 342
Iosebashvili, I., 243
Ireland, R. D., 83, 101, 102, 135, 206, 208, 243, 244, 341, 408
Isaacson, W., 307, 375
Ismail, Salim, C271
Isobe, T., 244
Ive, Jonathan, C26
Ivy, Lance, C187
Iyer, B., 174, 342

J

Jackson, E. M., 308
Jackson, M., 100

Jackson, Peter, C103
Jackson, S. E., 32
Jacobs, A., 174
Jacobs, Bonnie, C120
Jacobs, D. L., 57
Jacobs, Marc, C170, C172
Jager, Durk I., C198
Janis, Irving L., 428, 430, 437
Jannarone, J., C105
Jansen, P., C255
Janssens, M., 244
Jap, S. D., 101
Jargon, J., C93
Jarvis, J., 341
Jay, B., C144
Jean, S., 226, 244
Jeffries, A., C190
Jenks, John, 26
Jenner, Hartmut, 101
Jennings, L., C46
Jennings, Rebecca, C222
Jensen, Michael C., 308, 309
Jiang, Y., 309
Jicinsky, Terry, C13
Jimenez, Joseph, 11
Jin, B., 244
Jindra, B., 308
Joachimsthaler, E., 244
Jobs, Steven, 5, 61, 116, 135, 183, 284, C7, C8, C9,
    C10, C17, C19, C20, C21, C22, C23, C26, C27
Johannessen, J. A., 408
John, Daymond, C41
John, Prnce of England, C2
Johnson, A., C122
Johnson, David W., C237
Johnson, J., C27
Johnson, J. L., 289, 308
Johnson, M. W., 31, 243
Johnson, R. A., 309
Johnson, Ron, C26
Johnson, S., 67, 137
Joire, Myriam, C190
Jolie, Angelina, C64
Jones, A., C6, C27
Jones, C., C28
Jones, Curt, C106, C107, C109, C110, C111, C112
Jones, G., 135
Jones, Jim L., C16
Jones, L., C115
Jones, S. M., C56, C57
Jones, T. J., 31
Jordan, B. D., 437n
Josey, Ron, C78
Joshi, S., 207
Joyce, E., C212
Joyce, W. F., 31, 207, 340

K

Kafka, P., 381, C190
Kahn, J., 67
Kaiser, R. B., 136
Kale, P., 101, 245
Kamen, Dean, 388
Kampur, D., 216
Kane, Y. L., 261
Kang, E., 308
Kanter, Rosabeth Moss, 408
Kapalschinski, Christoph, C165

Kaplan, A., C62
Kaplan, D., 174
Kaplan, M., 88
Kaplan, R. E., 136
Kaplan, Robert S., 31, 92, 95, 102, 136
Kaplan, Steven, 296, 408
Kapur, D., 217
Karamchandani, A., 213
Kardashian, Kim, C64
Karri, R., 174
Kary, T., 30
Kasaks, Sally, C49
Kashwarski, T., 32
Kasten, Tom, 363
Katz, J. A., 274
Katz, J. H., 137
Katz, Jonathan, C243
Katzenbach, J. R., 342
Kaufman, A., C104
Kazanjian, R. K., 313, 340
Kean, Jim, 416
Keats, B., 340
Keazeney, A. T., C153
Kedia, B. L., 243
Keegan, R. W., 77
Keenan, F., 404
Keil, Thomas, 207, 308, 386, 408, 409
Keizer, G., C27
Kelleher, Herb, 5, 79, 86, C137, C138, C139,
    C140, C141, C142, C143, C144, C147
Keller, M., 44
Kelley, Brian, C256, C257
Kelley, C., C255
Kelly, Bill, 416
Kelly, Gary C., C137, C140, C142, C143
Kelly, K., C104
Kelly, Maureen, C66
Kelly, Michael A., C121
Kempf, Karl, 397
Kempiak, M., C212
Kengelbach, J., 208
Kennedy, A. A., 306
Kennedy, K., C57
Kenny, David, 120
Kenny, Katharine W., 80
Kent, Muhtar, 388
Kenworthy, T. P., 340
Kerin, Roger A., 175
Kerr, J., 307
Kerwin, K. R., 68
Kessler, S., 258
Ketchen, D. J., Jr., 68, 264, 275, 408
Kets de Vries, M. F. R., 32, 136, 341
Keynes, John Maynard, 27
Khaner, Lloyd, C45
Khanna, P., 307
Khanna, T., 208, 275, 309
Kharif, O., 156
Khavul, S., C87
Khermouch, G., C62
Khosla, S., 244
Khurana, Rakesh, C233
Kichen, S., 135
Kidd, J. B., 244
Kidwell, R. E., Jr., 308
Kiley, D., 301, C233, C234
Kilmann, R. H., 342
Kilpatrick, A., C255
Kim, B., 262

Kim, E., 175
Kim, Eric, C192
Kim, H. E., 341, 408
Kim, J., 309
Kim, L., 175
Kim, P. H., 274
Kim, W. C., 275
Kim, Y.-H., C195
Kimbrell, Duke, 316
Kimes, M., 373, C200
Kim Hyua-suk, C193
King, A. A., 68
King, I., 397
King, R., C27
King, Rollin, C137
Kingsbury, K., C57
Kirchhoff, David, C29, C31, C35
Kirkland, J., 67
Kirkman, B. L., 138
Kirn, S. P., 102
Kiron, D., 80
Kiss, C137
Klein, Jonathan, 292, 308
Klein, Zach, C186
Kleinbuam, Rob, C217
Kleinfeld, Klaus, 353
Klemmer, D., 208
Klemp, G., 374
Kletter, D., 409
Kline, D., 244
Kling, K., 306
Knowles, F., C233
Koch, Ed, C203
Koch, Jim, C129, C136
Koetsler, J., C190
Koogle, Tim, 254, C268, C272
Kopp, Wendy, 23
Koppel, B., 341
Koppenheffer, M., C56
Kopytoff, V. G., C273
Kor, Y. Y., 31
Korn, Helaine J., C29, C135, C220
Kosner, A. W., C37
Kosnik, R. D., 309
Kotabe, M., 208, 245, 275
Kotha, S., 275
Kotter, John P., 373
Kouzes, J. M., 360, 375
Koza, M. P., 245
Kozlowski, Dennis, 202
Kramer, Mark R., 32, C251, C254
Krantz, M., C16, C190
Krause, R., 269, 308, 309
Krauss, C., 308
Krill, Kay, C47, C48, C49, C53, C54, C55–C56
Kripalani, M., 217
Krisher, T., C234
Krishnan, H., 207
Krishnan, M. S., 101, 174
Krisnan, R. A., 207
Kroc, Ray A., C89
Kroll, M., 175, 274, 307
Kron, Steven, C88
Krug, Barbara, C83
Ku, G., 206
Kubzansky, M., 213
Kuemmerle, W., 341
Kulatilaka, N., 409
Kumar, M. V., 206

Kumar, N., 68
Kung, M., C104, C105
Kuperman, Jerome C., C39, C47
Kutaragi, Ken, 393
Kwak, M., 61, 68
Kwon, E. Y., C243
Kwon, S. W., 137
Kyriazis, D., 206
Kyunghan Jung, C193

L

Laamanen, T., 207, 308
LaBarre, P., 374
Labianca, G., 137
Labianca, Joe, 137
Lachenauer, Rob, 264, 265, 275
Lacity, M., 101
Lady Gaga, C185
Lafley, Alan G., 113, C196, C198, C199, C200, V198
LaForge, R. W., 175
Lal, R., 174
Lalwani, N., 213
Lam, K., 101
Lam, Y., 265
Lamadrid, Lorenzo, C129
Lambkin, M., 410
La Monica, P. R., 203
Lampel, Joseph, C2
Lance, M., C143
Landes, D. S., 243
Landinois, F., 405
Lane, C., C37
Lane, P. J., 206
Lanese, Lory, 113
Lang, Tom, C128
Laplume, A. O., 32
Largay, J. A., III, 375
Lareter, T., C212
Lash, J., 32
Lasseter, John, C7, C9, C10
Latham, G. P., 136, 307, 409
Lauinger, J., C212
Lavelle, M., 32
Laverty, K. J., 409
Lawler, E. E., III, 32, 373
Lawrence, Joanne, 196
Lawrence, T. B., 101
Lawton, C., 261
Lazandis, Michael, 384
Lazaris, Nick, C264, C266
Lazarus, D., C105
Lazarus, Michael, C148
Leana, C. R., 137, 375
Leavitt, P., 386
Lebesch, Jeff, C134
Leclair, Donat R., C224
Lee, E., C28
Lee, G., C57
Lee, G. K., 138
Lee, H. L., 17
Lee, J., 306, C37
Lee, Kun-Hee, 24
Lee, L., C46
Lee, M. J., C195
Lee, Minhyoul, C191
Lee, Spike, C203
Lee, T., C213
Leeman, John, C203

Lees, R. J., 31
Lee Yoon Woo, C194
Lei, D., 138, 175, 243
Leiber, N., 226
Leifer, R., 408
Lemer, J., C144
Lenzner, R., 136, 207
Leonard, D., C28
Leonard, Tom, C111
Leonard-Barton, Dorothy, 125, 137, 374
Leonhardt, D., C212
Lerner, J., 409
Lesnar, Brock, C70
Lester, P. B., 375
Lester, R. H., 308
Leu, C., 208
Leung, W., 31
Levchin, Max, C272
Levesque, L. C., 31, 340
Levin, D., 100, C233
Levine, D., 307
Levine-Weinberg, A., C153
Levit, A., 280
Levitt, Theodore, 225–226, 244
Levy, A., 258
Lewin, A. Y., 243
Lewis, Katherine, C36
Lewis, Ken, 202
Lewis, P., C195
Li, J. J., 101, 137, 208
Li, J. T., 244
Libert, B., 49, 67
Lichthental, John, 223
Liddy, Edward M., C5, C6
Lieberman, David, 331
Lieberman, M. B., 410
Liebeskind, Richard, Sr., C48
Liebeskind, Robert, C48
Light, D. A., 67, 137
Light, Larry, C92
Lim, Y., 175
Lin, H. C., 275
Lin, John, 137
Linblad, C., 307
Lindland, Rebecca, C216, C219
Ling, C. S., 31
Ling, Joe, 348
Ling, Y., 409
Linn, A., 170
Linton, Thomas, 79
Lipin, S., 206, 207
Lipparini, A., 101
Lipton, M., 33
Little, Arthur D., 207
Little, Mitch, 132
Liu, S. X. Y., 101
Lloréns-Montes, F. J., 373
Locke, Edwin A., 307
Loeb, M., 31
Loftus, P., C121
Lohr, S., 175
Loikkanen, V., C190
Lomax, A., C57
London, T., 31
Long, W., 274
Lopwz, Jose Ignacio, 136
Lorange, P., 66, 342, 374
Lorenzoni, G., 101
Lorsch, Jay W., 309, 374

Löscher, Peter, 353
Lotus, P., 373
Low, C. K., 289
Lowensohn, J., C27
Loyd, L., 204
Lu, J. W., 243, 275
Lubatkin, M. H., 409
Lublin, J. S., 116
Lucas, George W., Jr., C8
Lucchetti, A., 307
Luehrman, T. A., 102
Luhby, T., 110
Lumpkin, G. T., 137, 274, 384, 408, 410
Lund, S., 221
Lundberg, C. C., 436
Lunnan, R., 208
Luochs, K., 207
Luria, Gil, C78
Luthans, Fred, 374
Lutz, A., C57
Lutz, Robert A., 15, 32, C217
Lyons, D., 410

M

Ma, H., 174
Ma, Jack, C81, C84
Mabey, C., 136
MacArthur, Paul, C69
MacCormack, A., 31, 245
Machills, S., C212
MacMillan, A., C37
MacMillan, D., C83
MacMillan, J. C., 175, 243, 409, 410
Madhok, A., 244
Madoff, Bernard, 40, 365
Mahabubani, Manu, C166
Mahashwari, S., C56
Mahmood, I., 243
Maiello, M., 275, 309
Main, J., 375
Majluf, N. S., 207
Makino, S., 243, 244
Makri, M., 206
Malhotra, D., 206
Malik, O., C190
Mallas, S., 410
Malletier, Louis Vuitton, C166
Mallick, E. R., C190
Malone, John, 362
Malone, Michael S., 135
Malone, Tom, 120
Maloof, George, C15
Mandel, M., 67
Mandelker, G., 308
Mang, P. Y., 410
Mank, D. A., C27
Mankins, M. C., 430
Mann, J., 174
Manning, S., 243
Manville, B., 361
Mao Zedong, 349
March, J. G., 342, 409
Marcial, G., 68
Marcial, G. G., C38
Marcus, Bernard, 282
Mardy, Michael J., C256
Margolis, J. D., 32, 369
Markham, S. K., 409

Markides, C. C., 66, 174
Markkula, A. C. "Mike," Jr., C20
Markman, G. D., 306
Markosian, Suren, C126
Markovich, S., 318
Marks, M. S., 101, 176
Marriott, J. W., Jr., 144, 174
Martin, A., 208
Martin, J. A., 135, 136, 244, 340
Martin, J. E., 138
Martin, K. L., 31, 340
Martin, R. J., 374
Martin, Roger L., 425, 426, 427, 437
Martin, T., 174
Martin, X., 245
Martinez, Arthur, 2
Martinez, J., 207
Mass, N. J., 102
Massiliadis, Billy, C12
Massini, S., 243
Masters, B., C73
Matherne, Brett P., C94
Mathur, S. K., 67, 217
Matlack, C., 68
Matteson, S., C46
Matthews, C. H., 274
Mattioli, 110
Mauborgne, R., 275
Maurer, H., 307
May, R. C., 67
Mayer, J. D., 374
Mayer, Marissa, C268, C271, C272
Maynard, M., 100, C219, C233, C234
Mayo, Bud, C103
Mazumdar-Shaw, Kiran, 200
McAfee, A., 101
McArthur, Sarah, C10
McCarthy, D. J., 308
McCarthy, M., C16
McClennan, S., 199
McConnell, B., C144
McConnon, Aili, C213
McCracken, H., C27
McDaniel, Thom, C140, C142
McDermott, C. M., 408
McDonald, M. L., 206, 307
McDonald, Maurice, C89
McDonald, Richard, C89
McDonald, Robert, C196, C199–C200
McDonnel, Anne, C222
McDougall, P. P., 314n, 341
McEwen, Robert, 49
McGahan, Anita M., 68, 101
McGee, M., 341
McGeehan, P., 308
McGonagle, John J., 447
McGrath, C., 137
McGrath, J., 309
McGrath, Rita Gunther, 175, 243, 386, 408, 409, 410
McGregor, J., 213, 375
McKinnon, J. D., C6
McKnight, William, 363
McLaughlin, R., 208
McLaughlin, K. J., 341
McLean, B., C73
McLean, Bethany, 300, 309
McMahon, Linda, C68, C69, C70, C71
McMahon, Stephanie, C71

McMahon, Vince, C68, C69, C70, C71
McMillan, G., C190
McMullan, W. E., 274, 275
McNamara, G., 175, 197, 304
McNaughton, Edith, C222
McNaughton, Larry, C69
McNicol, J. P., 243
McQuilling, Andrew, C33, C37
McRay, G., C255
McVae, J., 32
McVey, Henry, 147
McWilliams, Larry S., C237
Means, Gardiner C., 290
Meckling, W. H., 308, 309
Meehan, Sean, 136
Mees, Charles, C151
Mehta, S. N., 174, 307
Meier, B., C122
Meier, D., 206
Meiland, D., 101
Meindl, J. R., 30
Meiners, Roger, 225
Melcher, R. A., 308
Mellick, Ethan, C185
Melrose, Ken, 360, 375
Mendelow, A. L., 409
Merchant, H., 245
Merrefield, D., C213
Merrick, A., C57
Meyer, A. D., 274
Meyer, K. E., 244
Meyer, Peter, 362, 375
Michael, D. C., 243
Michaels, Jillian, C31
Michaels, Shawn, C70
Michaelson, Steve, C202
Michel, J. G., 275
Michelangelo, 202
Michelle, S., C115
Mider, Z., 304
Miles, R. E., 332
Miller, A., 31, 174, 307, 340, 373, 375, 410
Miller, C. C., C273
Miller, D., 306, 341, 384
Miller, D. J., 207, 408
Miller, F. A., 137
Miller, J., 318
Miller, K. D., 410
Miller, W., 341
Miller-Kovach, Karen, C36
Milner, Alex, 223
Milner, Graham, 391
Minow, Neil, 14, 31, 288, 307, 308
Minter, S., 226
Mintzberg, Henry, 10, 11, 31, 278–279, 306, 436, C3
Misangyi, V. F., 31
Mitchell, R., 307
Mitroff, S., 262
Mitsuhashi, H., 208
Mittal, Lakshmi, 207
Mittal, Shefali, C137, C146
Mochari, I., 403
Mohammad, R., 174
Moin, D., C57
Moisse, K., C37
Mol, M. J., 408
Moliterno, T. P., 136
Mollick, E. R., C189

Monahan, J., 275
Monahan, Tom, 259
Monks, Robert, 14, 31, 288, 307, 308
Montenay, Françoise, C168
Montes-Sancho, M. J., 32
Montgomery, C. A., 101, 102
Montgomery, D. B., 341, 410
Monti, Mario, 6
Montijo, Eugenie de, C166
Moody, Keith F., C256
Moon, Y., 167, 175
Mooney, A. C., 437
Mooradian, D., C73
Moore, A., C57
Moore, Geoffrey A., 401, 410
Moore, J. F., 342
Moran, P., 137
Morates, David J., C74
Morison, R., 101
Morita, Akio, 19
Morris, B., 306
Morris, C., C184
Morris, E., 436
Morris, Jane, C147
Morrison, Denise, C135, C237, C238, C241
Morrissey, C. A., 408
Morrod, T., 261
Morrow, J. S., 176
Mors, M. L., 137
Morse, E. A., 101
Morse, G., 207
Mosey, Tom, C112
Moskin, J., C114
Moss, S. A., 374
Mouawad, J., 308
Mouio, A., 208
Mowery, D. C., 342
Moynihan, Brian, 105
Mozilo, Angelo, 289
Mudambi, R., 68, 208, 244, 275
Muir, Max, 265
Mulally, Alan, 22–23, 170, 171, C220, C221, C223, C224, C226, C227, C232, C233
Mullaney, T. J., 176, 404
Mulligan, J., C153
Mumm, J., 308
Munarriz, R. A., C46
Mundt, Kevin, C259, C267
Munk, N., 102
Munarriz, R. A., C46
Munk, N., 102
Munningham, J. K., 206
Murdoch, James, 302
Murdoch, Rupert, 302
Murningham, J. K., 206
Murphy, D., 374
Murphy, K., C114
Murphy, Kevin J., 309
Murphy, William, C237
Murply, P., 243
Murthy, N. R. Narayana, 350
Muse, Lamar, C137
Mushkin, Scott, C33
Mussberg, W., 341
Mutsuko, M., C184
Mutzabaugh, B., C144
Mysterio, Ray, C69

N

Nader, Ralph, 300
Nagarajan, G., 219

Nagaraju, B., 217
Nagourney, A., C16
Nagrath, Moheet, C198
Nahapiet, J., 135
Nair, H., 31, 243
Nair, Palmakumar, C85
Nalebuff, B. J., 59, 60, 68
Nam, D., 175
Napoleon III, C166
Narasimhan, O., 101
Narayan, A., 208, 240
Narayanan, V. K., 66, 67
Nasr, S. L., 388
Nasser, Jacques, C220, C227
Naughton, K., 54, C233, C234
Nayar, Vineet, 116
NcNerney, Jim, 311
Ndofor, H., 275
Needham, Charles, 7
Neeleman, David, C147–C148, C151,
    C152, C153
Neilson, G., 409
Neilson, G. L., 31, 340
Nelson, A. J., 436
Nelson, B., 39
Nelson, Randall E., C9
Nero, Emperor, C114
Ness, S. M., 38
Netessine, S., 307
Neuborne, E., 175
Newbert, S. L., 31, 101
Newman, R., 30
Nexon, M., 136
Niblack, J., 408
Nick, D., C190
Nidetch, Jean, C29, C30, C37
Niven, P., 102
Nixon, Cynthia, C203
Nmarus, J. A., 100
Nobel, Carmen, 369
Nobel, R., 244
Nohria, N., 138, 275, 408, 409
Nonaka, I., 135
Noorda, Raymond, 270
Noot, Walter, 91
Nordstrom, Dan, 76
Norrington, Lorie, C82
Norton, David P., 31, 92, 95, 102
Novak, David C., 415, C92
Novicki, C., 375
N Sync, C112
Nutt, P. C., 31
Nyberg, A. J., 308
Nystrom, H. E., C27

O

Obama, Barack, 327, C5, C189
Obodaru, O., 33
O'Brien, Chris, C83
O'Brien, J. M., 136
O'Brien, J. P., 409
O'Brien, William, 360
O'Connor, G. C., 408
O'Connor, M., 222
Odell, A. M., 110
Odlyzko, A., 67
O'Donnell, S. W., 245
Oestricher, D., C73

Ogren, E., C27
Oh, D. J., C194
Oh, H., 137
O'Hern, Mary Litogot, C222
Ohmae, Kenichi, 242, 342
Okie, Francis G., 282
O'Leary, Kevin, C41
O'Leary-Kelly, A. M., 307
Oliff, Michael, C137, C146
Oliver, C., 208
Olsen, B., 408
Olsen, Kenneth H., 40
Omidyar, Pierre, 384, C74, C77, C78, C79
O'Neal, Shaquille, C112
O'Neill, H. M., 340
Onstead, Kevin, C142
Ordonez, I., 204
Ordonez, L., 375
O'Reilly, B., 374
O'Reilly, Charles A., 136, 336, 342
Orey, M., 67
Orwall, B., C104
Orwell, George, C20
Oster, S. M., 207
Ouchi, William, 306, 307
Oviatt, B. M., 314n, 341
Oxley, J. E., 342
Ozzie, Raymond, 91

P

Paalanjian, A., 259
Padgett, T., 301
Page, Larry, 384, 392
Paine, Lynn S., 368, 369, 375
Palazzo, G., 307
Palladino, V., C27
Palmer, Amanda, C188
Palmer, T. B., 68
Palmeri, C., 174, C16
Palmisano, Samuel, 53, 389
Panaritis, Maria, C212
Pandit, Vikram, 292
Paranjpe, Nitin, 113
Pare, T. P., 206
Parise, S., 136, 138
Park, M., 44
Parke, Elizabeth, C222
Parker, James F., C141, C142
Parker, John, C137
Parkinson, Thomas, C208
Park Kang Ho, C191
Parmley, S., C16
Passariello, C., 271
Patel, Himanshu, C223
Patscot, Steven, 111
Patton, Paul, 76
Pauleen, D. J., 243
Pauling, Linus, 124
Paulson, Henry, C4
Pawlowski, Janina, 254
Paynter, B., C93
Pearce, J. A., II, 32, 175
Pearl Jam, 258
Pearson, A. E., 373
Pearson, D., 146
Pech, R., 265
Peck, S. I., 309
Peluso, M., 150

Peng, Mike W., 244, 309
Pennings, J. M., 408
Penske, Roger, 71
Pepitone, J., 274
Pepper, John, C198
Peridis, Theo, 138
Perkins, A. B., 135
Perlroth, N., C273
Perman, S., 401
Perna, G., C114
Perrenot, G., C37
Perrewe, P. L., 375
Perron, Kirk, C39
Pestana, Miguel, 150
Peteraf, M. A., 68, 137, 275
Peters, L. S., 408
Peters, S., 208, 245
Peters, Thomas J., 306
Peterson, K., 340
Petrucciani, Tony, 27
Pfeffer, Jeffrey, 31, 110, 135, 136, 325, 341, 374
Phadtare, Rohit R., C201
Phelan, Dan, 114–115
Phelps, C., 208
Phillips, C., 342
Phillips, R. A., 32
Picasso, Pablo, 123, 124
Picken, J. C., 73, 101, 130, 135, 175, 206, 207,
    306, 307, 342, 374
Pieper, Jurgen, 153
Pierantozzi, Ron, 380
Pil, F. K., 375
Pinchot, Gifford, 408
Pincus, Mark Jonathan, C123, C126
Pine, B. J., II, 175
Pinger, Markus, C157, C164
Pink, D. H., 132
Pinkham, Brian, C4
Pinkham, Brian C., C85
Pinto, J., 375
Pitts, R., 138
Pitts, R. A., 341
Plambeck, E., 17
Ployhart, R. E., 136
Pluhowski, John, C79
Pogue, D., 275, C27
Polanyi, M., 135
Polek, D., 208
Pollack, Lindsey, 110
Pollah, Reinhard, C157
Pollock A., 381
Pondy, L. R., 342
Pope, B., C234
Poppo, L., 137
Porizkova, Paulina, C203
Porras, J. I., 306, 402, 447
Port, O., 375
Porter, Michael E., 18, 31, 32, 49, 50, 55, 60, 65,
    67, 68, 72, 74, 77, 100, 102, 142, 144, 148,
    174, 175, 201, 206, 207, 208, 214, 215, 216,
    217, 243, 244, C251, C254
Portland, A., 137
Posner, B. Z., 360, 375
Potter, F., 252
Pottruck, D. A., 341
Poulfelt, F., 101, 102, 341, 374
Pound, J., 307
Poundstone, W., 307
Powell, B., 244

Powell, T. C., 174
Powers, E., 31, 340
Pozen, R. C., 308
Praet, N. V., C234
Prahalad, C. K., 35, 66, 106, 135, 174, 206, 207, 213, 244
Presley, Elvis, 37, C138
Preston, H. H., C122
Priddle, Alisa, C234
Priem, R. L., 67, 341
Prieto, I. M., 375
Prior, V., 67
Pritchard, David, 287
Protess, B., C57
Proud, Danya, C91
Prusak, L., 137, 409
Pucik, V., 410
Puffer, S. M., 308
Purda, L. D., 67
Puryear, R., 342
Putin, Vladimir, 220
Putnam, Howard, C138
Pylas, P., 31

Q

Quaas, Thomas-Bernd, C155, C157, C158, C160, C161
Quelch, John A., C61
Quigley, J. V., 33
Quinlan, Michael R., C89, C90
Quinn, James Brian, 135, 278–279, 306, 342, C3
Quinn, R. T., 102

R

Racamier, Henri, C166, C170
Radnofsky, L., C37
Rainer, Michaeli, 447
Raisinghani, D., 436
Rajiv, S., 101
Ramamurti, R., 216, 217
Raman, A. P., 242, 350
Ramirez, J., 26
Rampell, C., C273
Randall, D., 309
Randall, T., 155, 175
Rao, A. R., 174
Rao, R., 340
Rappaport, A., 207, C144
Rasheed, A. M. A., 67, 341
Rasheed, Abdul A., C4
Rashid, R., 137
Raths, D., 416
Ratliff, Rick, 171
Rattner, J., C37
Raum, T., C6
Raynor, M. E., 408
Rayport, J. F., 100
Rayport, Jeffrey, C66
Reagan, J., 170
Rechner, P. L., 437
Reed, S., 207
Reedy, E. J., 252
Reene, Michael, 120
Reeves, Terry, C112
Reeves, William T., C9
Regan, K., C212

Rehman, A., C27
Reinartz, W., 175
Reiner, C., 153
Reinert, U., 243
Reingen, P. H., 208
Reingold, J., C200
Reisinger, D., 61
Reiter, C., 100, 171
Reitzig, M., 342
Relan, Peter, C126
Renneboog, L. D. R., 306
Renz, Lee, C92
Ren Zhengfei, 349
Reuer, J. J., 208, 245
Reuss, Mark, C218
Reutzel, C. R., 309
Rexrode, C., 231
Rhodes, D., 174
Rhyne, E., C87
Rice, M. P., 408
Richard the Lionheart, C2
Richter, A., 410
Ricks, D., 245
Ridge, Garry, 261, 391
Ridge, J. W., 137
Rigas family, 202
Rigby, D. K., 207
Rihanna, C159
Riley, C., C254
Ring, P. S., 208
Ritter, Johannes, C165
Ritzman, L. P., 101
Rivington, James, C184
Rivkin, Jan W., 102, 244, 309
Robb, A., 252
Roberto, M. A., 374
Roberts, D., 68
Roberts, E. B., 408
Roberts, J., 410
Roberts, P. W., 135
Robin Hood, case, C2
Robins, J. A., 102
Robinson, Mark, 46
Robinson, R. B., 175
Robinson, S. L., 307
Robinson-Jacobs, K., 77, 338
Rock, the (Dwayne Johnson), C70
Rockefeller, Jay, C264
Rockoff, J. D., C121
Rocks, D., 226
Rocks,D., C195
Rodriguez, N., C212
Rodriguez, P., 243
Rogers, James, 113
Rogers, T. J., 23
Rollag, K., 136
Roman, M., C144
Romanelli, E., 275
Rondinelli, D. A., 31, 32
Ronstadt, R., 436
Roos, A., 208
Roos, J., 342
Root, Allan, 22
Rose, Charlie, 206
Rose, Doug, C65
Rose, Kevin, 246–247
Rosen, B., 138
Rosenberg, T., 397

Rosenblum, D., 68
Rosenzweig, Dan, 112
Rossetti, C., 341
Roth, David, 151
Roth, K., 102
Rothbort, Scott, C93
Rothenbuecher, J., 206
Rothhaermel, F. T., 275
Roundy, P. T., 206
Rouse, T., 243
Rowland, Kristan, C33
Rowley, I., 68
Rowley, T. J., 208
Rows, S. A., 437n
Roy, J. P., 208
Royer, I., 409
Rubin, Harry, C129
Rubin, Slava, C187
Rucci, A. J., 102
Rudden, E., 244
Rugman, Alan M., 234, 244
Ruisel, I., 374
Rukstad, M. G., 33
Rumelt, R. P., 341
Runyan, R., 410
Rush, Patrick, 105
Rusli, E., 206
Rusli, E. M., C273
Russo, M. V., 28
Russolillo, S., C28
Ruys, Thorny, C59
Ryan, L. V., 308
Ryan, M. K., 306
Rynecki, D., C37
Ryschkewitch, Mike, 361

S

Sacca, Chris, C271
Sachitanand, R., 217
Safferstone, T., 31
Saffo, P., 136
Safizadeh, M. H., 101
Sahlman, William A., 417
Saias, M. A., 341
St. John, W., 275
Saintvilus, R., C27
Sakaibara, M., 342
Salahi, L., C37
Salancik, G., 31
Salkever, A., C28
Salman, W. A., 68
Salomon, R., 244
Salvoney, P., 374
Sambol, David, 289
Sampson, R. C., 408
Samuelson, J., 31
Sanchez, Raymond, 429
Sandberg, W. R., 437
Sanders, P., C104
Sanders, W. G., 289
Sanderson, Rob, C270
Sandler, L., 30
Sandler, N., 243
Sandler, Ross, C271
Sanger, D. E., C219
Sant, Roger, 375
Sargent, David, C232

Sasseen, J., 309
Sauer, P. J., 430
Savage, Macho Man Randy, C69
Savner, Michael, C9
Sawhney, M., 244
Scarpello, L., 269
Schaefler, Leonard, 59
Schafer, S., 375
Schaffer, R. H., 374
Schandler, T., 375
Schawlow, Arthur, 117
Scheck, J., 307
Schecter, S. M., 176
Schein, Edgar H., 315, 340
Schendel, D., 245
Schendler, B., C27
Schenkel, M. T., 274
Scherer, A. G., 307
Scherzer, L., 102
Schiesel, S., C184
Schijven, M., 176, 197
Schiller, Philip, C26
Schindler, Pamela, 430
Schiro, Jim, 118
Schlangenstein, M., C144, C153
Schlender, B., C28
Schmidt, C., 135
Schmidt, Eric, 67
Schmidt, G., 175
Schmidt, Ulrich, C157, C164
Schneider, J., 66
Schneider, M., 308
Schneiderman, R. M., C73
Schoemaker, P. J. H., 66, 102
Schoenberger, C. R., C184, C212
Schoenherr, Tobias, 226
Schoettler, Steve, C187
Schol, M., 32
Schönen, Thomas, C165
Schoonhoven, C. B., 274
Schoppen, W., 308
Schreyoff, G., 66
Schrottke, J., 206
Schultz, Howard, 249
Schulz, Mark A., C232–C233
Schwartz, N. D., 244
Schweiger, D. M., 437
Schweitzer, M. E., 375
Schwert, G. William, 206
Scott, B. R., 340
Scott, F. S., 66
Scott, L., 68
Scott, Willard, C89
Scudamore, Brian, 126
Sculley, John, C19, C20
Segalla, M., 135
Segel, Joseph, C64
Seglin, J. L., 274
Seid, Michael, C90
Seijits, G. H., 136, 409
Sellers, P., 208, 242, 307
Semadini, M., 308, 309
Semel, Terry, C268, C270, C272
Sen, S., 32
Senge, Peter M., 8, 21, 31, 32, 358, 374
Serwer, A., 187, C144
Sethi, R., 410
Sexton, D. A., 33

Seybold, P., 175
Shah, B., 67
Shah, R. H., 208
Shamsie, Jamal, C7, C11, C58, C63, C68, C88,
    C116, C191, C196, C214, C268
Shanley, M., 68
Shapira, Z., 409
Shapiro, Andrew, C218
Shapiro, C., 68, 73
Shapiro, J., 136
Sharer, Kevin, 9
Sharma, A., 244, 408
Sharma, H., C27
Sharma, M., 240
Shaver, J. M., 275
Shaw, Peter, 184
Shaw, Robert, 187
Sheff, D., 375
Shen, Jia, C124
Shengyun Yang, C83
Shepherd, D. A., 274
Sher, Robert, C45, C46
Shetty, Ajit, C120
Shinar, Uri, 199
Shinn, S., C144
Shockley, R., 80
Shook, C., 136
Short, J. C., 68
Shrader, R. C., 274
Shrager, Gabrielle, C177
Shrestha, Shruti, C74, C201
Shubin, M., C105
Shukla, A., 17
Sidhu, Inder, 32, 90, 102
Siebel, Tom, 229, 244, 307
Siemers, E., 331
Sieracki, Eric, 289
Silva, C., 307
Silver, A., 308
Silverberg, Brad, 120
Silver-Greenberg, J., 135
Silverman, B. S., 342
Silverman, Henry, 91
Silvestri, L., 341
Simmons, Cal, 252
Simmons, Gene, C137
Simmons, P. J., 32
Simons, R., 306
Simpson, Jessica, C36
Sims, H. P., Jr., 375
Simsek, Z., 275, 409
Sinclair, M., C255
Sinder, N., C122
Singh, H., 207, 245
Singh, J. V., 101
Singh, K., 243
Singh, S., 219
Siracusa, J., C28
Sirmon, D. G., 101, 137, 176, 208, 309
Sirower, M. L., 207
Skin, J. K., C191
Skinner, Jim, C89, C91, C92
Skoll, Jeffrey, C77
Slater, D., 102
Slater, R., 115, 136
Sleeper, Nathan K., 198
Sleuwaegen, L., 342
Slevin, D. P., 342, 384, 410

Sloan, Alfred P., 21, 358
Sloan, G., C16
Slocum, J. W., Jr., 138, 175, 307
Slowinski, G., 342
Slywotsky, Adrian, 409, C259, C267
Smerd, J., C212
Smith, Alvy Ray, C7
Smith, B. R., 274
Smith, C., C212
Smith, Douglas K., 136, 332, 342
Smith, G., 243, 375
Smith, H., 271
Smith, K. G., 175, 264, 268, 275
Smith, R., C105
Smith, Stephen, 366
Smith, Thomasina, C222
Snell, J., C28
Snider, M., C105
Snow, C. C., 175, 264, 275, 332, 408
Snyder, Nancy, 22
Snyder, S. J., C190
Sole, Kenneth, 429
Solinsky, S., 338
Solomon, C., C10
Solomon, D., 388
Solomon, King, C114
Sonpar, K., 32
Sorkin, A. R., C273
Soros, George, C148
Sorrell, Martin, 126
Souers, Michael, 4
Soule, E., 375
Souter, D., 275
South, J., C46
Spainhour, J. Patrick, C47, C49
Spector, J., 49, 67
Spencer, J. W., 138
Sperling, John, 291
Spielberg, Steven, 362
Spindler, Michael, C19, C20
Spinelli, S., 249, 274
Spurlock, Morgan, C91
Srivastava, M., 239
Stabell, C. B., 100
Stadter, G., 102
Stafford, E. R., 208
Staley, O., 68
Stalk, George, Jr., 158, 175, 264, 265, 275
Stamboulidis, G., 265
Stanford, D., 21
Stanton, Andrew, C9
Stanton, S. A.., 375
Stanton, Steven, 359
Stark, Michael, C202
Staw, B. M., 374
Stead, D., 174
Stearns, T. M., 437
Stecklow, S., 307
Steens, H. K., 375
Steere, W. C., Jr., 408
Steere, William, 381
Steffens, P., 275
Steigrad, A., C56
Steinberg, B., C73
Steinman, Benj, C61
Stelter, D., 174
Stengel, Jim, C200
Sterling, T., C62

Sternberg, R. J., 374
Stetler, B., 101, 308
Stevens, J. M., 375
Stewart, C., 316, 381
Stewart, Thomas A., 108, 135, 136, 207, 274
Stewart, W. H., 67
Stibel, J. M., 174
Stieglitz, N., 68
Stienmann, H., 66
Stiller, Bob, C256
Stimpert, J. L., 175
Stoever, H., 308
Stoll, J., C233
Stone, A., 369
Stone, B., 88, C26, C28, C83
Strack, R., 135
Straus, S., 137
Streib, L., C37
Strickland, A. J., III, 307
Strickler, Yancey, C186, C187, C189, C190
Stringer, R., 409
Strom, S., C93
Stross, R. E., 243
Stuart, Keith, C184
Stuckey, J., 342
Stumpf, John, 13
Stürmlinger, Daniela, C165
Su, K. H., 275
Subasi, Ümit, C157, C164
Suchman, M., C254
Suddath, C., 174
Suer, Oral, C252
Sull, D. N., 33, 138, 409
Sullivan, John, C272
Sullivan, Trudy, C52
Summers, M., C56
Sun, J. J., 101
Sung, J.-A., C195
Sunoo, B. P., C38
Sunwyn, Mark, 110
Surette, T., C184
Sutcliffe, K. M., 66, 341
Swaminathan, A., 275
Swaminathan, V., 208
Swartz, J., 309, C273
Sweeney, J., 400
Sweo, R., 67
Swinney, J., 410
Sylvan, John, C264
Symonds, W. C., 174
Szobocsan, J., 138

T

Takahashi, D., 389
Takeda, Genyo, C179
Takeuchi, I., 135
Tallman, Joseph, 129
Tam, P.-W., C10
Tang, J., 67
Tang, Y., 208
Tanner, J., 175
Tao Yue, C83
Tapscott, D., 49
Task, A., 32, 208, 306
Tassi, Paul, C126
Tate, B., 374
Taub, E. A., 261
Taylor, A., C6

Taylor, A., III, 68, 174
Taylor, C., C190
Taylor, J. T., 375
Taylor, James, 363
Taylor, Norman O., C252
Taylor, Paul, C225
Taylor, Teresa, 357
Taylor, W. C., 138
Team, Trefis, C267
Teece, David, 131, 138
Teitelbaum, R., 307
Tekleab, A. G., 375
Teng, B. S., 342
Teramoto, Y., 244
Terdiman, D., C10
Terwiesch, C., 155, 175
Tesluk, P. E., 138, 375
Thain, John, 202, 208
Thakur, A., C104
Theoret, A., 436
Thoma, Wade, C91
Thomas, Dana, C176
Thomas, J. G., 32
Thomas, K., C121, C122
Thomas, R. J., 67, 137
Thompson, A. A., Jr., 307
Thompson, Don, C88, C89, C92, C93
Thompson, Scott, C78, C82, C271
Thornblad, David, C94
Thorndike, E. L., 374
Thornton, E., 174, 207
Thurm, S., 67
Tichy, Noel M., 374
Tierney, T., 138
Tierney, T. J., 374
Tietzen, Terry, 248
Tilin, A., 275
Timberlake, Justin, C90
Timmons, J. A., 249, 274
Tischler, L., 49, 68
Tiwana, A., 208
Tofel, K. C., C27
Tohme, N. S., 309
Tokuda, Lance, C124
Toman, N., 174
Tome, Carol B., 286
Tomlinson, D., 68
Tomlinson, R., C62
Toossi, M., 67
Torres, N. L., 274
Torvalds, Linus, 427
Tosano, Kaora, 243
Touryalai, H., 135
Townsend, M., 44
Travlos, D., C26
Tremblay, Diana D., C218
Tretter, M. J., 341
Trevino, L. K., 307
Triandis, H. C., 243
Trimble, C., 208, 341
Trimble, G., 391
Troianovski, A., 180
Troplowitz, Oscar, C155
Trotman, M., C144
Trudel, R., 32
Tsai, W., 275
Tsao, A., 67
Tserig, Jeff, C126
Tu, M., 175

Tucker, R., C56
Tuggle, C. S., 309
Tukiainen, T., 409
Tully, S., 180, 307, 341
Turk, T. A., 309
Turner, Fred L., C89
Turner, J., C57
Turner, S. F., 409
Turner, Ted, C68–C69
Tushman, Michael L., 336, 342
Tuttle, B., C104
Twain, Mark, 351
Tyrangiel, J., 138
Tyson, L. D., 67

U

Uhl-Bien, M., 307
Uhlenbruck, K., 243
Ulaga, W., 175
Ulrich, D., 101
Ulrich, K. T., 155, 175
Ultimate Warrior, C70
Unnikrishnan, M., C153
Uzoma, K., C37
Uzzi, B., 137

V

Vaaler, P. M., 175
Vaarnas, Markko, 447
Vagelos, P. Roy, 107
Vaishampayan, S., 371
Valdes-Dapena, P., 54, C234
Valeant-Yenichek, Julie, 44
Valikangas, L., 408
Van Aukun, P. M., 33
Van Boxmeer, Jean-François, C58, C59, C60–C61, C62
Van Buren, H. J., 137
Van Buren, M. E., 31
Vance, A., 405
Van Gogh, Vincent, 123, 124
Van Heck, Eric, C83
Van Hoven, M., 199
Van Looy, B., 244
Van Putten, A. S., 243
Van Wamelen, A., 221
Varian, H. R., 68, 73
Vascellaro, J. E., 265, 269, 408, C27, C273
Vega, T., C273
Veiga, J. F., 275, 409
Vella, Carolyn M., 447
Veloso, F. M., 408
Verbeke, Alain, 234, 244, 340
Verdú-Jover, A. J., 373
Verespej, M., 251
Vermeulen, F., 208
Verrier, R., C105
Very, P., 137
Veryzer, R. W., 408
Vesper, K. H., 274, 275
Vestring, T., 243
Victor, B., 341
Viguerie, P., 67
Vinh, K., C190
Vlasic, B., C219, C233, C234
Vogel, C., 275
Vogel, D. J., 32

Von, Hippel, Eric, 67
Vuitton, Georges, C166
Vuitton, Renée, C166

W

Waddock, S., 32
Wadia, A. S., C212
Wagner, M., 400
Wagner, S., 342
Wagoner, Rick, C216, C217, C218
Wagstaff, J., C27
Wakabayashi, D., 180
Walker, B. A., 208
Walker, Jay, 208, 274
Wall, S. J., 375
Wallace, B., 275
Wallace, J., 340
Walsh, Glenn, C211
Walsh, J. P., 309
Walters, B. A., 67, 208, 245, 274, 307
Walton, Sam, 16, 282
Wan, W. P., 244
Wang, E. Z., 309
Wang, L., 410
Wang, S. S., C121
Wang, William, 261
Warchol, G., C144
Ward, Elizabeth, C44
Warlick, Andy, 316
Warner, D., C56
Warner, F., 136
Warner, M., C93
Warnholz, J.-L., 243
Wasik, J., 254, 274
Wasserman, E., 417
Watercutter, A., C190
Waterman, Robert H., 306
Waters, J. A., 11
Wathieu, L., 174
Watkins, M. D., 67
Watson, R., 401
Watson, Thomas J., 21, 184, 358
Watts, Claire, C66
Watts, Colin, C37
Wauters, Robin, C83
Wayne, Ronald, C19
Weaver, G. R., 307
Weaver, K. M., 275
Webb, Reggie, C90
Webber, A. M., 135
Weber, J., 307
Weber, K., 66
Wei, James C., C157
Wei Jinping, 230
Weil, Laura, C56
Weilart, M., 341
Weinberg, D., 138
Weinberg, N., 309
Weiner, H., 341
Weinreb, E., 110
Weintraub, A., 404
Welch, D., 68, C219, C233, C234
Welch, Jack, 5, 79, 201, 208, 324

Weldon, William C., C116, C118, C120
Wellington, F., 32
Wells, R. M. J., 408
Welsch, Harold L., 274
Wen, S. H., 244
Werder, A. V., 307
Werhane, P. H., 203
Wernerfelt, B., 137
Wesley, Pamela, C77
Westerfeldt, R. W., 437n
Westergren, Tim, 258
Weston, J. S., 306
Weston, John F., 208
Weston, John S., 279
Westphal, J. D., 206, 307, 308, 374
Wetlaufer, S., 244, 307, 375
Wheelwright, S., 408
Whelan, D., 67
Whitacre, Edward E., Jr., C217
White, A., 271
White, D., 342
White, Dana, C71
White, I., 187
White, James D., C39, C40, C41, C42, C43, C44, C45
Whitman, Meg, 277, C77–C78, C79, C84, C187
Wiersema, F., 408
Wiersema, M. F., 102, 206
Wiggett, Jim, 76
Wiggins, J., C62
Willcocks, L. P., 101
Williams, A. D., 49
Williams, C. C., C62
Williams, G., 275, C37
Williams, M. A., 137
Williams, R., 375
Williams, S., C57
Williams, Venus, C42
Williamson, Oliver E., 207
Williamson, P., 242
Wilson, Chad, C110
Wilson, D., 174
Wilson, H. J., 138, 409
Wilson, K., 340
Wilson, M., C56
Wilson, Mackenzie, C185
Wilson, S., 261
Wilson, Sean, C185
Wind, Y., 244
Winder, Catherine, 392
Wingfield, N., 138, 208
Winkler, Annette, 71
Winston, A. S., 17, 348
Winter, C., 198, 244
Wirtz, J., 175
Wise, R., 68, 409
Wiseman, R., 304
Woellert, L., C16
Wojdyla, B., 68
Wolfenson, J., 67
Wolter, C., 408
Wong, Chris, C190
Wong, S.-S., 137
Wood, J., 101

Wood, R. C., 389
Woods, B., C212
Woodyard, C., C16
Woolley, S., 32
Worrell, D., 259
Worthan, J., C190
Wozniak, Steve, C19, C20
Wright, P., 175, 274, 307
Wriston, Walter, 201, 358
Wuestner, C., 171
Wurster, T. S., 67
Wyatt, E., C73
Wynn, Steve, 291, C12, C14
Wysocki, Bernard, Jr., 120, 137
Wyss, Hansjorg, 345–346

Y

Yakubovich, V., 307
Yamaguchi, Y., 240
Yang, Jerry, C270
Yang, Q., 244
Yao, X., 275
Yarow, J., 408
Yatsko, P., 17
Yeoh, P. L., 102
Yoffie, D. B., 61, 68
Yolton, Mark, 129
Yonekira, Hiromas, C193
Young, Bob, 427
Young, M. N., 309, 341
Yu, R., C195
Yukl, Gary, 373
Yun, S., 375
Yun Jong Yong, C191–C192, C193, C194
Yunus, Muhammad, C85, C87

Z

Zaccaro, S. J., 138
Zachadakis, A. L., 274
Zahra, S. A., 244, 408
Zajac, E. J., 307
Zardkoohi, A., 308, 409
Zaslav, David, 296
Zeitchik, S., C105
Zeleny, J., C219
Zell, D., 137
Zelleke, A., 309
Zellner, Wendy, 307, C144, C153
Zelman, K. M., C37
Zenger, J. H., 359, 374
Zetsche, Dieter, C220
Zhang, R., 375
Zhao, A., 252
Zhou, K. Z., 137
Zhu, D. H., 101
Ziegler, J., 251
Ziobro, P., C243
Zoe, Rachel, C64
Zollo, M., 206
Zongker, B., C254
Zozula, Sojna, 226
Zrike, Stephen, 165

Page numbers followed by n refer to notes.

A

Absolute customers, C168
Accessible customers, C168
Accounting, and Sarbanes-Oxley Act, 45
Achievable opportunities, 250
Acid-test ratio, 441
Acquisitions, 193; *see also* Mergers and
    acquisitions
    Abercrombie & Fitch by Limited Brands, C52
    AirTran by Southwest Airlines, C137, C143
    and antitakeover tactics, 202
    Beiersdorf AG, C157
    by Boston Beer Company, C129, C131
    Boston Proper by Chico, C52
    of Dippin' Dots Inc., C106
    by eBay, C78–C79, C79, C81, C83
    examples of success, 181
    GameHouse by RealNetworks, C125
    by Green Mountain Coffee Roasters,
        C256–C257, C260
    H. J. Heinz by Berkshire Hathaway, C241
    by Heineken, C58, C61–C62
    hostile takeovers, 202
    investor perception of value, 197
    J. Jill Group by Talbots, C52
    by Jamba Juice, C40
    by Johnson & Johnson, C117, C121
    by LVMH Group, C169–C170
    by McDonald's, C90
    means of diversification, 193–194
    NeXT by Apple Inc., C20
    Pillsbury by General Mills, C240–C241
    Pixar by Disney, C7
    Playfish by Electronic Arts, C126
    by QVC, C64, C66
    resulting in divestment, 181
    shareholder value destroyed by, 197
    SsangYong by SAIC, 210–212
    studies on disappointments, 180
    Talbott Teas by Jamba Juice, C41
    value destruction from, 180
    by World Wrestling Entertainment, C88–C89
    wrong motives for, 180
    by Yahoo!, C268, C270
Action plans
    Marks and Spencer, 286
    short-term, 285
Actions, 7, 9
Adaptability, 336
Adaptation
    versus cost reduction, 225–227
    in multidomestic strategy, 230, 231–232
    in transnational strategy, 232
Adaptive new entry, 259
    example, 259
    pitfalls, 259
    strategy choices, 259–260
Ad Meters, 77

Administrative costs in vertical integration, 188–189
Advertising
    Apple TV commercial of 1984, C20
    Campbell Soup Company, C237
    Dippin' Dots Inc., C110–C112
    Fresh Direct, C203
    Jamba Juice, C42
    lost by Yahoo!, C268
    mistakes by Google, 376–378
    misuse of cultural symbols, 223
    by movie exhibitors, C104
    in movie theaters, C99–C100
    product placement, 75–76, 153
    revenue for movie exhibitors, C98–C99
    Samsung Electronics, C192
    Super Bowl commercials, 77
    time allocated for pre-show ads, C101
    Weight Watchers, C35
    Zynga, C123
Advertising agencies, Google as threat to, 377
Affordable Nutrition Index, C242
Africa, population and Internet usage, C76
African Americans, 118
Agency costs, 334
Agency theory, 290
    and back-solver dilemma, 396–397
    and CEO duality, 297–298
Agents, 290, 397
Age of Paradox (Handy), 358
Age of Unreason (Handy), 328, 358
Aggregate demand
    in introduction stage, 165
    in maturity stage, 165
Aging population, 42
Agriculture, leading export destinations, C239
Airline industry
    bankruptcy, C147
    deregulation in 1978, C147
    effect of teleconferencing on, 53
    impact of terrorist attack, C147
    interline agreements, C152–C153
    JetBlue Airways, C146–C153
    low-fare carriers, C147
    main bases of competition, C147
    major airlines, C147
    mergers and acquisitions, 202
    mergers and consolidation, C147
    performance indicators, C152
    regional airlines, C147
    restructuring, C147
    Southwest Airlines, C137–C143
    stagnant market in U.S., C137
    terminology, C145, C154
    and Wright amendment, C142
Airport store locations, C43
Air Transport World, C149
Alcoholics Anonymous, C35
Alignment, 10, 336
Alternative solution, 419–421

Ambidexterity, 9
    combining alignment and adaptability, 10
    of managers, 9
Ambidextrous organizational designs, 336
    breakthrough projects, 336
    effectiveness, 337
    performance results, 336–337
American Heritage Dictionary, 290
American Journal of Preventive Medicine, C37
Americans with Disabilities Act, 44, 47
Analysis, 7, 9
Analysis-decision-action cycle; *see* Case analysis
Analytical tools, 419
Angel investors, 252
Antitakeover tactics, 202
    benefits to stakeholders, 203
    golden parachute, 202, 298
    greenmail, 202, 298
    poison pill, 202, 298
Antitrust law, France, 271
Apparel industry, 328
Apparel retailing industry
    Ann Taylor stores, C47–C51, C54–C56
    department stores, C51
    discount mass merchandisers, C51
    industry sectors, C51–C54
    specialty store chains, C51
Arbitrage opportunities, 217
    motive for international expansion, 217
Argo, C97
Asia
    emerging middle class, 46
    fortified drink market, 240
    population and Internet usage, C76
Asian Americans, number of, 118
Aspirational customers, C168
Asset management/turnover measures
    days' sales in inventory, 443
    days' sales in receivables, 444
    inventory turnover, 443
    receivables turnover, 444
    total asset turnover, 444
Asset restructuring, 190
Asset sales/dissolution, 197n
Asset surgery, 169
Asset utilization ratios, 93
Associating, 383, 384
Association of Southeast Asian Nations, 234
Atlantic City casino industry, C11–C16
Attractive opportunities, 250
Attrition, at Apple Inc., C26
Auctions
    earliest known, C75
    online, C76
    traditional, C75
Auditing failures, 299
Auditors, as control mechanism, 299
Austin Powers in Goldmember, 153
Australia, population and Internet usage, C76

Automated manufacturing, 154–155
Automobile industry
  best-selling cars, C231
  China's market for, 212
  Ford turnaround, 170, C220–C233
  market shares, C227
  Porsche, 171
  price cutting, 270
  SAIC in China, 210–212
  sales 2012 and 2013, C227–C229
  strategic groups, 61–62
  in United States, C232
  vehicle dependability rankings, C230
  vertical integration, 188
Autonomous work groups, 390
Autonomous work units, 399
Autonomy, 399
  independent action, 400
  at Johnson & Johnson, C118
  skunkworks, 400
Autorité de la Concurrence, France, 271
Avengers, The, C94, C96
Aviation Consumer Action Project, 300

B

Back-solver dilemma, 396
  and agency theory, 396–397
Backstage Following, C68
Backward integration, threat of, 52
Balanced scorecard, 94–96, **95**
  to assess new venture success, 394
  description and benefits
    customer perspective, 95
    financial perspective, 96
    innovation and learning perspective, 95
    internal business perspective, 95
  limitations and downsides, 96
Balance sheet
  Ann Taylor, C50
  Beiersdorf AG, C160
  Boston Beer Company, C130
  Campbell Soup Company, C242
  Ford Motor Company, C223–C224
  General Motors, C215
  Green Mountain Coffee Roasters, C258
  Heineken, C58
  Jamba Juice, C41
  Johnson & Johnson, C117
  McDonald's, C88
  Nintendo, C179
  Procter & Gamble, C197
  Samsung Electronics, C192
  Weight Watchers, C34
  Yahoo!, C269
  Zynga, C125
Bangladesh, origin of microfinance, C85
Bankruptcy
  airline industry, C147
  Borders, 3–4
  casino industry, C15
  Dippin' Dots Inc. in 2004, C106
  General Motors, C214, C216–C217
Banks
  as control mechanism, 299
  instability in European Union, 6
Bargaining power of buyers, 51
  few switching costs, 52
  in five-forces model, 51–52

impact of Internet, 55–57
increased by third-party services, 52
large purchases relative to seller sales, 51
legal services on Internet, 57
low profits, 52
potential backlash, 52
standard or undifferentiated products, 52
threat of backward integration, 52
unimportant quality, 52
Bargaining power of employees, 91
Bargaining power of managers, 91
Bargaining power of suppliers, 52
  differentiated products, 53
  few dominant companies, 52
  in five-forces model, 52–53
  high vs. low, 56
  impact of Internet, 57–58
  industry unimportant, 53
  lack of substitutes, 52
  products unimportant, 53
  switching costs for buyers, 53
  threat of forward integration, 53
  threat of substitute products and services, 56
Barrier-free organization, 325
  basic advantage, 324–325
  creating permeable internal boundaries, 325–326
  external constituencies, 326
  major shortcoming, 325
  potential downsides, 326–327
  pros and cons, 328
  risks and challenges, 326–327
Barriers to change, 350
  behavioral, 351
  overcoming, 350–352, 363
  personal time constraint, 351
  political, 351, 352
  resistance to innovation, 381
  systemic, 351
  vested interests in status quo, 350
Barriers to collaboration
  overcoming
    network lever, 123
    people lever, 123
    T-shaped management, 123
    unification lever, 123
  types of, 123
Barriers to entry
  capital requirements, 51
  for dot.com firms, 154
  industry dominance, 159
  low, 51
  low in online marketplace, C79
  one-time costs, 51
  product differentiation, 50–51
  for start-ups, 257
Barriers to mobility, 61
Beer industry
  Boston Beer Company, C128–C136
  brand recognition, C135–C136
  competitors, C133–C136
  consolidation, C60
  craft breweries, C128–C129
  distribution, C132
  domestic beer brands, C135
  dominant companies, C131
  and drinking habit changes, C131
  globalization, C59–C60
  Heineken, C58–C62
  leading brewers, C60

number of barrels sold in 2011, X131
three-tier system, C131–C132
top dollar sales, C133
top dollar sales of imports, C134
top ten brewers, C132
top ten categories, C133
total sales 2007–2012, C132
U.S. Open Beer Championship, C132
Behavioral barriers, 351
Behavioral control, 14, 279
  attaining
    improving efficiency and effectiveness, 285
    minimizing improper conduct, 286
    organizational culture, 281–282
    reward systems, 283–284
    setting boundaries and constraints, 284–286
    short-term objectives and action plans, 285
    strategic priorities, 284–285
  from boundaries and constraints to, 287–288
  with employees as free agents, 281
  focus on implementation, 281
  situational factors, 286–287
Benchmarking, 8, **362**
  competitive, 363
  functional, 363
  internal, 362
Best practices
  to attract millennials, 112
  for environmental sustainability, 326
  functional benchmarking for, 363
Better Business Bureau, 754
Better Homes & Gardens, 379
Biggest Loser, C35
Bloomberg BusinessWeek, 38, 88, 196, 246, 300, 379
Board of directors, 290–291, **292**
  Beiersdorf AG, C157–C158
  broad vision, 294
  in case analysis, 416
  and CEO departures, 292
  as CEO rubber stamp, 292
  changing face of, 1987–2011, 294
  in corporate governance, 14–15
  criticisms of, 15
  director independence, 293
  duties, 292
  expertise, 293
  focus on past, present, and future, 293
  full participation, 293
  General Motors, C217
  Heineken, C60–C61
  manageable size, 293
  managerial talent development, 294
  norms of transparency and trust, 294
  Sarbanes-Oxley Act on, 294
  stakeholders on, 221
  strong oversight, 292
  and succession planning, 293
Bond financing, 252
Bondholders of General Motors, C217
Bonus pay
  at AIG, C4–C6
  undeserved, 15
Book publishing
  demise of Borders, 3–4
  e-books, 4
  Internet sales, 4
Boom and bust cycles, 188
Bots, 58
Bottom of the pyramid population, 212–213

Boundaries and constraints, **284**
  focus on strategic priorities, 284–285
  improving efficiency and effectiveness, 285
  minimizing improper conduct, 286
  in nonprofit sector, 285
  providing short-term action plans, 285
  to rewards and culture, 287–288
Boundaryless, 324
Boundaryless organizational designs, 324
  barrier-free, 324–328
  common culture, 332–333
  communications in, 332
  coordination and integration, 332
  designing, 331–335
  horizontal operational structure, 333
  horizontal systems and processes, 333
  human resource practices, 332
  information technology for, 332
  internal and external relationships, 333–335
  modular organizations, 328–329
  problems at Boeing, 310–312
  Procter & Gamble, 334
  shared values, 333
  types of, 324
  virtual organizations, 329–331
Boundary types, 325
Box office receipts 2006–2011, C97
Box office revenues, C99
  opening weekend, C106
Bozo Filter, 111
Brainstorming, 326
Brand cannibalization, C55
Brand development, Samsung Electronics,
  C192–C193
Brand extension, 97
  in apparel industry, C51–C52
  Campbell Soup Company, C238
  Keurig, C265–C266
Brand identification, diluted by product-line
  extensions, 151
Brand identity
  Ann Taylor, C55–C56
  preservation at Jamba Juice, C45
  Weight Watchers, C35–C37
Brand management, Procter & Gamble, C198
Brand marketing, Jamba Juice, C40
Brand recognition, in beer industry, C135–C136
Brands
  Ann Taylor, C47
  in apparel industry, C51–C52
  Beiersdorf AG, C159–C160
  divested by General Motors, C217–C218
  domestic beer, C135
  globalization by Ford, C226
  Heineken, C59
  Johnson & Johnson, C120
  of leading brewers, C60
  Louis Vuitton, C170
  at QVC, C64
  updating at Procter & Gamble, C199
Breakaway positioning, 166
  Swatch Group, 167
Breakthrough projects, 336
Bridging relationships, 122
British Medical Journal, 240
Brokers
  online, 146–147
  on social networks, 124–125
Bullet train thinking, 348

Bureaucracy, cut at General Motors, C217
Bureaucratic control models, 120
Bureau of Labor Statistics, on millennials in
  workforce, 112
Businesses, effects of negative developments, 5–7
Business groups, 303
Business incubators, 390
  functions, 390–391
  to grow businesses, 390
Business-level strategy, 140–171, 142
  Ann Taylor, C47–C49, C55–C56
  Apple Inc., C17, C20–C26
  Boston Beer Company, C128–C131
  Campbell Soup Company, C235–C238,
    C242–C243
  in case analysis, 433–434
  change at Samsung Electronics, C191–C195
  for competitive advantage, 142–157
  Dippin' Dots Inc., C112–C114
  eBay, C79–C82
  Edward Marshall Boehm Inc., C3
  effect of Internet, 160–162
  Fresh Direct, C201–C202, C203–C204,
    C209–C212
  generic strategies, 142–157
  at Heineken, C61
  and industry life-cycle changes, 162–171
  at Jamba Juice, C39
  JetBlue Airways, C148–C150
  Louis Vuitton, C170–C173
  maintaining competitive strategies, 157–162
  McDonald's, C88–C89
  in microfinance, C85–C86
  mistakes at Hostess Inc., 141–142
  movie industry, C94–C104
  Pixar Animated Studios, C7–C10
  Procter & Gamble, C199
  purpose, 13
  QVC, C64–C67
  viability of, 142
  Weight Watchers International, C29–C37
  World Wrestling Entertainment, C69–C73
Business magazines, 300
Business model
  changes at JetBlue Airways, C149
  eBay, C74, C79–C81
  Fresh Direct, C203
  imitation of, 403
  JetBlue Airways, C146–C148
  rethinking at Southwest Airlines, C137
  at Weight Watchers, C32–C33, C36–C37
  of Zynga, C123
Business plan framework for case analysis, 417
Business process reengineering, 8
Business risk taking, 404
Business segments/units
  Campbell Soup Company, C235
  Keurig, C267
  Procter & Gamble, C196
Business services, by business incubators, 390
Business-to-business auctions, C76
Business-to-business model, Weight Watchers,
  C36, C37
Business-to-business purchasing, effects of
  Internet, 57
Business-to-consumer auctions, C76
Business-to-consumer purchasing, 56
Business websites, 450
BusinessWeek, 4

Buyer channel intermediaries, 57
Buyer needs, too much focus on, 154
Buyers; *see also* Bargaining power of buyers
  buyer channel intermediaries, 57
  end users, 56
  large volume, 51
  and low-cost position, 145
  perception of differentiation, 151

C

Cable networks, C102
Capabilities
  at Apple Inc., C20
  building, versus collaboration, 382
  criteria for assessing sustainability, 85
  Dell Inc., 90
  in human capital, 108
  organizational, 83, 84
  types of, 83
Capacity, augmented on large increments, 54
Capital expenditures, JetBlue Airways, C152
Capital intensity ratio, 93, 444
Capitalism, shared value concept, 18–19
Capital raising, by Dippin' Dots Inc., C109
Capital requirements, as barrier to entry, 51
Capital restructuring, 190
Career planning advice, 112
Career success, and social networks, 123
Case analysis, 413
  analysis-decision-action cycle
    business-level strategy, 433–434
    corporate entrepreneurship, 436
    corporate-level strategy, 434
    entrepreneurial strategies, 434–435
    ethical organization, 435–436
    external environment, 433
    intellectual assets, 433
    internal environment, 433
    international-level strategies, 434
    learning organization, 435–436
    organizational design, 435
    organizational goals and objectives, 432
    strategic control, 435
  analytical tools, 419
  asking the right questions, 414
  benefits from
    concise, 423
    critical self-analysis, 424
    drawing on personal experience, 423
    insights from other cases, 424
    learn from others, 423–424
    open mind, 422
    outside research, 424
    participate and persuade, 423
    taking a stand, 423
    think outside the box, 423
  business plan framework, 417
  company and industry information sources,
    447–452
  components of cases, 414
  conduct of
    alternative solutions, 419–421
    familiarity with material, 418
    problem identification, 418
    recommendations, 421
    role playing, 415–418
    strategic analysis, 419
  cycles of managerial activity, 415

decision-making techniques, 424–431
  conflict-inducing, 427–431
  integrative thinking, 425–426
differentiating skill, 414
integrating skill, 414
oral presentation, 422
plan of action based on, 414
ratio analysis as tool for, 420, 431, 437–447
reasons for, 413–415
Sapient Health Network, 416
skills required for, 414–415
speculating skill, 414
written presentation, 425
Case analysis teams, 429–430
Case problems, 418
Case symptoms, 418
Cash coverage ratio, 93, 443
Cash cows, 191–192
Cash flow statement
  Ann Taylor, C51
  Ford Motor Company, C225
  Weight Watchers, C34
Cash ratio, 93, 441
Casino industry, case
  bankruptcies, C15
  downturn in Las Vegas, C12
  effects of financial crisis, C11–C12
  growing threats
    Internet gambling, C15
    Native American casinos, C15
    racetrack gaming, C15
    riverboat gambling, C15
  history of growth, C12–C13
  increased competition, C14–C15
  Las Vegas/Atlantic City dominance,
    C13–C14
  leading operators, C14
  mergers and acquisitions in, C14
  Native American casinos by state, C12
  overseas competitors, C12
  prospects, C15–C16
  public view of, C13
  revenue breakdown by state, C11
  sources of growth, C13
  U.S. revenue 2002–2012, C11
  waterborne casinos, C12
Causal ambiguity, 87
Celebrate Your Mistakes (Holt), 364
Celebrity endorsements
  QVC, C65
  for Weight Watchers, C36–C37
Cell phones
  market, C23
  World Wrestling Entertainment on, C71
Center for Auto Safety, 300
Center for the Study of Responsive Law, 300
Center of Automotive Management, 171
CEO change
  Ann Taylor, C47, C49, C55–C56
  Apple Inc., C17, C20
  Beiersdorf AG, C155, C157
  Campbell Soup Company, C235
  Dippin' Dots Inc., C112
  eBay, C77–C78
  effect at Apple Inc., C26
  Ford Motor Company, C220–C223
  Fresh Direct, C202
  Green Mountain Coffee Roasters, C256
  Heineken, C59

Jamba Juice, C40, C42
JetBlue Airways, C152
Johnson & Johnson, C116–C117
Louis Vuitton, C166
McDonald's, C88–C90
Procter & Gamble, C198, C199–C200
Southwest Airlines, C141, C142
Yahoo!, C268, C270, C271
CEO compensation, 91, 303–304
  policies for, 296
  stock options, 296
  tied to performance, 303–304
CEO duality
  agency theory and, 297–298
  unity of command perspective, 297
CEOs
  as chairmen of board, 292
  effect of external environment, 5–7
  external control view of leadership, 5
  JetBlue Airways, C147–C148
  Louis Vuitton, C167
  Responsible Corporate Office Doctrine, 345
  rewards and incentives, 295–296
  romantic view of leadership, 4–5
  Southwest Airlines, C137–C138
  succession planning, 293
  termination of, 292
  of Zynga, C123, C126
Change
  in entrepreneurial cultures, 392
  from questioning status quo, 358–359
Change agents, 347
Change management, 378
Chapter 11 bankruptcy, C106
Charitable organizations
  competitors, C249–C252
  top ten in U.S., C251
  United Way Worldwide, C246–C254
  watchdog agencies, C253
Chief executive officer; *see* CEO *entries*
Childhood obesity, 44
China
  Apple manufacturing in, C22
  Beiersdorf AG in, C150
  Campbell Soup Company in, C236–C237
  eBay partnerships in, C74
  growing middle class, 10–11
  iPhone sales in, C24
  middle class, 217
  principal-principal conflicts, 301–302
  rising labor costs, 146
  Taobao, C82
  wage increases, 225
Cigarette pack warnings, 63
Closure, 121
Code of ethics, 39
Codes of conduct, 368–369
  elements of, 369
Coercive power, 352–353
Coffee consumption in United States, C259–C260
Coffee industry
  big three sellers, C259
  single-server brewing, C260–C267
  specialty, C259–C260
  trends in, C260
Cold War, end of, 168
Collaboration
  versus building capabilities, 382
  electronic teams for, 127–128

improved by social capital, 126
  at Johnson & Johnson, C118
  overcoming barriers to, 123
  at Pixar Animation Studios, C8
  in virtual organizations, 330, 331
Collaborative leaders, 116
College and university store locations, C43
Collusion, in soap business, 271
Combination strategies, 154
  automated and flexible manufacturing, 154–155
  extended value chain, 155
  and five-forces model, 155–156
  for Internet legal services, 163
  for new ventures, 262
  overall cost leadership-differentiation, 154–157
  pitfalls
    managerial time, 157
    miscalculating revenue sources, 157
    stuck-in-the-middle situation, 156
    underestimating value chain coordination, 156
  profit pool concept, 155, 156
  types of customers, 154
  Warby Parker, 263
Command-and-control decision process, 280
Commitment
  to excellence, 256
  irrational escalation of, 398
Commoditized products, 58
Common-size balance sheet, 437
Common-size income statement, 438
Communication, in boundaryless organizations, 333
Community values, eBay, C79
Company rankings, 450
Comparison shopping, on Internet, 162
Compensation, at Southwest Airlines, C140
Competencies
  to execute vertical integration, 188
  for innovation, 387
Competency companions, 359
Competition
  among divisions, 317
  among educational institutions, 369
  in apparel industry, C51–C54
  in book sales, 3–4
  broad context of, 40–41
  in casino industry
    Internet gambling, C15
    Native American casinos, C15
    from overseas casinos, C12
    racetrack gaming, C15
    riverboat gambling, C15
  for eBay
    Amazon, C82–C83
    Gmarket, C82
    Taobao, C82
    Yahoo!, C74, C82
  in focus strategy, 153–154
  Fresh Direct with supermarkets, C202
  intensifying for Southwest Airlines,
    C132–C143
  intensifying in maturity stage, 165–166
  for iTunes, C25
  for Jamba Juice, C40, C41, C44–C45
  for Kickstarter, C189
  within Las Vegas, C14
  Las Vegas vs. Atlantic City, C13–C15
  MP3 players, C22–C23
  not based on price, C22
  smartphone market, C23–C24

Competition—Cont.
in social media, 246–247
in software market, C25
tablet computers, C24–C25
for Weight Watchers, C30–C32
for World Wrestling Entertainment, C72
Competitive actions
Apple Inc., 269
defensive, 269
forms of, 270
frontal assaults, 267
guerrilla offensives, 267–268
strategic, 267–268
tactical, 267–268
Competitive advantage, 7
by Apple Inc., C22
Atlas Door case
conclusions on, 159–160
creation and results, 158
sustainability pros and cons, 159
and business performance, 143
codifying knowledge for, 128–129
from competitive analytics, 80
creating, 7
from dynamic capabilities, 131–132
effects of Internet, 160–162
eroding at Dell Inc., 90
from environmentally-friendly manufacturing, 75
from factor endowment, 214
gain in market share, 143
from general administration, 79
generic strategies, 142–157
in global markets
cost reduction vs. adaptation, 225–227
global strategy, 228–230
global vs. regional strategy, 223–234
international strategy, 228
multidomestic strategy, 230–232
transnational strategy, 232–233
and industry life cycle, 162–170
innovation essential for, 381
from intellectual property, 129–130
maintaining competitive strategies, 157–160
Pixar Animation Studios, C8–C9
related and supporting industries, 215
resources for, 85–89
return on investment, 143
sales growth, 143
short-lived, 157
strengths failing to lead to, 73
sustainable, 8
in time pacing for innovation, 385
from value-chain activities, 392
Competitive Advantage (Porter), 72
Competitive aggressiveness, 402
to combat industry trends, 402–403
damage to reputation, 403
expansion by eBay, C79
preannouncements, 403
SWOT analysis, 402
techniques
copying business model, 403
lower prices, 403
Competitive analysis, C2
checklist, 56
information resources, 450–452
Competitive analytics, 80
Competitive attack, responding to, 266–267
Competitive benchmarking, 363

Competitive dynamics, 13, 263
choosing not to react, 270
hardball strategies, 265
likelihood of competitive reaction, 269–270
model, 264
motivation and capacity to respond, 266–267
new competitive actions, 263–264
threat analysis, 264–266
types of competitive actions, 267–269
Competitive environment, 48
components, 48
effect of Internet on five-forces-model, 55–58
five-forces-model, 49–55
industry analysis, 59–63
strategic groups, 61–63
Competitive intelligence, 38
ethical guidelines, 39
examples, 38
failure to spot new competition, 39
information resources, 447
websites for, 38–39
Competitiveness; *see* Diamond of national advantage
Competitive parity, 143
failure to maintain, 144
Competitive position
enhanced by divestment, 198
marginal extensions, 61
Southwest Airlines, C137
Competitive reactions
choosing not to react, 270
and competitor's reputation, 270
and competitor's resources, 270
likelihood of, 269–270
and market dependence, 270
Competitive strategies
Atlas Door case, 158–160
effects of Internet, 160–162
maintaining, 157–160
Competitors
in airline industry, C147
in auto industry, C232
for Beiersdorf AG, C161–C164
for Boston Beer Company, C133–C135
for Campbell Soup Company, C239–C241
comparison of financial ratios, 94
competitive aggressiveness toward, 402
for Dippin' Dots Inc., C112
for Fresh Direct, C206, C207–C209
for JetBlue Airways, C152
for Keurig, C263–C264
for Louis Vuitton, C173–C176
for McDonald's, C88, C92–C93
numerous and equally balanced, 54
raising costs of, 265
resources of, 270
and threat of new entrants, 262–263
for United Way Worldwide, C249–C252
for Zynga, C1246–C126
Complementors, for Apple Inc., 61
Complements, 60
Compliance-based ethics programs, 366–368
Computer-aided design and manufacturing, 45, 154
Computer-animated films, C7–C10
Computer Bits, C205
Conde Nast Traveler, C149
Conflict-inducing techniques
devil's advocacy, 431
dialectical inquiry, 431
groupthink problem, 428–430

to improve decision making, 430–431
Conglomerate, 319
Connectors, 120–121
Consolidation
in airline industry, C147
of beer industry, C60
Consolidation strategy, 168
Consumer Council, Norway, C127
Consumer Electronics Show, C233
Consumer Price Index, 46
Consumer products, Procter & Gamble as icon
in, C196
Consumer Reports, 151, C31
Consumers
behavior in luxury goods industry, C169
and corporate social responsibility, 18
in movie theaters, C99
online information, 56
price-sensitive, C205–C206
worldwide homogeneity, 226
Contemporary approach to strategic control
behavioral control, 279
characteristics for effectiveness, 280
double-loop learning, 279–280
informational control, 279
Continuous improvement, 401
Continuous-replenishment system, 75
Contract-based outcomes, 291
Contracting out, Boston Beer Company, C129
Contracts, in vertical integration, 188
Control
based on feedback loop, 278
lost by licensing and franchising, 236–237
Control systems, 78
Cooperation, illegal, 271
Co-opetition, 276
Coordination
in boundaryless organizations, 332
of extended value chain, 155
Coordination costs, 225
Core competencies, 183
attained by mergers and acquisitions, 195
as collective learning, 183
criteria for synergy, 183
examples, 183–184
leveraging, 182–184
Core values
Beiersdorf AG, C156
eBay, C77
employee relationship with, 116–117
and performance evaluation, 115
Corporate Citizenship poll, 18
Corporate credos, 368–369
Corporate entrepreneurship, 14, 387
aims, 387–388
at Apple Inc., C20–C26
in case analysis, 436
determining new projects, 388
dispersed approaches
ability to change, 391–392
entrepreneurial culture, 392
idea sources, 391–392
product champions, 393
resource allotments, 392
factors affecting pursuit of new ventures,
388–389
focused approaches
business incubators, 390–391
new venture groups, 390

intrapreneuring, 388
measures of success, 393–394
at Microsoft, 405
need for entrepreneurial orientation, 389–404
uses of innovation, 387–388
Corporate ethical performance, 365
Corporate governance, 14, 288
and agency theory, 290–291
AIG, C4–C6
aligning interests of owners and managers, 291–296
board of directors role, 14–15
boards of directors, 292–294
and CEO duality
agency theory, 297–298
unity of command perspective, 297
and corporate performance, 289
effectiveness mechanisms, 15
examples of flawed governance, 289–290
external control mechanisms, 298–301
failure at United Way, C252–C253
and financial performance, 288
Heineken, C60–C61, C62
international perspective
business groups, 303
expropriation of minority shareholders, 303
principal-principal conflicts, 301–302
investment decisions, 288
key elements, 14, 15
management role, 14–15
managerial rewards and incentives, 295–296
and managerial self-interest, 291
in modern corporations, 290–291
primary participants, 288
problem of risk sharing, 291
problems at Hewlett-Packard, 276–277
Sarbanes-Oxley Act on, 300
shareholder activism, 295
and stakeholders, 288n
Corporate-level strategy, 178–204, **180**
achieving diversification
internal development, 200
joint ventures, 199–200
mergers and acquisitions, 192–199
strategic alliances, 199–200
Ann Taylor, C47–C48, C54–C55
and antitakeover tactics, 202–203
in case analysis, 434
casino industry, C11–C15
change at Samsung Electronics, C191–C192
Dippin' Dots Inc., C106–C107
eBay, C74, C78–C79, C80–C81
effect on Beiersdorf AG, C157–C158, C164–C165
erosion of value creation by managers, 201–202
Ford Motor Company, C220–C233
General Motors, C213–C219
at Heineken, C61–C62
Johnson & Johnson, C117–C118, C121
LVMH Group, C169–C170
making diversification work, 181–182
McDonald's, C88, C90–C92
merger and acquisition blunders, 180
problems at Cisco Systems, 178–180
purpose, 13
related diversification, 182–189
unrelated diversification, 189–193
World Wrestling Entertainment, C68–C69
Corporate parenting, 189

Corporate scandals, United Way Worldwide, C252–C253
Corporate social responsibility, 18
Corporate sustainability movement, 21
Corporations, 290
agency theory, 290–291
intrapreneuring, 388
patterns of growth, 312–314
proposed definitions, 290
separation of ownership and management, 290–291
stockholders, 290–291
Cost(s)
of divisional structure, 317
hidden in offshoring, 225
at Weight Watchers, C31
Cost advantage
erosion in focus strategy, 153
India, 216–217
obsolescence of bases of, 147
Cost argument, 118
Cost consciousness, Southwest Airlines, C140
Cost control, Fresh Direct, C201
Cost disadvantages, independent of scale, 51
Cost focus strategy, 152
Cost increase, at Southwest Airlines, C142
Cost parity, 148–149
Cost reduction
versus adaptation, 225–227
from digital distribution, C100
in global strategy, 229
at Jamba Juice, C44
from location of value-chain activities, 218
Cost savings, 184–185
deceptive in offshoring, 224–225
Cost structure, JetBlue Airways, C148
Cost surgery, 169
Counterfeiting, 220
extent of, 220
as growing problem, 222
Counterfeit software, 131
Counterproductive behavior, 284
Country Risk Ratings, 220, 221
Craft breweries, C128–C129
Creative abrasion, 125
Creative intelligence, 383–384
Creative thinking, 384
Creativity, 83, 401
enabling, 363–364
Pixar Animation Studios, C8–C9
Credit default swaps, C4
Critical skills, lost by outsourcing, 329
Cross-cultural dialogue, 356
Cross-functional skills, lost by outsourcing, 329
Cross-functional teams, 336
unsupported, 336
Crossing the Chasm (Moore), 401
Cross-selling strategy, 105
Crowdfunding
competitors, C187
concept, C185
evaluation guidelines, 254
and JOBS Act of 2010, C189
by Kickstarter, C185–C187
operation of, 253–254
Crowd gaming, C104
Crowdsourcing, 48
by Frito-Lay, 77
at Goldcorp, 49

for ideas at IBM, 389
Internet for, 46–48
for knowledge at SAP, 129
by strategic alliance, 199
well-known successes, 48
Cultural differences
challenge for managers, 223
between China and Korea, 211
and mergers and acquisitions, 196
and outsourcing, 226
Cultural symbols, 223
Culture of dissent, 363–364
Culture of experimentation, 364
Currency fluctuations
effect on mergers and acquisitions, 194
shekel, 222–223
United States dollar, 222
Currency risk, 222
Current ratio, 93, 441
Customer base, World Wrestling Entertainment, C68
Customer focus, Campbell Soup Company, C238
Customer mix, Weight Watchers, C36–C37
Customer perspective, 95
Customer perspective in balanced scorecard, 95
Customers
Ann Taylor stores, C47
complaints against Zynga, C127
information from, 363
Louis Vuitton, C171–C172
in luxury goods industry, C168–C169
of online grocers, C206
perception of differentiation, 147
of QVC, C66
in value chain, 80–81
Customer service, 76
Customer value, from core competencies, 183
Customization, Weight Watchers, C35, C36

D

Daily News Record, C51
Dark Knight Rises, C94, C96
Data analytics, 80
Data Protection Act, Norway, C127
Days' sales in inventory, 93, 443
Days' sales in receivables, 93, 444
Debt burden, Green Mountain Coffee Roasters, C257
Debt-equity ratio, 93, 442
Decentralized work models, 120
Decision agenda, 429
Decision making
command-and-control, 280
in divisional structure, 316
in functional structure, 315
and groupthink, 428–430
at Heineken, C62
managerial conceit, 397–398
for new ventures, 395–396
in simple structure, 314
stakeholders included in, 8
techniques for case analysis, 424
using conflict to improve
devil's advocacy, 431
dialectical inquiry, 431
using wisdom of employees, 361
Decisions, 7, 9

Decline stage, 166, 166–169
  and actions of rivals, 166
  harvesting, 168
  management time involved, 166
  occurrence of, 166–167
  strategies
    consolidation, 168
    maintaining, 168
    options, 167
    price-performance trade-off, 169
    retreating to defensible ground, 168–169
    using the new to improve the old, 169
Dedication, of entrepreneurs, 256
Defensive actions, 269
Demand, stabilizing, 188
Demand conditions, 215
  country variations, 214–215
  India, 216
Demographics
  of changing workplace, 117–118
  definition, 42
  Dippin' Dots customers, C110
  of future workplace, 112
  of gamblers, C13
  in luxury goods industry, C169
  of movie goers, C96
  Nintendo customers, C181
**Demographic segment of the general
    environment, 42,** 43
Demographic trends, 47
Denmark, demand conditions, 215
Department of Agriculture, C201
Department of Defense, 168
Department of Energy, 168
Department of Justice, 345, 349
Department stores, C51
Deregulation of airline industry, C147
Designers, employed at Samsung Electronics, C193
Designing the Organization, 348
Design process, Samsung Electronics, C193–C194
Desperate Housewives, C52
Developing countries
  emerging middle class, 46
  reverse innovation, 219
Development, tracking, 114–115
Developmental economics, and persistence of
    poverty, C85–C86
Devil's advocacy, 430, 431
Devil's Dictionary (Bierce), 290
Dialectical inquiry, 430, 431
Diamond of national advantage, 212
  demand conditions, 214–215
  factor endowment, 214
  firm structure, strategy, and rivalry, 215
  India's software industry, 216
  related and supporting industries, 215
Differentiation
  competitive parity as basis of, 143
  enhanced by related diversification, 185
  lack of parity in, 146–147
  in multidomestic strategy, 230
  too much, 150–151
  varying perceptions of, 151
Differentiation focus strategy, 152
Differentiation strategy, 142, 147
  cost parity, 148–149
  effects of Internet, 161
  examples, 149
  and five-forces model, 149–150

forms of, 147
integrated with overall cost leadership, 154–157
JetBlue Airways, C146
for new ventures, 260–261
pitfalls
  dilution of brand identity, 152
  easily imitated, 152
  price premium too high, 152
  summary, 152
  too much differentiation, 150–151
  uniqueness not valuable, 150
  varying perceptions by buyers and sellers, 151
price premium, 148
value-chain activities, 148
Digital projection techniques, C100–C101
Digital technologies, 160; *see also* Internet
Disconnected expert, 125
Discount mass merchandisers, C51
  sellers of packaged foods, C239
Discovery skills, 383
Disintermediation, 160
  by film studios, C97
  to lower transaction costs, 160
  by suppliers, 58
**Dispersed approaches to corporate
    entrepreneurship, 391**
  ability to change, 391–392
  entrepreneurial culture, 392
  idea sources, 391–392
  product champions, 393
  resource allotments, 392
Disruptive innovation, 380
  by Aereo, 381
Dissolution, 197n
Distribution
  by Fresh Direct, C211
  by Keurig, C263
  by Louis Vuitton, C169, C172
  in luxury goods industry, C169
  in movie industry, C97–C98
Distribution channels
  access by web-based businesses, 55
  access to, 51
  new, 268
  at QVC, C65
Diversification, 181; *see also* Related
    diversification; Unrelated diversification
  by Apple Inc., C20
  creating shareholder value, 181
  excessive, 298
  failure at Cisco Systems, 178–180
  failure at McDonald's, C90
  made to work, 171–182
  rejected by Samsung Electronics, C195
  risk reduction by, 192–193
  synergies from, 181
Diversity in workplace, 117–118
Diversity management
  areas for improvement, 118
  at Reckitt Benckiser, 119
Divestment, 196
  acquisitions resulting in, 181
  of brands at Ann Taylor, C52
  of brands at Ford, C224
  to enhance competitiveness, 198
  by Ford Motor Company, 170
  by McDonald's, C91
  means of, 197n
  objectives, 197

principles for success, 198–199
  of products by QVC, C66
  of Skype by eBay, C79
  by Talbots, C52
  Tyco International, 198
  well-known, 196
Divisional organizational structure, 313, 316;
    see also Holding company structure; Strategic
    business unit structure
  advantages, 316–317
  Ann Taylor, C47, C49
  Beiersdorf AG, C156–C157
  disadvantages, 317–318
  General Motors, 316
  Johnson & Johnson, C117–C118
  organizational chart, 317
  problems at ArcelorMittal, 318
Dogs, 191–192
Doing Both (Sidhu), 90
Dow Jones Industrial Average, 43
Dow Jones Sustainability Index, C241
Downsizing, Beiersdorf AG, C156
Drinking habit changes, C131
Drive, of entrepreneurs, 256
Dual-income families, C66
Durable opportunities, 250
DVD players, C102
DVD sales decline, C102
Dynamic capabilities, 131
  examples, 132
Dynamic pricing, C103

E

Earthquake and tsunami in Japan, 5–6
East Asia
  Heineken in, C58
  principal-principal conflicts, 301–302
E-books, 4
Echo Boom generation, 112
E-commerce
  in Asia, C76, C77
  in China, C74
  evolution of, C76–C77
  in North America, C76
Economic indicators, 45–46
Economic integration, regional vs. global, 234
Economic risk, 220
**Economic segment of the general environment,
    45–46**
Economic trends, 47
Economies of scale, 50
  augmented on large increments, 54
  cost advantages independent of, 51
  in five-forces model, 50
  in global strategy, 229
  from international expansion, 217
Economies of scope, 182
  from related diversification, 182
Economist, C172
Economy
  central role of knowledge, 106–119
  impact of government regulation, 44–45
  women as driving force in, 44
EDGAR database, 449
Education, of women, 44
Effectiveness, 9
Efficiency, 9
  at Louis Vuitton, C172–C173

Efficiency-effectiveness trade-off, 9
Egotism, 201
  effect on managers, 201
  examples of, 202
Electronic networks, 75, 80
Electronic storage, 58
Electronic teams, 127
  advantages, 127
  challenges, 127–128
  to enhance collaboration, 127
  process loss, 128
  versus traditional teams, 127–128
Electronics retailing, 156
Email, 126
Embedded options, 396
Embezzlement at United Way, C252
Emerging markets
  growth of, 212
  smartphone use in, C24
Emerging trends, 36–37
Emotional intelligence, 354
  components
    empathy, 355–356
    motivation, 355
    self-awareness, 354
    self-regulation, 354–355
    social skills, 356–357
  managing relationships, 355
  self-management skills, 355
  studies on, 354
Emotional Intelligence (Goleman), 354
Empathy, 355–356
  and tough decisions, 357
Employee database, Procter & Gamble, C198
Employee empowerment, 360–361
Employee involvement, 113
Employee mobility, 117
Employee morale, problem at Procter &
  Gamble, C196
Employee protests, Beiersdorf AG, C165
Employee recognition, at Southwest
  Airlines, C140
Employee relations, at Southwest Airlines,
  C139–C140
Employee retention
  challenging work, 117
  identifying with mission and core values, 116–117
  rewards and incentives, 117
  stimulating environment, 117
  task-first relationship, 117
Employees
  bargaining power, 91
  codes of conduct, 369
  in decision making, 361
  development at Pixar, C9
  exit costs, 91
  falloff in skills at McDonald's, C90
  as free agents, 281
  number of, in packaged-food industry, C240
  product champions, 393
  protected by Sarbanes-Oxley Act, 370
  replacement costs, 91
  time to think of new ventures, 392
  view of control systems, 280
End users, 56
Enforcement costs in vertical integration, 188
Enforcement in vertical integration, 188
Entrepreneur, C109, C111
Entrepreneurial culture, 392

Entrepreneurial ideas
  from employees, 392
  project definition, 393
  project impetus, 393
  sources, 392
Entrepreneurial leadership, 255, 255–256
  commitment to excellence, 256
  dedication and drive, 256
  vision, 256
Entrepreneurial opportunities
  contexts for value creation, 248
  discovery phase, 249
  environmental sustainability, 251
  evaluation phase, 249–250
  recognition phase, 249
  sources, 248–249
Entrepreneurial orientation, 389–404, 398
  at Apple Inc., C20–C26
  autonomy, 399–400
  competitive aggressiveness, 402–403
  innovativeness, 400–401
  proactiveness, 401–402
  risk raking, 403–404
Entrepreneurial projects; *see* Corporate
  entrepreneurship; New ventures
Entrepreneurial resources
  financial, 251–253
  government support, 255
  human capital, 254
  for Scottsdale Quarter, 271–272
  social capital, 254–255
Entrepreneurial strategy, 256
  in case analysis, 434–435
  for entry
    adaptive new entry, 259–260
    imitative new entry, 258–259
    pioneering new entry, 257–258
  examine barriers to entry, 257
  examples of failure, 246–247
  generic
    combination strategies, 262, 263
    differentiation, 260–261
    focus, 261–262
    overall cost leadership, 260
  industry analysis, 256
  ingredients, 256
  leadership, 255–256
  mistakes at Digg, 246–247
  opportunities, 248–251
  purpose, 13
  resources, 251–255
  and threat of retaliation, 257
Entrepreneurs; *see also* New ventures; Start-ups
  commitment to excellence, 256
  dedication and drive, 256
  example, 250
  risk minimization, 404
  vision, 256
Entrepreneurship, 248
  at Edward Marshall Boehm Inc., C3
  and innovation, 378
  at Johnson & Johnson, C117–C118
  and real options, 395
Entry modes; *see* International expansion
Entry strategies for new ventures
  adaptive new entry, 259–261
  imitative new entry, 258–259
  pioneering new entry, 257–258
Environmental analysis, requirements, 35–36

Environmental forecasting, 40
  industry- or firm-specific, 50
  poor predictions, 40
  underestimating uncertainty, 40
Environmental monitoring, 37
  hard trends, 37–38
  implications for strategy process, 37
  soft trends, *37*
Environmental responsibility, 110
Environmental revolution, 19
Environmental scanning, 36
  for emerging trends, 36–37
  spotting key trends, 36
Environmental sustainability
  best-practices forum, 326
  business case for, 21
  green plastics, 251
  measurable goals, 286
  and triple bottom line, 19–20
  in virtual organizations, 331
  vision at 3M Corporation, 348
Environmentally aware organizations
  analyses of external environment, 36–41
  Campbell Soup, C242
  Fresh Direct, C210
  keeping pace with changes, 36
Environmentally-friendly manufacturing, 75
Equity carve-outs, 197n
Equity financing, 252
Equity multiplier, 93, 442
Escalation of commitment, 398
Ethical behavior, commitment to, 349–350
Ethical organization, 14
  in case analysis, 435–436
  codes of conduct, 368–369
  corporate credos, 368–369
  individual vs. organizational ethics, 365–366
  integrity-based vs. compliance-based, 366–368
  policies and procedures, 370
  problems at Zynga, C126–C127
  reward and evaluation systems, 369–370
  role models, 368
Ethical orientation, 365
Ethics, 364
  individual vs. organizational, 365–366
  in international strategy, 239–240
  and leadership, 365
Ethics management, 367
Euromoney magazine, 220
Europe, population and Internet usage, C76
European Central Bank, 6
European Food Safety Authority, 239–240
European Union, 46, 234
  economic downturn, 6, 146, C162
Eurozone crisis, 6
Every Business Needs an Angel (Simmons), 252
Excellence, commitment to, 349–350
Excellent and ethical organizational culture, 349
Excessive product-market diversification, 298
Executive leaders, 21
Exit barriers
  high, 54
  types of, 54
Exit champion, 394
Exit cost of employees, 91
Expansion
  Fresh Direct, C210
  JetBlue Airways, C149–C150
Experience curve, 143

Experience vs. imitative, 382
Experimentation, 401
Experimenting, 383, 384
Expert power, 353
Expertise, 124
  on board of directors, 293
Explicit knowledge, 108, 128
Exporting, 235
  beachhead strategy, 235
  benefits, 235–236
  risks and limitations, 236
Exports, of U.S. in agriculture, C239
Expropriation of minority shareholders, 303
Extended value chain, 155
External analysis, for turnaround strategy, 169
External boundaries, 325
External constituencies, 326
External control view of leadership, 5
External environment
  analyzing
    competitive intelligence, 38–39
    environmental forecasting, 40
    environmental monitoring, 37–38
    environmental scanning, 36–37
    scenario analysis, 40–41
    spotting trends, 37–38
    SWOT analysis, 41–42
  in case analysis, 433
  changes leading to new opportunities, 249
  competitive environment
    effect of Internet of five-forces
      model, 55–58
    five-forces model, 49–55
    industry analysis, 59–63
    strategic groups, 61–63
  general environment
    demographic segment, 42
    economic segment, 45–46
    global segment, 46
    political/legal segment, 44–45
    relationship among elements of, 46–48
    sociocultural segment, 42–44
    technological segment, 45
  recognizing threats and opportunities in, 362
  in strategy analysis, 11–12
  too narrow focus of SWOT analysis, 73
External governance control mechanisms, 298
  auditors, 299
  banks, 299
  market for corporate control, 298
  at McDonald's, 301
  media, 300
  at Nike, Inc., 301
  public activists, 300
  regulatory bodies, 299–300
  stock analysts, 299
External information, 362–363
External relationships, of boundaryless
  organizations, 333–335
External staffing, 382

F

Factor endowments, 214
  India, 216
Factors of production
  creation in India, 216
  industry-specific, 214
Failure
  encouraging, 364

forums for, 364
  role in development, 364
Fast Company, C210
Fast-food market, fragmented, C88
Federal Communications Commission, C101
Feedback, from millennials, 112
Feedback loop, 278
Film studios
  distribution, C96
  financial risks, C96
  production, C96–C97
  Supreme Court ruling against, C98
  value chain activities, C96–C99
Financial crisis, in European Union, 6
Financial crisis of 2008, 5
  and American International Group, C4
  Bank of America in, 104–106
  collapse of financial institutions, 15
  effect on Beiersdorf AG, C160–C161
  Ford in, C220
  government bailouts, C4
  impact on Ann Taylor, C47, C49
  impact on casinos, C11–C12
Financial goals, 96
Financial intermediary, United Way Worldwide, C249
Financial leverage ratios, 93, 442
Financial performance
  Ann Taylor, C48
  apparel industry, C54
  Beiersdorf AG, C159–C161
  Campbell Soup Company, C240, C241
  and corporate governance, 288
  by divisions of Procter & Gamble, C197
  Ford Motor Company, C226
  Louis Vuitton, C170
  Southwest Airlines, C138
Financial perspective, 96
Financial ratio analysis, 92, 419
  changes over time, 92
  common-size balance sheet, 437
  common-size income statement, 438
  comparison with industry norms, 93–94
  comparison with key competitors, 94
  differing across industries, 94
  historical comparisons, 92–93
  ratio analysis measures, 440–447
  standard financial statements, 437
  summary of techniques, 420
  types of ratios, 92, 93
Financial ratios, 438; *see also* Ratio analysis
  Campbell Soup Company, C244
Financial resources, 83
  entrepreneurial
    angel investors, 252
    bank financing, 252
    crowdfunding, 253, 254
    factors in deciding on, 251
    family and friends, 252
    JOBS Act of 2012, 253
    venture capital, 252–253
    for entrepreneurs, 252
Financial rewards, 117
Financial risk taking, 404
Financial statements
  balance sheet, 437
  income statement, 438
  standard, 437
  United Way Worldwide, C250
Financial synergies, from unrelated diversification, 182
Financial vs. strategic goals, 394

Firm resources, 84
Firms; *see also* Corporations; Organizations;
  Resource-based view of the firm
  advantages of business groups for, 303
  assessing primary activities, 74
  assessing support activities, 76
  dynamic capabilities, 131–132
  entrepreneurial orientation, 389–404
  failures, 36
  indicators of emerging trends, 36–37
  information sources
    business websites, 450
    company rankings, 450
    competitive intelligence, 448
    guides and tutorials, 449
    public companies, 448
    public vs. private, 447–448
    search engines, 452
    Securities and Exchange Commission filings,
      449–450
    strategic and competitive analysis, 450–452
    subsidiaries or divisions, 447–448
  marketing to bottom of the pyramid, 212–213
  meaning of globalization, 233–234
  means of divestment, 197n
  moving from bureaucracy to decentralized
    work, 120
  performance and corporate governance, 289
  performance evaluation
    balanced scorecard, 94–96
    financial ratio analysis, 92–94
    principal-principal conflicts, 301–302
  recognized focus strategy, 153
  success from differentiation strategies, 149
  success from overall cost leadership, 145, 146
  view of customers, 80–81
Firm-specific knowledge, 214
Firm strategy, structure, and rivalry, 215
First-mover advantage, 165
  benefits, 401
  failures, 401–402
  PepsiCo in India, 239
Five-forces model of industry competition, 49
  bargaining power of buyers, 51–52
  bargaining power of suppliers, 52–53
  basic competitive forces, 49
  and combination strategies, 155–156
  and differentiation strategies, 149–150
  economies of scale, 50
  effect of Internet
    bargaining power of buyers, 55–57
    bargaining power of suppliers, 57–58
    intensity of rivalry, 58
    threat of new entrants, 55
    threat of substitutes, 58
  and focus strategy, *153*
  generic strategies to overcome, 142
  industry analysis, 59–63
  intensity of rivalry, 53–55
  and overall cost leadership, 145
  product differentiation, 50–51
  for profit potential, 50
  strategic groups, 61–63
  threat of new entrants, 50, 53
  zero-sum game assumption, 59
Fixed costs, high, 54
Flash Foresight (Burris), 37
Flexibility
  reduced, 147
  at Weight Watchers, C33

Flexible manufacturing, 154–155
Focused approaches to corporate entrepreneurship, 390
autonomous work groups, 390
business incubators, 390–391
new venture groups, 390
Focus strategy, 152
at BMW, 153
cost focus, 153
differentiation focus, 153
effects of Internet, 161–162
examples of success, 153
and five-forces model, 153
for new ventures, 261–262
pitfalls
erosion of cost advantage, 153
imitation and competition, 154
too focused on buyer needs, 154
Food and Drug Administration, 240, 344–345, C120, C121
Forbearance, 276
Forbes, 4
Formalists, 125
Fortified drink market, 240
Fortune, 38
Fortune, 4, 111, 165, 181, 196, 300, C17
Fortune 500, 276
membership changes, 2
Forward integration, threat of, 53
France
antitrust law, 271
tax increases, 6
Franchise Times, C111
Franchising, 236
benefits, 236
by Dippin' Dots Inc., C110
ice cream makers, C113
by Jamba Juice, C39–C40
McDonald's, C89–C92
risks and limitations, 236–237
Fraud at United Way, C252
Free agents, 118, 281
Frontal assaults, 267
Frozen dairy industry
consolidation in, C108–C109
consumer spending, C108
franchises in 2013, C113
industry giants, C108
overview, C107–C109
segmentation, C109
top ten brands in 2012, C108
Functional benchmarking, 363
Functional division, worldwide, 313
Functional organizational structure, 313, 314, 336
advantages, 315
characteristics, 315
disadvantages, 315–316
organizational chart, 315
Funding by business incubators, 390
Future of Work (Malone), 120

G

Game developers, C181
Game theory, value net concept, 59–60
General administration, 79
General Agreement on Tariffs and Trade, 46
General environment, 42
crowdsourcing, 46–48
demographic segment, 42, 43

economic segment, 32, 45–46
effects of changes on CEOs, 5–7
elements of, 11–12
global segment, 43, 46
political/legal segment, 32, 44–45
relationship among elements of, 46, 47
sociocultural segment, 42–44
technological segment, 42, 45
trends in, 47
General knowledge, 111
Generation Y, 112
Generic strategies, 142
differentiation strategy, 142, 147–152
effects of Internet
combination strategies, 162
differentiation strategy, 161
focus strategy, 161–162
overall cost leadership, 160–161
for entrepreneurs
combination strategies, 262
differentiation strategy, 260–261
focus strategy, 261–262
overall cost leadership, 260
focus strategy, 142, 152–154, 154–157
combination strategies, 142
overall cost leadership, 142, 143–147
to overcome five-forces model, 142
Geographic-area division structure, 313, 322
Geographic boundaries, 325
Getting from College to Career (Pollack), 110
Glass-Steagall Act of 1933, repeal of, 45–46
Global capitalism, 212
Global customer segments, 226
Global economy
bottom of the pyramid population, 212–213
comparisons of GDP per capita, 214
emerging markets, 212
global capitalism, 212
growth in trade, 212
rise of globalization, 212
varying income levels, 212
Global Entrepreneur, C237
Globalization, 212
of beer industry, C59–C60
cross-cultural dialogue, 356
effects on organizational structure, 314n
meaning for firms, 233–234
opportunities and risks in, 46
versus regionalization, 234
Global market ranking, Samsung Electronics, C192
Global markets
achieving competitive advantage
cost reduction vs. adaptation, 225–228
global strategy, 228–230
global vs. regional strategy, 229–230
international strategy, 228
multidomestic strategy, 230–232
transnational strategy, 232–233
challenges in, 4–5
Global segment of the general environment, 43, 46
Global start-ups, 322
circumstances for, 323
environmental sustainability, 323
examples, 323, 332
management challenges, 323
Global strategy, 228
cost-reduction pressures, 229
economies of scale, 229

risks and challenges, 229–230
standardized level of quality, 229
strengths and limitations, 230
Global trends, 47
Going green, 110
as marketing ploy, 366
Golden parachute, 202, 298
Good Morning America, 379, C42
Goods and services, demand in China, 11
Good to Great (Collins), 256
Gorillas in the Mist, 22
Government
request for proposals from, 386–387
support for start-ups, 255
Government bailout(s)
in financial crisis of 2008, C4
rejected by Ford, C220
Government contracting, 255
Government regulation
as control mechanism, 299–300
effect on mergers and acquisitions, 194
impact on economy, 44–45
Great Law of the Haudenosaunee, 28
Greece
bankruptcy, C162
economic crisis, 6
Green employment, 110
Green Lantern, C96
Green marketing, 21
Green movement, 21
Green plastics, 251
Greenmail, 202, 298
Greenwashing, 366
Gresham's law of planning, 351
Grocery industry; *see* Online grocery industry; Retail grocery industry
Gross domestic product
health care spending percent of, C30
knowledge-based, 106
Gross domestic product per capita, global comparisons, 214
Gross margin, packaged-food industry, C240
Groupthink, 125
characteristics, 428
symptoms and prevention, 428–430
Growth
as challenge for Southwest Airlines, C141
of eBay, C77
slowed at Procter & Gamble, C199
sources for casino industry, C13
strategy at Keurig, C266
Growth for growth's sake, 201
Growth/share matrix, 190–192
classifications, 191
strategic business units in, 191–192
Growth stage, 165
factors in, 164
lack of repeat purchasers, 165
requirements, 165
revenue increase, 165
selective demand, 165
Guerrilla offensives, 267–268

H

Hacker News, C126
Hard trends, 37
benefit at Mayo Clinic, 38
Hardball tactics
deceive competitors, 265
devastate rivals' profit sanctuaries, 265

Hardball tactics—*Cont.*
   massive overwhelming force, 265
   plagiarize, 265
   raising competitors' costs, 265
Harvard Business Review, 10, 19, 108–109, 354
Harvesting strategy, 168
Headhunters, 152
health care spending, C30
Health claims, 239–240
Health warnings, 63
Healthy Living Council, C44
Heroes-and-drones syndrome, 361
Hierarchical relationships, 181–182, 189
Hierarchy of goals, 23
High-definition TV, C101
High exit barriers, 54
High-tech industries, effects of legislation, 45
Hiring
   by Apple Inc., C26
   for attitude, training for skill, 111
   and behavioral control, 287
   bozo filter, 111
   at Jamba Juice, C44
   matching approach, 110–111
   poor practices, 109–110
   referrals, 111
   at Southwest Airlines, C139
   via personal networks, 120
Hispanic Americans
   number of, 118
   Weight Watchers customers, C36
Hispanics, targeted by Heineken, C61
Hoarding barrier, 123
Hobbit, The, C103
Holding company structure, 314, 319
   advantages, 319
   disadvantages, 319
   at Heineken, C60
   for unrelated diversification, 319
Home brewing, C132–C133
Home viewing
   content availability and timing, C102
   technology, C102
H1B visas, 45
Horizontal boundaries, 325
Horizontal organizational structures, 333
Horizontal relationships, 181
Horizontal systems and processes, 333
Hostile takeovers, 202, 298
Hours of work, at Southwest Airlines, C140
Human capital, 108
   attracting talent
      by going green, 110
      hire for attitude, 111
      input control, 110–111
      millennials, 112
      by networking, 111
      recruiting approach, 111
   creating sustainable advantages, 356
   developing, 111–116
      encouraging widespread involvement, 113
      evaluations, 116–117
      mentoring and sponsoring, 113–114
      monitoring progress, 114–116
      tracking development, 114–116
   entrepreneurial resource, 254
   free agents, 118
   lost by Bank of America, 105
   retaining

      challenging work, 117
      identifying with mission and values, 116–117
      rewards and incentives, 117
   technology for leveraging, 126–129
   three-way leveraging process, 109–110
   value creation through, 130
   and workforce diversity, 117–118
Human capital mobility, 120
Human Equation (Pfeffer), 325
Human resource departments, and LinkedIn, 152
Human resource management, 78
   differentiation strategy, 148
   overall cost leadership, 144
Human resource practices
   Bank of America, 105
   of boundaryless organizations, 333
   to capture value from innovation, 386
   dysfunctional, 125
   Procter & Gamble, C198
Human resource professionals, lock and key
      mentality, 110
Human resources, 83
Hurricane Katrina, 5
Hypercompetition (D'Aveni), 347

I

Ice Age 4, 217
Idea generation
   from customers of Procter & Gamble, C199
   Samsung Electronics, C194
Identification and combination activities, 128
Illegal activities, 344–345, 349
   examples, 289–290
   intensified by competition, 369–370
   Ponzi scheme, 365
   at United Way, C252–C253
   at Zynga, C126–C127
Illegal cooperation, 271
Illusion of control, 397–398
Illusion of invulnerability, 428
Imitation
   of business model, 403
   of differentiation, 151
   in focus strategy, 153–154
   in social media, 246–247
   of strategy, 146–147
   threat for low-cost leaders, 160–161
Imitative new entry, 258
   by established company, 258–259
Improper conduct, minimizing, 286
Inbound logistics, 74
   differentiation strategy, 148
   overall cost leadership, 144
Incentive programs; *see* Reward systems
Income statement
   Ann Taylor, C50
   Beiersdorf AG, C161
   Boston Beer Company, C130
   Campbell Soup Company, C243
   eBay, C75
   Ford Motor Company, C221
   General Motors, C214
   Green Mountain Coffee Roasters, C257
   Heineken, C58
   Jamba Juice, C40
   Johnson & Johnson, C116
   McDonald's, C88
   Nintendo, C178

   Procter & Gamble, C197
   QVC, C63
   Samsung Electronics, C191
   Weight Watchers, C33
   World Wrestling Entertainment, C71
   Yahoo!, C269
   Zynga, C124
Incremental innovation, 379, 380
   project time line, 385
Incremental management, 7
Incremental vs. preemptive launch, 382
India
   middle class, 217
   PepsiCo in, 239
   software industry, 216
Indian Gaming and Recreation Act of 1988, C15
Indirect costs, 225
Individual ethics, 365–366
Industry analysis
   caveats on, 59–60
   critical issues in
      root causes of profitability, 61
      time horizon, 59–60
      understand underpinnings of competition, 61
   information resources, 452
   not avoiding low-profit industry, 59
   by start-ups, 256–257
   as static analysis, 59
   strategic groups, 61–63
   unassailable assumptions, 61
   value net, 59–60
   variety of information needed, 59
   zero-sum game assumption, 59
Industry consolidation, promoted by mergers and
      acquisitions, 195
Industry environment, 12
Industry/Industries, 48; *see* Five-forces model of
      industry competition
   differing financial ratios, 94
   effect of demographic trends, 42
   information sources
      business websites, 450
      competitive intelligence, 447
      guidelines and tutorials, 449
      industry research analysis, 452
      search engines, 452
      strategic and competitive analysis, 450–452
   low-profit, 59
   primary value-chain activities, 74–76
   strategic groups, 61–63
   structure in beer industry, C131–C132
   trends in general environment, 47
   unimportant to suppliers, 53
Industry life cycle, 162
   decline stage strategies, 166–169
   growth stage strategies, 165
   illustrated, 164
   and international expansion, 218
   introduction stage strategies, 164–165
   limitations of concept, 163
   maturity stage strategies, 165–166
   and process innovation, 379
   reasons for importance, 162–163
   turnaround strategies, 169–171
Industry norms, 93–94
Industry-specific factors of production, 214
Industry-specific standards, 363
Inexperience, value of, 22
Influencers, 221

Infomediary services, 58
Information
  from customers, 363
  from Internet, 56
  sharing on social networks, 126
  from traditional sources, 362
Informational control, 14, 279
  responding to environmental change, 278–280
Information power, 353
Information technology
  in boundaryless organizations, 333
  to extend value chain, 155
Inherent morality of the group, 428
Inimitability
  of Amazon Prime, *88*
  of core competencies, 183
  of resources, 86
Initial public offering
  Ann Taylor, C48
  Boston Beer Company, C129
  eBay, C77
  JetBlue Airways, C148
  and microfinance, C86
  Pixar Animation Studios, C8
  by Zynga, C123
In-lobby dining, C103–C104
Innovation, 83, **378**; *see also* Corporate
    Entrepreneurship
  at Apple Inc., C20–C26
  attempts at Procter & Gamble, 383
  at Beiersdorf AG, C157–C158, C158–C159
  challenges of, 380–381
    resistance by companies, 381
    uncertain outcomes, 381
  company dilemmas
    building capabilities vs. collaboration, 382
    experience vs. initiative, 382
    incremental vs. preemptive launch, 382
    internal vs. external staffing, 382
    seeds vs. weeds, 382
  crowdsourcing for ideas, 389
  defining scope of
    focus on common technology, 385
    focus on market theme, 385
    questions about efforts, 385
    strategic envelope, 384–385
  disruptive, 380
  at Dutch Boy, 379
  at Edward Marshall Boehm Inc., C3
  and entrepreneurship, 378
  in external environment, 380
  flexibility for, 364
  human resource practices
    potentially counterproductive practices, 386
    staffing to capture value, 386
  incremental, 379–380
  in internal environment, 380
  at Louis Vuitton, C173
  managing pace of, 385–386
  at Microsoft, 405
  mistake by Google, 376–378
  need for entrepreneurial orientation, 389–404
  new industries from, 45
  perspective in balanced scorecard, 95
  at Pixar Animation Studios, C7–C10
  process innovation, 379
  at Procter & Gamble, C199
  product innovation, 378–379
  radical, 379–380

reverse, 218–219
single-server coffee brewing, C260–C263
sustaining, 380
technology as source of ideas for, 378
timing of, C45
Weight Watchers, C35–C37
Innovation and Entrepreneurship (Drucker), 404
Innovation and learning perspective, 95
Innovation Jam at IBM, 389
Innovation partners
  Coca-Cola Company and DEKA Research, 388
  competencies, 387
  identifying strengths and weaknesses, 387
  sharing of rewards, 387
  universities, 386–387
Innovation skills
  associating, 383, 384
  creative intelligence, 382–383
  discovery skills, 382
  experimenting, 383, 384
  networking, 383, 384
  observing, 383, 384
  patterns of action, 383–384
  questioning, 383, 384
Innovativeness, 400
  departure from existing practices, 400
  major pitfalls, 400
  risks, 400
  techniques
    continuous improvement, 401
    foster creativity and experimentation, 401
    investment in new technology, 401
    research and development, 401
Innovator's DNA, 384
Inputs, increased costs, 146
Insider information, 300
Institutional investors, 295
Intangible assets, critically important, 95
Intangible resources, 84
  Dell Inc., 90
  types of, 83
Integrated Workforce Experience, 126
Integration, in boundaryless organizations, 332
Integrative thinking, 425, 425–427
  architecture, 426
  causality, 426
  at Red Hat, Inc., 427
  resolution, 426
  salience, 426
Integrity-based ethical programs, 366–367
Intellectual assets
  in case analysis, 433
  protecting, 129–132
  in strategy analysis, 12–13
Intellectual capital, 107
  based on human capital, 109–118
Intellectual property, 106
  components, 130
  contrasted with physical property, 131
  development and costs, 131
  patent battles, 131
  protection of, 131, C264
Intellectual property rights, 131
  as cost in offshoring, 225
  and counterfeiting, 220, 222
  and piracy, 220
  and Zynga, C126–C127
Intended strategy, 10
  versus realized strategy, 10–11

**Intensity of rivalry among competitors in
    an industry, 53**
  advertising battles, 53
  and competitive dynamics, 262
  in five-forces model, 53–55
  high vs. low, 56
  impact of Internet, 58
  in India, 216
  at Pfizer, Inc., 55
  price competition, 53
  result of interacting factors, 54
  in search for new markets, 215
Interaction effect, 358
Interdivisional coordination, 326
Interest rates, 43
Internal analysis, for turnaround strategy, 169
Internal benchmarking, 362
Internal business perspective, 95
Internal constituencies, 326
Internal development, 200
  at Apple Inc., C21
  at Biocom, 200
  disadvantages, 200
  means of diversification, 193, 200
  at 3M Corporation, 200
  value creation, 200
Internal environment
  in case analysis, 433
  performance evaluation
    balanced scorecard, 94–96
    financial ration analysis, 92–94
    resource-based view of the firm, 82–92
  in strategy analysis, 12
  value-chain analysis, 72–82
Internal information, 361–362
Internal networkers, 21, 22
Internal relationships, of boundaryless
    organizations, 333–335
Internal staffing, 382
International Association of Machinists, C150
International Chamber of Commerce, 220
International Civil Aviation
    Organization, 362
International division, 313
International division structure, 322
International expansion
  Amazon, C83
  Beiersdorf AG, C155–C156
  Campbell Soup Company, C235
  by eBay
    Asia Pacific, C81
    Europe, C81–C82
  global start-ups, 322–323
  by Heineken, C58
  Jamba Juice, C43
  JetBlue Airways, C149
  modes of entry, 234–237
    exporting, 234–236
    franchising, 236–237
    joint ventures, 237–238
    licensing, 236–237
    strategic alliances, 237–238
    wholly owned subsidiaries, 238
  motivations
    arbitrage, 217
    explore reverse innovation, 218–219
    increase market size, 217
    optimize value-chain locations, 218
    product growth potential, 217–218

International expansion—*Cont.*
  outsourcing and offshoring, 223–225
  potential risks
    currency risk, 222–223
    economic risk, 220–222
    management risks, 223
    political risk, 220–222
  by QVC, C67
International operations
  implications for structure, 321–322
    contingencies, 322
    global strategy, 322
    multidomestic strategy, 322
  types of organizational structure, 313
International strategy, 228
  achieving competitive advantage, 225–234
  basis of, 228
  Beiersdorf AG, C156–C157
  Campbell Soup Company, C236–C237
  in case analysis, 434
  country risk ratings, 221–223
  diamond of national advantage, 214–215
  dispersal of value-chain activities, 223–225
  distinctive competencies, 228
  ethics for, 239–240
  Ford Motor Company, C226
  global economy, 212–213
  global strategy, 229–230
  growth of GDP per person 2001–2011, 213
  international strategy, 228
  Jamba Juice, C43
  lack of local adaptation, 228
  modes of expansion, 234–238
  motivations for expansion, 217–219
  multidomestic strategy, 230–232
  and organizational structure, 313
  PepsiCo in India, 239
  potential risks of expansion, 220–223
  problems for SAIC, 210–212
  purpose, 13
  risks and challenges, 228
  transnational strategy, 232–233
International trade
  agricultural exports, C239
  benefits of increase in, 46
  currency risk, 222–223
  increase in, 212
Internationalization of movie content, C97
Internet, 55
  for comparison shopping, 162
  for crowdfunding, C185–C189
  for crowdsourcing, 46–48
  impact on five-forces model
    bargaining power of buyers, 55–57
    bargaining power of suppliers, 57–58
    intensity of rivalry, 58
    threat of new entrants, 55
    threat of substitutes, 58
  legal services, 57, 163
  online auctions, C78
  popularity of e-commerce, C78–C79
  for price comparisons, 58
  for tracking information, 362
Internet browsers, C25
Internet gambling, C15
Internet marketing, 4
Internet Retailer Top 500 Guide, C203
Internet usage
  Africa, C76

  Asia Pacific, C83
  Australia, C76
  Europe, C76
  Latin America, C76
  Middle East, C76
  North America, C76
Interrelationships, 79–80
  among value chain activities,
    79–80
In-theater dining, C104
Intrapreneuring, 388
Introduction stage, 164
  challenge of, 164
  factors in, 164
  first-mover advantage, 165
  late-mover benefits, 165
Inventory, increase in, 225
Inventory turnover ratio, 93, 443
Investment
  crowdfunding, 253–254
  at Pixar Animation Studios, C8
  transaction-specific, 188, 189
Investment decisions
  agency problems, 397
  and corporate governance, 288
Investors
  angel investors, 252
  institutional, 295
  perception of value in acquisitions, 197
  venture capitalists, 252–253
Investors Business Daily, 300
Involvement of employees, 113
Ironman, 97
Iroquois Confederacy, 28
Irrational escalation of commitment, 398
Israel's shekel, 222–223
Italian Job, 153
Italy
  economic crisis, 6
  footwear industry, 215

J

Japan
  business groups, 303
  earthquake and tsunami of 2011, 5–6
  origin of just-in-time systems, 214
Jeopardy, 184
Job Corps, C44
Job losses
  Beiersdorf AG, C155
  Ford, C223
JOBS Act of 2012, 253, C189
Jobs added overseas, 46
Job security, at Southwest Airlines, C140
Joint ventures, 199
  benefits, 237
  to develop and diffuse technologies, 200
  eBay, C79, C81
  eBay in China, C74
  to enter new markets, 199
  means of diversification, 199
  potential downsides, 200
  to reduce value chain costs, 199–200
  risks and limitations, 237–238
  and virtual organizations, 331
Jumpstart Our Business Start-ups Act of 2012,
  253, C189
Just-in-time inventory systems, 8, 75, 158, 214

K

Key trends, 36
Knowledge
  codified for competitive advantage, 128–129
  critical role in economy, 106–109
  crowdsourcing for, 129
  firm-specific, 214
  redistributing
    external, 362–363
    internal, 361–362
  from socially complex processes, 108
  technology for leveraging, 126–129
  types of, 108
Knowledge-based GDP, 106
Knowledge economy, 107
  attracting top talent, 106
  examples, 106
  human capital, 108–118
  intellectual capital, 107–108
  protection of intellectual assets, 129–132
  social capital, 108, 118–126
  technology for leveraging human capital and
    knowledge, 126–129
Knowledge organization, Mayo Clinic, 38
Knowledge stocks, 129
Knowledge transfer, 233
Knowledge workers, 109
  and social capital, 118–119
Kung Fu Panda, C100

L

Labor abuses, China, C22
Labor costs, rising in China, 146
Labor unions
  and Fresh Direct, C210
  and JetBlue Airways, C150
  and Southwest Airlines, C141–C142
Large-volume buyers, 51
Las Vegas, casino industry, C11–C16
Late-mover benefits, 165
Latin America, population and Internet usage, C76
Leaders
  change agents, 347
  collaborative, 116
  development of vision, 23
  executives, 21
  four-step cross-training process, 359
  interaction effect, 358
  internal networkers, 21, 22
  local line, 21
Leadership, 346
  accumulating and sharing internal information,
    361–362
  challenging status quo, 363–364
  to correct unethical behavior, 371
  creating ethical organization
    codes of conduct, 368–369
    corporate credos, 368–369
    integrity-based vs. compliance-based
      programs, 366–368
    policies and procedures, 372
    reward and evaluation systems, 369–370
    role models, 368
  creating learning organization, 357–364
  developing competency companions, 357–364
  doing the right thing, 346–347
  effective uses of power, 351–353

emotional intelligence, 354–357
empowering employees, 360–361
enabling creativity, 363–364
entrepreneurial, 255–256
ethical orientation, 365
external control view of, 5
failure at AIG, C4–C6
gathering and integrating external information, 362–363
motivating, 360
overcoming barriers to change, 350–351, 352
Pixar Animated Studios, C7–C10
primary activities
  designing the organization, 348–349
  organizational culture, 349–350
  setting direction, 347–348
Responsible Corporate Office Doctrine, 345
Robin Hood, C2
role in strategy implementation, 13
romantic view of, 4–5
at Southwest Airlines, C138–C141
successes and failures, 407
Leadership Challenge (Kouzes & Posner), 360
Leadership traits, 354
Learning, 358–359
  perspective in balanced scorecard, 95
Learning from mistakes
  Bank of America, 104–106
  Boeing Company, 311
  control problems at Hewlett-Packard, 276–277
  Daimler AG, 70–71
  demise of Borders, 3–4
  entrepreneurial strategies at Digg, 246–247
  innovation problem at Google, 376–378
  JetBlue Airways, C151–C153
  SAIC in China, 210–212
  Salemi Industries, 31–35
  survival rate of companies, 2–4
  Synthes leadership problems, 344–346
  United Way, C252–C254
Learning organization, 14, 358, **360**
  accumulating and sharing internal information, 361–362
  benchmarking, 362, 363
  in case analysis, 435–436
  challenging status quo, 363–364
  critical requirement, 350
  culture of dissent, 363–364
  customer information, 363
  empowering employees, 360–361
  enabling creativity, 363–364
  gathering and integrating external information, 362–363
  key elements, 360
  risk-taking culture, 364
  using employee wisdom, 361
Legal services, on Internet, 57, 163
Legitimate power, 351–353
Leonardo Live, C103
Leverage ratios, 442
Leveraging core competencies, 182–184, 195
Licensing, 236
  benefits, 236
  Jamba Juice, C43, C44
  Keurig, C265
  risks and limitations, 236–237
Licensing Letter, C92

Linux operating system, 48
Liquidity ratios, 93
Litigation
  against Johnson & Johnson, C121
  over patents, C112
  Southwest Airlines, C137
  against Zynga, C123, C126, C127
Loan guarantee programs, 255
Loans
  by Banco Compartamos, C86
  traditional vs. microfinance, C85–C86
Location decisions
  for casino industry, C13–C14
  Jamba Juice, C42–C44
  value-chain activities, 232
  for value-chain activities, 218
Lock-in effects, 335
Logistics; *see also* Inbound logistics; Outbound logistics
  at QVC, C65
  tightly controlled, 158
Long-term perspective, 8–9
Long-term solvency ratios, 93
  cash coverage ratio, 442
  times interest earned, 442
  total debt ratio, 442
Los Angeles Times, C101
Losses, JetBlue Airways, C149
Low-cost leadership strategy
  JetBlue Airways, C148
  Southwest Airlines, C141
Low-fare airlines, C147
Low profits, 52
Luxury goods industry
  in China, C167–C168
  customer segments
    absolute, C168
    accessible, C168
    aspirational, C168
    changing demographics, C169
    differing behavior across markets, C169
  distribution, C169
  estimated growth, C168
  in Europe, C168
  growth rate, C167
  market share by region, C168
  pricing, C169
  projected revenue 2012, C167
  suppliers, C169
  in United States, C168

M

Machine age, 106
Main Event, C69
Making the Grass Greener on Your Side (Melrose), 360
Management
  Beiersdorf AG, C157, C164
  in corporate governance, 14–15
  diversion of profits to, 91
  at Heineken, C60–C61
  incremental vs.. strategic, 7
  innovations in, 8
  overhaul ay Yahoo!, C270–C271
  at Pixar Animation Studios, C7–C10
  reconfigured at Ann Taylor, C56
  reorganization at Ford, C224, C232–C233
  of World Wrestling Entertainment, C69–C71

Management change; *see also* CEO change
  Dippin' Dots Inc., C106–C107
  rejected by Samsung Electronics, C195
Management restructuring, 190
Management risk, 223
Management talent development, 294
Manager bargaining power, 91
Managerial conceit, 397
  at AIG, C4
  illusion of control, 397–398
  irrational escalation of commitment, 398
  overconfidence, 397–398
Managerial models, and behavioral control, 288
Managerial motives, 201
Managerial rewards and incentives, 295–296
Managers; *see also* CEO *entries*
  adaptability, 336
  and alignment, 336–337
  ambidexterity, 9
  in ambidextrous organizations, 336–337
  assumptions and biases, 35
  balanced scorecard use, 95–96
  caveats on industry analysis
    include low-profit industry, 59
    static analysis, 59–60
    value net, 59–60
    zero-sum game assumption, 59
  CEO duality, 297
  challenge of cultural differences, 223
  challenges from globalization and technology, 120
  credibility, ego, and sound decisions, 196
  erosion of valuation by motives of
    egotism, 201–202
    growth for growth's sake, 201
  examples of self-interest, 291
  excessive product-market diversification, 298
  golden parachutes, 202
  making transformational change, 22
  and market for corporate control, 298
  monitoring behavior of
    by board of directors, 292–294
    primary means, 291
    rewards and incentives, 295–296
    shareholder activism, 295
  on-the-job consumption, 298
  opportunistic behavior, 298
  opportunity recognition, 35
  reward and evaluation systems, 369–370
  shirking, 298
  training at Campbell Soup Company, C238
  view of control systems, 280
  in virtual organizations, 330
Managing change, 378
Manufacturing
  automated and flexible, 154–155
  Campbell Soup locations, C236
  cost reductions, 199–200
  environmentally-friendly, 75
  at Louis Vuitton, C172
  mass customization, 154
  offshoring, 223–225
  outsourcing, 223–225
  reshoring, 226
Manufacturing alliances, 255
Market capitalism, 212
Market capitalization
  Apple Inc., C17
  Campbell Soup Company, C240
  decline at Procter & Gamble, C198

Market capitalization—*Cont.*
  packaged-food industry, C240
  Samsung Electronics, C191
Market commonality, 266
Market dependence, 276
Market diversification, 221
Market environment, Beiersdorf AG,
  C161–C164
Market for corporate control, 298
Market niche
  at BMW, 153
  in focus strategy, 152
Market power, 185
  from related diversification, 182
  from unrelated diversification
    pooled negotiating power, 185–186
    vertical integration, 186–189
Market pruning, 169
Market responsiveness, reduced, 225
Market saturation, 165
Market segments
  Beiersdorf AG, C162
  casino industry, C13
  entered by mergers and acquisitions, 202
  undefined in introduction stage, 164
  Weight Watchers, C29–C30
Market share, 143
  auto industry, C227
  Beiersdorf AG, C163–C164
  Boston Beer Company, C129
  cell phones, C23
  General Motors, C214, C216
  ice cream brands, C108
  in online gaming, C124
  personal computers, C23
  smartphones, C24
  Yahoo!, C271
Market size
  motive for international expansion, 217
  online gaming, C123–C124
Market theme, 385
Market-to-book value/ratio, 93, 446
  and intellectual capital, 107–108
  in knowledge-intensive corporations, 107
Market value measures
  market-to-book ratio, 446
  price-earnings ratio, 445–446
Marketing and sales activities, 75
  to bottom of the pyramid, 212–213
  differentiation strategy, 148
  by Dippin' Dots Inc., C110–C112
  at Edward Marshall Boehm Inc., C3
  Fresh Direct, C203, C210–C211
  increased efforts in, 268
  by McDonald's, C92
  overall cost leadership, 144
  prosumer concept, 80–81
  unethical or illegal activities, 76
Marketing argument, 118
Marketplace, viability in, 250
Martial arts, C72
Mass customization, 154
  enabled by Internet, 161
Massive overwhelming force, 265
Matching approach to hiring, 110–111
Matrix organizational structure, 319
  advantages, 320
  disadvantages, 320–321
  multinational firms, 319–320
  organizational chart, 320

Procter & Gamble, C200
  worldwide, 313, 322
Maturity stage, 165
  aggregate demand softens, 165
  strategies
    breakaway positioning, 166
    reverse positioning, 166
  underidentification of rivalry, 165–166
Media, as control mechanism, 300–301
Men, Weight Watchers customers, C36
Mentoring
  benefits of, 113–114
  by business incubators, 391
  compared to sponsoring, 114
Mercosur, 234
Mergers, 193
  in airline industry, C147
  means of diversification, 193–194
  as strategic actions, 268
Mergers and acquisitions; *see also* Acquisitions
  and antitakeover tactics, 202
  Bank of America and Merrill Lynch,
    104–106
  in casino industry, C14
  and currency fluctuations, 194
  versus divestment, 196–199
  global value 2000–2012, 194
  and government regulation, 194
  Louis Vuitton and Moët Hennessy, C167
  motives and benefits
    attaining synergies, 194
    industry consolidation, 195
    new market segments, 195
    obtaining valuable resources, 194
  potential limitations
    cultural differences, 196
    imitation by competitors, 196
    manager credibility and ego, 196
    takeover premium, 195
  recent, 193
  value perceived by investors, 197
  well-know blunders, 180
  worldwide volatility, 193–194
Metropolitan Opera, C103
Mexico, microfinance in, C86
M-Form structure, 316
Microfinance, case
  Banco Compartamos, C86
  Bank Rakyat Indonesia, C86
  definition, C85
  Equity Bank,. Kenya, C86
  Grameen Bank, C85, C87
  growth of, C86–C87
  initial public offerings, C86
  origin of, C85
  pressure from nongovernmental organizations,
    C87
  profit, C85
  social collateral, C85
  successful use of, C86
Microloans by Boston Beer Company, C136
Middle class
  in China, 11
  in emerging economies, 46
  emerging in Asia, 217
Middle East, population and Internet
  usage, C76
Millennials
  attracting, 112
  social and environmental impact, 110

Mindguards, 430
Minority shareholders
  expropriation of, 303
  principal-agent conflicts, 302
  principal-principal conflicts, 302
Mission
  employee relationship with, 116–117
  United Way Worldwide, C253
Mission Impossible: Ghost Protocol,
  75–76
Mission statement, 25
  effective, 25–26
  examples, 24
  redefined, 26
  Southwest Airlines, C139
  stakeholder management in, 24
Mobile communication devices, C23–C24
Modular organization, 324, **328**
  apparel industry, 328
  conditions for success, 328–329
  outsourcing noncore functions, 328
  pros and cons, 330
  risks from outsourcing
    loss of control over suppliers, 329
    loss of critical skills, 329
    loss of cross-functional skills, 329
Monitoring
  programs, 114–115
  in vertical integration, 188
Mortgage-backed securities, 104
Motivation, 355
Movie exhibition industry in 2013, case
  audience demographics, C97
  box office receipts 1980–2012, C95
  challenges for exhibitors
    benefits from digital investments,
      C100–C101
    declining allure of theaters, C101
    home viewing, C101–C102
  domestic receipts 2000–2011, C97
  International receipts 2000–2011, C97
  leading U.S. theater chains, C98
  number of screens 2000–2011, C95
  opening weekend receipts, C100
  recent initiatives
    advertising, C104
    alternative content, C103
    on concessions, C103–C104
    dynamic pricing, C103
    expanded in-lobby dining, C103–C104
    in-theater dining, C104
    technological innovations, C103
    traditional innovations, C102
    upscale in-theater dining, C104
  revenue generation
    box office receipts, C99
    concessions, C99
    pre-movie ads, C99–C100
  revenues and expenses for 8-screen
    theater, C99
  ticket prices 1980–2012, C95
  top 25 releases in 2012, C94
  top studios and distributors, C96
  value chain activities, C96–C99
Movie exhibitors, theater chains, C97
Movie goers
  appeal of theaters for, C101
  demographics, C96
Movie industry
  computer-animated films, C7–C10

international sales, 217
World Wrestling Entertainment in, C72
Movie theaters
declining allure of, C101
MP3 market, C22–C23
Multichannel marketing by Keurig, C263
Multichannel sales approach, C54
Multidivisional structure, 316
Multidomestic strategy, 230
decentralized decisions, 230
geographic area divisions, 322
international divisions, 322
Procter & Gamble, 231
product names, 230
risks and challenges, 231–232
strengths and limitations, 232
worldwide matrix structure, 322
Multinational firms, 217
modes of international expansion, 234–239
monitored by nongovernmental organizations, 17
options in global strategy, 212
Multitiered department stores, C51

N

Nairobi Stock Exchange, C86
Nanotechnology, 45
National Aeronautics and Space Administration, 168, 361
National competitiveness; *see* Diamond of national advantage
National Hiring Day, C44
National Mediation Board, C150
Native American casinos
as competition, C15
federal law on, C15
by state, C12
Natural disasters, 5–6
impact on JetBlue Airways, C151–C152
Negotiating costs, 188
Net income
decline at Procter & Gamble, C196
General Motors, C216
JetBlue Airways, C146
packaged-food industry, C240
Net revenue, eBay 2010–2012, C80
Network lever, 123
Networking
by business incubators, 391
innovation skill, 383, 384
for recruiting, 111
Neuroscience, 384
New competitive action, 264
bases of, 264
hardball strategies, 265
reasons for, 263–264
New entrants; *see also* Threat of new entrants
and competitive dynamics
choosing not to react, 270
likelihood of competitive reaction, 269–270
motivation and ability to respond, 266–267
new competitive action, 263–264
threat analysis, 264–266
types of actions, 267–269
reactions from competitors, 262–266
New markets
entering, 199, 268
search intensified by rivalry, 215
New product development, Samsung Electronics, C193

New product launch, 268
Apple Inc., C19, C21, C22–C26
at Dippin' Dots Inc., C112–C114
failure at McDonald's, C90
by McDonald's, C91–C92
Nintendo, C177
Samsung Electronics, C191
New product lines, Samsung Electronics, C192
New product search, by QVC, C66
New venture group, 390
WD-40 Company, 391
New ventures; *see also* Start-ups
exit champions, 394–395
factors determining pursuit of, 388–389
idea sources, 392
measures of success, 394
Pixar Animation Studios, C7–C9
product champions, 394
project definition, 393
project impetus, 393
strategic decisions, 395–396
strategic reasons for undertaking, 394
Weight Watchers, C30
New York Institute of Technology, C7
New York Times, C42
Niche-differentiation strategy, 152, 153
Niche strategy
JetBlue Airways, C146
at Southwest Airlines, C140–C141
Nikkei, 5
Nineteen Eighty-Four (Orwell), C20
Nonfinancial rewards, 117
Nongovernmental organizations
and microfinance, C87
monitoring of multinational firms, 17
Non-invented-here barrier, 123
Nonprofit sector
strategic priorities, 285
watchdog agencies, C253
Nontraditional store locations, C43–C44
North America, population and Internet usage, C76
North American Free Trade Agreement, 46, 234
Norway, litigation against Zynga, C127

O

Obama, Barack, C189
Obama administration, C44, C217
Obesity, 44, C30–C31, C36, C37
Observing, 383, 384
Off-screen advertising, C104
Offshoring, 224; *see also* Outsourcing
coordination costs, 225
easily visible savings from, 224–225
hidden costs, 225
from increased inventory, 225
indirect costs, 225
wage inflation, 225
intellectual property rights, 225
recent explosion in volume of, 224
reduced market responsiveness, 225
versus reshoring, 226
by service sector, 224
wage inflation and, 225
Oil spill of 2010, 5
Online auctions
in China, C74
eBay, C77
strategic advantage, C76
Online brokers, 146–147

Online gaming
competitors, C124–C126
market size, C123–C124
number of daily users, C124
Zynga, C123–C124, C126–C127
Online grocery industry
competitors, C206–C209
price comparison, C207
price-sensitive customers, C205–C206
profiles, C207
sales, C205
types of shoppers, C206
Online marketing
at Dippin' Dots Inc., C114
Fresh Direct, C203–C204
by QVC, C64, C67
Online procurement, 57
Online travel agents, 337–338
On-screen advertising, C104
On-the-job consumption, 298
Open-sourcing model for talent, 117
Operating expenses, at Southwest Airlines, C142
Operational effectiveness, 8
Operational efficiency and effectiveness, 285
Operations, 75
Ann Taylor, C54–C55
Apple Inc., C21–C22
differentiation strategy, 148
Fresh Direct, C201–C202, C203
JetBlue Airways, C150
overall cost leadership, 144
QVC, C64–C66
Southwest Airlines 2008–2012, C138
Weight Watchers, C33–C37
World Wrestling Entertainment, C69–C72
Opportunistic behavior, 298
Opportunities
in crowdfunding, 254
in entrepreneurial cultures, 392
for entrepreneurs, 248–251
recognizing, 35
in retailing from obesity, 44
Opportunity evaluation, 249–250
Opportunity recognition, 249
Options, 395
Oral case presentation, 422
Order processing time, 158
Organizational bases of power, 351
coercive power, 352–353
information power, 353
legitimate power, 351–353
reward power, 352
Organizational boundaries, 14
Organizational buying, 57
Organizational capabilities, 84; *see also* Capabilities
Organizational conflicts, 335
Organizational culture, 281
in boundaryless organizations, 330–333
change at Procter & Gamble, C198
committed to excellence and ethical behavior, 349–350
culture of dissent, 363–364
entrepreneurial, 392
example, 282
Heineken, C62
Jamba Juice, C44
Pixar Animated Studios, C7–C10
rallies, 282
for risk-taking, 364

Organizational culture—*Cont.*
role in organizations, 282
self-governing, 280
setting boundaries, 282
Southwest Airlines, C138–C141
storytelling for, 282
studies on, 281
sustaining, 282
wolf culture, 349
Organizational design, 14
in case analysis, 435
leadership task, 348–349
Organizational ethics, 365, 365–366
compliance-based programs, 366–368
integrity-based programs, 366–368
Organizational flexibility argument, 118
Organizational goals and objectives, 8
Apple Inc., C26
Boston Beer Company, C129
in case analysis, 432–433
Edward Marshall Boehm Inc., C3
Jamba Juice, C39
Samsung Electronics, C195
in strategy analysis, 11
Organizational learning, experience curve, 143
Organizational resources, 83, **84**
Organizational structure, 312
ambidextrous design, 336–337
boundaryless organizational design, 324–335
Cisco Systems, 179
divisional structure, 313, 316–317, 320
dominant growth patterns, 312–314
effect of globalization, 314n
effect of lower transaction costs, 314n
functional structure, 313, 314–316
global start-ups, 322–323
Green Mountain Coffee Roasters, C267
holding company at Heineken, C60–C61, C62
holding company structure, 319
influence on strategy formulation, 324
for international markets, 313
international operations, 321–322
matrix structure, 319–321
online travel agents, 337–338
Robin Hood, C2
simple structure, 313, 314
strategic business unit structure, 318–319
strategy relationships, 312
types, 313–314
United Way Worldwide, C249
Organizational vision, 23–25
Organizational vs. individual rationality, 8
Organization for Economic Cooperation and
    Development, study on Asian Middle classes, 217
Organizations; *see also* Corporations;
    Environmentally aware organizations; Firms
barriers to change in, 350–351, 352
core values and performance evaluation, 115
diversity management, 118
hierarchy of goals, 23
integrative view of, 20–22
isolated departments, 315
key stakeholders and claims, 16
shared value concept, 18–19
situational factors in behavioral control,
    286–287
social responsibility, 17–18
stakeholder management, 15–17
structural holes, 122

tribal loyalty, 116
triple bottom line, 19–20
Orphan Drug Act of 1983, 228
Outbound logistics, 75
differentiation strategy, 148
overall cost leadership, 144
Outlets of McDonald's
cutbacks, C90
number of, C90
revamping plan, C92
worldwide distribution, C91
Outside consultant, 416
Outside the Ring, C68
Outsourcing, 8, **224**; *see also* Offshoring
by Ann Taylor, C55
by Apple Inc., C22
benefits and challenges, 312
by Boeing, 310–312
by modular organizations
    noncore functions, 328
    strategic risks, 329
recent explosion in volume of, 224
reversed at Louis Vuitton, C171
by service sector, 224
Overall cost leadership, 143
bases of, 142
competitive parity, 143–144
effects of Internet, 160–161
examples, 145
experience curve, 143
and five-forces model, 145
integrated with differentiation strategies, 154–157
interrelated tactics, 143
JetBlue Airways, C148
for new ventures, 260
pitfalls
    to easily imitated, 146–147
    increased cost of inputs, 146
    lack of parity in differentiation, 147
    obsolescence of basis of cost advantage, 147
    reduced flexibility, 147
    summary, 152
    too much focus on too few value-chain
        activities, 146
and process innovation, 379
Renault, 146
Southwest Airlines, C141
value-chain activities, 144
Vizio, Inc., 261
Overconfidence, 397–398

P

Packaged-food industry
discount sellers, C239
downsizing, C239
market capitalizations, C240
in United States, C238–C239
Parenting advantage, 189
from unrelated diversification, 182
Partnerships
Dippin' Dots Inc. and McDonald's, C110–C111
eBay and Yahoo!, C81
Keurig and Green Mountain, C265
Yahoo! and Microsoft, C271
Patent litigation
by Dippin' Dots Inc., C112
Samsung Electronics, C191
Patent protection, Keurig, C264

Patents
battles over, 131
litigation by Apple, C22
Path dependency, 86
Pension Rights Center, 300
Pentagon attack of 2001, C147
People for the Ethical Treatment of Animals, 301
People lever, 123
Performance appraisals, 112
Performance enhancement, from location of value-
    chain activities, 218
Performance evaluation
balanced scorecard, 94–96
and core values, 115
financial ratio analysis, 92–94
360-degree evaluation and feedback system, 115–116
Performance materials, 78
Permeable internal boundaries, 325–326
Personal agendas, 125–126
Personal bases of power, 353
expert power, 353
referent power, 353
Personal computers
competitors for Apple Inc., C22
market shares, C23
Personal digital entertainment devices, C22–C23
Personal risk taking, 404
Personal time constraints, 351
Physical resources, 83
Physical space, 390
Physical uniqueness of resources, 86
Piecemeal productivity improvements, 169
Pied Piper Effect, 120
Pioneering new entry, 257
disruptive of status quo, 257–258
Pandora, 258
pitfalls, 257
sustaining advantage, 257
Piracy
by counterfeiting, 220
of software, 220
Pirates of the Caribbean, C100
Plagiarize, 265
Plant closings at Ford, C223
Poison pill, 202, 298
Policies, ethical, 370
Political barriers, 351
Political barriers to change, overcoming, 352
**Political/legal segment of the general
    environment,** 43, **44–45**
Political/legal trends, 47
Political risk, 220
country risk ratings, 220, 221
examples, 220
managing
    by identifying key influencers, 221
    by market diversification, 221
    by stakeholder coalitions, 221
    by stakeholders on boards, 221
Ponzi scheme, 365
Pooled negotiating power, 185
potential downside, 186
Population
African Americans, 118
aging in United States, 42
Asian Americans, 118
Hispanic Americans, 117–118
and Internet usage worldwide, C76
of world in 2013, 217

Porter's five-forces model of industry competition;
  see Five-forces model of industry competition
Portfolio management, 190
  Campbell Soup Company, C28
  description and benefits, 190–192
  growth/share matrix approach, 190–192
  at Johnson & Johnson, C121
  limitations, 192
Portfolio of businesses, 189
Portugal
  economic crisis, 6
  emigration from, 6
Positioning strategies
  breakaway positioning, 166
  reverse positioning, 166
Poverty
  extent of, C85
  microfinance solution, C85–C87
Power, 351
  effective uses of, 351–353
  organizational bases, 352–353
  personal bases, 353
  from private information, 124–125
Preannouncements, 403
Preemptive launch, 382
Price(s)
  Apple computers, C20
  competition not based on, C22
  of online grocers, C207
Price comparison, on Internet, 58
Price cutting, 268
  automobile industry, 270
Price-earnings ratio, 93, 445–446
  packaged-food industry, C240
Price increases, 268
Price performance relationship, 53
Price-performance trade-off, 169
Price premium, 148
  too high, 151
Pricing policy
  Louis Vuitton, C169, C171
  in luxury goods industry, C169
  by McDonald's, C88–C89
  by movie exhibitors, C103
Primary activities, 72
  differentiation strategy, 148
  inbound logistics, 74–75
  marketing and sales, 75–76
  operations, 75
  outbound logistics, 75
  overall cost leadership, 144
  service, 76
  in service organizations, 81–82
  upstream, 232
Prime Time Live, 300
Principal-agent conflicts, versus principal-principal
  conflicts, 301–302
Principal-principal conflicts, 301
  conditions for, 303
  versus principal-agent conflicts, 301–302
Principals, 397
  in agency theory, 290–291
Private information, 123
  access to diverse skill sets, 124
  power from, 124–125
Proactiveness, 401
  examples of failure, 401–402
  first-mover advantage, 401
  pressure on competitors, 401

techniques
  new product introduction, 402
  new service offerings, 402
Problem identification, 418
Problem-solving argument, 118
Procedures, ethical, 370
Process for change, 346
Process innovation, 379
Process loss, 128
Procurement, 76–78
  differentiation strategy, 148
  at LG Electronics, 79
  online, 57
  overall cost leadership, 144
Product(s)
  in breakaway positioning, 166
  commoditized, 58
  complementors, 60
  counterfeit, 220
  in decline stage, 16–169
  Dippin' Dots Inc., C107
  in reverse positioning, 166
  stabilizing demand for, 188
  standardized or undifferentiated, 52
  unimportant to buyers, 53
  unimportant to quality, 52
  Zynga, C123–C124
Product categories
  eBay, C78–C79
  Yahoo!, C81
Product champion, 393
  contrasted with exit champion, 395
Product design, Louis Vuitton, C173
Product development, General Motors, C218
Product differentiation, 50
  access to distribution channels, 51
  capital requirements, 51
  cost disadvantages independent of scale, 51
  in five-forces model, 50–51
  lack of, 54
  switching costs, 51
Product division, worldwide, 313
Product growth potential, motive for international
  expansion, 217–218
Product innovation, 378
Product line
  Apple Inc., *C17,* C19, C21, C22–C26
  at Jamba Juice, C39, C41–C42
  reinvention at Campbell Soup, C236
  Samsung Electronics, C191
Product line extension
  Boston Beer Company, C129
  dilution of brand identity, 151
Product markets, separate divisions for, 316–317
Product names, 231
Product placement, 75–76
  by Dippin' Dots Inc., C111–C112
  in movies, 153
Product portfolio, change at Porsche, 171
Product pruning, 169
Product recall, by Johnson & Johnson, C116
Production
  capacity changes, 268
  customers included in, 80
  lowering unit costs, 228
  mass customization, 154
  process at Edward Marshall Boehm Inc., C3
Productivity, piecemeal improvements, 169
Profit centers, film studios, C96

Profit concentration, 155
Profit margin ratio, 93, 444–445
Profit pool, 155
  for combination strategies, 155
  in electronics retailing, 156
  miscalculating sources of, 157
Profit sanctuaries, 265
Profits
  diverted to top management, 91
  and employee bargaining power, 91
  and employee exit costs, 91
  and employee replacement costs, 91
  generation and distribution of, 90–91
  of Johnson & Johnson by segment, C117
  low, 52
  manager bargaining power, 91
  of online grocers, C207
  for vendors to QVC, C66
Profitability
  Louis Vuitton, C166
  of new ventures, 394
  underpinnings of, 80–81
Profitability measures
  profit margin, 444–445
  return on assets, 445
  return on equity, 445
Profitability ratios, 93
Project definition, 393
Project impetus, 393
Property rights, intellectual vs. physical property, 131
Proprietary information systems, 80
Proprietary software, 37
Prosumer concept, 80–81
  at Procter & Gamble, 81
Public activists, as control mechanism, 300–301
Public Company Accounting Oversight Board, 299
Public company information, 448
Public information, 123
Purchases, buyer bargaining power and size of, 51

Q

Quality
  in global strategy, 229
  versus growth, C10
  problems at Johnson & Johnson, C118–C120,
    C121
Quality assurance, at QVC, C66
Quality control
  Fresh Direct, C201
  Keurig, C265
  Louis Vuitton, C173
Question marks, 191–192
Questioning, 383, 384
Quick ratio, 93, 441

R

Racetrack gaming, C15
Radical innovation, 379, 380
  project time line, 385
Radio advertising, 376–378
Rare resources, 85
Ratatouille, C104
Ratio analysis
  asset management measures, 443–444
  categories, 440
  long-term solvency measures, 442–443
  market value measures, 445–446

Ratio analysis—*Cont.*
  problems with, 438–440
  profitability measures, 444–445
  questions about, 440
  short-term solvency measures, 440–442
  summary of, 446
Rationality, 8
Raw, C68
Raw Is War, C69
RBV; *see* Resource-based view of the firm
Real estate boom, Spain, 6
Real estate options, 395
Real options analysis, 395
  applications to strategic decisions, 395–396
  applied to entrepreneurs, 395
  at Intel, 397
  pitfalls
    agency theory and back-solver dilemma, 396–397
    and managerial conceit, 397–398
  wit property, 395
Reality-based TV shows, C68
Realized strategy, 11
  versus intended strategy, 10–11
Receivables turnover, 93, 444
Recession, effect on Procter & Gamble sales, C196
Recognition programs, 284
Recommendations, in case analysis, 421
Recruiting, 111
  at Fresh Direct, C201
  Robin Hood, C2
  at Southwest Airlines, C139
Reengineering, successful, 333
Reengineering the Corporation (Hammer & Champy), 333
Referent power, 353
Referrals, 111
Regional airlines, C147
Regionalization, 234
  versus globalization, 234
Reimaging, by McDonald's, C92
Reintermediation, 58
Related and supporting industries, 215
Related diversification, 182
  by Apple Inc., C20
  deriving cost savings, 184–185
  eBay, C79
  economies of scope, 182
  economies of scope from, 182
  enhancing revenue and differentiation, 185
  examples of success, 181
  leveraging core competencies, 182–184
  market power from, 182
    pooled negotiating power, 185–186
    vertical integration, 186–189
  sharing activities, 184–185
  value creation by, 181–182
Rents, 90
Repeat purchasers, 165
Replacement cost of employees, 91
Replacement demand, 171
Repositioning by Weight Watchers, C29–C30
Reputation, 83
  of competitors, 270
  damaged at JetBlue Airways, C151–152
  damaged by competitive aggressiveness, 403
Request for proposals, 386–387
Research and development
  by Apple Inc., C22
  at Beiersdorf AG, C158

  for innovativeness, 401
  for internal development, 200
  at Johnson & Johnson, C118, C120
  by Microsoft, 405
  Samsung Electronics, C193
  at Samsung Electronics, C193
Reshoring, 226
  by Apple Inc., C22
Resource acquisition argument, 118
Resource-based view of the firm, 82
  erosion of competitive advantage at Dell Inc., 89–90
  external analysis, 82
  generation and distribution of profits, 90–92
  internal analysis, 82
  and social capital, 119
  for sustainable competitive advantage
    causal ambiguity, 87
    inimitable resources, 86
    path dependency, 86
    physical uniqueness, 86
    rare resources, 85
    readily available resources, 87–89
    social complexity, 87
    valuable resources, 85
  types of resources, 83–84
Resource similarity, 266
Resources
  attributes for comparative advantage, 85
  without available substitutes, 87–89
  causal ambiguity, 87
  of competitors, 270
  criteria for assessing sustainability, 85
  inimitability, 86
  intangible, 84
  obtained by mergers and acquisitions, 194
  organizational capabilities, 84
  path dependency, 86
  physical uniqueness, 86
  rarity, 85
  social complexity, 87
  tangible, 83–84
  valuable, 85
Responsible Corporate Office Doctrine, 345
Restructuring, 189
  in airline industry, C147
  by Ann Taylor, C54–C55
  at Apple Inc., C26
  asset restructuring, 190
  at Beiersdorf AG, C155, C164–C165
  capital restructuring, 190
  drawback at Ford, C232–C233
  Ford Motor Company, C220–C233
  by Ford Motor Company, 170
  General Motors, C216
  Loews Corporation, 190
  management restructuring, 190
  at Procter & Gamble, C198
  from unrelated diversification, 182
Retail alliances, 255
Retail grocery industry
  inventories, C205
  online segment, C206–207
  sales in 2013, C205
  top ten chains, C205
Retailers/Retailing
  Apple Stores, C21
  at Edward Marshall Boehm Inc., C3
  electronics, 156
  by Jamba Juice, C40
  nontraditional store locations, C43–C44

  opportunities from obesity, 44
  used by Samsung Electronics, C192
  women's apparel, C47–C56
Retention bonuses, C4–C6
Retreating to more defensible ground, 168–169
Return on assets ratio, 93, 445
Return on book assets, 445
Return on book equity, 445
Return on equity ratio, 93, 445
Return on investment, 143
Return on sales, historical trends, 94
Revenue
  Boston Beer Company, C129
  of casinos by state, C11
  decline at Yahoo!, C268
  eBay in 2011, C74
  enhanced by related diversification, 185
  increase in growth stage, 165
  Jamba Juice, C40
  Louis Vuitton, C171
  miscalculating sources of, 157
  packaged-food industry, C240
  Pixar Animated Studios, C7
  from pre-show ads, C100
  QVC, C63
  Southwest Airlines, C141
  U.S. casino industry 2000–2012, C11
  Weight Watchers, C29, C33
  World Wrestling Entertainment, C71, C72
  of Zynga, C123
Revenue generation
  by eBay, C80–C81
  for Johnson & Johnson, C118
  movie exhibitors
    advertising, C99–C100
    box office sales, C99
    concessions, C99
Reverse innovation, 218
  in developing countries, 219
  examples, 219
  from international expansion, 218–219
  motivation and implications, 219
  products for emerging markets, 218–219
Reverse positioning, 166
  Commerce Bank, 167
Reward and compensation agreements, 291
Reward power, 352
Reward system, 283
  and behavioral control, 287, 288
  characteristics for effectiveness, 283–284
  as control mechanism, 283
  financial and nonfinancial, 117
  for innovation, 387
  potential downsides, 283
  problems across organizational units, 283
  at Southwest Airlines, C139–C140
Risk minimization, 404
Risk reduction
  goal of diversification, 192–193
  from location of value-chain activities, 218
Risk sharing, and agency theory, 291
Risk taking, 403
  potential pitfalls, 404
  techniques
    from other domains, 404
    research and assessment, 404
  types of, 404
Risk-taking culture, 364
Risks
  in exporting, 236

in global economy, 46
in international expansion
  currency risk, 222–223
  economic risk, 220–222
  management risks, 223
  political risk, 220–222
in joint ventures, 237–238
in licensing and franchising, 236–237
in strategic alliances, 236–237
in wholly owned subsidiaries, 238
Rivalry, 215
  intensifying in maturity stage, 165–166
Riverboat gambling, C15
Role models, 368
Role playing, in case analysis, 415–418
Romantic view of leadership, 4
Rule of law, 220
Russia, Campbell Soup Company in, C236–C237

S

Sales
  Ann Taylor, C49
  auto industry 2012–2013, C227–C229
  of beer in United States, C133
  of beer in U.S. 2007–2012, C132
  Campbell Soup Company, C235
  decline at McDonald's, C88
  Ford Motor Company, C226
  General Motors in 2011–2012, C216
  Green Mountain Coffee Roasters, C259
  Heineken, C59
  ice cream brands, C108
  of imported beers, C134
  of Johnson & Johnson by segment, C117
  by QVC, C63
Sales and leaseback, 169
Sales commission, 132
Sarbanes-Oxley Act, 45
  and boards of directors, 294
  on corporate governance, 300
  protection of whistle blowers, 370
Scenario analysis, 40
  context for, 40–41
  at PPG, 41
Scent of Mystery, 257
Search barrier, 123
Search costs, 160
  in vertical integration, 188
Search engines, 452
Securities and Exchange Commission
  Bank of America fine, 104
  as control mechanism, 299–300
  on crowdfunding, 253
  EDGAR database, 449
  filings, 449–450
Seeds vs. weeds, 382
Self-awareness, 354
Self-censorship, 428
Self-governing culture, 280
Self-regulation, 354–355
Sellers, perception of differentiation, 151
Sell-offs, 197n
Semiconductor business, 397
Separation of ownership and management, 290–291
Service organizations
  offshoring by, 224
  value chain applied to, 81–82
Services, 76
  differentiation strategy, 148

overall cost leadership, 144
Procter & Gamble expansion into, C199–C200
Setting a direction, 347–348
Shared value concept, 18–19
Shareholder activism, 291, 295
  institutional investors, 295
Shareholders, in corporate governance, 14, 15
Shareholder value, 9
  destroyed by acquisitions, 197
  from diversification, 181
  generating, 15–16
Sharing activities, 184
  attained by mergers and acquisitions, 195
  differentiation by means of, 185
  synergies from, 184–185
Shark Tank, C41
Shirking, 298
Shopping bots, 58
Shopping infomediaries, 58
Shopping malls, C43
Short-term objectives and action plans, 285
Short-term perspective, 8–9
Short-term solvency/liquidity measures, 440–442
  cash ratio, 442
  current ratio, 441
  quick/acid-test ratio, 441
Short-term solvency ratios, 93
Silos, 122, 315
Simple organizational structure, 313, 314
  advantages, 313
  disadvantages, 313
Single-serving coffee-brewing
  competition, C263–C264
  European roots, C260–C261
  Keurig, C256–C267
  pod-brewing market, C261–C263
Situational factors in organizational control, 286–287
Skilled human resource pool, 214
Skills
  lost in outsourcing, 329
  training for, 111
Skill sets, access to, 124
Skunkworks, 399, 400
Skyfall, 217, C94, C96
Slow industry growth, 54
Smackdown, C68, C69
Small Business Administration, 255, C109
Small Business Development Center, 255
Smartphone market, C23–C24
  competitors, C191
Soap opera origin, C198
Social capital, 108
  attracting and retaining talent, 120
  boundaryless organizations, 335
  entrepreneurial resource, 254
  example, 119
  generated by electronic teams, 126
  implications for career success, 122
  interdependence among group members, 121
  overcoming barriers to collaboration, 123
  Pied Piper Effect, 120
  potential downsides
    cost of socialization process, 125
    dysfunctional human resource practices, 125
    groupthink, 125
    not enough closure relationship, 126
    pursuit of personal agendas, 125–126
  and resource-based view of the firm, 119
  social networks for, 120–125

tying knowledge workers to firms, 118–119
value creation through, 130
Social complexity, 87
Social media
  imitation, 246–247
  LinkedIn, 152
Social network analysis, 121
  bridging relationships, 121–122
  closure relationships, 121–122
  communication patterns, 121
Social networks
  analysis of, 121–122
  brokers, 124–125
  connectors, 120–121
  implications for career success, 123
  network traps
    wrong behavior, 125
    wrong relationships, 125
    wrong structure, 125
  public vs. private information, 123–125
  for sharing information, 126
  structural holes, 122
Social responsibility, 17–18; *see also* Corporate
  social responsibility
  Apple Inc., C22
  demand for, 18
  Jamba Juice, C44
  shared value concept, 18–19
  triple bottom line, 19–20
Social skills, 356–357
Socialization process, costs of, 125
Socially complex processes, 108
Socially responsible investing, 20
**Sociocultural segment of the general
  environment, 42–44**
Sociocultural trends, 47
Soft power, 353
Soft trends, 37
  example, 37
Software market, C25
Software piracy, 220
Southeast Asia, poverty in, C85–C86
South Korea
  business groups, 303
  Gmarket, C82
Spain, economic crisis, 6
Specialty coffee industry, C259–C260
Specialty store chains, C51
Spin-offs, 197n
Split-ups, 197n
Sponsoring, advice on, 114
Staffing
  to capture value from innovation, 386
  for innovation success, 387
  internal vs. external, 382
Stakeholder coalitions, 221
Stakeholder management, 15
  generating shareholder value, 15–16
  key groups and claims, 16
  in mission statements, 26
  zero-sum vs. symbiosis, 16–17
Stakeholders, 8
  and balanced scorecard, 94–96
  benefits from antitakeover tactics, 203
  on board of directors, 221
  in boundaryless organizations, 333–335
  and corporate governance, 288n
  in decision making, 8
  impact of vertical integration, 188
  key groups, 16

Stakeholders—*Cont.*
  in Procter & Gamble, 17
  retention of profits, 92
  source of new venture ideas, 391
  in Walmart, 16
Standard and Poor's 500 index, 20
Standard financial statements, 437
Standardization, 226–227
Standardized products, 52
Stars, 191–192
Start-ups; *see also* Corporate Entrepreneurship;
    Entrepreneurs; New ventures
  capital sources, 252
  costs for ice cream franchises, C113
  criteria for viability, 250
  crowdfunding, 253–254
  Edward Marshall Boehm Inc., C3
  emigration of talent for form, 120
  entry strategies, 257–260
  financial resources, 251–254
  generic strategies, 260–262
  global, 322–323
  government contracting, 255
  government support, 255
  human capital, 254
  and JOBS Act of 2010, C189
  leadership in, 255–256
  in mature industries, 262
  opportunity evaluation, 249–250
  QVC as, C64
  social capital, 254–255
  sources of opportunities, 248–249
  strategic thinking for, 247–248
  threat of retaliation by incumbents, 257
  using microfinance, C85–C87
Static analysis, 59
Status quo
  challenging, 363–364
  dissatisfaction with, 346
  questioning, 358–359
  vested interests in, 350
Stereotyping, 428
Stock analysts, as control mechanism, 299
Stock market, 43
Stock options, 296, 395
Stock price performance
  Campbell Soup Company, C240, C241, C245
  changes at Apple Inc., C17
  decline after acquisition notice, 195
  of financial stocks, 15
  JetBlue Airways, C146, C152
Stock repurchase, General Motors, C219
Stockholders, 290
Storage costs, 54
Store-within-a-store, C43
Storytelling, in animated films, C9
Stove pipes, 122, 315
Strategic actions, 267
  types of, 268
Strategic alliances, 199
  Apple and Microsoft, C20
  benefits, 237
  crowdsourcing in, 199
  to develop and diffuse technologies, 200
  to enter new markets, 199
  JetBlue Airways and Aer Lingus, C149
  means of diversification, 193, 199–200
  potential downsides, 200
  to reduce value chain costs, 199–200

  risks and limitations, 237–238
  for start-ups, 254–255
    manufacturing, 255
    pitfalls, 255
    retailing, 255
    technology, 255
  as strategic actions, 268
Strategic analysis, 11, 419
  information resources, 450–452
Strategic business unit structure, 314, 318
  advantages, 319
  Apple Inc.
    App Store, C25–C26
    computers, C22
    iPad, C24–C25
    iPhone, C23–C24
    iPod, C22–C23
    iTunes, C25
    software, C25
  Campbell Soup Company, C236
  disadvantages, 319
  in growth/share matrix
    cash cows, 191–192
    dogs, 191–192
    question marks, 191–192
    stars, 191–192
  Johnson & Johnson, C117–C118
  Procter & Gamble, C196
Strategic control, 278
  alternative approaches, 287
  aspects of
    behavioral control, 278, 279
    corporate governance, 278
    informational control, 278, 279
  attaining behavioral control, 281–288
  based on feedback loop, 278
  in case analysis, 435
  contemporary approach, 279–280
  ensuring informational control, 278–280
  problems at Hewlett-Packard, 276–277
  role of corporate governance, 288–303
  traditional approach, 278–279
  types of, 14
  views of managers and employees, 280
Strategic decision makers, 415
Strategic decisions
  applications of real options analysis, 395–396
  embedded options, 396
  at Johnson Controls, 396
  tollgates, 396
Strategic direction
  creating sense of mission, 22–23
  hierarchy of goals, 23
  mission statements, 25–26
  strategic objectives, 26–27
  vision, 23–25
Strategic envelope, 384–385
Strategic groups, 61
  automobile industry, 62–63
  charting future strategies, 62
  classifying, 61–62
  identifying barriers to mobility, 62
  identifying competitive position, 62
  implications of each industry, 62
Strategic management, 7
  corporate governance, 14–15
  to create competitive advantage, 7–8
  decision dilemma, 28
  ensuring coherence in direction, 22–27

  hierarchy of goals, 23
  mission statement, 25–26
  strategic objectives, 26–27
  vision, 23–25
  integrative view of organization, 20–22
  key attributes
    efficiency-effectiveness trade-off, 9
    goals and objectives, 8
    short-term or long-term perspective, 8–9
    stakeholders in decision making, 8
  shared value concept, 18–19
  social responsibility, 17–18
  stakeholder management, 15–17
  triple bottom line, 19–20
Strategic management process, 9
  analyses, decisions, and actions, 9
  intended vs. realized strategy, 10–11
  ongoing, 7
  strategy analysis, 11–13
  strategy formulation, 13–14
Strategic objectives, 26
Strategic partnering, 387
Strategic plan, in virtual organizations, 331
Strategic priorities, 284–285
  at Jamba Juice, C39
Strategic resources, 84
Strategic thinking, 162
  for start-ups, 247–248
Strategic vs. financial goals, 394
Strategically equivalent valuable resources, 87
Strategy analysis, 11–13
  Robin Hood, C2
Strategy formulation, 13
  effect of organizational structure, 324
  summary of steps, 13
Strategy implementation, 13
  summary of steps, 13–14
Strategy objectives
  criteria for
    appropriate, 27
    measurable, 27
    realistic, 27
    specific, 27
    timely, 27
  financial, 26–27
  lack of focus from too many, 27
  nonfinancial, 26–27
Strategy/Strategies, 7
  at Apple Inc., C17
  Campbell Soup Company, C238
  change at Procter & Gamble, C200
  change at United Way Worldwide, C247
  charting future direction of, 61
  cross-selling, 105
  failure at Borders, 3–4
  going astray, 36
  intended vs. realized, 10–11
  overemphasis on single dimension of, 73
  reasons for failure, 10–11
  reinvention at Weight Watchers, C29
  requiring multiple types of resources, 85
  sources of implementation problems, 348–349
  too easily imitated, 146–147
  for turnaround at Ford, 170
  value of inexperience, 22
  Weight Watchers, C30
Strikes
  General Motors in 1970, C216
  United Food and Commercial Workers, 28

Structural holes, 122
Structure of Corporation Law (Eisenberg), 290
Stuck-in-the-middle problem, 142, 156
Subprime mortgage market, 371
Subsidiaries
  of Beiersdorf AG, C156
  Boston Beer Company, C129
  and corporate parenting, 189
  wholly owned, 238
Substitute products and services, 53
Substitutes
  available for resources, 86–88
  threat of, 53
Succession planning, 293
  and duality of command, 297
Super Bowl
  Apple's commercial of 1984, C20
  TV commercials, 77
Superficial networks, 125
Supplier base, 215
  India, 216
Suppliers; *see also* Bargaining power of suppliers
  to Apple Inc., C22
  disintermediation by, 58
  for General Motors, 59
  long-term relationships with, 59
  loss of control over, 329
  in luxury goods industry, C169
  problems for Boeing, 311
  to QVC, C66
  web based purchasing arrangements, 57
Supply chain
  Apple Inc., C17
  potential problem for Boston Beer Company, C131
Support activities, 72
  differentiation strategy, 148
  general administration, 79
  human resource management, 78
  overall cost leadership, 144
  procurement, 76–78
  technological development, 78
Sustainability, Campbell Soup Company, C241–C242
Sustainable competitive advantage, 8; *see also* Competitive advantage
  criteria for, 89
  no longer possible, 347
  resources for, 85–89
Sustainable global economy, 19
Sustaining competitive advantage, innovation for, 381
Sustaining innovation, 380
Switching costs, 51
  barrier to entry, 51
  built up for buyers, 53
  and buyer bargaining power, 52
  and intensity of rivalry, 58
  lack of, 54
  on web businesses, 56
SWOT analysis, 41, 85
  and competitive aggressiveness, 402
  limitations
    one-shot view of moving target, 73
    overemphasis on single dimension of strategy, 73
    strengths not leading to competitive advantage, 73
    too narrow a focus on external environment, 73
  not primary basis for internal analysis, 72

  for strategy, 42
  unpopularity of, 42
Symbiosis, role of stakeholders, 16–17
Synergies, 181
  core competencies as basis for, 183
  deriving cost savings, 184–185
  financial, 182
  imitated by competitors, 196
  main sources of, 189
  obtained by mergers and acquisitions, 195
  from sharing activities, 184–185
Systemic barriers, 351

T

Tablet computer market, C24–C25
Tacit knowledge, 108, 128
Tactical actions, 267
  for overall cost leadership, 143
  types of, 268
Takeover constraint, 298
Takeover premium, 195
Talent
  attracted and retained by social capital, 119
  attracting, 106, 110–112
  attracting and retaining, C10
  emigration to form start-ups, 120
  open-sourcing model for, 117
  role of empathy in retailing, 356
Tangible resources, 83
  Dell Inc., 90
  types of, 83
Target market of film studios, C96
Teams
  autonomous, 399
  autonomous work groups, 390
  in barrier-free organizations, 325–326
  in boundaryless organizations, 324, 332
  for case analysis, 429–430
  cross-functional, 336
  electronic vs. traditional, 127–128
  good vs. mediocre, 326
Technological resources, 83
Technological segment of the general environment, 43, **45**
Technological trends, 47
Technology
  contribution to decline stage, 168
  cutting edge at Pixar, C9
  developed and diffused by strategic alliances, 200
  focus for innovation, 385
  for hiring prepuces, 111
  for home viewing, C102
  investment in, 401
  for leveraging human capital and knowledge
    codifying knowledge, 128–129
    electronic teams, 127–128
    social networks, 126
  as source of new ideas, 378
  value creation through, 130
Technology advance
  digital projection techniques, C100–C101
  by movie exhibitors
    image quality, C103
    IMAX, C103
    sound systems, C103
  at Nintendo, C177, C180–C181
Technology alliances, 255

Technology development, 78
  Apple Inc., C17, C20–C26
  computer-animated films, C7–C10
  differentiation strategy, 148
  overall cost leadership, 144
  Pixar Animation Studios, C8–C9, C10
Ted, C97
Teleconferencing, 53
Television
  cable networks, C102
  home shopping by, C64
  reality-based shows, C68
  set sizes and features, C101
Television commercials
  Apple Inc. Super Bowl 1984, C20
  costs for Super Bowl, 77
Television industry, 381
Terrorist attack of 2001, 18, C147
Theater chains, C97
Theater screens in U.S. 2000–2012, C95
Theory of the business, 36
Threat analysis, 264, 264–266
  market commonality, 266
  resource similarity, 266
  strength of response based on, 266
Threat of new entrants, 50, 56
  in five-forces model, 50
  impact of Internet, 55
  by start-ups, 256–257
Threat of retaliation, Robin Hood, C2
Threat of retaliation for start-ups, 257
Threat of substitute products and services, 53, 56
  in five-forces model, 53
  impact of Internet, 58
360-degree evaluation and feedback system, 115
  at General Electric, 115
  at HCL, 116
Ticket prices, C95
Ticket sales
  increase vs. volume, C94
  in U.S. 1980–2012, C95
Time horizon in industry analysis, 60–61
Time pacing
  of innovation, 385–386, C45
  of production at Pixar, C9–C10
Times interest earned ratio, 93, 442
Tipping Point (Gladwell), 120
Tollgates, strategic decision makers, 396
Top-level executives, 21
Total asset turnover, 93, 444
Total debt ratio, 93, 442
Total performance indicators, 96
Total quality management, 8
Total wage costs, 225
Tourism, decline in European Union, 6
Trademark protection, Keurig, C264
Trade-offs
  efficiency-effectiveness, 9
  price-performance, 169
Trading blocs, 46, 234, **234**
Traditional approach to strategic control, 277–279, **278**
Training
  and behavioral control, 288
  Campbell Soup Company, C238
  for skill, 111
  and technology changes, 113

Transaction cost perspective, 188
Transaction costs, 334
  effects on organizational structure, 314n
  lowered by disintermediation, 160
  types of, 188
Transaction-specific investments, 188, 189
Transfer barrier, 123
Transformational change, 22
Transnational strategy, 232
  by Asea Brown Boveri, 232–233
  enhanced adaptation, 232
  location decisions for value chain, 232
  risks and limitations, 233
  strengths and limitations, 233
  value-chain activities, 232
Travel and Leisure, C149
Trend analysis, 36–38
  Samsung Electronics, C194
Trends
  in dietary eating, C31
  emerging, 36–37
  in general environment, 47
  hard, 37–38
  key, 36
  return on sales, 94
  weight-management industry, C29
Tribal loyalty, 116
Triple bottom line, 19
  and environmental revolution, 19
  environmental sustainability, 19–20
T-shaped management, 123
Turnaround strategy, 169
  asset and cost surgery, 169
  Dippin' Dots Inc., C106–C107
  external analysis for, 169
  Ford Motor Company, C220–C233
  at Ford Motor Company, 170
  at General Motors, C214, C217–C219
  internal analysis for, 169
  at Intuit, 169–170
  Jamba Juice, C45
  McDonald's, C88, C90–C92
  piecemeal productivity improvements, 169
  product and market pruning, 169
  and replacement demand, 171
  rescuing pockets of profit, 171
  Samsung Electronics, C191–C192
  at Yahoo!, C268–C273
Turnover measures, 443–444
Turnover ratios, 93

U

Uncertainty, underestimating, 40
Undifferentiated products, and buyer bargaining
  power, 52
Unemployment, in Spain, 6
Unethical behavior, 365
  in housing market, 371
  intensified by competition, 369–370
  minimizing, 286
Unification lever, 123
Uniqueness not valuable, 150
Unit costs, lowering, 228
United Auto Workers, 170, C216
United Food and Commercial Workers Union, 28,
  C210
United States
  aging population, 42

Beiersdorf AG in, C150
coffee consumption, C259–C260
history of gambling, C12–C13
leading agricultural exports, C239
number of franchisers, 236
packaged-food industry, C238–C239, C240
United States Bureau of Statistics, 42
United States Consumer Product Safety
  Commission, C263–C264
United States Supreme Court, ruling against film
  studios, C98
United States v. Paramount Pictures, C98
Unity of command, 297
Universities, as innovation partners, 387
Unrelated diversification, 189
  corporate parenting, 189
  Delta Air Lines, 203–204
  eBay, C79
  failure at Cisco Systems, 178–180
  hierarchical relationships, 189
  portfolio management, 190–192
  restructuring, 189–190
  risk reduction by, 192
  synergies from, 189
  value creation by, 181–182
Unsupported teams, 336
Upscale within-theater dining, C104
Upstream activities, 232
U.S. News & World Report, 369, C31
USA Today, 379, C42, C149
USA Today Super Bowl Ad Meter, 77
Using the new to improve the old, 169
Utility companies, greenwashing, 366

V

Valuable resources, 85
Value
  captured from innovation, 386
  definition, 72
Value chain, 72
  cost reductions, 199–200
  extended, 155
  global dispersal of, 223–225
  global dispersion of
    decline in transportation costs, 224
    example, 224
    offshoring, 224–225
    outsourcing, 224–225
    by service sector, 224
  integration at multiple points along, 149
  and reintermediation, 58
Value-chain activities
  at Campbell Soup, 75
  in decline stage, 168
  differentiation strategy, 148
  film studios
    distribution, C97–C98
    exhibition, C98–C99
    production, C96–C97
  for firms to consider
    primary activities, 74
    support activities, 76
  location in transnational strategy, 232
  optimizing location of, 218
  outsourced, 187
  overall cost leadership, 144
  primary, 72, 74–76
  source of competitive advantage, 392

  support, 72, 76–79
  too much focus on few, 146
  underestimating challenges, 156
Value-chain analysis, 72
  interrelationships among, 79–80
  primary activities, 72, 74–76
  prosumer concept, 80–81
  for service organizations, 81–82
  support activities, 72, 76–79
Value creation
  activities, 72
  from core competencies, 183
  from human capital, 130
  from intellectual processes, 106
  by internal development, 20
  from opportunities, 250
  from related diversification, 181–182
  from social capital, 130
  from technology, 130
  from unrelated diversification, 181–182,
    189–190
Value net, 59–60
Value of the firm
  in financial statements, 107
  market-to-book value, 107–108
Values
  in boundaryless organizations, 330–333
  decision dilemma, 28
Variance, estimation of, 396
Vehicle dependability rankings, C237
Venture capital, 253
Venture capitalists, 253
  for start-ups, 252–253
Vertical boundaries, 325
Vertical integration, 185, 186
  administrative costs, 188–189
  benefits and risks, 186–188
  issues to consider, 186–188
  market power, 186–189
  at Shaw Industries, 187
  transaction cost perspective, 188–189
Vested interest in the status quo, 350
Video game industry
  competitors, C177–C178, C181–C183
  game developers, C181
  Nintendo Wii, C177–C181, C183–C184
Video on demand, C102
Video rental business decline, 168
Vietnam, Procter & Gamble in, 231
Virtual organization, 324, 329, 329–331
  challenges and risks, 330–331
  collaboration in, 330, 331
  compared to modular type, 330
  pros and cons, 332
Visas for high-tech workers, 45
Vision, 23, 346
  anchored in reality, 24–25
  developed by leaders, 23
  downside, 24
  of entrepreneurs, 256
  of environmental sustainability, 348
  examples, 24
  Ford Motor Company, C220
  idealistic, 24
  irrelevant, 24
  setting a direction, 347–348
  sloganeering campaign, 24
  sources of implementation problems, 348–349
Vision statements, 24, 26

W

Wage inflation, 225
Wall Street Journal, 38, 120, 196, 266, 300, C42, C101, C173
Water purification system, 387
Watson supercomputer, 184
Websites
  business, 450
  for competitive intelligence, 38–39
  crowdfunding, 253
  for eBay, C74
  Weight Watchers, C30
  World Wrestling Entertainment, C70
West Side Story, C103
Wholly owned subsidiary, 238
  benefits, 238, 239
  risks and limitations, 238

Wisdom of Teams (Smith), 332
Wolf culture, 349
Women
  driving force in economy, 44
  educational attainments, 44
  involvement in microfinance, C85, C86
  in workforce, 42–44
Women's specialty retail stores, C52–C54
Women's Wear Daily, C48, C51
Work, challenging, 117
Workforce
  aging population of, 42
  changes at Procter & Gamble, C198
  diversity in, 117–118
  millennials in, 112
  women in, 42–44
Working Knowledge, 369
Working with Emotional Intelligence (Goleman), 354

Workplace, stimulating environment, 117
World Health Organization, C31
World Trade Center attack of 2001, C147
Worldwide functional divisions, 313
Worldwide functional structure, 322
Worldwide matrix structure, 313, **322**
Worldwide product division, 313
Worldwide product division structure, 322
Wrestling Perspective, C69
Wright amendment, C142
Written case analysis, 425

Z

Zero-sum game, 59, 317
Zero-sum role of stakeholders, 16–17